S0-AGL-238

Managing

A Competency-Based Approach

Don Hellriegel
Mays Business School
Texas A&M University

Susan E. Jackson
SMLR, Rutgers University
and GSBA-Zürich

John W. Slocum, Jr.
Edwin L. Cox School of Business
Southern Methodist University

THOMSON

SOUTH-WESTERN

Australia · Brazil · Canada · Mexico · Singapore · Spain · United Kingdom · United States

THOMSON

SOUTH-WESTERN

Managing: A Competency-Based Approach, Eleventh Edition
Don Hellriegel, Susan E. Jackson, John W. Slocum, Jr.

VP/Editorial Director:
Jack W. Calhoun

Editor-in-Chief:
Melissa S. Acuña

Senior Acquisitions Editor:
Joseph A. Sabatino

Developmental Editor:
John Abner

Editorial Assistant:
Ruth Belanger

Senior Marketing Manager:
Kimberly Kanakes

Marketing Coordinator:
Sarah Rose

Senior Marketing Communications Manager:
Jim Overly

Content Project Managers:
Marge Bril
Patrick Cosgrove

Manager, Editorial Media:
John Barans

Technology Project Manager:
Kristen Meere

Senior Manufacturing Coordinator:
Doug Wilke

Production House:
Lachina Publishing Services

Printer:
Transcontinental
Beauceville-Quebec, Canada G5X 3P3

Art Director:
Tippy McIntosh

Photography Manager:
Don Schlotman

Cover and Internal Designs:
Grannan Graphic Design Ltd.

Cover Images:
© Getty Images

COPYRIGHT © 2008, 2005
Thomson South-Western, a part of The
Thomson Corporation. Thomson, the Star
logo, and South-Western are trademarks used
herein under license.

Printed in Canada
1 2 3 4 5 10 09 08 07

Package: Student Edition:
ISBN 13: 978-0-324-42140-8
ISBN 10: 0-324-42140-0

Student Edition (core text only):
ISBN 13: 978-0-324-54393-3
ISBN 10: 0-324-54393-X

ALL RIGHTS RESERVED.
No part of this work covered by the copyright
hereon may be reproduced or used in any
form or by any means—graphic, electronic,
or mechanical, including photocopying,
recording, taping, Web distribution or information storage and retrieval systems, or in
any other manner—without the written
permission of the publisher.

For permission to use material from this text
or product, submit a request online at
http://www.thomsonrights.com.

Library of Congress Control Number:
2006939896

For more information about our products,
contact us at:
Thomson Learning Academic Resource
Center
1-800-423-0563

Thomson Higher Education
5191 Natorp Boulevard
Mason, OH 45040
USA

To Lois (DH)
To Randall (SEJ)
To Gail (JWS)

BRIEF CONTENTS

CONTENTS

Part 2: Managing in Turbulent Environments 75

Part 4: Organizing   355

OVERVIEW

Now in the eleventh edition, *Managing: A Competency-Based Approach* has been thoroughly revised, updated, and designed to guide the professional development of students. By focusing on the core competencies of effective managers, we seek to help students develop their management skills and the knowledge they will need to succeed in today's global organizations.

Editors at the *Wall Street Journal* asked recruiters what competencies they looked for when hiring college graduates. The top competencies that recruiters indicated were very important included communication and interpersonal skills, ability to work well within a team, personal ethics and integrity, leadership, and strategic thinking. Extensive research shows that these managerial competencies are needed by employees of many types—those in technical jobs, professional staff members, and line managers can all improve their effectiveness by developing these core competencies.

Similarly, in recognition of the importance of helping business students develop competencies, the American Association of Collegiate Schools of Business also identified in their Eligibility Procedures and Standards for Business Accreditation (AACSB International, 2006) the following:

▶ communication abilities,

▶ ethical understanding and reasoning abilities,

▶ analytical skills,

▶ multicultural and diversity training,

▶ reflective thinking skills,

▶ ethical and legal responsibilities in organizations and society,

▶ group and individual dynamics in organizations, and

▶ domestic and global environments of organizations.

For additional information on these and other learning standards for business accreditation by the AACSB International, go to *www.aacsb.edu.* *

In *Managing: A Competency-Based Approach*, we show how real-world managers use these general competencies as they address the daily challenges of managing and leading their organizations.

---

*AACSB International. *Eligibility Procedures and Accreditation Standards for Business Education*. Tampa, FL: AACSB International, 2006.

How will students use *Managing: A Competency-Based Approach* to develop their competencies? The text is filled with many types of learning opportunities. Each chapter begins with an organizational example that illustrates several of the major concepts that will be explained in the chapter. Throughout each chapter, managers from a variety of other organizations are featured in concise scenarios that illustrate their use of various managerial competencies. Discussion questions, experiential exercises, and interesting cases provide additional opportunities for students to develop and demonstrate their managerial competencies. We also offer a wide variety of support materials to assist instructors in teaching and guiding students as they learn about management. Information about these materials is presented in this preface and at the book's home page (*www.thomsonedu.com/management/hellriegel*), and is also available from your Thomson South-Western sales representative.

As you explore our home page and study this preface, you will see that this edition continues a long tradition of excellence. We introduced the competency-based approach in the eighth edition of *Managing*. We have continued to build on this approach with each subsequent revision. With the support of our editorial team at Thomson South-Western, we have created a student-oriented, integrated learning system that is engaging and stimulating to students from many backgrounds, including those with little or no work experience and those who are ready now to move into managerial roles.

OUR COMPETENCY-BASED APPROACH

Managing: A Competency-Based Approach and the learning system that supports it are intended for use in introductory management classes taught at any level in the university as well as community colleges. But so are many other books, so why should you use this one? To find out, read on.

Active Student Learning

We wrote this text to appeal to students who want to know about what's happening in organizations today, and are interested in what is likely to happen in the future. As employees in organizations, what challenges can they expect to face? As managers in organizations, how can they lead others to meet these challenges? Each chapter is filled with featured stories and current examples from organizations that students will recognize. Thus, this text shows students that essential management and leadership concepts are relevant in everyday work life.

Managing: A Competency-Based Approach is designed to engage students in active learning. Chapter 1 introduces the core managerial competencies that are examined throughout this textbook and explains what each one means. Chapter 1 also includes a Self-Assessment Inventory that students can use to measure their current standing on the six core managerial competencies that we feature throughout the book. After scoring their Self-Assessment Inventory, students will gain insight into their current areas of strength and be alerted to areas most needing improvement. With their heightened self-awareness, students will find it easy to connect personally with the material that follows in subsequent chapters.

NEW to this edition is a special feature called *Ethical Challenge*. To motivate students to consider the ethical managerial dilemmas that employees face, every chapter includes a featured situation that poses an ethical challenge. Real situations are described and students are asked to consider how they would respond if they were faced with such a situation. By addressing ethical concerns in every chapter, we show students the importance of thinking carefully about how the actions of managers can affect all organizational stakeholders.

Questions for Discussion and Reflective Thinking at the end of each chapter further encourage deeper thought and can be used to stimulate lively discussions. These questions call on students to engage in thoughtful analysis and reflection—not just restate what they have read. Several discussion questions require students to find additional information on the Internet and relate it to the material in the chapter. At the end of each chapter, an experiential exercise and a short case further challenge students to put their knowledge to work by diagnosing situations and thinking creatively about how to address real-life issues.

Managerial Competencies

We merge the concerns of managers with the managerial competencies that foster excellence. To appreciate the role of managers today and in the years ahead, a solid understanding of the competencies needed to manage and lead is essential. We focus on six core and vital managerial competencies:

▶ **communication,**

▶ **multicultural,**

▶ **planning and administration,**

▶ **self-management,**

▶ **strategic action, and**

▶ **teamwork.**

Managing: A Competency-Based Approach presents study materials, practice activities, and feedback directed at helping the student learn these competencies. Students benefit by having the competencies defined and clarified to foster early success in their careers. After completing the managerial competencies Self-Assessment Inventory in Chapter 1 (which is also accessible online using the access code included in new copies of the text), students can compare their development stages with those of hundreds of other students and practicing managers. Throughout the book, a series of specially designed competency features present students with examples of managerial competencies in action. We present a variety of ways in which they can assess their competencies and begin to develop their potential as effective managers and leaders.

Communication Competency. Competent managers lead others—they can't do so without being able to listen and share their ideas well. The communication competency involves listening, informing others, fostering open channels, and negotiating with others. The flow of information in an organization is its lifeblood. To maintain and improve the performance of an organization, information must freely flow in all directions. The communication competency strengthens the foundation for successful management. Communication is so fundamental that managers sometimes forget its significance to effective management. Through a series of cases and experiential exercises, students discover the importance of sharing information with others and of developing a culture in which they and others openly share information. Mastering the communication competency greatly expands a manager's influence and effectiveness.

Multicultural Competency. Competent managers stay abreast of important trends among and across nations that have potential impacts on their organizations. They diagnose how well their organizations are faring in global markets. This competency challenges students to recognize the impact of global trends on an organization's plans and growth. The challenges of global expansion and operating in various countries demand that students question their own leadership styles, values, and management practices within their own countries. The main factors for successfully doing business globally are being sensitive to key cultural, political, and economic differences in countries in which an organization operates and assessing the consequences of those differences for the organization.

Planning and Administration Competency. Competent managers understand that what worked well in the past may no longer serve the needs of an organization or its customers. This competency involves the regular review and adjustment of organizations to meet shifting internal and external needs and the changing competencies of employees. Work gets done when it is well planned, well coordinated, and well monitored. Competent managers lead by setting clear and challenging goals. When problems arise, they step in to help solve them. However, tasks may be neglected when managers spend too much time dealing with trivial problems. Similarly, employees may waste time because of inadequate controls, poor guidance, and slow decision making. Through a series of examples, students learn how effective managers use the planning and administration competency to create organizations that are responsive to customer demands and needs.

Self-Management Competency. Competent managers know that self-awareness is a crucial vantage point from which to view the operation of an organization and his or her role in that organization. Identification of one's strengths and developmental needs is an important first step in the process of learning to manage and lead others. Our presentation of the self-management competency assists students in identifying their own strengths and developmental needs in leadership, motivation, ethics, and other areas. We achieve this through the text material, experiential exercises, and cases. Besides learning about their current strengths and developmental needs, students gain an appreciation for the importance of continual self-assessment throughout their careers.

Strategic Action Competency. Competent managers craft creative strategies to guide an organization. Strategies are the major courses of action selected and implemented to achieve goals. Risk accompanies all strategic decisions, but the competent manager acts to devise contingency plans to minimize those risks. Our discussion of the strategic action competency demonstrates how managers of many types of organizations actually lead in the development and implementation of unique strategies to achieve a competitive advantage.

Teamwork Competency. Competent managers are able to cultivate an active network of relationships and to work well in diverse teams. The teamwork competency involves creating a healthy environment by forming give-and-take relationships, striving to enhance mutual understanding and respect, acknowledging the needs and feelings of others, and managing conflict productively. Competent managers rely on others to help them achieve organizational goals. Managers are forming and staffing teams and monitoring team performance. The right combination of talents is essential for teams to acquire the resources they need in order to be effective and to achieve their goals. Teamwork requires close collaboration, leadership and constant information sharing.

Guided Learning

Every chapter of *Managing: A Competency-Based Approach* includes features that make it teachable, readable, and learnable.

Learning Goals and a Fully Integrated Learning System. The text and all major support materials are organized around *Learning Goals* that form the basis of our easy-to-use integrated learning system. Along with the text, the *Test Bank*, *Instructor's Manual*, and *Web site* provide instructors and students with a fully integrated set of learning goals and content from which to teach and study.

Graphics. The text includes modern graphics that are colorful, reinforce chapter content, and very readable. We suggest that you quickly page through *Managing: A Competency-Based Approach*. You will discover that this book is appealing to look at and easy to read. Each figure and table is cited in the narrative and tied to the topic under discussion.

Challenge of Managing. Every chapter opens with a current, real-world account that sets the stage for the topics to be presented. These real-world accounts introduce chapter concepts, lead into the discussion, and whet students' appetites for what is to come. In the Chapter 1 *Challenge of Managing* feature, for example, students learn about some of the competencies of Anne Mulcahy, CEO of Xerox. In Chapter 15, students learn about the strong leadership abilities of John W. Thompson, CEO of Symantec. Among the other companies featured in other *Challenge of Managing* sections—all of which are **NEW** to this edition—are MTV, PepsiCo, Georgia Pacific, Lowe's, and Halliburton.

Competency features. Every chapter in *Managing: A Competency-Based Approach* contains four featured boxed inserts that relate the managerial competencies to chapter content. For example, in Chapter 14, the Teamwork Competency feature describes how chef Anthony Bourdain uses his teamwork skills to manage his kitchen staff. In Chapter 18, the Multicultural Competency feature describes how managers at Mercedes-Benz blended elements of German and American cultures at their auto plant in Vance, Alabama. With a few exceptions, the competency features are **NEW** in this edition. Those retained have been updated to reflect recent events.

Directly related in the text, the competency features reinforce the chapter concepts and enliven the learning process. The real-life examples help students apply basic concepts from the chapter, illustrate the value of developing one's core managerial competencies, and aid student learning. Questions in the *Test Bank* are provided for instructors who want to test material from these boxed features.

Snapshots. To further connect the concepts being taught to everyday life in organizations, each chapter includes at least four quotes—presented as margin inserts—that reveal unique insights and provide additional implications directly related to the text material where they appear. The Snapshot feature is **NEW** to this edition.

Key Terms and Concepts. Key terms and concepts are color highlighted in the text, making it easy for students to review the material and check their understanding. The definition of each term and concept is in italic to enhance clarity and student learning. A complete glossary is included on the product support Web site at *www.thomsonedu.com/management/hellriegel.*

Chapter Summaries. Every chapter ends with a summary that distills the chapter's main points. These summaries are organized around the chapter's *Learning Goals.* Thus, students can readily assess their mastery of the material presented for those goals.

Questions for Discussion and Reflective Thinking. Every chapter includes questions to stimulate discussion and encourage reflective thinking. These questions do more than simply ask students to repeat material from the chapter—they promote competency development by providing opportunities to apply and analyze important chapter concepts and related competencies. In addition, each chapter extends learning by encouraging students to venture into cyberspace to discover additional information relevant to the chapter. A number of questions are **NEW** to this edition or revised. Those that were retained have been reviewed for current relevance.

Developing Your Competencies: Experiential Exercises. To encourage students to engage in their own personal development, each chapter includes an experiential exercise that stimulates students to delve more deeply into the chapter's concepts. We have already described the managerial competencies Self-Assessment Inventory in Chapter 1. Other self-assessments in the *Experiential Exercise* section include questionnaires that provide feedback to students regarding their emotional intelligence, reactions to change, cultural values, and so on. Also included as experiential exercises are activities for small group discussions, personal planning activities, and knowledge quizzes. The highly effective and popular exercises have been retained, and many **NEW** ones have been added.

Developing Your Competencies: Cases to Develop Critical Thinking. Every chapter concludes with a substantive case study that challenges students to apply chapter concepts to an actual situation. Focused discussion questions at the end of each case ask students to analyze, evaluate, and suggest courses of action. These cases provide another opportunity for students to develop their managerial competencies through active learning. At the same time, students learn more about a wide variety of interesting organizations, including Wal-Mart, Harley-Davidson, FedEx, MTV, and the United Way. Most of the cases are **NEW** to this edition, and a few of the most highly effective ones have been retained.

Videos. All **NEW** videos are available for adopters of the eleventh edition for each chapter of *Managing: A Competency-Based Approach.* Featuring a wide variety of organizations, the videos illustrate key concepts in a chapter and provide students with an opportunity to improve their understanding of what managers actually do. By bringing management to life, the videos stimulate student interest and can be used to guide deeper analysis of the material covered in each chapter. Teaching notes and discussion questions to use with these videos are available in the *Instructor's Manual.*

Enrichment Materials

A comprehensive set of enrichment materials is available to instructors and students. We provide an overview of these materials in this section.

ThomsonNOW for Managing: A Competency-Based Approach

NEW to the eleventh edition, this powerful and fully integrated online teaching and learning system provides you with flexibility and control, saves you valuable time, and improves outcomes. Your students benefit by having choices in the way they learn through our unique personalized study path. All of this is made possible by using ThomsonNOW:

- ▶ homework, assignable and automatically graded,
- ▶ integrated e-book,
- ▶ personalized study paths,
- ▶ interactive course assignments,
- ▶ assessment options including *AACSB learning standards achievement reporting*,
- ▶ test delivery,
- ▶ course management tools, including a grade book, and
- ▶ WebCT and Blackboard integration.

Speak with your Thomson South-Western sales representative about integrating ThomsonNOW for *Managing: A Competency-Based Approach*, eleventh edition, into your courses! Visit *www.thomsonedu.com/thomsonnow* to learn more today!

Instructor's Manual (ISBN 0-324-53624-0)

Prepared by Susan Leshnower of Midland College, the *Instructor's Manual* emphasizes the integrated learning system. Each chapter includes (1) *Learning Goals*, (2) lecture outlines that are annotated with additional examples, (3) lecture-enhancing enrichment modules, (4) cross-references to text figures, (5) answers to all *Questions for Discussion and Reflective Thinking*, (6) answers to all experiential exercises and cases in the *Developing Your Competencies* sections, and (7) short cases related to the eleventh edition videos, with suggested answers to the case discussion questions.

Test Bank (ISBN 0-324-53626-7)

Prepared by Liesl Wesson of Texas A&M University, the substantially revised test bank is organized around the text's *Learning Goals*. **NEW** to the eleventh edition, the AACSB learning standards reflected in each *Test Bank* question have been identified to allow for the assessment of student achievement as it relates to these key measures. The *Test Bank* is available to instructors in print, on CD-ROM, and on the Web site. Tables at the beginning of each chapter classify each question according to type, difficulty level, and learning goal. This classification enables the instructor to create exams at the appropriate level with the desired mix of question types. Special questions aimed at the content of the text's *Challenge of Managing* features and competency features are designated throughout the *Test Bank*. The *Test Bank* contains more than 2,500 true/false, multiple-choice, and essay questions.

ExamView (ISBN 0-324-53625-9)

ExamView Computerized Testing Software, located on the *Instructor's Resource CD-ROM*, contains all of the questions in the printed *Test Bank*. This program is easy-to-use test creation software that is compatible with Microsoft Windows. Instructors can add or edit questions, instructions, and answers, and select questions by previewing them on the screen, selecting them randomly, or selecting them by number. Instructors can also create and administer quizzes online, whether over the Internet, a local-area network, or a wide-area network. Contact your Thomson South-Western sales representative for ordering information.

PowerPoint™ Presentation Slides

Prepared by Argie Butler of Texas A&M University, the **ALL-NEW** PowerPoint slides are available on the *Instructor's Resource CD-ROM* and online at *www.thomsonedu .com/management/hellriegel* to assist instructors by enhancing their lectures. Prepared in conjunction with the *Instructor's Manual*, more than 460 PowerPoint slides are available to supplement course content, adding structure and visual dimension to lectures. With a **NEW** lively design, these PowerPoint slides reflect the dynamic nature of management. All of the slides include meaningful captions that tie in directly to the concepts in the textbook, and they are easily printed to create customized transparencies.

Instructor's Resource CD-ROM (ISBN 0-324-53625-9)

This CD-ROM includes the key instructor support materials—*Instructor's Manual, Test Bank, ExamView*, and *PowerPoint Slides*—and provides instructors with a comprehensive capability for customizing lectures and presentations.

Comprehensive Video Package (ISBN 0-324-53619-4)

A **NEW** video library is available to users of the eleventh edition of *Managing: A Competency-Based Approach*. The videos bring action-based insights right into the classroom. They frame management issues in such a way that students must apply some aspect of chapter content to their analyses of the issues. This unique video package is on DVD to use as lecture launchers, discussion starters, topical introductions, or directed inquiries.

Product Support Web Site (www.thomsonedu.com/management/hellriegel)

An enriching Web site complements the text, providing many extras for students and instructors. The informative resources include (1) interactive quizzes, (2) downloadable support materials, and (3) text glossary and management dictionary.

InfoTrac College Edition

InfoTrac College Edition is packaged with every new copy of the textbook. It is a fully searchable online university library containing complete articles and their images. Its database allows access to hundreds of scholarly and popular publications—all reliable sources, including magazines, journals, encyclopedias, and newsletters.

ACKNOWLEDGMENTS

We give special thanks to Jerry R. Strawser, dean of Mays Business School; Duane Ireland, head of the Department of Management of Texas A&M University; Al Niemi, dean of the Cox School of Business of Southern Methodist University; and Barbara A. Lee, former dean of the School of Management and Labor Relations of Rutgers University. They have fostered work environments that made possible the completion of the eleventh edition of *Managing: A Competency-Based Approach*.

For their outstanding assistance with many of the essential tasks involved in manuscript preparation and review, we express our deep gratitude to Argie Butler of Texas A&M University and Tina Potter of Southern Methodist University. Their dedication and professionalism made this journey easier.

Many dedicated individuals at Thomson South-Western provided valuable professional advice and support in developing this text and the related supplemental materials that accompany it. Instructors and students who use these materials will be delighted by the outstanding results of their efforts to produce a lively and engaging integrated learning system. Those most directly involved at Thomson South-Western include Joe Sabatino, the thoughtful sponsoring editor for this book; Kimberly Kanakes, the creative marketing manager for the eleventh edition; John Abner, the developmental editor whose advice is reflected in every chapter and the enrichment materials; Marge Bril and Pat Cosgrove, the production editors who handled so superbly the many issues in the production process; Lorretta Palagi, the copyeditor whose expertise improved the flow and readability of the manuscript; Tippy McIntosh, who is chiefly responsible for the attractive and supportive art program; and Don Schlotman and Bryan Rinnert, who obtained the effective photos to enrich the written words.

Thanks also go to our excellent team of enrichment materials authors. Their many competencies and hard work are evident in the outstanding enrichment materials that foster student learning. These authors include:

Argie Butler	Susan Leshnower	Liesl Wesson
Texas A&M University	Midland College	Texas A&M University
PowerPoint Presentation Slides	*Instructor's Manual*	*Test Bank*

Our colleagues and friends at Texas A&M University, Rutgers University and GSBA–Zurich, and Southern Methodist University create environments that nurture our professional development, and we thank them for this. We are grateful to our families for their support and understanding also, as we devoted evenings and weekends to preparing this edition. With the completion of this edition, we look forward to spending more time with families and friends.

We extend a very special thanks to Marge Bril, who served as our production editor for the past several editions of the text. We wish Marge the very best upon her retirement from Thomson South-Western. Marge Bril has been the ultimate professional for the many years she worked with us. She has served as a role model for all us. Her calm and competent method of shepherding our manuscripts through the editorial and production process has helped ensure that *Managing: A Competency-Based Approach* is a top-quality product.

Many reviewers and colleagues made insightful comments as we prepared the eleventh edition. As to be expected, there were some differences among them as to what to include, modify, or delete. Regardless, their comments and suggestions resulted in substantial improvements. We are grateful to the following individuals for sharing their professional insights and suggestions.

Eileen Albright
Cinemark Theaters

Milorad M. Novicevic
University of Mississippi

Cecily Cooper
University of Miami

Peter Raad
Southern Methodist University

William Cron
Texas Christian University

William Riesel
St. Johns University

Michael Harvey
University of Mississippi

Charles Snow
Penn State University

William Joyce
Dartmouth College

Ralph Sorrentino
Deliotte Consulting

David Lei
Southern Methodist University

Ben Welch
Texas A&M University

Michael Murphy
Electronic Data Systems

Don Hellriegel
Texas A&M University

Susan E. Jackson
Rutgers University
and
GSBA–Zurich

John W. Slocum, Jr.
Southern Methodist University

Don Hellriegel

Don Hellriegel is Professor Emeritus of Management at the Mays Business School at Texas A&M University (TAMU). He received his B.S. and M.B.A. from Kent State University and his Ph.D. from the University of Washington. Dr. Hellriegel has been a member of the faculty at Texas A&M since 1975 and has served on the faculties of the Pennsylvania State University and the University of Colorado.

His research interests include corporate entrepreneurship, effect of organizational environments, and organizational innovation and strategic management processes. His research has been published in a number of leading journals.

Professor Hellriegel served as Vice President and Program Chair of the Academy of Management (1986), President Elect (1987), President (1988), and Past President (1989). In September 1999, he was elected to a three-year term as Dean of the Fellows Group of the Academy of Management. He served a term as Editor of the *Academy of Management Review* and served as a member of the Board of Governors of the Academy of Management (1979–1981 and 1982–1989). Dr. Hellriegel has occupied many other leadership roles, among which include President, Eastern Academy of Management; Division Chair, Organization and Management Theory Division; President, Brazos County United Way; Co-Consulting Editor, West Series in Management; Head (1976–1980 and 1989–1994), Department of Management, TAMU; Executive Associate Dean and Interim Dean, Mays Business School, TAMU; and Interim Executive Vice Chancellor, Texas A&M University System.

He has consulted with a variety of groups and organizations, including 3DI; Sun Ship Building; Penn Mutual Life Insurance; Texas A&M University System; Ministry of Industry and Commerce, Nation of Kuwait; Ministry of Agriculture, Nation of Dominican Republic; American Assembly of Collegiate Schools of Business, and Texas Innovation Group.

Susan E. Jackson

Susan E. Jackson is Professor of Human Resource Management in the School of Management and Labor Relations at Rutgers University and at GSBA–Zurich, Switzerland. She received her B.A. in psychology and sociology from the University of Minnesota and her Master's and Ph.D. in organizational psychology from the University of California, Berkeley, and has taught at the University of Maryland, New York University, and the University of Michigan.

Her primary area of expertise is the strategic management of human resources, and her special interests include managing knowledge-based organizations, teamwork, and workforce diversity. She has authored or co-authored more than 100 articles on these and related topics. In addition, she has published several books, including *Managing Knowledge for Sustained Competitive Advantage: Designing Strategies for Effective Human Resource Management* (with M. A. Hitt and A. S. DeNisi), *Managing Human Resources in Cross-Border Alliances* (with R. S. Schuler and Y. Luo), *Managing Human Resources through Strategic Partnership* (with R. S. Schuler), *Strategic Human Resource Management* (with R. S. Schuler), *Diversity in the Workplace: Human Resource Initiatives*, and *Creating Tomorrow's Organizations: A Handbook for Future Research in Organizational Behavior* (with C. L. Cooper).

Professor Jackson has held numerous positions in professional societies. In the Academy of Management, she is actively involved and currently serves on the editorial board of the *Academy of Management Journal*. She also has served as Consulting Editor and Editor of the *Academy of Management Review*, President of the Division of Organizational Behavior, Member-at-Large for the HRM Division, and Member of the Board of Governors. She is a Fellow of the Academy of Management and the Society for Industrial and Organizational Psychology, where she has served as Program Chair, and has served as a member of the editorial board of the Frontiers of Industrial & Organizational Psychology, the Scientific Affairs Committee, Member-at-Large/Long Range Planning Committee, and the Education and Training Committee. She also is a member of the International Association of Applied Psychology, where she has served as Program Co-Chair. In addition, she has served as a consultant to organizations such as General Electric, American Express, Merrill Lynch, Xerox, and the American Assembly of Collegiate Schools of Business.

John W. Slocum, Jr.

John Slocum holds the O. Paul Corley Professorship in Organizational Behavior at the Edwin L. Cox School of Business, Southern Methodist University (SMU). He has also taught on the facilities of the University of Washington, the Fisher School of Business at the Ohio State University, the Smeal School of Business at the Pennsylvania State University, the International University of Japan, and the Amos Tuck College at Dartmouth. He holds a B.B.A. from Westminster College, an M.B.A. from Kent State University, and a Ph.D. in organizational behavior from the University of Washington.

Professor Slocum has held a number of positions in professional societies. He was elected as a Fellow to the Academy of Management in 1976 for his outstanding contributions to the profession of management and a Fellow to the Decision Sciences Institute in 1984 for his research in behavioral decision theory. He was awarded the Alumni Citation for Professional Accomplishment by Westminster College, both the Nicolas Salgo and Rotunda Outstanding Teaching Awards from SMU, the Executive MBA Most Valuable Faculty Member Award, SMU Alumni Award for Outstanding Service to Alumni, and was the recipient of the inaugural Carl Sewell Distinguished Service and Distinguished University Citizen Awards by SMU. From 1975 to 1986, he served as a member of the Board of Governors, Academy of Management. In 1983–1984, he served as 39th President of the Academy and Chairman of the Board of Governors of that organization. Currently, he serves as Co-Editor of the *Journal of World Business, Organizational Dynamics*, and *Journal of Leadership and Organizational Studies*. He is the co-author of 24 books, the latest being *Organizational Behavior*, eleventh edition, South-Western Publishing Company, 2007, and has authored or co-authored 127 journal articles.

Professor Slocum has served as a consultant to such organizations as OxyChem, ARAMARK, The Associates First Capital Corporation, Fort Worth Museum of Science and History, Pier 1, Mack Trucks, Celanese, NASA, Lockheed Martin Corporation, and Key Span Energy. He is currently on the Board of Directors of Kisco Senior Living Communities of Carlsbad, California, the Japanese-American Dallas–Ft. Worth Association, the ViewCast Corporation, the Winston School of Dallas, Go-To-Learn (a nonprofit educational software corporation), Applied Management Sciences Institute of Houston, Texas, and the School of Business Management at the Bandung Institute of Technology in Indonesia.

PART 1

Overview of Management

Chapter 1
Developing Managerial
Competencies

Chapter 2
Learning from the History of
Management Thought

© BananaStock/Jupiter Images

Developing Managerial Competencies

Learning Goals

After studying this chapter, you should be able to:

1. Explain why managerial competencies are important.

2. Discuss the basic functions and levels of management.

3. Describe the competencies used in managerial work and assess your current competency levels.

Communication Competency

Planning and Administration Competency

Teamwork Competency

Managing Effectively

Self-Management Competency

Strategic Action Competency

Multicultural Competency

Challenge of Managing ....

Anne Mulcahy, CEO of Xerox

© William Taufic/www.williamtaufic.com

She never expected to become the CEO of Xerox. She had thought about quitting and spending more time with her boys. She had spent many years in the sales and human resources departments at Xerox, was head of the desktop business, and served as chief of staff for former CEO Paul Allair. Colleagues describe her as straightforward, persistent, disciplined, hardworking, and a person of high integrity. She is not afraid to hear bad news and is willing to work side by side with employees to solve problems.

When Xerox's board chose her to lead the company in 2002, the company was in terrible financial shape. It was $14 billion in debt and bankruptcy was a real problem. The only way to save the company was to make massive cuts. That meant downsizing the workforce, shutting down its consumer printer business, and spinning off its fabled Palo Alto Research Center (PARC). Today, under her leadership, Xerox is profitable and its income is growing at 14 percent a year. How did she accomplish this turnaround?

Mulcahy and her staff first examined what business Xerox was in. They determined that Xerox was not just selling copiers, but was in the business of managing the information flows for its customers by scanning and storing documents in digital form. Customers told Xerox salespeople that they were spending a fortune on IT (information technology), but it didn't pay off. Today, Xerox is in the business of helping its customers figure out how to optimize their flow of information rather than upgrading the technology as a solution. Xerox still uses the research capabilities of the PARC, along with Fujitsu, Canon, and Ricoh, to further its core competencies in imaging, search, and diagnostics. The spin-off of PARC, however, gave Xerox the financial ability to engage in research projects with new research partners. Second, Mulcahy personally negotiated the settlement of a long investigation into fraudulent accounting practices, insisting that her involvement was necessary to signal a new commitment to ethical business practices. Third, Xerox has successfully introduced numerous new products and services in high-growth areas such as digital technology, document services, color products, and consulting. This renewed emphasis on innovation signals that Mulcahy and her management team are concentrating on areas that should provide a solid

Learning Content

foundation for growth. Mulcahy and her team still face stiff competition from Hewlett-Packard, Canon, and other technology companies. She also must keep her management team focused on growth while maintaining the cost controls that made the company profitable.

What has Mulcahy learned about being the CEO of a major U.S. company? First, you need to listen and learn from customers. She asked senior managers to visit customers and learn how they use Xerox's products and the issues they face when using them. From these visits, they learned that, although Xerox had great technology, it didn't focus on customers' wants and needs. Second, she repositioned the company as a sales/solution company instead of a technology/copier company. By communicating with customers, Mulcahy and her team came to understand that Xerox didn't need more technology; it instead needed to focus on solving problems and understanding businesses from the customer perspective. Finally, she learned to value honest and candid assessments of what Xerox does well and poorly. She spends more than one-third of her time with customers talking about what matters to them.[1]

To learn more about this organization, visit *www.xerox.com.*

I.

Explain why managerial competencies are important.

Introductory Concepts

Effective managers such as Anne Mulcahy are essential to any organization's overall success, regardless of whether it is a global giant or a small start-up enterprise. Indeed, having talented people with the right competencies is so important to the success of a business that *Fortune* magazine includes "the ability to attract, develop, and keep talented people" as one of the key factors used to establish its list of most admired companies. A competency *is a combination of knowledge, skills, behaviors, and attitudes that contribute to personal effectiveness.*[2] Mulcahy has several competencies that enable her to perform effectively in her company's top managerial job.

What Are Managerial Competencies?

What are managerial competencies and why are these important to you? Managerial competencies *are sets of knowledge, skills, behaviors, and attitudes that a person needs to be effective in a wide range of positions and various types of organizations.* The nature of work is changing. You're being judged not just by how smart you are, but also by how well you handle yourself and manage others. Organizations take for granted that you are smart and have the technical know-how to do the job. Organizations hire people because they believe that they have the managerial competencies that will enable them to become star performers. If you are applying for a job, you are likely to be screened by a person in the human resources department for these managerial competencies. To advance in an organization, you need to continue to develop managerial competencies, so when you take a position in an organization you should consider how the organization will help you develop your competencies.

Managerial competencies can help people excel in different jobs. For instance, at Frito-Lay, successful customer service representatives need to exhibit high self-management and communication competencies. For a successful information technology person at Kraft Foods, Inc., the key competencies would also include planning and administration and teamwork. For Irene Rosenfeld, the CEO of Kraft Foods, she needs all of these in addition to multicultural and strategic competencies. For senior managers, a person must master a mix of competencies, not just one or two. Research has found that top senior managers are not just talented in teamwork, but they have strengths across the board. At Kraft Foods, for example, those managers who possessed strengths in all competencies, were far more likely to perform in the top third of the company than those who did not master these competencies.

How do you learn these competencies? Getting into a challenging situation like Mulcahy did at Xerox does not guarantee that you will learn the competencies needed to become successful. We believe that people can learn from experiences and by gaining feedback about their own behavior from others. We have seen many executives get derailed by their insensitivity to others because they didn't understand their weaknesses. Before reading further, please take time to complete the Experiential Exercise: Self-Assessment Inventory on pages 32–36. We have grouped into categories the scores of hundreds of students and practicing managers against which you can compare your competency scores. People use many types of competencies in their everyday lives, including those needed to be effective in leisure activities, in personal relationships, at work, and at school. In this book we focus on managerial competencies. Throughout, we emphasize the competencies that you will need for jobs having managerial responsibility. Specifically, our goal is to help you develop six key managerial competencies:

▶ communication,

▶ planning and administration,

▶ teamwork,

▶ strategic action,

▶ multicultural, and

▶ self-management.[3]

Figure 1.1 indicates how these six competencies are all interrelated. For now, an overview of what is involved in applying them is sufficient. Table 1.1 on the following page identifies several important aspects of each key managerial competency. In practice, knowing where one competency begins and another ends is difficult. You would seldom rely on just one at a time, so drawing sharp distinctions between them is valuable only for purposes of identification and description. Keeping these six managerial

Figure 1.1 A Model of Managerial Competencies

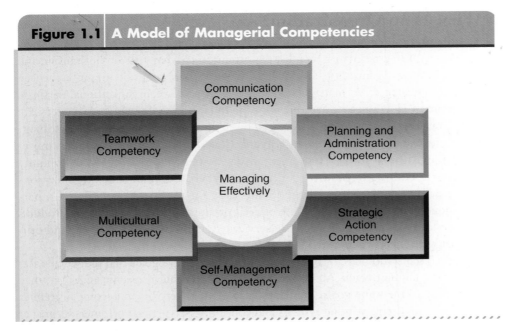

Table 1.1	Six Key Managerial Compentencies

COMMUNICATION COMPETENCY

Informal communication
Formal communication
Negotiation

PLANNING AND ADMINISTRATION COMPETENCY

Information gathering, analysis, and problem solving
Planning and organizing projects
Time management
Budgeting and financial management

TEAMWORK COMPETENCY

Designing teams
Creating a supportive environment
Managing team dynamics

STRATEGIC ACTION COMPETENCY

Understanding the industry
Understanding the organization
Taking strategic actions

MULTICULTURAL COMPETENCY

Cultural knowledge and understanding
Cultural openness and sensitivity

SELF-MANAGEMENT COMPETENCY

Integrity and ethical conduct
Personal drive and resilience
Balancing work and life demands
Self-awareness and development

competencies firmly in mind will help you think about how the material you are studying can improve your performance in jobs that require you to use them.

What Is an Organization?

An organization *is a formal and coordinated group of people who function to achieve particular goals.* Effective managers must pay attention to what goes on both inside and outside of their organizations. Regardless of where their attention might be focused at any particular time, managers are part and parcel of organizational settings. Profit-oriented businesses are one type of organization in which managers are found, but they aren't the only one. Undoubtedly, you could write your autobiography as a series of experiences with organizations such as hospitals, schools, museums, sports teams, stores, amusement parks, restaurants, orchestras, community groups and clubs, government agencies, and others. Some of these organizations were small, and others were large. Some were for-profit companies, and others were nonprofit organizations. Some offered products, some offered both products and services, and others offered only services. Some were well managed, and others struggled merely to survive.

Every organization has a structure and strives to achieve goals that individuals acting alone could not reach. All organizations strive to achieve specific goals, but they don't all have the same goals. For example, a goal at Xerox is to become a premier supplier of high-end printing systems and consulting services to customers. A goal at Sony is to create innovative cameras, whereas at Dell Computer a goal is to produce reliable, low-cost PCs and related computer products. All of these goals, however, are related to the overall goals of serving customers and earning profits.

Regardless of an organization's specific goals, the job of managers is to help guide the organization's achievement of these goals. In this book, we look at managers in organizations of all types and sizes that have many different goals and many different ways of achieving their goals. Our primary purposes are to help you understand how managers accomplish their goals and to help you develop some of the managerial competencies that you will need to be effective in whatever type of organization you find yourself. Many—indeed, most—of these competencies will be useful to you even if you never have a job with the word *manager* in the title.

What Is a Manager?

We've been talking about managers for several pages, so it's time to clarify exactly what the term means. A manager *is a person who plans, organizes, leads, and controls the allocation of human, material, financial, and information resources in pursuit of the organization's goals.* The many different types of managers include department managers, product managers, account managers, plant managers, division managers, district managers, and task force managers. What they all have in common is responsibility for the efforts of a group of people who share a goal and access to resources that the group can use in pursuing its goal.

You don't have to be called a manager to be a manager. Some managers have unique and creative titles, such as chief information officer (a person in charge of information systems) or team leader. People with the job titles of chief executive officer (CEO), president, managing director, supervisor, and coach also are responsible for helping groups of people achieve a common goal, so they too are managers.

Most employees contribute to organizations through their own work, not by directing other employees. Journalists, computer programmers, insurance agents, machine operators, newscasters, graphic designers, sales associates, stockbrokers, accountants, and lawyers are essential to helping organizations achieve their goals, but many people with these job titles aren't managers.

What sets managers apart, if not their job titles? Simply put, the difference between managers and individual contributors is that managers are evaluated on how well the people they direct do their jobs. Anne Mulcahy doesn't perform service calls at Xerox. She hires, trains, and motivates others to manage people who do that job. Similarly, Kevin Rollins, CEO of Dell Computers, doesn't assemble computers. His job is to position Dell in the marketplace by restructuring it to compete more effectively against Lenovo, IBM, and other competitors. He's accomplishing this by working with his management team to smoothly integrate the various departments at Dell.[4]

What Is Managing?

If managers are the people responsible for making sure that an organization achieves its goals, what does the term *management* mean? In everyday usage, people often refer to management as a group of managers in an organization. For example, the CEO and other high-level executives often are referred to as top management. The managers under them may be referred to as middle management, and so on.

The term can also be used to refer to the tasks that managers do. These tasks include planning, organizing, leading, and controlling the work of an organization. Recently General Electric (GE) divided GE Capital into six divisions—Commercial Finance, Healthcare, Industrial, Consumer Finance, Infrastructure, and NBC Universal—to ensure more clarity about what each manager's job within GE Capital entails. According to Jeff Immelt, CEO of GE, he wanted these businesses to operate separately for faster decision making and execution. Now, managers in GE

Snapshot

"We have traditionally marketed products in different parts of the world. To remain competitive against Sony, Samsung and Matsushita, we need to establish a global brand. We need to bring together marketing and distribution activities to be more efficient."
Gerard Kleisterlee, CEO, Philips Electronics

Consumer Finance focus on credit card services, such as J. C. Penney and global consumer financing, whereas managers in the GE Infrastructure division focus on providing fundamental technologies in aviation, rail, energy, oil, and gas to developing countries.

Managing *refers to making decisions to guide the organization through planning, organizing, leading, and controlling.* As you will see, people in many different jobs may be expected to do some management tasks, even if that isn't their main focus. For example, quality control programs such as the one at GE involve employees throughout the entire organization in developing plans for improving quality. When GE Consumer Finance looks for ways to reduce errors in the bills it sends to credit card customers, managers enlist the help of billing clerks and data processors. They will be empowered to reorganize some of their work and be expected to continue to look for new ways to control quality. In other words, they will be doing some management tasks, but they won't become managers. We reserve the use of the term *manager* to refer to people in jobs that primarily involve management tasks.

What Are the Types of Managers?

There are many types of managers and many ways in which managerial jobs differ from each other. One difference is the scope of activities involved. The scope of activities performed by functional managers is relatively narrow, whereas the scope of activities performed by general managers is quite broad.

Functional managers *supervise employees having expertise in one area, such as accounting, human resources, sales, finance, marketing, or production.* For example, Michael Brown is the head of a payroll department at Capstone Mortgage Corporation. He is a functional manager. He doesn't determine employee salaries, as a general manager might, but makes sure that payroll checks are issued on time and in the correct amounts. Usually, functional managers have a great deal of experience and technical expertise in the areas of operation they supervise. Their success as managers is due in part to the detailed knowledge they have about the work being done by the people they supervise, the problems those people are likely to face, and the resources they need to perform effectively. They rely on the communication, planning and administration, teamwork, and self-management competencies to accomplish their jobs.

General managers *are responsible for the operations of more complex units—for example, a company or a division.* Dan Buckley is a vice president for Groendyke Transportation in Enid, Oklahoma. As a general manager, Dan oversees the work of functional managers. General managers must have a broader range of well-developed managerial competencies than functional managers to do their jobs well. They also need to acquire multicultural and strategic action competencies. These competencies can be learned through a combination of formal training and various job assignments, or they can be learned simply in the course of trying to adapt and survive in a chosen area. Being adaptable enough to solve whatever problems he ran into has been critical for Buckley. He tries to bring freethinkers—the rebels—into his group to get more diversity in thinking. To increase their effectiveness, he doesn't require them to follow normal operating procedures as long as they do not violate ethical, legal, and safety requirements.

2.

Discuss the basic functions and levels of management.

Functions and Levels of Management

As we've described the various types of managers, we've given you some idea of what managers do. But these few examples don't show the whole picture by any means. Let's now consider systematically what managers do—the functions they perform and the specific tasks included in these functions.

Figure 1.2 | Basic Managerial Functions

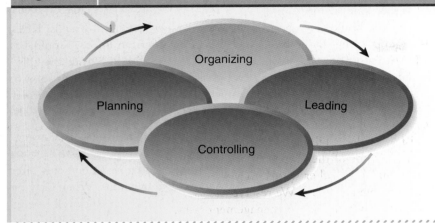

What Are the Basic Managerial Functions?

The successful manager capably performs four basic managerial functions: planning, organizing, leading, and controlling. However, as you will see, the amount of time a manager spends on each function depends on the level of the particular job. After further describing each of the four general managerial functions, we highlight the differences among managers at various levels in organizations.

Regardless of their level in an organization, most managers perform the four general functions more or less simultaneously—rather than in a rigid, preset order—to achieve organizational goals. Figure 1.2 illustrates this point graphically. In this section we briefly examine the four functions without looking specifically at their interrelationships. However, throughout this book we will refer to those interrelationships to help explain exactly how managers do their jobs.

Planning. Planning *involves determining organizational goals and the means to reach them.* Managers plan for three reasons: (1) to establish an overall direction for the organization's future, such as increased profit, expanded market share, and social responsibility; (2) to identify and commit the organization's resources to achieving its goals; and (3) to decide which tasks must be done to reach those goals. American Express CEO Kenneth Chenault is a good example of a manager who is good at planning.[5] Because of his in-depth knowledge of the financial services industry, he understood how important the financial services industry in China was going to be to the overall profitability of American Express by 2010. He also knew that in order for American Express to be competitive with Discover Card, Visa, and MasterCard, he needed to grow American Express's customer base, reduce its workforce, initiate proprietary cards, and establish global partners. He also needed to focus on cardholder's security needs after 9/11.

Organizing. After managers have prepared plans, they must translate those relatively abstract ideas into reality. Sound organization is essential to this effort. Organizing *is the process of deciding where decisions will be made, who will perform what jobs and tasks, and who will report to whom in the company.* By organizing effectively, managers can better coordinate human, material, and information resources.[6] Organizing involves creating a structure by setting up departments and job descriptions. For example, the U.S. Postal Service uses a structure that helps it deliver mail. At the U.S. Postal Service, most employees think of themselves as production workers, and the degree of job specialization is high. Relatively little attention is paid to the marketing

Snapshot

"The success you've enjoyed over time leads you into a rut. It's time to challenge managers to think out of the box. Strategic planning is one way to get managers to think out of the box."
Kenneth Chenault, CEO, American Express

function. Most of the decisions are made by top managers, with mail carriers and postal clerks having little to do with decision making. Carriers and clerks are promoted to other jobs as they gain seniority.

In contrast, YUM! Brands is organized into five distinct restaurant brands: KFC, Taco Bell, Pizza Hut, Long John Silver's, and A&W All-American Foods. Employees in each business attempt to serve customers in their business. David Novak, the CEO of YUM! Brands, believes that by having each restaurant be responsible for its own marketing, sales, and human resources functions it creates clearer lines of authority and responsibility and improves food quality and offers customers value-priced meals.

Leading. In addition to making plans, creating a structure, and hiring people, someone must lead the organization. Leading *involves getting others to perform the necessary tasks by motivating them to achieve the organization's goals.* Leading isn't done only after planning and organizing end; it is a crucial element of those functions. When Clayton Jones took over the reins at Rockwell Collins in 1995, he knew that Rockwell needed to change its direction from creating blockbuster commercial projects for Boeing to manufacturing products that would be used to fight the war on terrorism. Troops now fight with unmanned aircraft armed with transmitters that send information back to ground troops equipped with handheld global positioning system devices. Projects, however, were running 30 to 40 percent over budget. Jones immediately froze all hiring, trimmed corporate overhead, and consolidated the engineering, human resources, and purchasing departments. He also standardized the guts of navigational systems, instrument landing systems, and weather systems by requiring that managers in these divisions share technologies and components. By leading such changes, he saved millions of dollars and has restored Rockwell to the *Forbes*' Best Managed Companies list.[7]

Controlling. *The process by which a person, group, or organization consciously monitors performance and takes corrective action is* controlling. Just as a thermostat sends signals to a heating system that the room temperature is too high or too low, a managerial control system sends signals to managers that things aren't working out as planned and that corrective action is needed. Howard Schultz is CEO of Starbucks, the coffee company based in Seattle, with annual sales of more than $6.4 billion and coffee shops in more than 30 countries.[8] Schultz believes that Starbucks' success is due to its competitive spirit, ability to respond to customers' needs with diverse and genuine products, ability to attract and retain employees, and its managerial control system. The control procedures at Starbucks influence the criteria used to hire people, the type of beans used, the physical layout of each store, and relationships with suppliers, among other issues. In the control process at Starbucks, Amazon.com, Nike, and other organizations, managers

▶ set standards of performance,

▶ measure current performance against those standards,

▶ take action to correct any deviations, and

▶ adjust the standards if necessary.

The control system that makes FedEx unique is its central sorting facilities in Dallas, Memphis, and Indianapolis. All packages arrive at a location for sorting by midnight. A DC-10 with more than 50,000 pounds of packages (approximately 131,000 packages) is unloaded within 30 minutes. The packages are unloaded directly into a giant warehouse containing an elaborate system of conveyor belts. All packages must be sorted so that planes can leave for their destinations at 3:00 A.M. From the time a package is placed on one of the intake ramps, the conveyor system takes 6 minutes to scan, sort, and redirect the package to a container to be loaded onto an outgoing plane.[9]

What Are the Basic Levels of Management?

In telling you about the basic functions performed by managers in organizations, we've cited primarily examples of managers in large corporations. But managers and effective management are just as important in small organizations. When Stanford students David Filo and Gerry Yang founded Yahoo! in 1994, they started with a stack of three flat boxes to which Filo attached a sign reading "**DO NOT TOUCH.**" They hired Tim Koogle away from Motorola to help run the company. From this small beginning, Yahoo! now enables millions of customers to view Web pages each month. Yahoo! still doesn't own the servers; it rents them. Koogle, the former CEO of Yahoo!, knew that, in an intangible world, keeping Yahoo focused was crucial. At Yahoo! the primary resource is brainpower. Employees can start pursuing radically different tactics in the blink of an eye. The company's assets can become quickly and utterly uncoordinated unless top management constantly reinforces its strategic focus.

When Yahoo! first began, it was a small three-person organization. As a small organization, it had only one level of management. Large organizations usually have more than one level of management, with varying goals, tasks, responsibilities, and authority. A company's first-line store manager operates very differently than its CEO. Figure 1.3 shows the three basic management levels. We define them with a broad brush here, returning to add detail later in the chapter and throughout the book.

First-Line Managers. First-line managers *are directly responsible for the production of goods or services.* They may be called sales managers, section heads, production supervisors, or team leaders depending on the organization. Employees who report to them do the organization's basic production work—whether of goods or of services. For example, a first-line manager at a steel production plant supervises employees who make steel, operate and maintain machines, and write shipping orders. A sales manager at a U.S. automobile dealership supervises salespeople who sell cars to customers in the showroom. An automobile sales manager in Japan works in an office that has computers and telephones similar to a telemarketing center and supervises salespeople who go to people's homes to sell them cars.

This level of management is the link between the operations of each department and the rest of the organization. First-line managers in most companies spend little

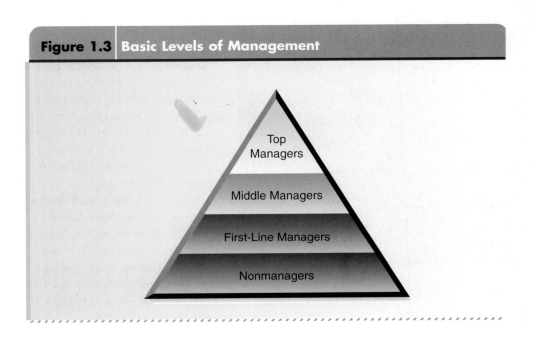

Figure 1.3 | **Basic Levels of Management**

time with higher management or with people from other organizations. Most of their time is spent with the people they supervise and with other first-line managers. First-line managers often lead hectic work lives full of pressure and having little glamour.[10]

First-line managers usually need strong technical expertise to teach subordinates and supervise their day-to-day tasks. Workers usually develop technical expertise before becoming managers. Sometimes, though, a first-line manager is a recent college graduate who is responsible for the work of both hourly employees and professionals. Such a first-line manager is likely to have little hands-on experience. The lack of experience isn't a problem if the new manager is willing to learn and has the competency to communicate with diverse types of people, to coach and counsel subordinates, and to provide constructive feedback.

Middle Managers.
Some managers at larger organizations must focus on coordinating employee activities, determining which products or services to provide, and deciding how to market these products or services to customers. Middle managers *are responsible for setting objectives that are consistent with top management's goals and translating them into specific goals and plans for first-line managers to implement*.[11] Middle managers typically have titles such as department head, plant manager, and director of finance. They are responsible for directing and coordinating the activities of first-line managers and, at times, such nonmanagerial personnel as clerks, receptionists, and staff assistants. Oftentimes middle managers try to resolve contradictions between what top management hopes to achieve and what first-line managers can actually do. As a section manager for State Farm Insurance Company, Eric Daly supervises agents who sell State Farm Insurance policies to people who live in Texas and Oklahoma. As a middle manager for State Farm, Daly must translate top management's strategy for growing State Farm into tangible goals for all agents in his section.[12]

Many middle managers began their careers and spent several years as first-line managers. Even so, promotion from the first level of management to middle management is often difficult and sometimes traumatic. The heavier emphases on managing group performance and allocating resources represent the most important differences between first-line and middle managers. The middle manager often is involved in reviewing the work plans of various groups, helping these groups set priorities, and negotiating and coordinating their activities. Middle managers are involved in establishing target dates for products or services to be completed; developing evaluation criteria for performance; deciding which projects should be given money, personnel, and materials; and translating top management's general goals into specific operational plans, schedules, and procedures.

© Court Mast/File/AP Photo

Larry Ellison has been Chief Executive Officer of the Oracle Corporation since he founded the company in 1977. The now multi-billion-dollar software giant is undergoing significant change to redirect the company's business strategy.

Middle managers carry out top management's directives primarily by delegating authority and responsibility to their subordinates and by coordinating schedules and resources with other managers. They often spend much of their day talking on the phone, attending committee meetings, and preparing and reviewing reports. Middle managers tend to be removed from the technical aspects of work, so whatever technical expertise they may have is of less direct help to them now. In many organizations today, developing subordinates and helping them move up in the organization is essential to being viewed as a successful manager. When middle managers fail to develop their people, low morale and high turnover are likely to follow.

Top Managers. *The overall direction of an organization is the responsibility of* top managers. Anne Mulcahy, CEO of Xerox, and Meg Whitman, CEO of eBay, are two such managers who lead large, successful companies. Typical titles of top managers are chief executive officer, president, chairman, division president, and executive vice president. Top managers develop goals, policies, and strategies for the entire organization.[13] The goals they set are handed down through the hierarchy, eventually reaching each worker.

The following Strategic Action Competency illustrates how Larry Ellison, the CEO of Oracle, has tried to redirect the strategy of Oracle, a $12 billion software company with more than 49,000 employees.[14] Oracle is in the midst of a significant change and it will take time to see if these changes will be successful. Oracle is second

Strategic Action Competency

Larry Ellison, CEO of Oracle

Ellison and his management team viewed Internet technology as an opportunity to expand Oracle's product line into software for customer relationship management, human resources management, supply chain management, and other applications. Ellison labeled this new system "Fusion Architecture" because it enabled Oracle to develop shared standards for the industry. These standards should make it easier for customers to share data between applications and protect and extend their technology investments. This change in strategy, however, put Oracle into competition with SAP, IBM, Siebel Systems, and SAS. Now, instead of selling a single product, Oracle's salespeople must become knowledgeable about a variety of products sold by these competitors. At first, salespeople lacked the competencies and knowledge to build long-term relationships with companies that had many needs and different systems.

To fully implement this strategy, Ellison realized that changes were needed. He created a "Fusion Strategy Council," an advisory board comprised of 20 customers' chief information officers, to review, validate, and provide input into Fusion's evolving strategy. Kevin Fitzgerald, who manages Oracle's government, education, and health business, reorganized his sales personnel so that each salesperson specialized in certain software applications that cut across various functions. Similarly, George Roberts reorganized his North American sales force so that salespeople who sell to major companies (e.g., Kodak, Boeing, 7-11) would specialize in particular Oracle products.

Ellison also realized that the compensation system needed to change. Salespeople would receive a flat commission and would not be rewarded for overstating a product's capabilities or pushing a product simply to make a monthly sales quota. The goal was to translate Oracle's reward system from a highly aggressive one to one that was more customer oriented. This required Oracle to publish a pricing policy for customers to avoid confusion over pricing options. Oracle even added an annual software licensing fee to make pricing decisions even simpler for customers. Oracle also created a customer relationship dashboard that lets customers continuously monitor the performance of Oracle's programs against the standards set by the contract, analyze exceptions, and enable Oracle to take immediate corrective action.

To learn more about this organization, visit *www.oracle.com*.

only to Microsoft in database management software and has been long known for its aggressive and knowledgeable sales force.

Top managers spend most of their day (more than 75 percent) planning and leading. They spend most of their leading time with key people in organizations other than their own. Top managers—like middle managers—spend little time directly controlling the work of others.

Pressures and demands on top managers can be intense. Tightly scheduled workdays, heavy travel requirements, and workweeks of 60 or more hours are common. A true break is a luxury. Lunch often is eaten during meetings with other managers, business associates, community representatives, or government officials. When there is some free time, eager subordinates vie for a piece of it. Top managers also face expanding public relations duties. They must be able to respond quickly to crises that may create image problems for their organizations. Imagine that you are Albert Stroucken, president of H. B. Fuller. Headquartered in St. Paul, Minnesota, Fuller manufactures industrial glues, coatings, and paints. Among its products is Resistol, glue used for making shoes. For many years children in Central America have sniffed Resistol because it provides a temporary euphoria that relieves hunger and hopelessness. The Federal Drug Administration (FDA) has evidence that Resistol's fumes are addictive and can cause brain damage. Fuller has tried to stop Resistol's use as a drug by reducing the toxicity of the glue and restricting its sales in Honduras and Guatemala. It has not added mustard oil, which causes vomiting, to the glue because the mustard oil affects the characteristics of the glue. Stroucken is faced with the issue of whether Fuller should do more to prevent abuse of its product, including withdrawing it from the market, or continue to make this highly profitable glue.[15]

Six Core Managerial Competencies

3.
Describe the competencies used in managerial work and assess your current competency levels.

We've introduced you to the six core managerial competencies and discussed the various levels of management and what managers do, but you may still be wondering about what it takes to be an effective (or even a great) manager. So, let's look more closely at the six core competencies that managers need in order to succeed.

What It Takes to Be a Great Manager

At the beginning of this chapter, we defined *managerial competencies* as sets of knowledge, skills, behaviors, and attitudes that a manager needs in order to be effective in a wide range of managerial jobs and various organizational settings. We identified six specific competencies as being particularly important: the communication, planning and administration, teamwork, strategic action, multicultural, and self competencies. These competencies are transferable from one organization to the next.[16] Managerial competencies useful to Jimmy McGill, State Farm Insurance Company sales manager responsible for southern Oklahoma, also would be useful if he took a job at the Government Employees Insurance Company (GEICO). They would be useful to the manager of a local coffee shop who is interested in increasing sales during the breakfast hour and to a project manager in Paris charged with developing a new multimedia game for children. Whether you supervise the work of a small team on the shop floor or serve as CEO of a global company, the odds are that with more experience, you will learn how to use these six competencies more effectively. Quite often, real learning comes from thinking about a challenging experience over time. Taking a challenging assignment doesn't guarantee that you will learn from it. For this to occur, managers need to create a situation in which other people are willing to play a constructive role in the learning process.

Regardless of when, where, or how you develop these competencies, you should be able to use them in the future in jobs that you can't yet even imagine holding—or that may not even exist today. One way to enhance your managerial competencies is by studying this book and completing the activities presented at the end of each chapter. By participating in extracurricular activities, you can develop competencies such as communication and teamwork that often can be transferred to a variety of jobs. By taking the appropriate courses and participating in international clubs and associations, you can broaden your knowledge of other countries and build your multicultural competency. By holding an office in a volunteer organization or taking responsibility for organizing a community event, such as spring cleanup day in the park, you can build your planning and administration competency. Because managerial competencies can be learned through such activities, in addition to on the job, campus recruiters pay a great deal of attention to students' involvement in them, instead of just looking at grade point averages.

Communication Competency

Communication competency is your ability to effectively transfer and exchange information that leads to understanding between yourself and others. Because managing involves getting work done through other people, communication competency is essential to effective managerial performance. It includes

- informal communication,
- formal communication, and
- negotiation.

Communication competency transcends the use of a particular communication medium. That is, good communication may involve having a face-to-face conversation, preparing a formal written document, participating in a global meeting via teleconferencing, giving a speech to an audience of several hundred people, or using e-mail to coordinate a project team whose members work in different regions of the country or the world. Scott Dietzen, president of Zimbra, is trying to help his company organize their e-mail system. Why? The average manager gets 470 e-mails a week and spends 15 hours dealing with them. He and his staff are designing a communication system that will enable managers to manage and distribute documents in their office over the Web.

Communication isn't something that you do *to* other people; it is something that you do *with* them. It is both informal and formal. Usually, it is a dynamic, give-and-take process that involves both receiving messages from others and sending messages to others. Besides speaking and writing, it involves listening, observing body language, and picking up on the subtle cues that people sometimes use to modify the meaning of their words. Cliff Hudson, CEO of Sonic, pays attention to all of these communication cues as he visits with employees on the job and with customers. As a member of numerous restaurant associations, he also applies his communication skills to network with other managers from other restaurants.

Of the six managerial competencies that we've identified, communication is perhaps the most fundamental. Unless you can express yourself and understand others in written, oral, and nonverbal (e.g., facial expression and body posture) communication, you can't use the other competencies effectively to accomplish tasks through other people. Nor can you effectively manage the vast network of relationships that link you to other people inside and outside of your organization.

The productive employment of workers of all ages, with varying types of work experience and expertise, of both genders and varied cultural and ethnic backgrounds, means that a basic level of communication competency is seldom enough these days. Managing effectively means getting all workers to contribute their best ideas and efforts to the goals of their organization. At Xerox, Anne Mulcahy knows that this effort requires plenty of spontaneous, informal communication that is sensitive to the different backgrounds and perspectives of employees and customers alike. Moreover, to be sure that you are understood, you need to become comfortable soliciting and accepting feedback.

Through *informal* communication, managers build a social network of contacts. In China, these connections are known as *guanxi*.[17] In Japan, they're called *kankei*, and in Korea they're called *kwankye*. Whatever language you say it in, maintaining social networks is especially important to managerial work. But in a Confucian society, the web of social contacts maintained through informal communication is central to success. In fact, when business leaders in China were asked to identify the factors most important to long-term business success, *guanxi* was the only factor chosen consistently—ahead of choosing the right business location, selecting the right business strategy, and competitive pricing. Through frequent informal communication, managers in all countries lay the groundwork for collaboration within and outside their organizations.

Being able to communicate in more formal situations also is important to managerial effectiveness. *Formal communication*, such as a newsletter, often is used to inform people of relevant events and activities and to keep people up to date on the status of ongoing projects. Public speeches are another example of formal communication. Whether the audience is company executives, professional peers, shareholders, or members of the community, high-impact public presentations can be used to address stakeholder concerns and enhance the firm's reputation.

Formal communication channels are often used by organizations announcing major decisions, such as an acquisition, merger, or downsizing. Downsizing *simply means a reduction in the number of employees employed by the organization.* Although downsizing has been used to improve the financial performance of an organization in the short run, several studies have shown that in the long run, the organization often winds up in worse financial shape. Regardless of its effectiveness, downsizing is a painful experience. The following presents an Ethical Challenge that Bill Ford, former CEO of the Ford Motor Company, faced. In 2006, he announced that the company, which his great-grandfather started, needed to lay off 30,000 employees out of its more than 123,000 in North America and close eight assembly plants in

Ethical Challenge

Plant Closings at Ford Motor Company

Bill Ford believed that nothing short of a cultural revolution would save the family firm. Ford Motor lost more than $4 billion in 2005 and because the company's financial fortunes have fallen, the former CEO of Ford had to take drastic measures. His own board members said, "Just cut away,"

and he did, resigning as CEO in September 2006. He would have liked to have chosen a different tactic, but he realized that Ford had to make some very tough decisions for it to become a better company. Ford was also facing the huge costs of benefits for its retired workers, such as health care, which account for $560 of the cost of each vehicle, compared to only $110 at Toyota. In 2005, Ford lost $258 for every car it produced, compared with a profit of $1,698 for Toyota.

The decision to close plants and lay off thousands of people will not save the Ford Motor Company. Bill Ford knows that the real question is whether his company can produce cars that have the quality, style, and value that drivers want. To survive, Ford must become innovative. During the 1980s and 1990s, Ford was lulled into complacency by the profits they earned from their SUVs and trucks. At the same time, the Japanese started making SUVs and trucks and this competition led to a decrease in profit margins. When the price of gas soared and SUV sales declined, Ford couldn't make a profit. When GM started its "employee pricing campaign" in 2005, Ford had to match it and profits became huge losses. To infuse a sense of innovation, a top-secret Piquette Project has begun. Named after the third floor where his grandfather invented the assembly line, the Piquette Project has put together a new management team. Members of this team have either come from other companies or have spent time overseas where they developed fresh perspectives. He hopes that this new project and Ford's new CEO, Alan Mulally, will save the company.

To learn more about this organization, visit *www.ford.com*.

order to remain competitive in the automobile business. Ford's share of the U.S. auto market had fallen from 24.1 percent in 2000 to 16.7 percent in 2006. Its stock price fell 39 percent in 2004 alone, wiping out more than $10 billion in shareholder value.[18]

Formal communication can also take place at a more personal level, such as during conversations with suppliers and clients. Among bankers, for example, formal communication is essential to managing client relationships. Rachel Cheeks, a manager at PepsiCo, is in charge of cultural diversity programs for PepsiCo. Her role as a diversity manager requires her to work with managers at Frito-Lay, Tropicana, and Quaker Oats to create programs that stimulate and reward cultural diversity programs within their divisions. Although she has traveled to more than 15 countries during the past five years, she isn't expected to be fluent in the language of every country she visits. But she must be able to communicate, often through an interpreter, in all of these cultures. In other words, for Rachel Cheeks, effective communication goes hand in hand with the multicultural perspective needed in a global firm.

Cheeks' job also involves *negotiating*—sometimes at great distances. One negotiation with a bottling plant in South Africa was particularly intense, with down-to-the-wire discussions stretching over days. Working from her hotel room, she needed to build consensus on goals and commitment to achieving them. Good negotiators learn to seek contrary opinions and find ways to respond to the divergent views they uncover. Building consensus and commitment is useful for negotiations with bosses, peers, and subordinates, as well as with clients. Managers also must be able to negotiate to obtain resources for their subordinates and to settle disputes that arise among various stakeholders.[19]

The following Communication Competency feature highlights how the Container Store communicates with its employees. Recognized in 2006 by *Fortune* magazine as one of America's Best Places to Work, the Container Store managers know how important it is to build trust and solid working relationships with employees. They also know that it's important for all managers to be seen as people who are committed to sharing information with others and developing a climate in which they and their employees have open information exchanges. Notice the various forms of communications that the Container Store uses to communicate with its employees.[20]

With employee turnover of greater than 100 percent in most retail stores but only 15 to 18 percent at the Container Store, how do its managers attract new employees and retain employees?

In 2005, sales exceeded $450 million for its 34 stores. How did it get this ranking? First, it invests in its employees. Every first-year, full-time employee gets an average of 241 hours of training. The Container Store hires people with passion, intelligence, enthusiasm, and attitude. If an employee recommends a person who is later hired, the employee who made the recommendation receives $200 for every person that they recruit. Once hired, they are given a performance review after 45 days. Tindell believes that in 45 days, managers will know if the person is a superstar or if he or she needs to be let go. Performance reviews are also provided both formally and informally by ongoing communication with managers, who not only ask what their people need to do their jobs well, but also regularly assess how to provide necessary assistance. Performance metrics, such as sales per hour and number of systems-hours, are discussed on a daily and weekly basis. Also, each employee is evaluated against 10 characteristics of a great employee at the Container Store, including attitude, passion for knowledge, and communication. Areas of strength and improvement are discussed.

Each store has a back room where new products are housed prior to display. Employees receive formal training on how to display these new products and how to communicate the products' benefits to customers. According to Garrett Boone and Kip Tindell, the Container Store's CEOs, "Nothing goes out on the sales floor until our people are ready for it." This program is coupled with extensive training programs designed to meet individual skills and job functions and team-based incentive programs. Moreover, a "super sales trainer" serves each store. These trainers are top sales performers who know how to sell the hard stuff and who have an aptitude for leadership and strong communication and presentation skills. These people give on-the-spot help to employees who ask, but employees are encouraged to take responsibility for their own development.

Guided by what Boone and Tindell call a "do-unto-others" philosophy, the Container Store's more than 4,000 employees, of whom 27 percent are minority and 60 percent are women, work in an environment that ensures open communication throughout the company, including regular discussions of store sales, company goals, and expansion plans. Once a year, Tindell gives a PowerPoint presentation to all employees. It is the same one that he gives to the board of directors. It includes a full disclosure of profits and losses, real estate investments trends, and the topics discussed by members of the Board.

To learn more about this organization, visit *www.containerstore.com*.

Because managers spend so much of their time communicating, recruiters look for people who can communicate effectively. In fact, we can't stress enough the importance of good communication. At a time when organizations increasingly expect employees to work with minimal supervision and show more initiative, competent oral, written, and electronic communication is essential. For more details about communication competency, refer to Table 1.2.

Planning and Administration Competency

Planning and administration competency *involves deciding what tasks need to be done, determining how they can be done, allocating resources to enable them to be done, and then monitoring progress to ensure that they are done.* For many people, planning and administration competency comes to mind first when they think about managers and managing. Included in this competency are

▶ information gathering, analysis, and problem solving;

▶ planning and organizing of projects;

Table 1.2   Dimensions of Communication Competency

INFORMAL COMMUNICATION

Promotes two-way communication by asking for feedback, listening, and creating a give-and-take conversation.
Has awareness of others' feelings.
Builds strong interpersonal relationships with people.

FORMAL COMMUNICATION

Informs people of relevant events and activities and keeps them up to date.
Makes persuasive, high-impact public presentations and handles questions well.
Writes clearly, concisely, and effectively, using a variety of computer-based resources.

NEGOTIATION

Negotiates effectively on behalf of a team over roles and resources.
Is skilled at developing relationships and exercising influence upward with superiors.
Takes decisive and fair actions when handling problem subordinates.

▶ time management; and

▶ budgeting and financial management.

When Cliff Hudson, CEO of Sonic, describes what his workday is like, he puts it this way: "Basically, the whole day comes down to a series of choices." To help him hone his planning and administration competency, Hudson and his staff analyzed his day, and his staff helped him reshape his management approach. Hudson instinctively knew that *information gathering, analysis, and problem solving* are important. He also recognized that customers are a rich source of useful information but that they can easily eat up a whole day. His staff helped him understand that he could delegate the handling of some types of customer phone calls in order to free up 25 percent of his time for meeting directly with customers.

Planning and organizing projects usually means working with employees to clarify broad objectives, discuss resource allocation, and agree to completion dates. Thus Hudson spends 40 percent of his day with employees and customers, 25 percent on the Internet, 10 percent on the telephone, and the rest on paperwork. Because there are more problems and opportunities than he possibly can attend to, Hudson needs to *manage his time* and delegate effectively.

Managers also are accountable for *budgeting and managing financial resources.* Boards of directors and shareholders of public corporations hold CEOs such as Anne Mulcahy of Xerox, Rick Wagoner of GM, and Bob Nardelli of Home Depot fiscally accountable. In nonprofit and government organizations, trustees, various regulatory bodies, and elected officials oversee fiscal management.

© Image Source/Getty

Effective planning of time and resources is crucial to running a successful organization.

Table 1.3	**Dimensions of Planning and Administration Competency**

INFORMATION GATHERING, ANALYSIS, AND PROBLEM SOLVING

Monitors information and uses it to identify symptoms, problems, and alternative solutions.
Makes timely decisions.
Takes calculated risks and anticipates the consequences.

PLANNING AND ORGANIZING PROJECTS

Develops plans and schedules to achieve goals efficiently.
Assigns priorities to tasks and delegates responsibility.
Determines, obtains, and organizes necessary resources to accomplish the task.

TIME MANAGEMENT

Handles several issues and projects at one time but doesn't spread self too thin.
Monitors and keeps to a schedule or changes schedule if needed.
Works effectively under time pressure.

BUDGETING AND FINANCIAL MANAGEMENT

Understands budgets, cash flows, financial reports, and annual reports and regularly uses such information to make decisions.
Keeps accurate and complete financial records.
Creates budgetary guidelines for others and works within the guidelines given by others.

In Table 1.3, we highlight the various dimensions that make up the planning and administration competency.

Teamwork Competency

Accomplishing tasks through small groups of people who are collectively responsible and whose job requires coordination is teamwork competency. Managers in organizations that utilize teams can become more effective by

▶ designing teams properly,

▶ creating a supportive team environment, and

▶ managing team dynamics appropriately.

In a study of more than 400 organizations and 80,000 managers, the Gallup Organization, a public opinion poll-taking company, found that the best managed companies used employees in teams.[21] Improving customer service was the main reason given for their use, followed by decreasing absenteeism and improving productivity. At Southwest Airlines, effective teamwork makes it possible for ground crews to turn around a plane at the gate in less than 20 minutes. Regardless of their job titles, all employees work together to get passengers unloaded and loaded. When necessary, pilots, flight attendants, and whoever else is available pitch in to ensure that a flight leaves the boarding gate on schedule.

When people think of teamwork, they often make a distinction between the team members and a team leader. We don't hold this view of teamwork. Instead, we view teamwork as a competency that involves taking the lead at times, supporting others who are taking the lead at other times, and collaborating with others in the organization on projects that don't even have a designated team leader. We hold this view of teamwork competency because most managerial work involves doing all of these activities simultaneously.

Designing the team is the first step for any team project and usually is the responsibility of a manager or team leader. But in self-managed teams, the entire team participates in the design. Team design involves formulating goals to be achieved, defining tasks to be done, and identifying the staffing needed to accomplish those tasks. Team members should identify with the team's goals and feel committed to accomplishing them. Members of a well-designed team understand its tasks and how its performance will be measured; they aren't confused about which tasks are theirs and which tasks belong to some other team. A well-designed team has just the right number of members. Having too many members leaves room for free riders; too few creates too much stress and leaves the team feeling incapable of successfully achieving its goals.

A well-designed team is capable of high performance, but it needs a *supportive environment* to achieve its full potential.[22] All team members should have the competencies needed to create a supportive environment. In a supportive environment, team members are empowered to take actions based on their best judgment, without always seeking approval first from the team leader or project manager. Support also involves eliciting contributions from members whose unique competencies are important for the team and recognizing, praising, and rewarding both minor victories and major successes. A manager having good teamwork competency respects other people and is respected and even liked by them in return. Managers who lack teamwork competency often are viewed as being rude, abrupt, and unsympathetic, making others feel inadequate and resentful. Fundamentally, creating a supportive environment involves coaching, counseling, and mentoring team members to improve their performance in the near term and prepare them for future challenges.

How an organization fosters teamwork is often just as important as teamwork itself. Managers with the greatest likelihood of developing their employees' teamwork competency are those who have input from all levels of the organization, including members of the team, employees who support the team, those who will administer the plan, and even customers. Managers need to pay attention to *managing team dynamics*. If team members remain ignorant about a process, they are more likely to reject it out of hand. People want to be involved. The Teamwork Competency feature highlights how teams work at Whole Foods.[23]

© Harry Cabluck/AP Photos

Employees at this Whole Foods Market in Austin, Texas, team up to provide better customer service because all work is teamwork.

Teams at Whole Foods

The Whole Foods Market culture is based on decentralized teamwork. Each of the stores is a profit center that typically has 10 self-managed teams—produce, grocery, prepared foods, and so on—with designated leaders and clear performance targets. The team leaders in each store are a team, store leaders in each region are a team, and the company's six regional presidents are a team. Three principles define how the company operates.

The first principle is *all work is teamwork*. Everyone who joins Whole Foods quickly grasps the importance of teamwork. That's because teams—and only teams—have the power to approve new hires for full-time jobs. Store leaders screen candidates and recommend them for a job on a specific team. But it takes a two-thirds vote of the team, after what is usually a 30-day trial period, for the candidate to become a full-time employee. Team members are tough on new hires for another reason: money. The company's gain-sharing program ties bonuses directly to team performance—specifically, to sales per labor hour, the most important productivity measurement at Whole Foods.

The second principle is *anything worth doing is worth measuring*. Whole Foods takes that simple principle to extremes—and then shares what it measures with everyone in the company. John Mackey, the CEO, calls it a "no-secrets" management philosophy. He states, "In most companies, management controls information and therefore controls people. By sharing information, we stay alighted to the vision of shared fate." The reports are indispensable to the teams, which make the decisions about labor spending, ordering, and pricing—the factors that determine profitability.

The third principle is *being your own toughest competitor*. "All-for-one" doesn't imply complacency. Whole Foods is serious about accountability. Teams are expected to set ambitious goals and achieve them. Teams compete against their own goals for sales, growth, and productivity.

To learn more about this organization, visit *www.wholefoods.com*.

Because more and more organizations are relying on teams to improve quality, productivity, and customer service, it becomes increasingly important for you to develop your teamwork competency and become a productive team member. Table 1.4 provides more detail about teamwork competency.

Table 1.4	Dimensions of Teamwork Competency

DESIGNING TEAMS

Formulates clear objectives that inspire team members to perform.
Appropriately staffs the team, taking into account the value of diverse ideas and technical skills needed.
Defines responsibilities for the team as a whole and assigns tasks and responsibilities to individual team members as appropriate.

CREATING A SUPPORTIVE ENVIRONMENT

Creates an environment in which effective teamwork is expected, recognized, praised, and rewarded.
Assists the team in identifying and acquiring the resources it needs to accomplish its goals.
Acts as a coach, counselor, and mentor, being patient with team members as they learn.

MANAGING TEAM DYNAMICS

Understands the strengths and weaknesses of team members and uses their strengths to accomplish tasks as a team.
Brings conflict and dissent into the open and uses it to enhance performance.
Shares credit with others.

Strategic Action Competency

Understanding the overall mission and values of the organization and ensuring that employees' actions match with them defines strategic action competency. Strategic action competency includes

- understanding the industry,
- understanding the organization, and
- taking strategic actions.

Today, employees at all levels and in all functional areas are being challenged to think strategically in order to perform their jobs better. They are expected to recognize that shifts in a company's strategic direction are to be expected—even anticipated. Managers and employees who understand the industry can accurately anticipate strategic trends and prepare for the future needs of the organization, and they are less likely to find themselves looking for new jobs when the organization changes direction.

One manager who has proved that he is extremely good at *understanding the industry* in which he operates is Robert Siegel, CEO of Lacoste, a global apparel company whose logo is a crocodile.[24] Siegel remembers when the elegant crocodile was worn by star athletes, students, and others on their polos. Since taking over the company in 2002, sales have grown 800 percent and Lacoste worldwide has developed into a more than $2 billion company.

When Siegel took over in 2002, the industry had changed and Lacoste hadn't kept up with the latest trends, so the brand had already been withdrawn from the American market because of its poor image. He redesigned the product to appeal to a younger crowd. With teenage girls in mind, he introduced the Lacoste stretch pique polo, a Lycra-cotton shirt with a sleeker fit, in 25 vibrant shades. Siegel knew that in order to revive the company, he needed to develop a premium brand and retool its sporty image. He signed top tennis contracts with Andy Roddick from the United States and French pros Richard Gasquet and Natalie Dechy. Siegel also signed Natalie Portman, Katie Couric, and other high-profile television people. Taking advice from retailers, he increased the price of new shirts, making them the most expensive polo shirt on the market. Siegel understood that luxury is now a mass market, but to keep up a luxury image, Lacoste sells to only high-end department stores, such as Barneys, Saks Fifth Avenue, and Neiman Marcus.

Strategic action competency also involves *understanding the organization*—not just the particular unit in which a manager works—as a system of interrelated parts. It includes comprehending how departments, functions, and divisions relate to one another and how a change in one can affect others. A manager with a well-developed strategic action competency can diagnose and assess different types of management problems and issues that might arise. Such a manager thinks in terms of relative priorities rather than ironclad goals and criteria. All managers, but especially top managers, need strategic action competency. Top managers, such as John Mackey of Whole Foods or Anne Mulcahy of Xerox, must perceive changes in the organization's environment and be prepared to *take strategic actions*. For more detail about strategic action competency, refer to Table 1.5.

© Mat Szwajkos/Getty Images

Robert Siegel, CEO of Lacoste, pictured here with tennis star Andy Roddick, revived the infamous crocodile, appealing to today's younger generations.

Snapshot

"Sony must sell off businesses that don't fit its core strategy of fusing gadgets with films, music, and game software. That means selling off its businesses in its Sony Financial Holdings, which are very profitable."

**Howard Stringer,
CEO, Sony**

Table 1.5	**Dimensions of Strategic Action Competency**

UNDERSTANDING THE INDUSTRY

Understands the industry and quickly recognizes when changes in the industry create significant threats and opportunities.

Stays informed of the actions of competitors and strategic partners.

Can analyze general trends in the industry and their implications for the future.

UNDERSTANDING THE ORGANIZATION

Understands the concerns of stakeholders.

Understands the strengths and limitations of various business strategies.

Understands the distinctive competencies of the organization.

TAKING STRATEGIC ACTIONS

Assigns priorities and makes decisions that are consistent with the firm's mission and strategic goals.

Recognizes the management challenges of alternative strategies and addresses them.

Establishes tactical and operational goals that facilitate strategy implementation.

Multicultural Competency

Multicultural competency *refers to understanding, appreciating, and responding to diverse political, cultural, and economic issues across and within nations.* Not all organizations have global markets for their products and services. Nor do all organizations need to set up operations in other countries to take advantage of tax laws and labor that is cheaper or better trained. Nevertheless, over the course of your career, you probably will work for an organization that has an international division or department. To be prepared for such opportunities, you should begin to develop your multicultural competency, which is reflected in

▶ cultural knowledge and understanding, and

▶ cultural openness and sensitivity.

In the course of growing up and being educated in a particular country or region, people naturally develop cultural knowledge and understanding of forces that shape their lives and the conduct of business.[25] These forces include geography and climate, political processes and orientations, economic systems and trends, history, religion, values, beliefs, and local customs. By the time you become a manager in your home country, your own culture has become second nature to you, so you don't need to devote much time to developing further general knowledge and awareness of it. However, unless you have traveled extensively, or have specifically studied other cultures as part of your education, you probably have much less general knowledge and understanding of other countries, except perhaps those that share a border with your own country. Yet because business is becoming global, many managers are now expected to develop *knowledge and an understanding* of at least a few other cultures, such as those where suppliers are located or those with newly emerging markets that can help sustain their companies.

Simply knowing about other cultures isn't sufficient; appropriate attitudes and skills are needed to translate this knowledge into effective performance. An open attitude about cultural differences and sensitivity to them are especially important for anyone who must operate across cultural boundaries. *Openness and sensitivity* involve, first and foremost, recognizing that culture makes a difference in how people think and act. You can't assume that everyone will think and act as you do, nor that everyone will automatically understand your point of view. Successful managers taking an international assignment find themselves asking more questions, making decisions on less information, tolerating different kinds of people, communicating more, and taking action without understanding how everything works. Second, openness and sensitivity mean actively considering how another culture might differ from your own and examining how your own culture affects your behavior. For example, is a gift expected and, if so, what kind of gift? Are flowers appropriate? What about the exchange of business cards? These and hundreds of others "little" things can make or break you on an international assignment.

Knowledge about other cultures and an open attitude and sensitivity about cultural differences set the stage for working with people from other backgrounds.[26] In any culture, appropriate language, social etiquette, and negotiation skills help in developing effective work relationships. Depending on your job, you may also need to learn country-specific laws, accounting methods, hiring techniques, and so on. Because there are so many cultures and because predicting which cultures will be most important to you in the future is so difficult, you shouldn't expect to develop multicultural competency relevant to many of the world's cultures. But neither can you put off beginning to build a good foundation.

Language and cultural differences require organizations to consider product names when selling in international markets. Inadequate translation can result in a negative image for the product and company. Global markets are complex and often difficult to understand. The following Multicultural Competency feature highlights some problems L'Oréal, a cosmetics company, faced when it entered the $9 billion Chinese market. As late as 1992, Chinese governmental officials discouraged women from using lipstick and other bourgeois displays of beauty. Today, however, some 90 million urban women in China spend 10 percent or more of their income on face cream, lipstick, mascara, and the like in Shanghai, Beijing, Hong Kong, and other urban centers.[27]

© Flying Colours Ltd./Digital Vision/Getty Images

Managers who take the initiative to learn about cultural differences greatly broaden their understanding of people. This helps them strengthen their connections, leading to future business opportunities.

Multicultural Competency

L'Oréal Goes to China

The Chinese tradition equates beauty with fine skin. Poems from the Tang dynasty and even a millennium earlier describe women as "jade white" and "creamy tinted." China's ancient tales have mothers giving their daughters pots of face cream to take on long journeys. Even in small villages today, grandmothers still drink a mixture of ground pearls mixed in water in the belief that it keeps their skin white. Herbal recipes for keeping Asians' faces translucent can be found in ancient imperial records. Unfortunately, the desire for whitening is sometimes mistaken as a desire to take on the trappings of Western beauty aesthetics in a country that decries breast implants, nose restructuring, and eye lifts.

Modernity versus tradition is a major battleground for the French-based L'Oréal. It has opened a new laboratory in Pudong, a suburb of

Shanghai, to develop pigments, waxes, and oils. Biochemists oversee the effectiveness of skin-whitening creams, the ovens that heat mixtures to test stability, and the two-way mirrors that enable them to observe the way Chinese women apply face creams and makeup. Chinese herbs, flowers, and roots are tested and researched to understand their impact on skin and hair. Hua jiap, the flower of the prickly ash tree, is reputed to clear up acne. It is mixed among the traditional whitening agents such as ginkgo leaf, ginseng, and mulberry. "We cannot separate the beauty and the culture," says Didier Saint-Leger, director of L'Oréal in China.

Selling to the masses in China is something entirely new for L'Oreal and other cosmetic companies. Retailing in rural China is badly managed, yet this market includes about 400 million women. L'Oréal needs to reach out to women who wash their hair once a week. For those who use only shampoo, the next step is to get them to buy conditioner and ultimately coloring, gel, and mousse. But, according to Paolo Gasparrini, president of L'Oréal China, it is extremely difficult to sell a product for $2 where the average household income varies between $37 and $50 a month.

To learn more about this organization, visit *www.loreal.com.*

Managers do not share the same cultural knowledge and understanding around the world. Global managers must understand other societies' religions, languages, values, laws, and ethics. Knowing the behaviors fostered by other cultures can help determine which course of action is most appropriate. For more detail about the multicultural competency, refer to Table 1.6.

Self-Management Competency

Self-management competency *refers to developing yourself and taking responsibility for your life at work and beyond.* Often, when things don't go well, people tend to blame their difficulties on the situations in which they find themselves or on others. Effective managers don't fall into this trap. The self-management competency includes

▶ integrity and ethical conduct,

▶ personal drive and resilience,

▶ balancing work and life issues, and

▶ self-awareness and development.

You may be thinking that developing your self-management competency really doesn't require much time and effort. Dee Hock would disagree. More than 1 billion people use Visa card, but did you know that Dee Hock is the man who built this

Table 1.6	Dimensions of Multicultural Competency

CULTURAL KNOWLEDGE AND UNDERSTANDING

Stays informed of political, social, and economic trends and events around the world.
Recognizes the impact of global events on the organization.
Understands, reads, and speaks more than one language fluently.

CULTURAL OPENNESS AND SENSITIVITY

Understands the nature of national, ethnic, and cultural differences and is open to examining these differences honestly and objectively.
Is sensitive to cultural cues and is able to adapt quickly in novel situations.
Appropriately adjusts own behavior when interacting with people from various national, ethnic, and cultural backgrounds.

worldwide powerhouse? Since 1970, when Hock founded Visa, the company has grown from an idea to a service that operates in more than 20 million locations in 150 countries processing more than 100 million credit and debit card purchases daily with annual revenues exceeding $1.5 trillion. Dee Hock, the man behind this phenomenal success story, isn't a household name, but his success as a manager is unquestioned—which is why he is such a popular speaker at CEO gatherings even though he has retired from Visa.[28]

Just as customers expect companies to behave ethically, organizations expect their employees to *show integrity and act ethically*. When recruiting entry-level employees—who don't yet have a long record of employment or much technical expertise—these qualities may be the most important ones that employers look for. According to a recent Gallup poll, when companies hire young employees, they are far more concerned with the employees' integrity and interest in the job than with their specific technical skills and aptitudes.

Personal drive and resilience are especially important when someone sets out to do something no one else has done and when that person faces setbacks and failures. As its founder, Jeff Bezos needed personal drive and resilience when he decided to start Amazon.com. Because there were no other online companies, banks and venture capital firms were not interested in funding him. It was his parents who originally gave him the $300,000 to start the company.

Future managers won't succeed unless they can find a way to *balance work and life issues*. According to a Catalyst Organization survey of 1,725 women-of-color managers and *Fortune* magazine's study of 1,735 business students, building a family is a top priority for the majority of the respondents. Hoping to have it all, 75 percent gave developing a career a top rating also.[29] These demands, which often conflict, and other family concerns led Congress to pass and the president to sign the Family and Medical Leave Act in 1993. In addition, many of the best companies to work for, including Southwest Airlines, Cisco Systems, SAS Institute, and Edward Jones, have family-friendly policies. The self-management competency is needed to decide when and how best to take advantage of such policies. New mothers and fathers alike may feel pressure to return to work soon after the arrival of a new family member, rather than take the entire leave allowed them. Having succumbed to work pressures, many parents experience pangs of guilt or anxiety when they look at the family photo sitting on the corner of the desk. Knowing your own work and life priorities, and finding a way to juggle them all, may be the most difficult management challenge many of you will face.

The dynamic work environment calls for *self-awareness and development* (as well as the ability continually to unlearn and relearn!). That includes both task-related learning and learning about you. On the one hand, task-related learning can directly improve your performance in your current job and prepare you to take on new jobs. Learning about yourself, on the other hand, can help you make wiser choices about which types of jobs you are likely to enjoy. With fewer opportunities for promotions and upward advancement, finding work that you enjoy doing is even more important today than in the past. Taking responsibility for your own career development—by understanding the type of work you find satisfying and developing the competencies that you will need—may be the best route to long-term success.[30]

Research shows that people who take advantage of the development and training opportunities that employers offer learn much from them and advance more quickly than those who don't take advantage of them. Derailment awaits managers who fail to develop their competencies. A derailed manager is one who has moved into a position of managerial responsibility but has little chance of future advancement or gaining new responsibilities. The most common reasons for derailment are (1) problems with interpersonal relationships and inability to lead a team (weak in teamwork competency);

Snapshot

"My strengths and weaknesses haven't changed a lot in 51 years. The important thing is to recognize the things you don't do well and build a team that reflects what you know the company needs."
Anne Mulcahy, CEO, Xerox

Irene Rosenfeld, CEO of Kraft Foods, Inc., has proven to be highly competent in several areas—self-management competency being one of these.

© Kraft Foods, Inc. HO/AP Photo

(2) inability to learn, develop, and adapt (weak in self-management competency); (3) performance problems (weak in planning and administration competency); and (4) having a narrow functional perspective (lacking strong strategic action and multicultural competencies).[31] Table 1.7 provides more detail about self-management competency.

Exploring Your Managerial Competencies

To those who want to become effective managers, the old saying "know thyself" is still a difficult task for many of us. We believe that until you know yourself—your strengths and weaknesses—you will not become an effective manager. Effective managers never lie to themselves, know their flaws as well as their strengths, and deal with their flaws directly.

Figure 1.4 gives you a road map of the book. Part 1 focuses on giving you an overview of management. You should be familiar with the six core competencies that we will feature throughout the book, the four functions that all managers play in organizations, the levels of management, and an example of the ethical challenge facing managers. In the next chapter, we will introduce you to some important viewpoints that have had staying power throughout the history of management. We also indicate how many of the concepts illus-

Table 1.7	Dimensions of Self-Management Competency

INTEGRITY AND ETHICAL CONDUCT

Has clear personal standards that serve as a foundation for maintaining a sense of integrity and ethical conduct.
Is willing to admit mistakes.
Accepts responsibility for own actions.

PERSONAL DRIVE AND RESILIENCE

Seeks responsibility and is ambitious and motivated to achieve objectives.
Works hard to get things done.
Shows perseverance in the face of obstacles and bounces back from failure.

BALANCING WORK AND LIFE ISSUES

Strikes a reasonable balance between work and other life activities so that neither aspect of living is neglected.
Takes good care of self, mentally and physically, and uses constructive outlets to vent frustration and reduce tension.
Assesses and establishes own life- and work-related goals.

SELF-AWARENESS AND DEVELOPMENT

Has clear personal and career goals.
Uses strengths to advantage while seeking to improve or compensate for weaknesses.
Analyzes and learns from work and life experiences.

Figure 1.4 | **Learning Framework for *Managing:* A Competency-Based Approach**

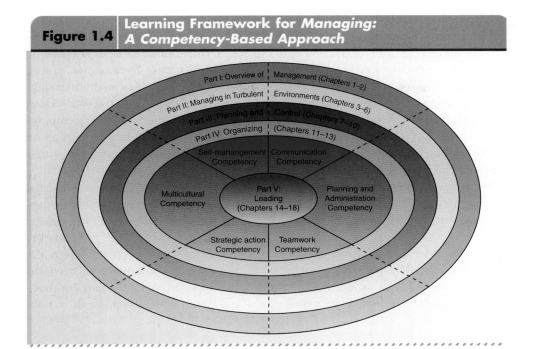

Part I: Overview of Management (Chapters 1–2)

Part II: Managing in Turbulent Environments (Chapters 3–6)

Part III: Planning and Control (Chapters 7–10)

Part IV: Organizing (Chapters 11–13)

Self-management Competency

Communication Competency

Multicultural Competency

Part V: Leading (Chapters 14–18)

Planning and Administration Competency

Strategic action Competency

Teamwork Competency

trated in these historical viewpoints are being used by practicing managers today to increase the effectiveness of their organization.

Part 2 introduces you to issues managers face in trying to navigate their organizations through turbulent environments. This part opens with a focus on the ethical and social responsibility challenges facing managers and their organizations. It continues with chapters that focus on how various environmental forces impact the management of organizations, issues that managers face when operating globally, and challenges facing entrepreneurs as they start up a new business.

Part 3 focuses on the planning and control functions of management. This part highlights the importance of choosing a corporate and business strategy to be competitive in its industry, various types of decisions managers usually make, and how various planning and decisions aids can help managers improve the effectiveness of their organization. The part concludes with a chapter that focuses on control processes used by managers to monitor the behavior of their employees and organization. We also discuss the role of corporate governance and how organizations use various controls to increase the effectiveness of their organization.

The chapters in Part 4 focus on how managers design their organizations to achieve their strategic goals. Basic types of organization are highlighted along with a discussion of how managers can change their organizations and introduce innovation to be more responsive to key stakeholders. This part concludes with a chapter on how organizations can effectively manage their human resources to increase employee retention and overall effectiveness.

Part 5 focuses on leading. It opens with a discussion of the motivational strategies that managers can use to increase the productivity of their employees. It then focuses on the leadership behaviors that managers can use to influence the behaviors of employees and the development strategies they can adopt to improve the performance of their employees. This part also focuses on the role that effective communication systems play in organizations. The role of teamwork is highlighted. Your ability to work effectively in teams is an important role that you need to master. Finally, we conclude this part with a discussion on organizational culture and cultural diversity.

Throughout this book, both in the text and in the exercises and cases at the end of each chapter, we present material to help you develop the six managerial competencies. In Figure 1.4, we indicate how these six management competencies are used by managers in carrying out their four basic managerial functions. For example, you've already read about how managers at the Container Store use their communication competency to help develop employees' passion for customer service. You've also seen how important teamwork is at Whole Foods and the competencies needed by employees to work in this organization. Examples such as these will help you develop an understanding of how all six competencies contribute to performance in jobs that involve managerial work.

We believe that continual development of your managerial competencies is essential because the challenges you will face on the job are constantly changing. In addition, fundamental changes in the business environment will continue to occur. To ensure that your organization keeps pace with these changes, you will want to improve its performance. Identifying your strengths and development needs is the first important step in the process of improving your managerial performance. To help you assess your strengths and weakness, we have included a self-assessment competency questionnaire on pages 33–38. We asked you to complete it earlier, but if you have not done so, please do so now.

Chapter Summary ....

In this chapter we introduced several concepts that you need to understand in order to be a successful manager in the years ahead. Because the nature and scope of management are changing so rapidly, no simple prescription can be given for how to manage. Rather, managers today and in the future need to develop six important competencies to enable them to lead dynamic organizations and tackle a variety of emerging organizational issues. You now should be able to do the following.

Learning Goals ....

1. Explain why managerial competencies are important.

Your ability to learn is central to becoming an effective manager. We are concerned with how you can develop the competencies needed to become more effective as a leader. Managers need to master six competencies: communication, planning and administration, teamwork, strategic action, multicultural, and self-management. Each competency was discussed independently, but in practice, it is hard to know where one stops and another starts. Improve & excel

2. Discuss the basic functions and levels of management.

The managerial functions—planning, organizing, leading, and controlling—are what managers do. Managers at different levels in an organization spend their time differently, but they all spend at least some time performing each function. The three basic levels of management are first line, middle, and top. First-line managers are directly responsible for the production of goods and services. They supervise workers and solve specific problems. Middle managers coordinate the work of several first-line managers or direct the operations of a functional department. They translate top management's goals into specific goals and programs for implementation. Top managers establish overall organizational goals and direct the activities of an entire organization or a major segment of an organization.

Managers at different levels divide their time among the managerial functions quite differently. First-line managers spend most of their time leading and controlling and the rest planning and organizing. Middle managers spend most of their time organizing and leading and the rest planning and controlling. Top managers spend most of their time planning and leading and very little time directly organizing and controlling. Managerial work also varies in scope, broadening at each higher level.

3. Describe the competencies used in managerial work and assess your current competency levels.

To be an effective manager in a dynamic environment, you will need to master the six managerial competencies discussed in this chapter. You can develop these competencies through study, training, and experience. By doing so, you can prepare yourself for a variety of jobs in various industries and countries. You can continue practicing your managerial competencies by completing the exercises at the end of this chapter.

Key Terms and Concepts

Communication competency	Manager	administration competency
Competency	Managerial competencies	Self-management competency
Controlling	Managing	
Downsizing	Middle managers	Strategic action competency
First-line managers	Multicultural competency	
Functional managers	Organization	Teamwork competency
General managers	Organizing	Top managers
Leading	Planning	
	Planning and	

Questions for Discussion and Reflective Thinking

1. What management functions does Anne Mulcahy perform as CEO of Xerox?

2. List the three managerial competencies that have led to your success so far in descending order. We have also suggested that for every strength, there can be a weakness. List your strengths and, for each strength listed, determine how that strength might get you into trouble.

3. Which competencies are needed for a person to work at L'Oréal in China?

4. Sally Zuponcic, group manager for Information Technology at PepsiCo Business Solutions, says, "The Internet and e-mail are making it easier to communicate with people across cultures." Do you agree or disagree? Why?

5. Think of a team of which you are a member. Using the Teamwork Competency section of the Experiential Exercise: Self-Assessment Inventory on pages 34–35, evaluate the team's effectiveness.

6. Why is it so difficult to become an effective middle manager?

7. What mix of competencies does Larry Ellison use at Oracle?

8. How does a person's background affect the development of his or her managerial competencies?

9. Describe some ways that you acquire new competencies that will help you be an effective manager.

10. When you think about your career, certain events stand out in your mind. What competencies stand out from these events?

DEVELOPING YOUR COMPETENCIES

Instructions (for self-administration)

Each of the five following statements describes a level of attainment on a dimension of a managerial competency. How well do you think each statement describes you? Following these statements is a list of 95 characteristics that are representative of effective, experienced managers. Next to each characteristic, fill in the number corresponding to the level-of-attainment statement that applies best to you. Presenting an accurate self-appraisal is important to understanding your current competencies and what you need to do to develop them further.

Level of Attainment

1. I have very little relevant experience. I have not yet begun to develop this characteristic.
2. I think that I am weak in this characteristic. I have had relevant experience, but I have not performed well.
3. I think that I am about average on this characteristic. It will take a good deal of focused effort for me to be consistently effective.
4. I think that I am above average on this characteristic. I need to develop this characteristic further in order to be highly effective.
5. I think that I am outstanding on this characteristic. I need to maintain my strong effectiveness on this characteristic.

Characteristic

___3___ 1. Seeks out and listens to others who have contrary opinions.

___5___ 2. In speaking with others, is able to make people feel comfortable in different situations.

___4___ 3. Varies communication approach when dealing with others from different backgrounds.

___3___ 4. Builds strong interpersonal relationships with a diverse range of people.

___4___ 5. Shows genuine sensitivity to the feelings of others.

___2___ 6. Informs people of events that are relevant to them.

___2___ 7. Makes persuasive, high-impact presentations before groups.

___2___ 8. When making formal presentations, handles questions from the audience well.

___4___ 9. Writes clearly and concisely.

___4___ 10. Communicates effectively using electronic media.

___4___ 11. Is comfortable using power associated with leadership roles.

___3___ 12. Skilled at influencing superiors.

___5___ 13. Skilled at influencing peers.

___4___ 14. When addressing problems, finds solutions that others perceive as fair.

___4___ 15. In conflict situations, helps parties move toward win-win situations.

___4___ 16. Monitors information that is relevant to ongoing projects and activities.

___5___ 17. Obtains and uses relevant information to identify symptoms and underlying problems.

___5___ 18. Makes decisions on time.

___4___ 19. When taking risks, is able to anticipate negative and positive consequences.

___5___ 20. Knows when expert knowledge is needed and seeks it out to solve problems.

___45___ 21. Develops plans and schedules to achieve specific goals efficiently.

___45___ 22. Prioritizes tasks in order to stay focused on those that are most important.

___3___ 23. Can organize people around specific tasks to help them work together toward a common objective.

___1___ 24. Is comfortable delegating responsibility for tasks to others.

___4___ 25. Anticipates possible problems and develops plans for how to deal with them.

___3___ 26. Handles several issues and projects at the same time but doesn't spread self too thin.

___4___ 27. Monitors and keeps to a schedule or negotiates changes in the schedule if needed.

___2___ 28. Works effectively under time pressure.

___2___ 29. Knows when to permit interruptions and when to screen them out.

___1___ 30. Knows when to renegotiate established deadlines in order to deliver satisfactory results.

_____1_____ 31. Understands budgets, cash flow, financial reports, and annual reports.

_____1_____ 32. Regularly uses budgets and financial reports to make decisions.

_____1_____ 33. Keeps accurate and complete financial records.

_____1_____ 34. Creates budgetary guidelines for others.

_____1_____ 35. Works well within the budgetary guidelines given by others.

_____4_____ 36. Formulates clear goals that inspire team members' commitment.

_____5_____ 37. Appropriately selects team members, taking into account diversity of viewpoints and technical skills.

_____5_____ 38. Provides team members with a clear vision of what is to be accomplished by the team as a whole.

_____5_____ 39. Assigns tasks and responsibilities to individual team members consistent with their competencies and interests.

_____3_____ 40. Creates a process for monitoring team performance.

_____5_____ 41. Creates a team setting in which team members feel that their suggestions make a difference.

_____3_____ 42. Recognizes, praises, and rewards team members for their contributions.

_____5_____ 43. Assists the team in acquiring the resources and support it needs to accomplish its goals.

_____4_____ 44. Acts as a coach, counselor, and mentor for team members.

_____5_____ 45. Is patient with team members as they learn new roles and develop their competencies.

_____5_____ 46. Is aware of team members' feelings.

_____5_____ 47. Understands the strengths and limitations of team members.

_____3_____ 48. Brings conflict and dissent within the team into the open and uses them to improve quality of decisions.

_____4_____ 49. Facilitates cooperative behavior among team members.

_____5_____ 50. Keeps the team moving toward its goals.

_____5_____ 51. Understands the history of the industry of which the organization is a part.

_____3_____ 52. Stays informed of the actions of competitors and strategic partners in the industry of which the organization is a part.

_____1_____ 53. Can analyze general industry trends and understand their implications for the future.

_____1_____ 54. Quickly recognizes when significant changes occur in the industry.

_____1_____ 55. Knows how organizations compete in the industry.

_____2_____ 56. Understands the concerns of all major stakeholders of the organization.

_____1_____ 57. Understands the strengths and limitations of various business strategies.

_____4_____ 58. Knows the distinctive strengths of the organization.

_____5_____ 59. Understands the organizational structure and how work really gets done.

_____5_____ 60. Is able to fit into the unique culture of the organization.

_____5_____ 61. Assigns priorities that are consistent with the organization's mission and strategic goals.

_____2_____ 62. Recognizes and resists pressures to behave in ways that are not consistent with the organization's mission and strategic goals.

_____5_____ 63. Considers the long-term implications of decisions on the organization.

_____3_____ 64. Establishes tactical and operational goals to implement strategies.

_____4_____ 65. Keeps the unit focused on its goals.

_____4_____ 66. Stays informed of political events around the world.

_____3_____ 67. Stays informed of economic events around the world.

_____3_____ 68. Recognizes the impact of global events on the organization.

_____1_____ 69. Travels to gain first-hand knowledge of other countries.

_____5_____ 70. Understands and speaks more than one language.

_____5_____ 71. Is sensitive to cultural cues and is able to adapt quickly in novel situations.

_____5_____ 72. Recognizes that there is great variation within any culture and avoids stereotyping.

_____5_____ 73. Appropriately adjusts behavior when interacting with people from various national, ethnic, and cultural backgrounds.

_____5_____ 74. Understands how own cultural background affects own attitudes and behaviors.

_____5_____ 75. Can empathize with those from different cultural backgrounds.

_____5_____ 76. Has clear personal standards that serve as a foundation for maintaining a sense of integrity and ethical conduct.

_____5_____ 77. Maintains personal ethical standards under fire.

_____5_____ 78. Is sincere and projects self-assurance; doesn't just tell people what they want to hear.

_5_ **79.** Recognizes own mistakes and admits to having made them.

_5_ **80.** Accepts responsibility for own actions.

_5_ **81.** Seeks responsibility beyond what is required by the job.

_5_ **82.** Is willing to innovate and take personal risks.

_5_ **83.** Ambitious and motivated to achieve goals.

_5_ **84.** Works hard to get things done.

_5_ **85.** Shows perseverance in the face of obstacles.

_5_ **86.** Strikes a reasonable balance between work and other life activities.

_5_ **87.** Takes good care of self mentally and emotionally.

_5_ **88.** Uses constructive outlets to vent frustration and reduce tension.

_4_ **89.** Exercises and eats properly.

_3_ **90.** Knows how to enjoy leisure time.

_5_ **91.** Has clear personal and career goals.

_5_ **92.** Knows own values, feelings, and areas of strengths and limitations.

_5_ **93.** Accepts responsibility for continuous self-development.

_5_ **94.** Develops plans and seeks opportunities for personal long-term growth.

_5_ **95.** Analyzes and learns from work and life experiences.

Scoring and Interpretation

The Experiential Exercise Self-Assessment Inventory measures characteristics that are representative of the core dimensions of the six basic managerial competencies. These managerial competencies are discussed on pages 14–30.

Transfer the number that you recorded next to each characteristic in the inventory to the corresponding competency dimension in the following list.

Communication Competency. Effective transfer and exchange of information that leads to understanding between yourself and others.

■ *Informal Communication Dimension:*
1 _4_ 2 _5_ 3 _5_ 4 _3_ 5 _4_
Add numbers recorded = _21_ / 5 = _4_, which equals your average self-assessment on this dimension.

■ *Formal Communication Dimension:*
6 _2_ 7 _4_ 8 _4_ 9 _4_ 10 _5_
Add numbers recorded = _19_ / 5 = _4_, which equals your average self-assessment on this dimension.

■ *Negotiation Dimension:*
11 _5_ 12 _4_ 13 _3_ 14 _4_ 15 _4_
Add numbers recorded = _20_ / 5 = _4_, which equals your average self-assessment on this dimension.

■ *Summary:*
Add the average scores for the three dimensions of this competency = _12_ / 3 = _4_, which is your overall average self-assessment for communication competency.

Planning and Administration Competency. Deciding what tasks need to be done, determining how they can be done, allocating resources to enable them to be done, and then monitoring progress to ensure that they are done.

■ *Information Gathering, Analysis, and Problem-Solving Dimension:*
16 _3_ 17 _3_ 18 _3_ 19 _3_ 20 _3_
Add numbers recorded = _15_ / 5 = _3_, which equals your average self-assessment on this dimension.

■ *Planning and Organizing Projects Dimension:*
21 _4_ 22 _4_ 23 _5_ 24 _1_ 25 _4_
Add numbers recorded = _18_ / 5 = _3.6_, which equals your average self-assessment on this dimension.

■ *Time Management Dimension:*
26 _3_ 27 _4_ 28 _2_ 29 _2_ 30 _1_
Add numbers recorded = _12_ / 5 = _2.7_, which equals your average self-assessment on this dimension.

■ *Budgeting and Financial Management Dimension:*
31 _1_ 32 _1_ 33 _1_ 34 _1_ 35 _1_
Add numbers recorded = _5_ / 5 = _1_, which equals your average self-assessment on this dimension.

■ *Summary:*
Add the average scores for the four dimensions of this competency = _10_ / 4 = _2.5_, which is your overall average self-assessment for planning and administration competency.

Teamwork Competency. Accomplishing tasks through small groups of people who are collectively responsible and whose work is interdependent.

■ *Designing Teams Dimension:*
36 _4_ 37 _5_ 38 _5_ 39 _5_ 40 _3_
Add numbers recorded = _22_ / 5 = _4.4_, which equals your average self-assessment on this dimension.

- *Creating a Supportive Environment Dimension:*
  41 _5_ 42 _3_ 43 _5_ 44 _4_ 45 _5_
  Add numbers recorded = _22_ / 5 = _4.87_, which equals your average self-assessment on this dimension.

- *Managing a Team Dynamics Dimension:*
  46 _5_ 47 _5_ 48 _3_ 49 _4_ 50 _5_
  Add numbers recorded = _22_ / 5 = _4.4_, which equals your average self-assessment on this dimension.

- *Summary:*
  Add the average scores for the three dimensions of this competency = _13.2_ / 3 = _4.4_, which is your overall average self-assessment for teamwork competency.

Strategic Action Competency. Understanding the overall mission(s) and values of the organization and ensuring that your actions and those of the people you manage are aligned with them.

- *Understanding the Industry Dimension:*
  51 _5_ 52 _3_ 53 _1_ 54 _1_ 55 _1_
  Add numbers recorded = _11_ / 5 = _2.2_, which equals your average self-assessment on this dimension.

- *Understanding the Organization Dimension:*
  56 _2_ 57 _1_ 58 _4_ 59 _5_ 60 _5_
  Add numbers recorded = _17_ / 5 = _3.4_, which equals your average self-assessment on this dimension.

- *Taking Strategic Actions Dimension:*
  61 _5_ 62 _2_ 63 _5_ 64 _3_ 65 _4_
  Add numbers recorded = _19_ / 5 = _3.8_, which equals your average self-assessment on this dimension.

- *Summary:*
  Add the average scores for the three dimensions of this competency = _9.4_ / 3 = _3.1_, which is your overall average self-assessment for strategic action competency.

Multicultural Competency. Refers to understanding, appreciating, and responding to diverse political, cultural, and economic issues across and within nations.

- *Cultural Knowledge and Understanding Dimension:*
  66 _4_ 67 _3_ 68 _3_ 69 _1_ 70 _5_
  Add numbers recorded = _16_ / 5 = _3.2_, which equals your average self-assessment on this dimension.

- *Cultural Openness and Sensitivity Dimension:*
  71 _5_ 72 _5_ 73 _5_ 74 _5_ 75 _5_
  Add numbers recorded = _25_ / 5 = _5_, which equals your average self-assessment on this dimension.

- *Summary:*
  Add the average scores for the three dimensions of this competency = _8.2_ / 2 = _4.1_, which is your overall average self-assessment for global awareness competency.

Self-Management Competency. Refers to developing yourself and taking responsibility for your life at work and beyond.

- *Integrity and Ethical Conduct Dimension:*
  76 _5_ 77 _5_ 78 _5_ 79 _5_ 80 _5_
  Add numbers recorded = _25_ / 5 = _5_, which equals your average self-assessment on this dimension.

- *Personal Drive and Resilience Dimension:*
  81 _5_ 82 _5_ 83 _5_ 84 _5_ 85 _5_
  Add numbers recorded = _25_ / 5 = _5_, which equals your average self-assessment on this dimension.

- *Balancing Work and Life Issues Dimension:*
  86 _5_ 87 _5_ 88 _5_ 89 _4_ 90 _3_
  Add numbers recorded = _22_ / 5 = _4.4_, which equals your average self-assessment on this dimension.

- *Self-Awareness and Development Dimension:*
  91 _5_ 92 _5_ 93 _5_ 94 _5_ 95 _5_
  Add numbers recorded = _25_ / 5 = _5_, which equals your average self-assessment on this dimension.

- *Summary:*
  Add the average scores for the three dimensions of this competency = _19.4_ / 4 = _4.85_, which is your overall average self-assessment for self-management competency.

Overall Profile

Instructions. Plot your overall profile of managerial competencies on the following grid, using the *summary average score* for each competency and multiplying the average score for each competency by 20. For example, if your average score on a competency is 3.2, you would multiply it by 20 to obtain a total score of 64 out of 100 possible points on that competency and mark that point on the grid. Then connect the points marked on each vertical line.

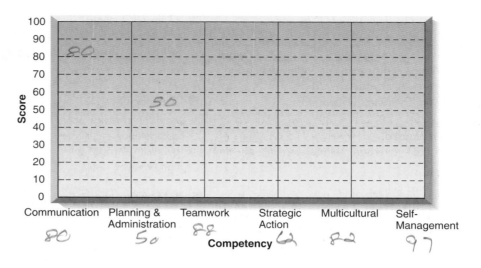

Handwritten annotations on graph: 80 (Communication), 50 (Planning & Administration), 88 (Teamwork), 62 (Strategic Action), 82 (Multicultural), 97 (Self-Management)

Overall Interpretations

Score	Meaning
20–39	*You have little relevant experience and are quite weak in this competency.*
40–59	*You are generally weak in this competency but are performing satisfactorily or better on a few characteristics.*
60–74	*You are generally about average in this competency and above average or better on some characteristics.*
75–89	*You are generally above average in this competency and outstanding on a number of characteristics.*
90–100	*You are generally outstanding in this competency.*

Questions

1. What does this profile suggest in relation to needed development in areas of your professional and personal life?

2. Based on the managerial competency in most need of development, identify three possible actions that you might take to reduce the gap between your current and desired level for that competency.

3. Would others who work with you closely or who otherwise know you well agree with your self-assessment profile? On what dimensions might their and your assessments be similar? Different?

4. How do your scores compare to those of hundreds of students and seasoned managers, as shown in the following graph?

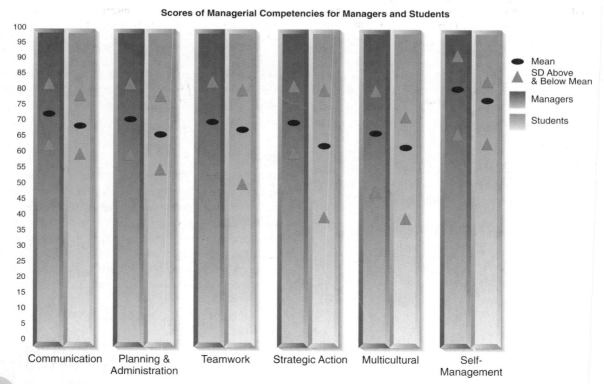

Scores of Managerial Competencies for Managers and Students

3M has been heralded as one of the great examples of success through change and innovation. Scotch tape and Post-It Notes are just two of its many product innovations. Over the years 3M has thrived by hiring talented scientists and researchers and encouraging them to spend part of every workweek (and some of the company's money) on projects that intrigued them. Small wonder, then, that some managers were concerned when they learned that, for the first time in 3M's 100-year history, an outsider was being brought in as CEO. The CEO, James McNerney, came from GE, a company known more for its disciplined execution than its freewheeling innovation.

Despite its long-term success, 3M's overhead costs had ballooned and overall growth had slowed by the time McNerney arrived. In fact, 3M hasn't had a commercial product success since Post-It Notes came out almost 25 years ago. The company was selling 50,000 industrial and consumer products, but a good number were merely size and color variations of basic items such as pink—not just yellow—Post-It Notes. McNerney imposed order by reorganizing the products under six broad categories: health care; specialty materials; industrial products; consumer and office products; electro and communications products; and transportation, graphics, and safety products.

Still, managers and employees were relieved to learn that while McNerney saw the need for changes, he also viewed 3M as a solid company with market-leading products. Rather than make major management changes, McNerney and his team sought ways to lower expenses through selective layoffs, shifting some production overseas, centralizing the purchasing process, cutting the supplier roster, and other cost-cutting measures. In one year, these moves shaved $600 million from 3M's expenses. To gain efficiency, he has enrolled a third of 3M's 67,000 employees in Six Sigma training, but it has not yet been accepted into 3M's culture. Six Sigma describes the defects in parts per million. In Jack Welch's transformation at GE, he used Six Sigma processes to dramatically improve the quality of GE's products.

Although product development had traditionally been 3M's strength, McNerney believed the company could do a better job of identifying the most promising new items and speeding them to market. In the past, 3M personnel were guided by the rule that "no market, no end product is so small as to be scorned." Sometimes the company would start building a plant for a new product even before the marketing department had finished analyzing the marketplace. Changes were needed to stay competitive in today's pressured business environment. In particular, McNerney wanted 3M employees to have "a more reality-based way of looking at the world." With about 1,500 products under consideration at any given moment—and a $1 billion research-and-development budget—R&D managers were challenged to change their approach as well. Instead of saying "yes" to most ideas and then letting the marketplace select winners and losers, R&D managers were asked to determine early in the development process which ideas had the highest business potential before moving ahead with additional investment.

While 3M managers were glad to hear McNerney say, "If I end up killing the entrepreneurial spirit (in 3M), I will have failed," many were nonetheless nervous about the push for accelerated product development, which meant bringing high-potential products to market in half the time. After all, no one predicted much demand for Post-It Notes until after the product was "smuggled" into the market and customers started requesting the product, which was not officially in production. How would middle managers help their subordinates understand the dual notion of "disciplined innovation" and learn to apply it in their areas of expertise?

To send a clear signal about the seriousness of these changes and reward managers who excelled in implementing them, McNerney revamped 3M's performance management and development practices. First, he abolished the company's seniority-based compensation plan in favor of a merit-based structure that offered more pay and promotions to outstanding employees and managers. Next, he established a leadership development school to prepare up-and-coming managers for more responsibility. These changes reinforced a sense of urgency throughout 3M's 70,000-strong workforce and ensured that high-performing managers at all levels would receive financial rewards. He sets high goals that can be measured, such as business-unit sales or the rate of product introductions, and demands that his managers meet them. He works with them as a dedicated coach to help them meet these goals.

More changes are ahead. McNerney pushed managers to move 3M into services, an area where the company has little experience, and senior managers now provide more direction on budget allocations to ensure that departments working on higher potential products receive sufficient resources. "I want people to start competing for resources around here again," McNerney commented.

In June 2005, McNerney left 3M to take the job of CEO at the Boeing Company and George Buckley became CEO in December of that same year. Born and educated in the United Kingdom, Buckley's appointment reflects 3M's strong desire to increase sales in the 60 countries in which it operates. 3M's sales were more than $20 billion in 2005, and 60 percent of these were from its foreign operations.

To learn more about this organization, visit *www.3m.com*.

Questions

1. What functions did McNerney perform?

2. What competencies did he display?

3. If you took a managerial position at 3M, what competencies would you need to develop to be successful?

chapter 2

© Brand X Pictures/Jupiter Images

Learning from the History of Management Thought

Learning Goals

After studying this chapter, you should be able to:

1. Describe the three branches of the traditional viewpoint of management: bureaucratic, scientific, and administrative.

2. Explain the behavioral viewpoint's contribution to management.

3. Describe how managers can use systems and quantitative techniques to improve employee performance.

4. State the two major components of the contingency viewpoint.

5. Explain the impact of the need for quality on management practices.

Communication Competency

Planning and Administration Competency

Teamwork Competency

Managing Effectively

Self-Management Competency

Strategic Action Competency

Multicultural Competency

Challenge of Managing ....

Starbucks

© Ben Margot/AP Photo

Howard Schultz, chairman and chief global strategist of Starbucks, indicated that his greatest challenge was to attract and manage a worldwide workforce. He believed that Starbucks could provide a human resources management system that would cut costs while maintaining high quality. Evidently, he has done just that. Since going public in 1992, the company's stock has risen by more than a thousand percent and its retail sales exceed $6 billion. Starbucks products can be found in restaurants, hotels, offices, and airlines, and it operates and licenses more than 8,500 stores in over 30 countries throughout the world. The company's long-term expansion plans are to grow to 15,000 outlets in the United States and 15,000 internationally, for a total of 30,000 outlets worldwide.

The Starbucks Support Center at Starbucks Coffee Company's headquarters in Seattle has associates involved in a robust blend of teamwork, sense of mission, and challenge. As one of *Fortune* magazine's "100 Best Companies to Work for in America," not to mention one of the world's fastest growing companies, Starbucks has been serving coffee since 1971.

Woven into the company's mission statement is this goal: "Provide a great work environment and treat each other with respect and dignity." It takes more than company declarations to motivate and inspire people. So how does a young, developing company on an aggressive growth track motivate more than 96,700 people and inspire a work/life balance and a team spirit?

Total pay is what Starbucks refers to as "your special blend" of compensation, stock, fringe benefits, savings, and partner perks. Starbucks developed these innovative work/life programs to foster a committed organizational culture—and a long-term partnership. In fact, employees at Starbucks are called *partners*. Because of these unique programs, Starbucks has comparatively low health-care costs, low absenteeism, and one of the highest retention rates in the industry. Moreover, employees reap the benefits of the company's ongoing success. The company's work/life program includes on-site fitness services, referral and educational support for child care and elder care, an info line for convenient information, and the Partner Connection—a program that links employees with shared interests and hobbies.

Learning Content

The Starbucks Foundation creates hope, discovery, and opportunity in communities where it does business with national nonprofits such as Jumpstart and America SCORES. Starbucks store partners (employees) have championed literacy efforts across America, and since 1997, the foundation has distributed more than $12 million to charitable organizations. The Starbucks Foundation has maintained a focus on improving young people's lives by supporting literacy programs for children and families.

While it continues to grow, Schultz and his top management team continuously face challenges from domestic competitors, such as Seattle's Best, Java City, and small local coffee shops. One challenge is to decide whether the company should expand into food service. In some pilot stores, its hot breakfast items are selling very well, but should it roll out these products to all of its stores? It has become a national retailer for CD burning. The company's HearMusic media bars offer customers more than 200,000 songs to burn into compact discs at its stores. What impact will this have on Starbucks' growth? Another challenge facing Starbucks is transporting its management viewpoint to other countries, such as France and China, where customers have a different set of values. In France, for example, the French like to sit in small cafes for a shot of espresso served in china cups rather than paper cups. Starbucks has not been able to establish a cult-like following in Germany, France, and many other European countries. In yet other European countries, Starbucks works with joint venture partners to operate its stores because of local laws and tariffs. In Spain, for example, it has had to partner with Grupo Vips to earn the profits that it has enjoyed in the United States. In other parts of the world, the challenges are different. For example, in Shanghai, the hours start at 8:00 A.M. and close early in the evening.[1]

To learn more about this organization, visit *www.starbucks.com*.

How would you like working at Starbucks? What are the positive features of working for this company? Does the company's philosophy of managing people appeal to you? These are just some of the questions that are the focus of this chapter.

Traditional Viewpoint

1.

Describe the three branches of the traditional viewpoint of management: bureaucratic, scientific, and administrative.

Working for a global company with plants scattered throughout the world is getting to be commonplace. In the past 10 years or so, companies such as Starbucks, Citigroup, Procter & Gamble (P&G), Marriott, and General Electric have challenged their managers to manage on a global scale. Managers now lead employees whom they seldom, if ever, see and who may know more about solving a problem than they do. Although new methods of managing employees are needed to keep pace with changes in today's organizations and technology, let's not discard the lessons from the history of management thought. Management today reflects the concepts, viewpoints, and experience gained over many decades.

During the 30 years following the end of the Civil War in 1885, the United States emerged as a leading industrial nation. The shift from an agrarian to an urban society was abrupt and, for many Americans, meant drastic adjustment. By the end of the century, a new corporate capitalism ruled by a prosperous professional class had arisen. Captains of industry freely wielded mergers and acquisitions and engaged in cutthroat competition as they created huge monopolies in the oil, meat, steel, sugar, and tobacco industries. The federal government did nothing to interfere with these monopolies. On the one hand, new technology born of the war effort offered the promise of progress and growth. On the other hand, rapid social change and a growing disparity between rich and poor caused increasing conflict and instability.

In 1886, several important turning points in business and management history occurred. Henry R. Towne (1844–1924), an engineer and cofounder of the Yale Lock Company, presented a paper titled "The Engineer as an Economist" to the American Society of Mechanical Engineers (ASME). In that paper Towne proposed that the ASME create an economic section to act as a clearinghouse and forum for "shop management" and "shop accounting." Shop management would deal with the subjects of organization, responsibility, reports, and the "executive management" of industrial works, mills, and factories. Shop accounting would treat the nuts and bolts of time and wage systems, cost determination and allocation, bookkeeping methods, and manufacturing accounting.

Other events in 1886 influenced the development of modern management thought and practice. During this boom period in U.S. business history, employers generally regarded labor as a commodity to be purchased as cheaply as possible and maintained at minimal expense. Thus it was also a peak period of labor unrest—during 1886 more than 600,000 employees were out of work because of strikes and lockouts. On May 4, 1886, a group of labor leaders led a demonstration in Chicago's Haymarket Square in support of an eight-hour workday. During the demonstration someone threw a bomb, killing seven bystanders. The Haymarket Affair was a setback for organized labor, because many people began to equate unionism with anarchy. In his pioneering study of labor history in 1886, *The Labor Movement in America*, Richard T. Ely advocated a less radical approach to labor–management relations. Ely cautioned labor to work within the existing economic and political system. One union that followed Ely's advice was the American Federation of Labor (AFL), organized in 1886 by Samuel Gompers and Adolph Strasser. A conservative, "bread and butter" union, the AFL avoided politics and industrial unionism and organized skilled workers along craft lines (carpenters, plumbers, bricklayers, and other trades). Like other early unions, the AFL protected its members from unfair management practices. Gompers' goal was to increase labor's bargaining power within the existing capitalistic framework. Under his leadership, the AFL dominated the American labor scene for almost half a century.

Chicago in 1886 also was the birthplace of an aspiring mail-order business called Sears, Roebuck and Company. From its beginning Sears, founded by railroad station agent Richard W. Sears, who sold watches to farmers in his area, characterized the mass distribution system that promoted the country's economic growth. For the first time, affordable fine goods were available to both rural and urban consumers. Also in 1886, the first Coca-Cola was served in Atlanta. This scarcely noticed event launched an enterprise that grew into a gigantic multinational corporation. Other companies that began in 1886 and remain in operation today include Avon Products, *Cosmopolitan* magazine, Johnson & Johnson, Munsingwear, and Westinghouse. Thus 1886 marked the origins of several well-known, large-scale enterprises, modern management thought and practice, and major labor unions.

Why are we recounting prior events in a book that presents modern management concepts? One reason is that many of the concepts and practices established in the early days of management are still used today. Many of the rules and regulations found in organizations today were originally created to protect managers from undue pressures to favor certain groups of people. Today FedEx, Wal-Mart, and Amazon.com, to name but a few, use rules and regulations for the same reason. A second reason is that the past is a good teacher, identifying concepts and practices that have been successful and those that no longer are effective. Recognizing that employees join organizations for social as well as economic reasons has led many organizations, such as Toyota, Dell, and

Analyzing business management strategies, successes, and failures of the past gives us insight to the present and future.

© RubberBall Productions/Jupiter Images

Southwest Airlines, to use teams to solve problems and base employee pay on team results. A third reason is that history gives us a feel for the types of problems for which managers long have struggled to find solutions. Many of these problems, such as low morale, high absenteeism, and poor quality, still exist in many organizations and continue to plague managers. By learning from the past, however, companies are able to avoid many of those problems.

Looking back also underscores the fact that professional management hasn't been around all that long. In earlier, preindustrial societies, men and women paced their work according to the sun, the seasons, and the demand for what they produced. Small communities encouraged personal, often familial, relationships between employers and employees. The explosive growth of urban industry—and the factory system in particular—changed the face of the workplace forever. Workers in cities were forced to adapt to the factory's formal structure and rules and to labor long hours for employers they never saw. Many were poorly educated and needed considerable oral instruction and hands-on training in unfamiliar tasks.

The emergence of large-scale business enterprises raised issues and created challenges that previously had applied only to governments. Businesses needed the equivalent of government leaders—managers—to hire and train employees and then to lead and motivate them. Managers also were needed to develop plans and design work units and, while doing so, make a profit—never a requirement for governments! In this chapter we briefly review how management viewpoints have evolved since 1886 to meet those needs.

During the past century, theorists have developed numerous responses to the same basic management question: What is the best way to manage an organization? We continue to study those responses because they still apply to the manager's job. In the following sections we discuss the five most widely accepted viewpoints of management that have evolved since about 1886: traditional (or classical), behavioral, systems, contingency, and quality. These viewpoints are based on different assumptions about the behavior of people in organizations, the key goals of an organization, the types of problems faced, and the methods that should be used to solve those problems. Figure 2.1 shows when each viewpoint emerged and began to gain popularity. As you can see, all five still influence managers' thinking. In fact, one important source of disagreement among today's managers is the emphasis that should be given to each of them. Thus a major purpose of this chapter is to show you not only how each has contributed to the historical evolution of modern management thought, but also how each can be used effectively in different circumstances now and in the future.

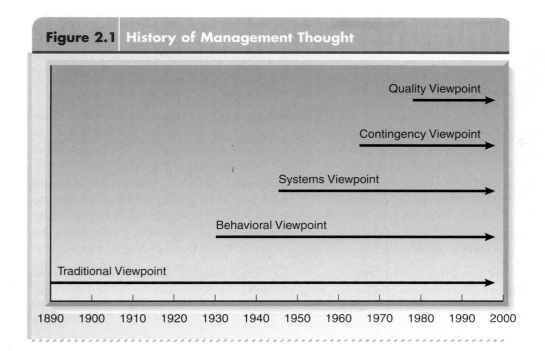

Figure 2.1 History of Management Thought

Quality Viewpoint

Contingency Viewpoint

Systems Viewpoint

Behavioral Viewpoint

Traditional Viewpoint

1890 1900 1910 1920 1930 1940 1950 1960 1970 1980 1990 2000

The oldest and perhaps most widely accepted view of management is the traditional (or classical) viewpoint. The traditional viewpoint *stresses one best way to manage by following certain prescriptions*. It is split into three main branches: bureaucratic management, scientific management, and administrative management. All three emerged during roughly the same time period, the late 1890s through the early 1900s, when engineers were trying to make organizations run like well-oiled machines. The founders of these three branches came from Germany, the United States, and France, respectively.

Bureaucratic Management

Bureaucratic management *refers to the use of rules, a set hierarchy, a clear division of labor, and detailed procedures*. Max Weber (1864–1920), a German social historian, is most closely associated with bureaucratic management (so named because Weber based his work on studies of Germany's government bureaucracy). Although Weber was one of the first theorists to deal with the problems of organizations, he wasn't widely recognized by managers and scholars in the United States until his work was translated into English in 1947. He was concerned primarily with the broad social and economic issues facing society; his writings on bureaucracy represent only part of his total contribution to social theory.[2]

Bureaucratic management provides a blueprint of how an entire organization should operate. It prescribes seven desirable characteristics: a formal system of rules, impersonality, division of labor, hierarchical structure, a detailed authority structure, lifelong career commitment, and rationality. Together these characteristics represent a formal, somewhat rigid method of managing. Let's take a look at this method, setting aside for the moment all of the negative connotations the word *bureaucracy* has today and focusing instead on the system's strengths, consistency, and predictability.

Rules. As *formal guidelines for the behavior of employees while they are on the job*, rules can help provide the discipline an organization needs if it is to reach its goals. Adherence to rules ensures uniformity of procedures and operations and helps maintain organizational stability, regardless of individual managers' or employees' personal desires.

Snapshot

"Each job has a policy manual detailing the rules that a person needs to follow to ensure efficiency. Drivers are told to walk to a customer's door at a brisk pace of 3 feet per second, carrying the package in the right hand and clipboard in the left. They should knock on the door so as not to lose valuable seconds searching for a doorbell."

Michael Eskew, Chairman and CEO, UPS

Impersonality. Impersonality *means that employees are evaluated according to rules and objective data, such as sales or units produced.* Although the word *impersonality* can also have negative connotations, Weber believed that this approach guaranteed fairness for all employees—an impersonal superior doesn't allow subjective personal or emotional considerations to color evaluations of subordinates.

Division of Labor. The division of labor *refers to the splitting of work into specialized positions.* It enables the organization to use personnel and job-training resources efficiently. Managers and employees are assigned and perform duties based on specialization and personal expertise. Unskilled employees can be assigned tasks that are relatively easy to learn and do. For example, employee turnover at fast-food restaurants such as McDonald's and Wendy's is more than 150 percent a year. Because of the narrow division of labor, most fast-food jobs can be learned quickly and require only unskilled labor. Thus high turnover in this type of business may not create serious service problems.

Hierarchical Structure. Kerr-McGee, a $5.5 billion Oklahoma-based company that explores for and produces oil and gas, uses a pyramid-shaped hierarchical structure, as shown in Figure 2.2.[3] A hierarchical structure *ranks jobs according to the amount of authority (the right to decide) in each job.* Typically, authority increases at each higher level to the top of the hierarchy. Those in lower level positions are under the control and direction of those in higher level positions. At Kerr-McGee, various directors of operations in the United States, United Kingdom, Far East, and Gulf of Mexico report to the senior vice president and chief of operations. If there is a problem in its chemical plant in Western Australia, the CEO knows whom to contact. According to Weber, a well-defined hierarchy helps control employee behavior by making clear exactly where each stands in relation to everyone else in the organization.

Authority Structure. A system based on rules, impersonal supervision, division of labor, and a hierarchical structure is tied together by an authority structure. Authority structure *refers to who has the right to make decisions.* Authority changes at different levels within the organization. At Kerr-McGee, the chief financial officer can make investment decisions involving plant and equipment that the treasurer cannot make.

Weber identified three types of authority structures: traditional, charismatic, and rational–legal.

▶ Traditional authority *is based on custom, ancestry, gender, birth order, and the like.* The divine right of kings and the magical influence of tribal witch doctors are examples of traditional authority.

▶ Charismatic authority *is evident when subordinates suspend their own judgment and comply voluntarily with a leader because of special personal qualities or abilities they perceive in that individual.* Charismatic leaders (e.g., Gandhi, Golda Meir, and Martin Luther King, Jr.) often head social, political, and religious movements. In contrast, business leaders seldom rely solely on charismatic authority, but some, such as Jeffrey Swartz, CEO of Timberland, and Oprah Winfrey, CEO of Harpo, have used their charisma to motivate and influence others.

▶ Rational–legal authority *refers to the use of established laws and rules that are applied uniformly.* A superior is obeyed because of the position occupied within the organization's hierarchy. This authority depends on employees' acceptance of the organization's rules.

Lifelong Career Commitment. In a bureaucratic management system, employment is viewed as a lifelong career commitment; that is, *both the employee and the organization view themselves as being committed to each other over the working life of the*

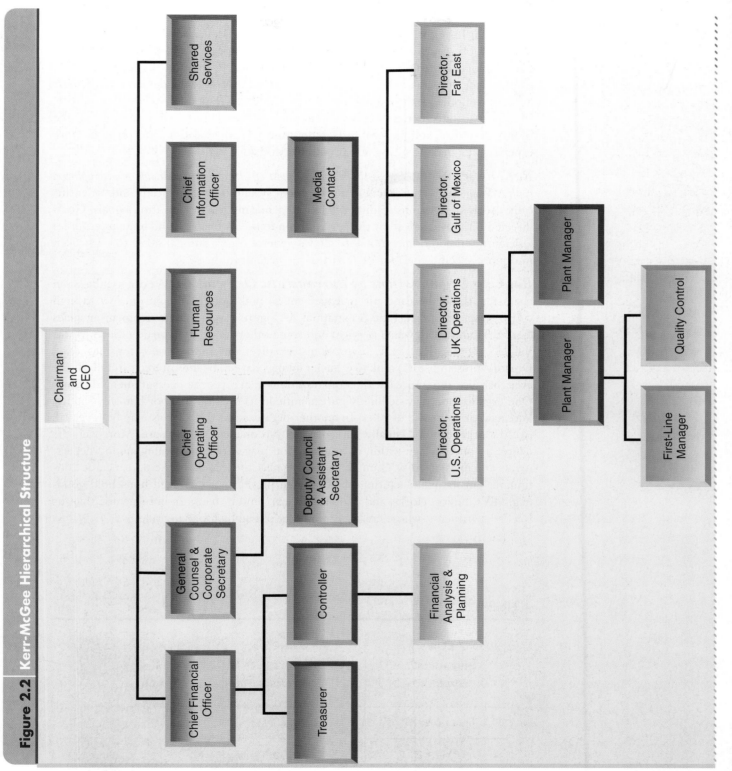

Figure 2.2 | Kerr-McGee Hierarchical Structure

Chairman and CEO

Chief Financial Officer
Treasurer
Controller
Financial Analysis & Planning

General Counsel & Corporate Secretary
Deputy Council & Assistant Secretary

Chief Operating Officer
Director, U.S. Operations
Director, UK Operations
Plant Manager
Plant Manager
First-Line Manager
Quality Control
Director, Gulf of Mexico
Director, Far East

Human Resources

Chief Information Officer
Media Contact

Shared Services

Source: From www.kerr-mcgee.com (June 2006).

employee. Traditionally, Asian organizations, such as NEC, Samsung, and Toyota, have hired key workers with the expectation—by both parties—that a permanent employment contract was being made. In general, lifelong career commitment means that job security is guaranteed as long as the employee is technically qualified and performs satisfactorily. Entrance requirements, such as level of education and experience, ensure that hiring is based on qualifications rather than connections. The organization uses job security, tenure, step-by-step salary increases, and pensions to ensure that employees satisfactorily perform assigned duties. Promotion is granted when an employee demonstrates the competencies required to handle the demands of the next higher position. Organizational level is assumed to correspond closely with expertise. Managers in bureaucratic organizations, such as the civil service, often rely on the results of written and physical tests, amount of formal education, and previous work experience in making hiring and promotion decisions.

Rationality. Rationality *is the use of the most efficient means available to accomplish a goal.* Managers in a bureaucratic management system operate logically and "scientifically," with all decisions leading directly to achieving the organization's goals. Goal-directed activities then allow the organization to use its financial and human resources efficiently. In addition, rationality allows general organizational goals to be broken into more specific goals for each part of the organization.

Ranking Organizations by Bureaucratic Orientation. We can use the seven characteristics of bureaucratic management to rank organizations from low to high with respect to bureaucratic orientation. As Figure 2.3 shows, government agencies (e.g., the Internal Revenue Service) and some others (e.g., McDonald's, State Motor Vehicle Registration) rank high. Some creative and innovative companies (e.g., DreamWorks and MP3) rank low. Such rankings have to be interpreted carefully, however, because differences within organizations make precise measurement difficult. One organization may be highly bureaucratic in its division of labor but only slightly bureaucratic in its use of rules. In another organization these levels may be reversed. Are the organizations equally bureaucratic? No one can say for sure. Moreover, the degree of bureaucracy within an organization may vary considerably among departments and divisions. For example, Sony falls near the middle of the bureaucratic continuum, but its manufacturing plants, which produce standardized household goods (e.g., TVs, radios, clocks, and digital cameras), tend to be more bureaucratic than its R&D departments, whose creativity would be stifled by too many rules.

Figure 2.3 Bureaucratic Continuum

LOW Bureaucratic Structure	MIDRANGE Bureaucratic Structure	HIGH Bureaucratic Structure
DreamWorks	Sony	IRS
MP3	PepsiCo	State Motor Vehicle Registration
R&D Thinktank	7-11	McDonald's

Benefits of Bureaucracy. The expected benefits of bureaucratic management are efficiency and consistency. A bureaucracy functions best when many routine tasks need to be done. Then lower level employees can handle the bulk of the work by simply following rules and procedures. The fruits of their labor should be of standard (high) quality and produced at the rate necessary to meet organizational goals. The following Planning and Administration Competency feature on Pulte Homes provides an excellent example of how bureaucracy can lead to efficiency in home building. In the United States, the top 10 home builders control just about 20 percent of this $375 billion industry. It is an industry dominated by more than 70,000 small local builders, each building an average of five homes a year. However, the goal of Pulte is to become efficient.[4]

© Joey Kottica/Creatas Images/Jupiter Images

A Pulte home under construction.

Pulte Homes

Richard Dugas, CEO of Pulte Homes, has built the company into a $12 billion sales company by following many of the basics of bureaucracy. Pulte builds 100 homes a day in 54 metro markets spanning 28 states. Managers from PepsiCo, Clorox, Disney, Wal-Mart, and other consumer product companies were hired to help Dugas grow his company. These managers led Pulte's marketing and sales employees through a detailed market research process, much like PepsiCo did when it divided up Pepsi and Mountain Dew drinkers. Using a rational decision process, they segmented the home market into 11 categories ranging from first-time homebuyers (ages 20 to early 30s), to homeowners looking to upgrade a second time (ages 40 to early 50s), to re-starters (single parents entering the market), to active adult retirees, that is, the baby boomers easing into retirement (ages 55 and up). Such detailed segmentation now drives every location decision. More than 200 people in the land acquisition department scout states, cities, and small neighborhoods to study their target customers. This team also conducts comprehensive demographic studies on what each segment wants, for example, houses that are near walking parks or that are a couple hours' drive from a major metropolitan area, medical facilities, recreation, and the like. The interviewers ask customers standardized questions to more fully understand their housing choice decisions.

Pulte has also used its extensive database to reduce the needless costs and the complexity of its supply chain management. For example, it discovered that 80 percent of its homebuyers end up selecting the same countertops, floors, carpets, toilets, and other options. Yet the company was offering a choice of 35 toilet models from six manufacturers, purchased windows from more than 17 suppliers, and offered customers more than 2,000 floor plans. Last year, Dugas hired a former supply chain manager from Wal-Mart to cut down the number of suppliers and costs. As a result, Pulte has reduced the number of floor plan options to less than 1,200 and has begun to standardize the options in each segment of homebuyers. All homes use nails, concrete, lumber, and so on purchased from an approved list of suppliers.

To learn more about this organization, visit *www.pulte.com*.

Costs of Bureaucracy. The same aspects of bureaucratic management that can increase one organization's efficiency can lead to great inefficiency in another. Managers at Brunswick, Zazzle, Embraer, and other organizations report that the orderliness of a bureaucracy often leads to inefficiencies that cannot be tolerated by companies operating in today's turbulent environment. The following are five, often unanticipated, drawbacks of bureaucratic management.

1. **Rigid rules and red tape.** Rigid adherence to rules and routines for their own sake is a frequent complaint of employees and customers of many organizations. Such a system leaves little room for individual freedom and creativity. This rigidity may foster low motivation, entrenched "career" employees, high turnover among the best employees, and shoddy work. A significant amount of time and money can be wasted.

2. **Protection of authority.** Managers in a bureaucratic organization may ignore issues of employee productivity while protecting and expanding their own authority. Caterpillar attacked the problem head-on. Management believed that the company couldn't afford to support a maze of corporate buck-passers, so it changed the system by focusing on customer satisfaction. Employees use their PCs to swap essential information and determine exactly what type of engine a customer wants. A computer-controlled monorail system and robots bring employees the engine, parts, and computer-generated information about what to do. This system requires 29 percent fewer people than the old system. Employees work on engines at their own pace and until they are satisfied that the job has been done right.[5]

3. **Slow decision making.** Large, complex organizations depend heavily on timely decisions. In a highly bureaucratic organization, however, adherence to rules and procedures may take precedence over effective, timely decision making. When that happens, rules take on lives of their own. Formality and ritual delay decisions at every level until all the red tape has been cleared, petty insistence on power and status privileges has been satisfied, and any chance of blame for errors in judgment has been minimized.

4. **Incompatibility with changing technology.** Advancing technology may make bureaucratic management inappropriate. Gerardo Gonzalez, chief operating officer at Dolex Dollar Express, believes that narrowly defined jobs based on rules and regulations generate little trust and sharing of information.[6] The technology changes rapidly, and employees must be able to go directly to the person who has the information they need to do their jobs.

5. **Incompatibility with workers' values.** More and more people are being hired by bureaucratic organizations to fill important decision-making positions. These workers' values include performing challenging work, serving clients and customers, and finding innovative solutions to problems. These values often are incompatible with the bureaucratic need for efficiency, order, and consistency. Bureaucratic authority is related to hierarchical position, but most professionals believe that authority stems from personal competence and technical knowledge. Cynthia Bland-Baker, Western regional VP of finance for Marriott International, says she has to rely more on the professionalism and commitment of her people than on rules and regulations. Marriott has developed a performance appraisal system that allows team members, peers, and customers to evaluate employees' work. The company has to do so because a manager might not know enough to evaluate a particular person's contributions.

Insights from Bureaucratic Management. As shown by the case of Pulte Homes, bureaucratic organizations are not always inefficient and unprofitable. In fact, bureaucratic management is still widely and successfully used. This approach is most effective when (1) large amounts of standard information have to be processed and an efficient processing method has been found (as in credit card and insurance companies, the IRS, and traffic courts); (2) the needs of the customer are known and aren't likely to change (as in the registration of drivers in most states); (3) the technology is routine and stable, so employees can be easily and quickly taught how to operate machines (as at Taco Bell and in toll booths); and (4) the organization has to coordinate the activities of numerous employees in order to deliver a standardized service or product to the customer (as is done by the IRS and the U.S. Postal Service).

Scientific Management

As manufacturing firms became larger and more complex in the late 1800s, not all managers could continue to be directly involved with production. Many began to spend more of their time on planning, scheduling, and staffing activities. Also, managers were hard-pressed to keep up with new technologies. As a result, a need was created for operations specialists who could solve the personnel and productivity problems that, if not addressed, could threaten operating efficiency.

Frederick W. Taylor. Thus the stage was set for Frederick Winslow Taylor (1856–1915) to do his pioneering work in scientific management.[7] Scientific management *is a philosophy and set of management practices that are based on fact and observation, not on hearsay or guesswork.* Scientific management is used by Microsoft, Kodak, Mattel, and other manufacturers in their plants, but it is also widely used in service-based organizations, such as FedEx, Southwest Airlines, and CIBC Oppenheimer to increase their efficiency.

Taylor, an American mechanical engineer, started out as a foreman at Midvale Steel Company in Philadelphia. He believed that increased productivity ultimately depended on finding ways to make workers more efficient by using objective, scientific techniques. When Taylor worked as a consultant to Bethlehem Steel, for example, he made a science of shoveling. Through observation and experimentation, he started a program that matched workers, shovel sizes, materials, and the like for each job. By the end of the third year, his program had reduced the number of shovelers needed from 600 to 140 while the average number of tons shoveled per worker per day had risen from 16 to 50. Workers' earnings also increased from $1.15 to $1.88 a day.

Taylor used time-and-motion studies to analyze work flows, supervisory techniques, and worker fatigue. A time-and-motion study *involves identifying and measuring a worker's physical movements when performing a task and then analyzing the results.* Movements that slow production are dropped. One goal of a time-and-motion study is to make a job highly routine and efficient. Eliminating wasted physical effort and specifying an exact sequence of activities reduce the amount of time, money, and effort needed to make a product. Taylor was convinced that having workers perform routine tasks that didn't require them to make decisions could increase efficiency. Performance goals expressed quantitatively (e.g.,

Henry Ford poses in his first car. Ford's success with the assembly line Model T is a tried-and-true example of scientific management.

© Ewing Galloway/Index Stock Imagery/Jupiter Images

number of units produced per shift) addressed a problem that had begun to trouble managers—how to judge whether an employee had put in a fair day's work. When Ford used Taylor's concepts in 1914 to assemble its Model T, it trimmed assembly time from almost 13 hours to less than 90 minutes.

Advocates of scientific management stress specialization. They believe that expertise is the only source of authority and that a single foreman couldn't be an expert at all of the tasks supervised. Each foreman's particular area of specialization therefore should become an area of authority. This solution is called functional foremanship, *a division of labor that assigned eight foremen to each work area*. Four of the foremen would handle planning, production scheduling, time-and-motion studies, and discipline. The other four would deal with machinery maintenance, machine speed, feeding material into the machine, and production on the shop floor.

What motivates employees to work to their capacity? Taylor believed that money was the answer. He supported the individual piecework system as the basis for pay. If workers met a certain production standard, they were to be paid at a standard wage rate. Workers who produced more than the standard were to be paid at a higher rate for all the pieces they produced, not just for those exceeding the standard. Taylor assumed that workers would be economically rational; that is, they would follow management's orders to produce more in response to financial incentives that allowed them to earn more money. Taylor argued that managers should use financial incentives if they were convinced that increases in productivity would more than offset higher employee earnings. Unions strongly opposed scientific management techniques because they believed that management might abuse their power to set the standards and piece rates too high.

The Gilbreths. Frank (1868–1924) and Lillian (1878–1972) Gilbreth formed an unusual husband-and-wife engineering team that made significant contributions to scientific management. Frank used a revolutionary new tool—motion pictures—to study workers' motions. For instance, he identified 18 individual motions that a bricklayer uses to lay bricks. By changing the bricklaying process, he reduced the 18 motions to 5, increasing a worker's overall productivity by more than 200 percent. Many of today's industrial engineers have combined Frank Gilbreth's methods with Taylor's to redesign jobs for greater efficiency.[8]

Lillian Gilbreth carried on Frank's work and raised their 12 children after his death. Concerned mainly with the human side of industrial engineering, she championed the idea that workers should have standard days, scheduled rest breaks, and normal lunch periods. Her work influenced the U.S. Congress to establish child-labor laws and develop rules for protecting workers from unsafe working conditions.

Henry Gantt. Taylor's associate, Henry Gantt (1861–1919), focused on "control" systems for production scheduling. His Gantt charts are still widely used to plan project timelines and have been adapted for computer scheduling applications. The Gantt chart *is a visual plan and progress report*. It identifies various stages of work that must be carried out to complete a project, sets a deadline for each stage, and documents accomplishments. Gantt also established quota systems and bonuses for workers who exceeded their quotas.[9]

Insight from Scientific Management. Taylor and other early proponents of scientific management would applaud the efforts of KFC, Honda, Canon, Intel, and other organizations that have successfully applied their concepts. Through time-and-motion studies, for example, KFC found that employees took almost two minutes to complete a customer's order. To improve performance, KFC instructed employees to acknowledge customers within 3 seconds of arriving at the drive-through window, fill a customer's order within 60 seconds, and arrive at an average service time of 90 seconds. To accomplish these objectives, KFC designed employees' workstations so that employees wouldn't need to take more than two steps to get what they needed, wouldn't lift anything, and from handy shelves could pull down napkins, straws, and other items needed to complete the order. Hundreds of other companies have used Taylor's principles to improve their employee selection and training processes and to seek the one best way to perform each task.

Unfortunately, most proponents of scientific management misread the human side of work. When Frederick Taylor and Frank Gilbreth formulated their principles and methods, they thought that workers were motivated primarily by a desire to earn money to satisfy their economic and physical needs. They failed to recognize that workers also have social needs and that working conditions and job satisfaction often are as important, if not more important, than money. For example, workers have struck to protest working conditions, speedup of an assembly line, or harassment by management, even when a fair financial incentive system was in place. Managers today can't assume that workers are interested only in higher wages. Dividing jobs into their simplest tasks and setting clear rules for accomplishing those tasks won't always lead to a quality product, high morale, and an effective organization. Today's employees often want to participate in decisions that affect their performance, and many want to be independent and hold jobs that give them self-fulfillment.[10]

Administrative Management

Administrative management *focuses on the manager and basic managerial functions*. Recall our discussion of the basic managerial functions—planning, organizing, controlling, and leading—that we outlined in Chapter 1. The administrative management viewpoint evolved early in the 1900s and is most closely identified with Henri Fayol (1841–1925), a French industrialist. Fayol credited his success as a manager to the methods he used rather than to his personal qualities. He felt strongly that, to be successful, managers had only to understand the basic managerial functions and apply certain management principles to them. He was the first person to group managers' functions in this way.[11]

Like the other traditionalists, Fayol emphasized formal structure and processes, believing that they are necessary for the adequate performance of all important tasks. In other words, if people are to work well together, they need a clear definition of what they're trying to accomplish and how their tasks help meet organizational goals.

Managers still use many of Fayol's principles of administrative management. For example, the unity of command principle *states that an employee should report to only one manager*. The reason for this principle was to avoid a person receiving conflicting work expectations from two different people. At Chapparal Steel the maintenance superintendent receives direction from the plant manager, the chief engineer, and the production manager—violating the unity of command principle. However, the maintenance superintendent has the authority to set priorities for plant maintenance. This illustrates the authority principle, *which states that managers have the right to give orders to get things done*.

Learning from the Traditional Viewpoint

Traditional management's three branches—bureaucratic, scientific, and administrative—still have their proponents, are often written about, and continue to be applied effectively. Table 2.1 highlights the points discussed.

Snapshot

"Walgreens is constantly pushing to drive costs down. It pioneered the application of satellite communications and computer technology and linked these to increase store efficiency. By using tried-and-proven management concepts, each of its 6,100 stores [is] able to process around 280 prescriptions a day and beat Wal-Mart by 27 cents and CVS by 94 cents on each prescription."

David Berbauer, CEO, Walgreens

Table 2.1 **Characteristics of Traditional Management**

BUREAUCRATIC MANAGEMENT	SCIENTIFIC MANAGEMENT	ADMINISTRATIVE MANAGEMENT
Rules	Training in routines and rules	Defining of management functions
Impersonality	"One best way"	
Division of labor	Financial motivation	Division of labor
Hierarchy		Hierarchy
Authority structure		Authority
Lifelong career commitment		Equity
Rationality		
FOCUS		
Whole organization	Employee	Manager
BENEFITS		
Consistency	Productivity	Clear structure
Efficiency	Efficiency	Professionalization of managerial roles
DRAWBACKS		
Rigidity	Overlooks social needs	Internal focus
Slowness		Overemphasizes rational behavior of managers

Let's summarize what the three branches have in common and what some of their drawbacks are. All three emphasize the formal aspects of organization. Traditionalists are concerned with the formal relations among an organization's departments, tasks, and processes. Weber, Taylor, the Gilbreths, Gantt, and Fayol replaced seat-of-the-pants management practices with sound theoretical and scientific principles. Managers began to stress the division of labor, hierarchical authority, rules, and decisions that would maximize economic rewards.

The manager's role in a hierarchy is crucial. In organizations, the relationship between expertise and organizational level is strong. Because of their higher position and presumed greater expertise, superiors are to be obeyed by subordinates. Administrative and scientific managements' emphases on logical processes and strict division of labor are based on similar reasoning.

Although they may recognize that people have feelings and are influenced by their friends at work, the overriding focus of traditionalists is on efficient and effective job performance. Taylor considered the human side of work in terms of eliminating bad feelings between workers and management and providing employees with financial incentives to increase productivity. Traditionalists consider job security, career progression, and protection of workers from employers' whims to be important. However, they do not recognize informal or social relationships among employees at work. Taylor and Frank Gilbreth focused on well-defined rules intended to ensure efficient performance, the primary standard against which employees were to be judged.

In assessing the work of the early traditional theorists, you need to keep in mind that they were influenced by the economic and societal conditions facing them at the time. The United States was becoming an industrial nation, unions were forming to protect workers' rights, and laws were being passed to eliminate unsafe working conditions. Even so, most organizations operated in a relatively stable environment with few competitors.

Behavioral Viewpoint

2.

Explain the behavioral viewpoint's contribution to management.

During the Great Depression of the 1930s, the federal government began to play a more influential role in people's lives. By the time President Franklin D. Roosevelt took office in 1933, the national economy was hovering on the brink of collapse. To provide employment the government undertook temporary public works projects—constructing dams, roads, and public buildings and improving national parks. It also created agencies such as the Social Security Administration to assist people who were elderly, unemployed, or had disabilities.

In one of the era's most dramatic changes, unskilled workers greatly increased their ability to influence management decisions though organization and membership in powerful labor unions. During the 1930s Congress aided unions by enacting legislation that deterred management from restricting union activities, legalized collective bargaining, and required management to bargain with unions. As a result the labor movement grew rapidly, and the Congress of Industrial Organizations (CIO) was formed. In 1937, the autoworkers and steelworkers won their first big contracts. Eventually professionals and skilled workers, as well as unskilled laborers, formed unions to bargain for better pay, increased benefits, and improved working conditions. Following the depression and World War II, a new wave of optimism swept the U.S. economy.

Against this backdrop of change and reform, managers were forced to recognize that people have needs, hold to values, and want respect. Managers were now leading workers who did not appear to exhibit what the early traditional management theorists had thought was rational economic behavior. That is, workers weren't always performing up to their physiological capabilities, as Taylor had predicted rational people would do. Nor were effective managers consistently following Fayol's principles. By exploring these inconsistencies, those who favored a behavioral (human relations) viewpoint of management gained recognition. The behavioral viewpoint *focuses on dealing effectively with the human aspects of organizations*. Its proponents look at how managers do what they do, how managers lead subordinates and communicate with them, and why managers need to change their assumptions about people if they want to lead high-performance teams and organizations.[12]

Follett's Contributions

Mary Parker Follett (1868–1933) made important contributions to the behavioral viewpoint of management. She *believed that management is a flowing, continuous process, not a static one, and that if a problem has been solved, the method used to solve it probably generated new problems*. She stressed (1) involvement of workers in solving problems and (2) the dynamics of management, rather than static principles. Both ideas contrasted sharply with the views of Weber, Taylor, and Fayol.[13]

Follett studied how managers did their jobs by observing them at work. Based on these observations, she concluded that coordination is vital to effective management. She developed four principles of coordination for managers to apply.

© Comstock Images/Jupiter Images

Management must deal effectively with the human aspects of an organization to maintain a high performing team.

1. Coordination is best achieved when the people responsible for making a decision are in direct contact.

2. Coordination during the early stages of planning and project implementation is essential.

3. Coordination should address all factors in a situation.

4. Coordination must be worked at continuously.

Follett believed that the people closest to the action could make the best decisions. For example, she was convinced that first-line managers are in the best position to coordinate production tasks. And by increasing communication among themselves and with workers, these managers can make better decisions regarding such tasks than managers up the hierarchy can. She also believed that first-line managers should not only plan and coordinate workers' activities, but also involve them in the process. Simply because managers told employees to do something a certain way, Follett argued, they shouldn't assume that the employees would do it. She argued further that managers at all levels should maintain good working relationships with their subordinates. One way to do so is to involve subordinates in the decision-making process whenever they will be affected by a decision. Drawing on psychology and sociology, Follett urged managers to recognize that each person is a collection of beliefs, emotions, and feelings.

Howard Shultz of Starbucks has had his ideas shaped by the philosophy of Follett. Starbucks is committed to providing an atmosphere that encourages respect and values the contributions that people make each day, regardless of who or at what level they are in the company. All partners who work a minimum 20 hours a week receive full medical and dental coverage, vacation days, and stock options as part of the Starbucks Bean Stock program. Eligible partners can choose health coverage from two managed care plans or a catastrophic plan. They also can select between two dental plans and a vision plan. Because of its young, healthy workforce, Starbucks can offer all of these benefits and still keep costs relatively low. The company's health-care costs are approximately 20 percent lower than the national average.

John Mackey, president of Whole Foods, a supermarket chain that sells only natural foods, believes that Follett's ideas have shaped his management practices.[14] Each Whole Foods Market typically employs between 60 and 140 people and is organized into various teams to develop a sense of cooperation. Each team is responsible for doing its own work and selecting new team members. A candidate must be voted on by the team and receive a two-thirds majority to become a team member. Every four weeks, each team meets to discuss problems and make decisions.

Barnard's Contributions

Chester Barnard (1886–1961) studied economics at Harvard but failed to graduate because he didn't finish a laboratory course in science. He was hired by AT&T, and in 1927 he became president of New Jersey Bell. Barnard made two significant contributions to management, which are detailed in his book, *The Functions of the Executive*.[15]

First, Barnard viewed organizations as social systems that require employee cooperation if they are to be effective. In other words, people should continually communicate with one another. According to Barnard, managers' main roles are to communicate with employees and motivate them to work hard to help achieve the organization's goals. In his view, successful management also depends on maintain-

Snapshot

Managers need to have a common touch and to be a team leader and not a drill sergeant. When their people shine, they shine."

Vickie Yoke, Senior Vice President, Alcatel

ing good relations with people outside the organization with whom managers deal regularly. He stressed the dependence of the organization on investors, suppliers, customers, and other outside interests. Barnard stressed the idea that managers have to examine the organization's external environment and adjust its internal structure to balance the two.

Second, Barnard proposed the acceptance theory of authority, *which holds that employees have free wills and thus choose whether to follow management's orders.* That is, employees will follow orders if they (1) understand what is required, (2) believe that the orders are consistent with organizational goals, and (3) see positive benefits to themselves in carrying out the orders.

The Hawthorne Contributions

The strongest support for the behavioral viewpoint emerged from studies carried out between 1924 and 1933 at Western Electric Company's Hawthorne plant in Chicago. The Hawthorne Illumination Tests, begun in November 1924 and conducted in three departments of the plant, initially were developed and directed by Hawthorne's engineers. They divided employees into two groups: a test group, whom they subjected to deliberate changes in lighting, and a control group, for whom lighting remained constant throughout the experiment. When lighting conditions for the test group were improved, the group's productivity increased, as expected. The engineers were mystified, though, by a similar jump in productivity upon reducing the test group's lighting to the point of twilight. To compound the mystery, the control group's output kept rising, even though its lighting condition didn't change. Western Electric called in Harvard professor Elton Mayo to investigate these peculiar and puzzling results.

Mayo and Harvard colleagues Fritz Roethlisberger and William Dickson devised a new experiment. They placed two groups of six women each in separate rooms. They changed various conditions for the test group and left conditions unchanged for the control group. The changes included shortening the test group's coffee breaks, allowing it to choose its own rest periods, and letting it have a say in other suggested changes. Once again, output of both the test group and the control group increased. The researchers decided that they could rule out financial incentives as a factor because they hadn't changed the payment schedule for either group.[16]

The researchers concluded that the increases in productivity weren't caused by a physical event but by a complex emotional chain reaction. Because employees in both groups had been singled out for special attention, they had developed a group pride that motivated them to improve their performance. The sympathetic supervision they received further reinforced that motivation. These experimental results led to Mayo's first important discovery: *When employees are given special attention, productivity is likely to change regardless of whether working conditions change.* This phenomenon became known as the Hawthorne effect.[17]

However, an important question remained unanswered: Why should a little special attention and the formation of group bonds produce such strong reactions? To find the answer, Mayo interviewed employees. These interviews yielded a highly significant discovery: Informal work groups, the social environment of employees, greatly influence productivity. Many Western Electric employees found their lives inside and outside the factory dull and meaningless. Their workplace friends, chosen in part because of mutual antagonism toward "the bosses," gave meaning to their working lives. Thus peer pressure, rather than management demands, had a significant influence on employee productivity.

The writings of Mayo, Roethlisberger, and Dickson that emerged from the Hawthorne studies helped outline the behavioral viewpoint of management. The researchers concluded that behavior on the job is determined by a complex set of factors. They found that the informal work group develops its own set of norms to satisfy the needs of individuals in the work setting and that the social system of such informal groups is maintained through symbols of prestige and power. As a result of their studies, the researchers recommended that managers consider the worker in a personal context (e.g., family situation, friendships, and membership in groups) in order to understand each employee's unique needs and sources of satisfaction. They also suggested that awareness of employee feelings and encouragement of employee participation in decision making can reduce resistance to change.

The following Teamwork Competency highlights how TDIndustries uses teams to recognize and reward people for directly contributing to the success of the organization. The importance of the relationship between the leaders and their subordinates is reinforced by the concept of servant leadership.[18]

Teamwork Competency

TDIndustries

Many organizations say that people are their most important assets, but TDIndustries (TDI) lives it. During the past 50 years, this organization has developed management practices that have enabled it to become one of America's most admired corporations, currently ranking among *Fortune* magazine's "100 Best Companies to Work for in America," a distinction that it has held for nine straight years. TDI has developed into a more than $234 million mechanical/electrical/plumbing company that employs some 1,500 people, many of whom have been with the company for more than 10 years. CEO Harold MacDowell believes that TDI's success can be related to its strong teamwork.

For TDI, creating a culture of teamwork that promotes high performance and longevity is based on the concept of *servant leadership*. The servant leader philosophy for TDI means that managers (servants) cultivate employees (leaders) by serving and meeting the needs of others. In his servant role, MacDowell answers his own phone, has no reserved parking space, and works in an 8- × 11-foot cubicle just like everybody else. Keys to the servant philosophy include the following.

▶ People should work together to build a company. They are partners.

▶ Employees ranging from foremen to sheet metal hangers to safety directors hold TDI stock.
▶ Managers have to earn the recognition and respect of employees.
▶ Managers assume that their followers are working with them and must see things through their eyes.
▶ Managers are people builders—they don't hold people down but lift them up.
▶ Managers can be led. They are not interested in having their own way, but finding the best way.

To keep servant leadership central to TDI's teamwork concept, new employees are assigned to servant leadership discussion groups, which meet weekly for six weeks to discuss various aspects of servant leadership, such as sharing power, listening, and trusting others—and how they can apply these concepts to their particular jobs. TDI has also started a mentoring program designed to give all new hires a positive start at the company. A mentor adopts a new employee for the first six months, and the relationship continues as long as both employees work together on the same job site. If the new hire changes job sites, a different mentor is assigned.

To learn more about this organization, visit *www.tdindustries.com.*

Lessons from the Behavioral Viewpoint Assessment

The behavioral viewpoint of management goes beyond the traditionalists' mechanical view of work by stressing the importance of group dynamics, complex human motivations, and the manager's leadership style. It emphasizes the employee's social and economic needs and the influence of the organization's social setting on the quality and quantity of work produced. The following are the basic assumptions of the behavioral viewpoint.

▶ Employees are motivated by social needs and get a sense of identity through their associations with one another.

▶ Employees are more responsive to the social forces exerted by their peers than to management's financial incentives and rules.

▶ Employees are most likely to respond to managers who can help them satisfy their needs.

▶ Managers need to involve subordinates in coordinating work to improve efficiency.

These assumptions don't always hold in practice, of course. Improving working conditions and managers' human relations skills won't always increase productivity. Economic aspects of work are still important to the employee, as Taylor believed. The major union contracts negotiated in recent years, for instance, focus on job security and wage incentives. And, although employees enjoy working with coworkers who are friendly, low salaries tend to lead to absenteeism and turnover. The negative effects of clumsy organizational structure, poor communication, and routine or boring tasks won't be overcome by the presence of pleasant coworkers. The human aspect of the job now is vastly more complex than those advocating the behavioral viewpoint in the 1930s could ever have imagined.

Snapshot

"Teamwork is one of the most beautiful experiences in life. Teamwork is our core value and a primary way that the Container Store enriches the quality of employees' work life."
Kip Tindell, President, The Container Store

Systems Viewpoint

During World War II the British assembled a team of mathematicians, physicists, and others to solve various wartime problems. These professionals formed the first operations research group. Initially, they were responsible for analyzing the makeup, routes, and speeds of convoys and probable locations of German submarines. The team developed ingenious ways to analyze complex problems that couldn't be handled solely by intuition, straightforward mathematics, or experience. The British and Americans further developed this approach (called *systems analysis*) throughout the war and applied it to many problems of war production and military logistics. Later, systems analysis became an accepted tool in the U.S. Department of Defense and the space program, as well as throughout private industry.[19]

3.
Describe how managers can use systems and quantitative techniques to improve performance.

System Concepts

A system *is an association of interrelated and interdependent parts*. The human body is a system with organs, muscles, bones, nerves, and a consciousness that links all of its parts. In the Challenge of Managing case, we described Starbucks as a system with employees, teams, and departments that are linked by its human resources management system to achieve its goals. An organization also is linked externally to suppliers, customers, shareholders, and regulatory agencies. A competent systems-oriented manager makes decisions only after identifying and analyzing how other managers, departments, customers, or others might be affected by the decisions.

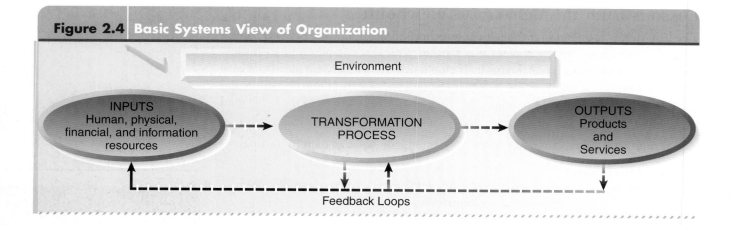

Figure 2.4 | Basic Systems View of Organization

Environment

INPUTS
Human, physical, financial, and information resources

TRANSFORMATION PROCESS

OUTPUTS
Products and Services

Feedback Loops

The systems viewpoint *of management represents an approach to solving problems by diagnosing them within a framework of inputs, transformation processes, outputs, and feedback.* A basic model is shown in Figure 2.4. The system involved may be an individual, a work group, a department, or an entire organization.

Inputs *are the human, physical, material, financial, and information resources that enter a transformation process.* At a university, for example, inputs include students, faculty, money, and buildings.

Transformation processes *comprise the technologies used to convert inputs into outputs.* Transformation processes at a university include lectures, reading assignments, lab experiments, term papers, and tests. Outputs *are the original inputs (human, physical, material, financial, and information resources) as changed by a transformation process.* Outputs at a university include the graduating students. For a system to operate effectively, it must also provide for feedback. Feedback *is information about a system's status and performance.* One form of feedback at a university is the ability of its graduates to get jobs. In an organization, feedback may take the form of marketing surveys, financial reports, production records, performance appraisals, and the like. A manager's role is to guide transformation processes by planning, organizing, leading, and controlling.

System Types

There are two types of systems: closed and open. A closed system *limits its interactions with its environment.* At the General Motors assembly plant in Arlington, Texas, the stamping department operates as a closed system, producing standardized products in an uninterrupted stream. An open system *interacts with the external environment.* Nike's marketing department constantly tries to identify new products and services to satisfy customers' telecommunications desires. It monitors what competitors are doing and then develops ways to deliver better quality and service at a lower price, constantly receiving feedback from customers as part of this process.

Communications processes—both internally with employees and externally with customers—are integral parts of a system.

Quantitative Techniques

While some advocates of systems analysis were suggesting that managers look at inputs, transformation processes, and outputs before making a decision, other systems advocates were developing quantitative techniques to aid in managerial decision making. Quantitative techniques have four basic characteristics.[20]

1. The primary focus is on decision making. Investigation identifies direct actions that managers can take, such as reducing inventory costs.

2. Alternatives are based on economic criteria. Alternative actions are presented in terms of measurable criteria, such as shipping costs, sales revenues, and profits.

3. Mathematical models are used. Situations are simulated and problems are analyzed by means of mathematical models.

4. Computers are essential. Computers are used to solve complex mathematical models, such as statistical process controls, that would be too costly and time consuming to process manually.

The range of quantitative decision-making tools available to management has expanded greatly during the past two decades. In the past, small businesses such as retail stores, medical offices, mom-and-pop restaurants, and farmers couldn't use systems analysis techniques—but today they can. Owners and managers now have inventory, statistical decision theory, linear programming, and many other aids for solving complex problems. Many of those tools are literally at their fingertips in the form of software that can be run on desktop computers. In the emergency room at Presbyterian Hospital in Dallas, a computer on the wall allows the staff to plug in different software modules. These modules relay the patient's functions to a display screen. Each type of sensor—pulse, blood pressure, and the like—is run by a piece of software in its module. Each computer has access to a high-speed local network, so that patient information can be monitored remotely. Thus each patient is monitored by a unique system of connected components that the staff can change as the medical needs of the patient change.

In the largest companies, groups of management scientists can tackle a broad range of business problems by devising their own sophisticated mathematical models for use on mainframe, networked, and personal computers. Such models help gambling casinos such as Caesar's Palace, Bally's, and Harrah's increase their profits and improve service. Casinos provide millions of dollars of complimentary services (e.g., food, rooms, and transportation) for high rollers. To reduce the cost of these services and improve the odds that these people will gamble—and probably lose—in their establishments, casino managers utilize sophisticated information systems that analyze customers' favorite games, betting patterns, accommodation preferences, food and drink choices, and other habits.

Learning from the Systems Viewpoint

Systems analysis and quantitative techniques have been used primarily for managing transformation processes and for the technical planning and decision-making aspects of management. These methods can also be used to improve managers' ability to deal with human resources issues. For example, sophisticated staffing models can be used to map the flow of people into and out of an organization.

Organizations no doubt will continue to develop more sophisticated systems in order to increase productivity. Such systems will require changes in many aspects of day-to-day operations. These changes will not come without struggle and pain. Yet for organizations to survive managers must use increasingly sophisticated systems in making decisions.

The use of systems to send information also has a dark side. Consider blogs, for example. A blog *is a journal that is available on the Web.* Blogs started a few years ago as a simple way for people to keep online journals. The first blog was set up on December 17, 1997. By 2003, the word *blog* had made its way into the *Oxford English*

Blogging: harmless fun turned lethal for corporations?

© Image Source/Jupiter Images

Dictionary. These virtual journals are created by individuals and typically updated daily using software that allows people with little technical background to maintain the blog. Today, 100,000 blogs are set up each day. More than 200 million U.S. Internet users visited a blog last year. So what is the dark side of blogs? It is estimated that employees wasted the equivalent of 551,000 work-years in 2005 reading blogs on the job. Suddenly blogs have become the new means of brand-bashing, personal attacks, political extremism, and smear campaigns. Often a bashing victim can't even figure out who the attacker is. This poses ethical challenges for major companies as well as individuals. Although bloggers are protected by the First Amendment, they are costing companies millions of dollars and tying up their computer systems. The following Ethical Challenge illustrates this problem.[21]

Ethical Challenge

Attack of the Blogs

Bash-the-company blogs provide information about a company that negatively affects their brand image. In 2004, bloggers posted videos showing how to break open a Kryptonite bike lock using a ballpoint pen. The blog accurately exposed a design flaw. However, the blog also spread bogus information—that all Kryptonite locks could be cracked with a pen and that Kryptonite knew about this and covered it up. Neither of these two claims was true, but Kryptonite spent millions replacing locks that were working perfectly. Even Microsoft isn't immune. Gay bloggers attacked Microsoft over its failure to support a gay rights bill in the state of Washington last year. Now Microsoft's public relations people have added blog-monitoring to their list of managerial duties. The company also has created a department, the "Blog Posse," to monitor blogs aimed at Microsoft.

Now some companies are using blogs as a weapon to attack their competitors. Bruce Fischman, a Miami lawyer, estimates that 50 to 60 percent of brand blog attacks are sponsored by competitors. The problem is that the company has only a few hours to respond before it can stop the blog from influencing sales. In 2005, Sara Radicati, a consultant, published a negative report on IBM's Notes e-mail product. That led to organized outrage from bloggers who were consultants and making money by installing Notes. Ed Brill, an IBMer who markets the Notes product and publishes his own blog, responded to her attack and questioned whether she had ties to Microsoft. Within days, bloggers had posted "investigative" articles exposing her as corrupt and unethical and claiming she took bribes from Microsoft. She countered saying these people were a bunch of "sickos."

Contingency Viewpoint

4. State the two major components of the contingency viewpoint.

The essence of the contingency viewpoint *(sometimes called the situational approach) is that management practices should be consistent with the requirements of the external environment, the technology used to make a product or provide a service, and capabilities of the people who work for the organization.*[22] The relationships among these variables are summarized in Figure 2.5. The contingency viewpoint of management emerged in the mid-1960s in response to the frustration of managers and others who had tried unsuccessfully to apply traditional and systems concepts to actual managerial problems. For example, why did providing workers with a bonus for being on time decrease lateness at one Marriott hotel but have little impact at another? Proponents of the contingency viewpoint contend that different situations require different practices. As one manager put it, the contingency viewpoint really means "it all depends."

Proponents of the contingency viewpoint advocate using the other three management viewpoints independently or in combination, as necessary, to deal with various situations. However, this viewpoint doesn't give managers free rein to indulge their personal biases and whims. Rather, managers are expected to determine which methods are likely to be more effective than others in a given situation.

Contingency Variables

The relative importance of each contingency variable—external environment, technology, and people—depends on the type of managerial problem being considered.

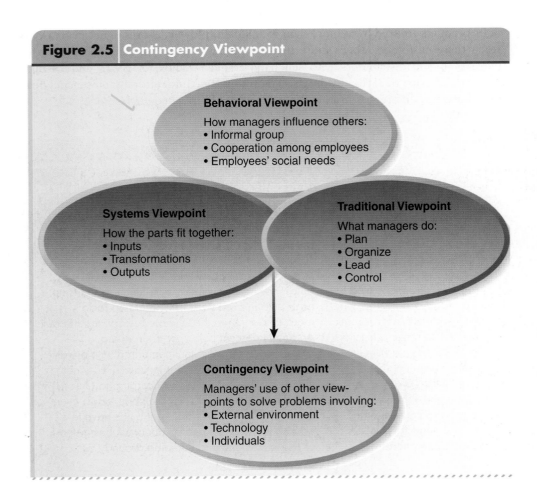

Figure 2.5 Contingency Viewpoint

Behavioral Viewpoint
How managers influence others:
• Informal group
• Cooperation among employees
• Employees' social needs

Systems Viewpoint
How the parts fit together:
• Inputs
• Transformations
• Outputs

Traditional Viewpoint
What managers do:
• Plan
• Organize
• Lead
• Control

Contingency Viewpoint
Managers' use of other viewpoints to solve problems involving:
• External environment
• Technology
• Individuals

For example, in designing an organization's structure a manager should consider the nature of the company's external environment and its ability to process customers' orders. Hence the IRS's structure is different from that of Starbucks. The IRS has a fairly stable set of customers, most of whom must file their tax returns by April 15 each year. It hires many part-time people during the peak tax season to process returns and answer questions and then lays them off after the peak has passed. In contrast, Starbucks has thousands of locations scattered throughout the world and a constantly changing set of customers whose demands for high-quality coffee/tea and service must be met every time coffee/tea is served.

Technology is the method used to transform organizational inputs into outputs. It is more than machinery; it also is the knowledge, tools, techniques, and actions applied to change raw materials into finished goods and services. The technologies that employees use range from the simple to the highly complex. A simple technology involves decision-making rules to help employees do routine jobs. For example, IRS clerks who enter tax information into computers perform routine tasks and work under such rules, requiring few (if any) independent decisions. A complex technology is one that requires employees to make numerous decisions, sometimes with limited information to guide them. A doctor treating an Alzheimer patient must answer many questions and make many decisions without having much guidance because the technology for treating the disease hasn't yet been perfected.

Royal Philips Electronics uses the contingency approach for manufacturing and marketing its products around the globe. In Shanghai, if you want a new cell phone plasma TV or iPod, you go to Yoko, a Chinese version of Best Buy. Last year, Royal Philips sold more than 80 percent of its Chinese electronics through Yoko-like hypermarkets. In India, less than 15 percent of Philips sales comes from big outlets. Most of its products are sold from more than 35,000 family-owned stores in urban areas. To reach these customers where more than 70 percent of the population lives, it uses more than 300 distributors who sell hand-cranked radios for $3.25 and 14-inch "starter" TVs for $125 to customers. The following Multicultural Competency feature illustrates differences in how Philips operates in these countries.[23]

Multicultural Competency

Royal Philips Electronics

In China, Philips has 35 factories and offices with more than 20,000 employees. It also has another 30,000 Chinese workers who are employed by subcontractors to Philips. Many of these are women who work 60 hours a week, make $78 U.S. a week, and live in company dorms. By contrast, the company's India investment is largely in its 1,500 software engineers who make a fraction ($500 to $600 a month) of what its workers in Silicon Valley make. These software engineers write the software for all of Philips' DVD players, most of its digital TV players, and some of its X-ray and magnetic resonance imaging machines. Another 250 accountants and financial analysts work to support its worldwide operations.

Philips faces different manufacturing and distribution in each country. In both countries, there are simple assembly lines where workers insert the filament and support wires into the shells of light bulbs moving down the line. A machine lights up each bulb in a quality test. The Indian factory is more efficient than the Chinese factory, turning out 460 incandescent bulbs per hour with a waste rate of less than 3 percent compared with a waste rate of more than 5 percent in China. Why not make more bulbs in India? According to Gerard Kleisterlee, Philips CEO, it's the poor roads. Even for shipments within India, light bulbs have to be packaged in corrugated cardboard tubes instead of thin boxes to avoid bumping around and breaking on India's rutted roads. India's shipyards also aren't equipped to handle the shipments needed for global distribution. Philips does not try to reach rural customers in China, but sells to big-box retailers like Yoko. Philips is using India as a test country to see if it can sell new products to rural "poor" people.

Philips has learned that Indian employees are more creative than Chinese employees at dreaming up new products and in the tradition of Gandhi rather than Mao, they are more concerned about the plight of the poor. In India, Philips partnered with Indian nongovernmental organizations to develop a van that is equipped with two doctors, a satellite dish, and medical equipment and supplies to take doctors into remote Indian villages and provide free medical care. In China, there are different local concerns. There Philips only sells high-end medical equipment, such as state-of-the-art X-ray, MRI, and heart-monitoring machines. Because the government is striving to improve the country's hospitals, it provides funding that makes it possible for new hospitals to purchase the latest medical technology.

To learn more about this organization, visit *www.china.philips.com.*

Learning from the Contingency Viewpoint

The contingency viewpoint of management is useful because of its diagnostic approach, which clearly departs from the one-best-way approach of the traditionalists. The contingency viewpoint encourages managers to analyze and understand situational differences and to choose the solution best suited to the organization, the process, and the people involved in each.

Critics argue that the contingency viewpoint really is nothing new. They say that it is merely a meshing of techniques from the other viewpoints of management. The contingency viewpoint does draw heavily from the other approaches. However, it is more flexible than the others, allowing managers to apply the principles and tools from those approaches selectively and where most appropriate. It holds that a manager can use principles from the traditional, behavioral, and systems viewpoints only after properly diagnosing the realities of the situation. Such a diagnosis looks at the nature of a situation and the means by which the manager can influence it.

Quality Viewpoint

5.

Explain the impact of the need for quality on management practices.

Today's organizations are dynamic and, whether large or small, local or global, face a host of new management challenges. Organizations feel pressure from customers and competitors to deliver high-quality products and/or services on time, reward ethical behavior of employees, and develop plans to manage highly diverse workforces effectively. Customer demand for high-quality products and services may be the dominant theme for the foreseeable future. Quality *is defined as how well a product or service does what it is supposed to do—how closely and reliably it satisfies the specifications to which it is built or provided.* Managers in successful organizations are quality conscious and understand the link between high-quality goods and/or services and competitive advantage.

Total quality management (TQM) *is a philosophy that makes quality values the driving force behind leadership, design, planning, and improvement initiatives.*[24] Quality must be stressed repeatedly so that it becomes second nature to everyone in an organization and its suppliers. Moreover, training, strategic planning, product design, management information systems, marketing, and other key activities all play a role in meeting quality goals. For example, the Ritz Carlton Hotel requires that all employees go through a training program to make sure that they understand the role of quality in their hotels.

The godfather of the quality movement was W. Edwards Deming (1900–1993).[25] Initially, U.S. managers rejected his ideas, and not until his ideas had helped rebuild Japan's industrial might after World War II were they accepted in the United States.

He taught eager Japanese managers how to use statistics to assess and improve quality. In 1951, Japan established the Deming Prize for corporate quality in his honor. Highly esteemed in Japan, this annual prize recognizes the company that has attained the highest level of quality that year. Deming believed that poor quality is 85 percent a management problem and 15 percent a worker problem. Westinghouse's Nuclear Fuel Division spends $18 million per year on training specifically devoted to quality improvement processes, principles, technology, and objectives of its managers.

The Quality Control Process

The quality control process generally focuses on measuring inputs (including customer expectations and requirements), operations, and outputs. The results of these measurements enable managers and employees to make decisions about product or service quality at each stage of the transformation process.

Inputs. Quality control generally begins with inputs, especially the raw materials and parts used in a transformation process. For services, the inputs are based on the information the client provides. Solectron, a manufacturer of printed circuit boards and networking products, emphasizes quality control by its suppliers. For almost all parts, Solectron uses only one or two suppliers for each location, which is consistent with one of Deming's prescriptions. Tom Kennedy, vice president for quality at Solectron, realizes that its products are only as good as the weakest link in its supply chain. As a result, it developed a set of practices for working with suppliers so that both Solectron and the suppliers learn faster.

Operations. Quality control inspections are made during and between successive transformation stages. Work-in-progress inspection can result in the reworking or rejecting of an item before the next operation is performed on it.

The use of statistical process control is one of Deming's key prescriptions. Statistical process control *is the use of quantitative methods and procedures to determine whether transformation operations are being done correctly, to detect any deviations, and, if there are any, to find and eliminate their causes.*[26] Statistical process control methods have been available for decades but only in the past 20 years have they been used to any significant extent. They serve primarily as preventive controls.

Sigma *is a unit of statistical measurement, which in this context is used to illustrate the quality of a process.* The sigma measurement scale (ranging from two to six) describes defects in parts per million. To simplify the concept, let's consider the application of six sigma to writing a text. If defects were measured in misspellings, four sigma would be equivalent to one misspelling per 30 pages of text; five sigma, one misspelling in a set of encyclopedias; and six sigma, only one misspelling in an entire small library, such as a high school library.

General Electric in its lighting product plants, for example, has adopted the quality goal of six sigma, which means eliminating defects to the level of 1 per 3.4 million opportunities—or a process that is 99.99966 percent defect free. Five sigma is 233 defects per million, and four sigma is 6,210 defects per million. Most firms operate at the four-sigma level. A key theme in six-sigma programs is the reduction of waste. GE trains all employees to seek opportunities to reduce waste in seven areas. They include

▶ waste of overproduction (also irregular production such as end-of-month or end-of-quarter surges),

▶ waste of time on hand (waiting),

▶ waste in transportation,

▶ waste of processing itself,

▸ waste of stock on hand (inventory),

▸ waste of movement, and

▸ waste of making defective products.

Outputs. The most traditional and familiar form of quality control is the assessment made after completion of a component or an entire product, or provision of a service. With goods, quality control tests may be made just before the items are shipped to customers. The number of items returned by customers because of shoddy workmanship or other problems is one indicator of the effectiveness of the quality control process. Service providers, such as barbers and hairdressers, usually involve their customers in checking the quality of outputs by asking if everything is okay. However, the satisfactory provision of a service often is more difficult to assess than the satisfactory quality of goods.[27]

Determining the amount or degree of the eight dimensions of quality shown in Table 2.2 is fundamental to quality control. The more accurate the measurement, the easier comparing actual to desired results becomes. Quality dimensions generally are measured by variable or by attribute. Measuring by variable *assesses product characteristics for which there are quantifiable standards (length, diameter, height, weight, or temperature).* Consider the quality control process and technology used on the Mercedes-Benz M-class sport utility vehicle at the Mercedes factory in Vance, Alabama.[28] Carmakers have traditionally tracked their body-building accuracy by taking sample vehicles off the assembly line and physically checking a large number of their dimensions with special equipment. Mercedes still does so, running about every 100th body through a measuring machine that checks 1,062 dimensions with sensitive touch probes in a process that takes about 4 hours.

Table 2.2	The Meaning of Quality		
		EXAMPLES	
QUALITY DIMENSION	DEFINITION	LEXUS	BANKAMERICA
Performance	Primary good or service characteristics	Miles per gallon, acceleration	Time to process customer requests
Features	Added touches, secondary characteristics	Level of road noise	Credit provisions, interest rates
Reliability	Consistency of performance over time	Number of miles to failure of parts	Variability of time to process customer requests
Durability	Useful life	Miles of useful life (with repair)	Timeliness of statements
Serviceability	Resolution of problems and complaints	Ease of repair	Resolution of errors, number of ATMs
Responsiveness	Person-to-person contact, including timeliness, courtesy, and professionalism	Courtesy of auto dealer, repairs completed as scheduled	Courtesy of teller
Aesthetics	Sensory effects, such as sound, feel, and look	Styling, interior finish	Appearance of lobby, location of branches
Reputation	Past performance and industry/customer regard	*Consumer Reports* ranking, owners' reviews	Advice of friends, *Kiplinger Magazine* ranking

To spot flaws that can develop between those elaborate inspections on every 100th body, Mercedes uses a new vision system. At the end of the body-building line, a body-in-white vehicle—factory language for an unpainted body minus doors, hood, and liftgate—arrives at the vision station. In a process that takes just 45 seconds, 38 laser cameras mounted on a superstructure check 84 key measurements. Slight dimensional flaws can be identified and corrected before any out-of-tolerance bodies get built. "Before laser gauging, carmakers couldn't do 100 percent inspection. Now we do it," stated Mike Hill, leader of the measurement team.

Measuring by attribute *evaluates product or service characteristics as acceptable or unacceptable.* Measuring by attribute usually is easier than measuring by variable. When Tom Stemberg founded Staples, the office supply superstore, he decided to track customer purchases as a measure of customer loyalty. His solution was to create a membership card good for discounts and special promotions. The company encouraged all of its customers to sign up and then entered their membership numbers at the cash register every time they made a purchase. If a customer forgot to bring the card, the cashier could access the account number simply by entering the customer's phone number. The membership application captured basic demographic information; cash-register data gave precise information about preferences, quantities, and frequency of purchase. Together the applications and purchase histories told Staples management which customers and customer segments accounted for most of each store's volume. Staples doesn't need mass mailings to entire geographic markets. Instead, it targets its coupons, mailings, and special promotions to specific customers who have purchased certain products.

Learning from the Quality Viewpoint

Producing high-quality products or services isn't an end in itself. Successfully offering high quality to customers typically results in three important benefits for the organization, as shown in Figure 2.6.[29]

Positive Company Image. A reputation for high-quality products creates a positive image for organizations, such as Maytag, Ritz Carlton Hotels, Nordstrom's, Southwest Airlines, Lexus, and others. A positive image eases recruiting of new employees, increasing sales, and obtaining funds from various lending agencies. A positive company image can influence new customers who have little direct experience with the company to shop there. The Container Store, Chick-fil-A, and Enterprise Rent-a-Car,

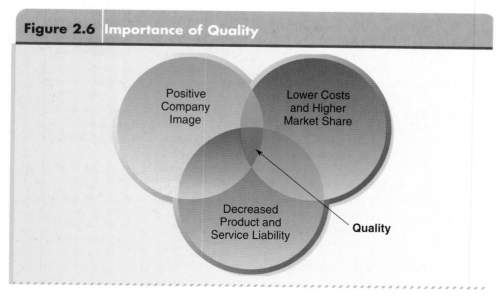

Figure 2.6 | Importance of Quality

among others, enjoy a positive company image that results in higher profits, lower employee turnover, and greater customer satisfaction than organizations with a poorer company image. The importance of a positive company image is a key management philosophy at Timberland as the following Self-Management feature illustrates.[30]

Self-Management Competency

Walking the Talk at Timberland

Jeffrey Swartz is a third-generation CEO whose grandfather founded Timberland in 1952. He is providing the leadership to use the resources and profits of this $1.5 billion company footwear-and-apparel company to combat social ills, help the environment, and improve conditions of workers around the world. The idea of helping others, he believes, is a vision around which he is creating a more committed, productive, efficient, and loyal workforce, which helps earn profits. During the past five years, the company, which sells outdoor-themed clothes, has seen sales grow at 9.7 percent a year, and its stock price has increased more than 64 percent. According to Kevin Martinez, Home Depot's Director of Community Affairs, "Timberland has one of the best business cultures of any retailer I know because it is built around service."

Swartz encountered a challenge that changed how he managed the company. Prior to 1989, he managed by the numbers. Alan Khazei, a member of a local charity, asked if Timberland would donate shoes to its workers. Swartz accepted the request and he and nine other employees cleaned up an old house used for troubled teens. While cleaning up this house, Swartz saw that his problems were small in comparison with the teens' emotional and physical struggles. Upon returning to the company after the project, he decided that Timberland would help those who were less fortunate. When he replaced his father as CEO in 1998, he was determined to make Timberland a living laboratory for a values-driven firm. The core values of humanity, humility, integrity, and excellence are practiced by all employees.

When employees arrive for work, they see Timberland's Community Impact Center where they can sign up for a host of volunteer projects or propose their own. One can also see a day-care center. Swartz created a Serva-a-Palooza day held in late September, a series of projects designed to clean up and reclaim public places around Lawrence, Massachusetts, and a plan to improve a center for kids with handicaps in Ho Chi Minh City, Vietnam. Swartz also invited Timberland's biggest customer, Foot Locker, to send employees to help with its projects.

Timberland posts signs through its plant touting ecometrics. Ecometrics *is a measure of the environmental impact of manufacturing a product on the planet.* One pair of its Miōn water sandals, for example, takes 2 kWh of electricity to make, produces no greenhouse gases, and is made with 100 percent renewable pieces.

In a recent survey of Timberland employees, more than 75 percent said that they would choose Timberland again as a place to work, and 79 percent indicated that the reputation of the company played a major part in their decision to work for the company.

Swartz's biggest challenge is getting investors to buy into Timberland's values. When Timberland's stock fell 18 percent recently, stockholders reminded Swartz that they expected financial results, so he shouldn't spend too much time and money on being nice to employees and people in the community.

To learn more about this organization, visit *www.timberland.com.*

Lower Costs and Higher Market Share. It is estimated that between 15 and 20 percent of every sales dollar is used for reworking, scrapping, inspections, tests, warranties, and repeated service. For a company with a well-run quality management program, these costs should be less than 2.5 percent. At Timberland, its well-run total quality program has increased productivity and lowered rework time, scrap costs, and warranty costs, resulting in increased profits. Improved performance features and product reliability at Toyota enabled Lexus to become the number one selling car in its class in the United States. Many have seen the TV advertisement for "The Lonely

Snapshot

"International operations aren't a backwater— they're a way to prove you can get quality on a global basis. To become a successful senior manager, you need to get involved with customer, manufacturing technologies and employees in different cultures and manufacture products that have high quality."

**Brian Sullivan,
Executive Recruiter,
Christian & Timbers**

Maytag Repairman." In service settings organizations, such as State Farm Insurance, USAA, and Mayo Clinic, higher quality service can be used to attract and retain new customers. People are willing to pay for excellent service.

Decreased Product and Service Liability. Product manufacturers and service providers increasingly face costly legal suits over damages caused by faulty, dangerous, and/or misrepresented products and services. Organizations that design and produce faulty products increasingly are being held liable in state courts for damages resulting from the use of such products. Successful TQM efforts typically result in improved products and product performance and lower product liability costs at Darden Restaurants, which operates the Olive Garden, Red Lobster, and other chains.

Decisions about quality should be an integral part of an organization's strategy—that is, how it competes in the marketplace. A core strategy of quality consistently provides the best possible products in their price ranges in the marketplace. Quality therefore must be a basic component of the structure and culture of the organization. Quality isn't simply a program that can be imposed on employees by top management; it is a way of operating that permeates an organization and the thinking of everyone in the organization.

Integration of Management Viewpoints and Competencies

In Chapter 1, we identified six management competencies that are essential to your future success as a manager. Each of the five managerial viewpoints discussed here stresses at least one of those competencies more than others. Table 2.3 shows the relationships between the management viewpoints and the competencies.

The traditional viewpoint sought to identify management competencies that efficiently organized the work of employees. Each level of management was assigned specific goals and tasks to accomplish in an allotted time period. The structure of the organization governed relations between manager and employee. It was the manager's job to plan, organize, and lay out the task for the employee; it was the employee's job to follow the manager's instructions. Employees were thought of as "rational" people who were motivated primarily by money.

The behavioral viewpoint focused on developing two competencies: communication and teamwork. It was the manager's job to acknowledge the social and emotional needs of employees and to develop harmonious relationships in the workplace. This viewpoint stressed that employees' behaviors are greatly affected by their interactions with peers. If managers communicated with employees and satisfied their workplace needs, the organization would be effective.

Table 2.3	Integration of Management Viewpoints and Competencies				
MANAGERIAL COMPETENCY	**MANAGEMENT VIEWPOINT**				
	TRADITIONAL	**BEHAVIORAL**	**SYSTEMS**	**CONTINGENCY**	**QUALITY**
Communication		X	X	X	X
Planning and administration	X			X	
Strategic action			X		X
Self-management					X
Multicultural			X		X
Teamwork		X		X	X

X = relatively high importance

The systems viewpoint stressed that managers should focus on how various inputs, transformation processes, and outputs are related to the organization's goals. The organization was viewed as a "whole," rather than simply the sum of its various departments or divisions. This wholeness requires managers to develop their communication, strategic thinking and action, and multicultural competencies. To develop these competencies, managers use quantitative models to help them understand complex organizational relationships and make appropriate decisions.

The contingency viewpoint draws from each of the other viewpoints and involves a somewhat different set of competencies. Deciding whether to draw on one set of skills in a competency or on several skills across competencies is the job of the manager. How an organization is designed depends on its external environment, the skills of its employees, and the technology used to transform raw materials into finished products. The use of teams, for example, tests the manager's communication and teamwork competencies.

The quality viewpoint stresses meeting customers' expectations in terms of the value (performance and quality) of goods and services. Top management is responsible for putting systems into place to achieve quality. One way for top management to gain the support of employees in such an effort is to design TQM practices that reward employees for meeting quality goals. The TQM philosophy requires a high level of coordination throughout the organization. One way to achieve that coordination is through teamwork. In quality-conscious organizations, teamwork means sharing both responsibility and decision making. Managers delegate decision-making authority to employees, permitting them to manage themselves—but only after they have received the necessary training. Deming's philosophy of statistical quality control not only provides a method for analyzing deviations from standards, but it also provides a way to increase communication among employees.

Today, many managers are using these five foundation viewpoints to create new ways of thinking about managing their organizations. For centuries, owners of family businesses have passed on their wisdom, experience, and contacts to their children; master craftsman have taught their ideas to apprentices; and employees have exchanged know-how about the job with their fellow coworkers. Throughout the book, we indicate that different viewpoints of knowledge management result in different management practices. Knowledge managers share information with others to achieve innovation and best practices. The roots of some of these practices can be traced to the contributions of managers who advocated the systems and quality viewpoints. The challenge facing managers is to draw on traditional viewpoints to become decisive and action oriented. Finally, since organizations are continuously changing, they must learn from the past in order to remain competitive.

Chapter Summary ....

In this chapter we introduced several influential viewpoints and approaches that have shaped managerial thinking during the past 100 years. Ideas from bureaucratic, scientific, and administrative management greatly influenced early managerial practices. Later, new ideas of managing stressed the human or behavioral aspects of managing. During World War II, industry and the armed forces developed sophisticated management systems to coordinate war efforts. Then, as organizations grew and became global, none of the earlier management concepts seemed to apply totally to various situations. The contingency approach stressed that these concepts could be applied under some conditions but not under others. Today's managers are concerned primarily with the quality viewpoint of management as a way to meet consumer demand throughout the world for quality products and services.

Learning Goals ....

1. Describe the three branches of the traditional viewpoint of management: bureaucratic, scientific, and administrative.

Max Weber developed a theory of bureaucratic management, which emphasizes the need for a strict hierarchy governed by clearly defined regulations and lines of authority. His theory contains seven principles: a formal system of rules, impersonal management, division of labor, a hierarchical structure, a detailed authority structure, lifelong career commitment, and rationality. Scientific management theorists tried to find ways to make workers more productive. Frederick Taylor thought that management's job was to make individual workers more efficient. That was to be accomplished by improving worker–machine relationships, based on time-and-motion studies. Frank and Lillian Gilbreth also studied how to make workers more efficient. Frank Gilbreth focused on the various physical motions workers used, and Lillian Gilbreth emphasized the welfare of workers. Henry Gantt thought that workers' performance could be charted and thus improved by setting deadlines. Administrative management theorists focused on principles that managers, rather than workers, could use to become more effective. Henry Fayol outlined four functions—planning, organizing, leading, and controlling—that he believed all successful managers use in their work.

2. Explain the behavioral viewpoint's contribution to management.

The behavioral viewpoint emphasizes employees' human and social needs. One of its first proponents, Mary Parker Follett, believed that management should coordinate the efforts of all employees to achieve organizational goals. Chester Barnard's contribution was similar to Follett's. He held, in part, that a manager doesn't have the authority to tell a worker what to do unless the worker accepts that authority. Studies conducted at the Hawthorne plant of the Western Electric Company led to the conclusion that social and human factors can be more important than physical and financial factors in influencing productivity.

3. Describe how managers can use systems and quantitative techniques to improve employee performance.

The systems viewpoint looks at organizations as a series of inputs, transformation processes, and outputs. A system may either be open or closed. Systems analysis advocates that managers use quantitative techniques to solve problems.

4. State the two major components of the contingency viewpoint.

The contingency viewpoint, or situational approach, encourages managers to use the concepts and methods of the traditional, behavioral, and systems viewpoints, depending on the circumstances they face at the time. The three key contingency variables that managers should consider before making a decision are the environment, technology, and people involved.

5. Explain the impact of the need for quality on management practices.

The quality viewpoint stresses the provision of high-quality products and services at all times. One of the founders of the quality movement was W. Edwards Deming. Long after he had helped Japanese managers make statistical analyses the basis for quality control improvements, his contributions were recognized by U.S. managers. His recommendations included planning for quality, striving for zero defects, using only a few suppliers who have demonstrated that they can deliver quality, and inspecting for quality during the process instead of after.

Key Terms and Concepts

Acceptance theory of
 authority
Administrative
 management
Authority principle
Authority structure
Behavioral viewpoint
Blog
Bureaucratic management
Charismatic authority
Closed system
Contingency viewpoint
Division of labor
Ecometrics
Feedback

Functional foremanship
Gantt chart
Hawthorne effect
Hierarchical structure
Impersonality
Inputs
Lifelong career
 commitment
Measuring by attribute
Measuring by variable
Open system
Outputs
Quality
Rationality
Rational–legal authority

Rules
Scientific management
Sigma
Statistical process control
System
Systems viewpoint
Technology
Time-and-motion study
Total quality management
Traditional authority
Traditional viewpoint
Transformation processes
Unity of command principle

Questions for Discussion and Reflective Thinking

1. Why should you know about the evolution of management?

2. Visit a Starbucks coffee shop and, using the quality attributes in Table 2.2, rate Starbucks' product and service quality. How does the store stack up against these criteria?

3. What competency is most critical in applying for a managerial position at Starbucks (*www.starbucks.com*)?

4. What competencies would you need to be employed at TDIndustries? Why? You might want to refer to *www.tdindustries.com* for help in answering this question.

5. How can managers use the concepts of the bureaucratic viewpoint to increase the efficiency of their operation?

6. What challenges face employees who are trying to implement aspects of the behavioral viewpoint in an organization?

7. Using systems concepts, describe the registration process used at your university to enroll students.

8. Visit a local fast-food restaurant. How has the store used principles of scientific management to help managers increase their store's efficiency?

9. What types of problems does systems analysis tackle?

10. How does Royal Philips Electronics (*www.philips.com/global*) use the concepts in the contingency viewpoint to manage its global operations?

11. What lessons did you take away from Timberland that you can apply to your career?

12. Why is quality important?

DEVELOPING YOUR COMPETENCIES

Although you might find it hard to do, try to answer each of the following 20 items with either a **mostly agree** or **mostly disagree** response. We'll talk about the scoring of the scale below.

	Mostly Agree	Mostly Disagree
1. I value stability in my job.	_____	_____
2. I like a predictable organization.	_____	_____
3. I enjoy working without the benefit of a carefully specific job description.	_____	_____
4. I'd enjoy working for a firm that promotes employees based on seniority.	_____	_____
5. Rules, policies, and procedures generally frustrate me.	_____	_____
6. I would enjoy working for a company that had 100,000 employees.	_____	_____
7. Being an entrepreneur would involve more risks than I'm willing to take.	_____	_____
8. Before accepting a position, I'd like to see a job description.	_____	_____
9. I'd prefer a job as a freelance landscape artist to one as a supervisor for the Department of Motor Vehicles.	_____	_____
10. Seniority should be as important as performance in determining pay promotions.	_____	_____
11. I'd be proud to work for the largest and most successful company in its field.	_____	_____
12. Given a choice, I'd rather make $90,000 a year as a VP in a small company than $100,000 a year as a middle manager in a large company.	_____	_____
13. I'd feel uncomfortable if I had to wear an employee badge with an ID number on it.	_____	_____
14. Parking spaces in a company lot should be assigned according to job level.	_____	_____
15. I'd generally prefer working as a specialist instead of performing lots of tasks.	_____	_____
16. Before accepting a job, I'd want to make sure that the company had a good program of employee benefits.	_____	_____
17. A firm won't be successful unless it has a clear set of rules and regulations.	_____	_____
18. I'd rather work in a department with a manager than on a team where managerial responsibility is shared.	_____	_____
19. You should respect people's rank.	_____	_____
20. Rules are meant to be broken.	_____	_____

Scoring: Give yourself a point for each time you answered **mostly agree** to the following items: 1, 2, 4, 6, 7, 8, 10, 11, 14, 16, 17, 18, and 19. Give yourself a point for each time you answered **mostly disagree** to the following items: 3, 5, 9, 12, 13, 15, and 20.

Interpretation: Some norms have been developed to help you interpret your total number of points:

- 0–7   You would most likely be frustrated by working in a very formal organization, especially a large bureaucracy.
- 8–14   You would experience a mix of satisfaction and disappointment from working in a large formal firm.
- 15–20 Large, formal firms are more compatible with your style and preferences.

Questions

1. What dimensions of the self-management competency are demonstrated in this exercise?

2. What dimensions of the planning and administration competency are demonstrated in this exercise?

For many years, people in England thought of Alliance Boots as a local pharmacy with well-stocked health items, cosmetics, and toiletries. Boots is the United Kingdom's and Ireland's largest drug chain with more than 1,400 stores. It also is a major retail brand that almost failed before Richard Baker took over in 2003.

Baker knew that Boots had become too bureaucratic. Its distribution and information technology systems were old; it also had high costs and inefficient management processes, its pricing structure was hopelessly mired in a maze of outdated rules and regulations, its stores were cluttered, and it had too many people at its headquarters in Nottingham. He also knew that the largest drug chain was facing stiff competition from Wal-Mart, which had recently acquired Asda to become a major force in the market along with Tesco. Boots' stores were also located in the cities and relied heavily on foot traffic, but in the United Kingdom, the population was moving to the suburbs. Baker knew that there would be no quick fixes, but Baker needed to radically change the way Boots was managed.

Baker had previously worked for Asda, a discount giant with a reputation for openness and innovation. Ideas that could provide useful change were encouraged and acted on quickly. Prior to his arrival at Boots, change was viewed as an enemy. According to Baker, "Boots operates in an extremely competitive environment where the pace of decision making and speed of implementation are critical to its success." He knew that Boots had its greatest success in an era when people signed on for lifetime careers at a company and expected to have a comfortable ride through the management ranks. With homegrown managers and a long tradition of doing things a certain way, Boots had grown immune to the changes that were taking place in the retail environment. Baker knew that there were three or four employees doing a job that one had done at Asda. Its top managers for years had tended to focus on current profits rather than on the future.

Baker immediately cut 900 jobs in headquarters to save more than $71 million. He also gave store managers freedom to make decisions about promotions and ordered managers at headquarters to spend some time in the stores. He also decided to focus on Boots' core business, drug stores and its international over-the-counter drugs. The company's Boots Healthcare International is a leading U.K. maker of the over-the-counter drugs such as Nurofen (ibuprofen) and Strepsils (sore throat remedy), which it sells in 130 countries. In the past, Boots had tried to extend its business into other areas, such as Wellbeing services and the Pure Beauty retail format. It sold off these businesses and used the money from the sales to modernize the stores and focus more effectively on the customer. Three hundred new pharmacists were hired and trained to become customer service oriented rather than technicians. Some Boots' stores are open 24 hours a day to give the customers more service. Boots has also rolled out a new pharmacy system, SmartScript, which will improve professional services and inventory management. The new pharmacy system is aimed at reducing the need to have large inventories in the stores and to utilize space more efficiently.

These changes have enabled Boots to grow sales by more than 5 percent a year and its revenue to top more than $10 billion. To learn more about this organization, visit *www.allianceboots.com*.

Questions

1. What viewpoint(s) has Richard Baker used to manage Boots? What are some of the limitations of this viewpoint(s)?

2. What are some of Baker's management competencies illustrated in this case?

3. How can you learn the competencies needed to work for a person like Baker?

PART 2
Managing in Turbulent Environments

chapter 3

© Tetra Images/Jupiter Images

Ethics and Social Responsibility

Learning Goals

After studying this chapter, you should be able to:

1. State the importance of ethics for individual employees and organizations.

2. Describe four influences that shape the ethical behaviors and decisions of individuals and organizations.

3. Describe three approaches that people use when making ethical judgments.

4. Explain stakeholder social responsibility and how it influences managers' ethical decisions and behaviors.

Communication Competency

Planning and Administration Competency

Teamwork Competency

Managing Effectively

Self-Management Competency

Strategic Action Competency

Multicultural Competency

Challenge of Managing ....

Halliburton

© AP Photo

David Lesar, CEO of Halliburton Co., answers a question for the media after an annual shareholders meeting in Duncan, Okla., May 2006.

Halliburton is one of the largest providers of products and services to the oil and gas industries. It employs more than 100,000 people in over 120 countries working in five major operating groups.

Some of the media, certain politicians, and various groups charge Halliburton with engaging in unethical and, at times, illegal behaviors and decisions. It is not our purpose here to find the firm innocent or guilty of these charges. Rather, we will note here and elsewhere in the chapter the challenges that management faces in dealing with these charges.

Halliburton Watch is one group that monitors Halliburton and reports on its alleged unethical and illegal behaviors and decisions. For example, outrage overflowed on Capitol Hill when members of Congress were told that Halliburton's dining halls in Iraq had repeatedly served spoiled food to unsuspecting troops. "This happened quite a bit," claimed Rory Mayberry, a former food manager with Halliburton's KBR subsidiary.

The outrage apparently doesn't end with spoiled food. Former Kellogg Brown & Root (KBR) employees and water quality specialists, Ben Carter and Ken May, told Halliburton Watch that KBR knowingly exposed troops and civilians to contaminated water from Iraq's Euphrates River. One internal KBR e-mail provided to Halliburton Watch says that, for "possibly a year," the level of contamination at one camp was two times the normal level for untreated water. Carter asserts "I discovered the water being delivered from the Euphrates for the military was not being treated properly and thousands were being exposed daily to numerous pathogenic organisms." Carter worked at Camp Ar Ramadi, located 70 miles west of Baghdad in the notoriously violent Sunni Triangle, but he claimed water contamination problems existed throughout Iraq's military camps.

In contrast, Halliburton spokeswoman Melissa Norcross said KBR "conducted its own inspection of the water at the site in question and has found no evidence to substantiate the allegations." Norcross noted that the "military's own records show that the water produced during this time period contained no bacteriological contamination and was suitable for these non-potable

Learning Content

purposes." A military spokesman told the Associated Press that a military medical unit visited the camp and found nothing out of the ordinary, and water quality records showed the water within normal parameters.[1]

To learn more about this organization, visit *www.halliburton.com*.

Importance of Ethics

This Challenge of Managing feature presents just two of a number of ethical charges against Halliburton. Regardless of the actual facts associated with these and other charges, it is clear that Halliburton management has experienced major challenges in coping with them. For a time, David Lesar, the chairman, president, and CEO of Halliburton, did not respond to them. But he and others at Halliburton eventually recognized the long-term importance of restoring in the public's mind and enforcing the ethical expectations of Halliburton. For example, in a recent letter to all employees, Lesar stated, in part:

> The Halliburton Company Code of Business Conduct is a guide for every Company Director, officer, employee and agent in applying legal and ethical practices to their everyday work. The Code describes not only our standards of integrity but also some of the specific principles and areas of the law that are most likely to affect us. There is no quality more important than integrity. This applies to a business just as it does to an individual. Integrity is a core value in our Code of Business Conduct.
>
> Compliance with the law and honesty and integrity in our dealings with others are not to be sacrificed in the name of profits. Management does not and will not condone any such action. Our success will be attained through compliance with the law, dealings evidencing fairness and integrity and a commitment to quality. We expect your wholehearted support of these Company values and principles.[2]

Clearly, this letter expresses the claimed importance of ethical and socially responsible behaviors and decisions at Halliburton. The key, of course, to ethical behavior is found in the actual day-to-day behavior of and decisions made by Halliburton's 100,000 employees, not simply written statements.

The importance of ethical issues facing managers and employees have been magnified in recent years due to the unethical and illegal conduct of some of the top executives in various major U.S. organizations, such as Enron, Tyco, and Adelphia. The notorious unethical and often illegal practices by the top executives of such organizations have resulted in bankruptcies, massive financial losses for shareholders, and loss of jobs by employees. The unethical behaviors in individual firms have spilled over to a general loss of trust in business leaders by the U.S. public. In a U.S. Roper poll, only 2 percent checked off "very trustworthy" to describe the chief executives of large U.S. companies. Only 9 percent of the respondents indicated they had full trust in U.S. financial services institutions. Also, 72 percent of respondents felt that wrongdoing was widespread in U.S. industry.[3]

The public's concern over the state of ethical behavior and decisions is not limited to executives. For example, a Gallup poll asked respondents to rate the ethical standards of people in 21 professions. The results put senators and congressmen near the bottom of the list—finishing behind lawyers and building contractors. Business executives also scored low, with only 16 percent of the public giving them a "high" or "very high" score for ethics. Journalists finished in the middle of the pack, above real estate agents and building contractors but trailing accountants and bankers. Nurses, doctors, and school teachers were ranked relatively high.[4]

A variety of studies suggest that ethical decisions and behaviors by managers and others are important to the long-term effectiveness of a company. An ethical organization is an important ingredient in achieving (1) stronger financial performance over the long run; (2) greater sales, brand image, and reputation; (3) more employee loyalty and commitment; (4) less vulnerability to activist pressure and boycotts; and (5) fewer or no fines, court-imposed remedies, and criminal charges.[5] The importance of company ethics to the economy and shareholders was succinctly expressed by Scott Burns, a syndicated business writer. He states "Modern capital markets run on trust and integrity. It could be argued that the American standard of doing business is higher than it has ever been. Whatever the current standard relative to our history, however, it fails to meet public expectations."[6]

The unethical and illegal actions of a single employee or small group of employees can tarnish the ethical reputation of a whole company. Recall our previous comments related to the challenges and efforts by Halliburton to restore its reputation. The *Wall Street Journal* published a brief article under the title of "Ex-Halliburton Employee Sentenced to Prison." Note the focus on "Halliburton." Brief excerpts from the story state:

> A former Halliburton Company worker was sentenced to 15 months in prison after pleading guilty in federal court in Illinois to taking more than $110,000 in kickbacks from an Iraqi company. The kickbacks were discovered by Halliburton's Kellogg Brown & Root (KBR) unit, which handles construction and government contracting, during an internal investigation. A Halliburton spokesperson stated "When the issue was discovered, KBR removed the company in question from consideration for any future work as a subcontractor. KBR also issued the government a credit for the amount of the improper payment.[7]

Although Halliburton discovered, took action, and reported the unethical and illegal behavior of the employee, the media's reporting focused on "Halliburton." This is another reason why top management at Halliburton and other companies must be proactive in preventing the unethical and illegal behaviors of its employees. David Lesar has been engaged in efforts within and outside of the firm to affirm and enforce ethical and legal behaviors among its employees. This is a major undertaking for the leader of such a large and complex global company.

In this chapter, we discuss four influences that shape ethical conduct; including cultural influences, legal and regulatory influences, organizational influences, and individual influences. Next, we invite you to consider your own approach to ethical issues. You will discover how much your personal judgments are influenced by utilitarian thinking, a concern for moral rights, and a belief in maintaining a sense of justice. Then, we review the stakeholder approach to the management of corporate social responsibility. Throughout the chapter, we address ways to encourage, expect, and enforce ethical conduct.

The top executives at General Electric, like those at Halliburton and many other companies, have increased their emphasis on the importance of ethical behaviors and decisions for employees at all levels. The Ethical Challenge feature on the following page provides a glimpse into the importance and challenges for General Electric in strengthening its compliance and ethical efforts.[8] General Electric (GE) is a large and complex organization with multiple divisions that provide such products as aircraft engines, plastics, appliances, lighting, nuclear reactors, financial services, and so on. GE operates throughout the world and has more than 300,000 employees.

Snapshot

"While the majority of corporate CEOs are honest leaders dedicated to building their companies, far too many got caught up in the quest for personal gain and wound up sacrificing their values and their stakeholders. Call it greed, because that's what it is. It threatens the very fabric of our system."

William W. George, Former CEO and Chairman, Medtronic, Inc.

© Adam Rountree/AP Photo

A view of the General Electric building at 30 Rockefeller Plaza, New York City.

General Electric's Compliance Training

General Electric has strengthened its compliance and ethics programs and training for all employees worldwide. GE executives say it is a particular challenge to reach small offices with only a handful of employees and to indoctrinate new employees. "It's not easy hiring and training 13,000 employees a year," says Jon Graham, GE's vice president of legal policy, who oversees compliance with its ethical and legal standards.

In most instances, GE employees undergo ethics and compliance training soon after joining the company. GE, like many companies, conducts much of the training online and tests employees on how to handle thorny issues, such as unusual requests by a customer for money or to ignore a government regulation. The company also holds small group meetings at which employees are encouraged to ask questions and raise concerns over potentially improper behavior.

To reinforce its commitment to compliance, GE developed a system to track employees' completion of its ethics courses. Every quarter, each business unit must tell the compliance department what percentage of its employees have completed the training sessions and what percentage have read and signed off on GE's "Spirit and Letter" ethics guide. The guide covers issues ranging from when it is permissible to work with a competitor to checking customers against terrorist watch lists. The results are audited. Graham states, "these results are part of the fabric of business leaders' reviews."

To learn more about this organization, see *www.ge.com*.

2.

Describe four influences that shape the ethical behaviors and decisions of individuals and organizations.

Shaping Ethical Conduct

In the most basic sense, ethics *is a set of values, principles, and rules that define right and wrong conduct.* These values, principles, and rules indicate when certain behaviors and decisions are acceptable and when they are unacceptable. What is considered ethical may depend on the perspective from which ethical issues are considered.[9] Figure 3.1 identifies the four basic influences that shape the ethical conduct of individuals and organizations. Rarely can the ethical implications of decisions or behaviors be understood by considering only one of these influences.

Cultural Influences

Culture *is the dominant pattern of living, thinking, and believing that is developed and transmitted by people, consciously or unconsciously, to subsequent generations.*[10] For a *culture* to exist, it must

▶ be shared by the vast majority of the members of a major group or entire society;

▶ be passed on from generation to generation; and

▶ shape behavior, decisions, and perceptions of the world.[11]

A key feature of a culture is its cultural values—*those consciously and subconsciously deeply held beliefs that specify general preferences and behaviors, and define what is right and wrong.* Cultural values are reflected in a society's morals, customs, and established practices. A significant part of what is considered ethical comes from cultural values and the specific norms and traditions that flow from them. Within the North American culture, fundamental personal values that are often cited as central to society and individuals include[12]

Figure 3.1 | Shaping Ethical Conduct

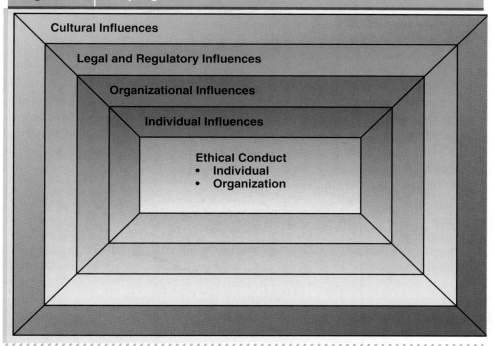

Cultural Influences

Legal and Regulatory Influences

Organizational Influences

Individual Influences

Ethical Conduct
- Individual
- Organization

▶ honesty,

▶ integrity,

▶ trustworthiness,

▶ respect for other people,

▶ self-respect,

▶ family,

▶ achievement,

▶ reliability,

▶ fairness, and

▶ loyalty.

A number of these values serve as anchors in ethical decision making and behavior. They reflect cultural ideals used to define ethical from unethical behaviors and decisions. Recall the comment by William George, the former chairman and CEO of Medtronic, Inc., in the previous Snapshot feature. We share another insightful comment from George here:

Our system of capitalism is built on investor trust—trust that corporate leaders and boards of directors will

© Triangle Images/Digital Vision/Getty Images

Discrimination against women and minorities was deemed unethical by our culture and subsequently made illegal in 1964.

be good stewards of their investments and provide investors with a fair return. There can be no doubt that the leaders of these corporations, and possibly many more, have violated that trust. As a result, investors are losing confidence and withdrawing from the market. In the process, everyone is getting hurt, not just the perpetrators of the egregious acts.[13]

Clearly, George is emphasizing the personal and cultural values of honesty, integrity, and trustworthiness in his remarks. Other impacts of cultural forces will be noted throughout the remainder of this chapter. Within the United States, some scholars suggest that the sense of national identity and dominant pattern of personal values are disappearing. The claim is that they are being replaced by a range of subnational and ethnic identities.[14] Regardless of this possible change, we contend that it is imperative for organizations—and our legal/justice system—to maintain and reinforce uniform ethical values, principles, and standards.

Legal and Regulatory Influences

What a society interprets as ethical or unethical frequently ends up being expressed in laws, government regulations, and court decisions. *Laws* are society's values and standards that are enforceable in the courts. The legality of actions and decisions doesn't necessarily make them ethical, however. At one time, for example, U.S. organizations could legally discriminate against women and minorities in hiring and promotions. A consensus developed that such discriminatory practices were unethical. For example, the Civil Rights Act of 1964 was passed to stop the practices and ensure equal employment opportunities for all citizens. The legal concept of employment-at-will provides another example of the interplay between changing societal ethical views and the law. *Employment-at-will* is a traditional common-law concept holding that employers are free to discharge employees for any reason at any time and that employees are free to quit their jobs for any reason at any time.[15] Historically, employers often dismissed employees without explanation (that is, "at will"). Courts and legislation have modified the freewheeling notion that employees can be fired for any reason. Table 3.1 lists a few of the lawful and unlawful reasons for dismissing employees.[16]

Table 3.1	Examples of Lawful and Unlawful Reasons for Dismissing Employees
SOME PERMISSIBLE REASONS	**SOME UNACCEPTABLE REASONS**
■ Incompetence in performance that does not respond to training or to accommodation	■ Blowing the whistle about illegal conduct by the employer
■ Gross or repeated insubordination	■ Reporting Occupational Safety and Health Administration violations
■ Civil rights violations such as engaging in harassment	■ Filing discrimination charges with the Equal Employment Opportunity Commission or a state or municipal fair employment agency
■ Illegal behavior such as theft or physical violence	■ Filing unfair labor practice charges with the National Labor Relations Board or a state agency
■ Repeated lateness or unexcused absences	■ Engaging in union activities, provided there is no violence or unlawful behavior
■ Drug activity or drunkenness on the job	■ Complaining or testifying about violations of equal pay, wage, or hour law

When behavior is clearly unethical *and* illegal, employees also have clear knowledge of what's right and what's wrong. In some areas of business, judgments about right and wrong fall within a gray area. How should employees behave when the laws are unclear or conflicting or when societal opinions have shifted and old laws are being questioned as unethical? Under these circumstances, employees must look to the standards, policies, and practices of their organization and to their personal values and beliefs.

During the past decade, a flurry of new laws and regulations have been passed within the United States at both the federal and state levels to reduce the discretion available to organizations and individuals as to what behaviors are both unethical and illegal. For example, the U.S. Congress enacted the Corporate and Criminal Fraud Accountability Act of 2002 in response to the numerous corporate scandals, such as those of Enron, WorldCom, Tyco, and Adelphia. It is part of the broader Sarbanes-Oxley Act, *which imposes rigorous auditing, financial disclosure, executive compensation, and corporate governance requirements on publicly traded companies.* The Sarbanes-Oxley Act does not merely reform and regulate corporate accounting practices—it has also created entirely new employment rights that expose both corporations and, in some cases, individual employees to civil and, under certain circumstances, even criminal liability.[17]

Section 806 of the act creates a new federal cause of action designed to protect employees of publicly traded companies who act as corporate whistle-blowers. It protects employees who, among other things, "provide information, cause information to be provided, or otherwise assist in an investigation regarding any conduct which the employee reasonably believes constitutes" a violation of federal securities law, SEC regulations, or "any provision of Federal law relating to fraud against shareholders."[18] The act also contains a strict antiretaliation provision (Section 1107). It protects any individual from being retaliated against for providing any truthful information to a law enforcement officer in connection with the commission of a federal offense. Individuals who violate this provision by attempting to retaliate against any individual are subject to a fine and/or imprisonment of up to 10 years. Other provisions of this legislation make criminal various behaviors and decisions that previously would have been considered unethical, but not illegal.

Snapshot

". . . today's compliance challenges are really information challenges. At its core, the Sarbanes-Oxley Act is about ensuring that data is turned into financial information in a way that enables accurate, reliable, transparent and timely financial reporting."
**Lee Dittmar,
Principal,
Deloitte Consulting
LLP**

Organizational Influences

Organizations influence employee actions both formally and informally. The Ethics Resource Center, headquartered in Washington, D.C., is a nonprofit, nonpartisan educational organization. Its mission is to be a leader in fostering ethical practices in individuals and organizations. In a recent *National Business Ethics Survey*, 3,000 employees were interviewed. A few key findings follow.

▶ 52 percent had observed one or more types of unethical conduct by their colleagues and 36 percent saw at least two events.

▶ 69 percent of employees said their companies have implemented ethics training. This is up from the 55 percent reported in a previous survey two years earlier.

▶ 19 percent of respondents observed "lying to employees, customers, vendors, or the public."

▶ 18 percent witnessed conflicts of interest.

▶ 12 percent reported observing discrimination based on race, color, gender, age, or similar categories.[19]

Importantly, this survey reported that at companies with a strong ethical culture and full formal ethics programs, employees are 36 percent less likely to observe misconduct.

An organization's code of ethics can help employees from diverse backgrounds work more effectively as a team.

© Digital Vision/Getty Images

Fostering an Ethical Organizational Culture. The basic informal source of guidance is top and middle management's day-to-day behaviors and decisions. They demonstrate the ethical principles and practices that are important to the organization. Unless top and middle managers send very clear signals, employees can easily misinterpret what the organization values. A few of the needed actions to foster the creation and day-to-day implementation of an ethical culture follow.[20]

▶ **Create a formal ethics system.** The organization should create and implement a formal ethics system, including procedures and policies that explicitly define ethical expectations regarding employee behaviors to guide them in their day-to-day decision making.

Examples of these systems include statements of values, codes of conduct, ethics policies and rules, ethics oversight committees, ethics surveys, employee "help lines," and other ethics management mechanisms.

▶ **Communicate ethical expectations.** Managers at all levels of the organization need to explicitly and implicitly communicate their expectations regarding employee behavior, reinforcing the explicit organizational expectations detailed through the formal ethics system and mechanisms. This includes the visible use of the ethics system in their own decision making and the requirement that subordinate employees do likewise.

▶ **Include ethical conduct as a measure on performance evaluations.** People do what is rewarded or measured. If the emphasis is on proactive, ethical behavior, there will be more of it. If it is an explicit goal, employees will think more about it. Managers from the top, starting with the board of directors, should (1) make the expectations for ethical conduct well known for each employee, (2) capture examples of ethical conduct to use when delivering a performance evaluation, and (3) provide some award or incentive for ethical performance. (One organization awarded certificates titled "Caught you . . . doing something good," which were delivered along with a gourmet cookie. Another presented small corporate commitment plaques for ethical conduct.)

▶ **Make it acceptable to talk about ethics.** Ethics has taken on a negative tone because of the multitude of scandals and ethical shortcomings reported in the press. These portray a depressing picture of individuals who skirt their responsibilities or ignore ethical guidelines for their own self-serving interests. In fact, there are countless examples of good ethical conduct that never see the light of day. Managers at all levels should (1) take time during a staff meeting or other group event to commend someone on demonstrated ethical conduct, (2) talk about ethical conduct routinely and encourage employees to seek guidance whenever they question whether or not an act is ethical, and (3) keep the lines of communication open. When someone wants to talk about an ethical issue, the time to talk about it is then—not at some future date. Pushing the discussion off to later diminishes the importance placed on ethics.

If an organization operates in different countries, local standards for ethical conduct may differ somewhat from one location to the next. Hence developing ethical guidelines that make sense in various settings can be a complex task. Increasingly, U.S. companies (e.g., Johnson & Johnson, Citigroup, and IBM) apply their U.S. standards for ethical conduct universally. They believe that this approach won't violate ethical principles elsewhere. They contend that the greater need is to avoid confusion among their employees as to what ethical standards apply from country to country. Other companies (e.g., Google) make some adaptation to local practices, arguing that ethical standards make sense only when considered within a particular societal context.

Importance of Codes of Ethics. To provide formal guidance for employees, an organization can state clear policies that define ethical and unethical conduct. A code of ethics *states the principles that employees are expected to follow when acting on behalf of the organization.* Codes of ethics are a necessity for public companies with a presence in the United States. The New York Stock Exchange and Nasdaq require listed companies to adopt and disclose a code of ethics. Additional regulatory requirements or expectations have been championed by various groups advancing the need for such codes. More importantly, an organization's code can clarify for all parties, internal and external, the principles and standards that govern its conduct. This helps convey its commitment to responsible practice wherever it operates.

Codes of ethics serve a variety of other practical purposes. They can help employees from diverse backgrounds work more effectively across geographic and cultural boundaries. A code may serve as a reference point for decision making. This enables organizations to operate with fewer layers of supervision and to respond quickly and uniformly to a crisis. It may even aid in recruitment by helping to attract individuals who want to work for an organization that advocates world-class principles and standards. A code that is enforced can also help an organization manage risk by reducing the likelihood of damaging misconduct.[21]

Table 3.2 on the following page presents a set of principles that have been suggested for the establishment of a world-class code of ethics. The eight principles set forth in Table 3.2 are based on the code of ethics guidelines suggested by a variety of professional and public organizations, such as the *Guidelines for Multinational Enterprises* advanced by the OECD (Organization for Economic Cooperation and Development). In addition, the principles were influenced by an examination of the codes of a number of leading and respected corporations. Each of the eight principles in Table 3.2 is accompanied by a number of more specific standards that apply to identified stakeholders, such as shareholders, employees, customers, suppliers, competitors, and the general public. A discussion of all of these standards is beyond our scope.

As suggested in the following Strategic Action Competency feature, Citigroup is an example of one organization that has elected to have a single code of ethics that applies to its 294,000 employees, which they refer to as a "Code of Conduct." Citigroup and its subsidiaries offer deposits and loans, credit cards, investment banking, brokerage, and a host of other financial services. It has 3,000 offices in the United States and 1,500 offices in about 100 other countries. On the following page, we present a few excerpts from the 19-page Citigroup Code of Conduct.[22]

Table 3.2 | **Suggested Principles in a World-Class Code of Ethics**

TYPE OF PRINCIPLE	PRINCIPLE
I Fiduciary Principle	Act as a fiduciary (representative) for the company and its investors. Carry out the company's business in a diligent and loyal manner, with the degree of candor expected of a trustee.
II Property Principle	Respect property and the rights of those who own it. Refrain from theft and misappropriation, avoid waste, and safeguard the property entrusted to you.
III Reliability Principle	Honor commitments. Be faithful to your word and follow through on promises, agreements, and other voluntary undertakings, whether or not embodied in legally enforceable contracts.
IV Transparency Principle	Conduct business in a truthful and open manner. Refrain from deceptive acts and practices, keep accurate records, and make timely disclosures of material information while respecting obligations of confidentiality and privacy.
V Dignity Principle	Respect the dignity of all people. Protect the health, safety, privacy, and human rights of others; refrain from coercion; and adopt practices that enhance human development in the workplace, the marketplace, and the community.
VI Fairness Principle	Engage in free and fair competition, deal with all parties fairly and equitably, and practice nondiscrimination in employment and contracting.
VII Citizenship Principle	Act as responsible citizens of the community. Respect the law, protect public goods, cooperate with public authorities, avoid improper involvement in politics and government, and contribute to community betterment.
VIII Responsiveness Principle	Engage with parties who may have legitimate claims and concerns relating to the company's activities, and be responsive to public needs while recognizing the government's role and jurisdiction in protecting the public interest.

Note: Each of these principles is accompanied by a set of more specific standards.
Source: Adapted from L. Paine, R. Deshpandé, J.D. Margolis, and K.E. Bettcher. Up to code: Does your company's conduct meet world-class standards? *Harvard Business Review*, 2005, 82(2), 122–133.

Strategic Action Competency

Citigroup's Code of Conduct

The worldwide Citigroup Code of Conduct outlines the principles, policies, and laws that govern the activities of the company, and to which its employees and others who work with or represent the firm must adhere. The code offers guidance under six main categories. We present these categories and one or two key points within each of them.

CATEGORIES	SAMPLE OF KEY POINTS
■ Responsibilities to Citigroup ■ Workplace Responsibilities ■ Representing Citigroup to Customers Other External Constituencies	■ We must identify, surface and resolve ethical issues with great speed. ■ We are committed to fair employment practices and a workplace free from any kind of discrimination, harassment or intimidation of employees. ■ We treat our customers, suppliers and competitors fairly.

CATEGORIES	SAMPLE OF KEY POINTS
■ Privacy/Confidentiality	■ We keep customer information secure at all times, as a sacred trust given to Citigroup by our customers, and have adopted the Citigroup Privacy Promise for Consumers to communicate additional protections that we provide to our consumer customers around the world.
■ Investments and Outside Activities	■ We must avoid real or perceived conflicts of interest in areas such as investments or outside business activities, among others.
■ Other Key Legal/Compliance Rules	■ Employees must report suspicious activity—for example, suspected insider and Issues trading, fraud, misappropriations of funds and money laundering—through proper channels to government authorities.

The Citigroup's code goes into much greater detail than presented here. Moreover, each new employee is required to sign a statement to (1) acknowledge having read the entire code, (2) express an understanding of the obligations as an employee, and (3) indicate agreement to adhere to it. In a cover letter to the code, the top 13 executives of Citigroup have jointly signed a letter, with their personal signatures reproduced. The letter sets forth the top leadership commitment to ethics and integrity, including several of the key values that are most relevant to the code. They state, in part:

History has shown how confidence in our markets can be easily undermined. To help ensure that we avoid unethical behavior, we ask you to read, enforce and adhere to this Code of Conduct as we ourselves have committed to do. To learn more about this organization, visit *www.citigroup.com*.

Individual Influences

Individuals have their own values and a sense of what is right or wrong. An individual's view of what is ethical may or may not agree with the views of their organization and society.

Stages of Moral Development. Lawrence Kohlberg (1927–1987) probably is the best known scholar in the field of the psychology of ethical decision making and behavior. Kohlberg's model of moral development is useful for exploring questions about how members of an organization regard ethical dilemmas, including how they determine what is right or wrong in a particular situation.[23] Kohlberg held that people develop morally, much as they do physically, from early childhood to adulthood. As they develop, their ethical criteria and patterns of moral reasoning go through stages, as suggested in Figure 3.2 on the next page. Stages of moral development *suggest that individuals evolve through various phases, ranging from the lowest (obedience and punishment orientation) to the highest (universal ethical principles)*. Kohlberg didn't assume that everyone progresses through all the stages. For example, an adult criminal could be stuck in the first stage.

A person at the *obedience and punishment stage* does the right thing mainly to avoid punishment or to obtain approval. In other words, only the immediate consequences of an action determine whether it's good or bad. An employee stuck at this stage might think that the only reason not to steal money from an employer is the certainty of getting caught and then fired or even arrested. Most organizations don't want employees who use such simple reasoning to guide their behavior when faced with ethical issues.

A person at the *instrumental stage* becomes aware that others also have needs and begins to defer to them to get what the individual wants. Proper behavior is what satisfies the person's self-interest. At times, self-interest can be satisfied by making deals or exchanges with other people. An employee at this stage might be willing to defer to the needs of the employer to reduce absenteeism, but only if the employer gives something in return.

A person at the *interpersonal stage* considers appropriate behavior as that which pleases or is approved by friends or family. Proper behavior exhibits conformity to conventional expectations, often of the majority. At this stage, being seen as a "good person" with basically good motives is important. An employee at this stage might focus on the importance of being a loyal employee and colleague who is always friendly and who avoids or smooths conflict. If absence creates conflicts or work overload for other employees, some people at this stage might be willing to reduce their absences even if that meant not using all of their allotted sick days.

A person at the *law and order stage* recognizes that ethical behavior is not determined only by reference to friends, family, coworkers, or others whose opinions the individual might value. Proper behavior consists of doing a person's duty, showing respect for authority, and maintaining the social order for its own sake. Loyalty to the nation and its laws are paramount. The person sees other people as individuals and also as parts of the larger social system that gives them their roles and obligations. An employee at this stage may rigidly adhere to organizational rules and regulations and legitimate orders from superiors. The employee is likely to resist or criticize the efforts of coworkers or superiors to bend or break the rules. In some organizations, employees commonly take paid sick days even when they aren't sick. Employees may even encourage each other to take all their sick days. They view these leave days as something the company owes them. However, the company policy or union contract may state that sick days are allowed only for legitimate illnesses. In this situation, employees at the law and order stage might resist peer pressure to take a day off if they aren't ill. They would view company rules or the union contract as overriding the somewhat selfish interests of their peers. At this stage of moral reasoning, rules are considered to be necessary for the effective functioning of the entire organization, and they should be followed even when it requires some self-sacrifices or resisting pressures from peers.

A person at the *social contract stage* is aware that people hold a variety of conflicting personal views that go beyond the letter of the law. A person at this stage understands that, although rules and laws may be agreed on and for the most part must be impersonally followed, they can be changed if necessary. Some absolute values, such as life and liberty, are held regardless of different individuals' values or even majority opinion. "The greatest good for the greatest number" is a key characteristic at this stage. People at this stage would recognize that employees of organizations are expected to follow the rules but would also

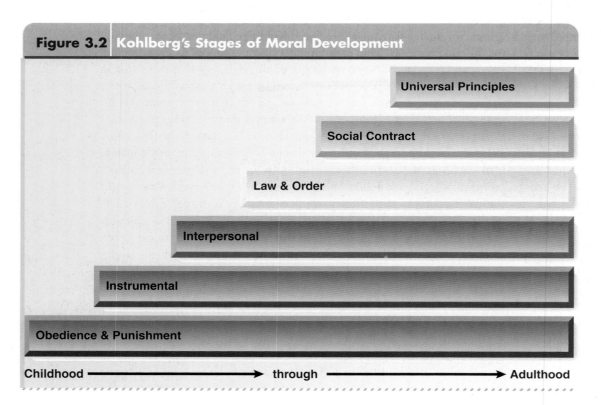

Figure 3.2 Kohlberg's Stages of Moral Development

Universal Principles

Social Contract

Law & Order

Interpersonal

Instrumental

Obedience & Punishment

Childhood ⟶ through ⟶ Adulthood

accept the notion of breaking the rules when those rules conflict with accepted social values. They might accept the notion of a company permitting employees to be absent for only a specified number of days. But if they believe that the absentee rules unduly restrict employees' freedoms, they might also feel justified in breaking the rule or might actively work to modify the rule to make it less restrictive. For example, they might encourage their employer to specify an allowable number of days off per year and allow employees to take these days for whatever reasons they choose.

Monica Gadsby, CEO of Tapestry, is considered an expert in her field of international marketing.

© Tapestry

Finally, someone at the *universal principles stage* views appropriate conduct as determined by a person's conscience, based on universal ethical principles. Kohlberg felt that universal principles are founded in justice, the public welfare, the equality of human rights, and respect for the dignity of individual human beings. In his model, people at the most advanced stage of ethical reasoning recognize these universal principles and act in accordance with them rather than rules or laws.

The following Multicultural Competency feature provides a brief profile of Monica Gadsby, CEO and managing director of Tapestry, an affiliate of Starcom MediaVest Group.[24] Tapestry is a multicultural contact agency that provides integrated media solutions for clients. It has experts specializing in Hispanic, African-American, Asian, and emerging markets consumers. The firm is headquartered in Chicago. This profile suggests her high level of moral development and multicultural competency. It is based on her receipt of the Media All-Star for Non-traditional Media Award.

Multicultural Competency

Monica Gadsby, CEO of Tapestry

Monica Gadsby is a 20-year veteran of multicultural marketing. She and her team have helped global marketers like Procter & Gamble and Coca-Cola reach their diverse customer bases.

She was brought up on three continents, is fluent in four languages, and was a founder of Hispanic units for Leo Burnett (advertising agency) and Starcom. Gadsby is considered one of the foremost authorities on marketing worldwide. *Vanidades* magazine named Gadsby one of the Top U.S. Hispanic Women. She was named Media Planning Executive of the Year by the Association of Hispanic Advertising Agencies.

Renetta McCann, global CEO of Starcom MediaVest Group, says Gadsby "recognized the importance of diversity from the very beginning, and not just diversity in the general sense. Her leadership has fostered diversity in ideas, in points of consumer contract and in client relationships. Gadsby is a pioneer in the multicultural media space. I have great respect for what she's done, not

only as a leader and a businesswoman, but also as an educator and mentor who infuses the same spirit of diversity in everyone and all the work she touches. Gadsby's role in the industry is even more important now as we shift toward the idea that the general market is truly a multicultural market."

Ivelisse Roche, a media manager with Kraft Foods, comments: "Gadsby always puts the client first. For all the power she wields in the marketplace, she uses that power very gracefully with our media partners."

Gadsby notes, "Most companies do not do as good a job reflecting, in their sampling and research, the complexity of the multicultural landscape today. So we've done a lot of work with clients trying to fill in the holes. . . . Tapestry's successes aren't just financial or competitive-wide recognition of the power of multicultural markets. It's not just the billings: It's what we stand for."

To learn more about this organization, see *www.tapestrypartners.com*.

Whistle-Blowing. Unethical conduct will never be eliminated, but there are ways to reduce it. As we have suggested, managers can implement a variety of organizational practices to support ethical conduct. Employees who find themselves in a position of knowing about unethical behavior must decide what to do about it.

Whistle-blowers *are employees who report unethical or illegal actions by their employers to other people or organizations that are capable of taking corrective action.* If you knew that a coworker was behaving illegally or unethically, would you report it to someone? If so, who would you tell—someone inside the company or someone on the outside?

When you see wrongdoing occur, your goal should be to find a way to stop it. Simply confronting the person involved may be all that you need to do. However, blowing the whistle yourself or encouraging others to blow the whistle doesn't always make sense. It is a step that you should take only after making other less drastic efforts to change the situation. That is, blow the whistle only as a last resort and when you're likely to achieve a useful outcome—and in full recognition of the possible consequences to yourself.[25] As reported previously in the chapter, the U.S. Sarbanes-Oxley Act of 2002 weaves a web of protections for employees of publicly traded companies who report violations of federal securities laws, the rules of the Securities Exchange Commission, or any provision of federal law relating to fraud against shareholders. Clearly, one intent of this law is to encourage whistle-blowing and protect whistle-blowers from personal adverse consequences with respect to the areas covered by it.[26]

© Pat Sullivan/AP Photo

In March 2006, prosecution witness and former Enron whistle-blower Sherron Watkins testified in the fraud and conspiracy trial of former Enron executives Kenneth Lay and Jeffrey Skilling.

Short of whistle-blowing, you might try to persuade other employees to act with you. Ignoring or firing a group of employees who report wrongdoing is more difficult than taking action against one person. Another alternative is to consider leaving the company. This action may not stop the wrongdoing, but at least it will ensure that you don't get caught up in the situation and possibly end up being drawn into the wrongdoing yourself. If the wrongful activity is causing serious harm to people, however, walking away from the situation may only result in feelings of guilt.

In addition to considering whether they will be effective whistle-blowers, employees should consider whether they are likely to experience retaliation for blowing the whistle. In addition to the federal laws, state laws also protect whistle-blowers from retaliation by employers. Some states protect only those whistle-blowers who go outside the company (e.g., telling a newspaper reporter) to report wrongdoing. Other states protect only those whistle-blowers who report wrongdoing to someone inside the company (e.g., writing a letter to the CEO). Regardless of such laws, fear of retaliation is a reasonable concern.[27]

Anyone thinking about whistle-blowing should ask themselves four important questions before doing so.[28]

▸ *Is this the only way?* Do not blow the whistle unless you have tried to correct the problem by reporting up the normal chain of command and gotten no results. Make sure your allegations are not minor complaints.

▸ *Do I have the evidence?* Gather documentary evidence that proves your case and keep it in a safe place. Keep good notes, perhaps even a daily diary. Make sure you are seeing fraud, not merely incompetence or sloppiness.

▶ *Why am I doing this?* Examine your motives. Do not act out of frustration or because you feel underappreciated or mistreated. Do not embellish your case and do not violate any confidentiality agreements you may have.

▶ *Am I ready?* Think through the impact on your family. Be prepared for unemployment and the possibility of being blacklisted in your profession. Last but not least, consult a lawyer.

Making Ethical Judgments

We have shown that an individual's ethical judgments can be shaped by many factors. How do you approach ethical questions? Table 3.3 on the next page will give you insights into your general approach to ethical behavior. Before continuing to study this chapter, please take a few moments to fill out the Managerial Values Profile questionnaire in Table 3.3.[29]

3.
Describe three approaches that people use when making ethical judgments.

Utilitarian Approach

If your approach to ethical dilemmas is to weigh all of the potentially positive outcomes of your action and compare them to all of the possible negative outcomes, you probably had a high utilitarian score. People guided by the utilitarian approach *focus on behaviors and their results, not on the motives for such actions.*[30] A manager or employee guided by this approach considers the potential effects of alternative actions from the perspective of the accepted social contract. The alternative chosen is supposed to benefit the greatest number of people, although such benefit may come at the expense of the few or those with little power. In other words, a good alternative may harm some people, but even more people will be helped in some way.

Classic capitalist theory is supported by the utilitarian approach. The primary managerial obligation is to maximize shareholders' profits and their long-term interests under the classical view of capitalism. Nobel Prize–winning economist Milton Friedman is probably the best known advocate of this approach. Friedman argues that using resources in ways that do not clearly maximize shareholder interests amounts to spending the owners' money without their consent—and is equivalent to stealing. According to Friedman, a manager can judge whether a decision is right or wrong by considering its consequences for the company's economic needs. The utilitarian approach prescribes ethical standards for managers and employees in the areas of organizational goals, efficiency, and conflicts of interests.[31]

Achieving Organizational Goals. Utilitarian managers think that businesses operating in a competitive market system can achieve the greatest good for the greatest number by maximizing profits. According to this logic, a company that achieves high profits can offer the highest quality products at the lowest prices for consumers. Profits are seen as the reward for satisfying consumers. If profits get too high, new competitors will enter the market, thereby increasing the supply of high-quality goods and pushing prices down.

According to Friedman, no firm *unilaterally* should go beyond what the law requires—to help preserve the environment, for example. Doing so would only reduce that firm's profits and would do nothing to eliminate the pollution caused by its competitors. Bill Ford, Jr., chairman of Ford Motor Company, must successfully argue against this logic as he strives to adopt environmentally friendly practices at Ford Motor Company. This is especially difficult for him during a period when the firm is struggling financially and attempting to stop the loss of market share to Toyota, Nissan, and others. Friedman contends that the government is responsible for

| Table 3.3 | Managerial Values Profile Questionnaire |

INSTRUCTIONS

Twelve pairs of statements or phrases follow. Read each pair and check the one that you most prefer. You may, of course, prefer neither statement; in that case, you should check off the statement that you most prefer, that is, the *lesser of the two evils*. It is essential that you select one and only one statement or phrase in each pair: Your Managerial Values Profile cannot be scored unless you do so.

_____ 1. The greatest good for the greatest number

✓ 2. The individual's right to private property

✓ 3. Adhering to rules designed to maximize benefits to all

_____ 4. Individuals' rights to complete liberty in action, as long as others' rights are similarly respected

✓ 5. The right of an individual to speak freely without fear of being fired

_____ 6. Engaging in technically illegal behavior in order to attain substantial benefits for all

✓ 7. Individuals' rights to personal privacy

_____ 8. The obligation to gather personal information to ensure that individuals are treated equitably

✓ 9. Helping those in danger when doing so would not unduly endanger oneself

_____ 10. The right of employees to know about any danger in the job setting

✓ 11. Minimizing inequities among employees in the job setting

_____ 12. Maintaining significant inequities among employees when the ultimate result is to benefit all

_____ 13. Organizations must not require employees to take actions that would restrict the freedom of others or cause other harm

✓ 14. Organizations must tell employees the full truth about work hazards

✓ 15. What is good is what helps the company attain ends that benefit everyone

_____ 16. What is good is equitable treatment for all employees of the company

_____ 17. Organizations must stay out of employees' private lives

✓ 18. Employees should act to achieve organizational goals that result in benefits to all

✓ 19. Questionable means are acceptable if they achieve good ends

_____ 20. Individuals must follow their own consciences, even if it hurts the organization

_____ 21. Safety of individual employees above all else

✓ 22. Obligation to aid those in great need

_____ 23. Employees should follow rules that preserve individuals' freedom of action while reducing inequities

✓ 24. Employees must do their best to follow rules designed to enhance organizational goal attainment

SCORING YOUR MANAGERIAL VALUES PROFILE

In the next column, circle the numbers of the statements or phrases that you checked off. When you have circled the numbers of all of your choices, add up the *number of circled items* in each column. Put this number in the row marked "Total." The total for any column can range from zero to eight. The higher your score, the more these values are important to you.

Utilitarian	Moral Rights	Justice
1	②	4
③	⑤	8
6	⑦	⑨
12	10	⑪
⑮	⑭	13
⑱	17	16
⑲	20	㉒
㉔	21	23
TOTAL 5	4	3

protecting the environment and should pass environmental laws and regulations that apply to *all* companies. Companies that voluntarily go beyond what is required by law may lose out in the long run because their competitors will have lower costs and thus lower prices.

Efficiency. Managers and employees alike should try to attain organizational goals as efficiently as possible. Efficiency is achieved by minimizing inputs (e.g., labor, land, and capital) and maximizing outputs. If technologies are available that allow an organization to produce goods or deliver services at a lower cost, it should use them. It should do so regardless of the consequences in terms of layoffs, retraining costs, or moving production overseas to obtain lower wages and be subject to fewer restrictive regulations.[32]

Conflicts of Interest. Managers and employees alike should not have personal interests that conflict with the organization's achievement of its goals. A purchasing agent having a significant financial interest in one of the firm's major suppliers faces a potential conflict of interest. Again, the reason for this proscription relates to profitability. In this case, the purchasing agent might be motivated to purchase from that supplier, even when the price or quality isn't the best available. In the case of accounting firms, such as PricewaterhouseCoopers (PWC) and Deloitte & Touche, employees owning stock in a company they audit may be inclined to issue a more favorable audit result than has been earned in order to maintain the value of their shares of stock. Therefore, the partners and employees are not allowed to own shares of stock in companies that the accounting firm audits. Indirect ownership is permitted if the stock is included in a broad-based mutual fund in which the employee has invested.

Conflicts of interest can sometimes be difficult to judge. At PWC, for example, many of the employees may think that the rules barring them from owning stock in companies that the firm audits are outdated and largely irrelevant today because stock ownership is so widespread. Identifying conflicts of interest can be even trickier when cultural differences are added to the mix, as one U.S. businessman discovered when on assignment in Russia. He was working with a senior Russian partner, who also happened to own some other businesses. When the Russian began to "borrow" company materials and equipment, the U.S. partner viewed his behavior as unethical. The Russian saw no conflict of interest; using the equipment interchangeably in two companies of which he was an owner seemed both reasonable and efficient.[33]

The utilitarian approach supports the values of profit maximization, self-interest, rewards based on abilities and achievements, sacrifice and hard work, and competition.[34] Many economists espouse the utilitarian approach, but it has received less support from the general public. During the past 40 years, utilitarian ethics have been increasingly challenged and tempered by the moral rights and justice approaches.

Moral Rights Approach

The moral rights approach *holds that decisions should be consistent with fundamental rights and privileges (e.g., life, freedom, health, and privacy).* These rights are set forth in documents such as the first 10 amendments to the U.S. Constitution (the Bill of Rights) and the United Nation's Declaration of Human Rights.[35] A number of U.S. laws require managers and other employees to consider these rights as guides and requirements for decision making and behaviors. Figure 3.3 on the following page suggests core interrelated elements in the moral rights approach, including life and safety, truthfulness, privacy, and freedom of conscience and speech.

Life and Safety. In the United States, many laws require businesses to comply with society's view of appropriate standards for quality of life and safety. Employees, customers, and the general public have the right *not* to have their lives and safety unknowingly and unnecessarily endangered. For example, this moral right in large part justifies the U.S. Occupational Safety and Health Act (OSHA) of 1970, which contains many requirements designed to increase the safety and healthfulness of the workplace. Among other things, OSHA and its implementing regulations restrict the

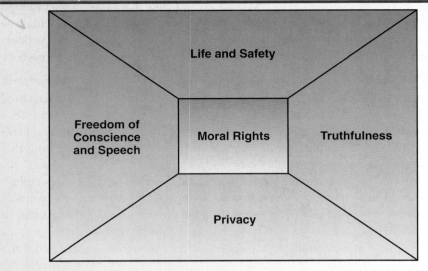

Figure 3.3 Common Interrelated Elements in the Moral Rights Approach

Life and Safety

Freedom of Conscience and Speech

Moral Rights

Truthfulness

Privacy

Snapshot

"If you are truly interested in teaching a grand and critically important concept like honesty, you must be willing to accept the awkward situations and inevitable flaring of human passions that are certain to occur. However, it's unquestionably worth the effort."

Tom Asacker, Business Consultant and author of Sandbox Wisdom

use of asbestos, lead-based paint, and various toxic chemicals in the workplace. Legislation is often introduced to modify, expand, or even restrict some of OSHA's policies and practices.[36]

We are mindful that this moral right is not often embraced when it requires the expenditure of monetary resources by businesses or even government. Years ago, automobile manufacturers firmly opposed legislation to require the installation of safety belts and, some years later, the legal requirement for air bags. At that time, the conventional wisdom was that these safety features were not desired by consumers and they did not want to pay for them. Now, safety features are often prominently displayed in the reviews and marketing of many automobiles. Typically, new safety systems—such as traction control, cornering, roll control, suspension control, anticipatory crash sensing, lane departure warning, and vision assist—are introduced in the most expensive vehicles first because of their cost before migrating slowly to other vehicles.[37]

The U.S. National Highway Traffic Safety Administration recently proposed new legislation to require stability-control systems on all vehicles and proposed a new performance standard for how a vehicle handles in sharp turns at highway speeds. Rollovers kill more than 10,000 people a year on U.S. highways. It is estimated that stability-control technology could save 7,000 lives a year. Eron Shostick, a spokesman for the Alliance of Automobile Manufacturers, suggest that the auto industry is likely to support this government mandate. He states: "It's an innovative technology that has been proven in the field."[38]

Truthfulness. Employees, customers, shareholders, and the general public have the right *not* to be intentionally deceived on matters about which they should be informed. The classic legal concept of *caveat emptor*—"let the buyer beware"—used to be the defense for a variety of shady business practices. During the 1950s and 1960s, an increasingly aware public began to challenge the ethics of such a position. Shifting societal attitudes and values concerning *appropriate* behavior by businesses have led to a flood of U.S. consumer legislation. Today, quality improvement practices and customer-oriented practices make such an approach to customer relations risky. Nevertheless, the rapid speed of change inevitably means that there are too often opportunities "legally" and otherwise to withhold or falsify information—and thereby deceive customers, shareholders, employees, and the general public.[39]

Privacy. The moral right of citizens to control access to personal information about themselves and its use by government agencies, employers, and others was the basis for the U.S. Privacy Act of 1974. The Privacy Act restricts the use of certain types of information by the federal government and limits those to whom this information can be released. The 1988 Video Privacy Protection Act is an example of a more specific law designed to ensure that privacy rights are respected. This act forbids retailers from disclosing video rental records without the customer's consent or a court order. For example, a customer who rents exercise videos from Blockbuster presumably need not worry about getting on mailing lists for exercise equipment catalogs, fitness magazines, and the like. Blockbuster is not allowed to sell or rent its customer lists, including their video preferences, without permission of the customer.

With the availability of new information technologies (especially computers and surveillance equipment), enormous concern has been expressed about invasions of privacy.[40] A few of these workplace and public privacy issues include drug testing, honesty testing, confidentiality of medical and psychological counseling records, monitoring of e-mail and work performed on computers, employee use of the Internet at work, access to credit records and "identity theft," and the gathering and sale of personal information gleaned from the Internet. Video monitoring is an example of the use of one technology that has become widespread at Wal-Mart, Exxon stations, Bank of America branches, and numerous other outlets. This monitoring is being done despite the negative reaction by many people to the idea of having everything they do recorded on a tape or DVD. People react in a similar way when they hear about software programs designed to keep track of which Web sites they have accessed via the Internet.[41]

Due to legal requirements and in response to customer expectations, a number of companies have established specific privacy policies and practices that are communicated to their customers on a regular basis. For example, the following Communication Competency feature presents a brief portion of how Fidelity forthrightly communicates its *Commitment to Privacy Policy*.[42] Fidelity Investments, headquartered in Boston, Mass, with key offices in a variety of locations, is an international provider of a wide array of financial services. Fidelity has approximately 37,000 employees.

Communication Competency

Fidelity's Public Commitment to Customer Privacy

Fidelity Investments and the Fidelity Funds have always been committed to maintaining the confidentiality, integrity and security of personal information about our current and prospective customers. We are proud of our privacy practices and want you to know how we protect this information and use it to service your account.

The privacy policies of Fidelity Investments and the Fidelity Funds are reviewed annually. Our printed and online notices are then updated to reflect any material changes. Fidelity has always considered the protection of sensitive information to be a foundation of customer trust and a sound business practice. We employ extensive physical, electronic and procedural controls and we regularly adapt these controls to respond to changing requirements and advances in technology.

Privacy, security and service in our online operations are just as critical as in the rest of our business. We, therefore, employ all of the safeguards described above, along with the following Internet-specific practices. Fidelity uses a variety of proven protections to maintain the security of your online session. For example, we make extensive use of firewall barriers, encryption techniques and authentication procedures. We may also place cookies and similar files on your hard drive for security purposes, to facilitate site navigation, and to personalize your experience on our site.

When you visit Fidelity's Internet sites, we may also collect technical and navigational information, such as computer browser type, Internet protocol address, pages visited, and average time spent on our Web sites. This information may be used, for example, to alert you to software compatibility issues, or it may be analyzed to improve our Web design and functionality.

Fidelity also clearly, and in detail, communicates the many other components of its privacy policies, practices, and safeguards.

To learn more about this organization, visit *www.fidelity.com.*

Freedom of Conscience and Speech. Speech is one way for expressing matters of conscience. So freedom of speech is closely related to freedom of conscience. Employees have the right to refrain from carrying out orders that violate their moral or religious beliefs. They also have the right to criticize the ethics or legality of their employers' actions, as long as the criticisms are conscientious and truthful and do not violate the rights of others within or outside the organization.

The freedoms of speech and conscience have often been at the center of ethical debates associated with new media, such as the Internet. Should executives at Yahoo! accept advertisements from companies engaged in pornographic activity? Advertisements for pornographic products and services have long been banished from broadcasts of the major television networks. The culture of the Internet, however, supports aggressive adherence to principles of free speech. Permitting such advertising may be consistent with the principle of free speech for advertisers. However, parents whose children are exposed to pornography on the Web often express other concerns. Knowing of these concerns, a manufacturer of snacks that knows its logo might appear next to a pornography ad needs to think carefully about whether to advertise on that Internet site.[43]

As a guide to ethical decision making in organizations, the moral rights approach serves as an effective counterweight that protects society from overenthusiastic business leaders who strictly follow the utilitarian approach. However, as a guide to ethical behavior in organizations, the moral rights approach says more about what organizations should *avoid* doing—that is, violating the moral rights of employees, customers, and members of society—than it does about what *to* do. The justice approach provides more guidance in this regard.

Justice Approach

The justice approach *involves evaluating decisions and behavior with regard to how equitably they distribute benefits and costs among individuals and groups.*[44] To ensure just decisions and behavior, the proponents of this approach argue that three principles should be followed when designing management systems and making organizational decisions: the distributive justice principle, the fairness principle, and the natural duty principle.

Distributive Justice Principle. The distributive justice principle *requires that individuals not be treated differently on the basis of arbitrarily defined characteristics.* It holds that (1) individuals who are similar in relevant respects should be treated similarly, and (2) individuals who differ in relevant respects should be treated differently in proportion to the differences among them. A legal regulation that supports the distributive justice principle is the U.S. Equal Pay Act of 1963. It made illegal the payment of different wages to women and men when their jobs require equal skill, effort, and responsibility and are performed under similar working conditions. Prior to the passage of this act, it was common for women to be paid at two-thirds the rate of men doing the same work. The practice of unequal pay for men and women doing equal work was a holdover from practices adopted during World War II, when many women entered the workforce to replace men who left the factories to go into the armed services. There is no suggestion that such discrepancies between men and women's pay for comparable positions have been eliminated.[45]

Perceptions about what constitutes distributive justice also are behind concerns over the growing disparity between the compensation packages that chief executive officers (CEOs) and other top executives receive and the pay levels of everyone else. Should the average daily compensation for CEOs be more than most workers make in an entire year? Is it fair for the average CEO's pay to be rising at a rate that is six or seven times the rate of increase for other workers? According to the distributive justice principle, these pay level rates of increase are ethical only if the contributions of a CEO are proportionately greater and if the value of the contributions has been increasing at a much faster rate than those of the average worker.[46]

Although it may have little direct impact on executive pay levels, the U.S. Securities and Exchange Commission recently changed it rules on corporate disclosure of executive pay by publicly traded firms. The new rules require public companies to provide a figure for total compensation—including perks, stock options, and retirement benefits—for each of its top five officers and all board members. The assumption is that increased disclosure will slow the rise of pay of its senior executive officers. Skeptics doubt this and note that the new rules do not give a greater voice to shareholders in setting pay packages.[47]

Fairness Principle. The fairness principle *requires employees to support the rules of the organization as long as the organization is just (or fair) and employees have voluntarily accepted some benefits or opportunities in order to further their own interests.* Employees are then expected to follow the organization's rules, even though those rules might restrict their individual choices. For example, if an applicant for a store clerk position at Wal-Mart was informed that accepting a job offer would involve being monitored via video, Wal-Mart could expect the employee to accept these conditions of employment. Under the fairness principle, both the organization and its employees have obligations and both should accept their responsibilities. Their mutual obligations can be considered fair as long as they were voluntarily agreed to, they were spelled out clearly, and they are consistent with a common interest in the survival of the organization.

Perceptions of fairness often reflect people's reactions to the procedures used to make decisions. Acceptable processes lead to perceived *procedural justice*. A company's management practices are more likely to be perceived as fair when a formal process is in place for investigating employees' grievances and taking remedial actions, when needed.[48]

Natural Duty Principle. In exchange for certain rights, people must accept certain responsibilities and duties. The natural duty principle *requires that decisions and behaviors be based on universal principles associated with being a responsible member of society.* Four universal duties are

▶ to help others who are in need or in jeopardy, provided that the help can be given without excessive personal risk or loss;

▶ not to harm or injure another;

▶ not to cause unnecessary suffering; and

▶ to support and comply with just institutions.

In exchange for accepting these duties or responsibilities, a person is entitled to certain rights. The natural duty principle complements the moral rights approach. For example, if a manager has the right to demand safety at work, as suggested by the moral rights approach, this right can best be ensured if employees also agree that they have a duty not to harm others. If everyone acted according to this principle, problems such as workplace violence would not occur. In addition, a manager's right to privacy should be complemented by a willingness to comply with privacy laws and regulations, as well as cultural norms regarding what constitutes invasions of privacy, in dealing with employees.

Combining Ethical Approaches

No approach to ethical decisions can be said to be the "best" approach. Each one has strengths and weaknesses.[49] Managers in many U.S. organizations regularly use the utilitarian approach when solving business problems. Consistent with this approach, which values the goals of efficiency, productivity, and profit maximization above all others, they consider issues of moral rights and justice only to the degree required by law. In many European countries, however, managers appear to be more likely to develop solutions that are relatively more consistent with the moral rights and justice approaches. These approaches give greater weight to long-term employee welfare than to quarterly profits. Although differences in cultural norms and values help explain some differences in how managers approach ethical decisions, there may be great variation among managers within any organization. Organizational cultures and differences in managers' personal perspectives help account for such differences.

As suggested in Figure 3.4, the use of all three approaches to ethical decision making increases the probability that decisions and behaviors will be judged as ethical by others holding a wide range of values and beliefs. Many organizational practices in the United States reflect solutions that were developed by managers who gave the most weight to the utilitarian approach but also believed that doing what was right was one way for the company to do well. Stakeholder social responsibility, as discussed in the next section, attempts to combine elements of all three ethical approaches.

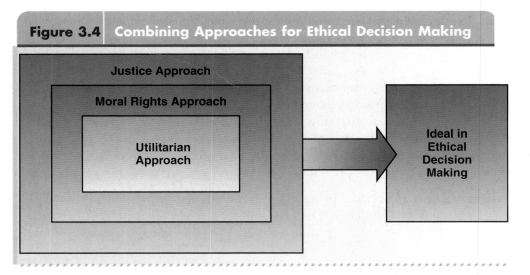

Figure 3.4 | Combining Approaches for Ethical Decision Making

4.

Explain stakeholder social responsibility and how it influences managers' ethical decisions and behaviors.

Stakeholder Social Responsibility

There is a preference for the utilitarian approach among many North American managers. However, most managers know that they also have many responsibilities for a wide range of activities. Even if they believe that the firm's financial considerations and shareholders must always be given highest priority, they recognize that long-term success requires attending to the concerns and demands of different groups of people.

A manager's job can be thought of as a series of attempts to address the concerns of these groups, or stakeholders.[50] Thus, *stakeholder social responsibility holds that managers and other employees have obligations to identifiable groups that are affected by or can affect the achievement of an organization's goals.*

Three primary reasons often are suggested for embracing stakeholder social responsibility: (1) enlightened self-interest, (2) sound investment, and (3) interference avoidance.[51] Under the rationale of enlightened self-interest, management uses social responsibility to justify numerous decisions and actions. The general idea is that a better society creates a better environment for business. Under the rationale of sound investment, management believes that social responsibility has a positive effect on a company's net worth. Socially responsible firms, such as Johnson & Johnson, appear to have superior financial performance compared to those of less socially responsible firms over the long run. Presumably, higher stock prices for socially responsible firms reduce the cost (interest rate) of capital and increase earnings. However, the studies on the relationship between social responsibility and financial performance conflict.[52] Under the rationale of interference avoidance, management aims to minimize the influence over company decisions by some stakeholders, such as government agencies. Industry self-regulation often is justified on the basis of interference avoidance.

Stakeholders

Stakeholders are individuals or groups that have interests, rights, or ownership in an organization and its activities. Those who have similar interests and rights are said to belong to the same stakeholder group. Customers, suppliers, employees, and shareholders are examples of primary stakeholder groups. Each has an interest in how an organization performs and interacts with them. These stakeholder groups can benefit from a company's successes and can be harmed by its mistakes. Similarly, an organization has an interest in maintaining the general well-being and effectiveness of stakeholder groups. If one or more stakeholder groups were to dissolve their relationships with the organization, the organization would suffer.

For any particular organization, some stakeholder groups may be relatively more important than others. The most important groups—the primary stakeholders—are those whose concerns the organization must address to ensure its own survival. They directly impact the financial resources available to the firm. At colleges and universities, these stakeholders include students, parents, faculty members, staff, and suppliers (e.g., food services, utilities, bookstores). They are directly impacted by various decisions of the top leadership of the colleges and universities. Secondary stakeholders are also important because they can take actions that can damage or assist the organization. Secondary stakeholders include governments (especially through regulatory agencies), unions, nongovernmental organizations, activists, political action groups, and the media.[53]

Figure 3.5 on the next page identifies the typical primary and secondary stakeholders that may have an interest in a particular organization. Of course, the relative importance of each stakeholder group varies from one organization to the next and as issues come and go.

© Mike Derer/AP Photo

William Weldon, president of Johnson & Johnson, poses in the company store at headquarters in New Brunswick, N.J. The company is a rare combination in the health-care business: a powerhouse in prescription drugs, consumer health products from Tylenol to the low-calorie sweetener Splenda, and diagnostic and medical devices.

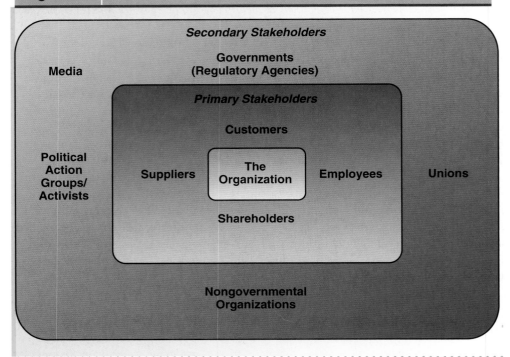

Figure 3.5 | **Common Stakeholders of Organizations**

Secondary Stakeholders

Media

Governments
(Regulatory Agencies)

Primary Stakeholders

Customers

Political
Action
Groups/
Activists

Suppliers

The
Organization

Employees

Unions

Shareholders

Nongovernmental
Organizations

The following Planning and Administration Competency feature reports on the important role of stakeholders to Johnson & Johnson's planning and decision-making processes as expressed through its credo.[54] Johnson & Johnson (J&J) invents, develops, and produces health-care products for the consumer, pharmaceutical, medical devices, and diagnostic markets. J&J is headquartered in New Brunswick, New Jersey, but operates with more than 200 subsidiary companies in 57 countries.[55] The firm has approximately 110,000 employees.

Planning and Administration Competency

Johnson & Johnson's Stakeholder Approach

William C. Weldon, chairman and CEO, comments "Johnson & Johnson is governed by the values set forth in our Credo, created by General Robert Wood Johnson in 1943. These principles have guided us for many years and will continue to set the tone of integrity for the entire Company. . . . Our Credo reminds us that if we serve patients and customers, our employees and our communities well, our shareholders will prosper." The J&J statement of *Our Credo* follows:

We believe our first responsibility is to the doctors, nurses and patients, to mothers and fathers and all others who use our products

and services. In meeting their needs, everything we do must be of high quality. We must constantly strive to reduce our costs in order to maintain reasonable prices. Customers' orders must be serviced promptly and accurately. Our suppliers and distributors must have an opportunity to make a fair profit.

We are responsible to our employees, the men and women who work with us throughout the world. Everyone must be considered as an individual. We must respect their dignity and recognize their merit. They must have a sense of security in their jobs.

Compensation must be fair and adequate, and working conditions clean, orderly and safe. We must be mindful of ways to help our employees fulfill their family responsibilities. Employees must feel free to make suggestions and complaints. There must be equal opportunity for employment, development and advancement for those qualified. We must provide competent management, and their actions must be just and ethical.

We are responsible to the communities in which we live and work and to the world community as well. We must be good citizens—support good works and charities and bear our fair share of taxes. We must encourage civic improvements and better health and education. We must maintain in good order the property we are privileged to use, protecting the environment and natural resources.

Our final responsibility is to our stockholders. Business must make a sound profit. We must experiment with new ideas. Research must be carried on, innovative programs developed and mistakes paid for. New equipment must be purchased, new facilities provided and new products launched. Reserves must be created to provide for adverse times. When we operate according to these principles, the stockholders should realize a fair return.

J&J has received numerous awards and honors in recognition that its *Our Credo* is real—not just a statement on paper—in guiding planning, decision making, and day-to-day behaviors throughout the organization.

To learn more about this organization, visit *www.jnj.com*.

Stakeholder Pressures

Each stakeholder group has somewhat different expectations of the organization. Each group cares more about some aspects of an organization's activities and less about others. As stated in its credo, Johnson & Johnson's commitments to stakeholders recognize the different viewpoints of its primary stakeholders in the organization: patients, customers, employees, suppliers, and shareholders. In this and other chapters, we discuss the importance of primary and secondary stakeholders as managers identify and assess the many pressures and issues that must be considered in the decision-making process. Table 3.4 on the next page provides examples of these general types of pressures. All of these stakeholders are demanding to be treated ethically; with renewed expectations and pressures for truthfulness and fairness.

Sustainable Development

The protection of the natural environment is one of the key areas of growing concern and interest to a number of primary and secondary stakeholders. Sustainable development *involves conducting business in a way that protects the natural environment while making economic progress, thus meeting the needs of the present generation without compromising the ability of future generations to meet their own needs.*[56] The issues addressed under the umbrella of sustainable development are wide ranging. For example, the United Nations Division of Sustainable Development identifies 41 broad categories under sustainable development. A few of these categories include atmosphere, climate change, consumption and production patterns, forests, freshwater, industry, land management, oceans and seas, sanitation, toxic chemicals, and waste.[57] Sustainable development is increasingly becoming an area of interest and commitment in both the private and public sectors. Businesses often make reference to *sustainability* rather than sustainable development, a term that dominates the public and academic sectors.[58]

Table 3.4	Examples of Types of Pressures from Primary Stakeholders

EMPLOYEES

- Pay and benefits
- Safety and health
- Rights at work/global labor standards
- Fair/ethical treatment in hiring, reviews, promotion, and related areas

SHAREHOLDERS

- Demands for efficiency/profitability
- Viability (sustainability)
- Growth of investment
- Ethical disclosure of financial information

CUSTOMERS

- Competitive prices
- Quality and safe products
- Respect for customers' privacy
- Concern for environment
- Truthful/ethical advertising and sales practices

SUPPLIES

- Meet commitments
- Repeat business
- Fair trade practices/ethical treatment

Snapshot

"Energy efficiency is a competitive advantage in the automotive industry and in the markets for everything from airplanes to refrigerators. It's high time we bring the same focus and competitive zeal—the same level of responsibility to the environment—to our (computer) industry."

Greg Papadopoulos, Chief Technology Officer, Sun Microsystems

On a practical level, sustainable development is based on the systems viewpoint (see Chapter 2 for a discussion of the viewpoint). It emphasizes that the economy exists within society, and both the economy and society exist within the natural environment. Sustainability *means managing all levels of systems—individual, group, organization, community, national, and global—in ways that ensure our economy and society can continue to exist and improve without destroying the natural environment on which we all rely.* In addition, it focuses on actually improving the natural environment.[59] Table 3.5 provides a summary of the key components of sustainable development and its partner, sustainability.

As might be expected, firms vary in the specific sustainability initiatives undertaken and how they go about implementing them. Consider this one example. Wells Fargo, headquartered in San Francisco, provides a broad range of financial services through its 3,000 branch banks. The firm recently committed to a 10-point plan for environmental sustainability. Mary Wenzel, the vice president for environmental affairs, commented: "We want to make sure Wells Fargo and our more than 80 businesses and 151,000 team members are committed to being environmentally responsible stewards in every community in which we do business."[60] Interestingly, environmental activists in San Francisco attacked Wells Fargo's 10-point plan because it did not address global warming, endangered ecosystems, and human rights issues.[61] We highlight 4 of the 10 points in Wells Fargo's commitment to environmental sustainability here.

▶ The company will provide more than $1 billion in lending, investments, and other financial commitments during the next five years to environmentally beneficial business opportunities including sustainable forestry, renewable energy, water resource management, waste management, energy efficiency, and "green" home construction and development. The company will solicit input from customers, industry groups, and environmental groups during the process.

Table 3.5   Components of Sustainable Development

- Integrated solutions to environmental, social, and economic needs.
- Helping to ensure that improvements to quality of life reach everyone, including those most in need.
- Operating within the environmental carrying capacity of the earth and its habitats.
- Using resources more efficiently and decoupling growth from environmental damage.
- Ensuring an equitable access to environmental resources.
- Recognizing that decisions and actions taken locally have global impacts.
- Acting now to address sustainable development concerns, many of which will be global and longterm in nature.
- Acting at all levels of society, including increased empowerment to act at a local level.
- Accepting that global issues are a local concern.
- Win–win–win solutions possible, rather than trade-offs between social, environmental, and economic issues.

Source: Adapted from World Wildlife Fund–UK. Sustainable development. *www.wwf.org.uk.* (February 2006); R. Steurer, M. E. Langer, A. Konrad, and A. Martinuzzi. Corporations, stakeholders and sustainable development I: A theoretical exploration of business-society relations. *Journal of Business Ethics,* 61, 2005, 263–281.

▶ To ensure the company's environmental decision making is thoughtful and thorough, it will adopt new environmental due diligence procedures and practices for middle-market and large corporate customers in environmentally sensitive industries. The company will solicit input from customers, industry groups, and environmental groups during the process.

▶ The company will adopt the *Equator Principles*, based on World Bank and International Finance Corporation guidelines, to improve environmental and social risk management in project financing. The company believes these principles are an important framework for guiding large-project development in environmentally sensitive areas.

▶ The company will increase efforts to conserve resources in its operations including companywide recycling and purchasing programs. The company will also collect data on energy and greenhouse gas emissions from all the facilities it owns and, where possible, those facilities it leases, to track and help minimize the effect on the environment from its operations.[62]

Organizations that actively address sustainability issues benefit in a variety of ways. Most obviously, they build reputations for being socially responsible. But they also develop new and valuable organizational capabilities. They learn to integrate the concerns of multiple stakeholders when planning and making key decisions. Moreover, they further develop abilities to innovate and learn.[63]

Evaluating Social Performance

With heightened public interest in social responsibility, many organizations are discovering that they can't avoid having people evaluate how well they perform in this respect. Business publications, such as *Fortune* and *Forbes* magazines, rank various aspects of organizational performance annually. Many stakeholders are pressuring business leaders to move away from the sole focus on the utilitarian approach with its overwhelming focus on profits and to instead contribute more actively to society. One approach to evaluating an organization's social and ethical performance is to consider whether it merely reacts to ethical pressures as they arise or anticipates and addresses ethical concerns proactively. The four major themes found in a firm with a commitment to evaluating its social performance and responsibility are as follows.[64]

Disclosure. The firm is transparent, providing comprehensive social and environmental information to the public. The firm produces reports annually that review, at least, its social and environmental policies, goals, and performance as well as financial performance, though it is rare for an organization to integrate social and financial reporting. The firm often provides additional social and environmental information on its company Web site or in other published materials.

A strong corporate responsibility report uses the Global Reporting Initiative (GRI) guidelines as a framework for reporting. The GRI suggests global standards that improve the consistency and comparability of reports. Some companies are now producing "In Accordance with GRI" reports. This is the highest level of disclosure recognized by the GRI. The firm also provides disclosure of goals and performance for key social and environmental metrics, such as workplace diversity data, workplace safety data, and energy consumption data.

Communication and Engagement. The firm actively seeks to communicate with various groups about its social and environmental performance. This allows the organization to present progress made and to learn from the groups about what future expectations may be. In some cases, the firm will have established a "road show" through which it meets with various stakeholder groups about social and environmental performance or developments areas of concern. The firm uses advisory committees to solicit regular input on key issues. Communication is a precursor to action. The firm takes what it learns from the interaction with stakeholder groups and works to ensure that business practices adapt to meet changing needs.

Proactive Management. The firm is committed to going beyond minimum compliance requirements and integrating corporate responsibility into board governance, executive compensation and incentives, and management policies. Compliance is no longer enough—if indeed it ever was. The organization integrates management of social and environmental issues into both day-to-day management and into its managerial, executive, and fiduciary governance. This can mean creating a stand-alone corporate responsibility department and a cross-functional executive committee. At the board level, the firm has a corporate responsibility committee to regularly evaluate and oversee social and environmental issues. It has a formal chain of command to handle these issues—from the board through line employees—to ensure that progress is not driven solely by crises.

The organization recognizes that these issues will not be managed properly unless they are included in management compensation incentives and reviews. There are ways to measure social and environmental progress, determining the proper metrics and setting up systems to collect relevant data, such as workforce diversity, employee turnover, employee safety, and energy consumption.

Creating Shareholder Value. The organization views corporate responsibility as central to its efforts to create shareholder value. It looks at how social and environmental issues can affect sales, costs, and reputation. For example, on the sales side, the firm recognizes that future sales depend on delivering products that are kinder to the environment, such as fuel-efficient cars or energy-efficient computers. The well-managed company recognizes the need for diverse workforces, managers, and boards to relate to the increasing diversity of its consumer base. From a cost perspective, it recognizes that proactive management of environmental and social risks can substantially lessen the uncertainties and liabilities created by changing regulatory requirements and new knowledge of emerging risks. Top management recognizes that it can cut costs through environmental initiatives, such as reducing energy intensity or minimizing waste. There is a recognition that its customers, suppliers, employees, and others would rather do business with a company that is mindful of its power and its ability to affect people's lives. Examples of such firms include General Electric, Johnson & Johnson, and Citigroup.

J&J's Self Assessment. Johnson & Johnson is a firm that mirrors the themes for evaluating social performance. One brief excerpt from the 42-page *Johnson & Johnson 2004 Sustainability Report* illustrates our contention[65]:

> Each of our companies and facilities is expected to go Beyond Compliance, striving to set the standard and be a leader among our peer companies rather than simply meeting minimum requirements. To conform to our definition of "Beyond Compliance," each Johnson & Johnson company will:
>
> ▶ Meet all Johnson & Johnson standards and regulatory requirements.
>
> ▶ Optimize the design of products, processes and facilities by incorporating quality, safety, environmental and engineering standards.
>
> ▶ Proactively partner with regulators and anticipate changes in regulations, standards and public expectations.
>
> ▶ Achieve operational excellence.
>
> We firmly believe that our Beyond Compliance culture creates competitive advantage for Johnson & Johnson.

Chapter Summary ·······································

This chapter examined ethical and socially responsible business decisions and behaviors. What is viewed as ethical or socially responsible varies, at times, among an organization's many stakeholders. Ultimately, individuals must accept responsibility for their own ethical conduct and decisions. Throughout the chapter, we presented concepts, approaches, policies, and examples of how to behave in ethical and socially responsible ways.

Learning Goals ·······································

1. State the importance of ethics for individual employees and organizations.

Concerns regarding ethics in business have recently been renewed. Many individuals say that they would prefer to work for organizations with good reputations for being ethical and socially responsible. At the same time, scandalous business practices have been revealed. Managers and other employees must recognize ethical issues and deal with them effectively by understanding the influences that shape ethical conduct and the key perspectives that can be used to make ethical decisions. Interestingly, there is some evidence that organizations with a reputation for being ethical tend to have competitive financial performance over the long run.

2. Describe four influences that shape the ethical behaviors and decisions of individuals and organizations.

The key categories of factors that shape a person's and an organization's ethical conduct are cultural influences, legal and regulatory influences, organizational influences, and individual influences. Cultural influences comprise shared values and norms that underlie standards for acceptable behavior. Legal and regulatory influences reflect societal standards that are enforceable by regulatory agencies and in the courts. Organizational influences include policies and practices—such as a code of ethics, cultural norms, ethics training, formal mechanisms for monitoring and enforcing ethical conduct, and how managers model ethical conduct and define acceptable employee performance. Finally, an individual's influence includes the view of what is right and wrong through the person's stages of moral development, and how that can influence a person's response.

3. Describe three approaches that people use when making ethical judgments.

Managers and employees commonly rely on one or some combination of three ethical approaches to guide decision making and behavior. The utilitarian approach focuses on decisions or behavior that are likely to affect an organization's profitability. For businesses, profits indicate financial and economic performance. The moral rights approach upholds a member of society's fundamental rights to life and safety, truthfulness, privacy, and freedom of conscience and speech. The justice approach advocates impartial, equitable distribution of benefits and costs among individuals and groups, according to three principles: distributive justice, fairness, and natural duty.

4. Explain stakeholder social responsibility and how it influences managers' ethical decisions and behaviors.

The diverse values and ethical approaches prevalent in advanced economies introduce a great deal of complexity for managers of organizations that attempt to act in socially responsible ways. One approach that managers can use to ensure socially responsible actions is to consider how the organization's actions affect important stakeholders. Each group of stakeholders has different concerns. Sometimes these concerns conflict; at other times they mesh. Thus finding solutions that address the concerns of multiple stakeholders becomes an important strategic task.

Key Terms and Concepts ....

Code of ethics

Cultural values

Culture

Distributive justice
  principle

Employment-at-will

Ethics

Fairness principle

Justice approach

Laws

Moral rights approach

Natural duty
  principle

Sarbanes-Oxley Act

Stages of moral
  development

Stakeholder social
  responsibility

Stakeholders

Sustainability

Sustainable development

Utilitarian approach

Whistle-blowers

Questions for Discussion and Reflective Thinking ....

1. In terms of the three approaches for making ethical judgments, what specific ethical concepts are illustrated in Johnson & Johnson's *Our Credo* as presented in the Planning and Administration Competency feature on page 100. You should relate specific statements in the code to specific ethical concepts.

2. In the opening Challenge of Managing feature and elsewhere in the chapter, we discussed several aspects of Halliburton in relation to the common view of some in the general public versus management's view of Halliburton's ethics and social responsibility. Go to *www.halliburton.com*. Find the firm's *Code of Business Conduct: Export Administration & International Economic Sanctions under Corportate Governance*. What influences that shape ethical conduct are illustrated in this code?

3. In our discussion of cultural influences, we identified 10 fundamental personal values that are often listed by individuals as central to them and the American culture. How would you rank these values in terms of their relative importance to you? What was the basis for your selection of the top three ranked values?

4. One way to simplify your approach to ethical decision making is to consider whether an action is legal or illegal. Is this a good approach to ethical conduct? Explain.

5. Think of an organization for which you have worked. Did this organization follow the actions recommended in this chapter to develop and ensure an ethical culture? Explain how it did or did not adhere to each of the recommended actions.

6. In one study, the Society for Human Resource Management found that approximately 50 percent of all job applications contained false information, 44 percent misrepresented their work experiences, 23 percent misrepresented credentials or licenses, and 41 percent misrepresented their education. What stage or stages of

moral development are suggested in these findings? What ethical concepts are being violated by these individuals? What types of rationalizations do you think these individuals are likely to offer for providing such false information?

7. Managers are important in setting the ethical tone for employees. If you work for an unethical manager, chances are you may eventually feel some pressure to act in ways that you consider unethical. Suppose that you suspect that your boss is not completely honest when reporting the sales figures for your unit. What would you do?

8. As the boundaries of the workplace have become more fuzzy and flexible, so have the boundaries of private life. Many people take work home with them and stay in almost constant touch with their colleagues or customers via e-mail or voice mail. Similarly, they may conduct some of their private business from their office at work. What types of personal activities are routinely conducted while you're at work, if any? Is it fair for employers to expect employees to be constantly "connected" to their workplace, but not allow them to make personal telephone calls or shop on the Internet while at work? Explain.

9. Organizations communicate their ethical principles in a variety of ways: through the behavior of leaders, in writing, by offering training programs, through performance assessment methods, and so on. Visit the home page of any major organization of interest to you. Are the ethical principles of the organization communicated to people who visit this site? Are the perspectives of potential customers, employees, shareholders, and suppliers considered?

10. As a student, you are almost certain to work in a team with other students on some class assignments—for this course or other courses. What can you and the members of your team do to manage the ethical conduct of your team? Would it be useful to develop a code of ethics for your team? Explain your answer.

DEVELOPING YOUR COMPETENCIES

Scenario 1

The U.S. Patent Office recently issued a patent to Tiger Automotive for a device that has been proven to increase the average car's gas mileage by 45 percent. Given that Tiger is protected from direct competition by this patent, it has decided to price the new product at $45 to auto parts dealers. The device costs less than $1 to produce and distribute.

How would you rate this action on the following five-point scale?

1 Strongly Disapprove	2 Disapprove	3 Neutral	4 Approve	5 Strongly Approve

What ethical approach is the basis of your rating for scenario 1?

Scenario 2

A friend of yours is the president of a company in a highly competitive industry. Your friend learns that a competitor has made an important scientific discovery that will give the competitor an advantage and will substantially reduce (but not eliminate) the profits of your friend's company for about a year. Your friend learns that there is a possibility of hiring one of this competitor's employees who knows the details of the discovery and proceeds to do so.

How would you rate this action on the following five-point scale?

1 Strongly Disapprove	2 Disapprove	3 Neutral	4 Approve	5 Strongly Approve

What ethical approach is the basis of your rating for scenario 2?

Scenario 3

Jack Ward works in product development for an auto parts contractor. Last summer Ward's firm won a big contract to manufacture transaxles for use in a new line of front-wheel-drive cars to be introduced by a major auto manufacturer in the near future. Winning the contract was very important to the firm. Just before getting the contract, the firm had scheduled half its employees, including Ward, for an indefinite layoff—a plan that was jettisoned with the award of the contract.

Final testing of the assemblies ended last Friday, and the first shipments are scheduled to be made in three weeks. The manufacturer's specifications call for the transaxle to carry 30 percent more than its rated capacity without failing. While examining the test reports, Ward discovers that the transaxle tended to fail when loaded to more than 20 percent over rated capacity and subjected to strong torsion forces. Such a condition could occur with a heavily loaded car braking hard for a curve while going down a mountain road. The consequences would be disastrous. Ward shows the test results to his supervisor and the company president, who both indicate that they are aware of the problem but have decided to ignore the report. Chances of transaxle failure in ordinary driving are low, and there isn't enough time to redesign the assembly. If the company doesn't deliver the assemblies on time, it will lose the contract. Ward decides not to show the test results to the auto manufacturer.

How would you rate this action on the following five-point scale?

1 Strongly Disapprove	2 Disapprove	3 Neutral	4 Approve	5 Strongly Approve

What ethical approach is the basis of your rating for scenario 3?

Interpretations

Scenario 1: *Strongly disapprove or disapprove*—reflects the justice approach. *Strongly approve or approve*—reflects the utilitarian ethical approach. *Neutral*—reflects no preference.

Scenario 2: *Strongly disapprove or disapprove*—reflects the moral rights approach. *Strongly approve or approve*—reflects the utilitarian approach. *Neutral*—reflects no preference.

Scenario 3: *Strongly disapprove or disapprove*—could reflect the utilitarian, moral rights, or justice approach. *Strongly approve or disapprove*—might reflect utilitarianism (Ward has no responsibility beyond telling his supervisor or the president or the risk of death or injury is too low to hold up the sale).

Wal-Mart Stores is the world's largest company, with 1.5 million employees and net annual sales of approximately $313 billion. Since its founding in 1962, Wal-Mart has expressed three basic principles stated by its founder, Sam Walton: (1) Provide value and service to customers by offering quality merchandise at low prices every day; (2) corporate dedication to a partnership between the company's associates (employees), ownership, management, and vendors; and (3) a commitment by Wal-Mart to the United States and the communities in which its stores and distribution centers are located. Each week, more than 140 million shoppers visit Wal-Mart stores to get "everyday low prices." Some groups and individuals claim these declared principles are not worth the paper that they are written on.

Charges against Wal-Mart

Wal-Mart has been the target of many groups over the years, including organized labor (unionization), feminists (gender discrimination in employment practices), human rights activists (overseas working conditions and wages in overseas apparel "sweatshops"), environmentalists, local businesses, and other antisprawl activists (new Wal-Mart stores). These groups have had a cumulative impact on the public's perceptions of Wal-Mart's corporate citizenship. We provide a small glimpse of these charges here.

Although Wal-Mart employees begin at the same salary level as unionized employees in the retail industry, it is claimed that, on average, they make 25 percent less than unionized retail workers after two years on the job. To qualify as a full-time employee, one must work a minimum of 28 hours per week; approximately 70 percent of Wal-Mart workers meet this minimum. Of those employees qualifying for health insurance, only 38 percent purchase it, possibly because employees are responsible for 35 percent of the overall cost. This is double the U.S. average for employee copayments. By keeping its deductibles high (the company does not cover flu shots, child vaccinations, or contraception, which many other firms include in their health-care coverage), Wal-Mart spends 30 percent less per employee on health care than its competitors. Giant and Safeway, unionized supermarket chains, estimate that, for every $3 they spend on health care for employees, Wal-Mart spends an average of $1. Furthermore, new full-time employees must wait for six months to be eligible for its health-care plan and the company does not cover any health-care benefits for retirees.

Wal-Mart, along with other "big-box" retailers such as Target, Lowes, and Home Depot, has become the focus of a national "antisprawl" movement. This has brought together environmentalists, local businesspeople, and residential homeowners in actively resisting what the National Trust for Historic Preservation (Washington, D.C.) defines as poorly planned, low-density, auto-oriented development that spreads out from the center of communities.

City officials in some states fear the arrival of the Wal-Mart Supercenters, believing that they place downward pressure on wages, because local businesses would need to reduce costs to compete, eliminate more jobs than create new ones, and leave more residents without health insurance. Wal-Mart critics point to the retailer's global pursuit of lower cost goods as contributing to the accelerating loss of U.S. manufacturing jobs to China and other low-wage-paying countries in Southeast Asia. One labor organizer in China alleges that Wal-Mart's supplier factories are notified before Wal-Mart inspectors arrive. These factories are alleged to clean up their operations, create fake time sheets for the auditors, and brief workers on what they should tell the inspectors. Wal-Mart is also charged with pitting one supplier against another, with the resulting competition for lower prices fueling longer employee working hours and lower wages. A critic describes the following competitive environment:

> . . . these factories often require employees to work as many as 80 hours per week during the busy season for $75 to $110 per month, violating Chinese labor laws. If Wal-Mart really wanted to monitor conditions among its suppliers, it could do so with surprise visits, longer inspections, and independent auditors. But if they did that, prices would definitely go up.

CEO Lee Scott's Perspectives

Lee Scott is the CEO of Wal-Mart. He has contrary views to the charges against Wal-Mart. We present a few of his views here.

> As one of the largest companies in the world, with an expanding global presence, environmental problems are OUR problems. The supply of natural products (fish, food, water) can only be sustained if the ecosystems that provide them are sustained and protected. There are not two worlds out there, a Wal-Mart world and some other world. . . . I believe, in fact, that being a good steward of the environment and in our communities, and being an efficient and profitable business, are not mutually exclusive. In fact, they are one in the same. . . . Our environmental goals at Wal-Mart are simple and straightforward:
>
> **1.** To be supplied 100 percent by renewable energy.
>
> **2.** To create zero waste.
>
> **3.** To sell products that sustain our resources and environment.
>
> Who better than Wal-Mart to make a kilowatt of electricity go twice as far, or a gallon of diesel [to] take our trucks twice the distance? Or three times? Who better than Wal-Mart to stretch our energy and material dollars farther than anyone ever has? To help lower our energy bills and gas prices for years to come? We didn't just get needed goods to Katrina victims—we did it less expensively than anyone.
>
> . . . . We will increase our fleet efficiency by 25 percent over the next 3 years and double it within 10 years. If implemented across our entire fleet by 2015, this would amount to savings of more than $310 million a year. . . .
>
> Wal-Mart can help restore balance to climate systems, reduce greenhouse gases, save money for our customers, and reduce dependence on oil, and we are committed to the following:
>
> **1.** Aggressively investing approximately $500 million annually in technologies and innovation to do the following:
>
> • Reducing greenhouse gases at our existing store, club and DC base around the world by 20 percent over the next 7 years.

- We have designed and opened a prototype store in McKinney, Texas, that is 25–30 percent more efficient and will produce up to 30 percent fewer greenhouse gas emissions. More of these energy efficient stores will be opened.

- Increasing our fleet efficiency by 25 percent in the next 3 years, and doubling efficiency in the next 10 years.

2. Aggressively pursuing regulatory and policy change that will create incentives for utilities to invest in energy efficiency and low or no greenhouse gas sources of electricity, and to reduce barriers to integrating these sources into the power grid. . . .

3. Initiating a program here in the U.S. that gives preference to suppliers who set their own goals and aggressively reduce their own emissions.

We are committed to further increasing our engagement concerning supplier factory conditions and becoming more transparent in this important area. For example:

1. We are currently reorganizing our global sourcing organization to separate the factor certification function from our buying organization so that these two organizations can focus completely on their respective missions.

2. We will continue to deepen our engagement and collaboration with industry, governments and leading community organizations on our sourcing practices in developing countries. . . .

3. In the interest of enhanced transparency, we are working towards an independent monitoring program to validate and provide additional credibility to our factory certification program.

For us, there is virtually no distinction between being a responsible citizen and a successful business . . . they are one in the same for Wal-Mart today.

Questions

1. Why do you think that Lee Scott, the CEO, felt that he needed to present Wal-Mart's stated commitment to stakeholder social responsibility to the public?

2. Do Lee Scott's remarks reflect stakeholder social responsibility? Explain.

3. What moral rights are at the heart of the charges against Wal-Mart?

4. What aspects of the justice approach serve as the basis for the charges against Wal-Mart?

5. How do you assess the ethics and social responsibility of Wal-Mart? For example, to obtain additional insights on Wal-Mart's initiatives, go to *www.walmartfacts.com*. Click on entries under "Environmental Sustainability." For contrary perspectives, go to Wal-Mart Watch at *http://walmartwatch.com*. Your assessment needs to draw on specific ethical and social responsibility concepts and practices presented in this chapter.1

© Creatas Images/Jupiter Images

chapter 4

Assessing the Environment

Learning Goals

After studying this chapter, you should be able to:

1. Explain how economic, demographic, and cultural factors affect organizations.

2. State the five competitive forces in an industry.

3. Describe the political and legal strategies managers use to cope with changes in the environment.

4. Explain how technology changes the structure of industries.

Communication Competency

Planning and Administration Competency

Teamwork Competency

Managing Effectively

Self-Management Competency

Strategic Action Competency

Multicultural Competency

Challenge of Managing ....

Home Video Game Industry

The Atari Flashback 2 recreates the classic home video gaming experience of decades past, offering gamers a nostalgic experience with Asteroids, Centipede, Pong, and other games. Instead of requiring cartridges like the original Atari, these games are programmed into the console.

© Paul Sakuma/AP Photo

The home video game industry began in 1972 with the founding of Atari. After riding a dramatic boom and bust in the early 1980s, most companies were squeezed from the business as Nintendo of Japan then rebuilt the industry—establishing a commanding worldwide position by the end of the decade. By 1990, Nintendo game systems could be found in one out of every three households in both Japan and the United States. The latest Entertainment Software Association survey shows that the average gamer is 29 years old and spends more time playing games than engaging in traditional forms of entertainment, such as watching TV or going to the movies. The typical gamer now has a full-time job and income to purchase video games.

The rise of video games as the entertainment outlet of choice had negative implications for TV and movies, especially in the critical age group of 18- to 34-year-olds. In 2005 alone, sales from video games were more than $9.9 billion, while the movie industry took in $8.4 billion—and the gap is widening. Consequently, film studios, bookstores, and media companies have been looking to get into the game (literally) through a slew of partnerships with game development companies. Nearly 60 percent of Sony's profits in 2005 were from sales of hardware and its latest video game console, PlayStation2. Barnes & Noble's GameStop, a video retailer, contributed as much profit as its bookstores. Without video games, Barnes & Noble would have reported a loss. Similarly, Paramount Pictures joined with Electronic Arts (EA) to develop a game in which the characters mimic the strategies of the Corleones, the mob family from the epic movie *The Godfather*. In addition, video games based on movies like *The Incredibles* were being used "to keep a story in consumers' minds" until a movie sequel could be developed.

As each new generation of game consoles is released, sales for existing games slow down. So, as sales of Sony's PlayStation2 (PS2), Microsoft's Xbox, and Nintendo's GameCube began to slow down, sales for PlayStation3, Xbox 360, and Nintendo Revolution started to grow. Worldwide sales of video games in 2004 were $24.5 billion and are projected to soar to $55 billion by 2008. Moreover, prices for game consoles have steadily declined. For example, the retail price for Sony's PS2 is now $149, about half its initial price. Sony's PS2 dominates the game console market with about 70 percent of global sales (Nintendo's GameCube and Microsoft's Xbox control about 15 percent each). The proverbial "good news" in these sales statistics was that demand for video game software is stronger than ever (up 7 percent to $6.2 billion in the United States, or 248 million units sold).

Sony's PlayStation3 was released in 2006, several months after Microsoft's Xbox 360, but before Nintendo's new Revolution console. Like the Xbox 360, PlayStation3 is more of a multimedia entertainment hub than a video game system; its computing power allows users to play a game, chat online, and listen to music all at the same time. It will also be able to render film-quality animations at a resolution that's equivalent to that of a cinematic digital projector.[1]

Explain how economic, demographic, and cultural factors affect organizations.

The Environment

Making money in the video game industry is difficult. While playing video games is constantly rated among the "most fun things to do," there are only a few companies selling video games. Why? The financial resources needed to enter this industry are huge, and the complexity of games has increased dramatically over time. The top three companies now generate more than 75 percent of all sales. Kazuo Hirai, president of Sony Computer Entertainment, observed that a company can have the best technology and the most advanced box, but with outdated software applications, the company will fail. The cost of designing software for a new game can easily exceed $6 million, employ hundreds of developers, and take years to create. Eighty percent of the games are sold within the first three months of their introduction. Therefore, companies need to recover the expenses very quickly before customers grow tired of the game.

The key driver of success is the ability (or good fortune) to choose the right game to finance and market. Another problem is that software designed for one game system will generally not work on the next-generation game system (e.g., Xbox and Xbox 360), even though it's made by the same company (e.g., Microsoft). So whenever a manufacturer introduces the next-generation machine, a decision must be made as to whether or not to enable the new machine to play existing games designed for the manufacturer's old system. When Sony introduced PlayStation3, owners of PlayStation2 could use their games on this new version. This enabled customers to have an instant library of software to use. It also increased the cost of developing new hardware because it must accommodate both PlayStation2 and PlayStation3 games.

The home video game industry illustrates how numerous environmental forces can impact industries. We have been selective in choosing the environmental forces to assess. For example, the international arena is certainly a key part of most managers' environments—today more than ever. However, we mention international forces here only briefly because we devote Chapter 5 to this topic. Also, various groups are pressing for new forms and higher levels of ethical behavior by managers and for increased social responsibility by organizations. We covered this aspect in Chapter 3. Generally, throughout this book, we discuss environmental forces and their management whenever they are relevant to the topic being considered.

We begin this chapter by introducing the basic features of the general environment within which organizations operate: economic and political systems, demographics, and cultural forces. We devote most of the chapter to three types of environmental forces that managers must monitor and diagnose because of their direct or indirect impact on organizations: competitive, political–legal, and technological forces.

The General Environment

The general environment, *sometimes called the macroenvironment, includes the external factors that usually affect all or most organizations.*[2] The general environment represents the broad collection of factors that directly or indirectly influence every organization in every industry. The general environment includes the type of economic system (capitalism, socialism, or communism) and economic conditions (expansionary and recessionary cycles and the general standard of living); type of political system (democracy, dictatorship, or monarchy); technology (hand crafted, mass production, and continuous process); demographics (age, gender, race, ethnic origin, and education level of the population); cultural background (values, beliefs, language, and religious influences); and competitors. Of course, managers cannot control factors in the general environment. Moreover, these factors are often difficult to predict with any real precision. Although numerous factors make up the general environment, we will consider developments in six areas as shown in Figure 4.1. All of these aspects of the general environment have fundamental implications for managing organizations.

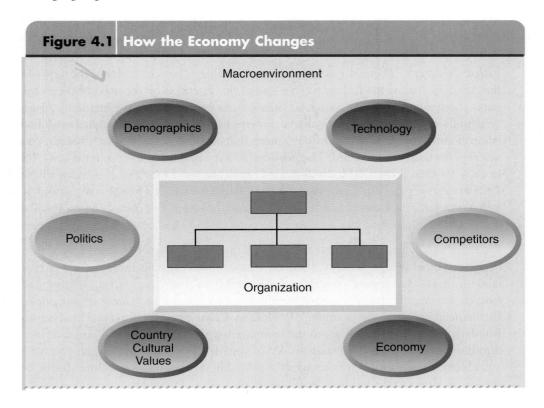

Figure 4.1 | How the Economy Changes

Macroenvironment

Demographics

Technology

Politics

Competitors

Organization

Country Cultural Values

Economy

The Economy

Economics *is the discipline that focuses on understanding how people or nations produce, distribute, and consume various goods and services.* Important economic issues are the wages paid to labor, inflation, the taxes paid by labor and organizations, the cost of materials used in the production process, and the prices at which goods and services are sold.[3] Free-market competition, private contracts, profit incentives, technological advancement, and organized labor with collective bargaining rights are essential elements of the U.S. economic system and those of a number of other countries. The government (part of the political system) acts as a watchdog over business, providing direction in antitrust, monetary policy, human rights, defense, and environmental matters. Particularly challenging economic and political conditions include the fluctuation of inflation, unemployment, taxes, and interest rates and the environmental and safety regulations covering both the workplace and goods produced. Government ownership of enterprises is the exception, rather than the norm. The U.S. economy is not centrally planned, as in North Korea or Cuba.

Thomas Friedman, author of the best-selling book *The World Is Flat*, describes 10 trends that are impacting all industries. Six of the most important management trends discussed by Friedman are shown in Table 4.1 and are illustrated in the following paragraphs.[4]

Table 4.1	New Age of Competition
OLD	**NEW**
Low-cost manufacturing	Value-added services
Self-reliance	Outsourcing
Made in U.S.A.	Borderless competition
Local knowledge	Customer convenience
Physical labor	Human capital, software, knowledge management
Smoke-stack industries	Environmental stewardship

Source: Adapted from T. L. Friedman, *The World Is Flat*. New York: Farrar, Straus & Giroux, 2005, 48–172.

Value Matters. There is a major emphasis on value. The economies of the past—in the Agrarian Age or the Industrial Age—were characterized by the mass of their outputs, whether crops or steel. Value has shifted from the tangible to the intangible, from steel mills to know-how. Today, manufacturers use more software and less unskilled labor. If you own a Toshiba laptop computer that is under warranty and it breaks, you call Toshiba to have it repaired. The Toshiba person will tell you to drop it off at a UPS store. UPS then ships it off to its dedicated repair shop in Louisville, Kentucky, where UPS workers repair your laptop and return it within 24 hours. The value to customers is that they have their computers back quickly and the number of complaints to Toshiba is low. UPS and Toshiba work collaboratively to create value for all parties.

Outsourcing. During the past few years, U.S. organizations have outsourced tens of thousands of jobs to India, China, and elsewhere to take advantage of lower cost labor in these developing countries. Outsourcing *is simply the shifting of work and business activities that were once performed inside the organization to other organizations.* In financial services, for example, JP Morgan Chase can hire financial analysts in Bombay, India, for $1,000 a month compared with $7,000 in the United States. Similarly, when Microsoft installs its MSN system on your computer and you have a problem, the customer service agent is probably stationed in Bangalore, India. In the home video game industry, software is created by knowledge workers who are located anywhere in the world. Managers are increasingly thinking in terms of the value they are creating by increasing their knowledge.

With the economy becoming less about goods and more about the transfer of information and delivery of service, companies in the new economy will focus on ideas and speed. According to Thomas Siems of the Federal Reserve, the number of jobs that have been outsourced for the past five years is 832,000. Many companies are also offshoring. Offshoring *refers to the situation in which a company takes one of its factories that is operating in one country and moves the entire factory to another country.* For example, Levi Strauss closed its jeans operation in San Antonio, Texas, and moved its entire factory to mainland China. In China, it produces the exact same pair of jeans, only with cheaper labor, lower taxes, subsidized energy, and lower health-care costs. It is estimated that 3.3 million American jobs will be offshored within the next 10 years. The challenge for U.S. companies and workers is to reinvent themselves and create the next generation of jobs, products, and services.[5]

© Eric Gay/AP Photo

In 2004, Levi Strauss & Co., whose trademark blue jeans have been an American clothing icon for generations, closed its last two sewing plants in the United States and relocated to China.

Borderless Competition. The limitations of geographic borders apply less and less. Firms can increasingly reach customers directly without regard to their own physical location or that of their customers. In an economy where almost everyone has a computer, the shortest distance between a customer and the company can be a single mouse click. The Internet is revolutionary because it has dramatically reduced the cost of communication and coordination in business and personal transactions. Firms such as Travelocity (travel), Wells Fargo (banking), and Charles Schwab (investments) are reaching out directly to customers across state and country borders. In the process, these companies are challenging distributors, traditional retailers, and geographic borders. Customers can easily search, evaluate, negotiate, pay for, and take delivery of products at different times and from different providers. Similarly, borderless competition has created new competitors. For example, in India, software companies such as Infosys Technologies, Wipro Technologies, and Saytan Computers are fast becoming global competitors to EDS, IBM, and Hewlett-Packard.

New companies have been formed to provide information and advice to customers so that they can make better decisions. For instance, *www.tietheknotevents.com* provides advice on wedding planning, including invitations, gift registries, honeymoons, and wedding-related travel. From *www.gardenguides.com*, customers can obtain gardening information, garden designs, gardening tips, and the like. More than 80 percent of new car buyers consult Edmund's or CarPoint on the Internet before purchasing a new car. Edmund's uses Autobytel for dealer searches and negotiations, GEICO for insurance, and Warranty Gold for extended warranties. Customers accessing Edmund's Web site (*www.edmunds.com*) can gather and evaluate information, negotiate price and terms, and finance, purchase, and insure a car—all from this single source.[6]

Wal-Mart's ability to move more than 2.3 billion merchandise cartons each year requires a state-of-the-art supply chain management system.[7] Its supply chain management system allows Wal-Mart to communicate directly with suppliers, its distribution centers, and stores. Being a supplier to Wal-Mart requires a company's commitment to excellence. Wal-Mart has introduced a new technology—radio-frequency identification (RFID) microchips. RFID microchips are attached to each pallet and merchandise box that comes into Wal-Mart, replacing bar codes. Wal-Mart requires that its top 100 suppliers ship all pallets to its distribution centers using RFID tags. According to Carolyn Walton, vice president for information technology, using RFID technology has enabled Wal-Mart to replenish its stock three times faster than it normally would have. Procter & Gamble (P&G) now provides Wal-Mart with daily information on what is selling in each of its stores. P&G, in return, restocks Wal-Mart's distribution centers as needed. Wal-Mart achieves greater sales because P&G products are not out of stock when a customer arrives and saves money because P&G carries the inventory. P&G increases its cash flow because it sends supplies only to those stores that need products, avoiding unnecessary distribution costs. Because Wal-Mart owns its own fleet of trucks and requires suppliers to deliver goods to its huge 2-million-square-foot warehouses scattered around the globe, Wal-Mart cuts out an average of 5 percent of its costs. Costs are passed on to consumers in terms of every-day low prices.

Customer Convenience. Organizations in the new economy will succeed by creating convenience for their customers. The online auction house eBay calls itself the world's largest personal trading community. This cyber-forum organization has more than 135 million registered users and sells merchandise in more than 45,000 categories in the United States, Korea, China, India, Spain, and other countries. It has 65 percent of the market share in the United States. Its competitors, Amazon.com, UBid, and Yahoo!, divide the rest. With nearly 1 million items on sale at any time and revenues exceeding $4.5 billion, eBay's Web site receives more than 50 million hits per month. More than 10 million people made purchases at online auction houses, making auction sales more than 10 percent of total e-commerce spending. What distinguishes eBay from your local flea market is not its sheer scale but the focus on convenience. The system is designed to allow buyers and sellers to search numerous categories and participate in auctions with as little friction as possible. Online tutorials lead customers through a simple four-step process: register, find stuff, bid, and sell. FedEx delivers the package and all financial transactions can be handled by PayPal, Inc. If buyers don't want to get involved, they can bring their goods to a Quick Drop. Quick Drop's employees put goods up for auction on e-Bay and handle all paperwork for the customer. The cost? Quick Drop takes a 30 percent commission. By bringing buyers and sellers together, eBay has created a huge market for resold goods, dramatically cutting the time needed for millions of buyers and sellers to find each other and transact business.[8]

Human Capital. In the old economy, the most important assets—capital, plant, and labor—were owned by the organization. To succeed in the new economy, organizations must manage knowledge, not just data or information. That is, knowledge is now an important asset too. Knowledge management *is the creation, protection, development, and sharing of information and intellectual assets.* In the new economy, human capital will have greater power because it is people who create and share knowledge. Knowledge workers in many organizations have positioned themselves to be independent entrepreneurs. Organizations will be forced to develop new ways to compensate employees because knowledge workers increasingly want to share in the wealth they create. Some 88 million N-Geners—the Net Generation (people between the ages of 2 and 22)—will enter the workforces in Canada and the United States between 2000 and 2020. The N-Geners thrive on collaboration and many find the notion of a "boss" somewhat bizarre.[9]

In the preceding sections, we noted that the U.S. economy has shifted from industrial production to services and information analysis. This shift means that jobs of all kinds are more likely to require some type of specialized skill. One result is that people with little education or training will continue to have a hard time finding meaningful and well-paying work and will experience long spells of "labor market inactivity." Currently, knowledge workers, such as physical therapists, computer engineers and scientists, special education teachers—all of whom must have education and training beyond high school—are among the workers in greatest demand.

Snapshot

"Our assets leave on the elevator every night. Organizations do not own human capital; they can only rent them. In today's world, human capital will have greater power than other resources because it is the people who create knowledge."

Andy Grove, Founder and CEO, Intel Corporation

Environmental Stewardship. Every firm exists in an environment. Although specific types of environmental forces and conditions vary from industry to industry, consider the rising consciousness of the need to protect the environment by all organizations. Consistent with our discussion of sustainable development in Chapter 3, environmental stewardship *is a policy that an organization adopts to protect or enhance the natural resources in the conduct of its activities.* Since 2003, the city of Calgary, Alberta, Canada, has installed more than 11,000 new lower wattage streetlights that saved residents of this Canadian city $2 million per year while reducing carbon dioxide emissions of gas and coal-burning generators. These new streetlights reduce light pollution (unnecessary light emitted into the sky) by using flat-lens fixtures that reduce the amount of excessive light shining onto private residences. These new lights also reduce glare, which increases a driver's visibility and cuts down on accidents. The city of Calgary has won the responsible lighting award from the Royal Astronomical Society of Canada for its improvements. The city has also mandated that only furniture made from recycled products be purchased by city employees.[10]

Organizations must address the concerns of environmental groups such as Greenpeace, the Sierra Club, and the Union of Concerned Scientists. These groups question whether designer crops can do much to clean up pollution. They also keep a close watch on the manufacture and use of herbicides and other synthetic products. The Audubon Society has broadened its efforts from protection of wildlife to actively monitoring business practices that affect native plants and animals. It was the first organization to propose legal agreements requiring removal of significant amounts of phosphate from the water used to refine sugar. The National Resources Defense Council has abandoned some of its earlier views—considered by some to be "fanatic and utopian"—and has displayed a greater understanding of the trade-offs involved in both economic and environmental survival. The organization has begun to move from confrontation to collaboration as a strategy. Nonetheless, some environmental organizations, such as Wise Use, continue to press legislators to adopt stricter laws and to urge regulatory boards that enforce land use and waste disposal regulations to tighten their procedures.[11]

This renewed interest in saving the environment poses numerous challenges to business. With the passage of the U.S. Clean Air Act of 1990 and the North American Free Trade Agreement (NAFTA), organizations faced more than a choice—they faced increasingly tough requirements. Meeting the requirements of such legislation may add costs to doing business. For manufacturers of steel, aluminum, and copper—Nucor, Alcoa, and Phelps-Dodge—meeting stringent new environmental standards has added millions of dollars to the cost of their products. It has also required them to design new manufacturing processes that will protect the environment.

Managers can take the following specific actions to respond to environmental concerns[12]:

▶ Give a senior-level person well-defined environmental responsibilities. This approach makes environmental concerns a strategic issue.

▶ Measure everything: waste, energy use, travel in personal vehicles, and the like. Set measurable goals and target dates for environmental improvements. Monitor progress.

© Image Ideas/Jupiter Images

Concern for the environment may drive some companies out of business, while opening new opportunities to others with earth friendly reputations.

▶ Consider reformulating products in order to use fewer toxic chemicals in the manufacturing process and cleanup. Try to use materials that won't harm the environment when the consumer eventually discards the product.

▶ Consider business opportunities for recycling or disposing of products, including having customers return them when the products have reached the end of their useful lives.

▶ Recognize that environmental regulations are here to stay and that they are likely to become more restrictive. Environmental awareness and behavior (*green behavior*) will have a lot to do with a firm's reputation in the future.

Environmental concerns have changed the way producers and consumers alike think about products, the raw materials used to make them, and the by-products of manufacturing processes. In fact, industries have developed a whole new generation of successful products in response to the Clean Air Act and reuse and recycling regulations. For example, Louisiana-Pacific makes various wood products, including particleboard, out of milling scraps. Cities like Calgary purchase products made by this company because of its green emphasis.

Impact of Changing Demographics on Organizations

Demographics *are the characteristics of a work group, an organization, a specific market, or various populations*, such as individuals between the ages of 18 and 22.[13] Demographics—and in particular, changes in demographics—play an important role in marketing, advertising, and human resource management. Let's consider a few of the broad demographic changes that have occurred in the United States recently and that are expected to continue for the foreseeable future.

Increasing Diversity. The U.S. workforce is becoming more diverse as we shall explore in depth in Chapter 13. In this chapter, we will just highlight some employment trends. People with disabilities—aided by passage of the Americans with Disabilities Act several years ago—have been finding more and more ways to become productive employees. Many gays and lesbians no longer try to hide their sexual orientation and want to be dealt with as employees who have rights equal to those of heterosexuals. Older employees want the right to refuse mandatory retirement and continue to work as long as they are productive. Obese people are beginning to expect and gain some rights to be treated fairly and equally in the workplace. By the end of this decade, more than 163 million people will be part of the U.S. labor force. The share of women in the U.S. workforce will increase from 46 percent in 2000 to 47.5 percent in 2012. By 2012, the percentage of Asians is expected to be at 5 percent, and the number of Hispanic Americans is expected to be at 13 percent, an increase from 10 percent in 2000.

Hispanic men have the highest workforce participation rate, while Hispanic women have the lowest. This growth will result from continued immigration of young adults, high birth rates, and relatively few retirees. About 23 million baby boomers—the generation of persons born between 1946 and 1964—will retire by 2012 and most of them will be white men. However, the share of the 55-and-older group will increase from 14.3 to 19.1 percent of the labor force by 2012. Women and people of color will gradually represent a larger share of the labor force. The overall rate of labor force participation will barely creep upward by 2012, from 66.6 percent in 2000 to 67.1 percent. By 2012, the number of African-American workers will increase by 12 percent from 2000. All of these trends will make the labor force much more diverse than it is today.[14]

By promoting diversity throughout their organizations, managers can promote and exchange ideas that can lead to new ways of doing business. For example, the Hispanic population is growing much faster than other ethnic groups and represents almost one-third of the population in many states such as California, Arizona, Texas, and New York. Hispanics currently make up one out of every seven Americans; by 2016, Hispanics and other minorities will make up one-third of the entire U.S. population. Many Hispanics working in the United States have traditionally sent cash home to their families living in Mexico. Because of the unreliability of this, Wal-Mart, Western Union, and American Express have all entered the money transfer market. This allows customers working in the United States to send money electronically to their outlets in Mexico where the relative can pick up the money.

Immigration brings enormous challenges to many U.S. organizations. High schools will soon be offering Hindi and Mandarin as more Asians come to America. MTV is already launching new channels; MTV Desi, MTV Chi, and MTV K are aimed at, respectively, South Asian, Chinese, and Korean immigrant teens. Many of these teens' parents are highly skilled workers who are looking for a better life in this country. Many companies located in California's Silicon Valley, for example, are staffed with new immigrants who have taken great risks to create and manage companies in biotechnology, software design, and other growth industries. At the same time, however, rising tides of immigrants, particularly those entering the United States illegally, pose another set of challenges for the U.S. economy. Many illegal immigrants provide an important source of low-cost labor in construction and service-based industries. Some people believe that these workers are siphoning away employment opportunities for U.S. citizens.

Managerial Challenges. Managers are likely to face new pressures from an increasingly diverse workforce. These challenges are discussed in more detail in Chapter 18. In response to the increasing diversity of the workforce, some organizations provide training to help employees at all levels be more tolerant of language, age, race, and ethnic differences but intolerant to sexual harassment; to identify and reject racial and gender preferences in hiring and promotion; and to be responsive to the needs of people with disabilities. Managers no longer can impose a traditional "Anglo male" organizational culture on workers. More and more workers from all backgrounds are interested in flexible scheduling that recognizes and accommodates the demands of modern families.

In addition, many new workers expect something more from their careers than simply earning a living—they want to feel that they are making a meaningful contribution to their employers and to society. These better educated employees want their individual and group needs recognized and met. They desire more control over their destiny, a say in decisions that affect them, and more flexibility in the terms and rewards of employment. They want a fair, open, flexible, and responsive work environment where they are productive, yet can also enjoy the workplace. Many expect to experience the excitement and stimulation of meeting challenging opportunities and problems and the security that comes from being appreciated and supported. People will be less willing to sacrifice personal and family life for career success.[15]

Why Is Culture Important to Managers?

Almost no organization is immune to the impact of culture. Most people do not realize the tremendous impact that national culture has on their interpretation of everyday events. The reality is that most organizations must increasingly cope with a diverse cross-cultural set of suppliers, customers, competitors, and employees. Because culture colors nearly every aspect of behavior, you will need to develop an appreciation for global mind-set. In Chapter 3, we defined culture (see page 80) as the dominant pattern of living and believing that is developed and transmitted by people.[16] Similarly, cultural values are those deeply held beliefs that specify general preferences and behavior, and define what is right and wrong. A value system *comprises multiple beliefs that are compatible and supportive of one another.* For example, beliefs in private enterprise and individual rights are mutually supportive. Cultural values aren't genetically transferred. People begin to learn their culture's values from the day they are born, and this learning continues throughout their lives. Throughout the book, we recognize that cultural values differ across countries, across organizations, and across ethnic groups.

Managers need to appreciate the significance of values and value systems, both their own and those of others. Values can greatly affect how a manager

▶ **views other people and groups, thus influencing interpersonal relationships.** In Japan male managers have traditionally believed that women should defer decision-making responsibilities to men. They belonged at home where they were responsible for raising and educating the children. Until recently, similar views prevailed in many U.S. organizations. But this situation has changed. Many more U.S. managers and government policies/laws view men and women as equals who should be recognized, consulted, and promoted because of their abilities and contributions, not their gender.

▶ **perceives situations and problems.** Many U.S. managers believe that conflict and competition can be managed and used constructively by employees to solve problems. In France, employees take their different perspectives to their bosses who will then issue orders for settling a situation.

▶ **goes about solving problems.** In Korea, managers at Samsung believe that team decision making can be effective. In Germany, managers at Hoechst Chemical believe that individuals should make decisions after thorough analysis and by following procedures.

▶ **determines what is and is not ethical behavior.** One manager might believe that ethics means doing only what is absolutely required by law. Another might view ethics as going well beyond minimum legal requirements to do what is morally right. In a country such as Nigeria, there are few ethical principles.

▶ **leads and controls employees.** In the United States, many managers believe in sharing information with employees and relying on mutual trust more than rigid controls. In Mexico, most managers emphasize rules, close supervision, and a rigid chain of command.[17]

The Internet battle between Yahoo, Google, and Microsoft and the Chinese government illustrates how different cultural values often clash and cause ethical challenges for CEOs of these companies. Hackers around the globe are trying to break through the "Golden Shield," a term they use to describe the filtering system that censors more than 400 million e-mails to China's 123 million Internet users. These hackers are trying to slip contraband words and ideas in and out of the country via mass e-mails on servers that have not been blocked out by the Chinese government and that aren't on government blacklists.[18] The following Ethical Challenge discusses some of these issues.

Ethical Challenge

Internet Battle in China

Imagine that you are Bill Gates, the chairman and chief software architect of Microsoft. His company cannot do business in China except on terms dictated by China's governmental authorities and that means zapping Web traffic that strays too far from the party line. If Microsoft, Google, and Yahoo comply, they become, in the eyes of Chinese dissenters, collaborators with an oppressive regime. Recently, Microsoft shut down a popular blog that had criticized the firing of an editor at a progressive newspaper in Beijing. Microsoft said that it had to shut down the blog based on explicit government notification. But when Microsoft shut down the blog, what law was it following? Yahoo also felt legally compelled to shut down its blog.

Google is also under attack for allowing its Chinese site to be controlled by Chinese authorities. Censorship is quite an industry in China. Many villages have spies that watch their neighbors; the mail and the old-fashioned "For Sale"-type bulletin boards also are watched. It is rumored that China has 40,000 Web police in Beijing alone looking over the words used by Web users and composing lists of banned words that cause the Web search to freeze up or a site to automatically be blocked. China has nine state-licensed Internet access providers, each of whom has one gateway to a foreign Internet. According to Open-Net Initiative, "China's Internet-filtering regime is the most sophisticated of its kind in the world."

Recently in a meeting before a congressional subcommittee on Global Human Rights, Gates and other Internet CEOs were called to answer questions about their operations in China. They indicated that they must comply with local (Chinese) laws, stating that they believe that it's better for Chinese citizens to be getting filtered access to the Web than none at all and that they hope for more openness in the future. Cisco's top managers claim that China's order for more than 800 million dollars' worth of Cisco routers was an important source of revenue for the company, and that Chinese employees altered its products to suit the "special needs" of the Chinese market.

Okay, if you were Bill Gates the chairman of Microsoft, what would you do? Follow the Chinese government's mandate or face leaving the Chinese market?

By diagnosing a culture's values, managers and employees can understand and predict others' expectations and avoid some cultural pitfalls. Otherwise, they risk inadvertently antagonizing fellow employees, customers, or other groups by breaking a sacred taboo (e.g., showing the bottom of a person's shoe to a Saudi, which is a sign of disrespect) or ignoring a time-honored tradition (e.g., preventing an employee from attending an important religious ceremony in Indonesia).

A framework of work-related values has been used in numerous studies of cultural differences among employees in more than 50 countries. Geert Hofstede, director of the Institute for Research on Intercultural Cooperation, developed the framework for research on intercultural cooperation in the Netherlands while an organizational researcher at IBM. The findings reported here are based on his surveys of thousands of IBM employees in 50 countries. Hofstede's studies uncovered some intriguing differences between countries across five value dimensions: power distance, uncertainty avoidance, individualism (versus collectivism), gender role orientation, and long-term orientation.[19] These are shown in Figure 4.2 on the following page.

To be open minded and to understand the cultures of different countries, you need to be able to compare your own culture with those of other countries. Before continuing to read this chapter, please take a few minutes to complete the questionnaire in the Experiential Exercise on pages 144–145 of this chapter. Think about the culture in which you now live and study.

The following discussion focuses primarily on Hofstede's ranking of four regions of the world with respect to each dimension. These rankings are based on the dominant value orientation in each country. Figure 4.3[20] on page 125 shows the rankings for Canada, Japan, France, and the United States.

Power Distance. *The degree to which less powerful members of society accept that influence is unequally divided is the measure of its* power distance. If most people in a society support an unequal distribution, the nation is ranked high. In societies ranked high (e.g., Mexico, France, Malaysia, and the Philippines), membership in a particular

Figure 4.2 Cultural Factors

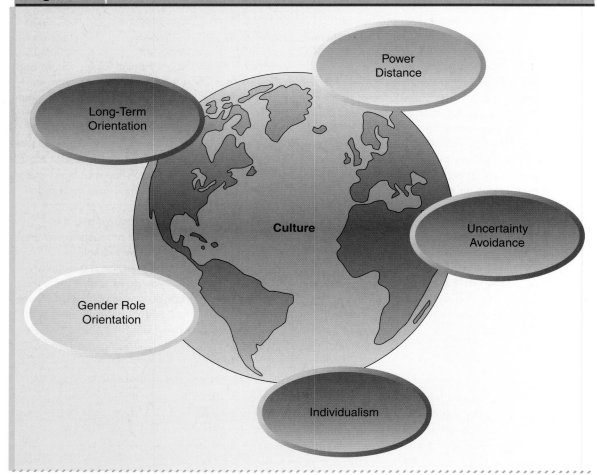

class or caste is crucial to an individual's opportunity for advancement. Societies ranked lower play down inequality. Individuals in the United States, Canada, Sweden, and Austria can achieve prestige, wealth, and social status, regardless of family background.

Managers operating in countries ranked low in power distance are expected to be generally supportive of equal rights and equal opportunity. For example, managers in Canada and the United States typically support participative management. In contrast, managers in Mexico, France, and India do not value the U.S. and Canadian style of participative management. Power is centralized and decisions are made from the top down. Managers in the United States and Canada try not to set themselves too much apart from subordinates by appearing to be superior or unique. In countries with high power distance, however, a more autocratic management style not only is common but also is expected by employees. There is also a wide gap between executives and workers' compensation.

Uncertainty Avoidance. *The extent to which members of a culture feel threatened by risky or unknown situations is the measure of its* uncertainty avoidance. Laws and rules try to prevent uncertainties in the behavior of other people. Individuals in cultures ranked low on this dimension generally are secure and don't expend a great deal of energy trying to avoid or minimize ambiguous situations. In France and other cultures with high uncertainty avoidance, individuals often try to make the future more predictable by

Figure 4.3 | Cultural Value Rankings

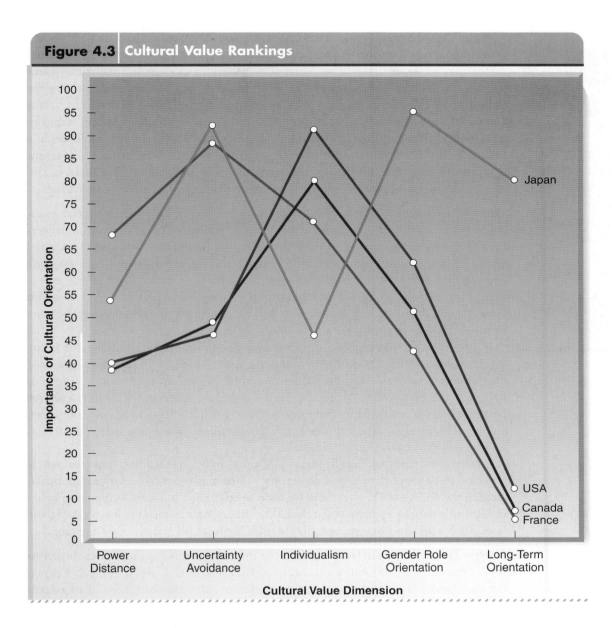

following established procedures and rules that foster tradition. In France, the younger person always approaches the older person for the *faire les bisous* or kiss. A violation of this formality is considered rude. In French organizations, such as Total Fina Elf and France Telecom, high uncertainty avoidance is often associated with built-in career stability (job security), numerous rules governing behavior, intolerance of deviant ideas and behavior, belief in absolute truths, and overreliance on expertise.

In the United States and Canada, employees and managers ranked low on uncertainty avoidance, sharing a relatively high tolerance for uncertainty, compared with workers and managers in Japan and France. Thus Canadian and U.S. managers are more likely to be receptive to changing rules, open competition, and new ideas than are their counterparts in Japan and France.

Individualism. Individualism is *a combination of the degree to which society expects people to take care of themselves and their immediate families and the degree to which individuals believe they are masters of their own destinies.* The opposite of individualism is collectivism, *which refers to a tight social framework in which group (family, clan, organization, and nation) members focus on the common welfare and feel strong loyalty toward one another.*

Snapshot

"What amazed me about Japan was how structured the society was. Little schoolchildren wear different-colored hats indicating gender and grade level. They also walk in line to school with girls following behind the boys."

Chris Koski, Vice President, nMetric

In the United States, France, and Canada, employees ranked high on individualism, a result that agrees with the frequent characterization of these countries as "I" societies rather than "we" societies. A strong sense of individualism supports and maintains a competitive market-based economic system. High individualism also is consistent with the individual merit and incentive pay systems favored in the United States and Canada. Conversely, group incentives and strong seniority systems are likely to exist in countries with low individualism (high collectivism), such as Japan. Managers and employees in a high-individualism culture move from organization to organization more frequently. They don't believe that their organizations are solely responsible for their welfare, nor do they expect decisions made by groups to be better than decisions made by individuals.

Gender role orientation. Gender role orientation *refers to the extent to which a society reinforces traditional norms of masculinity versus femininity.* This dimension reflects the division of labor among men and women in a society. Canada and the United States probably rank lower today on this dimension than they would have 20 years ago, largely because of the societal changes that have been taking place in role expectations for men and women. In recent years significant social pressures have begun to change stereotyped notions that men should be assertive and women should be nurturing or that gender roles should be clearly differentiated.

In high gender role orientation cultures (e.g., Mexico, Japan, Austria, and Italy), gender roles are clearly distinct. In many of these cultures, women still do not hold many managerial jobs. Men dominate most settings, and an organization's right to influence the private lives of its employees is widely accepted. Masculine cultures build a system of entitlements that often discourage what it takes to advance, improve, and to achieve. The dominant values in a masculine society are material success, money, and the acquisition of "things."

Mexico, for example, rigidly defines gender role expectations: The woman is expected to be supportive of and dependent on the man—not to do for herself, but to yield to the wishes of others, caring for their needs before her own. A common belief in Muslim countries is that women should be subordinate to men in all aspects of their lives. Such a system gives men privileges from birth simply because they are men.

Long-Term Orientation. This value dimension was originally developed to reflect the teaching of Confucius, a civil servant in China in about 500 B.C. Known for his wisdom, he developed a pragmatic set of rules for daily life.[21] Long-term orientation *reflects the extent to which a culture stresses that its members accept delayed gratification of material, social, and emotional needs.* In long-term oriented cultures (e.g., China, Hong Kong, Japan), families stress the importance of thrift, ordering relationships by status and observing this order, persistence, and education. We illustrate these rules by references to organizational life. First, the junior manager owes the senior manager respect and obedience; the senior manager owes the junior manager protection and consideration. Second, the family is the prototype of all social organizations. Members of organizations should learn to promote harmony by allowing others to maintain "face," that is, dignity, self-respect, and prestige, particularly in conducting business affairs. Third, people should treat others as they would like to be treated. First-line managers should encourage subordinates to acquire knowledge and skills to enable them to advance, just as these managers would like the middle managers above them to do. Finally, a person's tasks in life consist of acquiring skills and education, working hard, not spending more than necessary, being patient, and preserving the values of the society.

In cultures that score high on long-term orientation, management practices such as thrift, gift giving, good manners, and saving face are highly valued. Thrift leads to saving, which provides capital for reinvestment. Welcoming speeches by elder members of the organization and exchanges of small gifts prior to conducting business are important. Seniority is prized and is linked to the size of a person's office, pay, and other perquisites. Such practices emphasize the stability of authority relationships and respect. In the United States, Canada, and France, such management practices are not highly valued or practiced.

Managerial Implications. After reading this section and examining your scores on these five dimensions from the Experiential Exercise, some of you are probably questioning whether you have the ability to work in a foreign setting. We hope we have given you some information about key cultural differences among nations and how these differences influence the behaviors of its people. Understanding other cultures can make you a better manager even if you never leave your home country. [22] In an increasingly global market, managers in every country must think globally. Even in the United States, most products face tremendous foreign competition. Global competition is a reality, and the number of managers and workers taking assignments in countries other than their own is rapidly increasing. These workers bring aspects of their own

© Xinhua, Rao Aimin/AP Photo

For the opening ceremony of Hong Kong Disneyland in 2005, Mickey and Minnie welcome Hong Kong Chief Executive Donald Tsang, left, Walt Disney Company's then CEO Michael Eisner, China's Vice President Zeng Qinghong, and CEO-elect Bob Iger.

cultures into their organizations, neighborhoods, school systems, and homes. Learning how to integrate these workers and their values and ways of doing things into the organization is essential. Although various cultural behaviors may appear similar on the surface, their meanings in different cultures may be quite different. Realizing the importance of these differences helps managers understand their international partners and ultimately to be better managers.

The following Multicultural Competency feature highlights some of the challenges that Disney and the Magic Kingdom faced when entering China. With more than 300 million people under the age of 14 in China, Disney needed to enter that market if it wanted to continue to grow. Why? Recently Disney earned 22 percent of its revenues and 35 percent of its profits from foreign markets. ABC is the world's second largest media and entertainment conglomerate and it needed to have a market presence in the world's fastest growing economy. [23] In the following feature, we have put in parentheses the five cultural values where appropriate.

Magic Kingdom Goes to China

Robert Iger, the CEO of Disney, went to China to see firsthand the problems that Disney might encounter trying to enter China. He quickly learned that the Chinese government restricts media ownership and controls the news on all of China's 358 television stations and 2,119 newspapers (*power distance*). The government limits the ability of non-Chinese companies to sell, distribute, and identify the programs they produce. The messages broadcast by TV or printed in the newspapers are tightly controlled by the government. For example, the Chinese government has blacklisted any reference to the Tiananmen Square Massacre of June 4, 1989, and all June 4th related words, as well as any reference to Taiwan, Tibet Independence, and BBC.co.uk. (*uncertainty avoidance*). When Disney tried to mix its half-hour cartoon show with short segments produced in China, the government closed it down. Disney cannot call its Mickey Mouse Club by that name, so it airs as the Dragon Club, which reaches more than 380 million households. When Disney decided to build a Disneyland in Hong Kong complete with Main Street, Sleeping Beauty's Castle, and Tomorrowland, it had to go to great lengths to make sure that the architect heeded the advice of a master of feng shui, *which is the Chinese art of*

design and placement of buildings to represent the flow of energy and harmony. The feng shui master ordered that the entire park be laid out to foster harmony with the elements.

Because many mainland Chinese do not know who Mickey Mouse is, Disney has teamed up with the 70-million-member Communist Youth League to host a series of sessions aimed at aiding the reading skills and creativity of Chinese children. Disney also had performers go out to children in the local Guangdong province to tell stories using Disney characters (*collectivism*).

Disney has also had to confront piracy since entering China in 1997. Disney has released more than 500 DVD titles since then, but their sales are hurt by piracy. For example, *Finding Nemo*, which Disney claims is the number one selling DVD in China, sold only 284,000 copies. Legitimate DVDs sell for as much as 10 times the price of a knockoff and most Chinese consumers are not willing to pay that much.

To learn more about this organization, visit *www.disney.com.*

2.

State the five competitive forces in an industry.

Competitive Forces in an Industry

The general environment contains forces and development that affect all firms within the economy of a nation. You also know that developments in the general environment can have different effects on competitors within a single industry. The deregulation of the financial services industry has enabled companies such as Merrill Lynch and Fidelity Investments to offer services similar to that of BankAmerica, JP Morgan Chase, and other banks. Therefore, developments in the general environment can have unintended consequences for companies within and across different industries. As we illustrated in the video game industry, companies within that industry have had an impact on the number of people attending movie theaters and watching TV programs. The general environment is like a large pond in which hundreds of companies compete for customers. When a stone is tossed into the pond, it creates ripple effects that all firms feel—either directly or indirectly. Some organizations respond favorably, while others don't.

In this section of the chapter, we will explore those forces whose effects are limited to their immediate competitive environment. If Wal-Mart lowers its prices on household products, Target, Safeway, and other grocery chains will probably respond. Nordstrom's, Saks, and Barneys will not respond because they are not in Wal-Mart's competitive environment. The competitive environment *includes the forces shaping competition within an industry.* You can analyze the competitive environment of an industry by considering five forces: competitors, new entrants, substitute goods and services, customers, and suppliers.[24] The combined strength of these forces, shown in Figure 4.4, affects long-term profitability. Managers should monitor and diagnose each one, as well as their combined strength, before making decisions about future courses of action. In this section, we continue to examine the video game industry to illustrate how companies compete.

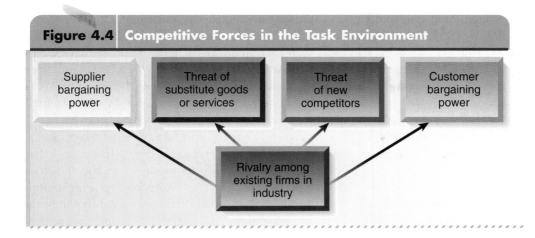

Figure 4.4 | Competitive Forces in the Task Environment

| Supplier bargaining power | Threat of substitute goods or services | Threat of new competitors | Customer bargaining power |

Rivalry among existing firms in industry

Competitors

Aside from customers, competitors are the single most important day-to-day force facing organizations. Bruce D. Henderson, founder and chairman of the Boston Consulting Group, comments: "For virtually all organizations the critical environment constraint is their actions in relation to competitors. Therefore any change in the environment that affects any competitor will have consequences that require some degree of adaptation. This requires continual change and adaptation by all competitors merely to maintain relative position."

In the Challenge of Managing case, we noted that the home video game industry has become fast paced and increasingly competitive.[25] As a result of changes in customer tastes, this situation creates cutthroat product rivalry with leading companies, such as Microsoft, Nintendo, Sony, and Electronic Art, attempting to gain market share through massive advertising and research and development campaigns. Designing home video games requires people with advanced skills in computer programming, digital animation, physics, and math.

New Entrants

The phrase new entrants *refers to the relative ease with which new firms can compete with established firms.* In an industry with low barriers to entry (e.g., the photocopy industry or the fast-food industry) competition will be fierce. The home video game industry is a particularly interesting case because it has had both high and low barriers to entry during the past 10 years. Economies of scale, product differentiation, capital requirements, and government regulation are four common factors that need to be diagnosed in assessing barriers to entry. Let's see how they have affected the video game industry.

Economies of scale *are achieved when increased volume lowers the unit cost of a good or service produced by a firm.* The potential for

© Bananastock/Jupiter Images

The home video game industry uses marketing to achieve product differentiation between brand names, such as Nintendo and PlayStation.

economies of scale in the video game software industry is substantial. During a recent holiday season, *Half-Life 2* sold 120 million copies during the first 24 hours. The video game *Grand Auto Theft* sold more than 1.4 million copies in the first three days at $48 each. Sports games, such as Electronic Arts' *Madden NFL Football*, can cost more than $1 million to produce. This game has sold more than 27 million copies since it was introduced in 1989, enough to supply the entire population of Peru. However, not all games are as successful, such as the *Incredibles*.

Product differentiation *is the uniqueness in quality, price, design, brand image, or customer service that gives one firm's product an edge over another firm's.* It is a tool that organizations can use to lock in customer loyalty to its products. In this industry, companies are differentiated by brand names, such as Nintendo and PlayStation. Sony's PlayStation has enabled it to leverage its quality and product differentiation to be significantly different from Nintendo and other PC game companies. Marketing is another way to achieve product differentiation. Celebrity status is important among teens and young adults, so using celebrities is one way to differentiate a product. John Madden's celebrity status, which resulted from his stint as an announcer on *Monday Night Football*, has been instrumental in promoting the Electronics Arts video games. Similarly, Sony's PlayStation has enabled it to leverage its quality and production differentiation to be significantly different from Nintendo and other PC game companies.

Capital requirements *are the dollars needed to finance equipment, purchase supplies, purchase or lease land, hire staff, and the like.* The demand for personnel to design games is great. Salaries often start at $60,000 a year, but people can quickly earn more than $100,000 if they're part of a team that makes a best-selling title. Although there is room for start-ups to enter this industry, three major manufacturers—Sony (PlayStation), Nintendo (GameCube), and Microsoft (Xbox)—have been able to capture a large share of the console (e.g., hardware) market. Start-up firms, such as Valve Software, focus mainly on software.

Government regulation *is a barrier to entry if it bars or severely restricts potential new entrants to an industry.* The home video game industry is not faced with as many government rules and regulations as is, say, the pharmaceutical industry.

Substitute Goods and Services

In a general sense, all competitors produce substitute goods or services, or goods or services that can easily replace another's goods or services. In the home video game industry, a major substitute is the movie rental and movie theater business. Amazon, Blockbuster, Wal-Mart, and Netflix, a web-based DVD rental firm, have all entered the billion-dollar-a-year video rental market. All of these companies rent DVDs that can be played through various outlets. Soon Netflix and TiVo plan to unveil a system that will permit people to download movies on demand that will impact the video game industry. Other substitutes for video games include watching TV, reading books, playing sports, and so on. In some instances, rental companies buy one copy of a game and then rent it for as many times as they can without additional residual income going back to the studio/publisher/developer. This practice is especially widespread in Shanghai, Beijing, Taipei, and other Asian cities.

Customers

Customers for goods or services naturally try to force down prices, obtain more or higher quality products (while holding price constant), and increase competition among sellers by playing one against the other. Customer bargaining power is likely to be relatively great under the following circumstances:

- **The customer purchases a large volume relative to the supplier's total sales.** People who buy home video games have little bargaining power over the prices charged by various manufacturers.

- **The product or service represents a significant expenditure by the customer.** Customers generally are motivated to cut costs that constitute large portions of their total costs. Buying home video games normally does not constitute a big expense for the customer.

- **Large customers pose a threat of backward integration.** Backward integration *is the purchase of one or more of its suppliers by a larger organization as a cost-cutting or quality-enhancing strategy.* In the home video game industry, there are clear examples of large companies, such as Paramount pictures and Barnes & Noble, buying into the video game industry.

- **Customers have readily available alternatives for the same services or products.** A consumer may not have a strong preference for one game over another. Therefore, they have a huge choice of which video game to buy as long as it will work on their console. This means that they have alternatives and lots of power.

Suppliers

The bargaining power of suppliers often controls how much they can raise prices above their costs or reduce the quality of goods and services they provide before losing customers. The video game industry uses many types of suppliers, including software employees, console manufacturers, celebrities, and advertising agencies.

The following Strategic Action Competency illustrates how Nintendo has crafted strategies over time to compete in the video game industry. A Japanese company, Nintendo, which loosely translated means "leave luck to heaven," started in 1889 as a manufacturer of handmade playing cards. Based in Kyoto, Japan, Nintendo is controlled by the old, established Yamauchi family. It is now the game software market leader and has sold more than 2 billion games since 1985.[26]

Strategic Action Competency

Nintendo

In 1977, Nintendo began making a home video game system in Japan under license from U.S. television manufacturer Magnavox. It teamed up with electronics giant Mitsubishi to launch a machine that played variations on *Pong*. The following year, Nintendo started putting out coin-operated video games. In 1981, Nintendo had its first smash hit with the coin-operated video game *Donkey Kong*.

By 1983, there were several players in the Japanese home video game industry, including Atari, Casio, and Sharp. The game systems sold for around $200 to $350. At Nintendo, Yamauchi was directing work on an entirely new video game

system that would be cheaper than the competition's, while at the same time having superior graphics and faster action. The strategy was to find a way of reproducing the "feel" of Nintendo's arcade games on a much less powerful home machine. A new video game system, the Famicom ("Family Computer"), was launched in 1983 in Japan. At a $100 price, widely believed to be sold at below cost, Famicom significantly undercut the competition. With its high-quality sound and graphics, Famicom sold 15.2 million consoles and more than 183 million game cartridges in Japan.

The company also developed games specially tailored to its new piece of hardware, such as the hits *The Legend of Zelda* and *Metroid*. In 1985, Nintendo released the smash hit *Super Mario Brothers*. That game grossed more than $7 billion for Nintendo—and "Nintendomania" had begun.

In 1980, Nintendo established a U.S. subsidiary, Nintendo of America (NOA), headquartered in Redmond, Washington. The operation was led by Yamauchi's son-in-law, who had previously studied and worked in the United States and Canada. NOA had a shaky start importing Nintendo coin-operated games in an attempt to gain a foothold in the U.S. arcade game business. But when *Donkey Kong* arrived from Japan, NOA's sales increased to more than $100 million in 1981.

By 1985, Nintendo started to sell the U.S. version of Famicom, now called Nintendo Entertainment System (NES). However, initial approaches to toy retailers met with an unenthusiastic response. The decision was made to reposition the video game system as a consumer electronics product rather than a toy. It was redesigned to look more like a computer and given a hi-tech package. NOA targeted electronics retailers and offered to stock stores for free,

with retailers having to pay for only what they had managed to sell after 90 days. To the surprise of the trade, consumer reaction was favorable. A national rollout followed in 1986.

As the market became saturated, Nintendo sought new products, launching handheld game devices such as Game Boy, Game Boy Pocket, Game Boy Advance, and Game Boy Advance SP. In 2004, the company introduced a two-screen, video game player called Nintendo DS (Nintendo Double Screen). They also updated their home video game system with the Super NES, Nintendo 64, and lastly Nintendo GameCube. Nintendo also plans to introduce a new game console dubbed "Revolution." Revolution is a game console first and not a digital entertainment hub. A strategic decision was made that the system would focus on just gaming. Revolution will not play DVDs and will require an add-on unit to do so. In addition to being backwards compatible with GameCube titles, players will also have access to an online library of popular classic Nintendo titles dating back to 1985.

To learn more about this organization, visit *www.nintendo.com*.

3.

Describe the political and legal strategies managers use to cope with changes in the environment.

Political–Legal Forces

Societies try to resolve conflicts over values and beliefs through their political and legal systems. For instance, in the United States and Canada the concepts of individual freedom, freedom of the press, property rights, and private enterprise are widely accepted. But legislative bodies, regulatory agencies, interest groups, and courts—often in conflict with one another—define the meaning and influence the actual interpretation of these concepts.

Many political and legal forces directly affect the way organizations operate. For the pharmaceutical industry in particular, changes in political forces have been especially significant during the past 25 years and will continue to be in the future. To achieve organizational goals, managers must accurately diagnose these forces and find useful ways to anticipate, respond to, or avoid the disturbances they cause.[27]

For many industries (e.g., financial services, pharmaceutical, chemical), government regulation is a central aspect of their environments. Consider, for example, how two federal credit laws affect lenders and borrowers in the United States:

▸ The *Equal Credit Opportunity Act* entitles the customer to be considered for credit without regard to race, color, age, gender, or marital status. Although the act doesn't guarantee that the customer will get credit, it does ensure that the credit grantor will apply tests of creditworthiness fairly and impartially.

▸ The *Truth in Lending Act* says that credit grantors must reveal the "true" cost of using credit—for instance, the annual interest rate the customer will be paying. In the case of a revolving charge account, the customer must also be told the monthly interest rate and the minimum monthly payment required.

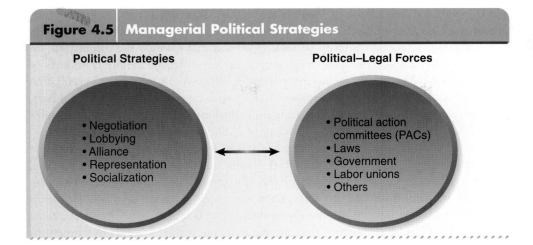

Figure 4.5 | **Managerial Political Strategies**

Political Strategies

- Negotiation
- Lobbying
- Alliance
- Representation
- Socialization

Political–Legal Forces

- Political action committees (PACs)
- Laws
- Government
- Labor unions
- Others

As shown in Figure 4.5, managers can use five basic political strategies to cope with turbulence in their environments: negotiation, lobbying, alliance, representation, and socialization. These strategies aren't mutually exclusive, are usually used in some combination, and each often contains elements of the others. Negotiation probably is the most important political strategy because each of the other four strategies involves to some degree the use of negotiation.

Negotiation *is the process by which two or more individuals or groups, having both common and conflicting goals, present and discuss proposals in an attempt to reach an agreement.*[28] Negotiation can take place only when the two parties believe that some form of agreement is possible and mutually beneficial. Recall that in 2005, management and the unions at Delta Airlines negotiated cuts in pay in an attempt to save the airline from bankruptcy. Negotiators representing the company and the union presented various proposals in an attempt to reach an agreement. Not until both parties realized that some agreement was necessary did they agree on and ratify a new contract. Unfortunately, it was too late to save Delta from bankruptcy.

Lobbying *is an attempt to influence government decisions by providing officials with information on the anticipated effects of legislation or regulatory rulings.*[29] Congress and regulatory agencies, such as the Securities and Exchange Commission, the Federal Communications Commission, and the Food and Drug Administration, are the targets of continual lobbying efforts by organizations affected by their decisions. Organizations whose stability, growth, and survival are directly affected by government decisions typically use their top managers to lobby for them. Motorola, Microsoft, and Coca-Cola, among others, lobbied Congress to allow favored nation trade status for China even after defiant student demonstrators were killed on Beijing's Tiananmen Square. These organizations agreed that human rights violations had occurred in China but that its market was too attractive to be ignored.

Only the largest organizations (e.g., NBC, AT&T, and Exxon) can afford to lobby for themselves. The most common form of lobbying for smaller companies is accomplished through membership in associations representing the interests of groups of individuals or organizations.[30] Approximately 4,000 national lobbying organizations maintain staffs in Washington, D.C. There are about 28,000 registered lobbyists. More than $2 billion, or $540,000 per day, was spent by lobbyists. Health care was the biggest issue with more than $173.2 million spent on Medicare drug and Medicaid plans in 2005.

Two of the largest associations representing business interests are the National Chamber of Commerce, with about 36,000 business and other organizational members,

"We are committed to doing whatever it takes to support the New Orleans business community in getting back on its feet. We are partnering with business leaders throughout the region to implement a recovery effort."

Melvin "Kip" Holden, Mayor, Baton Rouge

and the National Association of Manufacturers (NAM), which *Fortune* magazine calls one of the 10 most influential advocacy organizations in the United States. In 2005, NAM was able to lobby Congress to pass legislation that lowered the top tax rate on manufacturing income from 38.6 to 32 percent, saving its 12,000 members millions of dollars each. NAM annually spends more than $9 million on its lobbying efforts.[31] The American Association of Retired Persons (AARP), with more than 35 million members, is the largest U.S. association representing individual interests. The AARP spent more than $28 million in 2005 lobbying on behalf of U.S. citizens ages 50 and older.

Many citizens and organizations based in New Orleans, Mississippi, and Alabama urged the mayor of New Orleans, Ray Nagin, and the governor of Louisiana, Kathleen Blanco, to lobby the president and Congress to help them rebuild after the events of Hurricane Katrina in 2005. They were seeking more than $62 billion in relief. States that took in those who escaped from the flood, such as Texas, Arkansas, and Florida, also sent delegations to Congress lobbying for the federal government to help reimburse them for the costs they absorbed while helping victims of Katrina.[32]

An **alliance** *is a combined effort involving two or more organizations, groups, or individuals to achieve common goals with respect to a particular issue.*[33] Alliances, especially those created to influence government actions, typically form around issues of economic self-interest, such as reducing R&D costs in the pharmaceutical industry. Other issues include government policy (e.g., the control of raw materials or taxes), foreign relations (e.g., the control of foreign sales or investment in overseas plants), and labor relations (e.g., the control of industry wide salaries and benefits, as within the construction industry or the National Football League). Alliances often are used for the following purposes:

▶ **Oppose or support legislation, nomination of heads of regulatory agencies, and regulations issued by such agencies.** All companies involved in various aspects of high-definition television (HDTV) development—AT&T, Zenith, RCA, Phillips, and NBC—combined their various competing technologies into one Grand Alliance. The goal of this Grand Alliance is to gain agreement among all U.S. companies and pass legislation establishing a common digital standard for future HDTV broadcasts.

▶ **Improve competitiveness of two or more organizations through collaboration.** Qualcomm is collaborating with Nokia and Samsung to establish a digital standard that will be used in 90 percent of cell phones. This new standardized chip will enable cell phone users to "roam" around the globe.

▶ **Promote particular products or services, such as oranges, computers, and electricity.** For example, the Edison Electric Institute promotes both the use and conservation of electrical energy.

▶ **Construct facilities, such as new plants, that would be beyond the resources of any one organization to construct.** Sony and Samsung teamed up to build a leading-edge liquid-crystal display (LCD) screen plant because neither firm could afford to build a $2 billion plant by itself.

▶ **Represent the interests of specific groups, such as women, the elderly, minorities, and particular industries.** NAM lobbies Congress to pass legislation favorable to its members, including restricting imports of foreign goods such as shoes and automobiles, and trying to open new markets in foreign countries such as the sale of rice in Japan.

An alliance both broadens and limits managerial power. When an alliance makes possible the attainment of goals that a single individual or organization would be unable to attain, it broadens managerial power. When an alliance requires a commitment to making certain decisions jointly in the future, it limits managerial power. Members of the Organization of the Petroleum Exporting Companies (OPEC) periodically negotiate production levels and the price they will charge for oil. These agreements are intended to broaden OPEC's power by generating more revenue for its members. However, to be successful in this endeavor, OPEC members must abide by the agreed-on production limits.

A joint venture *typically involves two or more firms becoming partners to form a separate entity.* It is a common form of an alliance.[34] Each partner benefits from the other's expertise, which allows them to achieve their goals more quickly and efficiently. In the highly capital-intensive automobile industry, joint ventures are very common as firms seek to spread the high costs required to start a new plant. One of the most successful joint ventures involves the production of the European Airbus. The Airbus joint venture has become the world's second largest aircraft manufacturer. Various parts are manufactured by participating companies in the United Kingdom, Germany, and Spain and flown over to Toulouse, France, where the planes are assembled by a thoroughly international team of employees.

Representation *involves membership in an outside organization that serves the interests of the member's organization or group.* Representation strategy often is subtle and indirect. School administrators often receive paid time off and the use of school resources to participate in voluntary community associations that might support the school system, such as the PTA, Chamber of Commerce, Elks, Kiwanis, Moose, Rotary, and United Way. A more direct form of representation, often based on some legal requirement, occurs when a specific group selects representatives to give it a voice in an organization's decisions. For example, union members elect officers to represent them in dealing with management.

Corporate boards of directors, the top-level policy-making groups in firms, are elected by and legally required to represent shareholders' interests. The National Association of Corporate Directors, however, suggests a much broader role for board members: They should ensure that long-term strategic goals and plans are established; that a proper management structure (organization, systems, and people) is in place to achieve these goals; and that the organization acts to maintain its integrity, reputation, and responsibility to its various constituencies. The board's responsibility to monitor and control the actions of the chief executive officer and others in top management is essential to its representing the interests of the shareholders.

Socialization *is the process by which people learn the values held by an organization and the broader society.* The assumption is that people who accept and act in accordance with these basic values are less likely to sympathize with positions that threaten the organization or the society. The so-called American business creed stresses the idea that a decentralized, privately owned, and competitive system in which price is the major regulator should be continued and that citizens should oppose government actions that interfere with or threaten this system. Most U.S. and Canadian businesspeople subscribe to these beliefs and act on them.

Socialization includes formal and informal attempts by organizations to mold new employees to accept certain desired attitudes and ways of dealing with others and their jobs.[35] At its corporate executive education headquarters in Crotonville, New York, GE introduces thousands of its managers to the company's values and philosophy. These values include identifying and eliminating unproductive work in order to energize employees and encourage creativity and feelings of ownership at all levels. Conoco uses its virtual university to train managers. Employees can download courses from its Web site and/or attend courses at its location in Houston, Texas. Of course,

Lobbyists gather outside the Capitol in Jackson, Miss.

top management's attempts may be offset or reinforced by the expectations of and pressures exerted by workers or other groups within the organization.

The use of socialization strategies by organizations is subject to broader cultural forces. In the United States and Canada the importance of individualism limits the extent to which organizations can use socialization strategies. Too much of what may be perceived as the "wrong kind" of socialization is likely to be met with resistance and charges of invasion of privacy or violation of individual rights.

The AARP uses many of the political strategies just discussed to gain support for its programs. Founded in 1958 by Dr. Ethel Percy, it now has more than 35 million members. Its goal is to be one of the most successful organizations in America for positive social change by educating older Americans (50 years old or older) on issues that face them, asking political candidates for clarification of their positions on issues that affect senior citizens, and increasing voter participation. AARP does not endorse political candidates or contribute money to their campaigns. However, it does organize forums at which candidates can discuss particular issues for older Americans. Working with and through various other organizations, AARP advises members about health, auto, and home insurance, investment opportunities, mail-order pharmacy services, travel, and legal services, among others, and provides discounts for its members for some of these services.

As the leading advocate for older Americans, AARP engages in legislative and consumer advocacy on many subjects.[36] The following Planning and Administration Competency feature describes how AARP uses various political strategies to communicate its goals in three areas: Social Security, Medicare, and long-term care. The political strategies are indicated in parentheses.

Planning and Administration Competency

AARP's Political Strategies

Baby boomers in 2006 represented more than 36 million people, but by 2011, this population of people over age 65 will be growing faster than the rest of the U.S. population. Few currently retired people or those who will retire by 2010 will outlive their Social Security benefits under the program as it is now constituted. By 2011, the first generation of baby boomers will begin to retire. By 2027, the burden on Social Security will be greater than the payments going into the trust fund. Approximately 30 percent of the people receiving benefits today are under 65. Although Social Security was never intended to be a person's sole retirement, many people have no other income, and more than 50 percent of older people rely heavily on Social Security income. To ensure that the system is properly funded, AARP has pressured Congress

(lobbying strategy) to make adjustments in contribution rates, in annual cost of living adjustments, and investment of the trust fund. The organization has presented arguments against investing in the stock market, even though it routinely outperforms other investments, such as U.S. Treasury Bills. The argument presented is that most Americans with modest savings have little experience managing stock market investments and lack the skills needed to do so.

AARP was a driving force (representation strategy) for the 1997 Balanced Budget Act, which ensures that Medicare will be solvent through 2027. Under this act, Medicare makes regular monthly payments to certain health-care organizations that older people can use. It also supported the enactment of a medical savings account, which combines purchasing a catastrophic health

© Rogelio Solis/AP Photo

insurance policy with an individual medical plan, something like an IRA.

AARP is also concerned about long-term care. More than 6 million elderly people need some help in caring for themselves. As people grow old, they grow frail and often suffer from chronic and debilitating illnesses. To maintain a person in a nursing home, costs range from $110 to $210 per day, depending on the part of the country and other considerations. Medicare pays for such services only for a limited period of time after a person is released from a primary care facility (e.g., a hospital), and the remainder must come from a person's savings or from the person's family. Older people who go into a nursing home can be covered by Medicaid but only after they spend down their assets (e.g., sell their homes, stocks, and deplete almost all of their savings). AARP is trying to educate (*socialization strategy*) older people about different financing choices. But any financing program would require strong consumer protections and be easy for older people to understand and use. The organization is lobbying Congress to establish national standards to measure, assess, and ensure the quality of long-term care.

To learn more about this organization, visit *www.aarp.org*.

Technological Forces

In Chapter 2, we defined *technology* as a transformation process that changes organizational inputs into outputs. Thus technology is the knowledge, tools, techniques, and actions used to transform ideas, information, and materials into finished goods and services. A technology may be as simple as making coffee or as complicated as driving the Pathfinder on Mars.

Technological forces play an increasingly pivotal role in an organization's environment, building on the present and helping create the future. Many new technologies are radical enough to force organizations, especially in high-tech industries, to reconsider their purposes and methods of operation or face extinction. The United States and several other industrial societies have become information societies. This shift was made possible by the explosion of computer-based and telecommunications technologies. One example is the PC and its integration with mainframe computers and telecommunications systems to form supernets. Through them, organizations can collect, process, and transmit vast amounts of data quickly and economically. For instance, Kodak now supplies photographic dealers with a microcomputer and software system that enables them to order Kodak products directly rather than through wholesalers. The management of information technology is woven into various chapters of this book, but here we briefly examine technology's role in four areas: workplace, strategy, manufacturing, and distribution channels. These are shown in Figure 4.6 on the following page.

Technology's Impact in the Workplace

With each advance in technology, organizations need workers with even greater competencies to perform these new, technologically advanced jobs. In most jobs, little premium is placed on physical strength. Women can drive semi-tractor trailers today because of technology. Many farmers use GPS satellites to guide their tractors to make sure that all the rows are being planted straight. Moving from being a day laborer to a phone operator who helped people place calls was one thing, but in the 21st century, the phone operator's job has probably been outsourced to India and now that employee needs to be able to install and repair phone-mail systems or write software. These tasks require a whole new set of pattern recognition and complex problem-solving competencies.

4.

Explain how technology changes the structure of industries.

Snapshot

"With 135 million users selling goods in more than 45,000 categories in 27 international markets, eBay has left all competitors in the dust. Technology has really changed people's lives for the better."
Meg Whitman, CEO, eBay

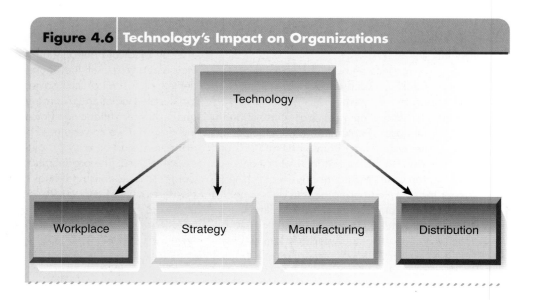

Figure 4.6 | Technology's Impact on Organizations

Technology

Workplace   Strategy   Manufacturing   Distribution

CapitalOne, the global credit card company, began outsourcing its phone call services to Wipro and Infosys in India several years ago to take advantage of the cost-savings opportunities that its competitors enjoyed. CapitalOne then developed a program of cross-training its computer programmers. The company took a programmer who specialized in mainframes and taught that person how to be a distributed systems programmer as well. As a result, employees who were eventually let go because of outsourcing were in a much better position to get another job because they had learned various, diverse technical skills that made them more employable. Similarly, Shell, Conoco, BP, and other global organizations have established virtual learning centers. The centers provide employees with lifetime learning opportunities and the ability to take online advanced university courses, both of which can be used to widen their skill base. The menu offered by online degree programs is enormous and the cost to the companies offering these educational options is very low. These organizations realize that science and math are the universal languages of technology and that technology drives standards of living. According to Tracy Koon, Intel's director of corporate affairs, "Unless today's kids understand the universal language, they will not be able to compete."

Technology's Impact on Strategy

Computer-based information technologies are now essential in most organizations, which is one reason why we included technological forces in this chapter. In the 1970s, one of every two watches sold in the United States was a Timex product. By the mid-1990s, however, the company's market share was less than 5 percent. Seiko, Citizen, Pulsar, and Swatch now dominate this market. Why? As the watch industry moved from mechanical to electronic, Timex didn't change its strategy and continued to build watches that relied on older technology. Innovations in quartz crystal chemistry and light-emitting diode semiconductors made Timex's technology obsolete. Electronic watches overwhelmed the marketplace and brought prices down, causing Timex to lose most of its market share. Similarly, in today's automobile industry, battery-powered engines and cars that run on hydrogen hold great promise for transforming this industry.

Information technology creates options for managers that simply weren't feasible with older technologies[37]:

- Solectron, a manufacturer of circuit boards used in PCs, uses computer-aided designs that enable it to have short production runs of custom designs with economies of scale approaching those of traditional large-scale manufacturing facilities.

- Consumers can shop via home pages on the Internet and "electronic shopping malls" more easily than using the Yellow Pages and telephones and going to shopping centers or individual outlets.

- With online, real-time financial management systems, managers can determine profit and loss positions daily, which was impossible with manual methods and earlier stages of computer technology.

- Retail banking customers can perform numerous banking functions from remote locations, including shopping centers, apartment building lobbies, and corporate offices, with their cell phones or PCs. With more than 200 million cell phones in the United States and 2 billion worldwide, people can now connect to their financial institution anytime, anyplace, and anywhere.

- The use of videoconferencing services is growing at 17 percent a year. Some companies, such as Frito-Lay and Hewlett-Packard, have reported savings as much as 45 percent of the company's travel account by using videoconferencing.

Elizabeth Charnock, CEO of Cataphora.

The following Self-Management Competency illustrates how two companies are using information technology to understand the day-to-day communications of their employees or voters.[38]

Self-Management Competency

Digital Sleuthing

According to Elizabeth Charnock, CEO of Cataphora, if you work for a sizable corporation, you can pretty much bet that all of your online communications—every e-mail, instant message, personal calendar—are stored for use in future lawsuits or government investigations. This creates an enormous resource for growing a number of "digital sleuths" who are paid to detect suspicious activity by making sense of those terabytes of data.

As a cofounder of Cataphora, this 73-person Silicon Valley company is serving more than 100 companies by combining the intelligence of human investigators with its own software to reconstruct the context that is vital to making sense of cryptic communications. Her company's software can figure out whether an e-mail that says "let's do it" means let's do lunch or let's commit securities fraud. Charnock says she learns more from what's omitted than from what's included and from noticing deviations from long-standing patterns. Her

software alerts investigators when people stop talking online and send e-mails that say "Let's talk in person."

Clay Johnson and his friends formed a company, Blue State Digital, that will use global positioning in the 2008 presidential election to target key voters in states, block by block. As the brain child of Governor Howard Dean that is designed for Democratic candidates, this software will automatically send messages to supporters to donate money. They will Google key words to find a candidate's supporters. "Wal-Mart has a record of every transaction of every customer, and that's something that each candidate will have," says Johnson. Knowing who's a Democrat and where they are living and integrating mapping technology so their firm can give a precinct captain a list of where to walk around a neighborhood and whose door to knock on is all based on GPS technology.

Technology's Impact on Manufacturing

Advances in design and manufacturing technology have made it possible to reduce substantially the amount of time required to introduce a new product into the market. The computers and statistical analyses used in manufacturing have also boosted quality, with machines and processes integrated by means of common databases and routines that simplify procedures and reduce the potential for human error.

Perhaps the most significant contribution of advanced manufacturing technologies is that of mass customization—that is, the ability to produce a wide variety of a product by using the same basic design and production equipment but making certain modifications to meet the demands of a broader market. For example, Levi Strauss has successfully used computer-assisted design systems to help design customized leather outfits and jeans for customers. Using an engineering workstation and advanced software, Levi Strauss can measure a customer's specific contours, body shape, weight, and preferences to create a customized pattern that becomes the basis for a perfectly fitting suit, pair of jeans, or dress in a short time. A customer's color and style preferences, as well as body measurements, are then directly fed into a computer that is electronically linked to a highly flexible stitching and finishing operation. Currently, most Levi Strauss outlets carry somewhere between 80 and 100 different varieties of jeans and outfits. With the use of new manufacturing and customization capabilities, company management believes that it will have between 400 and 500 variations on the shelves in the near future.[39]

Technology's Impact on Distribution

In the 1990s, perhaps the single greatest technological force was the change in the way goods and services were distributed. The strong presence of the Internet and the World Wide Web, which made possible online ordering, distribution, and sales, changed the way many organizations competed for customers. When Jeff Bezos created Amazon.com, suddenly the Internet threatened established retail booksellers, such as Barnes and Noble and Borders. Internet brokerage houses, such as Ameritrade and E*Trade, allow customers to access their accounts directly to buy and sell stocks. These services bypass those offered by traditional firms. Internet shopping also has replaced the department store for many customers. Combining Internet access and traditional catalog sales has enabled Lands' End, Early Winters, Touch of Class, and L. L. Bean to reach customers whose specialized needs are not effectively satisfied by existing "brick-and-mortar" department stores and discount chains.

Pitney Bowes, a company best known for making postage machines, faced a challenge from the rise of the Internet. Since 1920, Pitney Bowes has provided organizations with machines that allow them to affix the right amount of postage to letters and packages. In late 1998, companies such as E-Stamp and Stamp Master started designing Web sites that enable customers to pay for postage over the Internet, download customer-specific sets of coded data into their computers, and print out their own mailing labels and envelopes. In effect, the Internet, with permission of the U.S. Postal Service, now allows customers to print their own stamps. In response, Pitney Bowes introduced its own version of user-friendly, Internet-based software to help customers order prepaid postage with greater ease. Similarly, American Airlines and other carriers now permit travelers to print their boarding passes from their homes or place of business to avoid having to stand in lines.[40]

Building an international Information Superhighway now extends far beyond simple message systems and bulletin boards. Satellites, cellular towers, and fiber-optic telephone cables allow individuals and companies to exchange voice, data, and graphic messages in real time. Futurists speculate that within 5 to 10 years everyone will have personal numbers for all of the telecommunications devices they use; that wireless technology will replace twisted-pair, coaxial, and fiber-optic cable; and that telephone, fax, and computing will be integrated in handheld devices. In many countries, including the United States, Sweden, Japan, and the United Kingdom, telephone customers already have personal cards that they can slip into such a device and receive calls anywhere in their calling areas. Malaysia, China, and other developing countries are bypassing wired systems in favor of cellular technologies. PCs made by Toshiba, Sony, and others permit phone, fax, and computing with a pen-input screen. As a result, organizations have changed their business strategies to compete in the high-tech world.

The Information Superhighway via the Internet represents a significant change in technology for all companies. Like the computer-driven engineering technologies that revitalized manufacturing, the Information Superhighway has the ability to change the basic ways in which people communicate at work and home. Consider the International Cargo Management System. With this information system, Seal and other cargo carriers can send an electronic guard with cargo that will let the shipper visually inspect the product's location and condition. When the container is on land, the signal is sent via cellular carrier. When the cargo is at sea, the signal is sent via ship-to-shore radio or phone or global communication satellites. It is more than a cute gadget because theft is a major cost for shippers; more than $5 billion in losses are reported annually in the United States alone.[41]

The Information Superhighway will affect every organization in the years ahead. Because it represents new technology, this component of the environment undoubtedly will bring change to the political–legal arena, as customers and managers struggle with the problems of having confidential information travel around the world.

Chapter Summary

The purpose of this chapter was to help you develop your planning and administration, strategic action, multicultural, and self-management competencies with respect to an organization's environment. We discussed and presented examples of various practices that organizations can use in coping with their environments. We indicated that an organization's environment can be broken into four segments: economy and culture, competition, politics, and technology. Various competitive forces have impacts on these segments, creating both opportunities and threats that will challenge you to use all of the competencies you acquire.

Learning Goals

1. Explain how economic, demographic, and cultural factors affect organizations.

The environment includes the external factors that usually affect organizations, either directly or indirectly. It encompasses the economic system and current economic conditions, political system, natural resources, and the demographics of the population within which organizations operate. Cultural forces, primarily working through value systems, shape the viewpoints and decision-making processes of managers and employees alike. Hofstede's work-related value framework has five dimensions: power distance, uncertainty avoidance, individualism, gender role orientation, and long-term orientation.

2. State the five competitive forces in an industry.

Managers must assess and respond to five competitive forces in the environment: competitors, new entrants, substitute goods and services, customers, and suppliers. We used these five competitive forces to examine the hotly contested home video game market.

3. Describe the political and legal strategies managers use to cope with changes in the environment.

Political–legal issues, which used to be in the background, now often directly influence the way organizations operate. Five political strategies that managers use in coping with political–legal forces in the environment are negotiation, lobbying, alliances, representation, and socialization.

4. Explain how technology changes the structure of industries.

Technological forces in the environment are rapidly changing the specific knowledge, tools, and techniques used to transform materials, information, and other inputs into particular goods or services. We examined how technological changes affect four areas of an organization: the workplace, strategy, manufacturing, and distribution.

Key Terms and Concepts ....

Alliance
Backward integration
Capital requirements
Collectivism
Competitive environment
Demographics
Economics
Economies of scale
Environmental stewardship
Feng shui

Gender role orientation
General environment
Government regulation
Individualism
Joint venture
Knowledge management
Lobbying
Long-term orientation
Negotiation
New entrants

Offshoring
Outsourcing
Power distance
Product differentiation
Representation
Socialization
Uncertainty avoidance
Value system

Questions for Discussion and Reflective Thinking ....

1. How might the six trends in the new economy affect your job prospects?

2. Choose one of the following industries: chemical, lumber, or utility. Why is environmental stewardship a concern for managers in that industry?

3. What political strategies affecting international organizations are being used by Greenpeace (*www.greenpeace.org*)?

4. What implications do the changing demographic patterns in the United States have for managers in organizations such as Bank of America and Lowe's Home Improvement?

5. Pinault-Printemps-Redoute (*www.ppr.com*) is a fashion retail company with headquarters in France. What are some cultural values that you would need to be aware of in order to be a productive employee at Pinault-Printemps-Redoute? What management competencies might you need to develop?

6. Visit the Web site *www.hoovers.com*. Click on the pharmaceutical industry. Using the five-force industry model, describe the key competitive issues in that industry.

7. How has eBay used the Internet to change the retail industry?

8. What political strategies have U.S. Sugar, Imperial Sugar, or Tate & Lyle, all sugar companies, used to control imports into the United States? Have these strategies been successful? To learn more about these companies, consult *www.hoovers.com*.

9. What are the implications of the "aging" of America for you?

10. What are the ethical challenges facing Google, Microsoft, Yahoo, and other Internet companies doing business in China? For some background information, see *Forbes*, February 27, 2006, pp. 90–96, or go to *www.forbes.com/forbes*.

DEVELOPING YOUR COMPETENCIES

Instructions

In the following questionnaire, please indicate the extent to which you agree or disagree with each statement. For example, if you **strongly agree** with a particular statement, you would circle the **5** next to that statement.

1 Strongly disagree	2 Disagree	3 Neither agree nor disagree	4 Agree	5 Strongly agree

Questions

	Strongly disagree — Strongly agree		Strongly disagree — Strongly agree
1. It is important to have job requirements and instructions spelled out in detail so that employees always know what they are expected to do.	1 2 3 4 5	16. Employees should not disagree with management decisions.	1 2 3 4 5
2. Managers expect employees to follow instructions and procedures closely.	1 2 3 4 5	17. Managers should not delegate important tasks to employees.	1 2 3 4 5
3. Rules and regulations are important because they inform employees what the organization expects of them.	1 2 3 4 5	18. Managers should help employees with their family problems.	1 2 3 4 5
4. Standard operating procedures are helpful to employees on the job.	1 2 3 4 5	19. Management should see to it that workers are adequately clothed and fed.	1 2 3 4 5
5. Instructions for operations are important for employees on the job.	1 2 3 4 5	20. Managers should help employees solve their personal problems.	1 2 3 4 5
6. Group welfare is more important than individual rewards.	1 2 3 4 5	21. Managers should see that health care is provided to all employees.	1 2 3 4 5
7. Group success is more important than individual success.	1 2 3 4 5	22. Management should see that children of employees have an adequate education.	1 2 3 4 5
8. Being accepted by the members of the work group is very important.	1 2 3 4 5	23. Management should provide legal assistance for employees who get in trouble with the law.	1 2 3 4 5
9. Employees should only pursue their goals after considering the welfare of the group.	1 2 3 4 5	24. Management should take care of employees as they would treat their children.	1 2 3 4 5
10. Managers should encourage group loyalty even if individual goals suffer.	1 2 3 4 5	25. Meetings are usually run more effectively when they are chaired by a man.	1 2 3 4 5
11. Individuals should be expected to give up their goals in order to benefit group success.	1 2 3 4 5	26. It is more important for men to have professional careers than it is for women to have professional careers.	1 2 3 4 5
12. Managers should make most decisions without consulting subordinates.	1 2 3 4 5	27. Men usually solve problems with logical analysis; women usually solve problems with intuition.	1 2 3 4 5
13. Managers must often use authority and power when dealing with subordinates.	1 2 3 4 5	28. Solving organizational problems usually requires an active, forcible approach typical of men.	1 2 3 4 5
14. Managers should seldom ask for the opinions of employees.	1 2 3 4 5	29. It is preferable to have a man in a high-level position rather than a woman.	1 2 3 4 5
15. Managers should avoid off-the-job social contacts with employees.	1 2 3 4 5		

Interpretation

The questionnaire measures each of the five basic culture dimensions. Your score can range from 5 to 35. The numbers in parentheses that follow the title of the value are the question numbers. Add the scores for these questions to arrive at your total score for each cultural value. The higher your score, the more you demonstrate the cultural value.

Value 1: Uncertainly Avoidance (1, 2, 3, 4, 5). Your score _____. A high score indicates a culture in which people often try to make the future predictable by closely following rules and regulations. Organizations try to avoid uncertainty by creating rules and rituals that give the illusion of stability.

Value 2: Individualism/collectivism (6, 7, 8, 9, 10, 11). Your score _____. A high score indicates collectivism, or a culture in which people believe that group success is more important than individual achievement. Loyalty to the group comes before all else. Employees are loyal and emotionally dependent on their organization.

Value 3: Power Distance (12, 13, 14, 15, 16, 17). Your score _____. A high score indicates a culture in which people believe in the unequal distribution of power among segments of the culture. Employees fear disagreeing with their bosses and are seldom asked for their opinions by their bosses.

Value 4: Long-term orientation (18, 19, 20, 21, 22, 23, 24). Your score _____. A high score indicates a culture in which people value persistence, thrift, and respect for tradition. Young employees are expected to follow orders given to them by their elders and delay gratification of their material, social, and emotional needs.

Value 5: Gender role orientation (25, 26, 27, 28, 29). Your score _____. A high score indicates masculinity, or a culture in which people value the acquisition of money and other material things. Successful managers are viewed as aggressive, tough, and competitive. Earnings, recognition, and advancement are important. Quality of life and cooperation are not as highly prized.

Questions

1. What are your cultural values and how do they influence your behaviors?
2. Go to *www.chinatoday.com* and click on the China News Service icon. How do the stories shown depict the cultural values of China?

Since the late 1980s, movie theater attendance has fallen slowly partly because of rising DVD sales and the popularity of home video games. In 2002 an estimated 1.63 billion people went to the movies. In 2005, 1.5 billion people attended.

Why has attendance fallen? The industry is confronted by a number of competitors. Any leisure time activity can be considered a competitor, including college and major league sporting events.

Challenges from video rentals, cable TV, and satellite programming have all made inroads in the entertainment industry in an odd way. According to Eileen Albright, Lease Administrator–Western Region for Cinemark Theaters, people who rent and buy CDs, DVDs, and videos are more likely to attend movies than people who do not rent videos. Americans spend twice as much as buying and renting DVDs as they do going to the movies.

About 80 percent of U.S. households own a DVD player, up from 25 percent since 2002. It is estimated that there are more than 84 million DVDs in U.S. homes, and the forecast for the number in China will surpass that in the United States. With more people staying home, spending time with family, and keeping an eye on finances, the popularity of DVD players is expected to rise. As DVD players became more popular, the average price to purchase a DVD player has dropped dramatically from around $500 to less than $100. Many movie studios, such as Universal Studios Home Entertainment, Paramount Pictures, and 20th Century Fox, are releasing direct-to-DVD titles of their latest hits. Why? According to Kevin Kaska of New Line Home Entertainment, "There's just not enough time in the day to get out to the theater. We offer people more titles and they can stay home." A Nielsen study on the changing habits of moviegoers found that 41 percent of moviegoers still want to see the latest release on the "big" screen, but 76 percent of the least frequent attendees prefer to wait until the movie comes out on a DVD. JP Morgan analysts found that movie studios could make more money if they simultaneously released films in theaters and on DVD.

The video rental industry is also a vicious competitor for the moviegoers. Netflix claims to have more than 2.6 million subscribers, Blockbuster has 500,000, and Wal-Mart has more than 100,000. Netflix offers customers as many movies as they want for a flat fee. With no due date and late fees, it mails movies to its customers. Through its 30 distribution centers, 85 percent of its customers can be reached within a day.

The number of households with home theater systems has exploded. In 2005, home theater systems were the most asked-for (42 percent of new homeowners) technology systems in new homes. As ticket and concession prices continue to rise, more and more moviegoers have opted to build home theater systems that can play the latest DVDs. More than $23 billion were spent on HDTV last year. The technological line between watching movies in theaters and in the comfort of your home is becoming very blurred with the advent of big-screen HDTV. A Bose Lifestyle 48 DVD home entertainment system, for example, permits the user to adjust the acoustics in the room automatically to ensure a theater-like performance.

Cable television subscriptions are also growing rapidly in the United States. Between 2002 and 2006, the number of households that received basic cable grew from 63 million to more than 74 million with revenues exceeding $7 billion. In the United States, there are more than 9,000 cable systems (e.g., DirecTV, Comcast, SBC) that bring together more than 400 television stations. Some of these systems are directly targeted to an audience. For example, NTN Buzztime is mainly subscribed to by sports bars. Cable systems have also created new options for consumers through the convergence of telephone and computer technologies.

Market research has shown that four major factors determine consumer moviegoing: (1) the film itself, (2) the location of the theater, (3) the starting time of the film, and (4) the overall quality of the theater. Screen size is important to moviegoers but technological features, such as digital sound, and quality of service have a less significant impact on attendance than the first three items. Reductions in ticket price do not dramatically increase attendance.

Because film selection is the most important determinant of attendance, theater companies license films with great care. Family-oriented movies have made a major return to the movie theaters because of the popularity of computer animation and a more conservative audience after September 11, 2001. Negotiations to license a film contain provisions for a fee paid by the movie house to the movie studio. Some of the factors that determine the fees that a movie theater pays a movie studio include the intensity of competition between movie theaters in the same region, and the perceived box-office potential of a film. Well-promoted productions with big stars often receive higher rental fees. For a new film, the percentage can range from 60 to 70 percent of box-office receipts in the first week and gradually decrease to 30 percent after four to seven weeks. Experienced buyers cannot always predict which films would most appeal to moviegoers. Attendance is also influenced by the timing of the release relative to other movies. For example, when the 2005 blockbuster *Star Wars: Episode III, Revenge of the Sith* was released in mid-May, it coincided with the closing of many elementary and high schools in the United States. It grossed more the $380 million. Also, the attendance numbers for films such as *Brokeback Mountain* grew over time as a result of enthusiastic "word-of-mouth" recommendations and Academy Award nominations. Multiplex theaters offer a wide selection of films and reduce the pressure to pick "winners" when licensing.

Movie houses obtain most of their revenue from theater admissions (67 percent) and concession sales (26 percent). For the major movie houses, the average ticket price is $6.40. Ticket prices depend on location, whether the film is first run or not, the age of the customer, and whether the customer holds a discount pass. Admissions are difficult to predict. Therefore, multiplex theaters increase the flexibility of theater owners to balance screen capacity and moviegoer demand. At Carmike Cinemas, a large bag of popcorn costs $5 and the gross profit is $4.71; a small bag of popcorn costs $3.25 and the gross profit is $3.11. A large soda is $3.35 and the profit is $2.88. Nationwide the gross margin is 95 percent on popcorn and 90 percent on candy and beverages. Concessions costs run about 25 cents per patron. The remaining revenue comes from electronic games located in theater lobbies, the sale of DVDs (about 10 percent), and on-screen advertising. To increase concession sales, recently AMC Theaters partnered with Frito-Lay to create MovieNachos, and Burger King and Ben & Jerry's also have outlets in AMC's larger theaters.

The United States and Canada have more than 5,800 theaters, but most theater operators have fewer than 10 screens. The top companies control more than 50 percent of all screens. Mergers and acquisitions have dominated the industry for the last decade. Some new multiplexes have 24 screens. As the number of screens per location increases, the average attendance at each screen decreases. Some of the major movie theater operators include Regal Cinemas (*www.regalcinemas.com*), which has more than 6,273 screens in theaters; Carmike Cinemas (*www.carmike.com*), which has more than 2,469 screens in small to mid-sized communities with less than 100,000 people; AMC entertainment (*www.amctheatres.com*), which operates more than 5,672 screens in multiplex theatres; and Cinemark (*www.Cinemark.com*), which has 3,353 theaters.

Questions

1. Describe the five competitive forces in this industry.

2. Is this a good industry to enter? Explain why or why not.

3. How have demographics affected this industry?

chapter 5

© David Bartruff/Stock Connection/Jupiter Images

Managing Globally

Learning Goals

After studying this chapter, you should be able to:

1. State the trends affecting organizations in a global economy.

2. Describe how a country's culture can affect an organization's business practices.

3. Explain how political–legal forces impact global business.

4. Discuss how three major international trade agreements affect global competition and cooperation.

5. Describe six strategies used by organizations to grow globally.

Communication Competency

Planning and Administration Competency

Teamwork Competency

Self-Management Competency

Managing Effectively

Strategic Action Competency

Multicultural Competency

Challenge of Managing ....

Grupo Bimbo

© Rachel Weill/Nonstock/Jupiter Images

Grupo Bimbo (GB) was established in Mexico City, Mexico, in 1945 as a small bread production and delivery company. Today, GB is one of the top baking companies in the world and a leader among breadmakers in Mexico and Latin America with more than 80,500 employees. GB has expanded into the United States and 15 countries in Latin America and Europe, baking nearly 5,000 products. Some of its more than 100 brands are *Oroweat, Bimbo, Marinela, Tia Rosa,* and *Mrs. Baird's.* GB's 73 worldwide plants and 26,000-truck fleet allow products to reach the thousands of grocery stores that it serves.

Quality control has become an increasingly important aspect of food production. This is especially true in Mexico and Latin America where many consumers believe products to be of lesser quality than those produced in the United States. To date, GB has had more than 200 of its processes certified by the ISO (International Organization for Standardization, a world developer of manufacturing standards), and it has ISO 9002 certification for its plants. This certification helps to ensure quality control. It is the first bakery business in Latin America to receive these certifications. By committing resources to achieving certification, the company is attempting to exhibit a commitment to a healthy product and a commitment to international quality. GB sees production quality and international recognition as vehicles for strengthening value and its competitive position.

GB attempts to compete by producing bread and other products at a lower cost and by trying to reach customers more efficiently than its competitors. The massive quantities of bakery items that GB produces allow it to produce each unit at a lower cost than its competitors. GB's extensive distribution network creates another competitive advantage for the firm. The firm's extensive distribution network allows GB's products to reach more grocery stores than its competitors' products. GB products also reach the stores more quickly, making GB a fresher product.

GB has expanded into the United States through acquisitions and introduction of its brands to capture the growing U.S. Hispanic population. The increasing Hispanic population in the United States has opened the door for GB. Many American firms have taken advantage of lowered trade barriers and expanded into Mexican markets. Being a Mexico-based firm, GB entered the U.S. markets that have large Hispanic populations, such as Texas and California. Few Mexican firms have made a commitment to expand into the United States because they lack the resources needed to enter this fiercely competitive market.

Bimbo Bakeries USA, formed to control the Mrs. Baird's business it purchased in 1998, has become a leader in Texas and the southwestern United States with sales of more than $1.2 billion. GB currently operates 14 bakeries and distributes products through 3,000 routes throughout the United States. Expansion into U.S. markets has redefined GB's corporate strategy because the company now focuses on sales beyond its traditional markets. Significant resource commitment, vis-à-vis investment and acquisitions in the United States, exemplifies this new growth strategy at the international level.

GB has also capitalized on the expansion of U.S. firms into Mexico. GB's distribution capability has appealed to a number of American firms because it allows products to reach a broad consumer base. A major leap in the company's ability to compete on an international scope came when it won the exclusive contract to supply hamburger buns to Mexico's McDonald's restaurants.[1]

To learn more about this organization, visit *www.grupobimbo.com.mx.*

State the trends affecting organizations in a global economy.

The Global Economy

The Grupo Bimbo feature illustrates the effects of several global forces that an increasing number of companies are having to face: pressures on prices, the need for cost cutting, global expansion, and the impact of changes in the financial arena on profitability.

One of the unintended consequences of managing globally is that it puts different societies and cultures in much greater direct contact with one another. For example, Dell uses multiple suppliers for most of the 30 key components that go into its notebooks. That way, if one supplier breaks down or cannot meet the demand, Dell can continue to manufacture. If you own an Inspiron 600m, for example, the Intel microprocessor came from an Intel factory either in the Philippines, Costa Rica, Malaysia, or China. The memory came from Samsung, a Korean-owned company; the cooling fan from CCI, a Taiwanese-owned company; the keyboard from Alps, which is located in Tianjin, China; the hard disk drive from Seagate, an American-owned company operating out of Singapore, and so on.[2] Dell, Wal-Mart, and Philips, among other organizations, thrive on the sudden opportunities that globalization makes possible. They have designed their organizations to take advantage of these opportunities. Others, such as GM and Ford, feel threatened by globalization.

Table 5.1 highlights some of the more important trends in the global economy. In a global economy, products are shipped anywhere in the world in a matter of days, communication is instant, and foreign exchange rates can dramatically effect the financial status of an organization. For example, more than 20 percent of Wal-Mart's

Table 5.1	Global Economic Trends

Foreign exchange rates
Importance of exports and imports
Expanding nature of trade
Worldwide communication
Borderless organizations
Worldwide labor pool

revenue is generated by stores outside of the United States. Therefore, what happens in the financial markets in Asia, Europe, Latin America, and Africa is of vital interest to Wal-Mart. The fall of the euro against the U.S. dollar has been blamed for lower profits for Xerox, P&G, McDonald's, and Office Depot, among others.

Trade

Exports and imports of goods and services represent about 33 percent of the U.S. gross domestic product, up from less than 21 percent in 1992. Consider these 2006 statistics regarding global trade:

▶ The United States accounts for about 16 percent of the world's imported goods and 17 percent of the world's exported goods. The European Union (EU) exported more than the United States did recently.

▶ The EU had more direct investment in the United States than did the United States in the EU.

▶ The United States exported some $4.2 billion in goods to China, and imported $13.8 billion.[3]

Trade is now so important to the U.S. economy that one job in six depends on it. Yet a recent poll revealed that many people living in the United States thought that expanded trade led to a loss of U.S. jobs. When asked to identify the biggest threat to U.S. jobs, most people said that it was cheap foreign labor. This attitude reflects the fact that trade is often portrayed in the media as a war between nations in which countries that export more than they import win, whereas countries that import more than they export lose. However, imports have been growing at a faster rate than exports, in part because the U.S. economy has expanded, which gave its consumers more money to spend.

Increasingly, trade is taking place between different parts of the same corporation or through alliances (or joint ventures). Asking whether a product—computer, car, or shirt—has been "Made in the USA" or "Made in Canada" has become almost meaningless as evidenced by Dell Computer's multiple-supplier scenario discussed earlier. A&P, which operates 407 grocery stores in the central and eastern United States, is 57 percent owned by the

Container traffic through global ports increased by 52 percent between 2000 and 2005 (Containerisation International Magazine).

Tengelmann Group in Germany. Bayer, Inc., a major pharmaceutical company, is 100 percent owned by Bayer AG of Germany. Brach Candy is 100 percent owned by a Swiss Company, and Alcon Laboratories is 75 percent owned by Nestlé, S.A., of Switzerland. Although many executives tend to think in terms of managing a U.S. company overseas, they may well find themselves employed by a non-U.S. organization as a local manager to run its U.S. affiliate. The production of components for toys, vacuum cleaners, PCs, and many products is increasingly scattered around the world.[4]

Information Technology

Another driving force is the information revolution that now permits instantaneous worldwide communication. The globalization of business has placed a premium on information. Many organizations, especially in the United States, are spearheading the Internet boom, building fiber-optic networks and offering myriad new products and services on the World Wide Web. Sun Microsystems offers 24-hour technical assistance

Snapshot

"It is now possible for more people than ever to collaborate and compete in real time with more people on different kinds of work from different corners of the planet and on more equal footing than at any previous time in the history of the world using computers, e-mail, teleconferencing and dynamic software."

Thomas L. Friedman, Author, The World Is Flat

throughout the world with a single phone number drawing on employee teams in California, London, and Sydney. The teams coordinate their efforts electronically through a sophisticated information system. Within the next 15 years, the number of computers and communications satellites is projected to double. The number of wireless communications networks will increase to several billion as people who live in China, India, and other developing nations expand their communication networks. The number of Internet users is now estimated to be greater than 1.1 billion or 16 percent of the world's population. Internet use is increasing about 182 percent a year.[5] These figures are astounding when you realize that one-half of the world's population of 6.4 billion has never even used a phone!

Transparency

The drive for increased openness—both economically and politically—is happening. The collapse of communism in 1989 created a new group of rapid-growth countries in Central and Eastern Europe. Market institutions (e.g., banks and stock markets) that provide for effective corporate governance in many of these countries (e.g., Slovakia, Croatia, and Kazakhstan) have slowly started to develop. The lack of strong legal frameworks has allowed increases in bribery and corruption. The lack of well-defined property rights that convey ownership and transferability has also led to problems. However, the rapid and widespread adoption of market-based policies in these emerging economies has been significant.

Government Policies

Privatization permits organizations to adapt their strategies to meet the demands of the market and places the burden on top managers to manage their organizations effectively and efficiently. It also results in an increasing number of joint ventures with foreign firms and usually the adoption of more modern management practices. When GE created a joint venture with a manufacturer of light bulbs in Hungary, GE managers with global experience were called in to help the Hungarian company improve its production to world-class standards.

As domestic policies become more market oriented, governments are opening their countries to multinational trade and joining regional trade associations. New strategic partnerships between foreign and domestic organizations are emerging. Governments everywhere are pursuing market-based economic policies. Multinational corporations are accelerating the exchange of innovations across open borders. Global investors are pressuring companies to open their books. People are demanding stronger political and economic rights.

Labor Markets

One of the most important factors that has fueled the growth of the global economy is the prevalence of labor and resources in different parts of the world.[6] Many textile, housewares, and toy manufacturers have opened overseas operations to take advantage of low labor costs. Toy companies, such as Mattel and Hasbro, have significant production operations in China where the average worker earns US $78 per month. Such low labor costs enable these companies to offer high-quality toys at low cost. The presence of these companies has also helped stimulate the development of local economies.

Many U.S. firms are locating some of their operations in regions that have abundant sources of highly skilled, technical personnel, such as India. Bangalore, India, has become the call center operation of the world with more than 245,000 Indians answering phones from all over the world or dialing out to solicit people for credit cards or cell phone bargains. Ninety percent of call centers are owned by U.S. investors.

P. V. Kannan, CEO of 24/7, says that the majority of his newly hired employees start at $200 a month, which grows to $350 a month after six months. He also provides transportation, lunch and dinner, and life and medical insurance to employees. Everyone is also entitled to performance bonuses that range from 10 to 20 percent of their base salary. He also sponsors an MBA program for high performers on the weekends. Once hired, people must attend a training program. The program offers lessons on how to handle the specific processes of the company whose calls they will be taking, such as Delta Airlines, along with "accent neutralization classes." A language teacher prepares the Indian hires to disguise their Indian accents when speaking English or British, depending on the client company's location.[7]

We discuss these and other forces that are driving and restraining the global economy throughout this chapter. Although any type of organization may act globally, most that do are for-profit businesses. Therefore the material covered in this chapter applies primarily to them.

Cultural Forces

Each country has its own culture, norms, and taboos. The cultural forces that we discussed in Chapter 4 underlie the day-to-day behavior of people. Understanding cultural traditions, preferences, and behaviors can help managers avoid embarrassing mistakes and take advantage of cross-cultural opportunities. We have chosen five aspects of a culture that have direct implications for international management: views of social change, time orientation, language, value systems, and cultural distance. These five forces are shown in Figure 5.1.

2.

Describe how a country's culture can affect an organization's business practices.

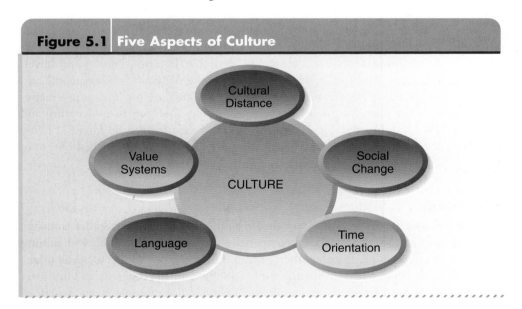

Figure 5.1 | Five Aspects of Culture

Views of Social Change

Different views of the need for social change and its pace can have a significant impact on an organization's plans for international operations.[8] The people of many non-Western cultures, such as those of India, Saudi Arabia, and China, view change as a slow, natural progression. For them change is part of the evolution of human beings and the universe, and the attitude toward it tends to be passive (or even reactive). In contrast, the people of Western cultures tend to view change differently. For them change can be shaped and controlled to achieve their own goals and aspirations, and the attitude toward it tends to be active. Therefore, Western managers assigned to non-Western countries often run into difficulty when trying to introduce innovations too rapidly. In cultures that hold a passive/reactive view of change, new ways of doing things often must go hand in hand with a painstaking concern for their effect on interpersonal relationships. Moreover, people in nations such as India, Italy, and Turkey that are characterized by high uncertainty avoidance also are likely to resist or react cautiously to social change. American managers plunged into these cultures have to recognize this viewpoint, plan for it, and manage change accordingly.

Time Orientation

Many people in the United States and Canada think of time as an extremely scarce commodity. They often say that "time is money" or that "there is too little time." Several popular books on time management show an almost frenetic concern with how managers should plan their days. The need to set and stick to tight deadlines for accomplishing tasks is a basic tenet of this style of management.

In some cultures, however, time is viewed more as an unlimited and unending resource.[9] For example, Hindus believe that time does not begin at birth or end at death. The Hindu belief in reincarnation gives life a nontemporal, everlasting dimension. Because of such attitudes, employees, customers, and suppliers in some cultures are quite casual about keeping appointments and meeting deadlines—an indifference that can be highly frustrating to Canadian and U.S. managers who have to work with them.

Traditionally, the Mexican attitude toward time can best be summed up by the word *mañana*, meaning "not today"—but not necessarily tomorrow either! A manager in Mexico might say, "Yes, your shipment will be ready on Tuesday." You arrive on Tuesday to pick it up but find that it isn't ready. No one is upset or embarrassed; they say politely that the paperwork hasn't been processed yet or offer some other explanation. Time commitments are considered desirable but not binding promises. However, this attitude toward time is changing among Mexican businesspeople and professionals. As lifestyles become more complex and pressures for greater productivity increase, many more people in Mexico are paying attention to punctuality and meeting time commitments. However, the disregard for time can be found in many government offices where most procedures require long forms to be filled out, long letters to be filed, and endless waits in long lines.

Language

Language serves to bind as well as to separate cultures.[10] Fluency in another language can give an international manager a competitive edge in understanding and gaining the acceptance of people from another culture. However, the ability to speak a language correctly isn't enough: A manager must also be able to recognize and interpret the nuances of phrases, sayings, and nonverbal gestures. For example, many American managers communicate a relaxed atmosphere by "putting their feet up." The manager with his feet on the desk is saying, "I'm relaxing, and you can, too." However, people from other cultures may consider this rude or even insulting. Most German managers would consider putting one's feet on the desk uncivilized, and showing the soles of the feet is one of the most outrageous insults to most Arabs.

Doing business in Japan can be confusing. In face-to-face communications, Japanese managers rarely say no. Thus, Americans tend to be impatient with having to spend time in polite conversation about the weather, sumo wrestling, or other such topics before getting down to business. When Japanese managers and American managers exchange business cards, the Americans typically give the Japanese cards a cursory glance and then stuff them in a pocket for later reference. Japanese managers will dutifully study the card during the greeting, carefully noting the organization's name and the giver's rank. They hand their cards to the most important person first, as a sign a respect.

In Mexico, managers are used to giving only positive feedback to their employees and to expressing views that only agree with their bosses. Mexican executives would consider it disrespectful of a subordinate to contradict them because they are essentially "people oriented." They judge superiors on their personal qualities. The Mexican employee must feel that his boss is a *buena gente* (e.g., nice guy) before they give him their whole-hearted support.[11]

© Ng Han Guan/AP Photos

A Chinese worker cleans the glass door of a KFC restaurant in Beijing. China's appetite for the colonel's chicken is robust, with 1,200 locations, soaring profits, and a menu that includes bamboo shoots and lotus roots.

Many global companies have had difficulty crossing the language barrier with results ranging from mild embarrassment to outright failure. Seemingly harmless brand names and advertising phrases can take on unintended or hidden meaning when translated into other languages. This poses a real challenge for global managers as illustrated in the following Ethical Challenge. As a global manager, how can you prevent such mistranslations?[12]

Watch Your Language

When Coca-Cola first marketed Coke in China in the 1920s, it developed a group of Chinese characters that when pronounced, sounded like Coke. Unfortunately, the characters actually translated to mean "bite the wax tadpole." Now, the characters on the Chinese Coke bottles translate as "happiness in the mouth." Coca-Cola made a similar blunder in Japan. Its ad "Coke adds life" was translated into Japanese to mean "Coke brings your ancestors back from the dead."

Several carmakers have had embarrassing advertisements. Chevy's Nova translated into Spanish as *no va*, which means that "it doesn't go." When Ford introduced its Fiera truck, it discovered that the name means "ugly women" in Spanish. Rolls-Royce avoided the name Silver Mist in German markets because *mist* translates to *manure* in German.

Travelers often encounter well-intentioned advice from service firms that takes on meanings very different from those intended. The menu in one Swiss restaurant stated "Our wines leave you nothing to hope for." Signs in a Japanese hotel stated: "You are invited to take advantage of our chambermaid." At a laundry in Rome, a sign read "Ladies, leave your clothes here and spend the afternoon having a good time." The Coors beer slogan "get loose with Coors" is translated in Spanish to mean "get the runs with Coors." In China where KFC is the number one selling brand for YUM! Brands, its slogan "finger licking good" came out "eat your fingers off." Frank Purdue's classic line "It takes a tough man to make a tender chicken" came out in Spanish meaning "It takes a sexually stimulated man to make a chicken affectionate." Finally, Kellogg had to rename Bran Buds cereal in Sweden because the name translates to "burned farmer."

Value Systems

In Chapter 4, we discussed the importance of value systems and described five value dimensions: power distance, uncertainty avoidance, individualism, gender role orientation, and long-term orientation. Obviously, differences in cultural values affect how managers and professionals function in international business.

Anyone who has managed employees from different countries knows that being an effective manager requires an understanding of the country's social customs. In China, for example, clocks, straw sandals, and the colors white, blue, and black are associated with death. In Brazil, you should avoid wearing yellow and green together (these are the colors of the Brazilian flag). In Sweden, Helene Curtis changed the name of its Every Night Shampoo to Every Day shampoo because Swedes usually wash their hair in the morning.

Figure 5.2 rates the differences in importance of cultural values between managers in Mexico and those in the United States.[13] What do these mean to you?

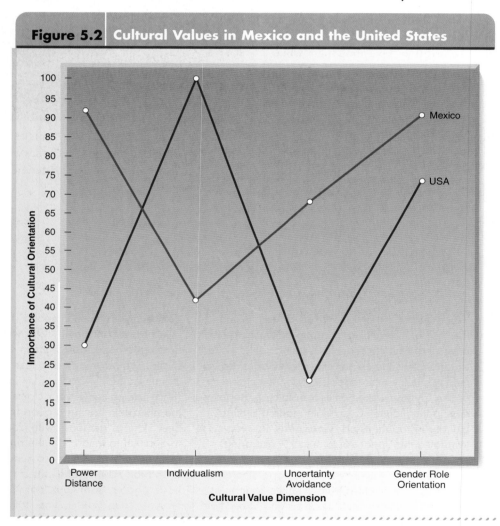

Figure 5.2 | Cultural Values in Mexico and the United States

Americans prefer small power distances, whereas Mexicans are comfortable with large power distances. Essentially, this implies that Americans believe inequalities should be minimized, that organizational hierarchies are established for convenience, and that bosses should be accessible. Middle and first-line managers usually answer their own phones and send their own e-mail. However, Mexicans view their relationships with their managers differently. The Mexican culture accepts large power distances between people. They believe that everyone has his or her place in an order of inequality. Managers and subordinates each view the other as different types of people. Subordinates believe that their managers are there to provide direction and approve decisions and that they should be inaccessible. Superiors have certain privileges (e.g., reserved parking, large offices, the ability to take long lunches, and the like) by right. For example, titles are valued as very important in Mexico. When Mexicans are answering phone calls, they normally identify themselves by title. Titles appear on business cards and elsewhere.

For an American manager to decentralize decision making to his Mexican subordinates would be inconsistent with Mexican values—managers make decisions rather than delegating them. The unintended result is that Mexican employees would feel uncomfortable if a manager attempted to delegate decisions and share information. These are strictly management rights. The implication for American managers is to use a more directive leadership style because it is expected. Strong leadership from the top is expected to make change. Furthermore, those in power should look as powerful as possible. The managerial implications for differences in power distance between the United States and Mexico are summarized in Table 5.2.

Table 5.2	Managerial Implications of Power Distance Differences	
ISSUE	**UNITED STATES**	**MEXICO**
Subordinates' dependence needs	Moderate dependence on supervisor	Heavy dependence on supervisor
Consultation	Expect to be consulted	Expect little consultation
Ideal superior	Democratic leadership	A benevolent autocrat or paternalistic father figure
Rules and regulations	Apply to all	Supervisors are above rules and regulations and take advantage of privileges
Status symbols	Are accepted as symbols of authority, but not necessary	Are very important evidence of the authority of superiors

Americans and Mexicans are also different with regard to uncertainty avoidance. Many Mexicans feel threatened by uncertain and ambiguous situations, and they struggle to develop security in their lives. In this regard, they feel a need for written rules and procedures and rely on experts to provide them guidance. They also seek consensus and social harmony. To preserve harmony, saving face is important. Therefore, Mexicans as a rule do not wish to admit that they do not know something or that certain tasks assigned were, in fact, not done. Elaborate stories can be told to explain why the outcome was different than expected. The combination of high uncertainty avoidance and power distance produces the desire to have a powerful manager who can be blamed or praised. This satisfies their desire to avoid uncertainty.[14]

The two cultures also appear different in relation to individualistic versus collectivist values. The typical American is more individualistic than the typical Mexican. Many people in Mexico place great emphasis on family and belonging to organizations. Friendships are determined by social relationships within their own social levels. There is an old saying in Mexico: "It is not what you know but who you know."

Snapshot

"Our way of working isn't hierarchical. We work through a small cadre of trusted executives, including my three sons. A good team can make companies profitable in a very short time."

Marco Antonio Slim Dormit, Chairperson, Inbursa

We opened the chapter with the story of Grupo Bimbo. The *Grupo* form of organization, in which individual families control many companies and decision making is centralized, is a reflection of collectivism. Status and titles are keys to developing relationships. Few relationships extend across social levels (e.g., subordinates and managers do not usually mix.)

Table 5.3 summarizes how the four value systems impact key managerial practices found in many organizations. If you do business in Latin America and Mexico, you will be constantly exposed to new cultural behaviors. Remember that there is no right way to run an organization. Although doing business in Latin American might require you to adapt some of your behaviors, the same issue is facing many Latin American managers who are conducting business in the United States for their organizations. Cultural values are a paintbrush of how people think about issues. That is, culture colors the way we view the world.

Table 5.3	Values and Managerial Characteristics	
CHARACTERISTIC	**UNITED STATES**	**MEXICO**
Decision making	Participation, delegation to employees	Centralized, concentrated at top
Responsibility	Employees assume responsibility for their own lives	Employees expect close paternalistic supervisors
Organization chart	Indicative of unequal competencies; reflects information flow in organization	Indicative of unequal roles; reflects power relationships of key family members
Hiring criteria	Demonstrated performance	Family or personal ties
Performance feedback	Employee accepts accountability	Critical feedback resented
Leadership pattern	Good communicator	Benevolent dictator
Planning process	Long term, proactive, formal	Short term, reactive, unstructured

Source: Adapted from T. H. Becker. *Doing Business in the New Latin America.* Westport, CT: Praeger, 2004, 135–136.

Cultural Distance

A country's cultural values determine how people interact with one another and with companies and institutions.[15] Cultural distance *refers to differences in religious beliefs, race, social norms, and language between two countries.* Some cultural differences between countries, such as language, are easily perceived and understood. Others are much more subtle. Social norms, the deeply rooted system of unspoken principles that guide individuals in their everyday behaviors, are often nearly invisible. In Mexico, for example, people are comfortable standing about eight inches from each other when speaking. If you move further away, the Mexican will move to close the gap. In North America, the comfortable distance is about two feet. Similarly in Mexico, nonverbal cues are very important, whereas in North America, managers use the spoken language to convey the message. Nonverbal cues may include the kind of clothing worn, facial expressions, hand and arm gestures, posture, eye contact, office size and trappings (e.g., windows, draperies, carpets), and display of family affiliations and educational attainments.

Cultural differences also influence the choices that consumers make. Table 5.4 gives examples of situations in which cultural distance matters and lists some of the industries affected by this cultural distance. Color tastes, for example, are closely linked to cultural values. The word *red* in Russia also means "beautiful." The Japanese prefer automobiles and household appliances to be small, reflecting a social norm that is common in countries where space is highly valued. Many families living in metropolitan Tokyo live in apartments of less than 700 square feet and commute to work in overcrowded subways. The food industry is particularly sensitive to religious attributes. Hindus, for example, do not eat beef because it is expressly forbidden by their religion.

Table 5.4	Examples of Cultural Distance and Industries Affected by It
ASPECTS OF DISTANCE	**INDUSTRIES AFFECTED BY CULTURAL DISTANCE INCLUDE:**
Different languages	Consumer foods
Different ethnicities	Tobacco products
Different religions	Products that have high linguistic content (TV)
Different social norms	Auto (size, features)

The following Multicultural Competency feature provides an additional perspective on the need to beware of how cultural forces influence worker behavior.[16] In the opening Challenge of Managing feature, we discussed some of the issues facing Grupo Bimbo as it expands its operations. Now we illustrate the motivational practices used by Grupo Bimbo in Mexico and the United States. You should be able to find illustrations of cultural differences between Mexico and the United States.

Multicultural Competency

Grupo Bimbo's Motivational Practices

Grupo Bimbo uses similar programs, such as the Employee-of-the-Month and Outstanding Safety Award, to recognize outstanding performance in both Mexico and the United States. The criteria for evaluating employees, however, are vastly different. In Mexico, stretch goals are used to motivate employees. Managers know that employees cannot attain these goals. Mexican employees believe that "you can't reach the stars without trying," and therefore they are evaluated on the basis of the means that they used to attempt to achieve these goals rather than the absolute achievement of the goals. If an employee pursues a goal with "leadership and passion," the employee is likely to be recognized for outstanding performance. In the United States, employees are likely to exhibit "leadership and passion" when they feel that the goals are difficult, but attainable. Only employees who reach or surpass the goal are eligible for an award.

Managers in Mexico use positive reinforcement to motivate employees to a greater extent than managers in the United States. A plant manager in Mexico was told that his plant needed to address an environmental emissions problem. He immediately called a group of managers together. If the group had not been able to solve the problem, they would have instead offered an elaborate explanation as to why it was not accomplished. Grupo Bimbo found that tying project completion to a financial incentive did little to increase the probability of its success; instead, it stimulated the excuses offered as to why the project was not completed. However, if the managers were assured that they had the ability to complete the project and that senior management was aware of the emissions problem, the likelihood of the project being completed was substantially increased. In the United States, if the manager cannot complete the project, then another person will be brought in who can accomplish the task.

Soccer fields are located next to many plants in Mexico. These fields are almost always in use and are highly valued by manufacturing employees.

Grupo Bimbo feels that having these fields contributes to a group mind-set, fosters pride and loyalty, and helps maintain a high-performance work culture. Award winners are also given a shirt with a Grupo Bimbo logo on it. Because the company is highly respected and held in high esteem by many Mexicans, this challenges other employees to win one. In the United States, there are few soccer fields, but Grupo Bimbo gives award winners access to health clubs. It also gives winners shirts, golf hats, etc., but these do not have the same status attached to them by most Americans.

To learn more about this organization, visit *www.grupobimbo.com.mx.*

3.

Explain how political–legal forces impact global business.

Political–Legal Forces

Organizations that engage in international business must cope with a web of political and legal issues. Therefore, management must diagnose these issues accurately in order to understand the risks and uncertainties involved in international business. In Chapter 4, we indicated that managers may use one or more of five political strategies—negotiation, lobbying, alliance, representation, and socialization—to reduce political risk.

Political risk *is the probability that governmental decisions or events in a country will negatively affect the long-term profitability of an investment.* Of concern to all international and global corporations is the political risk associated with resource commitments in foreign countries.[17]

Assessing Political Risk

Political risk factors may be grouped into five principal categories: domestic instability, foreign conflict, political climate, economic climate, and corruption. As Figure 5.3 shows, managers may estimate the seriousness of the political risk associated with conducting business in a country by assessing various factors in each category.

Domestic instability *is the amount of subversion, revolution, assassinations, guerrilla warfare, and government crisis in a country.* Haiti, Chad, and Fiji have histories of domestic instability that have generally discouraged foreign investment.

Foreign conflict *is the degree of hostility that one nation expresses to others.* Such hostility can range from the expulsion of diplomats to outright war. In 2003, President George W. Bush determined that the actions of the government of Iraq constituted an unusual and extraordinary threat to the national security and foreign policy of the United States. The government imposed a ban on trade with Iraq, which directly affected many firms, and requested that the United Nations send an inspection team into Iraq to look for weapons of mass

Countries with low-risk political and economic climates encourage foreign investment.

© Tetra Images/Jupiter Images

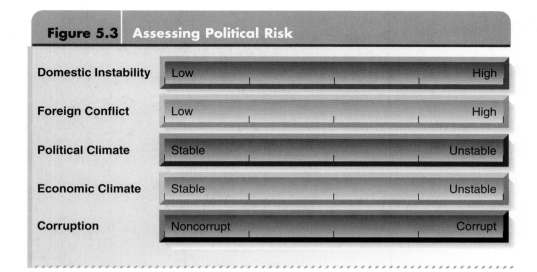

Figure 5.3 | **Assessing Political Risk**

Domestic Instability	Low	High
Foreign Conflict	Low	High
Political Climate	Stable	Unstable
Economic Climate	Stable	Unstable
Corruption	Noncorrupt	Corrupt

destruction. The United States waged war in Iraq on March 20, 2003; therefore, foreign conflict greatly increases the risk for doing business in Iraq.

Political climate *is the likelihood that a government will swing to the far left or far right politically.* Managers may evaluate variables such as the number and size of political parties, number of factions in the legislature, role of the military in the political process, amount of corruption in government, effectiveness of political leadership, influence of organized religion in politics, extent of racial and nationality tensions, and quality of the governmental bureaucracy. Currently, Chad is considered to have a risky political climate because of the instability of its government, opposing political forces, and widespread corruption.

The economic climate *reflects the extent of government control of markets and financial investments, as well as government support services and capabilities.* These factors include government regulatory and economic control policies (wages, prices, imports, and exports); government ability to manage its own economic affairs (inflation, budget surpluses or deficits, and amount of debt); government provision of support services and facilities (roads, airports, electricity, water, and refuse and sewage disposal), often referred to as *infrastructure*; and government capabilities in general. President Susilo B. Yudhoyono became Indonesia's first directly elected leader in 2005. He has been able to stabilize this ethically and politically divided country for the first time in decades. Yudhoyono has pledged to streamline the rampant corruption that was present in the previous government.

Corruption *refers to the degree to which institutions, including the government, are perceived to be untrustworthy, to be open to bribes, and to conduct fraudulent business practices.* Corruption in the United States, Canada, and other Western countries is viewed as wrong. Transparency International has compiled a Corruption Perception Index from research on 158 countries.[18] This list is based on perceptions rather than actual corruption, but the index is a good indicator for corruption in a country. This index is widely used by organizations and the U.S. government when making judgments about business practices in countries. As shown in Table 5.5, Iceland and some other countries are ranked as less corrupt than the United States, and Chad and Bangladesh are viewed as being among the most corrupt nations according to Transparency International.

Table 5.5	Perceptions of Country Corruption

COUNTRY RANK	COUNTRY SCORE*
1 (Least corrupt)	Iceland (9.7)
2	Finland and New Zealand (9.6)
6	Sweden (9.2)
14	Canada (8.4)
17	United States (7.6)
21	Japan and Chile (7.5)
40	Italy (5.0)
51	Costa Rica (4.2)
65	Mexico (3.5)
97	Argentina (2.8)
117	Philippines and Bolivia (2.5)
130	Venezuela (2.3)
158 (Most corrupt)	Bangladesh and Chad (1.7)

*Score relates to degree of corrupt behaviors by analysts. Scores can range from 10 (not corrupt) to 0 (highly corrupt).

Political Mechanisms

Governments and businesses utilize a variety of political strategies, as we discussed in Chapter 4, to cope with political and legal changes. In this section, we go beyond those strategies to explain two significant types of international political mechanisms: (1) protectionism and (2) bribery and extortion. We support neither but want you to be aware of actual practices that you may encounter someday in international business.

Protectionism. Protectionism *refers to the many mechanisms designed to help home-based industries or firms avoid (or reduce) potential (or actual) competitive or political threats from abroad.* Tariffs, quotas, subsidies, and cartels are among the most widely used political mechanisms. Protectionism has both strong advocates and opponents. Generally, it works against consumers' interests because it results in higher prices. Advocates claim that it protects home-country industries and jobs against unfair competition from countries with subsistence wages and special subsidies. Therefore, whether companies, business associations, and employee groups favor or oppose a particular protectionist measure depends on how it may affect their particular interests.

A tariff is *a government tax on goods or services entering the country. The primary purpose of a tariff is to raise the price of imported goods or services.* As a result, domestic goods and services gain a relative price advantage. In 2000, Congress passed the Continued Dumping and Subsidy Act, which allows manufacturers that successfully petition the U.S. Congress to impose tariffs on imports that they claim are being "dumped"—sold at less than fair market value. For example, China, the world's biggest candle-maker, had an antidumping tariff of 108 percent imposed by the U.S. government on candles made from palm oil. Consumers in the United States bought 60 percent of the total Chinese exports of candles.[19]

A quota is *a restriction on the quantity of a country's imports (or sometimes, on its exports).* Import quotas generally are intended to guarantee home-country manufacturers access to a certain percentage of the domestic market. Most experts agree that, if protectionism is politically unavoidable, tariffs are preferable to quotas. The reason is that quotas fix the levels of imports entering a country and thus freeze markets. Labor unions and members of Congress have argued against further opening of U.S. markets at a time of trade deficits, arguing that quotas protect U.S. industries from low-cost manufacturing abroad. However, if quotas were lifted, domestic producers would then have to become more productive and efficient to maintain market share. Quotas are a hidden tax on consumers, whereas tariffs are a more obvious tax. Recently, the United States Steelworkers Union and U.S. pipe manufacturers have lobbied Congress to get relief from Chinese manufacturers of pipe. They want the president to set a quota on the number of tons of pipe that can enter the United States from China.

A subsidy *is a direct or indirect payment by a government to domestic firms to make selling or investing abroad cheaper for them—and thus more profitable.* Indirect payments are illustrated by some of the activities of the Overseas Private Investment Corporation. This self-sustaining U.S. government agency helps qualified U.S. investors establish commercial projects in developing countries by offering reinvestment assistance and financing. Its political-risk insurance program provides coverage for eligible projects against losses from a foreign government's seizure of assets; nonconvertibility of local currency into U.S. dollars; and damage caused by war, revolution, insurrection, or strife.

Five of the world's largest sugar-exporting countries agreed to coordinate efforts to boost prices. Because this industry is dominated by large-scale sugar cane producers, Coca-Cola is lobbying for lower sugar prices, deregulation of the industry, scrapping of imports tariffs, and subsidies to small sugar cane producers. With such changes, Coke would pay a third less for the sugar used in its beverages.[20]

A cartel *is an alliance of producers engaged in the same type of business that is formed to limit or eliminate competition and control production and prices.* Governments impose tariffs and quotas and grant subsidies. In contrast, cartels operate under agreements negotiated between firms or governments, as in the case of OPEC (Organization of the Petroleum Exporting Countries). A primary goal of any cartel is to protect its members' revenues and profits by controlling output and therefore prices. International cartels currently exist in oil, copper, aluminum, natural rubber, and other raw materials. The best known cartel is OPEC, which was formed in 1960. The recent history of the oil industry and OPEC clearly demonstrates that cartels often face uncertainty and sometimes have to cope with rebellion among their members. OPEC's effectiveness in controlling oil production by member countries varies. Some members, especially Nigeria and Venezuela, can't always agree on prices or quantities to be produced. Law forbids U.S. firms from forming or participating directly in cartels because their purpose is at odds with preserving competitive markets and individual rights based on private property.

Bribery and Extortion.
A bribe *is an improper payment made to induce the recipient to do something for the payer.* Bribes are illegal in Canada and the United States but not in some countries, such as Italy and Brazil. By offering a bribe, the payer hopes to obtain a special favor in exchange for something of value (e.g., money, a trip, or a car). In recent years, the growing moral revulsion against bribery and other forms of corruption has swept politicians from office in China, Italy, and Japan. In China, for example, the bribes-for-promotion scheme in the city of Suihua involved so many governmental officials that authorities had to offer amnesty to people who pocketed less than $12,000 or else the entire city government would have ground to a halt. China's President Hu Jintao has promised to crack down on such behaviors.[21]

Extortion *is a payment made to ensure that the recipient doesn't harm the payer in some way.* The purpose of extortion is to obtain something of value by threatening harm to the payer. Recently, the United Nations launched an investigation into allegations that officials in Kenya were extorting thousands of dollars from refugees in exchange for settling them in America and Western Europe. If the refugees couldn't pay the extortion money, they were threatened and sometimes physically abused.[22]

Bribery and extortion are practiced throughout the world. These practices occur most frequently in Indonesia, Azerbaijan, Honduras, Tanzania, Yugoslavia, and several other countries. In fact, some countries culturally define certain forms of bribery and extortion as an acceptable, appropriate, and expected form of gift giving. Belgium, France, Sweden, Greece, and Germany allow or tolerate the tax deductibility of foreign bribes. The United Nations and the World Bank are attempting to get members to criminalize bribery and extortion—as has the U.S. government.

The U.S. Foreign Corrupt Practices Act of 1977 *prohibits the payment of "anything of value" to foreign officials, including employees of state-owned or controlled companies, or to political candidates or their parties for the purpose of securing improper influence or business advantages.* In some cases, companies can be held liable for payments made by third parties acting on their behalf, whether or not the company had actual knowledge of the payment.[23] The act established specific record-keeping requirements for publicly held corporations, making difficult the concealment of political payments prohibited by the act. Violators—both corporations and individuals—face stiff penalties. A company may be fined as much as $1 million, and a manager who directly participates in or has knowledge of any violations of the act faces up to 5 years in prison and/or $100,000 in fines. Furthermore, the act prohibits corporations from paying any fines imposed on their directors, managers, employees, or agents.

The act doesn't prohibit grease payments to employees of foreign governments whose duties are primarily procedural or clerical. Grease payments *are small payments—almost gratuities—used to get lower level government employees to speed up required paperwork.* Such payments may be required to persuade employees to perform their normal duties. Some examples where grease payments are permitted under U.S. law include paying people to obtain a license, processing government forms, such as visas or work orders, mail pickup and delivery, installing phone service, and the like.

4.

Discuss how three major international trade agreements affect global competition and cooperation.

International Trade Agreements

The world is shrinking rapidly with the advent of faster communication, transportation, and financial flows. Products developed in one country—Gucci purses, Mont Blanc pens, McDonald's hamburgers, KFC chicken—are finding enthusiastic acceptance in other countries. Before deciding whether to operate internationally, an organization must thoroughly understand the international environment. That environment has changed drastically in the past two decades, creating new opportunities and new problems. The world economy has globalized. World trade and investment have grown rapidly, with many new markets opening up in China, Eastern Europe, Russia, and elsewhere.

For an organization to consider expanding into these new markets, its managers must have a basic understanding of how global trade agreements can impact their ability to do business in these markets. In Chapter 4, we highlighted how competitors, new entrants, substitute goods and services, customers, and suppliers have impacted the home video game industry. These forces apply whether a firm competes locally (say, in the Denver, Colorado, area), nationally (say, in India), regionally (say, in Europe), or worldwide. In this section we briefly review three significant global trade agreements that directly affect one or more of the five competitive forces. These agreements heighten the competitive pressures on firms.

World Trade Organization

The World Trade Organization (*WTO*) was established in 1995 as an outgrowth of the General Agreement on Tariffs and Trade (GATT).[24] *WTO represents a series of negotiated understandings regarding trade and related issues among the participating countries.* Twenty-three countries signed the first GATT in 1947. Today, there are 149 member countries, accounting for more than 97 percent of the world trade. World trade in merchandise and commercial services now exceeds $9 trillion (1 trillion is 1,000 billion) and is growing by more than 6 percent annually.

The key functions of the WTO include

▶ administering WTO trade agreements,

▶ providing a forum for trade negotiations,

▶ handling trade disputes between nations,

▶ monitoring national trade policies,

▶ providing technical assistance and training for people in developing countries, and

▶ cooperating with other international organizations, such as the EU, the Association of South East Asian Nations (ASEAN), and the association formed as a result of the North American Free Trade Agreement.

WTO member countries receive many benefits:

▶ The agreement promotes peace by handling trade disputes constructively.

▶ Rules make life easier for all organizations to follow.

▶ Trade stimulates economic growth and reduces the cost of living.

▶ The system encourages good government.

Three principles are fundamental to WTO operations:

▶ The most favored nation principle *means that when country A grants a tariff concession to country B, the same concession automatically applies to all other countries that are members of WTO.*

▶ The reciprocity principle *means that each member country will not be forced to reduce tariffs unilaterally. A tariff concession is made only in return for comparable concessions from the other countries.*

▶ The transparency principle *means that tariffs are to be readily visible to all countries.*

Presumably, tariffs are the only permitted form of restriction. WTO doesn't allow internal taxes and regulations to be applied to imported goods if they aren't equally applied to domestic goods. However, there are exceptions to these principles. For example, the escape clause provides that, if a product is being imported into a country in such increased quantities that it causes or threatens to cause serious injury to domestic producers of that product, the importing country may temporarily increase the tariff on that product. This is how many organizations are lobbying Congress to respond to China's low wages and prices for products that range from eyeglass lenses, to cigarette lighters, to steel pipe. Industries that require huge R&D budgets and capital investment, such as aerospace and pharmaceuticals, haven't been impacted by China's entry into the WTO in 2001.

Snapshot

"Every morning in Africa, a gazelle wakes up and knows it must run faster than a lion or it will be killed. Every morning a lion wakes up and knows that it must outrun the slowest gazelle or it will starve to death. It doesn't matter whether or not you are a gazelle or lion. When the sun comes up, you better start running."
Jack Perkowski, Chairman and CEO, ASIMCO Technologies

Under WTO provisions, trade negotiations also may take place directly between two or more countries. One significant trade dispute between the United States and Thailand and Malaysia has focused on intellectual property rights and pirated videos of movies. A deputy director-general of Thailand's Intellectual Property Office stated that the government had declared war on piracy. Companies in the U.S. video game industry estimate that 75 percent of the Asian video industry is illegal. Government officials in both countries said a reward to encourage people to report pirates needs be introduced along with courts that are designed to hear and act on violations of intellectual property rights. Unfortunately, police rarely arrest street vendors who sell pirated DVDs. For example, three days after the film release of *Passion of the Christ*, one of your authors saw a DVD of the movie for sale for $1.25 on a street corner in Beijing.

North American Free Trade Agreement

The North American Free Trade Agreement *(NAFTA)* went into effect in 1994 to increase free trade among the United States, Canada, and Mexico. NAFTA *essentially created a giant free-trade zone among the United States, Canada, and Mexico by removing and reducing barriers to trade, such as tariffs, quotas, and licenses.* This free-trade zone covers more than 8.2 million square miles, 400 million consumers, and $650 billion in annual economic activity. NAFTA represents an extension of the Canada–United States Free Trade Agreement, which went into effect in 1993. When Congress approved NAFTA, trade between the United States and Mexico was $81 billion. Trade now exceeds $240 billion. U.S. exports to its NAFTA partners have increased more than 100 percent since 1993, whereas U.S. trade with the rest of the world grew only half as fast. Today, the United States exports more to Mexico and Canada than to the countries that combine to form the European Union.[25]

NAFTA was intended to reduce and eliminate numerous tariffs and most nontariff barriers among the three countries. Although full elimination of certain tariffs will not take place until 2009, more than 70 percent of the goods imported from Mexico may now enter the United States without tariffs. At the same time, more than 50 percent of U.S. exports to Mexico are now tariff free. The agreement also realizes long-held goals of fostering trade in services and liberalizing foreign investment rules. NAFTA tightens the protection of intellectual property (copyrights, trademarks, and patents, in particular). More than 80 percent of Mexico's exports are now to the United States and Canada.

The benefits of NAFTA to the United States and Canada are the ability of manufacturers to produce goods more cheaply, especially in *maquiladora* plants, and the ability to move raw materials easily among the three countries. *Maquiladora* plants *are foreign-owned industrial plants located in Mexico that border the U.S. states of Texas, New Mexico, Arizona, and California.* These plants employ more than 1.2 million people, account for roughly 40 percent of Mexico's manufacturing, and pay (from $15 to $20 a day) more than four times Mexico's minimum wage. Many small to medium-sized companies in the United States and Canada are moving to Tijuana and other border cities to gain cost efficiencies. These companies realize that it is not cost effective to move their operations to other parts of the world.[26]

Recently, organizations that produce electric and electronic goods have started to relocate their businesses from Mexico to China because of cheaper labor, which more than offsets the extra shipping charges. Managers at the *maquiladora* plants claim that the lack of clear regulations, increased tax costs, the deceleration of the U.S. economy, and the strength of the peso have all contributed to this relocation. Some of the companies that moved parts of their operations to Asia for cost efficiencies are now returning to the maquiladoras because employees have better educational backgrounds and quality control is better.

Although NAFTA further opened Canadian and U.S. markets, the most significant liberalization applies to Mexico. NAFTA expanded Canadian and U.S. companies' ability to establish or purchase businesses in Mexico and increased their ability to sell if they wanted to leave. NAFTA loosened previous restrictions on expanding operations in Mexico and removed restrictions on transferring profits to other countries. U.S. exports to Mexico and Canada now support almost 3 million American jobs.

Despite much liberalization, NAFTA retains certain protectionist provisions, some of which may persist with no time limit. NAFTA temporarily protects sensitive industries (e.g., agriculture, minerals, banking, textiles, and apparel) by stretching out the phase-in time for lifting restrictions that apply to them. NAFTA also contains other types of protection that are permanent and appear to raise trade barriers above pre-NAFTA levels. In some industries—notably automobiles, textiles, and apparel—NAFTA imposes higher North American content rules. For instance, under the previous Canada–United States Free Trade Agreement, automobiles could be imported duty free if they contained at least 50 percent Canadian and U.S. inputs. For auto imports to receive NAFTA benefits, the North American rule is now 62.5 percent. For textiles or apparel to qualify for "free" trade under NAFTA, all components—beginning with the yarn or fiber—must be produced in North America.

The service industries that received the most attention during NAFTA negotiations were finance, insurance, transportation, and telecommunications. NAFTA doesn't change requirements for foreign banks' entry into the United States and Canada. But the opening of the Mexican financial system is among the agreement's most significant achievements. Requirements for entry into brokerage, bonding, insurance, leasing, and warehousing were liberalized even more than they were for banking.

NAFTA and WTO certainly don't eliminate all trade problems among the member countries. But they do provide frameworks through which such problems can be resolved. By increasing the competitive forces that act on firms, the ultimate goals of WTO and NAFTA are to achieve greater efficiency and consumer satisfaction. However, as legal documents that were politically negotiated, they contain provisions, loopholes, and exceptions that will be tested over the decades to come. The provisions of these agreements no doubt will be welcomed or resisted, depending on their effect on a particular country, industry, labor organization, or firm.

The Planning and Administration Competency feature on the next page describes Mabe, a $1.8-billion-a-year manufacturer of appliances in Mexico that employs more than 15,000 people in its 13 plants. It has grown at annual rates of 15 to 20 percent since the passage of NAFTA.[27] Mabe exports refrigerators, ranges, heating elements, compressors, and washers to the United States, Canada, and Central and South American countries. If you buy a washing machine, stove, or refrigerator, there's a pretty good chance Mabe made it. Why? Mabe manufactures these products for a variety of companies, including GE, Easy, Serviplus, and IEM. It has been able to develop world-class manufacturing capabilities and innovative management practices under the CEO's leadership. This feature is based on remarks by Mabe's President and CEO Luis Berrondo, and highlights why Mabe is located in Mexico instead of other Latin American countries.

© Mark Segal/Workbook Stock/Jupiter Images

Television manufacturing assembly line, Tijuana, Mexico.

With the passage of NAFTA, Mexico has become a very competitive nation because of the low cost of labor, good relationships with unions, and well-trained engineers. To remain competitive, Mabe had to locate plants in areas of a country where there was an educated workforce. For example, Mabe had to have employees who could make products that met GE's demands for six-sigma quality. In Mexico, it is easy to find workers with at least a high school education. A high school education provides them with a basis of general knowledge and level of mathematics that allow them to be trained. The engineering programs at Mexican universities are first rate.

To ensure a high-quality workforce, Mabe invests heavily in training. At least 6 percent of an employee's working hours are spent in training. This emphasis on training allows employees to become more specialized in their areas of expertise or to develop managerial competencies. The average Mexican employee at Mabe works a 45-hour week. Therefore, in one year, that employee receives about three weeks of training. At the new $250 million Mabe factory designed to build side-by-side-door GE refrigerators for export to the United

States, employees are assigned to self-managed teams. Employees are trained in setting production objectives and learn how to assume responsibility for six-sigma-level quality. They measure defects, the amount of scrap, and take care of equipment maintenance. Mabe recently introduced the "Id System," a computerized intelligence system that makes washing machines run more efficiently with less water, gets clothes cleaner, and virtually eliminates the possibility of damaging clothes.

Mexico does not have labor unions whose goals are based on antimanagement ideologies, such as those found in some other Latin American countries. Currently, labor unions are focusing on promoting job stability for their members. The benefits for Mabe are that unions work with their members to help them arrive at work on time, be honest, and provide workplace stability. There is a sense of cooperation and consensus between management and unions. Mabe has also introduced scholarships for the unemployed in an area to help them develop the skills needed to enter or reenter the workforce.

To learn more about this organization, visit *www.mabe.com.mx.*

European Union

The European Union *is an organization with the goals of creating a single market among member countries through the removal of trade barriers (e.g., tariffs) and establishing the free movement of goods, people, services, and capital.* The European Union, called the European Community until 1994, currently has 25 members: Austria, Belgium, Czech Republic, Cyprus, Denmark, Estonia, Finland, France, Germany, Greece, Hungary, Ireland, Italy, Latvia, Lithuania, Luxembourg, Malta, the Netherlands, Poland, Portugal, Slovakia, Slovenia, Spain, Sweden, and the United Kingdom.[28] These countries are home to nearly 455 million consumers. In spite of the unemployment rate, the EU is hoping for full employment by 2010. The EU introduced a common currency, the euro, in 2001. Its valuation against the U.S. dollar is monitored by an independent central bank in Frankfurt, Germany. The EU and the U.S. together are responsible for 40 percent of the world's trade.

Implementation of activities to achieve the goals mentioned above officially began at the end of 1992. In addition, the changes go beyond economic interests to

© image100/Jupiter Images

The bridges on the reverse side of each euro symbolize close cooperation and communication between Europe and the world.

include social changes as well. Educational degrees have already been affected. The EU Council of Ministers issued a directive that recognizes diplomas of higher education across national boundaries. This action makes it easier for professionals to work in different countries. Most member countries have developed master's degree programs in business administration that are compatible with those of other member countries and of the United States.

The EU clearly is more than an economic union: It is a state of mind and a political force. Eventually, it intends to reduce interference in economic activities by governments in member countries. Meeting uniform quality standards and worker safety and environmental controls will be expected of all companies who trade in the EU.

An essential stage of the EU program is to complete formation of a common internal market. That involves eliminating

1. physical barriers at each country's borders, which prevent the free flow of goods and people;

2. technical barriers, which prevent goods and services produced or traded in one member nation from being sold in others;

3. fiscal barriers, such as red tape and the different national tax systems, which hinder cross-border trade; and

4. financial barriers, which prevent the free movement of investment capital.[29]

The European Commission is the EU's executive body and sole initiator of legislation. The commission claims that 95 percent of the legislative measures set out in the 1992 program have been adopted. In the EU summit of 2005, two of the toughest issues facing the 25-member EU were addressed: agreement on a common immigration policy, and intellectual property right violations. Some member nations are concerned that they will be flooded with immigrants as the result of an open-door policy. As unemployment has risen in Eastern Europe, the frontiers of the EU have been tightened. It is now virtually impossible to enter the member nations legally as an economic immigrant. An applicant rejected by one member nation can no longer apply to any other member nation. Members of the EU pledged to promote a strong and effective enforcement of intellectual property rights to reduce global piracy (especially of DVDs, computer software, and books) and counterfeiting and to foster public–private partnerships to protect intellectual property.

The EU has already increased market opportunities, fostered competition, and encouraged competition from the outside. The removal of transnational trade restrictions and the relaxation of border controls based on economic restraints have had a considerable impact on U.S. and Canadian companies. UPS has established a major hub in Cologne, Germany, and FedEx Kinko's has also established a major hub in Paris, France. DHL, a competitor of UPS and FedEx that is owned by the German government, has expanded its operations to include service to Eastern Europe, China, and the United States and has entered into an agreement with the United States Postal Service guaranteeing priority mail service across the Atlantic.

Many non-Europeans continue to be concerned that the free market of Europe will be anything but free to outsiders. The European Commission has pressured U.S. and Japanese firms to conduct more R&D and production in Europe or face the risk of increased tariffs and other barriers. Restrictions still apply to non-EU banks and security firms unless foreign countries (e.g., the United States, Canada, and Japan) grant reciprocal rights. These restrictions range from limiting the right to acquire banks in EU countries to special taxes on foreign banks operating there.

Various alternative strategies are available to U.S. and Canadian enterprises. One strategy is to export goods and services to the EU. In general, though, North

American firms have had only limited success in doing so. The most successful strategy has been to set up subsidiaries or branches in one or more of the EU countries. The advantages of subsidiaries have been demonstrated by well-established companies such as BMW, Ford, and IBM. Some companies have consolidated their previous positions in Europe.

5.

Describe six strategies used by organizations to grow globally.

Strategies for International Business

Managers in almost every imaginable industry need to think about strategies to serve worldwide markets. Rapidly changing technologies, the growth of the Internet, the rise of new competitors, and the availability of new raw material sources make global issues a critical consideration for managers. When organizations venture into the international arena, managers strive to formulate a global strategy that will enhance the effectiveness of their organization.

One decision managers face is choosing whether to emphasize global standardization or choose national responsiveness. Global standards, for example, requires the organization to understand the needs of new customers, perhaps build new facilities, and establish goodwill in these new markets, all of which are very time consuming. This also places a burden on managers to obtain a balance between meeting the different customers' needs in different parts of the world with maintaining a set of similar standards worldwide. Managers must decide whether they want each global organization to act independently or whether activities should be standardized across countries. These decisions are often at the core of choosing among various strategies for international business. We recognize that organizations operating in many national markets face different challenges than do organizations operating solely in one of two international markets.

Managers typically choose among six strategies for conducting international business.[30] These strategies range from low to high in complexity and in resource commitment, as shown in Figure 5.4 on the following page. *Complexity* refers to the structure of the organization (e.g., number of hierarchical levels, number of staff people, and number of departments) and the amount of coordination required to deliver a product or service to customers. *Resource commitment* refers to the amount of tangible assets (e.g., plants, finances, warehouses, personnel) and information support systems that the organization dedicates to its global strategy.

Exporting Strategy

The exporting strategy *involves maintaining facilities within a home country and shipping goods and services abroad for sale in foreign markets.* When a domestic firm decides that it wants to move toward global operations, its first priority should be to build a global customer base. All that is necessary is a Web page and some promotion to direct potential customers to its location.

Exporting is a practical means for small or medium-sized organizations with few financial resources to invest but who are facing increased competition in their domestic markets. For many such firms, exporting is the primary strategy of international operations. Tim Luberski, CEO of California Sunshine, uses this approach. California Sunshine is a leading exporter of U.S. dairy products, including milk, eggs, yogurt, and sour cream. Extended product dating and rapid delivery allow them to be sold virtually around the world. California Sunshine customers can order products directly on the Internet at *www.hiddenvilla.com*. With three large warehouses located next to international airports, California Sunshine guarantees product delivery within 72 hours.[31]

A variation on exporting (or importing) is countertrade, *an agreement that requires companies from the exporting nation to purchase products of equivalent value from the import-*

Figure 5.4 Strategies for International Operations

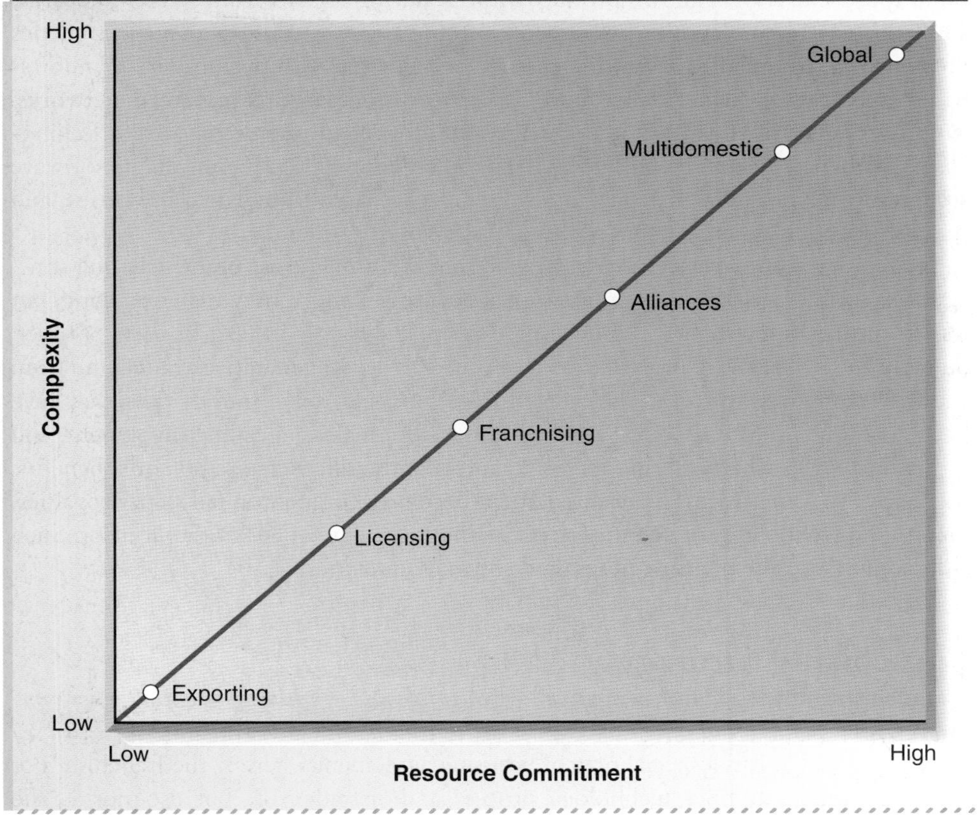
High
Low
Complexity
Low
High
Resource Commitment
Exporting
Licensing
Franchising
Alliances
Multidomestic
Global

ing nation. Countertrade continues to grow as a marketing tool for doing business in lesser developed countries.[32] The American Countertrade Association indicates that countertrade eases trade and investments into countries that either have (1) difficulties trading in hard currency or (2) impose certain counter purchase obligations on vendors that are selling their products into a country. For example, Pepsi sells its cola syrup to Russia for rubles and agrees to buy Russian-made Stolichnaya vodka for sale in the United States. Countertrade can also give a company a competitive advantage, improve customer relationships, and create goodwill with the importing country's government. However, countertrade agreements can become complex. For example, in Thailand, the government set a requirement that state projects worth more than 300 million bhat (US $7.03 million) would have to ask their foreign suppliers of equipment and services to accept at least half their payment in Thai products, such as frozen chicken, rice products, and furniture.

Licensing Strategy

A licensing strategy *involves a firm (the licensor) in one country giving other domestic or foreign firms (licensees) the right to use a patent, trademark, technology, production process, or product in return for the payment of a royalty or fee.*[33] This contractual arrangement also may involve the licensor in providing manufacturing, technical, or marketing expertise to the licensee. A simple licensing arrangement involves U.S. and Canadian book publishers giving foreign publishers the right to translate a book into another language and then publish, market, and distribute the translated book. The licensor doesn't have to worry about making large capital investments abroad or becoming involved in the details of daily production, marketing, or management. Many U.S.-based companies use this strategy because there is very little financial risk; the licensee gains production expertise or a well-known product without having to start from scratch. PepsiCo and Coca-Cola have licensing agreements with bottlers/distributors in most countries of the world. Microsoft has used licensing very effectively to promote its Windows-based operating system for use in PCs, servers, and large commercial networks. Microsoft gets a small royalty in exchange for allowing another firm, such as Beijing-based Lenovo, which makes all of IBM's laptop computers, to incorporate its software system into its product. In Japan, Budweiser beer is brewed by Kirin breweries, and Lady Borden ice cream is churned out at Meji Milk Product dairies.

Technological and market forces are combining to stimulate use of the licensing strategy. As a form of market entry, international licensing is more risky than exporting, but less risky than franchising. The licensor exports know-how instead of their product. Some of the reasons why organizations use a license are to generate extra income from existing technology, to spread the costs of R&D projects, to get into markets that have been closed or protected, to test new markets before making a capital investment, and to minimize risks when entering foreign markets. Although there are potential benefits, there are also some risks. The licensee might become a competitor, fail to pay royalties, imitate the technology, or sell the license without the agreement of the licensor. Such risks are likely in the pharmaceutical and software industries.

Franchising Strategy

A franchising strategy *involves a parent organization (the franchiser) granting other companies or individuals (franchisees) the right to use its trademarked name and to produce and sell its goods or services.* It is a special type of licensing agreement whereby the franchiser not only provides the product, technology, process, and/or trademark, but also most of the marketing program. It is similar to licensing, but the franchiser usually has more control over the franchisee. In nearly any major city around the world, you are likely to find Burger King, Kentucky Fried Chicken, or Marriott, among others. They are there because local entrepreneurs have bought franchises. Franchising permits companies to maintain marketing control while passing along many of the costs, risks, and responsibilities to the franchisees. The franchiser provides franchisees with a complete assortment of materials and services for a fee. Franchisees often function somewhat independently from the parent company but benefit from being part of a larger organization. However, the franchiser usually is actively involved in training, monitoring, and controlling certain actions of the franchisee to ensure that it conforms to the franchise agreement.[34]

To build its franchise system in Mexico, Singer relies on the franchisees' word-of-mouth to promote business rather, than large advertising campaigns.

© Hill Street Studios/Blend Images/Jupiter Images

Franchising has been used as a tactic to expand the market for goods and services dating back to 1850s when Singer Sewing Machine distributed its sewing machines. When Singer introduced its sewing machine in the 1850s, it did not have the capital to open a branch office or to hire sales people. As a result, Singer decided that the best way to market its machine was to use a network of commissioned sales agents to sell its then revolutionary machine. Today, Singer Sewing machines are sold in more than 190 countries through more than 58,000 franchise owners. The following Strategic Action Competency highlights how Singer used franchising to enter Mexico.[35]

Singer Sewing Machine

The first Singer Sewing Machine franchises in Mexico were established in the early 1980s and most of them were U.S.-based companies. Today, there are more than 800 franchises in Mexico. Singer knew that the fastest growth was in businesses that fulfilled the needs of working mothers, giving them support with personal, home, and children's services.

Singer learned that seamstresses and tailors across Mexico were stitching in the same way that their grandparents had been for decades—that is, using foot-powered machines. Owning a sewing machine was an impossible luxury that many could only dream about because most people use only cash to buy goods. To tap into a huge lower-middle-class market, Singer offered a lease-purchase plan to solve the cash problem faced by many customers who have income, but little access to credit cards or bank accounts. Singer offers machines from its basic $150 model to computerized machines starting at $3,000. Singer also understood that thanks to strong personal values (see pages 156–158) and

low transient rates, Mexicans will go to great lengths to avoid defaulting on monthly lease payments, thus avoiding the shame that would befall them if their machines were repossessed. That threat of social stigma has kept repossession rates down to less than 2 percent.

Singer chose to develop a franchise system whereby each franchisee would run their operation. The person in the local area would be highly committed to its success because Singer franchisees invest their own money and time in order to build and manage their outlet. Singer realized that having a highly committed local person would be vital because of their knowledge of customs and sewing circles. Sewers would be attracted to local events and it would be the franchisee's word-of-mouth connections rather than large advertising campaigns directed from its headquarters in New York City that would be important.

To learn more about this organization, visit *www.singer.com*.

Alliance Strategy

An alliance strategy *involves an agreement between two or more organizations to pool physical, financial, and human resources to achieve common goals.* Global strategic alliances *are joint ventures that involve actions taken internationally by two or more companies contributing an agreed-on amount of resources.* This approach may be preferred when competition is tough or technology and capital requirements are relatively large for one partner. In the beverage industry, Nestlé works with Coca-Cola to gain access to distribution channels in Europe. Nestlé and the French cosmetics company L'Oréal have an alliance to develop Inneov, a nutritional supplement intended to improve the health of skin. MTV Networks has alliances with companies in Brazil, Australia, and other countries to expand its global media presence.

The following factors have stimulated the formation of alliances, especially joint ventures[36]:

▶ The need to share and lower the costs of high-risk, technologically intensive development projects, such as computer-based information systems. IBM, for example, has created an alliance with Motorola and Toshiba to improve its semiconductor manufacturing skills in making super-dense chips. IBM and Motorola are also working together to develop new x-ray photolithography techniques that neither company can afford on its own. The partners are simultaneously owners investing capital, customers routing calls via satellites, and suppliers of technology to the venture.

▶ The desire to lower costs by sharing the large fixed-cost investments. An agreement between Robex Resources, Inc., a Canadian gold exploration and development company, and Geo Services International, an organization operating in Mali, enables the two firms to increase the success of gold exploration and drilling projects in certain areas.

▶ The desire to learn another firm's technology and special processes or to gain access to customers and distribution channels. The French publisher Hachette entered into an alliance with Pacific Publications of Australia to publish *Elle* and *Elle Cuisine* in Australia and New Zealand.

▶ The desire to participate in the evolution of competitive activity in growing global industries. Bayer AG of Germany entered into an alliance with Millennium Pharmaceuticals to develop cancer-fighting drugs. Both companies will work together to use computer simulations and advanced medical techniques to speed up the research on a new gene that causes tumors to form.

Alliances provide entry into markets that are risky because of strict political requirements or great economic uncertainty. For example, in Italy, distribution channels are fragmented and complex. Instead of large supermarkets and hypermarkets, such as Wal-Mart and Toys "R" Us, small family-owned retailers tend to control distribution channels. Numerous middlemen and wholesalers make it difficult for firms, such as Procter & Gamble, Colgate-Palmolive, and Unilever, to sell their products without forming an alliance with local Italian firms. These partners are likely to have a deeper understanding of how to deal with great political and economic complexity in the country. KFC entered Japan through an alliance with the Japanese conglomerate Mitsubishi. Mitsubishi is one of Japan's largest poultry producers and understands the Japanese culture.

Multidomestic Strategy

A multidomestic strategy *involves adjusting products, services, and practices to individual countries or regions* (e.g., Pacific Rim versus Western Europe versus North America).[37] A multidomestic strategy encourages the design, manufacturing, and marketing of a product to be tailored to meet the specific needs of each country. Pressures to respond to differences in customer demand, distribution channels, government demands, and/or employee needs drive this strategy. Domino's Pizza knows that the basics of crust, sauce, and cheese work for pizza everywhere, but the company also has more than 2,500 international restaurants. It offers more than 100 different pizza pies, including paneer pizza in India and mayo-jaga in Japan.

Procter & Gamble also uses a multidomestic strategy in its diaper business. Procter & Gamble learned that understanding the cultural values of a country is important to make their diapers acceptable to mothers. In Italy, for example, designing diapers that would cover the baby's naval was critical to success. Ogilvy & Mather has divided the world into four primary geographic regions because it has learned that advertising approaches need to be modified to fit the tastes, preferences, cultural, values, and government regulations in different parts of the world. In France, children cannot be used to advertise products, and in Germany, the competitive claims (e.g., cleaner, faster) made by U.S. companies cannot be shown on German television.

Under a multidomestic strategy, each major overseas subsidiary usually is somewhat independent. Often each is a profit center and contributes earnings and growth according to its market opportunity. A profit center *is an organizational unit that is accountable for both the revenues generated by its activities and the costs of those activities.* Its managers are responsible for generating revenues and minimizing costs to achieve the unit's profit goals. Frito-Lay uses a multidomestic strategy in tailoring its snack foods to taste preferences around the world. For example, Janjaree Thanma directs marketing research for Frito-Lay in Thailand. Interestingly, after testing 500 flavors for its chips with Thai consumers, the results showed that their preference was for U.S. flavors, such as barbecue.

Global Strategy

A global strategy *stresses worldwide consistency, standardization, and relatively low cost.*[38] Subsidiaries in various countries are highly interdependent in terms of goals, practices, and operations. As much as possible, top managers focus on coordination and mutual support of the firm's worldwide activities. For example, a Black & Decker subsidiary in one country might manufacture certain parts for families of products; subsidiaries in other countries do the same with regard to other parts. The subsidiaries then exchange components to complete assembly of their particular products. Profit targets vary for each subsidiary, reflecting its importance to the company's total system.

The customers of global firms have needs that are basically similar in many countries. Thus primary marketing strategies are highly transferable across national boundaries. For example, the marketing of Intel's Pentium chips to computer manufacturers in various countries has many similarities. Customers' technical standards are relatively compatible, and, for the most part, governments don't regulate computer chip production and sales practices. American Express Company also realizes the benefits of a global strategy by emphasizing the ideas of quality, security, and safety. One of American Express's goals is to create the world's most respected brand name. Travelers around the world recognize the reliability and quality symbolized by the American Express logo. Travelers who encounter trouble can go to any American Express office for emergency replacement of travelers' checks or lost or stolen credit cards. In addition, all offices are equipped to send emergency telegrams and messages to families, consulates, and other contacts for people in need of such services.

An increasing number of multinational corporations are using global strategies, including Caterpillar and Komatsu (heavy construction equipment), Kodak and Fuji (film), and Texas Instruments, Intel, and Hitachi (semiconductors). As demonstrated in the following Strategic Action Competency feature on Imperial Chemical Industries PLC, the global form of organization is not without pitfalls. You might not recognize the name of Imperial Chemical Industries, but you know its brands: Glidden, Alba, Dulux, and Color Your World. Located in London, it competes against Sherwin-Williams and Pittsburgh Plate Glass in coatings for cars, paint, liquid nails, and adhesives around the world.[39]

Snapshot

"Procter and Gamble chose a multidomestic strategy because we believe that this leads to superior understanding of consumers and their needs and it develops close relationships with suppliers. This structure also enables product divisions to share information and key activities."

A. G. Lafley, CEO and President, Procter and Gamble

Strategic Action Competency

Imperial Chemical Industries PLC

The sun never sets on the far-flung operations of Imperial Chemical Industries PLC (ICI). As one of the world's largest companies, ICI's sales exceed $10.7 billion. It has more than 200 manufacturing plants on six continents that make paints, chemicals, explosives, film, and polymers, among other products.

In 1983, ICI began to abandon its traditional country-by-country organization and instead formed worldwide business units. Today, the company focuses its resources in locations where it has the strongest competitive advantage. Since 1983, ICI has bought and sold more than 50 businesses in an attempt to position itself in the industry.

Today, it has four regional and industrial chemical centers. For example, of its more than $10.4 billion in sales, ICI gets more than 30 percent from sales in the United States. Therefore, ICI has established its U.S. headquarters near Cleveland, Ohio. From this location, it makes many of its paint products. From its operations in Argentina, ICI provides chemicals to the wine industry and other related chemicals. From its India operation, it manufactures explosives, pharmaceuticals, and rubber chemicals. In Pakistan, it manufactures fibers and soda ash, a major component for making glass.

To avoid overlapping research, labs are given lead roles near their markets. For example, leather dye research went to Pakistan and advanced materials research was assigned to the United States. As a result, employees had to be outsourced or moved to another country. According to High Miller, an American, "It's hard on people who have built national empires and now don't have such allegiance. We are asking people to be less nationalistic and more concerned with what happens outside their country." The payoff, says Miller, is more efficient decision making. "Before, each country would work up projects and you'd have warring factions competing in London for the same money. Now, with one person responsible for a global product line, it becomes immaterial where a project is located. Its profits will be the same. When you start operating in this manner, it takes a lot of steam out of country fiefdoms." In the wine industry, for example, better and quicker decision making from Argentina has helped ICI reduce the time it takes to introduce new chemicals used to fight insects that destroy grapes. These chemicals, subject to governmental approval, then can be used to fight insects in the United States, France, New Zealand, and other grape-growing regions of the world. Similarly, ICI has been able to reduce the time for introducing new drugs into the pharmaceutical industry from six years to one or two by having focused all of its pharmaceutical operations in India.

To learn more about this organization, visit *www.ici.com.*

Various needs must be addressed if a multinational's global strategy is to be successful.[40] The following are six such needs:

1. The firm needs to be a significant competitor in the world's most important regional markets: North America, Europe, and Asia.

2. Most new goods and services need to be developed for the whole world, such as American Express Company's financial services and Kodak's film and related products.

3. Profit targets need to be based on product lines, such as an ICI line of paint, rather than on countries or regions of the world.

4. Decisions about products, capital investment, R&D, and production need to be based on global considerations, such as ICI's choice of strategic locations for plants for producing chemicals and related products in various regions of the world.

5. Narrow-minded attitudes, such as "this isn't how we operate here," need to be overcome. Some ways to shape work-related attitudes and values include training employees to think globally, sending them to various countries for firsthand exposure, and giving them the latest information technology. Coca-Cola went so far as to ban the words *domestic* and *foreign* from its corporate vocabulary in order to bolster the image of a single global firm that had more than 80 percent of its sales from non-U.S. sources.

6. Foreign managers need to be promoted into senior ranks at corporate headquarters.

Chapter Summary ....

In this chapter, we focused on various global considerations for those engaging in international business. Organizations and individuals—both as employees and consumers—are increasingly touched by global forces and issues.

Learning Goals ....

1. State the trends affecting organizations in a global economy.

Organizations are becoming more global in their operations, and globalization of commerce will continue to accelerate. Societies also are becoming more global. During this next decade, these shifts will affect organizations in several important ways. First, as organizations become boundaryless, global trade will become increasingly important. Second, information technology is placing a premium on instant communication from anywhere in the world. Third, as global trade expands and information becomes more available, transactions between companies are becoming more transparent. Fourth, traditional closed economies are becoming more open and democratic to take advantage of the trading opportunities around the world. Finally, labor markets in China and India are taking many of the labor-intensive jobs traditionally performed in Mexico and other countries.

2. Describe how a country's culture can affect an organization's business practices.

The primary cultural factors that can influence how an organization is managed include views of social change, time, language, value systems, and cultural distance. Special attention was given to understanding how cultural issues have led to differences in the management systems in Mexico and the United States.

3. Explain how political–legal forces impact global business.

International business operations create new complexities, risks, and uncertainties. Broad political–legal issues include domestic instability, foreign conflict, political climate, economic climate, and corruption. Political mechanisms utilized in international business include tariffs, quotas, subsidies, cartels, bribes, and extortion.

4. Discuss how three major international trade agreements affect global competition and cooperation.

The World Trade Organization helps open markets and reduce trade barriers (e.g., tariffs) among its 149 member nations. The North American Free Trade Agreement further reduces barriers, encourages investment, and stimulates trade among Canada, Mexico, and the United States. The European Union is an organization of 25 member countries. Its primary goals are to create a single market and allow the free movement of goods, services, people, and capital among its members. The ultimate goal is to improve the standard of living and quality of life for the citizens of the member countries.

5. Describe six strategies used by organizations to grow globally.

The strategies used by many international businesses include exporting, licensing, franchising, alliances, multidomestic, and global. These strategies vary in terms of their relative complexity (reflected in organization design) and resource commitments required to effectively implement the strategy. Organizations use different strategies over time as they learn how to adjust their operations to the demands of their global marketplaces.

Key Terms and Concepts ....

Alliance strategy
Bribe
Cartel
Corruption
Countertrade
Cultural distance
Domestic instability
Economic climate
European Union (EU)
Exporting strategy
Extortion
Foreign conflict
Franchising strategy

Global strategic alliances
Global strategy
Grease payments
Licensing strategy
Maquiladora plants
Most favored nation
  principle
Multidomestic strategy
North American Free Trade
  Agreement (NAFTA)
Political climate
Political risk
Profit center

Protectionism
Quota
Reciprocity principle
Subsidy
Tariff
Tariff concession
Transparency principle
U.S. Foreign Corrupt
  Practices Act of 1977
World Trade Organization
  (WTO)

Questions for Discussion and Reflective Thinking ....

1. Identify at least three challenges facing Grupo Bimbo's global expansion.

2. What are some of the competencies you need to develop to become an effective global manager? How can your course work in school help you do so?

3. Describe the ways in which a rapidly changing competitive international environment has impacted global organizations.

4. What role does culture play in creating ethical challenges for people in global organizations?

5. Suppose that Microsoft wanted to open four new plants overseas. Name four countries that might represent a high degree of risk for such operations (go to *www.transparency.org*). What type of business strategy would minimize these risks?

6. Has NAFTA been good or bad for U.S. manufacturing companies? How are disputes settled in NAFTA? To answer these questions, go to *www.nafta.org*.

7. Has the EU stimulated trade in Europe? How has it affected nations that are not members of the EU? To answer these questions, go to *www.europa.eu*.

8. Singer Sewing Machine used a franchise strategy to increase sales globally. What are some limitations to this strategy? What other strategies might Singer have considered?

9. If you took an assignment with Kodak in Mexico, what behaviors and nonverbal gestures would be appropriate or offensive? To determine the business etiquette in Mexico, go to *www.AMCHAM.com.mx*.

10. China has recently been admitted to the WTO. Is this a good decision for U.S.-based companies?

DEVELOPING YOUR COMPETENCIES

Introduction

The Parking Garage Simulation is an exercise designed to illustrate the complexity of identifying an automobile with the manufacturer. Today's car is truly a global product developed from economic interdependencies. The exercise allows for testing what we know and provides a forum for learning.

Purpose

The purpose of this simulation is to raise levels of consciousness about the difficulty surrounding the identification of the true manufacturer of today's automobile. This simulation provides you with an opportunity to test your skill and knowledge as they relate to automobiles and their manufacturer.

As the Parking Garage Manager, you have the responsibility of admitting only American-made automobiles to the parking garage. Likewise, it is your responsibility to deny parking privileges to all employees driving any car with less than 75 percent domestic content.

This simulation sets the stage for discussion of economic interdependency. It illustrates the need to have sufficient knowledge before persons, groups, or organizations move toward trade barriers, tariffs, or laws of protectionism.

Goals of the Simulation

1. To understand the benefits of international competition in the context of the economic construct of "comparative advantage."

2. To explore the economic outcomes with international competition and the strategy of win–lose.

3. To explore the unproductive anxiety, emotionality, and ethnocentrism often associated with international competition.

4. To explore the 75 percent content rule in manufacturing within the U.S. auto industry.

Your Decision (Please Check)

Auto Seeking Entrance to Parking Facility

Facility	ADMIT	DENY	SCORE
1. Toyota F J Cruiser			
2. Ford Crown Victoria			
3. GMC Yukon XL			
4. Toyota Camry			
5. Mitsubishi Eclipse			
6. Mazda6			
7. Volkswagen Beetle			
8. Saturn Relay			
9. Chevrolet Corvette			
10. Honda Accord			
11. Chery			
12. Land Rover			

TOTAL _____

Scoring Sheet

	Rationale:	Correct Response:
1. Toyota F J Cruiser	Manufactured 100 percent in Japan	Deny
2. Ford Crown Victoria	Ford Motor Company top of the line, produced in Canada; 27 percent of parts come from Germany, Spain, Mexico, and Japan	Deny
3. GMC Yukon XL	Final assembly, Arlington, Texas, USA	Admit
4. Toyota Camry	Made 75 percent in Indiana, USA; 25 percent in Japan	Admit
5. Mitsubishi Eclipse	Manufactured in Illinois, USA, with 70 percent parts from USA; 30 percent parts from Japan	Deny
6. Mazda6	Produced by AutoAlliance, International (a joint venture with Ford); 75 percent U.S. content	Admit
7. Volkswagen Beetle	Built 100 percent in Puebla, Mexico.	Deny
8. Saturn Relay	Produced with 90 percent U.S. content in Tennessee	Admit
9. Chevrolet Corvette	Manufactured 100 percent in Bowling Green, Kentucky	Admit
10. Honda Accord	Manufactured and produced with 75 percent content in Marysville, Ohio, USA	Admit
11. Chery	Manufactured in China	Deny
12. Land Rover	Manufactured 100 percent in England	Deny

Scoring: To score, place the number 1 by *each* correct answer and sum for the total.

Your rating as an Auto Inspector-Rejecter:

Number of correct answers:

11–12 Auto expert
 9–10 Auto enthusiast
  7–8 Auto knowledge is fair

Questions

1. What political action tactics can U.S. automakers use to ease competition with imports?

2. According to Thomas Friedman, author of *The World Is Flat,* "The best companies are the best collaborators. In the new economy, more and more business will be done through collaboration than competition to create value." Do you agree with this statement? What are some roadblocks to achieving global collaboration in the automobile industry?

Yue Yuen is a city of 265,000 people that replaces the village young workers leave behind. Just like the farms from which these workers come, Yue Yuen has seasons and rhythms, but ones set by commercial dictates in countries thousands of miles away. Yue Yuen runs its own water treatment systems and power stations. Within each factory compound are dormitories and canteens, post office and phone company branches, medical clinics, and shops. One factory complex has a 100-bed hospital, a kindergarten, a 300-seat movie theater, and a performance troupe.

Zhang Qianqian, 21 years old, arrived at Yue Yuen three years ago. She says she left after 18 months because of conflicts with her boss and briefly returned home. She worked at an electronics factory last year before quitting to go home, this time for her grandmother's 80th birthday. Soon she rejoined Yue Yuen. "I've moved here and there, and I always seem to end up in this factory," she says.

One-third of the world's shoes are made in Guangdong, the province that borders Hong Kong. In this world, Yue Yuen is king. Established in 1989 by Pou Chen Corp. of Taiwan, Yue Yuen is the largest supplier to Nike, Adidas, Reebok, and other brands. The company runs three factory complexes in Gaobu, a suburb of Dongguan, and is one of the biggest employers in the province.

Yue Yuen runs some factories that make the raw materials for shoes and other factories that cut, stitch, and assemble these various parts. It employs designers to work with shoe companies to develop new styles. A Yue Yuen assembly line now takes 10 hours to make a shoe, from readying raw materials to having a finished product ready to ship, compared with 25 days four years ago.

In a world of change and uncertainty, Yue Yuen offers a stability that contrasts with the impermanence of migrant life. Many factories in the Pearl River Delta are unsafe and owe workers money. At Yue Yuen, the salary is average—about US $72 per month after deductions for room and board. The company has a reputation for long workdays and autocratic managers. But wages are paid on time. Work is capped at 11 hours a day and 60 hours a week, with Sundays off. Turnover is greater than 60 percent a year. Workers sleep 10 to a room with hot showers and adequate meals. Eighty-five percent of the workers at Yue Yuen are young women.

Factory society divides along provincial lines. Workers from the same province stick together, speaking dialects others can't understand. Local stereotypes color hiring. Many factory bosses refuse to hire people from Henan because they are considered untrustworthy, whereas those from Anhui are perceived as overly sly.

Almost all of the managers at Yue Yuen are migrants who started out on the factory floor. They're ranked by an intricate well-established hierarchy. There are 13 levels of managers, from manager trainee to managing director. There is a cafeteria exclusively for those in charge of production lines and another for chief supervisors, one step up the hierarchy.

Only line leaders and higher-up managers are permitted to live inside the factory with a child.

Zhang Qianqian had come to visit friends in Room 805 from a dorm down the hall. She wore jeans and a black sports watch. Ms. Zhang recalled mornings at home when her grandmother would make breakfast. "She calls me to come eat it and sometimes I am still sleeping. Then my father says to me, 'You are lying in bed, you won't even come to eat breakfast your grandmother has made for you.'" She frowned. "At home they are always criticizing you." Most workers have complex relationships with their homes. When they aren't there, they miss it. But when they spent time in their villages, they quickly got bored and longed to return to the city.

Back in their villages, families try to pressure the girls: Send money home; don't get a boyfriend; marry sooner; come back. For the most part, the girls do as they please. Many parents don't know their daughters' phone numbers inside the factory.

When the girls at Yue Yuen go home, their parents want them to rest rather than working on the farm, believing they already work too hard. The girls keep farmers' hours, rising at dawn and turning in early. But they spend most of their waking hours watching television. Time is not important in the village. At Yue Yuen, however, time is measured in precise increments. There is a plastic sign in front of every station noting how many seconds it takes that worker to complete a task. Employees are timed by supervisors with stopwatches. Productivity at Yue Yuen is up 10 percent in the past three years. An Adidas investigation into the impact of its drive to increase efficiency found that workers initially felt more stress but over time adapted.

One production line has 470 workers. An athletic shoe may pass through 200 stations. Workers in the cutting department stamp sheets of mesh fabric into pieces. Stitchers sew logos and shoelace eyelets onto these pieces to make the shoe upper. Stock fitters glue layers of rubber and plastic to make the sole. Assemblers press the sole and upper together, insert a foot-shaped plastic mold, called a last, and glue the two parts together. A machine applies 88 pounds of pressure to each shoe. Workers remove the lasts, check for flaws, and pack the shoes in boxes. Each shoe had a "Made in China" label on its tongue. Yue Yuen has 290 production lines in factories throughout China, each turning out 157.7 million pairs of shoes annually for companies such as Nike, New Balance, Timberland, and Rockport.

The Western companies that pushed factories to improve conditions also demanded lower prices. Workers now work fewer hours but are more exhausted because tasks are precisely parceled out to ensure almost no downtime. Brands now give factories 30 days to deliver an order; three years ago it was 60 days; a decade back it was 90. Orders are getting smaller, allowing designers to respond more rapidly to fashion changes.

Questions

1. What values are illustrated in this case? Are they similar to yours?

2. Would you like to work in this Chinese factory? Explain why or why not.

3. What competencies would you need to develop to manage employees in this factory?

chapter 6

© Gabe Palmer/Workbook Stock/Jupiter Images

Fostering Entrepreneurship

Learning Goals

After studying this chapter, you should be able to:

1. Explain the nature of entrepreneurship and the impact that the environment has on it.

2. Describe the competencies that contribute to entrepreneurs' success.

3. Outline the planning essentials for potential entrepreneurs.

4. Describe the basic essentials of corporate entrepreneurship.

Communication Competency

Planning and Administration Competency

Teamwork Competency

Managing Effectively

Self-Management Competency

Strategic Action Competency

Multicultural Competency

Challenge of Managing ....

Denise Devine, Founder of Devine Foods

© Dennis Gray/Cole Group/Photodisc Green/Getty Images

For Denise Devine, the entrepreneurial path was paved by what she considered a glaring need in the nutritional fare available for children. Devine is the president and CEO of Nutripharm, Inc., and Devine Foods, Inc., headquartered in Media (near Philadelphia), Pennsylvania. She said that motherhood was the spark that made her decide to take the chance on entrepreneurship. She was working as director of finance and investment strategy for Campbell Soup Company, but was dismayed by the lack of nutritious, convenient food for children.

Devine comments: "At the time, my children were very young. That was at the time the first food pyramid was released by the USDA and I was feeling quite frustrated working for a large food company. I was a frustrated consumer myself because I couldn't find nutritious food for my children. Being a busy working parent, it was even more difficult to find healthy, convenient food that you can pack in lunches for daycare or preschool. I began to do a lot of research and I began to get angry. I'm very passionate about this issue, and the only way I can describe it was that it was something I felt compelled to do."

Her initial idea was a healthy alternative to juice called Fruice. Packed with more vitamins and minerals, but without the excess sugar, Devine indicates that this idea was the catalyst for her new company. While she admits she "didn't have a clue" at first about how to start the company, she sought out others who could help. She consulted with a group of chemists and others at Cornell University who worked with her ideas and began developing them into products. At the same time, she received financial support from the Ben Franklin Technology Partners, a statewide network that fosters innovation to stimulate Pennsylvania's economic growth and prosperity.

Devine notes that her company's strategy has changed during the last couple years. Recently, they have worked with the U.S. Department of Agriculture to develop healthier products for school lunch programs. Devine Foods has entered into some other new development agreements with undisclosed large companies.

Devine indicates that there are many different avenues and goals for the budding entrepreneur. She is most proud of the fact

Learning Content

that her company is doing something positive for others. She said her entrepreneurial "itch" may be different than others. She comments: "I had an itch to arrange my life differently. I have always felt the need to be part of something that makes a difference. That's very gratifying to me."[1]

To learn more about this organization, visit *www.devinefoods.com*.

I.

Explain the nature of entrepreneurship and the impact that the environment has on it

Entrepreneurship: Its Meaning and Scope

What Is Entrepreneurship?

Entrepreneurship *is the creation of an innovative organization for the purpose of economic gain or growth under conditions of risk or uncertainty.* In launching a new business, entrepreneurs typically incorporate at least one of the following[2]:

▸ *Something new.* This could be a new product, service, or technology. Denise Devine spearheaded the development of a more nutritious drink, Fruice. As noted in the Challenge of Managing feature, Devine has led the development of a broad range of products and services since the founding of Devine Foods, Inc. This includes the formation of a holding company, Nutripharm, Inc., which holds and licenses 17 patents on nutritional and pharmaceutical products developed by Devine and her associates.

▸ *Something better.* This could be a significant and unique improvement on an existing product or service encompassing more features, greater reliability, faster speed, or increased convenience. Jake Burton Carpenter succeeded by improving on the design of a product that he first got to know as a 14-year-old. Shortly after college, he founded Burton Snowboards in Burlington, Vermont. He comments: "A lot of people think I invented snowboarding. But that's not true." The basic design for a snowboard had already been developed by Brunswick, the company that developed bowling alleys. But Brunswick never made the product a success. The philosophy of Burton Snowboards is to improve on what's available, based on an understanding of what customers really want. Burton states: "If the original product is a hassle for people, they'll fork over money for something that's better."[3] The firm is now the world's leading snowboard maker with 40 percent of the market. Burton Snowboards has diversified into the production and selling of snowboarding apparel, boots, and so on. At the 2006 Winter Olympics in Torino, Italy, Burton sponsored 19 riders, several of whom won gold and other medals.[4]

▸ *An underserved or new market.* This is a market for which there is greater demand than competitors can currently satisfy, an unserved location, or a small part of an overall market—a niche market—that hasn't yet been taken over by other competitors. Sometimes, markets become underserved when large companies abandon or neglect smaller portions of their current customer base. Todd Greene invented a razor designed specifically for men who shave their heads. He comments: "Shaving my head with a traditional razor was difficult, time consuming and I got plenty of cuts and nicks. I designed the HeadBlade to specifically address the contours of the scalp."[5] He tried to sell the concept to two large makers of men's grooming products, but was rejected outright. Greene decided to launch the innovative product on his own and formed

HeadBlade Co., headquartered in Culver City, California. He has three patents on HeadBlade and others pending in the United States and abroad. Sales come through the firm's Web site, *www.headblade.com*; and outlets such as Walgreens, Rite Aid, Sav-on, and CVS Pharmacy (online only). To complement its set of head-shaving razors, the firm introduced HeadLube, a lotion to moisturize the scalp.[6] HeadBlade also qualifies as "something new."

▶ *New delivery system or distribution channel.* New technologies, particularly the Internet, are allowing companies to reach customers more efficiently. This has opened up many new opportunities for businesses to provide products or services less expensively, to a wider geographic area, or with far greater choice. Kevin Grauman is founder, president, and CEO of The Outsource Group (TOG), headquartered in Walnut Creek, California. He was a recent recipient of one of the Ernst & Young Entrepreneur of the Year awards. Through heavy reliance on the Internet, TOG developed a new system for delivering human resource services, especially to small and medium-sized firms through the Internet. TOG has enabled its clients to substantially reduce the number of their employees devoted to increasingly complex human resource issues and to obtain virtually all of their needed specialized human resource services from one source. TOG is growing rapidly and serves more than 300 businesses. It provides a wide range of outsourced human resource services, including benefits administration, risk management, regulatory compliance, online training, and payroll administration. Its *Emportal* is an online self-service tool that lets managers and employees access and change personal information, manage performance reviews, and enroll in benefits, among other things.[7]

As these scenarios make clear, entrepreneurship is not limited to introducing something totally new. Successful entrepreneurs may begin by offering a higher quality product or service. They may make small modifications to what others are already doing. After they get started, they listen to customers or clients and come up with still other modifications. Then they quickly adapt what they're doing—and they repeat this process over and over. In brief, an entrepreneur is an innovator, decision maker, and organizational builder.[8] Typically, they get their inspiration through (1) previous work experience; (2) education or training; (3) hobbies, talents, or other personal interests; or (4) recognition of an unanswered need or market opportunity. Occasionally, the business idea comes from the experience of a relative or friend.

How Does the Environment Affect Entrepreneurship?

Chapters 3, 4, and 5 provided a number of insights on how the environment impacts all businesses, including those ventures launched by entrepreneurs. In this section, we focus on several external factors that are especially important to entrepreneurship.

Open and Free Markets. Entrepreneurship requires relatively open and free markets. Highly regulated and governmentally controlled markets severely limit opportunities for entrepreneurship. With the deregulation of markets in many countries during the past 20 years—including the United States, Canada, and other traditionally "free" and not so free (China and India, among others) market economies—the positive political climate for entrepreneurship has enabled millions of new entrepreneurs to flourish in the United States, Canada, and globally. There has been an explosion in venture formation by women, immigrants, and members of minority groups. Entrepreneurship—through new start-ups or new ventures within existing organizations—has been suggested as *the* defining trend of the 21st century.[9]

Economic and Technological Conditions. The rate of entrepreneurship ebbs and flows with economic and technological conditions. In the United States, entrepreneurship rates rose dramatically during the 1920s and then declined during the 1930s (a period of economic depression). They rose again after World War II but then declined from the 1950s and the late 1980s. The 1990s was another period of rising entrepreneurship, initiated by innovations in microelectronics, computers, telecommunications, and information technologies. The continuous development of the Internet, a technological condition, has fostered the creation of many new ventures. With the softening of the economy, the rate of entrepreneurship decreased in 2002 and 2003 and then increased again substantially in 2004 and continues.

The current support system for entrepreneurs also plays a role in the rate of new venture formation. The support system includes the availability of investment capital and loans, favorable tax rates and policies, and the availability of support services. The U.S. Small Business Administration, chambers of commerce, small business development centers, banks, venture capital firms, and other organizations provide a variety of services that are often helpful to entrepreneurs in the development, implementation, and growth of their ventures.

Business Incubation. According to the National Business Incubation Association, business incubation *is a business support process that accelerates the successful development of start-up and fledging companies by providing entrepreneurs with an array of targeted resources and services.*[10] These services are usually developed or orchestrated by the managers of the incubator and offered both in the business incubator and through its network of contacts. The main goal of business incubation is to produce successful firms that, when they leave the program, will become financially viable and freestanding. These incubator graduates have the potential to create jobs, revitalize neighborhoods, commercialize new technologies, and strengthen local and national economies. There are approximately 1,000 business incubators in the United States and about 4,000 worldwide. Local, regional, or state governments or other nonprofit organizations sponsor most incubators to stimulate economic development in their regions. Universities and colleges sponsor 25 percent of the incubators.[11]

Critical to the role of incubation is the provision of management guidance, technical assistance, networking, and consulting tailored to young, growing companies. Incubators also usually provide clients with access to appropriate rental space and flexible leases, shared basic business services and equipment, technology support services, and assistance in obtaining the financing necessary for company growth.

An important feature is the psychological or moral support that is fostered in an incubator. Often alone and unsure of themselves, entrepreneurs feel reduced anxiety and greater self-confidence when surrounded by a support system and other business owners experiencing similar struggles while starting a new venture.[12]

The incubator usually requires the entrepreneur to have a written business plan, evidence of adequate financing, and a commitment to relocate within the region upon leaving the facility. Most new ventures stay in an incubator for two or three years. At the end of this period, the business has either failed, chosen to expand within the incubator (if possible), or grown sufficiently enough to be able to move out of the incubator.

Small businesses can benefit from the support of the Small Business Administration, which was created by Congress in 1976 as an independent voice within the federal government on behalf of small businesses.

© Triangle Images/Workbook Stock/Jupiter Images

Is a Small Business an Entrepreneurial Firm?

A small business firm may be entrepreneurial but not all small businesses engage in entrepreneurship. If a small business owner undertakes one or more of the initiatives discussed previously, he or she is an entrepreneur. The U.S. Small Business Administration (SBA) defines a small business *as one that is independently owned and operated and which is not dominant in its field of operation.*[13] Over the years, the SBA has established and revised numerical definitions of what constitutes a small business in various industries. The SBA has published a 42-page *Table of Small Business Size Standards* where *size* is expressed in dollars of sales or number of employees. For example, a small business in the gold or mining industry is one with 500 or fewer employees. In contrast, a small business in the breakfast cereal manufacturing industry is one with 1,000 or fewer employees. A small business in other industries is defined by revenue (sales), such as $6.5 million or less in the child day-care services industry.[14] The SBA aids, counsels, assists, and protects the interest of small business concerns, and advocates on their behalf within the U.S. government. It also helps small-business victims of disasters. The SBA provides financial assistance, contractual assistance, and business development assistance. According to the SBA, more than 25 million small businesses are operating in the United States. Most of the employment growth in the United States continues to come from businesses with 500 or fewer employees.

Are Family Businesses Entrepreneurial Firms?

When people think of a small business, they may think of a family business run by an entrepreneur. Actually a family business may be either large or small. It may or may not be an entrepreneurial enterprise. A family business *is one owned and managed mostly by people who are related by blood and/or marriage.* Often these businesses are passed down from one generation to the next. Kohler Company, which is known for its kitchen and bath plumbing fixtures, is an example. Kohler was founded in 1873 by the inventor of the modern bathtub. Since then, the private company has diversified into furniture and accessories, small engines and generators, cabinetry and tile, and resort/recreation/real estate ventures. It is still controlled by the original family and employs many family members, including Herbert V. Kohler, Jr. He serves as the chairman of the board, CEO, and president.[15] The Kohler Company is a good example of a family business that is very entrepreneurial.

As we explain later in this chapter, pressures to expand, adapt, and innovate can create a great deal of stress for entrepreneurs and the people who work with and for them. When those people also are family members, knotty personal problems can arise. Some families handle these pressures by turning over management of their firms to professionals. Some families find ways to keep their businesses changing while maintaining management and ownership control. Some families sell their businesses or close down. Only about 30 percent of family businesses survive into the second generation of ownership. Twelve percent are still viable into the third generation. Only 3 percent operate into the fourth generation and beyond.[16]

Competencies of Successful Entrepreneurs

Few highly successful entrepreneurs start out with the goal of heading a rapidly growing company. When successful entrepreneurs were asked to explain why they started their own companies, they gave one or more of the following reasons:

▶ I wanted to work for myself and control my own life.

▶ I liked the challenge.

Snapshot

The U.S. Small Business Administration (SBA) administers the Small Business Development Center (SBDC) Program to provide management assistance to current and prospective small business owners. SBDCs offer one-stop assistance to individuals and small businesses by providing a wide variety of information and guidance in central and easily accessible branch locations. For extensive information on the SBA and SBDCs, go to www.sba.gov.

2.

Describe the competencies that contribute to entrepreneurs' success.

- I saw the demand for a product or service.
- I believed it was the best route to financial independence.
- I was frustrated or unhappy working for someone else.[17]

Recall our opening discussion of Denise Devine. She noted several of these reasons for starting her own business, including liking the challenge and seeing a need and demand for more nutritious children's food. In addition, she became frustrated and unhappy. Devine concluded the corporate world was not for her. Devine comments:

> I was getting to the point in my career where there was this endless waste of time—meetings and talking about things that never got done. There was a lot of politics involved, and if you don't particularly like to play politics, it's not a pleasant place to be. I know how to play the game but it just seemed like an incredible waste of energy.[18]

The many studies of entrepreneurs indicate that those who succeed have a cluster of attributes in common.[19] For the most part, these attributes fit within our general framework of managerial competencies, as adapted to some of the unique characteristics of entrepreneurs. The most important of these attributes relates to the self-management competency, as suggested in Figure 6.1.

Figure 6.1 | Common Attributes of Successful Entrepreneurs

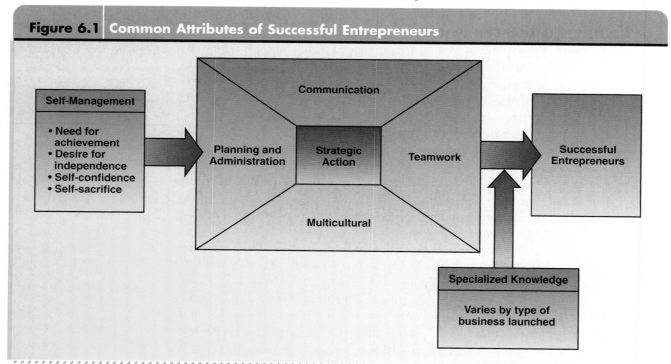

Self-Management Competency

A portfolio of attributes is embedded within the self-management competency. As suggested in Figure 6.1, those that many successful entrepreneurs share are a strong need for achievement, a desire to be independent, self-confidence, and the willingness to make sacrifices for the sake of the business.[20] You may be wondering whether you have what it takes to be a successful entrepreneur. Obviously, no one can predict your success as a potential entrepreneur. The characteristics that many entrepreneurs have in common—including family background, motivation, and personal attributes—may give you a rough idea of your potential. Complete the experiential exercise entitled Your Entrepreneurial Quotient at the end of this chapter in the Developing Your

Competencies section (see page 209). The questionnaire will help give you some idea of whether you see yourself as a natural for entrepreneurship.

Need for Achievement. The need for achievement—a person's desire either for excellence or to succeed in competitive situations—is a key personal attribute of successful entrepreneurs. High achievers take responsibility for attaining their goals, set moderately difficult goals, and want immediate feedback on how well they have performed. David McClelland and others have conducted extensive research into the human need for achievement. Their findings indicate that perhaps 10 percent of the U.S. population is characterized by a predominant need to achieve.[21] A strong drive to achieve is something that sets successful entrepreneurs apart from everyone else. Entrepreneurs set challenging but achievable goals for themselves and for their businesses. When they achieve these goals, they set new ones.

Desire for Independence. Entrepreneurs often seek independence from others. As a result, they may not be motivated to perform well in large, bureaucratic organizations. They have internal drive, are confident of their own abilities, and possess a great deal of self-respect.

Many of these feelings were familiar to Catherine Hughes, who now serves as chairperson of the board and founder of Radio One. She became the first African-American woman in the United States to head a publicly traded company. Hughes got started in business about 30 years ago. That's when she took on the challenge of running Howard University's ailing radio station. Within a few years, she had bought her own station, WOL-AM, with the help of a $600,000 loan. The cost of servicing the loan was so steep that she had to live at the radio station. Hiring adequate staff was also a problem, so she filled in as a DJ and talk show host. Despite these hardships, Hughes was happy, saying, "I was thinking of programming ideas, recruiting people, putting together sales packages. It was finally my show." Today, the show that Hughes runs is a $370 million business with 70 stations in 22 urban markets around the country and 14 million listeners each week.[22]

Self-Confidence. A successful track record does much to improve an entrepreneur's self-confidence and sense of optimism. It enables that person to be optimistic in representing the firm to employees and customers alike.[23] Expecting, obtaining, and rewarding high performance from employees is personally reinforcing, and it also provides a role model for others. Most people want an optimistic and enthusiastic leader—someone they can look up to. Because of the risks involved in running an entrepreneurial organization, having an "upbeat" attitude is essential. Optimists tend to interpret bad events as being only temporary ("We can get through this"), whereas pessimists interpret bad events as being permanent ("Our situation is hopeless. Why did I ever start this business?").[24]

Denise Devine, the focus of our Challenge of Managing feature, reflects on the importance of self-confidence and optimism in entrepreneurship:

> I think it's important to see this clear path and not be discouraged when people throw stones at it, because they will. You have to be willing to see the path, believe in it, and have the stamina and persistence to stick with it. You have to stand your ground and have confidence.[25]

Self-Sacrifice. Finally, successful entrepreneurs have to be self-sacrificing. They recognize that nothing worth having is free. That means giving up the two-week vacation, the golf game every Saturday, or the frequent trips to the mountains or shore. Success has a high price, and entrepreneurs are willing to pay it. For Catherine Hughes, living out of a sleeping bag at her radio station was a sacrifice. Having her car repossessed because she couldn't afford the payments on both her car and her station was a sacrifice. But perhaps her biggest sacrifice was selling a rare gold pocket watch because she needed the $5,000 it brought her. Made by slaves, the watch had belonged to her great-grandmother. Such sacrifices can be a tough reality for entrepreneurs.

Entrepreneurs: Made, Not Born. Although entrepreneurs are different than most people, they probably weren't born that way. They develop personal attributes over the years, but they acquire many of their key attributes early in life, with the family environment playing an important role. For example, women who were born first into a family tend to be more entrepreneurial than women born later into a family, perhaps because the first child receives special attention and thereby develops more self-confidence. Entrepreneurs also tend to have self-employed parents. The independent nature and flexibility shown by the self-employed mother or father is learned at an early stage. These parents are supportive and encourage independence, achievement, and responsibility.[26]

Jayson Home & Garden is a thriving business today because founder Jay Goltz was willing to take risks and make personal sacrifices.

Changing personal attributes isn't easy, especially by the time people reach adulthood. Nevertheless, doing so may well be worth the effort. The best way is to engage in entrepreneurial behavior. Successful entrepreneurial experiences can lead to development of new ways of thinking and spur motivation.

The following Self-Management Competency feature provides a brief profile of the personal attributes and struggles that are instrumental in the entrepreneurial success of Jay Goltz. He is the founder and CEO of the Goltz Group, headquartered in Chicago.[27] The Goltz Group consists of Chicago Art Source (an art gallery for corporate and residential customers—established in 1991), Artists' Frame Shop (the largest custom frame shop in the United States—established in 1978), and Jayson Home & Garden (a sophisticated furnishings and garden store with unique plants, flowers, and accessories—established in 1997).

Self-Management Competency

Jay Goltz, Founder of Goltz Group

Life got bad for Jay Goltz in the spring of 1997. It wasn't any one thing—it was everything: the huge cost overruns on the building he was renovating, the new business (Jayson Home & Garden) he was launching in an industry he didn't understand, the credit line he'd already maxed out, the suppliers he was stringing along because he couldn't pay them. In the midst of all this, Goltz had to fire his second chief financial officer in two years. He was also concerned with the problems his son was having in school. This raised questions in Goltz's mind about his own shortcomings as a parent.

It was, he says, the worst period of his life. He remembers lying in bed, tossing and turning, unable to sleep more than three hours a night.

Goltz comments: "I just had this horrible, dark feeling. I can't really describe it. It was circuit overload. I had so many things to worry about. Yes, my first start-up (Artists' Frame Shop) had been stressful, but this was different. This was self-imposed. I didn't *have* to buy that building and go into a business I knew nothing about. Was I out of my mind?"

Goltz survived the experience. Today, the store he launched that year, Jayson Home & Garden, is thriving, as are the other businesses that make up the Goltz Group. Oddly enough, the ordeal Goltz went through in 1997 is seen as a personal growth experience by him. It was the beginning of a major change in his perspective on business, forc-

ing him to start thinking about fundamental issues he'd never considered before—such as "How big is big enough?" And even "What is success?"

Not until the harrowing spring of 1997 did it dawn on Goltz that there might be something wrong with his endless need to do more. Goltz remarks: "Some successful entrepreneurs have a demon they have to get rid of. For me, it was having to do as much as I could. I always worried, 'Am I missing an opportunity? Am I leaving money on the table?' How do you turn that off? How do you keep the success bug from turning into the success disease?" In 2004, after the failure of an Internet business called FramerSelect, Goltz came to terms with himself and his goals. He stated: "I realized I'd been delusional. I'd been reckless with the money, and I didn't need to be. My other businesses were slowly but surely coming along and

doing just fine. I thought, *You know what? Having calm, controlled growth is good.* I would never have said that before. Never. I'd actually heard someone say it when I was in my twenties, and I'd thought, *You're a wimp.* I'd always thought that, for me to be happy, I had to have phenomenal growth and turn this into a giant company. It didn't occur to me that there are a lot of really happy people with very nice $10 million companies making good profits, and that those individuals are often way happier than ones with companies 10 times their size. That's what it comes down to. Happiness is not who's got the biggest company. Happiness is a whole lot of other things."

To learn more about this organization, visit *www.goltzgroup.com.*

The dimensions of the self-management competency illustrated through Jay Goltz include (1) willingness to admit mistakes, (2) showing perseverance in the face of obstacles and bouncing back from failure, (3) eventually striking a reasonable balance between work and other life activities so that neither aspect of living is neglected, and (4) analyzing and learning from work and life experiences.

Strategic Action Competency

Entrepreneurial success is often attributed to opportunistic behavior and being in the right place at the right time. Opportunity and luck may play some role in success, but sound strategic decisions also are important. Studies of long-term successful entrepreneurs reveal several strategic practices that include[28]

▸ delivering products and services that are perceived as high quality and that are seen by its customers or clients as adding value,

▸ developing or improving products and services on a regular basis,

▸ generating new customers or clients that expand revenue,

▸ focusing marketing expenditures and developing customer-oriented employees,

▸ maintaining financial control of the firm, and

▸ establishing a strong commitment to ethical practices.

These common strategic practices are not necessarily formulated early in the lives of these entrepreneurs' firms. Many of these practices emerged through the entrepreneurs' daily decisions. Making decisions that support growth is an ongoing activity that occurs day in and day out. Thus, a good approach is to treat a new venture like an experiment. It should be guided by a clear strategic plan focused on satisfying customers. Of course, decisions about how to achieve the goals should be based on trying various approaches and learning by observing what happens. Chapter 7 addresses various concepts and issues relevant to the strategic action competency for both entrepreneurs and managers of large established business firms.

Snapshot

"At the end of every day . . . I always ask myself two questions: Did we do what we said we were going to do? Was it what the customer wanted? Someone told me . . . you're not selling anything . . . you are finding a person who has a problem . . . and you're helping them solve their problem! This was a dramatic turning point in how I look at business!"

Carolyn A. Minerich, Founder and CEO, Carmin Industries, Alabama

Snapshot

"Do your homework prior to starting the business. Make sure the market truly needs your service or product. Finally, make sure you can differentiate your service or product from the competition in a way that is beneficial to the customer. Stay focused on your goals, but be flexible enough to modify your business plan to match what the market is truly asking for. As evidence of why this is important: 75 percent of my firm's revenue today is from services we did not offer in my original business plan."

Daniel Driesenga, Founder and CEO, Driesenga & Associates

INC. magazine recently administered the Test of Attentional and Interpersonal Style (TAIS) to successful *INC.* 500 CEO entrepreneurs. The TAIS is a 144-item instrument often used by large corporations, the U.S. military, and other groups.[29] According to the folklore, successful entrepreneurs are quick on their feet—great at making quick decisions in the heat of the moment, but not much good at long-term strategic thinking. Not so, according to the TAIS results.

The test divides people into three "attentional styles." These styles reflect how people see the world, process information, and come up with new ideas and solutions to problems. People high in "awareness" read people and situations and respond based on intuition. People high in "analysis" see the world as problems to be solved and tend to think strategically. "Action" people focus their attention narrowly on getting things done.

You'd think the *INC.* 500 CEO entrepreneurs would fall into the "action" category. In fact, their dominant attentional style is analysis—the group scores in the 92nd percentile on the ability to think strategically. Another surprise: They also scored 25 percent higher than chief executives in general on awareness, or the ability to read a situation. But that doesn't mean they're slow to act. These successful entrepreneurial leaders score higher than 84 percent of test-takers on decision-making speed.[30]

Planning and Administration Competency

Though plans typically have to be changed along the way, planning is nevertheless important for entrepreneurs and their companies.[31] Nearly 80 percent of successful entrepreneurs put their plans in writing. Their planning horizon is relatively short. Half the time it covers less than three years. Written monthly plans that cover periods of 12 to 24 months are common. As the time frame grows longer, the plans tend to become more general, such as by stating only annual goals.

Executing the plan is important, too. Staffing activities can be key in the start-up phase. When funds are scarce and the company has no track record, attracting top-notch employees can be difficult. Founders often do most of the crucial work themselves. But to grow, they must hire new talent. Once the talent has been brought on board, successful entrepreneurs tie a portion of their key employees' compensation to performance against the plan, on a semiannual or annual basis. They also use the plan to work with employees to set job performance standards.

Teamwork Competency

Successful entrepreneurs are extremely hard working and task oriented, but they aren't lone wolves—one person can do only so much alone. Unless they can build effective teams, their organization's growth will eventually reach a limit.[32] Successful entrepreneurs are self-starters who usually support subordinates enthusiastically. Entrepreneurs also maintain good relationships with their venture partners.

The dimensions of the teamwork competency discussed in Chapter 1 (see especially Table 1.4) are just as relevant to successful entrepreneurs of firms with a few employees as they are for managers in large-scale organizations such as General Electric or Toyota. Also, the presentation in Chapter 17, *Working in Teams*, provides many insights for fostering entrepreneurial success.

Texas Nameplate Co. (TNC) relies on a true team approach to run its successful small business.

© Texas Nameplate Company

Teamwork is a key ingredient of the work life and high-quality results achieved by the Texas Nameplate Co. (TNC), as discussed in the following Teamwork Competency feature.[33] Headquartered in Dallas, Texas, TNC is a small (43 employees), privately held family business that produces nameplates, identification tags, and labels for a variety of products, including high-pressure valves, oil field equipment, and computers. Through its chemical etching, screen printing, and photo engraving processes, the company places information—such as vendor names, model numbers, pressure limits, installation procedures, and safety warnings—on nameplates. It is the first small business to win the Malcolm Baldrige National Quality Award twice—1998 and 2004.

Teamwork Competency

Teams and Quality at TNC

Dale Crownover, the president and CEO of the Texas Nameplate Company (TNC), emphasizes that quality is everyone's responsibility at TNC. The company shuns the traditional, hierarchical approach to leadership in favor of a more flat approach. The company is not organized into a typical command structure of delegated authority or power. Rather, its leaders respect everyone's contributions as equally necessary, desirable, and valuable. Management and employees work together in teams.

John Darrouzet, the vice president and general counsel, comments: "We all have a role to play, so it's become a more flat organization. We call it next level leadership that's built on mutual respect. We guide the business based on the quote 'Fear is useless, what is needed is trust.' In the end, fear is useless if that's a company's only motivating force. Leaders need to trust their people and ensure their people trust them."

In an effort to deploy information visually, TNC has moved from selectively distributed paper reports to companywide, instantaneous data displays. TNC developed several intranet-based programs—the New Hotrod, the Real-Time Dashboard, and the Pipeline Dashboard—to collect and aggregate data for decision making and make data and information readily available to employees, customers, and suppliers.

The New Hotrod is the name of TNC's employee intranet. Besides hosting each employee's personal Web page, this site helps make company meetings transparent. The intranet site is projected onto the walls of meeting rooms. Also, the group uses Microsoft Front Page to take minutes, which become immediately available to everyone in the company. There's no paper involved, which has helped TNC become an almost paperless company. At informal and formal meetings, the leaders review documented processes as well as results—including charts with targeted goals, links throughout the intranet, and all other measures. The leaders share and invite comments about the significance of results at a variety of meetings. There is a continuing effort to encourage everyone to share what that they have learned with each other. TNC has a robust incentive program to reward team-based and individual-based performance. It is available to all employees.

To learn more about this organization, visit *www.nameplate.com.*

Communication Competency

For a budding entrepreneur with an idea and ambition, but little else to work with, being able to communicate effectively is essential to gaining the cooperation and support needed to turn a vision into reality.[34] The communication that occurs in larger companies often entails speeches, written reports, formal proposals, and scheduled reviews. In new ventures, much critical communication is face to face, informal, and unscheduled. All of the interpersonal communication concepts and techniques discussed in Chapter 16, *Communicating Effectively,* apply as much to the entrepreneur as to a manger in a large organization.

Recall our discussion of *INC.* magazine's profile of successful entrepreneurs. To assess communication skills, TAIS puts people into three categories based on whether their primary means of persuasion is to express ideas, criticism, or support. You might think that the successful entrepreneurs would fall primarily into the ideas camp. Successful entrepreneurs are often portrayed in the media as bold visionaries who lead by getting people to buy into their ambitious new ideas. You might also expect them to be highly critical of those who fail to deliver.

In fact, successful entrepreneurs score higher than 82 percent of the population on their ability to express support and encouragement. This is higher than any other group except high-performing salespeople. It also suggests that rather than conforming to the stereotype of the hard-charging, bullying entrepreneur, the *INC.* successful entrepreneurs succeeded by helping other people—their employees, partners, investors, suppliers—become successful themselves.[35]

The following Ethical Challenge feature reports on some of the communication challenges faced by Katie Sutliff Lang, who is an ethics officer for a small not-for-profit organization, the Ethics Resource Center, headquartered in Washington, D.C.[36] As you read about Sutliff Lang's experiences, think about the managerial competencies that seem to be important to her role.

Ethical Challenge

Katie Sutliff Lang, Ethics Officer, Ethics Resource Center

"I have tried to discipline myself so that, when people come talk with me, I actively ask whether they are talking with me just as a friend and colleague or whether they're coming to me as the ethics officer. Also, during a staff meeting, I let people know that I would be asking this question of them and I asked their help as well. Although we're still learning at it, the system really has helped. I feel comfortable asking people to tell me what they are looking for from a conversation. Often, my colleagues have come to me and, from the start said, 'I need to talk with you as our ethics officer.' It's a simple thing, but it definitely aids me in understanding what I should and should not do with what we discuss; it makes things much clearer for me. Whether it is my colleagues or I who initiate it, defining the purpose of the conversation gives us both piece of mind and enables me to better meet their needs.

"I make an effort to discuss with my coworker at some point in the conversation:

▶ After having a chance to talk through things, do you feel that any more needs to be done?

▶ Because it's always best to deal with situations at the lowest level possible, would you feel comfortable confronting him/her directly? If so, let's talk/think through what that conversation might be like.

▶ I can talk about this situation with him/her. I'll probably bring it up by saying things like. . . . Does that accurately represent and address your concern? Are you comfortable with that?

▶ (If necessary) I think this is something that Pat Moira (president) needs to know about. If you want to talk about it with her directly, I can go with you and help you talk/think through it beforehand. Or, if you'd prefer, I can tell her myself."

To learn more about this organization, visit *www.ethics.org*.

Multicultural Competency

Successful entrepreneurs often have to interact directly with employees, customers, suppliers, and others from diverse political, cultural, and economic backgrounds. These interactions often take place in the context of international business even for smaller entrepreneurial firms. Smaller firms are finding customers, suppliers, and partners across the globe. Typically, there are no layers of organization that can buffer the entrepreneur from having to understand, appreciate, and respond to such diversity.[37] Thus, the multicultural competency is critical to fostering relationships. As a reminder of the many types of diversity present within organizations and their immediate environments, refer back to Chapter 1 and Table 1.6, Dimensions of Multicultural Competency. The Small Business Administration has recognized the growing importance of international business to entrepreneurs through its employment of international trade officers who are located throughout the United States.[38]

Specialized Knowledge

Many entrepreneurs demonstrate specialized knowledge in a particular domain, often bringing some related experience to their new business ventures. Denise Devine's professional experiences and contacts as a result of working at Campbell Soup Company provided her with specialized knowledge related to launching Devine Foods and Nutripharm.

Joseph Sanda's passion for technology, his ability to envision its future, and his understanding of the importance of providing top-notch customer service are the keys that unlocked the doors to business success for his company, Astute Solutions. This firm is headquartered in Columbus, Ohio, and has grown from a 2-employee operation in 1995 to more than 45 employees with approximately $4 million in annual sales. The firm recently expanded its global reach by opening an office in London. Clients include McDonald's, GeorgiaPacific, and Kroger.

Astute Solutions specializes in consumer relationships management software and solutions for the unique needs of business-to-consumer (B2C) contact centers. The company helps firms manage customer relationships across multiple communication channels, including the Internet, phone, e-mail, and fax. Astute leverages Internet and telephony solutions for completely integrated technology-based B2C solutions. Sanda's specialized technical knowledge was essential to launching Astute Solutions.[39]

Planning Essentials for Entrepreneurs

3.

Outline the planning essentials for potential entrepreneurs.

The Business Plan

Before starting a business, entrepreneurs who are successful typically plan more carefully than those who fail.[40] One tool that helps them do so is the business plan. A business plan *describes the basic idea that is the foundation for the start-up and outlines how that idea can be turned into reality.* Table 6.1 shows the major components of a business plan for new ventures with a few of the guidelines for developing each component. Chapters 7, 8, and 9 present a number of concepts, models, and tools that are useful in the planning process whether it is being done for a start-up or established firm.

One of the challenges in developing a business start-up plan is to avoid exaggeration. Although somewhat tongue-in-check, we present four statements that are illustrative of this problem in statements by entrepreneurs within their business plans:

▶ "We took our best sales guess and divided by 2." *Reality:* We accidentally divided by 0.5.

▶ "We need only a 10 percent market share." *Reality:* So do the other 50 businesses getting funded.

▶ "Customers are clamoring for our product." *Reality:* We have not yet asked them to pay for it. Also, all of our current customers are relatives.

Prospective entrepreneurs must carefully examine factos such as expected revenue, initial investment, and level of competition.

© Photodisc/Photodisc Blue/Getty Images

"Someone once said: If you don't know where you're going, any road will take you there. You need to know exactly where you want to go, what route you're going to take, when you will arrive and what you are to do upon arrival—no guess-work at all. You need to determine whether there is a demand for your service and, if so, what constitutes your market."

Don Doggett, Management Counselor, Counselors to America's Small Business

Table 6.1	Essential Components of a Business Plan for New Ventures

I. Executive Summary
- What, how, why, where, and when must be summarized.

II. Business Description Component
- The name of the business.
- The potential and uniqueness of the new venture.

III. Marketing Component
- Convince investors that sales projections and competition can be met.
- Identify target market, market position, market share, pricing strategy.
- Evaluate all competition and state why and how you will be better than your competitors.
- Identify advertising plans with cost estimates.

IV. Location Component
- Describe the advantages of your location (zoning, tax laws, wage rates). List the production needs in terms of facilities (plant, storage, office space) and equipment (machinery, furnishings, supplies).
- Describe the access to transportation (for shipping and receiving) and labor.
- Indicate proximity to your suppliers.

V. Management Component
- Supply résumés of all key people in the management of your venture.
- Describe the legal structure of your venture (sole proprietorship, partnership, or corporation).
- Give information on how and how much everyone is to be compensated.

VI. Financial Component
- Describe the needed sources for your funds and the uses you intend for the money.
- Develop an estimated budget, cash flow statement, and profit and loss statement.
- Create stages of financing for purposes of allowing evaluation by investors at various points.

VII. Potential Critical-Risks Component
- Any potentially unfavorable industry wide trends, such as price cutting by competitors.
- Design or manufacturing costs in excess of estimates.
- Sales projections not achieved.
- Product development schedule not met.
- Provide some alternative courses of action.

VIII. Milestone Schedule Component
- Develop a timetable or chart to demonstrate when each phase of the venture is to be completed.

IX. Appendix or Bibliography

Adapted from D. F. Kuratko, J. S. Hornsby, and F. J. Sabatine, *The Breakthrough Experience: A Guide to Corporate Entrepreneurship* (Muncie, IN): The Midwest Entrepreneurial Education Center, College of Business, Ball State University, 1999.

▶ "The project is 98 percent complete." *Reality:* To complete the remaining 2 percent will take as long as it took to create the initial 98 percent but will cost twice as much.[41]

Next, we address several issues that are central to planning for and implementing a new business.

Deciding to Buy, Start, or Franchise a Business

Prospective entrepreneurs who have the option to "start or buy" begin by weighting the advantages and disadvantages of each alternative. Sometimes, of course, the decision to start a business is made for them. If they don't have the financial resources necessary to purchase an existing company, they have no choice but to start their own.

Even if they have the resources, suitable businesses may not be available. This situation is likely to be the case if an entrepreneur has a truly new idea.

Buy Strategy. If they have the resources, entrepreneurs often find that buying an existing company—perhaps one that the current owner is having difficulty managing—is a good idea. Leonard Riggio used this approach when he started Barnes & Noble in 1971. He secured a $1.2 million loan to purchase a failing 100-year-old bookstore on Fifth Avenue in New York City. Today, Barnes & Noble is the largest bookseller in the United States with approximately 42,000 full-time and part-time employees and more than 900 stores under the following names: Barnes & Noble, Bookstop, Bookstar, and B. Dalton. Through its stores and online operations (such as *www.barnes&noble.com*), the firm sells approximately 450 million books per year and stocks over 1 million unique titles in its warehouse.[42]

Buying an existing firm is tricky and may involve considerable risk. The seller may not reveal some hidden problems—and may not even be aware of others. Also, many a new owner has thought that he or she was buying goodwill, only to have the previous owner open a competing firm and lure away the established clientele. A prospective buyer is wise to specify, in the purchase agreement, restrictions limiting the previous owner's ability or right to compete with the new owner. Such restrictions may limit the types of businesses that the previous owner can operate in a certain area and/or for a stipulated period of time.

Learning about businesses available for purchase and negotiating the purchase agreement often require the assistance of experts. Bankers, accountants, attorneys, and other professionals may be aware of an opportunity to buy a business before it is publicly announced. A business broker may help the prospective owner find a firm and act as intermediary for the sale. Usually, an attorney prepares or reviews the sale documents.

Start-Up Strategy. As we discussed, new ventures may develop through business incubation where entrepreneurs develop the competencies and knowledge needed for launching their own businesses. When deciding what types of business to own, people should begin by examining their competencies and the contacts they can bring to their possible venture. Prospective entrepreneurs should carefully examine factors such as expected revenue, initial investment required, and intensity of competition. Such an analysis often turns up existing businesses that may be purchased. In addition to exploring the Internet, business magazines such as *INC.*, *Entrepreneur*, and *Venturing* can be good sources of ideas for new ventures. Much of our presentation in this chapter has focused on the start-up strategy.

Franchise Strategy. A middle ground between starting a business and buying an existing business is to invest in and run a franchise. A franchise *is a business operated by someone (the franchisee) to whom a franchiser grants the right to market a good or service*. It is estimated that approximately 800,000 establishments are operating within the United States in franchise systems.[43] The franchisee pays a franchise fee and a percentage of the sales to the franchiser. In return, the franchisee often receives financial help, training, guaranteed supplies, a protected market, and technical assistance in site selection, accounting, and operations management. McDonald's, Domino's Pizza, and Jiffy Lube, to name a few, all use franchises to market their products. Those who enter into a franchise agreement obtain a brand name that customers may know. However, franchisees are their own bosses only to a degree. They can't run their businesses as they please. They have to conform to standards set by a franchiser, pay a fee to the franchiser, and they may have to buy the franchiser's goods and services. But many people want to operate a franchise in the first place for these very reasons.

The success of the franchise strategy, just as with the start-up strategy, is improved if a well-developed business plan is in place. Moreover, the development of such a plan does not need to be a lonely process. For example, SCORE (Service Corps of Retired Executives) provides free and confidential counseling and low-cost workshop services to help individuals write a business plan, apply for a loan, and become more confident small business owners. SCORE has over 10,000 volunteer business counselors located throughout the United States, often in affiliation with Small Business Development Centers.

The following Planning and Administration Competency feature reports on how a SCORE counselor guided and assisted Shane Beard in the development of his business plan related to the purchase of a FASTSIGNS franchise.[44] FASTSIGNS has approximately 500 franchisees. The firm provides state-of-the-art computer technology to create custom signs, graphics, and more.[45]

Planning and Administration Competency

Shane Beard's FASTSIGNS Franchise Plan

When Shane Beard first met with a SCORE counselor, the counselor was not impressed. After reading Shane's business plan to purchase a FAST-SIGNS franchise in Naperville, Illinois (a suburb of Chicago)—a plan that had taken weeks to prepare—the counselor simply said, "Start over."

Shane recalls: "He kept calling my plan a 'scrapbook,' and said that it told him nothing about what I wanted to do. He didn't want to discuss the plan in detail, saying that I had to overhaul it first." A lot of conflicting emotions went through Shane's mind as he rode the train home. He had worked so hard to get to this point. After being downsized from his job, he had endured many frustrating months of job hunting until he found an opportunity to buy an existing FAST-SIGNS store almost literally in his backyard.

Not one to back away from a challenge, Shane set out to prove that he did indeed know what he was doing. He redrafted the plan by using most of the counselor's suggestions. Shane took his plan back to the SCORE counselor. This time, the response was markedly different. Shane comments: "He read the plan, looked up at me and said: 'This is what I wanted to see.' He admitted that while he didn't know the sign business specifically, he did know what makes a successful business, and what banks want to see before they lend money. My revised plan did just that."

The counselor revised a few sections, then sent Shane to the banks. He wasn't immediately successful—some lenders questioned whether Shane could revive a franchise that had not performed well in the past few years. On his fifth try, a banker said yes. Shane states: "I am so glad the counselor made those changes to my plan. Along with helping me get the loan, that business plan served as my calling card for securing the other services I needed, like a lawyer and a contract accountant."

After making the purchase and completing his management training, Shane took over the Naperville FASTSIGNS store in 1996. In his first 12 months, he boosted the store's sales by nearly 50 percent and has enjoyed increased success every year since. Recently, Shane moved to a new location in Naperville that features the new store décor adopted by the franchiser.

To learn more about this organization, visit www.fastsigns.com.

Other Options. Other options the prospective entrepreneur may consider are suggested in the following questions:

▶ Is there a way that I can begin the enterprise in stages or with a limited investment?

▶ Can I run the business at first from my home?

▶ Can I continue working for someone else and put in time on my own business after hours?

▶ To what extent can I draw on relatives to help me, perhaps simply by answering the phone while I work at my regular job?

Assessing Affordable Loss

Successful entrepreneurs often use the principle of affordable loss—*the conscious determination of the amount of resources (money, time, and effort) entrepreneurs are willing to commit to an idea, which, in turn, influences the choice of strategies and methods needed to generate early revenues.* The principle of affordable loss helps potential entrepreneurs resolve the tension between excessive analysis and quick action. Analysis increases a new business's chance of success but may decrease the probability of creating a business in the first place. Ironically, the endless search for more information and analysis may lead to more uncertainty and doubt about the opportunity.

In contrast, a bias toward quick action increases the probability of creating a business but decreases the probability of success. The rush to market often results in flawed strategies, poor goods and services, and insufficient resources. The principle of affordable loss helps entrepreneurs minimize risks while following their opportunity.[46] The dilemma facing potential entrepreneurs may be summed up by the saying "Paralysis by analysis or extinction by instinct."

The planning process and market assessment techniques described in Chapters 7 and 9 may be overlooked in planning for business ownership. Entrepreneurs may be so excited about their business ideas that they assume others will feel the same way. Their market research may consist of asking the opinions of a few friends or relatives about the salability of a product.

Finding Funds

Entrepreneurs are likely to overestimate their sales and underestimate their costs. The new-venture plan should identify anticipated costs of opening the business (e.g.,

deposits, fixtures, and incorporation fees). It should also include a month-by-month projection of the cost of goods or services sold and the firm's operating expenses for the first one to three years.

The entrepreneur must plan for obtaining funds to handle expenses associated with the start-up phase that revenues can't initially cover. Getting financial support is one of the most important activities that differentiates people who just think about starting their own business from those who actually start one.[47] Furthermore, the larger the amount of resources obtained, the better the odds are of being able to continue in business for the long term.[48] Common sources of funds and

The Eurotower building headquarters of the Central European Bank, Frankfurt, Germany.

© Jon Riley/Workbook Stock/Jupiter Images

support include (1) the entrepreneur and other members of the team, family, and friends; (2) financial institutions such as banks; (3) venture capital firms; and (4) business angels. Let's consider two of these here.

Venture Capitalist. A venture capitalist *typically provides equity (ownership) financing for start-up and young, rapidly growing enterprises.* In contrast, banks and other financial institutions provide debt (loan) financing. Venture capitalists get their funds and profits back if, and only if, their equity stake (ownership shares) rises in value or if sufficient dividends are paid. In brief, venture capitalists become part owners of the business by providing funds. Venture capitalists are organized as formal businesses, such as Top Gun in Palo Alto, California.

Because venture capitalists aren't subject to the same state and federal regulations as banks, they can take greater risks in making investments. Generally, venture capitalists expect their investments to provide returns of 25 to 35 percent annually. To increase the likelihood of this, they get much more actively involved in the businesses they fund than bankers do. Indeed, according to one recent study, venture capitalists spend 40 percent of their time monitoring businesses they have funded and serving as consultants or directors.[49]

Business Angel. A business angel *is a private individual who invests directly in firms and receives an equity stake in return.* Often such a person acts as a business adviser to the founder. Business angels may make less stringent demands than do venture capitalists on controlling the actions of the entrepreneur. Angels often truly enjoy seeing a business grow and watching a start-up venture mature into a viable business. Business angel Norm Brodsky has had this experience many times as an entrepreneur himself and now enjoys supporting others. "Yes, making money is important. I wouldn't go into deals unless I thought I could get my capital back and make a good return. But I really don't do this type of investing for the money anymore. I'm more interested in helping people get started in business."[50]

A sound business plan is essential for demonstrating to potential lenders and investors the viability of the proposed enterprise. Once funding has been obtained, entrepreneurs need to provide their financial backers with timely information and establish a trust relationship with them. This approach tends to reduce the extent to which investors intrude into the business, and it enhances the likelihood of their reinvesting in the future.

Going Global

Most new-venture entrepreneurs begin with a domestic focus. A growing number, however, establish their firms as global start-ups or enter the international market through export firms. Exports from small firms in the United States account for 31 percent of total merchandise and service export sales. The number of small firms engaged in exporting has more than tripled since 1987.[51] Because going global poses some special challenges to management, this strategic decision should be made only after very careful study and analysis. Figure 6.2 depicts the key factors affecting the decision about whether to establish a domestic or global start-up. Specific questions include the following[52]:

1. Are the best human resources available in several countries? If yes, it may be easier to operate as a global company than to convince potential employees to move to your hometown.

2. Would foreign financing be easier or more suitable? If yes, consider whether the advantages of foreign financing are sufficient to offset the advantages of relying on domestic sources to meet other resource needs.

Figure 6.2 Factors that Favor a Global Start-Up

3. Do target customers require a venture to be global? If yes, a global approach may be necessary to acquire a reasonable share of the market.

4. Will worldwide communication lead to quick responses from competitors in other countries? If yes, the best domestic defense may be an international offense.

5. Will worldwide sales be required to support the venture? If initial expenses (e.g., R&D, manufacturing) will be high, worldwide sales may be necessary to generate sufficient revenue to support the venture.

6. Will changing the government policies, procedures, product designs, and advertising strategies of your established domestic company be more difficult than building a globally effective firm from the beginning?

In going global, the importance of the multicultural competency is not to be underestimated. This is illustrated in the following Multicultural Competency feature. It presents a sampling of the learning experiences, from initial failure and eventual success, of the management team at the Henry Estate Winery and the firm's distributor.[53] This winery is headquartered in Umpqua, Oregon.

Multicultural Competency

Henry Estate Winery's Export Journey to China

Henry Estate Winery is no stranger to exporting. For a number of years, it has shipped cases to Canada, the United Kingdom, and Japan. So how much harder could it be to add China to the list? Several years ago, Doyle Hinman, the winery's marketing director, had some marketing materials translated into Mandarin, slapped some Chinese-language labels on the bottles, and found a distributor, Portland, Oregon–based American Pacific, with contacts in China. Soon, 700 cases of pinot noir were en route to China. Scott Henry III, the founder of the winery, comments: "We were prepared for the wine to sell. We were set to handle a demand of 500 cases a month."

But four months later, most of that wine was still on the shelves in Chinese stores. Hinman and American Pacific's Terry Protto flew to China to investigate. They were stunned by what they found. No one in China—not the local distributors, the retailers, or consumers—seemed to know much about red wine. For one thing, the Henry Estate wine, which is expensive, was being sold in the equivalent of convenience stores. Bottles were being delivered on the backs of motorcycles and were often left sitting in the sun for hours. Hinman remarks: "I thought some things about wine were just known. Not there."

Having botched their first export initiative to China, Henry Estate and American Pacific leaders were determined that their second effort would be more successful. Terry Protto of American Pacific comments: "Our new mantra was 'assume nothing.'" The first step was to get a better understanding of who their customers were and how to get the wine in their hands. Protto tapped one of his Chinese associates who began canvassing government officials, young banking and finance executives, owners of chic restaurants and bars, and Western expatriates—anyone who seemed likely to be a wine drinker. He discovered that

Chinese buyers are as interested in the status that wine confers as they are in the way it tastes. He also learned that the government-controlled Chinese Central Television network had launched a series of ads touting the health benefits of drinking red wine—which could provide a nice marketing bounce.

The Henry Estate team abandoned the small retail stores and used their Chinese connections to get the wine on menus at upscale hotels and restaurants in Beijing and Shanghai. Protto, who is fluent in Mandarin, gave tutorials to waiters, showing them how to use pinot noir wine with food. He developed an incentive plan to encourage servers to recommend Henry Estate. Turning their attention to merchandising, Henry Estate began packaging individual bottles and pairs of bottles in a rustic wooden box. Stenciled on the side was "Oregon Pinot Noir" and a pair of wineglasses. Hanging around the bottle's neck was an 18-minute DVD demonstrating how the wine is produced and how it should be consumed. "Chinese customers often whip out their mini-DVD players and watch the video right there at the table," Protto says. These and other efforts have paid off.

To learn more about this organization, visit *www.henryestate.com.*

Managing a Family-Owned Business

Family-owned businesses are an integral part of the U.S. economy. Unfortunately, a family business too often results in family feuds, which can destroy both the family and the business. For the employees of such a firm, getting caught in the cross fire is an occupational hazard that no one really knows how to prevent.[54] Family feuding often leaves employees wondering whether to look for new employment. Karen Langley (not her real name) explained why she eventually left the small family-owned company that she once worked for. The father, his sons, and their cousins fought constantly over the business, engaging in behavior that could best be described as backstabbing. "It was very uncomfortable," she says. Distrust within the family was high, and it eventually spread beyond the family. One family member began accusing employees of stealing and began lurking around trying to watch everyone. "It really became impossible for me to stay there," Langley explained.[55]

Not every family business has these problems, of course. Janice Bryant Howroyd started her family business ACT*1 Personnel Services, in part to serve her family. It is headquartered in Torrance, California. The firm has grown to 70 offices and 375 employees nationwide. She employs eight brothers, sisters, nieces, and nephews who handle everything from marketing and accounting to technology. Her three children own 49 percent of the business. Howroyd owns the other 51 percent.[56]

The Oasis Day Spa, headquartered in New York City, was founded by Marti and Bruce Schoenberg. When asked how they have been able to work together since successful spousal teams are rare, they responded:

▶ Bruce: "We have a 'firewall' between business and work. In addition, I don't go into her area, she doesn't come to my area. That's good."

▶ Marti: "Early on, Bruce and I established boundaries regarding our roles here. But at the same time, working together means we need to clearly communicate with each other, which in many ways is also the key to a successful marriage."[57]

Figure 6.3 outlines the interlocking set of recommendations that increase the likelihood of a successful family business and one that will prosper from one generation to the next. These recommendations include the following:

1. *Settle conflicts as they come up.* If a family member does something on the job that makes another angry, correcting the problem requires that it be brought into the open quickly. This requires the use of the communication and teamwork competencies. Particularly problematic is how to balance the need to make decisions that acknowledge both economic criteria and family obligation criteria. Various family members may feel differently about the importance of these two sets of criteria. This makes disagreements difficult to resolve through consensus if thought has not been given in advance as to how conflicts will be resolved quickly.

2. *Decide who is responsible for what and who has authority.* Jobs in family businesses probably shouldn't be too narrowly defined. Families should recognize each other's areas of expertise to determine who is best able to make decisions in various areas. Moreover, the types of decisions to be addressed by the family as a whole should be identified in advance.

3. *Agree on the hiring criteria to be used before considering any particular family member.* Being a daughter, son, spouse, uncle, etc., should not be enough. The competencies to ensure successful performance in the particular job must be present. It is better to experience the "hard feelings" that may come from not hiring a family member than the much greater harm to the business and "fights" involved in firing an unmotivated or incompetent family member.

4. *Use a board of advisers or board of directors to review and recommend key courses of action.* Outside advisers or board members can be especially helpful in providing guidance and a fresh perspective in assessing options.

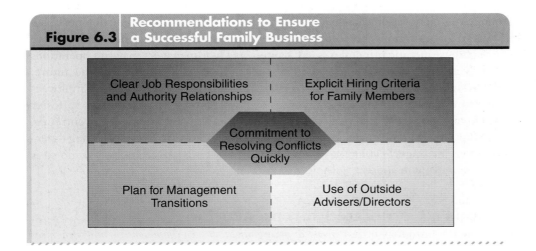

Figure 6.3 | Recommendations to Ensure a Successful Family Business

Clear Job Responsibilities and Authority Relationships

Explicit Hiring Criteria for Family Members

Commitment to Resolving Conflicts Quickly

Plan for Management Transitions

Use of Outside Advisers/Directors

5. *Plan for management transitions.* It might address issues such as succession during management transitions when the current head of the business steps down or dies; the conditions for disposing of or reallocating the equity in the business; policies in the determination of salary levels, bonuses, and dividend payments; and how a decision will be made on whether and when to sell the business.

The effective use of a board of directors (or advisers) can assist a family business in forming and implementing all of the recommendations presented. Of course, boards of directors are useful for all private companies, not just family businesses. When operating well, the greatest advantages of such boards include (1) providing unbiased and unflinching advice; (2) forcing the top executives to focus on short-term and long-term goals, not just day-to-day operational issues; and (3) serving as a source of specialty advice, contacts, and business referrals.[58]

4.

Describe the basic essentials of corporate entrepreneurship.

Corporate Entrepreneurship

What Is Corporate Entrepreneurship?

There is no single agreed-on definition of corporate entrepreneurship.[59] At its core, corporate entrepreneurship *refers to the development, promotion, and implementation of innovative initiatives in established firms for the purpose of generating growth and, thus, profits under risky or uncertain conditions.* Corporate entrepreneurship includes those components of entrepreneurship discussed in the first section of this chapter: (1) the development of new products, services, or technologies; (2) significant and novel improvements to the firm's existing products or services; (3) entering into unique, underserved, or new markets; and (4) developing new and novel delivery systems or distribution channels for the firm's products and services.[60]

Corporate entrepreneurship is now essential for the long-term survival of any established firm. Once considered a contradiction in terms, corporate entrepreneurship has become widely accepted in successful companies, such as General Electric, Disney, and Oracle.

Consider for a moment why an organization exists. It has a mission and goals to be accomplished, which require the efforts of more than one person. At the very least, a business has a long-term goal of satisfying customers so that it can become and remain profitable. Fundamental to organizing is dividing up the work. Managers may think that they have organized successfully when they have brought different people together, minimized conflict, increased stability, and reduced uncertainty. But they may overlook the effects of those organizing efforts on entrepreneurial tendencies. Is the new climate conducive to innovation change? Will disruption be tolerated? Is redirection possible?

Large organizations are often formally structured for efficiency and operate through bureaucratic principles (see Chapter 2). Their managers may run operations in such a way that the same activities will continue indefinitely into the future. Obviously, this approach often is at odds with innovation and change. Employees come to take the working environment for granted, and individual efforts to foster change may be met with resistance. What then can be done to encourage entrepreneurship when a company needs to be revitalized? The answer lies in changing—perhaps even inciting a revolution in—an organization's practices. One way to do so is for the company to support corporate entrepreneurship.

Who Is a Corporate Entrepreneur?

A corporate entrepreneur *is someone in an organization who champions turning new ideas into profitable realities.*[61] Lou Dobbs, creator of *CNNFN*, is an example of a corporate entreprenuer. *CNNFN* was Cable Network News' (CNN) financial news station until 2004. After that, it evolved into *CNN Money.com.* Lou Dobbs took the lead in creating *CNNFN.* He championed getting the station up and running. Initially, Dobbs served as the anchor for the channel's daily financial news program. He now serves as the anchor to *Lou Dobbs Tonight.*[62]

Not every employee can become a successful corporate entrepreneur. It requires unusually well-developed strategic action, teamwork, and communication competencies. For example, the person who is attempting to establish a new corporate venture must have a dream. Yet this dream may be at odds with what others in the organization are doing. So, to establish the new venture, the individual will have to sell that dream to top management while simultaneously challenging the organiza-

Lou Dobbs, left, creator of CNNFN and veteran CNN anchorman, is an example of a corporate entrepreneur. Dobbs speaks with Andy Parson, technical projects manager, prior to the show's debut in December of 1995. CNNFN was Cable Network News' (CNN) financial news station until 2004.

tion's beliefs and assumptions. Having successfully communicated a dream that others buy into, developing the venture requires that the corporate entrepreneur build a team to work on the venture, crossing departmental lines, structures, and reporting systems. Entrepreneurial activities can cause some disruption, particularly in large organizations where each manager's "turf" has been staked out carefully over the years, so being diplomatic and avoiding win–lose conflicts is essential. Even organizational diplomats aren't immune to the frustrations that occur throughout the establishment of any new entrepreneurial venture. Thus, a strong support team is needed to carry the corporate entrepreneur through endless trials and tribulations.

How Is Corporate Entrepreneurship Fostered?

Top management can foster an entrepreneurial culture by eliminating obstacles and providing incentives.[63] Organizations that redirect themselves through innovation have the following characteristics:

▶ *Commitment from senior management.* This commitment must include a willingness to tolerate failure. Top managers must regularly communicate their commitment to entrepreneurial activities—and back their words with actions.

▶ *Flexible organization design.* Entrepreneurial organizations are designed for fast action. Management gives information—and the authority to make decisions—to those best positioned to react to changing market conditions. These people often are first-line managers.

▶ *Autonomy of the venture team.* Closely aligned with flexibility is maintaining a hands-off policy in day-to-day management of the team charged with implementing an innovation. Successful corporate entrepreneurs usually are allowed considerable leeway in their actions.

▶ *Competent and talented people who exhibit entrepreneurial behaviors and attitudes.* A willingness to volunteer isn't sufficient reason to assign someone to a venture team—that person also must be competent in that or a related area. Competent volunteers usually have experience in, or have received training for, new-venture creation. Some companies conduct formal training programs; others establish mentor or coaching relationships. Even so, most entrepreneurs have experienced at least one failure before achieving successes that more than offset early losses.

▶ *Incentives and rewards for risk taking.* Corporate entrepreneurs may not be willing to risk their careers and undergo the frustration of forcing change only for the satisfaction of giving life to their ventures. The developers of successful ventures should be generously compensated. Entrepreneurship within the firm should not be a dead-end activity; rather, it should be linked to an identifiable career path of advancement.

▶ *An appropriately designed control system.* Nothing is more stifling to an entrepreneurial initiative than excessive red tape. Nevertheless, despite the potential contradiction between strong controls and the entrepreneurial spirit, senior management can't give up its accountability for new-venture projects. Controlling internal innovations means collecting and analyzing data that enable management to predict, to a reasonable degree, where the new-venture team is headed. It also involves ensuring that the team understands the difference between entrepreneurial behavior and irresponsible risk taking.

Chapter 12, *Guiding Organizational Change and Innovation*, provides more discussion about how to change an organization to encourage corporate entrepreneurship.

Chapter Summary . . . .

Entrepreneurial activity, whether through new business start-ups or corporate entrepreneurship, is one of the keys to long-term employment growth and rising standards of living.

Learning Goals . . . .

1. Explain the nature of entrepreneurship and the impact that the environment has on it.

Entrepreneurship involves the creation of new business activity in the economy. It is often done by starting a new company. Some entrepreneurs are creators of new business activity within a large organization. Entrepreneurs give various reasons for starting their own companies; two popular ones are that they want to be their own bosses and have more control over their lives. Rapid technological change, low interest rates, and high immigration rates all stimulate entrepreneurial activity. Local conditions that meet the needs of entrepreneurs—such as a good labor force and easy networking—also can stimulate entrepreneurial activity.

2. Describe the competencies that contribute to entrepreneurs' success.

As illustrated in the Self-Management Competency feature, the personal attributes of successful entrepreneurs include the need for achievement, desire for independence, self-confidence, and willingness to make personal sacrifices. These attributes often are developed early in life and seem to be shaped greatly by the family environment. Having a parent who was an entrepreneur and being involved in entrepreneurial activities increase the likelihood that a child will become an entrepreneur. Entrepreneurs often possess specialized knowledge, based on formal education and/or work experiences. All of the managerial competencies are as important for entrepreneurs as they are for other managers. Self-management, strategic action, planning and administration, teamwork, communication, and multicultural competencies are especially important for entrepreneurs.

3. Outline the planning essentials for potential entrepreneurs.

Entrepreneurs can improve their chances for success by creating a business plan and following it. A few of the questions a prospective entrepreneur must consider include these: (1) Have I developed a business plan that addresses all of the key issues? (2) Should I buy, start, or franchise a business? (3) What is my level of affordable loss? (4) How much will it cost, and where will I obtain the start-up funds? (5) Should I start a domestic or global organization? (6) What is involved in running a successful family business? Operating a family business leads to some unique opportunities and some special problems. Failure to manage them can spell doom for the firm as well as the family.

4. Describe the basic essentials of corporate entrepreneurship.

Corporate entrepreneurship often involves turning ideas into marketable products and services within large organizations. Fostering corporate entrepreneurship and successfully marketing new ventures require a commitment by top management, flexible organizational structures, autonomy of the venture team, competent and talented corporate entrepreneurs, incentives and rewards for risk taking, and appropriate control systems.

Key Terms and Concepts ....

Business angel	Corporate entrepreneurship	Principle of affordable loss
Business incubation	Entrepreneurship	Small business
Business plan	Family business	Venture capitalist
Corporate entrepreneur	Franchise	

Questions for Discussion and Reflective Thinking ....

1. "Opportunities rarely fall into an entrepreneur's lap; they must be discovered or created."[64] How did Denise Devine of Devine Foods and Nutripharm, Inc., discover or create her entrepreneurial opportunity?

2. What personal resources, other than money, did Denise Devine have that were vital to the success of Devine Foods and Nutripharm, Inc.?

3. How can business incubation improve the chances of a new venture's success? In addition to reviewing our text discussion, go to the National Business Incubation Association Web site at *www.nbia.org* to respond to this question.

4. Why is the owner of a small business not necessarily an entrepreneur?

5. The self-management competency is said to be the most fundamental of all of the competencies needed to be a successful entrepreneur. Why is that thought to be the case?

6. Complete the Your Entrepreneurial Quotient questionnaire found in the next section on Developing Your Competencies if you have not already done so. Do you think your entrepreneurial quotient is a reasonably accurate representation of whether you might have a head start or handicap if you go into business for yourself? Explain.

7. Why might someone prefer to start a franchise business rather than launch an entirely new business?

8. The International Franchise Association's (IFA's) mission is to enhance and to safeguard the business environment for franchising worldwide. Go to the IFA Web site at *www.franchise.org*. Do you think the content of this Web site reflects the pursuit and achievement of this mission? Explain.

9. Teamwork is important to any small business, including a family business. If you were to start a family business, what are three of the possible problems that *your* family business would likely experience when it comes to working together as a team? Considering the nature of your family in particular, develop a short list of recommendations for your family business to maintain a positive team atmosphere.

DEVELOPING YOUR COMPETENCIES

Instructions

Begin with the score of zero. Add or subtract from your score as you respond to each item.

1. Significantly high numbers of entrepreneurs are children of first-generation U.S. citizens. If your parents were immigrants, add 1. If not, subtract 1. _____

2. Successful entrepreneurs were not, as a rule, top achievers in school. If you were a top student, subtract 4. If not, add 4. _____

3. Entrepreneurs were not especially enthusiastic about participating in group activities in school. If you enjoyed group activities—clubs, team sports, and so on—subtract 1. If not, add 1. _____

4. Studies of entrepreneurs show that, as youngsters, they often preferred to be alone. Did you prefer to be alone as a youngster? If yes, add 1. If no, subtract 1. _____

5. If you started an enterprise during childhood—lemonade stands, family newspapers, greeting card sales—or ran for elected office at school, add 2 because enterprise usually appears at an early age. If you didn't initiate enterprises, subtract 2. _____

6. Stubbornness as a child seems to translate into determination to do things your own way—certainly a hallmark of proven entrepreneurs. So, if you were a stubborn child, add 1. If not, subtract 1. _____

7. Caution may involve an unwillingness to take risks, a handicap for those embarking into previously uncharted territory. Were you cautious as a youngster? If yes, subtract 4. If no, add 4. _____

8. If you were daring, add 4. _____

9. Entrepreneurs often speak of pursuing different paths—despite the opinions of others. If the opinions of others matter to you, subtract 1. If not, add 1. _____

10. Being bored with a daily routine is often a precipitating factor in an entrepreneur's decision to start an enterprise. If an important motivation for starting your own enterprise would be changing your daily routine, add 2. If not, subtract 2. _____

11. If you really enjoy work, are you willing to work long nights? If yes, add 2. If no, subtract 6. _____

12. If you would be willing to work "as long as it takes" with little or no sleep to finish a job, add 4. _____

13. Entrepreneurs generally enjoy their activity so much that they move from one project to another—nonstop. When you complete a project successfully, do you immediately start another? If yes, add 2. If no, subtract 2. _____

14. Successful entrepreneurs are willing to use their savings to start a project. If you would be willing to spend your savings to start a business, add 2. If not, subtract 2. _____

15. If you would be willing to borrow from others, too, add 2. If not, subtract 2. _____

16. If your business failed, would you immediately work to start another? If yes, add 4. If no, subtract 4. _____

17. If you would immediately start looking for a good paying job, subtract 1. _____

18. Do you believe entrepreneurship is "risky"? If yes, subtract 2. If no, add 2. _____

19. Many entrepreneurs put long-term and short-term goals in writing. If you do, add 1. If you don't, subtract 1. _____

20. Handling cash flow can be crucial to entrepreneurial success. If you believe that you have more knowledge and experience with cash flow than most people, add 2. If not, subtract 2. _____

21. Entrepreneurial personalities seem to be easily bored. If you are easily bored, add 2. If not, subtract 2. _____

22. Optimism can fuel the drive to press for success. If you're an optimist, add 2. If you're a pessimist, subtract 2. _____

Interpretation

A score of 35 or more: You have everything going for you. If you decide to become an entrepreneur, you ought to achieve spectacular success (barring natural disasters or other variables beyond your control).

A score of 15 to 34: Your background, skills, and talents give you an excellent chance for success in starting your own business. You should go far.

A score of 0 to 14: You have a head start on the ability and/or experience in running a business and ought to be successful in opening an enterprise of your own if you apply yourself and develop the necessary competencies to make it happen.

A score of minus 15 to minus 1: You might be able to make a go of it if you ventured out on your own, but you would have to work extra hard to compensate for a lack of advantages that give others a "leg up" in beginning their own business.

A score of minus 43 to minus 16: Your talents probably lie elsewhere. You ought to consider whether building your own business is what you really want to do because you may find yourself working against your true preference. Another work arrangement—such as working for someone else or developing a career in a profession or an area of technical expertise—may be far more attractive to you and therefore allow you to enjoy a lifestyle appropriate to your abilities and interests.

Gary Salomon, the founder of FASTSIGNS International, has proven that you don't have to invent a product to own it. He saw a technology and bought the rights to it from the inventor. With vision and sweat equity, he has grown a company that broke away from tradition and set a new standard in its industry.

The sign business is huge and diversified. People buy all types of signs but the ones you think of first are usually those that are installed permanently. Think Las Vegas and your mind fills with fantastic neon signs larger than you'll find anywhere else in the world. Think about driving down any commercial street in cities throughout the world and you see signs painted on buildings. At most strip malls, you'll often see a large freestanding sign where the shops located there are listed. These signs are permanent structures. They are often designed by mall architects and they are built out of materials to match the surrounding buildings.

Sign painting and sign building is not what FASTSIGNS does. FASTSIGNS centers use state-of-the-art computer technology to create custom signs, graphics, banners, trade show exhibits, vehicle graphics, and much more. Salomon's company created a niche in the sign industry by using technology that was previously unavailable. At one time, if a merchant wanted a sign, she might hire a painter to paint right on the window. The alternative would be to hand-write a sign or have a professional painter create a sign on paper or cardboard and display it in the window. Some of us may still see plenty of handmade signs in shop windows. FASTSIGNS makes professional signs for pennies on the dollar compared to what a sign painter would charge, so all of us can afford what used to be a luxury.

More people buy professionally made signs than ever before because they are so affordable. FASTSIGNS signs cost more than what you would spend on a piece of cardboard and a marker, but not that much more. Customers get a beautiful sign they are proud to post. FASTSIGNS has grown the sign industry. Salomon comments, "There's probably about $5 1/2 billion worth of revenue on an annual basis in the sign industry—at least that's what the trade associations tell us. The niche that we go after are the more temporary signs."

The professionally made temporary sign market hardly existed before FASTSIGNS.

Over breakfast one day, Gary and two others wrote the concept for opening the first FASTSIGNS. They decided if the one shop made money, they would franchise the idea. By putting personal savings and a small bank loan together, they had $40,000 to launch the venture. According to Salomon, "We operated a very lean, mean, effective machine. We didn't have the money to lose, so we made darn sure that we didn't, and there [were] quite a number of years where I didn't take any money out of the business."

Salomon honed his business concept and since the beginning has supported it with proven systems relating to operations, production, personnel management, financial management, customer service, marketing, and sales. Salomon remarks: "We never really sold a franchise to someone that had been in the sign business before. We were selling franchises to people that have been professional managers and marketers and salespeople. Now this technology will help you compete in an industry that you probably didn't know anything about before." It may sound weird to recruit people who had never made a sign before, but Salomon knew how to make signs and would teach those he believed could run their own operations. He was more interested in recruiting people with management and marketing skills because making the signs is the easy part.

When Salomon was asked why he thinks the company has been able to grow, he said "I think the bottom line is I don't have much of an ego. I'm not really interested in as much being right as I am interested in having the best result or the best solution. If it's not my idea, I really don't care. I'd rather it just be the best idea. When you have that attitude, people aren't afraid of giving you an opinion, because they know they're not going to be shot down."

Today, the initial investment by a franchisee in a FASTSIGNS center starts at about $205,000 including a franchisee fee of $20,000. The approximate minimum financial requirement for a franchisee is $240,000 net worth, $75,000 of which must be liquid.

Questions

1. What attributes make Gary Salomon an entrepreneur? For each attribute, identify the specific example(s) of it in the case.

2. Why is FASTSIGNS an example of entrepreneurship?

3. Why has franchising been effective for FASTSIGNS?

4. Go to the Web site for FASTSIGNS (*www.fastsigns.com*). Click on "About FASTSIGNS" and then "Why FASTSIGNS?" Do you think this is an effective statement? Why or why not?

PART 3

Planning and Control

chapter 7

© Image Source/Jupiter Images

Formulating Plans and Strategies

Learning Goals

After studying this chapter, you should be able to:

1. Describe the importance and core components of strategic and tactical planning.

2. Discuss the effects of organizational diversification strategies on planning.

3. Describe the basic levels of strategy and planning.

4. State the primary tasks of the strategic business-level planning process.

5. Explain the generic competitive strategies model.

6. Explain the integrated strategy model.

Communication Competency

Planning and Administration Competency

Teamwork Competency

Managing Effectively

Self-Management Competency

Strategic Action Competency

Multicultural Competency

Challenge of Managing ....

Judy McGrath, CEO of MTV Networks

© Scott Gries/Getty Images

Judy McGrath is the CEO and chairman of MTV Networks. Prior to this appointment in 2004, she served as a group president at MTV Networks. McGrath joined MTV in 1981 as a copyeditor for on-air promotions. As CEO and in several of her former positions, McGrath has been a leader in the continuous process of strategic planning at MTV Networks, including the development of new and revised strategies, as well as the specific actions for implementing them.

Upon her appointment as CEO and chairman in 2004, McGrath suggested the strategic direction of MTV Networks, both in terms of its culture and services this way:

I want to keep the culture vibrant and attractive to creative talent and up the incredible roll MTV Networks are on. I want to continue pushing ahead in new media, like cell phones, PVRs and the Internet. We need to continue to develop and create for that.

MTV Networks, headquartered in New York, is a subsidiary of Viacom. Viacom is primarily comprised of Black Entertainment Television, Paramount Pictures Corporation, and MTV Networks. MTV Networks is comprised of such units as MTV, Nickelodeon, VH1, Spike TV, Comedy Central, CMT (Country Music Television), and MTV Networks on Campus. McGrath and her other top executives are providing the strategic planning for a number of TV channels, Web sites, and wireless services. MTV Networks has approximately $7 billion in revenue and reaches 440 million households in 169 countries.

McGrath presents the firm's strategic direction as a "digital plan." The businesses within MTV Networks must now deliver services across new broadband channels, over cell phones, and via video games. McGrath comments: "Because MTV is so tapped into its consumers—we're more inside the heads of our audience than anybody else—advertisers will stay with MTV."

A significant thrust in MTV Networks' recent strategic direction is acquisitions and partnerships. A few of the recent strategic moves include the following.

▶ *Online communities.* It acquired Neopets, an online kids' network with 25 million members; IFILM, where amateur

Learning Content

filmmakers can show their short-form stuff; GameTrailers.com, a site for video gamers; and GoCityKids.com, for kid-friendly activities.

▸ *Broadband.* There are five broadband channels: Overdrive (MTV), TurboNick (Nickelodeon), Vspot (VH1), Motherload (Comedy Central), and mtvU Über (mtvU)—with more in the works.

▸ *Download.* URGE, a music service launched in partnership with Microsoft, includes exclusive MTV programs.

▸ *Wireless.* MTV has 57 wireless alliances worldwide reaching 750 million cell phone users. Amp'd Mobile shows programs from all of MTV's channels.

▸ *Video on demand.* MTV has agreements with Comcast and Charter to deliver on-demand programs from its channels.

▸ *Games.* MTV Games was created to launch new video game titles. Midway Games is a partner.

At a recent MTV Networks planning retreat, McGrath warned against complacency in the face of game-changing innovation triggered by the digital revolution. In speeches and side conversations, she pressed for the firm to shed its skin and reimagine itself. She comments: "Nobody wants to be who they used to be, including us." McGrath's strategic initiatives suggest that she has done so and is effectively leading those throughout the organization to do so.[1]

To learn more about this organization, visit *www.hoovers.com* (enter MTV Networks Company).

Some have suggested that McGrath's challenge is to make MTV Network unique amid the media culture. As with most strategic planning that involves novel and major strategies, the results of these initiatives are not likely to be known for several years.

In this chapter, we discuss some of the fundamentals of planning and the strategies employed by MTV Networks and other organizations. In Chapter 1, we noted that *planning* involves determining organizational goals and the means to reach them. We consider planning a basic managerial function because it sets the framework and direction for the organizing, leading, and controlling functions. In addition, the ability of an individual, team, or organization to plan is an integral part in each of the six managerial competencies that we develop throughout this book.

Importance and Types of Planning

1.

Describe the importance and core components of strategic and tactical planning.

Why Is Planning Important?

When used effectively, planning should assist leaders and managers to

▸ discover new opportunities,

▸ anticipate and avoid future problems,

▸ develop effective courses of action (strategies and tactics), and

▸ comprehend the uncertainties and risks with various options.

Planning should also improve the odds of achieving an organization's goals by creating desirable changes, improving productivity, and maintaining organizational stability. Realization of such goals enables the organization to achieve long-term growth, maintain profitability, and survive. If done properly, planning fosters organizationwide learning, including the discovery of key problems, opportunities, and new strategies.[2] A key goal of this chapter is to help you develop your planning and administration competency and strategic action competency.

Judy McGrath clearly demonstrated these competencies in the Challenge of Managing feature through the various initiatives related to MTV Networks' "digital plan." Moreover, she recognizes that the teamwork, communication, and other competencies all play a part in creating and implementing effective plans and strategies. McGrath suggests a variety of guidelines for leading a creative enterprise like MTV Networks. A few of McGrath's guidelines include these:

▶ Listen to all of your people.

▶ Make change part of your DNA.

▶ Companies don't innovate, people do.

▶ Use research as a tool for creativity.

Moreover, McGrath comments: "The smartest thing we can do when confronted by something truly creative is to get out of the way. The key is to create a space where people feel safe and unafraid to fail."[3]

What Is Strategic Planning?

Strategic planning *is the process of (1) diagnosing the organization's external and internal environments, (2) deciding on a vision and mission, (3) developing overall goals, (4) creating and selecting general strategies to be pursued, and (5) allocating resources to achieve the organization's goals.* Senior managers must take an organizationwide or divisionwide perspective in the process of strategic planning. Their focus is on developing strategies that deal effectively with opportunities and threats in relation to the organization's strengths and weaknesses.[4]

Contingency Planning. In most large organizations, such as IBM and General Electric, strategic planning includes contingency planning—*preparation for unexpected, major, and quick changes (positive or negative) in the environment that will have a significant impact on the organization and require immediate responses.* This process begins with managers developing scenarios of major environmental events that could occur. A contingency plan for a dramatic negative event could be developed for responding to a natural disaster (e.g., an earthquake, flood, or fire that destroys a company's manufacturing plant) or for managing a crisis (e.g., terrorist attack).[5] A contingency plan may also be developed for a positive event, such as an increase in customer demand for products (goods and/or services) that overwhelms the firm's current capacity. Generally, managers should plan for three to five potentially critical and unanticipated events. The attempt to consider more events is likely to make the contingency planning process too time consuming and unmanageable. Contingency planning forces managers to be aware of possibilities and to outline strategies to respond to them. It supports orderly and speedy adaptation, in contrast to panic-like reactions, to external events beyond the organization's direct control.[6]

If there was any doubt about the need to have a contingency plan to deal with the consequences of an unforeseen disaster, the tragic terrorist attacks of September 11, 2001, and the destruction wrought by Hurricanes Katrina and Rita in 2005 should put that doubt to rest. The following Planning and Administration Competency feature reports on how contingency planning at the Mississippi Power Company enabled it to respond to the ravages of Hurricane Katrina in 2005.[7] This firm, headquartered in

Snapshot

"The Internet is no longer about text. It's about video. We produce and own more video than anybody. This is a watershed moment for MTV Networks. We have an opportunity to build and execute the future, to reinvent this network once again. We are putting in place a whole set of strategies that will define the company's role, not just on TV, but in the digital world as well."

Michael J. Wolf, President and Chief Operating Officer, MTV Networks Company

Gulfport, Mississippi, provides electric service to approximately 190,000 residential, commercial, and industrial customers in the state of Mississippi. It is a wholly owned subsidiary of the Southern Company, which operates five regulated utilities in the southeastern United States.[8]

Mississippi Power's Contingency Plan and Katrina

The Mississippi Power Company has about 1,200 employees. Considering the relatively small workforce and customer base of this firm, the story of how it was able to restore power in just 12 days to its customers who could take power—all of whom lost power after landfall of Hurricane Katrina in 2005—is all the more amazing.

Kurt Brautigam, external communications manager for the company, comments: "In times of using our storm implementation plan, we have many, many employees doing something different from their everyday job. It's in our culture; we try very hard to allow our employees to do their job, and in case of severe circumstances, it becomes impossible to get a lot of approval. Depending on what the issues are, we want to empower our employees as much as possible. You do what you can to get the job done."

With its corporate headquarters flattened and its disaster response center taking on water, employees hired as marketing managers or salespeople became logicians and supply chain managers. Everyone assumed their emergency roles, and their roles were clearly defined. Most employees have had a logistical or storm contingency assignment for quite some time. Thus, some continuity is built in under emergency conditions.

Because of the location on the Gulf Coast, the company's crews have faced disruptions before. Brautigam remarks: "There are a couple of times a year where weather may threaten our service territory and we get geared up. Ice storms or other weather-related forecasts might require that we pull the storm team together and they take over their roles. We were extremely lucky to have our own internal radio communication system that was functioning—functioning at minimal capacity, but it was functioning, and we were able to talk to other Southern Company counterparts." Within a couple of days, the IT people were able to make strides in restoring e-mail and internal phone services in the 23-county, 150-mile service area.

The restoration process in Mississippi Power's contingency plan works as follows:

▶ They start at their power plants and work first on the large lines going out to the communities from the plants.

▶ While working on these main transmission lines, the focus goes to the next largest lines—the main feeders or distribution lines in a community, along with restoring power to essential services such as hospitals, water and sewer plants, and fire and police stations.

▶ Next, they repair damage that will return power to the greatest number of customers in the least amount of time.

▶ After these are repaired, smaller lines are repaired until the crews get down to the individual lines in the neighborhoods.

To learn more about this organization, visit *www.southernco.com.*

In Chapters 4 and 5, we discussed many domestic and global forces that managers and others must understand in strategic planning and the daily management of their organizations. As suggested in Figure 7.1, there are four interrelated core components in strategic planning that senior leaders can directly influence: vision and mission, organizational goals, strategies, and resource allocation.

Vision and Mission. A vision *expresses an organization's fundamental aspirations and purpose, usually by appealing to its members' hearts and minds.* A vision statement may add soul to a mission statement if it lacks one. Over time, traditional statements of mission (e.g., stating the business in which the organization is involved) may change, but the organization's vision may endure for generations.[9] The following statements represent the visions of three organizations[10]:

Figure 7.1 | Interrelated Core Components in Strategic Planning

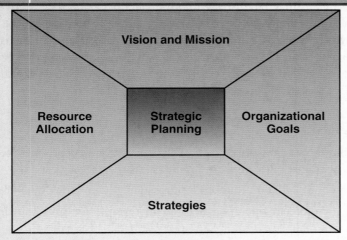

Vision and Mission

Resource Allocation

Strategic Planning

Organizational Goals

Strategies

▶ **Lowe's:** To be our Customer's first choice for home improvement in each and every market we serve.

▶ **eBay:** To pioneer new communities around the world built on commerce, sustained by trust, and inspired by opportunity.

▶ **Dell Computer:** To create a company culture where environmental excellence is second nature. Bringing value to customers and adding value to our company, our neighborhoods, our communities and our world through diversity, environmental, and global citizenship initiatives.

Many organizations don't have a vision statement. They may have a mission statement only. A mission *is the organization's purpose or reason for existing.* A mission statement often answers basic questions such as these: (1) What business are we in? (2) Who are we? (3) What are we about? A mission may describe the customer needs the firm aims to satisfy, the goods or service the firm supplies, or the markets the firm is currently serving or intends to serve in the future. Some mission statements are lengthy, but others are quite brief. The following statements illustrate how three organizations express their missions:

▶ **Lowe's:** To understand the needs of customers and develop business models to meet those needs.

▶ **eBay:** To serve as the world's online marketplace for the sale and payment of goods and services by a diverse community of individuals and businesses.

▶ **Dell Computer:** To fully integrate environmental stewardship into the business of providing quality products, best-in-class services, and the best customer experience at the best value.

A mission statement is meaningful only if it acts as a unifying force for guiding strategic decisions and achieving an organization's long-term goals. The mission statement should encourage the organization's members to think and act strategically—not just once a year but every day.

© Lynne Sladky/AP Photo

In September 2005, Hurricane Katrina left a tangled mess of downed power lines in the Gulf Coast area. The Mississippi Power Company expertly dealt with the emergency with its contingency plan in place.

Organizational Goals. Organizational goals *are the results that the managers and others have selected and are committed to achieving for the long-term survival and growth of the firm.* These goals may be expressed both qualitatively and quantitatively (what is to be achieved, how much is to be achieved, and by when it is to be achieved). Goodyear Tire & Rubber Company, headquartered in Akron, Ohio, has the stated vision "to become a market-focused tire company providing superior products and services to end-users and to our channel partners, leading to superior returns for our shareholders." A few of its corporate goals include[11]

▷ reducing company operating costs by $1 billion through 2009,

▷ simplifying the firm's supply chain and sales process,

▷ expanding the business through the introduction of new products so that 15 percent of annual sales are from products less than three years old,

▷ exporting up to 200,000 RunOnFlat tires annually in China by 2009, and

▷ earning a 5 percent operating margin on revenue for tires sold in North America.

Strategies. Strategies *are the major courses of action (choices) selected and implemented to achieve one or more goals.*[12] In Chapters 4 and 5, we reviewed several competitive strategies that managers can use to deal with threats and take advantage of opportunities in their business. They include forming alliances, exporting, licensing, developing a multidomestic strategy, or adopting a global strategy.

A key challenge is to develop strategies that are at least partially unique or to pursue strategies similar to those of competitors but in different ways, such as through quality, image, price, or service. Strategies will have the greatest impact when they position an organization to be different in one or more aspects from its competitors. Michael Porter, a professor at the Harvard Business School and widely regarded as one of the foremost thinkers on strategic management, comments:

> The essence of most good strategies is the need to make many choices that are all consistent—choices about production, service, design, and so on. Companies cannot randomly make a lot of choices that all turn out to be consistent. It's statistically impossible. That means companies need to grasp at least a part of the whole. As we study the histories of successful companies, we see that someone or some group developed insight into how a number of choices fit together. . . .[13]

A few of the good strategies implemented by Judy McGrath and her top leadership team at MTV Networks include

▷ acquiring other media companies and/or forming partnerships;

▷ building on digital-based technologies and the Internet for the delivery of its video products anyplace at anytime;

▷ initiating efforts to make MTV unique through each of its nine focused networks—such as MTV, VH1, and Comedy Central; and

▷ fostering a culture that supports creativity at all levels of the organization.

Resource Allocation. Resource allocation *involves assigning money, people, facilities, and other resources among various current and new business opportunities.* As part of the strategic planning process, resource allocation generally boils down to allocating money, through budgets, for various purposes. For example, Lowe's capital budget was $3.7 billion in a recent year. Most of this capital budget is for store expansion, renovation, and new distribution centers. Four hundred new store locations are planned for the next several years with approximately 150 new stores opening in a recent year. More than $700 million was spent in a recent year on its 1,200 plus existing stores. In addition, several state-of-the-art regional distribution centers were opened, increasing the total to eleven.[14] Each of these projects had a detailed capital budget associated with it, including specific dollar amounts for land, building, technology, and related costs.

What Is Tactical Planning?

Tactical planning *involves making decisions regarding what to do, who will do it, and how to do it—with a normal time horizon of one to two years or less.* Middle and first-line managers and teams often are heavily involved in tactical planning. It normally includes specific courses of action for implementing new initiatives or improving current operations. It is usually tightly integrated with the annual budget process for each department, division, and project within the guidelines set by higher level management.

Departmental managers and employee teams develop tactical plans to anticipate or cope with the actions of competitors; to coordinate with other departments, customers, and suppliers; and to implement strategic plans. The information presented in Table 7.1 demonstrates that tactical planning differs from strategic planning primarily in terms of shorter time frames, size of resource allocations, and level of detail. The two types of planning are closely linked in a well-designed planning process.

Snapshot

"As we manage our business, we are focused on meeting our financial targets the right way. Our actions are based on the company's long-term interests rather than on short-term, expedient solutions."

Kenneth I. Chenault, Chairman and CEO, American Express Company

Table 7.1   **Focus of Strategic and Tactical Planning**

DIMENSION	STRATEGIC PLANNING	TACTICAL PLANNING
Intended purpose	Ensure long-term effectiveness and growth	Means of implementing strategic plans
Nature of issues addressed	How to survive and compete	How to accomplish specific goals
Time horizon	Long term (usually two years or more)	Short term (usually one year or less)
How often done	Every one to three years	Every six months to one year
Condition under which decision making occurs	Uncertainty and risk	Low to moderate risk
Where plans are primarily developed	Middle to top management	Employees, up to middle management
Level of detail	Low to moderate	High

Diversification Strategies and Planning

Firms usually begin by just serving one or two market niches. At some point, many firms expand beyond their initial narrow base. They may expand their scope of operations to include different services, goods, or geographic regions within the same or different industries. In this section, we review key considerations involved in selecting diversification strategies. These strategies serve to define different types of firms and the complexity of planning associated with each type.

Questions in Considering Diversification

Diversification *refers to the variety of goods and/or services produced by an organization and the number of different markets it serves.* The degree of diversification directly affects the complexity of an organization's strategic planning.[15] Strategic changes in the degree

2.

Discuss the effects of organizational diversification strategies on planning.

Snapshot

"We are always looking for companies, products, or emerging technologies that will complement and strengthen our existing businesses, lead us into new therapeutic areas to address unmet medical needs, enhance our research and development capabilities, and, ultimately, further our strategy for growth. Each acquisition is different, and in each situation, we carefully examine the best way to integrate that technology, product, or organization into our family of companies."

William C. Weldon, Chairman and CEO, Johnson & Johnson

of diversification should be guided by answers to questions that help top managers identify the potential risks—and opportunities—that diversification presents. The following are four such strategic questions:

1. *What can we do better than other firms if we enter a new market?* Ideally, senior leaders are clear about what it is their firm can do better than their competitors. But, sometimes they base diversification decisions or new start-up decisions on vague definitions of their businesses rather than on a systematic analysis of what sets them apart from current or potential competitors.

   One of Johnson & Johnson's (J&J) strategic principles is to remain broadly based in human health care.[16] J&J has more than 200 companies in 57 countries that invent, develop, and sell health-care products in the consumer, pharmaceutical, medical devices, and medical diagnostics markets. J&J frequently makes acquisitions and develops alliances in the human health-care field. For example, J&J recently acquired the Animas Corporation for $515 million. This firm makes and develops external insulin pumps as well as insulin accessories—insulin cartridges, infusion sets, and batteries. J&J did not make insulin pumps.[17]

2. *What strategic resources—human, financial, and others—do we need to succeed in the new market?* Excelling in one market doesn't guarantee success in a new one. The capabilities required to be competitive in one type of business may not transfer to another type of business. One of the keys to J&J acquisitions is that they are broadly based human health-care companies. Acquisitions by some firms, especially when they involve significantly diversifying from what they do well, often do not work.[18] When that problem is recognized, a firm may engage in downscoping—*a divestiture, spin-off, or some means of eliminating divisions and business lines that are unrelated to a firm's core businesses.*[19] DaimlerChrysler has been divesting itself of some businesses. It sold Detroit Diesel Corporation, its off-highway diesel unit.[20] A recent DaimlerChrysler management report states: "We consistently continued our strategy of focusing on our core competencies by disposing of operations that are not part of our core business."[21]

3. *Will we simply be a player in the new market or will we emerge a winner?* Diversifying or new start-up companies may be outmaneuvered by current competitors. The reason is that managers may have failed to consider whether their organizations' resources can be easily imitated, purchased on the open market, or replaced by other competitors. The entry by the firm may stimulate the current competitors to become much more competitive. For example, several years ago, Toys "R" Us, with more than 1,400 stores worldwide, responded aggressively when several Internet-based toy retailers entered the market. The firm established its own Internet-based retailing arm. This provided the firm with a greater capability in meeting customer needs. If there were problems with an Internet order, a customer could go to one of its "brick-and-mortar" stores to return it.[22] This approach eliminated the need for customers to return items through the mail. With its buying power, Toys "R" Us was able to meet head on the price competition of the new Internet-based competitors. Most of its online competitors have now gone out of business. However, Toys "R" Us soon fell on hard times as a result of intense competition from Wal-Mart and Target. This led to the acquisition of Toys "R" Us by a group of private equity firms. Gerald Storch, a highly respected former executive with Target, was hired in 2006 to lead a turnaround strategy for Toys "R" Us.[23]

4. *What can we learn by diversifying, and are we sufficiently organized to learn it?* Astute managers know how to make diversification a learning experience. They

anticipate how new businesses can help improve existing businesses, act as stepping stones to markets previously out of reach, or improve efficiency. Dell diversified from initially being a provider of just desktop PCs to a provider of laptops, network servers, workstations, printers, storage systems, handheld computers, digital music players, LCD and plasma televisions, and other products or services needed to assemble and run computer networks. The addition of these products and services is interrelated in various ways and has been added over a number of years. One common theme is that all of Dell's products are sold direct through the Internet, phone, or mail.[24]

Types of Diversification Strategies

An organization may follow a single-business strategy, dominant-business strategy, related-business strategy, or unrelated-business strategy. Figure 7.2 indicates that the level of diversification and the complexity of strategic planning are directly related. A firm that produces varied goods or services for unrelated markets often must have a complex planning process. In contrast, a firm involved in a single product line or service needs a less elaborate planning process.

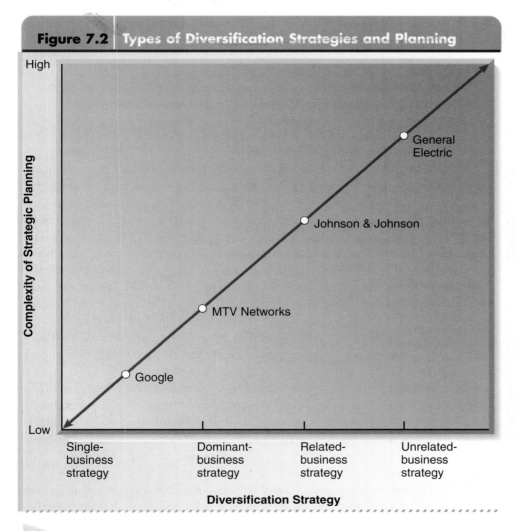

Figure 7.2 Types of Diversification Strategies and Planning

A single-business strategy *involves providing a limited number of goods or services to one particular market*. Google's mission is to organize the world's information and make it universally accessible and useful. The firm operates a Web site at *www.google.com* that is recognized by some as the world's best search engine. It offers targeted search results from more than 8 billion Web pages and attracts an audience of 80 million people in English-speaking markets. Google also offers search results in 35 other languages. The firm is headquartered in Mountain View, California.[25]

A **dominant-business** strategy *involves serving various segments of a market.* The term *market* refers collectively to the various users of a product line. MTV Networks, which we discuss in several sections of this chapter, approximates the use of a dominant-business strategy. MTV Networks serves a number of niches in the video entertainment market through its nine television networks, Web sites, and wireless services. The mtvU network (*www.mtvu.com*) is an example of MTV Networks' service to the college-age segment of the video-based entertainment and information market. It is available at about 730 campuses, reaching almost 7 million students in dining halls, student lounges, fitness centers, and dorm rooms or apartments.[26]

A **related-business** strategy *involves providing a variety of complementary goods and/or services.* Its divisions generally operate in the same or similar markets or use similar technologies, or share common distribution channels, or benefit from common strategic assets. Johnson & Johnson is a related-business firm. As noted previously, it is a comprehensive and broadly based provider of health-care products and services. J&J's 200 companies are organized primarily into three major segments by markets served:

▶ The consumer segment makes nonprescription drugs, products for skin and hair care, baby care, oral care, first aid, women's health, and nutrition.

▶ The medical devices and diagnostics segment makes products such as surgical equipment, medical monitoring devices, and disposable contact lenses.

▶ The pharmaceutical segment makes ethical pharmaceutical drugs for a vast array of ailments that are prescribed by health-care professionals.[27]

An **unrelated-business** strategy *involves providing diverse products (goods and/or services) to many different types of markets.* Often referred to as a *conglomerate,* such a firm usually consists of distinct companies that have little or no relation to each other in terms of goods, services, or customers served. Unrelated-business firms are not common, although they are typically very large. Yahoo! Finance, a Web site that provides information on businesses, lists 210 conglomerates worldwide; including Siemens AG, Teledyne, Textron, and 3M Company to name a few.[28] For the most part, the volume and diversity of information needed to plan for and manage such firms are enormous. As a result, their top managers often revert to planning and controls through financial data that focus on the past and near term for making strategic decisions. These factors help to account for the relatively few successful unrelated businesses and the tendency of firms to have to downscope over time if they diversify too much from their core businesses.

General Electric (GE) is among the successful unrelated-business firms. GE is a diversified services, technology, and manufacturing company with approximately 300,000 employees worldwide and more than $160 billion in annual sales. GE is made of six primary businesses each with its own divisions: GE Commercial Finance, GE Consumer Finance, GE Healthcare, GE Industrial, GE Infrastructure, and NBC Universal.[29]

GE has received many awards and accolades as an outstanding organization with outstanding leaders over the years. For example, GE, once again, was recently recognized as America's Most Admired Company by *Fortune* magazine.[30] The following Strategic Action Competency presents a glimpse of the perspectives by Jeffrey R. Immelt, chairman of the Board and chief executive officer, on GE's business model.[31]

General Electric's CEO Jeffrey R. Immelt is known for adequately investing and planning to manage growth.

© Jim McKnight/AP Photo

Jeff Immelt on GE's Business Model

"We are a fast-growth, multi-business enterprise that is expanding around the world. Our goal is not just to be big, but to use our size to be great. But accomplishing this goal is harder than it sounds. Size with complexity breeds bureaucracy. Size without a face makes you the target of cynicism. Size with no heart will turn away the best people. Size can insulate a company from failure until it is too late to change. The corporate landscape is littered with companies that allowed themselves to be trapped by size. But GE has thrived because we use our size to help us grow. Our depth allows us to lead in big markets by providing unmatched solutions for our customers; our breadth allows us to spread concepts across the Company, leveraging one small idea to create a big financial gain; and our strength allows us to take the risks required to grow. We make size an advantage without ever allowing it to be a disadvantage. . . .

There are many companies that have been created through acquisitions that are frequently compared to GE, called conglomerates. However, our business model is designed to achieve superior performance through the synergies of a large, multi-business company structure. The following strategic imperatives provide the foundation for creating shareowner value:

1. Sustain a strong portfolio of leading businesses that fit together to grow consistently through the cycles;
2. Drive common initiatives across the company that accelerate growth, satisfy customers and expand margins; and
3. Develop people to grow a common culture that is adaptive, ethical, and drives execution.

It is our profound commitment to the integration of the elements mentioned above that makes GE different. It is not an easy model to copy, as it requires financial and cultural commitments over decades."

GE recently launched initiatives to achieve 8 percent organic growth per year, which is about twice the rate of GE's industrial and financial peers. One of the initiatives to achieve is to develop great people in a strong culture. Immelt continues: "Developing and motivating people is the most important part of my job. I spend one third of my time on people. We invest $1 billion each year in training to make them better. . . . We are committed to teach our leaders new skills that make them contemporary in every area. Consistent with our initiatives, we are teaching them to be growth leaders."

To learn more about this organization, visit *www.ge.com.*

Strategic Levels and Planning

Plans and the competitive strategies embedded in them are normally developed at three primary levels in firms with a dominant-business (e.g., MTV Networks), related-business (e.g., Johnson & Johnson), or unrelated-business (e.g., General Electric) diversification strategy. Figure 7.3 shows some of the executives involved in planning at these levels for GE. For single-business strategy firms, plans and competitive strategies are developed at two primary levels—the business level and the functional level.

3.
Describe the basic levels of strategy and planning.

Corporate-Level Strategy

Core Focus. Corporate-level planning and strategy guides the overall direction of firms having more than one line of business. The amount of diversification determines the complexity and scope of planning and strategy formulation required. Corporate-level strategy *focuses on the types of businesses the firm wants to be in, ways to acquire or divest businesses, allocation of resources among the businesses, and ways to develop learning and synergy among those businesses.* Top corporate managers then determine the role of each separate business within the organization.[32]

Figure 7.3 | General Electric's Strategic and Planning Levels

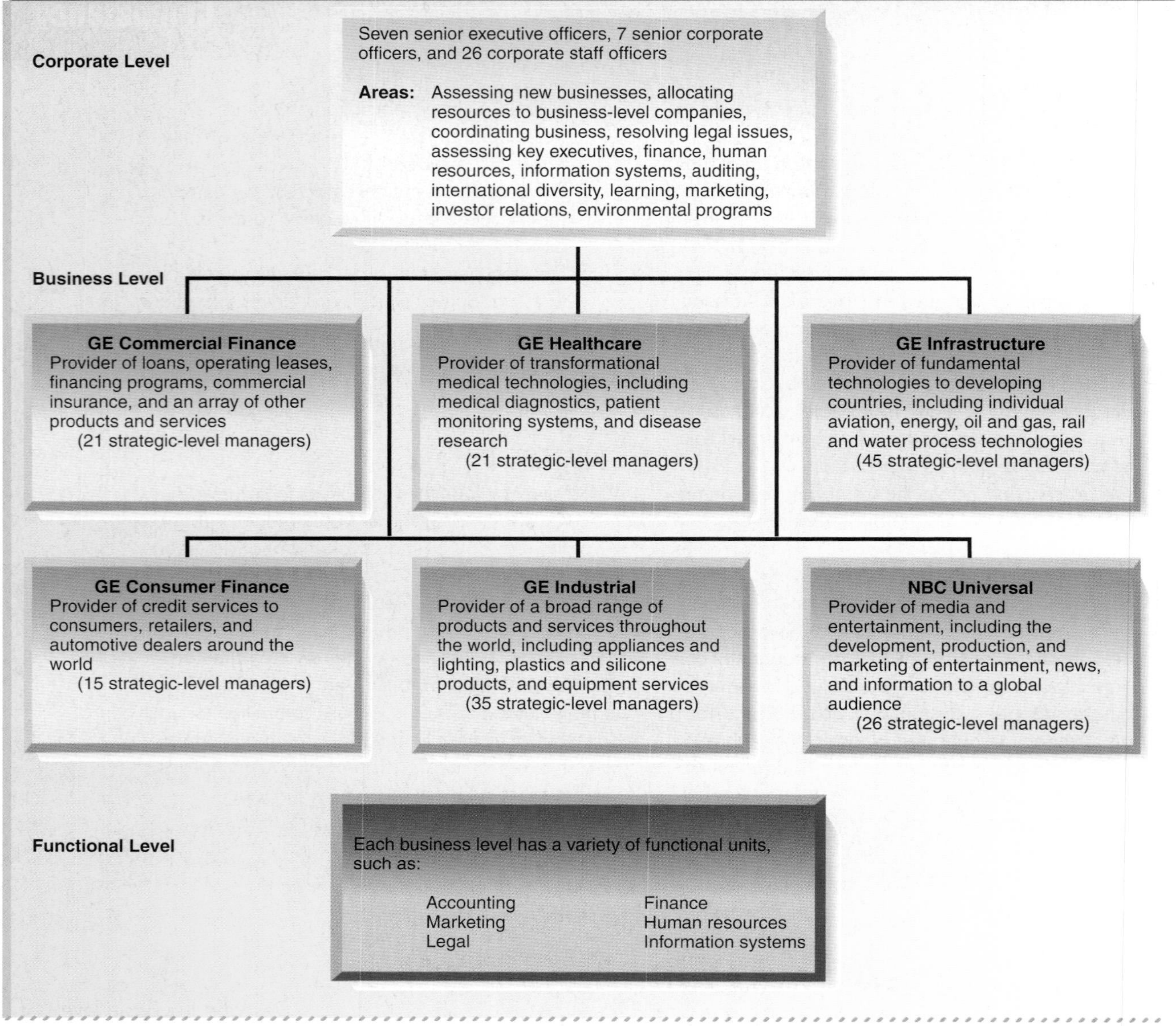

Corporate Level

Seven senior executive officers, 7 senior corporate officers, and 26 corporate staff officers

Areas: Assessing new businesses, allocating resources to business-level companies, coordinating business, resolving legal issues, assessing key executives, finance, human resources, information systems, auditing, international diversity, learning, marketing, investor relations, environmental programs

Business Level

GE Commercial Finance
Provider of loans, operating leases, financing programs, commercial insurance, and an array of other products and services
(21 strategic-level managers)

GE Healthcare
Provider of transformational medical technologies, including medical diagnostics, patient monitoring systems, and disease research
(21 strategic-level managers)

GE Infrastructure
Provider of fundamental technologies to developing countries, including individual aviation, energy, oil and gas, rail and water process technologies
(45 strategic-level managers)

GE Consumer Finance
Provider of credit services to consumers, retailers, and automotive dealers around the world
(15 strategic-level managers)

GE Industrial
Provider of a broad range of products and services throughout the world, including appliances and lighting, plastics and silicone products, and equipment services
(35 strategic-level managers)

NBC Universal
Provider of media and entertainment, including the development, production, and marketing of entertainment, news, and information to a global audience
(26 strategic-level managers)

Functional Level

Each business level has a variety of functional units, such as:

Accounting	Finance
Marketing	Human resources
Legal	Information systems

Source: Developed from *GE 2005 Annual Report. www.ge.com* (March 2006).

Several of GE's corporate-level strategic imperatives were presented in the previous Strategic Action Competency feature. Another recently launched corporate-level strategy is GE's *Ecomagination*. This strategy is focused on applying GE technology to drive energy efficiency and improve environmental performance. Three of the corporate-level *ecomagination* goals that involve all of GE are

▶ from 2005 to 2010, double revenue from eco products to $20 billion annually,

▶ from 2005 to 2010, double eco-related research and development investments to $1.5 billion annually, and

▶ from 2005 to 2008, decrease GE's greenhouse gas intensity by 30 percent with a 1 percent absolute reduction by 2012 (even though GE plans to have a number of new and expanded facilities). Without this strategic initiative, it is estimated that GE's greenhouse gas emissions would have risen by 40 percent annually in 2012.[33]

One of the functions of corporate-level management is to guide and review the performance of strategic business units. A **strategic business unit (SBU)** *is a division or subsidiary of a firm that provides a related set of products or services and usually has its own mission and goals.* An SBU may have a well-defined set of customers and/or cover a specific geographic area. An SBU is normally evaluated on the basis of its own income statement and balance sheet. The top managers of each SBU are responsible for developing plans and strategies for their units. These proposals normally are submitted to corporate headquarters for review. Top corporate management, as at GE, is involved in determining which SBUs to start, acquire, or divest. Corporate-level management also decides whether to allocate the same, less, or more financial and human resources to the various SBUs.[34]

Corporate Growth Strategies. Managers can use a variety of corporate-level growth strategies to reach their organizational goals. As suggested in Figure 7.4, five of the more common corporate-level strategies are forward integration, backward integration, horizontal integration, related diversification, conglomerate diversification, and organic. Organic simply refers to initiatives to grow the firm's current businesses.

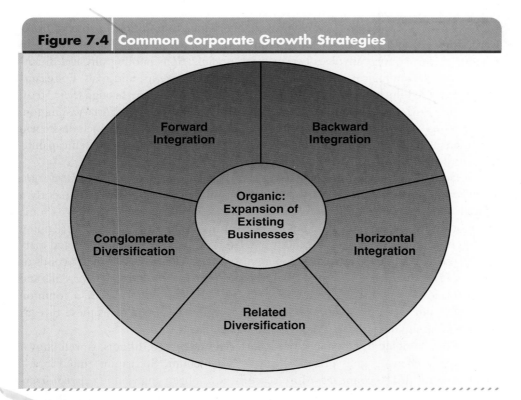

Figure 7.4   Common Corporate Growth Strategies

A forward integration strategy *refers to entering the business of its customers, moving it closer to the ultimate consumer.* For example, Cisco Systems, headquartered in San Jose, California, is a major provider of routers and switches used to link networks and power the Internet. It primarily sells to other firms. To further extend its reach into homes, Cisco recently purchased Scientific-Atlanta, which is one of the largest makers of home-based boxes used by cable subscribers to receive TV programming and interactive online services such as movies-on-demand, e-mail, and Web communications. Cisco acquired Scientific-Atlanta for about $7 billion to gain a greater direct presence in the "digital home" of the 21st century.[35]

A backward integration strategy *refers to entering the business of its suppliers, usually to control component quality, ensure on-time delivery, or stabilize prices.* Examples of these strategies are the purchase of suppliers or the creation of new businesses that provide

These managers show their delight at the announcement of the team-based bonuses for the year.

© PureStock/Jupiter Images

the same goods or services as the organization's suppliers. IBM makes use of this strategy through the acquisition of software and service vendors. For example, IBM recently acquired Micromuse, Inc., headquartered in San Francisco, for $865 million. Micromuse is a maker of back-office software that monitors and manages computer networks.[36]

A horizontal integration strategy *refers to acquiring one or more competitors to consolidate and extend its market share.* SBC Communications, headquartered in San Antonio, Texas, used this strategy in acquiring AT&T Corporation in 2005 for $16 billion. Soon thereafter, SBC changed its name to AT&T Inc. In 2006, AT&T acquired BellSouth for $67 billion, which was another example of the horizontal integration strategy. All of these firms are in the telecommunications industry. The new AT&T has 49 million access lines in service and 54 million subscribers to its Cingular Wireless service.[37]

A growing alternative to traditional forms of backward, forward, and horizontal integration is the *alliance strategy.* As suggested in Chapter 5, this strategy involves two or more organizations pooling physical, financial, human, technological, and/or other resources to achieve specific goals. For example, Johnson & Johnson has a strategic alliance with Merck & Co. through their 50/50 joint venture, Merck Consumer Pharmaceuticals, headquartered in Fort Washington, Pennsylvania. This firm's prescription and over-the-counter products include Pepcid Complete and Pepcid AC. This alliance combines Merck's clinical research capabilities with J&J's sales and marketing expertise.[38]

A related diversification strategy *refers to acquiring or starting a business related to the organization's existing business in terms of technology, markets, or products.* Frequently a related-business enterprise acquires another company or starts a new venture. Some common thread or threads must link the two firms. Examples of these overlapping threads include one or more of the following: (1) a common set of customers and markets, (2) shared technology, (3) overlapping distribution channels, (4) similar goods or services, (5) common suppliers and raw materials sources, (6) common labor skills and competencies, (7) similar operating methods, and (8) the ability to share a common sales force and other marketing methods. The greater the number of these threads that are naturally interwoven, the greater the relatedness.[39]

The Wm. Wrigley Jr. Company, headquartered in Chicago, Illinois, is well known for its many chewing gum brands—such as Doublemint, Spearmint, and Extra— which are sold in 180 countries. More recently, it has been engaged in related diversification. For example, Wrigley's acquired various confectionery assets from Kraft Foods for about $1.5 billion. A few of the brands acquired include Altoids, LifeSavers, Crème Savers, and Sugus. William Wrigley Jr., the CEO, comments on the relatedness of the acquisition from Kraft Foods in these words:

> With our confectionery expertise and focus, we look for these newly acquired brands to flourish under Wrigley's global umbrella. They have a rich heritage and are well-loved and well-known as quality brands by our customers and consumers. This transaction represents a significant reinforcement of our position as a world-class confectionery company.[40]

Wrigley's primary corporate growth strategy is through organic growth. The firm opened a global innovation center in Chicago to serve as the firm's creative hub to expand research and development activities—including new and used products, packaging, and designs. Since the center's opening in 2005, Wrigley has launched 72 new products and brand extensions.[41]

A conglomerate diversification strategy *refers to adding unrelated goods or services to its line of businesses.* A firm may acquire another company or start a venture in a totally new field. Diversified enterprises operating unrelated businesses most often purchase established companies. As mentioned previously, this corporate-level strategy is usually viewed with skepticism by financial and management experts. The acquiring firm seeks organizations that can enhance its growth, overall stability, or balance in the firm's total portfolio of companies, especially in terms of better use and generation of resources.

General Electric and Berkshire Hathaway are among the few firms that have successfully used this strategy. Berkshire Hathaway, Inc., headquartered in Omaha, Nebraska, has approximately 35 subsidiaries engaged in a number of unrelated business activities. A few of these include Acme Brick Company, Benjamin Moore Co., Fruit of the Loom, GEICO Corporation, H. H. Brown Shoe Company, International Dairy Queen, Inc., John Manville Corporation, See's Candies, and Star Furniture.[42] Warren Buffet has been a key shareholder and chairman of the board of Berkshire Hathaway since 1965 and has recently decided to step out of that role.[43] One of Berkshire Hathaway's recent unrelated acquisitions is Business Wire for approximately $550 million. Business Wire electronically distributes company press releases and other company information to news media, online services, and databases worldwide.[44]

Executive Compensation and Corporate Growth.

With corporate growth that leads to higher stock prices and reported profits, top-level corporate and business executives are often richly rewarded through increases in salary, higher annual bonuses, and lucrative stock options.[45] In brief, a stock option *is a contractual right granted by a company to the employee to purchase a defined number of shares of the company's stock at a fixed price within a specified period of time.*[46] Most options give the employee the right to buy the stock at a future point in time at the market price on the day the option is granted, often up to 10 years into the future. Stock options and other incentive-based programs often serve as effective mechanisms to motivate executives to work on behalf of serving the interests of shareholders through increasing the per share value of the stock. During the past 15 years, stock option grants have emerged as the single largest component of executive compensation in the United States.[47]

With appropriate design and corporate board oversight, the incentive-based executive compensation programs that are designed to foster growth in sales, profits, and share prices are often effective. However, there are many notable exceptions, as evidenced by the scandals of executive greed and even illegal behavior that have been played out before the public in recent years.

The 2001 bankruptcy and eventual failure of the Enron Corporation, an energy-related firm that was headquartered in Houston, Texas, is often presented as a prime example of the unrestrained unethical and illegal behaviors by a number of the firm's top executives. The questionable design and poorly monitored executive compensation program is often cited as one of the key factors in motivating the top executives to make short-term decisions to enrich themselves at the long-term costs to the firm's other stakeholders—customers, employees, suppliers, shareholders, and others.[48] A number of its top executives pleaded guilty to or were found guilty by the courts of various forms of fraud and conspiracy to deceive shareholders, the government, and others.

The following Ethical Challenge reports on some of the testimony by Sherron Watkins, a former vice president at Enron, at the 2006 trial for Kenneth L. Lay,

Enron's former chairman, and Jeffrey K. Skilling, Enron's former chief executive officer.[49] They were on trial for fraud and conspiracy that contributed to Enron's bankruptcy. Both were found guilty by a jury of multiple charges. Not long after the trial, Kenneth Lay died unexpectedly of a heart attack, prior to sentencing. What do you think were the ethical challenges experienced by Watkins at the time of her employment at Enron?

Ethical Challenge

Sherron Watkins' Enron-Related Court Testimony

In June 2001, Watkins went to work for then–chief financial officer Andrew Fastow and was assigned to examine assets the company might sell. What she found, she said, was that Fastow's LJM side company had already gotten its money back with profit, leaving the failing Raptors owing Enron $500 million it didn't have to pay out. At Enron, "Raptors" was the code name for special-purpose entities. They were intended to shield Enron from market losses in its growing equity business. (Fastow later pleaded guilty in a plea bargain that involved a 10-year prison sentence.) "Accounting just doesn't get that creative," she said. Her concern was mounting, she said, when in mid-August Jeff Skilling resigned as the company's CEO. Watkins stated "It told me he was a smart man . . . this stuff I stumbled across, he knows it. He knows it's bad and he's getting out."

On questioning by prosecutor John Hueston, she said she trusted Lay and thought he didn't know about the Raptors, so she decided to warn him. She wrote her famous seven-page memo August 15, 2001, leaving it anonymous at first, then met with Lay on August 22 and revealed that she had authored the memo. Her memo stated, in part: "It sure looks to the layman on the street that we are hiding losses in a related company. I am incredibly nervous that we will implode in a wave of accounting scandals." She had about 30 minutes with Lay in which she asked him to "come clean" about Fastow's side deals for the company's sake. "I did most of the talking. He seemed kind of surprised these things could be problems," she said. Watkins said Lay winced when he read that an employee said: "'I wish we would get caught, we are such a crooked company.'" She said she thought Lay took her seriously. He asked if she'd told anyone outside the company about her concerns and she said no.

Watkins indicated that she asked Lay to investigate without using Houston law firm Vinson & Elkins and Enron auditors Arthur Andersen, because those professionals had already signed off on questionable deals. But Lay did use Vinson & Elkins for the investigation. Watkins contended the law firm lied to her when claiming it had checked the accounting. She noted that the law firm did not satisfy a duty to its client in this case.

Watkins testified how she trusted Lay before she went to him with her memo in August 2001. But she said he later lied to analysts in a conference call in October 2001 about the Raptors established through Fastow's LJM side company. "It was a blatant lie . . . to say these could have been done with anyone else," Watkins said of the many overvalued Enron assets hedged in Fastow's financial vehicles. "You don't make statements like that, they're misleading." She said Lay also misled employees that same day. Lay kept making upbeat public statements that were inconsistent with her perception of deep financial troubles. She told the jury: "I was surprised that . . . he could make those statements. If my allegations were true, then those statements would be very, very false."

Business-Level Strategy

Business-level strategy *refers to the resources allocated and actions taken to achieve desired goals in serving a specific market with a highly interrelated set of goods and/or services.* The focus is on using the firm's present and continuously developing organizational capabilities in specific markets.[50] Business-level strategies are developed for each of the businesses within J&J, GE, and MTV Networks. For a single-business firm, there is no distinction between business-level and corporate-level strategies. For example, the top managers at Lowe's focus primarily on business-level strategies because its activities and services are highly related.

Top managers of a firm or SBU focus on planning and formulating strategies for (1) maintaining or gaining a competitive edge in serving its customers, (2) determining how each functional area (e.g., production, human resources, marketing, and finance) can best contribute to its overall effectiveness, and (3) allocating resources for expansion and among its functions.[51] A focus on customers is the foundation of successful business-level plans and strategies. This focus requires attention to three basic questions:

1. *Who will be served?* Customer needs and demand may vary according to demographic characteristics (e.g., age, gender, income, occupation, education, race, nationality, and social class), geographic location, lifestyle choices (e.g., single or married, with or without children), type of customer (e.g., manufacturers, wholesalers, retailers, or end customers), and so on. Lowe's focuses on selling to *do-it-yourself* customers, *do-it-for-me* customers, remodeling firms, and small-scale builders. It is estimated that Lowe's serves approximately 12 million customers each week.[52]

2. *What customer needs will be satisfied?* Lowe's serves primarily the needs of homeowners who want to beautify, maintain, repair, or enlarge their homes. Renters are served as well, but they do not purchase as wide of a range of Lowe's products and services. Remodeling firms and small-scale builders purchase items with the intent of serving homeowners and, to a lesser extent, small-scale businesses engaged in repair or renovation projects.

3. *How will customers' needs be satisfied?* Lowe's strives to satisfy customers by providing large, bright, clean, and well-organized stores with a comprehensive array of products and services to meet virtually all home improvement needs.[53] A variety of special in-store services are offered, such as (1) professional installation services if the homeowner does not want to do it; (2) home delivery seven days a week; (3) free how-to-do it clinics, customer color matching, free computer-based designs for kitchens, decks, and storage buildings; (4) custom cutting of lumber, miniblinds, pipe, rope, chain, and more; and (5) employee assembly of items.

Functional-Level Strategy

Functional-level strategy *refers to the actions and resource commitments established for operations, marketing, human resources, finance, legal services, accounting, and the organization's other functional areas.* Functional-level plans and strategies should support business-level strategies and plans. At the functional level, these tasks often involve a combination of strategic and tactical planning. Table 7.2 on the following page provides examples of the issues that management in various types of firms usually address when developing functional-level plans and strategies.

Operations strategies *specify how the firm will develop and utilize its production capabilities to support the firm's business-level strategies.* Marketing strategies *address how the firm will distribute and sell its goods and services.* Finance strategies *identify how best to obtain and allocate the firm's financial resources.*

In Chapter 13, we discuss a number of issues central to developing a functional plan and strategy in human resource management. Among others, these issues include the legal and regulatory environment, staffing, training and development, performance appraisals, and compensation.[54] For example, Lowe's human resource department develops and updates job descriptions and helps to recruit in 36 functional areas, such

Table 7.2	**Examples of Issues Addressed in Developing Functional Strategies**

SAMPLE FUNCTIONS	SAMPLE KEY ISSUES
Human resources	■ What type of reward system is needed? ■ How should the performance of employees be reviewed? ■ What approach should be used to recruit qualified personnel? ■ How is affirmative and fair treatment ensured for women, minorities, and the disabled?
Finance	■ What is the desired mixture of borrowed funds and equity funds? ■ What portion of profits should be reinvested and what portion paid out as dividends? ■ What criteria should be used in allocating financial and human resources to projects? ■ What should be the criteria for issuing credit to customers?
Marketing	■ What goods or services should be emphasized? ■ How should products be distributed (e.g., direct selling, wholesalers, retailers, etc.)? ■ Should competition be primarily on price or on other factors? ■ What corporate image and product features should be emphasized to customers?
Operations (manufacturing)	■ What should be the level of commitment to total quality? ■ How should suppliers be selected? ■ Should the focus be on production runs for inventory or producing primarily in response to customer orders? ■ What production operations should be changed (e.g., automated or laid out differently) to improve productivity?

as accounting/finance, business development, distribution/transportation, information technology, merchandising, and store management.[55] Lowe's has a sophisticated online system for posting positions. It represents a joint effort of the firm's human resource and information technology functions.

4.

State the primary tasks of the strategic business-level planning process.

Business-Level Strategic Planning Tasks and Process

The planning process that we present applies primarily to single-business firms, SBUs, and highly related-business firms. It comprises a sequence of eight primary tasks, which are summarized in Figure 7.5. However, these tasks and the process do not necessarily have to be undertaken in the sequence we show to be successful. In practice, managers and teams, such as at Lowe's, involved in business-level planning often jump back and forth between tasks, or even skip tasks, as they develop their plans.

Task 1: Develop Vision, Mission, and Goals

We noted previously that an organization's vision, mission(s), and goals are guided by considering questions such as these: What business are we in? What are we committed

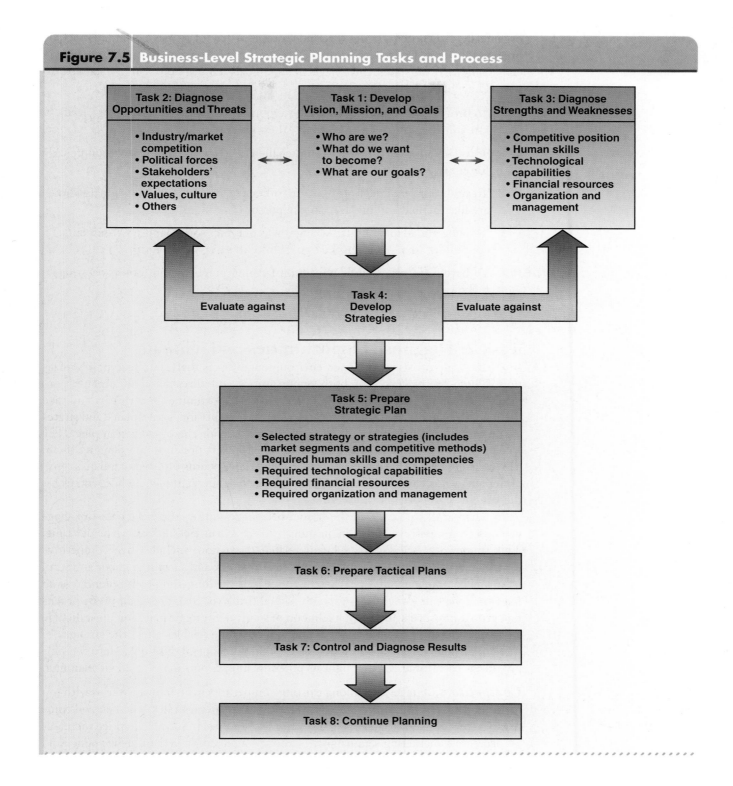

Figure 7.5 | **Business-Level Strategic Planning Tasks and Process**

Task 2: Diagnose Opportunities and Threats
- Industry/market competition
- Political forces
- Stakeholders' expectations
- Values, culture
- Others

Task 1: Develop Vision, Mission, and Goals
- Who are we?
- What do we want to become?
- What are our goals?

Task 3: Diagnose Strengths and Weaknesses
- Competitive position
- Human skills
- Technological capabilities
- Financial resources
- Organization and management

Evaluate against → **Task 4: Develop Strategies** ← Evaluate against

Task 5: Prepare Strategic Plan
- Selected strategy or strategies (includes market segments and competitive methods)
- Required human skills and competencies
- Required technological capabilities
- Required financial resources
- Required organization and management

Task 6: Prepare Tactical Plans

Task 7: Control and Diagnose Results

Task 8: Continue Planning

to? What results do we want to achieve? General goals provide a sense of direction for decision making and may not change from year to year. The vision, mission(s), and goals are not developed in isolation. They are affected by an assessment of external opportunities and threats (task 2) and strengths and weaknesses (task 3).

Eden Foods, headquartered in Clinton, Michigan, is a producer and distributor of 250 organically grown and processed foods. Eden's products are made from ingredients grown by 300 certified-organic North American farms. It also imports some organically grown items from Asia and Europe. A few of its EDEN brands include organic tomatoes, Quinoa, vinegar, oils, mustard, and Artesian Spring Water. Eden's *Our Company Goals* statement reflects general goals that do not change from year to year. They include the following[56]:

▶ To provide the highest quality life supporting food and to disseminate accurate information about these foods, their uses and benefits.

▶ To maintain a healthy, respectful, challenging, and rewarding environment for employees.

▶ To cultivate sound relationships with other organizations and individuals who are like minded and involved in like pursuits.

▶ To cultivate adaptability to change in economic, social, and environmental conditions, to allow Eden the opportunity to survive long term.

▶ To have a strong, positive impact on farming practices and food processing techniques throughout the world.

▶ To contribute to peaceful evolution on Earth.

Task 2: Diagnose Opportunities and Threats

In Chapters 4 and 5, we discussed environmental forces that can affect an organization. These forces represent both opportunities and threats for an organization. Strategic planning helps managers identify these opportunities and threats and take them into account when developing an organization's mission, goals, plans, and strategies. Political forces and stakeholders within and outside the organization play a key role in determining its mission and goals and also exert pressure for changing them. Top managers negotiate with powerful stakeholders (boards of directors, banks, governments, major customers, and suppliers) in an attempt to influence those forces for the benefit of the organization.

In Chapter 4, we reviewed the framework suggested by Michael Porter for diagnosing the competitive forces in an industry that a firm faces at any particular time. This framework (see Figure 4.4 and related discussion) includes five competitive forces: competitors, new entrants, customers, suppliers, and substitute goods and services. The combined strength of these forces affects the long-run profit potential of an industry. That, in turn, affects each individual firm's (or SBU's) overall profit potential, growth prospects, and even likelihood of survival. Strategic planning must include an assessment of these five forces. Numerous specific variables affect the strength of each force, but a review of all variables is beyond the scope of this book. Here, we simply review each force and highlight its potential impact on a firm's strategic planning.

Competitors. The rivalry among existing competitors in an industry varies with top management's view of threats or opportunities, the strategies a firm pursues, and competitors' reactions to those strategies. A few of these reactions include price increases or decreases, marketing campaigns, introduction of improved or new goods, and changes in customer service. Three of the variables affecting the strength of rivalry among competitors are the number of firms in the industry, the rate of industry growth, and the level of fixed costs.

The many manufacturers (mostly assemblers) of personal computers, growth in demand for PCs, and ever improving computer-based capabilities have combined to create intense rivalry among firms in the PC industry. Through endless combinations of price cuts, improved features, and service enhancements, global and local suppliers of PCs have attempted to gain a competitive edge over their competitors. Some of the global PC firms operating today include Dell, Hewlett-Packard, and Lenovo.

New Entrants. The entry of new competitors into an industry is often in response to high profits earned by established firms and/or rapid growth in an industry. The difficulties that new competitors experience are influenced by the barriers to entry and the reactions of established competitors. Barriers to entry are factors that make entering an industry relatively easy or relatively difficult. Two important barriers are economies of scale (lower costs as volumes increase) and capital requirements to enter the industry. The nuclear power and pharmaceutical industries have significant barriers to entry, including government rules and regulations, capital requirements, and patent approvals. The opening of a local Subway sandwich store has few barriers to entry.

The Internet has created a revolution of new firms entering the market of traditional firms. For example, many brick-and-mortar travel agencies have closed, merged, downsized, or changed their strategies as a result of online travel services—such as Expedia.com, Travelocity.com, and Travelzoo.com—and the major development of online passenger reservation systems by airlines.

The primary tasks of the strategic business-level planning process help managers and teams plan for ongoing changes in their business environments.

Customers. The bargaining power of customers depends on their relative ability to play one firm against another in order to force down prices, obtain higher quality, or buy more goods or services for the same price. As a result of deregulation, new computer-based technologies, digital convergence, and new competitors, the power of customers in purchasing telecommunications services has increased substantially during the past dozen years.

The bargaining power of customers is likely to be great in the following situations:

▶ *A small number of customers purchase relatively large volumes from the seller.* For instance, major automobile manufacturing firms buy tires from a few makers, for example, Goodyear, Michelin, and Bridgestone.

▶ *Customers purchase standard and undifferentiated goods or services.* Customers may perceive few differences between many telecommunications services, such as different long-distance and wireless services.

▶ *Customers can easily switch from one seller to another.* Credit card providers often make switching easy.

Suppliers. The bargaining power of suppliers increases when they can raise or protect market share, increase prices, or eliminate certain features of their goods or services with little fear of losing customers. The situations that tend to make suppliers more powerful are similar to those that make customers more powerful. The bargaining power of suppliers is likely to be great in the following situations:

▶ *A small number of suppliers sell to a large number of customers in an industry.* Several years ago, Microsoft was found guilty by a federal court of abusing its supplier power.

▶ *Suppliers don't have to worry about substitute goods or services that their customers can readily buy.* Enron was found guilty of manipulating and distorting the availability of electrical power in several markets to artificially raise prices to its customers, who had little choice in the short term other than to pay the increased price and attempt to conserve electrical energy.

> *Supplier's goods or services are differentiated by quality, image, and service, among others.* Intel attempts to differentiate its microprocessors (computer chips) through mass advertising to PC purchasers. In contrast, Lexus attempts to appeal to a limited portion of automobile purchasers by differentiating itself from competitors—such as Cadillac, BMW, Audi, and Mercedes-Benz—through style, quality, and service.

Substitute Goods or Services. The threat of substitute goods or services depends on the ability and willingness of customers to change their buying habits. Substitutes limit the price that firms in a particular industry can charge for their products without risking a loss in sales. Cable television providers are being challenged by providers of digital satellite television transmission, such as DirecTV and Dish. Brinks and other armored car and guard operators were threatened by the increase in the number of electronic surveillance firms. As a result, Brinks and other traditional security firms have rapidly diversified into providing a wide range of technology-based security services, including those for the home.

Task 3: Diagnose Strengths and Weaknesses

Core Competencies. The diagnosis of strengths and weaknesses enables managers to identify an organization's core competencies and to determine which need to be improved. This diagnosis includes the organization's market share, ability to adapt and innovate, human resource skills, technological capabilities, financial resources, managerial depth, and the values and background of its key employees. Core competencies *are the strengths that make an organization distinctive and competitive by providing goods or services that have unique value to its customers.* Core competencies fall into three broad groups: superior technological know-how, reliable processes, and close relationships with external stakeholders. A *reliable process* involves delivering an expected result quickly, consistently, and efficiently with the least inconvenience to customers.[57] Ideally, a firm's core competencies make imitation difficult for competitors. Core organizational competencies represent strengths. Most managers find that assessing their organization's strengths is easier than assessing its weaknesses. Weaknesses often are blamed on specific managers, employees, or events. As a result, statements of organizational weaknesses may be perceived as personal threats to their positions, influence, and self-esteem. But weaknesses are not self-correcting and are likely to become worse if not fully addressed in the strategic planning process.

Ted Rouse directs the Global Business Practice of Bain and Company, a highly respected consulting firm. This organization has the mission of helping to make companies more valuable. Bain has 31 offices in 19 countries. Rouse comments[58]:

> If you look at most of the corporate tragedies in the last five years, you'll also discover that many of them were companies moving into other businesses they really shouldn't have moved into, that weren't close to their core business and competencies, including Enron, Kmart, and Worldcom. If you're having problems in your core business and think you can move to another business, it's not going to work. You have to have strong assets you can build on. The farther away people got from their core business and competencies, the lower their rate of success.[59]

Table 7.3 provides a basic framework for beginning the assessment of some organizational strengths and weaknesses. In some firms, senior-, middle-, and first-level managers develop statements of opportunities, threats, strengths, and weaknesses for their areas of responsibility. Issues assessed by midlevel plant managers usually are quite different from those considered by top managers. Plant managers are likely to focus on manufacturing opportunities, threats, strengths, and weaknesses, whereas top managers are likely to focus on current and potential competitors, legislation and government regulations, societal trends, and the like. The key issues, regardless of their source, need to be addressed in the organization's strategic plan.

Table 7.3	Sample Factors in Diagnosing Strengths and Weaknesses

Instructions: Evaluate each issue on the basis of the following scale.

A = Superior to most competitors (top 10%).
B = Better than average. Good performance. No immediate problems.
C = Average. Equal to most competitors.
D = Problems here. Not as good as it should be. Deteriorating. Must be improved.
F = Major cause for concern. Crisis. Take immediate action to improve.

		Scale				
Category	**Issue**	**A**	**B**	**C**	**D**	**F**
Information technologies	Networking capabilities	___	___	___	___	___
	Service to customers	___	___	___	___	___
	Product features	___	___	___	___	___
Human resources	Employee competencies	___	___	___	___	___
	Reward systems	___	___	___	___	___
	Team orientation	___	___	___	___	___
Marketing	Channels of distribution	___	___	___	___	___
	Advertising effectiveness	___	___	___	___	___
	Customer satisfaction	___	___	___	___	___
Finance	Ability to obtain loans	___	___	___	___	___
	Debt-equity relationship	___	___	___	___	___
	Inventory turnover	___	___	___	___	___
Manufacturing	Per unit cost	___	___	___	___	___
	Inventory control	___	___	___	___	___
	Quality process	___	___	___	___	___

Outsourcing Strategy. An increasing number of firms are outsourcing part or all the tasks and functions that are not core competencies (e.g., strengths) or represent a current or potential weakness. As you will recall from Chapter 4, the *outsourcing strategy* means contracting with other organizations to perform a needed service and/or manufacture needed parts or products that had previously been provided within the firm. Drivers for outsourcing include (1) expense reduction (including fewer employees), (2) better production quality, (3) improved reporting uniformity and regulatory compliance, (4) more effective use of expensive talent so that they can spend more of their time on innovating, (5) expanded global capabilities, and (6) more effective business process management. Although all of these are reasons for outsourcing, 80 percent of companies surveyed cite expense reduction as the main driver.[60] For example, many well-known companies—such as General Electric, British Petroleum, and Procter & Gamble—have contracted outsourcing service providers to manage significant pieces of their finance and accounting business processes.[61]

A few of the work processes that are being outsourced by some organizations, include the following.[62]

> *Finance and accounting:* such as accounts payable, billing, and financial and tax statements.

> *Manufacturing:* such as contract production of everything from electronics to medical devices.

> *Customer service:* such as call centers for technical support, airline bookings, and bill collection.

> *Information technology:* such as software development, technical support, Web site design, and IT infrastructure.

> *Human resources:* such as payroll administration, benefits, and training programs.

> *Analysis:* such as market research, financial assessment, and risk calculation.

Task 4: Develop Strategies

The development of strategies must be evaluated in terms of (1) external opportunities and threats, (2) internal strengths and weaknesses, and (3) the likelihood that the strategies will help the organization achieve its mission and goals. Firms such as J&J, GE, and Berkshire Hathaway have a number of strategic business units. Thus, the development of corporate-level and business-level strategies for these organizations is typically a complex process.

As noted in Figure 7.6, business-level planning has three primary organic and growth strategies: market penetration, market development, and product development.

A market penetration strategy *involves seeking growth in current markets with current products or services.* A single-business firm or strategic business unit might increase

Figure 7.6 | **Organic Growth Strategies in Business-Level Planning**

market penetration by (1) encouraging greater use of its goods or services (e.g., getting current United Airlines customers to fly it or one of its partners by taking advantage of its Mileage Plus award travel programs), (2) attracting competitors' customers (e.g., getting Citibank credit card customers to switch to a Capital One Visa credit card), and (3) buying a competitor (e.g., Thor Industries, a recreational vehicle (RV) manufacturer, purchased ten RV companies during the past two decades with such brand names as Airstream, Mandalay, and Thor America).

A market development strategy *involves seeking new markets for current goods or services.* A single-business firm or strategic business unit might do this by (1) entering new geographic markets (e.g., Lowe's opening of stores in new cities and states), (2) entering strategic markets (e.g., with more than 9,000 brick-and-mortar stores, Blockbuster's decision—as a result of intense competition from Netflix—to begin an online DVD rental service), and (3) expanding uses for current products and facilities (e.g., Time Warner Cable's use of its cable lines to carry new multimedia, phone, and high-speed online services, rather than just television signals).

A product development strategy *involves developing new or improved goods or services for current markets.* A single-business firm or SBU within a corporation might do this by (1) improving features (e.g., Toyota Highlander's new hybrid model with improved gas mileage); (2) increasing quality in terms of reliability, speed, safety, or durability (e.g., Honda Accord's new model with more agile handling, a peppier V6 engine, and better crash test results); (3) enhancing aesthetic appeal (e.g., Infinity's M35 midsize luxury sedan with a new contemporary design); and (4) introducing new models (e.g., Ford's redesigned Ford Explorer model with many new features).

Task 5: Prepare Strategic Plan

After developing alternative strategies and selecting among them, management is ready to prepare the written strategic plan. *Plan Ware*, among others, is a useful online site (*www.planware.org*) that provides additional details on how to write a business plan.[63] The written plan should contain sections that address

▶ organizational vision, mission, and goals;

▶ goods and/or services offered, including what makes them unique;

▶ market analysis and strategies, including opportunities and threats and contingency plans if things don't go as expected;

▶ strategies for obtaining and utilizing the necessary technological, manufacturing, marketing, financial, and human resources to achieve the stated goals, including capitalizing on strengths and overcoming weaknesses as well as contingency plans in these areas;

▶ strategies for developing and utilizing organizational and employee competencies; and

▶ financial statements, including profit-and-loss, cash flow, and break-even projections.

Task 6: Prepare Tactical Plans

Tactical plans are intended to help implement strategic plans. As suggested in Task 6 of Figure 7.5, middle and first-line managers and employee teams normally base tactical plans on the organization's strategic plan. (See Table 7.1 for a summary of the features of tactical planning.) Four factors are important in determining the successful implementation of a tactical plan: (1) achieving it at or under budget, (2) executing it by or under the scheduled time frame, (3) meeting or exceeding the stated goals, and

(4) perhaps most importantly a clear communication of the key elements of the strategic plan itself throughout the organization.[64] Some research suggests that, on average, more than 90 percent of employees are unaware of or do not understand the organization's corporate or business-level strategies. This helps to explain why such strategies may fail to be implemented successfully.[65]

The following Communication Competency feature provides a few of the features of the communication program developed by Bombardier, Inc., to engage its employees with business priorities and strategies.[66] Among other products, Bombardier manufactures and services aviation and light rail products. The firm has approximately 60,000 employees worldwide under such brand names as Bombardier, Learjet, and Challenger. The firm is headquartered in Montreal, Quebec.[67]

Communication Competency

Bombardier's Strategic Employee Engagement

The need to address the issue of employee engagement at Bombardier Aerospace began in earnest in 2001 when the aerospace industry took a nosedive. "Bombardier Aerospace had enjoyed 10 to 15 years of uninterrupted growth," says Lise St-Arnaud, director of internal communication at Bombardier. "Suddenly instead of hiring people, we were laying people off—our employees weren't used to that."

Employee engagement now forms one of the company's three business priorities. The goal, says St-Arnaud, is simple: to make sure people have the knowledge and understanding of business priorities to guide their decisions and actions, and the capability—in terms of skills, tools, processes, and overall organizational culture—to contribute to those goals. This definition demands two primary areas of focus: building intellectual engagement through knowledge, and maintaining emotional engagement through organizational culture.

On the intellectual side, tough industry times made it apparent that a simple lack of business acumen was limiting employees' ability to mobilize against new industry threats. St-Arnaud states: "We realized that employees just didn't really understand the strategic challenges faced by the industry as a whole, or what they represented for us as an organization." To help leaders and managers cascade business-critical information, the communication function provides a series of tools. For example:

▶ *Quarterly results.* The chief operating officer (COO) initially shares the quarterly results with top managers via a videoconference. He runs through a series of slides relating the results to the company's key business priorities, and within this context talks about challenges, issues, and areas of focus for the coming months. Managers get the chance for Q&A at the end of the session.

After the meeting, the slides are sent to all middle-level managers so they can pull from the main document the information of most importance for their teams, focusing on the areas where they can make the most impact. The communication unit provides additional key messages to support the cascade process, and communication specialists located within various countries and business units are available to provide further support.

▶ *Major events or announcements.* Any major organizational announcement is carefully planned to make sure all messages are consistent, timely (delivered internally before or at the same time as any external announcements are made), distributed simultaneously (bearing in mind geographical time differences), and focused on the company's strategy and business priorities.

A plan is drawn up by the communication function detailing when the announcement will be made to different audiences, and who is responsible for each element of communication. All senior managers involved—as well as union representatives—are given a chance to go over the plan and provide input before announcements are made.

To learn more about this organization, visit *www.bombardier.com*.

Task 7: Control and Diagnose Results

Controls are needed to ensure implementation of plans as intended and to evaluate the results achieved through those plans. If the plans haven't produced the desired results, managers and teams may need to change the mission and goals, revise the strategies, develop new tactical plans, or change the controls utilized. A thorough assessment of results will reveal specific changes that need to be incorporated in the next planning cycle. In Chapter 10, we discuss various types of organizational controls. Controls help to reduce and correct deviations from plans and provide useful information to the ongoing planning process.

Task 8: Continue Planning

Planning is a continuing and ongoing process. The external (e.g., new competitors) and internal (e.g., expectations of new employees) environments are constantly changing. Sometimes these changes are gradual and foreseeable. At other times, they are abrupt and unpredictable, which was experienced by Bank of New York, American Express, and numerous other firms due to the acts of terrorism perpetrated on September 11, 2001.

Generic Competitive Strategies Model

5.

Explain the generic competitive strategies model.

Competitive strategies must be based on some source of comparative advantage to be successful. Companies build comparative advantage when they take actions that enable them to gain an edge relative to their competitors in attracting customers. These actions may vary from making the highest quality product to providing outstanding customer service to producing a product at the lowest cost. Regardless of the actions selected to build a comparative advantage, customers must perceive superior value than that offered by competitors.

Organizations have attempted to build comparative advantage through an infinite number of ways. The generic competitive strategies model *provides a framework of four basic business-level strategies for a variety of organizations in diverse industries.*[68] This model is called *generic* because all types of organizations can use it, whether they are involved in manufacturing, distribution, or services. Figure 7.7 on the next page shows the basic parts of this model. The *strategic target* dimension (vertical axis) indicates how widely the good or service is intended to compete—industrywide or within a particular market segment of the industry. The *source of advantage* dimension (horizontal axis) indicates the basis on which the good or service is intended to compete—uniqueness as perceived by the customer or low cost (price) to the customer. The various combinations of these two variables, strategic target and source of advantage, suggest four different generic competitive strategies: differentiation strategy, focused differentiation strategy, cost leadership strategy, and focused cost leadership strategy. The three basic growth strategies for a single-business firm or SBU—market penetration, market development, and product development—can be used within each of these generic competitive strategies.

Differentiation Strategy

The differentiation strategy *involves competing by offering goods or services that customers perceive to be unique in ways that are important to them.* This strategy is dominant in much of the auto industry. Most automakers attempt to create unique value (benefits) by influencing customer perceptions and/or providing real differences for each automobile make and model. They use various strategies, including innovative product design (BMW), high quality (Infiniti), unique brand image (Mercedes-Benz), technological leadership (Honda's hybrid model), customer service leadership (Lexus), an

Figure 7.7 | Generic Competitive Strategies Model

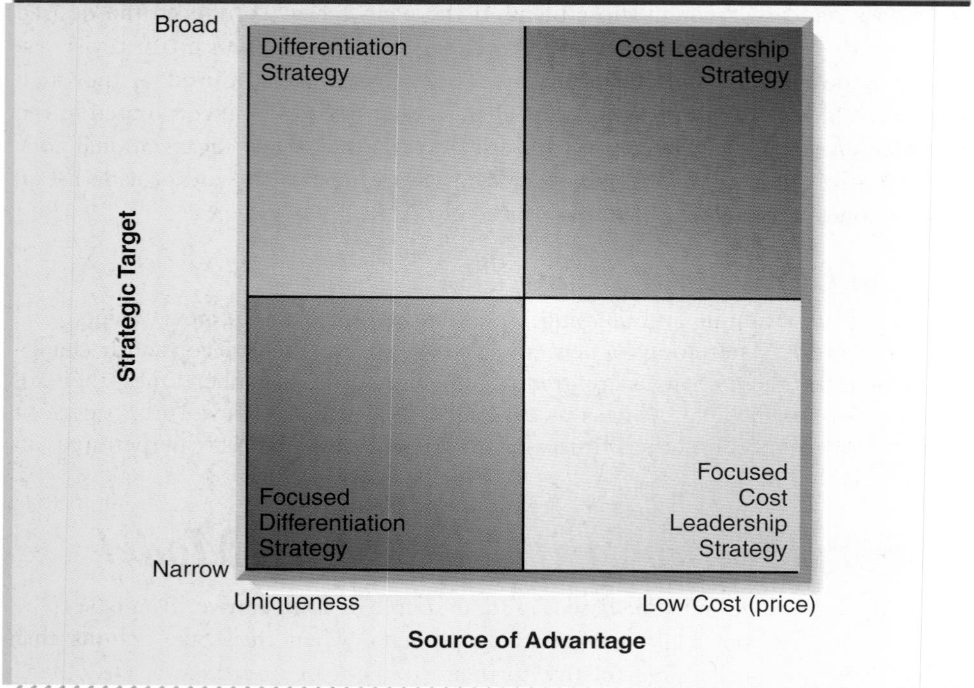

Source of Advantage diagram with axes: Strategic Target (Broad to Narrow) vs. Source of Advantage (Uniqueness to Low Cost (price)). Quadrants: Differentiation Strategy, Cost Leadership Strategy, Focused Differentiation Strategy, Focused Cost Leadership Strategy.

Snapshot

"The best strategy for a smaller business is to divide demand into manageable market niches. Small operations can then offer specialized goods and services attractive to a specific group of prospective buyers. . . . Try to find the right configuration of products, services, quality and price that will ensure the least direct competition."

Ron Consolino, Management Counselor, Counselors to America's Small Business

extensive dealer network (Ford and GM), and product warranty (Hyundai's five-year, 60,000-mile bumper-to-bumper warranty). The long-term effectiveness of the differentiation strategy depends on how easily competitors can copy the unique benefits provided by the firm. As soon as most or all competitors imitate the offering (such as bumper-to-bumper car warranties), it is no longer an effective means of differentiation.

A few of the requirements for implementing the differentiation strategy include (1) strong marketing, (2) effective integration among functions, (3) creative and innovative employees, (4) continuous development of new or improved products and services, and (5) a reputation for quality and a commitment to continuous improvement in it. If successful, several benefits of this strategy include (1) fewer price wars, (2) loyal customers who are less sensitive to price competition, (3) increased market share, and (4) greater difficulty for competitors trying to copy the firm's goods or services.

Focused Differentiation Strategy

The focused differentiation strategy *involves competing in a specific niche by serving the unique needs of certain customers or a specific geographic market. A niche* is a specialized group of customers (e.g., undergraduate college students, heart surgeons, or military retirees) or a narrowly defined market segment that competitors may overlook, ignore, or have difficulty serving (e.g., an inner-city area being redeveloped or rehabilitated). Organizations attempt to create a unique image for their products by catering to the specific demands of the selected niche and ignoring other potential customers. Strategic actions associated with the focused differentiation strategy are adaptations of those associated with differentiation, but are applied to a specific market niche. This strategy is often critical to the success of smaller businesses, as we suggested in Chapter 6, *Fostering Entrepreneurship.*

Within the auto industry, several firms produce and sell cars that emphasize the focused differentiation strategy. Bugatti Automobiles S.A.S., headquartered in Molsheim, France, is one such firm. For example, one of its models, the Bugatti Veyron 16.4, is priced at approximately $1.2 million. It is available direct from the factory—produced to order—and purchased or serviced through top-of-the-line dealerships such as Bentley and Mercedes-Benz. One U.S. dealer touts it as "the car for billionaires."

The following Multicultural Competency reports on one entrepreneur's use of the focused differentiation strategy, which required the development and use of her multicultural competency.[69]

Amanda Knauer, Founder of Qara Argentina

Fresh out of college and living in a tiny apartment in Manhattan, New York, Amanda Knauer concluded that she wouldn't land her dream job—combining fashion design with the adventure of international business—at her age. So, Knauer decided to go to Buenos Aires, Argentina, often called the Paris of South America, in 2004 at the age of 24. She arrived with one suitcase, $45,000 in the bank, and a conversational knowledge of Spanish. She explored the city streets for inspiration, and it didn't take long to find her opportunity: Argentine leather.

Within months, she launched Qara Argentina, a luxury leather-accessories company that makes hand-crafted calfskin wallets, messenger bags, and other leather trimmings, targeting what she deems an underserved market: 25- to 40-year-old urban men.

For an entrepreneur establishing a business in a foreign country—or even setting up an overseas unit—it is easy to make a mistake if you assume what would work well at home would work in another country. Knauer comments: "Everything reverts back to the cultural divide, which is also what makes it interesting. You can't come here as an American and expect to do business as an American. You have to observe and immerse yourself and study the Argentine way of doing business and more or less mimic it."

Knauer had to quickly master unfamiliar business approaches without a partner, as well as craft an authentic Argentine persona for her company so that she'd receive the same treatment from suppliers as an indigenous operation would. She immediately contacted a lawyer, whom she found through friends back home, and incorporated in both countries. Her lawyer also helped her find an "on-paper-only" Argentine partner. The arrangement cost money, but having such a partner made it much easier to incorporate in Argentina.

Knauer initially used well-known leather manufacturers, but they had trouble translating her ideas into goods that met her standards. Seven months after Qara's creation, she rented a 1,200-square-foot space in the heart of Buenos Aires for $365 a month, bought second-hand machines, and found artisans through advertising in the local paper.

When she discovered that several leather tanneries she visited were inflating their prices to her, Knauer says "I realized . . . what I needed to do was hire more Argentines to go as my cultural brokers. There were linguistic subtleties that an American would just miss, as well as cultural issues."

Qara's goods retail anywhere from $60 for a calfskin credit-card holder and $65 for an iBook laptop cover, to $286 for a leather messenger bag and $650 for a weekend bag. Qara's line is currently available through its Web site, as well as a boutique, Foley + Corinna, in Manhattan. Knauer is seeking department-store shelves to bring her brand to the next level.

To learn more about this organization, visit *www.qara.com*.

The biggest risk with this strategy is that the underlying market may shift. Distinctive tastes and product characteristics may blur over time, thus reducing the defensibility of the niche. In home building, large U.S. home builders, such as Pulte Homes, Toll Brothers, and Centex, are beginning to invest in new technologies that allow customers to create their own home designs. In effect, this creates more direct competition for custom home builders. Finally, customers can quickly fall out of love with a product if the focused differentiation strategy is compromised to expand sales. When Krispy Kreme opened its stores in the 1980s, an almost "cult-like" following among very committed customers began. Customers would line up early in the morning for fresh-from-the-oven doughnuts. As they made their doughnuts available at gas stations and grocery stores, the cult-like status and freshness of Krispy Kreme doughnuts disappeared. Customers quickly fell out of love with their product and sales rapidly declined.

Cost Leadership Strategy

The cost leadership strategy *means competing by providing goods or services at a price as low as or lower than competitors' prices.* This strategy requires a constant concern with efficiency (e.g., reduction in per unit costs). A few of the requirements for implementing the cost leadership strategy include (1) utilizing facilities or equipment that yield high economies of scale; (2) constantly striving to reduce per unit overhead, manufacturing, marketing, labor, and follow-up service costs; (3) minimizing labor-intensive personal services and sales forces; and (4) avoiding customers whose demands would result in high personal selling or service costs. High volume and/or rapid growth often are needed for profitability with the cost leadership strategy. Wal-Mart, for example, has been able to keep potential direct competitors out of their market through its low-price strategy. Its "everyday low prices" generate substantial obstacles for companies trying to compete in this segment of the retail industry.

Online personal investing and financial services firms, such as E*Trade Financial Corporation, use the cost leadership strategy. E*Trade emphasizes its low commission and margin rates on its Web site by advertising statements such as "No annual fees," "No account minimums," "Customizable, no-fee trading platform," "Trade from $6.99–9.99 + 75 cents option contracts," and "Free cash management tools including checking and bill paying."[70]

Several potential benefits of a cost leadership strategy are that it (1) results in higher market share, (2) imposes discipline on competitors to not start price wars because they know there will be an immediate response, and (3) detracts competitors from entering the market because of the need to achieve very low costs in producing the good or service.

Focused Cost Leadership Strategy

The focused cost leadership strategy *refers to competing in a specific customer or geographic niche by providing goods and services at a price as low as or lower than competitors' prices.* The requirements implementing this strategy are aligned with those of cost leadership, but the focus is on serving a subset of customers in an industry, such as furniture buyers, or set of customers in a particular geographic area, such as a local furniture store that focuses on low price. Gallery Furniture in Houston, Texas, is one such example of the latter.

IKEA, the Swedish home furniture retailer, pursues a focused cost leadership strategy. IKEA vision states, in part[71]:

> The IKEA business idea is to offer a wide range of home furnishings with good design and function at prices so low that as many people as possible will be able to afford them. And still have money left!

IKEA's key strategy is to keep making furniture less expensive, without making it cheap. In addition to appearance and utility, IKEA's designers and engineers focus on using materials as efficiently as possible and analyze the function of every furniture surface. This is done to determine which materials, finishes, and construction techniques will work best for the least amount of money. The company-designed furniture is made by about 1,500 suppliers in more than 50 countries. There are many other aspects to IKEA's focused cost leadership strategy. For example, its products are designed to ship disassembled, flat enough to be slipped into an SUV or safely tied to the roof of an auto.[72]

The cost leadership strategy is not without risks. A major risk is the high level of resource commitment. To deliver a product/service at a low cost often requires firms to invest considerable sums into inflexible production and distribution channels that are difficult to use with other goods or services. This was the case with Motorola when, during the late 1990s, the company's analog-based cell phones were no longer competitive with the changing digital world. Another limitation is that other firms copy or imitate the product. Cost advantages, particularly in standardized products, are usually short lived as many U.S. steel manufacturers found out when China's Boa Steel Corporation started to compete against them in world-class steel projects.

There is no guarantee that any one strategy ensures success. A successful firm tends to develop and utilize a set of strategies that integrate functions, resources, and competencies to meet market demands, just as a symphony orchestra requires a score and conductor to integrate its many components to play in harmony.[73]

Integrated Strategy Model

6.

Explain the integrated strategy model.

Don Hambrick and Jim Fredrickson have presented a useful and acclaimed integrated strategy model, *which is a model consisting of five interrelated elements that attempt to provide answers to five questions.* These elements and questions are as follows:

▸ *Arenas*—where will the firm be active?

▸ *Vehicles*—how will the firm get there?

▸ *Differentiators*—how will the firm excel?

▸ *Staging*—what will be the firm's speed and sequence of moves?

▸ *Economic logic*—how will the firm obtain profits?

Figure 7.8 provides a representation of the interrelatedness of these elements and questions. Much of this chapter has focused on various facets of these elements and questions. Our discussion here serves to enrich and integrate our presentation in previous sections. Thus, we focus on the key points and concepts related to the model shown in Figure 7.8 on the following page rather than presenting examples and applications. This discussion is adopted from Hambrick and Fredrickson.[74]

Arenas

The most fundamental choices leaders make are those of where, or in what arenas, the business will be active. In defining arenas, it is important to be as specific as possible about the product categories, market segments, geographic areas, and core technologies, as well as the value-adding stages (e.g., product design, manufacturing, selling, servicing, distribution) the business intends to take on.

At Yum! Brands, the company has chosen to be in the quick-food-service arena through its strategic business units: KFC, Pizza Hut, Long John Silvers, Taco Bell, and A&W. It has chosen not to compete in the casual dining arena where Brinkers (e.g., Chili's, Romano's Macaroni Grill, On-the-Border), Carlson Restaurants (e.g., Friday's) and Outback Steakhouse, among others, compete for customers.

Figure 7.8 | **Integrated Strategy Model**

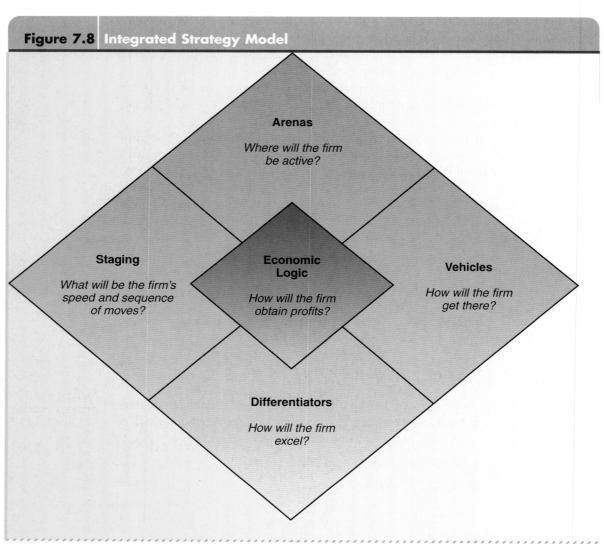

Arenas

Where will the firm be active?

Staging

What will be the firm's speed and sequence of moves?

Economic Logic

How will the firm obtain profits?

Vehicles

How will the firm get there?

Differentiators

How will the firm excel?

Source: Adapted from D. C. Hambrick and J. W. Fredrickson. Are you sure you have a strategy? Reprinted in *Academy of Management Executive*, 15(4), 2005, 54.

In choosing arenas, leaders need to indicate not only where the business will be active, but also how much emphasis will be placed on each. Some market segments, for instance, might be identified as centrally important, while others are deemed secondary. A strategy might reasonably be centered on one product category, with others—although necessary for defensive purposes or for offering customers a full line—being of less importance.

Vehicles

The means (vehicles) for attaining the needed presence in a particular product category, market segment, geographic area, or value-creation stage should be the result of deliberate strategic choice. If the leaders have decided to expand a product range, are they going to accomplish that by relying on internal product development, joint ventures, or acquisitions? If the leaders are committed to international expansion, what should be the primary modes, or vehicles—exporting, new start-up operations, local acquisitions, licensing, or joint ventures?

Differentiators

Differentiators focus on how the firm will succeed in the marketplace—how it will get customers to come its way. In a competitive world, success is the result of differentiators and they don't just happen. Leaders need to make up-front, conscious choices about which competitive strategies will be used to obtain customers, revenues, and profits. For example, Gillette uses its proprietary product and process technology to develop superior razor products, which the company further differentiates through a distinctive, aggressively advertised brand image. Regardless of the intended differentiators—image, customization, price, product styling, after-sale services, or others—the critical issue for leaders is to make up-front, deliberate choices.

Staging

Staging is the speed and sequence of major moves taken in order to heighten the likelihood of success. Most strategies do not call for equal, balanced initiatives on all fronts at all times. Instead, usually some initiatives must come first, followed only then by others, and then still others. In erecting a great building, the foundation must be laid, followed by walls, and only then the roof.

Decisions about staging can be driven by a number of factors. One, of course, is resources. Funding and staffing every envisioned initiative, at the needed levels, is generally not possible at the outset of a new strategic campaign. Urgency is a second factor affecting staging; some elements of a strategy may face brief windows of opportunity, requiring that they be pursued first and aggressively. A third factor is the achievement of credibility. Attaining certain results—in specific arenas, differentiators, or vehicles—can be critically valuable for attracting resources and stakeholders that are needed for other parts of the strategy. A fourth factor is the pursuit of early successes. It may be far wiser to effectively tackle a part of the strategy that is relatively doable before attempting more challenging or unfamiliar initiatives.

Economic Logic

At the heart of a business strategy must be a clear idea of how profits will be generated—not just some profits, but profits above the firm's cost of capital. The most successful strategies have a central economic logic that serves as the fulcrum for profit creation. In some cases, the economic key may be to obtain premium prices by offering customers a difficult-to-match product.

In other instances, the economic logic might reside on the cost side of the profit equation. ARAMARK is a leader in providing food, hospitality, and facility management services. Many stadiums and company cafeterias use ARAMARK services. By adding to its pricing leverage, via its huge scale of operations and presence in multiple market segments (business, educational, health care, and correctional-system food service), ARAMARK is able to achieve a sizable cost advantage in food purchases—an advantage that competitors (e.g., Sodexho) cannot easily duplicate.

Need for Unity

Table 7.4 on the next page provides a set of key criteria for evaluating the quality of a firm's proposed overarching strategy. All five elements must align with and support each other. All five require certain capabilities that cannot be generated spontaneously. All five elements are required to effectively design all of the other supporting activities—functional policies, organizational arrangements, operating programs, and processes—that are needed to reinforce the strategy. The five elements of the strategy diamond of Figure 7.8 can be considered the hub or central nodes for designing an integrated unifying strategy model.

Table 7.4	Criteria for Evaluating the Quality of a Firm's Integrated Strategy

■ Does the strategy fit with what's going on in the environment?
   1. Is there a healthy profit potential where the firm's headed?
   2. Does the strategy align with the key success factors of the chosen environment?

■ Does the strategy exploit the firm's key resources?
   1. With the firm's particular mix of resources, does this strategy give it a good head start on competitors?
   2. Can this strategy be pursued more economically than competitors can pursue their strategies?

■ Will the differentiators be sustainable?
   1. Will competitors have difficulty matching the firm?
   2. If not, does the strategy call for innovation and opportunity creation?

■ Are the elements of the strategy internally consistent?
   1. Have the leaders made choices of arenas, vehicles, differentiators, staging, and economic logic?
   2. Do they all fit and mutually reinforce each other?

■ Are there enough resources to pursue this strategy?
   1. Does the firm have the money, managerial competencies, and other capabilities to implement the strategy?
   2. Are the leaders sure that they are not spreading the firm's resources too thinly, only to be left with a collection of positions?

■ Is the strategy implementable?
   1. Will the key stakeholders allow the firm to pursue this strategy?
   2. Can the organization make it through the transition?
   3. Is the management team able and willing to lead the required changes?

Source: Adapted from D. C. Hambrick and J. W. Fredrickson. Are you sure you have a strategy? Reprinted in *Academy of Management Executive,* 19(4), 2005, 61.

Chapter Summary ....

This chapter focused on the development of your planning and administration and strategic action competencies. The formulation of plans and strategies at the corporate and business level was emphasized.

Learning Goals ....

1. Describe the importance and core components of strategic and tactical planning.

Planning is the most basic managerial function. It helps managers identify opportunities, anticipate problems, and develop appropriate strategies and tactics. If done properly, planning identifies threats and opportunities, facilitates entrepreneurship and innovations, and fosters learning.

Strategic planning focuses on the development of an organization's mission and vision, goals, general strategies, and major resource allocations. Tactical planning focuses on the shorter term detailed decisions regarding what to do, who will do it, and how to do it. Tactical planning specifies the actions for implementing strategic plans.

2. Discuss the effects of organizational diversification strategies on planning.

The primary organization-level diversification strategies vary from single-business strategy to dominant-business strategy, related-business strategy, and unrelated-businesses strategy. The complexity of strategic planning increases as an organization becomes more unrelated in terms of the range of differences in the goods and services the firm provides and the differences in the markets it serves.

3. Describe the basic levels of strategy and planning.

Corporate-level strategy focuses on the activities of various businesses (or product lines) within a parent organization. Corporate-level growth strategies include forward integration, backward integration, horizontal integration, related diversification, and conglomerate diversification. The organic strategy simply refers to initiatives to grow the firm's current businesses. Business-level strategy focuses on the operations and performance of a single-business firm or strategic business unit. Functional-level strategy focuses on the actions for managing each specialized area, such as accounting, finance, marketing, information systems, and human resources. It specifies how each function will contribute to the organization's business-level strategies and goals.

4. State the primary tasks of the strategic business-level planning process.

The planning process includes eight interrelated tasks: (1) develop the organization's vision, mission, and goals; (2) diagnose opportunities and threats; (3) diagnose strengths and weaknesses; (4) develop strategies; (5) prepare a strategic plan; (6) prepare tactical plans; (7) control and diagnose the results of both strategic and tactical plans; and (8) continue the planning process. Typical organic growth strategies in business-level planning include market penetration, market development, and product development.

5. Explain the generic competitive strategies model.

The generic competitive strategies model provides a framework of four basic business-level strategies (differentiation, focused differentiation, cost leadership, and focused cost leadership) that are applicable to various sizes and types of organizations in diverse industries.

6. Explain the integrated strategy model.

The integrated strategy model consists of five interrelated elements that attempt to provide answers to five major questions: (1) arenas—where will the firm be active? (2) vehicles—how will the firm get there? (3) differentiators—how will the firm excel in the marketplace? (4) staging—what will be the firm's speed and sequence of moves? and (5) economic logic—how will the firm obtain profits?

Key Terms and Concepts

Backward integration
strategy
Business-level strategy
Conglomerate diversifica-
tion strategy
Contingency planning
Core competencies
Corporate-level strategy
Cost leadership strategy
Differentiation strategy
Diversification
Dominant-business
strategy
Downscoping
Finance strategies
Focused cost leadership
strategy

Focused differentiation
strategy
Forward integration
strategy
Functional-level strategy
Generic competitive strate-
gies model
Horizontal integration
strategy
Integrated strategy model
Market development
strategy
Market penetration strategy
Marketing strategies
Mission
Operations strategies
Organizational goals

Product development
strategy
Related-business strategy
Related diversification
strategy
Resource allocation
Single-business strategy
Stock option
Strategic business unit
(SBU)
Strategic planning
Strategies
Tactical planning
Unrelated-business strategy
Vision

Questions for Discussion and Reflective Thinking

1. Review the Challenge of Managing feature on Judy McGrath, CEO of MTV Networks, and our other discussions on her within the chapter. What manageri-al competencies did she display?

2. Southwest Airlines states: "The mission of Southwest Airlines is dedication to the highest quality of customer service delivered with a sense of warmth, friendliness, individual pride and company spirit. To our employees: We are committed to pro-vide a stable work environment with equal opportunity for learning and personal growth. Creativity and innovation are encouraged for improving the effectiveness of Southwest Airlines. Above all, employees will be provided the same concern, respect and caring attitude within the organization that they are expected to share externally with every Southwest customer." Is this a good mission statement? Explain.

3. Think of the unit of an organization for which you have worked. Based on your experience, what seemed to be four of the elements of the tactical plan for that unit?

4. Review the Strategic Action Competency on Jeff Immelt's discussion of GE's business model. What aspects of corporate-level, business-level, and functional-level strategy are suggested in his comments?

5. Think of a firm for which you have worked. What were its strengths and weak-nesses? What were its opportunities and threats?

6. Consumer products giant Procter & Gamble (P&G) has an array of established brands (e.g., Tide, Crest, Ivory Soap) that people use to perform mostly basic

tasks. Assume that you are a member of P&G's top management team. What strategic factors and issues would you want to consider in deciding how to market and operate in various countries? Identify four strategies that P&G likely finds to be useful. Explain your selection of those strategies. For more information on Procter & Gamble, visit the firm's home page at *www.pg.com*.

7. Does Lowe's effectively address the three basic questions of (1) Who will be served? (2) What customer needs will be satisfied? and (3) How will customers' needs be satisfied? Explain. For more information on Lowe's, visit the firm's home page at *www.lowes.com*.

8. Think of a firm for which you have worked. What was its generic competitive strategy? Did it seem to be effective? Explain.

9. Examples abound of firms that have suffered because they lacked an effective strategy at one time or another—General Motors, Sears, Enron, Kmart, U.S. Air, and numerous others. Why might the use of the integrated strategy model have been helpful to the leaders of these organizations in avoiding or reducing the severity of their strategic problems?

DEVELOPING YOUR COMPETENCIES

Instructions

The business-level strategic planning tasks and process, as summarized in Figure 7.5, has a number of parallels with your own personal strategic planning. To provide you with insights into these tasks and process as applied to you, we would like you to "put on" your creative and innovative "hat" by thinking of yourself as a "strategic business unit" and consider ways by which the tasks and process in Figure 7.5 are relevant to you. We recognize that there are differences in how Figure 7.5 applies to a business versus an individual. For now, we want you to focus on the parallels. To assist in discussing those parallels, we have provided some adaptations in the tasks shown in Figure 7.5 below. This is a demanding exercise that takes time when fully undertaken. A general sense of the parallels may be achieved by generating one or two responses to each of the tasks shown below.

- *Task 1: Develop your vision, mission, and goals.* Who are you? What do you want to become? What are your goals?

- *Task 2: Diagnose your opportunities and threats.* What are they both personally and professionally? Will most of the new jobs in your chosen career field be outsourced to other countries? Are there technologies on the horizon that will reduce or eliminate the growth of positions in your chosen career field?

- *Task 3: Diagnose your strengths and weaknesses.* What are they, both personally and professionally (especially in relation to the managerial competencies presented in Chapter 1 and throughout this book)?

- *Task 4: Develop personal and professional strategies.* How do you evaluate them against (in relation to) the self-diagnosis of your own opportunities, threats, strengths, and weaknesses?

- *Task 5: Develop your strategic plan.* What strategies (courses of action) will you attempt to implement over the next three to five years? What are the skills and competencies needed by you to implement those strategies? Do you have them? If not, what is your own human resource functional strategy for developing them? What are the required financial resources for implementing your personal and professional strategies? Do you have them? If not, how will you go about obtaining the needed financial resources?

- *Task 6: Prepare your tactical plan.* What specific decisions do you need to make and what actions do you need to engage in over the next year to implement your strategic plan?

- *Task 7: Control and diagnose results.* What benchmarks, standards, and measures will you establish for yourself to determine if you are making progress in implementing your tactical and strategic plans?

- *Task 8: Continue planning.* What changes, if any, need to be made in your strategic plan based on a reassessment of tasks 1, 2, and 3? At a minimum, this careful reassessment should occur once per year.

Harley-Davidson, Inc., headquartered in Milwaukee, Wisconsin, is the only major U.S. maker of motorcycles and the number one seller of heavyweight motorcycles in the United States. The company offers 33 models of touring and custom Harleys through a worldwide network of more than 1,300 dealers. The firm has approximately 9,700 employees and $5.5 billion in annual sales. Motorcycles sold annually exceed 350,000 units.

Mission

Harley states its mission, as follows:

> We fulfill dreams through the experiences of motorcycling, by providing to motorcyclists and to the general public an expanding line of motorcycles and branded products and services in selected market segments.

The firm reflects on its mission in these words: "It takes more than just building and selling motorcycles to fulfill the dreams of our customers. It takes unforgettable experiences. . . . If there's one secret to our enduring brand and the passion it ignites in our riders, it's that we deliver these experiences, rather than merely a collection of products and services. And we're dedicated to creating experiences and developing relationships with all of our stakeholders—customers, employees, investors, suppliers, governments and society."

Core Values

The stated core values of Harley are:

- Tell the truth.

- Be fair.

- Keep your promises.

- Respect the individual.

- Encourage intellectual curiosity.

The firm comments on its values in these words:

> These are our values. They are the heart of how we run our business. They guide our actions and serve as the framework for the decisions and contributions our employees make at every level of the Company. More than just a list of "feel good" buzzwords, our values define the character of Harley-Davidson

just as much as the motorcycles that bear the Harley-Davidson name. They reflect how we relate to each other and to all of our stakeholders, including our customers, dealers and suppliers. The company fosters these values by actively communicating their importance and encouraging employee involvement and development. We believe that our business will be most successful if we tap the contributions of each of our people.

Business Segments

Harley-Davidson, Inc., is the parent company for the group of companies doing business as Harley-Davidson Motor Company, Buell Motorcycle Company, and Harley-Davidson Financial Services (HDFS). In addition to its heavyweight motorcycles, Harley-Davidson Motor Company offers a complete line of motorcycle parts, accessories, apparel, and general merchandise. Harley models include the Sportster, Electra Glide, and the Fat Boy. Buell Motorcycle Company produces sport motorcycles. Harley-Davidson Financial Services provides wholesale and retail financing and insurance programs to Harley-Davidson dealers and customers.

Harley Owners Group

The Harley Owners Group, or H.O.G., is the largest sponsored motorcycle club in the world. Through local chapters sponsored by authorized Harley-Davidson dealers, H.O.G. enhances the motorcycling experience for enthusiasts worldwide. Year-long programs and events provide the opportunity for customers to gather at their local dealerships to shop, ride, and have fun.

Changing Demographics

Changing demographics have resulted in Harley's effort to obtain new customers among women, blacks, and Hispanics. These groups have not been traditional Harley-Davidson riders.

The effort has involved the development and rollout of new products, such as the 883 Sportster Low—which is built for smaller, lighter riders—and new marketing efforts, such as Harley's TV ad campaign during recent NCAA tournaments. Today's biggest challenge for Harley, according to Joanne Bischmann, marketing vice president, is to continue to harness the brand's mystique and traditional customer base, while reaching out to new groups.

Questions

1. Based on this case and other information about Harley at *www.harley-davidson.com* and other sources, what do you think are its major strengths and weaknesses?

2. What are several of the potential opportunities and threats facing Harley?

3. Does Harley have a clear and well-stated mission?

4. In terms of the generic competitive strategies model, which of the four strategies does Harley appear to be following? Explain.

5. What corporate-level diversification strategy or strategies are emphasized at Harley?

chapter 8

© Jon Feingersh Photography/Blend Images/Jupiter Images

Fundamentals of Decision Making

Learning Goals

After studying this chapter, you should be able to:

1. Explain certainty, risk, and uncertainty and how they affect decision making.

2. Describe the characteristics of routine, adaptive, and innovative decisions.

3. Discuss the rational and bounded rationality models of managerial decision making.

4. Explain the features of political managerial decision making.

Communication Competency

Planning and Administration Competency

Teamwork Competency

Managing Effectively

Self-Management Competency

Strategic Action Competency

Multicultural Competency

Challenge of Managing ....

David Hoover, CEO of Ball Corporation

© Creatas/Creatas Images/Jupiter Images

The Ball Corporation, headquartered in Broomfield, Colorado, is a provider of metal and plastic packaging, primarily for beverages and foods, and of aerospace and other technologies and services to commercial and governmental customers. The company employs approximately 13,000 people in 90 locations worldwide—9,000 in the U.S. and 4,000 in other countries. The firm has five major business segments: North American Metal Beverage Packaging, North American International Packaging, Metal Food Packaging, North American Plastic Packaging, and Aerospace and Technologies. One of its long-term goals is to achieve 10 to 15 percent annual growth in earnings per share.

R. David Hoover is chairman, chief executive officer, and president of the Ball Corporation. The following are excerpts from an in-depth interview of Hoover in which he comments on the decision process, problems, and challenges faced by him and the members of the Ball Leadership Team (BLT).

The BLT consists of 15 people or so, primarily business unit heads and corporate officers, who get together monthly to discuss where we are, what we're doing, and where we are going. There is, of course, a continuing list of issues we monitor. We identify critical issues, identify owners of those issues, and report against them periodically, usually quarterly. They can be anything from improving the image of the can to making acquisitions to improving the overall cost benefit of the employee benefits programs we have. For an issue to become a critical one, it's got to be something we really need to tackle. We have a dozen of those right now that we're working on.

About a year ago, sensing a need for renewal, the BLT met to explore the questions "Why is there a Ball? Why are we here?" I was a little worried some of the operations people might leave, because that delved into the philosophical side of life. However, none of that happened and everyone was very participative. As a result, we came up with a new core purpose statement. We then shifted to the core values we believe drive our company and generated a list of a half-dozen or so. Integrity was at the top of the list; that's important, particularly these days. We want it to be clear that integrity is important to us, and to reinforce that throughout the company. Recently, we met off-site and talked about potential areas of diversification. We looked not necessarily at specific opportunities, but of a half-dozen or so, some were pretty far afield and some were pretty close. We decided to stay close, if we can. We also pledged to stay disciplined.

In another 25 years, I think we'll be involved in some businesses we currently are not, although I don't think you'll see us in the car making business or selling cosmetics. I suspect we'll still be in packaging but have a broader offering, that we'll still be making beverage and food cans and PET bottles, and that we'll still be in the aerospace business.

We've got lots of challenges ahead of us. I spend about 75% of my time solving problems of one sort or another. The other 25% is really wonderful, though. Watching people grow, develop, achieve, and do good things and seeing the company succeed is very rewarding and lots of fun."[1]

To learn more about this organization, visit *www.ball.com*.

Decision making is a daily fact of life for each of us. Of course, most of the time we are making decisions that do not have major life or profit consequences—such as deciding on a class schedule for the following semester. Senior executives are engaged on a daily basis in addressing issues that require major decisions in the near term that are likely to have major consequences—negative or positive—on one or more stakeholder groups. As implied by David Hoover's remarks, thoughtful decision making typically involves the foundational elements of defining the problem, gathering information, identifying and assessing alternatives, and deciding what to do. Hoover's comments also suggest that a process is needed for addressing these foundational elements. At the Ball Corporation, one way to address them is through the Ball Leadership Team. Recall that Hoover calls the 15-member BLT together monthly to "discuss where we are, what we're doing, and where we are going." Hoover continues by noting that they identify and monitor critical issues (problems) and that the BLT is working on a dozen of those types of issues.

Decision making *includes defining problems, gathering information, generating alternatives, and choosing a course of action.* We discuss how managers and employees can base various types of decisions on the nature of the problem to be solved, the possible solutions available, and the degree of risk involved.[2]

Effective managers rely on several managerial competencies to make and implement decisions. Decision making provides a foundation for most managerial competencies. For example, Hoover uses a decision-making process to develop strategies for achieving goals, which reflects the strategic action competency. He uses his teamwork competency through the formation and ongoing use of the BLT to address critical issues. Recall Hoover's discussion of how the BLT met at an off-site retreat to explore these core questions: "Why is there a Ball?" "Why are we here?" He noted that everyone participated and they came up with a new core purpose statement, which is as follows[3]:

Ball Corporation is in business to add value to all of its stakeholders, whether it is providing quality products and services to customers, an attractive return on investment to shareholders, a meaningful work life for employees or a contribution of time, effort and resources to our communities. In all of our interactions, we ask how we can get better—how we can make it better, be better and do better, for our own good and the good of those who have a stake in our success.

If the senior executives and other employees at the Ball Corporation take this core purpose to heart, it will serve as an anchor for their decision making. For example, there is an explicit recognition that alternatives being considered should take into account their impact on multiple stakeholders, such as employees, customers, and shareholders.

Decision-Making Conditions

1.
Explain certainty, risk, and uncertainty and how they affect decision making.

Numerous developments and events—often outside of the control of individuals—influence the individual's decision-making process and decisions. In Chapters 4 and 5, we identified and discussed a number of domestic and global competitive, political, and cultural forces that must be considered when managers and employees make decisions. A number of these forces are beyond their direct control. In Chapter 3, we noted the impact that key stakeholders can have on decisions involving ethical and social responsibility issues. Decisions are affected by many factors. In addition to identifying and measuring the strength of these factors, managers must estimate their potential impact. The Ball Corporation has, for the most part, been successful with its acquisition strategy. However, as Hoover indicates, there may be strong forces that create unanticipated adverse impacts. He comments: ". . . we acquired a business in China in the 1990s and the market unexpectedly turned down. In large part, successful acquisitions depend on execution, but they also depend on good fortune and timing. You've got to have a little luck along the way to make them work. That being said, if part of your strategy for growth is to acquire, you really have to be good at it."[4]

The conditions under which decisions are made can be classified as certainty, risk, and uncertainty.[5] These conditions are shown as a continuum in Figure 8.1. When individuals can identify developments and events and their potential impact with total predictability, they can then make decisions under the condition of certainty. As information dwindles and becomes ambiguous, the condition of risk enters into the decision-making process. Individuals begin to base their decisions on either objective (clear) or subjective (intuition and judgment) probabilities. The decision by the top management of the Ball Corporation to acquire a business in China was based on the expected subjective probability that the market would continue to grow. In fact, it turned down. In the condition of uncertainty, the decision maker has little or no information about developments and forces on which to base a decision. Because of that uncertainty, decision makers may be able to make only a reasonable guess as to possible outcomes from the decision.

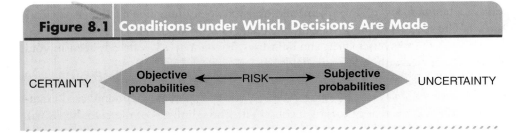

Figure 8.1 | **Conditions under Which Decisions Are Made**

CERTAINTY — Objective probabilities ← RISK → Subjective probabilities — UNCERTAINTY

What Is Certainty?

Certainty is the condition under which individuals are fully informed about a problem, alternative solutions are known, and the results of each solution are known. This condition means that both the problem and alternative solutions are totally known and well defined. Once an individual has identified alternative solutions and their expected results, making the decision is relatively easy. The decision maker simply chooses the solution with the best result.

Decision making under the condition of certainty is the exception for most managers. First-line managers often make some day-to-day decisions under conditions of certainty or near certainty. Avis Rent A Car System, Inc., headquartered in Parsippany, New Jersey, is a wholly owned subsidiary of the Cendant Corporation, which also owns Budget Rent A Car. It has attempted to make the entire rental process as certain as possible. The process has been broken down into more than 100 incremental and prescribed steps. These steps are designed to take out the risk and uncertainty in decision making for both employees and customers at its 2,000 locations in the United States, Canada, and four other countries. In addition, Avis has marketing agreements with Avis Europe PLC, a separately owned U.K. company with more than 3,000 locations in Europe, the Middle East, and Africa. Employees know exactly what to do and how to deal with problems that have already been anticipated. Customers know what to expect. F. Robert Salerno, the president and CEO, notes: "Without our employees' strong commitment to consistently exceeding customer service standards, 'We Try Harder' would just be an empty slogan."[6] For a number of years, Avis has continued to be at the top if its category in the Brand Keys customer loyalty index. Brand Keys, a market research firm, surveys 16,000 consumers twice a year on their attitudes toward 222 brands in 35 categories.[7]

Managers analyze the amount of risk involved to estimate the potential impact of their decisions.

© Tetra Images/Jupiter Images

What Is Risk?

Risk *refers to the condition under which individuals can define a problem, specify the probability of certain events, identify alternative solutions, and state the probability of each solution leading to a result.* Risk generally means that the problem and alternative solutions fall somewhere between the extremes of being certain and being unusual and ambiguous. In its day-to-day meaning, *risk* is usually thought of as the potential harm that may arise from some decision or decision process (e.g., a safety procedure for handling chemicals) or future event (e.g., a fire). In general, *harm* may be physical (e.g., destruction of a building, loss of investment) and/or psychological/emotional to a person (work stress). The specific meaning, measurement, and assessment of risk varies widely across different professions, disciplines, and industries, as you may have already seen in your academic courses within different fields.[8]

Probability *is the percentage of times that a specific result would occur if an individual were to make the same decision a large number of times.* The most commonly used example of probability is that of tossing a coin: With enough tosses of the coin, heads will show up 50 percent of the time and tails the other 50 percent. Insurance companies make use of probabilities in setting all kinds of premium rates. The probability of a specific event is a measure between 0 (impossible) and 1 (certainty) of whether the event is likely to happen.[9]

The quality of information available to an individual about the relevant decision-making condition can vary widely—as can the individual's estimates of risk. The type, amount, and reliability of information influence the level of risk and whether the decision maker can use objective or subjective probability in estimating the result (see Figure 8.1).

Objective Probability. Objective probability *is the likelihood that a specific result will occur, based on hard facts and numbers.* Sometimes an individual can determine the likely result of a decision by examining past records. For example, although State Farm, Prudential, and other life insurance companies can't determine the year in which each policyholder will die, they can calculate objective probabilities that specific numbers of policyholders, at various ages and with other characteristics (e.g., male or female, smoker or nonsmoker) will die in a particular year. These objective probabilities are based on the expectation that past death rates for those with a specific set of characteristics will be repeated in the future.

Subjective Probability. Subjective probability *is the likelihood that a specific result will occur, based on personal judgment.* Judgments vary among individuals, depending on their intuition, previous experience with similar situations, expertise, and personality traits (e.g., preference for risk taking or risk avoidance).

The leaders of the Ball Corporation recognize many risks—and uncertainties—in their business. In the filing of its annual 10-K form with the Securities and Exchange Commission, Ball Corporation management annually identifies "risk factors," which actually include uncertainties as well, for review by all interested parties. Five of the 17 general risk factors—including uncertainties—that the Ball Corporation management set forth recently were as follows[10]:

▶ The loss of a customer could have a significant negative impact on our sales. Brief excerpt of explanation: "While we have diversified our customer base, we do sell a majority of our packaging products to relatively few major beverage and packaged food companies."

▶ We face competitive risks from many sources (e.g., foreign competitors) that may negatively impact our profitability.

▶ We are subject to risks due to competition from alternative products (e.g., paper packaging) that could result in lower profits and reduced cash flows.

▶ We are vulnerable to fluctuations in the supply and price of raw materials.

▶ Our significant debt could adversely affect our financial health and prevent us from fulfilling our obligations under the notes (loan and bond agreements).

What Is Uncertainty?

Uncertainty *is the condition under which an individual does not have the necessary information to assign probabilities to the outcomes of alternative solutions.* In fact, the individual may not even be able to define the problem, much less identify alternative solutions and possible outcomes.[11] As suggested in the risks and uncertainties identified by the Ball Corporation, the problems and alternative solutions are often both ambiguous and highly unusual. Dealing with uncertainty is an important part of the jobs for many managers and various professionals, such as R&D engineers, market researchers, and strategic planners. Managers, teams, and other professionals often need to resolve uncertainty by using their intuition, creativity, and all available information to make a judgment regarding the course of action (decision) to take.

Table 8.1 on the next page provides examples of possible crises that may be sources of uncertainty and high risk for organizations. Seventy-five percent of the *Fortune 500* companies are not prepared to handle unfamiliar crises (e.g., Hurricane Katrina, 9/11). These crises involve uncertainty in terms of their likelihood of occurrence, potential impact, and means for dealing with them should they occur. Businesses often prepare to handle only the types of crises they've already suffered, and not even all of those.[12] The potential crises facing an organization, such as those listed in Table 8.1, can't be totally eliminated. Through crisis anticipation and preparation, their likelihood of occurrence or severity of consequences can be reduced.

Table 8.1	Possible Crises That May Be Sources of Uncertainty and High Risk
ECONOMIC CRISES Recessions Stock market crashes Hostile takeovers	**INFORMATION CRISES** Theft of proprietary information Tampering with company records Cyberattacks
PHYSICAL CRISES Industrial accidents Supply breakdowns Product failures	**REPUTATION CRISES** Rumormongering or slander Logo tampering
PERSONNEL CRISES Strikes Exodus of key employees Workplace violence	**NATURAL DISASTERS** Fires Floods Earthquakes
CRIMINAL CRISES Theft of money or goods Product tampering Kidnapping or hostage taking	

Sources: Adapted from I. I. Mitroff and M. C. Alpaslan. Preparing for evil. *Harvard Business Review*, April 2003, pp. 109–115; I. I. Mitroff. *Crisis Leadership: Planning for the Unthinkable.* New York: John Wiley & Sons, 2003.

The following Strategic Action Competency reports on how Matthew Smith, the founder of Shoes For Crews, which is headquartered in West Palm Beach, Florida, developed a unique warranty as a way to reduce customers' sense of uncertainty and risk regarding the company's shoes.[13] Most individual customers have no idea how to assign a probability of being injured due to slipping on the job. For those customers, slipping and injuring themselves represents a condition of uncertainty. Smith attributes this unique warranty as a critical factor in the company's success. The firm has 160 employees and annual revenue of about $100 million.

Strategic Action Competency

Shoes For Crews Reduces Uncertainty

Offering a $5,000 warranty on a $50 product sounds insane. Matthew Smith, whose shoe company has honored that warranty for a decade, thinks that this promise was the smartest move he ever made. Shoes For Crews makes work shoes that are guaranteed not to slip. It had few sales before offering this unique warranty. It covers medical expenses and workers' compensation costs up to $5,000 if an employee slips and encounters an injury while wearing a pair of the company's shoes.

Smith thought slip injuries involving his shoes were unlikely. He started the uncertainty reduction warranty with a $500 cap and moved up to $5,000 eventually. In a recent year, Shoes For Crews honored several hundred claims—ranging from a few hundred dollars for an ambulance ride to $5,000 for an accident involving broken bones.

Smith considers it a cost of doing business. He comments: "Paying $15,000 a year in claims on a $2 million account is nothing."

Kurt Leisure, a vice president at the Cheesecake Factory, a chain of restaurants based in Calabasas, California, encourages all 25,000 employees to buy their shoes at Shoes For Crews and nearly all of them do. That's about 30,000 shoe orders a year. Leisure says he would be a fan of Shoes For Crews for safety reasons alone. The shoes, he says, have helped the chain cut slip accidents 87 percent over five years. He doubts he would have done business with Smith in the first place if not for the guarantee. He comments: "The warranty is obviously a big incentive for us to get as many employees as possible into their shoes. It's very shrewd business on their part."

Smith's guarantee helped get Shoes For Crews out of a serious marketing quandary. For years, the shoes, which cost between $20 and $75, were sold mainly through payroll deduction plans, in which employers would deduct the cost of the shoes directly from workers' paychecks. Workers could also buy work shoes directly from Wal-Mart and Sears. Smith needed to convince factory and restaurant managers to market his shoes to their employees. It was difficult getting managers to care about where their employees shopped for work shoes. However, managers did care immensely about preventing injuries and workers' compensation claims because injuries increase costs. So Smith began promising managers that if a worker slipped while wearing his shoes, Shoes For Crews would help pay the claim. A decade after launching the program, 9 of the 10 largest restaurant chains in the country either buy the Shoes For Crews brand for their workers or urge them to do so.

To learn more about this organization, visit *www.shoesforcrews.com.*

Basic Types of Decisions

2. Describe the characteristics of routine, adaptive, and innovative decisions.

No single decision-making method can be used in all situations faced by managers and employees. As a start, the decision maker needs to define accurately the problem at hand, move on to generating and evaluating alternative solutions, and finally make a decision. Doing so, however, is not this simple in reality.

The considerations of certainty, risk, and uncertainty provide an underpinning to the basic types of decisions—routine, adaptive, and innovative. They reflect the types of problems encountered and the types of solutions considered. Figure 8.2 on the next page presents the different combinations of problem types (vertical axis) and solution types (horizontal axis) that result in the three types of decisions. The diagonal line from lower left to upper right shows the related conditions of certainty, risk, and uncertainty.

Types of Problems

The types of problems that managers and others deal with range from the relatively common and well defined to the unusual and ambiguous. The bank teller with an out-of-balance cash drawer at the end of the day faces a common and well-defined problem. In contrast, senior executives at the Ball Corporation and other organizations must deal with unusual and ambiguous problems. For the Ball Corporation, a major problem would be what to do if there were a reduction in the scope of their contracts with key customers due to unanticipated changes in their customers' requirements or budget constraints. When the number of such problems escalates with short time frames for resolution, a pattern of *fire fighting* may occur with linked elements, such as the following, creating unsatisfactory results.

▶ *Solutions are incomplete.* Too many problems are patched, not solved. That is, superficial effects are dealt with, but the underlying causes are not fixed.

▶ *Problems recur and cascade.* Incomplete solutions cause old problems to reemerge or actually create new problems, sometimes elsewhere in the organization.

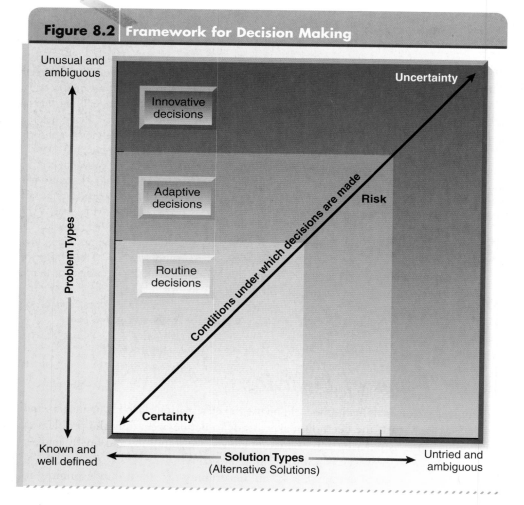

Figure 8.2 | Framework for Decision Making

Unusual and ambiguous

Innovative decisions

Adaptive decisions

Routine decisions

Problem Types

Uncertainty

Risk

Conditions under which decisions are made

Certainty

Known and well defined

Solution Types
(Alternative Solutions)

Untried and ambiguous

▶ *Urgency supersedes importance.* Ongoing problem-solving efforts and long-range activities, such as developing new processes, are repeatedly interrupted or deferred because fires must be extinguished.

▶ *Some problems become crises.* Problems smolder until they flare up, often just before a deadline.[14]

Types of Solutions

The types of solutions available range from the known and well defined to the untried and ambiguous. What happens when a bank teller at a Bank of America branch has an out-of-balance cash drawer? In brief, the teller follows a specific, well-defined procedure: Check all deposit slips against deposit receipts and cash tickets and recount all the cash. In contrast, managers often must develop solutions that are untried and ambiguous. More and more firms are finding it necessary to provide tailored solutions to fit customer preferences.

A few home builders and suppliers are developing, at customers' requests, new products and techniques to construct homes that are strengthened well beyond what the building codes require. In certain geographic areas, some home buyers want to reduce the consequences of the risks and uncertainties associated with powerful hurricanes, tornadoes, earthquakes, and fires. Joe Redburn, a home builder in Fort Meyer, Florida, says it costs an extra $15,000 to fortify and make highly energy efficient a $200,000 home in his market area.[15]

Routine Decisions

Routine decisions *are the standard choices made in response to relatively well-defined and common problems and alternative solutions.* As suggested in Figure 8.2, routine decisions are typically made under conditions of certainty through risk with objective probabilities. How to make various routine decisions is often covered by established rules or standard operating procedures or, increasingly by computer software, such as computerized airline reservation systems. Placing orders online, cleaning buildings, processing payroll vouchers, packing and shipping customers' orders, and making travel arrangements are but a few examples of tasks requiring routine decisions.

Managers and employees need to guard against the tendency to make routine decisions when a problem actually calls for an adaptive or innovative decision.[16] Doing so results in active inertia—*the rigid devotion to the status quo by attempting to do more of the same old thing better.* At times, even major companies, such as American Airlines, become stuck in the routine ways of thinking and working that brought them initial success. When the competition changes, their once winning formulas bring stagnation, declining profits and shareholder value, or even failure.

Effective application of complex and sophisticated standards for routine decisions at Four Seasons Hotels and Resorts, headquartered in Toronto, Ontario, is one example. Four Seasons is a leading operator of midsize—200 to 400 guest rooms and suites—luxury hotels and resorts. The firm manages 70 properties in 31 countries. To ensure that routine decisions are made in standardized ways, Four Seasons has established seven service culture standards expected of all staff all over the world at all times.

▶ *Smile:* Employees will actively greet guests, smile, and speak clearly in a friendly manner.

▶ *Eye:* Employees will make eye contact, even in passing, with an acknowledgment.

▶ *Recognition:* All staff will create a sense of recognition by using the guest's name, when known, in a natural and discreet manner.

▶ *Voice:* Staff will speak to guests in an attentive, natural, and courteous manner, avoiding pretension and in a clear voice.

▶ *Informed:* All guest contact staff will be well informed about their hotel, their product, will take ownership of simple requests, and will not refer guests elsewhere.

▶ *Clean:* Staff will always appear clean, crisp, well-groomed, and well-fitted.

▶ *Everyone:* Everyone, everywhere, all the time, will show their care for our guests.

These standards set the framework for making routine decisions. In addition to its service culture standards, Four Seasons has 270 core worldwide operating standards (routine decision rules). Table 8.2 on the next page provides some examples of these standards, all of which encourage routine decision making. These routine decision rules are recognized by Four Seasons managers and employees as setting *minimum* expectations. Employees are told repeatedly: "If you can do something for a client that goes beyond the standards, do it."[17]

Adaptive Decisions

Adaptive decisions *refer to choices made in response to a combination of moderately unusual problems and alternative solutions.* Adaptive decisions typically involve modifying and

Table 8.2

Examples of Decision Rules at Four Seasons Hotels and Resorts

RESERVATIONS

- Phone service will be highly efficient, including: answered before the fourth ring; no hold longer than 15 seconds; or, in case of longer holds, call-backs offered, then provided in less than three minutes.
- After establishing the reason for the guest visit, reservationist automatically describes the guest room colorfully, attempting to have the guests picture themselves in the room.

HOTEL ARRIVAL

- The doorman (or first-contact employee) will actively greet guests, smile, make eye contact, and speak clearly in a friendly manner.
- The staff will be aware of arriving vehicles and will move toward them, opening doors within 30 seconds.
- Guests will be welcomed at the curbside with the words "welcome" and "Four Seasons" (or hotel name), and given directions to the reception desk.
- No guest will wait longer than 60 seconds in line at the reception desk.

HOTEL DEPARTURE

- No guest will wait longer than five minutes for baggage assistance, once the bellman is called (eight minutes in resorts).
- No guest will wait longer than 60 seconds in line at the cashier's desk.
- Staff will create a sense of recognition by using the guest's name, when known, in a natural and discreet manner.

MESSAGES AND PAGING

- Phone service will be highly efficient, including: answered before the fourth ring; no longer than 15 seconds.
- Callers requesting guest room extensions between 1 A.M. and 6 A.M. will be advised of the local time and offered the option of leaving a message or putting the call through.
- Unanswered guest room phones will be picked up within five rings, or 20 seconds.
- Guests will be offered the option of voice mail; they will not automatically be routed to voice mail or they will have a clear option to return to the operator.

Source: Adapted from R. Hallowell, D. E. Bowen, and C. I. Knoop. Four seasons goes to Paris. *Academy of Management Executive*, 16(4), 2002, pp. 7–24.

Snapshot

"Visa continuously strives against outages and defects on two broad fronts. Its physical processing operations are protected by multiple layers of redundancy and backups. The company's IT staff continuously conducts extensive and refined software testing. We make 2,500 system changes to VisaNet per month and modify 2 million lines of code annually."

Richard Knight, Senior VP for Global Operations, Inovant LLC, a Visa Subsidiary

improving on past routine decisions and practices. As suggested in Figure 8.2, they are typically made under conditions of risk that may range from objective probabilities to subjective probabilities.

Convergence. Adaptive decisions may reflect the concept of convergence—*a business shift in which two connections with the customer that were previously viewed as competing or separate (e.g., brick-and-mortar bookstores and Internet bookstores) come to be seen as complementary.* Those customer connections can include previously competing or separate sales channels, product categories, distribution channels, applications, features, and the like. Consider this application of convergence as an example of adaptive decision making.

Philips Consumer Electronics recently developed a remote control, the RC9800i, that eliminates all other remotes. It controls all traditional audio and video equipment as well as the new universal plug-and-play devices. This allows the transfer of PC content, such as MP3 files and photos, to the entertainment system. This product offers one-button activity-based control of the entertainment experience. This blends (converges) the most frequently used functions into activities, such as *watching DVD* or *listening to CD*. It automatically blends a series of commands into a single activity.[18]

Continuous Improvement. Adaptive decisions also reflect the concept of continuous improvement—*which refers to a management philosophy that approaches the challenge of product and process enhancements as an ongoing effort to increase the levels of quality and excellence.*[19] Continuous improvement involves a series of adaptive organizational decisions made over time that result in a large number of incremental improvements year after year. The process resembles the wheel in a hamster cage—a ladder wrapped onto a cylinder, with no beginning and no end. Each "turn of the wheel" improves an existing product and/or process. Year after year the organization's products and processes keep getting better, more reliable, and less expensive. Continuous improvement is driven by the goals of providing better quality, improving efficiency, and being responsive to customers.[20]

Consistent with the concepts of *convergence* and *continuous improvements,* senior leaders may adapt their current strategies through a partial imitation of their competitors' processes, goods, or services. The following Planning and Administration Competency feature reports on the recent adaptive decisions by Dunkin' Donuts to partially imitate Starbucks and other firms.[21] Dunkin' Donuts is one of the largest coffee and baked goods chains in the world with nearly 6,500 stores worldwide in 30 countries with 4,400 of them in 36 states within the United States. Dunkin' Donuts is a subsidiary of Dunkin Brands, headquartered in Canton, Massachusetts, which also owns and franchises Baskin-Robbins shops and Togo's Subs.[22]

© Jennifer Boggs/FoodPix/Jupiter

Planning and Administration Competency

Dunkin' Donuts' Adaptive Decisions

Dunkin' Donuts plans to modify its 4,400 U.S. stores by 2010 and triple the number of stores by 2020. The chain is attempting to adapt its brand as a quick and appealing alternative to specialty coffee shops, such as Starbucks and Seattle's Best, and fast-food chains, such as McDonald's and Burger King. Dunkin executives insist they aren't trying to copy Starbucks, but their makeovers will include some similarities to it. A new prototype Dunkin' store in Euclid, Ohio, located outside of Cleveland, features rounded granite-style coffee bars where workers make espresso drinks face-to-face with customers. Open-air pastry cases contain yogurt parfaits and fresh fruit. A carefully selected pop-music soundtrack is heard throughout the store.

Dunkin' built itself on serving simple fare to working-class customers. Inching upscale without alienating that base is tricky. There will be no couches in the new stores. Dunkin' renamed a new hot sandwich a "stuffed melt" after customers complained that calling it a "panini" was too fancy.

Dunkin' Donuts hopes to counter Starbucks by expanding its menu beyond breakfast with snacks that can substitute for meals, like smoothies and dough-wrapped pork bites. The new Euclid store is doing three times the sales of other stores in its area, partly because more customers are coming after 11 A.M. for new gourmet cookies and

Dunkin' Dawgs, hot dogs wrapped in dough, says Matt Zaroslinski, the store's director of operations.

Dunkin' executives made dozens of decisions, ranging from where to put the espresso machines to how much of its signature pink and orange color scheme to retain to where to display its fresh-baked goods. They decided early on that Dunkin' would keep its goal of moving customers through its cash register line in two minutes; Starbucks, by comparison, has a goal of three minutes. Dunkin' customers said they didn't want any changes in store design to result in longer waiting times.

Out went the square laminate tables, to be replaced by round imitation-granite tabletops and sleek chairs. Dunkin' covered store walls in espresso brown and dialed down the pink and orange tones. Executives considered but held off on installing wireless Internet access because customers "just don't feel it's Dunkin' Donuts," says Joe Scafido, Duncan's chief creative and innovation officer. Executives continue to discuss dropping the word "donut" from its signs to convey that its menu is now broader. Franchisees are paying for the $150,000 cost to remodel each store.

To learn more about this organization, visit *www.dunkindonuts.com.*

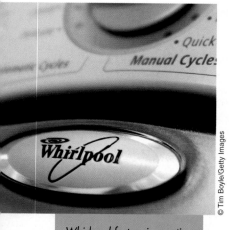

Snapshot

"You have to innovate and optimize at the same time. After all, you're under pressure to optimize 24 hours a day, but no one is pushing you to innovate. In order for us to be able to compete over a long period of time, we give everyone in our organization all of the information needed so they can make decisions that will drive innovation throughout our company."

Jack Stack, CEO, Springfield ReManufacturing Corporation

© Tim Boyle/Getty Images

Whirlpool fosters innovative decisions with the goal of "innovation from everyone, everywhere."

Innovative Decisions

Innovative decisions *are choices based on the discovery, identification, and diagnosis of unusual and ambiguous problems and/or the development of unique or creative alternative solutions.* As suggested in Figure 8.2, they are typically made under conditions that vary from risk with subjective probabilities to uncertainty. Major and novel solutions may involve a series of small, interrelated decisions made over a period of months or even years. In particular, leading-edge innovations may take years to develop and involve numerous professionals and teams. Because innovative decisions usually represent a sharp break with the past, they normally don't happen in a logical, orderly sequence. Such decisions are typically based on incomplete and rapidly changing information. Moreover, they may be made before problems are fully defined and understood. To be effective, decision makers therefore must be especially careful to define the right problem and recognize that earlier actions can significantly affect later decisions.[23] As we discussed in Chapter 6, most successful entrepreneurial ventures are launched by entrepreneurs making innovative decisions.

Economic progress is driven by three forms of innovation:

▶ *Institutional innovation*, which includes the legal and institutional framework for business;

▶ *Technological innovation*, which creates the possibility of new products, services, and production methods; and

▶ *Management innovation*, which includes changes in the way organizations are structured, departures from traditional management principles and processes, and changes in how managers perform their functions. [24]

Major innovation typically comes from looking at the world through a slightly different lens. **Innovators** *are those individuals or organizations who do one or more of the following: change customer expectations, change the bases for competition in an industry, or change the economic efficiency of an industry.* Let's consider several characteristics of innovators.

▶ *They challenge the prevailing dogmas and practices.* Michael Dell questioned the need for dealers to sell its PCs. Charles Schwab questioned the need for high commissioned brokers to trade stocks. When most people think about the future, they often take 98 percent of current products and practices as a given.

▶ *They spot changing trends that have gone unnoticed by others.* It has been suggested that managers should spend some time on the fringe—the fringe of technology, entertainment, fashion, and politics. Why? It's on the fringe where new possibilities are often found. Jeff Bezos founded Amazon.com after attending a book publishers' show in Los Angeles. He wondered why books were not being sold over the Internet instead of just bookstores.

▶ *They learn to live inside the "skin" of potential customers.* Innovation often doesn't come from an expressed need. It comes from insights and understanding of people's frustrations or desires. Dell, Starbucks, and Amazon.com were not created by simply asking potential customers if they would like the goods or services.[25]

The following Teamwork Competency feature reports on how David Whitwam, the recently retired CEO of Whirlpool Corporation, initiated the goal of "innovation from everyone, everywhere."[26] Jeff Fettig succeeded Whitwam as chairman and CEO. Fettig worked closely with Whitwam in fostering Whirlpool's innovation process. Whirlpool Corporation, headquartered in Boston Harbor, Michigan, is a global manufacturer and marketer of major home appliances. The firm has approximately 68,000 employees. Whirlpool senior leadership launched a worldwide effort involving teams and individual employees to instill innovation as a core competency throughout the organization. Whirlpool sees innovation as its differentiating strategy.[27]

Teamwork Competency

Whirlpool's Process Innovation

Frustrated by chronically low levels of brand loyalty among appliance buyers, Dave Whitwam issued a challenge to his leadership team: Turn Whirlpool into a model of rule-breaking, customer-pleasing innovation. From the outset, it was clear that Whitwam's goal of "innovation from everyone, everywhere" would require major changes in the company's management processes, which had been designed to drive operational efficiency.

Nancy Snyder, a corporate vice president and Whirlpool's first innovation leader, rallied employees around what would become a five-year effort to reinvent the company's management processes. Key changes included these:

▶ Making innovation a central topic in Whirlpool's leadership development programs.

▶ Setting aside a substantial share of capital spending every year for projects that meet a certain tough standard of innovativeness.

▶ Requiring every product development plan to contain a sizable component of new-to-market innovation.

▶ Training more than 600 innovation mentors to encourage innovation on their work teams throughout the company.

▶ Enrolling every salaried employee in an online course on business innovation.

▶ Establishing innovation as a large part of top management's long-term bonus plan.

▶ Setting aside time in quarterly business team review meetings for an in-depth discussion of each unit's innovation performance.

▶ Building an innovation portal that grants Whirlpool's employees and teams all over the world access to an array of innovation tools and data on the company's global innovation pipeline.

▶ Developing a set of metrics to track innovation inputs (such as the number of engineering hours devoted to innovative projects), throughputs (such as the number of new ideas entering the company's innovation pipeline), and outputs (such as the pricing advantages gained from more distinctive products and higher customer loyalty).

Whirlpool didn't make all these changes at once. There were plenty of false starts and detours along the way. Translating a novel management ideal (like innovation from everyone, everywhere) into new and deeply rooted management practices required a sustained and broad-based effort, but the payoff was substantial. Jeff Fettig, Whirlpool's current chairman, estimates that by 2008, the innovation program will add more than $500 million a year to the company's sales and help to protect current sales.

To learn more about this organization, visit www.whirlpool.com.

Process of Rational Managerial Decision Making

Our presentation to this point in the chapter has provided the foundation for presenting two models that address somewhat different, but related, processes of managerial

3. Discuss the rational and bounded rationality models of managerial decision making.

decision making: the rational model and the bounded rationality model. Each model provides valuable insights.

Rational Model

The rational model *prescribes a set of phases that individuals or teams should follow to increase the likelihood that their decisions will be logical and optimal. A rational decision results in the maximum achievement of a goal in a situation.* The rational model usually focuses on means—how best to achieve one or more goals. Moreover, this process may be used to assist in identifying, evaluating, and selecting the goals to be pursued.[28]

Figure 8.3 shows the rational model of decision making as a seven-step process. It starts with defining and diagnosing the problem and moves through successive steps to following up and controlling. When making routine decisions, individuals can follow these steps easily. In addition, people are most likely to utilize this process in situations involving low risk. That is, when they can assign objective probabilities to outcomes. Routine decisions under conditions that approximate certainty obviously don't require using all of the steps in the model. For example, if a particular problem tends to recur, decisions (solutions) may be written as standard operating procedures or rules. Moreover, individuals or teams rarely follow these seven steps in a strict sequence when making adaptive or innovative decisions.[29]

Step 1: Define and Diagnose the Problem. The rational model is based on the assumption that effective decisions (solutions) are not likely if people haven't iden-

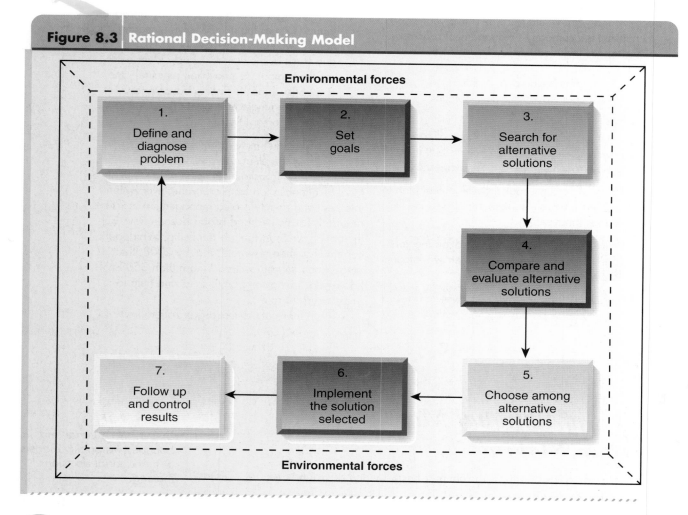

Figure 8.3 | **Rational Decision-Making Model**

tified the real problems and their possible causes. The task of problem definition and diagnosis involves three skills that are part of a manager's planning and administration competency: noticing, interpreting, and incorporating. *Noticing* involves identifying and monitoring numerous external and internal environmental factors and deciding which ones are contributing to the problem(s). *Interpreting* requires assessing the factors noticed and determining which are causes, not merely symptoms, of the real problem(s). Finally, *incorporating* calls for relating those interpretations to the current or desired goals (step 2) of an individual department or the organization as a whole. If noticing, interpreting, and incorporating are done haphazardly or incorrectly, people are likely to incorrectly define and diagnose the problem.

A basic part of effective problem definition and diagnosis is asking probing questions. Consider the meaning of the word *question*. Our use of the word goes beyond the dictionary definition—an act or instance of asking—and is closer to the multiple meanings expressed by creativity experts:

▶ A question is an invitation to creativity.

▶ A question is an unsettled and unsettling issue.

▶ A question is a beginning of adventure.

▶ A question is a disguised answer.

▶ A question pokes and prods that which has not yet been poked and prodded.

▶ A question is a point of departure.

▶ A question has no end and no beginning.[30]

Let's consider an example of the critical importance of careful problem definition and diagnosis. In the mid-1990s, Internet-based brokers seemed to invade the market of Edward Jones, a traditional office-based brokerage firm, with headquarters in St. Louis, Missouri. The leadership of Edward Jones wondered if this development was a major problem that needed to be addressed by entering into Internet-based brokerage sales. After questioning, they decided not to enter the Internet brokerage business. Instead, Edward Jones focused on improving value-added products for its targeted customers and on investing in its highly personal, face-to-face services in offices across the country. Edward Jones has increased its number of offices from 300 in 1980 to almost 9,000 today (more than any other U.S. brokerage firm) and has nearly 6 million clients. The company continues with its one-broker office strategy, which runs counter to that of virtually every other major U.S. securities organization. A managing partner, John Bachmann, stated: "You will not buy securities over the Internet at Edward Jones. That's going to be true as far as I can see into the future. . . . If you aren't interested in a relationship and you just want a transaction, then you could go to E*Trade if you want a good price. We just aren't in that business."[31]

Step 2: Set Goals. Goals *are results to be attained and indicate the direction toward which decisions and actions should be aimed.* General goals *provide broad direction for decision making in qualitative terms.* General goals for you may be to obtain a quality education and a good job upon graduation. One of the general goals of the Smithsonian Institute in Washington, D.C., is to serve as an educational resource for the people of the United States and the rest of the world. Operational goals *state what is to be achieved in quantitative terms, for whom, and within what time period.* A simple operational goal is "to reduce my weight by 15 pounds within three months." It specifies what in quantitative terms (15 pounds of weight), for whom (me), and a measurable time period (three months). Recall the expressed operational goal of the Ball Corporation in the

Challenge of Managing feature: "to achieve 10 to 15 percent (amount) annual (time period) growth in earnings per share" (what) by the Ball Corporation (whom).

Management usually tries to link goals between organizational levels and across units. This is no easy task and can be the source of many conflicts. A hierarchy of goals *represents the formal linking of goals between organizational levels.* A successful hierarchy-of-goals approach requires meeting the goal of the lowest level units in order to achieve goals at the next higher organizational level, and so on, until the goals of the organization as a whole are achieved.[32]

Figure 8.4 presents a simple hierarchy of goals for an organization with five organizational levels. It illustrates the use of operational goals. Figure 8.4 also shows that goals for the lowest level organizational units tend to become more detailed, narrower in scope, and easier to measure. The arrows pointing in both directions indicate that top management should not unilaterally set goals and impose them on employees. Setting goals often involves the back-and-forth flow of decisions between organizational levels, as well as across units at any given level.

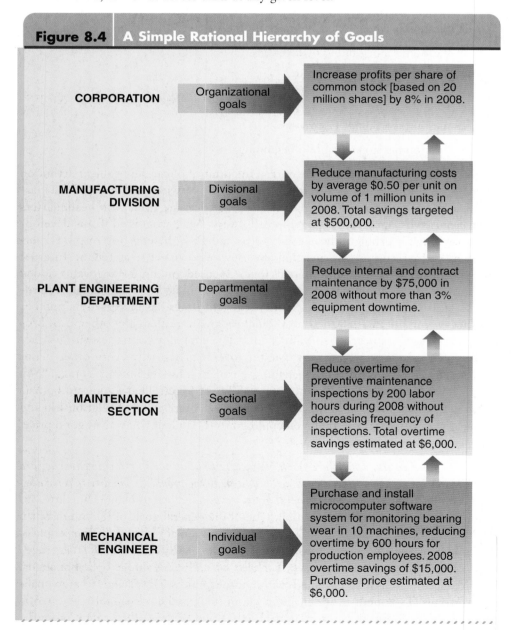

Figure 8.4   A Simple Rational Hierarchy of Goals

CORPORATION — Organizational goals → Increase profits per share of common stock [based on 20 million shares] by 8% in 2008.

MANUFACTURING DIVISION — Divisional goals → Reduce manufacturing costs by average $0.50 per unit on volume of 1 million units in 2008. Total savings targeted at $500,000.

PLANT ENGINEERING DEPARTMENT — Departmental goals → Reduce internal and contract maintenance by $75,000 in 2008 without more than 3% equipment downtime.

MAINTENANCE SECTION — Sectional goals → Reduce overtime for preventive maintenance inspections by 200 labor hours during 2008 without decreasing frequency of inspections. Total overtime savings estimated at $6,000.

MECHANICAL ENGINEER — Individual goals → Purchase and install microcomputer software system for monitoring bearing wear in 10 machines, reducing overtime by 600 hours for production employees. 2008 overtime savings of $15,000. Purchase price estimated at $6,000.

We deliberately kept Figure 8.4 simple by *not* showing several aspects of setting goals. It doesn't show all of the performance goals normally found at each organizational level. Nor does it show the interaction between units at the same level, such as production and marketing.

Goals aren't set in a vacuum. Various stakeholders (e.g., customers, shareholders, suppliers, and government agencies) have an impact on an organization's goals. This impact is felt in the goal-revision process. As suggested previously in Figure 8.3, stakeholders play a crucial role in shaping the problems identified, goals selected, alternatives considered, and decisions made by managers and employees. The relative range of choices that organizations have in setting goals varies greatly, depending on the magnitude of stakeholder power.[33]

DuPont, headquartered in Wilmington, Delaware, is a major chemical manufacturer. The firm faced pressures from governmental agencies and environmental groups to reduce pollution from its various chemical plants. DuPont has set a new general goal for its research center, named the Experimental Station, with 2,000 scientists and engineers, to "make real differences in everyday life by providing advances that help make the world a safer and better place." To do this, the center has developed more specific goals for achieving breakthroughs in nanotechnology, emerging displays technologies, fuel cell energy sources, and biomaterials produced from renewable resources such as corn. These developments could lead to foods that help prevent diseases and brittle bones, "smart" materials that can adjust performance on their own, microorganisms that produce biodegradable products, and innovative materials for personal protection.[34]

Step 3: Search for Alternative Solutions.

Individuals or teams must look for alternative ways to achieve a goal. This step might involve seeking additional information, thinking creatively, consulting experts, and undertaking research. In the following chapter, we discuss the creative decision-making process for visualizing, generating, and identifying new and novel alternatives.

Gary Tooker is the former CEO and then chairman of the board of directors at Motorola. Motorola, headquartered in Schaumburg, Illinois, is a major manufacturer of integrated communications and electronic solutions used in products such as cell phones, pagers, digital video, and semiconductors. Tooker's reflections on the importance of searching for alternative solutions are instructive for all of us:

> . . . I think many people in a rush to make a decision do not have enough of
> the alternatives out in the open. So they have two of the alternatives and say,
> "Okay, I'm going this way" but they didn't think through it enough when
> there were possibly three or four alternatives. One of the hidden ones might
> have been the best, and so the issue is making sure that either all or enough of
> the alternatives are out in the open to allow you to make the best decision.[35]

Step 4: Compare and Evaluate Alternative Solutions.

After individuals or teams have identified alternative solutions, they must compare and evaluate these alternatives. This step emphasizes determining expected results and the relative cost of each alternative.

The consequences of inadequately comparing and evaluating alternative solutions are illustrated by British Airways' experience with its baggage handling system. Some British Airways customers at London's Heathrow Airport asked a baggage handler how they could obtain yellow and black tags for their bags. The baggage handler asked them why they wanted these tags. They told him that bags with yellow and black tags always arrived at the luggage carousel first. Thus, they wanted their baggage tagged that way. The baggage handler came to the realization that the people asking about the tags were first-class passengers. They deplaned first and were the first to arrive at the luggage carousel. However, first-class customers had to wait on their bags while other passengers received their bags first.

The baggage handler didn't just ignore the problem. He asked questions about why this was happening. The answer from the operations people indicated that the stand-by and late passengers were the last to board the plane. Their luggage was loaded last and then unloaded first. Ironically, stand-by and late passengers were receiving first-class luggage service. First-class passengers, who are highly profitable to the airline, had to watch and wait for their bags. The baggage handler offered a simple alternative solution. First-class luggage should be loaded last. Airline managers recognized the merit in his solution. The implementation of this solution required changing the British Airways luggage-handling procedures in airports all over the world. This would take time and money. Eventually, the procedures were changed. The average time for transporting first-class luggage from plane to carousel dropped from an average of 20 minutes to less than 10 minutes at all of the airports served by British Airways.[36]

Step 5: Choose among Alternative Solutions.
Decision making is sometimes viewed as having made a final choice. Selecting a solution, as illustrated in the baggage-handling incident at British Airways, is only one step in the rational decision-making process.

Many managers complain that when recent college graduates receive a project assignment, they tend to present and propose only one solution. Instead of identifying and evaluating several feasible alternatives, the new graduate presents the manager with the option only of accepting or rejecting the alternative presented. The ability to select among alternative solutions might appear to be straightforward; however, this may prove to be difficult when the problem is highly complex and ambiguous.

This was the case for David Hoover and his management team when they met off-site to talk about areas of diversification. Recall Hoover's comment in the Challenge of Managing feature: "We looked not necessarily at specific, real opportunities, but of a half-dozen or so, some were pretty far afield and some were pretty close. We decided to stay close if we can. We also pledged to stay disciplined."

Step 6: Implement the Solution Selected.
A well-chosen solution isn't always successful. A technically correct decision has to be accepted and supported by those responsible for implementing it if the decision is to be acted on effectively. If the selected solution cannot be implemented for some reason, another one should be considered. We explore the importance of participation in making a decision by those charged with implementing it in Chapters 15 and 17. The success of Whirlpool's management innovation strategy was a direct result of all of the key changes made to implement the concept of "innovation from everyone, everywhere." The previous Teamwork Competency feature presented the numerous changes in management processes that were required to implement Whirlpool's innovation strategy.

Step 7: Follow Up and Control the Results.
Implementing the preferred solution won't automatically achieve the desired goal. Individuals or teams must control implementation activities and eventually follow up by evaluating the results of the decision. If implementation isn't producing satisfactory results, corrective action will be needed. Because environmental forces affecting decisions change continually, follow-up and control may indicate a need to redefine the problem or review the original goal. Feedback from this step could even suggest the need to start over and repeat the entire decision-making process.[37]

The rational model might be thought of as an ideal, nudging individuals or teams closer to making rational decisions. At best, though, human decision making rarely approximates this ideal, especially under conditions of high risk or uncertainty. When dealing with some types of problems, people don't even attempt to follow the rational model's seven phases.[38] Instead, they apply the bounded rationality or a political model, which is the focus of the last part in this chapter. Observations of actual decision-making processes in organizations suggest that individuals may modify or even ignore the rational model, especially when faced with making certain types of adaptive and innovative decisions.

Bounded Rationality Model

The bounded rationality model *contends that the capacity of the human mind for formulating and solving complex problems is small compared with what is needed for objectively rational behavior.*[39] Herbert Simon, a management scholar, introduced this model in the mid-1950s. It contributed significantly to the Swedish Academy of Sciences' decision to award him the 1978 Nobel Prize in economics for his "pioneering research into the decision-making process within economic organizations." This model emphasizes the limitations of rationality and thus provides a better picture of the day-to-day decision-making processes often used by managers and others. It partially explains why different individuals make different decisions when they have exactly the same information. Figure 8.5 presents the key factors in the bounded rationality model.

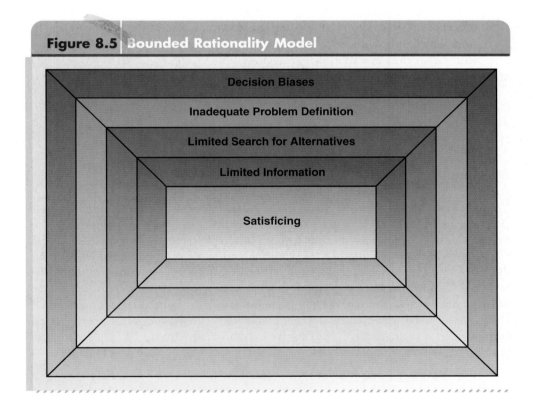

Figure 8.5 Bounded Rationality Model

Decision Biases

Inadequate Problem Definition

Limited Search for Alternatives

Limited Information

Satisficing

Decision Biases. People often fall prey to various biases when they engage in decision making. These biases cause individuals to use inadequate information in decision making. They can even influence what problems are recognized and how they are interpreted. The potential for such biases are most likely under conditions of high risk and uncertainty. A few of the biases that can influence one or more of the other elements in this model, or any model of decision making, include the following[40]:

- The availability bias *refers to easy recall of specific instances of an event that may lead individuals to overestimate how frequently the event occurs and, thus, becomes a problem.* People who have recently seen a serious automobile accident often overestimate the frequency of such accidents.

- The selective perception bias *refers to people seeing what they expect to see.* People tend to seek information consistent with their own views and downplay conflicting information, thereby influencing what problems are perceived. Some people eagerly leap from a tower 100 feet above the ground with only a bungee cord between them and certain death. Yet these same people may not be willing to live near a closed plant that has been declared a completed Superfund cleanup site.

- The concrete information bias *refers to the recollection of a vivid, direct experience usually prevailing over more objective and complete information.* A single personal experience may outweigh statistical evidence. An initial bad experience on the job may lead an employee to conclude that most managers can't be trusted and are simply out to exploit their subordinates and, thus, are seen as problems for them.

- The law of small numbers bias *refers to the tendency to view a few incidents or cases as representative of a larger population (i.e., a few cases "prove the rule") even when they aren't.* Widely publicized, but infrequent, events of excessive use of force by a few police officers often trigger characterizations of most police officers as people who regularly engage in extreme use of force and aggression. Thus, police officers are likely to be seen as a problem to be reckoned with rather than as a source of protection.

- The gambler's fallacy bias *refers to people seeing an unexpected number of similar events that lead them to the conviction that an event not seen will occur.* For example, after observing nine successive reds turn up on a roulette wheel, a player might incorrectly think that chances for a black on the next spin are greater than chance. They aren't! Thus, the event not seen is interpreted as an opportunity rather than the continuing problem of having to deal with a random chance.

Competent and experienced decision makers attempt to minimize these biases. Past experience enables them to quickly gain an accurate sense of what's going on in the situation. They recognize typical and effective ways of reacting to problems. Their past experience enables them to see patterns and anomalies that serve as warning signs. Successful managers do not settle on the first thought—definition of the problem or solution—that comes to mind. They have typically encountered the adverse consequences of this approach in the past and have thus learned from experience.[41] On the other hand, experienced decision makers have to guard against preconceived notions. This is suggested by Jeffrey McKeever, the chairman and CEO of MicroAge. He comments on the importance of guarding against biases in decision making:

> ...When someone comes to you, you often have a bias about what they are talking about. If you have been in business for 20 to 30 years, chances are you've been there and done that. Their idea is generally not so new or innovative as they think. You have a strong prejudice about outcomes. That is a dangerous thing. One of the things you have to do very cognitively to be a good leader is not let your biases or your filters totally cloud the message someone's trying to deliver.[42]

Inadequate Problem Definition. As might be expected, all of the decision biases just reviewed may lead to inadequate problem definition. In addition, problems often reoccur or new problems are viewed as being just like the old problems that needed solving. Thus, decisions from the past are used to solve similar problems as they reoccur, but they may lose their effectiveness over time because the initial problems may become symptoms of the new and real problems. For example, poorly performing employees may be seen as the source of the problem for poor quality. The initial solution may be thought to be to change the selection process or increase training. That may work for a time to relieve—but not solve—the quality problem. Eventually, it is discovered that poor leadership and management practices are the real problem, resulting in inadequate quality.

It has been suggested that the greatest weakness in problem definition is laziness. Problems get expressed in obvious and familiar ways. Even worse, they may get defined by the most powerful individual, such as an executive, who may know much less about the true nature of the problem than those at lower levels in the organization. But, the executive is not willing to take the time to listen carefully to these subordinates and to seek their inputs.

Limited Search for Alternatives. According to the bounded rationality model, individuals usually do not make an exhaustive search for possible goals or alternative solutions to a problem. They tend to consider options until they find one that seems adequate. For example, when trying to choose the "best" job, college seniors can't evaluate every available job in their field. If they tried to, they probably would reach retirement age before determining every job possibility. In applying the bounded rationality model, students would stop searching for jobs as soon as they found an acceptable one.

Some research suggests that searching for more alternatives does not always yield better decisions. This result can be caused by several factors: the tendency to focus on problems that may only represent symptoms, the inability to process all of the information needed to evaluate a large number of alternatives, or the additional costs of searching for and evaluating a large number of alternatives that may not sufficiently improve the quality of the decision to justify those additional costs.[43] However, the greater limitation is with the limited search for alternatives. As suggested in the adjacent Snapshot, personal experience can be valuable in guiding decision making and searching for alternatives. However, it can also be a source of blinders.

Limited Information. Bounded rationality suggests that people frequently have inadequate information about the precise nature of the problems facing them and the consequences of each alternative.[44] These conditions create a condition of *ignorance—the lack of relevant information or the incorrect interpretation of the information that is available.*

S. C. Johnson Wax took advantage of the ignorance of its competitors when estimating sales potential in Central and Eastern Europe. Its competitors used official government data, which showed that Russia and Poland rank below Spain on per capita gross domestic product. However, the actual purchasing power in most East European countries is much higher than that reported in government figures. The official data do not take into account unreported income and sales in that region. Unreported income is estimated to generate between 25 and 50 percent of all income. S. C. Johnson Wax capitalized on its competitors' ignorance of this fact. After just 5 years, its sales volume in Poland is already 50 percent of that in Spain where it has operated for more than 30 years.[45]

Satisficing. Satisficing *is the practice of selecting an acceptable goal or alternative solution rather than searching extensively for the best goal or solution.* An acceptable goal might be easier to identify and achieve, less controversial, or otherwise safer than the best available

Snapshot

"Leaders who differentiate themselves time and again are the ones who trust their instincts but also use properly researched evidence to make decisions. . . . [A]t times, there is nothing more difficult than to challenge a leader with evidence that contradicts their opinions. But I would contend that we owe it to all our stakeholders, no matter how large or small the company, to insist on the facts at every opportunity."
Chris Hyman, Chief Executive, Serco Group

goals. As revealed previously in Figure 8.5, the factors that culminate in a satisficing decision are decision biases, inadequate or incorrect problem definition, limited search for alternatives, and limited information.

In an interview on the bounded rationality model, Herbert Simon explained satisficing this way:

> Satisficing is intended to be used in contrast to the classical economist's idea that in making decisions in business or anywhere in real life, you somehow pick, or somebody gives you, a set of alternatives from which you select the best one—maximize. The satisficing idea is that first of all, you don't have the alternatives, you've got to go out and scratch for them—and that you have mighty shaky ways of evaluating them when you do find them. So you look for alternatives until you get one from which, in terms of your experience and in terms of what you have reason to expect, you will get a reasonable result.[46]

Consider this basic example of satisficing. A team spends hours projecting and developing the next fiscal year's budget. After hours of discussion, they eventually reach an apparent consensus on the budget only to have one person speak up and question if the projections are really correct. When the team becomes upset at the question, it is not because this person is wrong to ask, but rather because they have come up with projections that work in developing the budget. The projections may not be what will actually come, but most agree that the projections are good enough to develop the budget.[47]

The following Ethical Challenge feature puts you in a scenario as a manager of having to make a decision under urgent conditions.[48]

Ethical Challenge

Your Bounded Decision

Your weekend staff is faced with a dilemma: The computers are down and a critical deadline is six hours away. The company's contract for computer repair has a minimum charge of $1,000 to get the system back on line for a weekend emergency. Just last week you were humiliated by your manager's scathing criticism for going over budget; he lectured you about the fact that margins are thin and money is tight. Your manager is now out of town for a brief vacation break. You are hesitant to approve this new expenditure on your own, but you also don't want your manager to think that you can't make a decision under urgent conditions.

An employee who is trying to be helpful suggests going around the service contractor by calling in his neighbor, who does the same work for another vendor, knows your computer system, will charge a lot less, and is available now. What should you do? What ethical issues are involved? What aspects of bounded rationality are apparent in this brief scenario?

Satisficing doesn't necessarily mean that managers have to be satisfied with whatever alternative pops up in their minds or in their computers and let it go at that. The level of satisficing can be raised—by personal determination, by setting higher individual or organizational standards (goals), by the use of an increasing range of sophisticated management science and computer-based decision-making and problem-solving techniques, and by following the seven steps in the rational model we discussed.[49]

Process of Political Managerial Decision Making

4.
Explain the features of political managerial decision making.

The political model *represents the decision-making process in terms of the self-interests and goals of powerful stakeholders.* Before considering this model, however, we need to define power. Power *is the ability to influence or control individual, team, departmental, or organizational decisions and goals.* To have power is to be able to influence or control the (1) definition of the problem, (2) choice of goals, (3) consideration of alternative solutions, (4) selection of the alternative to be implemented, and ultimately (5) actions and success of the organization. Political decision-making processes are most likely to be used when issues involve powerful stakeholders who have a

- ▶ divergence in problem definition, or
- ▶ divergence in goals, and/or
- ▶ divergence in preferred solutions.[50]

Figure 8.6 presents a simplified political model of decision making. The factors in this model are highly interrelated.

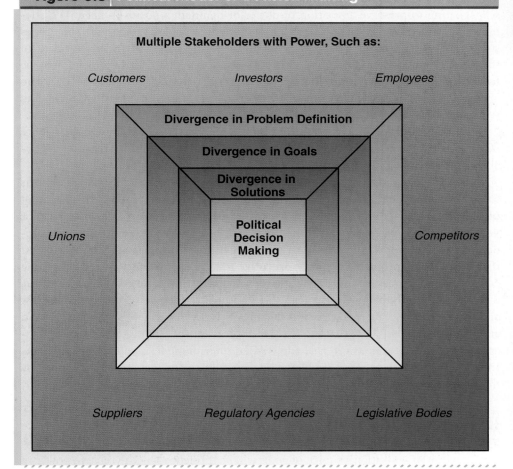

Figure 8.6 | Political Model of Decision Making

Multiple Stakeholders with Power, Such as:

Customers   Investors   Employees

Divergence in Problem Definition

Divergence in Goals

Divergence in Solutions

Political Decision Making

Unions   Competitors

Suppliers   Regulatory Agencies   Legislative Bodies

Snapshot

"Recognize up front the amount of time and attention to organizational politics, the informal systems and processes that influence so much about how things actually get done in an organization. . . . Politics, by the way, is not a bad thing. Any enterprise has its own political system, if we can call it that. But, I think what makes the difference is the curiosity and the inquiry by you to learn how the political system works."

Eliza Hermann, Vice President for Human Resources Strategy, BP PLC

Let's briefly review our discussions in previous chapters related to political decision making. In Chapter 3, we discussed the potential importance of diverse stakeholder pressures with respect to achieving stakeholder social responsibility. Table 3.4 in Chapter 3, for example, illustrates the diverse types of pressures from a firm's primary stakeholders. In Chapter 4, we noted that societies try to resolve conflicts over values and beliefs through their political and legal systems. We presented the use of five basic political strategies used by managers to cope with turbulence in their environments: negotiation, lobbying, alliance, representation, and socialization. These strategies are also used *within* organizations as part of the political model. In Chapter 5, we reviewed several of the political–legal forces of international business, including political risk factors and two significant types of international political mechanisms utilized by some governments and businesses: protectionism and bribery and extortion. Our discussion here of the political model of managerial decision making represents an extension of the political dimensions presented in those previous chapters.

Divergence in Problem Definition

In the political model, external and internal stakeholders attempt to define problems to their own advantage. Conflicts occur when various stakeholders have different perceptions about the nature and sources of problems.

When things go wrong in a politically based organization, one or more individuals may be singled out as the cause of the problem. Scapegoating *is the casting of blame for problems or shortcomings on an innocent or only partially responsible individual, team, or department.* By implication, the other people who might be responsible for the problem are considered to be free from blame. Individuals or organizational units may use scapegoating to preserve a position of power or maintain a positive image. Whistleblowers, who report what they see as wrongdoing to outside agencies, are sometimes subject to scapegoating. This has been of concern to the American Institute of Certified Public Accountants. The institute's position is that whistle-blowing may be necessary to meet the ethical standards of the certified public accountant (CPA), who is employed by the firm. That very act, however, too often results in the CPAs being scapegoated as the real problem by higher management and labeled as "snitches," "disgruntled employees," or "poor team players." Of course, this situation is more likely to occur when higher management is the source of the misleading or questionable practices and statements.[51]

When corporations lose money for several quarters or years, there may be efforts to lay blame for the problems on external sources. For example, the top management of General Motors often suggests rising health-care and pension costs due to labor demands, global overcapacity, falling prices, unstable fuel prices, and increasing competition as the problems that have triggered its financial problems.[52] Others suggest that GM's major problems are poor executive leadership; nonresponses to changing consumer preferences for more style and fuel efficiency in vehicles; too many car lines, which reduces production efficiencies; lagging quality relative to competitors; slow and excessively bureaucratic decision making with too many levels of management; and so forth. You will note that the first set of problems presented by the senior management of GM is seen as external and beyond their immediate control or influence. In contrast, the second set of problems is seen as due to the actions and inactions by the senior management of GM over a period of years.

Divergence in Goals

The political model recognizes the likelihood of conflicting goals among stakeholders. Thus, an organization's choice of goals will be influenced by the relative power of these stakeholders. Often no clear "winner" will emerge. If power is concentrated in one stakeholder, the organization's primary goals will likely reflect that stakeholder's goals.

A balance of power among several stakeholders may lead to negotiation and compromise in the decision-making process. Although a balance of power may lead to compromise, as in most union–management negotiations, it also may lead to stalemate. Recall that a common political strategy is to form a coalition (alliance) when no one person, group, or organization has sufficient power to select or implement its preferred goal. Many health-related organizations and associations—such as the American Cancer Society, American Heart Association, and American Medical Association—have formed an informal coalition with Congress to fight smoking and the tobacco interests.

Divergence in Solutions

Some goals or the means used to achieve them may be perceived as win–lose situations; that is, my gain is your loss, and your gain is my loss. In such a situation, stakeholders often distort and selectively withhold information to further their own interests. Such actions can severely limit the ability to make adaptive and innovative decisions, which, by definition, require utilizing all relevant information, as well as exploring a full range of alternative solutions.

Stakeholders within the organization often view information as a major source of power and use it accordingly. The rational decision-making model calls for all employees to present all relevant information openly. However, managers and employees operating under the political model would view free disclosure as naïve, making achievement of their personal, team, or departmental goals more difficult.[53] To complicate the picture, information often is (1) piecemeal and based on informal communication (Did you know that. . .?); (2) subjective rather than based on hard facts (Those computer printouts don't really matter around here.); and (3) defined by what powerful stakeholders consider to be important (What does the boss think? or How will the board respond?).

Co-optation is one of the common political strategies used by stakeholders to achieve their goals. Co-optation *refers to bringing stakeholder representatives into the strategic decision-making process as a way to avert threats to an organization's stability or existence.*[54] An example is Lockheed Martin placing retired military generals on its board of directors to foster lobbying within the Defense Department to aid in selling the department military equipment and services offered by Lockheed. IBM and State Farm, among others, have created junior executive committees as a way to involve middle managers in selected strategic issues and to gain their support in implementing a chosen course of action.

Despite the common view, the political model is not necessarily bad. As with the other two models—rational and bounded rationality—it can be useful and appropriate, especially for resolving conflicts among stakeholders with divergent goals and/or divergent preferences for actions to be taken. If the political model is implemented with an underpinning of basic ethical principles as discussed in Chapter 3, it is likely to lead to constructive decisions and outcomes.

The following Communication Competency feature reports on negative examples of political interpersonal communications experienced by John Wade, the chief information officer at Saint Luke's Health System in Kansas City, Missouri, and his own positive political coping tactics.[55]

© ImageShop/Jupiter Images

Motivated individuals do not allow themselves to be held back by the poor leadership of bad bosses. Instead they find a way to improve their situation.

John Wade and Bad Bosses

When John Wade started his first information technology position at the Polaroid Corporation, he soon discovered the downside of his manager's style. Though extroverted and a master politician with his peers and superiors, he didn't support his team. Wade comments: "You felt like you were just floundering." Although the people on the team commiserated among themselves, they considered it politically unwise to take their complaints outside their circle. "We didn't try to end-run him because we figured his boss must think he's doing a good job," Wade says.

Wade wanted to continue working at Polaroid. Instead of suffering in the shadow cast by his manager, he decided to let his competencies shine through to anyone who might notice. Wade remarks: "I figured, 'This guy isn't going to help me; I have to redouble my efforts to be successful and outperform on my own.'" Eventually, after a change of management at the company, the manager was transferred to a different department. The replacement manager was tough, but a person who inspired his team to give 110 percent.

When Wade accepted a managerial job at Children's Hospital Boston, he was not overly impressed with his executive. Wade saw great growth potential at the hospital and the atmosphere was interesting. "I figured I'd demonstrate to myself that I'd learned to turn around a bad situation and that in five years, this guy will move on," Wade says. Despite the positive attitude, Wade's first seven months were "absolute hell," he recounts. The executive would inevitably find reasons several times a week to call "emergency" meetings at 4:30 P.M. for the entire IT management group—and then not even stay for the entire meeting. Wade comments: "The meetings would run three hours, and this guy would leave at 6:15." Wade's interpretation was that his superior didn't feel competent to solve the problems that came up and figured if he got all the managers together, they'd get the problems fixed.

One day, Wade took a risky stand. He walked into the executive's office and said, "When you're not there providing leadership, we come out of these meetings without much more [direction] than what we went in with. So next time there's a crisis meeting, I'll have a letter in my hand, and it'll be my resignation." The tactic worked. After that, when the executive called a meeting, and there were fewer of them, it was better planned and better timed. He was there to provide guidance. Wade states: "It was almost like by channeling the guy, he became more effective." The executive was eventually let go, and Wade became the chief information officer at the hospital.

Chapter Summary

This chapter presented the basics of decision making, especially as related to managers. We discussed foundational decision-making concepts and models that are used by managers and other professionals in organizations. Decision making involves identifying problems, gathering information, considering alternatives, and choosing a course of action from the alternatives generated. Decision-making abilities are needed to develop and implement all six managerial competencies—communication, planning and administration, teamwork, strategic action, multicultural, and self-management.

Learning Goals

1. *Explain certainty, risk, and uncertainty and how they affect decision making.*

Individuals make decisions under circumstances that represent the probability of events occurring over which they have no control but that may affect the outcomes of those decisions. Such conditions may be viewed as a continuum from certainty to risk to uncertainty. Decision making becomes more challenging with increasing levels of risk and uncertainty.

2. Describe the characteristics of routine, adaptive, and innovative decisions.

Routine decisions are relatively well defined and address common problems and solutions. Adaptive decisions address somewhat unusual problems and/or solutions of low to moderate risk. Innovative decisions address very unusual and ambiguous problems and/or solutions of high risk or uncertainty. In general, managers and professionals become more highly valued as they increase their ability to make effective adaptive and innovative decisions.

3. Discuss the rational and bounded rationality models of managerial decision making.

The rational model prescribes a sequence of seven phases for making decisions: (1) define and diagnose the problem, (2) set goals, (3) search for alternative solutions, (4) compare and evaluate alternative solutions, (5) choose among alternative solutions, (6) implement the solution selected, and (7) follow up and control the results. In contrast, the bounded rationality model describes a pattern that tends to be more descriptive of how managers and others may attempt to make what they consider to be rational decisions. It represents tendencies to satisfice, engage in a limited search for alternative solutions, have limited information, and use various biases to obtain and process information. This model recognizes the practical limitations of individuals when they attempt to make rational decisions. This model recognizes that, over time, the level of satisficing can be raised through various actions.

4. Explain the features of political managerial decision making.

The political model emphasizes the impact of multiple stakeholders who have the power to make decisions. Political decision making is triggered when stakeholders hold divergent views about problem definitions, desired goals, and/or preferred solutions. In addition to those presented in previous chapters, various political strategies, including co-optation and scapegoating, may come into play under such circumstances.

Key Terms and Concepts

Active inertia	General goals	Probability
Adaptive decisions	Goals	Rational decision
Availability bias	Hierarchy of goals	Rational model
Bounded rationality model	Ignorance	Risk
Certainty	Innovative decisions	Routine decisions
Concrete information bias	Innovators	Satisficing
Continuous improvement	Law of small numbers bias	Scapegoating
Convergence	Objective probability	Selective perception bias
Co-optation	Operational goals	Subjective probability
Decision making	Political model	Uncertainty
Gambler's fallacy bias	Power	

Questions for Discussion and Reflective Thinking

1. Reread the Challenge of Managing feature regarding David Hoover, CEO of Ball Corporation. What examples of decision making under uncertainty are reflected in Hoover's comments?

2. Are any of Hoover's comments consistent with the bounded rationality model of decision making? Explain.

3. Reread the "Shoes For Crews Reduces Uncertainty" Strategic Action Competency feature. Visit the company's Web site at *www.shoesforcrews.com*. Has this firm effectively communicated to its potential customers how it reduces safety uncertainty and risks for employees and firms?

4. Go to the Web site for Visa at *www.visa.com*. Click on the relevant country Visa Web site. Click on the section that addresses "Visa Security and Protection." What routine decisions does Visa prescribe for individuals to help protect themselves from the risk and uncertainty of identity theft and fraud?

5. Give three examples of a "personal" problem that you have encountered: one that involved the condition of certainty, one that involved risk, and one that involved uncertainty.

6. What is your assessment of the adaptive decisions being made by Dunkin' Donuts? Reread the Planning and Administrative Competency feature on Dunkin' Donuts and go to the firm's Web site at *www.dunkindonuts.com*. It presents more information on the adaptive decisions being made at Dunkin' Donuts.

7. Why can managers, who are limited by the concept of bounded rationality, be expected to make reasonably *rational* decisions at times?

8. See the current General Motors Corporation Annual Report, which is available at its Web site. Go to *www.gm.com*. Read the "Letter to Stockholders." What decision-making concepts are illustrated in this letter?

9. Think of an important decision that you have made during the past year or so. In what ways did your process of making the decision match or vary from each factor in the political model of decision making?

DEVELOPING YOUR COMPETENCIES

Instructions

The following incidents are used in ethics training programs at various companies. Select the preferred judgment (the choices are listed below each incident) for each of the four incidents presented below. Then respond to the questions that follow the four incidents. This exercise can also be undertaken with the addition of a team format by having the individuals share and explain their judgments as well as their responses to the questions. The team may seek to arrive at consensus judgments and responses to each incident.

1. At a Global Energy board meeting, the CEO reports that he received an anonymous letter three months ago in which an employee complained about misleading financial disclosures. The CEO notes that he gave the letter to the company's outside law firm, which investigated it and concluded that the allegations were without merit. The CEO then goes on to the next agenda item. Wendy, an independent director, is troubled that none of her fellow directors asked to read either the letter or the law firm's report, and that the CEO waited three months to tell anyone on the board about the letter. As a board member, what is Wendy's best option?
   a. Let it pass, because the issue seems to have resolved itself.
   b. Raise the question privately with the CEO to get a satisfactory answer.
   c. Ask for time during the meeting for an executive session to discuss the issue.
   d. Personally call the outside law firm for a more detailed explanation.

2. One evening after work, you're scanning the investment message boards on the Internet. To your surprise, someone is spreading information about your company that just isn't true. They are saying that your company is going to fall far short of expectations. You know that, in fact, the company will exceed them. You're afraid that this rumormonger will hurt the stock price. You are tempted to set the record straight. What do you do?
   a. Hold your tongue.
   b. Post the real numbers but don't volunteer your identity.
   c. Post the real numbers and add that you are in a position to know.
   d. Refute the rumor but don't post any numbers.

3. You've been a manager at your company for five years and have developed an excellent reputation. Your future looks bright, which is a good thing since you have a family to support. Yesterday a fellow employee, Kim, came to you with a problem. Kim, a woman of color who used to report to you, had just been turned down for a promotion. You believe she was very qualified for the position and perfectly capable of doing it with excellence. The candidate chosen was a white male with good qualifications. But, he did not have as much experience or, in your opinion, capability as Kim. Steve, the manager who did not select Kim, happens to be "a rising star" you've known for years and the two of you get along pretty well. Steve couldn't make you CEO and couldn't get you fired. But, he is in a position to help or hinder your career. What do you do?
   a. Encourage Kim to speak to the appropriate person in the human resources department and offer to speak to them as well about your excellent opinion of Kim.
   b. Talk to Steve.
   c. Tell Kim that many (legitimate) factors go into a promotion decision and that such a decision can't be judged from the outside.
   d. Talk to Steve's supervisor.

4. Jeff has just been appointed to the board of Worldwide International. During his first meeting, the board hears a presentation about new product development from one of the company's senior managers, who is black. After the manager leaves, the CEO comments, "He's the smartest one of his people I've ever met. I'm glad we have him." Jeff should:
   a. Confirm that the manager's career has not been hurt by the CEO's apparent racism.
   b. Confront the CEO about his apparent racism in front of the rest of the board.
   c. Speak to the CEO privately about the matter later.
   d. None of the above.

Questions

1. For each of the four incidents, identify the decision-making condition it likely represents for the decision maker: certainty, risk (objective probability or subjective probability), or uncertainty. Explain.

2. For each of the four judgments you selected, what type of decision did it likely represent for the decision maker: routine, adaptive, or innovative? Explain.

3. What model of decision making seemed to be dominant in the judgment selected for each of the four incidents: rational, bounded rationality, or political? Explain.

Advanced Build-It is a small cabinet-making operation consisting of a six-person workshop. Build-It contracts "outside crews" from local companies to do the delivery and installation work. It is normal to have four or five different projects in progress at the same time, with deliveries being made to various job sites in the Windsor to Toronto, Ontario, Canada, market area.

Two jobs requiring "rush" deliveries for on-time installation were ready for shipping on Friday morning. One was black acid-proof plastic laboratory units for a renovation project in Strathroy, Ontario. The other was for kindergarten cabinets made in the school colors, gray and pink, destined for University Heights Elementary School in London, Ontario.

The delivery truck was privately owned by another small business operator who specialized in reasonably priced, fast delivery. The loading of the cabinets took up most of Friday morning. By 1 P.M., Dan, the owner/driver, and Rick, his laborer helper, were ready to depart. The units completely filled the delivery truck. By skillfully arranging the contents, only one trip would be necessary. Installation crews had been contracted and scheduled for each job site. They were to begin first thing on Saturday so as to meet the Monday openings for each project.

Saturday Morning

The scene is the home of Jerry Day, owner of Advanced Build-It.

While sitting at the kitchen table, leisurely reading the paper and lingering over a second cup of coffee, I reached to answer the phone. During the next 10 minutes, the phone is almost smoking during several calls. People are mad!

University Heights crew supervisor:	"Where's my stuff to install? I have no cabinets at this school! What do you want us to do?"
Me:	"What! They were shipped yesterday. Stay there. I'll get back to you."
Strathroy crew supervisor:	"Where do I install the gray cabinets? I don't see them on the floor plans you gave us."
Me, choking on my coffee:	"What gray cabinets? All the Strathroy lab stuff is black!"
Strathroy crew supervisor:	"Well, I have 12 gray and pink lockers and sink units here and I can't figure out where to put them."

That was the statement that did it! I knew what had happened. My suspicions were confirmed when I roused Dan out of bed at his home by phone that Saturday morning.

Dan: "We didn't get to Strathroy till after 3 P.M. yesterday. We had a flat tire. I had a golf date with Sue at 5:00 P.M., so I figured the sooner we were empty, the sooner we were done for the day. Your guys didn't mention anything about two different delivery locations when we were loading the truck."

Dan and Rick had unloaded everything at the Strathroy job site and taken the truck and trailer, empty, all the way past London to Woodstock where he lived. In his haste, Dan had not looked at the delivery sheets. Also, he had not noticed or cared that the cabinets were two very different sets in color and design. Dan's mind had obviously been on other things.

SNAFU (Situation Normal All Fouled UP) was quickly becoming FUBAR (Fouled UP Beyond Recognition)!

As the owner of Advanced Build-It, both of the prebuilt jobs we had completed had been carefully costed and we had been awarded the contracts for quality cabinets at very low prices. It would have been impossible for us to reduce any of the costs. Suddenly, I had incurred jobs I knew I would have to pay for, but had never allowed for in my estimated costs. At least a half day's wages would be required for the University Heights crew who did no work Saturday morning. Thankfully, the Strathroy crew chief had not tried to install the cabinets that did not belong at that site.

Sunday wages would be required if the University Heights kindergarten was to be ready for Monday. It would require two men plus a large truck for most of Saturday to "rescue" the kindergarten cabinets from Strathroy and deliver them to the London site. If Dan were to do the job, he and his truck had to come all of the way from Woodstock!

Questions

Put yourself in the position of Jerry Day, the owner of Advanced Build-It.

1. What are the immediate and underlying problems in this case?
2. Who was in error here? Why?
3. How would you solve the immediate problems?
4. What model of decision making was dominant in arriving at your solution? Explain.

chapter 9

© Andersen Ross/Brand X Pictures/Jupiter Images

Using Planning and Decision Aids

Learning Goals

After studying this chapter, you should be able to:

1. Explain the essentials of knowledge management and how it is used to create value for organizations.

2. Describe the features and uses of the Delphi method, simulation, and scenario forecasting aids.

3. Discuss the creative process and how to use Osborn's creativity model.

4. Explain and apply three quality improvement aids: benchmarking, the Deming cycle, and the Baldrige quality program.

Communication Competency

Planning and Administration Competency

Teamwork Competency

Managing Effectively

Self-Management Competency

Strategic Action Competency

Multicultural Competency

Challenge of Managing ....

OMR Architects

© Rubberball Productions/Jupiter Images

OMR Architects (formally known as the Office of Michael Rosenfeld, Inc. Architects) is headquartered in West Acton, Massachusetts. The firm provides full architectural services and is organized into five specialty groups: educational, religious, residential, municipal, and corporate. The 30-plus professionals are from eight countries and work in a casual and goal-oriented environment. Michael Rosenfeld, the founder, contends the firm's diversity serves as a competitive advantage: Different cultures, backgrounds, talents, experiences, and perspectives support the organizational mission.

Paul Woyda is the firm's chief information technologist. In an industry that calls for extensive teamwork, his job is to find and deliver the software and hardware solutions OMR needs to successfully design, develop, and construct its projects. Woyda faced the challenge of improving the ability to (1) share knowledge and information among the professionals and other staff, (2) prevent "data chaos" during updates and changes, and (3) make data and documents easier to use. He comments: "When we are working on a project as large as a $65 million, 350,000-square-foot public high school, there are dozens of people involved at each stage and thousands of details to track."

Newburyport High School, located in Newburyport, Rhode Island, was a special challenge: The old school was gutted right back to the frame, with only the historic brick facades left intact. Everything from the gym floor to the chemistry lab tables had to be rethought, redesigned, and constructed anew. Architects, engineers, contractors, subcontractors, site supervisors, secretaries, and, of course, school officials all had to work together, stay informed, and have access to the very latest and most accurate data.

The OMR team is highly mobile, sometimes working in the office, sometimes at the project site, and sometimes on the road. On a typical OMR project, the clients and contractors have separate offices in separate cities or even across the country.

The firm had tried construction-specific software applications. Woyda and his team found, however, that such software demanded time-consuming employee training, customization, and technical support, and was just too complex for everyday use. The software wasn't always that helpful in communicating with contractors, clients, and outside members of the OMR team. Woyda sought a solution that would be powerful enough to organize a $100 million project, yet simple enough that the whole firm could use it anytime, anywhere.

He found a knowledge management software package that was (1) easy to use, (2) provided 24/7 online access, (3) improved teamwork and accountability, and (4) was scalable to any project size. In this case, the knowledge management (KM) software selected was QuickBase for Small Business.

The KM software selected is one of an increasing number of several options that provide a user-friendly Web-based approach. The KM software organizes and shares all documents, drawings, specifications, and contracts during a project's design and construction phases. Clients and contractors can also share and update data and other information along with the OMR professionals. A separate database is set up for each new project, with varying access permissions given to appropriate individuals.

Woyda comments: "Everyone authorized can submit drawings and specs without having to track people down or waste time playing phone or fax tag." The automatic e-mail notification feature alerts the right staff members when updates are made. The whole team has access to the very latest information, 24 hours a day.[1]

To learn more about this organization, visit *www.omr-architects.com.*

OMR Architects had a positive work environment and was a successful organization prior to its adoption of knowledge management (KM) software. The KM software provided a variety of positive results for OMR Architects, including (1) saving time and money, (2) improving the quality and speed of communications to enable more timely decision making, (3) reducing confusion and stress when developing and changing plans, and (4) improving coordination among all of the members on a project team (which includes those both within and outside of the firm) to develop better decisions. This was possible because the firm's employees, clients, and contractors accepted the use of the KM technology. As you will learn, knowledge management is about much more than technology, although that is typically an essential ingredient.

In this chapter, we highlight and describe the features of KM, especially its role in supporting more effective planning and decision making. We also present eight planning and decision aids that can be used (1) at various organizational levels, (2) in virtually all functional areas (e.g., marketing, finance, human resources, and auditing), and (3) for aiding planning and decision making with many types of organizational issues and problems.

We begin by discussing the fundamental features and uses of knowledge management, which increases the likelihood of the effective application of the other aids. We present one of the more comprehensive frameworks of knowledge management, namely, the balanced scorecard model. Next, we review the basics and uses of forecasting as well as the essentials of three forecasting techniques: the Delphi method, simulation, and scenarios. Then we address the need and uses for creativity in many situations by reviewing—from among dozens of aids—Osborn's creativity model. We conclude the chapter with a discussion of the features and uses of three aids that are designed specifically to improve quality: benchmarking, the Deming cycle, and the Baldrige quality program.

Using Knowledge Management

Explain the essentials of knowledge management and how it is used to create value for organizations.

What Is Knowledge Management?

Knowledge management (KM) *involves recognizing, generating, documenting, distributing, and transferring among persons useful information, know-how, and expertise to improve organizational effectiveness.* It requires developing a system for collecting and maintaining data, information, experiences, and lessons, as well as improving communication.[2] Decision making and planning have always benefited from having the right knowledge at the right place and at the right time. Knowledge management helps to achieve this. According to one estimate, 81 percent of the leading companies in North America and Europe are utilizing some form of KM. A few of these companies include Accenture, DaimlerChrysler, Hewlett-Packard, IBM, and Unilever.[3]

Main Components. Knowledge management is generally viewed as consisting of three main components[4]:

▶ *Explicit knowledge:* published in internally generated reports and manuals, books, magazines, journals, government data and reports, online services newsfeeds, and the like. The KM software adopted by OMR Architects provided for 24/7 access to and updating of documents, drawings, specifications, and contracts for each project.

▶ *Tacit knowledge:* the information, competencies, and experience possessed by employees, including professional contacts and interpersonal information sharing. This knowledge may be difficult to express, is often developed from direct experiences and action, and is typically shared through conversations involving storytelling and shared experiences. OMR Architects recognized the importance of tacit knowledge by organizing into five specialty groups so that its professionals in each group can develop deep insights, contacts, and relationships. Also, the firm's embracing of many forms of diversity—cultural, educational backgrounds, talents, experiences, and perspectives—is believed to provide knowledge that supports the mission of OMR Architects.

▶ *Enabling technologies:* intranets, the Internet, search engines, work-flow software. OMR Architects' adoption of KM software and related technologies enabled the firm to take a major step in fostering knowledge management on a 24/7 basis for those involved in each project. You will recall that Web-based (Internet) KM software substantially improved the work flow of each project.

Information Age Drivers. The Information Age has replaced the Industrial age. The balance sheet typically measures physical assets (e.g., land, factories, equipment, and cash). Managers, shareholders, and others are increasingly recognizing a new asset—knowledge. Knowledge is becoming more valuable than physical or financial assets, or even natural resources in many cases. Information and knowledge are the new competitive weapons.

The serious risks of not taking steps to manage knowledge assets and processes are driving organizations to reevaluate their knowledge strategies. In doing so, they are finding some rather severe shortcomings in their systems, including the following:

▶ *Productivity and opportunity loss:* a lack of knowledge where and when it is needed; a knowledge base that is not usable by employees and customers;

▶ *Information overload:* too much unsorted and nontargeted information;

- *Knowledge attrition:* according to some estimates, the typical organization loses half its knowledge base every 5 to 10 years through obsolescence and employee and customer turnover; and

- *Reinventing the wheel:* lack of standards and a means for creating, capturing, sharing, and applying best practices or lessons learned.

Strategic importance must be placed on overcoming these and other such shortcomings to ensure that the right knowledge is available to the right person at the right time.[5]

Knowledge Management Targets

The application of KM has three natural targets: an organization's teams, customers, and workforce.[6]

Teams. Collaboration is often crucial to ensuring that goods and services are designed to meet customer or client needs. By obtaining input from sales, marketing, engineering, design, and other groups, KM provides a method for both the sharing of ideas and the identification of best practices across teams. By bringing together the ideas and information of each team, a project team can move ahead more quickly and efficiently. It becomes aware of work being done elsewhere in the organization, thereby reducing duplication and enhancing interteam problem solving.

Some years ago, knowledge management for Xerox's service technicians was as simple as giving them two-way radios. They could confer with each other from different locations while dealing with a challenging problem when repairing a broken machine. More recently, Xerox developed a repair database for technicians that can be accessed through the Internet on a 24/7 basis. Julian Orr, an anthropologist for Xerox, recalls: "At first, the technicians were reluctant to submit tips. They didn't find it natural to write down what they knew." Managers "seeded" the database with suggestions from engineers at headquarters. Some managers offered rewards, including cash and t-shirts, for submitting tips. Managers also featured the names of people who contributed, resulting in "thank yous" from colleagues around the world. Today, Xerox's "Eureka" system holds about 70,000 suggestions and saves the company millions of dollars a year in service costs.[7]

Customers. Satisfied customers are the foundation of a company's continuing success. Tracking customers—their issues, buying patterns, and expectations—is essential for developing and improving those relationships. Knowledge management can help in this process. Organizations are challenged constantly to revise strategies affecting every area, from the supply room to the executive suite.

First Franklin is a mortgage lender with headquarters in San Jose, California. The company needed to improve and tailor various communications for three initiatives: direct communication with customers, communication with customers and other external groups through an extranet, and communication with employees through an intranet. Gaurav Kohli, an applications manager at First Franklin, comments: "One of the major initiatives we have as a mortgage lender is to entice mortgage brokers to our site. To do that, we provide an array of services including e-mails that are sent to brokers as the loan goes through its life cycle." The message content varies depending on the status of the loan being processed. Content for the notification e-mails is stored with metadata that allows the right message to be picked up by the notification application. The content of the message is determined by KM software. Personalization is accomplished based on login types, which define user categories. Kohli continues: "We leverage the ability to push content to various destinations in a personalized way quite a bit. More and more, people are looking for ways to put together content contextually, creating Web sites specific to particular user groups."[8]

Knowledge management technologies are not without the potential ethical challenge of sacrificing too much customer privacy. As you will recall from Chapter 3, the moral rights approach to making ethical judgments holds that decisions should be consistent with the fundamental right and privilege of privacy—along with life and safety, truthfulness, and freedom of conscience and speech. A variety of technologies are being introduced that create challenges for managers in determining when these technologies are too invasive of customers' privacy. The recent introduction and increasing use of radio-frequency identification tags is an example of a challenge for managers. Radio-frequency identification (RFID) *is an automatic identification method that relies on storing and remotely retrieving data using devices called RFID tags or transponders.* An RFID tag is a small object that can be attached to or incorporated into a product, animal, or person. These tags contain silicon chips and antennas to enable them to receive and respond to radio-frequency signals from an RFID transceiver. Passive tags require no internal power source, whereas active tags require a power source. Most RFID tags are passive, such as those attached to clothing or books.[9]

The following Ethical Challenge feature discusses RFID technology, which serves as a tool in the larger knowledge management process, and its relationship to customer privacy.[10]

Ethical Challenge

RFID Technology and Customer Privacy

A U.S. Government Accountability Office's report on RFID concluded that "once a tagged item is associated with a particular individual, personally identifiable information can be obtained and then aggregated to develop a profile." Retailers today routinely link bar codes on items shoppers buy with personally identifiable information from their credit, debit, or store-loyalty cards. This practice is likely to continue as radio tags replace bar codes. With tags on every item you own, from shoes to hats, all of them are capable of broadcasting to a database that can be linked to your credit card. The result is that the potential for privacy invasion by corporate and government organizations has risen to a new level.

A U.S. patent assigned to IBM, which provides RFID systems, describes exactly how radio-tag person-tracking would work. The patent application from IBM stated: "When a person enters a retail store, a shopping mall, an airport, or any location where a person can roam, an RFID tag scanner located therein scans all identifiable RFID tags carried on the person. The collection of items is assigned a tracking number that can be correlated with sales transaction records to identify the person being tracked and the person tracking unit may keep records of different locations where the person has visited as well as the visitation times."

Mark Roberti, editor of *RFID Journal,* asserts: "Corporations, even if they're self-interested, know that the way to make money generally is to do the right thing, so they won't alienate customers by violating their privacy." Do you agree with Roberti's comment? Explain. Do you think there is a need for RFID regulation to protect consumer privacy? Explain.

To learn more about RFID, visit *www.rfidjournal.com* or *www.rfidbusiness.org.*

Workforce. An organization's single most valuable asset is its workforce.[11] Knowledge management can track employees' competencies, facilitate performance reviews, deliver training, provide up-to-date company information, manage benefits, improve employee knowledge and morale, and help employees learn from one another. Rapidly changing market conditions can catch a company short in terms of needed valuable employee skills. Knowledge management systems should be able to anticipate and identify skill gaps and provide mechanisms for training employees in new competencies. Also, KM enables employees within the same organization or different organizations who are working on the same project to work together more effectively.[12] This was demonstrated in our presentation of the KM process at OMR Architects and through Xerox's "Eureka" system.

Snapshot

"The most valuable assets of a 20th-century company were its production equipment. The most valuable asset of a 21st-century institution, whether business or nonbusiness, will be its knowledge workers and their productivity. In the society into which we are moving very fast, knowledge is the key resource."

Peter Drucker (1909–2005), author of Management Challenges for the 21st Century and of many other pioneering books on management

Consider the experiences by the leadership of BECU (formerly known as Boeing Employees' Union) in developing its KM system, known as "The Source."[13] BECU, headquartered in Seattle, has approximately 415,000 credit union members and 830 employees. Sheri Sala, the BECU performance support manager, led the development of "The Source" to improve employee productivity and satisfaction, as well as enable them to know and have easy access to the large amount of complex information needed to service the credit union members.

The implementation of the KM system has been a significant undertaking. BECU is still working to determine what best practices to adopt, who should own what content, and how that content should be managed. Sala comments: "Where do we find the resources to do the updating, writing, editing and publication? I think that that's probably everybody's greatest struggle. We have all of this content, but how do we then centrally put in some controls so that we have content management. That's been our point of pain."

At BECU, the knowledge management system has become the repository for training materials. Sala states: "We don't print paper manuals anymore. It's all in The Source." In training, we've reinforced that you don't have to know everything—you just have to know where to find it." In the past, trainers would create training manuals that were paper based and quickly outdated. Now, everybody has access to the same information through the online resource and it is much more efficient for everybody.

According to Sala, getting staff to use the KM system has not really been a problem. She continues: "They were very drawn to it even in the early stages, including a willingness to share their own knowledge. There was concern in the beginning that [getting people to share] was going to be a problem—knowledge is power they say. But, what we are trying to say is that 'the power of knowledge is the sharing' and our staff seem to be OK with that."

Enabling Technology

Technology is one of the KM enablers. It provides the foundation for solutions that automate and centralize the sharing of knowledge and fostering innovation. All of the examples of KM systems presented—OMR Architects, Xerox's "Eureka," First Franklin, and BECU's "The Source"—involved the integration of specific technologies, including the use of various software applications.

Choosing a set of technologies on which to build KM should involve addressing at least two critical issues.[14] First, the technologies should deliver only the relevant information to users, but quickly and from every feasible source. A by-product of the speed at which technologies change is the creation and storage of knowledge in many different places. The technology used should support exploration of new ideas and solutions to problems and make existing knowledge easily available to both developers and users. Xerox's Eureka is an example of such technology. Second, because of the increasing mobility of knowledge workers, technologies used need to comprise a variety of devices—from telephones to laptop computers. The ability to obtain and deliver information is useless if it cannot be transmitted to the place where a decision needs to be made and on a timely basis. We have identified some of these enabling technologies in this and previous chapters—the Internet, Web sites, extranets, intranets, RFID tags, etc. The numerous types of KM software are enabling technologies as well. In this section, we comment on the use of two of many enabling technologies—expert systems and wiki.

Expert Systems. Computer-based technologies have been developed to perform functions normally associated with human intelligence, such as comprehending spoken language, making judgments, and even learning.[15] Most business applications of such technologies involve what is called an expert system. An expert system *is a com-*

puter program based on the decision-making processes of people with specialized knowledge and skills that stores, retrieves, and manipulates data, diagnoses problems, and makes limited decisions based on detailed information about a particular problem. It helps users find solutions by posing a series of questions about a specific situation and then offering solutions based on the information it receives in response. The primary characteristics of an expert system include the following:

▶ It is programmed to use factual knowledge, if–then rules, and specific procedures to solve certain problems. If–then rules are logical steps of progression toward a solution.

▶ It is based on the decision-making process used by effective managers or specialists when they search among possible alternatives for a "good enough" solution.

▶ It provides programmed explanations, so the user can follow the assumptions, line of reasoning, and process leading to the recommended alternative.[16]

Expert systems have problem-solving capabilities within a specific area of knowledge. They vary in complexity, both in terms of knowledge and technology. An example of the simplest type of system is a personal budgeting system running on a PC. The thrust of basic expert systems is to improve personal decision making and thereby increase productivity. In contrast, strategic impact expert systems involve high levels of knowledge and technological complexity.

DeepGreen Financial, which is owned by Lightyear Capital, was founded in 2000 as the first fully automated home equity lender in the country specializing in home equity lines of credit and loans. Since its inception, it has closed 65,000 loans for approximately $5 billion. DeepGreen was designed from the ground up around expert system decision technology for home equity loans. Customers can complete an application within five minutes, and an expert system process goes into action. The system pulls a credit report, applies a scoring algorithm, accesses an online valuation of the property, checks fraud and flood insurance, and then makes a loan decision. About 80 percent of the time, the customer receives a final decision within two minutes. The system automatically selects a local notary, and the customer completes the process by choosing a closing date. A positive loan decision is subject to follow-up verification of the information submitted by the loan applicant. This is explicitly stated on the Web site.[17]

Wiki. Wiki *is a type of Web site that allows users to easily add, remove, or edit all content, very quickly and easily, sometimes without the need for registration.*[18] This ease of interaction and operation makes a wiki an effective tool for collaboration and knowledge sharing. In Hawaiian, the word *wiki* means "quick." The term *wiki* can also refer to the collaborative software itself (wiki engine) that facilitates the operation of such a Web site. There are a number of facets to wiki, but they go beyond our scope. To experience the process, feel, and philosophy of *wiki* as a knowledge management aid, we suggest you read about *Wikipedia* (at *http://en.wikipedia.org*). It is an example of a public wiki. Wikipedia contains approximately 4 million articles in many languages, including more than 1.1 million in the English-language version. It is written collaboratively by volunteers, allowing most articles to be changed and added to by anyone with access to a computer, Web browser, and Internet connection. Now let's take a look at a business application of a wiki.

© AP Graphics Bank

Wikipedia is one type of public wiki.

Tom Wilkinson is a vice president of Black & McDonald, a construction and maintenance contractor with headquarters in Toronto, Ontario, Canada. His firm's wiki has proven to be an ideal way to store information and communicate with its staff of 3,000. What was the impetus for adopting this technology? Managers were tired of wrestling with the public folders they were using to avoid sending scores of bulky e-mails to staff. Information was scattered in files all over the place. Wilkinson comments: "There was no global search feature, so you had to go through all 90 public folders to locate specific information. Once you did, a lot of it was out of date."

When a member of Wilkinson's information technology team suggested a wiki might fix this problem, he was receptive. A wiki, using TWiki, a free software program, was quickly created. The firm uses the wiki primarily to store knowledge needed by more than one person, such as service operation manuals, staff phone numbers and safety information. Wilkinson says it is highly efficient because staff make changes to a single, centralized document. The wiki search engine means "what would have taken an hour to find before takes 20 seconds now." The firm uses password controls to limit who's allowed to view and edit certain pages. Wilkinson states: "The revision control works, and people don't change things for no reason."[19]

Enabling Corporate Culture

Organizations consistently identify cultural issues as the greatest barriers to the successful implementation of KM.[20] There is an old saying that "knowledge is power." To overcome the hoarding of information as a source of power, an appropriate organizational culture needs to be in place or created. In later chapters, particularly Chapter 18, we discuss many facets of the type of culture and management practices that are necessary to ensure that knowledge management will flourish. As a start, a sense of trust in the organization is essential for members to actively share knowledge, especially tacit knowledge from one network member to another. There needs to be a belief that sharing one's expertise with another member will not be used against oneself.

The following Multicultural Competency feature provides a glimpse into Lafarge's corporate culture and its implementation of knowledge management across nations.[21] In this feature, our emphasis is on multicultural competency as an attribute of the firm's culture. Lafarge, headquartered in Paris, France, is organized into four divisions: cement, aggregates and concrete, roofing, and gypsum. It has 80,000 employees and operations in 75 countries, including extensive operations throughout North America.

Multicultural Competency

Lafarge's Culture and Knowledge Management

Lafarge's leadership strives to advance what it calls a "multilocal" culture—one that builds on both its local and global strengths. Several years ago, Lafarge launched a global initiative that included all of the reasons for implementing KM that we have discussed. For example, the *Knowledge Sharing Handbook*—developed by Lafarge's corporate knowledge manager and global steering committee—states: "Knowledge sharing is about people using technology to enable more efficient processes to capture, store, retrieve, use, re-use and share knowledge for the improvement of business performance."

The Lafarge vision for knowledge management is to become the undisputed world leader in building materials by

- generating value for key stakeholders through the widespread sharing and application of expertise and best practices;

- providing operations in 75 countries with a simple way to access knowledge and know-how, find experts, and work collaboratively on solutions that leverage and apply the knowledge of the company; and

▶ providing tools that will analyze knowledge and turn it into actionable business intelligence to further enable performance improvements for each operation and customers in each country.

One example, among others, of the importance of the multicultural competency at Lafarge is the *Langkawi story*. It has been shared a number of times within Lafarge to illustrate the vital communications between Lafarge's relatively recent knowledge management process and its culture. The story goes like this. A cement plant in Malaysia wanted to increase its use of petrol-coke, an effi-

cient energy source that can be used by cement kilns. The technical director was facing challenges with the buildup of residue in the kiln as a result of burning petrol-coke. Using the firm's technical center and the knowledge sharing databases, he discovered that a best practice had been developed by another cement plant in Turkey. A dialogue was organized between personnel in the two plants. The learning curve was sped up thanks to this exchange of knowledge. Petrol-coke had been used in the past at 32 percent efficiency by the Langkawi plant in Malaysia. One year later, it was used at a level of 80 percent efficiency by the same plant, reducing the energy costs and increasing the returns in a shorter period of time.

To learn more about this organization, visit *www.lafarge.com.*

Balanced Scorecard Model

The balanced scorecard model *provides a process for an organization to gain deeper knowledge and understanding of its strategic decisions by considering the role of finances, customers, internal processes, and learning/growth.*[22] Many leading organizations have adopted some version of the balanced scorecard to provide a broader perspective of the factors, issues, and goals considered in planning and decision making. A few of these organizations include Caterpillar, Inc., Chemical Bank, DaimlerChrysler, DuPont, Hilton Hotels Corporation, and Verizon Communications.

The model takes into account financial and nonfinancial measures, internal improvements, past outcomes, and ongoing requirements as indicators of future performance. The balanced scorecard model attempts to measure and provide feedback to management in implementing overall goals and strategies. The model contends that long-term organizational excellence and quality can be achieved only by taking a broad approach, not by focusing solely on financials. The model can include the performance of an entire organization or each of the business units. The balanced scorecard model is future oriented, not a review of past performance, as is often the case with traditional financial reports such as income and balance sheet statements. The shift to a services and knowledge economy has increased the interest in the *intangibles* that are so important to organizational effectiveness.

Four Knowledge Perspectives. As illustrated in Figure 9.1 on the following page, the balanced scorecard model requires managers to look at their organizations' planning and decision making from four perspectives.[23] Vision and strategies are at the center of the model. Unlike traditional performance measurement systems that have financial controls at their core in the decision-making process, the balanced scorecard begins with an organization's vision and strategies. The model attempts to translate the vision and strategies into performance measures that can be tracked and used to assess the effectiveness of their implementation. The intent is to link and balance the goals and related measures for each perspective to one another. The financial and customer knowledge perspectives are viewed as focusing on *outcomes*. The internal and learning/growth knowledge perspectives are viewed as focusing on *activities*. Examples of the factors and questions addressed in each knowledge perspective include the following:

▶ *Financial perspective:* profitability, revenue growth, market value of firm, return on investment relative to the best in the industry, the extent of compliance with financial reporting laws and regulations, asset utilization, and so on. What are our shareholders' expectations for financial performance and compliance with transparent financing reporting?

▶ *Customer perspective:* meeting and exceeding expectations for service and product quality, reputation for trustworthiness, loyalty through repeat business by customers, and so on. To reach our financial goals, how do we create value for our customers?

▶ *Internal perspective:* improvements in efficiency and quality, use of improved production technologies, use of appropriate rules and procedures, employee rate of defects/errors, safety record, pattern of adhering to ethical behaviors and practices, and so on. What processes must we excel at in order to satisfy our customers, shareholders, and other stakeholders?

▶ *Learning and growth perspective:* human capital (employee skills and competencies, creativity, training, etc.), information capital (access to information and knowledge management capabilities), and organizational capital—the ability to change and sustain success (culture, teamwork, etc.). This perspective enables everything else on the balanced scorecard. How do we align and develop our intangible assets—people, systems, and culture—to achieve the desired outcomes?

Assessment. The financial perspective of an organization is fundamental to its survival and success. An overemphasis on financial performance in planning and decision

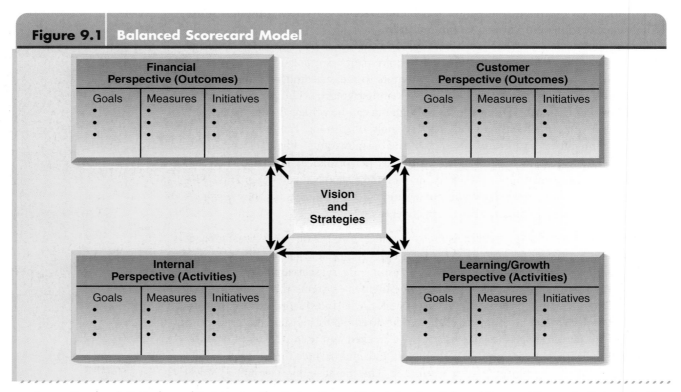

Figure 9.1 | **Balanced Scorecard Model**

Source: Based on R. S. Kaplan and D. P. Norton. *The Strategy-Focused Orientation: How Balanced Scorecard Companies Thrive in the New Business Environment.* Boston: Harvard Business School Publishing, 2000. P. R. Niven. Driving focus and alignment with the balanced scorecard. *Journal for Quality and Participation.* 28(4), 2005, 21–25.

making, however, has two key limitations. First, financial figures are historical. Although they tell us what has happened financially in the past, they may not tell us what is currently happening and they may not be good indicators of future performance. Second, it is common for the current market value of an organization to exceed the reported value of its book assets. The excess value can be thought of as intangible assets. The value of intangible assets (e.g., employees, patents, customer loyalty) is not measured by normal financial reporting, yet they are vital to the firm's long-term survival. The balanced scorecard attempts to present deeper and more comprehensive knowledge that goes beyond financial reporting of the firm's outcomes and activities. It is assumed that this enlarged knowledge profile will assist managers in making better decisions and plans.

In brief, the potential benefits of the balanced scorecard include that it

▶ helps align key performance goals and measures with strategy at all levels of an organization,

▶ provides management with a comprehensive picture of business operations,

▶ facilitates communication and understanding of business goals and strategies at all levels of an organization, and

▶ fosters strategic feedback and learning.[24]

The balanced scorecard model is consistent with one of the themes of our book: No one perspective or emphasis is adequate for creating a high-performance, quality organization. This model has the potential to serve managers well by requiring them to integrate important nonfinancial goals and measures into the planning and decision-making process.

The following Strategic Action Competency feature reports on the introduction of the balanced scorecard for ground crews at Southwest Airlines, which is headquartered in Dallas, Texas.[25]

Snapshot

"We had an overemphasis on financial indicators, and we were struggling to report quality and cost-effectiveness data to the board of directors. So we adopted a scorecard approach at the highest level of the organization to balance the financial indicators with quality measures and other indicators. We then drove it down to the department level, to the point where the scorecards become very targeted.
George G. Pepetti III, Executive Vice President and COO, Silver Cross Hospital, Joliet, Illinois

Strategic Action Competency

Southwest Airlines' Balanced Scorecard

Southwest Airlines employs a number of scorecards, one of which relates ground-crew performance to company profitability. It arranges the four quadrants of the balanced scorecard in this way: financial, customer, internal, and learning/growth. The scorecard suggests that the goals and measures in each perspective need to relate to one another.

A financial measure, such as "lower costs," is related to an operations measure, such as "fast ground turnaround." This is a relatively new idea according to Mike Van de Ven, vice president of financial planning and analysis. He states: "Historically, the budget system was the primary system to monitor costs. If you were an accountant, you got it. But if you were an operations person, you weren't used to cost centers, general ledgers and budget-to-actual variances. They didn't make any sense to you."

The operations people had hundreds of measures dealing with things such as on-time performance or baggage delivery, but they weren't linked directly to the financial measures or the budget system. Van de Ven comments: "So what we have been doing over the past several years is putting these things together, and that neatly rolls into this balanced scorecard concept." Another advantage of the balanced scorecard approach is that it retains the hundreds of detailed measures for front-line supervisors but gives top management a "dashboard" displaying a few key measures. Van de Ven remarks: "We are trying to get more focused on key measurements that we want to stay on top of."

Sample goals and measures used in the Southwest Airlines balanced scorecard, primarily as it relates to ground crews, are as follows:

▶ *Financial perspective.* General goals: profitability, increased revenue, lower costs; measures: market value with operational goal of 30 percent compound annual growth rate; seat revenue with operational goal of 20 percent compound annual growth rate; plane lease cost with operational goal of 5 percent compound annual growth rate.

▶ *Customer perspective.* General goals: on-time flights and lowest prices; measures: Federal Aviation Authority on-time arrival rating with the operational goal of being ranked number one; customer ranking based on market surveys with the operational goal of being ranked number one.

▶ *Internal perspective.* General goal: fast ground turnaround; measures: time on

ground with the operational goal of 30 minutes; on-time departure with the operational goal of 90 percent on-time departures.

▶ *Learning and growth perspective.* General goal: ground-crew alignment with company goals; measures: percent ground crew who own Southwest Airlines shares with the operational goals of 70 percent in year 1, 90 percent in year 3, and 100 percent in year 5; percent ground crew with training beyond new employee training with the operational goals of 70 percent in year 1, 90 percent in year 3, and 100 percent in year 5.

To date, Southwest Airlines has found the balanced scorecard approach to be effective in linking the four perspectives and related goals/measures to maintain and increase quality and profitability over the long run.

To learn more about this organization, visit *www.southwest.com.*

There are concerns with the balanced scorecard model. We note several of them here:

▶ The learning/growth perspective is internal, so why does it warrant a box separate from the internal process perspective?

▶ Why aren't other stakeholders represented? Aren't financial measures also relevant to customers? In which case, why is finance on its own? Every organization has many internal processes. Which ones should be chosen for this perspective?

▶ Goals must be set for each of the four perspectives, but managers are not provided with any specific methodology or rationale on how to do that. They are left to their own devices.[26]

These concerns, in our judgment, are useful in recognizing that the balanced scorecard model has limitations. Of course, this is the case with all of the planning and decision-making aids. As with all aids, the balanced scorecard can become a measurement "straightjacket" if used mechanistically.

2.

Describe the features and uses of the Delphi method, simulation, and scenario forecasting aids.

Using Forecasting Aids

Forecasting *involves projecting or estimating future events or conditions in an organization's environment.* Forecasting is concerned primarily with external events or conditions beyond the organization's control that are important to its survival and growth. A team of experts at Battelle, a renowned technology organization based in Columbus, Ohio, has developed a list of the 10 most strategic technological trends that will shape business and the world by the year 2020. A presentation of these 10 strategic technologies is available at *www.battelle.org/forecasts.* As an overview to identifying these strategic technologies, Stephen Millett, manager of Battelle's technology forecasts, remarks:

The 20th century was the time of big technologies, mass production, mass wars, and mass politics. But in the years ahead, new technologies will become much more personalized, and they will closely affect almost every aspect of our lives. We see advances in information and biological technologies bringing us into a more intimate relationship with nature and with each other. From cloned human organs, to personalized public transportation, to computers and sensors embedded in our bodies, we will become intertwined with technology.[27]

Most forecasting is based on some form of extrapolation, which is certainly an important factor in Battelle's forecasts of strategic technologies by the year 2020. Extrapolation *is the projection of some trend or tendency from the past or present into the future.* The simplest, and at times most misleading, form of extrapolation is a linear, or straight-line, projection of a past trend into the future.[28] For years, experts had forecasted the failure of the levees in New Orleans in the face of a major hurricane, yet the extrapolation was that the next hurricane season would be like those in the past. That extrapolation was proven wrong in 2005.

Cheryl Russell, a well-respected demographer and forecaster, warns of four forecasting pitfalls:

▶ *Listening to the media.* Tracking trends through headlines is asking for trouble. The media often distort trends, blow fads up into trends, or completely miss trends.

▶ *Assuming that things are going to return to the way they used to be.* The belief that trends are like a swinging pendulum—going one way, then the other—is a nice concept, but things really don't work that way.

▶ *Hearsay.* The neighbors are doing it, or everyone says that they know someone doing it, so therefore a trend must exist.

▶ *Tunnel vision.* The business media provide only a narrow view of what's going on in the world. Reading or obtaining material in other ways about other aspects of life provides an expanded view of the world.[29]

Even though forecasting is risky, it's still necessary. Managers and teams at all levels have to use whatever is available to them when trying to anticipate future events and conditions. Numerous forecasting aids are available.[30] We will discuss three forecasting aids—the Delphi method, simulation, and scenarios—that are often used in planning and decision making. Because all of them focus on understanding possible futures, they aren't mutually exclusive and may well be used with one another.

Delphi Method

The Delphi method *is a forecasting and decision-making aid for seeking consensus by a panel of experts.* The experts refine their judgments phase by phase, until they reach a consensus or near consensus. Because the method relies on judgments, it obviously isn't foolproof. The consensus arrived at tends to be more accurate than a single expert's opinion. The Delphi process replaces face-to-face communication and debate with a carefully planned, orderly program of sequential impersonal exchanges.

An early decision that has to be made involves the selection of a group of experts.[31] The number of participating experts may range from only a few to more than 100, depending on the scope of the issue. A range of 15 to 30 is recommended per issue. As the sample size (number of experts) increases, the amount of coordination required also increases, as do costs.

Delphi Questionnaires. The heart of the Delphi technique is a series of questionnaires. The first questionnaire may include generally worded questions. In each later

Snapshot

"We separate financial forecasting from target setting and performance management. You never will get accurate and honest forecasts if bonuses and performance appraisal of people are linked in some way with these forecasts. So we introduced rolling financial forecasting that looked beyond the fiscal year. We implemented it as an independent tool and process, independent from target setting and performance management."

Rainer Gunz, Head, Controlling and Cost Accounting, Borealis GmbH

phase, the questions become more specific because they are built on responses to the previous questionnaire.

Phases. The Delphi method typically involves at least three phases:

1. *A questionnaire is sent to a group of experts.* This used to be sent through the mail, but now often involves responses through the use of a Web site. Experts remain unknown to one another. The questionnaire requests numerical estimates of specific technological or market possibilities. It asks for expected dates (years) and an assignment of probabilities to each of these possibilities. Respondents are asked to provide reasons for their judgments.

2. *A summary of the first phase is prepared.* This report may show the median and ranges of the responses. The report, along with a revised questionnaire, is sent to those who completed the first questionnaire. They are asked to revise their earlier estimates, if appropriate, or to justify their original judgments. The reasons for the possibilities presented in the first phase by the experts are critiqued by fellow respondents in writing. The technique emphasizes informed judgment. It attempts to improve on the panel or committee approach by subjecting the views of individual experts to others' reactions in ways that avoid face-to-face confrontation and provide anonymity of judgments and of perspectives advanced in defense of them.

3. *A summary of the second phase is prepared.* This report often shows that some consensus is developing. The experts are then asked in a third questionnaire to indicate whether they support this emerging consensus and the explanations that accompany it. At this phase, the participants are encouraged to find reasons for *not* joining the consensus.

Three phases generally are recommended. The participants often begin dropping out after the third phase because of other time commitments. The following Planning and Administration Competency feature reports on the use of the Delphi method to forecast trends in globalization.[32] A brief sampling of the findings are included.

Planning and Administration Competency

Forecast of Globalization: A Delphi Study

The selection criteria for participation as an expert were (1) active career in international business for at least 10 years, (2) a leadership role within the participant's organization, (3) a global vision beyond local and temporary concerns, and (4) accessibility and willingness to engage in intellectual dialogue.

A list of 45 global experts with 15 each in the policy, business, and research fields was developed. Of these, 33 were contacted to ensure that there were 11 representatives each from the three geographic areas chosen. At the policy level, the representatives were current or former members of the legislative and executive branches of government. The business leaders approached were typically either corporate presidents or vice presidents for international operations. The academic participants were professors and program directors specializing in international business. Although most of the experts invited to join the panel participated in the first round, duties, travel, illness, and time constraints eliminated some of them in the second and third rounds. Twenty-five experts participated in all rounds of the study.

The Delphi study started out with an open-ended questionnaire asking for "the identification of international business dimensions subject to change in the next 10 years." In addition, respondents were requested to "highlight the corporate and policy responses to these changes." Issues and responses were to be rated for their impact on a 10-point scale, ranging from very low to very high. This first round resulted in 36 pages of issues and trends. In most instances, respondents provided ratings for an issue or trend heading, and then added substantial comments that elaborated on that dimension. The various comments were grouped into categories. In addition, predicted changes were linked with specific corporate responses.

In the second round of the Delphi, the panelists were presented with these categories and comments and were asked to elaborate on the statements, and to indicate the level of their agreement or disagreement. In addition, the respondents were requested to rate the impact such a change would have on corporations and policy makers. The third, and final round, focused on those statements for which there continued to be disagreement between the panelists.

There were numerous results. We are only able to share several highlights from this Delphi study here:

▶ Globalization issues will increasingly be understood to go far beyond the economic dimension and be much broader than "Americanization."
▶ There is likely to be a swinging back of the pendulum from a global strategy with the development of a major regional or even local focus in firm strategy. Global expertise and best practices can still be leveraged; however, a main emphasis on local adaptation and implementation is likely to be a key to success.
▶ A worldwide push for more corporate transparency and accountability is emerging. Quick, ongoing, and public action against unethical business practices by the industrialized nations is essential for world acceptance of globalization and market forces.

Simulation

A simulation *is a representation of how a real system performs.* A simulation

1. imitates something real,

2. is not real itself, and

3. can be altered by its users.[33]

A simulation model usually describes the behavior of the real system (or some aspect of it) in quantitative and/or qualitative terms. Simulation often is used to forecast the effects of environmental changes and internal management decisions on an organization, department, or strategic business unit. The goal of simulation is to reproduce or test reality without actually experiencing it. Most simulations are intended to let management ask numerous "what if" questions. For example, *What* profits can we anticipate next year *if* inflation is 8 percent and we continue current pricing policies? Or *What* profits can we expect next year *if* inflation is 2 percent and we open two new plants? To answer such questions, analysts often develop complex equations and use computers to perform many of the step-by-step computations required. Such models can be used to simulate virtually any issue of interest (e.g., profits, sales, and earnings per share) for which a forecast is needed. Table 9.1 lists the common types of business simulation models.

Spreadsheet Simulations. Spreadsheets are often used to create hypothetical financial reports so that planners can experiment with how the future might look based on different sets of financial assumptions. They are simulations when used to create *pro forma* income statements and balance sheets, instead of real income statements and balance sheets.

Table 9.1   Examples of Business Simulation

BUDGET MODELS
- All levels of organization

OPERATIONS MODELS
- Inventory costs
- Materials costs
- Production costs

TREASURY AND FINANCIAL MODELS
- Cash management
- Income statements
- Cash flow projections
- Stock and commodity prices

HUMAN RESOURCES MODELS
- Compensation
- Optimum staffing levels
- Measurements of productivity

MARKETING MODELS
- Sales budgets
- Pricing
- Market share projections
- Advertising and marketing plans

STRATEGIC PLANNING MODELS
- Scenario planning
- Political/economic forecasts
- Business war-gaming

ExperCorp is a business-planning consulting firm located in Naperville, Illinois. The company specializes in new venture strategy and marketing research for entrepreneurs entering the recreation and sporting goods markets. A key to small business planning is the development of good risk and reward estimates.[34]

First, the consultants estimate the size of the available target market. Then, they develop realistic assumptions for sales, selling price, production costs, and operating expenses in the first year of operation. An income statement spreadsheet is developed to create appropriate estimations for sales, production costs, operating expenses, and profit/losses.

The most critical and difficult aspect of venture planning is developing estimates of cash flow. Developing realistic statements for the first and subsequent years of operation along with determination of cash reserves is a task that all planners must face. This task is simplified with cash flow templates that plug into spreadsheets. The intent is to increase the precision of cash flow forecasts through these spreadsheet simulations.

Scenarios

Scenarios *are descriptive narratives that help people recognize and adapt to plausible changing and uncertain alternative futures.* Scenarios provide a way to identify alternative paths that may exist for an organization in the future and the actions that are likely to be involved in going down each path.[35] They are intended to be provocative and helpful in strategic planning and decision making.

"What If" Questions. Scenarios often involve considering multiple "what if" questions. For example, "Considering the most pressing competitive and political forces our organization is likely to face, how can we weave in the risks and uncertainties of a future world to create new perspectives?" Scenario planning differs in several ways from contingency planning in that the latter normally takes into account one specific source of uncertainty. Scenario planning considers combinations of uncertainties and questions in each scenario. Also, there is an attempt to develop plausible combinations of economic, technological, political, and cultural developments.[36]

A competitor scenario *presents a discussion that considers what a competitor (or set of competitors) might do over some specified time period, how the competitors would do it, and why they would choose to do so.* As with all scenarios, a competitor scenario presents a possible future. It is not a prediction of what the competitor or set of competitors will do.[37] Table 9.2 presents the cluster of questions that might be used in developing a "what if" competitor scenario.

Table 9.2	Typical Questions in a "What-If" Competitor Scenario

- What if the competitor (or set of competitors) commits to a diversification of its product line (new products for existing and new customers) through a combination of current and new technologies?
- What if the competitor launches a series of new products?
- What if the competitor launches a sequence of extensions to its current product lines (with the specific aim of attracting new customers to the market)?
- What if the competitor suddenly divests a number of its product lines and/or pulls out of a number of geographic regions?
- What if the competitor fundamentally changes how it competes to win customers in the marketplace, such as moving from a differentiation strategy to a cost leadership strategy (see Chapter 7)?
- What if the competitor commits to gaining significant market share (and to do so as quickly as possible) without apparent regard to its long-term consequences (either for the firm itself or for the marketplace), such as through aggressive price cutting?

Source: Adapted from L. Fahey. Competitor scenarios. *Strategy & Leadership,* 31(1), 2003, 32–44.

Some of the most creative, convention-breaking thinking occurs during the mapping of extreme scenarios—for instance, a fundamentally different but better world. However, the number of scenarios under consideration should be limited to prevent decision making from becoming unwieldy. The three most common categories of scenarios used in organizational planning are (1) the company's worst nightmare, (2) a fundamentally different but better world, and (3) more of the same (equivalent to the status quo) but better. Scenarios are quite useful in forcing managers to evaluate preliminary plans against future possibilities.

Scenario Planning Process. A few of the guidelines for undertaking scenario planning in a single business firm are as follows[38]:

▶ *Establish a core planning team.* Developing scenarios and analyzing their strategic implications is best done in teams. The creative dynamics of an effective team are likely to provide the type of breakthroughs that will make the scenario process worthwhile. What seems obvious to one person will be surprising to another. A good rule of thumb is to have 7 to 12 (at most) people in the core planning team.

▶ *Get a cross section of professionals.* Include the heads of major functional areas—marketing, operations, purchasing, information technology, personnel, etc. Include individuals beyond the top executives. This injects new perspectives.

▶ *Include outside information and outside people.* Focus on injecting interesting and challenging perspectives into the discussion. In a team composed solely of insiders, it will be hard to achieve breakthrough insights. Outsiders may be customers, suppliers, or consultants. If possible, there might even be an executive from another line of business.

Shell International, the multinational energy firm, has been a leader for more than 30 years in developing global scenarios for use in its strategic planning process.[39] Shell recently published a book entitled *Shell Global Scenarios to 2025*. A 45-page document that presents the executive summary and excerpts from this book is available on the firm's Web site.[40] We present a brief glimpse into Shell's three scenarios and the rationale for them.

According to Shell, the terrorist events of September 11, 2001, and the crisis of trust in the market arising from corporate scandals have brought profound changes in the business environment, which the *Shell Global Scenarios to 2025* book explores. The feelings of insecurity and mistrust that have arisen in the light of these events have led to new barriers to the free movement of people, goods, and capital. Also, there is a stronger role for the state in protecting national security and restoring trust in the market.

These changes make the interactions between business firms, governments, and society more complex. The Shell scenarios provide a way of navigating through that complexity by outlining three sets of forces—market incentives, the force of community, and coercion and regulation—and discussing how these drive companies toward three different goals: efficiency, social cohesion, and security. These goals are, at times, incompatible and the scenarios explore the resulting trade-offs that are needed to reconcile them, setting out what is called a *Trilemma Triangle*. The scenarios that the Shell team developed provide insights on the kinds of strategy different groups may adopt in different environments.

A thumbnail sketch of the three possible futures represented by Shell is as follows:

▸ *Low trust globalization*. This is a legalistic world in which the emphasis is on security and efficiency, even at the expense of cultural unity and cohesion.

▸ *Open doors*. This is a pragmatic world that emphasizes cultural unity and cohesion and efficiency. The marketplace provides "built-in" solutions to the crises of security and trust.

▸ *Flags*. This is a dogmatic world where security and community values are emphasized at the expense of efficiency. Trust is fragmented with an emphasis on nationalism and conflicting causes by special interest groups.

Jeron Van Der, the chief executive of the Shell Group, provides insight into the role of scenario planning in general. He comments: "Scenarios are different from forecasts in that they provide a tool that helps us to explore the many complex business environments in which we work, the factors that drive changes, and developments in those environments."

3.

Discuss the creative process and how to use Osborn's creativity model.

Using Creativity Aids

All planning and decision making needs to be supported by creativity. Creativity *is the ability to visualize, generate, and implement new ideas or concepts or new associations between existing ideas or concepts that are novel and useful.*[41] Creative thinking increases the quality of solutions to many types of problems, helps stimulate innovation, revitalizes motivation and commitment by challenging individuals, and serves as a catalyst for effective team performance. For organizations, creativity is no longer optional—it is imperative. In particular, for innovative initiatives to succeed, managers and employees alike need creative thinking skills.

The creative process, as suggested in Figure 9.2, usually involves five interconnected stages: preparation, concentration, incubation, illumination, and verification.[42]

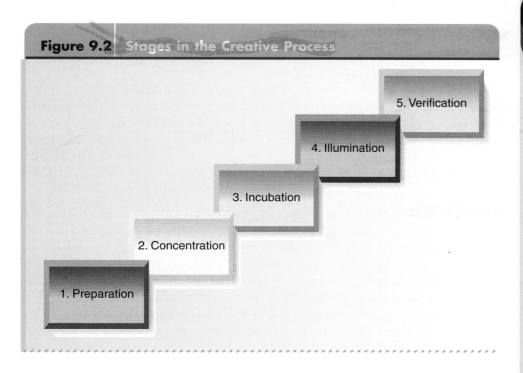

Figure 9.2 Stages in the Creative Process

5. Verification

4. Illumination

3. Incubation

2. Concentration

1. Preparation

Snapshot

"SAS has developed a unique framework for managing creativity, one that rests on three guiding principles: Help employees to do their best work by keeping them intellectually engaged and by removing distractions. Make managers responsible for sparking creativity and eliminate arbitrary distinctions between 'suits' and 'creatives.' And engage customers as creative partners so you can deliver superior products."
Jim Goodnight, Chief Executive Officer, SAS Institute

The *preparation stage* involves thoroughly investigating an issue or problem to ensure that all of its aspects have been identified and understood. This stage involves searching for and collecting facts and ideas. Extensive formal education or many years of relevant experience are needed to develop the expertise required to identify substantive issues and problems. The preparation and concentration stages are consistent with Thomas Edison's statement that "Creativity is 90 percent perspiration and 10 percent inspiration." Edison was responsible for more than a thousand patents, the most famous of which is the electric light bulb in 1879.[43]

The *concentration stage* involves focusing energies and resources on identifying and solving an issue or problem. A commitment must be made at this stage to implement a solution.

The *incubation stage* is an internal and unconscious ordering of information. This stage may involve an unconscious personal or team conflict between what is currently accepted as reality and what may be possible. Relaxing, sometimes distancing oneself or the team from the issue, and allowing the mind to search for possible issues or problems and solutions is important. A successful incubation stage yields fresh ideas and new ways of thinking about the nature of an issue or a problem and alternative solutions.

The *illumination stage* is the moment of discovery, the instant of recognition, as when a light bulb seems to be turned on mentally. The mind instantly connects an issue or a problem to a solution through a remembered observation or occurrence.

The *verification stage* is the testing of the created solution or idea. At this stage, confirmation and acceptance of the new approach is sought. The knowledge and insights obtained from each stage of the creative process are often useful in addressing new issues and problems at the next *preparation stage*.

The Personal Creativity Inventory at the end of this chapter is a way for you to assess barriers to your own creative thought and innovative action. For now, we present

A. F. Osborn's creativity model as an aid to teams for fostering creative planning and decision making in organizations.

Osborn's Creativity Model

Osborn's creativity model *is a three-phase decision-making process that involves fact finding, idea finding, and solution finding.* It is designed to help overcome blocks to creativity and innovation, which may occur for a variety of reasons. It is intended to stimulate free-wheeling thinking, novel ideas, curiosity, and cooperation that in turn lead to innovative decisions.[44] It can be used with all types of groups and teams. Sufficient time and freedom must be allowed for the model to work well, and some degree of external pressure and self-generated tension are helpful. However, too much pressure or threats from the wrong sources (e.g., an order from top management for the team to determine within 10 days why quality has deteriorated) can easily undermine the process.

Fact-Finding Phase. Fact finding involves defining the issue or problem and gathering and analyzing relevant data. Although the Osborn creativity model provides some fact-finding procedures, they aren't nearly as well developed as the idea-finding procedures.[45] One way to improve fact finding is to begin with a broad view of the issue or problem and then proceed to define subissues or subproblems. This phase requires making a distinction between a symptom of an issue or a problem and an actual issue or problem. For example, a manager might claim that low morale is a problem. A deeper investigation might reveal that low morale is only a symptom of a festering issue. The issue may be a lack of any positive feedback to employees when they are performing well.

Idea-Finding Phase. Idea finding starts by generating tentative ideas and possible leads. Then the most likely of these ideas are modified, combined, and added to, if necessary. Osborn maintained that individuals can generate more good ideas by following two principles. First, defer judgment. Individuals can think up almost twice as many good ideas in the same length of time if they defer judgment on any idea until after they create a list of possible leads to a solution. Second, quantity breeds quality: The more ideas that individuals think up, the more likely they are to arrive at the potentially best leads to a solution.

To encourage uninhibited thinking and generate lots of ideas, Osborn developed 75 general questions to use when brainstorming a problem. Brainstorming *is an unrestrained flow of ideas in a group or team with all critical judgments suspended.* The group or team leader must decide which of the 75 questions are most appropriate to the issue or problem being addressed. Moreover, the leader isn't expected to use all of the questions in a single session. The following are examples of questions that could be used in a brainstorming session:

▶ How can this issue, idea, or thing be put to other uses?

▶ How can it be modified?

▶ How can it be substituted for something else, or can something else be substituted for part of it?

▶ How could it be reversed?

▶ How could it be combined with other things?[46]

A brainstorming session should follow four basic rules:

1. *Criticism is ruled out.* Participants must withhold critical judgment of ideas until later.

2. *Freewheeling is welcomed.* The wilder the idea, the better; taming down an idea is easier than thinking up new ones.

3. *Quantity is wanted.* The greater the number of ideas, the greater the likelihood that some will be useful.

4. *Combination and improvement are sought.* In addition to contributing ideas of their own, participants should suggest how ideas of others can be turned into better ideas or how two or more ideas can be merged into still another idea.[47]

These rules are intended to separate creative imagination from judgment. The two are incompatible and relate to different aspects of the decision-making process. The leader of one brainstorming group put it this way: "If you try to get hot and cold water out of the same faucet at the same time, you will get only lukewarm water. And if you try to criticize and create at the same time, you will not do either very well. So let us stick solely to *ideas*—let us cut out *all* criticism during this session."[48]

A brainstorming session should have from 5 to 12 or so participants in order to generate diverse ideas. This size range permits each member to maintain a sense of identification and involvement with the group or team. A session should normally run not less than 20 minutes or more than an hour. However, brainstorming could consist of several idea-generating sessions. For example, follow-up sessions could address individually each of the ideas previously generated. Table 9.3 presents the guidelines for leading a brainstorming session.[49]

Table 9.3	**Guidelines for Leading a Brainstorming Session**
BASIC LEADERSHIP ROLE	■ Make a brief statement of the four basic rules.
	■ State the time limit for the session.
	■ Read the problem and/or related question to be discussed and ask, "What are your ideas?"
	■ When an idea is given, summarize it by using the speaker's words insofar as possible. Have the idea recorded by a participant or on an audiotape machine. Follow your summary with the single word "Next."
	■ Say little else. Whenever the leader participates as a brainstormer, group productivity usually falls.
HANDLING PROBLEMS	■ When someone talks too long, wait until he or she takes a breath (everyone must stop to inhale sometime), break into the monologue, summarize what was said for the recorder, point to another participant, and say "Next."
	■ When someone becomes judgmental or starts to argue, stop him or her. Say, for example, "That will cost you one coffee or soda for each member of the group."
	■ When the discussion stops, relax and let the silence continue. Say nothing. The pause should be broken by the group and not the leader. This period of silence is called the *mental pause* because it is a change in thinking. All the obvious ideas are exhausted; the participants are now forced to rely on their creativity to produce new ideas.
	■ When someone states a problem rather than idea, repeat the problem, raise your hand with five fingers extended, and say, "Let's have five ideas on this problem." You may get only 1 or you may get 10, but you're back in the business of creative thinking.

Brainstorming sessions are often engaging, stimulating, and fun.

© Image Source/Jupiter Images

Solution-Finding Phase. Solution finding involves generating and evaluating possible courses of action and deciding how to implement the chosen course of action. This phase relies on judgment, analysis, and criticism. A variety of planning and decision aids—such as those presented in this chapter and elsewhere in the book—can be used. To initiate the solution-finding phase, the leader could ask the team to identify from one to five of the most important ideas generated. The participants might be asked to jot down these ideas individually on a piece of paper and evaluate them. A very important idea might get five points, a moderately important idea could get three points, and an unimportant idea could be assigned one point. The highest combined scores may indicate the actions or ideas to be investigated further.

Osborn's creativity model has been modified often and applied in a variety of ways. The following Teamwork Competency feature highlights how IDEO Product Development, headquartered in Palo Alto, California, uses brainstorming.[50] The company is a renowned professional services firm that helps clients design and develop new products and, in the process, become more innovative. The creative process at IDEO is fostered through the extensive use of empowered design teams. These teams are staffed to take advantage of diverse perspectives, technical and creative skills, and ability to achieve goals jointly. Diverse views are encouraged and used to enhance the quality and creativity of decisions. At the same time, cooperation is fostered, and the teams are kept moving toward their goals.

Teamwork Competency

IDEO Brainstorms

IDEO projects last from a few weeks to several years, with the average being 10 to 12 months. Depending on the client's needs, results can range from sketches of products to crude working models to complete new products. Clients vary from venture-funded start-ups to multinational corporations in North America, Europe, and Japan. IDEO has developed part or all of more than 3,000 products in dozens of industries, including Apple's first computer mouse, the Palm V, Polaroid's I-Zone pocket camera, and Oral B's "Squish Grip" toothbrushes for children.

IDEO is unique in that it encourages clients to participate in brainstorming sessions conducted by its design teams. By going to a "brainstormer," clients gain insight and learn because they join IDEO designers in the creative process. Brainstorming sessions usually are initiated by a design team. The team members then invite other IDEO designers to help generate ideas for the project. These sessions are held in rooms with five brainstorming rules written on the walls: (1) Defer judgment, (2) build on the ideas of others, (3) one conversation at a time, (4) stay focused on the topic, and (5) encourage wild ideas.

Designers who are also skilled facilitators lead the brainstorming sessions, enforce rules, write suggestions on the board, and encourage creativity and fun. Nearly all of the designers are experienced at brainstorming. Typically, project members (or clients) introduce the project and describe the design issue or problem they face (e.g., How do you make fishing more fun and easier for neophytes?). Participants then generate ideas (e.g., use the "slingshot" method to launch lures), often sketching them on paper or whiteboards. Many new projects start with a flurry of brainstorming sessions. Clients often attend them to describe their existing products and the new products that they want designed. Clients may also give detailed demonstrations before a brainstormer to explain the product or service, such as when clients from a chain of hair salons did haircuts at the Palo Alto office to demonstrate their work process. Twenty or so IDEO employees may be invited to brainstorming sessions in the early weeks of a project.

Effectiveness. The Osborn creativity model is based on the assumption that most people have the potential for greater creativity and innovation in decision making than they use. Some research suggests that the same number of individuals working alone may generate more ideas and more creative ideas than do groups.[51] Whether group brainstorming in a work setting is more or less effective than individuals working alone to generate ideas remains an open question.

Some evidence suggests that, under certain conditions, electronic brainstorming may be a better way to generate ideas than face-to-face brainstorming.[52] One condition is when individuals from different organizational levels are in the same brainstorming group. For example, lower level employees may be reluctant to spontaneously express novel ideas if they think their superiors in the group might view those ideas as dumb or might not support them, especially if the ideas could be seen as indirect criticisms of their superiors. Electronic brainstorming *makes use of personal computers that are networked to input and automatically disseminate ideas in real time to all team members, each of whom may be stimulated to generate additional ideas.* For example, individuals may input ideas via the keyboard as they think of them. Every time an idea is entered, the team's ideas appear in random order on each person's screen. An individual can continue to see new sets of ideas in random order by pressing the appropriate key.[53] The random order format of the system prevents identifying who generates each idea.

Using Quality Improvement Aids

4.
Explain and apply three quality improvement aids: benchmarking, the Deming cycle, and the Baldrige quality program.

In Chapter 2, we defined *quality* as how well a product or service does what it is supposed to do—how closely and reliably it satisfies the specifications to which it is built or provided. The most common meaning of *quality* is the extent to which a good or service meets and/or exceeds customers' expectations.[54] Consumers often apply the value dimension of quality when making purchasing decisions. *Consumer Reports* ranks goods and services on both quality and price to arrive at recommendations of "best buys." The various perspectives of quality are, of course, appropriate in different circumstances. We review three planning and decision aids that focus on improving quality: benchmarking, the Deming cycle, and the Baldrige quality program.

Benchmarking

Benchmarking *is a systematic and continuous process of measuring and comparing an organization's goods, services, and practices against industry leaders anywhere in the world to gain information that will help the organization improve performance.*[55] By identifying how leading organizations achieved excellence in particular areas or processes, other organizations can determine how to develop their own strategic or tactical plans and processes to reach or exceed those levels. At the most fundamental level, benchmarking helps managers and employees learn from others.

Stages. As noted in Figure 9.3 on the following page, benchmarking includes seven stages.[56] Stage 1 focuses on *defining the domain* to be benchmarked. This stage includes a careful assessment of the organization's own products and processes that are to be compared to benchmark products and processes. For example, common benchmarks used by airlines and rating services are percentages of on-time arrivals and amount of lost or misrouted baggage.

Manufacturing, finance, marketing, inventory management, transportation, accounting, legal services, human resources, and marketing processes may be benchmarked. Each function may be broken into more specific categories of processes for that purpose. For example, benchmarking in human resources may include the processes of recruiting, diversity enhancement, training, compensation, performance appraisal, recognition programs, and job design.

Figure 9.3   **The Benchmarking Process**

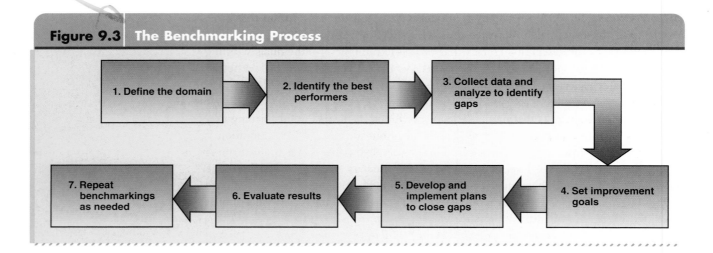

Benchmarking can be expensive and time consuming. Some experts recommend that benchmarking be directed at the specific issues and processes that are likely to yield the greatest competitive advantage for the organization. At Southwest Airlines, the ability to turn around a plane quickly and safely was one area of competitive advantage. Others, such as the American Society for Quality, suggest that benchmarking or related quality processes be applied to all functions and processes to instill total quality throughout the organization.[57]

Stage 2 focuses on *identifying the best performers*, or best-in-class, for each function, process, and product to be benchmarked. They may include organizations in the firm's own industry or in other industries. For example, Xerox compared its warehousing and distribution process to that of L. L. Bean, the catalog and online sales company, because of Bean's excellent reputation in this area. Southwest Airlines benchmarked successful NASCAR pit crews because the amount of time spent in the pits is one key indicator of effective competition in a race.

Stage 3 focuses on *collecting and analyzing data to identify gaps*, if any, between the function, product, or process being evaluated and that of the best-in-class organizations. The data collected need to focus on specific methods utilized, not simply on the results obtained. It is one thing to know that Wal-Mart has a superb warehouse distribution system, yet it is another thing to learn how Wal-Mart has achieved this level of excellence. Many sources of information are available for learning about best-in-class organizations. They include customers, suppliers, distributors, trade journals, company publications, newspapers, books on quality, consultants, presentations at professional meetings, and even on-site interviews with people at the best-in-class organizations. This last source usually is easier to tap if the organizations aren't direct competitors.

The remaining steps are consistent with the typical planning phases: Stage 4 focuses on *setting improvement goals*; stage 5, *developing and implementing plans to close gaps*; stage 6, *evaluating results*; and stage 7, *repeating benchmarking* as necessary. Stage 7 suggests that benchmarking needs to be an ongoing process. Over time, the things benchmarked may remain the same or need to be revised. Revisions may include dropping and/or adding functions, products, or processes as issues, conditions, technology, and markets change.

Effectiveness. Benchmarking always looks at the present in terms of how some process or quality dimension is being achieved by others. However, this approach may not be adequate for determining what should be done in the future or whether an organization should retain a function or process or contract it out. For example, an organization could contract out its computer operations to IBM or some other firm. When used simply to copy the best-in-class competitors, benchmarking may only lead to short-term competitive advantage. Finally, benchmarking needs to be used to complement and aid, not to substitute for, the creative and innovative efforts of the organization's own employees.[58] Benchmarking is often used to help an organization adapt, but less commonly to innovate.

The Deming Cycle

We provided some information on W. Edwards Deming, considered by some to be the "godfather" of the quality movement, in Chapter 2 (in the Quality Viewpoint section). One of the aids he advocated for improving quality is commonly known as the *Deming cycle*. Others refer to it as the *PDSA cycle* because it involves the four stages of plan (P), do (D), study (S), and act (A). As Figure 9.4 suggests, these stages unfold in sequence and continuously. Thus the Deming cycle *comprises four stages—plan, do, study, and act—that should be repeated over time to ensure continuous learning and improvements in a function, product, or process.*[59]

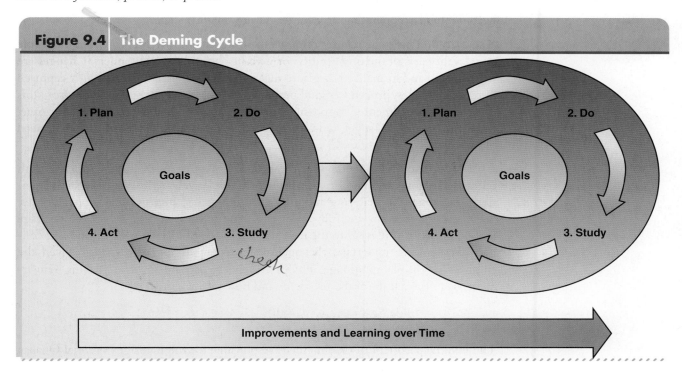

Figure 9.4 | The Deming Cycle

Plan Stage. In the Deming cycle, planning is the foundation for the successful implementation of projects.[60] It is imperative to analyze the current situation and potential impacts of any desired changes before doing anything. Think ahead about what to measure. Plan to include measurements as part of the execution. Do not leave thinking about what to measure until a later stage. Develop an implementation plan, and staff it fully with all process owners. Ask the following questions:

1. Who does this plan impact (specifically, with what characteristics or qualifications)?

2. What is the purpose of the relationship? What are we trying to accomplish (goals)? What changes can we make that will result in improvement?

3. Why does this support the end purpose of the system (i.e., the "vision")?

4. Where will this take place (addressing all characteristics of the intended location)?

5. When is it to occur (i.e., earliest start/end, latest start/end, sequence/timing of steps/subprocesses)?
6. How—a step-by-step procedure to convert any and all system/process inputs to all system outputs. How will we know that the change is an improvement?

Do Stage. This stage involves testing alternatives experimentally in a laboratory, establishing a pilot production process, or trying it out with a small number of customers or suppliers. During this stage, it is necessary to (1) follow the plan, (2) document any changes to the plan along with the rationale for the change, (3) measure progress relative to goals from both the client's and the firm's perspectives, and (4) document results. These steps maximize the learning from the implementation experience.

Study Stage. This stage requires determining whether the trial or process is working as intended, whether any revisions are needed, or whether it should be scrapped. There is an effort to determine (1) what was learned, (2) what can be generalized for use in future improvement activities, and (3) what, if anything, remains ineffective. Even successfully implemented plans may still require some fine-tuning before they become standard operating procedures during the next stage.

Act Stage. This stage focuses on implementing the improvements within the whole or relevant parts of the organization or with its customers and suppliers. Changes are documented and formalized to ensure that the progress made is permanently captured in revised policies, procedures, and processes. The experiences and learning from this cycle are also documented for possible use in future improvement projects. Over time, the Deming cycle, as suggested in Figure 9.4, is repeated when another area in need of improvement is identified.

Effectiveness. The Deming cycle can be an effective aid.[61] First, consistent with rational decision-making processes, it provides a relatively logical set of recommendations/guidelines for analyzing and implementing quality improvement opportunities. Second, by proceeding logically from one stage to the next, the *output* of one stage flows naturally as the *input* to the next stage. This helps to reduce confusion and conflict over how to undertake the quality improvement initiative. Third, given the emphasis on the planning stage, it helps prevent the participants from rushing to judgments as to the nature of the problems and how to solve them.

Baldrige Quality Program

The U.S. Department of Commerce is responsible for the Baldrige National Quality Program and the Baldrige award. The National Institute of Standards and Technology (NIST), an agency of the Department of Commerce's Technology Administration, manages the program. NIST promotes U.S. economic growth by working with industry to develop and deliver the high-quality measurement tools, data, and services necessary for the nation's technology infrastructure. The Baldrige quality program *provides a systems perspective for managing an organization and its key processes to achieve the result of performance excellence.*[62]

Quality Award. One component of this program is *Malcolm Baldrige National Quality Award*, named after the 26th Secretary of Commerce of the United States. This award, and quality program, was established by the U.S. Congress in 1987 to enhance the competitiveness and performance of U.S. businesses. The program was expanded in 1998 to include education and health-care organizations. The award promotes excellence in organizational performance, recognizes the quality and performance achievements of U.S. organizations, and publicizes successful performance strategies. In 2007, the award may be presented to six types of organizations: manufacturers, service companies, small businesses, education, health-care, and nonprofit organizations. The award is not given for specific products or services. Sixty-eight Baldrige awards have been presented to 64 organizations since 1988.

Systems Perspective. The systems perspective for the comprehensive Baldrige Quality Program for Performance Excellence is outlined in Figure 9.5. In some respects, this program reflects a number of the concepts, perspectives, and themes presented throughout this book. Thus, we only highlight several of the key features of the Baldrige Quality Program (BQP) here.

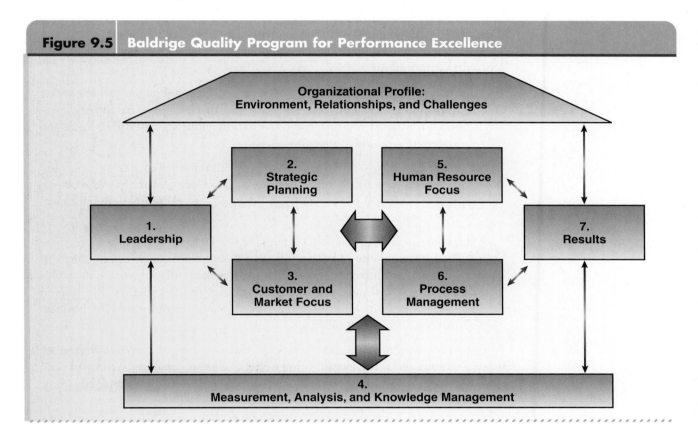

Figure 9.5 | Baldrige Quality Program for Performance Excellence

The *Organizational Profile* (top of Figure 9.5) sets the context for the way the organization operates. The environment, key working relationships, and strategic challenges serve as an overarching guide for the organizational performance management system. Applicants are expected to answer up to 31 questions, depending on their relevance, related to the organizational profile. Three of these 31 questions follow: (1) What are your stated vision, mission, and values? (2) What are your key customer and stakeholder groups and market segments? (3) What is your competitive position?

Baldrige Categories. The seven Baldrige categories listed in Figure 9.5 form the building blocks for the system. However, successful management of overall performance in this program requires organization-specific *synthesis, alignment,* and *integration. Synthesis* means looking at the organization as a whole and building on key business requirements, including the strategic goals and action plans. *Alignment* means using the key links among requirements given in the Baldrige categories to ensure consistency of plans, processes, measures, and actions. *Integration* builds on alignment, so that the individual components of the performance management system operate in a fully interconnected manner.

A systems perspective includes the senior leaders' focus on strategic directions and on customers. It means that senior leaders monitor, respond to, and manage performance based on results. A systems perspective also includes using measures, indicators, and organizational knowledge to build key strategies. It means linking these strategies with key processes and aligning resources to improve overall performance and satisfy customers and stakeholders. Thus, a systems perspective means managing the whole organization, as well as its components, to achieve success.

Applicants for the Baldrige award must follow a rigorous process for consideration as set forth in a 70-page document entitled *Baldrige National Quality Program: Criteria for Performance Excellence*. Each category, which includes multiple "items of interest" and specific questions to be answered, is given a maximum potential point value with a total maximum potential of 1,000 points for all categories combined.

The core meaning and maximum potential points for each category when judging a business firm follow:

▶ *Leadership—120 points (category 1):* Examines how the organization's senior leaders guide and sustain the organization. Also examined are the organization's governance and how the organization addresses its ethical, legal, and community responsibilities.

▶ *Strategic planning—85 points (category 2):* Examines how the organization develops strategic goals and action plans. Also examined are how the chosen strategic goals and action plans are deployed and changed if circumstances require, and how progress is measured.

▶ *Customer and market focus—85 points (category 3):* Examines how the organization determines the requirements, needs, expectations, and preferences of customers and markets. Also examined is how the organization builds relationships with customers and determines the key factors that lead to customer acquisition, satisfaction, loyalty, and retention and to business expansion and sustainability.

▶ *Measurement, analysis and knowledge management—90 points (category 4):* Examines how the organization selects, gathers, analyzes, manages, and improves its data, information, and knowledge assets. Also examined is how the organization reviews its performance.

▶ *Human resource focus—85 points (category 5):* Examines how the organization's work systems and employee learning and motivation enable all employees to develop and utilize their full potential in alignment with the organization's overall goals, strategy, and action plan. Also examined are the organization's efforts to build and maintain a work environment and employee support climate conducive to performance excellence and to personal and organizational growth.

▶ *Process management—85 points (category 6):* Examines the key aspects of the organization's process management, including key product, service, and organizational processes for creating customer and organizational value and key support processes. This category encompasses all key processes and all work units.

▶ *Results—450 points (category 7):* Examines the organization's performance and improvement in all key areas: product and service outcomes, customer satisfaction, financial and marketplace performance, human resource outcomes, operational performance, and leadership and social responsibility. Performance levels are examined relative to those of competitors and other organizations providing similar products and services.

Cooperative Process. The cooperative nature of this joint government/private-sector process is perhaps best captured by the award's Board of Examiners. In 2006, almost 550 experts from industry, educational institutions, governments at all levels, and nonprofit organizations volunteered countless hours reviewing applications for the award, conducting site visits, and providing each applicant with an extensive feedback report citing strengths and opportunities to improve.

The following Communication Competency feature reports on one recent recipient of the Malcolm Baldrige National Quality Award. This feature focuses on the quality communication process and effectiveness of Sunny Fresh Foods (SFF), Inc.[63] Sunny Fresh is headquartered in Monticello, Minnesota, with plants in Minnesota, Michigan, and Iowa. The firm is a wholly owned subsidiary of Cargill, Inc. The company provides more than 160 egg-based food products to more than 2,000 customers, including quick-service restaurants, business and institutional food services, schools, and the military. The company's 620 employees produce and package products ranging from refrigerated and frozen liquid pasteurized eggs to precooked egg entrees to scrambled egg mixes, cholesterol-free and fat-free egg products, and peeled hard-cooked eggs.[64]

© Mannie Garcia/AP Photo

Vice President Dick Cheney, left, shakes hands with Warren Staley, Chairman and CEO of Cargill, Inc., parent company of Sunny Fresh, while being honored wih a Baldridge award.

Communication Competency

Sunny Fresh Foods

Sunny Fresh Foods (SFF) ensures quality through leadership that continually focuses people and business processes on the company's core purpose ("to be the supplier of choice to our customers worldwide") and core values (customer focus, safety, quality, stakeholder focus, and ethics). These tenets guide all company activities, from customer service and stakeholder training to strategic planning and new product development. The company's leadership structure includes a Management Committee, comprising SFF's senior managers, and a Business Leadership Team that includes representatives from all functional areas of the company. The structure helps to ensure that everyone in the organization knows how to apply the company's core purpose and values in daily operations.

To build and maintain channels of communication, Management Committee members hold small group and department meetings throughout the company each year to discuss the annual business plan, capture concerns, and answer employee questions. Internal communication also is fostered through an orientation program, presentations during continuous improvement training, bimonthly recognition meetings, and the SFF internal newsletter, *The Eggceptional News*.

External communication is equally important. SFF brings value to customers through a variety of personal interactions that aim to build long-term business relationships based on trust and understanding. The same philosophy guides communication with suppliers, local communities, regulatory agencies, and others.

SFF monitors customer satisfaction through direct feedback. Several key customers regularly provide formal scorecards. Sales representatives follow up on delivered orders to assess satisfaction with products, services, and relationships. By measuring specific performance items and designing action plans to improve performance, SFF has achieved remarkable results. SFF's rate of on-time deliveries reached 99.8 percent, and customer complaint levels are maintained at better than world-class standards. Even as product complexity has increased, customer satisfaction has remained near 100 percent. For all products, the length of time to resolve customer complaints has declined from 2.8 days in 1997 to 0.8 day.

To learn more about this organization, visit *www.sunnyfreshfoods.com*.

Effectiveness. The Baldrige quality program has the potential to be highly effective, as experienced by most of the organizations who have submitted applications for the Malcolm Baldrige National Quality Award. It is the most comprehensive and complex of the planning and decision aids presented in this chapter. Because of the enormous scope and complexity of the Baldrige quality program, its implementation requires major commitments from all areas and levels of the organization. If a long-term commitment to the Baldrige quality program at all levels exists or is developed, the organization will benefit. There can be no half-hearted commitment for program effectiveness.

Relation to ISO 9000. ISO 9000 *is a set of international standards that define the requirements for an effective quality management system.*[65] These standards are maintained and published by the International Organization for Standardization (ISO), headquartered in Geneva, Switzerland. ISO certification is administered by accreditation and certification bodies within the country where the firm operates. Conformity with ISO standards is valuable for several reasons: (1) it helps conscientious manufacturers and service providers to distinguish themselves from less reputable firms; (2) some government agencies and firms will not do business with suppliers unless they have ISO certification; (3) it provides consumers with more confidence in products or services that bear a mark or certificate that attests to quality, safety, or other desirable characteristics; and (4) it provides regulators with a partial means of enforcing health, safety, and environmental legislation.

One of the ISO 9000 standards, ISO 9000-1, states that the standards have five quality goals, as follows:

▶ Achieve, maintain, and seek to continuously improve product quality. The standards define a *product* as the output of any process. Thus, this term also applies to *services*, whether internal or external to the organization.

▶ Improve quality of operations to continually meet all customers' and other stakeholders' stated and implied needs.

▶ Provide confidence to internal management and other employees that requirements for quality are being fulfilled and maintained, and that quality improvement is taking place.

▶ Provide confidence to customers and stakeholders that requirements for quality are being, or will be, achieved in the delivered product.

▶ Provide confidence that quality system requirements are being fulfilled.

Virtually all leading companies—such as Carrier, Hewlett-Packard, PepsiCo, and Toyota—use ISO standards to help maintain their quality conformance programs. The standards describe the need for an effective quality system, for ensuring that measuring and testing equipment is calibrated regularly, and for maintaining an adequate record-keeping system. ISO 9000 registration determines whether a company complies with its own quality system.

Overall, ISO 9000 registration covers less than 10 percent of the Baldrige award criteria. The Baldrige categories focus on results and continuous improvement. They provide a systems framework for designing, implementing, and assessing a process for managing all business operations. ISO 9000 is narrower in scope. It may be and is often used as standards within the Baldrige categories.

Chapter Summary

In this chapter, we focused on the features and uses of eight of the literally hundreds of planning and decision aids. They are aids that specifically foster knowledge management, forecasting, creativity, and quality management. These aids are useful in virtually all types of organizations, at all organizational levels, and in all functional areas.

Learning Goals

1. Explain the essentials of knowledge management and how it is used to create value for organizations.

Knowledge management (KM) is the art and practice of obtaining and transforming information and utilizing intellectual assets to create value for an organization's employees and customers or clients. A supportive organizational culture is a prerequisite for the introduction and use of KM. Its three major components are an information base, enabling technologies, and the skills and abilities of employees. Information and knowledge are key assets and competitive weapons, perhaps more than an organization's physical assets. Knowledge management is most often applied to (1) collaboration among teams and departments; (2) improving service to customers or clients; and (3) tracking employees' capabilities, improving employee training, and performing other human resource functions. The balanced scorecard is a KM aid.

2. Describe the features and uses of the Delphi method, simulation, and scenario forecasting aids.

Forecasting is the process of estimating future events and conditions in an organization's environment. The Delphi method is a process of consensus building among experts to arrive at such estimates. Simulation involves the use of models of real systems to test alternatives, often on a computer. Scenarios are written descriptions of possible futures. All three methods are especially relevant as aids in the strategic planning process.

3. Discuss the creative process and how to use Osborn's creativity model.

Creativity is the ability to visualize, generate, and implement new ideas. The creative process usually involves five interconnected stages: preparation, concentration, incubation, illumination, and verification. Osborn's creativity model attempts to stimulate creativity and innovation by overcoming the blocks that often hinder free thinking. It helps decision makers address unstructured and ambiguous problems.

4. Explain and apply three quality improvement aids: benchmarking, the Deming cycle, and the Baldrige quality program.

Quality management is concerned with improving how well a good, service, or process does what it is supposed to do and also with raising the standards and specifications for what it is supposed to do. In brief, benchmarking involves comparing an organization's functions, products, or processes with those of best-in-class organizations. This ongoing process is a sequence of seven stages: defining the domain, identifying the best performers, collecting and analyzing data to identify gaps, setting improvement goals, developing and implementing plans to close gaps, evaluating results, and repeating the evaluations. The Deming cycle, also known as the PDSA cycle, includes four stages—plan, do, study, and act—that should be repeated over time to ensure continuous learning and improvement in functions, products, and processes.

The Baldrige quality program provides a systems perspective for managing an organization and its key processes to achieve performance excellence. Seven Baldrige categories, as shown in Figure 9.5, are the building blocks and integrating mechanism for the system. It is a comprehensive and complex program that requires a long-term commitment from all levels of the organization for successful implementation.

Key Terms and Concepts

Balanced scorecard model
Baldrige quality program
Benchmarking
Brainstorming
Competitor scenario
Creativity
Delphi method

Deming cycle
Electronic brainstorming
Expert system
Extrapolation
Forecasting
ISO 9000
Knowledge management

Osborn's creativity model
Radio frequency identification (RFID)
Scenarios
Simulation
Wiki

Questions for Discussion and Reflective Thinking

1. Review the Challenge of Managing feature on OMR Architects. How does OMR's system serve the three natural targets of knowledge management (KM): teams, customers, and workforce?

2. Review the Ethical Challenge feature on technology and customer privacy. Do you think legislation should be enacted that controls the use of radio-frequency identification (RFID) by firms? Justify your position.

3. *Wikipedia: The Free Encyclopedia* exists as a wiki, which enables visitors to edit its content. What is the process for editing Wikipedia's content and how is this controlled? Go to Wikipedia, at *http://en.wikipedia.org/wiki*, to answer this question.

4. In what ways has an organization for which you have worked used or failed to use KM? Explain.

5. The Balanced Scorecard Institute provides training, consulting, and guidance in the use of the balanced scorecard. Go to this organization's Web site at *www.balancedscorecard.org*. Click on "Basic concepts." What insights are provided beyond those presented in the chapter in the discussion of "What is a balanced scorecard?"?

6. How might the Delphi method be used to develop a forecast of the possible impacts of the Internet on higher education?

7. Describe a personal experience that you've had with playing a computer game. Which of its features might apply in a business setting?

8. Develop a negative scenario on the impact of the Internet on the work environment for college graduates in 2020.

9. Describe a personal situation that occurred within the past six months for which Osborn's creativity model would have been useful. Why would it have been useful?

10. Explain how benchmarking could be used to help plan improvements in one service or process (e.g., registration, advising, or financial aid) at your college or university. Who might you benchmark? Explain why.

DEVELOPING YOUR COMPETENCIES

This inventory provides you the opportunity to assess, reflect on, and reduce possible personal barriers to creativity. For each of the statements in the questionnaire, use the following scale to express which number best corresponds to your agreement or disagreement with the statement. Write that number in the blank to the left of each statement. Please do not skip any statements.

1 Strongly Agree	2 Agree Somewhat	3 Agree	4 Diagree	5 Strongly Approve

Disagree

___3___ 1. I evaluate criticism to determine how it can be useful to me.

___4___ 2. When solving problems, I attempt to apply new concepts or methods.

___3___ 3. I can shift gears or change emphasis in what I am doing.

___4___ 4. I get enthusiastic about problems outside of my specialized area of concentration.

___3___ 5. I always give a problem my best effort, even if it seems trivial or fails to arouse enthusiasm.

___5___ 6. I set aside periods of time without interruptions.

___2___ 7. It is not difficult for me to have my ideas criticized.

___1___ 8. In the past, I have taken calculated risks and I would do so again.

___4___ 9. I dream, daydream, and fantasize easily.

___3___ 10. I know how to simplify and organize my observations.

___2___ 11. Occasionally, I try a so-called unworkable answer in hopes that it will prove to be workable.

___2___ 12. I can and do consistently guard my personal periods of privacy.

___1___ 13. I feel at ease with peers even when my ideas or plans meet with public criticisms or rejection.

___1___ 14. I frequently read opinions contrary to my own to learn what the opposition is thinking.

___5___ 15. I translate symbols into concrete ideas or action steps.

___2___ 16. I see many ideas because I enjoy having alternative possibilities.

___3___ 17. In the idea-formulation stage of a project, I withhold critical judgment.

___3___ 18. I determine whether an imposed limitation is reasonable or unreasonable.

___1___ 19. I would modify an idea, plan, or design, even if doing so would meet with opposition.

___1___ 20. I feel comfortable expressing my ideas even if they are in the minority.

___2___ 21. I enjoy participating in nonverbal, symbolic, or visual activities.

___2___ 22. I feel the excitement and challenge of finding solutions to problems.

___5___ 23. I keep a file of discarded ideas.

___3___ 24. I make reasonable demands for good physical facilities and surroundings.

___3___ 25. I would feel no serious loss of status or prestige if management publicly rejected my plan.

___2___ 26. I frequently question the policies, goals, values, or ideas of an organization.

___3___ 27. I deliberately exercise my visual and symbolic skills in order to strengthen them.

___5___ 28. I can accept my thinking when it seems illogical.

___2___ 29. I seldom reject ambiguous ideas that are not directly related to the problem.

___1___ 30. I distinguish between trivial and important physical distractions.

___4___ 31. I feel uncomfortable making waves for a worthwhile idea even if it threatens team harmony.

___1___ 32. I am willing to present a truly original approach even if there is a chance it could fail.

___4___ **33.** I can recognize the times when symbolism or visualization would work best for me.

___3___ **34.** I try to make an uninteresting problem stimulating.

___2___ **35.** I consciously attempt to use new approaches toward routine tasks.

___2___ **36.** In the past, I have determined when to leave an undesirable environment and when to stay and change the environment (including self-growth).

Scoring

Transfer your responses to the statements above and record them in the blanks provided below. Then add the numbers in each column, and record the column totals

	A		B		C		D		E		F
1.	3	2.	4	3.	3	4.	4	5.	3	6.	5
7.	2	8.	1	9.	4	10.	3	11.	2	12.	2
13.	1	14.	1	15.	5	16.	2	17.	3	18.	3
19.	1	20.	1	21.	2	22.	2	23.	5	24.	3
25.	3	26.	2	27.	3	28.	5	29.	2	30.	1
31.	4	32.	1	33.	4	34.	3	35.	2	36.	2
Totals:	14		10		21		19		17		16

Interpretation

Take your scores from the scoring sheet and mark them with a dot in the score categories (cells) on the following graph. The vertical axis, which represents the possible column totals, ranges from 6 to 36. The horizontal axis represents the columns on your scoring sheet and ranges from A to F. The Key to Barriers legend at the end of this exercise identifies the category of barriers in each column. Connect the dots you have marked with a line. The high points represent your possible barriers to creativity as you see them. The higher the number in each column, the greater the barrier that factor represents in realizing your creative potential.

Key to Barriers

A = Barriers related to self-confidence and risk taking
B = Barriers related to need for conformity
C = Barriers related to use of the abstract
D = Barriers related to use of systematic analysis
E = Barriers related to task achievement
F = Barriers related to physical environment

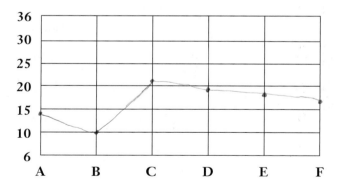

Questions

1. Based on these results, are there any actions that you can and want to take to improve your creativity?

2. What managerial competencies are most linked to your potential creativity?

Since 1993, DynMcDermott Petroleum Operations Company, headquartered in New Orleans, has operated and maintained the U.S. Department of Energy's (DOE's) U.S. Strategic Petroleum Reserve (SPR). The DOE's oil reserve was designed as "energy insurance" against disruptions to the availability of crude oil.

With a budget of $113 million and just over 500 employees in Louisiana, Texas, and Mississippi, DynMcDermott works exclusively for DOE. This firm, which is privately owned, recently received the Malcolm Baldrige National Quality Award.

The SPR stores 700 million barrels of crude oil in 62 underground salt caverns at sites along the U.S. gulf coast. These storage caverns, which each hold from about 7 million to 35 million barrels of crude oil, were created by hollowing out salt domes with fresh water injected at high pressure. This approach has won engineering awards for being safer and less expensive than other large-scale above-ground storage methods. It is considered a global benchmark that has been studied by other countries.

Each of the SPR's storage sites uses state-of-the-art automated systems to conduct operations from a central control room and to monitor conditions such as temperature, pressure, and vibration. Each site also has an advanced fire protection system, emergency response personnel and equipment, and specialized security. DynMcDermott routinely updates its oil storage and operations technology to tap new technologies, such as using cement linings for brine disposal pipelines to reduce corrosion and erosion.

For DynMcDermott, priority number one is operational readiness. In the event of oil supply interruption and following an order from the president of the United States, the SPR is ready to distribute crude oil to refineries. Called "drawdown," this is DynMcDermott's primary mission. Another key process, "fill," consists of filling the SPR to specified capacities. DynMcDermott conducts oil storage, oil movement, and field-operating functions at the SPR sites in Louisiana and Texas.

During the past decade, DynMcDermott has continually improved its Operational Readiness System, a strategic planning and organizational tool to ensure the company can conduct its drawdown and fill processes efficiently, securely, and safely. Each site is run as a separate business unit under the operational control of a site director. This allows maximum decision-making capability at the field level.

DynMcDermott's approach has worked well. Drawdown system availability has sustained a 98 percent or better performance level and has exceeded DOE expectations in each year and at each site since 2001. The drawdown rate has been sustained at the target level since 2000 and meets the DOE drawdown target of 4.4 million barrels per day. Overall distribution capability as a percentage of drawdown rate has been sustained at 153 percent. This compares to the DOE goal of 120 percent. Drawdown readiness has steadily improved from 95 percent in 1999 to 99 percent or better, exceeding DOE's target of 95 percent. DynMcDermott has conducted three major drawdown exercises in recent years.

Fulfilling its other major task, in August 2005, DynMcDermott completed a "fill" of the SPR to its authorized capacity of 700 million barrels as ordered by President Bush following the terrorist event on September 11, 2001.

In 2005, DynMcDermott's response to Hurricanes Katrina and Rita demonstrated the company's operational readiness, emergency planning, and emergency response. Both hurricanes directly impacted several company sites, displacing employees. But, less than five days after Hurricane Katrina hit the Gulf Coast, DynMcDermott restored operations and was able to provide oil to refiners. DynMcDermott's response included rerouting the primary SPR computer networks to a storage site in Louisiana to support the Emergency Operation Center (EOC) in Texas. Just a month later, Hurricane Rita forced an EOC evacuation and relocation to a second planned alternate site. During this period, President Bush declared a drawdown from the SPR, an action that has occurred only twice in 30 years. Although the EOC had to be relocated over 200 miles, DynMcDermott made its first drawdown oil delivery just three days after Hurricane Rita.

DynMcDermott has achieved success by aligning its purpose, vision, mission, and values to match those of its customer, DOE. The two organizations hold joint planning and performance reviews and share computer networks and critical information. DynMcDermott's values-based strategic planning process is integrated with the DOE planning process. DynMcDermott employees are involved in the DOE strategic planning activities.

This close interaction has allowed both DynMcDermott and DOE to continually assess progress, leading to improvements and positive results across the SPR. Since 2001, performance levels have been well above average. In 2003, DynMcDermott successfully competed to renew its DOE contract, which currently runs through 2008 and contains renewal options through 2013.

To further ensure a high-performing and safe organization, DynMcDermott employees are trained in workplace safety, environmental stewardship, ethical business practices, and management and leadership development. DynMcDermott's rate of workdays lost due to injury per 200,000 worker hours was 0.6 compared to the Bureau of Labor Statistics average of 4.8. Overall, employee satisfaction increased from 74 percent in 2000 to 83 percent, which compares favorably to the 43 percent benchmark determined by Business Research Laboratory. (BRL conducts employee satisfaction surveys for about 300 organizations and establishes industry norms.) Employee understanding of DynMcDermott's mission was in the excellent range, well above the Society for Human Resources Management norm of 72 percent and the BRL benchmark of 82 percent.

DynMcDermott's management of the SPR not only must be efficient, it also must be environmentally sound. DynMcDermott is focused on ways to better identify, reduce, and eliminate waste produced by the SPR. Since 2000, DynMcDermott has decreased the SPR's total pounds of hazardous waste from 3,802 to 515 pounds, compared to the DOE goal of 539 pounds. Since 2001, DynMcDermott also has maintained certifications for the ISO 9000:2000 quality management system and the ISO environmental management standards (ISO 14001).

To learn more about this organization, visit *www.dynmcdermott.com*.

Questions

1. How does DynMcDermott use the concepts, practices, and tools of knowledge management?

2. Based on the balanced scorecard model, how do the specific management practices link to the perspectives in the balanced scorecard model?

3. Identify specific examples and applications in this case that link to the categories and organizational profile of the Baldrige quality program for performance excellence as summarized in Figure 9.5.

4. In what ways does DynMcDermott make use of benchmarking?

chapter 10

© Leland Bobbe/Stone/Getty Images

Achieving Organizational Control

Learning Goals

After studying this chapter, you should be able to:

1. Explain the foundations of control.

2. Identify the six phases of the corrective control model.

3. Describe the primary methods of organizational control.

4. Explain key corporate governance issues and control mechanisms.

Communication Competency

Planning and Administration Competency

Teamwork Competency

Managing Effectively

Self-Management Competency

Strategic Action Competency

Multicultural Competency

Challenge of Managing ....

PepsiCo's Corporate Governance

© AP Graphics Bank

PepsiCo, with headquarters in Purchase, New York, is the world's number two soft-drink maker. PepsiCo also makes Tropicana juice brands, Gatorade, and Aquafina water drinks and owns Frito-Lay. The firm has 153,000 employees.

PepsiCo recently received the Alexander Hamilton Corporate Governance Award from *Treasury & Risk Management,* a major publication for chief financial officers, treasurers, and controllers. This award recognizes excellence in corporate governance. We provide a few perspectives from the recognition citation.

One of PepsiCo's strongest corporate governance attributes is its independent corporate board that, if needed, can keep management in check. Twelve of its 14 directors are independent (e.g., not employees of PepsiCo), including the presiding director. Shareholders vote on the full board each year. Rice Marshall, chief analyst of the watchdog group *The Corporate Library,* comments: "It is a very conservative board for what they are paying themselves, given the size of the company."

Recently, PepsiCo implemented multilevel Web-based training programs for 25,000 senior employees and others in key positions around the world where ethical conflicts and issues could emerge. These employees must certify each year that they are in compliance with PepsiCo's code of conduct. The new Web site also tests their understanding of issues like insider trading, sexual harassment and safety using real-world scenarios. A separate series of Web-based courses are being offered to executives on business ethics and other compliance-related issues.

The company is also making it easier for international employees to report misconduct by establishing an Internet reporting process and acquiring dedicated international phone lines so employees can call a toll-free phone number. "We want people to come forward and ask questions, to create a culture where people are willing to raise issues and challenge behavior," says Pam McGuire, PepsiCo's senior vice president and deputy general counsel of business practices and compliance. "We have an open door and are encouraging people to speak openly and honestly." Perhaps the compliance office's most ambitious program involves a database and case management system that will allow for better monitoring and tracing of complaints at the facility level, enabling the company to identify causes quickly. Compliance reports are shared regularly with the audit committee.

Learning Content

Each division (e.g., Pepsi, Frito-Lay, Gatorade) has a coordination team in place to oversee financial control testing and reporting results. Once those results are signed off on, they go to a separate corporate-level team for review before the results are shared with senior management.

PepsiCo conducts an annual survey of about 100 senior executives to help demonstrate the condition of its control culture. Conducted by the company's internal auditors, the questionnaire probes hiring practices, employee evaluation, contract solicitation, incident reporting, objective setting, and other issues.[1]

To learn more about this organization, see *www.pepsico.com.*

Explain the foundations of control.

Foundations of Control

The Challenge of Managing feature reflects the increased importance of achieving organizational control from the board of directors level all the way to first-level employees. Control *involves the processes for ensuring that behaviors and decisions conform to an organization's standards and legal requirements, including its rules, policies, procedures, and goals.*[2] To most people, the word *control* has a negative connotation—of restraining, forcing, delimiting, watching, or manipulating. Given the 21st-century's ever-present threats of terrorism, governments and business firms have substantially accelerated their use of security-based controls, especially through the increased use of security guards, surveillance cameras, computer monitoring, telephone monitoring, personal searches at airports, and scanning. Although some people accept these control methods as necessary, others feel they have become too intrusive and threaten individual rights of privacy.

Organizational controls are both useful and necessary. Effective control is viewed as one of PepsiCo's criteria for its long-term success. We can illustrate the need for controls by describing how control interacts with planning:

▶ Planning is the formal process of developing goals, strategies, tactics, and standards and allocating resources. Controls help ensure that decisions, actions, and results are consistent with those plans.

▶ Planning prescribes desired behaviors and results. Controls help maintain or redirect *actual* behaviors and results.

▶ Managers and employees cannot effectively plan without accurate and timely information. Controls provide much of this essential information.

▶ Plans indicate the purposes to be served by controls. Controls help ensure that plans are implemented as intended. Thus, planning and control complement and support each other.

Preventive and Corrective Controls

The two general types of organizational controls are preventive and corrective.[3] Preventive controls *are mechanisms intended to reduce the likelihood of an unwanted event and thereby minimize the need for corrective action.* A key factor in PepsiCo's receipt of the Alexander Hamilton Corporate Governance Award was its focus on the development of and continued use of effective preventive controls. A few examples of PepsiCo's preventive controls reported on in the opening feature include:

▶ The use of an independent board of directors to prevent top management from gaining too much control over the use and allocation of resources.

- The introduction of multilevel Web-based training to ensure that employees at all levels know what is and is not permissible in a number of areas so as to help prevent errors, ethical lapses, violations of rules, and illegal acts.

- The annual certification by employees through their personal signatures that they are in compliance with PepsiCo's code of conduct, which employees are expected to read each year prior to signing the certification form.

- The use of division-level and corporate-level teams to oversee financial controls and reporting results so that all employees know of the monitoring and are thereby less likely to engage in violations of requirements.

- Documentation and controls testing to ensure sound processes and avoidance of conflicts of interest.

- Stricter prior approvals by senior-level managers for third-party services. For example, PepsiCo may pay an executive recruiting firm a percentage of the applicant's starting salary once the person is hired by PepsiCo.

Rules and regulations, standards, recruitment and selection procedures, and training and development programs function primarily as preventive controls. They direct and limit the behaviors of managers and employees alike. The assumption is that, if managers and employees comply with these requirements, the organization is likely to achieve its goals. Thus, preventive controls are needed to ensure that rules, regulations, and standards are being followed and are working.

Corrective controls *are mechanisms intended to reduce or eliminate unwanted behaviors or results and thereby return the situation to conformity with the organization's regulations and standards.* PepsiCo has many corrective controls, only a few of which are presented in the Challenge of Managing feature. A few examples of PepsiCo's corrective controls include:

- The development of an Internet-based reporting process and the establishment of dedicated (toll-free) international phone lines so that international employees can more easily report misconduct. This enables higher level management to investigate and take corrective action, if appropriate.

- Division-level and corporate-level teams that oversee financial control testing and reporting results and initiate corrective actions if they find violations and discrepancies. The presence of these teams also serves as a preventive control, as noted previously.

- Improvements in the compliance office's ability to monitor and trace complaints to enable quicker identification of causes and the implementation of corrective actions. In the case of theft, a corrective action may be dismissal of the violating employee.

Sources of Control

The four primary sources of control in most organizations are stakeholders, the organization itself, groups, and individuals. These sources are shown in Table 10.1 on the next page, along with examples of preventive and corrective controls for each.

Stakeholder Controls. Stakeholder controls *are expressed as pressures from sources and entities on organizations to maintain or change their behaviors and decisions.* Stakeholders may be unions, government agencies, customers, shareholders, and others who have direct interests in the well-being of an organization.[4] For instance, during the past decade or so, organizations have been increasingly pressured to change

Table 10.1	Examples of Different Sources and Types of Control	
	TYPES OF CONTROL	
Source of Control	**Preventive**	**Corrective**
Stakeholders	Maintaining quotas for hiring personnel in protected classes	Changing recruitment policies to attract qualified personnel
Organization	Using budgets to guide expenditures	Disciplining an employee for violating a "No Smoking" safety regulation in a hazardous area
Group	Advising a new employee about the group's norm in relation to expected level of output	Harassing and socially isolating a worker who doesn't conform to group norms
Individual	Deciding to skip lunch in order to complete a project on time	Revising a report you have written because you are dissatisfied with it

their behaviors to reduce pollution, save energy, pursue sustainability, and produce more environmentally safe goods.

The mission of the U.S. Environmental Protection Agency (EPA) is to protect human health and the environment. The EPA employs 18,000 people across the country. One of the things the EPA does is develop and enforce regulations that implement environmental laws enacted by Congress. The EPA is responsible for researching and setting national standards for a variety of environmental programs. It delegates to states and Indian tribes the responsibility for issuing permits and for monitoring and enforcing compliance with those permits. Where national standards are not met, the EPA can issue sanctions and take other steps to assist the states and tribes in reaching the desired levels of environmental quality. For example, a regulation issued by the EPA to implement the Clean Air Act might state what levels of a pollutant—such as sulfur dioxide—are safe. It then tells industries how much sulfur dioxide they can legally emit into the air, and what the penalty will be if they emit too much. Once a regulation is in effect, the EPA then works with industries to assist with compliance (preventive controls) and to enforce the regulation when there is noncompliance (corrective controls). Enforcement may be through civil action, required cleanup, or even criminal action.[5] From the perspective of business leaders, this agency creates preventive controls for the firm by prescribing what should not be done to the natural environment—air, water, and land—and it creates corrective controls by prescribing needed reductions in air, water, or land pollution by the firm.

Organizational Controls. Organizational controls *comprise the formal policies, rules, procedures, and records for preventing or correcting deviations from plans and for achieving desired goals.* As indicated in the Challenge of Managing feature, many of the initiatives by PepsiCo involve preventive and corrective organizational controls. Much of this chapter focuses on organizational controls.

Group Controls. Group controls *comprise the norms and values that group or team members share and maintain through rewards and punishments.*[6] Examples include acceptance by the group or team and punishments, such as giving group members the silent treatment. A number of aspects of group or team control are discussed in Chapters 17 and 18.

Individual Self-Controls. Individual self-controls *comprise the guiding mechanisms that operate consciously and unconsciously within each person.* Standards of professionalism are becoming an increasingly important aspect of individual self-control. Becoming a professional involves acquiring detailed knowledge, specialized skills, and specific attitudes and ways of behaving. The entire process may take years of study and socialization. In doing their work, certified public accountants, lawyers, engineers, business school graduates, and physicians, among others, are expected to exercise individual self-control based on the guiding standards of their professions.[7]

Stakeholder, organizational, group, and individual controls form patterns that differ widely from one organization to another. A strong organizational culture, the characteristics of which we describe in Chapter 18, usually produces mutually supportive controls and reinforces organizational, group, and individual controls.

Linkage to Strategic Goals

Controls should be linked to the strategic goals of the organization. These strategic goals often include increasing profits, improving customer service, protecting the organization's assets, and improving the quality of the goods and/or services it produces. As suggested in Figure 10.1, an effective organizational control system has features that support the achievement of strategic goals. These features include being objective, complete, timely, and acceptable.

Figure 10.1 | Features of an Effective Organizational Control System

Objective Controls. Objective controls are impartial and cannot be manipulated by employees for personal gain. In the United States, the Financial Accounting Standards Board (FASB) and several government agencies devote a great deal of effort to developing and monitoring principles and practices that attempt to ensure that financial statements reflect reality as objectively and as accurately as possible. As discussed in previous chapters, the executives of some major corporations (e.g., Enron, Tyco, WorldCom) manipulated financial and accounting procedures and practices for their personal gain. The controls exerted by various external stakeholder groups did, eventually, lead to exposing the illegal and unethical practices by the top executives at such firms.

Complete Controls. A complete system of controls encompasses all of the behaviors and goals desired by the organization. A purchasing manager evaluated solely on the basis of cost per order may allow quality to slip. A software salesperson at Oracle evaluated only on the basis of sales volume may ignore after-sales service. Thus, Oracle balances quantitative (measurable) and qualitative (subjective) controls.

Timely Controls. Timely controls provide information when it is needed most. Timeliness may be measured in seconds for evaluating the safe movement of trains and planes or in terms of months for evaluating employee performance. Computer-based information systems have played a major role in increasing the timely flow of information. The computerized cash registers at Target, Kohl's, JC Penney, and many other major retailers give store managers and top-level executives data on a daily basis regarding each department's sales, costs, and profitability measures for the entire store.

Acceptable Controls. To be effective, controls must be recognized as necessary and appropriate. If controls are widely ignored, managers need to find out why. Perhaps the controls should be dropped or modified, should be backed up with rewards for compliance and punishments for noncompliance, or should be linked more closely to desired results. T. J. Rodgers is the founder, president, CEO, and director of Cypress Semiconductor, which is headquartered in San Jose, California. The firm is a supplier of a broad array of semiconductors and related products. Several years ago, Rodgers implemented computer-based controls for the firm's employees, dubbed *killer software*. It tracked detailed and daily goals and deadlines for each employee. When targets were missed, the software shut down the offending department's computers and canceled the manager's next paycheck. Rodgers ditched the scheme several years ago after realizing that it encouraged dishonesty and turned some employees into "checklist robots."[8]

The following Planning and Administration Competency feature reports on PepsiCo's control policy related to business gifts and payments.[9] This feature links to PepsiCo's strategic goals. It represents preventive policy controls that are designed to be objective, complete in the area of business gifts and payments, timely, and acceptable.

Planning and Administration Competency

PepsiCo's Preventive Policy Controls for Gifts

"Our business decisions are made on merit. Therefore, we will never give or offer, directly or indirectly, anything of value to a government official to influence any discretionary decision by such official in his or her official capacity. Giving gifts or entertainment to governmental officials and employees is highly regulated and often prohibited. Such gifts and entertainment should not be provided unless you have determined that they are permitted by law and your business unit's policies.

In circumstances where it would not create an appearance of impropriety, employees may provide existing or potential customers with reasonable entertainment or gifts. However, the gifts must be permitted by local law, the customer's own policies and your business unit's policies.

Employees may not accept a gift, favor, loan, special service, payment or special treatment of any kind from any individual or organization which conducts or seeks to conduct business with the Company, or which competes with the Company, unless:

▶ It would be consistent with good business practices;

▶ It could not be considered a business inducement;

▶ It is of nominal value as set forth in your Division's policy;

▶ Public disclosure of the transaction would not embarrass PepsiCo.

All business-related gifts, which exceed your Division's definition of nominal value, should be reported to your immediate supervisor as soon as they are received."

To learn more about this organization, visit *www.pepsico.com*.

How Much Organizational Control?

One way to assess the amount of needed formal organizational controls is to compare the cost and benefits. Such a cost–benefit analysis addresses three basic questions:

1. For what desired behaviors and results should organizational controls be developed?

2. What are the costs and benefits of the organizational controls required to achieve the desired behaviors and results?

3. What are the costs and benefits of utilizing alternative controls to obtain the desired behaviors and results, such as greater reliance on self-managed teams, informal peer control, or individual self-control?

Although the optimal amount of control is difficult to calculate, effective managers probably come closer to achieving it than do ineffective managers. Managers have to consider trade-offs that affect the amount of organizational control to use. With too little control, costs exceed benefits and the controls are ineffective. As the amount of control increases, effectiveness also increases—up to a point. Beyond a certain point, effectiveness declines with further increases in the amount of control exercised.[10] For example, an organization might benefit from reducing the average managerial span of control from 30 to 16 employees. However, to reduce it further to 8 employees would require doubling the number of managers. The costs of the increased control (managers' salaries) might far outweigh the expected benefits. Such a move might also make workers feel micromanaged. That, in turn, could lead to increased dissatisfaction, absenteeism, and turnover. Obviously, some of these costs and benefits can be difficult to quantify.

Internal Control

Preventive controls, corrective controls, and the sources of control discussed—stakeholder, organizational, group, and individual—are encompassed in internal control. Internal control *is a process—effected by an organization's board of directors, management, and other personnel—designed to provide reasonable assurance regarding the achievement of goals in the various categories.*[11] These categories include (1) effectiveness and efficiency of operations, (2) reliability of financial reporting, and (3) compliance with applicable laws and regulations.

As noted in Figure 10.2 on the next page, internal control consists of five interrelated components and layers. These are based on the way management runs a business, and are integrated with the management process. Although the components apply to all organizations, small and mid-sized companies may implement them differently than large ones. Smaller companies' controls may be less formal and less structured, yet they can still have effective internal control.

Control Environment. The control environment sets the tone of an organization, influencing the control consciousness of its people. It is the foundation for all other components of internal control, providing discipline and structure. Control environment factors include the integrity, ethical values, and competence of the entity's employees; management's philosophy and operating style; the way management assigns authority and responsibility and how it organizes and develops its employees; and the attention and direction provided by the board of directors.

Risk Assessment. Every organization faces a variety of risks from external and internal sources that must be assessed. A precondition to risk assessment is the establishment of goals linked at different levels and internally consistent. Risk assessment is the

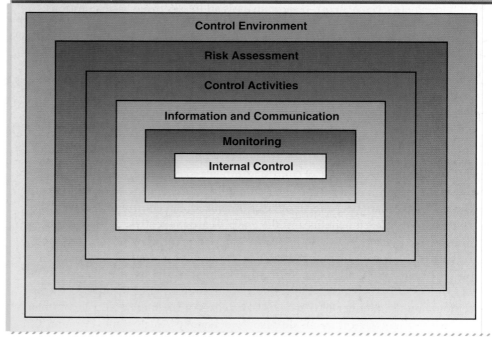

Figure 10.2 | Interrelated Components and Layers of Internal Control

Control Environment

Risk Assessment

Control Activities

Information and Communication

Monitoring

Internal Control

identification and analysis of relevant risks that could affect the achievement of goals. This assessment provides a basis for determining how the risks should be managed. Because economic, industry, regulatory, and operating conditions will continue to change, mechanisms are needed to identify and deal with the special risks associated with change.

Control Activities. Control activities are the policies and procedures that help ensure management directives are accomplished. They help ensure that necessary actions are taken to address risks to achievement of the entity's goals. Control activities occur throughout the organization, at all levels and in all functions. They include a range of activities as diverse as approvals, authorizations, verifications, reconciliations, reviews of operating performance, securing of assets, and segregation of duties.

Information and Communication. Pertinent information must be identified, captured, and communicated in a form and time frame that enable people to carry out their responsibilities. Information systems produce reports containing operational, financial, and compliance-related information that make it possible to run and control the business. They deal not only with internally generated data, but also with information about external events, activities, and conditions necessary to informed business decision making and external reporting. Effective communication also must occur in a broader sense, flowing down, across, and up the organization. All personnel must receive a clear message from top management that control responsibilities must be taken seriously. They must understand their own role in the internal control system, as well as how individual activities relate to the work of others. They must have a means of communicating significant information upstream. There also needs to be effective communication with external parties, such as customers, suppliers, regulators, and shareholders.

Monitoring. Internal control systems need to be monitored—a process that assesses the quality of the system's performance over time. This is accomplished through ongoing monitoring activities, separate evaluations, or a combination of the two. Ongoing monitoring occurs in the course of operations. It includes regular management and supervisory activities, and other actions personnel take in performing their duties. The scope and frequency of separate evaluations will depend primarily on an assessment of risks and the effectiveness of ongoing monitoring procedures. Internal control deficiencies should be reported upstream, with serious matters reported to top management and the board.

Synergy. There needs to be coordination among these components, forming an integrated system that adjusts to changing conditions. The internal control system is an important part of the organization's operating activities and exists for good business reasons. Internal control is most effective when controls are built into the whole organization. "Built-in" controls support quality and empowerment initiatives, avoid unnecessary costs, and enable quick response to changing conditions. Internal control can help an organization achieve its performance and profitability goals and prevent loss of resources. It can help ensure reliable financial reporting. And it can help ensure that the enterprise complies with laws and regulations, avoiding damage to its reputation and other consequences. In sum, it can help an organization get to where it wants to go, and avoid pitfalls and surprises along the way.

Limitations of Internal Control. Even effective internal control can only help an organization achieve its goals. It can provide management information about the organization's progress, or lack of it, toward their achievement. But internal control cannot change a poor manager into a good one. In addition, shifts in government policy or programs, competitors' actions, or economic conditions can be beyond management's control. Therefore, internal control cannot ensure success or even survival.

An internal control system, no matter how well thought out and operated, can provide only partial—not absolute—assurance to management and the board regarding achievement of an entity's goals. The likelihood of achievement is affected by limitations inherent in all internal control systems. These include the realities that judgments in decision making can be faulty. Breakdowns can occur because of simple error or mistake. Controls can be circumvented by the collusion of two or more people. Management has the ability to override the system. There are resource constraints, and the benefits of controls must be considered relative to their costs. Thus, while internal control can help an entity achieve its goals, it is not a panacea.

Corrective Control Model

The corrective control model *is a process for detecting and eliminating or reducing deviations from an organization's established standards.* This process relies heavily on information feedback and responses to it.[12] As shown in Figure 10.3 on the following page, the corrective control model has six interconnected phases: (1) define the system (an individual, a department, or a process), (2) identify the key characteristics to be measured, (3) set standards, (4) collect information, (5) make comparisons, and (6) diagnose problems and make corrections.

Define the System

Formal controls might be created and maintained for an employee, a work team, a department, a process, or an entire organization. The controls could focus on inputs, transformation processes, or outputs. *Input* controls often limit the amount by which raw materials used in the transformation process can vary from the organization's standards. For example, breweries use elaborate preventive controls (including inspections and laboratory testing) to guarantee that the water and grains they use to make

"Fundamentally, control exists only to mitigate risk. So every internal control framework has to start with a systematic approach to identifying risk. . . . Look at some of the major recent corporate failures. Where did the problems fundamentally arise? They occurred primarily because of breakdowns in the control environment."
Larry Rittenberg, Chairman, COSO– Committee of Sponsoring Organizations of the Treadway Commission

2.
Identify the six phases of the corrective control model.

Figure 10.3 Corrective Control Model

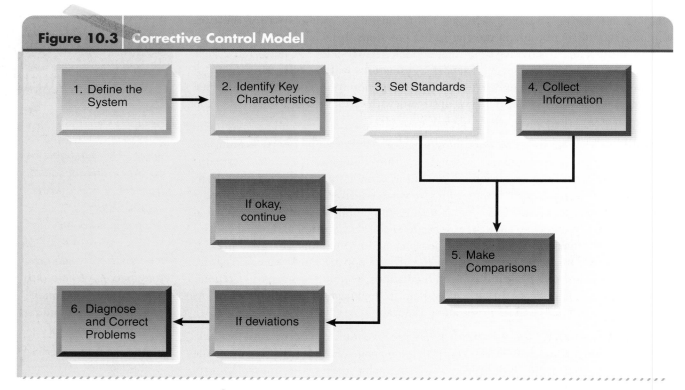

beer meet predetermined standards. Such controls ensure that the correct quantity and quality of inputs enter the production process.

Many formal corrective controls are applied during production (the *transformation* process). For Budweiser, Coors, Miller, and other brewers, they include timing the cooking of the brew, monitoring the temperature in the vats, sampling and laboratory testing of the brew at each stage of the process, and visual inspection of the beer prior to final packing. Finally, *output* controls are used. For brewers, they range from specifying the levels of distributor inventories to monitoring consumer attitudes toward the beer and its marketing.

The corrective control model relies heavily on information feedback and responses to it.

Identify Key Characteristics

The key types of information to be obtained about a person, team, department, or organization must be identified. Establishing formal corrective controls requires early determination of the characteristics that can be measured, the costs and benefits of obtaining information about each characteristic, and whether variations in each characteristic are likely to affect performance.

After identifying them, managers must choose the characteristics to be measured. The principle of selectivity *(also known as Pareto's principle) holds that a small number of characteristics always account for a large number of effects.* In brewing beer, three characteristics that greatly influence the final product's quality are water quality, temperature, and length of brewing time. Failing to control these few vital characteristics can account for large variations in results. This is sometimes stated as the 80/20 rule, which suggests that, with any product or

© Image Source/Jupiter Images

service, a few of its aspects (20 percent) are vital, while the rest of them (80 percent) are minor.[13]

Set Standards

Standards *are criteria for evaluating qualitative and quantitative characteristics and should be set for each characteristic measured.* There are literally thousands of organizations that set thousands of standards.[14] For example, the International Organization for Standardization (ISO), which we briefly discussed in Chapter 9 with respect to ISO 9000, publishes thousands of standards in numerous categories, ranging from very specific contexts (ISO 2171—cereals and milled cereal products—determination of total ash) to general contexts (ISO 9000—quality management system in production environments).[15]

ISO standards and those of other international standards organizations, such as the International Electrotechnical Commission and International Telecommunication Union, are intended to be used on a worldwide basis. These organizations have no authority to enforce their standards, whereas the authority of the U.S. Environmental Protection Agency to enforce its standards is well known.

Cultural Influences. Cultural and cross-cultural differences may influence differences in the standards set, some of which are not written in a document. However, major corporations, such as PepsiCo, increasingly have codes of conduct standards, financial standards, safety standards, and the like that are designed to apply to their employees and operations throughout the world. In other areas, PepsiCo and many other organizations give discretion to *acting locally.*[16] Different time standards are reflected in differing approaches to work. U.S. and Canadian executives often (not always) expect meetings to begin and end at certain times. In contrast, Indonesians have "rubber time." To them, time is elastic. If something comes up that is more important than business, such as a wedding, business gets postponed. In Nigeria, starting time for a meeting is only an approximation, and "tardiness" is readily accepted. Thus, global organizations must observe standards set by the local cultures, rather than apply the standards the organizations are accustomed to and would prefer to set.[17]

Performance standards. Increasingly, controls are being based on performance standards (outcome controls), of which many types are possible.[18] Let's look at examples from five different functional areas:

1. *Inventory.* Monthly finished goods inventory should be maintained at the sales level forecast for the following two-month period.

2. *Accounts receivable.* Monthly accounts receivable should be no more than the dollar value of the previous month's sales, except for the month of December.

3. *Sales productivity.* The dollar value of sales per salesperson should be $1,500 greater than the comparable month for the previous year and $18,000 greater in the current year.

4. *Employee turnover.* The turnover of field sales personnel should be no more than 2 per 100 salespeople per month and no more than 24 per 100 salespeople annually.

5. *Production waste.* Waste should amount to no more than $200 per month per full-time production worker, or no more than $2,400 per year per full-time production worker.

Collect Information

Information on each of the standards can be collected manually or automatically. The electronic counting devices used at Disney World to count the number of people who

Snapshot

"Many large companies suffer the ravages of fiefdoms, turf wars and bureaucracy. It's a problem that begins when individuals, groups, or divisions try to protect their turfs, reshaping their environments to gain as much control as possible. . . . . Ultimately, fiefdoms lose their ability to act consistently on behalf of the greater good of the company."

Robert J. Herbold, Former Chief Operating Officer of Microsoft, and author of *The Fiefdom Syndrome*

use each ride or the turnstiles at many sports facilities that count the number of people who enter are examples.

If the individual or group whose performance is to be controlled collects information, its validity must be checked. Employees and managers sometimes have an incentive to distort or conceal information if they will be criticized or punished for negative results. Moreover, when formal controls emphasize punishment, strong group controls (see Chapter 17) may emerge to distort the information reported to management. Such reporting may obscure responsibility for failure to meet standards or achieve goals.

Of course, rewards tied to performance also create the possibility of individuals distorting information or groups pressuring others to avoid full disclosure of information. Consider what happened at Fannie Mae (Federal National Mortgage Association), which is headquartered in Washington, D.C. Fannie Mae is a public company that raises funds from investors and purchases mortgages from lenders. Fannie's regulator, the Office of Federal Housing Enterprise Oversight (OFHEO), identified more than a dozen accounting and financial reporting problems. The reporting scandal forced the departures of Chief Executive Franklin Raines and Chief Financial Officer Timothy Howard. The OFHEO report concluded that Fannie Mae's executives manipulated earnings to meet exact earnings targets and that executive bonuses were tied to meeting targets. The report finds that Fannie doctored its earnings for six years so that top executives could collect hundreds of millions of dollars in bonuses.

OFHEO found that Fannie Mae was infected by a belief that "we're smarter than anyone else." The company failed to invest in computer systems and expertise to ensure that it could comply with accounting rules and keep its books accurate. Fannie Mae agreed to a consent order with OFHEO under which the company will undertake remedial actions to address all the recommendations contained in the OFHEO special examination report, including accounting practices, internal controls, governance, capital plans, corporate culture, disclosure, personnel oversight and compensation, and oversight of certain corporate activities. Fannie Mae agreed to pay $400 million in penalties related to its accounting and financial reporting problems.

The oversight agency report condemned the company's board of directors for lax oversight. It concluded that Fannie's board actually contributed to the accounting errors and earnings manipulation by failing to act independently of Raines (CEO) and Howard (CFO), and by failing to correct accounting and internal control problems even after similar problems emerged previously at Freddie Mac, Fannie Mae's chief competitor.

James Lockhart, the director of OFHEO, comments:

> The image of Fannie Mae as one of the lowest risk and "best in class" institutions was a façade. Our examination found an environment where the ends justified the means. Senior management manipulated accounting; reaped maximum, undeserved bonuses; and prevented the rest of the world from knowing. They co-opted their internal auditors. They stonewalled OFHEO. Fannie Mae's executives were precisely managing earnings to the one-hundredth of a penny to maximize their bonuses while neglecting investments in systems internal controls and risk management. The combination of earnings manipulation, mismanagement and unconstrained growth resulted in an estimated $10.6 billion of losses, well over a billion dollars in expenses to fix the problems, and ill-gotten bonuses in the hundreds of millions of dollars.[19]

Make Comparisons

Comparisons are needed to determine whether what is happening is what should be happening. In other words, information about actual results must be compared with performance standards. Such comparisons allow managers and team members to concentrate on deviations or exceptions. Such comparisons are also made by external stakeholders, especially regulatory agencies like the EPA and OFHEO. For example, the 326-page OFHEO report on Fannie Mae makes many comparisons as to how Fannie Mae failed to follow generally accepted accounting principles and standards, including the broader components of internal control that we reviewed in a previous section of this chapter.

© AP Graphics Bank

Fannie Mae struggled with resolving internal manipulation of earnings to meet targets by top executives.

Diagnose and Correct Problems

Diagnosis involves assessing the types, amounts, and causes of deviations from standards. Action can then be taken to eliminate those deviations and correct problems.

The following Communication Competency feature presents the proactive and positive communications of the new leadership at the board and executive levels with regard to how Fannie Mae is addressing the OFHEO report—*Report of the Special Examination of Fannie Mae.*[20]

Communication Competency

Fannie Mae's Leadership Addresses Problems

Stephen Ashley, chairman of the board, announced that Fannie Mae agreed to the comprehensive settlements with the OFHEO as well as the Securities and Exchange Commission (SEC). Ashley comments:

We are pleased that we have been able to reach a comprehensive agreement and bring these matters to a conclusion. This important step today builds on some of the changes and progress we have made over the past 18 months to rebuild the company and restore the confidence of our shareholders and stakeholders.

The Board has read the report and is committed to implementing the terms of the settlement. The company has undertaken a number of remedial steps. Over the course of the past two years, the Board has made a number of changes in its structure and membership, and its relationship to the company. We are also pleased with the steps Dan Mudd has taken as President and CEO and are confident in his leadership. He has established a new leadership team, restructured the finance, controllers, internal audit and compliance organizations and functions, and begun to change the corporate culture, repair relationships with our regulators, and refocus the business to serve the company's affordable housing mission. The Board and new management team are fully committed to working closely and cooperatively with our regulators to ensure that the progress made so far will continue and that the future of our company remains bright for our shareholders, investors and employees.

Dan Mudd adds:

We are glad to resolve these matters. We have all learned some powerful lessons here about getting things right and about hubris and humility. We are a much different company than before. But we also recognize that we have a long road ahead of us. We pledge to continue to work closely and cooperatively with our regulators as we continue to move forward with remedial measures, carry out the terms of our regulatory agreements, complete our restatement and build a better company. A lot of people are counting on us to build a company that is worthy of our public purpose to help the housing finance system serve affordable housing.

To learn more about this organization, visit *www.fanniemae.com.*

3.

Describe the primary methods of organizational control.

Primary Methods of Control

Throughout this textbook, we have discussed various aspects of control and have indicated how a firm's strategy helps focus (control) employee behavior. Compared to the Marriott's Ritz-Carlton, a very exclusive and expensive hotel, Marriott's Fairfield Inn properties provide low-cost accommodations. Therefore, Marriott's control systems for the Fairfield Inn properties focus on maintaining a low-cost strategy. In terms of human resource management, performance appraisal systems help managers assess the behaviors of employees and compare them to performance standards. Deviations are noted and corrective controls are used to reduce or eliminate problems.

In this section, we explore five primary methods of organizational control. Two are basic to the type of organization: mechanistic and organic controls. One reflects external considerations: market controls. One is functional: financial controls. And one is technological: automation controls. We also provide examples of specific control methods utilized by organizations.

As Figure 10.4 illustrates, all organizations utilize some combination of mechanistic controls and organic controls in conjunction with their market, financial, and automation-based controls. The methods available have the potential for complementing one another or working against one another. Thus, management should select and assess control methods in relation to one another when deciding which to apply. All of these methods involve various combinations and degrees of emphasis on preventive control and corrective control.

| Figure 10.4 | Primary Organizational Control Methods |

Mechanistic and Organic Controls

Mechanistic controls *involve the extensive use of rules and procedures, top-down authority, tightly written job descriptions, and other formal methods for preventing and correcting deviations from desired behaviors and results.* Mechanistic controls are an important part of bureaucratic management (see Chapters 2, 11, and 18).[21] In contrast, **organic controls** *involve the use of flexible authority, relatively loose job descriptions, individual self-controls, and other informal methods for preventing and correcting deviations from desired behaviors and results.*[22]

Organic controls are consistent with a clan culture (see Chapter 18). In clan-type organizational cultures, such as Johnson & Johnson and Accenture, members share pride in membership and a strong sense of identification with management. In addition, peer pressure to adhere to certain norms is considerable. Teams of self-managed employees control themselves on a day-to-day basis with less direct detailed control from higher management. These self-managed teams use many organic controls, which create a supportive environment for members to learn new tasks. Table 10.2 contrasts the use of mechanistic and organic control methods.

Table 10.2	**Mechanistic and Organic Control Methods**
MECHANISTIC CONTROL METHODS	**ORGANIC CONTROL METHODS**
Use of detailed rules and procedures whenever possible	Use of detailed rules and procedures only when necessary
Top-down authority, with emphasis on positional power	Flexible authority, with emphasis on expert power and networks of influence
Activity-based job descriptions that prescribe day-to-day behaviors	Results-based job descriptions that emphasize goals to be achieved
Emphasis on extrinsic rewards (wages, pensions, status symbols)	Emphasis on both extrinsic and intrinsic rewards (meaningful work)
Distrust of teams, based on an assumption that team goals conflict with organizational goals	Use of teams, based on an assumption that team goals and norms assist in achieving organizational goals

Snapshot

"As soon as people start to figure out they're being monitored and tracked, pretty much, you get what you ask for. If people feel they're the victims of bean counters who ignore quality and focus solely on numbers, they'll figure out how to drive numbers up without putting effort into quality. Metrics are a great thing to have. It's just you have to think about how they're being used."

Carla Lorek, Manager, Integrated Strategy & Planning, Xerox

PepsiCo and other major organizations have large numbers of departments, which can differ widely in their use of mechanistic or organic controls. The use of mechanistic controls in certain departments and organic controls in others does not necessarily reduce a firm's overall effectiveness. At PepsiCo, the syrup production plants operate in a relatively stable environment, whereas the marketing units operate in a changing environment. Managers of these different types of units use different ways to divide and manage the work. The syrup production managers use more mechanistic controls, whereas the marketing managers are subject to more organic controls. One consequence of use of the organic controls is that marketing managers are given more control over making decisions because consumers in different countries do not use or perceive Pepsi in exactly the same way in all countries. For example, in Spain, refrigerators are smaller than in other countries. As a result, two-liter bottles do not fit in the refrigerators. Thus, containers in Spain are a somewhat different size than in North America.[23] Moreover, marketing managers in each country are given more control over the messages and marketing techniques targeted to the specific country. For example, PepsiCo has thirteen country- and language-specific Web sites in Europe and Northern Asia as well as three country- and language-specific Web sites in: China, Japan, and India.[24]

Market Controls

Market controls *involve the collection and evaluation of data related to sales, prices, costs, and profits for guiding decisions and evaluating results.* The idea of market control emerged from economics. Dollar amounts provide standards of comparison. To be effective, market controls generally require mechanisms that enable

- the costs of the resources used in producing outputs to be measured monetarily,
- the value of the goods and services produced to be defined clearly and priced monetarily, and
- the prices of the goods and services produced to be set competitively.[25]

Two of the control mechanisms that can satisfy these requirements are incentive compensation and customer monitoring.

Incentive Compensation. Incentive compensation *provides various types of financial rewards based on achievement of defined performance outcomes.* The performance outcomes may be for a strategic business unit, a division, a store in a chain, a team, or a department. They are primarily a source of preventive control and outcome-based control. Incentive compensation may be effective if it serves to

- increase employee identification with the organization's performance goals, allowing greater reliance on individual self-control and group controls;
- achieve a more flexible wage structure, reflecting the company's actual economic position and controlling labor costs;
- attract and retain workers more easily, improving control of selection and lowering turnover costs; and
- establish a more equitable reward system, helping to develop an organizational culture that recognizes achievement and performance.[26]

There are many types of incentive compensation.[27] One of the more common types is **profit sharing**, *which means an individual's compensation may be increased, based on a predetermined formula, according to the level of earnings by the firm or each of its subsidiaries.* At least three important factors influence whether the goals of a profit-sharing plan can be achieved. First, employees must think that the plan is based on a reasonable, accurate, and equitable formula. The formula, in turn, must be based on valid, consistently, and honestly reported financial and operating information. Recall the problems with the profit-sharing incentives for top executives at Fannie Mae because they were able to distort and manipulate reported profits. Second, employees must think that their efforts and achievements contribute to profitability. Third, employees must think that the size of profit-based incentives will increase on the basis of a formula as profitability increases.[28]

Customer Monitoring. Customer monitoring *consists of ongoing efforts to obtain feedback from customers concerning the quality of goods and services.* Such monitoring is done to prevent problems or learn of their existence and solve them. Customer monitoring is being used increasingly by organizations in their attempt to correct problems with service and quality.[29] Based on such assessments, management may take action to prevent the loss of further business because of customer dissatisfaction.

Service providers use customer monitoring often. Fairfield Inn, a limited service motel chain and division of Marriott, focuses on a basic customer monitoring process. Guests are encouraged to rate three core aspects of service: cleanliness, friendliness, and efficiency. The three scores are aggregated to give an overall guest score. The accumulation of these guest scores may affect bonuses for everyone at a property—from guest room attendant to inn manager. The use of the guest scores to affect individual bonuses is left to the discretion of inn managers.[30] After purchases of their goods or services, Club Corporation, Hospital Corporation of America, and many other organizations follow up with telephone interviews or Web-based mail questionnaires to obtain feedback from customers.

Financial Controls

Financial controls *include the mechanisms for preventing or correcting the misuse and misallocation of resources, especially monetary resources.*[31] The chief financial officer (CFO) *of a company is the corporate officer primarily responsible for the strategic management of financial risks and controls of a business.*[32] This executive is also responsible for financial planning and record keeping. In recent years, however, the role has expanded to encompass communicating financial performance and forecasts to the analyst community. The CFO typically reports to the chief executive officer, and is frequently a member of the board of directors.

External auditors, usually certified public accounting firms (e.g., Ernst & Young and KPMG) and/or internal auditing departments (e.g., accounting, controller, and treasurer), monitor the effectiveness of financial controls. The primary responsibility of external auditors is to the shareholders. The auditors' role is to assure shareholders that the firm's financial statements present its true financial position and are in conformity with generally accepted accounting principles and the regulatory requirements of government agencies.

Because so many financial control mechanisms exist, we focus on only two of them: comparative financial control and budgeting.

Comparative Financial Control. *Evaluation of a firm's financial condition for two or more time periods is called* comparative financial control. When data are available from similar firms, they are used in making preventive and corrective control comparisons.[33] Industry trade associations often collect information from their members and publish it in summary form. Publicly owned firms publish income statements, balance sheets, and other financial statements. These sources often are used by managers and outsiders to assess changes in the firm's financial indicators and to compare its financial health with that of other firms in the same industry. Companies that have multiple production facilities (e.g., Toyota and Bridgestone/Firestone), retail outlets (e.g., Pier 1 and Target), restaurants (e.g., Taco Bell and Olive Garden), and hotels (e.g., Marriott and Sheraton) compare the financial results among its units for control purposes.

One of the commonly used financial control techniques is ratio analysis. Ratio analysis *typically involves selecting two significant figures (or a combination of a number of figures), expressing their relationship as a fraction or percent, and comparing the value for two or more periods of time.* The comparison of ratios may be within the same organization, over periods of time, with other specific organizations, or with the industry as a whole (such as fast-food industry). Some ratios may be monitored and analyzed on a daily, weekly, monthly, quarterly, and annual basis. There are numerous possible ratios. We present five of the more common ones here[34]:

▶ The return on investment (ROI) ratio *is net profit before tax divided by net worth and is a measure of the efficiency of total assets in generating net profits.* A return on investment ratio of 15 percent means that for every $1 invested in net worth, the firm is generating 15¢ in net profit before tax. It is considered by some as the most important profitability ratio because it indicates how efficiently and effectively the organization is using its resources.

▶ The current ratio *is current assets divided by current liabilities and is a measure of short-term liquidity.* A current ratio of 1.5 means that for every $1 of current

Snapshot

"Our annual budget process has two layers. The first includes the business as usual activities. The business units develop their forecasts based on assumptions that business will continue as usual. The second layer involves budgeting for new initiatives and for areas where we're going to have dramatic changes to existing initiatives."

Sandy King, Vice President and Director, Corporate Reporting & Financial Compliance, Citizens Banking Corporation

liabilities, the firm has $1.50 in current assets with which to pay. It may indicate the organization's ability or inability to pay bills on time.

▶ The debt-to-worth ratio *is total liabilities divided by net worth and is a measure of financial risk.* A debt-to-worth ratio of 2.0 means that for every $1 of net worth the owners have invested, the firm has $2 of debt with its creditors. This ratio aids in assessing the organization's ability to meet its long-term financial commitments.

▶ The sales-to-assets ratio *is sales divided by total assets and is a measure of asset efficiency in generating sales.* A sales-to-assets ratio of 20 means that for every $1 invested in total assets, the firm generates $20 in sales.

▶ The inventory turnover ratio *is cost of goods sold divided by dollar value of inventory and is a measure of internal performance.* An inventory turnover ratio of 12 means that the average dollar volume of inventory is used up 12 times during the fiscal year, or once per month on average.

Financial ratios have little value unless managers know how to interpret them. For example, an ROI of 10 percent doesn't mean much unless it is compared to the ROIs of other organizations, especially those in the same industry. A firm with an ROI of 7 percent in an industry where the average ROI is 12 percent appears to be performing poorly. An inventory turnover rate of 5 per year at Pep Boys, Chief Auto Parts, and other auto-supply stores might be excellent. However, it would be disastrous for Kroger, Safeway, and other large supermarkets for which an inventory turnover rate of 15 per year is common.

Budgetary Control. Budgetary control *is the process of monitoring, comparing, and evaluating actual expenditure levels in various categories in relation to budgeted amounts, and making changes as needed during the budget time period.*[35] Before discussing the control assets of budgets, a few comments on budgeting are needed.

Budgets usually express the dollar costs of various tasks or resources. For example, at Toyota, production budgets may be based on hours of labor per car produced, machine downtime per thousand hours of running time, wage rates, and similar information. The main budget categories usually include labor, supplies and materials, and facilities (property, buildings, and equipment).

Budgeting has three primary purposes: (1) to help in planning work effectively, (2) to assist in allocating resources, and (3) to aid in controlling and monitoring resource utilization during the budget period. When managers assign dollar costs to the resources needed, they sometimes realize that proposed tasks are not worth the cost; they can then modify or abandon the proposals.

Budgeting for completely new tasks usually requires that conditions be forecast and costs estimated. Budgeting for established tasks is easier because historical cost data are available. In either case, those who prepare budgets must exercise judgment about what is likely to happen and how it will affect the organization. Budgets often are developed for a year and then broken down by month. Managers are, thus, able to track progress in meeting a budget as the year unfolds—and to take corrective action as necessary.

The control aspect of budgeting may be either corrective or preventive. When budgeting is used as a corrective control, the emphasis is on identifying the deviations from the budget. Deviations indicate the need to identify and correct their causes or to change the budget itself.

The power of a budget, especially when used as a preventive control, depends on whether it is viewed as an understanding that has been discussed or a club to bludgeon those who do not stay strictly within their budgets.[36] Most managers and employees who must live by budgets accept their use by top management as a control mechanism. Some managers and employees view budgets with fear and hostility. This reaction usually occurs when an organization focuses on budget controls as a means of threat and punishment.[37]

There is no single classification system for budgets. Specific individuals, sections, projects, teams, committees, departments, divisions, or SBUs may be given budgets within which they are expected to operate. The following are common types of budgets used in business:

- *Sales budget*—a forecast of expected revenues, generally stated by product line on a monthly basis and revised at least annually.

- *Materials budget*—expected purchases, generally stated by specific categories, which may vary from month to month because of seasonal variations and inventory levels.

- *Labor budget*—expected staffing and benefits levels, generally stated by number of individuals and dollars for each job category.

- *Capital budget*—targeted spending for major tangible assets (e.g., new or renovated headquarters building, new factory, or major equipment), often requiring a time horizon beyond a year.

- *Research and development budget*—targeted spending for the development or refinement of products, materials, and processes.

- *Cash budget*—expected flow of monetary receipts and expenditures (cash flow), generally developed at least once a year for each month of the year.

The types of budgets and budget categories used are strongly influenced by organizational design and organizational culture. An organization having a functional design usually has a budget for each function (e.g., marketing, production, finance, and human resources). However, an organization having a product design usually has a budget for each product line. For example, Dell Computers has a variety of product lines—servers, notebooks, computers, workstations, switches, desktop PCs, printers, and so on. Product-line budgeting enables Dell's control system to measure the contributions of each product line to sales, costs, and profits.

The Strategic Action Competency feature on the next page reports on how the budgeting process was changed at Western Container Corporation to make it more of a preventive and corrective control process that is embraced throughout the company.[38] Western Container Corporation is a subsidiary of Coca-Cola Enterprises. It is headquartered in Midland, Texas. This firm manufactures low-cost plastic bottles at seven sites in Arizona, California, Mississippi, Texas, and Washington for Coca-Cola bottlers. Dale Hosack joined the Western Corporation as its chief financial officer. We provide his comments on some of the strategic changes made in the budgeting process at Western Container Corporation.

Assigning dollar amounts to the resources needed for a project helps managers realize if the proposed task is worth the cost.

Automation-Based Controls

Automation *involves the use of self-regulating devices and processes that operate independently of people.*[39] Automation usually involves linking machines with other machines to perform tasks. Machine control *utilizes self-regulating instruments or devices to prevent and correct deviations from preset standards.* The use of machines in business has gone

Western Container's Changes to Their Budgeting Process

Dale Hosack, the chief financial officer, reports on the changes in Western Container's budgeting process in these words:

A number of significant changes were made to our budgeting process. The plants got ownership of their budget. Our plant general managers now do their own entry of everything, and they have become budgeting gurus. They're much more effective as far as knowing what they budgeted, how they budgeted. In the past, we were never able to upload a real budget into our general ledger, so the plant general managers always just received a big lump sum for what they were supposed to spend that year.

Our plant in Big Spring, Texas, was over budget in repairs and supplies. The director of operations immediately called up the GM and said, "Hey, you guys are over budget in two months. The way you're spending, you're going to be more than a million dollars over budget this year." The plant leadership put in a whole new system to track and monitor their spending (something they should have already been doing but weren't), and now they're under budget. In the past, they wouldn't have known right away that they went over budget. They would have kept spending that way all year because we didn't have the detail to compare actuals with what they said they were going to do.

The whole budget process has become much better. We have standards, so everything looks exactly the same. We do a lot of comparisons of how plants are spending their money. Because we all look at the numbers the same exact way now, we can compare apples to apples between plants. In the past, we didn't know what we were really comparing. A big portion of our discretionary spending is on repairs and supplies because we have a lot of equipment—so this is an area in which we want to compare different plants. But in the past, what one plant called a repair, another plant might call a supply. So it was hard to say, "Well, you're spending too much on supplies or too much on repairs." Now, with the line-item detail we create in Microsoft Forecaster, we can say, "This is what you're buying." It's not just that supplies are allotted $50,000 a month, but water system supplies are budgeted at $4,000 a month, while individual items for the blow machine get $2,000 a month. We can really see what people are putting behind their budget, versus just the totals.

During the budget review process, we put together a concise document that shows everybody's expenses on a per-thousand-unit basis so that they can say, "OK, here's where we've got to cut." People who are good want to be better and want competition. The budget helps them understand what they're competing with when it comes to cost.

Western Container Corporation is a subsidiary of Coca-Cola Enterprises and does not have its own Web site.

through several significant stages of development. Machines initially increased productivity by giving employees better physical control over certain manufacturing tasks. Eventually, the coordination of employee and machine created a mutual control system. Then a new threshold was reached with automation. Machine control of other machines takes over part of the managerial control function. That is, machines can now participate in the control process with managers. For example, computers in oil refineries collect data, monitor, and make automatic adjustments during refining processes.[40]

A steady shift toward machine control in production operations has occurred. It began with machines being given control of some production tasks, such as when automatic sensors replaced visual inspection in steel production. With the advent of assembly lines and mass-production technology, machines supplemented rules and regulations as a way of directly controlling production workers. In continuous process or robotic operations, machines actually control other machines.

Air Products and Chemicals, Inc., is headquartered in Allentown, Pennsylvania. One of its product lines is gases such as argon, hydrogen, nitrogen, and oxygen. These gases are provided to manufacturers, health-care facilities, and other industries. The company often distributes industrial gases by building on-site plants. At many of these on-site plants, Air Products and Chemicals uses what it calls a *lights-out system*, which is defined as an "unattended operation with remote access." The company no longer needs full-time operators at its many small plants that produce gases fed directly into larger, neighboring factories, such as steel mills and chemical plants. Instead, the company's machines send a signal to alert operators miles away when a motor overheats or a valve sticks. Safety systems automatically shut the plant down if a problem poses imminent danger. An operator working from home and assigned to monitor several plants scattered in his region first will try to fix the problem from a computer at home by sending signals through a telephone line to restart processes, just as the operator would from inside the plant's control room. If that fails, the operator then drives to the site to fix the problem. "We can leverage one individual over a large geography this way," says David Fritz, general manager of North American product supply for Air Products.[41]

Corporate Governance

Explain key corporate governance issues and control mechanisms.

A *corporation is a government-approved form of organization that allows different parties to contribute capital, expertise, and labor for the benefit of all of them.* It is a legal entity separate from the owners, board members, executives, and other employees. Corporations have many other legal features, such as limited liability, but they are beyond the scope of our discussion. Most of the examples throughout this text are from firms organized as corporations.

What Is Corporate Governance?

Corporate governance is the pattern of relations and controls between the stockholders, the board of directors, and the top management of a company.[42] David Richards, president of the Institute of Internal Auditors, sums up the essence of corporate governance this way:

> Corporate governance is all about three words: *expectations, communications* and *accountability.*

> ▶ *Expectations* are set by the organization through policies, procedures, practices and guidelines that essentially say, 'This is what we expect you to do.' Good governance puts in place the kinds of activities, policies and procedures that drive people to do the right kinds of things.

> ▶ *Communication* is about making sure that expectations get communicated throughout the organization, and that there is proper training so that people understand what we mean by, say, 'conflict of interest,' and how that applies to them on their job on a day-to-day basis. If that is not done, the governance of the organization is going to fail.

> ▶ *Accountability* is being able to hold people accountable for meeting the expectations that have been set. You cannot hide under a rock or get away with something when there is an accountability and monitoring process in place.[43]

The relations and controls in corporate governance are set by the corporate charter, bylaws, formal policy, governmental laws and regulations, and the courts.[44] A few of the other terms that are central to corporate governance are defined as follows:

- Annual meeting—*a company gathering, usually held at the end of each fiscal year, at which shareholders and management discuss the previous year and the outlook for the future, directors are elected, and other shareholder concerns are addressed.*

- Annual report—*an audited document issued annually by all publicly listed corporations to their shareholders in accordance with Securities and Exchange Commission regulations and those of other regulatory bodies, as relevant.* Contains information on financial results and overall performance of the previous fiscal year and comments on future outlook.

- Board of directors—*the collective group of individuals elected by the shareholders of a corporation to oversee the management of the corporation.*

- Bylaws—*a document stating the rules of internal governance for a corporation as adopted by its board of directors.*

- Disclosure—*the public dissemination of important market-influencing information.* (Market influencing means that shareholders, government agencies, and others will act and make decisions based on the information provided by the firm.)

- Proxy statement—*a document sent by publicly listed corporations to their shareholders that provides material information on corporate matters subject to vote at the general shareholders' meeting.*[45]

Corporate governance includes a wide variety of issues and activities, such as (1) strategic and business planning, (2) risk management associated with major capital investments and the purchase of another firm or sale of a company/division, (3) performance assessment of the top executive and the firm as a whole, (4) compensation and benefits paid to executives and higher level managers, (5) CEO/management succession and appointment, (6) disclosure and reporting to stockholders and government agencies, (7) corporate values and corporate culture, (8) independent inputs from members of the board of directors, and (9) organization design.[46]

As suggested in our opening Challenge of Managing feature related to PepsiCo, many complex issues and activities fall under the umbrella of corporate governance. Our focus in this section is to provide a snapshot of the control aspects of corporate governance, as these relate to top executives and boards of directors. The control aspects of corporate governance include *external* and *internal* mechanisms.[47]

A few of the external control mechanisms include (1) laws and regulatory agencies, (2) the possibility of being acquired by other firms, (3) proxy statements in which stockholders vote on issues of interest to top executives, and (4) the possibility of being sued in the courts by stockholders or other stakeholders. A few of the internal control mechanisms include boards of directors, compensation contracts that attempt to align the interests of top executives with those of stockholders, and corporate bylaws that set ground rules for the responsibilities of top executives and board members. In the remainder of this section, we highlight several aspects of *external* and *internal* governance that apply particularly to publicly traded corporations in which there is a separation between the ownership and management of the firm. When a single individual or small set of individuals owns a firm, the issues of corporate governance are much less complex and problematic.

External Control: Sarbanes-Oxley Act

A variety of external control mechanisms are used in corporate governance. One of these mechanisms is enacted through the provisions of the Sarbanes-Oxley Act, which was passed by the U.S. Congress and signed by the president in 2002. This legislation, which is 66 pages in length, was prompted by the corporate scandals related to the extreme self-serving actions of some corporate executives (e.g., Enron, Tyco, Adelphia) and the lack of monitoring and control by some boards of directors. Many of the provisions of this act focus on defining the responsibilities of top executives and boards of directors to stockholders and the public at large. The act also defines the penalties for the failure to fulfill these responsibilities. In brief, executives and boards are required to be better agents or representatives of the interests of stockholders and the public.[48]

General Provisions. The act, which is named after its primary architects, Senator Paul Sarbanes (D-Maryland) and Representative Michael Oxley (R-Ohio), is organized into 11 sections. These sections deal with such issues as auditor independence, corporate responsibility, enhanced financial disclosures, conflicts of interest, and corporate accountability. The act also establishes a public company accounting oversight board.

The requirements of Sarbanes-Oxley may be divided into three categories: *certification*, *auditability*, and *disclosure*. Perhaps the best known provisions concern top management. It requires CEOs and CFOs (chief financial officers) of publicly traded companies to *certify* financial statements. Those who knowingly certify falsely are liable for criminal and civil penalties. This certification is the CEO's and CFO's personal guarantee that valid financial/accounting processes have been established to ensure the proper flow of financial disclosure.

The second mandate, *auditability*, requires companies to develop and publish internal processes so that outsiders can confirm the existence of appropriate controls. Finally, under the act's *disclosure* mandates, companies must report financial results and material changes in corporate financial condition or operations "on a rapid and current basis."

Accuracy and visibility are the two touchstones of Sarbanes-Oxley. *Accuracy* refers to the quality of the financial information a company reports to the public. *Visibility* means that the internal information processes that make accuracy possible must be transparent.[49]

The U.S. Securities and Exchange Commission (SEC) has been charged with developing detailed rules and regulations to implement this legislation. This includes the establishment of a five-member Public Company Accounting Oversight Board. The purpose of this board is to oversee the audit of public companies to protect the interests of investors and further the public interest in the preparation of informative, accurate, and independent audit reports.[50]

Criminal Accountability. Criminal penalties for destroying, concealing, covering up, or falsifying records or documents may result in individual fines, imprisonment up to 20 years, or both. Fines against individual corporate officers can reach up to $5 million. These potential penalties are intended to serve as a strong preventive control mechanism to increase the likelihood of full compliance by corporate executives with the provisions of this act. If they fail as a preventive control, the penalties applied to those convicted of wrongdoing are intended to serve as a form of corrective control.

Whistle-Blower Protection. The Sarbanes-Oxley Act also protects employees of publicly traded companies who provide evidence of fraud on any rule or regulation of the SEC. The act has a number of provisions

© Michael Rowe/DK Stock/Getty Images

Whistle-blowers can be protected under federal law, but there are grey areas for interpreting that law.

that serve to protect whistle-blowers from retaliation or harm. For example, an employee who provides information regarding a possible violation of this legislation or a regulation of the SEC may not be dismissed, demoted, suspended, threatened, harassed, or in any other manner discriminated against in the terms and conditions of employment. An employee who is so discriminated against may seek relief through the Secretary of Labor or through the appropriate U.S. district court. Relief may include (1) the amount of back pay with interest; (2) reinstatement with the same status; (3) compensation for litigation costs, expert witness fees, and reasonable attorney fees; and (4) compensation for any other special damages.

Although the ethical foundation for whistle-blower protection in the act may seem obvious, the legal interpretations that have followed its implementation are anything but clear-cut. In the following Ethical Challenge feature, we present one issue related to the diverse administrative law judges' interpretations of this act and the federal Department of Labor regulations that implement it.[51]

Ethical Challenge

Interpretations of Whistle-Blower Protection

The case law on corporate whistle-blowing to date is very mixed on several key issues, including which employees are covered, whether the law applies to subsidiaries of U.S. corporations located in other countries, what constitutes whistle-blowing, and what constitutes retaliation. We briefly address one of these issues here.

Administrative law judges (ALJs), who hear cases of discrimination or retaliation at the Department of Labor, are all over the map as to whether employees of subsidiaries of publicly traded companies are protected. Some ALJs (and one court) appear to find employees of a subsidiary to be covered *per se* if the parent is publicly traded. For instance, one ALJ explained that "A publicly traded corporation is, for Sarbanes-Oxley purposes, the sum of its constituent units." In another case, the ALJ summarily considered the parent company and subsidiary sufficiently connected without discussing their relationship.

At the opposite end of the spectrum, other ALJs have required a showing of facts sufficient to "pierce the corporate veil." For instance, one ALJ dismissed a claim because the complainant failed to name a publicly traded company and the ALJ found no indication that the parent companies were sufficiently involved in the management and employment relations of the subsidiary to justify piercing the corporate veil.

If the standard for protection and liability is defined by reference to corporate law principles of "piercing the corporate veil," the effect may be to bar a large proportion of whistle-blower claims. Corporations often operate through subsidiaries and take care to observe the corporate formalities—precisely in order to insulate other entities in the corporate structure from legal claims and liabilities. As a result, persons seeking to pierce the veil typically have substantial hurdles to overcome.

What ethical justification might these administrative law judges offer *for* or *against* including employees of subsidiaries under this legislation and related regulations? What ethical justifications might executives offer for claiming that employees of their subsidiaries should not be included under whistle-blower protection that holds the corporation liable?

To learn more about whistle-blower protection under the Sarbanes-Oxley Act, visit *www.whistleblowers.org/html/sarbanes-oxley.htm*.

Internal Control: Boards of Directors

Boards of directors are elected by stockholders. They are expected to act in the owners' interests by monitoring and controlling the top-level executives. Many proposals and new requirements have been created to increase the accountability of boards of directors, especially in relation to their control role of top executives. Let's consider a few that may serve as an effective source of internal control.[52]

Independent Directors. The board should be composed of a substantial majority of independent directors. *Independence* means the director is not currently or formerly employed by the company, nor does the director have any significant financial or personal tie to the company or its management that could compromise the director's objectivity and loyalty to the shareholders. The board's three major committees—audit, compensation, and nominating and/or governance committees—should consist entirely of independent directors. All monetary arrangements with directors for services outside normal board activities should be approved by a committee of the board that is composed of independent directors and should be reported in the proxy statement.

Boards of directors are elected by stockholders. They are expected to monitor and control top level executives.

Self-Assessment. The board should have ways to evaluate and improve its ability to represent the shareholders. At a minimum, there should be an annual review by the board of its overall performance, including the effectiveness of its committees. These committees should be evaluated against criteria defined in committee bylaws. The board should hold periodic executive sessions during which management, including the CEO, is not present.

Executive Compensation. Control of the executive compensation process is critically important. In one sense, it represents a window through which the effectiveness of the board may be viewed by shareholders and the public. The board should ensure that a fair compensation program is in place. Conversely, weak compensation practices—clearly excessive pay, unfairly enriching stock plans, or loose and subjective bonus awards for top executives—are likely to suggest a weak board. The board should ensure that the company describes clearly its overall compensation philosophy in the proxy statement to shareholders. It also should explain the rationale for the salary levels, incentive payments, and stock options granted to top executive officers.

Evaluation of CEO. Ensuring continuity of top-level leadership is also a primary responsibility of the board of directors. Accordingly, the evaluation of a corporation's chief executive officer is critical. A clear understanding between the board and the CEO regarding the expected performance and how that performance will be measured is essential. The board should establish a specific set of performance goals with the CEO annually. These should include concerns of shareholders, other investors, employees, customers, and the communities in which the company operates. Performance goals should include both annual and multiyear time periods. The board should establish an annual review process that incorporates CEO performance evaluation in executive session.

Resource Allocation. Every company needs to plan strategically to ensure future economic success. The strategic allocation of corporate resources to each of the company's businesses is critical to its future success and to the increased shareholder value needed for efficient capital formation. The board should discuss and evaluate the strategic plan of each of the company's major businesses at least annually.

Fiduciary Responsibility and Control. The board has a primary duty to exercise its fiduciary responsibility and control in the best interests of the corporation and its shareholders. This includes periodic review to ensure that corporate resources are used only for appropriate business purposes. To address some of the most important areas of fiduciary responsibility, the board should do the following:

Snapshot

"Board members must combine judgment, integrity and courage. They should be people who do speak up and won't back down if they don't get the answers to their questions. . . . After Enron, directors sat straighter in their chairs and the audit committee had an incentive to look at the work papers. This meant longer meetings, more substantive meetings, and audit committees that were more vigilant. There was more care in the boardroom."

Barbara Hackman Franklin, Member, Board of Directors, Dow Chemical Co., GenVec, Inc., MedImmune, Inc., and Washington Mutual Investor Fund

▶ Ensure a corporate environment of strong internal controls, fiscal accountability, high ethical standards, and compliance with all applicable laws and regulations.

▶ Develop appropriate procedures to ensure the board is advised on a timely basis of alleged or suspected violations of corporate standards of noncompliance and how management handled these violations.

▶ Appoint an audit committee of at least three independent directors, all of whom have financial expertise. This is now required by rules of the New York Stock Exchange and the National Association of Securities Dealers. The audit committee should develop its statement of responsibilities and publish it in the company's proxy statement. The audit committee has both the authority and the responsibility to (1) select and evaluate the outside auditor and ensure its independence, (2) review quarterly and annual audit statements, and (3) assess the adequacy of internal controls and internal risk management processes.

▶ Install a mechanism to review corporate operating and expense reimbursement policies and practices (e.g., travel and entertainment policy, executive perquisites) to ensure proper use of corporate resources.

We opened this chapter with a discussion of PepsiCo's corporate governance and followed it with a Planning and Administration Competency feature on PepsiCo's control policy related to business gifts and features. We conclude the text portion of the chapter with a Strategic Action Competency feature on a portion of PepsiCo's corporate governance principles (guidelines) for its board of directors.[53] You will note how these guidelines mirror many of the proposals and requirements just discussed for effective boards of directors. You will recall that PepsiCo was a recent recipient of the Alexander Hamilton Corporate Governance Award and was recently recognized by *Fortune Magazine* as one of the best run companies in the world.[54]

Strategic Action Competency

Corporate Governance Guidelines for PepsiCo's Board

The Board of Directors (the "Board") of PepsiCo, Inc. (the "Corporation"), acting on the recommendation of its Nominating and Corporate Governance Committee, has developed and adopted certain corporate governance principles (the "Guidelines") establishing a common set of expectations to assist the Board and its committees in performing their duties in compliance with applicable requirements. In recognition of the continuing discussions about corporate governance, the Board will review and, if appropriate, revise these Guidelines from time to time.

▶ Director Responsibilities
1. Represent the interests of the Corporation's shareholders in maintaining and enhancing the success of the Corporation's business, including optimiz-

ing long-term returns to increase shareholder value.

2. Selection and evaluation of a well-qualified Chief Executive Officer ("CEO") of high integrity, and approval of other members of the senior management team.

3. Oversee and interact with senior management with respect to key aspects of the business including strategic planning, management development and succession, operating performance, and shareholder returns.

4. Provide general advice and counsel to the Corporation's CEO and senior executives.

5. Adopt and oversee compliance with the Corporation's Worldwide Code of Conduct. Promptly disclose any waivers of the Code of Conduct for Directors or executive officers.

6. Hold regularly scheduled executive sessions of independent directors. Designate and publicly disclose the name of the Director who will preside at such meetings. Formally evaluate the performance of the CEO and senior management each year in executive sessions.

7. Regular attendance at Board meetings is mandatory. Meeting materials should be reviewed in advance.

8. Duty of Care: In discharging the duties of a Director, including duties as a Committee member, the state law where PepsiCo is incorporated requires that a Director shall act: (1) in good faith; (2) with care an ordinary prudent person in a like position would exercise under similar circumstances and (3) in a manner he or she believes to be in the best interests of the Corporation.

The other major sections of the corporate governance guidelines for the board of directors address the following:

▶ Director qualification standards

▶ Board committees

▶ Director compensation

▶ Director access to management and independent advisers (For example, a portion of this section indicates that directors are granted access to the name, location, and phone number of all employees of the corporation.)

▶ Director orientation and continuing education (For example, a portion of this section states: "Directors are required to continue educating themselves with respect to international markets, accounting and finance, leadership, crisis response, industry practices, general management, and strategic planning.")

▶ Management succession and CEO compensation

▶ Annual performance evaluation of the board

To learn more about this organization, visit *www.pepsico.com.*

Chapter Summary ....

In this chapter, we examined how organizations use various controls to achieve their goals and strategies. We considered the basic foundations of control. Next, we looked at a corrective control model and detailed the steps involved in its use. We then discussed primary types of financial and nonfinancial controls. We concluded with a discussion of corporate governance with the primary emphasis on selected external and internal control mechanisms.

Learning Goals

1. Explain the foundations of control.

The foundations of organizational control are (1) the type of control, (2) the source of control, (3) the pattern of control, (4) the purpose of control, (5) linkage of controls to strategic goals, and (6) the costs versus benefits of organizational controls. Preventive controls, such as rules, standards, and training programs, are designed to reduce the number and severity of deviations that require corrective action. In contrast, corrective controls are designed to bring unwanted results and behaviors in line with established standards or goals. The four sources of organizational control are stakeholders, the organization itself, groups, and individuals. Patterns of the different kinds of control vary from mutually reinforcing to independently operating to conflicting.

2. Identify the six phases of the corrective control model.

The corrective control model comprises six interconnected phases: (1) define the subsystem, (2) identify the characteristics to be measured, (3) set standards, (4) collect information, (5) make comparisons, and (6) diagnose and correct any problems.

3. Describe the primary methods of organizational control.

The primary methods of organizational control are (1) mechanistic, (2) organic, (3) market, (4) financial, and (5) automation-based controls. Effective managerial control usually requires using multiple methods of control in combination.

4. Explain key corporate governance issues and control mechanisms.

Corporate governance focuses on the system of relations and controls between the stockholders, the board of directors, and the top management of a company. A wide variety of issues and activities are often included in corporate governance. A few of the internal and external control mechanisms, especially those related to the control of top executives, were noted. Key provisions of the Sarbanes-Oxley Act of 2002, which created new external controls, were discussed. The board of directors was discussed as a key source of internal control on top executives. Some of the key characteristics of effective boards were reviewed.

Key Terms and Concepts

Annual meeting	Corrective controls	Organic controls
Annual report	Current ratio	Organizational controls
Automation	Customer monitoring	Preventive controls
Board of directors	Debt-to-worth ratio	Principle of selectivity
Budgetary control	Disclosure	Profit sharing
Bylaws	Financial controls	Proxy statement
Chief financial officer (CFO)	Group controls	Ratio analysis
Comparative financial control	Incentive compensation	Return on investment (ROI) ratio
Control	Individual self-controls	Sales-to-assets ratio
Corporate governance	Internal control	Stakeholder controls
Corporation	Inventory turnover ratio	Standards
Corrective control model	Machine control	
	Market controls	
	Mechanistic controls	

Questions for Discussion and Reflective Thinking ....

1. We presented some of the specific mechanisms that serve as controls at PepsiCo in the Challenge of Managing feature and elsewhere in the chapter. Go to PepsiCo's Web site at *www.pepsico.com*. Click on "Careers" and then click on "taste the success." What does this presentation reveal about methods of control at Pepsico?

2. Do you think shareholders have too much corporate governance control relative to other stakeholder groups? Explain.

3. One of the features on an effective control system is objective formal controls. Why is it so difficult, if not impossible, to establish totally objective controls as seen through the eyes of all stakeholders?

4. Evaluate PepsiCo's formal controls related to business gifts and payments in terms of the criteria for effective controls, including *objective*, *complete*, *timely*, and *acceptable*.

5. Give three examples of organizational control in an organization in which you have worked or are now working. Within the same organization, give three examples of group and/or individual self-control that were/are present.

6. Based on the examples presented in Question 5, did any of these sources of control reinforce or conflict with one another? Explain.

7. Based on the cost–benefit perspective, did the organization you identified in Question 5 have too much, too little, or ineffective control mechanisms? Explain.

8. Review the mechanistic and organic control methods in Table 10.2. Based on the organization you identified in Question 5, what was its relative emphasis on mechanistic versus organic control methods? Do you think that relative emphasis was effective? Explain.

9. Think of an experience in which you were highly dissatisfied and complained as a customer. What control mechanisms were used in dealing with your complaint? Was your complaint resolved to your satisfaction?

10. Issues of corporate governance are often in the business and general news because of the revelations about extreme self-serving interests by some top executives at the expense of stockholders and other stakeholders. How can boards of directors do more to control and reduce such self-serving? Explain.

DEVELOPING YOUR COMPETENCIES

Introduction

The company's annual meeting provides its shareholders an opportunity to ask questions of management and the board. This instrument presents a variety of questions related to corporate governance. For each question, you should indicate if it is acceptable to ask the question and to expect to get an answer at the annual shareholders meeting. Circle "Yes" or "No" if each question is acceptable and should be acceptable to ask.

Questions

Overall Governance

	Acceptable	Should Expect an Answer
1. Is the board of directors' membership and practices compliant with the Sarbanes-Oxley Act and the NYSE and NASDAQ governance rules?	Yes No	Yes No
2. Does the board have a written statement of its own governance principles that it reevaluates on a regular basis?	Yes No	Yes No
3. Does the board have a committee responsible for overall board governance, including compensation, size, composition, and performance?	Yes No	Yes No
4. How do the company's governance practices compare with best practices recommended by groups such as the National Association of Corporate Directors, the Business Roundtable, and the Commission on Public Trust and Private Enterprise?	Yes No	Yes No
5. Do the company's code of conduct and conflict-of-interest policies for officers and employees also cover outside directors?	Yes No	Yes No

Size, Composition, Qualifications

6. Has the board reevaluated whether its members have the right set of qualifications?	Yes No	Yes No
7. What initiatives has the company taken to promote diversity within the board and executive management?	Yes No	Yes No
8. Does the company's former CEO serve on the board of directors?	Yes No	Yes No
9. How much training do board members receive annually to help them meet their responsibilities?	Yes No	Yes No
10. Have any directors sold company stock during the past year?	Yes No	Yes No
11. Does the board have a policy of rotating directors through committees?	Yes No	Yes No

Recruitment

12. Does the company have a committee of independent directors for nominating candidates for board membership?	Yes No	Yes No
13. What qualifications are required for prospective board members?	Yes No	Yes No
14. How does the committee ensure that those nominated represent the interests of all shareholders?	Yes No	Yes No

Independence, Conflicts of Interest

15. Does the company plan to add more outside directors and/or reduce the number of management or inside directors?   Yes No   Yes No

16. Why are members of management also on the board of directors?   Yes No   Yes No

17. Is *independence* defined?   Yes No   Yes No

18. Are any of the company's outside attorneys also officers, directors, or shareholders of the company?   Yes No   Yes No

19. Are any major lenders represented on the board?   Yes No   Yes No

20. Does any director have a potential conflict of interest because of membership on another board?   Yes No   Yes No

21. Does the company require directors and officers to submit conflict-of-interest statements?   Yes No   Yes No

22. Do the nonmanagement directors meet in regularly scheduled sessions without management?   Yes No   Yes No

Compensation

23. Do directors receive their fees if they do not attend meetings?   Yes No   Yes No

24. Does the company grant stock options to directors?   Yes No   Yes No

25. Does the company provide pension benefits or life or health insurance for directors?   Yes No   Yes No

26. Does the company have a compensation committee composed entirely of independent directors?   Yes No   Yes No

Meetings and Attendance

27. Did the board of directors meet this year?   Yes No   Yes No

28. Did all board members attend?   Yes No   Yes No

Board of Directors—Other

29. Does the board monitor significant business transactions and arrangements?   Yes No   Yes No

30. Does the company have a policy on the number of outside boards its directors can be on?   Yes No   Yes No

31. Do the CEO and other senior executives of the company serve on the boards of other companies?   Yes No   Yes No

32. Does the company have a policy on the number of outside boards its senior executives can be on?   Yes No   Yes No

33. Does the board understand and discuss the major risks the company faces?   Yes No   Yes No

34. Have there been disagreements between inside and outside directors?   Yes No   Yes No

35. Does the full board meet separately with the external auditors?   Yes No   Yes No

Internal Control

36. Does management establish an appropriate "tone at the top" regarding its commitment to internal control?   Yes No   Yes No

37. Does management assess the adequacy of internal control?   Yes No   Yes No

38. Does the audit committee monitor the company's internal control?   Yes No   Yes No

39. Is there an ongoing self-assessment program to review and revise internal control as the company's operations change?   Yes No   Yes No

40. Does the company's reporting system provide appropriate information for timely identification of potential major financial or operational difficulties?   Yes No   Yes No

41. Does the audit committee receive the same comments on internal control from the auditors as management receives?   Yes No   Yes No

Fraud and Illegal Acts

42. Does the company have a fraud prevention and detection program?   Yes No   Yes No

43.	Are there adequate controls to protect the company's technology, trade secrets, and other sensitive records?	Yes No	Yes No
44.	Are internal control policies and procedures adequate to identify potential errors, fraud, or illegal acts?	Yes No	Yes No
45.	Does the audit committee have a process to focus specifically on the risk of fraud?	Yes No	Yes No
46.	Was any fraud or illegal act reported to the audit committee during the year through the whistle-blowing process or otherwise?	Yes No	Yes No
47.	Were any violations of insider trading rules identified this year?	Yes No	Yes No
48.	Does the company have policies and procedures for voluntarily reporting violations of federal procurement laws to appropriate governmental agencies?	Yes No	Yes No

External Auditors

49.	Do the external auditors meet with the audit committee?	Yes No	Yes No
50.	Does the audit committee review the scope of external audit activities in advance?	Yes No	Yes No
51.	Does the audit committee take steps to oversee the independence of the external auditors?	Yes No	Yes No
52.	Do the external auditors have any relationships with management or the board of directors that may be viewed as a conflict of interest?	Yes No	Yes No
53.	Did any members of management come from the external audit firm?	Yes No	Yes No
54.	Have any offers of employment been made to members of the current audit engagement team?	Yes No	Yes No
55.	What nonaudit services were provided by the external auditors?	Yes No	Yes No

Interpretation. Add up your replies and insert below. Each "Yes" or "No" is worth one point.

Acceptable	Should Expect an Answer
_____Yes; _____No	_____Yes; _____No

Questions

1. Is it considered acceptable to ask all of the questions, and many others, at the annual shareholders' meeting?

2. If you thought any of the questions should not be acceptable, what was your reasoning for thinking so?

3. Compare your scores to others in the class. What does this show you about the role of shareholders in corporate governance?

"You can't keep us here like this!"

"Yes, I can; no one is leaving this room until we find out where the missing money is."

Over two hours had passed since the three front office employees who also served as cashiers had been ordered by their supervisor to meet in one of the hotel's guest rooms at the end of their shift. Everyone was beginning to show the strain of continuously discussing the missing $200 and no one seemed to have any clues as to where it was or if it was really missing.

None of them were more frustrated than the front office manager, Chad Reynolds. During the past three weeks, the cash drawer shared by all three employees when they worked the same shift had been short by exactly $100 on four different occasions. They had counted and recounted the cash on each occasion and verified that the drawer was short by exactly $100. The drawer didn't always balance, but to be short by $200 on this shift after the other round number shortages was simply not a coincidence as far as Chad was concerned.

Although they had all worked together for almost seven months with no problems until recently, he was sure one of them was stealing the money and he was determined to identify the culprit! Acting on instincts without consulting anyone else, he ordered all three employees who worked the shift in question to meet him in an unoccupied fifth floor room. He laid out the facts as he knew them, telling them that as far as he was concerned the only answer for the shortage was theft by one of them.

Multiple explanations were offered ranging from someone other than the employees working behind the front desk gaining access to the cash drawer to the possibility of mistakes in making change at the busy front desk. After all, cash transactions at this 300-room luxury hotel often topped $5,000 during their busy morning shift where they shared check-in and check-out responsibilities. No one in the room could account for the missing money, and each one of them vehemently denied any wrongdoing. In exasperation, one of the employees even suggested taking a polygraph test, and they all chimed in that this sounded like a good way to clear up the matter.

Chad was beginning to second-guess himself. Maybe it was because he had been watching too many legal shows on television that the questions started swirling in his mind. Perhaps his instincts had been wrong and he should let them leave. Had he made the right decision by ordering everyone up to the room and accusing one or all of them of stealing the money? What if he had made a mistake and no one in the room had taken the money? Had he been within his rights to keep them confined so long? What should he do now?

Questions

1. What problems are evident in the internal control procedures in this situation?

2. What recommendations for better internal controls would you make?

3. Do you think Chad has created ethical problems by his actions? Explain.

4. If Chad were concerned that he might have placed either himself and/or the hotel in legal jeopardy, what steps could he or one of his superiors take to protect themselves and the hotel from potential legal problems?

PART 4
Organizing

chapter 11

© Digital Vision/Getty Images

Designing Organizations

Learning Goals

After studying this chapter, you should be able to:

1. Explain the two fundamental principles of designing organizations.

2. State the major concepts of vertical organizational design.

3. Describe four types of horizontal organizational design.

4. Describe the major options for achieving organizational integration.

Communication Competency

Planning and Administration Competency

Teamwork Competency

Managing Effectively

Self-Management Competency

Strategic Action Competency

Multicultural Competency

Challenge of Managing ....

Lowe's Companies

© Justin Sullivan/Getty Images

In 1946, Carl Buchan transformed North Wilkesboro Hardware into Lowe's by eliminating some general merchandise lines and concentrating on hardware and building materials. By the mid-1950s, the stores had grown and the slogan "Lowe's Low Prices" was adopted. The single store had expanded into a chain of 15 stores by 1960, operating primarily in North Carolina, Tennessee, and West Virginia, and selling lumber, tools, and hardware to contractors in these three states. Today, Lowe's Companies has evolved to become a nationwide chain of home improvement stores with more than 185,000 employees and revenues of more than $43 billion. More than 12 million customers a week visit its 1,250 stores.

In 1980 when housing starts fell, company profits dropped sharply. At the same time, Home Depot introduced its low-price warehouse concept. To survive, Lowe's changed its stores' layouts. By 1982, half of the stores had been redesigned to be more oriented toward the do-it-yourself consumer. These new store designs featured softer lighting and displays of entire room layouts to appeal to women. This was a significant shift away from its traditional contractor-oriented store, but the shift was needed to offset the ups and downs caused by swings in housing starts.

Today, Home Depot is the leader in number of stores (2,000) and sales ($82 billion) and Lowe's is number 2 with 1,250 stores. Lowe's has stores in 49 states and has announced plans to build 6 to 10 stores in the Toronto, Canada, area during 2007 and operate 90 more throughout Canada in the future. The company's stores sells about 40,000 products for do-it-yourselfers and professional contractors in the business of making home improvements and doing repair projects. Lowe's also offers name-brand appliances (for which the company holds a 13 percent share of the market) and furniture. Although Home Depot also sells these products, Lowe's sells more washers, dryers, refrigerators, stoves, and dishwashers than Home Depot.

At the beginning, Lowe's focused on small and medium-sized markets. Now Lowe's is expanding into metropolitan markets with populations of 500,000 or more. But the company is not forgetting its roots and plans to open half of its 150 new stores in rural markets to serve farmers and small business owners. To improve its geographic presence, Lowe's purchased a 38-store chain, Eagle Hardware and Garden. To supply all of these stores, Lowe's is expanding its distribution network. Recently, Lowe's spent $2.4

Learning Content

billion on building new warehouses in Oregon, Georgia, Indiana, Missouri, and North Carolina.

Lowe's is also trying to take advantage of major trends, three of which relate to its organization design and its vision and mission as we discussed in Chapter 7. First, Lowe's is putting an emphasis on installation services in more than 40 categories, such as flooring, cabinets, and appliances. Lowe's second goal is trying to appeal to urban customers. In 2004, Lowe's opened its first urban store, with a focus on the needs of city dwellers and building superintendents, in Brooklyn, New York. This is consistent with its market development strategy. Third, to keep the professional home builder as a customer, Lowe's entered into a joint venture to sell an exclusive line of Kobalt-brand professional mechanics' tools produced by Snap-on. Finally Lowe's wants to attract more baby boomers who want less hassle, one-stop shopping, and someone they can trust to help with home improvement projects. Baby boomers don't like to waste time shopping and appreciate convenience, trust, and technology.[1]

To learn more about this organization, visit *www.lowes.com.*

Most of you have probably visited a Lowe's store. The information in the Challenge of Managing feature provides some insights into Lowe's successes and plans for the future. While it does not go into every problem facing Robert Niblock, the CEO of Lowe's, the case does highlight the important issues that we will cover in this chapter. In Chapter 7, we indicated that the strategy of an organization has a major influence on how an organization is structured.[2] Niblock and his top management teams at Lowe's are working hard to make certain that low-cost strategy and structure are aligned with each other.

In Chapter 1, we defined *organizing* as the process of creating a structure of jobs that enables employees to implement management's goals and plans. Organizing was presented as one of the four general managerial functions, the others being planning, controlling, and leading. The process by which management forms jobs and relationships is termed **organization design**, *which means quite simply the decisions and actions that result in a structure.*[3] Organizations use various organization designs to help them achieve their purpose and goals. Nearly every firm has undergone some organization design changes to meet the challenges it faces. These changes are needed to reflect new strategies or respond to competitors. In fact, the existence of structure is most visible in the familiar organization chart, but it is somewhat like the tip of an iceberg. Figure 11.1 shows the vertical and horizontal organization designs of Lowe's.

Fundamentals of Organizing

1.

Explain the two fundamental principles of designing organizations.

Managers often describe the structure of their organization by looking at its organization chart. The concept of an organization chart has been around for centuries. The **organization chart** *is a diagram that illustrates the reporting lines between units and people within the organization.* We use the term *units* to refer to teams, groups, departments, or divisions. Basically, the organization chart is the skeleton of an organization. Figure 11.1 shows the general organization of Lowe's. This figure shows that the CEO has five executive vice presidents reporting to him. Note that the chart conveys four kinds of information:

1. The boxes represent different units (marketing, human resources).
2. The titles in each box show the work performed by that person.
3. Reporting relationships are shown by the lines connecting superiors and subordinates.

Figure 11.1 | **Organization Chart for Lowe's**

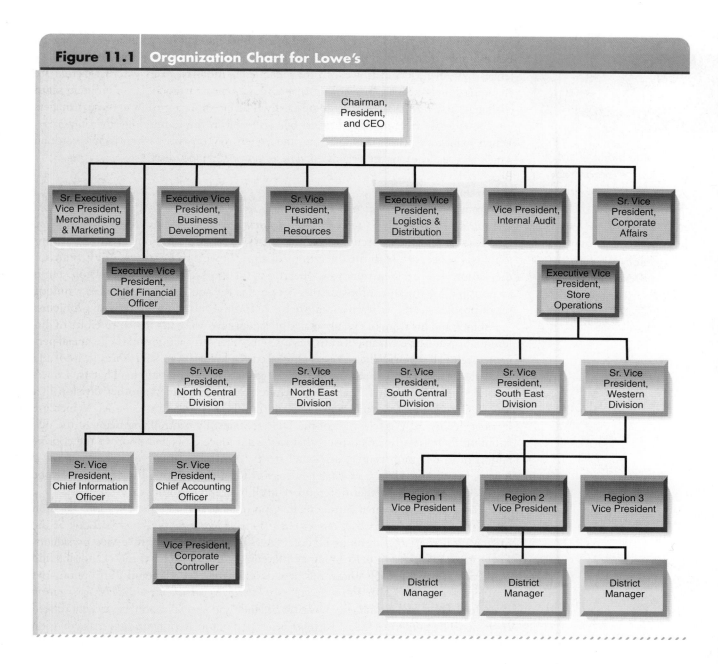

4. Levels of the organization are indicated by the number of vertical layers in the chart.

In this chart, we show four levels at Lowe's. For example, all five senior vice presidents of the various divisions (North Central, North East, South Central, South East, and Western) report to the executive vice president of store operations, who in turn reports to the chairman, president, and CEO. Store managers in various regions report to their respective district manager, who in turn reports to the regional vice presidents, who report to the divisional senior vice presidents.

An organization chart provides several benefits. First, it gives some insight into how the entire organization fits together. That is, it indicates how the various positions relate to the whole organization. Thus everyone presumably knows who reports to whom and where to go with a particular problem. Second, the chart may indicate gaps or duplication of activities. A limitation of the chart is that it's just a picture and doesn't show how things really get done in the organization. For example, it cannot highlight what function has the most or least amount of political clout or how information flows between functional areas.

"I've often thought that after you get organized, you ought to throw away the organization chart. It really doesn't show who has the power and how things really work."

David Packard, Cofounder, Hewlett-Packard

In Chapters 4, 5, and 7, we illustrated many different environments facing managers. For example, managers in the rapidly changing video game industry face different challenges than managers at Lowe's. In the video game industry, many external factors are changing simultaneously. Similarly, managers at Google and Yahoo! face a different set of challenges in China than they do domestically. The question confronting these managers is: "How do we organize our firm to be successful in these differing environments?" When managers answer this question, they often rely on two basic principles around which all organizations are organized: *differentiation* and *integration*.[4]

Differentiation

Differentiation *means that the organization is composed of units that work on specialized tasks using different work methods and requiring employees with unique competencies.* Charles Canter is the executive vice president for store operations at Lowe's. In his job, he is concerned with the operations of all of Lowe's 1,250 stores. Bill Edwards is the senior vice president for store operations for the North Central Division. He is responsible for the operations of all stores in his region. Each person faces a unique set of problems, and each will organize his unit differently to handle these problems.

Niblock and his team of executive vice presidents are using the basic principles of differentiation at Lowe's in an effort to increase customer satisfaction and the financial performance of all stores. When Lowe's purchased Eagle Hardware's 38 stores in 1999 and converted these stores into Lowe's, it was an act of differentiation. That is, Lowe's expanded into the Western part of the United States and added another division that reported to Canter. By combining and acquiring these stores, Lowe's hoped to increase its presence in the Western part of the United States. By centralizing many of the distribution functions, Lowe's expects that this will reduce costs and improve the coordination of distribution centers across all stores. Another example of differentiation is Lowe's recent move into Canada, a new market for Lowe's. If this decision proves to be a success, Lowe's will further differentiate itself by adding another division.

Differentiation is created through a division of labor and job specialization. Division of labor *means that the work of the organization is divided into smaller tasks.* Look at the organization chart of Lowe's in Figure 11.1. There are five executive vice presidents. Each one is in charge of performing a different set of tasks, such as merchandising and marketing, chief financial officer, business development, logistics and distribution, and store operations. Specialization *is the process of identifying particular tasks and assigning them to departments, teams, or divisions.* Division of labor and specialization are closely related concepts. The numerous tasks that must be carried out in an organization make division of labor and specialization necessary. Otherwise, the complexity of running the entire organization would be too great for any one person.

Integration

Integration *means that the various units coordinate their work to achieve common goals.* Rules and procedures are one means used by managers to coordinate the ongoing activities of an organization's various units. If departments have common goals, are organized similarly, and work together to achieve the organization's goals, the organization is highly integrated.

As organizations differentiate their designs, managers are also concerned with issues of integration. An organization is more than the sum of its parts; it is an integration of its parts. Because different units are part of the larger organization, some degree of coordination is needed among them for an organization to be effective. When Lowe's grew during the mid-1990s, for example, merchandising decisions were made by various regional presidents. With Home Depot, TrueValue, Ace Hardware, and other organizations entering the market, senior management recognized that

Lowe's needed to become more efficient in its merchandising function. Therefore, they coordinated all merchandising decisions at Lowe's headquarters and put a senior executive vice president in charge of this function.

Now that we have introduced you to the two basic principles of organizing, we will discuss the vertical structure of an organization. In one sense, an organization's vertical structure acts as a "harness" to guide employees' decision-making activities.

There are few hard and fast rules for designing or redesigning an organization. An organization's vertical structure is often the result of many decisions and its past. It may reflect political biases, the preferences of powerful external stakeholders, and historical circumstances.

Vertical Design

An organization's design should ease the communication among employees and departments to accomplish the goals of the organization. That is, employees at lower levels should carry out activities consistent with senior managers' goals, and senior managers need to be informed about the activities and accomplishments of lower level employees. Organizations may use any one of five ways to achieve these results.

2.
State the major concepts of vertical organizational design.

Hierarchy

In Chapter 1, we introduced how organizations are designed. The hierarchy *is a pyramid showing relationships among levels.* The CEO occupies the top position and is the senior member of top management. The CEO and members of the top management team set the strategic direction of the organization. In Figure 11.1, this would include the CEO and the five senior executive vice presidents at Lowe's. Reporting to these people are senior vice presidents in charge of specific areas, such as chief information officer, accounting, human resources, and corporate affairs. At the next level are various vice presidents (internal audit and corporate controller). The Western Division's senior vice president is responsible for three regional managers who manage six district managers (only three are shown in the figure). Each district manager is responsible for eight stores.

During the past few years, many U.S. companies, including GE, Wells Fargo Bank, and Farmers Insurance, have reduced the number of hierarchical levels in their organizations.[5] For example, GE used to have more than 20 hierarchical levels between the CEO and its first-line employees. Today, it has 5. Why? Most executives think that having fewer layers creates a more efficient organization that can react faster to competition and is more cost effective. According to Andy Kohlberg, president of Kisco Senior Living Communities, with fewer levels, top managers can hear "bad" news more frequently and quickly and, hence, take quicker corrective action to solve the problem before it spins out of control. Also, having fewer hierarchical levels permits more people to participate in the decision-making processes.

Span of Control

Span of control *refers to the number of employees directly reporting to a person.* In the case of Lowe's, the CEO has a span of control of five. The implications for different spans of control on the vertical design of an organization are clear. By holding size constant, narrow spans of control

The purpose of a company establishing a vertical design is to perpetuate consistency throughout an organization.

© IT Stock Free/Jupiter Images

lead to more hierarchical levels. Wider spans create a flatter organization with fewer hierarchical levels. The span of control can either be too wide, too narrow, or appropriate. The optimal span of control is not so narrow that the manager "micro-manages" subordinates or too broad so that the manager loses the ability to lead subordinates.

What is the optimal number of subordinates? There is no "correct" number of subordinates that a manager can supervise effectively. The following four key factors can influence the span of control in any situation[6]:

1. *The competence of both the manager and the employee.* If managers and/or employees are new to a task, they require more supervision than do knowledgeable veteran managers and employees.

2. *The similarity or dissimilarity of tasks being supervised.* At Starbucks, the span of control in the retail store area is broad because all managers can focus on one main product: coffee and its accessories. The more numerous and dissimilar the products, the narrower the span of control should be.

3. *The incidence of new problems in the manager's department.* A manager should know enough about the operations of the department to understand precisely the problems that subordinates are likely to face. The more the manager knows about these factors, the broader the span of control can be.

4. *The extent of clear operating standards and rules.* Clear rules and standard operating procedures (SOPs) leave less to chance and reduce the need for improvisation. At Lowe's, rules govern the tasks and behaviors of store employees in serving customers. For example, when a customer wants to exchange an item, the store clerk should know the procedure to follow. This makes it possible for managers to have larger spans of control. The greater the reliance on rules and SOPs, the broader the span of control may be because the rules do part of the controlling for the manager.

Authority, Responsibility, and Accountability

Authority *is the right to make a decision.* Authority is the glue that holds the vertical and horizontal parts together.[7] Generally, but not always, people at higher levels have the authority to make decisions and tell lower level people what to do. For example, the manager of the paint department at Lowe's has the authority to schedule worker overtime. The manager of the store has the authority to review the overtime scheduled by the paint manager. Robert Niblock, the CEO of Lowe's, has the authority to make decisions that require spending money opening stores in Canada.

Authority implies both responsibility and accountability. That is, by exercising authority, employees accept the responsibility for acting and are willing to be held accountable for success or failure. **Responsibility** *is an employee's duty to perform the assigned task.* Employees take on this obligation when they accept a job assignment. When giving an employee responsibility, the manager should give the subordinate enough authority to get the job done. Oftentimes, a manager is not able to give the person sufficient authority to get a job done. Under these conditions, the subordinate must use her informal influence instead of relying on formal authority.

When a manager delegates authority and responsibility to an employee, that person is accountable for achieving the desired results. **Accountability** *is the manager's expectation that the employee will accept credit or blame for his work.* No manager can check everything an employee does. Therefore managers normally establish guidelines and performance standards within which responsibilities are carried out. As such, accountability flows from the bottom to the top. The manager of the garden department at Lowe's is accountable to the store managers for their operation. Accountability is the point at which authority and responsibility meet and is essential for high performance. When either authority or responsibility is lacking, managers cannot judge a subordinate's accomplishments fairly. When managers are reluctant to hold their subordinates accountable, subordinates can easily pass the buck for nonperformance onto others.[8]

While these three concepts seem simple to understand, a close look at business practices at Enron, one of America's biggest business failures, illustrates that these concepts are often difficult to implement. In Chapter 7, we discussed the ethical challenges facing Sherron Watkins, the whistle-blower whose memo to Ken Lay started the investigation of Enron. Now, after several years and mountains of conflicting testimony by Jeff Skilling, Andy Fastow, Ken Lay, and other top managers at Enron, a picture had emerged that indicates these people often didn't follow the basic principles of accountability, responsibility, and authority. Who are senior managers accountable to? Who has the authority to make decisions? Who is responsible for making a decision? We have asked questions to highlight these three basic management principles in the following Ethical Challenge feature.[9]

Snapshot

"Ken Lay, you have completely failed at the job you were hired to perform. If this lack of accountability would have occurred farther down the organization, no one would hesitate to fire the person."

Jim Schwieger, former Enron Employee

Ethical Challenge

Enron

One of the more interesting testimonies in the Enron trial occurred right after Jeffrey Skilling resigned in August 2001. Greg Whalley, the company's soon-to-be president, after meeting with worried investors in New York, flew home to Houston so he didn't have to lie too much if he stayed in New York. Who is a president accountable to?

Both Fastow and former Enron treasurer Ben Glisan testified at a meeting of Enron's top executives in September 2001 that the company was roughly $500 million short of its earnings target. Whalley said "Don't worry about it. I'll cover it with reserves." Whalley had asked an employee to hide hundreds of millions of dollars in losses in a separate account. Unfortunately for Whalley, this employee gave the government some of the most powerful testimony against Whalley, Skilling, Fastow, and Lay during the trial. Did Whalley have the authority to make the decision to cover the reserves?

The poor financial condition of Enron's international assets and its water business was another issue that arose during the trial. Whalley said that all of the heads of the international business division should be fired because they had done billions of dollars worth of bad deals. Skilling disagreed and no one was fired when Skilling overvalued the assets by billions of dollars to hide the losses. Skilling told Ken Lay that everything was fine.

Merrill Lynch agreed to buy three Nigerian power barges from Enron. A verbal guarantee had been made that the three barges would be repurchased six months later at a guaranteed profit for Merrill Lynch. Jeff McMahon, who was working for Fastow at the time, was in charge of the deal. After six months, there was no profit and losses were mounting. McMahon told Fastow of the problem. The money Fastow got to pay off Merrill Lynch came from "offshore" deals that he and other senior managers at Enron had made off the books. Fastow and Skilling told Lay that "you can always hit the earnings target. We just need to sell more business." Who is responsible for the power barge losses?

While admitting to two major business mistakes—Enron's failed broadband venture and its inability to unload its international assets—Skilling and Lay passionately maintain that they did nothing wrong with a company they called the "finest in the world" back in August 2001. Skilling claimed that most of the people who testified against him were really lying when they say that he committed crimes at Enron.

In May 2006 a jury convicted both Skilling and Lay, who died on July 5, 2006, on many counts of fraud and unethical behaviors. Is Skilling still accountable for Enron's future?

Delegation

Delegation *is the process of giving authority to a person (or group or team) to make decisions and act in certain situations.* In addition to holding an employee accountable for the performance of certain job responsibilities, the manager should give the employee the authority to carry out the responsibilities effectively. Delegation starts when the design of the organization is being established and work is divided. Delegation continues as new jobs and tasks are added during day-to-day operations.

Effective Delegation. Delegation should occur in conjunction with the assignment of responsibilities, such as when a company president assigns to an executive assistant the task of preparing a formal statement for presentation to a congressional committee or when the head of a computer department instructs a programmer to debug a new management reporting system. In each case, the manager is delegating authority to a subordinate. The following practices are useful for achieving effective delegation[10]: *include:*

1. *Establish goals and standards.* Individuals or teams should participate in developing the goals that they will be expected to meet. Ideally, they should also agree to the standards that will be used to measure their performance.

2. *Ensure clarity.* Individuals or teams should clearly understand the work delegated to them, recognize the scope of their authority, and accept their accountability for results.

3. *Involvement.* The challenge of the work itself won't always encourage individuals or groups to accept and perform delegated tasks well. Managers can motivate them by involving them in decision making, by keeping them informed, and by helping them improve their skills and abilities.

4. *Expect completed work.* Individuals or teams should be expected to carry a task through to completion. The manager's job is to provide guidance, help, and information—not to finish the task.

5. *Provide training.* Delegation is only as effective as the ability of people to make the decisions necessary to perform the work and then actually to do the work. Managers should continually appraise delegated responsibilities and provide training aimed at building on strengths and overcoming deficiencies.

6. *Timely feedback.* Timely, accurate feedback should be provided to individuals or teams so that they can compare their performance to stated expectations and correct any deficiencies.

Barriers to Delegation. Delegation is only as effective as the ability of managers to delegate. The greatest psychological barrier to delegation is fear. A manager may be afraid that if subordinates don't do the job properly, the manager's own reputation will suffer. Such a manager may rationalize: "I can do it better myself" or "My subordinates aren't capable enough" or "It takes too much time to explain what I want done." In addition, some managers also may be reluctant to delegate because they fear that subordinates will do the work their own way, or do it too well and outshine them!

Among the organizational barriers that may block delegation is a failure to define authority and responsibility clearly. If managers themselves don't know what is expected or what to do, they can't properly delegate authority and responsibility to others.

The six practices for achieving effective delegation that we presented earlier provide a strong foundation for reducing barriers to delegation. In addition, managers need to accept that there are several different ways to deal with problems and that their particular way of dealing with a problem is not necessarily the way their subordinates will choose to deal with it. Employees will make mistakes, but, whenever possible, they should be allowed to develop their own solutions to problems and learn from their mistakes.

Another barrier to delegation is culture.[11] Japanese managers tend not to delegate decisions to others because of Japan's high power distance ranking (see Chapter 4, page 125). Most Japanese organizations operate like centralized hubs into which information flows and decisions are announced by managers. Nearly all senior management positions in Japanese companies are held by Japanese managers who rarely give foreign managers access to decision-making processes. Many U.S. and other foreign employees complain about the "bamboo ceiling," a term used to refer to the exclusion of foreigners from key decision-making roles.

The following Multicultural Competency feature highlights how American Standard, based in the United States and specializing in the manufacture and sale of plumbing fixtures, air conditioners, and bath fixtures, used its multicultural competencies when it invested in Bulgaria. Why did this $10 billion company from New Jersey choose Bulgaria to build its plant? One of the reasons was because Bulgaria is strategically located to provide easy access to Western Europe and the Middle East. Bulgaria has labor costs about one-tenth of those in Western Europe. American Standard knew that it faced challenges ranging from streets filled with horse-drawn carts and Russian-made cars (Ladas) to managers who were short on international experience, but it still made the decision to go to Bulgaria.[12]

Multicultural Competency

American Standard

When American Standard entered Bulgaria, top management knew the company would face significant political risks. To respond to these diverse political risks, the company followed six management practices. First, it relied heavily on local suppliers. As a significant buyer, it has been able to convince suppliers from Germany, Austria, Spain, and Italy to open operations in Bulgaria to ensure rapid and dependable supply.

Second, American Standard had pursued direct contacts with the national government. These contacts had two major goals: management of day-to-day needs, such as licenses and certificate requirements, and lobbying activities that affected preferred tax and custom policies. American Standard also sponsored nonbusiness activities that showed the government in a positive light. The transformation from communist dictatorship to a free-market democracy had been rocky. Just a few years ago, inflation was 2,000 percent a year and the country was about to suffer an economic collapse. American Standard's work with the International Monetary Fund was important to bail out the country. It also has been actively supporting Bulgaria's attempts to join the European Union.

A third management practice was to develop strong relationships with local stakeholders. American Standard is one of the few foreign investors not located in the capital, Sofia. Instead, they are in Sevlievo, a rural area. The company is recognized as a major force for development in this struggling area. Jobs at the plants are so plentiful that workers have to be bused in by the company from towns as far away as 35 miles. This benefits not only local governmental agencies interested in development, but also local cultural and recreational organizations that benefit from the growth in wages.

Fourth, American Standard has created strong ties with its unions, employees, and other workers in the region. It employs more than 3,700 workers at its plants and indirectly employs about five times that many, including truck drivers and construction workers. The average salary is $2.00 an hour, which compares favorably to Bulgaria's national average of $1.75. Skilled workers can make about $500 per month. American Standard has invested in improving working conditions, pay scales, and social services for its workers.

Fifth, it learned quickly that it had to trust local managers and to keep existing managers. "We found a good group of people who were talented and willing to learn and wanted to be better," says Frederic Poses, the CEO of American Standard.

Finally, the factories lacked modern manufacturing practices. The plant had no gas-fired kilns to bake clay forms into shiny white bidets and sinks. American Standard solved that problem by helping a Bulgarian utility finance a new pipeline. One fringe benefit is that now the residents of Sevlievo can cook and heat with gas. The sour smell of coal soot that marks so many Eastern European cities is now gone. Until recently, fittings were still polished by hand. Today, workers are using computer terminals to work on design of the next generation of gold-plated faucets.

To learn more about this organization, visit *www.americanstandard.com*.

Centralization and Decentralization

Centralization and decentralization of authority are basic, overall management philosophies that indicate where decisions are to be made. **Centralization** *is the concentration of authority at the top of an organization or department.* **Decentralization** *is the delegation of authority to lower level employees or departments.* Decentralization is an approach that requires managers to decide what and when to delegate, to select and train personnel carefully, and to formulate adequate controls.

No Absolutes. Neither centralization nor decentralization is absolute in an organization.[13] No one manager makes all the decisions, even in a highly centralized setting such as the IRS. Total centralization would end the need for middle and first-line managers. Thus there are only degrees of centralization and decentralization. In many organizations, some tasks are relatively centralized (e.g., payroll systems, purchasing, and human resource policies), whereas others are relatively decentralized (e.g., marketing and production).

Potential benefits to decentralization include the following:

1. It frees top managers to develop organizational plans and strategies. Lower level managers and employees handle routine, day-to-day decisions.

2. It develops lower level managers' self-management and planning and administration competencies.

3. Because subordinates often are closer to the action than higher level managers, they may have a better grasp of the facts. This knowledge may enable them to make sound decisions quickly. Valuable time can be lost when a subordinate or team must check everything with a manager.

4. It fosters a healthy, achievement-oriented atmosphere among employees.

Many organizations choose to centralize some functions and tasks and decentralize others.

© David Buffington/Blend Images/Jupiter Images

Key Factors. A variety of factors can affect management's decisions to centralize or decentralize authority in various areas of decision making. We briefly consider five of these factors:

1. *Cost of decisions.* Cost is perhaps the most important factor in determining the extent of centralization. As a general rule, the more costly the outcome, the more likely top management is to centralize the authority to make the final decision.

2. *Uniformity of policy.* Managers who value consistency favor centralization of authority. These managers may want to assure customers that everyone is treated equally in terms of quality, price, credit, delivery, and service. At Lowe's, for example, a nationwide home improvement sales promotion on paint requires that all stores charge the same price. Uniform policies have definite advantages for cost accounting, production, and financial departments. They also enable managers to compare the relative

effciencies of various departments. In organizations with unions, such as Delta, United Airlines, and Northwest Airlines, uniform policies also aid in the administration of labor agreements regarding wages, promotions, fringe benefits, and other human resource matters.

3. *Competency levels.* Many organizations work hard to ensure an adequate supply of competent managers and employees—an absolute necessity for decentralization. Royal Dutch Shell, Harley-Davidson, and Brinker, among others, recognize that extensive training and practical experiences are essential to developing the competencies needed by people in a decentralized organization. These organizations decentralize many decisions to employees because managers are willing to permit employees to make mistakes involving small costs so as to learn from them.

4. *Control mechanisms.* Even the most avid proponents of decentralization, such as Philips, Cisco, and Marriott, insist on controls and procedures to prevent costly mistakes and to determine whether actual events are meeting expectations. For example, each Marriott Hotel centralizes the analysis of key data, including number of beds occupied, employee turnover, number of meals served, and the average amount that guests spend on food and beverages. Analysis of these data helps managers control important aspects of the hotel's operation and compare it against the performance of others in the chain. If a hotel's operations don't fall within certain guidelines, top management may step in to diagnose the situation.

5. *Environmental influences.* External factors (e.g., unions, federal and state regulatory agencies, and tax policies) affect the degree of centralization in an organization. For example, laws and government regulations regarding hours, wages, working conditions, and safety make it difficult to decentralize authority in those areas.

The following Teamwork Competency feature illustrates how Kate and Andy Spade, a husband-and-wife team, work together to make their upscale company, Kate Spade, successful. It has taken them working together for more than 13 years to build their company into a $275 million company.[14]

Teamwork Competency

Kate Spade

Finding a business partner is never an easy job. Finding someone you can share a home and a company with is almost impossible. Why? Because of the problems surrounding authority and responsibility. When they started the business in 1993, Kate Spade was to be the editor and designer, and her husband Andy was to be the big-idea guy who pushed the boundaries, who took risks, and shaped the brand. But which of them is responsible for exactly what? Who has the final authority on big decisions?

Kate and Andy have developed four principles to help them run their company:

▸ Be clear about job definitions. Which decisions is each partner going to handle,

and which decisions are to be shared? After many years, they have it down pat: Andy provides the big picture or vision and Kate enjoys dotting the *i*'s and crossing the *t*'s and making sure the products conform to her exacting detail.

▸ Figure out how to maintain boundaries in your personal life. They used to talk business in bed, but now they don't talk about business until they get back to the office.

▸ Establish guidelines for professional behavior. As team members, they try not to barge in on each other's business. They do not interrupt each other on the phone.

Decide who has the final say if there are differences of opinion. After a healthy debate, the person who is most passionate wins. For example, in 1996, they had to settle a major difference regarding developing freestanding stores versus selling primarily to upscale department stores. Andy felt it was time to develop stores, but Kate felt differently. The result: The partner who feels the most passionate gets to make the call. So they began with a tiny 300-square-foot store in the SoHo district of New York City that is now 10 times bigger. End of discussion.

Working together and using these four principles, the couple identified a void in the market, combined their competencies, and designed six simple handbag shapes that emphasized utility, color, and fabric. These six original designs continue to be the company's signature styles. Their business has now grown from just selling handbags to selling home furnishings, shoes, stationery, eyewear, and even baby carriages. They have more than 20 stores in the United States and 9 in Asia and also sell their merchandise in Neiman Marcus, Saks Fifth Avenue, and other upscale department stores. They have plans to increase their stores to 50 within the next three to five years.

To learn more about this organization, visit *www.katespade.com.*

Designer Kate Spade is a prime example of an entrepreneur who has made a name for herself and her products.

© Bebeto Matthews/AP Photo

In this section, we examined the five basic vertical parts of an organization. Issues of hierarchy, span of control, authority, delegation, and centralization/decentralization are important because they give you an idea of how managers and employees relate to each other at different levels. These five parts can be combined in many different ways to build a vertical design. Accordingly, managers need the right combination of hierarchical levels, spans of control, and delegation to implement the organization's strategy. Managers can use a number of practices, procedures, or rules to achieve consistent performance.

Horizontal Design

The basis for a successful organization design rests on people working together in an organization. They must be able to understand its strengths and limitations. As we indicated in Chapter 7, a company's choice of a particular structure will go a long way toward supporting its strategy. In this section, we will illustrate four basic designs and provide guidelines for using them. The four most commonly used types of horizontal design are (1) functional, (2) product, (3) geographical, and (4) network. Each of these designs involves different choices with respect to the vertical integration factors that you have just read about.

3.

Describe four types of horizontal organizational design.

Functional Design

Functional design *means grouping managers and employees according to their areas of expertise and the resources they use to perform their jobs.* Functions vary widely according to the type of organization. For example, Presbyterian Hospital doesn't have a production unit, but it has functional units for admitting, emergency rooms, surgery, and maintenance. Similarly, Boeing has production units, but doesn't have admitting and emergency rooms. Functional units are usually found in organizations that produce a high volume of a narrow range of products, such as oil and mining. Functional units are also particularly suited for small organizations.

As shown in Figure 11.2, Harley-Davidson has chosen a functional form of departmentalization.[15] Harley has more than 1,300 worldwide dealers, produces 33 different models of motorcycles, and has eight functional vice presidents as shown in Figure 11.2. Grouping activities by way of a functional structure is efficient and cost effective. That is, a set of functional managers oversees activities for each major area of the organization.

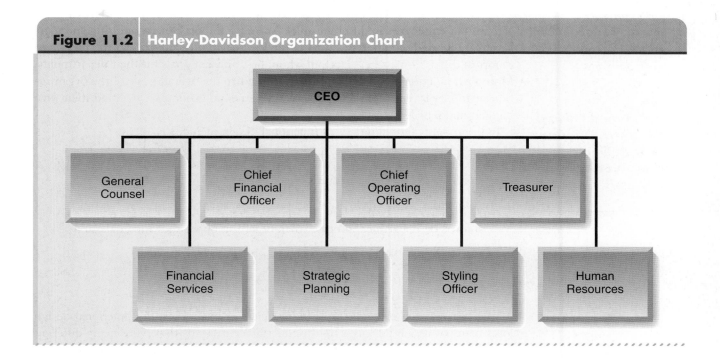

Figure 11.2 | Harley-Davidson Organization Chart

Potential Benefits. Designing by function is economical because it results in a simple design. Management creates one department for each primary function to be performed (e.g., production, marketing, and human resources). This design keeps administrative expenses low because everyone in a department shares training, experience, and resources. Senior managers can easily identify and promote those people who have the necessary competencies to manage their particular functional unit. Also, employees can see clearly defined career paths within their own departments. As a result, the organization can more easily hire and promote employees who have or develop good problem-solving skills in each area of specialization.

In brief, the potential benefits of functional design include

▶ supporting skill specialization,

▶ reducing duplication of resources and increasing coordination within the functional area,

▶ enhancing career development and training within the functional area,

▶ allowing superiors and subordinates to share common expertise, and

▶ promoting high-quality technical decision making.

Potential Pitfalls. The pitfalls of functional design become apparent when an organization provides highly diverse products (goods and/or services) or serves highly diverse

Snapshot

"A hierarchical organization structured around functions develops competing empires. Collaboration on creative approaches to customer problems is unthinkable and, at best, forced."

**David Falvey,
Executive Director,
British Geological
Survey, Nottingham,
United Kingdom**

customers. Making decisions quickly becomes difficult when employees have to coordinate with other units. For example, a sales rep at Harley-Davidson in Chicago, Illinois, may lose a sale because he or she has to wait for the sales manager to get the production manager in Kansas City to make a scheduling decision. In addition, when friction exists between units, managers have to spend time resolving the issues involved. Pinpointing the accountability and performance levels of employees who are performing separate functions may also be difficult. In other words, a top manager may not be able to determine easily which department—production, sales, or credit—is responsible for delays and declining profits.

Another pitfall is that top management may have a hard time coordinating the activities of employees in different units. At Pier 1 Imports, merchandising and marketing are located on different floors of the Pier 1 building in Fort Worth, Texas, and report to different managers, each of whom has different goals for their departments. Moreover, functional designs tend to de-emphasize the overall goals of the organization, with employees often focusing on departmental goals (e.g., meeting their own budgets and schedules).

In brief, the potential pitfalls of functional design include

▶ inadequate communication between units,

▶ conflicts over product priorities,

▶ difficulties with coordination between departments,

▶ a focus on departmental rather than organizational issues and goals, and

▶ developing managers who are experts only in narrow fields.

Product Design

As the organization expands into new products or businesses, the functional design loses many of its advantages. High product diversity leads to serving many different kinds of customers and a variety of geographic regions of the world. Many organizations group all of their functions into a single product line or division. Product design *means that all functions that contribute to a product are organized under one manager.* Product designs (sometimes labeled divisional structures) simply divide the organization into self-contained units that are responsible for developing, producing, and selling their own products and services to their own markets. As illustrated in Figure 11.3, General Dynamics is organized into four product lines. Each product competes against competitors in its own market.[16]

Product design is the most commonly used design for companies in the Fortune 500. In large companies, such as Komatsu, General Dynamics, or Procter & Gamble, these divisions remain fairly autonomous. Thus, managers and employees assigned to a particular product often become expert about that division's products and markets. Each product also has its own functional specialists and resources needed to support the product. Therefore, a product design encourages decentralization of authority to the product manager by tailoring functional activities to the needs of the particular product. In the case of General Dynamics, the manager in charge of the Bath Iron Works has various functional managers, such as manufacturing, finance, and human resources, reporting to him.

Product designs are evaluated on the basis of their profit contributions to the entire organization. Because each division represents a product or group of products, senior management can measure the financial performance of each division. For example, at General Dynamics, the profitability of Bath Iron Works can be compared against the profitability of the Electric Boat division to see which division is more profitable. In

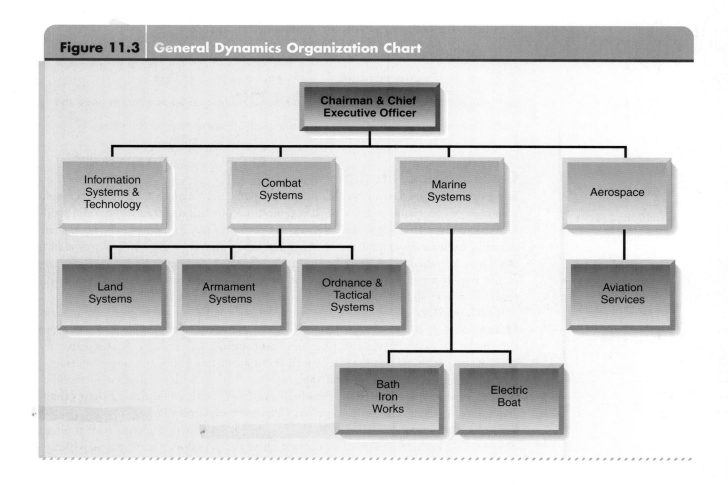

Figure 11.3 | **General Dynamics Organization Chart**

many respects, separate divisions act almost as separate businesses and work independently to accomplish their goals and those of the organization.

Potential Benefits. This form of organization enables managers and employees to become specialized and expert in a particular product (good or service) line. This benefit lessens only as the number and diversity of products provided by an organization increase. Management also can pinpoint costs, profits, problems, and successes accurately for each product line.

In brief, the potential benefits of product design include

▶ permitting fast changes in a product line,

▶ allowing greater product line visibility,

▶ fostering a concern for customer demands,

▶ clearly defining responsibilities for each product line, and

▶ developing managers who can think across functional lines.

Potential Pitfalls. Because some or many functions are duplicated for each product line, resource utilization may be relatively inefficient. In addition, products with seasonal highs and lows in sales volumes may result in higher personnel costs. Coordination across product lines usually is difficult. Employees tend to focus on the goals for their particular products, rather than on broader company goals. This situation may create unhealthy competition within an organization for scarce resources.

In brief, the potential pitfalls for product design include

▶ not allowing efficient utilization of skills and resources,

▶ not fostering coordination of activities across product lines,

▶ encouraging politics and conflicts in resource allocation across product lines, and

▶ limiting career mobility for personnel outside their own product lines.[17]

Geographical Design

Some organizations, such as Nestlé, Sheraton Hotels, and Celanese Chemical, operate in a number of geographic regions. Such organizations often find that functional and product designs are inefficient because they do not provide a way for managers to coordinate activities within a geographic region. Geographical design *organizes activities around location.* Geographical designs allow organizations to develop competitive advantage in a particular region according to that area's customers, competitors, and other factors. This form of horizontal design permits managers to specialize in particular markets.

If each manager is in close contact with customers in his or her market, the manager can quickly adapt to changing market conditions. Geographical designs are extremely versatile. Thus, the practices, procedures, and standards used can vary according to regional conditions, as well as the priorities senior management assigns to each region. Managers at local sites become familiar with local labor force practices, governmental requirements, and cultural norms that could impact their operations. For manufacturing firms, such as Celanese and Motorola, locating plants near the source of raw materials saves transportation costs. As in the case with product designs, geographical designs also contain all of the necessary functional activities to reach the organization's goals.

Potential Benefits. Geographical designs allow an organization to focus on customer needs within a relatively small geographic area and to minimize the costs associated with transportation of goods or services. In brief, the potential benefits of geographical design include

▶ having facilities and the equipment used for production and/or distribution all in one place, saving time and costs;

▶ being able to develop expertise in solving problems unique to one location;

▶ gaining an understanding of customers' problems and desires; and

▶ getting production closer to raw materials and suppliers.

Potential Pitfalls. Organizing by location typically increases problems of control and coordination for top management. To ensure uniformity and coordination, organizations that use geographical designs, such as Starbucks and the IRS, make extensive use of rules that apply to all locations. One reason for doing so is to guarantee a standard level of quality regardless of location, which would be difficult if units in various locations went their own separate ways.

In brief, the potential pitfalls of geographical design include

▶ duplication of functions, to varying degrees, at each regional or individual unit location;

▶ conflict between each location's goals and the organization's goals; and

▶ added levels of management and extensive use of rules and regulations to coordinate and ensure uniformity of quality among locations.[18]

Network Design

Recently, a number of organizations have started to rely on a network design. A network design *subcontracts some or many of its operations to other firms and coordinates them to accomplish specific goals.*[19] Sometimes also called a virtual organization, managers need to coordinate and link up people (from many organizations) to perform activities in many locations. Contacts and working relationships in the network are facilitated by electronic means, as well as through face-to-face meetings. The use of computer-based technologies permits managers to coordinate suppliers, designers, manufacturers, distributors, and others on an instantaneous, real-time basis. Often, managers in a network design work as closely with their suppliers and customers as they do with their own employees.

By connecting people regardless of their location, the network design enhances fast communications so that people can act together. Numerous organizations in the fashion, toy, publishing, software design, and motion picture industries use this design. Organizing as a network design allows the organization to compete on the basis of speed and ability to quickly transfer knowledge. For example, Cisco Systems outsources most of its manufacturing to other organizations that are better able to manage this function than Cisco. In turn, Cisco focuses exclusively on product development and customer relationships.

Potential Benefits. All organizations seek to combine the stability and efficiency of their existing designs with a capability for fast response to competitors. However, relying on functional, product, or geographical designs to attain such a balance is very difficult. To meet the dual needs of high efficiency and fast response, many organizations are becoming much more focused and specialized in what they will do in-house. As a result, some activities that used to be performed within the organization are now given to other firms.

The network design offers many potential benefits for an organization. First, the organization brings together the special knowledge and skills of others to create value rather than hiring employees to perform this task. The network design enables managers to focus on one set of activities and rely on others to contribute. Second, the network design has the advantage of bringing together people with different insights into teams that work exclusively on a given project. Thus, network designs enhance the search for new ideas and creative solutions. Yet, it is important for employees working on such a project to have strong self-management, teamwork, communication, and planning and administration competencies. When a given project is completed, these teams will be disassembled. Third, organizations choosing a network design can work with a wide variety of different suppliers, customers, and other organizations. This gives managers a high degree of flexibility to respond to different circumstances.

Potential Pitfalls. With many people working from different locations and often linked by electronic means, potential pitfalls exist. First, other organizations can sometimes fail to live up to the deadlines that were established. Because network designs work in real time, a delay in one part of the process has ripple effects throughout the system. How many times have you waited for a doctor in an office? In instances where time is critical, delays can be very costly because the entire system must wait until a decision is made. Thus, dependence on other organizations can create an operational risk. Often, additional resources or coordination is needed, thus increasing the cost to the consumer. Second, since the network design does not provide managers with knowledge to complete the process on their own, they must constantly monitor the quality of work provided by those in other organizations. Knowledge resides in people's minds. Thus, the network organization is only as competitive as the quality and resources assigned to the project by another organization. Assigning employees with weak communication and planning and administration competencies, for example, can lead to reduced effectiveness. Third, employees in the outsourced organization may not commit to the same values and sense of time urgency

Snapshot

"We want to be global and local, big and small, radically decentralized with centralized reporting and control. If we resolve those contradictions, we create real organizational advantage."
Percy Barnevik, former, CEO, Asea-Brown-Boveri

to which employees in the networked organization are committed. Therefore, it is crucial that all people working in a network organization understand the critical nature of the project. Last, the network design involves managers working with many organizations. Lines of authority, responsibility, and accountability are not always clear. Projects may be delayed and cost overruns can occur.

The production of movies has for a long time illustrated many characteristics of the network design. Filmmakers, directors, producers, actors, agents, makeup artists, costume designers, special-effects artists, technicians, and lawyers come together from many different organizations and agencies to produce a film. Although they are all independent, the producer and director need to closely orchestrate and communicate with each of these to produce a film according to very exact specifications. After the production is complete and the film is released, these various people disband and then regroup (often with different people) to produce another film with a different set of actors, producers, directors, and so forth. Thus, the movie industry is actually composed of many different specialized organizations, each of which is critically dependent on the people, knowledge, and skills of other organizations to create a product that is often beyond the scope, capabilities, and means of any one firm.

The following Communication Competency feature illustrates how DreamWorks SKG uses a network design to make movies.[20] Created in 1994 by Steven Spielberg, Jeffrey Katzenberg, and David Geffen, this multibillion-dollar company produced such mega box office hits as *Old School, Chicken Run, Shrek 2,* and *A Beautiful Mind.*

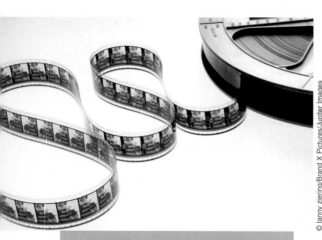

The company also produced other movies, such as *Amistad* and *Mouse Hunt,* that had mediocre box office sales. While *Shrek 2* sold more than $430 million at the box office, sales quickly fell off for DVDs. Retailers returned unsold copies to the company to make room for newer titles.

DreamWorks has also produced television shows, as well as music albums for a number of pop artists, and it produced a string of TV flops before producing Michael Fox's successful comedy *Spin City.* In 2003, the company had to exit the music business because of lagging sales and high costs. After facing a multitude of environmental protests, cost overruns, and construction delays, the three founders sold DreamWorks to Paramount Pictures in 2006. Stacey Snider, former chairman of Universal Pictures, was appointed chairman and CEO of DreamWorks.

The entertainment industry is composed of contributors with many different competencies. These contributors are highly dependent on each other to create a product that is beyond the scope of what DreamWorks can do alone. Some of the benefits and pitfalls of the network design are illustrated in this example.

© Ianny ziering/Brand X Pictures/Jupiter Images

For each product it undertakes, "DreamWorks" senior management assembles a team of competent freelancers to complete a project, and then disbands the group once the project is finished.

Communication Competency

DreamWorks SKG

At DreamWorks, senior managers divide their responsibilities by function. Bill Damaschke is the head of creative production and development, Derek Chan is the head of digital operations, Nancy Bernstein is the head of production, Terry Press is the head of worldwide marketing, and Andy Hendrickson is the head of production technology. These people and a few more comprise the senior management circle shown in Figure 11.4.

Figure 11.4 | **DreamWorks SKG Network Design**

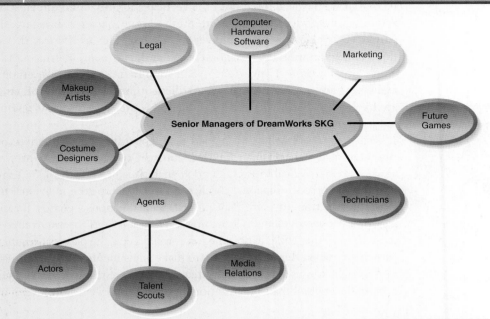

DreamWorks relies heavily on many other organizations to provide the critical resources, people, and skills needed to produce a film. As shown in Figure 11.4, makeup artists, costume designers, actors, and agents are not a part of DreamWorks. These people are hired at the time they are needed. Likewise, DreamWorks hires other specialized organizations to develop many of the newest technologies used to create computer-generated, animated films. A central management task for the senior managers of the company is communicating with people from different backgrounds, expertise, and competencies to produce blockbuster entertainment. It is the job of senior management to rapidly find the competencies needed to complete a project on time and within budget, assemble the team(s), and then disband the team when the project is finished.

DreamWorks signed with computer giant Hewlett-Packard (HP) to develop cutting-edge technologies for new forms of animation. HP provided all of the computing resources for DreamWorks' next-generation digital studio at its Glendale, California, location. Working with HP permitted DreamWorks to create the latest computer-designed animation more quickly and more cost effectively than previous technology. HP also supplied all of the workstations, servers, printers, and networking devices needed. HP also helped

DreamWorks develop technologies that fostered closer collaboration among producers, directors, animators, and other technicians working from many distant locations. Hewlett-Packard had effectively become a key provider of computer hardware and other technologies that allowed DreamWorks, which could not develop the technology as effectively or in as timely a manner on its own, to produce even more realistic animation.

Many of DreamWorks' popular movies have become the basis for the newest video game ideas. Yet, DreamWorks does not currently seek to invest in this industry by itself, especially after having encountered some product failures in the late 1990s. DreamWorks realizes that it does not have the skills or the resources to successfully invest in or compete in the video game industry. Yet, DreamWorks recognizes that the video game market is a new channel that could help spark interest in both current and future DreamWorks films. So DreamWorks signed a deal with Activision to publish games based on three DreamWorks films: *Sharkslayer, Madagascar,* and *Over the Hedge.* In this relationship, Activision has helped DreamWorks develop a video game franchise for interactive entertainment, but DreamWorks will not actually be developing the games.

To learn more about this organization, visit *www.DreamWorksAnimation.com.*

Describe the major options for achieving organizational integration.

Organizational Integration

Now that we have explored both the vertical and horizontal dimensions of an organization's design, we can turn our attention to how managers integrate the efforts of all employees. Specialization and division of labor refer to the fact that employees will think and act in ways that are good for their department, but may not be good for the entire organization. However, to achieve organizational goals, employees, projects, and tasks have to be coordinated regardless of the task. Without it, employees' efforts are likely to result in delay, frustration, and waste. Integration is one of the basic elements of organizing.

Many managers believe that good people can make any organization design work. Although such managers may be overstating the case, employees who work well together are extremely valuable assets. A good analogy is basketball, where teamwork is essential. During practice sessions, coaches try to transform the individual players into one smoothly functioning team. Players learn their functions—guards, forwards, center—as part of a cooperative effort, learn how each task relates to every other task, and relate these tasks to the whole. Coordination is required as the players execute their functions, particularly when they are called on to make adjustments in a game situation.

Managers can use a variety of systems to integrate the activities of their employees to achieve the goals of their organization. In this section, we review several of these systems.

Integration through Mechanistic and Organic Systems

We have identified two types of systems—mechanistic and organic—for integrating employees and the tasks they perform.[21] A mechanistic system *is one in which management breaks activities into separate, highly specialized tasks, relies extensively on standardized rules, and centralizes decision making at the top.* This type of system may be most appropriate when an organization's environment is stable and predictable. Table 11.1 highlights these characteristics.

Snapshot

"Coordination is like professional sports: It looks easy, but when you're on the field, you see how difficult it is. The more people need to work with each other to reach the organization's goal, the more coordination is needed. However, there is a cost (meeting time, travel, uniform policies) to achieving integration."

Mike Lazaridis, President, Research in Motion, Waterloo, Ontario, Canada

Table 11.1   **Organic Versus Mechanistic Systems**

ORGANIC	MECHANISTIC
■ Tasks tend to be interdependent.	■ Tasks are highly specialized.
■ Tasks are continually adjusted and redefined through interaction and as situations change.	■ Tasks tend to remain rigidly defined unless changed by top management.
■ Generalized roles (responsibility for task accomplishment beyond specific role definition) are accepted.	■ Specific roles (rights, obligations, and technical methods) are prescribed for each employee.
■ Network structure of control, authority, and communication.	■ Hierarchical structure of control, authority, and communication.
■ Communication and decision making are both vertical and horizontal, depending on where needed information and expertise reside.	■ Communication and decision making are primarily vertical, top-down.
■ Communication emphasizes the form of mutual influence and advice among all levels.	■ Communication emphasizes directions and decisions issued by superiors.

An *organic system encourages managers and subordinates to work together in teams and to communicate openly with each other.* In fact, employees are encouraged to communicate with anyone who might help them solve a problem. Decision making tends to be decentralized. Authority, responsibility, and accountability flow to employees having the expertise required to solve problems as they arise. As a result, an organic organization is well suited to a changing environment. Table 11.1 summarizes the characteristics of an organic system.

Michael Marks, chairman of Flextronics International, has used many of the ideas of an organic system to create a very successful organization that manufactures and assembles printed circuit boards for Motorola, Xerox, Ericsson, and other networking and telecommunications equipment companies. Located in Singapore, the organization employees more than 92,000 people in more than 20 countries located in the Americas, Asia, and Europe. In the past 10 years, its revenues have gone from $93 million to more than $15.9 billion by acquiring competitors. Let's read the following Self-Management Competency feature to learn about how his management style has created an organic system at Flextronics.[22]

Self-Management Competency

Michael Marks

Ask Michael Marks about his organization's procedures for making big capital investments and he is likely to refer you to the corporate policy manual. It has 80 pages—all of them blank. Sometimes Marks lets subordinates do multimillion-dollar acquisitions without showing him the paperwork. He asks four questions: One, what is their line of business; two, what is their manufacturing capacity; three, how big and what is their customer base; and four, what are their cultural values? If his managers answer all of these questions, then the acquisition is verbally agreed on and as far as Marks is concerned, it's a done deal. He hates staff meetings and has refused to draw up an organization chart outlining his managers' responsibilities.

As Marks sees it, the business of global contract manufacturing is all about speed. The time it takes to get a prototype in mass production and onto retail shelves across the globe can determine whether or not the digital gadget succeeds or flops. Marks thinks the biggest mistake is to miss important opportunities rather than make a mistake or two. So he doesn't want to tie down his top managers with bureaucracy. This means that Flextronics' global managers can utilize the company's worldwide information technology to solve a local customer's problem or send a project to other global managers to solve without going through a lot of red tape.

The basketball hoops hanging in Marks' modest, somewhat messy office seem to sum up his organization. Marks is a passionate player, even though he's 5 feet 2 inches tall. He's convinced that he can retain the agile management style of a start-up, while making Flextronics a global organization.

To learn more about this organization, visit *www.flextronics.com*.

Integration through Types of Interdependence

An organization's need for coordination has a significant impact on how managers pull together the organization's various activities because of the requirement for technological interdependence. Interdependence *is the degree of coordination required between individuals and units to transform information and raw materials into goods and services.*[23] There are three types of interdependence: pooled, sequential, and reciprocal. Figure 11.5 on the following page shows how they operate to coordinate the efforts of employees in order to achieve desired results.

Figure 11.5 | Three Types of Interdependence

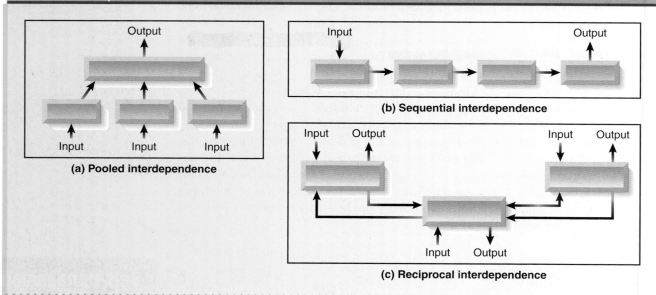

(a) Pooled interdependence

(b) Sequential interdependence

(c) Reciprocal interdependence

Pooled Interdependence. Illustrated in Figure 11.5(a), pooled interdependence *involves little sharing of information or resources among individuals within a unit or among units in the performance of tasks.* Although various departments contribute to overall organizational efforts, they work on their own specialized tasks. At a Bank of America branch, for example, the savings, consumer loan, and commercial loan departments work independently of one another. Bank of America achieves coordination by requiring each department to meet certain standards and follow certain rules. These rules are consistent for all of its banks in various states and apply to all routine transactions, such as check cashing and receiving deposits, with few exceptions. Lowe's, Home Depot, and other organizations designed by function use pooled interdependence to coordinate various activities.

Sequential Interdependence. Illustrated in Figure 11.5(b), sequential interdependence *involves the orderly step-by-step flow of information, tasks, and resources from one individual or team to another within the same unit or from one unit to another.* That is, the output from department A becomes the input for department B, the output from department B becomes the input for department C, and so on. General Motors uses standard methods and procedures at its Lansing, Michigan, plant to manufacture its Saturn Outlook and Buick Enclave. These methods and procedures spell out the single exact and proper way to do every task. They were drawn up by engineers and posted at workstations for easy reference. Everything is spelled out, down to the proper way to tighten a lug nut. When an employee is finished with a hammer, guides (e.g., chalk body outlines) indicate exactly where it is to be laid. To ensure coordination of its workstations, managers must carefully schedule when parts arrive and leave each workstation.

Reciprocal Interdependence. Illustrated in Figure 11.5(c), reciprocal interdependence *involves the need for every individual and unit to work with every other individual and unit; information and resources flow back and forth freely until the goal is achieved.* For example, hospitals use resources from several departments (e.g., X-ray, nursing, surgery, and physical therapy) to restore a patient's health. Each specialist and department supplies some of the resources needed to help the patient. Doctors and professionals from each specialized area meet to discuss the patient's recovery. The method of coordination is mutual adjustment, achieved through team meetings.

Designing an organization to handle reciprocal interdependence and then managing it are extremely challenging tasks as DreamWorks discovered. The design of the organization must allow for frequent communication among individuals and units, and planning is essential. Because management can't easily anticipate all customer demands or solve all of the problems that arise, managers must continually communicate to be sure that they understand the nature and scope of issues and problems—and to devise effective solutions. Usually managers choose a network design if various units are reciprocally interdependent.

Chapter Summary

In this chapter, we highlighted some of the basics of designing an organization. The two fundamentals of organizing, differentiation and integration, along with the vertical and horizontal ways of designing the organization were discussed. Various methods that organizations can use to integrate its activities were also highlighted. We also indicated that no organization is simply a static set of boxes and charts. Organizations are like motion pictures—they constantly change according to the demands placed on them by competitors, employees, governments, and many other stakeholders.

Learning Goals

1. Explain the two fundamental principles of designing organizations.

There are two fundamentals of organizing: differentiation and integration. Differentiation is created through a division of labor and job specialization. As organizations grow, they create departments to handle certain activities, such as payroll, manufacturing, and human resources. Because different units are part of the larger organization, some degree of integration (coordination) is needed among them for an organization to be effective. Integration is achieved through the use of systems and technology.

2. State the major concepts of vertical organizational design.

The vertical design of an organization has five major parts. The hierarchy shows relationships among the various management levels in an organization. These relationships are shown in the organization chart. The span of control refers to the number of subordinates reporting to each manager. Authority, responsibility, and accountability are the glue that holds an organization together because these indicate who has the right to make a decision, who will be held responsible for the decision, and who is accountable for the results. Delegation is the process of giving authority to a person (or group) to make decisions. Delegation should go hand in hand with responsibility and accountability. Centralization/decentralization refers to the overall philosophy of management as to where decisions are to be made.

3. Describe four types of horizontal organizational design.

The four primary types of design are (1) functional design—groups employees according to common tasks to be performed; (2) product design—groups employees by product or service in self-contained units, each responsible for its own goods or services; (3) geographical design—groups functions and employees by location; and (4) network design—subcontracts some or many of its operations to other organizations and coordinates them to accomplish specific goals.

4. Describe the major options for achieving organizational integration.

Ideally, an organization's design will help management to implement the development of key integration practices. We reviewed basic ways in which an organization can integrate its activities. Mechanistic and organic systems refer to the use or absence of rules and regulations. Mechanistic bureaucratic systems are used when customers' demands are well known and do not change. Organic systems use few rules and regulations. These systems are usually found in organizations that must respond rapidly to changes in customer tastes, competitors' pressures, and the like. Three types of interdependence are pooled, sequential, and reciprocal. Pooled interdependence requires little sharing of information and other resources among individuals who work on specialized tasks. Sequential task interdependence serializes the flow of information and other resources between individual and departments to accomplish tasks. Reciprocal task interdependence encourages the constant flow of information and resources back and forth between individuals, teams, and departments to accomplish tasks.

Key Terms and Concepts

Accountability	Geographical design	Organization design
Authority	Hierarchy	Pooled interdependence
Centralization	Integration	Product design
Decentralization	Interdependence	Reciprocal interdependence
Delegation	Mechanistic system	Responsibility
Differentiation	Network design	Sequential interdependence
Division of labor	Organic system	Span of control
Functional design	Organization chart	Specialization

Questions for Discussion and Reflective Thinking

1. We discussed many features of Lowe's organizational design. If Lowe's continues to grow, what are some of the possible changes that might be considered in its organization design?

2. Could a large firm, such as Lowe's, function without an organizational chart?

3. How is your university or college organized?

4. Go to *www.starbucks.com*. How is this company organized?

5. Give examples of authority, accountability, and responsibility for a course in which you have been enrolled.

6. Think of a manager you have worked for. Based on the guidelines presented for effective delegation, did this manager do a good job of delegating? Explain your answer.

7. What are some advantages and disadvantages of organizing by product?

8. What are some warning signs that an organization's design is not working?

9. What implications for managerial spans of control can be expected as organizations downsize? What additional managerial competencies might be placed on the managers who remain in a downsized organization?

10. Name sports that use each of the three types of interdependence. What does this suggest for the design of effective organizations? What managerial competencies would be most useful for each type of interdependence?

11. If an organization's structure reflects the ideas and values of its leader, how have the values of Kate and Andy Spade impacted the design of their organization?

Experiential Exercise | What Type of Design Is Your Organization?[24]

In this exercise you are to focus on either your university or an organization for which you currently work in a full- or part-time capacity or for which you have worked in the past. Please circle the letter on the scale indicating the degree to which you agree or disagree with each statement. There is no "right" answer; simply respond according to how you see the organization.

Strongly Agree (SA)	Agree (A)	Neutral (N)	Diagree (D)	Strongly Disagree (SD)

1. People in this organization are urged to be innovative.

   SA   A   N   D   SD

2. There are a lot of rules to follow in this organization.

   SA   A   N   D   SD

3. People who pay attention to details are likely to get ahead in this organization.

   SA   A   N   D   SD

4. A person has a secure job in this organization.

   SA   A   N   D   SD

5. Precision in one's work is valued by the organization.

   SA   A   N   D   SD

6. This company operates with a stable set of competitors.

   SA   A   N   D   SD

7. People in this organization are urged to take risks and experiment with new ways of doing things.

   SA   A   N   D   SD

8. Jobs in this organization are very predictable.

   SA   A   N   D   SD

9. There are few rules in this organization.

   SA   A   N   D   SD

10. Employees are very careful in performing their work.

    SA   A   N   D   SD

11. Employees are treated impersonally by managers in this organization.

    SA   A   N   D   SD

12. Lines of authority are closely followed in this organization.

    SA   A   N   D   SD

13. Job opportunities in this organization are limited to employees who play by the rules.

    SA   A   N   D   SD

14. Being highly organized is expected and rewarded in this organization.

    SA   A   N   D   SD

15. Being people oriented is a characteristic of this organization.

    SA   A   N   D   SD

16. People are not constrained by many rules in this organization.

    SA   A   N   D   SD

Scoring. On the scoring grid, circle the number that corresponds to your response to each of the 16 questions. Add the numbers in each column. Enter the total for each column on the line at the bottom of each column. Add the column totals and enter as a total score. This is your organization's score.

Interpretation. A high score (90–64 points) indicates that your organization has many of the features characteristic of the mechanistic system. A low score (32–16 points) indicates that your organization has more features usually associated with the organic system. A score in the middle range (63–33 points) indicates that your organization incorporates features of both.

	Strongly Agree (SA)	Agree (A)	Neutral (N)	Disagree (D)	Strongly Disagree (SD)
1.	1	2	3	4	5
2.	5	4	3	2	1
3.	5	4	3	2	1
4.	5	4	3	2	1
5.	5	4	3	2	1
6.	5	4	3	2	1
7.	1	2	3	4	5
8.	5	4	3	2	1
9.	1	2	3	4	5
10.	5	4	3	2	1
11.	5	4	3	2	1
12.	5	4	3	2	1
13.	5	4	3	2	1
14.	5	4	3	2	1
15.	1	2	3	4	5
16.	1	2	3	4	5

Scores: _____ _____ _____ _____ _____

Total Score = _____

Kinko's (now FedEx Kinko's) has come a long way since its humble beginnings as a college town copy shop. It was the creation of Paul Orfalea, who started selling pencils and spiral notebooks on the campus of the University of California, Santa Barbara, in 1970. However, when he realized that it cost 10 cents per page to use the photocopy machine in the library, he realized that selling copies would be more profitable than pencils and notebooks. He borrowed $5,000 and opened his first Kinko's shop in a tiny office measuring 100 square feet. He sold school supplies and made copies on a copy machine that he moved outside when it was in use because the shop was so small.

When Orfalea decided to expand his business into college towns nationwide, he didn't seek out local entrepreneurs to buy franchise rights. Rather, he invited his friends and relatives to become his partners. These partners enjoyed a large share of the store's profits, usually around 50 percent. Many of the partners shared profits with their employees. By 1979 Kinko's had expanded to more than 80 stores in 28 states. Then in the early 1990s, Kinko's was no longer just serving colleges and small businesses. It established a partnership with Federal Express, and FedEx drop boxes were handily placed in all Kinko's outlets following a shift in focus to the growing home office market. By then Kinko's had 420 stores.

In 1996, Orfalea started looking for a group of investors who were interested in reorganizing his company. He realized his organization had become somewhat unmanageable because it had outgrown its original design. Orfalea, himself, was the hub around which the business ran. His partners relied on interpersonal relationships instead of formal authority and responsibility. Orfalea's charismatic leadership style had worked early on because very little coordination was needed among the partners.

Clayton Dubilier & Rice (CD&R) was a private investment firm that could see bright prospects for Kinko's, as long as some organization design changes were made. This new structure was created in 1997. Kinko's established a highly integrated organization. Many of the decisions that had been made in the stores were now being made by top management. The company was reorganized by geographical region—East, West, Central, and International. Kinko's shops had been located in Japan and the Netherlands since 1992. Partners who owned the largest group of stores headed up their regional divisions.

After the reorganization, a search was begun for a new CEO. Gary Kusin joined the company in 2001 in that position. Kusin decided to relocate the company headquarters from Ventura, California, to Dallas, Texas. The move was completed in 2002. Dallas was chosen because it was more centrally located in the United States and a less expensive city in which to do business than was Southern California.

All but three of Kinko's top executives had been replaced by the end of 2002. The common thread in the new top team was that each person was a strong team player, had previously been with a successful organization, and each held jobs with high accountability. The team members had diverse managerial competencies. Their primary job was to implement the programs that Kusin and his team had put together to improve the overall performance of Kinko's.

The team zeroed in on improving efficiency and reducing corporate overhead in each store in order to reduce costs. Management layers in the company's hierarchy were reduced from 12 to 6. An executive vice president of operations was named for the retail side of the business. The vice president of marketing and two general managers for retail operations, operations support, and real estate reported directly to him. These general managers were put in charge of 18 operations directors, each of whom was responsible for the profit and loss in a distinct geographical market. Seventy-four district managers and the human resource and technology staff report directly to these operations directors. All 1,100 branches of Kinko are reported up through the individual districts.

Further expansion of Kinko's commercial business depended on its ability to utilize its store network. The stores had been reorganized into a hub-and-spoke configuration. Spokes were small stores that reported to larger facilities that had extensive capabilities and were open 24 hours a day. Each hub had one or two spokes. Kinko's also added two other categories to their stores: a flagship and a node. Flagship stores were large hubs in high-demand areas and each one had a broad range of technologies. Nodes were smaller stores that were staffed by one person. The nodes were designed for small and sporadic walk-in customers. They sometimes occupied only a corner in an office building. Nodes had low volume, but they were convenient to use and exposed more and more customers to Kinko's.

Large, commercial customers were not forgotten during the organizational redesign. Stand-alone locked facilities were built for large batch jobs. By 2003, four of these large facilities were in use, with four per district planned for the future. All stores were connected through the Internet so that jobs could be allocated, distributed, or shared, as the need arose. This was possible because Kinko's had calibrated all machines in these facilities so that all color copies were identical, regardless of where they were produced.

The senior vice president of sales had 18 sales directors reporting directly to him. Each sales director was responsible for profit and loss in his geographical district. Twenty-four digital sales consultants were added to call on clients and suggest money-saving processes to customers. These consultants reported to the sales directors. Ten engagement managers had been located on-site at the largest Kinko's facility, and there were 74 sales managers, all organized by district, who reported to the sales directors.

FedEx purchased Kinko's in 2004 and changed the company's name to FedEx Kinko's Office and Print Services, Inc. Kusin stepped down in 2006 and was replaced by company executive Kenneth May. Today, FedEx Kinko's operates more than 1,300 locations in 11 countries and has 22,000 team members worldwide serving more than 100 million customers each year. They are the only brand that offers customers 24-hour-a-day, seven-days-a-week, walk-in access to a full range of office and shipping services in more than 400 of their locations. All of their efforts have resulted in an earnings growth with sales in 2005 of more than $2 billion.

Questions

1. What aspects of differentiation and integration are illustrated in this case?

2. What concepts of vertical design are highlighted?

3. Does Kinko's use an organic or mechanistic system to achieve integration?

4. How has the interdependence between the stores changed over time?

chapter 12

© PureStock/Jupiter Images

Guiding Organizational Change and Innovation

Learning Goals

After studying this chapter, you should be able to:

1. Describe four types of organizational change.

2. Explain the planning process for organizational change.

3. Identify four methods of organizational change.

4. Describe how innovation relates to organizational change.

5. Discuss how learning organizations foster change.

Communication Competency

Planning and Administration Competency

Teamwork Competency

Managing Effectively

Self-Management Competency

Strategic Action Competency

Multicultural Competency

Challenge of Managing ....

Georgia-Pacific

© AP Graphics Bank

Located in Atlanta, Georgia-Pacific manufactures and markets tissue, packaging, paper, and building products. Founded 80 years ago as a lumber company, it is now a division of Koch Industries that employs 55,000 people in 300 locations throughout North America and Europe. With Wal-Mart as its biggest customer, it must continually improve in order to retain that account and stay competitive.

To change continuously for the better, Georgia-Pacific relies heavily on teamwork. The goal is to create targeted change quickly, and to do so continuously. A Mill Improvement Process team, located in the Engineering Department, coordinates all of the change projects going on throughout the company. To initiate a change, this group conducts some preliminary diagnostic work. The diagnosis helps the group make decisions about which particular types of changes are needed in specific mills. Then the group works with the managers of each mill to initiate a change effort. If a mill is targeted for change, the process begins with the formation of a mill steering committee. At the Container-board Mill, for example, the steering committee might include five section heads who understand all aspects of manufacturing in that particular mill. The first task of this committee is to conduct a more thorough diagnosis of the mill. After talking to employees to get ideas, the steering committee selects about a dozen specific changes that are needed.

For each needed change at a mill, a special project team is created. Each project team focuses on making a targeted change in a period of 10 weeks. A team leader is appointed to each team and this becomes that person's full-time responsibility. The 10-week periods of targeted change are called *waves*. A wave begins with each project team conducting an all-day kick-off meeting to set a specific goal, establish the methods they will use to track changes, and set up a work plan to achieve the goal. As an example, at the Lehigh Valley Dixie plant, where they manufacture paper cups and plastic lids, a team set a goal of finding new equipment that could produce products more efficiently at a cost that was affordable for the plant. After setting their goals, project teams review them with the mill steering committee. Then project teams work on their own to implement specific changes.

In the case of locating new equipment, the team investigated all of the requirements the new equipment would have to meet, discussed the implications of using a new technology, and conducted an analysis to determine if the required investment was justified.

At the end of 10 weeks, the wave concludes with teams reporting their results to the steering committee. Then, the whole cycle starts over with a new set of project teams working on a new set of issues. To ensure that the same people are not always called on for these intensive projects, the company has a set of rules that helps ensure rotating involvement in the process.

At Georgia-Pacific, the basic process for creating change is highly structured. Each mill has a great deal of independence to implement the process in its own unique way, however. Often project teams create logos for their projects, print identifying t-shirts, and in general find ways to take ownership of the process. At the end of each wave, rewards and recognition may be given to celebrate the achievements of the project teams. During the past decade, thousands of change projects have been carried out, and the Mill Improvement Process has contributed hundreds of thousands of dollars to the company's bottom line. Just as important, the process helped Georgia-Pacific become a learning organization that is capable of thriving in a highly competitive industry.[1]

To learn more about this organization, visit *www.gp.com*.

Describe four types of organizational change.

Types of Organizational Change

Organizational change *refers to any transformation in the design or functioning of an organization.*[2] Effective managers understand when change is needed and are able to guide their organizations through the change process. Often, they learn by watching what other organizations are doing. Other times, the environment jolts the organization into making major changes. Recently, for example, development of the Internet has required managers in almost every industry to rethink and radically change the way their organizations function.

Degree of Change

Massive changes in the way an organization operates occur occasionally, but more often change occurs in small steps. The desire to improve performance continuously in order to stay ahead of competitors is a common reason for smaller organizational changes.[3] Georgia-Pacific understands that small, continuous improvements are essential to remaining competitive. Their Mill Improvement Process is a method for ensuring continuous small change. Over time, the effect is to create large-scale change without experiencing major disruptions. Successful organizations are equally adept at making both radical and incremental changes.

Radical. Radical change *occurs when organizations make major innovations in the ways they do business.* Adopting a new organization design, merging with another organization, and changing from a privately held to a publicly traded company are all examples of radical change. Radical change is relatively infrequent and generally takes a long time to complete. It can be stimulated by changes in the environment, by persistent performance declines, by significant personnel changes, or by a combination of all three factors.

YRC (formerly Yellow Roadway Corporation) underwent radical change after Bill Zollars became CEO. The company had just finished one of its worst years in its 70-year history. It had suffered losses of $30 million, two rounds of layoffs, and a major strike by the teamsters. Zollars was hired to help save the company. He visited terminals all over the country and talked to thousands of dock workers, sales staff, and office employees to convince employees that the company could survive only if it went through a process of radical change. From a company that used to think of itself as just delivering goods, YRC has transformed itself into a high-tech, customer-focused delivery and service business. Due to the changes Zollars spearheaded, a sophisticated information system is now used to implement YRC's new customer-focused strategy. Customers place their orders, track shipments, and review their accounts online. Dock workers and drivers can communicate instantly with each other and easily access schedule and delivery information using wireless, mobile data terminals. Using these same means of communications, sales representatives can learn instantly about a customer's company, the type of loading dock it has, and who needs to sign for deliveries, among other things. Throughout the company, YRC employees are now able to quickly spot and solve problems as they strive to satisfy customers.[4]

Figure 12.1 illustrates a common framework for describing radical organizational change. Although it was introduced more than 50 years ago, most modern accounts of organizational change reflect the basic ideas shown. Developed by social scientist Kurt Lewin, the framework divides the change process into roughly three stages: unfreezing, transitioning, and refreezing.[5]

In stage 1—unfreezing—management plans and prepares the members of the organization for a major transformation. A primary objective in this stage is to convince members of the organization of the need for change and to reduce their tendency to resist the change. In stage 2—transitioning—most of the actual change occurs. Often this stage is described as the implementation process. Finally, in stage 3—refreezing—the

Figure 12.1 | Stages of Radical Change

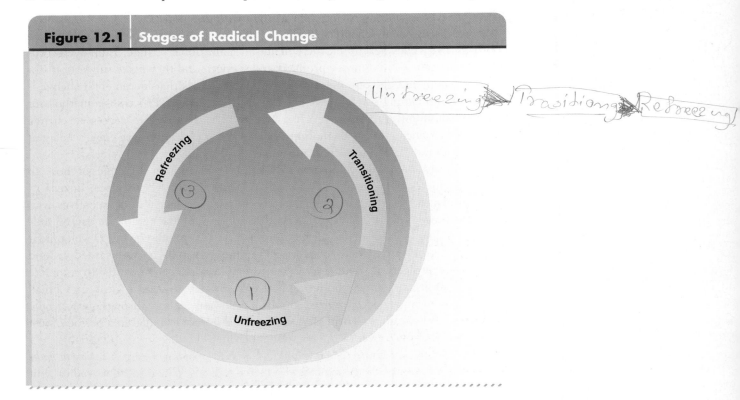

change is solidified. Ideally, changes remain in place once they have been made. But people tend to be creatures of habit, and habits are difficult to change. During refreezing, therefore, monitoring the intended outcomes and providing support for new behaviors are essential to minimize relapses to the old way of doing things.[6]

When implementing a strategy to turn around Boston's Beth Israel Deaconess Medical Center, CEO Paul Levy planned carefully for each of these three stages of change. To unfreeze the organization and convince people of the need for change, he informed the staff of the dire financial situation they faced: Unless the hospital was successful in its effort to improve, it would have to be sold to a for-profit chain and would lose its status as a Harvard teaching hospital. To provide hard evidence that the situation was truly dire, Levy circulated a report prepared by a consultant, which exposed all of the problems they would have to begin dealing with. The change itself was multifaceted. Layoffs were required as part of a restructuring process, and many operational changes were put in place to improve efficiency. Finally, Levy had to deal with the challenge of refreezing the organization. The objective during this phase was to avoid the problem of backsliding, where employees slip back into their old bad habits. In this phase, Levy developed a set of guidelines for behavior for his senior staff (e.g., "disagree without being disagreeable" and "state your objections"), led a discussion about the guidelines and the importance of following them, and made an effort to personally monitor how well individuals followed the guidelines. Employees who behaved according to the new guidelines were recognized and praised; those who slipped back into their old habits were reprimanded. Within three years, Levy had succeeded in returning the medical center to a state of fiscal health, and at the same time improved employee morale.[7]

Incremental. Radical change suggests that one "big bang" can transform an organization into something new. In contrast, incremental change *is an ongoing process of evolution over time, during which many small adjustments occur routinely.* After enough time has passed, the cumulative effect of these adjustments may be to transform the organization totally. Yet while they are occurring, the adjustments seem to be just a normal aspect of revising and improving the way that work gets done.

As we discussed in Chapters 2 and 9, total quality management (TQM) is an approach that relies heavily on incremental organizational change. Employees routinely look for ways to improve products and services, and they make suggestions for changes day in and day out. Georgia-Pacific understands that incremental change is essential to remaining competitive. Their Mill Improvement Process is a method for ensuring continuous small change. Over time, the effect is to create large-scale change without experiencing major disruptions. Successful organizations are equally adept at making both radical and incremental changes.

The World Bank's Development Marketplace is another example of how to encourage incremental change. At the first Development Marketplace, dozens of teams displayed ideas and answered questions from managers and executives who made on-the-spot decisions about which ideas to fund. By the end of the day, $3 million in funding was given to 11 new projects. At each subsequent Development Marketplace (they are held about every 18 months), $5 million was awarded to fund 50 to 60 new projects. By 2006, more than $40 million had been invested to complete about 250 projects ranging from using native freshwater mussels to clean up China's lakes, to establishing a decentralized supply of renewable energy throughout Rwanda, to using LED light units to bring lighting to tribal homes in India. In a period of just a few years, the total effect of the many small changes has become substantial.[8]

People who strive to create radical change but do so by prodding an organization to make many small incremental changes are called tempered radicals.[9] Their ideas are radical, but their approach is tempered. Tempered radicals understand that they can get more done by working as an insider, rather than an outsider, in the system they want to change. Robert Redford, the well-known movie actor and director, is an example of a tempered radical. For two decades, he has worked to increase the diversity of films produced by supporting independent filmmakers at Sundance Institute, an artists' community and film production studio located in Utah. Redford feels he has learned a great deal about creating change. His advice for how other tempered radicals can be successful in creating change is summarized in Table 12.1.[10]

Table 12.1	Advice for Tempered Radicals from Robert Redford

1. Earn credibility first, and then leverage it. If no one will listen to your ideas, it will be impossible to change the system.
2. Gather and accept support from others along the way. People who see you succeeding will want to join you.
3. Develop grassroots initiatives and be willing to share the stage with supporters.
4. Chip away at standard operating procedures little by little over time until you achieve real success.
5. Accept small changes as making progress.
6. Develop your ability to compromise as well as persuade.
7. Be persistent.

Bonnie Nixon-Gardiner at Hewlett-Packard is another tempered radical. As described in the Ethical Challenge feature, Nixon-Gardiner seeks to improve the working conditions of employees in overseas high-tech factories. She seeks to create industry-wide changes by setting standards for her employer, and she also seeks to influence what other companies in the industry do. She is passionate about her concerns, but her approach to creating change is practical. She understands that she cannot change the world in a day, a week, or even a year. If she can stimulate small changes over the course on a decade, she will feel she has made a significant contribution.[11]

Ethical Challenge

Bonnie Nixon-Gardiner

A middle-level manager at Hewlett-Packard, Bonnie Nixon-Gardiner cares about how companies treat employees. To show how serious she is, she recently showed up unannounced in Long Hua, China, to inspect the working conditions at the massive manufacturing plant of one of HP's key suppliers. When company executives tried to steer her into a conference room, she simply refused to be diverted from her mission to see firsthand how the company's 200,000 employees were treated. After all, as the program manager for HP's Supply Chain Social and Environmental Responsibility unit, touring the plant was her responsibility.

When the tech industry began outsourcing manufacturing to low-wage countries she worried about the sweatshop conditions that had been exposed in offshore plants such as those that produced athletic gear for Nike and other apparel companies. To address those concerns, she began by benchmarking how other companies monitored their suppliers. Then she set high standards for HP's partners.

Today HP has a system of 70 auditors who inspect 200 factories owned by 150 of their suppliers. Nixon-Gardiner also uses education to create change. For example, HP recently introduced a training program to teach Chinese manufacturers how to prevent labor and environmental abuses.

But Nixon-Gardiner was not content to monitor HP's suppliers. She wants to help the whole industry meet its ethical responsibilities. "My 10-year vision is for consumers to know that when you touch a technology product, you are guaranteed it was made in a socially and environmentally responsible way," she explains. From her position within HP, Nixon-Gardiner realized that she could help create industry-wide change. When a human rights watchdog group began to put the spotlight on high-tech companies, she and her counterparts at Dell, IBM, Intel, and other companies quietly formulated the Electronic Industry Code of Conduct. Briefly, the code bans abuses such as forced labor, child labor, and excessive overtime. It also requires manufacturers to adhere to some basic standards for environmental protection and participate in an inspection system for monitoring working conditions in the plants.

Gradually, Nixon-Gardiner's effort is paying off. After six visits to one plant, she could see the results of her work. The supplier had addressed her concerns one-by-one, which eventually meant they spent tens of thousands of dollars to reduce employees' exposure to dangerous equipment and harmful noise. A manager at the plant described the experience this way: "Dealing with Nixon-Gardiner is like being kissed and slapped at the same time. It can make you psychotic—but it needs to be done."

To learn more about the Electronic Industry Code of Conduct, visit *www.eicc.info*.

Created by tempered radicals within the high-tech industry, the Electronic Industry Code of Conduct monitors employee working conditions.

© Mark Gibson/Workbook Stock/Jupiter Images

Timing of Change

In addition to the differences in the magnitude of change are differences in the timing of change. Organizations may make radical changes in response to a crisis or because leaders have a bold new vision of what the future *could* be like. Similarly, organizations may make incremental changes as a reaction to past events or in anticipation of trends that have just begun to develop. Figure 12.2 illustrates how the degree and timing of change combine to form different types of change.

Reactive. Reactive change *occurs when an organization is forced to adapt or innovate in response to some event in the external or internal environment.* New strategic moves made by competitors and new scientific or technological discoveries are common reasons for reactive change. Declining organizational performance is another common trigger for reactive change. When a business is in severe decline, often a new top management team is hired to develop and implement a turnaround plan.[12] As Wal-Mart expanded, for example, Kmart had to pursue a reactive change strategy. Its declining performance required it to close hundreds of stores, fire the CEO, and rethink its business strategy. Similarly, now that Wal-Mart is the world's biggest grocery chain, Safeway, Kroger, and other competitors are reacting to Wal-Mart's low-price strategy by offering upscale products and services to retain customers.

Reactive change can be incremental or radical. If an organization adapts to a change in the environment without undergoing a substantial reorientation in its strategy or values, the change is reactive and incremental.

At General Electric, Avery-Denison, and many other organizations, managers are encouraged to make incremental reactive change through a process called *Work-Out*. In a Work-Out session, groups of managers and employees from around the company work together in

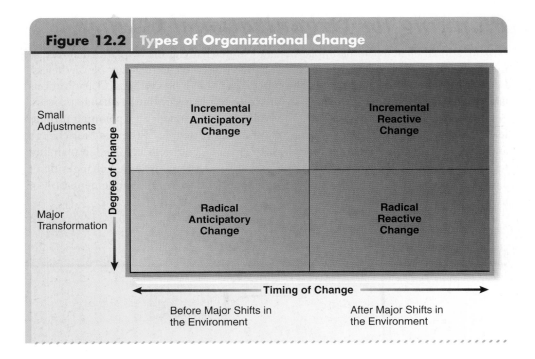

Figure 12.2 | Types of Organizational Change

Degree of Change

Small Adjustments

Major Transformation

| Incremental Anticipatory Change | Incremental Reactive Change |
| Radical Anticipatory Change | Radical Reactive Change |

Timing of Change

Before Major Shifts in the Environment

After Major Shifts in the Environment

small teams to address problems. Often the teams focus on how to reduce unnecessary work. That is, they try to find ways to get work out of the system—for example, by reducing red tape and finding ways to be more efficient. Small teams work to develop solutions to problems, and then present their ideas in a Town Meeting. Attending the Town Meeting are other small teams and a senior manager with the authority needed to agree to implement the suggestions. During the Town Meeting, the manager discusses the ideas with everyone and makes a decision on the spot about whether to accept each solution that is recommended. If a change is to be made, volunteers are given assignments immediately and they are expected to be sure that the changes get implemented.[13] As described in the opening Challenge of Managing feature, Georgia-Pacific uses a process similar to Work-Out to constantly reduce costs and improve efficiency.

Anticipatory Change. As the term suggests, anticipatory change *occurs when managers make organizational modifications based on forecasts of upcoming events or early in the cycle of a new trend.* The best-run organizations always look for better ways to do things in order to stay ahead of the competition. They constantly fine-tune their policies and practices, introduce technological improvements, and set new standards for customer satisfaction. Often, anticipatory change is incremental and results from constant tinkering and improvements. Occasionally, anticipatory change is discontinuous, however. Visionary leaders within the organization become convinced that major changes are needed even though there is no apparent crisis. Because there is no crisis, the change can be planned carefully and implemented gradually. For example, Cisco Systems, Procter & Gamble, and Bank of America all are rethinking their use of office space. Offices are very expensive for companies. With new technologies that make it easier for employees to work from home, on the road, or even at the local Starbucks coffeehouse, forward-looking CEOs are beginning to realize that they can cut costs by supporting employees who can and want to work at locations other than the company office. Over time, these companies are initiating changes that focus more attention on what their employees accomplish and less on where and when they do their work.[14]

Planning for Organizational Change

Organizational change can be unplanned and somewhat chaotic or planned and relatively smooth. By its very nature, chaotic change is difficult to manage. Nevertheless, large-scale organizational changes seldom occur without a bit of chaos. Organizations usually strive to minimize that chaos by imposing some order on the change process.

Change is most likely to be orderly when it has been planned. The planning process itself can help unfreeze the organization by convincing people of the need for change and involving them in decisions about how to change. The steps involved in planning for organizational change are shown in Figure 12.3. Although planned changes don't always proceed exactly as shown, planning generally precedes the implementation of major change initiatives.[15]

The Process of Organizational Change

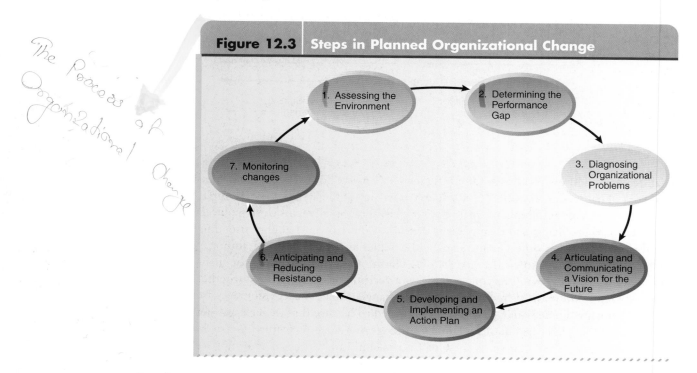

Figure 12.3   Steps in Planned Organizational Change

1. Assessing the Environment
2. Determining the Performance Gap
3. Diagnosing Organizational Problems
4. Articulating and Communicating a Vision for the Future
5. Developing and Implementing an Action Plan
6. Anticipating and Reducing Resistance
7. Monitoring changes

Assessing the Environment

As we described in Chapter 4, both the degree and rate of change in the environment have implications for organizations. The four environmental factors most responsible for stimulating organizational change are customers, technology, competitors, and the workforce. Other factors that may pressure organizations to change include globalization, technological advances, and the actions of important stakeholders, such as shareholders, government regulators, unions, and political action groups.

Environmental scanning activities ensure that organizations become aware of changes as they occur. Marriott Hotels and Bank of America, among other firms, use customer satisfaction surveys and other forms of market research to assess customers' changing preferences. Similarly, employee surveys are a method of scanning the internal environment to assess the concerns of the workforce.

At PepsiCo, the maker of soft drinks and snack foods, environmental scanning helped the company recognize that customers were beginning to switch from carbonated to noncarbonated drinks. That insight meant the company began early to build market share in bottled water and sports drinks, under their Gatorade brand. More recently, PepsiCo's environmental scanning processes led it to form an alliance with

Starbucks, and now it dominates the bottled-coffee market.[16] Many other aspects of PepsiCo were addressed in Chapter 10.

Determining the Performance Gap

A performance gap *is the difference between what the organization wants to do and what it actually does.* By determining the performance gap, managers provide clear answers to the question "What is wrong?" At Georgia-Pacific, teams of employees have responsibility for determining performance gaps. At the corporate level, a Mill Process Improvement team assesses the performance gaps of specific mills. This information is used to decide which mills are most in need of improvement. Then for each mill, a local steering committee conducts more detailed diagnoses to identify particular aspects of the production process where performance improvements are needed. For example, at the Dixie plant, performance improvements were needed on the lines that produced paper cups and lids in order to reduce the costs of these particular products.

Diagnosing Organizational Problems

The aim of organizational diagnosis *is to identify the nature and extent of problems before taking action in order to develop an understanding of the reasons behind gaps in performance.* They answer the question "Why do we have performance gaps?" At Georgia-Pacific, teams concluded that the high production costs were due to outdated technology, and not to the high cost of raw materials or packaging. The idea that diagnosis should precede action may seem obvious, but its importance is often underestimated. All too often results-oriented managers prematurely begin the change process and impatiently push for solutions before the nature of the problem itself is clear.

Organizations often hire outside consultants to assist with problem diagnosis. For example, interpersonal problems often require gathering sensitive information from employees. Outside consultants may be better able to conduct interviews and interpret data in an unbiased manner than insiders. In addition, consultants often have the expertise in implementing change processes. Georgia-Pacific used consultants to help it design its approach to creating small, rapid changes.

Articulating and Communicating a Vision for the Future

Successful change efforts are guided by a clear vision for the future. Until leaders formulate a clear vision and persuade others to join them in being dedicated to that vision, they won't be able to generate the enthusiasm and resources needed for large-scale cultural change.[17]

To communicate the leader's vision, messages should be sent consistently and repeatedly through varying organizational channels by credible sources.[18] Communicating his vision for YRC was one of the most important items on Bill Zollars' agenda during his first year as CEO. He went on a tour and visited sites all around the country. Zollars used face-to-face communication because he believed employees needed to hear directly from him about his vision. He spent 18 months traveling to different locations and holding small on-site meetings to explain his new vision to employees.[19]

Developing and Implementing an Action Plan

Although investments made in planning often produce significant improvements in productivity, many companies begin substantial change efforts without a thoughtful, integrated plan of action. For major change efforts, the organization's action plan can

Snapshot

"Visibility is incredibly important. It's hard to lead through e-mail. When I first got to YRC we were in a bad state. So I spent 85 percent of my time on the road talking to people one on one or in small groups. I would start off in the morning with the sales force, and then the people on the docks and then have a customer dinner. I would say the same thing to every group ad nauseam. You have to be relentless in your message."

Bill Zollars, CEO and Chairman, YRC

be quite complex and not easily understood by most employees because it includes proposals for all levels and all units involved in the change effort. However, in an organization structured by functional department, each department should develop a more focused action plan based on the overall plan. In an organization structured by region, more detailed plans for each region should be developed, and so on. At Georgia-Pacific, where changes typically are completed within a period of just 10 weeks, each project team develops its own plan for implementing change.

Regardless of the approach used, the action plan should be adopted only after considering the full range of alternative methods for fostering change, which we describe in more detail later in this chapter. An action plan articulates the goals for change and describes the specific measures to be used to monitor and evaluate progress toward those goals. Finally, the action plan provides a timetable for implementation and evaluation.

Consider Alternatives. When developing an action plan, management should consider all feasible alternatives, along with their advantages and disadvantages. In recent years, for example, many U.S. companies have had to cope with declining business due to a weak economy. To cut costs, many companies have resorted to laying off their employees. But some companies understand that the long-term effects of laying people off can be very negative, so they have used other methods of cutting costs. Some alternatives to layoffs include:

- Reducing the hours in a standard workweek, so everyone works and earns a little less,

- Encouraging employees to take temporary leaves,

- Not renewing contracts for temporary and part-time workers,

- Job sharing, and

- Reducing executive salaries and bonuses.

These alternatives to layoffs can reduce costs without imposing job losses on workers. When layoffs cannot be avoided, the best companies help their employees adjust to the change. At Ben & Jerry's, layoffs were needed after the company was acquired by Unilever. To ease the disruption of this change, Unilever gave the 52 affected employees one full year of advance notice and helped them find new jobs.[20]

Early Involvement. For a plan to be effective, those who will be affected must buy into it. The best way to ensure that is through early involvement.[21] That employees should be involved in planning change seems obvious, but even experienced managers often forget this principle.

Task forces, focus groups, surveys, hot lines, and informal conversations are but a few of the ways that managers can involve employees and other stakeholders in assessing the alternatives for change. There is little disagreement among change experts about the importance of involvement. How you get people involved is less important than doing it.

Set Goals. For change to be effective, goals should be set before the change effort is started. If possible, the goals should be (1) stated in clear and measurable terms, (2) consistent with the organization's overall goals and policies, and (3) realistically attainable. For example, when a take-out pizza business in Virginia decided that it needed to improve driver safety, it began by collecting systematic information about driving behaviors (e.g., the extent to which drivers came to complete stops at intersections). Management shared the information with employees and asked them to set specific goals for improvement. During the months that followed, driving behavior was monitored and charts were used to inform employees of their progress toward meeting those goals. Employees participating in goal setting showed improvement in several areas of behavior, including some for which they hadn't even set specific goals.[22]

Anticipating and Reducing Resistance

Few planned change efforts go as smoothly as managers would like. As we have already noted, most run into some amount of resistance. Although we often are stimulated by change, most people react negatively when faced with too much change. How do you react to change? To gain more awareness of your own feelings about change, complete the self-diagnostic questionnaire presented in the Self-Management Competency feature.

Self-Management Competency

Reactions to Change

For each item, circle "T" if the statement is true or circle "F" if the statement is false. There are no right or wrong answers. Rather, the intent is to help you explore your attitudes about change.

Statement

(T) F 1. Among my friends, I'm usually the first person to try out a new idea or method.

T (F) 2. When I take vacations, I prefer to return to places I have been to already and know I will like.

T (F) 3. Compared to other people, I tend to change the way I look (hair, clothes) fairly often.

(T) F 4. I enjoy trying new foods, even if I'm not sure about the ingredients.

T (F) 5. I would prefer to work for many different companies rather than just a few during the course of my career.

(T) F 6. I am happiest when I'm working on problems that I'm quite sure I can solve.

T (F) 7. At work I get annoyed by people who seem to always have suggestions for how to change the way things are done.

(T) F 8. I seldom follow rules that I think are silly or ineffective.

(T) F 9. I believe that taking needless risks is irresponsible.

(T) F 10. I would prefer a job that I can master and become a real expert at doing, rather than one where I am always doing something new.

T (F) 11. Most of my friends are pretty similar to me in their general interests and backgrounds.

(T) F 12. In five years, I am likely to be working at something that is so different I can't even imagine doing it today.

T (F) 13. If I'm working on something new and run into a problem, I prefer to keep trying to solve the problem on my own rather than ask someone else for help.

Scoring

A. For the following items, circle those you answered "True." Then give yourself one point for each item you circled:

1
3
4
5
8
12

Total Points for Part A: ___4___

B. For the following items, circle those you answered "False." Then give yourself one point for each item you circled.

2
6
7
9
10
11
13

Total Points for Part B: ___4___

C. Add your points for parts A and B to get your total score:

___4___ + ___4___ = ___8___ (Total Points)

Interpretation

The higher your score, the more you enjoy change and the uncertainty associated with change. If you scored 10 or higher, you would enjoy working in an organization that offers cutting-edge products or services. Radical change drives you.

If you scored 4 through 9, you welcome incremental changes that do not disrupt your life. You would enjoy organizations that reward calculated risk-taking and prefer improving products rather than designing new ones.

If you scored 3 or less, you react to change as a burden and try to avoid changes that will cause you frustration. You would most enjoy working for organizations that provide clear performance measures and career guidelines.

After you have calculated your score, discuss it with a few of your classmates. Does everyone react to change the same way you do?

Change looks easy on paper, but can be hard to implement and maintain. This is why employees need continuous guidance during the initial stages of change within an organization.

© Steven Puetzer/Nonstock/Jupiter Images

To deal successfully with the resistance they are likely to encounter, managers must learn to anticipate people's reactions to change and address their concerns. Experienced managers are all too aware of the various forms that resistance can take: immediate criticism, malicious compliance, sabotage, insincere agreement, silence, deflection, and in-your-face defiance, strikes, and output restrictions are just a few examples.[23] Some managers don't even initiate needed changes because they feel incapable of overcoming expected resistance. Successful managers understand why people resist change and what can be done to overcome such resistance.

Some resistance to change may actually be useful. Employees can operate as a check-and-balance mechanism to ensure that management properly plans and implements change. Justifiable resistance that causes management to think through its proposed changes more carefully may result in better decisions. Effective change efforts rest on the ability of managers to overcome resistance. The commonly used methods for doing so are education, participation, and incentives.

In general, individuals—and sometimes even entire organizations—tend to resist change for four reasons: fear, vested interests, misunderstandings, and cynicism.[24]

Fear. To be able to reduce resistance to change, managers first of all must not be afraid of resistance—and then help employees not to be afraid of change or its consequences. Some people resist change because they fear that they'll be unable to develop the competencies required to be effective in the new situation. A common obstacle to organizational change is the reluctance of managers and employees to change their attitudes and learn the new behaviors that the organization requires.

When Unilever acquired Ben & Jerry's, employees feared that their quirky culture would be destroyed and their organization would lose its unique appeal as a great place to work. To help counteract those fears, Unilever allowed Ben & Jerry's employees to choose the human resource policies it wanted to retain. And when Ben & Jerry's did adopt a Unilever policy, it was permitted to modify it to fit the company culture.[25]

Vested Interests. Fear often goes hand in hand with vested interests. People who have vested interests in maintaining things as they are often resist change. This behavior seems to occur even when these people recognize the need for change. Convincing people that change is needed for the good of the organization does not necessarily reduce their resistance to it. They are likely to continue to resist the change if they believe that it conflicts with their own self-interests.[26]

Some managers initiate change believing that anyone with the same information would make the same decision. This assumption isn't always correct. Often top-level managers see change as a way to improve the organization. They may also believe that change will offer them new opportunities to develop their own competencies as they tackle new challenges. In contrast, employees may view proposed changes as upsetting the agreements between themselves and their employer. They may expect increased workloads and longer hours to be the only rewards for staying around to help implement a major organizational change. As Georgia-Pacific understands, empowering workers and giving them some control over the change process is an effective way to reduce the stress that employees experience during a change effort.

Misunderstandings. People resist change when they don't understand its implications. Unless quickly addressed, misunderstandings and lack of trust build resistance. Top managers must be visible during the change process to spell out clearly the new direction for the organization and what it will mean for everyone involved. Getting employees to discuss their problems openly is crucial to overcoming resistance to change. When wide-ranging changes are planned, managers should anticipate that misunderstandings will develop and take steps to minimize them.

Cynicism. In some organizations, initiating change efforts is seen simply as something that new managers do to make their mark. Over time, employees see change efforts come and go much like the seasons of the year, as managers implement one fad after the other. Eventually, cynicism sets in and employees refuse to support yet another change "program." Without employee support the change efforts fail, which further contributes to cynicism.[27]

One way to reduce cynicism is to make *successful* change a normal part of daily life in the organization. Employees who are more accustomed to seeing changes occur around them become more open to new change initiatives.[28] Another way to reduce cynicism is by involving employees throughout the change process. Research shows that participation, especially when it is voluntary, usually leads to commitment.[29] Involving employees in the change process provides them with an opportunity to help control their own destiny. It encourages people to take ownership and accept responsibility for helping to shape the new future in which they will work. Georgia-Pacific relies on informal communications among employees as a way to minimize misunderstandings that might arise during the process of change. Georgia-Pacific's Mill Improvement Process involves employees from all levels and all areas in planning and carrying out change. Problems of misunderstanding are minimized because members of project teams are involved in every step of the change process. When employees who are not part of the project team have questions, they can easily get answers by asking a coworker who is directly involved.

Monitoring Change

As the process of change unfolds, managers need to monitor employees' reactions as well as results. Measures of employee stress, customer satisfaction, new-product development, market share, profitability, and other results should be tracked to assess both short-term and long-term consequences. The speed, degree, and duration of improvement should all be monitored. Ideally, the measures used for monitoring and follow-up should be closely tied to the goals and timetables established in the action plan.

Because the continuous monitoring of change is costly and time consuming, assessments typically are made at predetermined intervals. If possible, the first assessment should be made before the change has been implemented. If that is not possible, it should be made as soon as the change process begins. To avoid jumping to premature

Snapshot

"When I need to announce a change, I go to my top performers first. I give as much information as I possibly can to help them understand the reasons behind the change. I prefer one-on-one communication, particularly if it is an important change."

Teresa Robinson, Senior Manager of Best Practices and Risk Management, Aflac

conclusions, management should make another assessment later. Sometimes the second assessment reveals that the positive effects of change have worn off. Alternatively, a second assessment could reveal delayed positive effects.

At Georgia-Pacific, the initial diagnosis is the first assessment. All project teams also conduct an assessment after 5 weeks, which is typically the midpoint of the change process. Another assessment occurs at the end of the 10-week wave. Monitoring of the results is then done on an as-needed basis to ensure that the changes have taken hold permanently.

3.

Identify four methods of organizational change.

Implementing Change

Having decided that change is needed, managers have available to them many methods that they can use to make it happen. Here we discuss the four major methods depicted in Figure 12.4. Although we describe each method separately, some combination of these approaches is involved in most large organizational change efforts. Seldom can significant change be based on one of these approaches alone.[30]

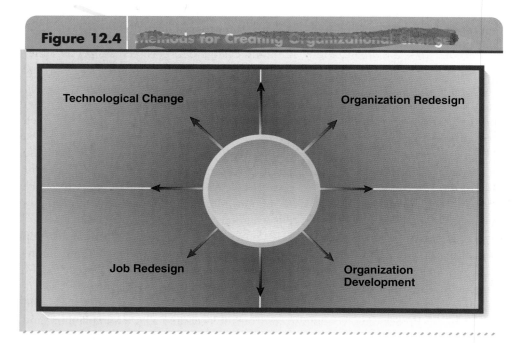

Figure 12.4 Methods for Creating Organizational Change

Technological Change

Organization Redesign

Job Redesign

Organization Development

Technological Change

Technological change *involves incremental adjustments or radical innovations that affect workflows, production methods, materials, and information systems.* In 1908, Henry Ford changed the workplace by demonstrating how effectively assembly-line technologies could be used to produce cars. In that new age of mass consumption, the revolutionary assembly-line technology was ideal for making identical goods in volume.

Today, technological change often involves new forms of information technology—the complex networks of computers, telecommunications systems, and remote-controlled devices that are the glue of modern organization. As information technology continues to evolve, it is becoming increasingly easy for organizations to build links between suppliers, producers, distributors, and customers. At YRC, information technology allows customers, drivers, and service representatives to stay in continuous communication with each other. In the retail industry, electronic cash registers monitor the goods sold, their prices, and the amounts remaining on hand (inventory). If the system recognizes that a store is low on a particular product, the system can order it from the nearest distribution center. Information technology also allows customers to provide comments and feedback to companies on their Web sites. Companies, in turn, can use their Web sites to inform customers about changes in an organization's products and services. At the Yahoo! Web site, employees and customers hold a continuing electronic conversation about both the changes that customers request and the actions that Yahoo! takes in response.

A very recent technological change is open-source software, *which refers to computer software that is available with its source code. Whereas the source code for traditional software (e.g., Microsoft Office) is typically kept secret and protected by patents that prevent others from altering or selling it, open-source software allows anybody to acquire it, copy it, revise it, share and market it.* The Linux computer operating system is probably the best-known example of open-source software. Since Linux first began to reinvent the process of software development, however, dozens of other programs have become available. IBM has been a major force in the promotion of open-source software. It has spent billions developing the Linux operating system because it saw this as an opportunity to leverage the talents of thousands of talented programmers. Then, in 2004, IBM offered 500 of its software patents to programmers. It now offers all of its patents royalty-free to anyone designing software standards for health or education. The idea is to encourage faster development of software that works effectively across a wide range of products.[31]

Organization Redesign

Organization redesign *involves incremental adjustments or radical innovations focused on realigning departments, changing who makes decisions, and merging or reorganizing departments that sell the organization's products.* Recall our discussion of the fundamentals of organization design in Chapter 11. The organization redesign approach may mean moving from one form of organization to another—for example, from functional to product departmentalization. At Emerson, an electronics business based in St. Louis, Missouri, an organization redesign involved setting up account teams to deal with big customers who buy from several of the company's different divisions. With more and more goods being sold through very large, "big-box" retailers, Emerson is just one of many manufacturing companies that have implemented this type of organization redesign.[32]

Two basic approaches to organization redesign are changing the organization's structure and changing the organization's processes. Occasionally, a truly radical idea shapes the organization's design, as was the case with Visa, the credit card company. Visa was the world's first virtual company. It began as a consortium of banks offering a credit card service and has grown into a worldwide brand. Today, it is a network organization made up of a web of connections between 27,000 financial institutions and about 1.3 billion cardholders. Visa not only invented a new type of organization, it reinvented the credit card business.[33]

Regardless of the redesign chosen, the intent usually is to clarify what gives the organization its leadership position with its customers. In other words, organization design changes should capitalize on the capabilities that differentiate the organization from its competitors. Businesses, goods, or services that don't contribute to this goal are candidates for elimination or sale.

Structural Redesign. Restructuring *typically means reconfiguring the distribution of authority, responsibility, and control in an organization.* Authority, responsibility, and control change radically when entire businesses or divisions are combined or spun off, such as when IBM sold its laptop computer business to Lenovo.

Downsizing is another familiar approach to structural redesign. Downsizing is usually a reactive response to poor organizational performance. This often-used method of change doesn't necessarily work, however. When Colgate Palmolive offered incentives to 400 senior managers to resign, it was looking to reduce costs. When more than 300 managers decided to leave, however, the company lost many more of its most experienced managers that it had planned for. Although downsizing may improve financial performance in the short run, several studies have indicated that downsized firms end up in worse financial shape later.[34] However, no one knows whether such firms would have even survived without the changes undertaken. Regardless of how effective it may be in the long run, downsizing is a painful experience for both those who are let go and those who survive the cuts. The survivors often feel guilty because, somehow, they have been spared, but they also are anxious because they might be next. Survivors often have trouble maintaining a commitment to an organization when they might be "doing time" until the next round of layoffs is announced.[35]

Reengineering. When organizations want to improve their efficiency and the quality of their products and services, they often examine their internal production processes. If they decide to change those processes, they may create change through reengineering, *which refers to the radical redesigning of an organization's functions and business processes.* The change usually involves reorganizing from a structure based on functional departments to one that is based around key production processes and/or service processes. Reengineering often involves redesigning processes related to logistics, manufacturing, and distribution. The goal is to design the most effective process for making and delivering a product or service.[36] Effective processes are those that cost the least while at the same time rapidly producing goods and providing services of excellent quality. The starting point is to assess current processes from the customer's point of view.

Often, reengineering is interrelated with other key activities. Recall that many organizations are structured by function and that employees' reactions to change typically are based on its effect on their departments. Reengineering requires employees to think across functions. Reengineering can reduce the amount of "handoffs" between departments by increasing the amount of resources that are brought together simultaneously to meet customers' needs. Benefits may include faster delivery time, more accurate billing, and fewer defective products that must be returned. By reengineering its insurance claims processes, National Grange Mutual & Insurance Company, a subsidiary of Main Street America Group, was able to reduce its response time by 55 percent. This means that customers receive their money faster and with less hassle. After reengineering, customer satisfaction improved as did the company's overall growth rate.[37]

Job Redesign

Job redesign *involves modifying specific employee job responsibilities and tasks.* Whenever a job is modified—whether because of new technology or an organizational redesign—job designs also change. Two dramatically different ways of changing job designs are job simplification and job enrichment.

The oldest task approach to change is job simplification. Job simplification *involves the scientific analysis of tasks performed by employees in order to discover procedures that produce the maximum output for the minimum input.* The goal of job simplification is to find the most efficient way to get work done. It identifies the tasks to be performed and the work methods to be used to achieve an efficient workflow process. Like reengineering, job simplification is founded on engineering concepts.

Recall that the scientific management techniques developed by Frederick Taylor defined jobs and designed tasks on the basis of time-and-motion studies (see Chapter 2). But there is a big difference between these two approaches to change. Reengineering focuses on an entire process, which may involve many employees working in many parts of the organization. In contrast, the focus of job simplification is the work done by employees in a particular job. For example, if McDonald's restaurants reengineered its facilities, it would redesign the entire stores—including the order-taking technology, kitchen design, and eating areas. However, if how the job of cashier needed to be changed, the company could simply undergo a job simplification.

The downside of job simplification is that it leads to low employee commitment and high turnover. Most current competitive challenges require a committed and involved workforce that is able to make decisions and experiment with new ways of doing things. Many people seek jobs that allow greater discretion and offer more of a challenge. Thus designing jobs with employee needs in mind requires a different approach. *Changing job specifications to broaden and add challenge to the tasks required and to increase productivity is called* job enrichment. Job enrichment has four unique aspects. First, it changes the basic relationships between employees and their work. Job enrichment is based on the assumption that interesting and challenging work can be a source of employee satisfaction, involvement, and increased performance.

Second, job enrichment directly changes employee behaviors in ways that gradually lead to more positive attitudes about the organization and a better self-image. Because enriched jobs usually increase feelings of autonomy and personal freedom, employees are likely to develop attitudes that support the new job-related behaviors.

Third, job enrichment offers numerous opportunities for initiating other types of organizational change. Technical problems are likely to surface when jobs are changed. This offers management an opportunity to refine the technology used. Interpersonal problems almost inevitably arise between managers and subordinates and sometimes among coworkers who have to relate to one another in different ways. These situations offer opportunities for developing teamwork and communication competencies.

Finally, job enrichment can humanize an organization. Individuals can experience the psychological lift that comes from developing new competencies and doing a job well. Individuals are encouraged to grow and push themselves.

Organization Development

Many people-oriented methods for changing organizations are commonly grouped under the broad label of organization development. Organization development (OD) *is a planned, long-range behavioral science strategy for understanding, changing, and developing an organization's workforce in order to improve its effectiveness.*[38] Although OD methods frequently include design, technological, and task changes, their primary focus is on changing people. Of the many OD methods available, three of the most commonly used are focus groups, survey feedback, and team building.

Focus Groups. When focus groups are used for organizational development, the goal is usually to learn about how employees feel about the current situation in their organization. Understanding the perspective of employees is important when designing change efforts. A focus group discussion *is a carefully planned discussion among several employees about a specific topic or issue of interest, which is led by a trained facilitator.* The facilitator's role is to create an open, nonthreatening environment and to keep the discussion on track. Because the goal is to collect information systematically, several focus groups are conducted throughout the organization, and notes are taken at each focus group meeting. Figure 12.5 shows a typical setup for a focus group discussion.[39]

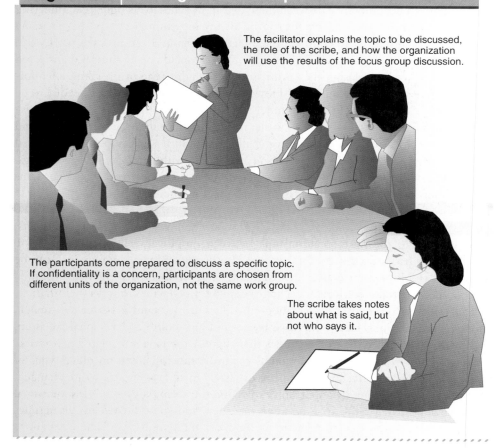

Figure 12.5 | Running a Focus Group Discussion

The facilitator explains the topic to be discussed, the role of the scribe, and how the organization will use the results of the focus group discussion.

The participants come prepared to discuss a specific topic. If confidentiality is a concern, participants are chosen from different units of the organization, not the same work group.

The scribe takes notes about what is said, but not who says it.

Survey Feedback. Focus groups can reveal a great deal about how employees think and feel, but they are not practical for gathering data from a large number of employees. When managers want to hear from several hundred or even thousands of employees, they may find that it is more practical to use survey feedback as a method for organization development. Survey feedback *is a process that allows managers and employees to report their thoughts and feelings about the organization and to learn about how others think and feel about their own behaviors.*[40] Such information becomes the basis for group discussion and the stimulus for change. Accurate feedback from others about behaviors and job performance is one of the primary bases of OD.

Feedback is obtained by means of a questionnaire developed and distributed to all employees, who complete it and turn it in anonymously. The content of the questionnaire depends on the areas of most concern to the organization. Typically, however, employee surveys tap into employees' feelings of commitment and satisfaction, their assessments of the climate for innovation, the degree to which they feel that the organization is customer oriented, and their attitudes toward supervision and management practices. When employee surveys are designed to address issues of strategic importance, they can be used to enhance the organization's competitive advantage.

When companies such as Intel, GE, and IBM conduct employee surveys, the company's employees respond over the Web. Results from the survey are reported separately for each business unit around the world. After studying and discussing their results, and making comparisons to other units, managers are expected to develop action plans for making improvements within their units. Most large U.S. companies conduct employee surveys annually as a way to monitor employee satisfaction and morale.

Team Building. As organizations become flatter and rely more on teams to get work done, the importance of team building has also grown. Team building *is a process that develops the ability of team members to collaborate effectively so they can perform the tasks assigned to them.* Team building activities often emphasize the importance of developing a group climate that is safe, where people trust each other and feel free to express their feelings and share their perceptions about daily experiences and hassles. Outdoor challenge courses and various types of physical activities are popular approaches to team building. Hiding feelings or not being accepted by the group diminishes the individual's willingness to work constructively toward solutions to problems. Openness can be risky, but it also promotes creativity and can usually help people effectively plan solutions to problems and carry them out.[41]

Combining Methods of Change

Organizational change is a complex undertaking. Usually, large-scale change efforts involve a combination of methods. Because information is integral to the functioning of most organizations, any restructuring effort is likely to have implications for the design and use of information systems.

Purchasing and installing enterprise resource planning (ERP) software is a management decision that often involves many forms of organizational change. ERP software is designed to be an enterprise-wide solution to all the information technology needs a company might have. It can pull together information about the company's financial performance, customer relations, human resources, manufacturing, distribution, and so on. Usually, it is extremely costly and it can be difficult to implement well. Changing to an ERP system involves more than having employees learn a new software program. They often must also learn to do a variety of new administrative tasks. For example, salespeople may be asked to record information about the source of all new customers and the reasons for customers canceling their orders. The information doesn't help the salesperson directly, but marketing uses it to assess the productivity of advertising campaigns.

When managers decide to purchase ERP software, they may think they are just making a change in the company's IT system. But that's a mistake. As described in the following Communication Competency feature, installing new information technologies can be a form of radical change. To succeed, employees need to embrace the new technologies. Fairchild Semiconductor understands that involving employees in the design of new technologies goes a long way toward gaining employee support and cooperation.[42]

Fairchild Semiconductor

When Fairchild Semiconductor introduced the first integrated circuit back in the 1960s, it began a revolution in information technology. Since its founding, it has undergone many transformations, including being acquired by National Semiconductor, and subsequently being spun off again. After it was spun off from National, one of its first goals was to transition from National's data management system to one of its own. It chose an ERP application from PeopleSoft, and then set about adapting its processes to meet the software's requirements. The first step was to form teams of employees from all over the world to rework the company's business processes in finance, manufacturing, logistics, and human resources. The goal was to replace all of the customized business processes throughout the company with "plain vanilla" processes that fit the generic software system.

Once new processes were designed, extensive training was needed before and after the rollout of the new system. Besides teaching employees the new tasks they would be expected to perform, the training sessions explained why these new tasks were important. The goal was to ensure that employees understood how their own work was related to the overall business processes. The company felt that employees would be less likely to take shortcuts to reduce their own workloads if they understood how their own contributions affected other people in the company and the bottom line. To build employees' confidence in their ability to use the new system, training sessions provided plenty of time for people to practice using the software and receive feedback.

Fairchild's installation of ERP software turned out to be the first step in an ongoing and long-term process of change. Once they had software in place to manage day-to-day activities, the company began another major change effort. This time the goal was to design and deploy a comprehensive solution for forecasting demand and man-

aging their supply chain. Fairchild needed to reengineer its core business processes and implement world-class supply chain management practices for all plants and divisions. Working with IBM as their strategic partner, Fairchild used a similar approach for managing this change effort. To build on its past achievements, the new system would not introduce new data sources. Instead it would use data captured by the existing ERP system. When completed, the new system would change the company's methods of demand forecasting, supply and demand matching, strategic capacity planning, factory loading, allocation management, inventory transfers, warehouse management, and order promising.

Once again, involving key employees facilitated acceptance of the new system. A series of workshops was held with key people from various Fairchild organizations around the world. During these workshops, company experts documented their current business processes and the planning data they were using. IBM used the documentation to create prototypes for the new system. When the prototypes were ready, employees were involved in testing them and providing feedback and suggestions for revision. During a period of three years, a process of documenting what "is," developing prototypes for the new system, testing the prototypes on site, giving feedback, and making revisions eventually resulted in a new system that Fairchild's managers endorsed and were eager to begin using.

To learn more about this organization, visit *www.fairchildsemi.com.*

Role of Innovation in Organizational Change

4.

Describe how innovation relates to organizational change.

As discussed in Chapter 8, innovation *is the discovery, identification, and diagnosis of unusual and ambiguous problems and/or the development of unique or creative solutions.*[43] When Jeff Bezos founded Amazon.com, he invented a new way for people to purchase books—over the Internet. The new ideas that lead to innovation may come from inside the company, but often they come from somewhere else. For example, many companies copied Bezos's new invention and began selling products other than books over the Internet.

Strategic Importance of Innovation

A dynamic, changing environment makes innovation and change as important—if not more important—for established organizations as they are for new organizations. Successful organizations can't rest on their prior successes. If they become complacent, competitors are sure to woo customers away. Organizational decline and even extinction may follow.

Procter & Gamble's CEO, Alan G. Lafley, avoided these problems by supporting innovation at P&G. As described in the Strategic Action Competency feature, Lafley leads a company that lets customers inspire the innovation process.[44] His approach to managing innovation reflects his deep understanding of the company he leads. Lafley has spent most of his career at P&G, so he has years of personal experience on which to draw. But he didn't rely on his personal opinions to revitalize P&G. When he became CEO, he spent his first three months on the road talking to P&G employees, customers, and suppliers. One thing he learned from these discussions was that P&G's employees did not have a clear vision of the company's mission or the priorities for their own work. "We had outstanding people . . . who felt they had so much to do every day and weren't really clear about the one or two things that would really make a difference," he recalled. Under Lafley's leadership, P&G has regained its focus. Now employees understand that their job is to focus on customers—learn everything that's possible about what customers want, and then deliver products that they will love. With customers in 160 countries, P&G employees must innovate continually to meet this challenge.[45]

© Al Behrman/AP Photo

A.G. Lafley, president of P&G, speaks at an annual shareholders meeting in Cincinnati.

Strategic Action Competency

Alan G. Lafley of Procter & Gamble

When Alan G. Lafley was appointed CEO of P&G, he was a total unknown outside the company. The day his promotion was announced, the company's stock price fell, suggesting that investors were not confident in his ability to lead P&G in a time of change. But after five years at the helm, profits were up nearly 70 percent and investors seemed happy. Apparently the 25 years Lafley had spent working his way up through the company had prepared him for his new role.

Innovation is a key element in Lafley's strategy for P&G, and customers are the focus of attention. Lafley explains: "I wanted to put consumers front and center and get back to asking, Who are they and what do they want? Find out what they want and give it them. I have this incredibly simple saying, 'The consumer is the boss.'" Today, most of P&G's products are invented and developed in-house, but Lafley is in the process of changing that. His goal is to develop connections to external sources of new products. Eventually, he wants only 50 percent of P&G's new products to be created internally. The rest would come from outside initially and then be fine-tuned in P&G's labs.

Toward this end, Lafley has cultivated relationships with designers worldwide. He also restructured the company's R&D activities so that product development processes occur near customers all around the world. More recently, he orchestrated the acquisition of Gillette, another consumer products company known for its ability to innovate. Lafley hopes the Gillette acquisition will stimulate new ideas and new products. "They're mechanical engineers and we're chemical engineers. I'm very hopeful that we'll learn a lot from each other," he says. At P&G, innovation is something that happens everyday, and it creates the need for continuing incremental change.

To learn more about this organization, visit *www.pg.com.*

refers to the creating of new goods and services.

Types of Innovation

Because new ideas can take many forms, many types of innovation are possible. Three basic types of innovation are technical, process, and administrative.

Technical. *The creation of new goods and services is one main type of innovation, and is often referred to as* technical innovation. Many technical innovations occur through basic R&D efforts intended to satisfy demanding customers who are always seeking new, better, faster, and/or cheaper products. At P&G, technical innovations are the basis for many of the company's new products. Even in the absence of a new product, innovation can still occur, however.

Process. Process innovation *involves creating a new way of producing, selling, and/or distributing an existing good or service.* The introduction of do-it-yourself online stock trading represents a process innovation. At Toyota, *oobeya* (pronounced ooh-bay-yuh) was a process innovation that enabled the company to dramatically lower the cost of producing automobiles. In Japanese, oobeya means "big open office." At Toyota, oobeya brings together big teams of people involved in all aspects of the business to discuss how to cut costs out of the design, production, and sales processes. Before oobeya was introduced, each unit was given a budget. All they were expected to do was not go over their budget. With oobeya, cutting costs without reducing quality became the goal. By encouraging everyone to work together to cut costs, Toyota succeeds in producing high-quality cars that cost substantially less than similar models offered by competitors.[46]

Administrative. Administrative innovation *occurs when creation of a new organization design better supports the development, production, and delivery of goods and services.* At P&G, the worldwide redistribution of R&D activities was an administrative innovation. Other forms of administrative innovations that organizations have experimented with include flexible work schedules, telecommuting, and virtual work teams. Network organizations (see Chapter 11) and virtual organizations also are examples of administrative innovations. As noted earlier in this chapter, adopting these innovative ways of working such as telecommuting often means that an organization must find innovative ways to supervise and coordinate the work of employees who communicate electronically and seldom have face-to-face conversations with each other.[47]

Convergence of Forms. Various types of innovation often go hand in hand. For example, the rapid development of business-to-business e-commerce represents process innovation. This new process required numerous technical innovations in computer hardware and software. As organizations began to use business-to-business e-commerce, administrative innovations soon followed. Implementation of process innovations, in turn, often stimulated the creation of new organization designs.[48] By necessity, doing something new means doing things differently. Thus innovation and organizational change go hand in hand.

Architecture for Innovation

Because innovation is so important to success in a variety of industries, managers in all types of organizations are expected to help build infrastructures that encourage and support innovation and change. If an organization's basic infrastructure is in place before specific change initiatives are planned, the organization will be prepared to transform itself as needed. One of management's primary concerns should be to ensure that the organization maintains a state of readiness so that it can move quickly and effectively when innovation is needed. Building an infrastructure and maintain-

Snapshot

"Champion was an old-line paper manufacturing company with classic characteristics solidly in place. We had a traditional management structure, an adversarial relationship with unions, and information systems that reflected that type of thinking. [Now] we've changed our hierarchy, opened up our information systems, developed cooperative partnering with unions, and established accountability within supervisory groups."

Mark Childers, Senior VP of Organizational Development, Champion International, a subsidiary of International Paper

ing a state of readiness require an architecture for innovation. Organizations such as Citigroup, Coca-Cola, Hershey, Kellogg, Newell Rubbermaid, and Humana have put senior executives with titles such as chief innovation officer in charge of creating the conditions needed for innovation.[49] Figure 12.6 summarizes several key features of that architecture. Briefly, managers should

- develop a learning environment and a learning orientation among employees,
- provide a support system for innovation , and
- foster workforce resilience.[50]

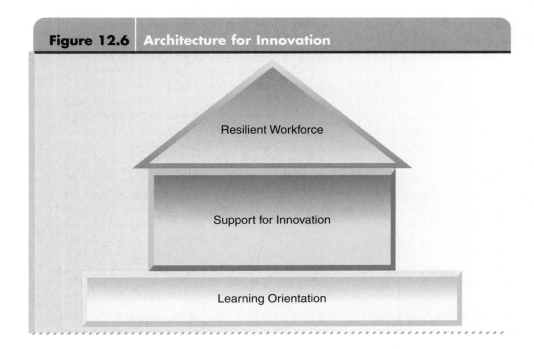

Figure 12.6 | **Architecture for Innovation**

Resilient Workforce

Support for Innovation

Learning Orientation

Learning Organizations

A learning organization *has both the drive and the capabilities to modify or transform itself and improve its performance continuously.* It learns from past experiences, it learns from customers, it learns from various parts of the company, and it learns from other companies.[51] In learning organizations, successful innovation and change aren't events with clear-cut beginnings and endings. Rather, they are never-ending processes that have become part of the daily routine. Innovation and change are not infrequent and special—they are simply a way of organizational life. As one manager observed, this way of life helps a learning organization avoid organizational stupidity.

The Hewlett-Packard Company strives to be a learning organization. Continuous learning is especially important at HP Labs, the company's central research unit. HP Labs recently underwent change to improve its learning capacity. As described in the Planning and Administration Competency feature on the following page, the goal was to become the best industrial research center in the world.[52]

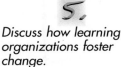

5.

Discuss how learning organizations foster change.

With 1,200 employees located in the United States, Japan, and the United Kingdom, HP Labs is the innovation engine of the Hewlett-Packard Company. Lab employees include more than 900 engineers and scientists charged with discovering and developing products that will fuel the company's long-term growth. To ensure that HP Labs can deliver what the company needs, HP's top managers challenged it to implement whatever changes were needed in order for the lab to become the world's leading R&D facility.

The change process began with a comprehensive discussion that involved everyone in the lab—managers and technical professionals as well as support staff. Using a variety of communication technologies, including surveys, electronic groupware, and face-to-face discussions, HP Labs employees assessed their current situation and agreed on a set of indicators to use to assess their progress toward their goal of becoming the best lab in the world. Among these indicators were the behaviors people in the lab displayed. Behaviors that they wanted to see more of in the lab included listening to each other's suggestions, questioning each other in order to explore how people's ideas differ, encouraging others to think "outside the box," encouraging risk taking, and collaborating across traditional functional boundaries.

After much discussion, HP Labs decided to use communities-of-practice to help create change in the organization. Initially, 36 communities-of-practice were formed. These were informal groups of people who were interested in tackling a specific problem. For example, one community focused on the problem of creating better communications between engineers. This community of practice formed to solve a problem that some of the engineers themselves identified—namely, the tendency of people to focus on their own work and "never talk to each other." The solution to this problem was something called *Chalk Talks.* Chalk Talks took place on Friday afternoons, when time was set aside for people to meet and talk about the projects they were working on that week. Another community-of-practice tackled the issue of worklife quality. This group included mostly secretaries, who felt there were many tasks they could be performing more effectively, and that doing things differently would make their work more enjoyable. During the course of a year, this community-of-practice rewrote the corporate shipping manual, reduced the number of forms needed to enroll employees in the company's benefits plans from 13 to 1, and started a self-development seminar program for the secretarial staff.

Four years after this change process began at HP Labs, several significant results have been documented by the company, including a substantial increase in collaborative work, more use of lateral communication instead of vertical communication, the creation of more than 100 results-oriented improvement programs, and agreement on a clear vision for the lab.

Today, making changes such as these is an ongoing and self-supporting process. People have learned that making organizational improvements is their responsibility. When employees identify problems, they know that they can create communities-of-practice to help find solutions. By sharing their concerns with each other and discussing ideas for change, employees have discovered that they have a great deal of control over their work situation.

To learn more about this organization, visit *www.hp.com.*

Through continuous innovation and change, a learning organization creates a sustainable competitive advantage in its industry.[53] When an organization's environment is unstable, learning may require a lot of exploration and experimentation. Failures may be frequent, but so are unexpected achievements. When an organization's environment is more stable, learning is more likely to occur through a systematic process of testing alternative approaches.[54] In either situation, however, learning organizations change at a rate at least as fast as—or even faster than—the rate of change in their environments. For engineers at HP Labs, changes in technology and the development of new products by competitors, and new customer demands create an unstable organizational environment. Communities-of-practice offer a mechanism for employees to respond quickly to such changes. For example, when a survey of HP customers revealed that they were dissatisfied with the quality of products and services provided, a community-of-practice organized to solve the problem. Their solution was to develop a set of standards for measuring quality and then ensuring that these standards were adopted and measured in all of the company's lab facilities.

Today, HP Labs exhibits many of the five features of a learning organization. As shown in Figure 12.7 and discussed in the following sections, these features are

▶ shared leadership,

▶ culture of innovation,

▶ customer-focused strategy,

▶ organic organization design, and

▶ intensive use of information.

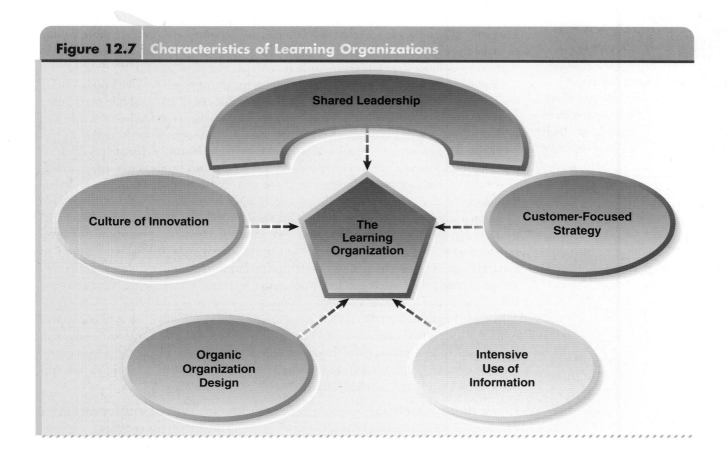

Figure 12.7 | **Characteristics of Learning Organizations**

Shared Leadership

In learning organizations, responsibility for making decisions, directing operations, and achieving organizational goals is shared among all employees. These leadership tasks aren't the responsibility of top-level managers alone. *Everyone* is encouraged to find ways to improve the organization and its products.[55] Georgia-Pacific's Mill Improvement Process and the communities-of-practice at HP Labs are two different examples of how organizations can use shared leadership to create change.

Snapshot

"We all make mistakes. It's not as though at any given time, Dell doesn't have some part of its business that's not working for us as it should. But we have a culture of continuous improvement. We train employees to constantly ask themselves, 'How do we grow faster? How do we lower our cost structure? How do we improve service for customers?'"

Michael Dell, Chairman and Cofounder, Dell Computer

Culture of Innovation

Shared leadership goes hand in hand with a culture of innovation. For learning organizations, successful innovation is a never-ending process that becomes part of the daily routine. Instead of being an infrequent and special event that takes people's attention away from the central work of the organization, it *is* the central work of the organization. At P&G and at HP, employees are always thinking about how to make products that customers will find more appealing. At Georgia-Pacific, they are thinking about how to be more efficient. At Southwest Airlines, employees are always looking for better ways to meet customers' needs for low-cost, reliable air travel.

Community. To support innovation, learning organizations nurture a sense of community and trust. Everyone works together, respecting each other and being able to communicate openly and honestly. Problems can't be avoided or handled by just passing them along to another department or up the hierarchy. Conflict and debate are accepted as responsible forms of communication. People willingly share the information and knowledge they have, so others can benefit from it.[56]

A sense of community also gives employees the feeling that they are important and are being treated fairly. Employees cooperate because they want to, not because they have to.[57] When people feel that they are part of a community, they are more willing to make the extra effort needed to find and fix problems. They also are more likely to share their solutions with their coworkers.

Consistent with our discussion in Chapter 1 of the use of teams, Whole Foods Market has built a sense of community that supports innovations of all types. While many other grocery stores have focused on lowering their costs, Whole Foods has become the most profitable company in the industry by catering to health-conscious shoppers. In this team-based organization, small teams of employees manage departments such as seafood, fresh produce, and bakery goods. Teams have considerable autonomy to experiment and try out new ideas. And they have access to extensive financial data, which they can use to evaluate whether their ideas are working. The entire operation is designed to maintain a strong sense of community. That sense of community is considered essential to the company's evolution and survival. Incremental progress is a core value at Whole Foods Market, and a strong sense of community supports the risk taking required to make change. The company aims to continually improve "through unleashing the collective creativity and intelligence of our Team Members. We recognize that everyone has a contribution to make. We keep getting better at what we do."[58]

In some organizations, Web logs (*blogs*) are used to help build a sense of community. At the law firm of Latham & Watkins, for example, lawyers are experimenting with using blogs to share knowledge among the firm's various practice areas. Lawyers and staff are encouraged to use blogs to tell stories that communicate what they are learning so new knowledge is quickly disseminated around the firm.[59]

Continuous Learning. A learning organization can't succeed without employees who are willing to learn and change. Hence learning organizations encourage individual learning in numerous ways. One of the most successful ways is through empowerment, which places responsibility on employees for problem finding and problem solving.[60] Empowerment requires more involvement and learning than does simply having someone else make all the decisions. At HP Labs, engineers and secretaries are empowered to identify problems and find solutions to those problems. At Dell Computers, managers are empowered to figure out how to achieve success within their business units. They are held responsible for being successful, but how they achieve that success is not dictated by higher level executives. Instead, the company relies on open sharing of information and a culture that encourages people to ask questions, ask for help when needed, and share ideas when asked.[61]

The flat, team-based structure found in learning organizations facilitates learning because employees are involved in a broad range of activities and work with others from whom they can learn. Formal training is another way to ensure continuous learning. For managers, in particular, continuous learning is essential to develop the competencies needed by generalists who are knowledgeable in several areas, as opposed to specialists who understand only finance, production, marketing, or some other function.

Customer-Focused Strategy

Learning organizations add value for customers by identifying their needs—in some instances, even before customers have done so—and then developing ways to satisfy those needs. Customer-focused strategies reflect a clear understanding of how important customers are to the organization's long-term success and serve as the basis for aligning all of its major activities. The changes at YRC described earlier helped that company implement a customer-focused strategy. P&G uses innovative consumer research to support its customer-focused strategy. To keep the company's leaders attuned to customers, Lafley even sent the four vice chairmen, the presidents of operating units, and heads of functions out to spend at least half a day in consumers' homes to watch how they use company products. Once a year, he also sends all of the country and business leaders out for a day of shopping with families, so they can observe people make their purchasing decisions. At HP Labs, when satisfying customer's demands for excellent product and service quality was recognized as an important issue, a community-of-practice spent an entire year designing a set of measures that HP Labs now uses to monitor this aspect of its performance.

Organic Organization Design

The design of learning organizations often reflects their emphasis on organic rather than mechanistic systems. In particular, they emphasize the use of multidisciplinary teams, communities-of-practice, and network organizational designs.

In learning organizations, employees with dissimilar expertise form multidisciplinary teams. To encourage the free flow of ideas, these teams may be formed only as needed, on a project-by-project basis. "Bosses" may be practically nonexistent. Team members have considerable autonomy to make key decisions and can take action without waiting for requests to crawl through a bureaucratic decision-making process. Compared to functional organizational designs, team-based structures are more flexible and fluid. Knowledge flows more easily among members of the organization, which contributes to learning and creates opportunities for innovation.

In addition to experimenting on their own, many learning organizations use strategic alliances with suppliers, customers, and even competitors as a method of learning.[62] Often, a web of such relationships leads to an organization with a network structure. As we described in Chapter 11, a network structure maximizes the links among collaborating organizations. Such links provide learning opportunities and generate innovation in goods and services. Network structures seem to work in part because they create a sense of community among a larger pool of people who share their diverse knowledge and expertise, using it to find creative solutions to difficult problems.[63]

Intensive Use of Information

Information is the lifeblood of learning organizations. To be effective, they must undertake extensive environmental scanning, be measurement oriented, and foster communication about shared problems and solutions.

Scanning the Environment. In learning organizations, managers strive to be creators of change. Staying attuned to emerging trends is their passion. To ensure that they don't miss an important trend or change, managers in learning organizations aggressively scan both the external and internal environments for information. As a result, large amounts of information are obtained from the external environment about how customers are reacting to current goods and services, how customers compare them to those of competitors, and whether new competitors may be entering the market. Such information is essential to judgments concerning the need to create new products to meet customer demand. Information obtained from the internal environment indicates how employees feel about the organization, whether their attention is focused on customers, whether they feel energized to solve difficult problems, and whether key employees are likely to defect to competitors.

Measurement Oriented. Organizations learn in order to improve. To judge improvement, an organization needs to know where it was before and where it is now. Systematic measurement makes assessing improvement possible.[64] In learning organizations, such as Dell Computers and Whole Foods Market, employees have access to data about customer satisfaction, profit and loss, market share, employee commitment, and competitors' strategies, among other things. Data are gathered, monitored, disseminated, and used throughout the organization.

Pharmaceutical companies are good examples of learning organizations, because without continuous learning they would have no new products to offer the public. The process of developing new products and bringing them to market takes about eight years, on average. Throughout this time, pharmaceutical companies typically measure their learning progress in a variety of ways. For example, Pfizer, Sanofi, and Merck all keep track of the expertise of their scientists and engineers, the number of scientific papers published by their scientists, patent applications, and FDA drug approvals, among many other things. By monitoring measures such as these, pharmaceutical firms can better predict in advance how many new products they are likely to be able to introduce in future years.[65]

Communication. Numerical data (measurements) aren't the only type of information considered important in learning organizations. "Soft" information—sometimes referred to as tacit knowledge or gossip—is valued too. Employees who serve customers day in and day out may not need to read the results of monthly customer satisfaction surveys to know where problems lie. The anecdotal evidence they gather through dozens of service encounters may be enough to begin seeing a pattern of pieces that all seem to fit together, make sense, and suggest needed improvements. When Xerox wanted to improve its service for customers, it hired an anthropologist to study how service reps went about their jobs. The anthropologist concluded that informal storytelling and conversations around the water cooler were important activities for sharing problems and solutions.[66] By sharing information about the problems they face and the solutions they discover, employees minimize the number of times they reinvent the wheel and speed up the process of organizational learning.[67]

Chapter Summary

Whether they are newly established or mature, organizations maintain their vitality by innovating, changing, and learning from their experiences. As their external environments become increasingly competitive and turbulent, the most effective organizations will be those that build innovation, change, and learning into their normal operations.

Learning Goals ....

1. Describe four types of organizational change.

Organizational changes vary in both degree and timing. In terms of degree, change can be radical or incremental. In terms of timing, change can be reactive or anticipatory. As shown in Figure 12.2, combinations of these possibilities create four basic types of change: radical reactive change, radical anticipatory change, incremental reactive change, and incremental anticipatory change.

2. Explain the planning process for organizational change.

Although change often involves a bit of chaos, organizations can usually reduce its amount and impact by carefully planning for major change. Through planning, the organization begins to unfreeze and prepare for the change. The key planning activities are (1) assessing the environment; (2) determining whether a performance gap exists and, if so, its nature and magnitude; (3) diagnosing organizational problems; (4) articulating and communicating a vision for the future; (5) developing and implementing an action plan; (6) anticipating and making plans to reduce resistance; and (7) monitoring change and following up after the main initiatives have been implemented.

3. Identify four methods of organizational change.

Many approaches to implementing change are possible. Four general methods are technological change, organization redesign, job redesign, and organization development. Technological change often involves changing the way work is done by adopting new information technologies. The organization redesign method may involve changing the organizational structure and/or organizational processes. It normally affects large portions of an organization. Downsizing and reengineering are examples of this method. Job redesign involves changing employees' jobs by either simplifying or enriching them. Organization development can be used to change employee attitudes and behaviors. Focus groups and survey feedback permit managers and employees to provide information about a range of topics, including job satisfaction, organizational commitment, and perceptions of supervisory and managerial behaviors. Team building is used to improve the functioning of people who must work together to achieve assigned tasks. Change efforts often involve a combination of these methods.

4. Describe how innovation relates to organizational change.

Innovation is the process of creating and implementing a new idea. Three basic types of innovation are technical, process, and administrative. Organizational change refers to any transformation in the design or functioning of an organization. Generally, innovations require organizational change. Innovation and change are important to both new and established organizations, owing to the dynamic nature of the external environments of most organizations.

5. Discuss how learning organizations foster change.

Organizations are redesigning themselves to become learning organizations capable of quickly adapting their practices to satisfy the needs of their customers. The basic features of such organizations are leadership that is shared, a culture that supports innovation, a strategy focused on customers, an organic organization design, and an intensive use of information. In a learning organization, change is not a special event; it's a natural part of the organization's continuous attempts to satisfy customers.

Key Terms and Concepts

Administrative innovation
Anticipatory change
Focus group discussion
Incremental change
Innovation
Job enrichment
Job redesign
Job simplification
Learning organization

Open-source software
Organization development
Organization redesign
Organizational change
Organizational diagnosis
Performance gap
Process innovation
Radical change
Reactive change

Reengineering
Restructuring
Survey feedback
Team building
Technical innovation
Technological change
Tempered radicals

Questions for Discussion and Reflective Thinking

1. Which type of change did Georgia-Pacific undergo: radical change or incremental change? Explain.

2. The company that is now General Motors began more than a century ago, in 1887. Since then it has undergone many changes. To review the major historical events in this company's history, go to *www.gm.com.* Under "The Company," click on "Corporate Information" and then "History." Choose three examples of change at this company that you find interesting. For each example, describe the type of change that occurred (refer to Figure 12.2 on page 391.)

3. Learn more about the Electronics Industry Code of Conduct by visiting *www.eicc.info.* After reading about what is expected of its members, consider how adopting this code might affect the operation of a small manufacturing company that is based in the United States. Assume the company purchases some of its supplies from China and is not currently monitoring its foreign suppliers in any way. Do you think it would be wise for a small U.S. company to voluntarily adopt the code? If the company did adopt the code, would it be likely to require radical or incremental change? Explain your reasoning.

4. Is the way you react to innovation and change based on your personality, which is relatively stable? Or do you think you can develop the competencies needed to be effective in an organization that constantly changes? Explain.

5. No matter how much planning you do, the process of organizational change is unpredictable. This can be frustrating, but does it mean that planning is a useless exercise? How can planning help the change process even when almost nothing goes as planned?

6. Schools and colleges are supposed to be places of learning, but many fall short of being learning organizations. Choose a school or college with which you are familiar and explain how it could use one or more of the four basic change methods described in this chapter to become a more effective learning organization.

7. Effective communication is essential to any change effort, but in large organizations it is impossible for a CEO to speak personally to everyone. Can e-mail solve this problem? Describe the advantages and disadvantages of using face-to-face versus electronic communication channels during times of change.

8. Samsung is a successful electronics company that manufactures TVs, digital cameras, DVDs, VCRs, and audio systems. A key weapon of Samsung's success is the Value Innovation Center. Using an Internet search engine of your choice, learn more about Samsung's Value Innovation Center. Could HP Labs use some of these same ideas to become even more effective? Explain why or why not.

DEVELOPING YOUR COMPETENCIES

By any measure, change in organizations has grown tremendously in the past decade. As more and more organizations are pushed to reduce costs while improving the quality of products and services, change is inevitable. Major changes have helped some organizations improve their financial and marketplace condition, but in many situations, improvements have been disappointing. Managers and employees have reported being burned out, scared, or frustrated. As change agents, managers must define what the future looks like, align people with that vision, and inspire them to make things happen despite the obstacles that will occur along the way. One of the critical issues that you will face is to understand the tactics that you can use to manage change.

We have found that managers who are trying to achieve change in their organizations usually use several tactics to successfully bring it about. This exercise is designed to enable you to assess your own style in response to 10 critical incidents. Your responses to these 10 incidents are illustrative of the options available to managers to achieve change.

Instructions

Ten critical incidents follow that require you to react in some way. For each incident, three alternative actions have been provided for your consideration. *Rank order the options for each item* to indicate what you would probably do in these situations. Write "1" in front of your first choice, "2" for your second choice, and "3" for your least preferred choice. Do not omit any items.

Incidents

1. You receive a telephone call that is a request for you to settle a dispute between the caller and another person. You say:
_____ a. "How do you feel about the situation?"
_____ b. "You should talk with the other person first."
_____ c. "Could you give me some background information?"

2. After hearing your academic credentials incorrectly represented, you:
_____ a. Let the incident go unnoticed to avoid embarrassment to the person(s) talking about you.
_____ b. Set the record straight.
_____ c. Analyze with the other person(s) later how the data about you were distorted.

3. In an interview, the manager discloses that your friend's job is in jeopardy. You:
_____ a. Explore the manager's dilemma and feelings.
_____ b. Test the manager's willingness to deal with the situation openly.
_____ c. Explore alternative actions the manager might consider.

4. A manager calls you to ask your assessment of a colleague who has recently attended one of your training sessions. You say:
_____ a. "I feel good about your taking an interest in your people."
_____ b. "You're talking to the wrong person."
_____ c. "Let's explore the implications of evaluating a person in this way."

5. Immediately prior to conducting a highly important event, you experience a personally traumatic occurrence. You:
_____ a. Say to yourself, "The show must go on."
_____ b. Postpone the event.
_____ c. Consult with others to explore options.

6. You have spent a significant amount of effort in preparing for a job interview. Afterward, you learn that the "winning" candidate had inside information that was not made available to you. You:
_____ a. Chastise yourself for your naïveté.
_____ b. Demand a full explanation.
_____ c. Reconstruct the bidding process to look for possible learnings for yourself.

7. During a break between sessions (or classes), one of the members makes a sexual overture toward you. You:
_____ a. Thank the person for the compliment and politely change the subject.
_____ b. Confront the need to explore the relationship within the group session.
_____ c. Solicit feedback on how you may have behaved to create such an interest.

8. In a team building session, the members are "ganging up" on one person, bombarding that person with negative feedback. You say to the individual:
_____ a. "You must be feeling under attack."
_____ b. "You don't have to be a target right now unless you want to."
_____ c. "What would be useful for you right now?"

9. In a meeting of a team of managers, one member whose department is far behind schedule, begins to cry. You:
_____ a. Assure the person that it is understandable to be upset.
_____ b. Announce a break so that you can work with the person individually.
_____ c. Explore with the entire team what can be done to improve the situation.

10. You have become increasingly concerned that your organization is engaging in illegal practices in hiring employees. In a meeting of the executive team, sexist and racist attitudes are expressed. You:
_____ a. Say nothing lest you be perceived as judgmental.
_____ b. Confront the team with your concerns about its policies.
_____ c. Suggest that the team discuss ways in which the organization might ensure fairness in hiring.

Scoring and Interpretation Sheet

Scoring instructions: Sum the points you assigned to the alternative "a" for the 10 items, and then do the same for "b" and "c." Enter these totals in the boxes below.

☐ a. Support

☐ b. Direction

☐ c. Problem Solving

Total 60

Interpretation

The major options available to a manager in response to critical situations can be classified as follows:

Support: Being sensitive to the feelings of the others.
Direction: Controlling situations through confrontation and leadership.
Problem Solving: Assisting others through exploring facts, options, and strategies.

Look at your lowest score. This is your most probable, or "knee-jerk," response in difficult situations. Your middle score represents your most likely backup style. Your highest score, of course, indicates your least-often-used strategy. Although this rank ordering may be situation specific, it can give you an overall picture of your change management style.

Consider the distances between your scores. These can be thought of as a crude index of the "thickness" of your "up-front" and backup responses. A large score gap can indicate that you will persist for some time before changing to the approaches represented by higher scores.

Questions

1. If you want to change your style, what behaviors might you engage in to accomplish this?

2. Is your score on these three dimensions a fixed part of your personality? Explain.

3. Given your profile, what stage in the planning for organizational change do you feel this profile would be most successful?

In Chapter 7, we discussed several of MTV's strategic initiatives and aspects of Judy McGrath's leadership. With this case, we extend that discussion to consider McGrath's approach to managing innovation and change.

As chairman and CEO of MTV Networks, Judy McGrath is responsible for managing such well-known brands as Comedy Central, Nickelodeon, Spike TV, CMT, Noggin, LOGO, VH1, and, of course, MTV. When MTV celebrated its 25th year, she was one of the few people there who had been with the company since its beginning. With a degree in English literature, she first worked as a promotions copy editor, but since then she has become a driving force in MTV's success. Rising through the ranks gradually, she now oversees operations valued at $7 billion plus a talented cast of celebrities ranging from SpongeBob SquarePants to Jon Stewart.

How does Judy McGrath manage a company that lives or dies on how quickly it can innovate and change? Communicating is a big part of McGrath's job. Her most important communications are with MTV employees—talent is the core asset that makes MTV click. She starts off many days meeting with MTV President Michael J. Wolf to discuss possible deals and recent developments. Wolf, who came to MTV after stints at McKinsey and Booz Allen Hamilton, seems to be the opposite of McGrath. Together they merge his left-brain skills with her right-brain skills to form an impressive leadership team.

McGrath's approach to managing her creative staff is to foster an inclusive culture where all ideas are welcome. MTV's cofounder, Bob Pittman, explains it like this: "There is less testosterone. It's not the system of the old Hollywood moguls where they are throwing chairs at each other. It's about listening and accepting ideas wherever and whoever they come from."

McGrath understands that good ideas can come from anywhere. When she was in the trenches, she had her share of good ideas—like inviting Bill Clinton to appear and giving Jon Stewart a second chance after his earlier series had been canceled. Fortunately her bosses listened to her, and then let her run with her ideas. Her experiences taught her that "the smartest thing we can do when confronted with something truly creative is get out of the way."

A fan of pop culture, one friend described McGrath as "a 16-year-old boy trapped inside an adult woman's body." But the "creatives" at MTV refer to her as one of the "suits." As a "suit," McGrath faces the challenge of ensuring that MTV maintains its place as a cutting-edge trendsetter that can compete in a world of iPods, BlackBerries, broadband entertainment, and electronic social networks. For most of McGrath's career, MTV has focused on developing and delivering television programming. Going forward, it will have to expand into and perhaps create new interactive media channels. (For more details about McGrath's strategic plans, see Chapter 7, pages 213–214.) Hiring great talent and just getting out of their way may not prove to be as successful in the future as it has been in the past.

MTV is becoming increasingly reliant on partnerships with other companies that have complementary skills and competencies. Her strategy for ensuring that MTV innovates and changes with the times is to stay connected—to everyone and everything that might possibly result in creating the next great brand. McGrath communicates constantly with people throughout the entertainment and media world. During Grammy Awards week, she might find herself meeting with CEOs of IFILM and DreamWorks, one or two Indie film directors, a few cable distributors, and a video game designer. Seeing that change is clearly on the horizon, veterans of MTV may begin to worry: Are they secure in their jobs? Is television no longer the soul of MTV? Will they be able to compete successfully against the next generation of new media stars?

McGrath seems unconcerned about such worries and is confident she can lead MTV through the changes ahead. She thinks one of her greatest assets is perseverance. "It's a really undervalued asset," she says. "It's not sexy, but if you really want something, you've got to hang in there. I never phoned it in. I've given my share of dogs' lives to MTV." She expects everyone else at MTV to do the same.

To learn more about this organization, visit *www.viacom.com*.

Questions

1. MTV is aggressively expanding its offerings beyond television. Will this require the organization to undergo radical or incremental change?

2. How can McGrath prepare MTV employees for the changes that are on the way? Is it possible to plan for a future that is almost completely unknown?

3. If MTV begins to form strategic alliances with new-media companies, is this likely to be viewed as threatening to the "creatives" that are the stars in the company today, or are they likely to see it as an opportunity for personal growth and development? Explain.

chapter 13

© Big Cheese Photo/Jupiter Images

Managing Human Resources

Learning Goals

After studying this chapter, you should be able to:

1. Explain the strategic importance of managing human resources effectively.

2. Describe several important laws and government regulations that affect how organizations manage their human resources.

3. Explain the objective of human resource planning and describe how organizations respond to the unpredictability of future business needs.

4. Describe the hiring process.

5. Describe several types of training and development programs.

6. Describe several principles for improving the accuracy of managers' appraisals of employee performance.

7. Describe the basic elements of a monetary compensation package.

Communication Competency

Planning and Administration Competency

Teamwork Competency

Managing Effectively

Self-Management Competency

Strategic Action Competency

Multicultural Competency

Challenge of Managing ....

Schlumberger

© Peter & Georgina Bowater/Stock Connection/ Jupiter Images

Schlumberger uses complex technologies to search for and retrieve the petroleum that drives its business, but its core values are simple: *people* who thrive on the challenge of excelling in any environment and are dedicated to safety and customer service worldwide, a commitment to *technology,* and a determination to produce superior *profits.* What types of people does this high-tech company need to reach its goals? Mostly engineers, researchers, and scientists, but also electrical and mechanical technicians and equipment operators—and they're needed all around the world. With only 1,500 petroleum engineers enrolled in U.S. colleges, the war for the talent it needs is fierce.

To help get the talent it needs, high-level Schlumberger executives serve as "ambassadors" to 44 of the best engineering programs around the world. As ambassadors, these executives can help fund university research projects and in the process develop relationships with faculty and their students. When the Nigeria University of Ibadan was struggling, a Schlumberger ambassador saw to it that the university received several million dollars to create a petroleum learning center. As a result of that investment, Schlumberger now has more Nigerian-trained engineers working around the world than it has employees in Nigeria itself.

When it comes to finding talent, Schlumberger is in better shape than most oil companies these days. Many competitors hired and fired talent as the industry went through earlier cycles of boom and bust. Schlumberger focused on keeping its talent and developing people to build up its bench strength. According to CEO Andrew Gould, "The capacity to develop talent from anywhere in the world is one of our key strengths." The task is aided by a sophisticated information system that tracks vital employee information. Using the system, a human resource professional can search a database that contains "career networking profiles" as well as performance and salary data for employees working in dozens of countries. Written by each employee, a career networking profile describes career goals, past assignments, professional affiliations, patents, hobbies, and so on. If a country manager is needed in Brazil, for example, the system can immediately identify current employees who are qualified for the job and potentially interested in making the move.

Learning Content

In the short run, keeping talent and developing their competencies seems costly. Consider the training required for the engineers Schlumberger hires: Those who will be sent to work out in the oil fields must first complete three years of education within the company. The process includes rotating between on-the-job projects and classroom learning sessions. In the third year, they must demonstrate their knowledge by completing and presenting a major project of their own. The education is not a cake walk—about 40 percent who start the process drop out before completing it. But those who do finish have the skills Schlumberger needs and are grateful for the experience.

Does all this focus on people pay off? It seems to. Engineers appreciate having opportunities to develop and move up throughout their careers. Of the company's top managers today, 80 percent were recruited right out of school and have remained loyal employees throughout their entire careers. Shareholders also benefit. According to recent studies, the best performing firms are much more likely to have homegrown CEOs. In poor performing firms, CEOs are more likely to have been hired externally. Schlumberger has returned 240 percent to shareholders during the past decade, beating the S&P 500 and most of its competitors.

CEO Gould seems to understand the value of keeping the people pipeline filled. He's spent much of his time ensuring that the firm's human resource department is effective. Whenever the firm loses a high-performing employee, the company conducts an exit interview to understand the reason and posts the information online where all managers can see it. As one manager explained, "We essentially treat attrition, especially if someone has high potential, as a catastrophic incident."[1]

To learn more about this organization, visit *www.slb.com.*

Explain the strategic importance of managing human resources effectively.

Strategic Importance

Human resource management (HRM) *refers to the philosophies, policies, and practices that an organization uses to affect the behaviors of people who work for the organization.* It includes activities related to planning, hiring, training and development, performance review and evaluation, and compensation. The strategic use of all of these activities can improve organizational effectiveness. In fact, companies with state-of-the-art HRM produce about 10 percent more revenue per employee compared to average companies.[2] This chapter describes several of the most valuable human resources practices used by the best employers.

Activities related to managing human resources (HR) occur in all organizations, from the smallest to the largest. At a minimum, every company has jobs, which comprise a set of responsibilities. To get these jobs done, people are hired and compensated in return for the work they do. Few employers continue to pay a person who cannot or will not perform satisfactorily, so at least some measurement of performance generally occurs—even if it is just to keep track of how many hours were worked. To ensure that people know what they are supposed to do, some instruction and training are usually given, though these may be minimal.

Who Is Responsible for Human Resources?

In large firms like Schlumberger, HR professionals working in the company have responsibility for the design and use of most of the firm's people management practices. Human resource professionals *are people with substantial specialized and technical knowledge of HR issues, laws, policies, and practices.* The leaders of HR units and the people who work within the department usually are HR professionals. In small and medium firms, consultants and other vendors that specialize in providing HR services may design and administer some of the practices.[3] Regardless of how the organization's HR practices are developed, managers always share responsibility for carrying them out. The special expertise of HR professionals is used by, and in cooperation with, the expertise of line managers, other administrative staff, and all first-line employees in every department.

In small businesses, owners must have HR expertise as they build the company from the ground up. Usually, the founder makes all hiring and pay decisions when the company is first getting started. Performance appraisals are likely to occur on the spot whenever there seems to be a performance problem. Formal policies may not exist at all! This reality is clearly reflected in the various popular magazines targeted to small-business owners—for example, *INC., Money, Success,* and *Entrepreneurship.* These publications devote a great deal of space to discussing issues related to managing the people who make up a small company.

Eventually, as a company grows, the owner may contract out some of the administrative aspects related to managing people (e.g., payroll), or delegate some responsibilities to a specialist, or both. If the company grows larger, more specialists may be hired, either as permanent staff or on a contract basis to work on special projects, such as designing a new pay system. As with other business activities, these specialists assist the company, but responsibility for the work remains with the company managers.

Regardless of their particular jobs, all employees in an organization share some of the responsibility for effective human resource management. Some employees write their own job descriptions and even design their own jobs. Many employees provide input for the appraisal of their own performance or the performance of their colleagues and supervisors, or both. Many organizations ask employees to participate in annual surveys where they can express their likes and dislikes about the organization's approach to managing people. Perhaps most significant, employees assess their own needs and values and must manage their own careers in accordance with these. Doing so effectively involves understanding many aspects of their employer's human resource management practices. Table 13.1 on the following page summarizes some of the major HR responsibilities of these three key players: line managers, HR professionals, and employees.[4]

Gaining and Sustaining Competitive Advantage

As described in Chapter 7, a firm has a competitive advantage when all or part of the market prefers the firm's products and/or services. Companies seek ways to compete that can last a long time and cannot easily be imitated by competitors. Firms such as Google, J. M. Smucker, and The Container Store use their approaches to managing human resources to gain a sustainable competitive advantage.

Successful organizations view their employees as assets that need to be managed conscientiously and in tune with the organization's needs. Tomorrow's most successful organizations are working now to ensure that they have available tomorrow and a decade from now employees who are eager and able to address competitive challenges. Increasingly this means attracting superior talent and stimulating employees to perform at peak levels. Several large research projects have generated substantial evidence linking human resource management practices to bottom-line profitability and productivity gains. One study involved asking thousands of employees to describe their job and their organizations. The responses were used to form an index to reflect how much emphasis was placed on managing human resources. The research results

Snapshot

"I serve the board of directors, executive management, general office employees, retirees, production and salespeople across the country, every type of function—and they all view HR slightly differently based on their backgrounds, their needs and their histories. That has told me there isn't a one-size-fits-all solution. I've got to listen and ask questions, so that we can ultimately do something that's fair for everybody. HR can be very challenging because what we do can affect people at the most personal level and we can't lose sight of that."

Janet Brady, Vice President of Human Resources, The Clorox Company

Table 13.1	Shared Responsibilities for Managing Human Resources	

LINE MANAGERS	HR PROFESSIONALS	EMPLOYEES
Planning		
Include HR professionals in the formulation and implementation of business strategy and discussions of its HR implications.	Stay informed of the latest technical principles for managing human resources.	Accept responsibility for managing their own behavior and careers in organizations.
Recruitment and Selection		
Help disseminate information about open positions to all potentially qualified internal applicants. Understand and abide by all legal regulations. Interview applicants. May administer some selection tests. May make final selection decision.	Develop a recruiting plan to guarantee a diverse pool of applicants. Provide training to line managers and employees involved in recruitment and selection. Develop and administer a selection procedure. Monitor retention patterns and use exit interviews to diagnose potential problems.	Participate in recruiting by making referrals and answering questions about the organization. May participate in selection process by interviewing job applicants.
Training and Development		
Work with employees to identify their training and development needs. Provide on-the-job socialization and training.	Develop and administer training and development programs. Inform employees of opportunities for training and development.	Identify own training and development needs. Actively seek out and participate in activities that help build own competencies. Assist in socialization and training of other employees.
Performance Appraisal		
Help develop performance measures. Conduct performance appraisals. Use performance information to make decisions about pay raises, promotions, firing, etc. Provide feedback to employees to help them improve future performance.	Develop performance appraisal tools and train managers to use them. Train managers in how to conduct performance review sessions. Monitor managers' decisions to be sure they are performance based.	Candidly appraise the performance of others when asked to participate in 360-degree appraisals. Seek and use honest feedback to improve own performance.
Compensation		
Assist in developing incentive and bonus plans.	Establish appropriate rates of base pay in compliance with legal requirements. Work with managers to design and develop incentives and bonus plans. Work with accounting and financial staff to monitor compensation costs.	Develop an accurate understanding of all elements of the organization's pay practices. Be alert to dysfunctional and possible unethical attempts to "game" performance-based pay practices.

showed a strong association between using state-of-the-art approaches to HRM and profitability in subsequent years. Other research shows that the value of excellent human resource management can be especially great in firms that are growing rapidly and, thus, hiring large numbers of new employees.[5]

To gain sustainable competitive advantage by managing human resources effectively, three conditions must be met:

▸ Employees must be a source of added value.

▸ Employees must be "rare" or unique in some way.

Competitors must not be able to easily copy or imitate the company's approach to human resource management.

Employees Who Add Value. Like most intangibles, the value of an organization's employees doesn't appear on a balance sheet. Yet, intangibles such as the knowledge that employees have and the way employees feel and behave can be used to predict financial performance. At Schlumberger, the three years of specialized training completed by field engineers ensures that these employees have deep knowledge of their industry and its challenges. At the same time these employees are being educated, they also are developing strong personal bonds with their peers and a feeling of loyalty to the company. Investors seek companies with satisfied employees. They understand that employees who hate their jobs can't give the best possible service to customers. Conversely, when customers are happy, employees feel a sense of pride and satisfaction at being part of the company.[6]

Employees Who Are Rare. To be a source of sustainable competitive advantage, human resources must also be rare. If competitors can easily hire the same people, there is no competitive advantage. When Lincoln Electric Company in Cleveland, Ohio, announced it was planning to hire 200 production workers, it received more than 20,000 responses. When BMW announced that it had selected Spartanburg, South Carolina, as the site for its first U.S. production facility, it received more than 25,000 unsolicited requests for employment. Numbers this large make it more feasible for Lincoln Electric and BMW to hire employees who are two to three times more productive than their counterparts in other manufacturing firms.

By being an employer of choice, organizations can gain access to the best available talent. In other words, "the best get the best." Books and articles that purport to identify the "best" places to work are especially popular among students graduating from college, who view firms high in the rankings as desirable places to land their first post-graduation job. Dissatisfied workers who are looking for better employment situations read these lists too. Over time, a good reputation for attracting, developing, and keeping good talent acts like a magnet drawing the best talent to the firm.

An Approach That Cannot Be Copied. Business practices that are easy for competitors to copy don't provide sources of sustained competitive advantage. Approaches to human resource management that have evolved over a long period of time to meet the specific needs of the organization are the most difficult to copy. The HR practices at General Electric (GE) are an example. GE is widely regarded as a leader in managing people, and many firms have tried to copy their HR practices. Copying GE may bring some improvements to other organizations, but GE's HR practices work well for GE because they have been developed over time to fit the company's specific needs. As GE has evolved and changed, it has changed its HR practices to align them with the needs of the organization. Currently, for example, GE's CEO, Jeffry Immelt, is trying to shift the mind-set of employees to encourage greater innovation. After two decades of focusing relentlessly on continuous quality improvements, cost cutting, and efficiency, Immelt believes the company has lost its ability to innovate. How can Immelt change the culture of GE to encourage more innovation? He's doing it by changing many of the company's HR practices. Among the changes he has made are (1) recruiting more managers from outside the company, (2) hiring more employees from the countries where GE sells its products and services, (3) setting goals for managers to develop creative new business ideas and tying compensation to meeting these goals, (4) rewarding managers for revenue growth and customer satisfaction instead of just bottom-line financial performance, and (5) urging people to stay in their jobs longer so they can develop deeper knowledge of their industry.[7]

Bottom-Line Consequences

Estimating the dollar value of investments in human resources is a topic of increasing interest to accountants and financial analysts. "Everyone understands that the quality of people is the key differentiating factor—whether they're great as individuals or because they've set up systems that work best," says Peter Cappelli, professor of management and director of the Center for Human Resources at the Wharton School at the University of Pennsylvania. "The hard part is how do you measure it?"[8]

Investors' judgments about the value of a company's human resources often are informed by reputation rankings, such as those published by *Fortune*, *Forbes*, and *Black Enterprise*, and by other forms of the public recognition for excellence. For example, the Catalyst Award is given to organizations with outstanding initiatives that foster women's advancement into senior management. Another form of recognition for excellence in managing human resources is receipt of awards from professional organizations. For example, J. M. Smucker & Co. won the 2006 Ethical Practice Award, sponsored by *Workforce Management* magazine, for its use of several HRM practices aimed at ensuring that employees meet high ethical standards. The approach used by Smucker's is described in the Ethical Challenge feature.[9]

© Al Behrman/AP Photo

Employees may tend to agree that "with a name like Smucker, it's got to be good," thanks to the company's favorable HR practices.

Ethical Challenge

J. M. Smucker & Co.

J. M. Smucker is a fourth-generation family business in Orville, Ohio, that wants its name to stand for integrity. When James Monroe Smucker started the company in 1897, he personally inspected every jar of apple butter he produced. Today, with nearly 4,000 employees making jams, peanut butter, fruit spreads, shortening, and ice cream toppings in 45 countries, that level of personal involvement by the co-CEOs, Timothy and Richard Smucker, isn't possible. Instead, they rely on a system of HRM practices to ensure ethical conduct.

During job interviews, applicants hear Smucker executives refer frequently to the company's basic beliefs: ethics, quality, people, independence, and growth. In the interview, applicants hear specific information about how ethics relates to the job they want. For applicants who do well in the interview, the next stage is reference checking. Here too, the company asks prior employers and other people serving as references to specifically address the applicant's ethical conduct. Those who pass this hurdle are hired and then immediately

attend a training session that includes executive presentations, videos, and group discussions on moral awareness, moral courage, and values.

Smucker's training programs presents employees with examples of the choices they may have to make—for example, making decisions that are good in the short term versus the long term, being honest versus being loyal, and doing what's best for an individual versus doing what's best for the community. Throughout the training, employees learn about different approaches they can use to address the ethical dilemmas they face at work: the utilitarian approach, which involves seeking to do the greatest good for the greatest number of people; a rules-based approach, which involves making decisions based on rules others have created; and the Golden Rule, which means treating others as you would want them to treat you. After completing their initial training, and once a year thereafter, employees sign a nine-page ethics contract. Needless to say, ethical violations are all it takes to get fired from this company. To ensure that employees remember the lessons they learn as new hires, they also take refresher ethics training every three to five years.

Employees seem to respond well to the company's ethical commitment. According to *Fortune*, Smucker has consistently been ranked as one of the "100 Best Companies to Work For." By using effective HRM practices, this company hopes to prevent unethical employee behaviors that will harm the company.

To learn more about this organization, visit *www.smuckers.com*.

Social Value

The financial consequences of how organizations manage human resources have received a great deal of attention in recent years, but these are not the only consequences that matter. During an era of seemingly constant restructuring and downsizing, many people have become more aware of the social consequences of different approaches to managing human resources. When a large employer in a community is forced to downsize because of declining sales and profits, the change can affect the entire community. Similarly, if employers discriminate unfairly against some groups when making hiring decisions, the consequences of those discriminatory practices can ripple through the community for many years.

Within the United States, society often judges organizations in terms of the fairness with which they treat their employees. People believe that fairness is a desirable social condition—we want to be treated fairly, and we want others to view us as being fair.[10] Companies that rank high as the best places to work generally emphasize fairness as part of their corporate culture because fairness creates the feeling of trust that is needed to "hold a good workplace together." When deciding which company to work for, a potential employee evaluates whether a company pays a fair wage. If they feel unfairly treated after being hired, employees are likely to "vote with their feet" and seek employment elsewhere.[11] Some companies make a point of addressing basic concerns such as fairness even when doing so is costly and perhaps even reduces profitability. In addition, many legal regulations are intended to protect members of society from HRM practices that are unfair and potentially harmful.

The Legal and Regulatory Environment

Through elected government representatives, members of the labor force initiate and ultimately create federal and state laws. Through their tax payments, employees pay for the operations of a vast array of government agencies and courts that are responsible for interpreting and enforcing the laws. Thus, employment laws should be thought of not only as legal constraints; they are also sources of information about the issues that potential employees are likely thinking about as they decide whether to join or leave an organization. Some of the most important regulations affecting human resource management are described in Table 13.2 on the following page.

The numerous laws and regulations that affect how organizations manage human resources cannot all be discussed here, but two major categories that deserve comment are equal employment opportunity and compensation and benefits.

Equal Employment Opportunity

The principle of equal employment opportunity (EEO) *states that job applicants and employees should be judged on characteristics that are related to the work that they are being hired to do and on their job performance after being hired, and that they should be protected from discrimination based on their personal background characteristics, such as gender, race,*

Snapshot

"Our aim is to treat our job candidates as well as we treat our customers, to do something memorable for them. You can't treat people shabbily, especially in a world where there are far more open jobs than there is available talent to fill them. We strive to put the humanity back into the recruiting experience."

**Jason S. Warner,
Director of North American Recruiting, Starbucks Corporation**

2.

Describe several important laws and government regulations that affect how organizations manage their human resources.

Table 13.2	**Major Federal Employment Laws and Regulations**	

ACT	**JURISDICTION**	**BASIC PROVISIONS**
National Labor Relations Act (Wagner Act; 1935)	Most nonmanagerial employees in private industry	Provides right to organize, provides for collective bargaining; requires employers to bargain; requires unions to represent all members equally.
Fair Labor Standards Act (FLSA; 1938)	Most nonmanagerial employees in private industry	Establishes a minimum wage; controls hours through premium pay for overtime; controls working hours for children.
Equal Pay Act (1963)	Most employers	Prohibits unequal pay for males and females with equal skill, effort, and responsibility working under similar working conditions.
Title VII of the Civil Rights Act (1964, 1991)	Employers with 15 or more employees; employment agencies; unions	Prevents discrimination on the basis of race, color, religion, sex, or national origin; establishes the EEOC; provides reinstatement, back pay, compensatory, and punitive damages; permits jury trials.
Age Discrimination in Employment Act (ADEA; 1967)	Employers with more than 20 employees	Prevents discrimination against persons age 40 and over; states compulsory retirement for some employees.
Occupational Safety and Health Act (OSHA; 1970)	Most employers involved in interstate commerce	Ensures as far as possible safe and healthy working conditions and the preservation of our human resources.
The Pregnancy Discrimination Act (1978)	Employers with 15 or more employees	Identifies pregnancy as a disability and entitles the woman to the same benefits as any other disability.
Worker Adjustment and Retraining Notification Act (WARN; 1988)	Employers with more than 100 employees	Requires 60 days notice of plant or office closing or substantial layoffs.
Americans with Disabilities Act (ADA; 1990)	Employers with 15 or more employees	Prohibits discrimination against individuals with disabilities.
The Family and Medical Leave Act (1993)	Employers with 50 or more employees	Allows workers to take up to 12 weeks unpaid leave for childbirth, adoption, or illness of employee or a close family member.

ethnicity, religion, and so forth. This general principle is the foundation of several federal and state laws that govern employment practices. In recent years, the number of EEO charges filed against employers has averaged about 75,000.[12]

One especially important EEO law has been Title VII of the Civil Rights Act. *As originally enacted in 1964, Title VII prohibited discrimination by employers, employment agencies, and unions on the basis of race, color, religion, sex, or national origin.* A 1978 amendment prohibited discrimination against pregnant women. In 1991, a new version of the Civil Rights Act went into effect. The 1991 law reinforces the intent of the Civil Rights Acts of 1964 but states more specifically how cases brought under the act should proceed. Other important employment discrimination laws shown in Table 13.2 protect employees from discrimination on the basis of age and pregnancy.

Enforcement of U.S. EEO Laws. Power to enforce Title VII of the Civil Rights Act rests with the Equal Employment Opportunity Commission (EEOC). In carrying out their duties, the EEOC has the authority to make rules, conduct investigations, make judgments about guilt, and impose sanctions. In practice, this means that the EEOC has the responsibility and authority to prosecute companies that it believes are in violation of the law.

When employers don't comply with EEO laws, they can lose in court and lose employee loyalty.

Following the terrorist attacks on September 11, 2001, employees thought to be of Middle Eastern ethnicity suddenly became targets of discrimination in the workplace, as well as elsewhere. This problem became so pervasive so quickly that dealing with it was already the top priority of the EEOC by December of that year. The EEOC quickly alerted employers to the responsibility they had to prevent any such discrimination in their organizations.

Failure to comply with EEO laws exposes a company to lawsuits. For example, the EEOC joined in a lawsuit against Wal-Mart alleging widespread discrimination against women, who earn less than men in similar jobs and are underrepresented in the company's managerial ranks. That suit has not yet been settled, but it has already cost Wal-Mart millions of dollars to defend itself to the courts as well as to customers. After the EEOC brought a racial discrimination lawsuit against Texaco, that company eventually agreed to pay some $140 million to current and former aggrieved employees—the largest settlement ever for a case of racial discrimination.

EEO in the Global Arena. The challenge is even greater for international organizations because laws take dozens of different forms in countries around the world. To provide a flavor for the international legal environment, consider the situation faced by Cirque du Soleil. When making hiring decisions around the world, Cirque du Soleil must understand the legal constraints that apply in each country, as well as cultural factors. Wherever it hires employees—which it does in every country where it performs—the company must ensure that it adheres to all local labor laws. If the local regulations don't seem sufficient, Cirque du Soleil establishes its own minimal standards to ensure people are treated fairly. Typically, these standards comply at least with major U.S. employment laws, such as the Civil Rights Act.[13] Table 13.3 on the following page illustrates differences in discrimination laws—just one aspect of employment conditions.[14]

Compensation and Benefits

Compensation and benefits practices are shaped by numerous laws and regulations. These cover topics such as taxation, nondiscrimination, fair wages, the protection of children, hardship and overtime pay, and pension and welfare benefits. Here we describe two of the most far-reaching laws affecting compensation practices in the United States.

Table 13.3	**Who Is Protected Where?**								
Country	Race or Color	Sex	Religion	Age	Disability	Sexual Orientation	Political Ideology	National Origin	Marital or Family Status
United States	✓	✓	✓	✓	✓	No	No	✓	No
France	✓	✓	✓	✓	✓	✓	✓	✓	No
India	✓	✓	✓	No	✓	No	No	No	No
Brazil	✓	✓	No	✓	No	No	No	No	✓
Canada	✓	✓	✓	✓	✓	✓	No	✓	✓
China	✓	✓	✓	No	No	No	No	✓	No
Japan	No	✓	✓	✓	No	No	No	✓	No
Indonesia	No	✓	No	No	No	No	No	No	No
United Kingdom	✓	✓	✓	No	✓	✓	✓	✓	✓
Singapore	No	✓	No	✓	No	No	No	No	No
Mexico	✓	✓	✓	✓	✓	✓	✓	✓	✓
Turkey	No	✓	No	No	✓	No	No	No	No

Fair Labor Standards Act. Of the several laws that influence compensation and benefits practices, the primary one is the Fair Labor Standards Act (FLSA) of 1938. The Fair Labor Standards Act *is a federal law that specifies a national minimum wage rate and requires payment for overtime work by covered employees.* In 1938, the federal minimum wage was set at $0.25/hour. In 2006, it was $5.15—and it had been at that same level since 1997. Individual states can, and often do, set higher standards than those set at the federal level. The FLSA also includes provisions to protect children. For example, it prohibits minors under the age of 18 from working in hazardous occupations.

Equal Pay Act. Another important regulation affecting compensation practices is the Equal Pay Act of 1963. The Equal Pay Act *requires men and women to be paid equally when they are doing equal work (in terms of skill, effort, responsibility, and working conditions) in the same organization.* Suppose for example, that a software company had mostly male programmers designing computer games and mostly female programmers designing Web sites for those games. If the levels of skill, effort, and responsibility are similar in these two jobs, the male and female programmers should be paid equally—despite the fact that they aren't doing identical work.

Many states have extended the logic of the Equal Pay Act to require that men and women be paid equally for doing *comparable* work. Comparable worth *legislation requires employers to assess the worth of all jobs and ensure that jobs of comparable worth are paid similarly.* These state laws go beyond the narrow language of the federal law to state that work that appears to be quite dissimilar (e.g., nurses and engineers) can be of comparable worth. If one occupation (e.g., nursing) tends to be dominated by women and the other (e.g., tree surgeons) by men, chances are high that the occupation dominated by women will be paid less. Such discrepancies may be due to historical factors, discrimination, or labor market conditions. For organizations covered by comparable worth laws, employers must demonstrate that pay discrepancies between men and women reflect differences in factors such as the skills and responsibilities associated with their work.

Many other laws and regulations put constraints on how employers manage their human resources. Failure to comply with such laws can be costly. In addition to legal fees required to defend the company against lawsuits are the costs of any fines the company must pay and damage to the company's reputation. By ensuring their managers know and follow all relevant employment laws, companies such as Cirque du Soleil, GE, and Schlumberger can reduce their exposure to lawsuits and keep their attention focused on managing people effectively.

Human Resource Planning

3.
Explain the objective of human resource planning and describe how organizations respond to the unpredictability of future business needs.

Central to managing human resources effectively is the process of planning. Human resource planning *involves forecasting the organization's human resources needs and developing the steps to be taken to meet them.* The primary objective is ensuring that the right number and type of individuals are available at the appropriate time and place to meet the organization's needs. Human resources planning is tied directly to strategic planning (see Chapter 7).

Typically, strategic goals are established first, followed by goals for managing human resources that are consistent with the broader goals. At Hewlett-Packard (HP), the computer company, human resource planning became a top priority after the firm acquired Compaq. Through planning, HP determined which employees would stay in the new HP and who would have to leave. More recently, HP has been focusing on how their move into the digital entertainment market will influence the types of employees they will need. HP's planning process is described in the Strategic Action Competency feature.[15]

Strategic Action Competency

HP's Workforce Plan

HP has been through a lot of changes in recent years, and it knows the future will hold just as many surprises as the past. But uncertainty about what the future holds doesn't stop the company from planning for it. One thing is certain: The company will need new competencies to continue to innovate and succeed. As Gerard Boussard, vice president of global workforce planning at HP, explained: "HP operates in a rapidly changing environment. It's critical to be agile and respond to change faster than our competition. A new set of products [digital entertainment] and a new set of customers requires a radical workforce change."

To plan for its future workforce needs, HP uses a six-step process. Briefly, these steps are:

Step 1. Business leaders scan the environment to detect business trends, and HR professionals scan the environment to learn about demographic changes, workforce trends, and political trends.

Step 2. Business leaders describe the high-level workforce implications of business strategies. For example, if the strategy calls for growing the market in China, this step reveals that the company will have to have a sales force in place in China

and it identifies the regions of China where growth will occur.

Step 3. Business leaders describe in general terms their current workforce. What types of competencies do they have in place today? Where are these competencies located?

Step 4. The next task is to understand the implications of the projected trends. Given the business strategies and an understanding of the current workforce, what changes are needed by HP in the next three years? Where will the company need to be finding new talent? What new competencies are needed? Where are new competencies needed?

Step 5. Here the focus shifts to operational issues. Now the big-picture trends that were identified in earlier steps are quantified with specific numbers and dates. Questions about how to achieve the changes (e.g., Retrain current employees? Hire new employees? Conduct layoffs?) also are addressed.

Step 6. The final step involves focusing on the short-term. Given the three year plan, what needs to get done in the next six months? If hiring is needed, who will be used for recruiting and where will the applicants come from? If layoffs are expected, how will this be communicated to employees?

Gerard Boussard knows he and his colleagues can't predict the future perfectly. Any long-term plan is likely to change. But the planning process is valuable nevertheless because it keeps everyone thinking about how human resource management contributes to the firm's long-term success.

To learn more about this organization, visit *www.hp.com.*

At the heart of HP's planning are two tasks: determining an organization's future human resource needs and developing a strategy to meet those needs. HP relies on its own managers to forecast the company's future needs. Many other companies use outside experts to help them forecast HR needs. Regardless of who makes them, forecasts about the future may not be accurate. During times of growth, it is difficult to foresee changing conditions that may cause a downturn in the business. It's just as difficult to predict when another business boom will occur. Realizing that the future is uncertain, some organizations stay flexible by hiring contingent workers that can be hired and fired as needed.

Contingent Workers

Instead of hiring permanent workers to meet the demands of a growing business, many companies hire contingent workers. Contingent workers *are employees who are hired by companies for specific tasks or short periods of time with the understanding that their employment may be ended at any time.* Included among contingent workers are part-timers, freelancers, subcontractors, and independent professionals of many types. A 2005 Census Population Survey conducted by the Bureau of Labor Statistics estimated that the number of contingent workers is about 11 percent of the U.S. workforce.[16]

At Trader Joe's, the grocery store chain, part-time contingent workers are central to the firm's success. As described in the Planning and Administration Compentency feature, employing part-time employees is one way the company ensures it can provide career opportunities to a smaller core of full-time employees.[17]

Planning and Administration Competency

Trader Joe's

At Trader Joe's, the mission is "to bring our customers the best food and beverage values and the information to make informed buying decisions." If you've ever shopped at Trader Joe's, you know it's different from most grocery stores. The stores tend to be small and you won't find every imaginable food product available. What you will find are more than 2,000 unique grocery items carrying the Trader Joe's label, offered at relatively low prices. You'll also find very friendly employees in all of its 217 stores around the country. The story goes that former CEO John Shields wouldn't hire anyone who didn't smile during the first 30 seconds of their job interview. Besides being friendly,

Trader Joe's also looks for people who are familiar with their products and enthusiastic salespeople. The application process includes describing what you like best about the Trader Joe's store where you shop. If you don't already know the company and shop at one of its stores, chances are pretty good you won't get hired.

Trader Joe's can be picky about who it hires because so many people want to work there. Besides offering a casual and friendly culture, the company pays well. Part-time clerks earn between $8 and $12 per hour. Full-time clerks earn an average of about $16 per hour in their first year—about 30 percent more than the industry average. In addition to their regular wages, they typically receive annual bonuses of $950 and another $6,300 in contributions to their retirement. The compensation for store managers, who are never hired from outside the company, totals approximately $132,000—comparable to what managers at other chains would earn if they were in charge of a store six to seven times as large. To further motivate staff to keep up with the company's changing products, the company offers employees a 10 percent store discount.

To learn more about this organization, visit *www.traderjoes.com*.

Members of the contingent workforce understand that they'll be frequently entering into and exiting from employment relationships. Temporary assignments generally last 3 to 12 months. One benefit of being a contingent worker is that while working on temporary assignments, they develop connections to a wide range of possible future employers.

Many employers use contingent employees as a recruiting source for regular employment, a practice that is commonly called *temp-to-hire*. John Sullivan, T-Mobile area director of engineering and operations, says of contingent workers, "Many of them are not necessarily interested in full-time work; but for those that are, it's a chance for us to see who's a fit and it gives them a chance to see this is a pretty good place." In effect, contingent workers must continually maintain their status as a member of the applicant pool in order to ensure their continued employment.[18]

© Ric Francis/AP Photo

Contingent workers are key to Trader Joe's success. The company and employees both benefit from this flexible arrangement.

Layoffs

When business is slow, many companies reduce their workforce by laying off employees. During business downturns, companies may lay off 5, 10, or even 15 percent of their employees within a matter of weeks. Typically, the people who lose their jobs are those who were most recently hired or those whose performance is the least desirable. Layoffs are a short-term solution to difficult economic conditions or an expected decline in the company's business.

Often, sooner than expected, companies that have conducted layoffs find that they need to rehire these same people. According to one large study, approximately 25 percent of the companies that had trimmed their workforces were rehiring people the next year—either for their former jobs or for new permanent jobs. The problem seems to be that managers use layoffs as a quick method of cost cutting. In the longer term, however, layoffs create problems because the overall trend is that the size of the labor force is growing very slowly. The historical trend is shown in Figure 13.1 on the following page.[19] Therefore, as soon as business conditions improve, employers who have conducted layoffs quickly find that they must compete even harder to find new workers.[20]

Experienced managers understand that layoffs should be a strategy of last resort. To rehire a laid-off staff person, a company may have to offer higher pay. And, although they may be paid better, such employees now feel less loyalty to the firm. So, if a better opportunity comes along, they may be more willing to change jobs than to stay put in anticipation of a promotion or pay raise.

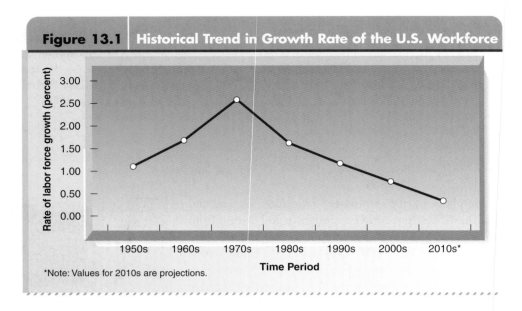

Figure 13.1 | **Historical Trend in Growth Rate of the U.S. Workforce**

*Note: Values for 2010s are projections.

Figure 13.2 shows some of the other consequences of laying off workers. By laying off workers, companies may save some money in the short term, but in the longer term they may find that morale goes down and labor costs go up.[21]

Competency Inventories

In addition to matching the number of employees to the amount of work that needs to be done, human resources planning ensures that a company has the right types of employees—those with the competencies needed by the organization. One way to keep track of the skills present in a company's workforce is to use competency inventories. A competency inventory *is a detailed file maintained for each employee that lists level of education, training, experience, length of service, current job title and salary, and performance history.* At Schlumberger, the Career Networking Profiles that employees prepare are an element in the company's competency inventory. Also included are assessments of the employee's competency levels in terms of the factors includ-

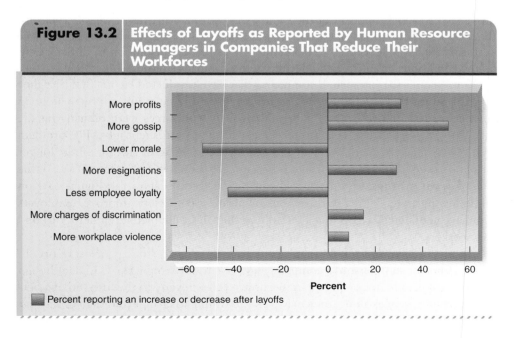

Figure 13.2 | **Effects of Layoffs as Reported by Human Resource Managers in Companies That Reduce Their Workforces**

Percent reporting an increase or decrease after layoffs

ed in the competency model used throughout this book.[22] Our competency model is only one of many that could be used. In fact, a survey of 217 companies revealed a total of 148 different competency models in use. Of course, a great deal of overlap exists among the models. The purpose of all of these competency models is the same: to keep track of the talent in the organization so that it can be nurtured and used effectively.[23]

Like Schlumberger, many organizations use computerized human resources information systems for storage and easy retrieval of such vital job-related information. These files help the firm's top managers spot human resources gaps. When gaps exist between the human resource needs of the organization and the current supply of talent in the organization, managers can use a variety of other human resource activities to fill the gaps. They can hire more (or fewer) people or they can begin hiring people with different competencies. If the organization has the right number of people, but they need new competencies, training activities may be used to address the gap. In the remainder of this chapter, we discuss these and other HR activities in more detail.

The Hiring Process

4.
Describe the hiring process.

The hiring process *includes activities related to the recruitment of applicants to fill open positions in an organization and the selection of the best applicants for a position.* Through hiring activities, employers ensure that the right person is in the right job.

As illustrated in Figure 13.3, recruitment and selection are stimulated by a vacancy in the organization. These vacancies may occur because employees leave the organization (turnover), because they have been moved to another position within the organization, or because the organization is growing and needs more people to do the work. At Trader Joe's, for example, recruitment and selection are stimulated mostly by growth—they open between 8 and 25 stores per year. By effectively communicating its values and key behaviors during recruitment and selection, Trader Joe's avoids hiring people who will not work out as long-term employees. At their existing stores, they retain productive employees as long as possible, reducing the number of vacancies created by employee turnover.

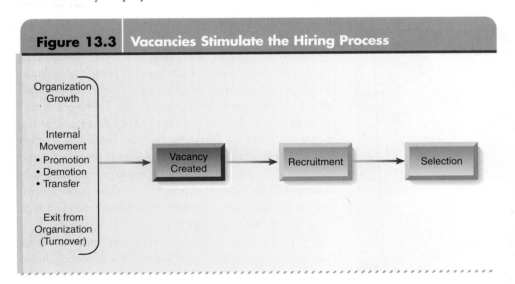

Figure 13.3 | **Vacancies Stimulate the Hiring Process**

Advanced Financial Solutions (AFS) is another company that understands the links between recruitment, selection, and retention. Located in Oklahoma City, Advanced Financial Solutions must compete with the glamour of cities like New York, San

Francisco, Boston, and even Paris, Brussels, and Tokyo when hiring software technicians. Yet employee turnover averages only about 1 percent. How does AFS make sure that the professionals it hires will like Oklahoma City and their new jobs well enough to stay put? They invest heavily in recruitment and selection. Applicants participate in lengthy telephone interviews, and detailed reference checks are conducted. When the company thinks it has found a good candidate, he or she is invited to spend one week visiting the company. Spouses are invited, too. Prospective employees visit all departments and meet everyone from the CEO to the support staff. Spouses are shown around the town and company volunteers make an effort to answer their questions about life in Oklahoma City: How are the schools? What religious organizations are there? How good are the sports facilities? And so on. No job offers are made until applicants complete their one-week visit. The approach costs AFS about $7,500 per hire, and the company feels the investment is well worth it.[24]

Recruitment

Recruitment *is the process of searching, both inside and outside the organization, for people to fill vacant positions.* During recruitment, the organization develops a pool of job candidates from which to select qualified employees. After recruiting candidates, the organization selects those who are most likely to perform well on the job.[25]

In some organizations, recruitment activities are centralized in the human resources department, and professional HR staff members do most of the recruiting. In less centralized organizations, however, line managers often have most of the responsibility for recruitment. At Advanced Financial Solutions, even the CEO is active in recruiting and hiring the technical professionals that are so vital to the success of that company.

The initial recruiting experience—when an employee is first considered for a position in the organization—is an employee's first exposure to the organization's recruiting activities, but it is not the last one. Employees may again become involved in recruiting activities as they help (or hinder) their employers' efforts to attract others to the company. When employees eventually consider applying for other jobs in the organization, they again become actively involved in recruitment activities. These experiences with the organization's recruiting activities may be especially important in determining whether talented employees are retained.

Employers inform potential applicants about employment opportunities using a variety of methods. They place ads, post notices on the company bulletin board, accept applications from people who simply walk into their recruiting offices, and so on. Different methods may reach different sources of applicants. Posting announcements on company bulletin boards is a good way to recruit employees who are already working at the company but may be ready to move to another job. Placing ads in local newspapers, in trade publications, and on the Internet are common methods used to reach those in the external labor market.

Instead of using just one recruiting method, most employers use multiple methods. This approach helps the organization generate a large, diverse pool of applicants. Southwest Airlines tries to be creative when it comes to recruiting. They seek out applicants in unlikely places—they prefer schoolteachers and police officers over industry veterans, for example. Many of their appli-

Once potential employees are recruited, they face a selection process that is based on their individual competencies.

cants learn about the company through the reality TV series called *Airline*, which shows the work life of Southwest employees at four airports. For every job opening, Southwest Airlines receives nearly 100 applications.

Electronic and Other Media. Virtually every company has a Web site that applicants can go to and learn about the company. Many of these sites have specific information about job postings, required competencies, career progression programs, mentoring, diversity initiatives, and benefits. Increasingly, company Web sites encourage electronic applications, which save a great deal of time and cost and usually result in more applicants applying because of their ease of use.

Continental Airlines uses a Web-based screening process to improve the quality of its new hires. If you're interested in becoming a flight attendant, for example, you begin the application process by answering 41 questions designed to screen out people who are clearly not suitable for such jobs. The same questions are asked of all applicants around the world.[26]

Web-based recruiting is not a panacea, however. According to a study of business school graduates who were looking for jobs, poorly designed electronic recruiting sites can cause frustration. Figure 13.4 describes some of the most common problems encountered by electronic job searchers. How many of these problems would you put up with before deciding not to make a job application?[27]

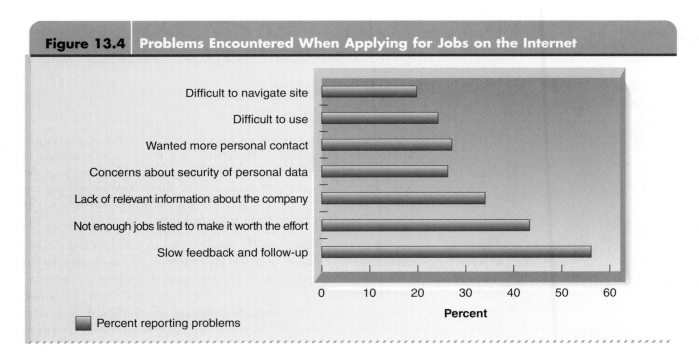

Figure 13.4 | Problems Encountered When Applying for Jobs on the Internet

Difficult to navigate site
Difficult to use
Wanted more personal contact
Concerns about security of personal data
Lack of relevant information about the company
Not enough jobs listed to make it worth the effort
Slow feedback and follow-up

Percent

☐ Percent reporting problems

Job Postings. A job posting *prominently displays current job openings to all employees in an organization.* They are usually found on bulletin boards (cork as well as electronic). Job postings provide complete job descriptions, explain the competencies needed, and may also provide information about compensation and performance standards. Savvy employees observe postings over time to gain information about turnover rates in various departments, as well as information about the competencies that are most in demand.

Employee Referrals. Employee referrals *occur when current employees inform people they know about openings and encourage them to apply.* Many firms that recruit accountants and auditors encourage employee referrals. Especially at senior levels, there are too few qualified accountants for projected need in coming years. Employees can help the firm tap into the supply of talent and also help prescreen potential applicants. KPMG offers bonuses to employees who make referrals that lead to hiring, and 50 percent of their new hires come from employee referrals.[28] Quicken loans has a team of full-time talent scouts whose only job is encouraging employees to refer their friends and classmates. Quicken even provides training to remind employees that part of their job is to help recruit new employees.[29]

Employee referrals are a very low-cost approach to recruiting, but low cost is not the only reason for using this method. Employee referrals usually result in the highest one-year retention rates. One explanation for this success is that employees provide a balanced view of organizational life. The more information that is available, the better the referral decision is likely to be. Another explanation is that employees tend to recruit applicants who are similar to them in interests and motivations. Because employees are already adjusted to the organizational culture, this matching process increases the likelihood that applicants also will fit.[30]

Selection

Through recruitment, a company finds people who are potential employees. **Employee selection** *is a process that involves deciding which of these recruits should actually be hired and for which positions.*[31] The decision about who to select often takes into account a person's competencies and how well they fit into the organization. The most common sources of information for making selection decisions are

- résumés,
- reference checks,
- interviews, and
- tests.

Employers use the information they gain from these sources to select the best potential employees from a pool of applicants. Applicants, in turn, may draw inferences about the organization and the requirements of a job based on both the content of the selection procedures and the way the organization treats applicants throughout the selection process. Well-qualified applicants who react negatively to either the content or process used during selection may decline the organization's job offer.[32]

Résumés. A well-written résumé is clear, concise, and easy to read and understand. It gives (1) personal data; (2) career objectives; (3) education; (4) work experience, highlighting special skills and responsibilities; (5) descriptions of relevant competencies, activities, and personal information; and (6) the names, addresses, telephone numbers, and e-mail addresses of references. Many companies that accept electronic résumés specify the format you must use or provide an electronic form to complete. In such cases, complying with all the requirements for submitting your résumé is especially important because some of the companies also use software programs designed to scan for information and route your résumé to the appropriate person.

Reference Checks. Because résumés can be falsified easily, managers may request references and conduct reference checks. Many employers routinely check educational qualifications, including schools attended, majors, degrees awarded, and dates. Unfortunately, such checking often reveals that applicants have lied about their backgrounds.[33] An applicant's work experience is more difficult to check because employers often are reluctant to provide performance evaluations of former employees. Their concern stems from cases in which employees successfully sued their former employers for giving negative references. In fact, by law, organizations are required to provide only the job title and dates of employment of a former employee.

Interviews. In making a final selection, most organizations rely on a combination of interviews and tests. At Jet Blue, the people you are going to work with conduct some of the interviews. One objective is to find people who will live the company's values: safety, caring, integrity, fun, and passion.

Although commonly used, interviews don't always predict on-the-job performance accurately. An experienced applicant who knows how to manage the interview process may be able to create a favorable impression of herself even if she is not well-qualified for the job.[34] Managers who conduct very structured interviews may be less susceptible to such tactics, but even experienced managers make judgments about people based on non-job-related cues. An example of the questions that might be asked in a structured interview are shown in Table 13.4.

Table 13.4	Examples of Questions to Use in a Structured Interview

COMPETENCY BEING ASSESSED: TEAMWORK

1. Sketch out two or three key strengths you have in working as part of a work team. Can you illustrate the first strength with a recent example? [repeat this question and the following probes for each strength]:
   Probes:

   When did this example take place?
   What possible negative outcomes were avoided by the way you handled the situation?
   How often do situations like this happen?
   What happened the next time it came up?

2. Tell me about a time when you used your teamwork competency to solve a problem with a customer.
   Probes:

   Where did this take place?
   What did the customer say?
   What did you tell your teammates?
   Did the team have any problems dealing with the situation? Explain.
   How did the customer respond?

Snapshot

"If you're being considered as a pilot, one of your interviews is with a pilot. The interviewers keep notes and the interview is scored. The pilot, along with the recruiter and someone from the line leadership, all put their scores together and, as a group, decide if a person is going to be hired or take the next step. Our posture in this is to help [employees] get people [they] would want to work with."

Vincent Stabile, Vice President of People, Jet Blue Airways

Most interviewers decide about a person early in the interview and then spend the rest of the time seeking information to support that decision. Too often, managers form favorable impressions of candidates simply because they share superficial similarities with the manager, for example, where they grew up or where they went to school. Managers may also let their stereotypes affect their judgments about individual candidates. Problems like these were what made Home Depot decide to automate its hiring process. By using a computerized approach to screening all job applicants, it is now much more likely that a qualified woman, for example, will end up in a job that uses all of her competencies instead of being put into a job that fits an interviewer's stereotype about what types of jobs women do best.[35]

Despite their potential drawbacks, well-structured interviews can be useful.[36] When you first enter the world of work, you probably will be interviewed many times before you're in a position to conduct interviews yourself.

Tests. Many organizations use tests to screen and select candidates. The cognitive ability test *is a test that employers use to measure general intelligence; verbal, numerical, and reasoning ability; and the like.* Such tests have proved to be relatively successful in predicting which applicants are qualified for certain jobs.[37]

Written tests can also be used to measure personality. A **personality** test *assesses the unique blend of characteristics that define an individual.* In jobs that involve a great deal of contact with other people, such as sales agents and many types of service jobs, a personality characteristic referred to as *extraversion* is a good predictor of future job performance. Extraverts tend to be talkative, good natured, and gregarious. They are good at communicating with customers and clients. Another personality characteristic of interest to many employers is conscientiousness. Conscientious people seem to have a strong sense of purpose, obligation, and persistence—all of which lead to high performance in almost any type of work situation.[38]

A **performance** test *requires a candidate to perform simulations of actual job tasks.* One example is a code-writing test for computer programmers. Another example is an in-basket exercise. In this case, job candidates receive a stack of letters, notes, memos, telephone messages, faxes, and other items and are told to imagine that they have been promoted to a new position. They are given a specific amount of time to deal appropriately with these items. In most cases they will have the opportunity to explain or discuss their decisions in a follow-up interview.

Regardless of the specific procedures used to select employees, employers should be concerned with how applicants view them. It is important that hiring procedures *be* fair and also that they *feel* fair to applicants.

5. *Training and Development*

Describe several types of training and development programs.

When unemployment levels are high, it's relatively easy for employers to simply hire people who have the competencies needed to perform well in a job. But during labor shortages, it becomes much more difficult to solve problems by simply hiring new people. For Schlumberger, the shortage of engineers with relevant experience is the reason they provide up to three years of rigorous training before sending people to work in the oil field. Like Schlumberger, employers provide training and development to help their employees develop the competencies needed by the company. **Training** *refers to activities that help employees overcome limitations and improve performance in their current jobs.* **Development** *refers to practices that help employees gain the competencies they will need in the future in order to advance in their careers.*

Even if a company hired only the very most qualified people available, they would probably still need to invest in training and development. The activities can range from a one-day orientation session to a personalized, long-term career development plan. Different approaches generally are used to achieve different purposes.

Orientation Training

Almost all new hires need to "learn the ropes." Every company has its own ways of doing things, which are important for all employees to understand. A few hours of training during the first day or two on the job helps ease new hires into the company's way of doing things.[39] At Jet Blue, orientation begins on the first day with the company when a new employee spends an hour listening to the CEO explain how the company makes money. For pilots and flight attendants, the orientation session also includes a session on "crew resource management," which explains the company's system for communicating with each other in flight.[40]

For many firms with a strong set of values and clear strategic objectives, orientation training provides the direction that new employees need in order to be successful in their jobs. As described in the following Teamwork Competency feature, orientation and job-specific training is extensive for new employees of the Ritz-Carlton Hotel Company. This company has become so widely recognized for its ability to use HR practices to support quality service that it decided to teach other companies how they can improve. Interested managers and executives can attend classes and presentations at the firm's leadership training center and buy consulting services.[41]

Teamwork Competency

Ritz-Carlton Hotel Company

Employees who work for the Ritz-Carlton Hotel Company are proud of the fact that the company is a two-time winner of the Baldrige National Quality Award and consistently earns top ratings in the travel and leisure industry. The awards and the excellent customer service they represent don't happen by accident. It begins with the belief that "At the Ritz-Carlton, our Ladies & Gentlemen are the most important resource in our service commitment to our guests." Excellent hiring practices are the next step. The company knows what types of people perform well in each job, and it is careful to employ only the right people. Orientation comes next. This is the first step in creating a team of employees who all share the same vision and goals. During orientation, the company infuses new employees with the company's "soul," according to Horst Schultz, the former COO, president, and vice chairman. During orientation, Schultz would explain that every employee was essential to the company's success. If they didn't make checking in a pleasure, keep the rooms clean, and respond to the guests' every need, the company would suffer. In comparison, if Schultz didn't show one day for work, it made very little difference!

After a general orientation program, Ritz-Carlton provides more specific training. Some principles of conduct all employees must learn—for example, when a guest asks for directions, always escort them rather than just pointing, and answer the phone with a "smile." Training for specific jobs is designed and delivered by the five best employees in each job category. Working together, those who are best at doing each job develop a set of principles that everyone in that job needs to understand to perform it well. And the training never stops. For the first 10 minutes of each day, all employees participate together in the "line-up," which is used to remind all team members that they should strive to live the company's values throughout their workday. By constantly reminding employees what the company strives to achieve, it teaches them habits that will serve the guests and the company well. Each year, employees attend additional training to earn their annual training certificate.

To learn more about this organization, visit *www.ritzcarlton.com*.

Basic Skills Training

Basic skills training may be needed by employees who are unable to read, write, do arithmetic, or solve problems well enough to perform even simple tasks. Such employees can't write letters to customers, read warning labels on chemical containers, or understand machine operating symbols. Some employees may also need training to perform basic behavioral skills, such as how to work safely and how to talk to customers. Organizations spend large sums of money on remedial training for employees because they believe that, if employees can master certain basic skills, they can perform a variety of jobs and be able to deal with some of the new technologies.[42]

Increasingly, language training is being offered to employees around the world working in customer service jobs. As described in the Multicultural Competency feature on the following page, the widespread outsourcing of such jobs to India has stimulated a huge demand for such training.[43]

BPO Ltd.

Every six months, hundreds of new employees converge on BPO Ltd., a business process outsourcing firm in Bangalore, India. They are there to improve their customer service and communication skills so they can support BPO Ltd.'s twenty-two global clients. BPO Ltd.'s clients include firms in banking, telecommunication, and financial services. The firm's employees handle home mortgage information, overdraft issues, telephone repair problems, and other customer service tasks.

To prepare for these jobs, employees attend a boot camp training program. The skills they will master include accent neutralization and sales. English accents in India vary tremendously depending on one's native language. There are at least 18 different spoken languages across India. Most of BPO Ltd.'s new hires need to improve their general communication skills, too. Language is not the only concern. According to Nandita Gurjar,

vice president and head of human resources, "In terms of their ability to interact with people from different cultures, they have absolutely no experience."

Employees hired to answer the phone, rather than communicate only by e-mail, devote two hours daily for six weeks striving to neutralize their accents. Training includes recording their voices and then rewinding and analyzing the tape. In addition, new hires learn about their client's business. For some employees who handle sophisticated transactions, training can last as long as eight weeks. They immerse themselves in their client's world, learning their history, their jargon, and the latest news in order to better connect with customers and develop their own knowledge.

To learn more about this organization, visit *www.infosys.com/bpo*.

Snapshot

"When you're in a business like ours, the HR dynamic is incredibly important. Education—training and teaching others—are key elements of our culture. It's a consistent theme. If our organization doesn't continue to evolve, it will fail."

Richard Mott, CEO, Kyphon, Inc.

E-Learning

Regardless of *what* is being learned, many companies are using electronic media to deliver training, instead of relying on traditional classroom approaches. *When training is delivered using electronic-based technologies, it is commonly referred to as* e-learning. Reflecting the great proliferation of computer technology, e-learning applications and processes include Web-based learning, computer-based learning, virtual classrooms, and digital collaboration. It includes the delivery of content via the Internet, intranet/extranet, audio- and videotape, satellite broadcast, interactive TV, CDs, and even video games. An estimated 30 percent of all company training is now delivered using these technologies instead of instructor-led classroom training.[44]

A major advantage of e-learning technology is it allows employees to develop their competencies at their own pace and at a time that is personally convenient. For companies, it is less expensive than sending everyone to traditional classroom training. When LEGO, the toy company, conducts employee attitude surveys, it uses e-learning to teach all managers how to interpret the results of the surveys. When Intuit signs on new distributors of its tax software programs, it combines e-learning with traditional approaches to train them. First the distributors meet face to face with Intuit staff. Subsequently, they meet in monthly virtual classes to learn about special features of the software, for troubleshooting sessions, and for sales demonstrations. At Cold Stone Creamery, an ice cream store in California, a Web-based video game teaches employees portion control so they don't serve too much or too little ice cream in each scoop. One employee commented: "It's so much fun, I e-mailed it to everyone."[45]

At Kyphon, Inc., effective training can make the difference between life and death. Kyphon produces and sells a patented device than is used to correct painful spinal conditions. The firm's salespeople teach surgeons how to use it in the operating room. So, in addition to offering the more usual types of training to people in accounting, operations, and so on, Kyphon provides medical training to its sales force. Kyphon's zeal for training doesn't stop there, however. They view learning as the life blood of the company. Employees are encouraged to pursue training in any form that suits them—from technical and business courses to lifestyle management. The philosophy is that everyone needs to be continuously learning and developing to support a company that is evolving and changing as new technologies become available.[46]

Career Development

Most employees would not be satisfied doing the same job year after year. They want to grow in order to move into new jobs.[47] The intent of development programs is to improve an employee's competencies in preparation for future jobs. Before sending an employee to a development program, a needs analysis is conducted to identify that person's particular strengths and developmental needs. For beginning supervisors and managers, developmental needs often include inability to set goals with others and learning how to negotiate interpersonal conflicts.

Colgate-Palmolive is one company that takes development seriously. Its People Development unit conducted an extensive analysis of the external environment and had experts forecast Colgate's future personnel needs. Then they developed a profile of required leadership competencies, such as business savvy, use of personal influence, global perspective, strong character, people management skills, and entrepreneurial action. With a clear view of the types of leaders needed by the company, the People Development unit laid out a strategy for getting such people into place. The success of that strategy required (1) a commitment to identifying "high-potential" employees and giving them job assignments that develop their leadership competencies, and (2) the active involvement of high-potential employees in their own career management. Table 13.5 describes the components of a tool kit developed to assist high-potential employees with their career management.

Table 13.5	**Components of a Tool Kit for Individual Development at Colgate-Palmolive**

I. Overview of the Individual Development Process
- Assess individual competencies and values.
- Define personal strengths, development needs, and options for career growth. Identify developmental actions.
- Craft individual development plan.
- Meet with manager to decide a course of action (based on preceding analysis).
- Accept the challenge of implementing the plan.

II. Worksheets for Individual Assessment
- Competency assessment worksheet: assesses strengths and weaknesses for a specified set of competencies.
- Personal values survey: assesses preferences for types of work environments, work relationships, work tasks, lifestyle needs, and personal needs.
- Development activities chart: describes on-the-job and off-the-job learning opportunities that can be used to develop key competencies.
- Global training grid: lists all formal training programs offered by the company and explains how each relates to key competencies.
- Individual development plan: developed by the employee, this describes specific development goals and a course of action to be taken to achieve those goals.

III. Defining and Understanding Global Competencies
This section of the tool kit is like a dictionary. It lists all the competencies considered to be important for various types of jobs throughout the company and describes the meaning of each competency. This section serves as a reference guide and encourages people across the company to use a common set of terms when discussing competencies and career development issues.

Many large companies, such as GE, McDonald's, Motorola, and Siemens, provide so many hours of development activities to so many employees that they have built company "universities," complete with classrooms, "dorm" rooms, and other amenities of a typical college campus. Organizations may encourage employees to attend these "universities" as part of a long-term strategy for developing a cadre of high-potential employees who, several years in the future, may eventually become upper-level managers. The development experiences are intended to broaden these managers' perspectives and prepare them for general (as opposed to functional) management positions. A key objective often is to develop managers' strategic action competency.

One-on-One Mentoring and Coaching

Besides training employees in groups, some companies use a more personal approach that includes one-on-one mentoring and coaching.

Mentoring. Mentoring *occurs when an established employee guides the development of a less experienced worker, or protégé, to increase that employee's competencies, achievement, and understanding of the organization.* At Intel, the mentoring program is designed to help less experienced employees (called partners) develop specific knowledge or skills with the help of an expert (the mentor). Mentors, in turn, often learn from the less experienced employees they are supposed to assist. The company's intranet is used to match up partners and mentors, who then work together an average of six months. Increasingly, these are "virtual" relationships between employees in different countries, with mentoring discussions taking place via e-mail or telephone. Responsibility for setting up meetings, deciding what to talk about, and deciding when to end the relationship is in the hands of the partner and mentor.

Coaching. For high-level executives and other employees who hold visible and somewhat unique jobs, traditional forms of on-the-job training are impractical. Yet, these employees often need to develop new competencies in order to be fully effective. In recent years, more and more executives have turned to personal coaching to address their training needs. With coaching, *an expert observes the employee in his or her job over a period of weeks or months and provides continuous feedback and guidance on how to improve.* Most coaches also encourage their "trainees" to discuss difficult situations as they arise and work through alternative scenarios for dealing with those situations. Although coaching is rapidly growing in popularity, it's a relatively new technique and few guidelines are available to evaluate whether a potential coaching relationship is likely to succeed.

6.
Describe several principles for improving the accuracy of managers' appraisals of employee performance.

Performance Appraisal

Performance appraisal *refers to a formal, structured system for evaluating an employee's job performance.* Its focus is on documenting how productive the employee is and which areas of performance could be improved. One of the primary responsibilities of managers is appraising the performance of their employees. Increasingly, employees also are being asked to appraise the performance of their managers.[48]

Uses of Performance Appraisal Results

Performance appraisal is generally used in two ways. On the one hand, performance appraisal is an evaluation of the past. Appraisal results are used in making decisions about who will be promoted, demoted, transferred, or dismissed, and the size of raises to give employees. On the other hand, performance appraisal is a means for moving into a more productive future.

[handwritten margin note:] Results influence who is promoted demoted transferred, dismissed and the size of raises that employees receive.

For performance appraisals to improve the future performance of employees, it is not sufficient to just *do* them; employees must *act* on them. Usually, supervisors have responsibility for communicating the results of appraisals to their subordinates and helping their subordinates improve in the future. Conversely, subordinates usually have responsibility for seeking honest feedback and using it to improve their performance.[49]

In performance feedback sessions, *managers and their subordinates meet to exchange performance information and discuss how to improve future performance.* In many organizations, the performance information that is discussed includes the employee's own assessments of his or her performance, the assessment of teammates, and even information from customers. Regular assessment of progress toward attaining goals helps employees remain motivated and solve problems as they arise. Regular feedback also encourages periodic reexamination of goals to determine whether they should be adjusted. This is true regardless of whether the manager is giving the feedback—or getting it! In a study that tracked the performance of managers over five years, researchers found that some managers who received appraisals by subordinates improved more than others. The managers who improved the most were the ones who met with their direct reports to discuss the appraisal results and what they could do to improve.[50]

Much of the value of performance appraisals depends on their accuracy. In order for managers and their subordinates to accept the decisions that are based on performance appraisals, such as who should be promoted or how much of a bonus an employee has earned, they must believe that the results of the performance appraisal process are accurate.

Performance Appraisal Accuracy

During the past 50 years, hundreds of studies have been conducted to learn about how to improve the accuracy of managers' performance appraisals. Studies have examined the judgmental errors that managers make, problems that can be created by poorly designed appraisal forms, and even how employees use tactics such as ingratiation to influence their supervisors' evaluations of their performance.[51] A basic lesson that has been learned from all of this research is this: It is very difficult for managers to accurately assess the performance of their subordinates. Fortunately, there are several things organizations can do to help managers be more accurate when conducting performance appraisals. Providing appropriate rating scales and using multiple raters are two approaches to improving the accuracy of performance appraisals.

Rating Scale Format. A performance rating scale *is used by managers to record their judgments of employee performance.* The rating process is similar to assigning a grade. At Sun Microsystems, for example, employees are rated as "Superior," "Sun Standard," or "Underperforming."[52] Performance ratings tend to be more accurate when the rating scales are precise. At TRW, a global business with nearly 100,000 employees, rating scales provide very specific descriptions of what each level of performance means. The same rating system is used worldwide. When designing their system, a major objective at TRW was to use the rating scales to communicate the behaviors needed for the company's profitability. These behaviors include creating trust, energizing people, embracing change, building teamwork, and being customer oriented. Managers rated their subordinates' performance against these key behaviors. For each point on the scale, a paragraph explains what that rating means. For example, two of the possible ratings that might appear at the high and low ends of a rating scale are:

> **7 Far Exceeds Expectations** (highest possible rating): *Organizational contributions and excellent work are widely recognized. Performance consistently exceeds all defined expectations, producing important and impactful results through superior*

planning, execution and creativity. Employee consistently demonstrated the rated TRW behaviors and/or initiatives at higher levels than expected.

1 Needs Improvement (lowest possible rating): *Performance falls below expectations on one or more critical position competencies, objectives or tasks. While some responsibilities may be executed in a generally satisfactory manner, improvement is required for performance to become fully competent. Demonstration of the TRW Behaviors and/or Initiatives is inconsistent or at lower levels than expected.*

In another section, managers describe the subordinate's performance goals and professional development activities for the upcoming year. The subordinate's perspective is recorded too. Subordinates describe their strengths and the areas where they feel they can improve. They assess their own future potential and possible future positions.

Multiple Raters. One popular way to assess performance is to have several raters provide their input using a 360-degree appraisal. A 360-degree appraisal *measures performance by obtaining assessments of the employee from a variety of sources: supervisors, subordinates, colleagues inside the company, people outside the organization with whom the employee does business, and even a self-appraisal by the employee.* The identities of specific individual assessors aren't disclosed to the employee. Multiple raters acting as a group may be especially effective in producing accurate ratings because discussion among members of the group helps overcome the various errors and biases of individuals.[53]

Many organizations use the 360-degree appraisal method as a means of providing feedback that employees can use to improve their performance and long-term career success. YUM! Brands uses 360s to create a "customer maniac" culture. With 850,000 employees working at 33,000 Pizza Hut, Taco Bell, KFC, A&W, and Long John Silver franchises, YUM! relies on a Web-based 360-degree appraisal tool. It works in 50 different languages and is easy to use for managers all over the world. It works like this: To begin the process, an e-mail is sent to employees asking them to submit a list of people who could serve as raters. Supervisors review the list and settle on about a dozen people. Questionnaires are sent to these raters, and their ratings and comments are used to create a report. Managers and the employee then have a discussion about the results, with managers taking on the role of coach. Even the CEO uses the 360-degree process to get feedback. When he asked a broad array of people to provide feedback on his own performance, 120 people responded and the CEO received a report that was 65 pages long. Like everyone else, he'll use this information to improve his future performance.[54]

Performance Appraisals for Teams

Teams frequently take full responsibility for constructing and conducting their own performance appraisals. Team members are well acquainted with each other's strengths and weaknesses, so it makes sense for them to be the primary performance evaluators. But team performance appraisal is fraught with challenges. When team members evaluate each other, they become concerned about creating conflict and hurting people's feelings. Because they will be working closely together in the future, fear of disrupting the team may be greater than the desire to provide accurate performance assessments. Using the team appraisal also is difficult. How should they use the information to provide feedback? Should someone outside the team conduct the feedback session? Should a team leader be designated for this task? Or should everyone on the team be involved in every feedback session?

The reality is that different teams handle appraisals and feedback in different ways. At Con-Way, everyone on the team participates in providing feedback to everyone else, and feedback is provided in a group discussion format. The goal is to incorporate feedback sessions into the normal work routine. Many other organizations provide feedback in a more private setting. Often the manager to whom the team reports is responsible for collecting performance information from the team and discussing it with each team member privately.

More important than who delivers the feedback is how they deliver it. Ideally, anyone who gives feedback has been trained in how to do so effectively. At Con-Way, teams are learning this invaluable skill by involving a professional facilitator in their feedback sessions. With sufficient practice and guidance, Con-Way teams may eventually develop enough skill and self-confidence to hold feedback sessions spontaneously and unassisted.

Compensation

At most companies, the total compensation that employees receive for the work they do includes a mix of both monetary and nonmonetary compensation. Nonmonetary compensation *includes many forms of social and psychological rewards, such as recognition and respect from others and opportunities for self-development.* Nonmonetary compensation is certainly important to employees. As we describe in Chapter 14, money alone does not usually keep employees satisfied and motivated to do their best. In fact, nonmonetary compensation practices are central to employee satisfaction[55] and for creating an organization's unique culture (discussed in Chapter 18). The focus of our discussion here, however, is monetary compensation.

Monetary compensation *includes direct payments such as salary, wages, and bonuses, as well as benefits such as covering the costs of insurance plans.* Like many other aspects of an organization's approach to managing human resources, monetary compensation can facilitate (or interfere with) achieving various organizational objectives. Two objectives of particular relevance to compensation are attracting and retaining the talent required for a sustainable competitive advantage and maximizing productivity. In conjunction with an organization's recruitment and selection efforts, monetary compensation can help ensure that the rewards offered are sufficient to attract the right people at the right time for the right jobs. Pay practices also are used to help retain the best workers.[56]

Importance of Pay Fairness

Effective compensation systems appeal to employees' sense of fairness. Pay fairness *refers to what people believe they deserve to be paid in relation to what others deserve to be paid.* Unless the compensation is perceived as externally competitive, the organization will have a difficult time attracting the best applicants. And unless it is internally fair, good employees (those the organization wants to retain) are likely to leave.[57]

When evaluating whether a company's pay is fair, employees consider three basic components of the pay system: base pay, incentive pay, and benefits.

Base Pay. In most organizations, being hired means that you are guaranteed some basic level of pay, assuming you come to work and perform adequately. *The guaranteed pay offered for a job is called the* base pay. Employees who receive base pay that is on par with the market average, or even above the market, are more likely to feel fairly paid than those who are paid below the going rate. As described earlier in this chapter, Trader Joe's believes that it can beat its competitors in part by paying higher wages that attract better talent. Costco has a similar philosophy. Costco employees earn an average of about $17 per hour, compared to a national average of $11 per hour for U.S. retailers. The high pay is one reason that Costco's annual turnover rate is only 6 percent, compared to an industry average of 59 percent.[58]

According to a recent study, inadequate compensation is the top reason people give for leaving a company. Such turnover is expensive. The cost of replacing someone who leaves is equal to about 27 percent of their annual salary. Yet most employees say they would likely stay in their current job if they were offered a small raise of 10 to 15 percent.[59] Clearly, paying a little more to keep good employees makes sense.

Incentives. *When monetary compensation is linked to the level of performance exhibited by employees it is referred to as* incentive pay. Incentive pay is intended to encourage superior performance. Commissions, bonuses, and profit sharing are all forms of incentive pay. When pay is linked to strategically important behaviors and outcomes, it improves organizational productivity.[60]

Costco gives bonuses twice a year, based on length of service and hours worked. Hartford Insurance Company gives bonuses for individual performance, and it also recognizes the performance of whole divisions and the entire company. When an individual, their division, or the company achieves specific business goals, employees are rewarded with additional compensation beyond their base salary. Hartford believes this approach helps to attract the best talent, motivates them to perform well, and keeps them satisfied so they will stay with the company.[61] High performers are more motivated to stay with an organization when they are rewarded more generously than poor performers.

Bank of America is another company that believes in the power of annual bonuses. In a program they call Rewarding Success, Bank of America distributes bonuses of $500 to $3,000 to approximately 150,000 employees. An employee can receive the bonus directly as a cash payment or the company will make a direct contribution to the employee's 401(k) retirement account. The company began this new program after learning from an employee survey that people wanted to feel that they could share in the company's success.[62] Using pay to reward performance can be cost effective. Savings result from productivity improvements and from the organization's ability to match compensation costs to performance levels.

Benefits. Employee benefits *are generally defined as in-kind payments or services provided to employees for their membership in the organization.* Some benefits are required by law, so all U.S. employers offer them. These include Social Security contributions, unemployment compensation, and workers' compensation. Other benefits are offered voluntarily by employers. Typically, larger organizations voluntarily offer health care, life insurance, disability insurance, and retirement pensions or savings plans. Benefits programs also include pay for time not at work: vacations, holidays, sick days and absences, and short breaks during regular work days. Figure 13.5 on the following page illustrates the cost of benefits as a share of total labor costs for the "average" U.S. employee.[63]

Unlike direct compensation, which differs according to the job a person holds, full-time employees in an organization generally all receive the same benefits. In some organizations, including Starbucks where two-thirds of employees work part time, part-time employees also receive these same benefits. But Starbucks is unusual. It is more typical for part-time employees to receive fewer benefits. At Costco, which is generous with benefits, part-time workers receive most of the benefits offered to full-time workers. Nearly all of Costco's workers receive health insurance and most participate in a retirement plan. They don't receive store discounts, but they do receive a free Costco membership card.

Choosing which benefits to offer employees is a complex and very important strategic issue. Generous benefits such as those offered by Costco and Starbucks help attract and retain the best employees. Attracting and keeping talent is essential for firms like these that are growing and expanding year after year. But generous benefits packages are expensive: Starbucks spends about as much on health-care costs as it spends for coffee! According to Dave Pace, vice president of partner resources at Starbucks, the company is very clear about how its approach to compensation fits the

Figure 13.5 | **Average Hourly Cost of Monetary Benefits and Earnings**

Retirement and Savings ($0.67) 3.0%

Legally Required Benefits ($1.93) 8.5%

Other Benefits ($0.03) 0.1%

Insurance ($1.57) 6.9%

Supplemental Pay ($0.64) 2.8%

Paid Leave ($1.46) 6.5%

Wages and Salaries ($16.31) 72.1%

company's needs. "We're successful because we're giving to our people. We believe it's a fundamental way to run our business. We're in business and we need to deliver to our shareholders. The difficult decision is, do I spend money and risk profitability, or do I make cuts? We go with what's best for the long-term health of the organization. Without partner stability, we couldn't grow so fast."[64]

Chapter Summary

Through human resource management activities, organizations influence the behaviors of their employees in many ways. Because the behaviors of employees have so many consequences for organizations, managing human resources is critical to their success. The more effectively a firm manages its human resources, the more successful the firm is going to be. The complexity of managing human resources means that no one person can manage this task alone. Instead, managers, HR professionals, and all other employees in the organization must work together to conduct activities such as carrying out HR planning, hiring employees and providing them with training, conducting performance appraisals, and making decisions about how to compensate employees for their work.

Learning Goals

1. Explain the strategic importance of managing human resources effectively.

Human resources management (HRM) is concerned with the philosophies, policies, and practices that affect the people who work for an organization. The various HRM activities should help the organization achieve its strategic goals and achieve a sustained competitive advantage. Effective HRM has a positive impact on an organization's financial bottom line, employees, and the life of people in the local communities and the larger society.

2. Describe several important laws and government regulations that affect how organizations manage their human resources.

Many laws and regulations govern human resources management. Two major categories of laws and regulation are those that are intended to ensure equal employment opportunity and those that provide oversight of compensation and benefits. A few of the major U.S. laws that managers need to understand are Title VII of the Civil Rights Act, the Fair Labor Standards Act, and the Equal Pay Act.

3. Explain the objective of human resource planning and describe how organizations respond to the unpredictability of future business needs.

Human resource planning should ensure that the right number and type of individuals are available at the appropriate time and place to fulfill organizational needs. At the heart of planning are two tasks: determining an organization's future human resource needs and developing a strategy to meet those needs. To stay flexible, some organizations hire contingent workers who are hired and fired as needed. An alternative is to maintain a workforce of more permanent employees, but this strategy often means that layoffs become necessary when business declines.

4. Describe the hiring process.

The hiring process includes two major activities: recruitment of job applicants and selection of the best applicants. When labor is in short supply, recruitment activities become more important. Selecting the right people to hire from the pool of applicants helps improve productivity and reduce turnover. When selecting who to hire, the most common sources of information used are résumés, reference checks, interviews, and numerous types of tests. Of these, tests generally do the best job of predicting performance.

5. Describe several types of training and development programs.

Training programs help employees develop the competencies they need to perform their best in their current jobs. Orientation training and basic skills training are examples of programs that help organizations improve the performance of their workforce. Development programs help employees develop competencies that will enable them to continue to advance in their career over the longer term. They often provide employees with tools to assess their own strengths and weaknesses and develop personal plans for improvement.

6. Describe several principles for improving the accuracy of managers' appraisals of employee performance.

Performance appraisal is a formal, structured system for measuring job performance. During performance feedback sessions, managers and their subordinates meet to exchange performance information and discuss how to improve future performance. Performance appraisal and feedback are most effective when managers make accurate judgments of performance and when employees work with managers to performance appraisal information as a basis for developing plans for performance improvement.

7. Describe the basic elements of a monetary compensation package.

Monetary compensation includes wages, salaries, incentives, and bonuses as well as several types of benefits, such as health insurance. Social Security, unemployment compensation, and workers' compensation are benefits that employers must provide. Insurance and vacation pay are commonly offered benefits that are not required by law. When choosing how to pay employees, employers must consider both the strategic needs of the business and the costs associated with compensation. Effective pay practices help the organization achieve its long-term objectives.

Key Terms and Concepts

- 360-Degree appraisal system
- Base pay
- Coaching
- Cognitive ability test
- Comparable worth
- Competency inventory
- Contingent workers
- Development
- E-learning
- Employee benefits
- Employee referrals
- Employee selection
- Equal employment opportunity
- Equal Pay Act
- Fair Labor Standards Act
- Hiring process
- Human resource management
- Human resource planning
- Human resource professionals
- Incentive pay
- Job posting
- Mentoring
- Monetary compensation
- Nonmonetary compensation
- Pay fairness
- Performance appraisal
- Performance feedback sessions
- Performance rating scale
- Performance test
- Personality test
- Recruitment
- Title VII of the Civil Rights Act
- Training

Questions for Discussion and Reflective Thinking

1. How does effective human resource management address shareholders' concerns?

2. How can organizations ensure that managers understand and abide by the primary laws and regulations that govern the hiring process?

3. Which types of training and development programs are likely to be most important for (a) Starbucks and (b) Costco? If you are not familiar with these organizations, visit their Web sites at *www.starbucks.com* and *www.costco.com*.

4. Some people believe that having their peers and coworkers participate in 360-degree performance appraisal is a bad idea, especially if pay and promotion decisions might be affected. They worry about office politics and the effects on friendships, among other things. Do you think managers or other employees are likely to intentionally give inaccurate 360-degree performance ratings? If you think this happens, explain why. To learn more about this topic, you may want to visit *www.humanresources .about.com* and search for articles using the key phrase "360 feedback."

5. Do you think the federal minimum wage level should be raised? Why or why not? What about the minimum wage in your state? For most states, you can learn about the minimum wage by visiting the Web site for the state's labor office. A complete list of these offices is provided by the federal Department of Labor at *www.dol.gov/esa/contacts*.

6. Describe the ideal compensation package that you would like to receive. Which elements of the package are most important to you? Why?

7. Assume that you are a senior partner in KPMG, a consulting firm. You are writing a proposal for an assignment in Indonesia. As part of the proposal, you describe the members of the team who will work with your client, who you know has very "traditional" views about men and women. The person with the most expertise on the client's problem is a woman, so you list her as one of the team members. Your potential client states that a woman team member is unacceptable. Describe what you would do and why. Consider the ethical, legal, and business consequences of keeping her on the team versus removing her from consideration.

8. Suppose a company decided to accept job applications online *only*. What are the advantages and disadvantages of such a policy for the company? What are the advantages and disadvantages of such a policy for job applicants?

DEVELOPING YOUR COMPETENCIES

Experiential Exercise | Interviewing Job Applicants

The following 10 questions might be asked during an employment interview. Some of them are illegal and should never be asked. Employers who ask illegal questions may be subject to legal prosecution for employment discrimination. Place a check mark in the appropriate column to indicate whether the question is legal or illegal. Before taking this quiz, visit the home page of the Equal Employment Opportunity Commission (EEOC) at *www.eeoc.gov*.

	Legal	Illegal
1. How old are you?	_____	_____
2. Have you ever been arrested	_____	_____
3. Do any of your relatives work for this organization?	_____	_____
4. Do you have children, and if you do, what kind of child-care arrangements do you have?	_____	_____

	Legal	Illegal
5. Do you have any handicaps?	_____	_____
6. Are you married?	_____	_____
7. Where were you born?	_____	_____
8. What organizations do you belong to?	_____	_____
9. Do you get along well with other men [or women]?	_____	_____
10. What languages can you speak and/or write fluently?	_____	_____

Note: Answers on the following page.

The State Bank is located in a Midwestern town of about 50,000 people. It is one of four banks in the area and has the reputation of being the most progressive. Russell Duncan has been the president of the bank for 15 years. Before coming to State Bank, Duncan worked for a large Detroit bank for 10 years. Duncan has implemented a number of changes that have earned him a great deal of respect and admiration from both bank employees and townspeople alike. For example, in response to a growing number of Spanish-speaking people in the area, he hired Latinos to work as loan officers and tellers. He organized and staffed the city's only agricultural loan center to meet the needs of the area's farmers. In addition, he established the state's first "uniline" system for handling customers waiting in line for a teller.

Perhaps more than anything else, Duncan is known for establishing progressive personnel practices. He strongly believes that the bank's employees are its most important asset and continually searches for ways to increase both employee satisfaction and productivity. He feels that all employees should strive to continually improve their skills and abilities; hence, he cross-trains employees and sends many of them to courses and conferences sponsored by banking groups such as the American Institute of Banking.

With regard to employee compensation, Duncan firmly believes that employees should be paid according to their contribution to organizational success. Ten years ago, he implemented a performance-based pay system under which employees could earn raises from 0 to 12 percent each year, depending on their job performance. Raises are typically determined by the bank's HR Committee during February and are granted to employees on March 1 of each year. In addition to granting employees merit raises, six years ago the bank also began giving cost-of-living raises. Duncan had been opposed to this idea originally but saw no alternative to it. A cost-of-living raise is set to equal the local rate of inflation, which is about 3 percent. So, with this system, in recent years the best performers would have received raises of up to 15 percent.

This year, another bank in town conducted a wage survey to determine the average compensation of bank employees in the city. The management of the State Bank received a copy of the results and was surprised to learn that its 23 tellers, as a group, were being paid an average of $35 per week more than were tellers at other banks. The survey also showed that employees holding other positions in the bank (e.g., branch managers, loan officers, and file clerks) were being paid wages similar to those paid by other banks. Only the tellers made more.

After receiving the report, the HR Committee of the bank met to determine what should be done regarding the tellers' raises. They knew that none of the tellers had been told how much their raises would be but that they were all expecting raises. They also realized that, if other employees learned that the tellers were being overpaid, friction could develop and morale might suffer. They knew that it was costing the bank more than $40,000 extra to pay the tellers more than competitors were paying. Finally, they knew that as a group the bank's tellers were highly competent, and they did not want to lose any of them.

Questions

1. Should State Bank give the tellers raises using criteria similar to that used in past years? Why or why not?

2. If State Bank wants to reduce its compensation costs for tellers, what are their options? Is there any way to reduce these costs and still give their "normal" pay raises?

3. Suppose you were one of the bank's top-performing tellers. You learn that the bank will be giving smaller raises this year because it believes tellers are overpaid. How would you respond?

Answers (previous page)

The following evaluations provide clarification rather than strict legal interpretation because employment laws and regulations are constantly changing.

1. How old are you?
   This question is legal but inadvisable. An applicant's date of birth or age can be asked, but telling the applicant that federal and state laws prohibit age discrimination is essential. Avoid focusing on age, unless an occupation requires extraordinary physical ability or training and a valid age-related rule is in effect.

2. Have you ever been arrested?
   This question is illegal unless an inquiry about arrests is justified by the specific nature of the organization—for instance, law enforcement or handling controlled substances. Questions about arrests generally are considered to be suspect because they may tend to disqualify some groups. Convictions should be the basis for rejection of an applicant only if their number, nature, or recent occurrence renders the applicant unsuitable. In that case the question(s) should be specific. For example: Have you ever been convicted for theft? Have you been convicted within the past year on drug-related charges?

3. Do any of your relatives work for this organization?
   This question is legal if the intent is to discover nepotism.

4. Do you have children, and if you do, what kind of child-care arrangements do you have?
   Both parts of this question are currently illegal; they should not be asked in any form because the answers would not be job related. In addition, they might imply gender discrimination.

5. Do you have any handicaps?
   This question is illegal as phrased here. An applicant doesn't have to divulge handicaps or health conditions that don't relate reasonably to fitness to perform the job.

6. Are you married?
   This question is legal, but may be discriminatory. Marriage has nothing directly to do with job performance.

7. Where were you born?
   This question is legal, but it might indicate discrimination on the basis of national origin.

8. What organizations do you belong to?
   As stated, this question is legal; it is permissible to ask about organizational membership in a general sense. It is illegal to ask about membership in a specific organization when the name of that organization would indicate the race, color, creed, gender, marital status, religion, or national origin or ancestry of its members.

9. Do you get along well with other men [or women]?
   This question is illegal; it seems to perpetuate sexism.

10. What languages can you speak and/or write fluently?
    Although this question is legal, it might be perceived as a roundabout way of determining an individual's national origin. Asking how a particular language was learned isn't permissible.

PART 5
Leading

© Dave & Les Jacobs/Blend Images/Jupiter Images

chapter 14

Motivating Employees

Learning Goals

After studying this chapter, you should be able to:

1. Describe four approaches that can be used to explain employee motivation and satisfaction.

2. Explain how managers can use goals and rewards to improve performance.

3. Describe how jobs can be designed to be motivating and satisfying.

4. State how the organization context affects motivation and satisfaction.

5. Describe how the needs of individuals can affect their work.

6. Describe how understanding motivation can help managers improve employee performance and satisfaction.

Communication Competency

Planning and Administration Competency

Teamwork Competency

Managing Effectively

Self-Management Competency

Strategic Action Competency

Multicultural Competency

Challenge of Managing ....

Johnson Space Center

©/NASA

Tom Holloway began working for Johnson Space Center as an aerospace technician in 1963. He worked on the *Apollo* and space shuttle programs and eventually became manager of the International Space Station. He was excited and engaged in his work most of the 39 years he worked at the center before eventually retiring. He summed up his views like this: "I can truthfully say, I've always thought I had the best job in town." Reflecting on his experiences as an astronaut, Neil Armstrong, known for his historic moon walk, recalled Johnson Space Center as a place where "everybody involved was, one, interested, two, dedicated, and three fascinated by the job they were doing."

Located in Houston, Texas, Johnson Space Center is the home of NASA's mission control for its space exploration program. Being involved in the space program is something many people dream about, but only a few lucky people get these jobs. NASA doesn't expect its 3,000 employees to stay motivated year after year just because they have great jobs, however. It helps that employees feel they are all part of a big extended family, but even that is not enough to keep people energized all of the time. After all, the realities of working in a government bureaucracy can be frustrating at times. When a mission goes wrong, everyone suffers.

To sustain the initial enthusiasm the employees bring to their jobs, space center managers work hard to support a culture built around the values of safety, teamwork, mission success, and integrity. Central to this culture is their rewards program, which is designed to recognize the achievements of employees working as members of space crews, maintenance crews, public relations, and so on. According to Natalie Suiz, director of human resources at the center, the goal is to use awards to recognize *all* types of work.

As a federal agency, regulations prohibit the center from giving employees gifts or merchandise, but monetary awards are okay. For routine activities, GEM awards are given on the spot by managers who observe someone "Going the Extra Mile." Many other awards are given out with greater ceremony, with family and friends invited to share the spotlight. These events focus attention on the recipients and give everyone a chance to applaud their peers. The many types of awards employees receive at these ceremonies include the Distinguished Service Medal, length-of-service awards, technical achievement awards, and group achievement awards. When Hurricane Rita threatened the Center, they were forced to evacuate and close everything down. All operations were temporarily transferred to the center's partners near Moscow. The large team of people who worked on making that transition, and then later returning operations back to Houston, were recognized at a ceremony for a group award as well as several individual awards. Awards like these are greatly appreciated by employees—in fact, they are one reason that the Johnson Space Center is considered one of the "Best Places to Work in the Federal Government." Reflecting on his years at the center, Tom Holloway observed, "Over the years, I've become more and more convinced that the best organization is one where the entire team and all of the people are fully appreciated."[1]

To learn more about this organization, visit *www.spacecenter.org.*

Understanding Motivation and Satisfaction

l.

Describe four approaches that can be used to explain employee motivation and satisfaction.

Motivation *is a psychological state that exists whenever internal and/or external forces stimulate, direct, or maintain behaviors.* In organizations, the employee behaviors of interest include both productive and unproductive behaviors. Productive behaviors include staying focused on the most important aspects of your job as well as being a good corporate citizen. Unproductive behaviors include simply goofing around instead of working, as well as being antisocial, hostile, or even violent toward coworkers. By understanding employee motivation, managers can increase productive behaviors, such as arriving on time and putting in extra effort, and decrease disruptive behaviors, such as tardiness, theft, and loafing.[2]

Satisfaction *is a psychological state that indicates how people feel about their situation, based on their evaluation of the situation.* Many managers assume that employee motivation goes hand in hand with employee satisfaction. As the saying goes, "a happy worker is a productive worker." As this chapter explains, the relationship between employee motivation and employee satisfaction is a bit more complicated than that. Satisfied employees do perform their jobs somewhat better that dissatisfied employees.[3] But understanding satisfaction also is important for other reasons. For example, a dissatisfied employee may perform at an acceptable level while searching for another job at the same time.

Understanding employee motivation and satisfaction has long been of interest to managers and researchers alike because it is so important to managing effectively. It also has been a topic of much debate, because there are no easy answers. We have grouped the many different theories of employee motivation and satisfaction into four general approaches: the managerial approach, the job design approach, the organization approach, and the individual differences approach.

As illustrated in Figure 14.1, all four approaches help explain employee motivation and satisfaction. Figure 14.1 also suggests why managers care about employee motivation and satisfaction; namely, because motivation and satisfaction lead to other important consequences.[4] Creating an organization filled with satisfied and motivated employees is not an end in and of itself. It is a means for achieving business success. Highly motivated employees outperform those who are less motivated. Research also shows that employee satisfaction results in higher customer satisfaction, lower employee turnover, improved safety, and greater profitability.[5]

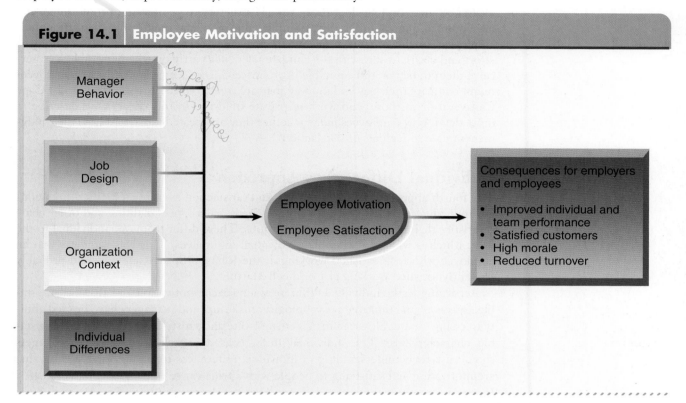

| Figure 14.1 | Employee Motivation and Satisfaction |

- Manager Behavior
- Job Design
- Organization Context
- Individual Differences

→ Employee Motivation / Employee Satisfaction →

Consequences for employers and employees

- Improved individual and team performance
- Satisfied customers
- High morale
- Reduced turnover

Managerial Approach

The managerial approach to understanding motivation focuses on how the behaviors of managers influence the satisfaction and motivation of their employees. Managers can directly motivate and satisfy employees through personal communication, by setting realistic goals, and by offering recognition, praise, and monetary rewards to employees who achieve those goals. According to this approach, the dedication of employees at the Johnson Space Center can be at least partly explained by the fact that managers make an effort to recognize employees who do outstanding work.

Job Design Approach

A second approach to motivating employees empha- sizes the design of jobs. Managers can sometimes design the jobs of the people they supervise, but not always. Often the design of jobs is determined by fac- tors that cannot be easily changed without changing the technology or the structure of an entire work unit. As described in Chapter 12, enriched jobs are more motivating than jobs that are narrow in scope. Later in this chapter, we describe in greater detail how sev- eral aspects of job design determine whether employees experience their jobs as motivating and satisfying.

© Walter Lockwood Photography/Workbook Stock/Jupiter Images

Effective managers understand what motivates employees and strive to keep them satisfied.

Organization Approach

The broader organizational context also is important. As described in Chapter 13, human resource management policies and practices are generally an important aspect of the organizational context. The appropriate benefits (e.g., paid vacations, sick leave, insurance, and child or elder care), reward structure (e.g., bonuses, promotions), and development opportunities (e.g., training, education, and mentoring) may attract new employees to the organization. Whether such policies serve to increase employee effort and desire to stay with the company depends partly on whether employees perceive them to be fair and equitable. At Johnson Space Center, for example, employees might compare their pay and the way they are treated to employees who work at Cape Canaveral or to those who work in private industry. In this chapter, we describe in more detail how employees judge whether they are treated fairly, and how their judgments relate to feelings of satisfaction.

Individual Differences Approach

The fourth approach treats motivation and satisfaction as characteristics of individuals. Individual differences are the unique needs, values, personalities, and other characteristics that employees bring to their jobs. These differ from one individual to the next, which is why they are called individual differences. This view suggests that an employee who feels satisfied working at the Johnson Space Center would probably feel fairly satisfied working at Lockheed Martin.

According to the individual differences approach, motivation and attitudes are stable aspects of an employee's psychological make-up, and managers have limited ability to change them. How can managers motivate and satisfy employees if these are stable characteristics? The individual differences approach suggests that managers should use their understanding of individual differences to create organizations that are motivating and satisfying to people with a wide range of personal characteristics. Instead of treating everyone alike, managers should attempt to find employees whose values and preferences fit the job and organizational conditions.[6]

2.

Explain how managers can use goals and rewards to improve performance.

Managerial Approach

Managers who are in direct contact with employees may be the most important influences on the motivation and satisfaction of employees. When the Gallup Organization interviewed 80,000 people about their work, they found that employees tolerate a lot of negative aspects of their work (low pay, ugly offices) if they work for a good manager. And if they have a bad manager, they are likely to look for another job.[7] Good managers understand the unique characteristics of each employee and are responsive to these. But they also understand that there are a few basic principles they can follow to ensure that all employees are motivated to perform their jobs well. Good managers don't just make employees feel comfortable—they help them be productive. Three practical things managers can do to enhance the motivation of their employees are to (1) inspire employees through one-on-one communication, (2) be sure that employees have specific and challenging goals that they accept and will strive to achieve, and (3) provide employees with praise, recognition, or other rewards so they feel good about achieving those goals.

Communication Comes First

As we have seen throughout this book, effective communication is central to many aspects of managerial work. This is definitely the case when it comes to motivating employees. As a space shuttle commander, Colonel Eileen Collins understands that effective communication is essential to ensuring that everyone involved in a shuttle mission is motivated to do whatever it takes to ensure safe and successful flights. As a commander, her communication style is what everyone calls "nice." By that they mean that she never seems to make negative comments about anyone. She feels a big part of her job is to "listen, listen, listen"—and then decide, communicate the decision, and get everyone to work together to get the job done.

Setting Goals

Besides instilling a sense of purpose, managers can further motivate employees through the use of goal setting. Put simply, goal-setting theory *states that managers can direct the performance of their employees by assigning specific, difficult goals that employees accept and are willing to commit to.* Done correctly, goal setting has been shown to be effective for increasing the performance of people working in a wide range of jobs. Today, many of the basic principles from this theory are accepted as standard management practice.[8] As described in Chapter 9, setting goals is central to the business planning process.

Successful managers are also successful communicators and are people with whom employees feel comfortable.

UMB Financial, a Midwestern bank, provides just one example of a company that uses goals to align the behavior of employees with business plans. Goal-setting principles are at the heart of the electronic management scorecards that the company uses to track performance and motivate the workforce. Business-unit goals are set for managers each quarter, and managers in turn are expected to motivate employees to meet those goals. When the employees are successful in meeting the goals—for example, for product sales, number of customer calls made, and service quality—they are rewarded with higher pay.[9]

At NCCI, a nonprofit consortium that provides workplace injury data to its customers, the use of goal-setting principles is credited with the company's success in turning around its performance, which had begun to deteriorate after 75 years in business. Members of NCCI include insurance companies, insurance brokers, and state officials in 40 states. When customers began to express concerns about the service they were receiving, and when annual employee turnover reached 26 percent, NCCI developed a new approach to motivating employees. NCCI's goal-setting system is designed to align the efforts of employees with the organization's business objectives. The board and senior management set the corporate objectives. Then each department identifies what it can do to contribute to meeting those objectives, and finds ways to measure those contributions. Each individual's goals are then linked directly to the department's goals. Employees meet with their managers twice a year to develop goals to achieve during the next 12 months. At the first meeting, goals specific to the job are set. A billing analyst might have a goal of completing 100 percent of invoices on time. A marketing manager might have a goal of completing a project by a specific date and within a certain budget. Six months later at a second meeting, focus is on the employee's extra contributions to the organization. If a corporate goal is to streamline performance to improve the bottom line, a billing analyst's extra contribution might be to seek efficiencies in the billing process to improve cycle time.[10]

Figure 14.2 on the next page illustrates how goal setting works. It shows that effective goals are specific, difficult, and accepted by employees. The exhibit also illustrates the four ways through which goals can result in better performance.

Figure 14.2 | **How Goal Setting Works**

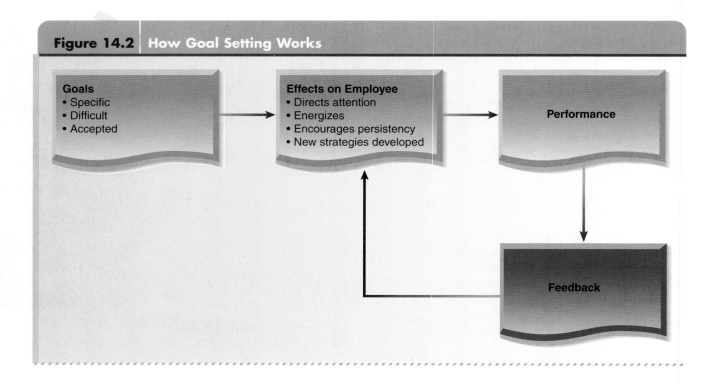

How to Set Effective Goals. Numerous studies have documented that performance is improved when managers set goals that are specific and difficult. In addition, employees must accept the goals as reasonable—so they shouldn't be so difficult that they are considered impossible to achieve.

In one of the most famous studies, goals were used to improve the efficiency of truck drivers hauling logs to Weyerhaeuser lumber mills. Before goals were introduced, loggers were carrying loads that were well below their trucks' legal weight capacities. Goals were introduced to encourage the loggers to transport fuller loads. At first, drivers were given a vague, easy goal that was stated as "do your best." This goal had almost no effect on the size of loads the drivers hauled. Three months later, drivers were given the *specific* goal of carrying loads that were 94 percent of their trucks' capacities. Within a month, the average load had increased from less than 60 percent to more than 80 percent of capacity. Six months later, truckers were carrying loads that averaged over 90 percent of capacity. Specific goals also make it easier for employees to gauge how well they're doing. If a goal is specific, employees can quickly judge whether their efforts are paying off in terms of performance. Employees can then use this feedback to decide whether to continue using the same methods or try new approaches.[11]

Besides being specific, goals should be *difficult.* If goals are too easy, they don't give the employee any reason to exert extra effort. Difficult goals must also be *accepted* by employees, however, so they should not be too difficult. If employees reject their goals as impossible, they won't even bother trying to achieve them.[12] When judging whether a goal is too difficult, managers and employees have no easy rules to follow. One way that managers try to be sure goals are accepted by employees is to involve the employees in the goal-setting process.

If they accept the difficult goals and believe they are *attainable,* employees will put in more effort and usually perform better. They may also feel a bit more fatigued by their jobs, but employees who enjoy achieving outstanding results will feel satisfied as a consequence of having performed well.[13]

Pitfalls. Goal setting can be a powerful motivational technique, but it is not a panacea. Table 14.1 shows some of the potential problems associated with goal setting, as well as some solutions to these problems.[14]

Table 14.1	Goal-Setting Pitfalls and Solutions

PITFALLS	SOLUTIONS
■ Focusing on performance may reduce learning.	■ Include goals that recognize the importance of learning as well as maximizing performance.
■ Employees may feel stressed.	■ Be sure employees have the training and resources they need to achieve their goals.
■ Individual goals can create conflict among members of a team.	■ Establish group goals and a shared vision. ■ Put proper controls in place.
■ People may be tempted to cheat, especially if they are close to achieving their goals but expect to ultimately fail.	■ Establish a culture that values ethical behavior.
■ Focusing on goals may mean some other aspects of performance are ignored.	■ Set goals for all important aspects of performance.

Some of the pitfalls of goal setting can be avoided by careful use of management by objectives *(MBO), which is a participative goal-setting technique.* Generally, the MBO process begins with a conversation between manager and employee. During this conversation, past performance is reviewed and objectives (goals) for the future are identified. The manager and employee agree to a set of goals that both parties accept as appropriate, with the understanding that future performance evaluations and rewards will reflect the employee's progress toward the agreed-on goals. NCCI is one example of an organization that uses MBO.

When employees are very competent and empowered, they may set their own goals. Because people generally feel committed to achieving goals they set themselves, this approach ensures goal acceptance. Universal Technical Institute (UTI), based in Phoenix, Arizona, believes in letting employees set their own goals. UTI provides technical training for people who work as automotive repair technicians. Thus, a BMW dealer might send repair technicians to UTI courses to learn how to service the cars' air conditioning and heating system. When UTI decided to change its strategy, top executives didn't sit down and draw up a list of goals for its 1,100 employees. Instead, they set the objective of finding new ways to generate revenue and then involved all employees in creating a new strategic plan and developing accountability measures. When employees feel that they are capable of high performance, their self-set goals may actually be higher than those that a manager would assign. UTI's highly participative approach to goal setting helped increase profits by 44 percent while also improving employee morale.[15]

How Goals Work. First, goals help *direct* the attention of employees toward the most important work activities and away from irrelevant tasks. This is why effective managers invest so much time in communicating company goals. Second, goals *energize* employees to exert more effort. When employees accept a goal as something to strive for and then commit to achieving that goal, they essentially agree to exert the amount of effort required to do so. Assuming employees have the competencies needed to achieve the goals, then exerting greater effort usually leads to better performance.

Third, goals encourage employees to *persist* in their work efforts. For example, the desire to achieve a specific goal may encourage an employee to work extra hours instead of just putting in the minimum time required. Fourth, when employees are striving to achieve specific goals, they are more likely to *think about alternative strategies* to achieve that goal. If one approach doesn't work, they will try another approach in order to achieve their goal.[16]

Feedback. Goal setting works best when employees receive timely feedback about the progress they are making toward achieving their goals. As we explained in Chapter 13, performance feedback helps employees improve their performance. Even very simple forms of feedback (e.g., how well employees are doing compared to their goals) can be effective. Unsolicited feedback that is not job related or directed at employee's performance is likely to be ignored, however.[17] When managers provide feedback that employees see as valuable, they take the initiative to actively see it out.[18]

When employees can see that they aren't performing well enough to reach their goals, they're likely to consider why and then change their methods or behaviors. One way is simply to try harder. If putting out more effort doesn't help, another way is to approach tasks differently.[19] Feedback is a signal that tells employees that they are doing well and should continue with their current approaches or that they aren't doing very well and should try new approaches.[20]

Team Goal Setting. Just as goals can improve the performance of individual employees, team goals can improve group performance. Like individual goals, team goals work best if they are difficult, yet doable. To keep a team focused, it is best not to set too many team goals—usually no more than three to five. Also important in setting team goals is being sure that employees understand why it's important for them to achieve the goals.

The copper mining company of Phelps Dodge uses team goals throughout its six locations in North America. For truck maintenance workers, for example, a team goal is to shorten the time that trucks are off-line for maintenance. The goal is set participatively, using input from the maintenance crews and their supervisors. Miners at each location also have team goals designed to improve productivity. For achieving their team goals, employees receive extra compensation above their typical salary.[21]

Performance versus Learning Goals

In most organizations, the goals employees work toward focus their attention on performance. That is, they work toward goals related to production, sales, service, and so on. For many people work is increasingly knowledge based. Thus, learning at work is becoming as important as doing. Does setting goals for learning increase employees' ability to learn? The answer is yes. When the goal is to improve learning, employees should be encouraged to focus on developing their knowledge and focus less on the end result. The focus of a learning goal is to increase one's knowledge and ability; the focus of a performance goal is to increase one's motivation to implement that knowledge. Therefore, both learning and performance goals are needed for employees to be successful.[22]

Offering Incentives and Rewards

In some situations, managers can use goal setting to improve performance even if they don't offer any significant rewards to employees for achieving the goals. The idea of simply beating the goal may be all the motivation that some employees need. In most work situations, however, goals become more powerful when achieving them results in some type of tangible reward. Rewards for goal achievement increase motivation and performance because they strengthen the level of commitment that employees feel. Another explanation for the effectiveness of rewards is provided by reinforcement theory.

Reinforcement theory *states that behavior is a function of its consequences.* Positive consequences are referred to as rewards, and negative consequences are referred to as punishments. Psychologist B. F. Skinner developed and extended much of this approach to understanding what motivates behavior.[23] Skinner gained much public attention—and generated considerable controversy—when he revealed that he raised his children strictly by reinforcement principles.

Behaviors, Not Outcomes.
Whereas goal setting focuses directly on improving performance outcomes, reinforcement focuses on changing behaviors. For this reason, *when the principles of reinforcement theory are used, it is sometimes referred to as* behavior modification. A manager who follows the principles of reinforcement will almost certainly be able to modify employee behaviors to some extent. Whether those changes in behavior result in better performance, however, depends on whether the manager actually knows which behaviors result in better performance.[24]

The basic principles of reinforcement are simple. They state that behavior followed by pleasant consequences is more likely to be repeated and that behavior followed by unpleasant consequences is less likely to be repeated. For instance, suppose that your job involves helping modify the company's Web site. You come to a staff meeting with a proposal for letting customers search the Web site using everyday language instead of the high-tech jargon used by the company's employees. If your manager praises your initiative and creativity, your behavior is rewarded. You probably will be motivated to come up with other innovations. However, if your manager gives you a disapproving look and says that the firm is perfectly happy with existing methods, you probably would feel put down or embarrassed in front of your colleagues. In effect, your behavior has been punished, indicating that you should modify that behavior in the future.

Figure 14.3 shows the process by which pleasant and unpleasant consequences influence behavior. A manager who wants to change an employee's behavior must change the specific consequences of that behavior.

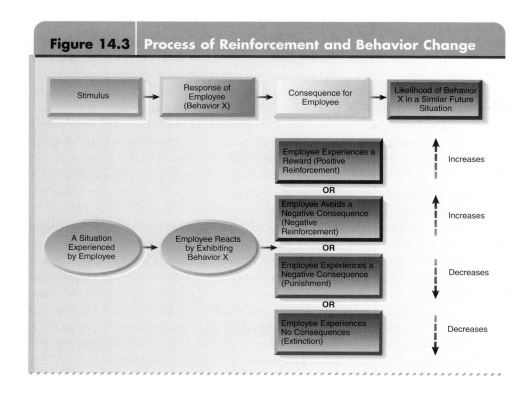

Figure 14.3 Process of Reinforcement and Behavior Change

Reinforcement principles don't require that managers actually tell employees what they should strive to accomplish. The theory assumes that employees will learn what is expected of them simply by experiencing the consequences of their behaviors. Employees also learn by observing what happens to others in the organization. Fortunately, not everyone has to be punished before most learn that some behaviors are best avoided. According to reinforcement theory, the behaviors of employees (e.g., helping each other out) occur because employees are being reinforced for them. If undesirable behaviors occur (e.g., harassment), it's because there are positive consequences for employees who engage in the undesirable behaviors. If desirable behaviors are absent (e.g., reporting harassment behavior), it is because those behaviors lead to no positive consequences for employees.

While it may be true that employees can learn what is expected simply by experiencing various outcomes and observing what happens to others, good managers recognize that it is important to communicate their expectations as clearly as possible. This is a simple matter of fairness. Employees should be told what they can do to receive reinforcement. If there are some behaviors that will be punished, employees should be told what those behaviors are and why they will be punished.

Behaviors that managers can most easily change by using reinforcement principles are those that can be easily measured.[25] Measurable behavior is action that can be observed and counted. Examples include smiling when a customer approaches, using a seat belt when driving a delivery truck, and wiping up spills when they occur on the shop floor. As Figure 14.3 suggests, a manager may increase the frequency of any of these behaviors by using positive reinforcement or negative reinforcement. To decrease any of these behaviors, a manager may use punishment or extinction. The concepts of reinforcement and punishment are easily understood because most individuals can readily recall at least one instance of a behavior being reinforced or punished. The concepts of negative reinforcement and extinction are sometimes more difficult to grasp, however.

Positive Reinforcement.
Positive reinforcement *increases the likelihood that a behavior will be repeated by creating a pleasant consequence.* Any reward that encourages an individual to repeat a behavior can be classified as a positive reinforcer. Some common positive reinforcers used by organizations are praise, recognition of accomplishment, and salary increases. John Farrell, a senior director at Carlson Marketing Group, thinks that recognition is like oxygen to employees; without recognition, they can't survive.

Recognition and award programs such as those in place at the Johnson Space Center are one common means to provide more positive consequences to employees who do a good job. GEM is a way for managers to acknowledge employees' efforts with small gifts and awards, without worrying about the many administrative and legal issues associated with awarding bonuses or salary increases. When a garment factory decided it needed to improve employee attendance, it created a recognition program to provide several positive consequences to employees who came to work every day. For attending every day of the month, an employee's name was posted with a gold star for others to see. If perfect attendance continued for the entire quarter, the employee received a letter of recognition. At the end of the year, employees with perfect attendance were recognized at a plant-wide meeting where they were presented with a small gift (a silver necklace or penknife). Because the company wanted to see if this program was effective, they introduced it into only one of their plant locations. When they compared this plant to other locations, they found that absenteeism decreased 52 percent in six months. This compared to almost no change at the other locations.[26] Compared to the cost of absenteeism, which is estimated to cost about $1,000 per employee per year, on average, the cost of recognition programs is worth the investment.[27]

Snapshot

"The problem with reward and recognition as it's typically done is that it tends to violate everything that we know about positive reinforcement from a scientific perspective. . . . Much of [what managers do] is based on their own personal experiences rather than any systematic ways of approaching them to sort out fact from fiction."

Aubrey Daniels, Founder, Aubrey Daniels International

Punishment. Punishment *involves creating a negative consequence to discourage a behavior whenever it occurs.* For example, disciplinary actions may be taken against an employee who comes to work late, fails to clean up the work area, or turns out too many defective parts. The disciplinary action might take the form of a verbal reprimand, a monetary fine, a demotion, or, if the employee persists, a suspension—all with the intention of discouraging the behavior.

Weyco, a health-care company in Michigan, uses punishment to discourage smoking among employees: Employees caught smoking are fired! The CEO says he turned to punishment because the company's other approaches to eliminating smoking (e.g., paying for health club memberships) weren't 100 percent effective. Sprint also uses punishment to deter smokers. At Sprint, smokers are charged higher premiums for their health-care insurance.[28]

Punishment is sometimes a useful way of eliminating unwanted behaviors, but it must be done carefully. Managers should avoid punishment that humiliates or embarrasses employees. Doing so will reduce the likelihood of the employee feeling resentment and possibly retaliating against the company.

Extinction. Extinction *is the absence of any consequence—either positive reinforcement or punishment—following the occurrence of a behavior.* Usually, extinction occurs when the positive reinforcement that once normally resulted from the behavior is removed. Because the behavior no longer produces reinforcement, the employee stops engaging in it.

When extinction results in the decline of a disruptive behavior, the organization usually benefits. But extinction of beneficial behaviors occurs just as often, as illustrated in the following example. Jan Smith, a 7-11 store manager who seeks to reduce tardiness, puts in place a plan to reward employees for coming to work and not taking days off. Smith begins to offer a small monetary bonus for perfect attendance. Absenteeism goes down, as planned. Then Smith feels pressured to reduce costs and decides to eliminate the bonus program. Soon absenteeism is higher than ever. What happened? Unfortunately, Smith has gotten everyone to overcome any barriers they encountered in getting to work on time in order to receive their bonuses. Removing the bonus they received for doing so caused extinction of the behavior.

Negative Reinforcement. Notice that punishment, positive reinforcement, and extinction can be used only after a behavior has actually occurred. Employees experience negative reinforcement *when they engage in a behavior in anticipation of avoiding unpleasant consequences in the future.* Most students come to class on time to avoid a possible reprimand from the instructor. Similarly, most employees follow coffee break and lunch hour guidelines to avoid the disapproval of managers or coworkers. In both cases, these individuals are acting to avoid unpleasant results; when they are successful they are negatively reinforced. Whereas punishment causes a behavior to occur less frequently, negative reinforcement causes the behavior to be repeated.

Self-Management. Just as managers can use the principles of goal setting and reinforcement to change the behavior and performance of employees, so too can employees. With a bit of training, employees can learn to set their own goals, provide their own reinforcements, and even monitor their results over time. Taking an active self-management approach to job performance and career progress is one way to improve long-term outcomes, such as quicker promotions and higher salary levels.[29] People who have confidence in their own ability to achieve their self-set goals can improve their performance in a variety of domains. Besides improving their work performance, they can improve their performance at school, they can perform better in athletic competitions, and they can even improve their own health outcomes.[30]

Using Goals and Reward Expectations to Motivate Employees

Experienced managers understand that keeping employees motivated and satisfied requires them to use a combination of goal setting and offering incentives and rewards. This combined approach to motivation and satisfaction is evident in expectancy theory.

Expectancy theory *states that people tend to choose behaviors that they believe will help them achieve their personal goals (e.g., a promotion or job security) and avoid behaviors that they believe will lead to undesirable personal consequences (e.g., a demotion or criticism).* Examples of choices that are related to work performance include whether to go to work or call in sick, whether to leave work at the official quitting time or stay late, and whether to exert a great deal of effort or to work at a more relaxed pace. Notice that these same behaviors might be explained by reinforcement principles. The two theories are somewhat similar, but there is one subtle difference to keep in mind. Reinforcement theory emphasizes changing behaviors *after* they occur, whereas expectancy theory emphasizes the initial decision to engage in a behavior.

As you can see, expectancy theory also includes some elements of goal-setting theory. But again, there are some subtle differences. One difference is that goal-setting theory emphasizes the importance of work-related goals, whereas expectancy theory emphasizes the personal goals of employees. Another difference is that goal-setting theory assumes that goals alone are motivating—they can influence performance even if there are no rewards or punishments tied to goal achievement.

Figure 14.4 illustrates how expectancy theory can be used to understand an employee's decision to exert more effort at work. When making such a decision, an employee would normally consider three questions:

1. *The expectancy question:* If I make an effort, will I be able to perform the behavior?

2. *The instrumentality question:* If I perform the behavior, what will be the consequences?

3. *The valence question:* How much do I value the consequences associated with the behavior?

Expectancy. Expectancy *refers to a person's estimate of how likely a certain level of effort will lead to the intended behavior or performance result.* Effort is the amount of physical and/or mental energy exerted to perform a task or to learn something new. At Saks Fifth Avenue department stores, a salesperson's attempt to find a petite-sized pair of slacks for a short customer is an example of effort. Effort refers solely to the energy expended—not how successful it is. At Saks, performance could involve making more sales, creating a satisfied customer, and/or helping another salesperson do his or her job more effectively.

Employees who believe that exerting more effort results in better performance experience expectancy. When feelings of expectancy are strong, employees generally perform better, compared to employees who don't believe that their efforts will pay off.[31] When employees feel their effort is not likely to result in better performance, they don't even bother to put in the effort. For example, after Saks decided to shift its focus to younger, fashion-conscious customers, it decided to stop carrying the petite sizes that shorter women often look for so salespeople quickly stopped putting in the effort needed to satisfy those customers; they knew their efforts just wouldn't pay off.

Instrumentality. To be willing to expend the effort needed to achieve the desired performance, employees must also believe that the performance will have some type

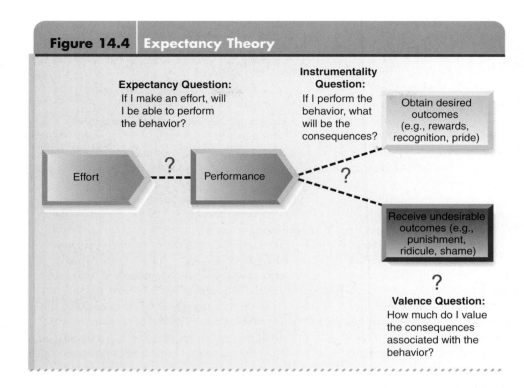

Figure 14.4 | Expectancy Theory

Expectancy Question:
If I make an effort, will I be able to perform the behavior?

Instrumentality Question:
If I perform the behavior, what will be the consequences?

Effort —— **?** ——▶ Performance

Obtain desired outcomes (e.g., rewards, recognition, pride)

Receive undesirable outcomes (e.g., punishment, ridicule, shame)

?

Valence Question:
How much do I value the consequences associated with the behavior?

of payoff. Instrumentality *refers to a person's perception of how useful the intended behavior or performance is for obtaining desired outcomes (or avoiding undesired outcomes)*. If Jackie develops an innovative product design at Texas Instruments, will she receive public recognition for this accomplishment? If Juan arrives at work on time at UPS, rather than being a few minutes late, will anyone else really care? If Max's employee's performance rating is outstanding at Texaco, will he be paid more? According to a survey of U.S. workers, only about 35 percent of employees see a clear link between their job performance and important outcomes such as their pay.[32] Among that 35 percent, many are likely to be managers, because managers appear to see their extra work effort as leading to higher compensation.[33]

Incentive pay and bonuses are intended to create perceptions of high instrumentality. They don't always succeed, however. For managers whose pay is tied to movement in the company's share price, unpredictable market conditions or a single bad decision by the CEO can have devastating consequences for the company's bonus pool, despite overall excellent performance by most managers. Such events may result in a manager having a feeling of low instrumentality. When incentives are tied to the performance of a work team, a similar problem may occur; that is, individual team members may feel that the link between their own individual performance and their rewards is weaker. This problem seems to be more severe in larger work teams.[34]

At McDonald's, increasing perceptions of instrumentality among senior managers was a strategic concern for corporate headquarters. As described in the Strategic Action Competency feature on the next page, to strengthen the link that store managers saw between how they performed and the rewards they received, McDonald's decided to change the way it calculated store managers' compensation.[35]

© George Widman/File/AP Photo

McDonald's responded to its managers quitting because of the lack of performance related compensation.

With more than 30,000 restaurants worldwide, and more than 400,000 managers and senior staff in charge of making sure those restaurants are profitable, McDonald's understands the need to ensure that there is a link between how managers perform their jobs and the rewards those managers receive from the company. The challenge is especially difficult when employees are scattered across 118 countries. In 2003, the company decided that managers were leaving the company in part because they saw too little relationship between how well they performed and how much they were paid. To correct the problem, McDonald's overhauled its compensation approach. The new system—called "Plan to Win"—was launched in 2004. Now managers "plan" by setting goals in areas such as customer service, marketing, and restaurant reimaging. Corporate headquarters identifies general areas such as these that they want to emphasize each year, and then gives managers autonomy to set specific goals for success in their local markets.

By allowing managers to participate in setting their goals, McDonald's ensures that managers accept the goals. To ensure that managers establish goals that improve financial performance, McDonald's pays incentives that are based partly on the business unit's operating income, partly on the region's success, and partly on each person's individual performance. Managers "win" when they perform well personally, when their business generates income, and when the entire region meets its business goals. By 2006, McDonald's could see that the new pay was beginning to work. Their annual survey revealed a 5 percent increase in the number of employees who said they believed they were paid fairly. McDonald's hopes the new pay plan will also help it attract and retain better managers in the future.

To learn more about this organization, visit *www.mcdonalds.com*.

Valence. Valence *is the value (weight) that an employee attaches to a consequence.* Because money is appreciated by most employees, it is often used by companies to reward employees for desired behaviors and for good performance. But money is not the only thing that employees value.

Valences are personal; the same outcome (e.g., a bonus) may have a high valence for one person and a low valence for another. For example, for Charlie Walter at the Fort Worth Museum of Science and History, a promotion from senior curator to the higher paying position of museum director would be appealing if he values (places a high valence on) financial gain and increased responsibility; it would be less appealing if he values creativity and independence.

In the Air Force, the opportunity to accumulate hours of flying time is very valuable to young pilots. When the Air Force was preparing for war in Iraq, it was faced with the challenge of conducting a large number of unmanned reconnaissance flights, which are guided by remote control. The Air Force believed that trained pilots would perform these jobs best, but it was not easy to convince pilots to spend their time sitting at a desk. To motivate pilots to volunteer for the required training, the Air Force needed to find a way to link something of value to participating in the training program. The solution was to allow some of the time spent training for unmanned flights as "flying time." This meant that pilots could accumulate the flying hours they valued so highly in a new way—by flying via remote control.[36]

Applying Expectancy Theory. Expectancy theory gives great weight to how people think about the future. By understanding how employees think about the future, managers can find solutions to troublesome behavior problems, like theft. Theft is a major problem for many U.S. employers. The annual cost of theft for a forest products company in the Northwest was $1 million—or $833 per employee! The theft problem concerned the company managers because it cost nearly $1 million per year and had a significant impact on the bottom line. The theft problem concerned the union because their members had started to complain that they too were often the victims of theft. But getting answers from employees about what was going on proved difficult. No one was talking. To find a solution to their theft problem, the company enlisted the help of a consultant—an expert on employee motivation. The consultant suggested a procedure designed to discover how employees thought about theft. To find out, he interviewed employees, asking them questions such as these:

▶ What positive outcomes do you personally expect for honest behavior (at work)? Where is the win for you to be honest?

▶ What are the negative outcomes that you can expect for being honest? How will you get hurt for being honest? What are the downsides?

▶ What are the positive outcomes for you personally to steal (from the company)? What are the "wins" for you to steal? How will you come out ahead?

▶ What are the negative outcomes you can expect for engaging in theft? How might you get hurt? How might you lose?

The consultant used the employees' answers to create a scoreboard like the one shown in Figure 14.5. Given the employees' responses shown in Figure 14.5, what should the mill managers do to reduce theft? What would you do? Put in cameras for surveillance? Hire a private detective to masquerade as an employee? These were some of the ideas suggested by company managers. But the consultant believed these solutions might make the problem worse. His reasoning was that surveillance cameras and private detectives would simply make it more difficult to steal. And increasing the challenge might actually motivate the thieves even more. After all, as the challenge becomes greater, so does the thrill of succeeding.

Snapshot

Baptist Health Care helps managers learn about what subordinates value by asking questions in their employee survey. Using the survey results, a manager can determine what type of reward or recognition is likely to have the most impact on a particular employee. Managers are encouraged to use this information in a personalized motivation process.

J. Sullivan, Personalizing motivation, Workforce Management, March 27, 2006, p.50.

Figure 14.5	Scoreboard for Understanding What Motivated Employees to Steal

	Responses to the Question "What Are the Positive Outcomes You Expect?"	Responses to the Question "What Are the Negative Outcomes You Expect?"
For Honesty	• "Nothing." • "You can look yourself in the mirror when you get out of bed in the morning." • "It is the right thing to do." • "I can live with myself." Cell 1	• "If you want to get along here, you better play the game." • "There's no harm. The company spills more milk at breakfast than you and I can steal in a year." • "See no evil, hear no evil." Cell 2
For Stealing	• "We are so good, we could steal a head-rig [which weighs more than a ton] from a sawmill." • "Doc, tell us what you want and we will get it out within 45 days." • "It takes real teamwork." • "It's a real thrill." Cell 3	• "If we got caught, we would get temporarily suspended." • "If someone got suspended, the guys would take a collection [to cover that person's pay loss]." Cell 4

After considering various options, the managers finally focused on the responses shown in cells 2 (negative consequences of honesty) and 3 (positive consequences of theft). Their solution was to set up a "library" system that allowed employees to borrow any type of tool or equipment that had previously been stolen. Employees did not steal things in order to sell them; they stole things to use them and for the fun of it. The library system removed the thrill and also made it easier for employees to get access to things that they might find useful to borrow for a home project. The company also created an amnesty day on which employees could return stolen material with no questions asked. On Amnesty Day, everyone would assume that the person returning an item was doing it for "a friend," and no one would be expected to disclose the friend's name. The solution was a huge success. Employees returned truckloads of stolen items—so much was being returned that the company extended amnesty for three days. Almost everything that had been stolen was returned. Theft dropped to near zero and was still that low after three years. No other negative behaviors—such as graffiti or vandalism—crept up after the problem of theft had been resolved.[37]

As the scoreboard shown in Figure 14.5 revealed, employees who stole made rational choices about how to behave using the information available to them. Included in that information was some knowledge about how likely their efforts would affect their performance (as thieves) and how their performance (theft) would be related to certain outcomes, such as feeling "thrilled." Similarly, employees who knew about the theft but said nothing were thinking about their future and how people would react to someone who squealed.[38]

Danger: Motivated Employees Ahead. Expectancy theory recognizes that tying monetary rewards to performance can be a powerful way to change how employees behave. Like any powerful instrument, it can be dangerous when used incorrectly. Poorly designed incentive systems sometimes lead to behavior that is unethical and/or illegal. Nucor, the steel producer, knows the power of money and uses it to encourage employees to produce defect-free steel. At Nucor, two-thirds of a steelworker's pay is tied to meeting production goals. Bonuses are calculated for every order and paid out every two weeks. But the company doesn't want employees to just produce as much as possible—it wants them to produce only high-quality steel. To ensure that steelworkers don't let bad steel get passed on to customers just to increase their pay, Nucor incorporates some penalties. If workers catch a bad batch of steel, they get no bonus for that batch. But if they don't catch a bad batch at the production stage and the batch is later found to have defects, it costs the steelworkers three times the bonus. With this system, Nucor hopes to minimize any temptation employees might have to reward themselves at the expense of customers.[39]

The potential dangers of poorly designed incentives are widely recognized, but you may be surprised to learn that highly motivated employees might cheat to achieve their goals even when there is no reward for doing so. Goals alone can be so motivating that employees are willing to lie or break the rules to achieve them.[40]

How susceptible are you to the temptation to cheat a little in order to achieve your goals? To find out, take a few minutes to consider the situations posed in the Ethical Challenge feature. When employees feel it is okay to cheat in order to meet their goals and obtain the rewards offered by their employer, whose responsibility is it? Are the employees at fault? Is their manager responsible? Or is it just "the system" that is to blame?

Achieving Peak Performance

Read each situation. Then indicate how tempted you feel to act in ways that might be viewed as questionable. Try to be candid. Your answers will help you recognize tempting situations when they present themselves.

Situation

How Tempted Are You?

| Not at All; Would Not Cheat | | | | | Very Tempted; Probably Would Cheat |

1. You work in a retail store selling clothes. Your goal for the week is to sell $4,000 of merchandise. Achieving your goal earns you a red recognition ribbon for your name badge. You have sold $3,950 with one hour of time left. A colleague is in a similar situation and proposes that you each spend $50 to purchase items from each other to achieve your goals. Do you go along with your friend's suggestion?

    1 2 3 4 5 6 7

2. The situation is almost the same as #1 above, but the reward is different. Besides the recognition ribbon, you will receive a $100 bonus if you meet your goal. Do you agree to work with your friend to reach the sales goal?

    1 2 3 4 5 6 7

3. You work in a call center for a catalog company. The company monitors calls to measure service quality and also gives extra points to employees who process calls quickly. Your service quality is excellent but your speed is too slow. Your sister offers to help by posing as a caller. She'll keep calling until she gets you, and then ask a simple question so you can have a few fast calls. She says she learned this trick where she works, where people do it all the time. Do you tell her to call you?

    1 2 3 4 5 6 7

4. You clean windows in homes during the summer to help pay for your college costs. You are paid by the size and number of windows you clean. You are responsible for counting the number of windows and estimating the sizes. Most of the homes you work on have a *lot* of windows. You are pretty sure the home owners don't really know how many windows they have. You suspect that you could easily charge for two extra windows without being caught. Do you do it?

    1 2 3 4 5 6 7

5. You deliver frozen food products to grocery stores. To maximize profits, your employer sets goals for a variety of performance metrics. One measure used is fuel efficiency. You find it difficult to meet the fuel goals, but have figured out that one solution is to carry more products on each trip. The only space available is the passenger seat, but if you use that space you cannot keep products at the lower temperature required by state food safety regulations. You learn that other truck drivers bring their own coolers and use them to carry products in the passenger seat. They say it is the only way anyone can meet the fuel goals. Do you bring a cooler to store food on the passenger seat?

1   2   3   4   5   6   7

After answering all of the questions, review your answers. Most people admit that they would be tempted to cheat in some of these situations. In which types of situations were you most tempted: When the reward was large? When the degree of cheating seemed minor? When you believed you wouldn't get caught? In situations like these, what can managers do to reduce the likelihood their employees will be tempted to cheat?

3.

Describe how jobs can be designed to be motivating and satisfying.

Job Design Approach

We have described how individual managers can affect motivation and satisfaction without saying much about how a specific job is performed by an employee. Characteristics of jobs also influence satisfaction and motivation. Job characteristics theory is the most popular and extensively tested approach to designing jobs that employees enjoy and feel motivated to perform well. Figure 14.6 illustrates the components of this theory.[41]

Job characteristics theory *states that employees are more satisfied and motivated when their jobs are meaningful, when jobs create a feeling of responsibility, and when jobs are designed to ensure that some feedback is available.* In essence, jobs should be designed to provide work that employees enjoy doing. People who enjoy doing their jobs may not need the extra motivation of high pay and impressive job titles. In fact, according to a survey of 1,200 U.S. employees, the nature of the work they did was the most important factor (ahead of direct and indirect financial rewards and career concerns) in determining how people felt about staying with their current employer and how motivated they were to work hard.[42]

Critical Psychological States

The job characteristics theory describes three critical psychological states that are needed to create high levels of motivation in the workplace.

Experienced meaningfulness *is a critical psychological state that refers to whether employees perceive their work as valuable and worthwhile.* For example, people working in health care understand that their efforts can help save lives and improve the quality of people's lives. At Johnson Space Center, managers know that astronauts are dedicated to space exploration and experience their work as meaningful, but they must ensure that employees in less glamorous jobs feel the same way. Rewards and recognitions help communicate that all types of work contribute to the success of the space program.

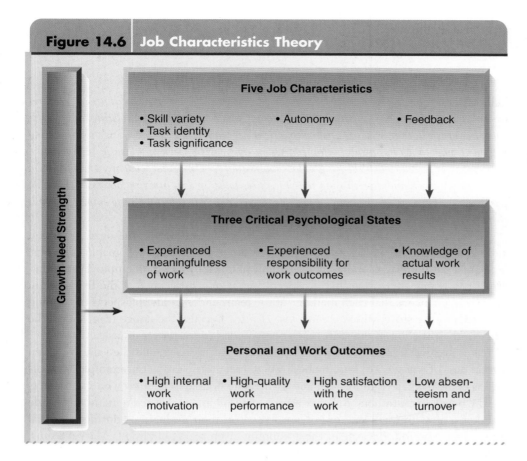

Figure 14.6 | Job Characteristics Theory

Growth Need Strength

Five Job Characteristics

- Skill variety
- Task identity
- Task significance
- Autonomy
- Feedback

Three Critical Psychological States

- Experienced meaningfulness of work
- Experienced responsibility for work outcomes
- Knowledge of actual work results

Personal and Work Outcomes

- High internal work motivation
- High-quality work performance
- High satisfaction with the work
- Low absenteeism and turnover

Experienced responsibility *is a critical psychological state that refers to whether employees feel personally responsible for the quantity and quality of their work.* A surgeon who specializes in orthopedics is likely to experience a feeling of responsibility for the amount and quality of her or his work. Have you ever found a slip of paper among the packaging material of something you bought that said something like "This product was inspected by Stacy Stamford"? Attaching a person's name to their work is one way that some companies use to increase employees' feelings of responsibility.

Knowledge of results *is a critical psychological state that refers to the extent to which employees receive feedback about how well they are doing.* Feedback can come from the task itself (e.g., successfully reviving a heart attack victim) or from other sources (e.g., the comments of colleagues or patient satisfaction surveys). At Lincoln Electric, knowledge of results can come directly from customers. When Lincoln Electric ships out an electric motor, for example, it includes the name of the employee who built it. If a customer has any complaints about the quality of the product, the employee who made it is informed of the problem and required to make the repairs.

Key Job Characteristics

Look again at Figure 14.6. How should jobs be designed to create the three critical psychological states? Job characteristics theory states that the critical psychological states are affected by five key job characteristics. **Key job characteristics** *are objective aspects of the job design that can be changed to improve the critical psychological states.* The five key job characteristics are:

▶ skill variety,

▶ task identity,

- task significance,
- autonomy, and
- feedback.

Skill variety is the degree to which the job involves many different work activities or requires several skills and talents. Task identity is present when a job involves completing an identifiable piece of work, that is, doing a job with a clear beginning and outcome. Task significance is present when a job has a substantial impact on the goals or work of others in the company. Autonomy is present when the job provides substantial freedom, independence, and discretion in scheduling work and determining the procedures to be used in carrying out tasks. Finally, feedback is present when the outcome provides direct and clear information to employees about their performance.

At Whole Foods Market, having jobs that are motivating fits the overall mission and values of the organization. The jobs are organized around self-managed teams. They're a natural extension of a management philosophy based on employee empowerment.[43] Teams are responsible for specific areas of a store, such as the fish section. One consequence is that each member of the team understands all aspects of running their area of the store, which creates *task identity*. Because the entire team shares the work in their section of the store, each person performs a *variety* of tasks.

Teams are given goals that they're responsible for meeting, and then they're given a great deal of *autonomy* to find the best way to meet those goals. For example, if a holiday is coming up, a team decides how to arrange holiday schedules while also meeting the needs of customers. Another aspect of autonomy is that team members decide whether a new hire will stay on a team, based on their evaluations during an initial probationary period. Because of the autonomy given to Whole Foods Market teams, feelings of *responsibility* seem to follow naturally.

Teams also get *feedback* about their results. If a team comes in under budget, the team gets to keep the difference and split it among the team members. If it comes in over budget, it builds up debt within the company, which can be erased by coming up with a plan to address the problem and showing some improvement. People get personal feedback, also. Team leaders know that they can be voted out at any time. To ensure that this doesn't happen very often, team members let leaders know clearly how the team feels about them, and leaders make the effort to get feedback without actually having to take a vote. Feedback in the form of financial results is plentiful, too. In fact, employees get so much financial information that they are "insiders" according to the Securities and Exchange Commission's definition.

Research conducted on employees in the Unites States shows that employees who work in jobs that include all five key job characteristics feel involved in their work and exert more effort, compared to those working in poorly designed jobs.[44] Studies in other countries reveal some cultural differences, however. For example, in Bulgaria, feedback seems to be less important than it is in the United States. For Dutch workers, task variety and task identity appear to be less important.[45] Clearly, managers working in counties outside the United States must be aware of such differences in order to be effective in motivating employees.

Growth Need Strength

Job characteristics theory considers individual differences to be important in determining how employees react to job content. In particular, employees' growth needs influence how they react to their jobs. Growth need strength *is a desire for personal challenge, accomplishment, and learning.* Employees with a strong growth need respond

Snapshot

"We recruit the best people we can to become part of our team. We empower them to make their own decisions, creating a respectful workplace where people are treated fairly and are highly motivated to succeed."

Excerpt from Whole Foods Market Web Site

more favorably to enriched jobs, whereas employees with a weak growth need may experience enriched jobs as frustrating and dissatisfying. In other words, enriched jobs aren't for everyone. Nevertheless, many people thrive in an environment characterized by jobs designed to give them a sense of responsibility and meaningfulness.

People with strong growth needs are just the type of people that Jamba Juice looks for when hiring general managers to run its stores. In selection interviews, the interviewers look for people who "think the glass is half full"—that is, they see opportunities and are eager to make the most of them. When it finds the right people, Jamba Juice puts them in a situation that guarantees they'll feel a sense of responsibility. Besides the challenging task of being in charge of Jamba Juice stores—retail outlets that sell made-to-order smoothies and a variety of healthy foods—general managers who succeed at expanding their businesses also experience significant personal financial gain.[46]

Organization Approach

The organization context includes many different elements, such as the organization's design, pay plans, the organizational culture, and so on. Here we focus on a few elements of the organization context that are most important to understanding motivation and satisfaction. For small and medium-sized organizations, the organization context is usually similar for most employees working within a specific organization, regardless of what job a person has. In very large firms, such as Procter & Gamble and PepsiCo, the organization context may vary among different divisions or business units. To understand employee motivation and satisfaction, the immediate work context that an employee experiences on a daily basis is most relevant.

4.
State how the organization context affects motivation and satisfaction.

Herzberg's Two-Factor Theory

According to Frederick Herzberg, the relationship between job satisfaction and motivation is a complicated one.[47] To gain an understanding of that relationship, Herzberg interviewed 200 accountants and engineers. He asked them to describe job experiences that produced good and bad feelings about their jobs. He discovered that the presence of a particular job characteristic, such as responsibility, might increase job satisfaction. However, the lack of responsibility didn't necessarily produce dissatisfaction. Conversely, if lack of job security produced dissatisfaction, high job security didn't necessarily lead to satisfaction.

The study's results led to Herzberg's two-factor theory, *which states that two separate and distinct aspects of the work context are responsible for motivating and satisfying employees.* He used the terms *hygiene factors* and *motivator factors* to refer to these two aspects of context. Figure 14.7 on the following page illustrates these basic components of Herzberg's two-factor theory.

Hygiene Factors. The two-factor theory states that hygiene factors determine how satisfied employees feel. Hygiene factors *are the nontask characteristics of the work environment—the organizational context—that create dissatisfaction.* They include compensation, level of responsibility, working conditions, company policies, supervision, coworkers, salary, formal status, and job security. Hygiene factors need to be present, at least to some extent, to avoid dissatisfaction. Which work conditions are most important to your satisfaction? Table 14.2 lists 20 factors that might be important to you. Take a minute now to rank order them according to how important they are to you personally.

As described in Chapter 13, many of the fringe benefits offered by employers are attempts to remove potential sources of employee dissatisfaction.

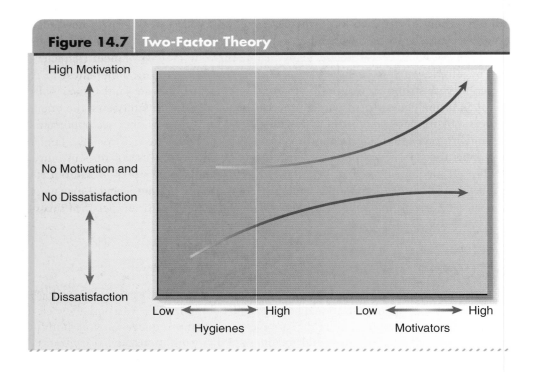

Figure 14.7 | **Two-Factor Theory**

High Motivation

No Motivation and

No Dissatisfaction

Dissatisfaction

Low ←→ High   Low ←→ High
   Hygienes   Motivators

Table 14.2   **What Matters to You?**

Review the job conditions listed below. Think about what is important to your job satisfaction. Rank order the items, using a 1 to indicate "most important" and 20 to indicate "least important."

RANK

_____ Autonomy and independence
_____ Benefits
_____ Career advancement opportunities
_____ Career development opportunities
_____ Communication between employees and senior management
_____ Compensation
_____ Contribution of your work to organization's goals
_____ Feeling safe at work
_____ Flexibility to balance work/life issues
_____ Job security
_____ Job-specific training
_____ Management recognition of employee performance
_____ Meaningfulness of job
_____ Opportunities to use skills and abilities
_____ Organization's commitment to your development
_____ Overall corporate culture
_____ Relationship with immediate supervisor
_____ Relationships with coworkers
_____ The work itself
_____ Variety of work

The Planning and Administration Competency feature on the next page illustrates the approach Jack in the Box used to reduce the dissatisfaction that was causing its employees to leave the company and look for work elsewhere.[48]

Jack in the Box

When the original Jack in the Box restaurant opened in San Diego in 1951, a hamburger cost just 18 cents and McDonald's was unknown. Today, more than 2,000 Jack in the Box restaurants operate in 17 states, serving hamburgers, sandwiches on ciabatta bread, and tacos. Jack in the Box wants its employees to be passionate about their jobs—a tall order for a quick-service restaurant.

Jack in the Box restaurants learned the hard way that dissatisfaction with hygiene factors causes much of the employee turnover experienced by fast-food restaurants. Turnover is problematic for the industry because it reduces the level of service customers receive and it increases labor costs. But in an industry where companies live and die on the basis of their costs, keeping employees passionate about their work and loyal to their employer is a big challenge. Prior to 1991, Jack in the Box offered employees health insurance. But because competitors like McDonald's and Burger King generally did not offer such insurance, Jack in the Box stopped offering it to new crew members. During the next 15 years, they found that the turnover rate for crew members without health insurance was 10 times the rate for insured crew members. An analysis revealed that the cost of turnover was higher than the cost of insurance, so today Jack in the Box is again offering medical, dental, and vision insurance. Without these hygiene factors, it seems, Jack in the Box employees were simply too dissatisfied.

As an indication of the success of their new approach, Jack in the Box was named as the winner of the National Restaurant Association Educational Foundation's Spirit Award for the category of quick-service restaurants. According to Mary M. Adolf, president and chief operating officer of the association, "Spirit Award winners have developed outstanding recruitment and retention programs that can serve as a model for operators in every segment as restaurateurs throughout the industry constantly seek ways to enhance employee satisfaction. We commend these restaurant companies for their inspiring commitment to their people."

To learn more about this company, visit *www.jackinthebox.com*.

The absence of dissatisfaction is an essential, but not sufficient, condition for creating a motivated workforce. Hygiene factors won't generate feelings of excitement about the job and organization. Nevertheless, hygiene factors help create a work setting that makes it possible to motivate employees.

Motivator Factors. Assuming hygiene factors are present and employees feel satisfied, then the presence of motivator factors results in employees who feel excited about their work. Motivator factors *are aspects of the organizational context that create positive feelings among employees.* Achievement, the challenge of the work itself, responsibility, recognition, advancement, and growth are all motivator factors. The presence of motivators alone doesn't guarantee that employees will be productive. Motivators lead to superior performance *only* if no dissatisfiers are present. At Intuit, employees are generally satisfied, so motivator factors are used to increase motivation. Because employees are both satisfied and motivated, Intuit is one of *Fortune*'s Best Companies to Work For.

© AP Graphics Bank

Jack in the Box discovered that cutting benefits for new employees cost more money in the long run; the benefits were reinstated and employee retention improved.

The two-factor theory is based on the assumption that motivator and hygiene factors are similar for all employees. Individual differences among employees aren't recognized as being important. Therefore, in Herzberg's view, employers should be able to motivate all employees in the same way—by ensuring the presence of both hygiene and motivator factors. Studies that compare the importance of motivator and hygiene factors among different types of employees (e.g., those who work in the private sector versus the public sector or those who work in lower skill versus higher skill jobs) support this view.[49]

Recognizing the Power of Recognition. Perhaps you noticed that Herzberg's two-factor theory considers compensation a hygiene factor, whereas recognition is considered a motivator. In other words, the theory states that a person's compensation might cause him or her to feel more or less satisfied, but recognition is more effective for motivating employees. Some people argue that recognition programs are just a way for employers to avoid spending a lot of money on pay raises. Of course, spending *any* money on recognition programs would be a waste of money if they were not effective. But the evidence indicates that noncash recognition programs can be effective motivators.[50]

At Knott's Berry Farm, a theme park in California, employees' name badges are used to recognize those who give outstanding customer service, with gold and silver badges indicating the best service. At Wells Fargo Internet Service Group, employees can nominate each other for e-wards by going online and completing a form that explains what actions deserve special recognition. Managers review the nominations and if they approve, employees receive electronic thank-you cards. More than 3,000 e-cards are sent annually.[51]

Intuit also uses recognition to motivate employees. As described in the Communication Competency feature, managers at Intuit understand that there are many ways besides a simple "thank-you" to communicate how much they appreciate the efforts of their employees.[52]

Communication Competency

Intuit

Headquartered in Silicon Valley, Intuit is the maker of well-known software programs such as Quicken and Turbo-Tax. But one program you may not have heard about is the company's Thanks Program.

With nearly 7,000 employees, the company has offices in 13 states throughout the United States, the United Kingdom, and Canada. At each site, giving out small awards is part of every manager's job. The company's philosophy is that awards should be given only to people who perform well above what is expected. Getting an award is special—it is a way to recognize excellence and communicate appreciation. Managers decide the criteria that will be used for giving awards, and they decide what awards to give. Examples of awards given include gift certificates to restaurants, movie tickets, written thank-you notes, and a Night-on-the-Town. Why do employees get these awards? Some employees get awards for going beyond the call of duty to help out their colleagues. Some get awards for making suggestions

that reduce bureaucracy. Some get awards for technical programming achievements, or even for outstanding service to the community. Intuit gives managers the authority to make these decisions.

To make sure managers use good judgment when giving awards, Intuit developed a Web site designed to help them. It explains the importance of linking the awards they give to achieving business objectives. It also helps managers ensure that the awards given out are valued by employees. To monitor how employees feel about the Thanks Program, Intuit includes a question in the employee satisfaction survey that reads "I am rewarded and recognized when I do a great job." As long as employees continue to agree with that statement, Intuit can be sure the Thanks Program is working and helping to earn the company recognition as one of America's best companies to work for.

To learn more about this organization, visit *www.intuit.com*.

Treating People Fairly

As Herzberg's two-factor theory suggests, employees are sensitive to many aspects of the organizational context. But the theory does not go into much detail about how employees think about all of these elements. According to equity theory, people evaluate their work experiences much like an accountant might. They consider everything they put into their work, everything they get out of their work, and then make a judgment about whether the balance of inputs and outcomes is fair. Even when the job itself is enjoyable and motivating, people will probably be upset if they feel that they're not being treated fairly.

In Chapter 13, we noted that compensation practices are one aspect of the organizational context that employees consider when evaluating whether they are fairly treated. When evaluating pay, they consider their salary or wage rate, bonuses and incentive pay, and the package of benefits offered by the organization. If their pay is judged as unfair, employees are likely to feel unmotivated and dissatisfied. But how exactly do employees decide what is fair?

According to equity theory, *employees judge whether they've been treated fairly by comparing the ratio of their outcomes and inputs to the ratios of others doing similar work.* Inputs are what an employee gives to the job (e.g., time, effort, education, and commitment to the organization). Outcomes are what people get out of doing the job (e.g., the feelings of meaningfulness and responsibility associated with jobs, promotions, and increased pay).[53] Equity theory explains how employees think and behave when they feel unfairly treated at work.[54]

Equity Ratios. Examples of equity ratios are shown in Table 14.3. In these examples, the outcomes and inputs are simply money and time. These are easy to quantify and the examples are easy to understand. In reality, the ratios and comparison can be quite complex. Employees consider many factors that are quite difficult to quantify and compare.

Table 14.3	**Examples of Equity Perceptions**				
	Andy	**Ally**	**Comparison**	**Andy's Equity Perception**	**Ally's Equity Perception**
Situation A	Outcome: $500 Input: 50 hours work	Outcome: $800 Input: 80 hours work	$500/50 = $800/80 = $10/hour	Equitable	Equitable
Situation B	Outcome: $500 Input: 50 hours work	Outcome: $500 Input: 60 hours	$500/50 > $500/60	Feels over-rewarded (inequitable)	Feels under-rewarded (inequitable)

In Situation A, Andy evaluates the pay he received and compares it to what Ally received. Ally received more pay, but she also worked more hours. Because the pay-per-hour worked is equal for Andy and Ally, Andy feels it is equitable and fair. In Situation B, Andy also compares his pay to Ally. In this example, Andy received the same pay as Ally. Both Andy and Ally know this. They also know that Andy worked fewer hours than Ally. Consequently, when Andy compares himself to Ally, he should feel overrewarded. When Ally makes the comparison, she is likely to feel underrewarded. In other words, Ally and Andy both view the situation as inequitable.

Feelings of being overrewarded are probably rare. Overrewarded employees tend to perform better in their jobs and are better members of the organization than employees who haven't been so well rewarded.[55] More typical are situations that result in employees feeling underrewarded. In those situations, employees feel dissatisfied and unmotivated.

Comparison Targets. As Table 14.3 makes clear, equity is a relative concept. Equity theory states that employees must make comparisons in order to decide

When Microsoft eliminated some low-cost perks—like towel service for workers who used the locker room after bike rides or workouts—employees were furious. One employee wrote in an e-mail to the company, "Small things like this chip away at employee loyalty and morale and in the long run do more harm than benefit."

Anonymous Employee, Microsoft.

whether their current balance of outputs-to-inputs is fair. Employees compare their pay to people who are similar, such as people in the same occupation or same organization. Employees also compare their pay to people who are dissimilar, such as people in other occupations and or in other organizations that they know about.[56] Two common targets of comparisons are other employees and past situations you have experienced.

Perceived inequities often occur when employees compare outcomes such as their promotions, pay raises, and perquisites (perks) to those received by others. Sometimes, these comparisons are quite simple, as in the example of Andy and Ally. The comparisons to others can become much more complicated, however. For example, imagine you are a U.S. manager working for Cisco as an expatriate in China. The business you work in is a joint venture between Cisco and a local Chinese company. When evaluating whether your pay is fair, you probably make the following comparisons: (1) Your pay compared to the pay of other expatriate managers you know who are working for Cisco but in other countries, (2) local Chinese managers working in the same joint ventures as you, and (3) managers working in other state-owned Chinese businesses in your industry. If you give great weight to (1), you might feel underrewarded, because expatriates working in other countries would probably be paid more than you. But if you give more weight to (2) and (3), you would feel overrewarded, because U.S. expatriates working in China typically are paid considerably more than local Chinese managers.

When employees make comparisons to others, they understand that not everyone deserves to receive exactly the same outcomes. Nevertheless, when their comparisons reveal that others are getting more, employees may question whether the inputs of other employees justify the better outcomes that those employees receive. When lower level employees compare their own pay and perks to those of the executives, they usually acknowledge that executives deserve more than they do. But how much more? In addition to salaries worth hundreds of thousands of dollars and bonuses worth millions, high-ranking executives in many companies receive extravagant perks (daily limousine service, lavish lunches, offices adorned with expensive artwork, etc.). Can executives put in 500 times as much effort as someone lower in the hierarchy? Can they work 500 times as many hours? Can they have 500 times as much skill? If so, perhaps they deserve rewards worth 500 times more. But if not, people lower in the organization may feel underrewarded when they make the comparison. Herb Baum, CEO of Dial Corporation in Scottsdale, Arizona, recognized this when he said, "If you draw the line on your own greed, and your employees see it, they will be incredibly loyal and perform much better for you."[57]

Feelings of (in)equity can be stimulated by making comparisons between oneself and others, but such comparisons are not the only basis for judging whether your employer is treating you fairly. Another type of comparison employees make is how their current employer treats them compared to other employers in the past, or even the same employer in the past. Consider the situation faced by the thousands of people who have been laid off during the recent economic decline. Because jobs were few and far between, many laid-off employees felt they had to accept new jobs that paid less. When these recently laid-off employees compare their new situation to their old situation, two facts are salient: One fact is that they still have the same (or perhaps greater) level of competency, education, and experience that they had previously. In other words, their inputs to their work have not changed. The second fact is that their outcomes (pay) are less than they were in their previous job. Together, these two facts naturally lead such employees to experience feelings of inequity and dissatisfaction.[58]

Reactions to Perceived Inequity. Inequity can arise due to being either under-rewarded or overrewarded. Either situation causes people to feel dissatisfied. When people are dissatisfied, they usually do something about it. How do employees react to inequity? Generally, six alternatives are available to employees who want to reduce their feelings of inequity. They can:

- increase their inputs (e.g., time and effort) to justify higher rewards when they feel that they are overrewarded compared to others;

- decrease their inputs to compensate for lower rewards when they feel under-rewarded;

- change the compensation they receive through legal or other actions (e.g., forming a union, filing a grievance, or leaving work early);

- modify their comparisons by choosing another person to compare themselves against;

- distort reality by rationalizing that the inequities are justified; or

- leave the situation (quit the job) if the inequities cannot be resolved.

Clearly, most of these reactions are harmful to the organization. For example, it can be quite costly to employers when high performers who feel that their pay is too low leave the organization. Not only does the company lose their productive talent, it must spend time and money to find replacement talent. If dissatisfied employees stay, they may react by withholding effort in order to restrict output or lower quality. Customers are not the only ones who suffer from such behavior; the morale of coworkers is also likely to suffer. Because feelings of inequity often cause frustration, they also lead people to behave in hostile and aggressive ways.

To be effective in their roles, managers must strive to treat all members of the organization fairly. Doing so can pay huge dividends. Employees who are paid and treated fairly are more likely to believe in and be committed to what they do. In turn, they will become more trusting, honorable, and loyal employees and will work harder to exceed the expectations that managers have of them. In team situations, equitable treatment improves cooperation among team members.[59]

Individual Differences Approach

People differ from each other in many ways, having different abilities, personalities, values, and needs. During the past century, psychologists have conducted thousands of studies designed to improve understanding of such differences.[60] Here, we describe one popular view of how individual differences affect employee motivation and satisfaction. This approach considers employees' needs to be the basis for differences in motivation and satisfaction.

5.
Describe how the needs of individuals can affect their work.

Types of Needs

A need *is a strong feeling of deficiency in some aspect of a person's life that creates an uncomfortable tension*. That tension becomes a motivating force, causing the individual to take actions to satisfy the need, reduce the tension, and diminish the intensity of the motivating force.

Hierarchy of Needs. Psychologist Abraham Maslow believed that people have five types of needs, as shown in Figure 14.8 on the following page: physiological (at the base), security, affiliation, esteem, and self-actualization (at the top). He arranged these in a hierarchy of needs, *which describes the order in which people seek to satisfy their desires*. Satisfying the needs at the bottom level of the hierarchy comes first. As a person satisfies each level of needs, motivation shifts to satisfying the next higher level of needs.[61]

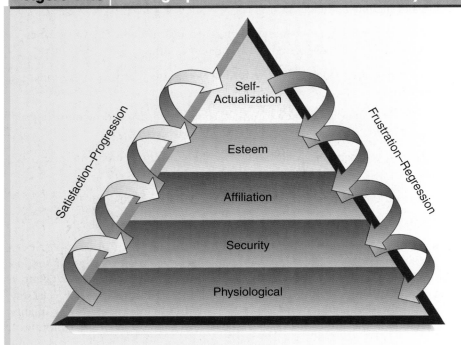

Figure 14.8 | Moving Up and Down the Needs Hierarchy

Physiological needs *are those for food, clothing, and shelter, which people try to satisfy before all others.* For example, the primary motivation of many Hurricane Katrina flood victims was to obtain food rather than, say, gain recognition for achievements. Thus people work for wages that will allow them to meet their physiological needs first.

Security needs *include the desire for safety and stability, and the absence of pain, threat, and illness.* As we saw during the Katrina disaster, people who were deprived of the means to satisfy security needs were motivated to fulfill those needs, even if it means leaving behind everything they have and moving to another city to live with strangers. Some workers express their security needs as a desire for a stable job with adequate medical, unemployment, and retirement benefits. Such people are likely to be frustrated with current flexible staffing practices (e.g., emphasis on temporary workers to avoid providing benefits). Other workers express security needs as a desire for work that builds their competencies and ensures their long-term employability, and this concern is often more important than getting a bigger salary.

Affiliation needs *are the desire for friendship, love, and belonging.* Employees with high affiliation needs enjoy working closely with others. Employees with low affiliation needs may be content to work on tasks by themselves. When an organization doesn't meet affiliation needs, an employee's dissatisfaction may be expressed in terms of frequent absenteeism, low productivity, stress-related behaviors, and even emotional breakdown. A manager who recognizes that a subordinate is striving to satisfy affiliation needs might encourage others to work more closely with the employee and suggest that the employee participate in the organization's social activities.

Esteem needs *are the desire for self-respect, a sense of personal achievement, and recognition from others.* To satisfy these needs, people seek opportunities for achievement, promotion, prestige, and status—all of which symbolize their competence and worth. When the need for esteem is dominant, managers can promote job satisfaction and high-quality performance by providing opportunities for exciting, challenging work and recognition for accomplishments.

Self-actualization needs *are the desire for personal growth, self-fulfillment, and the realization of the individual's full potential.* Richard Branson, chairman of the Virgin Group, seems to be strongly motivated by the need for self-actualization. When explaining why he founded Virgin Atlantic Airlines and Virgin Records, he admits that part of the reason was to have fun but also important was to change things and make a difference. In the process of building new businesses, Branson himself developed and grew.[62]

Managers who recognize these needs in employees can help them discover the growth opportunities available in their jobs or create special growth opportunities for them. For example, at Merck, scientists can attend law school and become patent attorneys; at Hewlett-Packard, a parallel technical ladder was established so scientists can earn higher salaries without taking on management tasks. At both companies, managers also can offer employees special assignments, such as working on a task force that reports to top management. Such assignments often represent growth opportunities through which employees can develop their managerial competencies while continuing to utilize to the fullest their technical knowledge and skills.

Chef Anthony Bourdain is well aware of these needs and their consequences for his employees. Bourdain knows that his employees appreciate knowing that he is concerned about their needs and is looking after them. By addressing employees' needs, he motivates them to perform effectively as a team. His approach to managing is described in the Teamwork Competency feature.[63]

Teamwork Competency

Chef Anthony Bourdain

If you watch the Food Network channel, you know Chef Anthony Bourdain as the star of shows such as *A Cook's Tour* or *Anthony Bourdain: No Reservations*. But if you've visited New York, you may know him as the owner of Les Halles, his popular brasserie. Les Halles' kitchen operates according to the classical French model, which has been described as "the brigade." The hierarchy is clear, with the chef firmly in control. Jobs are specialized, the rules are rigid, and compliance with the rules is absolutely mandatory. When the rules are followed, the result is that every dish the kitchen serves is excellent. In this environment, what motivates the kitchen staff?

Bourdain believes that he makes the stressful life of working in his profession satisfying by attending to the needs of his staff. "It's important that the crew knows I care about them and will take care of them. They know that they can come to me and say, 'I got drunk last night . . . got into a fight . . . and the police are after me,' and I will help them out." By showing sincere concern about the difficulties employees face in their personal lives—Bourdain offers more than a secure paycheck to employees. In fact, he believes that the camaraderie enjoyed among staff is one of the most satisfying aspects of working in a professional kitchen. "The kitchen's a place where you spend so much of your time that everyone knows everything about you. You're totally exposed, but also protected. In my kitchen, the intricacies and anomalies of one's love life are generally common knowledge—and openly discussed. Resentments are not allowed to simmer. . . . People are forced to get along, to cooperate, to come to understand one another."

Teamwork drives the system, and in the process of building a team that is strong enough to get through any crisis, the staff members become friends. What about esteem needs? These are satisfied each time a cook "makes a really beautiful plate of food and puts in up in the window—the pass—to be taken into the dining room." The satisfaction doesn't come from the customer; it comes just before the food leaves the kitchen, when the kitchen staff see how perfect it is. When everything goes well, people feel a sense of achievement. One of the best feelings is sitting at the bar after a long night, enjoying a free drink, and reviewing the evening's events. "It's golden," says Bourdain.

To learn more about Anthony Bourdain, see *www.anthonybourdain.com*. To learn more about his restaurant, visit *www.leshalles.net*.

Moving through the Needs Hierarchy

Snapshot

At Timberland, employees with one or more years of service can take a three- to six-month paid sabbatical with a nonprofit group of their choice if they already have a relationship with the nonprofit group. The company sees sabbaticals as a means to allow employees to strive toward self-fulfillment by sharing their skills and energy to create lasting community change.

People often equate individual differences with fixed traits that don't change much over time. In contrast to this view, Maslow believed that people move through the needs hierarchy by considering which needs have been satisfied and which needs remain to be satisfied. For any specific person, a need that was dominant three months ago may no longer be dominant, and a need that is dominant today may not be dominant next year. In Maslow's original formulation of the needs hierarchy, he viewed movement as occurring much as it does when people are moving up on an escalator—the only way to go is up. However, later research showed that movement through the hierarchy could actually go in both directions.

Moving Up. To explain which need is dominant for someone at a particular time, Maslow proposed the satisfaction–progression hypothesis. The satisfaction–progression hypothesis *states that a need is a motivator until it becomes satisfied.* When a need is satisfied, it ceases to be a motivator and another need emerges to take its place. In general, lower level needs must be satisfied before higher level needs become strong enough to motivate behavior. Research supports Maslow's view that, until their *basic* needs are satisfied, people won't be concerned with higher level needs. Many employers understand that employees' needs for self-actualization can be difficult to satisfy on the job. To help build employee loyalty and keep those who are searching for self-actualizing experiences, employers such as McDonald's, Intel, Nike, Goldman Sachs, and Timberland offer sabbatical leaves.[64]

Moving Down. Maslow focused on the dynamics of satisfaction–progression. Later research showed that people can also move down the hierarchy.[65] The frustration–regression hypothesis *holds that when an individual is frustrated in meeting higher level needs, the next lower level needs reemerge and again direct behavior.* For example, a finish carpenter who does highly creative trim work in houses may work for a contractor who builds from a limited number of floor plans with few trim options. Because the job doesn't provide a creative outlet, the frustrated carpenter may stop pursuing satisfaction of growth needs at work and instead regress to pursuing activities that satisfy his relatedness needs. An example would be socializing with other construction workers.

The frustration–regression hypothesis suggests that managers should try to determine the cause of an employee's frustration and, if possible, work to remove impediments to needs satisfaction. If impediments can't be removed, managers should try to redirect the employee's behavior toward satisfying a lower level need. For example, a company's production technology may limit the growth opportunities for people in their jobs. If employees are frustrated because they can't be creative or develop new skills, they could be encouraged to focus on relating to their coworkers, which can also generate feelings of satisfaction.

6.

Describe how understanding motivation can help managers improve employee performance and satisfaction.

Guidelines for Managers

Managers who understand what motivates employees and what detracts from employee motivation have a good basis for diagnosing and rectifying the causes of performance problems and dissatisfaction. Here we summarize some of the practical lessons suggested by the theories and research described in this chapter.

▶ **Clearly communicate the organization's mission and explain how employees' contribution to the organization will help the organization realize its mission.** Effective managers understand that motivating employees involves two steps. The first step is setting a clear direction. Only when everyone is working for the same results will their combined efforts move the organization forward. Assuming employees understand the big picture and how they fit into it, increasing the effort they exert should improve the effectiveness of the organization.

▶ **State the behaviors and performance achievements that are desired and explain how they will be rewarded.** By working with employees to set specific and measurable goals, managers can clarify their expectations for employees. These goals may include job-specific performance goals as well as behaviors that extend beyond job tasks but are necessary for the organization to function effectively. When setting goals, managers should be careful not to fall into the trap of focusing only on goals that are easily quantified, such as sales or absenteeism. They should also set goals for "soft" objectives, such as teamwork and being customer focused.[66]

▶ **Design jobs with high motivating potential.** Jobs designed to meet the principles of job characteristics theory tend to be more satisfying than other jobs. To determine whether jobs need to be redesigned, managers should assess the degree to which employees experience their work as meaningful, feel personally responsible for their work outcomes, and receive adequate feedback.

▶ **Provide frequent and constructive feedback.** When employees are performing well, telling them so spurs them on. When employees are performing poorly, telling them so suggests that they consider a different approach to the task or intensify their efforts. Giving appropriate feedback can be difficult, however. As a general rule, feedback should focus on task performance and be given immediately; avoid criticizing personal characteristics that are difficult for employees to change.[67]

▶ **Provide rewards for desired behaviors and outcomes.** Employees tend to repeat behaviors that are rewarded, and they strive to achieve goals to which rewards are attached. When a gap exists between actual and desired behaviors and goal achievement, rewards and punishments are likely to be misaligned. Effective managers ensure that the formal and informal rewards and punishments experienced by employees are aligned with the organization's desired behaviors and goal achievement.

▶ **Provide rewards that employees value.** To be motivators, rewards must reflect the things that employees value. The rewards that employees want can be determined simply by asking them. Some employees value monetary rewards above everything else, whereas others value scheduling flexibility, the opportunity to work on special projects, training and development opportunities, and so on. Whenever possible, effective managers find ways to use various rewards to motivate a variety of employees.

▶ **Provide equitable rewards.** Employees make two types of comparisons when evaluating whether they have been rewarded fairly. One involves assessing their own accomplishments in terms of the rewards they receive. The second involves assessing their own accomplishments and rewards in terms of those of other employees. Effective managers recognize that employees' assessments of equity and fairness are basically subjective perceptions. Perceptions may partially reflect objective facts, but inaccurate assumptions and beliefs often play a role, too. Effective communication about rewards is essential. A well-designed reward system will have little motivational value if employees misunderstand the system and rely on inferences and rumor when assessing whether the system is fair.

Snapshot

"In our employee surveys, workers always say that this is the one thing they love most about working for Nucor. They know what their bonus structure is down to the penny and there are no politics."
Jim Coblin, Vice President, Human Resources, Nucor Corporation

▶ **Recognize that each person is unique.** The principles just stated should, on average, result in employees who are more motivated and more satisfied. But effective managers also must recognize the individual differences that make each person unique. Differences in employees' needs mean that rewards valued by one employee may not be valued by another employee. Similarly, although most employees seem to like enriched jobs, some employees find such jobs to be more stressful. Because individual differences play a part in shaping motivation and satisfaction, a manager needs to understand each employee.

Chapter Summary ....

Ensuring that employees are motivated to work effectively is a primary managerial responsibility. Managers who are able to do so will be rewarded for their efforts with a workforce that expresses little dissatisfaction and exerts high levels of effort. To be effective, managers must understand the many factors that, in combination, can enhance or squelch motivation.

Learning Goals ....

1. Describe four approaches that can be used to explain employee motivation and satisfaction.

The four approaches used to understand the motivation and satisfaction of employees are the managerial approach, the job design approach, the organization approach, and the individual differences approach. None of these influences alone can fully explain employee motivation and satisfaction. Effective managers understand that the four approaches are most useful when used in combination.

2. Explain how managers can use goals and rewards to improve performance.

To use goals and rewards effectively, managers must begin by communicating a general direction to employees. To improve performance in a specific job, managers should set goals for employees. Performance improves when employees have specific, difficult goals that they accept and are committed to. Providing feedback to employees about their progress toward those goals is important to their effectiveness. Reinforcement theory states that behavior is a function of its consequences. Positive and negative reinforcement should be used to encourage desired work behaviors, whereas punishment and extinction should be applied to discourage undesired work behaviors. Expectancy theory provides a framework for combining the principles of goal setting and reinforcement, while also taking into account the specific rewards that each employee values most. Expectancy theory states that motivation is highest when employees feel that their efforts lead to improved performance (expectancy) and when performance is rewarded with outcomes that they value (instrumentality).

3. Describe how jobs can be designed to be motivating and satisfying.

Job characteristics theory states that three critical psychological states—experienced meaningfulness, experienced responsibility, and knowledge of results—lead to high motivation and job satisfaction. These critical psychological states are created by well-designed jobs. Specifically, five job characteristics of job design are important: skill variety, task identity and significance, autonomy, and feedback. Individuals with strong growth needs are likely to respond positively to jobs having these characteristics.

4. State how the organization context affects motivation and satisfaction.

Herzberg's two-factor model states that factors in the work situation strongly influence satisfaction and performance. Motivator factors such as challenging work, responsibility, recognition, achievement, and growth create high levels of motivation. The presence of motivators should enhance performance. Hygiene factors, such as good working conditions and benefits, are important determinants of satisfaction and dissatisfaction. Hygiene factors can hurt employee performance if not present but don't necessarily increase performance when present. Equity theory is based on the assumption that employees want to be treated fairly. Employees judge fairness by comparing their own inputs and outcomes to those of others in the workplace. When inequities exist, employees feel dissatisfied and their performance drops.

5. Describe how the needs of individuals can affect their work.

Maslow's hierarchy of needs includes physiological, security, affiliation, esteem, and self-actualization needs. Need satisfaction causes people to move up the hierarchy and need frustration causes them to move down. The importance of a category of needs at any specific time in a person's life determines how strongly it influences a person's behavior.

6. Describe how understanding motivation can help managers improve employee performance and satisfaction.

An understanding of employee motivation and satisfaction provides guidance concerning how managers should behave in their daily interactions, how to design jobs and organizations, and how to intervene when employees seem unmotivated or unsatisfied. To improve the performance and satisfaction of employees, managers should clearly communicate the organization's mission, clearly state what employees are expected to do, design jobs with high motivating potential, provide feedback as well as rewards, and attend to employees' equity perceptions. In addition, they must recognize that each employee is unique. Due to individual differences among employees, their reactions to these approaches will not be identical.

Key Terms and Concepts

Affiliation needs
Autonomy
Behavior modification
Equity theory
Esteem needs
Expectancy
Expectancy theory
Experienced
 meaningfulness
Experienced responsibility
Extinction
Feedback
Frustration–regression
 hypothesis

Goal-setting theory
Growth need strength
Hierarchy of needs
Hygiene factors
Instrumentality
Job characteristics theory
Key job characteristics
Knowledge of results
Management by objectives
Motivation
Motivator factors
Need
Negative reinforcement
Physiological needs

Positive reinforcement
Punishment
Reinforcement theory
Satisfaction
Satisfaction–progression
 hypothesis
Security needs
Self-actualization needs
Skill variety
Task identity
Task significance
Two-factor theory
Valence

Questions for Discussion and Reflective Thinking

1. Review the description of Johnson Space Center in the opening Challenge of Managing feature. Which approaches to motivation best explain how employees at the center feel about their work? Explain.

2. At Maxi's Health Club, customers have been complaining that the locker rooms look sloppy. Customers want the towels picked up, litter removed from lockers, and cleaner shower stalls. The health inspector has also indicated that the club needs to improve. Using the principles of goal setting and reinforcement theory, develop a three-month plan to help Maxi's improve locker room cleanliness and customer satisfaction without spending substantial sums of monetary rewards.

3. When have you been motivated by specific, difficult goals? In that situation, were any of the pitfalls listed in Table 14.1 present? What were the consequences of those pitfalls?

4. Think about a specific job that you've had. Use expectancy theory to explain your motivation to perform the job well. What aspects of the situation were motivating for you? What aspects of the situation interfered with your performance? How could a manager have used expectancy theory to improve your motivation and/or your performance?

5. When organizations downsize and lay off employees, the survivors of the downsizing often have increased workloads. According to equity theory, what are some of the possible reactions of the survivors that managers should expect? What can managers do to discourage negative reactions that employees may have if they feel that they're being treated unfairly?

6. Use job characteristics theory to analyze the motivational aspects of this course. What could your instructor do to enhance your feelings of meaningfulness, responsibility, or knowledge of results?

7. Review the five categories of needs shown in Figure 14.8. Which of these needs do you feel have been satisfied for you at this point in your life? Which needs are you still striving to satisfy?

8. List three things you could tell your manager about how your need satisfaction (or frustration) is likely to affect you at work. What could a manager do (or not do) to show that she is taking your needs into account?

9. Share your rankings of the items in Table 14.2 with two or three classmates. How similar are your rankings? Where you find differences, discuss what might explain your different views. Then think about the management implications of your results. Describe three ways that a manager could use your rankings to motivate you at work.

DEVELOPING YOUR COMPETENCIES

You can develop a plan to change your own behavior and performance by taking the following steps. You may choose to focus on behavior related to your life at work, at school, or at home. Most important is that you focus on something fairly specific.

Step 1. Choose a behavior that you really would like to change (e.g., walking more and driving less). Briefly, I want to change this behavior:

_____
_____
_____
_____
_____
_____
_____
_____
_____

Step 2. State a specific short-term goal for changing the behavior (e.g., within six months, I'll increase the number of times I walk to work from one to five times per week):

_____
_____
_____
_____
_____
_____
_____
_____
_____

Step 3. Develop a procedure for monitoring the behavior (e.g., I'll make a chart and tape it to my bathroom mirror):

_____
_____
_____
_____
_____
_____
_____
_____
_____

Step 4. Create a plan to reward yourself for making progress toward your goal (e.g., each day I walk, I'll put $5 in a special reward fund, to be spent at the end of each month. Each day I drive, I'll remove $6):

_____
_____
_____
_____
_____
_____
_____
_____

Step 5. Write a contract with yourself, specifically stating your goals, your plan for how to change, and any contingencies that you might want to consider (e.g., one of my contingencies is that on days when I have to travel beyond the office, I'll drive without removing any funds.):

_____
_____
_____
_____
_____
_____
_____
_____
_____
_____
_____

Step 6. Develop a plan for how you will deal with difficult obstacles (list five) that may interfere with progress toward your goal (e.g., I don't like to walk in the rain, so I'll purchase rain gear that makes it less of a problem for me to do so):

_____
_____
_____
_____
_____
_____
_____
_____
_____
_____
_____

You probably know that BMW is a German automaker, but do you know what BMW stands for? If your answer is Bayerische Motoren Werke you're right. Or maybe you said BMW stands for "The Ultimate Driving Machine." That would be true too (although competitors such as Jaguar, Porsche, and Alfa Romeo may disagree!). Because BMW's reputation for excellent performance and design is so widely recognized, some people questioned the company's decision to build its Mini car in an old Rover plant. But the decision turned out to be a good one.

Located in Oxford, England, BMW's Mini factory produces one of the company's hottest new products. It's a big change from a few years ago, when Rover owned the factory. Then the buildings were crumbling and the plant was often half-empty. After acquiring the Rover factory, the first challenge for BMW was modernizing the facilities. They installed the newest production technology, expanded the parking lot, created more appealing landscapes, and in other ways created a more pleasant work environment. As employee Bernard Moss explained, "We had an open day for old employees and they just couldn't believe the transformation of the plant."

The improvements were badly needed, but they were costly, too. For the plant to become profitable, productivity had to improve. BMW emphasizes quality at every stage of the manufacturing process, from product conception to customer feedback. Their quality control system means that quality audits are conducted at every stage of the manufacturing process. Every member of staff is fully responsible for the quality of their work. When quality problems are found, the goal is to correct them immediately.

BMW relies on the factory workers themselves to find ways to improve quality as well as cutting costs and boosting output. To motivate their employees and align their efforts with the needs of the business, BMW managers and union leaders designed a new pay system. It offers all employees an annual bonus of £260 (approximately $400) for their ideas. In order for the employees to receive the full bonus, they must come up with an average of three ideas per employee and the ideas must save an average of £800. There were other changes in the way employees were paid, also. Under the old system, when production stopped and employees didn't come to work, they were paid anyway. And when the plant was extra busy, they earned overtime pay. Now, when the plant is closed, employees are paid, but there is a new twist. The agreement is that they will make up the time by putting in extra hours when needed. When things are busy, the workers are expected to put in longer hours; but instead of overtime pay, they build up an account of extra days off.

Of course, the pay scheme is no magic bullet. To ensure the pay scheme works, managers are expected to be in regular contact with their team members, providing guidance and feedback. Some of the feedback is formalized in a performance management process. Once a year, managers and employees review the past year's performance against the objectives that had been set, and they establish new performance objectives for the coming year. Through discussions, managers also help employees identify training and development needs, and develop action plans to build on strengths, address weaknesses.

Today the plant is more productive, and employees have offered more than 10,000 ideas for improvements, saving the company £6 million. But morale is a concern to managers. Some workers resent the new pay arrangements. "I would like to see the camaraderie back. If people are happy, they are more efficient. If they are unhappy, they are not going to bother [making] suggestions," says Moss. Despite any morale problems, BMW planned to invest another $188 million to expand the Mini plant and create 200 new jobs. The goals are to boost Mini output from the current 189,000 units annually to more than 200,000 cars by 2007.

Questions

1. Using at least two of the different approaches to motivation described in this chapter, analyze the changes made at the plant. Which aspects of the pay scheme would be most motivating to *you*? Explain why.

2. Some workers are happy with the new pay arrangements, but many are not. What explains these different reactions?

3. As a manager at this plant, would you be concerned about morale given that production has improved? Explain.

©Digital Vision/Getty Images

chapter 15

Dynamics of Leadership

Learning Goals

After studying this chapter, you should be able to:

1. Explain what leadership means.

2. Describe the personal characteristics that enable leaders to be effective.

3. Describe the types of behaviors required for leadership.

4. Identify the contingencies that may shape how leaders behave.

5. State the key characteristics and behaviors of transformational leadership.

6. Describe how organizations develop leaders.

Communication Competency

Planning and Administration Competency

Teamwork Competency

Managing Effectively

Self-Management Competency

Strategic Action Competency

Multicultural Competency

Challenge of Managing

John W. Thompson, CEO of Symantec

© Justin Sullivan/Getty Images

Operating in more than 40 countries, Symantec provides a broad range of information security and storage products that make it easier for companies to manage their IT infrastructure. Under the leadership of CEO and Chairman John W. Thompson, Symantec has grown from a $632 million consumer antivirus company to an enterprise security player with $4.1 billion in annual sales. Today, almost every Fortune 500 firm uses Symantec products.

John W. Thompson grew up in Florida, where his mother was a teacher and his father was a postal worker. "My mom and dad believed very much in the concepts of working hard for what you want and making sure you're properly prepared for what your pursuits are," he recalls. After college, he went to work as a salesman for IBM. By the time he left—28 years later—people were thinking he might someday be CEO of IBM. Thompson didn't think that was likely to ever happen, however. Instead, he chose to become CEO of Symantec.

When Thompson arrived at Symantec, it was known mostly for its Norton AntiVirus program. The company was struggling financially and its business strategy was unclear. Everyone knew that change was needed if the company was to survive. With a reputation for taking calculated risks that paid off, Thompson seemed like a good choice to lead the company forward. Besides having good business skills, he also was known to be ambitious, likable, and very persuasive. For Thompson, the Symantec job offered a chance to be a true leader. "It's one thing to be a part of a great team, recognized as doing well in the industry. It's another to be a leader of the team trying to create an image for the company and its product," he explained.

Thompson quickly refocused Symantec on its data security business. He sold or shut down several units and replaced more than half of the company's original 2,300 employees, including most top managers. Within three years, he was being recognized as one of the country's best managers, and *BlackEngineer.com* listed him as one of the 50 Most Important African-Americans in Technology. Subsequently, one of Thompson's biggest tests as a leader involved the acquisition and integration of Veritas Software. In addition to persuading

Learning Content

investors that the combination made sense, he led the company through significant change: The merger doubled the size of his company. Experts viewed the deal as risky, and Thompson faced a lot of difficult questioning. But he believed the company was well prepared for the change and eventually succeeded in convincing critics that the potential payoff would be significant. Thompson's leadership was a big factor in persuading investors to support the deal. "When it comes down to it, I really believe in the guy," said one.

During this challenging time, Thompson's confidence and resolve served him well. "He did not back off [for] one moment on everything he said about Veritas and the need and the value of that acquisition, despite the pressure that he was under," observed Bruce Chizen, CEO of Adobe in San Jose, who met Thompson through a Silicon Valley CEO peer group. "He did not cave. The leadership he demonstrated under difficult circumstances was admirable." In fact, Chizen was so impressed with Thompson's leadership skills that he later sought Thompson's advice and support. "I continue to ask him to share with me his experience, and that has helped me form my own opinions on how to move ahead with Macromedia," Chizen says. "I learned a great deal from the experiences he had." Today, Symantec's strategy focuses on providing sophisticated software to protect against threats introduced by e-mail, instant messaging, voice-over-Internet technology, and online collaboration.

As a leader, Thompson's style is friendly and easygoing. He's a good storyteller, and the kind of person people describe as charismatic. Based on three decades of business experience, Thompson thinks he understands what it takes to be a good leader. Besides being able to work with numbers, he says, leaders need personal integrity and a relentless focus on people. Leaders also need to take time to rest and reflect. "You cannot run 24/7, 365 days a year. You need to take time to enjoy the fruits of your labors." Thompson tries to keep a healthy balance between working hard and having fun. He enjoys fine wines, home cooking, fast cars, horseback riding, and hunting. He likes to host so-called Bordeaux-and-Barbecue dinners, where he might serve ribs and beans with a $500 bottle of Bordeaux wine. When asked how others can achieve what he has achieved, Thompson points to the important role of mentors. Reflecting on his own experience, he observed: "I had the belief that if I could produce good results, the rest would take care of itself. But along the way, I also was fortunate enough to have support from some really well-placed people who took an interest in my career. . . . Success is a combination of hard work and a good support structure that helps to get you going, but it's determination along the way that keeps you moving along. I had enough of all of those to get me where I am today."

With his own future secure, Thompson has begun spending more of his time encouraging young African Americans to pursue engineering careers. He takes this responsibility personally, inviting young talent to his home and treating them to a barbecue. Periodically he also coaches students at Florida A&M University, his alma mater.[1]

To learn more about this company, visit www.symantec.com.

The Meaning of Leadership

Explain what leadership means.

When people think of "leaders," they often think of famous people in positions of power, like John Thompson and other CEOs. But not all leaders are as famous and powerful as the CEOs of America's largest companies. Leaders can be found at all levels of an organization and in all spheres of life. Although we focus here on leaders in business, much of what has been learned about leadership has come from observations and research on political leaders, religious leaders, and even students. Leadership *is an influence relationship between leaders and followers who strive for real change and outcomes that reflect their shared purposes.*[2] It takes many forms and can be used for a wide variety of purposes.

Bases of Influence

Managers can use many means to influence subordinates. They often use the authority of their *formal position* to influence subordinates. As CEO, John Thompson clearly can use his formal position to influence Symantec employees to do as he wishes. He and other managers in the company also use *rewards* to influence subordinates. As we described in Chapter 14, appropriate use of rewards is an effective way to direct employee's attention and motivate them to do their best work.

Some managers also use *coercion* to influence subordinates. These managers obtain compliance by creating fear, and generally are not considered to be good bosses to have. Most leaders realize that using coercion to gain compliance is not a sound approach. When Stanley O'Neal, CEO of Merrill Lynch, was asked whether it is better for a leader to be loved or feared, he said "No right-thinking person wants to be feared. Fear is a negative emotion. It is one that inhibits performance. Who wants to be feared? I think it is better to be respected."[3]

Expertise is another source of influence that managers can use. If subordinates believe their managers have more knowledge or technical skill than they do, they will accept the manager's view more easily.

Finally, leaders can influence others through personal *charisma*. John Thompson is a charismatic leader. Later in this chapter, we return to the role of charisma in effective leadership.

The means that leaders use to influence others determines their effectiveness. Figure 15.1 on the following page illustrates how employees are likely to respond to each type of influence tactic.[4] Coercion often results in employee resistance. Rewards and legitimate influence usually result in compliance, but may not create feelings of strong commitment.

Leaders who use their expertise and charisma to influence followers are most effective in creating a sense of commitment. Steve Jobs, CEO of Apple Computer, is a leader who relies on both charisma and expertise. Using his expertise in electronics and design, he takes personal responsibility for what Apple makes and how the products look and feel. Through charisma, he keeps his employees motivated to aspire for perfection even when they seem to be underdogs in the computer wars. Later in this chapter, we will discuss charismatic leaders in more detail.

Shared Purposes

Effective leaders understand that they need to do more than simply convince people to follow them. They strive to create a vision that reflects the concerns and aspirations of the people with whom they work. When a leader and his or her staff and colleagues have shared purposes, each can count on the other to act in ways that move everyone toward the common goal.[5]

Figure 15.1 | **How Followers Respond to the Influence Tactics of Leaders**

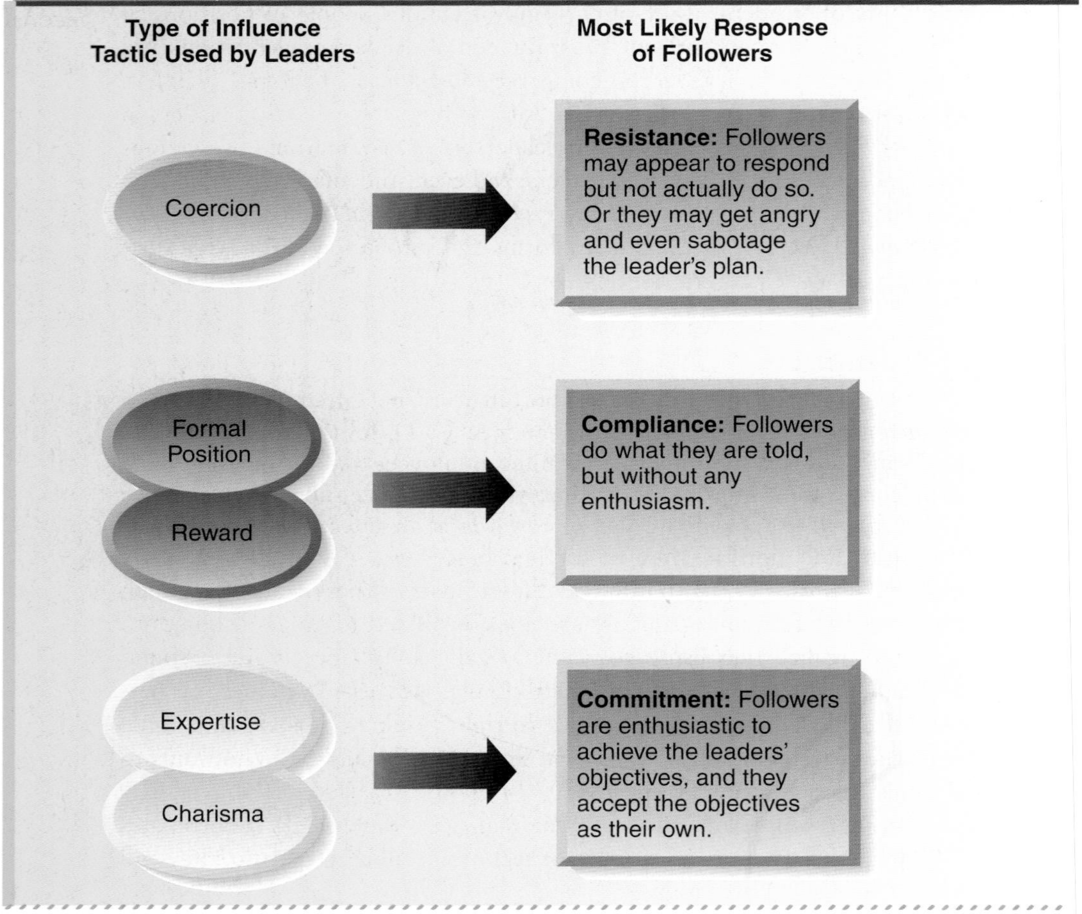

Type of Influence Tactic Used by Leaders

Most Likely Response of Followers

Coercion

Resistance: Followers may appear to respond but not actually do so. Or they may get angry and even sabotage the leader's plan.

Formal Position

Reward

Compliance: Followers do what they are told, but without any enthusiasm.

Expertise

Charisma

Commitment: Followers are enthusiastic to achieve the leaders' objectives, and they accept the objectives as their own.

Creating Change

Change is the third key element in our definition of leadership. As described in Chapter 12, the need for change seems to be constant in modern organizations. At Symantec, John Thompson has been leading his organization through a series of changes ever since becoming CEO. The changes began when he redefined the company's strategy, and since then they have continued as employees execute the new strategy. At Symantec, restructuring, downsizing, and mergers have all been sources of significant change.

Kenneth Chenault, CEO of American Express, is another leader who has been effective at leading his company through significant change. As the new CEO in 2001, he worked with the outgoing CEO and chairman of the board, Harvey Golub, to develop a new growth strategy for the company's future. The plan called for expanding the company's card network through banks and financial institutions; expanding its financial and investment services; and increasing its market share in specialty segments, including small businesses and overseas markets. Executing this strategy has meant transforming the company in a variety of ways. One major change involved reducing the workforce by 15 percent. Another change involved putting technology at the center of the company's business. Yet another change required envisioning a whole new market. In the years since Chenault took the helm, the company has arranged deals with luxury apartment buildings in New York City to allow customers to charge their monthly rent and earn reward points while they're at it. The vision now is to make it possible to use the American Express card for everything that you buy, especially big-ticket items that generate significant fees. To make it easy,

Chenault has invested in the development of a new system called ExpressPay. Customers just wave a small device across a reader and the payment process is finished. Since being introduced, this new technology has begun to spread elsewhere. Leading change seems to be one of Chenault's greatest strengths. Chenault understands that his role is to help employees understand his vision and what it means for them. "Leaders must focus an organization on facing reality. Then they give them the confidence and support to inspire them to change that reality," he says.[6]

In the remainder of this chapter, we present various leadership models that explain and prescribe how effective leaders influence others. There is no single or simple answer to which leadership approach works best. We have grouped the models into four main categories: personal characteristics, behavioral, contingency, and transformational. Each model provides some useful insights into what effective leadership involves. After explaining these models, we describe how organizations and individuals can develop their leadership capabilities.

Personal Characteristics of Effective Leaders

2.
Describe the personal characteristics that enable leaders to be effective.

The personal characteristics of leaders are the relatively stable attributes that make each person unique, including their physical, social, and psychological traits. A person can change some of his or her personal characteristics, but it is not easy. Taken together, personal characteristics generally result in fairly predictable behavior over time and in various situations. Personal characteristics also create images in the minds of other people, and some of these images fit the stereotype of an effective leader.[7]

In recent years, the term *emotional intelligence* has received much attention for describing the personal characteristics of effective leaders.[8] Emotional intelligence *is a set of abilities that enable individuals to recognize and understand their own and others' feelings and emotions and to use these insights to guide their own thinking and actions.*[9] Emotional intelligence may be affected by some aspects of our physiology. Not everyone is capable of being a mathematical genius, and not everyone can reach the highest levels of emotional intelligence. On the other hand, emotional intelligence is not fixed at birth. It develops over a period of many years as a person encounters various experiences and matures. Because emotional intelligence takes so long to develop, it is not easy for adults to change this aspect of their personal makeup.

As shown in Figure 15.2 on the following page, emotional intelligence has four components—two that refer to awareness and two that address action. The model also recognizes two referents of awareness and action—one's self (e.g., the leader) and others (e.g., the followers).

Self-Awareness

The first component of emotional intelligence is self-awareness. Self awareness *is the ability to recognize and understand your moods, emotions, and drives, as well as their impact on others.* To be effective as a leader, one must "know thyself"—that includes the good, the bad, and the ugly! Self-aware people might know that social events create feelings of anxiety, and that deadlines make them short tempered. They also understand that those emotional reactions can have a negative impact on subordinates. Self-awareness also extends to understanding one's own motivation and goals. Self-aware people know what they want from their jobs and from life in general. They are honest with themselves and are able to see where two different goals may be in conflict with each other. They recognize that the desire to have it all can put stress on the people they care about most deeply.

© Rubberball Productions/Jupiter Images

True leaders are perceptive about themselves and others, and then use what they know to produce desired results.

Figure 15.2 | **Four Components of Emotional Intelligence**

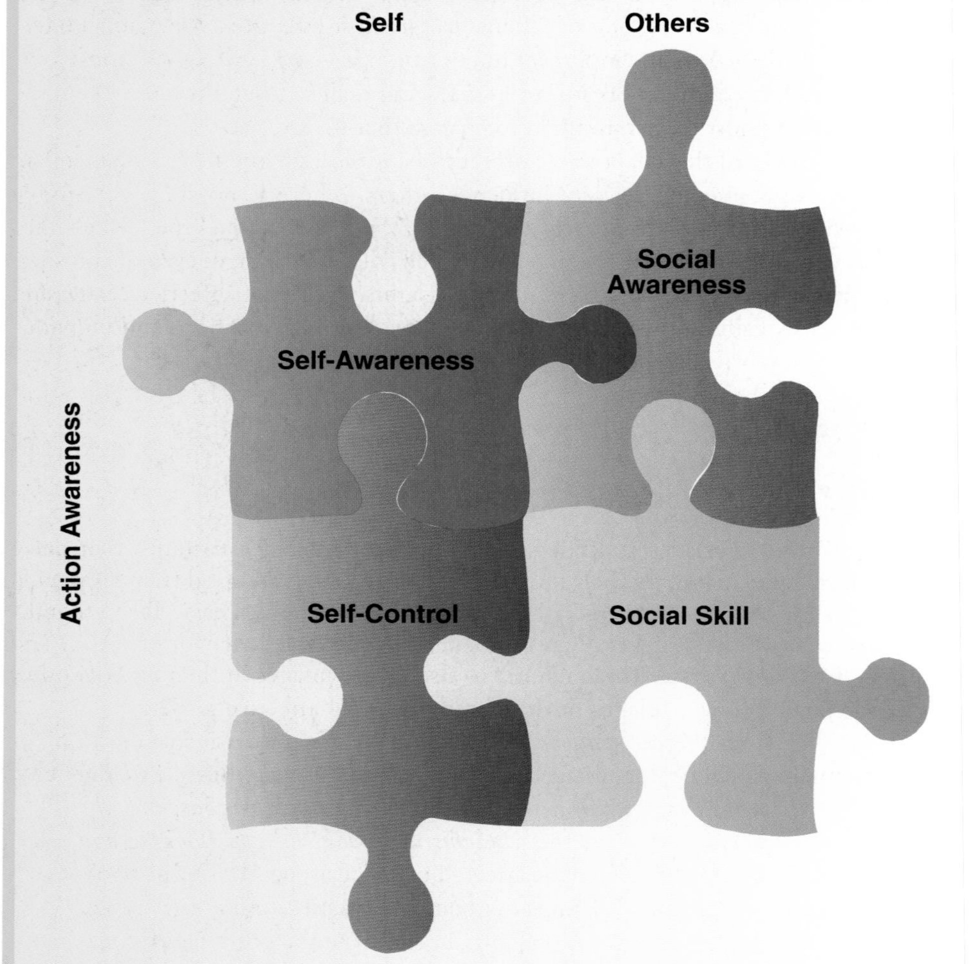

After receiving 360-degree feedback on her leadership style, Lorrie Browning, a general manager at U.S. Brands, developed deeper self-awareness. From the feedback, she learned that she had a blind spot around listening. "I know that I pay attention to everything, but I was received as not listening. I learned that I need to stop what I am doing, look a person in the eye and focus only on them when we talk."

Sylvia Montero developed self-awareness at an early age, and it continues to serve her well today as an executive at Pfizer, the pharmaceutical company. Montero's self-awareness is one of the things that help her stay motivated and confident that she can meet the challenges she faces as a senior leader. Her experiences are described in the Self-Management Competency feature.[10]

Self-Management Competency

Sylvia Montero of Pfizer

Growing up on a farm in Puerto Rico seems like a tough way to start out life, but as a young child, Sylvia Montero didn't feel it was a burden: "We were poor," she said. "We just didn't know it." At the age of eight, she and her family moved to New York City. It was then that she first realized she was poor, and it was then that she began to see herself as a member of an ethnic minority group. Her childhood experiences did little to help her develop a sense of self-confidence. "Children internalize subtle messages. I had a sense that I couldn't compete with people who were more prosperous," she recalled. But Montero did well in high school and her abilities were recognized by others.

As a high school student, Montero had the benefit of an effective mentor—the high school counselor who encouraged her to attend college and helped her apply for financial assistance. A full scholarship paid for her college tuition. Nevertheless, she had to live at home and commute by subway to school. She married in her freshman year and became a mother as a sophomore. "I lived between two worlds," she said, "a co-ed by day and a married mother who lived in a drug-infested tenement by night." She was still poor, and that's when she realized things had to change. "I chose to actively participate in what happened to me." After a divorce, she returned to Puerto Rico and taught literature for several years.

When a job at a small pharmaceutical firm became available, she jumped at the chance to start a new career. She stayed with that small company for 15 years, and during that time both she and the company grew. She had "numerous opportunities for growth. I traveled around the world and had the chance to live abroad, including China, where I set up the company's first HR function." Moving up the corporate ladder, she was often the first female or first Hispanic in the job. She recalls being deeply aware of being a minority, and that concern often held her back. But her self-awareness also served to keep her motivated to press on. "I purposely decided that I was not going to allow it to be an obstacle."

When Pfizer eventually bought the company, Montero stayed on. To help her meet the new challenges she faced, she began to work with a management coach, and has continued to work with this person for several years. She describes her coach as a "thinking partner, someone who challenges me and helps me work through strategies," she said. To stay up with the demands of her job, she also asks a lot of questions and does a lot of listening. Today as a senior executive at Pfizer, Montero is responsible for the overall strategy and development of companywide human resource policies. As part of her job, she oversees leadership development for the company's 120,000 worldwide employees.

Have Montero's experiences changed her from the day she first arrived in New York City as a young child? "Yes, but not in the way you might think." Having once been poor, she thinks she probably takes more risks because she knows that even if she lost her job and the wealth that goes with it, "it wouldn't be scary because I have done without."

To learn more about Pfizer, visit *www.pfizer.com.*

Self-Control

Being aware of one's emotions and how they can affect others is essential to the development of emotional intelligence, but it is just the beginning. Emotional intelligence also requires an ability to control your emotions. Thus, the second component of emotional intelligence is self-control, *which is the ability to regulate and redirect one's own impulses, moods, and desires.* All of us experience negative moods and emotions. At times we feel frustrated and angry. At times our level of energy is low, and we may feel that the challenges ahead are almost overwhelming. Effective leaders are not immune from such feelings. But when these feelings arise, they do not let the feelings take control. Instead, they take control of their feelings and use them for constructive purposes. When they feel angry, emotionally intelligent leaders analyze the causes of the anger and look for ways to remove those causes. When they feel overwhelmed by the amount of work that must get done, emotionally intelligent leaders take time out to reflect on their commitment to the objectives they set out and rejuvenate their enthusiasm.

With help from Pfizer's management coach, Sylvia Montero challenged herself to improve her skills as a leader. She is now a senior executive for the company.

© Mark Lennihan/AP Photo

Social Awareness

So far, we have focused on how emotionally intelligent leaders view and control their own emotions. Next we consider how they attend to the emotional states and needs of others. Social awareness *is the ability to understand the emotional makeup of other people, and the skill to treat people according to their emotional reactions.* Just as they are able to recognize their own emotional reactions, emotionally intelligent leaders have empathy for the feelings of their followers. They can read the signs of distress on people's faces. They anticipate the feelings of anxiety that followers will experience as they encounter major changes at work—and their actions take these emotional reactions into account.

Social Skill

The final component of emotional intelligence is social skill. Social skill is not simply the ability to get along well with others, nor is it mere popularity. Social skill *is the ability to build interpersonal networks, manage relationships, find common ground, and build rapport.* Socially skilled leaders like John Thompson are generally well liked and have a wide circle of acquaintances, but they are not satisfied with just being a friend. They use their relationships with people to get everyone moving in the same direction, which results in better organizational performance.[11] They seem to have a knack for finding common ground. This doesn't just happen by luck. Socially skilled leaders use their emotional insights to understand people's concerns, motivations, feelings, and aspirations. This understanding, along with their ability for self-control, enables emotionally intelligent leaders to build collaborative relationships and effectively manage large teams of followers.[12]

Are you interested in assessing your own emotional intelligence? If so, complete the questionnaire given in the experiential exercise at the end of the chapter. Your scores will give you an estimate of how emotionally intelligent you think you are. Of course, other people may not agree with your self-assessment. When someone's emotional intelligence is assessed in a work setting, a neutral third party should conduct a 360-degree assessment to gain a more accurate view.

3.

Describe the types of behaviors required for leadership.

Leadership Behaviors

Behavioral models of leadership *focus on describing differences in the actions of effective and ineffective leaders.* They seek to identify and understand what leaders actually do.[13] Behavioral models of leadership assume that most people can learn to be effective leaders. Because effective behaviors can be learned, most individuals can become effective leaders with the proper encouragement and support.

Theory X and Theory Y

The behavior of leaders is often influenced by their assumptions and beliefs about followers and what motivates their followers. Thus, differences in the behaviors of effective and ineffective leaders can be understood by looking at the different assumptions they make. One of the most widely cited and recognized models for describing differences in these assumptions was developed by Douglas McGregor in 1957. He coined the labels "Theory X" and "Theory Y" as a way to contrast two sets of assumptions and beliefs held by leaders. Theory X and Theory Y managers both understand that they are responsible for the resources in their units—money, materials, equipment, and people—in the interest of achieving organizational goals. What draws them apart are their assumptions about what motivates their subordinates and what are the best ways to carry out management responsibilities. Figure 15.3 on the following page summarizes the beliefs and assumptions of leaders who subscribe to Theory X and those who subscribe to Theory Y.

Theory X. When McGregor developed his model of effective leadership, he knew many managers with the Theory X point of view. Theory X *is a composite of propositions*

Figure 15.3 | Assumptions Associated with Theory X and Theory Y

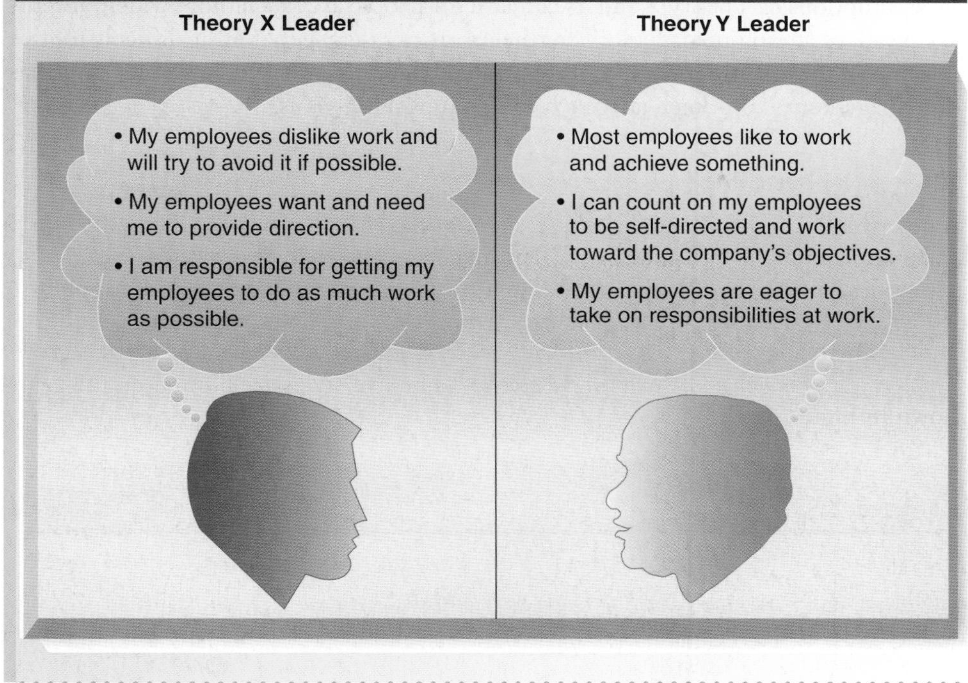

Theory X Leader

- My employees dislike work and will try to avoid it if possible.
- My employees want and need me to provide direction.
- I am responsible for getting my employees to do as much work as possible.

Theory Y Leader

- Most employees like to work and achieve something.
- I can count on my employees to be self-directed and work toward the company's objectives.
- My employees are eager to take on responsibilities at work.

and underlying beliefs that take a command-and-control view of management based on a negative view of human nature. Theory X managers view management as a process that involves directing, controlling, and modifying their subordinates' behaviors to fit the needs of the organization. They view employees as basically lazy and self-centered. This perspective assumes that, without the intervention of managers, most employees would be passive—even resistant—to organizational needs. Therefore, employees must be persuaded, rewarded, punished, and their activities tightly controlled. Doing so is management's primary task.[14]

McGregor believed that Theory X managers could be found everywhere in organizations, and that was a problem. According to him, management by direction and control was largely ineffective because it ignored the social, egoistic, and self-fulfillment needs of most employees.

Theory Y. McGregor concluded that a different view of managing employees was needed—one based on more adequate assumptions about human nature and human motivation. Theory Y *is a composite of propositions and beliefs that take a leadership and empowering view of management based on a positive view of human nature.* According to this view, employees are not *by nature* passive or resistant to organizational needs. They have become so as a result of their experiences in organizations. The motivation, the potential for development, the capacity for assuming responsibility, and the readiness to direct behavior toward organizational goals are all present in employees. Management does not put them there. It is management's responsibility to make it possible for people to recognize and develop these human characteristics for themselves.

Whereas Theory X managers attempt to gain control over their subordinates, Theory Y managers rely on the self-control and self-direction of their subordinates. Robert Eckert, CEO of Mattel, the toy company, is a Theory Y manager. "Workers are not dummies," he says. "They knew what had to be done [when the company was in trouble]. It was management that stood in the way. These are very hard workers," he says of his employees.

Snapshot

"People want to win. And if people think they've been given the capability to win and are with winners, that's how you get people in the game. People who want to build things and like who they work with will stay with us. If you like building stuff and you like who you work with, this is a pretty energizing place."
Jeffrey Immelt, CEO, General Electric

McGregor's descriptions of the Theory X and Theory Y perspectives spawned many new leadership models, concepts, and approaches. Compared to 50 years ago, the assumptions of Theory Y and its concern for people are much more widely accepted nowadays among managers. Nevertheless, many managers find it difficult to give up some of the assumptions that make up the Theory X perspective and its emphasis on management's top-down approach to accomplishing goals.

Managerial Grid

In describing Theory X and Theory Y assumptions, McGregor described only two leadership perspectives. He assumed that managers behaved according to the assumptions of Theory X *or* Theory Y; that is, managers could not hold both points of view. A decade later, Robert Blake and Jane Mouton elaborated a more complex model. The managerial grid *identifies five leadership styles that combine different degrees of concern for production and concern for people.*[15] The five styles are plotted on the grid shown in Figure 15.4.

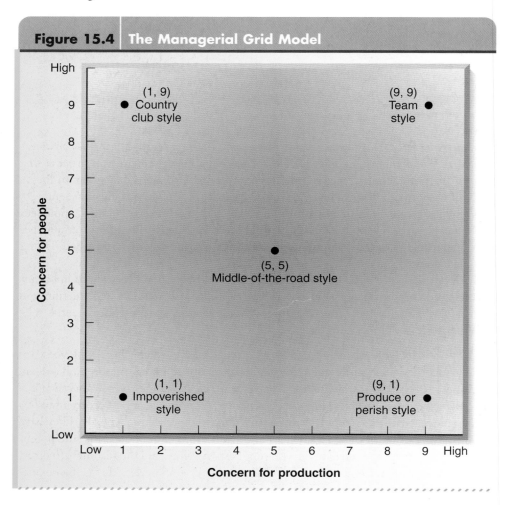

Figure 15.4 | **The Managerial Grid Model**

Impoverished. At the lower left-hand corner of the grid is the *impoverished style*, which is characterized by low concern for both people and production. The primary goal of managers who use this style is to stay out of trouble. They pass orders along to employees, go with the flow, and make sure that they can't be held accountable for mistakes. They exert the minimum effort required to get the work done and avoid being demoted or fired.

Country Club. At the upper left-hand corner of the grid is the *country club style*, which is characterized by a high concern for people and a low concern for production. Managers who use this style try to create a secure, comfortable atmosphere and trust that their subordinates will respond with high performance. Attention to the need for satisfying relationships leads to a friendly, if not necessarily productive, atmosphere and work tempo.

Produce or Perish. A high concern for production and a low concern for people are reflected in the *produce or perish style* at the lower right-hand corner of the grid. This style is consistent with Theory X. Managers who use this style don't consider employees' personal needs to be very relevant to achieving the organization's objectives. In addition to tying pay to performance, they use legitimate influence tactics to pressure subordinates to meet production goals. They believe that operational efficiency results from arranging the work so that employees merely have to follow orders. When a company's profitability is falling, showing more concern for production may seem like the best thing a manager can do to turn the company around.

Home Depot's CEO, Robert Nardelli, uses this command-and-control leadership style approach. Whereas the founders of Home Depot allowed managers to have a great deal of autonomy, Nardelli imposes his decisions on them. According to Joe DeAngelo, executive vice president of Home Depot Supply, "There's no question: Bob's the general." Nardelli feels his approach is appropriate for the company, which needs to improve its performance. But some members of the staff say this "culture of fear" is demoralizing for people. Although it may lead to improved efficiencies, the new culture at Home Depot could be a problem for Nardelli, who hopes to improve customer service in his stores.[16]

Middle of the Road. At the middle of the grid is the *middle-of-the-road style*. Managers who use this style believe that the needs of people and organizations are in conflict so it is difficult to satisfy both. The best one can do is to find an acceptable balance between workers' needs and the organization's productivity goals. Adequate performance is obtained by maintaining employee morale at a level sufficient to get an adequate amount of the work done.

Team. Finally, at the upper right-hand corner of the grid is the *team style*. It reflects high levels of concern for both people and production. Consistent with Theory Y, leaders who use this style attempt to establish teamwork and foster feelings of commitment among workers. By introducing a "common stake" in the organization's purpose, the leader builds relationships of trust and respect.

Mattel's Robert Eckert treats his workforce as a team. During his first six years as CEO, he had lunch with thousands of employees around the world as a way to learn their views. As often as possible when he visited a company facility he would go to the cafeteria and join a small group of 10 or so employees for lunch. Usually, the employees had been invited in advance to represent the diverse jobs and backgrounds of the workforce. Eckert used these meetings for his own learning, and also to encourage employees to take ownership in transforming the company.[17]

Behavioral models have added to the understanding and practice of leadership. The focus has grown from who leaders *are* (personal characteristics) to what leaders *do* (behaviors). However, leadership behaviors that are effective in one situation aren't necessarily effective in another. Certainly there are some cross-cultural differences in the behavior of effective leaders. For example, North American employees generally prefer leaders

©Image Source/Jupiter Images

The managerial grid identifies multiple styles of management. The team approach seems to be a popular model in corporate environments, as well as others.

who give their followers great autonomy, but in China leaders who delegate too much are viewed as less competent.[18] Even within the United States, the same set of leader behaviors is not equally effective in all situations. Because behavioral models of leadership failed to uncover leadership styles that were effective in all situations, more complex models of leadership emerged. The next stage in the evolution of knowledge about leadership was the creation of contingency models.

Contingencies for Leadership Behavior

4.

Identify the contingencies that may shape how leaders behave.

According to contingency models of leadership, *situational factors determine the best style of leadership to use.*[19] These models assume that leaders can change the way they behave from one situation to the next. Effective leaders choose the behaviors that are most effective in a given situation. Leonard Shaeffer, former CEO of BlueCross of California, understands the importance of contingencies for leadership behavior. Looking back over his 30-year career, he made the following observations:

> I've come to understand that leadership is about more than heavy-handed action from the top. Its defining characteristics change according to the needs and vagaries of the individual, the organization, the industry, and the world at large. In other words, leadership is . . . a journey. There aren't always sharp lines between one style of leadership and another—an autocratic leader sometimes has to be participative, and a reformer sometimes has to act like an autocrat. But by thinking clearly about the different roles I've needed to assume at different times, I've been able to tailor the way I make decisions, communicate with people, and manage my time so that I can address the most pressing needs of the organization at the moment.[20]

As Schaeffer realized, several factors in situations may determine the best leadership style to use. No single contingency model of leadership addresses all of these situational factors in detail. Here we discuss two contingency models of leadership. The first model we discuss considers only one situational contingency, while the second model considers many more.

Situational Leadership® Model

The Situational Leadership® Model *states that the style of leadership used should be matched to the level of readiness of the followers.*[21] Like other contingency models of leadership, this one contains three basic components: a set of several possible leadership styles, a description of several alternative situations that leaders might encounter, and recommendations for which leadership styles are most effective in each situation.

Leadership Styles. According to the model, leaders can choose from among four leadership styles. These four leadership styles involve various combinations of task behavior and relationship behavior. Task behavior is similar to showing concern for production, and relationship behavior is similar to showing concern for people, as described in the managerial grid. More specifically, task behavior *includes using one-way communication, spelling out duties, and telling followers what to do and where, when, and how to do it.* Effective leaders might use a high degree of task behavior in some situations and only a moderate amount in other situations. Relationship behavior *includes using two-way communication, listening, encouraging, and involving followers in decision making, and giving emotional support.* Again, an effective leader may sometimes use a high degree of relationship behavior, and at other times use less. By combining different amounts of task behavior with different amounts of relationship behavior, effective leaders use four different leadership styles. The four leadership styles are called telling, selling, participating, and delegating. These styles are shown in Figure 15.5.[22]

Figure 15.5 | The Situational Leadership® Model

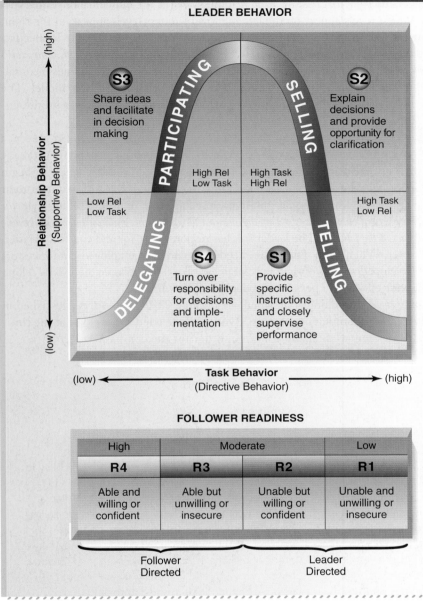

LEADER BEHAVIOR

FOLLOWER READINESS

High	Moderate		Low
R4	R3	R2	R1
Able and willing or confident	Able but unwilling or insecure	Unable but willing or confident	Unable and unwilling or insecure

Follower Directed   Leader Directed

Source: P. Hersey, K. H. Blanchard, and D. E. Johnson. *Management of Organizational Behavior: Leading Human Resources*, 8th ed. (Upper Saddle River, NJ: Prentice Hall, 2001), 182. Copyright © 2001, Center for Leadership Studies, Escondido, CA. Used with permission.

Situational Contingency. According to this model, leaders should consider the situation before deciding which leadership style to use. The situational contingency in this model is the degree of follower readiness. Readiness *is a follower's ability to set high but attainable task-related goals and a willingness to accept responsibility for reaching them.* Readiness is not a fixed characteristic of followers—it depends on the task. The same group of followers may have a high degree of readiness for some tasks, but a low degree of readiness for others. The readiness level of followers depends on how much training they have received, how committed they are to the organization, their technical expertise, experience with the specific task, and so on.

Choosing a Leadership Style. As Figure 15.5 shows, the appropriate leadership style depends on the level of follower readiness. The curve running through the graph indicates the leadership style that best fits each readiness level of the individual or team. Note that high readiness levels appear on the left and low readiness levels appear on the right.

For followers who are low in readiness (R1, shown in red), a telling style is effective. In using a telling style, *the leader provides clear instructions, gives specific directions, and supervises the work closely.* When employees first enter an organization, their readiness is usually low, so the telling leadership style is most appropriate according to this model. The telling style helps ensure that new employees perform well, which provides a solid foundation for their success and satisfaction.

As employees learn their jobs and their readiness increases (R2, shown in green), a leader needs to continue using some task behavior because the employees aren't yet ready to assume total responsibility for doing their jobs. In addition, a leader needs to begin using supportive behaviors in order to build employees' confidence and maintain their enthusiasm. That is, the leader should shift to use a selling style. In using a selling style *the leader provides direction, encourages two-way communication, and helps build confidence and motivation on the part of the follower.* The leader still has responsibility for and controls decision making, however. When John Thompson needed to convince employees and investors that he had developed an appropriate new strategic plan for Symantec, he used a selling style and was very effective in persuading people to follow his lead.

Andrea Jung used the selling style when she became CEO of Avon. As described in the Communication Competency feature, Avon really needed a makeover at the time, and Jung felt she knew what changes were in order for the company.[23]

Communication Competency

Andrea Jung, CEO of Avon

It may be hard to believe, but when Andrea Jung became CEO of Avon in 1999, she was the first woman to head this 115-year-old company, whose workforce is almost all female. The company was in deep financial trouble at the time. The stock price had plummeted and people were questioning whether the company's business model of door-to-door sales had become obsolete. Within two years, the stock price, revenues, and profits were all growing again. Since then, the company has continued to evolve. Today, 70 percent of Avon representatives do some of their business online—something that was unheard of when Jung became CEO. At the same time, Avon continues to build its face-to-face business. Jung estimates that there is an Avon representative present in over 80 percent of the business offices in the United States. She had proved that an Avon Lady could also be a world-class leader overseeing a business that spans 50 countries.

It was Jung's experience as an Avon Lady that helped her understand the company's problems and know how to fix them. Those experiences also gave her plenty of opportunity to hone her ability to communicate effectively and persuade others to take the actions she wanted them to take. After mapping out a turnaround plan, Jung began selling it to Wall Street analysts, her board, and her employees. The plan included cutting costs by hundreds of millions of dollars, developing new blockbuster products, and launching a new line of business. At first, analysts seemed to doubt the plan would work. When an initiative to sell Avon products through retail stores stumbled, Jung didn't blink. She kept selling her ideas: "I'm not changing any of our thinking. This turnaround is far from complete." One successful change involved an idea that had been kicked around for years at the company, but no one else had ever sold it as well as Jung did. Referred to as "Leadership," the initiative was designed to grow the ranks of sales reps by providing rewards to reps who recruited new reps.

Today, no one questions Jung's leadership style. Avon has regained its footing and remains the world's largest direct seller. Year after year, this $8 billion company receives widespread recognition for its excellence, being named a Most Admired Company, one of the Best Companies to Work For, a Top 100 Global Brand, and one of the 100 Best Corporate Citizens, among others.

To learn more about this organization, visit *www.avon.com*.

When followers feel confident performing their tasks and are ready to do so (R3, shown in purple), the leader no longer needs to be directive. The leader maintains open communication by actively listening and assisting in followers' efforts to use what they have learned. In using a participating style, *the leader encourages followers to share ideas and facilitates the work by being encouraging and helpful to subordinates.*

Ann Mulcahy, CEO of Xerox, uses a participating style. As described in Chapter 1, Mulcahy led Xerox through a major transformation. When she became CEO, one of her tasks was to cut costs quickly. She believed employees had a great deal of useful knowledge that could be used to cut costs and improve the organization's effectiveness. When Xerox got ready to cut costs, Mulcahy made sure everyone understood that cost reductions were needed and then she challenged everyone to look for cost-cutting opportunities. "You can never depend on filtering information up through the company," she says. "You have to talk to front-line employees. The bottom line is that it's all about getting your people aligned around a common set of objectives. At Xerox, that was the difference between success and failure." Together, Mulcahy and her employees succeeded in cutting the costs of operations as well as the cost of Xerox products, putting the company back on the road to profitability.[24]

Andrea Jung's persistant selling style has made this former Avon lady a successful CEO.

Finally, for employees at a high level of readiness (R4, shown in blue), effective leadership involves more delegation. In using a delegating style, *the leader turns over responsibility for making and implementing decisions to followers.* Delegating is effective in this situation because followers are both competent and motivated to take full responsibility for their work. Even though the leader may still identify problems, the responsibility for carrying out plans is given to these mature followers. They are permitted to manage projects and decide how, when, and where tasks are to be done. Carlos Ghosn, CEO of Nissan Motors, uses a delegating style with his top-level executives. He spends only one week a month at Nissan headquarters and one week a month at Renault headquarters. The other two weeks he travels around the world to other plant locations. Members of his team may see him for as little as one hour a month. Most of the time, he leaves them to make and implement decisions on their own.

Assessment. The Situational Leadership® Model helps leaders recognize that the same leadership style may be effective in some situations but not others. Furthermore, it highlights the importance of considering the followers' readiness level when choosing a leadership style. It has generated quite a bit of interest among practitioners and researchers.[25] The idea that leaders should be flexible with respect to the leadership style they use is appealing. An inexperienced employee may perform as well as an experienced employee if properly directed and closely supervised. An appropriate leadership style should also help followers gain more experience and become more competent. Thus, as a leader helps followers develop higher levels of readiness, the leader's style also needs to evolve. Therefore, this model requires the leader to be constantly monitoring the readiness level of followers in order to determine the combination of task and relationship behaviors that is most appropriate.

Like other contingency models, this one assumes that managers can accurately assess each situation and change their leadership styles to match different situations. Some people can read situations and adapt their leadership style more effectively than others. For those who can't, what are the costs of training them to be able to do so? Do these costs exceed the potential benefits? Before an organization adopts a management training program to teach managers to use this model of leadership, they need to answer questions such as those just posed.

Vroom–Jago Leadership Model

We next consider another contingency model of leadership—one that is even more complex. Like other contingency models, this one states that leaders should evaluate a set of situational factors and then decide how to behave. The Vroom–Jago model also recognizes that various leadership styles have different costs and benefits associated with them. Some styles of leadership may save time and money in the short run, but in doing so they are less effective for developing followers. Others styles have the longer term benefit of being more effective for developing followers, but they require more resources (e.g., time) in the short term. The Vroom–Jago leadership model *states that leaders should choose among five leadership styles based on seven contingency variables, while also recognizing the time requirements and other costs associated with each style.*[26]

Leadership Styles. The focus of this model is on how leaders involve a team of followers when making decisions. This model identifies five basic leadership styles. These five leadership styles represent different ways in which leaders can involve the team members when making work-related decisions. Keep in mind that none of the five approaches to decision making is best under all circumstances. These five styles that leaders can choose among are as follows:

▶ **Decide style**—*The leader makes the decision and either announces or sells it to the team.* The leader may use his or her expertise and/or collect information from the team or others whom the leader believes can help solve the problem. The role of employees is clearly one of providing specific information that the leader requests, rather than generating or evaluating solutions.

▶ **Consult individually style**—*The leader presents the problem to team members individually, getting their ideas and suggestions without bringing them together as a group, and then makes the decision.* This decision may or may not reflect the team members' influence.

▶ **Consult team style**—*The leader presents the problem to team members in a meeting, gets their suggestions, and then makes the decision.* This decision may or may not reflect the team members' suggestions.

▶ **Facilitate style**—*The leader presents the problem to the team in a meeting and acts as a facilitator, defining the problem to be solved and the constraints within which the decision must be made.* The goal is to get concurrence on a decision. Above all, the leader takes care to ensure that his or her ideas are not given any greater weight than those of others simply because of position on the team. The leader's role is much like that of chairperson, coordinating the discussion, keeping it focused on the problem, and being sure that all the essential issues are discussed. The leader doesn't try to influence the team to adopt a particular solution and is willing to accept and implement any solution that the entire team supports.

▶ **Delegate style**—*The leader permits the team to make the decision within prescribed limits.* The team undertakes the identification and diagnosis of the problem, developing alternative procedures for solving it and deciding on

Snapshot

"To retain and attract the best people, it's necessary to provide them with autonomy and independence to make decisions. When people are spending all of their time writing up reports on their activity, we lose a lot of their productivity."

Charles (Ed) Haldeman, CEO, Putnam Investments

one or more alternative solutions. The leader doesn't enter into the team's deliberations unless explicitly asked, but behind the scenes plays an important role, providing needed resources and encouragement. This style represents the highest level of subordinate discretion and participation.

Situational Contingencies. The Vroom–Jago leadership model includes seven contingency factors that leaders should assess before choosing which leadership style to use. The situational factors to be considered by leaders are as follows:

▶ *Decision significance*—How important is the technical quality of this decision?

▶ *Importance of commitment*—How important is it for followers to be committed to the decision? Can the decision be implemented even if followers don't agree that it is the best decision?

▶ *Leader expertise*—Does the leader have the relevant information and competencies to understand the problem fully and select the best solution?

▶ *Likelihood of commitment*—If the leader makes the decision, will followers trust the leader's judgment? Would they be committed to implementing a decision made by the leader?

▶ *Team support*—Do the followers share the goals to be achieved by solving this problem? Are the followers' interests aligned with those of the organization as a whole?

▶ *Team expertise*—Does the leader believe that followers have the abilities and information to make a high-quality decision?

▶ *Team competence*—Are the followers capable of handling their own decision-making process?

Choosing a Leadership Style. The matrix shown in Figure 15.6 on the following page integrates the model's seven situational contingencies with its five leadership styles.[27] In effect, the matrix represents a decision tree. The column headings identify each situational contingency that may or may not be present. The process of deciding which leadership style to use begins with the leader evaluating the significance of the problem—high (H) or low (L). Proceeding across the matrix, the leader records an H or L for only those contingencies that call for a judgment, until the recommended leadership style is reached.

To illustrate how you would use the tree, imagine you are in the following situation[28]:

You are the newly appointed director of a repertory theater company, with full responsibility for the financial and artistic health of the organization. You were a drama major in college and have 20 years of acting and directing experience. Your understanding of financial issues is fairly good because you recently spent a year heading up a task force charged with developing a long-term strategy that will ensure the theater company's long-term financial viability. Shortly after the task force disbanded, the former director left the company and you replaced her. The four other members of your management team, who all report to you, are in charge of production, marketing, development, and administration. In addition, the theater company employs about 30 artists with a variety of special skills. They are a talented and very committed team. You have been implementing various suggestions of the task force and things seem to be going relatively well. You face one big problem, however. Production and labor costs have been rising faster than you expected. And audience size has been somewhat smaller than you expected. You believe the weak economy has kept some people from buying tickets. Because your mission is to serve the

Figure 15.6 Model for Determining an Appropriate Decision-Making Style

PROBLEM STATEMENT	Decision Significance?	Importance of Commitment?	Leader Expertise?	Likelihood of Commitment?	Team Support?	Team Expertise?	Team Competence?	
	H	H	H	H	—	—	—	Decide
				L	H	H	H	Delegate
							L	
						L	—	Consult (Group)
					L	—	—	
		H	L	H	H	H	H	Facilitate
							L	
						L	—	Consult (Individually)
					L	—	—	
				L	H	H	H	Facilitate
							L	
						L	—	Consult (Group)
					L	—	—	
		L	H	—	—	—	—	Decide
			L	—	H	H	H	Facilitate
							L	
						L	—	Consult (Individually)
					L	—	—	
	L	H	—	H	—	—	—	Decide
				L	—	—	H	Delegate
							L	Facilitate
		L	—	—	—	—	—	Decide

Source: Reprinted from *Organizational Dynamics,* Spring 2000, Vol. 28, Victor H. Vroom, Leadership and the Decision-Making Process, 62–94, © 2000, with permission from Elsevier.

community, you've kept ticket prices low despite the rising costs. You need to decide what to do in order to resolve this situation.

Using the matrix shown in Figure 15.6, you might proceed as follows:

1. First, you consider the significance of the decision. You rate it as highly important.

2. Next, you consider whether it is important that your management feel committed to whatever solution you choose. You feel that their commitment is essential.

3. You evaluate your expertise. Before the problem arose, you thought it was pretty high, but now you feel much less confident. You rate your expertise as somewhat low.

4. Now you consider whether it is likely that people would accept your decision if they were not involved in formulating the solution. You conclude the likelihood is low.

5. The next question to consider is whether your management team is strongly committed to the mission and goals of the theater. You know that they are very committed, so you rate this as high.

6. You consider next the issue of how much expertise is present among the members of your management team. You rate their expertise as quite high. Each has different skills, but they all have many years of experience working in their professions.

7. Finally, you consider how well your management team works together. Your top managers actually do not work well together. There have been many conflicts during the past several months, and the team has been unable to resolve them. They all have very strong views and have not learned to collaborate and compromise when needed. You rate team competence as low.

Having evaluated these seven situational factors, you can see that the recommended decision style is the consult team style. That is, you should present the problem to the team, have them offer suggestions, and then make a decision. You may have two or three team meetings as you narrow down the options, but everyone understands that you will make the final decision. You will not delegate the problem and expect the management team to resolve the problem on its own.

To make it easier for leaders to use this matrix, Victor Vroom developed a computer program called Expert System. The program records the leader's judgments about each of the seven situational contingencies using a five-point rating scale. The program then uses these ratings to recommend the best leadership style.

Prioritizing Costs and Benefits. The matrix shown in Figure 15.6 should be used by leaders who are concerned about making decisions under time pressure. The matrix is designed to help leaders make a decision of acceptable quality with the maximum speed. Leaders often must make decisions when time is of the essence. For example, a decision about whether or not to purchase a particular software package may need to be made quickly because an attractive low price is being offered for only a short time. Should the leader act alone and make a very quick decision? Or, consult the team first and then decide? Or, delegate the decision and let the team decide on its own? When choosing a leadership style for this decision, the speed of the decision will be given high priority because there is a penalty for not deciding quickly enough.

Speed is not always the most important consideration when making decisions, however. Other priorities may be more important in some situations. For example, when there is less time pressure, a leader may give more priority to choosing a style that has the benefit of developing the followers. By using a more participative style, a leader can develop the technical and managerial competencies of employees, build teamwork, foster loyalty and commitment to organizational goals, and more effectively use the talents of a diverse team to find creative solutions to problems.[29] Here we have discussed in detail only the time-driven decision matrix. Other matrices are also available for leaders to use. Thus, a leader who wishes to give greater priority to developing followers could use a matrix for choosing the best style when development is of more concern than speed.

Assessment. If leaders can diagnose contingencies correctly, choosing the best leadership style for those situations becomes easier. These choices, in turn, will enable them to make high-quality, timely decisions. If the situation requires delegation, the leader must learn how to establish the desired goals and limitations and then let employees determine how best to achieve the goals within those limitations. If the situation calls for the leader alone to make the decision, the leader should be aware of potential positive and negative consequences of not asking others for their input.[30]

This model does have limitations. First, most American employees have a strong desire to participate in decisions affecting their jobs, regardless of the model's recommendation of a leadership style. If subordinates aren't involved in a decision, they are more likely to become frustrated and not be committed to the decision. In China, Mexico, and other countries, this desire to participate may not be as strong due to different cultural values. Second, certain competencies of the leader play a key role in determining the relative effectiveness of the model. In situations involving conflict, for example, only leaders skilled in conflict resolution may be able to use the kind of participative decision-making strategy suggested by the model.[31] A leader who hasn't developed this competency may obtain better results with a more directive style, even though this style is different from the style that the model proposes. The importance of having the right competencies in place may be one reason why senior executives tend to involve their staff in decision-making processes much more than do lower level supervisors and managers.[32]

5.

State the key characteristics and behaviors of transformational leadership.

Transformational Leadership

The leaders of some organizations have increasingly realized that leadership is more than a matter of personal characteristics, specific behaviors, or particular contingencies. It is all of those things, and much more. The people needed to guide organizations through needed changes are often called transformational leaders.

Transformational leaders *inspire others with their vision, often promote this vision over opposition, and demonstrate confidence in themselves and their views.*[33] They take an active and personal approach to influencing others. Transformational leaders alter the feelings, desires, and expectations of others.[34] They change perceptions of the possible and desirable. These leaders develop new approaches to long-standing problems and new options to open issues. Transformational leaders reflect excitement and enthusiasm and generate the same in others. They embrace risks to pursue new opportunities. They are empathetic and intuitive in their ability to relate with others and, in general, are high in emotional intelligence. As a result, they are highly trusted and their organizations perform better.[35]

Figure 15.7 outlines the interrelated characteristics and behaviors of transformational leaders. Each transformational leader is a unique mosaic of these characteristics. Each transformational leader may be stronger in terms of some characteristics than others, but all are likely to be present.[36]

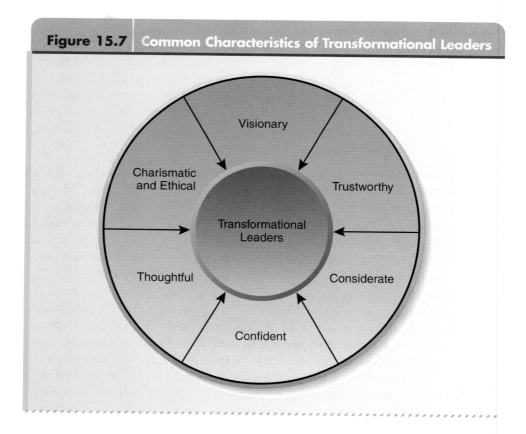

Figure 15.7 | **Common Characteristics of Transformational Leaders**

Visionary

Charismatic and Ethical

Trustworthy

Transformational Leaders

Thoughtful

Considerate

Confident

Visionary

Perhaps the dominant characteristic that transformational leaders possess is their ability to create a *vision* that binds people to each other and creates a new future. Dr. Martin Luther King's famous "I Have a Dream" speech in 1963 galvanized a generation to support the civil rights movement in the United States. Business leaders can also galvanize people to act. Dr. Irwin Redlener's vision was to establish a "medical home" for every child who lacks continuous access to high-quality, comprehensive health care. A pediatrician, his vision is to "use health care as a lever to address the global needs of the most disadvantaged kids . . . [he wants to] unlock the future for millions of kids with no sense of hope . . . to ignite the imaginations of children and change their lives." Redlener's vision has become a reality at the Children's Hospital at Montefiore, in New York. The hospital combines Carl Sagan's cosmic world view with cutting-edge medical technology and the elaborate design artistry of a professional theatrical production. While being treated, children can learn about poetry, painting, chemistry, space, oceanography, and many other topics in an interactive bed-side environment.[37]

Transformational leaders have more than just a vision. They also have a road map for attaining it. What is important is that followers "buy into" that vision and that the leader has a plan to energize them to reach it. Visionaries challenge old beliefs and ways of doing things. They strongly believe in their ideas, are able to communicate them clearly, and use them to excite others.

Charismatic and Ethical

Transformational leaders are charismatic, but not all charismatic leaders are transformational leaders. A charismatic leader *is a person who has the ability to influence others because of his or her inspirational qualities.* The Greek word *kharisma* means "divine gift." Leaders with charisma, like Symantec's John Thompson, have the power to obtain the cooperation and devotion of followers. Followers of charismatic leaders attribute heroic and extraordinary abilities to them.[38]

Charismatic leaders may benefit or harm an organization or society. Adolph Hitler was a charismatic leader to his followers but not to most people. He was an unethical, unbalanced, and immoral charismatic leader who focused on his own needs and was not open to criticism or suggestions. In contrast, consider Martin Luther King. King also was a charismatic leader, but his vision and ability to communicate inspired a nation to make significant and positive social changes. Transformational leaders like King are charismatic *and* ethical.

Over time, transformational leaders inspire and develop their followers to become leaders. These leaders do not make fun of the opinions of others, regardless of their status and position. In essence, transformational leaders are role models for followers to emulate. Leaders who attain higher levels of moral development create organizations with more ethical cultures. Ethical leadership is also a good predictor of employee satisfaction and dedication.[39]

Trustworthy

Because transformational leaders strive to be ethical in their relationships, they are viewed as trustworthy. Employees who do not trust a leader will hesitate to follow the leader's expressed vision and will interpret inspirational messages with skepticism. These leaders are often known for their honesty under pressure, including straight talking and keeping commitments. They "walk the talk."

In addition to being perceived as trustworthy, transformational leaders show trust in their followers. These leaders empower and delegate tasks to followers. They actively encourage a two-way flow of information.[40]

Snapshot

"If you look around Hollywood and say, 'Which of these companies are really trying new things and looking at new models?' It's an awfully short list. "It's not inherent in our industry to be entrepreneurial. [But] we view innovation and taking chances as part of our business. If we don't do it, someone else will, and they'll knock us down."
Mark Cuban, CEO and Cofounder, 2929 Entertainment

Carlos Ghosn transformed Nissan by involving employees in the decision-making process and showing respect for their ideas.

© Paul Sancya/AP Photo

Thoughtful

Transformational leaders are thoughtful. They challenge followers to build on their vision by offering innovative solutions and new ideas. They encourage positive thinking and problem solving. These leaders embrace taking risks, but base their actions on thoughtful analysis and discussion. Creativity is encouraged. Followers are expected and encouraged to question long-standing assumptions and practices. These leaders often focus on the "what" and "why" of problems, rather than on the "who" for placing blame. For these leaders, nothing is too good, too fixed, or too political that it can't be challenged or changed.

Carlos Ghosn is known as a thoughtful leader. As CEO of both Nissan and Renault, his responsibilities keep him busy traveling between Japan and Paris. Others may view his travel schedule as grueling, but he appreciates the time it gives him to think, as described in the Strategic Action Competency feature.[41]

Strategic Action Competency

Carlos Ghosn, CEO of Nissan Motors

When Carlos Ghosn became CEO of Nissan Motors, the company was in serious trouble. Ghosn succeeded in turning that company around so successfully that few people remember it ever had a problem. More recently, he has been working to transform Renault in much the same way. Ghosn's intellect, unwavering focus, and effective decision making are among the major reasons for his effectiveness as a leader. At both Nissan and Renault, Ghosn motivates employees to continuously strive to improve. In a recent broadcast to Renault, he warned employees against getting caught in the cyclical trap of boom-and-bust that has damaged so many auto companies, "Success breeds complacency and sometimes arrogance," he tells employees. Then when they find themselves at the bottom of the cycle, they wonder "What happened to us?"

To avoid that fate, Ghosn pushes himself and his executives to analyze situations carefully and then be decisive in their actions. "What I'm trying to explain at both Nissan and Renault is that we have to choose the moment, and we have to choose the field, and we have to choose the circumstances in which to fight the battles. If not, it will take us much more energy and resources to get the same result."

Spending an average of 48 hours a month traveling gives him plenty of time to think—about what questions to be asking, what strategic directions to pursue, and how to influence employees to take the actions needed. Commenting on his flights [via private jet] between Tokyo and Paris, Ghosn notes, "When you are alone, it's a great time for critical analysis. You never have this kind of time alone in the office or at home." Ghosn also wants his employees to be thoughtful.

Although he's always involved in key strategic decisions, Ghosn relies heavily on his top-level managers, who run the day-to-day operations and debate the alternative perspectives that inform most decisions. "What I hate are meetings where people hide their opinions," he says. "If you don't see different aspects of a decision and different options, you can't make a good decision." To encourage other people to think "outside the box," Ghosn emphasizes cross-functional and cross-cultural teamwork. And he isn't afraid to go against long-standing traditions. At Nissan, he did the unthinkable of making English the official language, brought in outsiders to take on some high-level positions, and broke up the company's supplier network, which was based on family ties and friendships. He has brought this same style to Renault, but it is too soon to see if the results will be equally good. When the company's new Twingo hits the market in 2008, customers will decide whether Ghosn's thoughtful approach is equally good for Renault.

To learn about these two organizations, visit *www.nissanusa.com* and *www.renault.com*.

Considerate

Transformational leaders care about the needs of others and have a great capacity for empathy. They actively listen to concerns of employees, customers, suppliers, and the public. They are willing to accept responsibility when mistakes inevitably occur and do not look for scapegoats. They respect and value the contributions of all employees. Transformational leaders are often willing to sacrifice immediate personal gain for the benefit of others. They use their sources of power to move individuals and teams toward their visions but avoid the use of power for personal gain.[42]

Bill Greehy, CEO of Valero Energy, the nation's top oil refiner, is considerate. He maintains a no-layoff policy and is enthusiastic about ensuring the safety of his employees. He tells employees they come first—before customers and shareholders. When Hurricane Katrina hit New Orleans in August 2005, Greehy ordered 60 mobile homes for employees whose own homes were destroyed. He also established the Valero SAFE Fund, which provided up to $10,000 to employees in need, and provided free fuel to Valero employees as well as the local police. Despite the devastation, Valero kept every employee on the payroll. Bob Pena, a Valero manager, was grateful: "If it wasn't for Valero, God knows where I'd be," he said.[43]

Confident

Transformational leaders project optimism and self-confidence. John Thompson's confidence helped him persist in pursuing a new strategy even when others were skeptical. Recall what Bruce Chizen, CEO of Adobe, said: "He [Thompson] did not back off [for] one moment on everything he said about Veritas and the need and the value of that acquisition, despite the pressure that he was under. He did not cave. The leadership he demonstrated under difficult circumstances was admirable." It was also very effective.

Jeff Immelt, CEO of GE, also has confidence. Before Immelt became CEO, his boss, Jack Welch, told him that he would fire him if he made one more big mistake. At the time, Immelt felt that he was the only person who believed he had a future with the company. "It was like you see people in a meeting looking at you and covering their eyes thinking, 'Dead meat walking.' I recognized that I had made a few mistakes and I recognized that I was the only one who could get us out of [the problem]. I knew I was a good guy. I realized that sometimes bad things happen to good people. I was able to play through it, fix it, and it gave me a lot more confidence to face other things."[44]

Followers have to see that a leader is passionate about a vision and confident that it can be achieved—but not arrogant. Such leaders also exhibit confidence in their followers. They recognize that mistakes will be made and know that if errors are not tolerated, followers will become too risk adverse.

As these examples illustrate, transformational leaders demonstrate a unique profile of personal characteristics, behaviors, and competencies. But transformational leaders aren't found only in top management positions in business organizations. They also are found in charitable organizations, civic and community groups, schools, student organizations, government agencies, small and large businesses, and every other type of organization. Chances are, you've been inspired by one at some time in your life.

Leadership Development

A poll of 700 employees working in dozens of different companies found that 83 percent believed there was a leadership vacuum in their organizations. Another study found that only 45 percent of employees have confidence in the job being done by their top executives. Trust in senior management has been falling steadily during the past few years.[45] Even many CEOs acknowledge that it is unclear who will be the future leaders of their companies.[46] Where are all the good leaders? How can organizations address the need for better leaders?

Snapshot

"What we have found is that the more you do for your employees, the more they do for the shareholders and the more they do for the community. I see this cycle with companies where they fire and they hire and they fire and they hire. I think it's just poor management. Fear does not motivate people."

Bill Greehy, CEO, Valero Energy Corporation

6.

Describe how organizations develop leaders.

Some people believe that leaders are born, not made. Other people believe that a person's leadership capacity is learned during childhood and is pretty much set by the time they are working as managers. Xerox's Ann Mulcahy believes that her general approach to leading has not changed a great deal over the years: "I don't think I'm a different leader today than I was when I had my first management job. I'm very direct. I'm less into management than I am into working with teams and solving problems. So I'm very engaged and involved." But that doesn't mean Mulcahy is the same today as she was 20 years ago. As she moved from one job to the next and up the organizational hierarchy, she developed a much better understanding of the business. She also learned to have confidence in her ability to lead others.[47]

John Thompson also believes that leadership is something people can develop. That's why he periodically returns to Florida A&M to help coach college students. It also is the reason he hosts barbecues in his home for young African Americans who see him as a role model and value the mentoring he provides.

If leadership skills couldn't be developed and improved, all an organization could do is to search for good leaders and hope to find them somewhere. Most CEOs seem to believe that leadership can be improved through personal experiences, and research supports this view. That's why CEOs invest both personal time and company resources in efforts to develop the leadership capacity of their employees. These investments fall into four general categories: (1) assigning people to positions to promote learning on the job, (2) offering assistance through coaching and mentoring, (3) sending employees to formal leadership assessment and training programs, and (4) sending them on special assignments. Of course, many organizations use a combination of these approaches in the hopes of having the talent they'll need to lead the organization many years from now.[48]

On-the-Job Learning

As we noted in Chapter 1, on-the-job learning is important for all aspects of managerial work, and that includes learning leadership. Developing leadership on the job requires that employees take jobs or project assignments that include leadership responsibilities. Early in a person's career, working as an individual contributor on team projects provides many opportunities for learning how to be an effective leader. Being a formal leader of a project allows an employee to use different types of influence tactics and observe how people react to those influence attempts. Team leaders also can ask team members for candid feedback and suggestions for how to improve. Team members who aren't designated as the formal leader also can learn by observing the relationship between the leader and team.

On-the-job learning is most effective for people who take personal responsibility for their own development. You will learn more through this approach if you understand your current approach to leadership, develop an action plan for improvement, and focus on carrying out the plan. Throughout this book, we have given you an opportunity to learn about yourself by completing various questionnaires, addressing various discussion questions, analyzing various cases, and reflecting on the textbook's various competency features. We hope that these activities are helping you develop your own leadership abilities.

Formal Assessment and Training

Leadership assessment and training *generally involves evaluating an individual's style of leadership and providing educational experiences designed to improve the individual's effectiveness as a leader.* Assessing a person's strengths and weaknesses helps set the stage for a formal training program.

Formal programs for developing leadership typically are built around the company's own view of what is required of its managers and leaders. The 3M Company used the opinions of its own executives to develop its leadership model. The CEO uses 3M's leadership model when he conducts his annual review of top executives, and managers at lower levels use the model as a guide when choosing developmental activities and assignments. Executives and managers also use the company's leadership model when setting performance expectations, judging performance, and discussing the development needs of their employees. The dimensions of leadership that 3M identified and now uses for developing future leaders are organized into three categories, as shown here:

1. **Fundamental Leadership Competencies.** New employees should possess these competencies when hired and refine them through experience in successive managerial assignments:

    ▶ Ethics and Integrity

    ▶ Intellectual Capacity

    ▶ Maturity and Judgment

2. **Essential Leadership Competencies.** These competencies are developed through experience leading a function or department, and set the stage for more complex executive positions:

    ▶ Customer Orientation

    ▶ Developing People

    ▶ Inspiring Others

    ▶ Business Health and Results

3. **Visionary Leadership Competencies.** These competencies develop as executives take on responsibilities that require them to operate beyond the boundaries of a particular organizational unit, and are used extensively in higher level positions:

    ▶ Global Perspective

    ▶ Vision and Strategy

    ▶ Nurturing Innovation

    ▶ Building Alliances

    ▶ Organizational Agility

As you can see, 3M's model of managerial competencies is similar to the one we use in this book. To assess their employees' leadership capabilities, organizations like Hasbro, 3M, and IBM use trained experts, self-assessments, and 360-degree feedback. For employees in roles that involve leadership, providing feedback is a good way to improve their effectiveness. Not surprisingly, most leaders see themselves in a more positive light than their followers do. The best leaders have realistic self-perceptions and use feedback about their behavior to make improvements. Formal assessment and training may be conducted at the organization's own educational facilities, at a college or university, or by organizations such as the Center for Creative Leadership, a non-profit organization dedicated to leadership research and education.

Weyerhaeuser offers leadership assessments and training through its corporate university. As described in the Ethical Challenge feature on the following page, developing ethical leaders is a top priority.[49]

Weyerhaeuser

There has been much discussion and concern about unethical business behavior in recent years, and business is starting to get the point. Simply relying on employees to use their best judgment does not seem to be enough to ensure that people in leadership positions behavior ethically. In fact, a recent survey of more than 3,000 U.S. workers revealed that a variety of unethical behaviors still occur too frequently: At least one out of six workers reported that they observed managers who were abusive or intimidating, lied to customers and employees, and/or tolerated safety violations that could result in harm. Weyerhaeuser Co. doesn't want its leaders—or any other employee—engaging in these or other unethical behaviors.

Founded in 1900, Weyerhaeuser is a $22 billion producer of forest products and services with employees in 19 countries. For years, it has included ethics training as part of its formal leadership training. The company's philosophy is that remarkable leaders can inspire and motivate others to accomplish great tasks. From the beginning, effective leadership has been highly valued at the Weyerhaeuser Company. And effective leadership has always meant ethical leadership. To help managers spot and think through tough ethical situations, the company's top executives serve as the teachers. During training programs, managers are asked to read and discuss several case studies that present realistic ethical challenges. Leaders present several choices for managers to consider, including one or two good ones. A group discussion gives managers a chance to explain how they think about the situation, how they would behave, and why.

"Pulp Fiction" is the title of one case that Weyerhaeuser uses to teach ethics. In this case, Lena is an employee at a pulp mill. When the maintenance contractor employed by the plant begins to do shoddy work, her boss, Donna, asks her to recommend another contractor to perform the needed maintenance tasks. Lena hears that the current maintenance contractor employs the son-in-law of Donna, the mill's maintenance manager. What would you do? Here are some options:

1. Ask a coworker if she has the correct information—is the man really Donna's son-in-law?

2. Tell the plant manager about the potential conflict.

3. Ask the contractor about the situation.

4. Ask Donna about whether her son-in-law works for the maintenance contractor.

Leaders and managers discuss how each choice might affect the various people involved as well as the company. Very few managers will ever face this particular situation—that's not the point. The point of these discussions is to help managers develop an approach to thinking about the ethical issues they might face. What would you do if you were Lena, and why?

To learn more about this organization, visit *www.weyerhaeuser.com.*

Coaching and Mentoring

Coaching involves providing one-on-one, personalized feedback and advice for the purpose of enhancing the manager's performance and the organization's performance.[50] John Thompson believes that the coaching and mentoring he received early in life helped him succeed later in life. "I . . . was fortunate enough to have support from some really well-placed people who took an interest in my career. . . . Success is a combination of hard work and good support structure that helps to get you going," he said.

A relatively new approach to leadership development is the use of personal coaches. As described earlier in the Self-Management Competency feature, Sylvia Montero uses a coach who helps her think through strategic issues. Sometimes bosses are good coaches. GE's Jeff Immelt credits his former boss, Jack Welch, with being a great coach to him.

At Ericsson, the telecommunications company, managers spend huge amounts of time coaching each employee. Managers work with each employee to draw up a performance contract, which includes an assessment of the employee's strengths and weaknesses. To monitor progress, managers meet with each employee six times in the following year holding one-on-one coaching sessions that last about 90 minutes each. It is rare for managers to provide so much intensive coaching for every employee, but Ericsson believes the investment will pay off. After all, the most important thing that managers manage is their people.[51]

When managers or other people who are not professional coaches provide coaching, people often call it *mentoring.* For many managers, learning from a mentor is more feasible than hiring a professional coach. Mentors most often are managers or senior colleagues in the organization who provide advice and guidance about a variety of career-related concerns. Grace Lieblein, a chief engineer at GM, is a mentor who is especially interested in helping female engineers to manage their careers. As a mentor, she helps them find assignments that develop their potential for long-term advancement to become either technical leaders or CEOs. "I strongly encourage folks I mentor to get a very strong foundation of experiences that find your career potential. I definitely think a broad foundation of experiences is really important," she said.[52]

The U.S. Army also uses peer-to-peer mentoring. For managers and army officers, talking with mentors about how to develop more effective leader behaviors is important to career advancement. Mentors can help managers understand how others respond to their behaviors and point out weaknesses or blind spots. Mentors also serve as role models that individuals can emulate, and they provide valuable advice concerning the styles of leadership favored in the organization. Finally, mentors often assist managers in developing leadership capabilities by helping them obtain assignments that will foster on-the-job learning.[53]

When Avon's CEO Andrea Jung began working at Bloomingdale's her first year after college, she sought out executive Joan Vass to act as her mentor. Vass had a fast-paced career, which she successfully balanced with a quiet family life. Jung saw Vass as an ideal role model who could teach her how to be tactfully aggressive, so she sought Vass out as a mentor.

Special Assignments

Providing managers with very challenging special assignments is another method some organizations use to develop leaders. Such assignments are especially useful for helping people develop multicultural competencies. Globalization affects almost every American corporation today. One of the many consequences of globalization is that business leaders are having to learn to be effective in several different cultures and countries. As globalization spreads, many companies are finding out that they do not have the global leaders they need now or for the future. One survey found that fully 85 percent of Fortune 500 companies report a shortage of competent global managers and leaders.

What does it take to be an effective global leader? The first step is to understand how employees in different cultures think about leadership—effective leadership in the United States may not be effective elsewhere. In fact, recent research on global leadership shows that leadership takes different forms in different countries. Figure 15.8 summarizes a few of the research findings.[54] As Figure 15.8 shows, some behaviors facilitate effective leadership in almost all cultures; and yet other behaviors interfere with effective leadership almost anywhere. But there also are behaviors that are effective in some cultures and ineffective in others. PricewaterhouseCoopers (PwC) knows that understanding these culturally contingent leadership behaviors is essential for global leaders. To help its managers develop their global leadership skills, PwC sends them abroad in a program call Ulysses, which is described in the Multicultural Competency feature on the following page.[55]

Figure 15.8 | Views of Leadership across Cultures

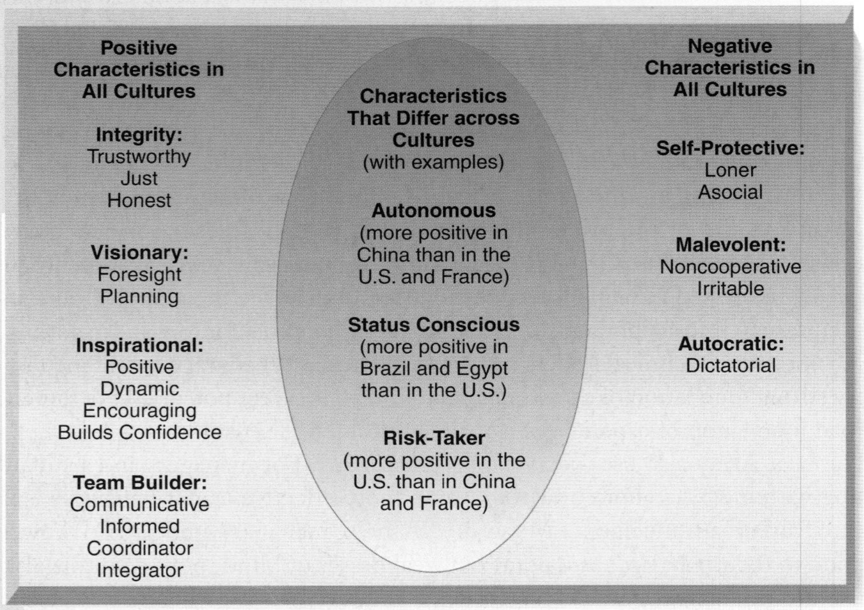

Positive Characteristics in All Cultures

Integrity:
Trustworthy
Just
Honest

Visionary:
Foresight
Planning

Inspirational:
Positive
Dynamic
Encouraging
Builds Confidence

Team Builder:
Communicative
Informed
Coordinator
Integrator

Characteristics That Differ across Cultures
(with examples)

Autonomous
(more positive in China than in the U.S. and France)

Status Conscious
(more positive in Brazil and Egypt than in the U.S.)

Risk-Taker
(more positive in the U.S. than in China and France)

Negative Characteristics in All Cultures

Self-Protective:
Loner
Asocial

Malevolent:
Noncooperative
Irritable

Autocratic:
Dictatorial

Multicultural Competency

PriceWaterhouseCoopers

Tahir Ayub is a partner at Pricewaterhouse-Coopers (PwC), and he needs to be able to "think global, act local." PwC helped him develop this competency by sending him to Namibia, a country being devastated by HIV/AIDS. PwC arranged for the trip and Ayub's stay there as part of their Ulysses Program to develop global leaders. As part of the program, each year the company sends 17 partners to work in small teams on projects in developing countries. The partners "go local"—they are stripped of all the comforts they have grown to take for granted and given a specific task to complete. They must rely on their own resourcefulness to succeed. PwC believes such hands-on experience is essential to developing global leaders.

On arrival, Ayub paired up with two other PwC partners whom he had never met before—one from The Netherlands and the other from Mexico. Having grown up in the United Kingdom and having gone to college in Vancouver, it was a life-changing experience: "When you work in a [culturally diverse] place like Vancouver, you work with people from different backgrounds and you think you are culturally aware," he recalled. But

working as part of the Namibia team, he was less sure of his open-mindedness. He also learned that "perhaps the way you see things isn't necessarily the best way"—a humbling experience for someone as successful as a PwC partner.

Two years after returning from Namibia, Ayub says he can still see the faces of the orphans he met, whose parents had died from AIDS. PwC says it can see that Ayub benefited from the experience. Today, he recognizes the importance of listening to different perspectives before making decisions. "Before, when I came across an issue that I thought I knew how to deal with, I would say that I didn't have a lot of time to listen to everyone involved to make sure it was the right way to go. Now I am much more open to listening and to other people's points of view," he says. As more and more of its partners work through such experiences, the firm knows it will improve the company's global effectiveness. In 10 years, they expect to really begin to see the results of this long-term investment.

To learn more about this organization, visit *www.pwc.com.*

Chapter Summary ....

Leadership is central to the effectiveness of organizations. Employees at all levels of an organization can exercise leadership, which takes many forms. Because effective leadership is so important, numerous studies have been conducted in attempts to understand its nature. Each of numerous models explains some—but not all—aspects of effective leadership. Organizations interested in developing effective leaders often use these models as the basis for leadership development activities.

Learning Goals ....

1. Explain what leadership means.

Leadership is an influence relationship among leaders and followers who strive for real change and outcomes that reflect their shared purposes. Leaders can influence others by using their formal position, rewards, coercion, expertise, and charisma. The most effective use of influence tactics results in followers who are committed to the leader's goals. The improper use of influence may result in mere compliance or even resistance.

2. Describe the personal characteristics that enable leaders to be effective.

A leader's personal characteristics include his or her physical, social, and personal attributes. Personal characteristics are not easy to change, and they generally result in fairly predictable behavior over a period of time. The presence and absence of certain individual characteristics enable some leaders to be more effective than others. Emotional intelligence is a set of four personal characteristics that appear to be useful for effective leadership. These characteristics are self-awareness, self-control, social awareness, and social skill.

3. Describe the types of behaviors required for leadership.

Behavioral models of leadership provide a way of identifying effective leaders by their actions. The Theory X and Theory Y model states that leaders' behaviors reflect their basic assumptions about people. Theory X and Theory Y represent two quite different ways that leaders view their subordinates and thus manage them. The managerial grid model identifies various combinations of concern for people and production. They provide the basis for deriving five different styles of leadership: country club, impoverished, produce or perish, middle of the road, and team. In this model the team style is viewed as the ideal leadership style to strive for.

4. Identify the contingencies that may shape how leaders behave.

The Situational Leadership® Model indicates that leaders must adapt their leadership style to the readiness level of their followers. This model prescribes different combinations of directive and supportive leader behaviors for different levels of subordinates' readiness. It suggests four leadership styles: telling, selling, participating, and delegating. The Vroom–Jago leadership model prescribes a leader's choices among five leadership styles based on seven contingency variables, recognizing the time requirements and other costs associated with each style. The five core leadership styles are decide, consult individually, consult team, facilitate, and delegate. Contingencies models assume that leaders can be highly flexible in their use of leadership styles.

5. State the key characteristics and behaviors of transformational leadership.

The transformational model of leadership views it as involving a combination of personal characteristics, behaviors, and contingencies. It is all of these things combined in unique ways. People who guide organizations through needed changes are often called transformational leaders. They inspire others with their vision, promote this vision over opposition, and demonstrate confidence in themselves and their views. In addition to having a vision for the future, they use their charisma to achieve ethical objectives, and they are thoughtful, considerate, trustworthy, and confident.

6. Describe how organizations develop leaders.

Organizations use three major approaches to develop leaders: placing employees in positions that promote learning on the job, providing employees with formal leadership assessments and training, offering mentoring and coaching, and sending them on special assignments. Organizations invest in these leadership development activities because they understand that leaders are made, not born.

Key Terms and Concepts

Behavioral models of leadership
Charismatic leader
Contingency models of leadership
Delegating style
Emotional intelligence
Leadership
Leadership assessment and training

Managerial grid
Participating style
Readiness
Relationship behavior
Self-awareness
Self-control
Selling style
Situational Leadership® Model
Social awareness

Social skill
Task behavior
Telling style
Theory X
Theory Y
Transformational leaders
Vroom–Jago leadership model

Questions for Discussion and Reflective Thinking

1. Do you think John Thompson, CEO of Symantec, has emotional intelligence? Assess this leader on the four elements of emotional intelligence.

2. Think of a leader that you know. Give examples of how this person influences others using formal authority, expertise, rewards, coercion, and charisma. Do you respond in different ways to these influence tactics? Explain.

3. Describe a manager you have worked for in terms of Theory X or Theory Y. Give some examples of this manager's behaviors and attitudes that seem to be consistent with Theory X or Theory Y.

4. When Robert Eckert became CEO of Mattel, he knew the company needed to dismantle the organizational silos that kept people from different parts of the company from collaborating. He wanted to create a flatter, more team-based organization. A major decision that had to be made was whether to combine the boys' and girls' divisions into a single unit. Use the Vroom–Jago leadership model to analyze this situation (refer to Figure 15.6). What approach does the model suggest Eckert should use? Assume that Eckert will involve his top management

team in the decision-making process. He does not feel pressured to make a speedy decision and is concerned about developing the members of his management. Explain how you arrived at your conclusion. You can learn more about Mattel at *www.mattel.com.*

5. Numerous organizations offer leadership development programs. Investigate the leadership training program offered by the Center for Creative Leadership by visiting their Web site at *www.ccl.org.* Which of the following does this organization offer: on-the-job learning, leadership assessment, formal leadership training, coaching and/or mentoring, global leadership training?

6. Several professional organizations now offer online mentoring services that make it easy for people to find mentors they may never meet in person. For examples, visit *www.asabe.org* and *www.ieee.org.* What do you feel are the strengths and weaknesses of online mentoring? Would you consider trying it? Why or why not?

7. Describe three things you could do during the next year to develop your competencies as a global leader. Consider only things that really are feasible for you. How motivated are you to do these three things? Explain.

DEVELOPING YOUR COMPETENCIES

Instructions

Indicate how well the statements below describe you, using the following scale:

1 Strongly disagree	2 Somewhat disagree	3 Somewhat agree	5 Strongly agree

___1. I know when to speak about my personal problems to others.

___2. When I'm faced with obstacles, I remember times I faced similar obstacles and overcame them.

___3. I expect that I will do well on most things.

___4. Other people find it easy to confide in me.

___5. I find it easy to understand the nonverbal messages of other people.

___6. Some of the major events of my life have led me to reevaluate what is important and not important.

___7. When my mood changes, I see new possibilities.

___8. Emotions are one of the things that make life worth living.

___9. I am aware of my emotions as I experience them.

___10. I expect good things to happen.

___11. I like to share my emotions with other people.

___12. When I experience a positive emotion, I know how to make it last.

___13. I arrange events others enjoy.

___14. I seek out activities that make me happy.

___15. I am aware of the nonverbal messages I send to others.

___16. I present myself in a way that makes a good impression on others.

___17. When I am in a positive mood, solving problems is easy for me.

___18. By looking at facial expressions, I can recognize the emotions that others are feeling.

___19. I know why my emotions change.

___20. When I am in a positive mood, I am able to come up with new ideas.

___21. I have control over my emotions.

___22. I easily recognize my emotions as I experience them.

___23. I motivate myself by imagining a good outcome to the tasks I do.

___24. I compliment others when they have done something well.

___25. I am aware of the nonverbal message other people send.

___26. When another person tells me about an important event in their life, I almost feel as though I have experienced this event myself.

___27. When I feel a change in emotions, I tend to come up with new ideas.

___28. When I am faced with a challenge, I usually rise to the occasion.

___29. I know what other people are feeling just by looking at them.

___30. I help other people feel better when they are down.

___31. I use good moods to help myself keep trying in the face of obstacles.

___32. I can tell how people are feeling by listening to the tone of their voices.

Scoring

1. Add your responses to questions 1, 6, 7, 8, 12, 14, 17, 19, 20, 22, 23, and 27. Put this total here ____. This is your *self-awareness* score.

2. Add your responses to questions 4, 15, 18, 25, 29, and 32. Put this total here ____. This is your *social awareness* score.

3. Add your responses to questions 2, 3, 9, 10, 16, 21, 28, and 31. Put this total here ____. This is your *self-control* score.

4. Add your responses to questions 5, 11, 13, 24, 26, and 30. Put this total here ____. This is your *social skills* score.

Interpretation

Emotional intelligence refers to how well an individual handles herself and others rather than how smart she is or how capable she is in terms of technical skills. Emotional intelligence includes the attributes of self-awareness, self-control, social awareness, and social skill. The higher your score is in each of these four areas, the more emotionally intelligent you are. People who score high (greater than 36) in *self-awareness* recognize their emotions and their effects on others, accurately assess their strengths and limitations, and have a strong sense of their self-worth and capabilities. People who score high (greater than 18) in *social awareness* are good at understanding others, taking an active interest in their concerns, and empathizing with them, and recognize the needs others have at work. People who score high (greater than 24) in self-control can keep their disruptive emotions and impulses under control, maintain standards of integrity and honesty, are conscientious, adapt their behaviors to changing situations, and have internal standards of excellence that guide their behaviors. People who have high (greater than 18) *social skills* sense others' developmental needs, inspire and lead groups, send clear and convincing messages, build effective interpersonal relationships, and work well with others to achieve shared goals.

Questions

1. What insights did you gain about your approach to leadership? What is your area of greatest strength?

2. Choose one aspect of your emotional intelligence that you could improve. List three things that you can do to develop and improve.

Case to Develop Critical Thinking | Sam Palmisano, CEO of IBM[57]

Before Sam Palmisano became CEO of IBM in 2002, Big Blue (as the company is known) had spent more than a decade pulling itself back from the brink. A firm that revolutionized computing earlier in the 20th century seemed to have lost its way as that century came to a close. By the time Palmisano took the reins, IBM no longer needed a life support system. But it still needed a vision for how to become a truly great company again.

Palmisano is leading IBM back to greatness. He believes his industry is poised for another revolution and envisions IBM as the one-stop provider of on-demand e-business computing. In the new era, he believes businesses will want efficient, extremely powerful, consolidated systems that run on open standards and meet the specific needs of an industry. The radical new idea is that a company will no longer own and house its own computing system. Instead, it will purchase computing power directly from a provider that manages and distributes computing power. To serve these companies, IBM plans to manage and distribute computing power in a way that's similar to what we now do with electrical power. Coupled with the new technology will be powerful new software that captures and distributes an organization's base of knowledge. According to Palmisano, the new, emerging model is collaborative innovation, which will include more open-source tools and different kinds of ownership—and IBM will be a major player in changing the way the industry works.

Palmisano didn't develop this vision alone. He asked his top management team to join him in coming up with an idea that would be the type of major breakthrough that IBM made when it developed a mainframe computer 40 years earlier. The new vision is so radical that today most of the technology needed is not even available—it still has to be invented.

To make the IBM vision a reality, Palmisano must rely on other executives. One of his first moves as CEO was to abolish the bureaucratic corporate executive committee that held monthly meetings and oversaw every strategic initiative. He created teams made up of people from all levels in the company and put them in charge of operations, strategy, and technology. He believes teams will be the engines of creativity at IBM. "Creativity in any large organization does not come from one individual, the celebrity CEO. That stuff's B.S. Creativity starts where the action is—either in the laboratory, or in R&D sites, at a customer place, in manufacturing."

When he first began leading with this new (to IBM) approach, heads were spinning, according to one executive. They weren't used to a CEO who reached deep into the organization asking questions. They weren't used to collaborating across organizational boundaries. They weren't used to working in teams that were responsible for their own destiny. And they weren't used to partnering with and forming alliances with customers. The old IBM culture was collegial and friendly, but the hierarchy was clear. Decisions tended to be made at the top, communicated downward, and then implemented. Now, those days are just a memory.

To learn more about this organization, visit www.ibm.com.

Questions

1. Review the characteristics and behaviors of transformational leaders. Which of these does Sam Palmisano seem to have?

2. Assume you are a midlevel manager at IBM in charge of a unit with 30 employees whose work involves evaluating and monitoring purchasing decisions. Would the new culture at IBM be likely to change the way you manage your unit? Explain.

3. Review the models of leadership described in this chapter. Which model would you adopt to guide you in this position? Explain your choice.

© Triangle Images/Digital Vision/Getty Images

Communicating Effectively

Learning Goals

After studying this chapter, you should be able to:

1. Explain the communication process.

2. Identify hurdles to communication.

3. State ways to eliminate communication hurdles and improve your communications.

4. Discuss two ethical issues in communications.

Communication Competency

Planning and Administration Competency

Teamwork Competency

Managing Effectively

Self-Management Competency

Strategic Action Competency

Multicultural Competency

Challenge of Managing ....

Staples

When Shira Goodman took over as Staples' executive vice president for marketing, the ratio of complaints to kudos was 8 to 1. Customers griped that items were often out of stock and said that the sales staff was unhelpful. After weeks of talking with customers, she had a revelation: "Customers want an easier shopping experience." Rather than bombarding customers with a new slogan, she and her staff led a companywide effort to actually simplify the shopping experience. The marketing department created a red icon, the Easy Button, to communicate to customers that shopping would be easy at Staples. The five-year communication plan has helped make Staples a leader in office retail. Sales exceed $16 billion and profits have risen tremendously. Today, the ratio of complaints to kudos is 1 to 2.

The change effort that Goodman and her staff undertook involved communicating with employees, customers, and suppliers. At first, Goodman and her team shopped at competitors, like OfficeMax, and discovered that they had everything in stock. Customers told her team that price wasn't the only factor in their selection of a store. Customers wanted a straightforward shopping experience. They wanted knowledgeable and helpful associates and a hassle-free environment.

To accomplish these changes, Staples removed more than 800 slow-moving items from its stores. Because customers revealed that the availability of printer cartridges was one of their biggest concerns, the company introduced an in-stock guarantee on printer cartridges. A four-paragraph letter to prospective new customers was cut to just two sentences focusing on an easy shopping experience and a helpful staff with an image of the Easy Button.

The first TV advertisement using the Easy Button aired in January 2005 and aired during the Super Bowl a month later. In one ad, called "The Wall," an emperor uses the button to erect a giant barrier as invaders approach; another ad shows an office worker causing printer cartridges to rain down from above. Online, Staples created a downloadable Easy Button toolbar, which guided shoppers directly to www.staples.com. As a result of the advertising campaign, customers began asking about buying

Easy Buttons. Staples immediately started selling these for $5. When pushed, the button says "That was easy." Staples donates $1 million to charity each year from the profits it earns from selling the Easy Button. By selling the Easy Button, Staples is turning its customers into advertisers. Homegrown movies starring the button have appeared on the video-sharing site YouTube, while a blogger at Sexy Red-Headed Nuns hacked the button to create a garage door opener.

Goodman knows that there is no guarantee that the Easy Button communications push can maintain its momentum. Recently, it introduced a new back-to-school TV campaign featuring the Easy Button. While customers' recall of having seen an ad for the Easy Button has reached over 70 percent, if sales lag, ad budgets are usually the first thing to be cut. Staples spent more than $160 million on advertising recently and as long as the stock price is high, shareholders are happy.[1]

To learn more about this organization, visit *www.staples.com*.

Goodman knows that even the best companies have trouble sustaining themselves because, once successful, they become sloppy and a little complacent. To make sure that this doesn't happen at Staples, she constantly communicates with customers and employees both verbally and through e-mails. She answers the customer's hotline and can be seen greeting customers as they walk into a Staples store to keep in touch. She constantly asks her staff: "What do you think customers want?" When they answer, she asks them to think out of the box. She also knows that the "buck stops" with her. For example, she ended Staples' relationship with an ad agency in mid-2004 because she believed that Staples needed to rethink its TV advertising strategy. Staples hired McCann-Erickson Worldwide, which had created MasterCard's "Priceless" campaign. It was during a brainstorming session that a staff member mentioned how easy it would be if she could just push a button to come up with a great ad so they could go to lunch. With that simple statement, the Easy Button was born.

Explain the communication process.

The Communication Process

Whether the organization is an office supply firm, bank, transportation system, or manufacturing plant, effective communication is essential. Communication is to an organization what the bloodstream is to a person. Just as a person can develop hardening of the arteries, which impairs physical efficiency, an organization can develop blockages of communication channels, which impair its effectiveness. Just as heart bypass surgery may be necessary to save a person's life, an organization may have to revamp its communications system to survive. And, just as heart patients can do more harm than good if they overreact to their health problems by exercising too strenuously, an organization may go overboard trying to repair a history of poor communication with employees.

Without *effective* communication, managers can accomplish little, which is why we included communication as one of the six core managerial competencies. Communication can be formal or informal, verbal or nonverbal, and may take many forms, including face-to-face interactions, phone calls, faxes, e-mail, notes posted on bulletin boards, letters, memos, reports, videos, and oral presentations. In this chapter, we examine how organizational communication takes place, identify key hurdles to communication, explore ways of improving communication in organizations, and highlight two ethical issues.

Communication *is the transfer and exchange of information and understanding from one person to another through meaningful symbols.*[2] It is a process of sending, receiving, and sharing ideas, attitudes, values, opinions, and facts. Communication requires both a sender, who begins the process, and a receiver, who completes the communication link. When the receiver provides feedback that the message was received as intended, the communication cycle is complete.

In organizations, managers use the communication process to carry out their four functions (planning, organizing, leading, and controlling). Because they must have access to relevant information in order to make sound decisions, effective managers build networks of contacts that facilitate information gathering, interpretation, and dissemination. These contacts help managers become the nerve centers of their organizations. Much like radar screens, managers scan the environment for changes that could affect the organization and share this information with others. Once made, decisions are quickly disseminated to those who will help carry them out.

In contrast, ineffective managers often leave employees in the dark about what is happening. Poor communication seems to be a particular problem during downsizing, when managers' and employees' stress levels soar. Poor communication allows rumors to replace facts, fosters animosities between departments and teams, and impedes successful organizational change. Under such circumstances, poor communication seems to be the single most important reason for poor strategy implementation.[3]

Most managers spend a large part of their working day communicating with superiors, peers, customers, and others; writing and answering e-mails, letters, and reports; and talking with others on the phone. In doing so, they are engaged in the communication process, which involves six basic elements: sender (encoder), receiver (decoder), message, channels, feedback, and perception.

Figure 16.1 shows how these elements interact during the communication process.[4] Managers and employees who are concerned with improving their communication competency need to be aware of these elements and how they contribute to successful communication. We discuss the roles of the sender and the receiver first because they are the actors in the process.

Snapshot

"People pooh-poohed our idea for more than a year. I took it to mean that either we weren't explaining it well or we were dead wrong. I realized that we needed to communicate our idea better by connecting the dots more clearly. We did that by finding a metaphor that explained what our company does."

Gibu Thomas, CEO, Sharpcast

Figure 16.1 | The Communication Process

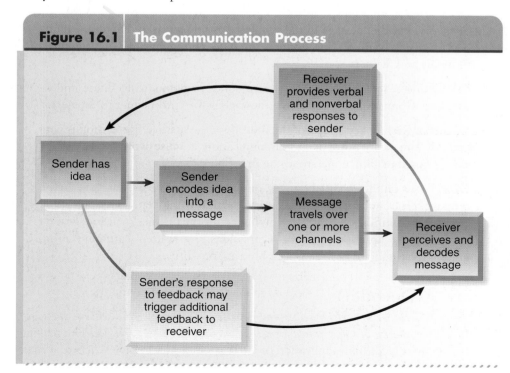

Sender (Encoder)

The **sender** *is the source of information and the initiator of the communication process.* The sender tries to choose the type of message and the channel that will be most effective. The sender then encodes the message.

Encoding *is the process of translating thoughts or feelings into a medium—written, visual, or spoken—that conveys the meaning intended.* Imagine that you are planning to apply for a summer job. You will get the best response by first learning about the channels of communication used by the organization. Many employers now prefer to accept applications via the Internet, so you should begin by visiting the organization's Web site. From there, you often can determine which job openings exist and the procedures that the company uses to process applications for employment. If the organization accepts electronic applications, you're likely to get a faster response to your inquiry by using this method. If the organization has no Web site, you can begin the process by calling to find out whether an opening exists, then writing a letter, and then phoning again to confirm that your letter has been received.

Regardless of whether you apply electronically or use a traditional letter, your application should convey certain ideas and impressions. For example, you should explain why you're interested in that particular company. You also need to provide background information about your qualifications for the job and explain how you think the job will further your career. When you transfer these ideas into speech or to an electronic memo or to paper, you are encoding your message. To increase encoding accuracy, apply the five principles of communication to the form of communication you're using:

1. *Relevancy.* Make the message meaningful and significant, carefully selecting the words, symbols, or gestures to be used.

2. *Simplicity.* Put the message in the simplest possible terms, reducing the number of words, symbols, or gestures used to communicate your intended thoughts and feelings.

3. *Organization.* Arrange the message as a series of points to facilitate understanding. Complete each point in a message before proceeding to the next.

4. *Repetition.* Restate key points of the message at least twice. Repetition is particularly important in spoken communication because words may not be clearly heard or fully understood the first time.

5. *Focus.* Focus on the essential aspects, or key points, of the message. Make the message clear and avoid unnecessary detail. In spoken communication, emphasize significant points by changing your tone of voice, pausing, gesturing, or using appropriate facial expressions. In written communication, underline or italicize key sentences, phrases, or words.

Receiver (Decoder)

The **receiver** *is the person who receives and decodes (or interprets) the sender's message.* **Decoding** *is translating messages into a form that has meaning to the receiver.* The person who receives your electronic application or letter about a summer job reacts to it first on the basis of whether the organization has any openings. If it doesn't, the receiver

Every message has two sides, what is sent (encoded) and what is received (decoded). How we interpret messages varies according to our backgrounds and perceptions.

© Stewart Charles Cohen/Workbook Stock/Jupiter Images

probably won't pay much attention to your inquiry. If there are openings, the receiver probably will compare what you wrote about yourself to the type of person that the organization wants to hire. Ralph Sorrentino, a partner at Deloitte Consulting, is responsible for recruiting at more than 15 colleges and universities. He's learned to decode messages efficiently. He takes no more than a half a minute to judge a résumé. He prefers a standard résumé—if he receives one printed on pink paper with a color photo, he'll "try to look beyond it." He searches for key information, including job experience, campus leadership, grades, and hometown. Why hometown? He says that it helps him judge the likelihood of a student's accepting a job in one of the cities where Deloitte has offices.[5]

Gender Differences. Both encoding and decoding are influenced by personal factors, such as education, personality, socioeconomic status, family, work history, culture, and gender. Some research suggests that women are more concerned with the feelings and reactions of the person with whom they're speaking than men are.[6] When women talk with each other, they often talk about their private lives. They also stick to one topic for a long time, let all people finish their sentences, and try to have everyone participate in the communication. Men rarely talk about their personal relationships and feelings, but rather seem to be in competition to prove themselves better informed on a variety of subjects. Research has shown that men gain the floor more often and keep the floor for longer periods of time, regardless of their status in the organization. Men are more likely than women to interrupt other people while they are speaking, and they are more likely to interrupt women than they are to interrupt men. Women are less likely to resist the interruption than men.

Women strive to build connections and intimacy through their communications. They seem to be most effective when they are in informal or collaborative settings where people jointly build ideas. Their relationship style of communication may put them at a disadvantage in some organizations. Women tend to use less assertive styles of speech, using questions such as "I really like this idea, don't you?", disclaimers such as "I may be wrong, but . . . ," and "Won't you create that report?" They focus on seeking and giving more support and they try to gain consensus. When men use qualifiers such as *perhaps, maybe, sort of,* or *I guess,* they are often perceived as warm and polite; when women use such qualifiers, they are often perceived as weak and unassertive. Some of the important communication differences between men and women are shown in Table 16.1.

Snapshot

"Women use more adverbs and are more sensitive to nonverbal messages in face-to-face meetings than men. Women also tend to discuss their personal experiences and problems to develop a personal closeness to the other person."
Ellen Collins, Corporate Sales Manager, Rock Resorts

Table 16.1	Communication Differences between Men and Women

1. Men are less likely to ask for information or directions in a public situation that would reveal their lack of knowledge.
2. In decision making, women are more likely to downplay their certainty; men are more likely to downplay their doubts.
3. Women tend to apologize even when they have done nothing wrong. Men tend to avoid apologies as signs of weakness or concession.
4. Women tend to accept blame as a way of smoothing awkward situations. Men tend to ignore blame and place it elsewhere.
5. Women tend to temper criticism with positive buffers. Men tend to give criticism directly.
6. Women tend to insert unnecessary and unwarranted thank-yous in conversations. Men may avoid thanks altogether as a sign of weakness.
7. Men tend to usurp (take) ideas stated by women and claim them as their own. Women tend to allow this process to take place without protest.
8. Women use softer voice volume to encourage persuasion and approval. Men use louder voice volume to attract attention and maintain control.

One of the main requirements of the receiver is the ability to listen. Listening *involves paying attention to the message, not merely hearing it.* Of the 75 percent or more of their time that managers spend in communicating, about half is spent listening to others. Becoming a better listener is an important way for people to improve their communication skills. Studies have shown that most people can recall immediately only about 50 percent of what someone tells them. Two months later, they can recall only about 25 percent. That's why effective communication often involves the use of several media, such as written reports, memos, newsletters, and e-mails, in addition to the telephone, face-to-face conversations, and speeches.

Ten guidelines for effective listening are presented in Table 16.2. Try using them the next time you're having a conversation with someone. You'll be surprised at how much effective listening improves the communication process.

Table 16.2	**Guidelines for Effective Listening**

1. Remember that listening is not just about receiving information—how you listen also sends a message back to the message sender.
2. Stop talking! You can't listen if you're talking.
3. Show a talker that you want to listen. Paraphrase what's been said to show that you understand.
4. Remove distractions.
5. Avoid prejudging what the person thinks or feels. Listen first, then make judgments later.
6. Try to see the other person's point of view.
7. Listen for total meaning. This includes both the content of the words and the feeling or attitude underlying the words.
8. Attend to both verbal and nonverbal cues.
9. Go easy on argument and criticism, which put people on the defensive and may make them "clam up" or become angry.
10. Before each person leaves, confirm what has been said.

Message

The message *refers to the verbal (spoken and written) symbols and nonverbal cues representing the information that the sender wants to convey to the receiver.* Like a coin, a message has two sides, and the message sent and the message received aren't necessarily the same. Why? First, encoding and decoding of the message may vary because of differences in the sender's and the receiver's backgrounds and viewpoints. Second, the sender may be sending more than one message.

Managers and employees generally use three types of messages: nonverbal, verbal, and written. The use of nonverbal messages is extremely important, although many individuals don't recognize this fact. Accordingly, we discuss nonverbal messages at greater length than the other two types.

Nonverbal Messages. All messages not spoken or written constitute nonverbal messages. Nonverbal messages *are facial expressions, eye contact, body movement, gestures, and physical contact (collectively often called* body language) *that convey meaning.* When people communicate in person, as much as 60 percent of the content of the message is transmitted through facial expressions and other methods of nonverbal communication.[7]

Ralph Sorrentino of Deloitte Consulting sees each candidate for only 30 minutes, so every bit of information he can get is important. A smile and a strong handshake create an excellent first impression. Sorrentino admits that first impressions based on nonverbal cues can be misleading but that they are hard to ignore. He uses his understanding of nonverbal communication to gather information about the candidate during the interview.[8] The ability to interpret facial expressions is an important part of communication. Eye contact is a direct and powerful way of communicating nonverbally. In the United States, social rules suggest that in many social situations brief eye contact is appropriate. However, if eye contact is too brief, people may interpret it as a sign of aloofness or untrustworthiness. Conversely, people often interpret prolonged eye contact as either a threat or a sign of romantic interest, depending on the context. A good poker player watches the eyes of the other players as new cards are dealt. Pupil dilation often betrays whether the card(s) just dealt improved the player's hand.

With regard to *body language*, the body and its movement—particularly movements of the face and eyes, which are very expressive—tell a lot about a person. As much as 50 percent of the content of a message may be communicated by facial expression and body posture and another 30 percent by inflection and the tone of speech. The words themselves may account for only 20 percent of the content of a message.[9]

The meaning of nonverbal communication varies by cultures.[10] For example, a smile on the face of a candidate may indicate happiness or pleasure in the United States, but for Asians, it can also be a sign of embarrassment or discomfort. In the United States, maintaining eye contact is the sign of a good communicator; in the Middle East, it is an integral part of successful communication; but for the Chinese and Japanese, it can indicate distrust. Many Americans shake hands to greet people, whereas Middle Easterners of the same sex kiss on the cheek. Chinese never greet each other with kisses on the cheeks, nor do they exchange hugs. Flying arms or moving hands are perceived as bad manners, as are physical displays of frustration and enthusiastic slaps on the back. Business cards are always presented with two hands because it shows greater respect than presenting it with just one.

With regard to *space*, how close you are to another person, where you sit or stand, and how you arrange your office can have a significant impact on communication. **Proxemics** *is the study of ways in which people use physical space to convey messages.* Think about how you would feel if you walked into class midway through the term and someone was sitting in "your" seat. You'd probably feel angry because your space, or territory, had been invaded. To test how important your territory is to you, complete the questionnaire shown in Figure 16.2 on the following page.[11]

The distances at which people feel comfortable when communicating vary greatly by culture. South Americans and Southern and Eastern Europeans prefer closeness. Asians, Northern Europeans, and North Americans prefer not to be as close. These behaviors reflect a culture's overall tendency to be *high context* or *low context*. People in high-context cultures like to stand close and touch each other. High-context cultures usually are located in warmer climates; there people tend to have greater interpersonal orientation and are perceived as interpersonally "friendly." Those from low-context cultures prefer to stand farther apart and touch infrequently. These cultures are often found in cooler climates, in which people tend to be task oriented and interpersonally "cool." Figure 16.3 on page 535 shows the approximate placement of various countries along the high- to low-context culture continuum. For example, in Japan, strict rules of etiquette guide seating behavior. If businesspeople are traveling together on a train, the most senior executive sits next to the window, facing the direction in which the train is moving. In a taxi, the "top" seat is behind the driver and the most junior seat is next to the driver. In elevators, the senior person stands in the rear in the center facing the door and the most junior person stands near the buttons.[12]

Spatial arrangements in corporate offices in North America send many signals to members of an organization.[13] In some organizations, such as Kimberly-Clark, JC Penney, and EDS, top managers have larger offices, windows with better views, plusher carpets, and higher quality furnishings than do middle managers. Having a personal assistant, a seat at the head of the table at meetings, a chauffeured limousine, use of

Figure 16.2 | **How Territorial Are You?**

Instructions: Circle one number to answer each question as follows:

1. Strongly agree
2. Agree
3. Not sure
4. Disagree
5. Strongly disagree

1. If I arrive at my apartment (room) and find my roommate sitting in my chair, I am annoyed if he/she doesn't at least offer to get up immediately.	1	2	3	4	5
2. I do not like anyone to remove anything from my desk without first asking me.	1	2	3	4	5
3. If a stranger puts a hand on my shoulder when talking to me, I feel uncomfortable.	1	2	3	4	5
4. If my suit jacket is lying on the back of a chair and another student comes in and chooses to sit in the chair, I feel that he or she should ask me to move my jacket or choose another seat.	1	2	3	4	5
5. If I enter a classroom and "reserve" a chair with a notebook, I am annoyed and offended upon my return to find my book moved and someone sitting in "my" seat.	1	2	3	4	5
6. If a person who is not a close friend of mine gets within a foot from my face to talk to me, I will either back off or uncomfortably hold my ground.	1	2	3	4	5
7. I do not like strangers walking into my room (apartment).	1	2	3	4	5
8. If I lived in an apartment, I would not want the landlord to enter for any reason without my permission.	1	2	3	4	5
9. I do not like my friends or family borrowing my clothes without asking me first.	1	2	3	4	5
10. If I notice someone staring at me in a restaurant, I become annoyed and uncomfortable.	1	2	3	4	5

To score and interpret your responses, add the numbers you circled for all 10 statements. Then compare your total with the following definitions:

10–25 points: *Highly territorial.* Your instincts for staking out and protecting what you consider yours are high. You strongly believe in your territorial rights.

26–39 points: *Ambiguous but territorial.* You may act territorial in some circumstances but not in others. You feel differently about different types of space.

40–50 points: *Not territorial.* You disagree with the entire concept of territoriality. You dislike possessiveness, protectiveness, and jealousy. The concept of private ownership is not central to your philosophy of life.

a private dining room, and the ability to summon employees for discussion all send messages via the use of space. Organizations that seek to treat people more equally, such as Whole Foods, Dollar General, and Starbucks, intentionally avoid these status symbols. Most managers don't have the opportunity to plan and design the buildings in which employees work. However, many do have the opportunity to plan floor lay-

Figure 16.3 | **Examples of Cultures on the Cultural Context Continuum**

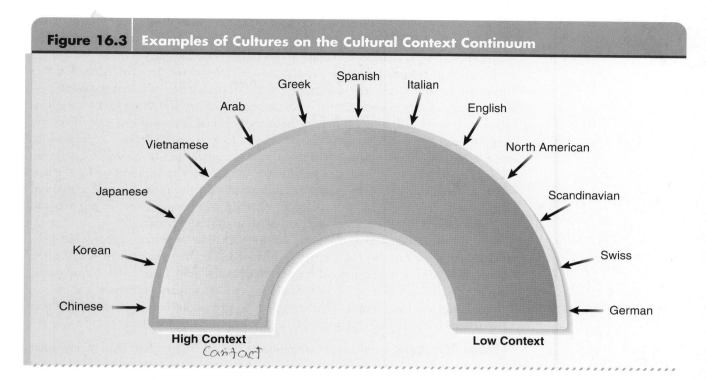

outs and the style and arrangement of office furniture, the tables and chairs used to furnish meeting rooms, and similar elements of work space.

Recently, some organizations, such as Citibank in Sydney, Australia, Lanyon Phillips in Vancouver, British Columbia, and Concord Hospital in Concord, New Hampshire, have turned to feng shui to foster better communications. Feng shui *is a system for arranging everything around you in such a way that your environment works for you and with you.* Nearly 4,000 years ago, farmers in southern China recognized that how they arranged their fields, their crops, and their homes had significant effects on their lives.[14] For example, they noticed that families whose huts faced north were hit by dust storms, whereas those with huts facing south were protected from wind and dust and enjoyed the warmth and light of the sun. Today, many Chinese businesspeople believe that organizations need to seek a balance between social and economic relationships. The emphasis on harmony is critical to the success of the business. The same principles have been adapted by managers to increase the flow of communications.

Feng shui (pronounced "fung schway") is all about increasing chi ("chee") or energy and making sure it flows in the right direction. Donald Trump hired an expert in feng shui to consult on the layout and design of his Trump International Hotel and Tower in New York City. Among other recommendations, the expert suggested that the building's entrance face Central Park, in order to achieve balance with nature. Similarly, to improve communications, Northern Ontario first arranged its office furniture to encourage people to informally communicate with each other.[15] Sitting rooms were arranged so people could more easily communicate with each other. The less obstructed a person's view, the more likely communication is to take place. Second, because the office is right across from the Canadian Pacific railway tracks, a concrete planter with evergreens was built. This buffered the noise from the passing trains and added some color to the walls. Third, offices were arranged so that people do not sit with their backs to the door, so they can see if someone is approaching. If a person cannot see who is approaching, he or she might become anxious and fearful. Employees' computer monitors were positioned to avoid glare, which strains the eye. Employees were asked to remove clutter from their desks because clutter means that

Chapter 16 *Communicating Effectively* 537

they are surrounded by a bunch of decisions that have been postponed. Fourth, when a manager has been in an office for a long period of time and has to move to another office, the office is changed to adjust to this person's needs.

In terms of *personal appearance*, you've undoubtedly heard the expression "Clothes make the person." Style consultants for major corporations believe that the way a person dresses definitely communicates something to others. You should ask yourself: Is the way I'm dressed going to hurt or help my business relationships? Like it or not, people judge you partly on the basis of how you look. If you're dressed appropriately, customers and others may see you as a more competent person than someone who dresses inappropriately. This is especially true for people who are meeting for the first time. Of course, what is *appropriate* depends on the organization. A conservative suit fits in well on Wall Street, but looks out of place in a Staples store. In the arts and entertainment industry, fashionable clothes are more appropriate.

Posture also communicates meaning by signaling a person's degree of self-confidence or interest in what is being discussed. The more interested you are, the more likely you are to lean toward the person who is talking. Conversely, leaning away may communicate a lack of interest. Similarly, tension and anxiety typically show in a person's legs and feet. People often are able to hide tension from the waist up but may give themselves away by crossing their legs tightly and tapping their feet.[16]

Verbal Messages. Employees communicate verbally more often than in any other way. Spoken communication takes place face to face, over the telephone, and via other electronic media. Most people prefer face-to-face communication because nonverbal messages are an important part of it. But some people prefer written communications because it allows them to choose and weigh their words more carefully before sending the message. When emotions run high, or someone is writing in a second language, weighing words carefully can be advantageous.

Effective verbal communication requires the sender to (1) encode the message in words (and nonverbal cues) that will convey it accurately to the receiver, (2) convey the message in a well-organized manner, and (3) try to eliminate distractions. At Bank of America, loan officers must be especially good at sending verbal messages. Many customer transactions involve the use of long written documents, filled with legal and financial jargon. Loan officers assume that most customers won't read these documents, even though they are required to sign them. Therefore, sales associates take responsibility for conveying verbally the messages contained in the written documents. They translate the jargon into everyday language and then summarize what the documents mean for the customer, checking to be sure that the customer understands the key points.

Written Messages. Although spoken communication is quicker than written communication and allows the sender and receiver to interact, organizations use many forms of written messages (e.g., reports, memoranda, letters, e-mail, and newsletters). Such messages are most appropriate when information has to be collected from or distributed to many people at scattered locations and when keeping a record of what was sent is necessary. The following are some guidelines for preparing effective written messages:

1. The message should be drafted with the receiver clearly in mind.

2. The contents of the message should be well thought out ahead of time.

3. The message should be as brief as possible, without extraneous words and ideas.

4. Important messages should be prepared in draft form first and then polished. If the message has to be long, a brief summary should be presented on the

first page. This summary should clarify the main points and contain page references to details on each item.

5. The message should be carefully organized. The most important point should be stated first, then the next most important point, and so on. Thus, even if the receiver reads only the first few points, the essentials of the message will get across. Giving the message a title makes the subject clear. Using simple words and short, clear sentences make the message more readable and easily understood.

What happens when people do not communicate clearly is illustrated in the following Ethical Challenge between New Balance and one of its Chinese operators.[17] Before reading this feature, remember that all communication takes place within a cultural context. Behind every written document is a series of cultural codes that are important to understand. China is a high-context country. That means that the message can only be understood in relation to its environment. Managers in high-context cultures tend to be much less literal and much more personal than managers in low-context cultures (e.g., United States).

Ethical Challenge

New Balance

New Balance has annual sales of more than $1.6 billion. Executives at New Balance are proud that they still own five plants in New England that manufacture footwear. Even so, about 70 percent of its shoes are now made in China, another 5 percent in Vietnam, and the rest in the United States. Horace Chang, a businessperson who opened a factory near Hong Kong, employs more than 4,000 people to manufacture and distribute New Balance products in China. He had signed a contract protecting New Balance's intellectual property rights. The contract banned him from selling the shoes without the permission of New Balance. Chang then started to manufacture an inexpensive "classic" shoe and within the first year, sold more than 250,000 pairs. The shoe looked like the New Balance brand.

New Balance notified him that it was terminating his company's right to make and distribute classics. He was supposed to return to New Balance all of its confidential technical information, production molds, and marketing plans, but he didn't. At New Balance's request, China's

Administration of Industry and Commerce seized about 100,000 pairs of shoes from his factories and discovered that Chang had launched his own brand of "classics" called Henkees. He marked them with a logo on the saddle that was supposed to be a distortion of "Hi." At a glance, customers thought that it looked a lot like New Balance's block N. He had obtained a trademark on the Hi logo from China without informing New Balance.

New Balance took Chang to court in Hong Kong. New Balance senior managers knew that judges are elected locally, promoted locally, and fired locally. They also knew that if New Balance won the suit, it had the potential to cost thousands of local factory workers their jobs. The court found that while New Balance had terminated its agreement with Chang's Hong Kong factory, it failed to do so in his other factories. The court also found that the agreement between Chang and New Balance carried an implied license to distribute shoes without paying any royalties.

To learn more about this organization, visit *www.newbalance.com.*

Channels

The channel *is the path a message follows from the sender to the receiver.* Information richness *is the information-carrying capacity of the channel.* Not all channels can carry the same richness of information.[18] Written communications are low in richness. Customer and employee surveys are a form of written communication that many organizations rely on heavily despite their lack of information richness. Surveys usually ask people to express their opinions about various topics by choosing from multiple-choice options. Customers might be asked to indicate whether they were delighted, just satisfied, or disappointed with the customer service they received. Employees might be asked to indicate whether they strongly agree, agree, disagree, or strongly disagree with a statement such as "My manager treats me with respect." This form of communication facilitates quantitative analyses, but it limits the type and amount of information received from customers and employees. Only the information written down is received. A channel low in richness is considered to be *lean* because it is effective mainly for sending specific data and facts.

As Figure 16.4 indicates, face-to-face communication is the richest communication channel. It conveys several clues simultaneously, including spoken and nonverbal information. Face-to-face communication also provides immediate feedback so that understanding can be checked and misinterpretations corrected. Managers can gather additional information about how customers and employees feel about the organization and its products by speaking with them personally. Focus groups are a structured form of rich face-to-face communication that often is used to gauge customers' reactions to products. The telephone is somewhat less rich than face-to-face communication, but not as lean as written surveys. When Goodman joined Staples in 2001, she changed Staples' approach to customer satisfaction surveys in order to obtain richer information. She discontinued its mail survey and began to walk into stores and talk to customers. Directly hearing the voices of customers added richness and perspective to the information provided.

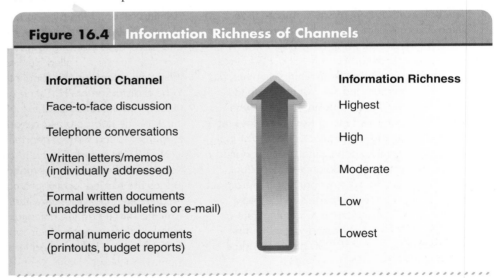

Figure 16.4   Information Richness of Channels

Information Channel		Information Richness
Face-to-face discussion		Highest
Telephone conversations		High
Written letters/memos (individually addressed)		Moderate
Formal written documents (unaddressed bulletins or e-mail)		Low
Formal numeric documents (printouts, budget reports)		Lowest

In addition to selecting a channel that fits the level of information richness they need, individuals must choose among several *types* of channels for communicating with others. They include downward, upward, and horizontal formal channels as well as informal channels, such as the grapevine and networking or caucus groups.

Downward Channels. Downward channels *involve all the means of sending messages from management to employees.* For instance, the Freeport, Maine, mail-order headquarters of L. L. Bean, the $1.4 billion apparel and sporting goods cataloger, receives more than 350,000 communications (e.g., phones calls, faxes, and e-mail messages) a day during the holiday season for 16,000 outdoor items ranging from socks to flannel shirts to hunting bows to tents.[19] It sends out more than 200 million catalogs a year from which it receives 80 percent of its sales and has more than 3 million visitors annually to its Freeport, Maine, store. L. L. Bean recently opened a Japanese version of its e-commerce site (*www.llbean.co.jp*) that includes a Japanese pronunciation database for customer service representatives in Freeport and has an online payment system for the yen.

To communicate effectively with L. L. Bean's 3,900 employees, managers use downward channels to convey

- ▶ how to handle special promotional items;

- ▶ job descriptions, detailing duties and responsibilities;

- ▶ policies and procedures, explaining what is expected of employees and the organization's rules and employee benefits;

- ▶ feedback about an individual's job performance; and

- ▶ news of activities and events that management believes employees should participate in (charitable organizations, blood drives, and the like).

Managers frequently use downward communication effectively as a channel, but it may be the most misused channel because it provides little opportunity for employees to respond. In fact, the fundamental problem with downward communication is that it is too often one way. It's a lean channel that doesn't encourage feedback from those on the receiving end. To correct this problem, managers should urge employees to use upward channels.

Upward Channels. Some managers don't see the value of encouraging employees to participate in setting goals, planning, and formulating policies. The result is a failure to use upward channels of communication. Upward channels *are all the means used by employees to send messages to management.* Such channels may be the only formal means that employees have for communicating with higher level managers in the organization. Upward communication includes providing feedback on how well employees understand the messages they have received via downward channels. Moreover, it enables employees to voice their opinions and ideas. If effective, upward communication can provide an emotional release. At the same time, it gives employees a chance to participate, the feeling that they are being listened to, and a sense of personal worth. Most important, employees and customers often have excellent suggestions for improving efficiency and effectiveness. That is why Staples' Goodman frequently receives hotline calls, talks with customers, and chats with sales associates.

At Cirque du Soleil, upward channels are as strong as downward channels.[20] Specific methods for communicating upward include direct personal contacts and three publications circulated regularly within the company. One publication is *The Ball*, which features a column that enables employees to complain, gripe, and rib without censorship. "This is part of the way we do things," explained Marc Gagnon, executive vice president of business services and development. One message indicated that the writer felt that the Dutch employees were being treated better than the Canadians. This information was quite useful because it allowed the company to head off certain issues before they could become crises. *The Ball* also informs employees of events and activities taking place at company locations around the world.

Besides its publications, Cirque du Soleil uses employee focus groups to help design new initiatives and develop new policies. "We look for three things," explained Gagnon:

- ▶ Make sure the proposed policy is clear and employees understand it.

- ▶ See if they agree with it, or if they disagree with it, why.

- ▶ See if we have any chance to get employees to use it. Employees are allowed to say "no" to a policy.

Snapshot

"Sell good merchandise at a reasonable profit; treat your customers like human beings, and they will always come back for more. Tell them honestly about the product and give them great service. Give employees straight answers to their questions and the business will grow."
Leon Leonwood Bean, Founder, L. L. Bean

Upward channels provide many benefits, but managers need to be aware of the problems that can plague upward communication. First, most employees don't want their superiors to learn anything negative about them, so they may screen out bad news. Most employees try to impress their superiors by emphasizing their contributions to the organization. Some may even try to make themselves look better by putting others down. Second, an employee's personal anxieties, aspirations, and attitudes almost always color what is communicated. Would you tell a potential employer of the bad things you've heard about the organization? If you really wanted the job, you probably wouldn't be so bold. Finally, the employee may be competing for the manager's job and thus remains silent in the hope of being recommended for it when the manager is promoted and moves to another position.

Realizing that employees aren't always comfortable giving direct upward feedback has led many companies to provide another alternative—anonymously contacting a third party. At Pillsbury, employees can call a recording machine and sound off. Verbatim transcripts are prepared of each call and forwarded to the CEO and other top-level managers, with no identification about the gender or any other detectable caller characteristics. The objective is to let the company's senior managers hear the views of employees, without causing employees to be fearful of what might happen to them for voicing their concerns and criticisms. Employees began using the service to share all sorts of information. They noted that a clock in one bakery always ran five minutes fast, identified locations that didn't carry particular products on the shelves, suggested new pizza toppings, and complained so much about slow expense reimbursements that the company overhauled some of its accounting procedures. By calling to express their appreciation, employees also made a hero of a manager who closed down operations during a snowstorm.[21] Companies that have also encouraged upward communication include TDIndustries, Crocs, and Brinker. In each case, the CEO encourages open griping and pays particular attention when the same comment is made repeatedly.

Horizontal Channels. Horizontal channels *are all the means used to send and receive messages across departmental lines, with suppliers, or with customers.* This type of channel is especially important in network organizations (see Chapter 11). Essential to the success of a network organization is maintaining effective communication among customers, suppliers, and employees inside and those working outside of the organization. New Balance outsources 75 percent of its manufacturing of athletic shoes and apparel. It needs effective horizontal communication channels to link suppliers with information about market demand in order to schedule production and shipping efficiently.

Horizontal channels are formal if they follow prescribed organizational paths. Messages communicated horizontally usually are related to coordinating activities, sharing information, and solving problems. Horizontal channels are extremely important in today's team-based organizations, where employees must often communicate among themselves to solve their clients' production or process problems.

Informal Channels. So far we have concentrated on formal channels of communication. Equally important, however, are informal channels of communication. Informal channels *represent all of the informal means for sender and receiver to communicate downward, upward, and horizontally.* The grapevine *is an organization's informal communication system, along which information can travel in any direction.* The term comes from a Civil War practice of hanging telegraph lines loosely from tree to tree, like a grapevine. In organizations, the path that messages follow along the grapevine is based on social interaction, not organization charts.

At Xerox's Palo Alto Research Center, informal channels are essential to its success. The company learned just how important informal channels were when it began looking for ways to boost productivity. Management hired a social anthropologist to observe closely the behavior of technicians who repaired copiers (tech reps) in an effort to improve efficiency. The consultant saw that tech reps often made a point of spending time with each other but not with customers. They would hang around the parts warehouse or the coffee pot and swap stories from the field. The consultant recognized the importance of these informal conversations to tech rep performance. Through their stories, the reps shared knowledge and generated new insights about how to repair machines better. Xerox concluded that tech rep performance could be improved by increasing this type of communication, so the company issued two-way radio headsets to the reps.[22]

Informal channels of communication have been recognized by many organizations as so important that they encourage and provide support for employees' efforts to strengthen them. Employee network groups *are informal groups that organize regularly scheduled social activities to promote informal communication among employees who share a common interest or concern.* In many organizations, network groups form to bring together employees who share common interests and concerns. For example, at Sara Lee, Motorola, IBM, and many other large organizations, numerous network groups (also called affinity groups) exist for members of particular ethnic groups. The main goal of social network groups is to create a communication channel to exchange ideas.[23] According to a survey of Fortune 500 companies, affinity groups have grown rapidly during the past decade. Participants benefit from the business information shared during meetings, as well as from the friendships they form and the contacts they make. At Sara Lee, women's leadership councils operate within specific divisions of the company to support career development and offer networking opportunities for women. To ensure their effectiveness, Ellen Turner, president of Sara Lee Foods, regularly reviews developmental activities of female and minority employees.

External Networking. Managers and employees also spend considerable time meeting with peers and others outside the organization. They attend meetings of professional associations, trade shows, and other gatherings. As a result, they may develop various close, informal relationships with talented and interesting people outside the organization. People use these networks to help each other, trading favors and calling on each other's resources for career advancement or other types of information and support.

The following Communication Competency feature illustrates how social networks carry information that influences millions of people. Personal connections, forged through words, pictures, video, and audio posted on Web sites, are the core of a social network. These types of Web sites provide real peer-to-peer communication that is very credible in the eyes of users. Users of social networks produce and freely share a whole universe of content for others to use. According to Bradley Horowitz, director of technology development for Yahoo!, "Social networking is the concept of leaving value for others. That value starts with expression." For example, Pet Talk provides pet owners the opportunity to upload photos of pets and share stories. The company sponsoring Pet Talk found that when it sends surveys to thousands of members, response rates are much higher and the data more useful because pet owners feel a part of a community. The expansion of social networks will be driven not just by the technology, but also by the various causes of people who use it.[24]

Social Networks through MySpace

More than 100 million people use MySpace and millions more use social networks where people share one category, such as Flickr (photos), Digg (new stories), Wikipedia (encyclopedia articles), and YouTube (video). Some of these social networks are art, journalism, or just a great deal of fun. MySpace and Flickr are targeting the 18- to 34-year-old audience and connecting them to real action, as opposed to "fake" action on TV. The influence of social networks on communications is important because networked consumers are not passive participants in the communication process. It's easier than ever for them to uncover independent information about companies or events and to post their own opinion about the same issue.

It should be no surprise that a political protest on MySpace was one of the first real-world demonstrations of the power of social networks. Activists are able to use the power of social networks because these Web sites mesh their goals of connecting and empowering individuals. For example, on Monday, March 27, 2006, about 40,000 mainly Latino high school students in Los Angeles played hooky to protest the Senate's proposed bill to crack down on illegal immigration. On May 1, 2006, in metropolitan areas all across the United States, millions of people demonstrated against this proposed bill.

Rupert Murdoch, the chairman and managing director of News Corporation, paid more than $580 million to buy MySpace, because it enables the News Corporation to place ads where millions of teens visit. Murdoch hopes that the site will not only generate revenues, but will serve as a gold mine for new ideas and tastes and for finding new talent. His idea is to build relationships with "panels" of thousands of users who will become part of the decision-making process and give feedback on their ideas.

To learn more about this organization, visit *www.myspace.com.*

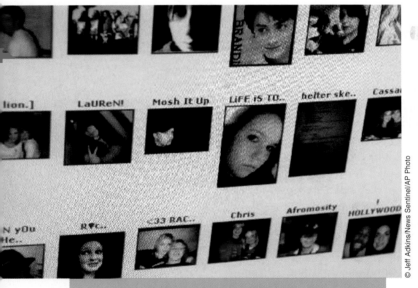

Social networks on the Internet have quickly become powerful, valuable tools, which was especially apparent when Google acquired YouTube for $1.65 billion in stock in late 2006.

© Jeff Adkins/News Sentinel/AP Photo

Feedback

Feedback *is the receiver's response to the sender's message.* The communication cycle isn't complete until the sender receives feedback from the receiver. It's the best way to show that a message has been received and to indicate whether it has been understood. As Shira Goodman and her top managers found out at Staples, lots of information gets filtered and lost between top management and those salespeople who see customers. As senior managers at New Balance learned in dealing with Horace Chang in China, one shouldn't assume that everything you say or write will be understood exactly as you intend it to be. If you don't encourage feedback, you're likely to misjudge how much others understand you. Thus you'll be less effective than those who encourage feedback.

When managers are asked to rank the communication skills they find crucial to their success on the job, they consistently place feedback at the top of the list. Managers spend more than half their time listening to others. Because most people speak at a rate of 100 to 150 words per minute and the brain is capable of thinking at a rate of 400 to 500 words per minute, people often daydream. Therefore, feedback is needed to ensure that messages sent are accurately received. The following Self-Management Competency feature allows you to assess your openness to receiving feedback.[25]

Whenever a message is sent, the actions of the sender affect the reactions of the receiver. The reactions of the receiver, in turn, affect later actions of the sender. If the sender receives no response, the message was never received or the receiver chose not to respond. In either case, the sender is alerted to the need to find out why the receiver didn't respond. Upon receiving rewarding feedback, the sender continues to produce the same kind of message. When feedback is *not* rewarding, the sender eventually changes the type of message.

Self-Management Competency

Are You Open to Feedback?

When answering these 11 questions, use the following rating scale:

1. Strongly disagree
2. Disagree
3. Slightly disagree
4. Slightly agree
5. Agree
6. Strongly agree

_____ 1. I seek information about my strengths and weaknesses from others as a basis for self-improvement.

_____ 2. When I receive negative feedback about myself from others, I do not get angry or defensive.

_____ 3. In order to improve, I am willing to be self-disclosing to others (i.e., share my feelings and beliefs).

_____ 4. I am very much aware of my personal style of gathering information and making decisions.

_____ 5. I am very much aware of my own interpersonal needs when it comes to forming relationships with other people.

_____ 6. I have a good sense of how I cope with situations that are ambiguous and uncertain.

_____ 7. I have a well-developed set of personal standards and principles that guide my behavior.

_____ 8. I feel very much in charge of what happens to me, good and bad.

_____ 9. I seldom, if ever, feel angry, depressed, or anxious without knowing why.

_____ 10. I am conscious of the areas in which conflict and friction most frequently arise in my interactions with others.

_____ 11. I have a close personal relationship with at least one other person with whom I can share personal information and personal feelings.

SCORING KEY

Skill Area	Total
Self-disclosure and openness to feedback from others (items 1, 2, 3, 9, 11)	_____
Awareness of own values, cognitive style, change orientation, and interpersonal orientation (items 4, 5, 6, 7, 8, 10)	_____
Grand Total	_____

COMPARISON DATA

Compare your scores to three standards: (1) the maximum possible (66); (2) the scores of other students in your class; and (3) the scores of a norm group consisting of more than 500 business students. In comparison to the norm group, if you scored

55 or above,	you are in the top quartile.
52–54,	you are in the second quartile.
48–51,	you are in the third quartile.
47 or below,	you are in the bottom quartile.

Receiver reactions also tell the sender how well goals are being achieved or tasks are being accomplished. However, in this case the receiver exerts control over the sender by the type of feedback provided. The sender must rely on the receiver for an indication of whether the message was received and understood. Such feedback assures the sender that things are going as planned or brings to light problems that have to be solved. Companies often have guidelines in place for providing effective feedback. According to these guidelines, feedback should have the following characteristics[26]:

1. *It should be helpful.* If the receiver of the message provides feedback that adds to the sender's information, the feedback is likely to be seen as constructive.

2. *It should be descriptive rather than evaluative.* If the receiver responds to the message in a descriptive manner, the feedback is likely to be effective. If the receiver is highly critical (or judgmental), the feedback is likely to be ineffective or even cause a breakdown in communication.

3. *It should be specific rather than general.* The receiver should respond specifically to points raised and questions asked in the message. If the receiver responds in generalities, the feedback may indicate evasion or lack of understanding.

4. *It should be well timed.* The reception—and thus the effectiveness—of feedback is affected by the context in which it occurs. Giving performance feedback to a person during a round of golf or at a luncheon is different from giving the same person this feedback in the office. Informal settings usually are reserved for social activities as opposed to performance-based feedback.

5. *It should not overwhelm.* Spoken communication depends heavily on memory. Accordingly, when large amounts of information are involved, spoken feedback is less effective than written feedback. People tend to "tune in and out" of conversations. They may fail to grasp what the speaker is saying if the message is too long and complex.

Perception

Perception *is the meaning given to a message by either sender or receiver.* Perceptions are influenced by what people see, by the ways they organize these elements in memory, and by the meanings they attach to them. The ability to perceive varies from person to person. Some people, having entered a room only once, can later describe it in detail, whereas others can barely remember anything about it. Thus the mental ability to notice and remember is important. How people interpret what they perceive is affected by their pasts. A clenched fist raised in the air by an employee on strike and walking the picket line could be interpreted as either an angry threat to the organization *or* as an expression of union solidarity and accomplishment. The attitudes that people bring to a situation color their perceptions of it.

Some problems in communication can be traced to two problems of perception: selective perception and stereotyping. Selective perception *is the process of screening out information that a person wants or needs to avoid.* Many people "tune out" TV commercials. Most everyone has been accused at one time or another of listening only to what they want to hear. Both are examples of selective perception. In organizations, employees sometimes do the same thing. Manufacturing employees pay close attention to manufacturing problems, and accounting employees pay close attention to debits and credits. Such employees tend to filter out information about other areas of the organization and focus on information that is directly related to their own jobs.

Stereotyping *is the process of making assumptions about individuals on the basis of their belonging to a certain gender, race, age, or other category.* Stereotyping distorts reality by suggesting that all people in a category have similar characteristics, which simply isn't true. Look at the photo. What is your stereotype of those in the photo? Can you identify one of the world's richest men in this photo? See page 556 for answer.

Stereotyping is not only unfair, but leads to inaccurate conclusions about people and their capabilities.

© Microsoft

During the 1990s, organizations became increasingly sensitive to the potential negative consequences of stereotyping based on a person's gender, race, ethnicity, age, or sexual orientation. As they have sought to manage workforce diversity more effectively, many organizations—including State Farm Insurance and Citigroup—have developed training programs and other initiatives to reduce the negative personal and organizational consequences of stereotyping. We discuss workforce diversity further in Chapter 18.

In summary, then, the message sent, the channel of communication used, and the ability to respond all depend on a person's perceptions. Encoding and decoding skills are based on a person's ability to perceive a message and situation accurately. Developing the ability to send and receive messages accurately is central to developing your communication competency.

Hurdles to Effective Communication

One of the first steps in communicating more effectively is to identify hurdles to the process. These hurdles hinder the sending and receiving of messages by distorting, or sometimes even completely blocking, intended meanings. We have divided these impediments into organizational and individual hurdles—although there is obviously some overlap—and listed them in Table 16.3.

2.
Identify hurdles to communication.

Table 16.3	Hurdles to Communication

Organizational
Authority and status levels
Specialization of task functions by members
Different goals
Status relationships among members

Individual
Semantics
Emotions

Organizational Hurdles

Channels of communication, both formal and informal, are largely determined by organization design. Hierarchical organizations have more levels of authority and greater differences in status (e.g., reserved parking spaces, larger offices) among their members. Flat organizations have relatively few authority levels, tend to be more democratic, and have fewer status differences. The degree of specialization present in the organization also may affect clear communication, as can the presence of conflicting goals.

Authority and Status Levels. A person holding a higher formal position than another person has a higher level of authority. A person who is held in higher esteem than another person, regardless of their positions, has a higher status. Authority level and status often go hand in hand, but not always. Status *is a person's social rank in a group.* This is often determined by a person's characteristics, in addition to the person's formal position. When status and authority level differ, communication problems are likely to occur.

The more levels in the organization—and the farther the receiver is from the sender—the more difficult effective communication becomes. Figure 16.5 on the next page illustrates the loss of understanding as messages are sent downward through a formal communication channel. To minimize this problem, top managers increasingly

Snapshot

"Be honest, open, and direct and recognize that for every employee who might like what you are doing there could be another who doesn't, and you're not going to make everybody happy. You need to minimize status differences between people."

**Bruce Chizen,
CEO, Adobe**

are using live video presentations to deliver the same message to employees at all of an organization's locations. In doing so, these managers use both verbal and nonverbal messages. Videos also increase the probability that the original messages will be received intact. Many organizations use videos to smooth the transition of managers to new locations. Such presentations can introduce the managers, reinforce the reason(s) for the relocation, and emphasize the need for employee cooperation during the changeover.

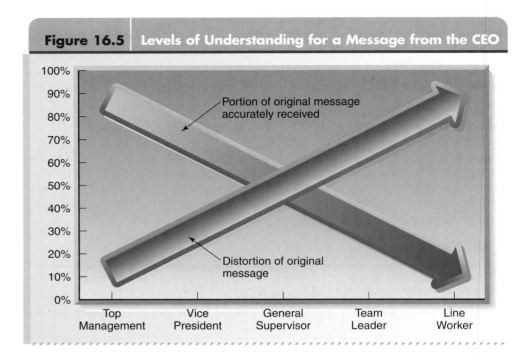

Figure 16.5 Levels of Understanding for a Message from the CEO

Even when communicating with others at the same level of authority, status can interfere with the process. In group discussions, members having higher status speak more and have more influence than members having lower status. This phenomenon is difficult to overcome, and it has been observed in exchanges of e-mail messages and face-to-face discussion groups. When computer-mediated group discussions were first introduced, many people expected them to decrease the effects of status on communication. Instead such information technologies often reinforce existing status relationships and magnify their effects on communication.

In organizations with flat hierarchies, such as Sun Hydraulics and Chaparral Steel, authority levels may not interfere with communication, but status is likely to come into play. Temporary employees, for example, often report feeling as if they are treated as second-class workers. Often they are excluded from meetings, not invited to social functions, and denied team-based rewards. They seldom hear news as it travels through the grapevine and miss the many advantages of being part of informal communication networks. Not surprisingly, then, nearly one of four managers reports that friction between permanent and temporary workers is a significant disadvantage of relying on temporary employees to create flexible staffing levels and reduce costs.[27]

Specialization. As knowledge becomes more specialized, professionals in many fields develop their own jargon, or shorthand, to simplify communication among themselves. That often makes communication with people outside a particular field difficult. For example, a tax accountant and a marketing research manager might have trouble communicating successfully. Moreover, in an attempt to make themselves powerful, some people intentionally use the language of specialization to obscure what's going on. Employees often use specialized language when trying to "snow" others. When a plumber wrote to the U.S. Department of Housing and Urban Development (HUD) to find out whether using hydrochloric acid to unclog drains was safe, a HUD bureaucrat wrote back: "The efficacy of hydrochloric acid is indisputable, but corrosive acid is incompatible with metallic permanence." The plumber wrote back saying he agreed and was using it. A fax message from the bureaucrat arrived immediately at the plumber's shop. It read: "Don't use hydrochloric acid. It eats the hell out of pipes." Then the plumber understood.

Different Goals. If each department has its own goals, these goals can interfere with the organization's overall performance.[28] David Neeleman, president of JetBlue Airways, doesn't set departmental goals because he believes that they would create conflicts between departments. The maintenance department might want to take a plane out of service for maintenance, while the operations managers might need the plane. Such conflicts can be direct consequences of competing interests, or they may simply arise from misunderstandings created by the different perspectives of the people involved. However, open communication between people with differing goals speeds problem solving and improves the quality of solutions. At ARAMARK, a large managed-services organization, each of its seven divisions—campus dining, business dining, sports and recreation, facilities management, maintenance, hospital, and correctional—has its own goals for revenue, account retention, and gaining new accounts. The goal of the campus-dining director is to serve student dining needs. Some colleges also outsource their maintenance and facilities needs, so it would be logical for the campus-dining director to look into a campus's needs in these other two areas. Unfortunately, most campus-dining directors narrowly focus on their own goals and neglect reaching out to help the organization reach its overall goals in the other areas. Why? Because their rewards are based on achieving their own unit's goals, not those of the entire organization.

Individual Hurdles

The Center for Creative Leadership at Greensboro, North Carolina, estimates that half of all managers and 30 percent of top managers have some difficulty communicating with others.[29] Through an intense training session at the center, managers can learn how to improve their communication competencies. The center's staff works with participants who believe that their messages are clear and effective when, in fact, they aren't. Their words, phrases, and references may be clear to some individuals, puzzling to others, and obscure to still others. These problems can be caused by semantics and emotions.

Semantics. *The study of the way words are used and the meanings they convey is called* semantics. Misinterpretation of word meanings can play a large role in communication failure. When two people attribute different meanings to the same words but don't realize it, a communication hurdle exists. Consider what happened when a sales rep phoned in a special order to her company's shipping department. She asked that it be shipped "as soon as possible," expecting these words to ensure that the order was given top priority. Five days later, the sales rep got a call from the irate customer wanting to know when the order would be delivered. Upon checking with the shipping department, the sales rep found that the order was being shipped that day. After some shouting, she realized that, in the shipping department, "as soon as possible" meant that the request did *not* need to be given top priority.

To avoid such blunders, companies should routinely have messages translated back to the original language to ensure the accuracy of the original translation—a process called *backtranslation*. If the original message and the backtranslation version agree, the translated version probably will not have the unexpected meaning. Even backtranslation is not foolproof, however, because the meanings of words often depend on the context in which they are used, especially in high-context cultures (e.g., Arabic, Japanese, and Chinese). In these cultures, communication involves sending and receiving many subtle cues. Nonverbal cues, slang subtleties, and inferences are all essential aspects of communication. The Japanese often talk around a point without ever stating it directly. From their perspective, it is the responsibility of the listener to discern the message from the context. German, Scandanavian, and Anglo cultures are low-context cultures that place more emphasis on the precise meanings of words and terms.

Emotions. An emotion *is a subjective reaction or feeling.* Remembering experiences, an individual recalls not only events but also the feelings that accompanied them. Thus when people communicate, they convey emotions as well as facts and opinions. The senders' feelings influence encoding of the message and may or may not be apparent to the receiver. The receivers' feelings affect decoding of the message and the nature of the response.

Misunderstandings owing to differences in what arouses people's emotions often accompany cross-cultural communication. In Japan, for example, feelings of embarrassment and shame are more easily aroused during social interactions than they are in Western cultures. Furthermore, these emotions aren't easily detected by people not socialized in the Japanese culture. Consequently, Westerners are likely to create situations that cause their Japanese counterparts to feel embarrassment and shame without realizing it—and thus seem insensitive.

Although there are many other cultural differences in how people experience and express emotions, there are also many similarities. Rather than being hurdles to communication, these similarities aid communication. In particular, the antecedents of some emotions—anger, happiness, disgust, fear, sadness, and surprise—seem to be similar in most cultures, as are the facial expressions that accompany the emotions. These similarities mean that nonverbal cues are less likely to be misinterpreted when emotions are involved.[30]

Listening and choosing words wisely and selectively can be enormously helpful when dealing with people from other countries. Steve Morris, CEO of Singapore-based Steve Morris Associates, found that the inabilities to listen and communicate effectively are major causes of poor leadership and management decisions in Asia. He indicates that listening more and talking less can act as a huge advantage because there is less potential for a person to say the wrong thing. The following Multicultural Competency feature highlights some ways that non–Chinese-speaking people can improve their communications while doing business in China. Melanie Hayden was former vice president of organizational development and communications with Citibank Asia Pacific.[31]

Multicultural Competency

Melanie Hayden

The Chinese style of communications is generally indirect. Chinese show a remarkable resistance to counterfactual thinking. Telling someone what they should have done is a less effective form of communication than simply telling the person what they must do in detail. Chinese may talk around the point and hedge their speech with softening modifiers, such as *maybe* or *perhaps,* because

they must protect their social face and respect social roles (e.g., manager, subordinate). The Chinese will lose social face if they fail to understand what is being asked or cannot do what is requested. The Chinese are also concerned about protecting the asking person's face. Therefore, by being vague, Chinese businesspeople save face and can continue to build and maintain relationships. For example, when the Chinese say "Let me look into this further," it is simply a way to avoid a direct no. Many Americans find that Chinese partners apparently agree to certain terms or conditions but then fail to follow through (see the Ethical Challenge on page 537).

Hayden offers this advice for communicating with the Chinese:

▷ Use "softening" words, such as *maybe*, *perhaps*, or *could be*. Say "What do you think about this project?" instead of "Is this project acceptable?"

▷ Use a group to gain more active participation. Chinese employees are more willing to speak for the group than for themselves.

▷ Where possible, use oral (preferably face-to-face) rather than written communication.

▷ Balance criticism with confidence building; give credit to others.

▷ Always start with a positive statement.

▷ Showing anger is a no-no.

▷ Be patient.

▷ Respect politeness; be humble.

▷ Try to avoid "yes" or "no" questions.

▷ Avoid Western idioms.

▷ Do not tell jokes because they are likely to be misunderstood.

Fostering Effective Communication

3.

State ways to eliminate communication hurdles and improve your communications.

Eliminating Hurdles

Regardless of how much information is needed to create feelings of overload in individuals, every organization is capable of producing a great volume of information and more. One way of doing so is to ask others to bring you information only when significant deviations from goals and plans occur (known as *exception reporting*). When everything is going as planned, managers don't need a report. To empower subordinates, managers should let them know that they don't need to copy you on *all* of those e-mail messages.

Regulate the Flow of Information. If you receive too much information, you will suffer from information overload. How much information is too much varies from one person to the next and may even be different for today's X-Generation. The X-Generation has grown up in an environment where 10- to 30-second TV commercials are normal and students do homework with iPods turned on. MTV and video games that can lead to information overload for older people are normal for today's students.

Regardless of how much information is needed to create the sensation of information overload, every organization is capable of producing volumes of information. Therefore, managers should set up a system that identifies priority messages for immediate attention. Some e-mail software packages allow senders to put "red flags" next to their messages, indicating urgency to recipients. In spite of this, between 35 and 50 percent of all e-mail received is regarded as unimportant. There is a lot of "spamming" going on. E-mail usage has been associated with a decrease in face-to-face communications and a feeling of employees being less connected to the organization.

Encourage Feedback. You should follow up to determine whether important messages have been understood. Feedback lets you know whether the other person understands the message accurately.[32] The sales manager who describes desired changes in the monthly sales planning report receives feedback from the report itself when it is turned in. If it contains the proper changes, the manager knows that the message was received and understood. Similarly, when you talk to a group of people, look for nonverbal feedback that will tell you whether you are getting through to them.

Simplify the Language. Because language can be a hurdle, you should choose words that others will understand. Your sentences should be concise, less than 15 words. Avoid jargon that others won't understand or that may be misleading. In general, understanding is improved by simplifying the language used—consistent, of course, with the nature of your intended audience.

Listen Actively. You need to become a good listener as well as a good message sender. Some organizations offer training programs to improve employee listening. Such programs emphasize that listening is an active process in which listeners and speakers share equal responsibility for successful communication. The following are some characteristics of active listeners[33]:

▶ *Appreciative:* Listens in a relaxed manner, seeking enjoyment, knowledge, or inspiration.

▶ *Empathic:* Listens without judging, is supportive of the speaker, and learns from the experiences of others.

▶ *Comprehensive:* Listens in order to organize and make sense of information by understanding relationships among ideas.

▶ *Discerning:* Listens to get complete information, understand the main message, and determine important details.

▶ *Evaluative:* Listens in order to make a decision based on the information provided.

Restrain Negative Emotions. Like everyone else, you convey emotions when communicating, but negative emotions can distort the content of the message. When emotionally upset, you are more likely than at other times to phrase a message poorly. When you or others get angry and upset, call a halt until you and the other people involved can restrain your emotions—that is, until all of you can be more descriptive than evaluative.

Use Nonverbal Cues. You should use nonverbal cues to emphasize points and express feelings. Recall the methods of nonverbal communication that we've presented. You need to be sure that your actions reinforce your words so that they don't send mixed messages.

Use the Grapevine. As a manager, you couldn't get rid of the grapevine in an organization even if you tried, so you should use it to send information rapidly, test reactions before announcing a final decision, and obtain valuable feedback. Also, the grapevine frequently carries destructive rumors, reducing employee morale and organizational effectiveness. By being "plugged into" the grapevine, you can partially counteract this negative effect by being sure that relevant, accurate, meaningful, and timely information gets to others.

Improving Your Personal Communications Competencies

To be an effective communicator, you must understand not only the communication process depicted earlier in Figure 16.1, but also the guidelines for fostering effective communication. These guidelines, presented throughout the chapter, are summarized in the following list. We have expressed them in terms of the American Management

Association's seven guidelines that you can use to improve your communication skills[34]: *Fostering Effective Communication*

▶ *Clarify your ideas before communicating.* Analyze the topic or problem to clarify it in your mind before sending a message. Communication often is ineffective because the message is inadequately planned. Part of good message planning is considering the goals and attitudes of those who will receive the message.

▶ *Examine the true purpose of the communication.* Before you send a message, ask yourself what you really want to accomplish with it. Decide whether you want to obtain information, convey a decision, or persuade someone to take action.

▶ *Consider the setting in which the communication will take place.* You convey meanings and intent by more than words alone. Trying to communicate with a person in another location is more difficult than doing so face to face.

▶ *Consult with others, when appropriate, in planning communications.* Encourage the participation of those who will be affected by the message. They can often provide a viewpoint that you might not have considered.

▶ *Be mindful of the nonverbal messages you send.* Tone of voice, facial expression, eye contact, personal appearance, and physical surroundings all influence the communication process. The receiver considers both the words and the nonverbal cues that comprise your message.

▶ *Take the opportunity to convey something helpful to the receiver.* Considering the other person's interests and needs often presents opportunities to the sender. You can make your message clearer by imagining yourself in the other's position. Effective communicators really try to understand the message from the listener's point of view.

▶ *Follow up on the communication.* Your best efforts at communication can be wasted unless you succeed in getting your message across. You should follow up and ask for feedback to find out whether you succeeded. You can't assume that the receiver understands your message; feedback in some form is necessary.

If you follow these recommendations, you will improve your ability to communicate effectively. Unfortunately, when communication does break down, people often waste time and energy trying to figure out who is at fault, provoking a defensive reaction that further inhibits effective communication. Oftentimes defensive behavior occurs in times of stress, such as during as downsizings, plant closings, or workplace aggression.

Ethical Issues in Communications

4.

Discuss two ethical issues in communications.

Earlier in this chapter, we described how social networks have changed the way in which people communicate and develop cyber communities. Given the fact that these networks have an influence on the way people communicate, many organizations are finding that their real competitive edge comes from their employees' ability to use real-time information found in social networks and databases. The ability to use real-time information to make decisions raises two major ethical issues: computer ethics and privacy.

Because databases and other forms of information can be accessed from anywhere around the world, many employees no longer have a need to come to work everyday. Their ability to work at home or away from their office has been aided by technology. Many employees contend that this has enabled them to be more independent and productive. In fact, Eli Lilly & Company recently asked employees about what hours they preferred to work and found out that a normal work day (e.g., 9-to-5) was outdated. Many employees didn't want the commute to work, but wanted the flexibility to work at home or offsite from another location. The price for increased employee independence has led some organizations to monitor employee's work. Also, it is tempting for employees to engage in personal activities, such as checking stock quotes, shopping, or looking for another job, while on the job. Advances in communications are likely to increase the pressures on both management and employees to develop a code of ethics.

Computer Ethics

Computer ethics *is concerned with the nature and social impact of information technologies and the formulation of policies for their appropriate use.*[35] An increasing number of individuals and organizations are concerned with computer ethics. The ethical issues surrounding computers arise from their unique technological characteristics, including the following:

▶ Computers make mistakes that no human being would make.

▶ Computers communicate over great distances at high speed and low cost.

▶ Computers have huge capacities to store, copy, erase, retrieve, transmit, and manipulate information quickly and economically.

▶ Computers have the effect of radically distancing (depersonalizing) originators, users, and subjects of programs and data from each other.

▶ Computers may collect and store data for one purpose that can easily be used for another purpose and be kept for long periods of time.

The Computer Ethics Institute, a professional association headquartered in Washington, D.C., was formed because of growing concerns with the ethical use of computer technology. It has issued a "ten commandments" of computer ethics, which are listed in Table 16.4.[36] The commandments provide an ethical code of conduct for guidance in situations that may not be covered by law.

Other than the occasional urge to throw our computers out the window due to technical glitches, most of us regard them as old friends—and some people take it a step further by making their computers accomplices in their unethical behavior.

©image 100/Jupiter Images

Table 16.4	Computer Ethics

1. Thou shalt not use a computer to harm other people.
2. Thou shalt not interfere with other people's computer work.
3. Thou shalt not snoop around in other people's files.
4. Thou shalt not use a computer to steal.
5. Thou shalt not use a computer to bear false witness.
6. Thou shalt not copy or use proprietary software for which you have not paid.
7. Thou shalt not use other people's computer resources without authorization or proper compensation.
8. Thou shalt not appropriate other people's intellectual output.
9. Thou shalt think about the social consequences of the program you are writing or the system you design.
10. Thou shalt use a computer in ways that show consideration and respect for your fellow humans.

The following Self-Management Competency feature gives you an opportunity to assess and develop further your understanding of computer ethics.[37] With the ability to send text messages, download music into iPods, and receive and send e-mails from almost anywhere in the world, we now have the ability to access lots of information. In many schools and organizations, the emphasis is on learning and creating knowledge and not just on getting the assignment or project completed. With this explosion of information, some ethical questions have arisen as discussed next.

Self-Management Competency

Ethics and Information Technology

Instructions: Twenty statements appear in this survey. You should evaluate each statement by using the following five-point scale:

1 True
2 Somewhat True
3 Neither True nor False
4 Somewhat False
5 False

If you think that a statement is *true*, record a 1 next to it. If you think that a statement is *neither true nor false*, place a 3 next to it, and so on. Don't skip any statement.

_____ 1. Somehow it seems easier to cross the line in e-mail than it does elsewhere in your life.

_____ 2. Employees are usually informed by employers if their voice mail is going to be monitored.

_____ 3. If you supply a false e-mail address just to get someone out of your hair, you're committing an ethical violation.

_____ 4. Most organizations have clear written policies and procedures for deletions of text in e-mails or inserting short phases in brackets for clarification.

_____ 5. The confidentiality of e-mail and text messaging is generally well maintained.

_____ 6. People often claim that they do not understand the message when they actually do.

_____ 7. Many people claim that they did reply to an e-mail message when they actually did not.

_____ 8. People often send e-mails from another's account without permission for the purpose of deceiving someone.

_____ 9. People often edit the headers or forwarded messages so as to misrepresent the time, date, and author.

_____ 10. The best way to deter unethical behavior in the use of computers is through professional codes of conduct.

_____ 11. People often intentionally omit someone from a "To" list for the purposes of harm or harassment.

_____ 12. Many people intentionally delay sending a message so as to deprive the recipient of time-critical opportunities or information.

_____ 13. Oftentimes people send a text message to embarrass the recipient.

_____ 14. People borrow other people's words a lot.

_____ 15. MySpace and other social networks are fairly well "policed" and do not contain potentially harmful information.

_____ 16. The statement "I have not given or received aid . . ." deters e-mail fraud.

_____ 17. Someone borrows a friend's password to gain access to a library.

_____ 18. Students think that if they get it off the Internet, it's free.

_____ 19. The issue of the public's trust of intellectual property is high.

_____ 20. Employees routinely play computer games on company time.

Scoring

Discuss your answers with a friend. What have you learned about your computer ethics? How easy was it to defend your answers?

Privacy Issues

The amount and types of information available about most individuals in the United States and Canada to just about any business (or individual in that business) or government agency are astounding. Some of this information starts to be gathered when people borrow money, participate in a government program, or purchase goods with a credit card. Consumers and borrowers routinely give information voluntarily to retailers and creditors so that they can purchase goods on credit. At least once a month, banks, retailers, credit card companies, and mail-order houses send computer tapes or other electronic files detailing their customers' purchases and payment activities to credit bureaus.

The three large credit rating companies—Experian, TransUnion, and Equifax—maintain credit information on more than 200 million people in the United States. This information is accessible in a matter of seconds to merchants, clerks, and, in essence, just about anyone. In addition to credit ratings, a large amount of information on nearly everyone in the United States—ranging from medical histories and insurance information to buying habits—is stored in computer-readable form and widely disseminated among credit bureaus, resellers of data purchased from bureaus, and many businesses. The information that used to be inaccessible or very difficult to obtain is now instantly available for use by almost anyone. Protection of privacy through the legal system, organizational and managerial policies and practices, self-regulation through professional and trade associations, and consumer groups hasn't caught up with technological developments as we noted in Chapter 3 on ethics and social responsibility.

One step in the direction of trying to reestablish online "rights of privacy" was taken by the Council of Better Business Bureaus, headquartered in Arlington, Virginia.[38] One component of their initiative is the "Privacy Seal Program," which participating and approved companies can use and display on their Web sites. For consumers, the program is designed to help Internet users identify companies that stand behind their privacy policies and have met the program requirements of notice, choice, access, and security in the use of personally identifiable information. Among other things, the program requires a site to disclose how it intends to use the information being collected, mandates that consumers be allowed to opt out of data collection, and requires site operators to obtain parental permission to collect data on children. The nation's largest online advertising agency, DoubleClick Inc., has been banned from tracking users without their knowledge. Though the company will continue tracking the movement of online visitors, it must now reveal its methods for retrieving and using this information and give individuals access to the profiles created about them.[39]

Some critics of the online invasion of privacy crisis assert that such voluntary industry efforts are inadequate. They contend that more governmental regulation and enforcement of privacy protections are needed for both consumers and employees. However, with the increased threat of terrorism since September 11, 2001, the efforts of the U.S. government have focused more on gaining access to private information than on protecting privacy.

Answer for photo on page 546: lower left is Bill Gates, Chairman of Microsoft.

Chapter Summary ....

Effective communication is essential to many aspects of human endeavor, including organizational life. For managers, the communication competency is the foundation on which managerial effectiveness is built. Through communication, managers gather and interpret information that they then use to plan, set goals, and make strategic decisions. Strategic decisions, in turn, must be communicated throughout the organization, where they are used to guide planning and team activities. In cross-cultural situations, the multicultural competency supports effective communication.

Learning Goals ....

1. Explain the communication process.

The communication process comprises six elements: the sender (encoder), the receiver (decoder), the message, channels, feedback, and perception. Of the many possible forms of nonverbal communication, managers should be particularly aware of—and able to use effectively—space, physical appearance, and body language. Channels of communication are both formal and informal. Formal channels are downward, upward, and horizontal. Managers most frequently use downward channels to send messages to the various levels of the organization. Upward channels allow employee participation in decision making and provide feedback to management. Horizontal channels are used among peers in different departments and are especially important in network organizations. Informal channels—the grapevine and network groups— often are as important as formal channels of communication. Managers can never eliminate the grapevine and thus should learn to use it to send messages and receive feedback.

2. Identify hurdles to communication.

Hurdles to communication hinder the sending and receiving of messages by distorting or even blocking intended meanings. Hurdles can be either organizational or individual. Organizational hurdles may result from the design of the organization itself, from differences in status, from the jargon that often grows up around highly specialized tasks, and from differing goals. Individual hurdles may result from conflicting assumptions on the part of the sender and receiver, from misinterpretation of meaning, and from misunderstanding of emotional reactions.

3. State ways to eliminate communication hurdles and improve your communications.

Ways to improve your communication effectiveness include regulating the flow of information you send to others, encouraging others to give you feedback on whether your message has been understood, using language that the receiver understands, actively listening to what others are saying, restraining your negative emotions, and paying special attention to nonverbal cues that others are sending you. Guidelines for effective communication include clarifying ideas, examining the purpose of communicating, considering the setting, consulting with others, being mindful of nonverbal messages, taking the opportunity to convey something helpful to the receiver, following up, and being sure that actions taken support the communication.

4. Discuss two ethical issues in communications.

Many ethical issues arise from unique characteristics of computers and information technologies. The "ten commandments" of computer ethics reflect the need for radically different attitudes and actions of individuals. These commandments provide an ethical code of conduct for situations not covered by law. Privacy issues are also becoming more important because more and more individuals have access to information once considered private.

Key Terms and Concepts

Channel
Communication
Computer ethics
Decoding
Downward channels
Emotion
Employee network groups
Encoding
Feedback

Feng shui
Grapevine
Horizontal channels
Informal channels
Information richness
Listening
Message
Nonverbal messages
Perception

Proxemics
Receiver
Selective perception
Semantics
Sender
Status
Stereotyping
Upward channels

Questions for Discussion and Reflective Thinking

1. What type of communication channels did Shira Goodman of Staples use? When is each channel most effective?

2. Why are some people defensive about receiving feedback about their performance?

3. How do your friends deal with computer privacy?

4. How does upbringing contribute to the communication differences between men and women?

5. The world is a busy and confusing place, and people are constantly bombarded by multiple messages. How do you simplify these messages in order to reduce the confusion?

6. How do cultural expectations of a society impact both verbal and nonverbal communications?

7. Besides taking foreign language lessons, what other activities could you participate in to avoid communication blunders overseas? What benefits would be associated with improving this competency?

8. Go to the *www.chacocanyon.com/pointlookout/050406.shtml* Web site and download the newsletter by Rick Brenner on e-mail ethics. Do you support his statements?

9. Relationships between a manager and subordinates are critical to good communication. What obstacles have you observed that hinder good communications between managers and subordinates?

10. What specific actions do you need to take to improve your communications competency?

DEVELOPING YOUR COMPETENCIES

The following statements relate to how your manager and you communicate on the job. There are no right or wrong answers. Respond honestly to the statement, using the following scale:

1 Strongly Agree	2 Agree	3 Uncertain	4 Disagree	5 Strongly disagree

____ 1. My manager criticizes my work without allowing me to explain.

____ 2. My manager allows me as much creativity as possible in my job.

____ 3. My manager always judges the actions of his or her subordinates.

____ 4. My manager allows flexibility on the job.

____ 5. My manager criticizes my work in the presence of others.

____ 6. My manager is willing to try new ideas and to accept other points of view.

____ 7. My manager believes that he or she must control how I do my work.

____ 8. My manager understands the problems that I encounter in my job.

____ 9. My manager is always trying to change other people's attitudes and behaviors to suit his or her own.

____ 10. My manager respects my feelings and values.

____ 11. My manager always needs to be in charge of the situation.

____ 12. My manager listens to my problems with interest.

____ 13. My manager tries to manipulate subordinates to get what he or she wants or to make himself or herself look good.

____ 14. My manager does not try to make me feel inferior.

____ 15. I have to be careful when talking to my manager so that I will not be misinterpreted.

____ 16. My manager participates in meetings with employees without projecting his or her higher status or power.

____ 17. I seldom say what really is on my mind because it might be twisted and distorted by my manager.

____ 18. My manager treats me with respect.

____ 19. My manager seldom becomes involved in employee conflicts.

____ 20. My manager does not have hidden motives in dealing with me.

____ 21. My manager is not interested in employee problems.

____ 22. I feel that I can be honest and straightforward with my manager.

____ 23. My manager rarely offers moral support during a personal crisis.

____ 24. I feel that I can express my opinions and ideas honestly to my manager.

____ 25. My manager tries to make me feel inadequate.

____ 26. My manager defines problems so that they can be understood but does not insist that his or her subordinates agree.

____ 27. My manager makes it clear that he or she is in charge.

____ 28. I feel free to talk to my manager.

____ 29. My manager believes that if a job is to be done right, he or she must oversee it or do it.

____ 30. My manager defines problems and makes his or her subordinates aware of them.

____ 31. My manager cannot admit that he or she makes mistakes.

____ 32. My manager tried to describe situations fairly without labeling them as good or bad.

____ 33. My manager is dogmatic; it is useless for me to voice an opposing point of view.

____ 34. My manager presents his or her feelings and perceptions without implying that a similar response is expected from me.

____ 35. My manager thinks that he or she is always right.

____ 36. My manager attempts to explain situations clearly and without personal bias.

Communication Inventory Scoring and Interpretation Sheet

Place the numbers that you assigned to each statement in the appropriate blanks. Now add them to determine a subtotal for each communication category. Place the subtotals in the proper blanks and add your scores.

Part I: Defensive Scores

Evaluation		**Neutrality**	
Question 1	_____	Question 19	_____
Question 3	_____	Question 21	_____
Question 5	_____	Question 23	_____
Subtotal	_____	Subtotal	_____

Control		**Superiority**	
Question 7	_____	Question 25	_____
Question 9	_____	Question 27	_____
Question 11	_____	Question 29	_____
Subtotal	_____	Subtotal	_____

Strategy		**Certainty**	
Question 13	_____	Question 31	_____
Question 15	_____	Question 33	_____
Question 17	_____	Question 35	_____
Subtotal	_____	Subtotal	_____

Subtotals for Defensive Scores

Evaluation	_____	Neutrality	_____
Control	_____	Superiority	_____
Strategy	_____	Certainty	_____

Total _____

Place an X on the graph to indicate what your perception is of your organization or department's communication. You may wish to discuss with others their own perceptions and interpretations.

18 25 30 35 40 45 50 55 60 65 70 75 80 85 90
Defensive Defensive to Neutral Neutral to Supportive Supportive

Part II: Supportive Scores

Provisionalism		**Spontaneity**	
Question 2	_____	Question 20	_____
Question 4	_____	Question 22	_____
Question 6	_____	Question 24	_____
Subtotal	_____	Subtotal	_____

Empathy		**Problem Orientation**	
Question 8	_____	Question 26	_____
Question 10	_____	Question 28	_____
Question 12	_____	Question 30	_____
Subtotal	_____	Subtotal	_____

Equality		**Description**	
Question 14	_____	Question 32	_____
Question 16	_____	Question 34	_____
Question 18	_____	Question 36	_____
Subtotal	_____	Subtotal	_____

Subtotals for Supportive Scores

Provisionalism	_____	Spontaneity	_____
Empathy	_____	Problem Orientation	_____
Equality	_____	Description	_____

Total _____

Place an X on the graph to indicate what your perception is of your organization or department's communication. You may wish to discuss with others their own perceptions and interpretations.

18 25 30 35 40 45 50 55 60 65 70 75 80 85 90
Supportive Supportive to Neutral Neutral to Defensive Defensive

Questions

1. What communication skills would you like to improve?

2. What did you learn about your communication competency from this exercise?

3. What steps will you take to become a more effective communicator?

Going to the hospital is no fun. Nobody likes to do it. The experience is unnerving, often frightening, and a symbol of our own mortality. Also, it is difficult for the average person to judge the "quality" of the hospital, based on direct evidence. Therefore, it is important to learn as much as possible about the competence, care, and integrity of a medical facility before entering it.

The Mayo Clinic doesn't leave this information to chance. Mayo tells a consistent and compelling story of its services to potential "customers." At Mayo Clinic, the patient always comes first. Hospital employees are hired and trained and facilities are designed with that in mind. Mayo offers patients and their family's concrete and convincing evidence of its strengths and values: competence, care, and integrity. Communicating these values to patients has resulted in exceptional positive word of mouth, and abiding customer loyalty has enabled Mayo Clinic to build the most powerful name in health care. It was done with very little advertising. It's called evidence management, an organized, explicit approach to presenting customers with easy-to-understand information and honest communication of the hospital's abilities. Evidence management is much like advertising, except that it turns Mayo Clinic into a living, breathing advertisement for it. And it's all done through communication.

A study was done on the communication process at Mayo Clinic. Researchers interviewed 1,000 Mayo employees and patients and observed hundreds of doctor–patient visits at Mayo. They even checked themselves in as patients. They got the message that Mayo was communicating: The patient comes first. However, verbal communication is not the only type of communication that works. Mayo Clinic has effectively designed a communication system that coordinates doctors' needs and patients' requests. The clinic communicates with patients and visitors through careful planning of space, light, color, sound, and the attitudes and personal appearance of staff members.

Many Mayo patients describe their care as being organized around their personal needs rather than the doctor's schedule, the hospital's processes, or any other factor. Mayo staff members clearly signal the patient-first focus. Patients are reassured by the kindness and concern shown by the staff. Their caring attitude is clearly communicated. The caring attitude applies not only to doctors and nurses, but is embodied by all staff members, including the receptionists when patients check in. This is due to the fact that Mayo consistently hires people who genuinely embrace the organization's values of quality, competence, integrity, and caring. This is reinforced to employees through training and ongoing seminars. William Mayo, one of the founders, stated in 1910, "The best interest of the patient is the only interest to be considered." This statement guides hiring practices and decisions to this day. People are not hired at Mayo because of intellect or technical skill alone. Those things are important, of course, but individual personality, personal values, and life experiences are equally important in the hiring process.

A story is told of a young woman whose wedding was scheduled to take place at a time when her mother became critically ill. The mother was not expected to live to attend her daughter's wedding in several weeks. Mayo came through. Nurses and staff members decorated the hospital's atrium for the wedding, provided a cake, nurses handled makeup and a hairstyle for the ill mother and wheeled her bed to the atrium. The hospital chaplain performed the ceremony, while hospital staff, family, and friends watched from the atrium balconies. The bride said they looked "like angels from above." That wedding signaled not only evidence of caring to the patient and her family, but also a strong reminder to the staff that the patients really do come first.

Because medical services are so intangible and technically so complex, patients are especially attentive to what they can see and understand in the physical environment. The questions for the Mayo Clinic's top administrators were "What does the Mayo Clinic communicate to customers?" "Do these clues convey the optimal message about our service?" From public spaces to exam rooms to laboratories, Mayo facilities have been designed explicitly to relieve stress, offer a place of refuge, create positive distractions, and convey caring and respect. For example, the outpatient facilities include quiet, darkened private areas for patients to rest between appointments. The pediatric unit located in Mayo's St. Mary's Hospital Emergency Department, for example, transformed artwork by local schoolchildren into a colorful arrangement of wall and ceiling tiles. The resuscitation equipment in the examination rooms is hidden behind a large picture, which slides out of the way when the equipment is needed. Public spaces are made softer with natural light, color, artwork, music, and fountains.

The architect who designed Mayo Rochester's 20-story Gonda building said, "I would like the patients to feel a little better before they see their doctors." Mayo has used careful planning of space as a means of communicating that it cares about the people occupying that space. A well-designed physical environment also has a positive impact on employees, reducing physical and emotional stress—which is of value to patients as well. Visible employee stress communicates the wrong signals to patients. Mayo does not wish to convey the wrong signals. For example, on the main floor of the Gonda building, there is a multimedia Cancer Education Center. Its location was chosen to help take the stigma out of having cancer.

Mayo understands that the way employees present themselves also sends signals to patients. Doctors do not wear casual attire, nor do they wear the typical medical white coats. Instead, the more than 2,500 staff physicians wear business suits, unless, of course, they are wearing surgical scrubs. The suits convey professionalism and expertise and also communicate respect to patients and their families. The physicians' area is near patients' rooms and has a large sofa to hold the patient and family members. This arrangement removes the desk as a barrier to communication. The patient also may use the sofa to lie down while waiting for the doctor. This design helps communicate care, comfort, and compassion, showing commitment to patient well-being before the patient meets the doctor. The environment also inspires health-care professionals to deliver the high quality of care the patient is seeking.

Years ago, a young laboratory employee went to work one morning and her supervisor noticed and commented that the woman's white shoelaces were soiled. She was told to clean the shoelaces and to be more careful in the future. That young woman has since progressed to administrator of General Service and the Office of Patient Affairs. Her name is Mary Ann Morris, and she said, "Though I was initially offended, I realized over time that everything I do, down to my shoelaces, represents and communicates my commitment to our patients and visitors. Twenty-eight years later, I still use the dirty shoelace story to set the standard for the service level I aspire to for myself and my coworkers." Mayo believes that the personal appearance of its staff conveys the message of respect for the patient and instills a feeling of pride in the employees.

A dirty shoelace may seem minor, given the overall picture of caring for the patient, but a shoelace is something that a patient (customer) can see, while medical expertise and technical ability are not. It is a small part of the story that Mayo communicates to its customers—a story that puts each patient in a starring role—a story that communicates not only competence, but great caring, as well. What Mayo Clinic has done is identify a simple, consistent message and then manage the evidence—the buildings, the approach to care, and even the shoelaces—to support that message, day in and day out, year after year.

Questions

1. What channels of communications are illustrated in this case?

2. What are the nonverbal clues that the clinic uses to communicate its mission to patients and their families?

3. What communication competencies are illustrated in this case?

chapter 17

© Comstock Images/Jupiter Images

Working in Teams

Learning Goals

After studying this chapter, you should be able to:

1. Explain the importance of work teams.

2. Identify five types of work teams.

3. State the meaning and determinants of team effectiveness.

4. Describe the internal team processes that can affect team performance.

5. Explain how to diagnose and remove barriers to poor team performance.

Communication Competency

Planning and Administration Competency

Teamwork Competency

Managing Effectively

Self-Management Competency

Strategic Action Competency

Multicultural Competency

Challenge of Managing ....

W. L. Gore & Associates

© Roberto Borea/AP Photo

When Wilbert L. Gore launched his business in 1958, he had 17 years of experience as an engineer at DuPont and understood how traditional, large businesses were run. He thought that many big organizations took risks and were committed to change only when they faced a crisis. To deal with crises, they formed task forces, overrode established hierarchies, and finally got things done. "Why should we have to wait for a crisis?" Gore asked himself. His company would be different. In the following years, he created a company with hardly any hierarchy and few titles or bosses. Gore believed in the power of small autonomous teams, open communication, and a strong commitment to innovation and change. He organized his company as if it were a collection of self-administered task forces.

At Gore, teams are the nucleus of a successful strategy of innovation that has yielded products such as the famous Gore-Tex fabric, the dental floss Glide, and Elixir guitar strings. Almost 50 years later, W. L. Gore & Associates still feels like a small company. Yet it has grown into a $1.58 billion enterprise with over 6,300 employees. Each of Gore's manufacturing facilities has only 150 to 200 employees. The small size of each facility ensures that people are familiar with each other and consider themselves a team. Everyone knows who works on what and they have a good sense of each person's strengths and weaknesses. Multidisciplinary work teams include R&D technicians, salespeople, and production workers. Because there are no standard job descriptions, employees can decide for themselves what "commitments" they take on in their teams. Most decisions are made on a team basis. For example, compensation decisions are made by evaluation committees that carefully assess each individual's contribution to their team's success.

CEO and President Terri Kelly is proud of Gore's reputation as one of the Best Companies to Work For. Much of the company's appeal is due to its team-based culture. When new associates are hired, they are chosen to work in general areas, not specific jobs. Their sponsors (not bosses) help them identify opportunities to use their talents to help meet team objectives, and associates then commit to projects that match their skills. The culture

Learning Content

provides associates with a great deal of freedom and in return expects them to work cooperatively.

To be successful, associates learn to embrace four guiding principles that were set down by Bill Gore:

▶ Fairness to each other and everyone with whom they come in contact

▶ Freedom to encourage, help, and allow other associates to grow in knowledge, skill, and scope of responsibility

▶ The ability to make one's own commitments and keep them

▶ Consultation with other associates before undertaking actions that could impact the reputation of the company.

For those joining the organization from other companies, Gore's team-centered approach requires some getting used to.[1]

To learn more about this organization, visit *www.gore.com*.

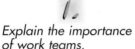

Explain the importance of work teams.

Work Teams and Other Groups

In everyday conversation, the terms *group* and *team* often are used interchangeably, but in this chapter we distinguish between the two. Here, *group* is the more general term, and *team* is a special type of group. Teams and groups are both important to organizational life, but for different reasons.

Organizational Groups

A **group** *is two or more individuals who come into personal and meaningful contact on a continuing basis.* Many types of groups can be found in most organizations. Some of these are formal groups responsible for doing the work of the organization. Among the formal organizational groups that you learned about in Chapter 11 are departments, divisions, and business units.

Informal groups—such as bowling leagues and parent-support groups—can also be found in organizations. An **informal group** *consists of a small number of individuals who frequently participate together in activities and share feelings for the purpose of meeting their mutual needs.* Informal groups have little to do with completing tasks required by the employer. In the last chapter, you learned about affinity groups. In most organizations, affinity groups are a type of informal group the company supports even though the activities of the group are not directly related to people's work responsibilities.

Five employees who by chance happen to sit at the same lunch table in their company's cafeteria one day are not a group. Although they have personal contact, it isn't likely to be highly meaningful and most likely is just a brief, one-time event. Suppose, however, that the same five employees regularly seek each other out and almost always eat lunch together. As their interactions become more meaningful and they develop expectations for each other's behavior, the five employees become an informal group.

Informal groups may support, oppose, or have no interest in organizational goals, rules, or higher authority. When informal groups become very cohesive, however, they can pose special challenges if the employees feel dissatisfied.[2] Pilots working for major airlines often form cohesive informal groups. United Airlines discovered how powerful those informal groups were when the pilots decided not to work overtime because top management had not negotiated a new contract with them. The pilots banded together in informal groups at United's major hubs in Denver, Chicago, and Los Angeles, and agreed to refuse to fly overtime. Angry customers who were left stranded at airports vowed never to fly United Airlines again.

Organizations like W. L. Gore and Whole Foods encourage employees to participate in positive informal groups, such as those based on shared hobbies or other interests. The friendships formed in such informal groups are greatly valued by many employees and may result in their feeling a greater sense of loyalty toward their employer. Members of work teams may develop close friendships that bind them together emotionally and increase their sense of loyalty, but this is not the primary objective of organizing employees into work teams.

Work Teams

Work teams are generally much smaller than formal organizational groups and their purpose is to serve the company. A work team *consists of a small number of employees with complementary skills who collaborate on a project, are committed to a common purpose, and are jointly accountable for performing tasks that contribute to achieving an organization's goals.*

To illustrate how organizational groups differ from work teams, consider how auto repair garages can be organized. In a traditional garage located at a Subaru dealership, the employees who provide maintenance and repair services belong to an organizational group with its own identity. Usually, the service manager controls the flow of their work assignments. As repair jobs come in, the service manager decides which technician will work on each job, and in what order they will do their work. Technicians often perform their jobs in relative isolation. Each technician has a task to do, and the various technicians who work on a particular repair are not held jointly responsible for the finished product. In a garage with this traditional organization, mechanics are members of a group but they don't work as a true team.

In a team-based garage at a Lexus dealership, technicians work in small teams of about six people. A repair job is assigned to the whole team. Technicians do not specialize in specific repairs. The service manager's role is to act as a coach-player. He or she helps the team with special problems that arise and gives advice about how the team can be more effective. When the repair is finished, the team as a whole is held accountable for the parts they used, the time they billed, and for the customer's satisfaction. A study that compared traditional repair garages to team-based garages found that team-based garages were more profitable and their customers were more satisfied.[3]

To be a work team, the members must have a shared goal that they can achieve only if they communicate and collaborate with each other. At Gore, teams often focus their efforts on developing new products. One team was formed when an associate wondered about whether industrial fibers could be used to clean teeth. The result? They developed Glide dental floss.

The importance of work teams is reflected in the amount of time that managers and others spend in team meetings. Many top managers report spending 50 percent or more of their time in team meetings; first-line managers and professionals may spend between 20 and 50 percent of their time in such meetings. These team meetings range from quick huddles in someone's office to voice-mail exchanges to retreats that last several days. A few of the terms used to describe the many types of work teams found in organizations are shown in Figure 17.1 on the following page.

In some organizations, the importance of team meetings drives the physical design of the work space. As described in the Planning and Administration Competency feature, the architecture of Google's headquarters in Mountain View, California, was created to meet the requirements of the company's many work teams.[4]

Snapshot

"When I arrived at Gore I didn't know who did what. Who was my boss? Then I realized your team is your boss, because you don't want to let them down. Everyone is your boss and no one is your boss."

**Diane Davidson,
Sales Executive,
W. L. Gore**

Figure 17.1 | Terms for Work Teams

Empowered teams
Autonomous work groups
Crews
Self-managing teams
Cross-functional teams
Quality circles
Project teams
Task forces
High-performance teams
Emergency response teams
Committees
Councils

Googleplex

If you tour Google's corporate headquarters in Mountain View, California, you may be a bit puzzled at first. Called Googleplex, this company compound is very different from other company headquarters you might have seen. Located near the Shoreline Regional Park wetlands natural reserve, Googleplex might remind you of a somewhat quirky holiday resort. Lava lamps, electric skooters, and heated lap pools are just part of the fun. On a sunny day, employees might be playing roller hockey in the parking lot or competing in a game of beach volleyball. When the weather is cold and wet, employees may prefer spending time in the company's workout center, or at the Ping Pong and pool tables. Having fun is intentional at Google.

Although you might not realize it at first, "form follows function" at Googleplex. The design of Googleplex perfectly supports the way the company is organized. Outdoor activities and games help build team spirit and camaradie among employees. The work spaces at Google are spacious and comfortable, too. Snack rooms and a state-of-the-art cafeteria offer free, healthy lunches and refreshments along with many opportunities to meet and exchange ideas. Typically, three or four employees share a lounge area with couches and common tables. Inspired by their extraordinary work environment, Google's employees have plenty of room to meet and thrash out new ideas. Indeed, most work gets done in small, project-focused teams, called "Googlettes." From the work of Googlettes have come many of the company's most innovative products—including Google Earth and Gmail.

Of course, formal planning and administration meetings take place, too. Marrissa Mayer is Google's vice president for search products and user experiences. Like a university professor, she holds office hours several times a week. Her staff members use these office hours to chat about their new ideas, propose new projects, review financial issues, and so on. Before a new feature is adopted, it must survive a grueling process of critique and review, managed by Mayer.

To learn more about this organization, visit *www.google.com.*

Why Organizations Use Work Teams

Automakers estimate that developing a new model requires as many as 7 million engineering hours. The design and development of a new car at Toyota or Honda requires as many as 1,000 engineers working together for one to two years. At Google, creating a new product like Gmail may involve dozens of people. Management's first challenge is figuring out how to divide the work involved in such complex projects. Its second challenge is integrating the efforts of the individuals and teams working on the projects to ensure that they achieve the organization's goals.

The specific goals to be achieved differ from team to team and organization to organization. The goals depend partly on the needs of the particular customers being served. The main reasons that managers give for organizing work around teams are serving customers better through innovation, speed, cost reduction, and quality improvement.

A Google employee enjoys coconut milk from a coconut at the Pacific Cafe at the Googleplex.

Innovation and Creativity. Bringing together people who have a variety of experiences and expertise to address a common problem or task can increase creativity, which is the bedrock of new products.[5] At W. L. Gore, Google, and many other companies that thrive by creating new products, teams allow employees to brainstorm and imagine things that don't yet exist. In teams, employees bring together diverse knowledge and skills to create new designs, solve design problems, develop production methods, and develop marketing campaigns.

Speed. In addition to introducing more ideas, teams can reduce the time required for product development. They do so by replacing serial development with parallel development. In the pharmaceutical industry, being first to market with a new pharmaceutical product is absolutely essential to recovering the costs of developing the product and for generating profits from investments in R&D. In the past, the drug developmental process involved completion by one function (e.g., basic research) of its task and then forwarding the item to the next function (e.g., marketing). With parallel development, many tasks are done at the same time and are closely coordinated among the functions. Parallel development cuts the amount of time spent in the developmental cycle, or what is often called *time to market.*

Cost. At Questar Energy Services, teams help keep costs low. Recently, a team of IT specialists redesigned and launched the company's new customer information system. As the team worked on this project, they understood that improving communications with customers was one goal. But keeping the company's costs low also was very important. In the end, the new system cost the company only $25 per customer—that was about $20 per customer less than their competitors were spending. Vice President and COO Shahab Saeed credited teamwork for the success of the project and the competitive advantage they gained. According to Saeed, "Anybody can replicate your infrastructure, but nobody can replicate your human capital."[6]

Quality. Excellent quality is a primary goal of some work teams. At Bang & Olufsen, which offers high-end electronics to home users, providing high-quality products takes priority over reducing costs. Product development is the responsibility of teams of people who bring together a wide range of expertise. For these teams, the standard to be met is not simply to develop a new product—the product should advance the field in design, sound, picture, and user interaction.

Types of Work Teams

Just as the goals to be achieved by work teams can differ greatly, many types of work teams are found in organizations. Some work teams complete their work quickly and then disband; other teams stay together for years. A short-lived team comprising lawyers, investment bankers, and other specialists might be formed to help a company go public and then disband after the initial public offering (IPO). On the other hand, NASA's mission control team has been in existence for several decades.

The membership of work teams also can differ greatly from one situation to another. Sometimes all members of a team work in the same department or field of specialization. The Questar team that designed their customer information system was made up mostly of IT specialists. At other times, work teams include employees from several different departments or even people from different organizations. Product development teams at Bang & Olufsen typically include a designer, a psychologist, a software developer, a narrator, and other experts as needed to create something that is truly unique.

Different types of work teams suit different situations. Problem-solving, functional, multidisciplinary, self-managing, and virtual work teams are five common types found in organizations. Many organizations use all five types.

Problem-Solving Work Teams

A **problem-solving work team** *consists of employees from different areas of an organization whose goal is to consider how something can be done better.* Such a team may meet one or two hours a week on a continuing basis to discuss ways to improve quality, safety, productivity, or morale. Not all problem-solving teams have indefinite life spans, however. Temporary task forces are a familiar example of problem-solving teams that exist just long enough to deal with a specific problem. When Xerox needed to find a solution to a design problem for a product using photoreceptors that had to "rest" for 24 hours in the dark, it turned to a problem-solving team. The team discovered the causes of the problem, developed an improved design, and saved the company $266,000 the first year.

Quality Circles. A **quality circle** *(also called a TQM team) is a group of employees who meet regularly to identify, analyze, and propose solutions to various types of workplace problems.* Meetings usually lasting an hour or so are held once every week or two during or after regular working hours. Quality circles at Navistar International, Johnson & Johnson, and Exxon/Mobil, among others, don't address just one problem and then disband. They are expected to look for and propose solutions to quality-related problems *continually.* Members often receive several hours of formal training in decision-making and team processes, which they apply in their meetings. Quality circles normally don't have the authority to implement their proposed solutions. Instead, they present their solutions to management for further consideration and action.

Task Forces. A **task force** *is a team that is formed to accomplish a specific, highly important goal for an organization.* Task forces often meet intensively during the course of a few weeks or months and then disband. Task force members usually are expected to continue working at their normal jobs for the duration of the task force's existence. Also typical of task forces is diversity in the backgrounds and expertise of the mem-

Snapshot

In its Hutchinson, Minnesota, facility, 3M was able to increase its production gains by 300 percent after organizing its workforce into self-directed teams that were empowered to take corrective actions to resolve day-to-day problems.

R. Williams, self-directed work teams: A competitive advantage, www.qualitydigest .com

bers. Managers often create task forces to help achieve such goals as strategic reorientation, gathering data about the external environment, and designing approaches for implementing a new strategy.

Functional Work Teams

A functional work team *includes members from a single department who have the common goal of considering issues and solving problems within their area of responsibility and expertise.* Functional work teams formed for the purpose of completing their daily tasks are quite stable, enduring for as long as the organization maintains its same basic structure. In contrast, a functional work team brought together as a task force to look at a specific issue or problem disbands as soon as it completes its specific assignment.

At ConAgra, a diversified international food company, a functional team might consist of the purchasing manager and the purchasing agents in the department. Their goals might include minimizing costs and ensuring that beef supplies are available to stores when needed. To achieve their goals, these team members need to coordinate their activities constantly, sharing information on price changes and demand for various products. Radius, a Boston restaurant, also organizes the work around functional teams. There's a meat team, a fish team, a pastry team, and so on. Each team is responsible for everything related to its specialty. The fish team, for example, buys, cleans, and prepares the fish.

Multidisciplinary Work Teams

A multidisciplinary work team *consists of employees from various functional areas and sometimes several organizational levels who collectively work on specific tasks.* In this respect, multidisciplinary teams are like task forces. However, they differ from task forces in one important way: They are the primary means for accomplishing the core work of the organization. The work assigned to multidisciplinary teams at Lockheed Martin includes designing technology, meeting with customers and suppliers, and developing new products for the U.S. Navy. The use of such teams is spreading rapidly and crosses all types of organizational boundaries.[7]

A product development team is a common type of multidisciplinary work team. It exists for the period of time required to bring a product to market, which could vary from a couple of months to several years. Roche, Pfizer, Merck, and other pharmaceutical companies use multidisciplinary teams to speed up the process of bringing new drugs to the marketplace. In the telecommunications and electronics industries, multidisciplinary R&D teams bring together experts having a variety of knowledge and backgrounds to generate ideas for new products and services. To ensure that the products appeal to customers, the work teams may include representatives from marketing and the products' eventual end users. The following Strategic Action Competency feature describes how Roche used multidisciplinatory research teams to keep up with developments in the field of genomics.[8]

Strategic Action Competency

The Roche Group

Genomics, the study of DNA, is one of the biggest revolutions occurring in the pharmaceutical industry. Using genomics, researchers are making more effective, customized medicines and creating new ways to diagnose diseases. Until recently, Roche's diagnostics and pharmaceutical businesses didn't have much in common. Scientists working on new approaches to diagnosis focused on their speciality and didn't concern themselves with developments related to new treatments. Because scientists were in competition with each other for resources, they seldom shared their expertise with other teams fearing that it would damage their own chances of success. Roche's old competitive approach to teamwork was counterproductive. But genomics has changed that. Scientists at Roche are no longer divided into competing teams that focus on their own projects and fight each other to gain resources.

To prosper in the era of genomics, cross-disciplinary communication is essential, so multi-disciplinary research teams are used. For exam-ple, the Genomics Oncology (GO) team includes seven researchers with specialties such as immunology, statistics, genetics, and oncology. Elsewhere in the company, new teams bring together plant geneticists, chemists, and diagnosti-cians. Restructuring into multidisciplinary teams wasn't easy. The new team structure meant the company had to create a new culture to support collaboration. Now it even looks for a different type of researcher. Instead of someone with 20 years of experience in their area of specialty, Roche wants people who can reinvent themselves as opportunities change. For Roche and many other pharmaceutical companies, genomics has changed everything.

To learn more about this organization, visit *www.roche.com.*

Self-managing work teams decide how to get their work done with little or no input from a team leader.

Self-Managing Work Teams

A self-managing work team *consists of employees who have nearly complete responsibility and authority for working together to make an entire product or deliver an entire serv-ice.* The members may all be from a single functional area, but more often such teams are multidisciplinary. In the United States, manufacturers have been steadily moving to self-managing work teams during the past two decades.[9]

The jet engine–building teams at GE/Durham are self-managing work teams. Each team "owns" the engines it builds—from the beginning of the assembly process to getting the engine loaded on a truck for deliv-ery. As a team begins each engine, about the only instruc-tion it receives is the date on which the engine is to be shipped from the plant. Besides producing an 8.5-ton jet engine from 10,000 individual parts, team members order tools and parts; schedule their training; adjust the produc-tion process to improve efficiency; and monitor quality. Decisions about these and all other issues that the teams face are made by consensus.

The distinctive feature of a self-managing work team is the level of responsibility that the team itself has for various managerial tasks. To a large extent, the team as a whole—not just its leader—decides what the team needs to do and how to do it, including:

▸ scheduling members' work and vacations,

▸ rotating job tasks and assignments among members,

▸ ordering materials,

▸ deciding on team leadership (which may rotate among members),

▸ providing feedback to team members,

▸ setting performance goals, and

▸ monitoring progress toward team goals.

When it is truly empowered, a self-managing team does more than simply take over administrative duties. It also has a strong commitment to the organization's mission, the autonomy needed to control its own activities, belief in itself, and a chance to see directly the impact of its efforts. Research shows that fully empowered teams provide better service and are more productive.[10]

Virtual Teams

A virtual work team *meets and does its tasks without everyone being physically present in the same place or even at the same time*. In virtual teams, team members usually work in widely scattered geographic locations and often across time zones. They may occasionally have face-to-face meetings, but more often they communicate using e-mail, electronically mediated groupware, voice mail, videoconferencing, and other technologies that allow team members to work together even though they are separated by physical and cultural boundaries.[11] As described in Chapter 11, such teams are becoming more and more important as companies evolve toward network forms of organizations. Virtual work teams can be functional, problem solving, multidisciplinary, or self-managing. Figure 17.2 illustrates a virtual team that also is a self-managing team.

Figure 17.2 | **A Self-Managing Virtual Team**

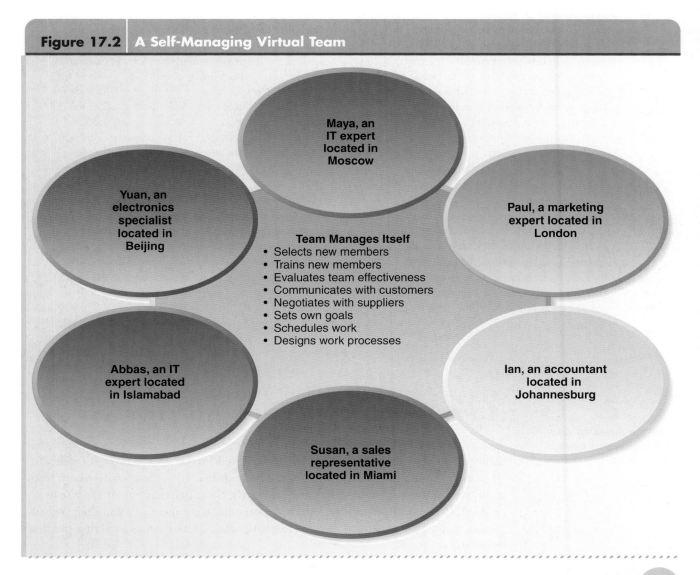

Maya, an IT expert located in Moscow

Yuan, an electronics specialist located in Beijing

Paul, a marketing expert located in London

Team Manages Itself
- Selects new members
- Trains new members
- Evaluates team effectiveness
- Communicates with customers
- Negotiates with suppliers
- Sets own goals
- Schedules work
- Designs work processes

Abbas, an IT expert located in Islamabad

Ian, an accountant located in Johannesburg

Susan, a sales representative located in Miami

MySQL, a software company, relies on virtual teams. Its 320 employees live in 25 countries and most work from home. Even the company's annual holiday party is virtual. One year, Thomas Basil, director of support, played an online Santa who dispensed virtual gifts and drinks while staffers chatted and shared jokes electronically. "When a company is as spread out as this one, you have to think of virtual ways to imitate the dynamics of what goes on in a more familiar employment situation," he explained. As organizations expand into global consumer and labor markets, managing virtual work teams that cross international borders will be an increasingly important managerial responsibility. The Multicultural Competency feature describes some of the challenges experienced by members of virtual global teams at Intel.[12]

Multicultural Competency

Global Teams at Intel

Intel, the world's largest chip maker and a leading manufacturer of computer, networking, and communications products, is a truly global organization: The company employs some 85,000 people in more than 50 countries. Intel generates more than 75 percent of its revenue outside the Americas. Intel relies on virtual international teams to manage a wide range of its projects. It is not unusual for people from six or seven different nationalities and functional backgrounds to work together on the design of a new chip or on a sales campaign for a new product. Making the work of these teams even more complex is the fact that information is scattered across a fragmented technical environment. Using teleconferencing, online collaboration platforms, and videoconferencing, Intel's teams span great geographic and cultural distances.

One reason for Intel's success with globally staffed teams is that they have learned to use a few simple, basic processes and procedures throughout the company. For example, work is coordinated and tracked using electronic documents that everyone can see. This helps people

who are working on multiple teams and multiple tasks coordinate their work and be sure the team's work is completed within an appropriate time frame. To help individuals manage their work on multiple teams, they can create their own personal task lists and calendars that integrate the work being done on multiple teams.

Despite all of the available electronic support for project management, global teams at Intel face many challenges. One of the biggest challenges for individual employees is mastering all of the different project management tools being used throughout the company. The company does not yet have a single integrated system that works equally well for all types of teams and is used in all locations. So an engineer who works on three different team projects may be using three different suites of project management tools. So, in addition to working with people who speak different languages and work at different times, Intel's global teams also must find ways to bridge the diversity of technical cultures present in the firm.

To learn more about this organization, visit *www.intel.com*.

3.

State the meaning and determinants of team effectiveness.

A Framework for Team Effectiveness

The increasing popularity of team-based organizational designs reflects the view that teams can achieve goals that could not be achieved by the same number of individuals working alone. But as many organizations are discovering, the positive payoff from teams isn't automatic. Although teams offer great potential, that potential isn't always realized. Even when teams do fulfill their potential, team members and their organizations may experience unanticipated negative side effects, such as lingering political fights and turnover.

Effectiveness Criteria

The first step in fostering team effectiveness involves stating what *effectiveness* means. Figure 17.3[13] shows several effectiveness criteria for evaluating work teams. Effectiveness criteria *are used to measure the outcomes achieved by individual members and the team as a whole.* A particular work team may be effective in some respects and ineffective in others. Typically, organizations strive to ensure that work teams are effective on all four of the dimensions shown. In addition, they are able to adapt to changing circumstances, which improves their long-term success as a team. Effective teams also develop satisfying social relationships that can serve as a foundation for working together again in the future. And, finally, in effective teams, the group experience contributes positively to the learning and personal well-being of each individual team member.[14]

Figure 17.3	Effectiveness Criteria for Work Teams		
Team Processes	**Team Performance**	**Team Preparedness for Future**	**Satisfaction of Individual Members**
• Cohesiveness	• Innovation	• Trust in team	• With team process
• Trust	• Quality	• Ability to adapt to change	• With team members
• Managing conflict	• Speed		• With own development
• Decision making	• Cost		

For a team of scientists from Adidas and Bayer, the most important measure of team effectiveness was the roundness of the World Cup soccer ball they produced. The Adidas scientists brought expertise in sports equipment to the project, and the Bayer scientists contributed their expertise in materials. Experts from these two companies have collaborated on making the World Cup soccer ball for more than two decades. Until the new ball was created, the ball used in the World Cup had a somewhat imperfect shape, so it bounced differently depending on how the ball hit the ground. The new ball is both rounder, which is good for the game, and it is also smoother and glossier, which Adidas hopes will be good for sales.[15]

Effectiveness Determinants

Once a team's goals have been established and it is clear how their effectiveness will be measured, the second step in achieving team effectiveness involves knowing the various factors that will determine the team's effectiveness. Figure 17.4 on the following page illustrates several factors that work in combination to determine work team effectiveness. Three main influences on effectiveness are the external support context in which the team operates, team design, and internal team processes.

Teamwork always presents challenges. Managers who understand its nature and challenges are in the best position to take advantage of teamwork and anticipate some of the problems that often crop up when teams are used. Internal problems—such as too much conflict—may be the most immediate cause of performance problems. When a team experiences internal problems, the root cause of those problems may lie

Snapshot

"As we attract, retain, and develop the best talent, we have to assess employees on a continuing basis for flexibility and adaptability to work in a virtual environment— that is the 21st-century workplace."

Joy Gaetano, Senior Vice President, USFilter, Palm Desert, California

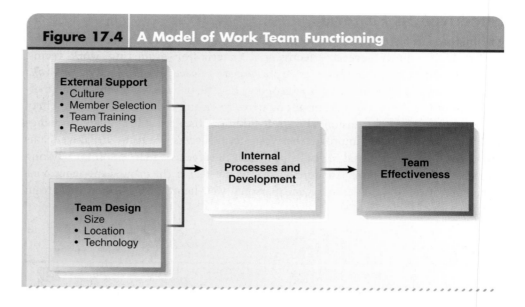

Figure 17.4 | A Model of Work Team Functioning

External Support
- Culture
- Member Selection
- Team Training
- Rewards

Team Design
- Size
- Location
- Technology

Internal Processes and Development

Team Effectiveness

elsewhere. The team members may be doing the best they can, but under adverse circumstances. Their internal problems may be due to the design of the team or to aspects of the external context. When teams are ineffective, managers must be able to diagnose and correct the causes of the teams' problems.[16]

4.
Describe the internal team processes that can affect team performance.

Internal Team Processes

Internal team processes *include the development of the work team over time, personal feelings, and behavioral norms.* In effective work teams, these processes support cooperation among team members and coordination of their work. When a team leader and individual team members learn how to manage the team's internal processes, they improve the likelihood of the team's being effective.[17]

Developmental Stages

People with little experience working in teams often expect a team to be fully functioning immediately, but that rarely happens. Observations of newly formed work teams reveal that coordination and good team processes tend to develop over a period of time. Team members usually need to spend some time together before the team can jell—knowing this fact of team life reduces needless frustration. The establishment of trust and clear behavioral norms usually precede effective task completion.[18]

The developmental stages that teams commonly go through are shown in Figure 17.5. The vertical axis indicates that work teams develop along a *continuum of maturity*, which ranges from low, or immature (e.g., inefficient and ineffective), to high, or mature (e.g., efficient and effective). The horizontal axis represents a *continuum of time together*, which ranges from start (e.g., the first team encounter) to end (e.g., the point at which the team adjourns).[19] In general, the speed of team development seems to reflect the team's deadlines. Work teams tend to develop slowly at first. Then, as deadlines approach, team members feel more pressure to perform and often respond by resolving or setting aside personal differences in order to complete the task.[20]

No particular period of time is needed for a team to progress from one stage to the next. A work team whose members have effective interpersonal skills and high initial commitment to the team's goals could move rapidly to the performing stage. In con-

Figure 17.5 | The Development of Work Teams

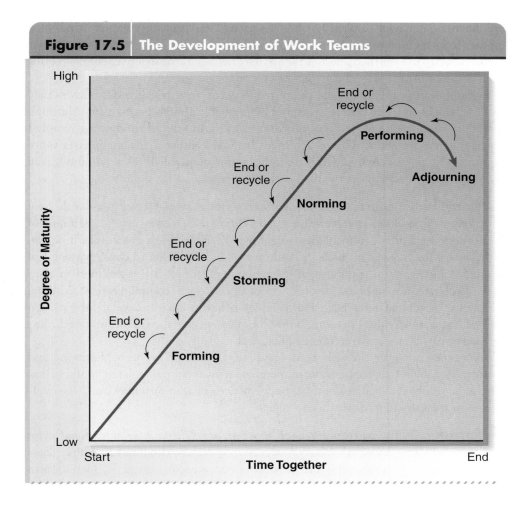

trast, a committee that is skeptical about whether its work is really valued by the organization and which also experiences early conflict among its members may never make much progress and may even disband without producing a recommendation or report.

Figure 17.5 also shows the possibility of a team ending at each stage or recycling to a previous stage. For example, a mature work team could lose the majority of its members in a short period of time due to promotion, retirement, and/or rotation of membership. With so many new members, the team may recycle to an earlier stage of development. The stages identified represent general tendencies, and teams may develop by going through repeated cycles rather than linearly, as shown. Each stage simply reveals the *primary* issues facing team members. Behaviors from other stages may occur at times within each stage.

Forming. During the forming stage, *a work team focuses on orientation to its goals and procedures.* Members may be anxious about what the team and what they are supposed to do. In newly formed teams, relationships often are guarded, cautious, and noncommittal. Understanding leadership roles and getting acquainted with other team members facilitate development. In global teams, the forming stage may also involve learning about the differing cultural backgrounds of the members.

Storming. The storming stage *begins when competitive or strained behaviors emerge.* Initially, the storming process may involve resistance and impatience with the lack of progress. A few dominant members may begin to force an agenda without regard for the needs of other team members. Team members may challenge the leader, or they may isolate themselves from team discussion. If conflict spreads, frustration, anger,

Snapshot

"My advice for any new team: Don't short-change your startup. Take time to understand what you're going to do and how you're going to deal with the possible bumps along the way."

Jeanie Duck, Senior Vice President, The Boston Consulting Group

and defensive behavior (especially the self-serving "look out for yourself" kind) may appear. Team members might think: Our problem is that we don't want to resolve our conflicts; we thrive on them, and though it may be counterproductive, conflict seems to be a way of life for now.

If conflict is suppressed and not permitted to occur, resentment and bitterness may result, which in turn can lead to apathy or lack of commitment to the team. Although conflict resolution often is the goal of work teams during the storming stage, conflict management generally is what is achieved. In fact, conflict management is a more appropriate goal because maintaining conflict at a manageable level is a desirable way to encourage a work team's growth and development.

Norming. In the norming stage, *team members become increasingly positive about the team as a whole, the other members as individuals, and what the team is doing.* At the beginning of the norming stage, the dominant view might be: We are in this together, like it or not, so let's make the most of it. Thus the team members may begin to develop a sense of belonging and renewed commitment. Members increasingly are committed to their team. Problems are resolved through cooperation, open communication, and the acceptance of mutual influence. The rules of behavior that are widely shared and enforced by team members develop. If the work team gets to the end of this stage, most members may like their involvement a great deal.

Sometimes, however, the work team focuses too much on "we-ness," harmony, and conformity. When that happens, team members may avoid task-related conflicts that need to be resolved to achieve optimal performance. That in turn may cause the quality and/or quantity of performance to slip.

Performing. By the performing stage, *members usually have come to trust and accept each other and are focused on accomplishing their goals.* As deadlines and due dates approach, teams often shift into a mode of productive performance.[21] To accomplish tasks, diversity of viewpoints (rather than we-ness) is supported and encouraged. Members are willing to risk presenting "wild" ideas without fear of being put down by the team. Careful listening and giving accurate feedback to others will focus team members on the team's tasks and reinforce a sense of clear and shared goals. Leadership within the team is flexible and may shift among members in terms of who is most capable of solving a particular problem. The team accepts the reality of differences and disagreements and works on them cooperatively and enthusiastically. The team tries to reach consensus on important issues and to avoid internal politics. The following characteristics lead to high levels of team performance:

▶ Members direct their energies toward the twin goals of getting things done (task behaviors) and building constructive interpersonal ties and processes (relationship behaviors).

▶ Members use procedures for making decisions, including how to share leadership.

▶ Members trust each other and are open among themselves.

▶ Members receive help from and give help to one another.

▶ Members are free to be themselves while feeling a sense of belonging with others.

▶ Members accept and deal with conflicts.

▶ Members diagnose and improve their own functioning.[22]

Teams that diagnose and improve their own functioning are especially valued because they can adapt to changing circumstances. Important adaptive behaviors include handling unpredictable work situations, emergencies, and crises; managing interactions across team boundaries; handling work stress; solving problems creatively; and learning new technologies and procedures. Teams that make good use of the diversity on the team tend to be more able to adapt, and teams that are more adaptive tend to be more successful.[23]

Adjourning. The adjourning stage *involves terminating task behaviors and disengaging from relationships.* This stage isn't always planned and may be rather abrupt. However, a planned team conclusion often involves recognition for participation and achievement as well as an opportunity for members to say personal goodbyes. Adjournment of a work team charged with a particular task should be set for a specific time and have a recognizable ending point. However, many work teams (e.g., the executive committee of an organization's board of directors) are ongoing. As members turn over, some recycling through earlier stages rather than adjournment may occur. Staggered terms of appointment can minimize the amount of recycling required.

Throughout the entire life of a team, communication is a key activity. Effective communication helps ensure the team will achieve its objectives. The Communication Competency feature illustrates the importance of communication in the R&D team that developed Motorola's RAZR phone.[24]

© M. Spencer Green/AP Photo

At Motorola, a multidisciplinary team knew it was effective when it had a feasible design for the world's thinnest phone.

Communication Competency

Motorola's RAZR

The team that developed Motorola's RAZR phone helped put that company back on the road to financial health. Initially, this was a skunkworks project—team members kept their ideas and progress top secret. They broke the rules as needed and made sure no one knew what they were up to until they were pretty sure they would succeed.

When the team formed in 2003, Nokia dominated the market with its "candy bar" phone design. But engineers at Motorola were thinking thin. They had made a mock-up design of an ultra-thin phone and Roger Jellicone became the leader of a team charged with the task of creating the thinnest phone ever in less than a year. The goal was to introduce the phone at the Academy Awards ceremony in February. Jellicone invited a long-time friend to join him and together the two of them pulled together a team of 20 of the most talented people in the company. The designers worried about how the phone would look and the engineers worried about making it work. Near the

end of each day, they all met to provide updates on their progress and haggle over decisions. During these meetings, the designers and engineers were like partners in a dance, contemplating the details of each feature. The designers knew how they wanted the new phone to look—thin, sleek, modern—and the engineers knew what they wanted the phone to do. After each problem was solved by one group, the others would respond and pose another problem. The placement of the antenna meant the earplug had to be redesigned. The external caller ID display made the phone too thick, so something else would have to go. According to designer Chris Arnholt, "Design is really about communication. Sometimes my ideas are tough to communicate." Day after day, the give and take among team members continued until the team finally created the thinnest phone in the world.

To learn more about this organization, visit *www.motorola.com.*

Feelings

Throughout the stages of a work team's development, team members experience a variety of emotions or feelings. As we use the term here, feelings *refers to the emotional climate of a group.* The four feelings most likely to influence work team effectiveness and productivity are trust, openness, freedom, and interdependence. The more these feelings are present, the more likely the work team will be effective and the members will be satisfied.[25] These feelings probably are present in a formal or informal group to which you belong if you *agree* with the following statements:

▶ *Trust:* Members have confidence in each other.

▶ *Openness:* Members are really interested in what others have to say.

▶ *Freedom:* Members do what they do out of a sense of responsibility to the group, not because of pressure from others.

▶ *Interdependence:* Members coordinate and work together to achieve common goals.

The greater the degree to which the four feelings are present, the greater the level of group cohesiveness.

Cohesiveness *is the strength of members' desires to remain on the team and their commitment to it.* It is a reflection of the members' feelings toward one another and the team as a whole. In cohesive teams, the members like each other and feel attached to the group. In fact, team members may feel strongly committed to the team, even if they don't feel strongly committed to the organization.[26] Usually, however, cohesive teams also share a commitment to the group's task and they feel pride in what the team represents.[27] Cohesiveness can't be dictated by managers, team leaders, or others.

Ken Neishi, vice president of operations at Michael Foods, understood that managing feelings within teams can be essential to business success. When Michael Foods acquired one of its major competitors, Papetti's Hygrade Egg Products of New Jersey, his task was to gradually create a new business that incorporated the best aspects of each company. Knowing that the two companies' organizational cultures were vastly different—Papetti's was a family-run business, and the owners did not share much information with employees, whereas Michael Foods was a big corporation that valued open communication—he allowed time for the members of the two companies to build relationships and to learn to trust each other. He started the process by visiting Papetti's plant and getting to know the top-level managers. The next step was to organize a team-building session. So as not to create differences among the two parties, it was held at a neutral location and co-led by representatives of both sides. When the session began, "It was like a union negotiation, with eight guys on one side of the table and eight guys on the other staring each other down," Neishi recalled. Many more of these sessions had to follow until team spirit evolved. Although the process was painful at first, the leaders gradually helped the group accept the norms of allowing everyone to talk and showing respect for everyone's ideas. Today it is impossible to tell who came from Papetti's and who came from Michael Food.[28]

Behavioral Norms

How people feel is an important aspect of teamwork. How people actually behave may be even more important. Behavioral norms *are the rules of behavior that are widely shared and enforced by members of a work team.* Their main function is to regulate and standardize the behaviors viewed as important by team members.

Norms may specify how much work to do, how customers should be treated, the importance of high quality, what members should wear, what kinds of jokes are acceptable, how members should feel about the organization, how they should deal with their managers, and so on. When members of a team share a common understanding of what they need to get done and how they can work together to achieve their goals, they tend to be more effective.[29] Two important types of norms are those governing performance and those governing how team members deal with conflict.

Performance Norms. A performance norm exists when three criteria have been met.[30] First, there is a standard of appropriate behavior for team members. Second, members must generally agree on the standard. If most members have widely varying opinions about how much work is enough, for example, the team doesn't have a productivity norm. Third, the members must be aware that the team supports the particular standard through a system of rewards and punishments. Norms such as these reduce the chances of one team member being a free rider. A free rider *is a team member who isn't contributing fully to team performance but still shares in team rewards.* Students who are assigned to work in teams for grades often express concern about the possibility of having a team member who is a free rider. Effective teams realize that they can reduce this problem by developing strong norms that make it clear what is expected and put pressure on everyone to pull their weight in the team. Most students want to be accepted by their peers and do not intend to take advantage of others. But if the team norms aren't clear, they may simply not realize what is expected of them.

Norms for Managing Conflicts. Norms concerning how to handle conflicts within the team are important for teams engaged in a lot of problem solving and decision making. Social pressures to maintain friendships and avoid disagreements can lead to work team members agreeing to a decision based more on personal feelings than on facts and analysis. When team norms stifle conflict, groupthink can develop. Groupthink *is an agreement-at-any-cost mentality that results in ineffective work team decision making and may lead to poor solutions.* The fundamental problem underlying groupthink is pressure on members to concede and accept what other members think. The likelihood of groupthink increases when

> ▸ peer pressure to conform is great,
>
> ▸ a highly directive leader presses for a particular interpretation of the problem and course of action,
>
> ▸ the need to process a complex and unstructured issue under crisis conditions exists, and
>
> ▸ the group is isolated.[31]

Instead of stifling conflict, a better approach to handling disagreements is to engage in productive controversy. Productive controversy *occurs when team members value different points of view and seek to draw them out to facilitate creative problem solving.* To ensure productive controversy, work team members must establish ground rules to keep them focused on issues rather than people and defer decisions until various issues and ideas are explored. They should frame decisions as collaborations aimed at achieving the best possible results and follow procedures that equalize sharing of power and responsibility. By following these norms, team members can focus on their common goal and avoid becoming embroiled in battles of egos.

A study of executive teams revealed that norms concerning conflict differed greatly from one team to the next. About half the teams studied reported that the team members argued most of the time. In these teams, everyone felt free to voice opinions and share ideas. One executive described his team's pattern for handling conflict this way: "We scream a lot, then laugh, and then resolve the issues." In several other teams, however, there was little open conflict—in fact, some teams actually had too little conflict.[32]

Snapshot

Each year, Seagate Technology sends about 200 employees off to participate in Eco Seagate, a week-long team-building event dreamed up by CEO Bill Watkins. A recent expedition headed off to New Zealand for kayaking, foot races, biking, and more. To Watkins, the cost of nearly $2 million is worthwhile because it has helped his company create a culture that is "open, honest, and encourages people to work together."

William D. Watkins, CEO, Seagate Technologies

Managers Help Establish Norms. Effective managers understand that they can shape the norms that develop within work teams. At Google, the physical space helps shape the norms for teamwork. During team-building sessions at Michael Foods, the managers helped the team establish norms that ensured everyone's ideas would be listened to and considered respectfully. At AeroMexico, CEO Arturo Barahona and his top management team wrote their norms on paper. They came up with a list of 10 things they agreed were important. Barahona gave the list to everyone and had them sign it. When one of the team members violated a norm, Barahona pulled out his list and said, "What you did violated Norm #3 right here." After a few instances like this, he never had to do it again.[33]

In internationally staffed teams, establishing norms can be an especially big challenge.[34] From what we know, teams need norms that all members can relate to. We also know that norms can differ from one culture to another. What is common practice in one culture might be considered unethical or illegal in another. For example, the norms that guide the way men and women relate to each other varies greatly around the world. So, whose gender norms should be used by the team as a whole? Should the team adopt the gender norms from the culture or region from which the majority of the team members come? Should the team adopt the gender norms for the country in which the company is headquartered? If the company is headquartered in the United States, but the team is working in China, should the team's norms be based on Chinese culture? Or, should international teams create new norms that reflect a mixture of all the cultures represented in the team? As the Ethical Challenge feature highlights, it is sometimes hard for managers to find behavioral norms that are plausible and acceptable to all team members.

Ethical Challenge

When in Rome, Do as the Romans Do?

Imagine you are an American working for FedEx/Kinko in Bangkok, Thailand. You are heading a team of both local and U.S. managers to organize the supply chain for one of your company's most important customers, an international car-manufacturing group. A large shipment of engine parts is scheduled to arrive shortly and your customer has already expressed severe concern about supply shortages. You are under pressure and extremely relieved when you hear that the shipment has finally arrived at the port. The port authorities inform you that due to a temporary lack of personnel, the customs department has to hold your shipment for longer than usual. It might take up to four additional days until your freight is released! You and your customer cannot afford to lose four days.

Annoyed and desperate, you call for an emergency meeting with your team to solve the prob-

lem. After 30 minutes of fruitless discussion, a local manager makes a suggestion: Do it the local way and "help" a bit with the administrative procedures. One of the veteran expatriates in your team agrees: "This is the way it works here—a small grease payment (i.e., kickback) to one of the customs officers and we'll have our engines in minutes." Besides, "all the other companies around here do it as well." A bit embarrassed, the remaining local managers agree. Only one U.S. manager opposes the idea. "This is strictly against our corporate policy and violates everything we stand for. What we would not do in the United States, we should not do here." You are not sure what to do. You believe in your company's norms and values, but you can see that it may be necessary to adapt them to local conditions. What would you do? How would you decide which norms to follow?

Diagnosing the Causes of Poor Team Performance

5.

Explain how to diagnose and remove barriers to poor team performance.

When teams fail to perform as well as they are supposed to, many reasons may be at fault. Internal team processes are the first thing that people usually think about as the cause of poor performance. Effective teams and their leaders consider whether negative internal team processes are responsible for poor performance, but they don't stop there. Teams don't exist in a vacuum, and their internal processes don't unfold in isolation. The external system acting on a team may also be the cause of team performance problems. A team's external system *comprises outside conditions and influences that exist before and after the team is formed.* Important features of the external system to consider include team design, culture, team member selection, team training, and the reward system.[35]

Team Design

The design choices involved in creating a work team are numerous. When teams are designed well, they are more effective in managing their work, their members are more satisfied, and they perform better.[36] We have already discussed the importance of choices concerning team goals, team duration, and team membership. Here we focus on two additional design choices: team size and team location.

Team Size. As the number of team members increases, changes occur in the team's internal decision-making processes. A good rule of thumb to remember is that understaffed teams tend to outperform overstaffed teams.[37] Members of teams with more than a dozen members generally have difficulty communicating with each other. Increasing team size also causes the following effects:

▶ Demands on leader time and attention are greater. The leader becomes more psychologically distant from the other team members. This problem is most serious in self-managing work teams, where more than one person can take on leader roles.

▶ The team's tolerance of direction from the leader is greater, and the team's decision making becomes more centralized.

▶ The team atmosphere is less friendly, the communications are less personal, more cliques form within the team, and, in general, team members are less satisfied.

▶ The team's rules and procedures become more formalized.

▶ The likelihood of some members being free riders increases.[38]

For innovative decision making, the ideal work team size is probably between five and nine members.[39] If a work team has more than nine members, separate cliques might form. If larger teams are required for some reason, the use of subteams may be a solution to the problem of size. The purpose of subteams is to encourage all team members to share ideas when analyzing problems, information, and alternative solutions. The full team can then meet to discuss subteam assessments and recommendations. In some instances, different subteams work on the same set of problems and then share and discuss their conclusions with the entire team. The leader of a large work team needs to be aware of the possibility that subteams, or cliques, may form on their own, each with its own leader and agenda. Although more resources are available to large teams, these resources can create a backlash that hurts overall team effectiveness if each unofficial subteam or clique lobbies strongly for its own position.

Team Location. Team proximity *refers to the location of a team's members.* Two aspects of team location are (1) proximity to other work teams and members of the organization and (2) team members' proximity to each other.

The location of team members may depend on where the talent needed for a task happens to be. As explained earlier in this chapter, virtual work teams are used when people who have the talent needed by a team are not physically co-located. As described in Chapter 11, virtual teams often are essential to the functioning of network organizations. Many of the principles of effective teamwork that apply to face-to-face team activities also apply to virtual work teams. However, the challenges associated with managing virtual teams with members from many different cultures and living in many different time zones are often greater than those faced by teams that operate within the same geographical and cultural boundaries.

The ideal proximity *among* teams depends on the work being done. When many teams are working together on a single project, close coordination among the teams is needed. At Microsoft, teams benefit from being near others in the organization. Members of different teams can meet at the snack shop or water cooler to fill each other in on developments within their respective teams. Problem solving readily occurs as the need arises.

For some work teams, performance is improved when the team is removed from the daily activities of the organization. Recall the discussion of corporate entrepreneurship in Chapter 6. Innovation and creativity are essential to successful entrepreneurship, but the bureaucracy and political intrigue often found in large corporations can stifle them. Consequently, teams at 3M, Apple, and Motorola frequently set up skunkworks operations in a remote location. At Motorola, the RAZR team's skunkworks operation allowed it to get away with ignoring some of the company's standard operating procedures and instead do whatever worked best for the project. Isolated from outside distractions, the entrepreneurs are able to focus on the future without having to battle the status quo.

Culture

The societal cultures within which work teams operate are important aspects of the external context.[40] Differences in the language people use to describe work teams and differences in norms for team behavior often reflect differences in national culture. In some cultures, such as China, Malaysia, and Thailand, societal values support striving for harmony and cohesiveness and avoiding open conflict. In the more individualistic cultures of the United States and Canada, people feel more comfortable when they are able to express their opinions and have their views taken seriously by other team members. At the same time, U.S. and Canadian cultures value friendly relationships among coworkers, so too much conflict feels uncomfortable. In an international work team, the natural tendency of team members is to behave according to the norms of their countries. When different cultures are present, misunderstandings are the likely result if team members are not familiar with the cultures represented on the team.[41]

Regardless of national cultures, work teams can function well if they are supported by the organization's culture. Whole Foods, Mayo Clinic, and other organizations that support participation by lower level employees increase the likelihood that work teams will embrace organizational goals and authority relations, rather than attempt to undermine them. When individualistic employees are empowered through self-managing work teams, they gain more control and influence over their work. Because having control is important in individualistic cultures, employees working in self-managing teams often report being very satisfied with their work.

Team Member Selection

The characteristics needed in an employee who works in relative isolation are different from those needed in an employee who must work in a team environment. In work teams, the personality traits of *agreeableness* and *conscientiousness* seem to be especially important.[42] People with agreeable personalities seek to find areas of common understanding with the members of the team. When areas of agreement are known, team members may also be able to accept their differences more easily. People who are conscientious tend to stay focused on the task and seem to be good at organizing and coordinating activities.

At Worthington Industries, a steel company, the personalities of new team members are evaluated by those already on the team. New hires must have the necessary skills to get a job. But when hired, they are put on "probation" for 90 days. Their teammates use this probation period to evaluate the new hire's personality and teamwork competencies and *they* decide whether the new hire is allowed to stay on the team.[43]

Of our six managerial competencies, communication and teamwork are essential for working in *all* types of teams. If the team is self-managed and everyone shares all aspects of a task, more technical skills often are needed by each team member. The planning and administration competency also is extremely important for members of self-managing teams. When teams are used to coordinate the activities of organizational units spread throughout the world, the global awareness competency is especially important.

Personality traits are difficult to change, and both technical skills and managerial competencies develop slowly over time. For these reasons, team-based organizations often use intensive and sophisticated selection procedures when hiring new employees. The GE/Durham plant is a good example. When the plant was started, management decided that all job candidates would have to be FAA-certified mechanics. FAA certification requires 2 years of training and is something that no other GE plant requires of all job candidates. First-rate mechanical skills are just one of the 11 areas that job applicants must possess to get a job. Others include helping skills, teamwork, communication, coaching, and flexibility. As one current employee remembers, the interview process—lasting 8 hours—was especially grueling: "That was one heck of an experience. I talked to five different people. I participated in three group activities with job candidates. I even had to do a presentation: I had 15 minutes to prepare a 5-minute presentation." Through these activities, GE assessed the teamwork and communication competencies that these mechanics would have to rely on day in and day out in doing their new jobs.

The value of paying attention to teamwork competencies appears to hold for many types of teams. When Roche redesigned its research activities around multidisciplinary teams, they realized they would also need a different type of scientist to work on those teams. Paying attention to teamwork competencies pays off despite the level of technical skill involved in the work. A study of cardiac surgery teams found that the process used to select members of the team predicted the team's subsequent performance. When team members participated more in the selection of new members, and when they took both teamwork competency and technical skills into account, cardiac surgery teams were more effective.[44]

Team Training

Even in organizations that do a good job of selecting employees who are capable of working well in teams, additional team training can be beneficial for improving team effectiveness. Perhaps more than any other organization, NASA understands that training comes before effective teamwork. Before astronauts are sent into space to live in a community that relies heavily on teamwork for survival, NASA has them working together every day for a year or two in order to become a team. They share office space, spend countless hours together in flight simulators, and rehearse everything from stowing their flight suits to troubleshooting malfunctions. Formal training in procedures is part of the experience, but it isn't everything. NASA realizes that teamwork training also involves helping teammates get to know each other and develop confidence in each other.

To help teams learn to deal with the types of life and death situations they'll eventually face, NASA also uses outdoor survival training. The *Discovery* space shuttle crew spent several days mountain climbing through a snowstorm. The conditions were so bad that the team eventually decided to cut their climb short and forego continuing on up to the summit. Helping the crew throughout the process was a team trainer. His role was to help the leader and the team understand how to work together when making life-and-death decisions to ensure that the entire team believed they made the right decision and was committed to whatever decision it made. Those were skills NASA wanted the team to master *before* they began their shuttle flight, not while they were facing a crisis in space.[45]

Most organizations can't afford to give team members a year or two of training before teams begin working to achieve their goals. They look for quicker ways to achieve the same goals that NASA has for its training program. Regardless of how many hours of team training organizations require, their goals usually are the same: to train team members to perform a variety of managerial and leadership activities and to enhance team cohesiveness. Among the managerial tasks that effective teams know how to perform for themselves are setting goals, learning how to measure results, and deciding what needs to be measured. Teams that are proficient at such team tasks tend to perform better.[46] Organizations that invest resources to train teams can increase both team and organizational effectiveness.[47]

Management and Leadership Training. Work teams of all types are being empowered to perform tasks that previously weren't employees' responsibility. Figure 17.6 shows a wide range of tasks that may be assigned to a work team. The vertical axis indicates the degree to which the team is self-managing. The greater the degree of self-management, the more the team has authority, responsibility, and general decision-making discretion for tasks. The horizontal axis indicates the amount and range of competencies required of team members for handling an increasing number and complexity of tasks. The more self-managing a team is, the more important it is for team members to receive training that will enhance all of their management competencies. The more confident team members feel about the team's ability to perform, the more likely it is that the team actually will perform well.[48]

We've already described leadership development in some detail in Chapter 15. That discussion applies particularly to situations where there is one designated team leader. Managers who are responsible for a work team often select the team members, structure and plan the team's work, set goals for the team and provide them with the resources they need, monitor their performance, and so on.[49] As organizations have become flatter, however, these leadership roles have moved into the team itself. That is, the task of leadership is shared among all members of the team. In such circumstances, all can benefit from a discussion of the key leadership responsibilities that they'll be sharing, which include the following:

▸ *Managing meetings.* People who resist teamwork often point to time wasted in meetings as a big source of dissatisfaction. True, teams do need to meet, one way or another, but team meetings should never be a waste of time. Training

Figure 17.6 | **Training Can Help Self-Managing Teams Develop the Managerial Competencies They Need to be Effective**

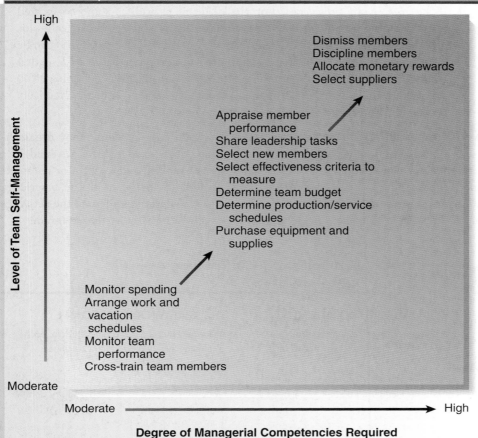

High

Level of Team Self-Management

Dismiss members
Discipline members
Allocate monetary rewards
Select suppliers

Appraise member
  performance
Share leadership tasks
Select new members
Select effectiveness criteria to
  measure
Determine team budget
Determine production/service
  schedules
Purchase equipment and
  supplies

Monitor spending
Arrange work and
  vacation
  schedules
Monitor team
  performance
Cross-train team members

Moderate

Moderate   High

Degree of Managerial Competencies Required

team members to run meetings properly can make meetings more efficient. Team members can then share the key leadership role (e.g., scheduling a meeting, developing an agenda, recording ideas and decisions, and communicating with others outside the team), rotating through these responsibilities during the life of the team.

▶ *Supporting disagreement.* A skillful team leader supports disagreement that stimulates innovative solutions while minimizing the risk of bad feelings. Disagreement can be productive if members are open to differences within the team and if they separate idea generation from idea evaluation. Team members also need to understand that the absence of disagreement on a work team may be as destructive as too much disagreement to the team's proper functioning. The use of decision-making aids, such as brainstorming, the nominal group technique, devil's advocacy, and dialectical inquiry, creates productive controversy and can result in better quality decisions that team members can fully accept.[50]

▶ *Committing to a team decision.* Making a final decision when team members disagree can be relatively easy if final decisions ultimately rest with a team leader. Reaching a final decision that everyone will endorse is more difficult when there is no designated leader. For teams that make most decisions by reaching a consensus, it is helpful to train the team in how to come to a consensus and the importance of moving ahead once the consensus is reached. Such training helps team members understand that they won't be allowed to moan or drag their feet after the team's decision has been made.

▶ *Using group-based technologies.* For virtual teams as well as some co-located teams, training may be needed to develop the teams' abilities to use technologies that support their work. Group decision support systems (GDSS) can be particularly useful. A GDSS is an interactive, computer-based system that combines communication, computer, and decision-making technologies to support group meetings. Using such a system can help a team effectively process information when making a group decision.[51]

Building Team Cohesiveness. To develop team cohesiveness, many organizations use experientially based adventure training. Such training often is held in a camplike environment and includes navigating river rapids, scaling cliffs, or completing a ropes course. After each activity, trainers lead a discussion about the experience to identify the lesson to be learned from it. Table 17.1 describes a few of the activities and associated lessons from one company's specially designed one-day program.

Table 17.1	**Examples of Team Training Activities and Objectives**
THE CHALLENGING ACTIVITY	**THE TEAMWORK LESSON**
Juggle several objects simultaneously (e.g., tennis balls, hackey sacs, and Koosh balls) as a team.	Although everyone has a different role, each person touches and affects the outcome.
Find the path hidden in a carpet maze and move each member through it in a limited amount of time.	Teams must find and use each individual's hidden strengths (e.g., a good memory and the abilitiy to move quickly). Doing so allows the team as a whole to succeed.
Balance 14 nails on the head of a nail that has been pounded into a supporting block of wood, creating a free-standing structure without supports.	Things that may seem impossible can be achieved when people work together.
Draw a vehicle that represents the training team and signify which part of the vehicle each member represents.	Each member has different strengths and bringing these strengths together leads to task success.

Experiential training is an effective way to develop cohesiveness, but used alone it isn't likely to result in optimal teamwork. Teams can also benefit from more formal training. In addition to covering organization-specific procedures for obtaining resources, cost accounting, progress reports, and the like, team members may benefit from learning about the stages of team development. If they understand how teams normally develop, they are less likely to become easily frustrated during the early forming and storming stages of their own team's development. Formal team training can also help members realize the importance of norms to their performance and stimulate the team to develop norms that aid rather than hinder it.

At some companies, such as GE, Intel, and Siemens, the excitement of experiential training is combined with the goal of more rigorous learning by providing teams with opportunities for action-based training. Siemens gives responsibility for solving real business problems to analysts and engineers from around the world who work together in "student" teams. One team was sent to Mexico for a week with the assignment of developing a plan for introducing a new product. Instead of teaching students in a classroom about product design, marketing, budgets, and so on, the team members were expected to learn from each other and use whatever other resources they could to complete their assignment. Teams such as these learn by doing, and in the process they often develop friendships that last long after the training ends.

Reward Systems

As described in Chapters 13 and 14, reward systems inform employees about how to direct their energies and reinforce them for making valuable contributions to the organization. When employees work in a single team most of the time and it is essentially the employee's entire job, establishing team performance measures and using them to determine rates of pay is relatively easy. In most organizations, however, people aren't assigned full time to a single team. Their primary responsibilities may derive from a job that they perform essentially as an individual, with work team participation added to their regular duties. Or most of a person's regular duties may require working on teams. Over the course of a year, the person may serve on five or six different teams.

Most experts agree that different team designs call for different reward systems. Thus, rather than prescribing a specific approach to rewarding work teams, understanding the basic choices involved in tailoring a reward system to an organization's situation is more useful. For Motorola's RAZR team, generous stock options were the reward. At Gore, the pay raises of team members reflect the ratings they receive from their peers. Regardless of the details of a team-based reward system, employees need to understand it and managers need to endorse and support it.[52] Table 17.2 lists several questions that managers should consider when designing and evaluating team reward systems. With so many choices, perhaps the best way to develop an appropriate reward system is to assign the task to an empowered, multidisciplinary, well-trained work team.

Table 17.2	Choices in Designing Reward Systems for Work Teams

- How can nonmonetary rewards be used to recognize excellent team performance?
- What portion of a person's total monetary rewards should be linked to performance of the team (versus the performance of the individual or the business unit)?
- If rewards are to be linked to results, which effectiveness criteria should be used to evaluate team results? Individual results?
- How should rewards be distributed among the members of a team? Should they all receive equal rewards? If not, on what basis should people receive differential rewards?
- Who should be responsible for the allocation of rewards among team members: team members, a team leader, someone outside the team?
- For global teams, how should cultural differences among members of the team and the pay systems used in different countries be addressed?

Chapter Summary

One of the most striking things about today's organizations is their reliance on work teams. The trend toward greater reliance on team-based structures is the reason that teamwork competency is one of the six key managerial competencies. The discussion of work team functioning presented in this chapter is intended to help you improve your teamwork competency.

Learning Goals

1. Explain the importance of work teams.

The popularity of team-based organizational structures reflects the belief that teamwork offers the potential to achieve outcomes that couldn't be achieved by individuals working in isolation. Several strategic objectives lead organizations to design their structures around work teams, including customers' demands for innovation, faster response times, better quality, and lower prices.

2. Identify five types of work teams.

A work team is a special type of group. Most work teams consist of a small number of identifiable, interdependent employees who are held accountable for performing tasks that contribute to achieving an organization's goals. Members of a work team have a shared goal and must interact with each other to achieve it. The five common types of work teams are problem-solving, functional, multidisciplinary, self-managing, and virtual. Three key differences among work teams are the nature of their goals, their duration, and their membership. Different types of work teams suit different organizational purposes.

3. State the meaning and determinants of team effectiveness.

The primary components of a model of work team functioning are the external system, team design, internal team processes, and criteria for assessing the team's effectiveness. Effectiveness criteria measure the outcomes achieved by individual members and the team as a whole. A particular work team may be effective in some respects and not in others. Internal processes include the development of the work team over time, personal feelings, and behavioral norms. Through these processes, team members develop and integrate their behaviors. The choices involved in creating a team, including goals, membership, size, location, and duration, are numerous. Virtual work teams are an increasingly common choice in global and high-tech organizations. A team's external system comprises outside conditions and influences that exist before and after the team is formed. Its components include the societal and organizational culture, member selection, team training, and reward system.

4. Describe the internal team processes that can affect team performance.

Teams develop over time, moving through several developmental stages. These stages include forming, storming, norming, performing, and adjourning. Teams may move through these stages in a variety of ways. In effective teams, members develop feelings of trust, openness, freedom, and interdependence. These feelings allow team members to cooperate and coordinate their actions. Behavioral norms also develop within a work team. They function to regulate and standardize behaviors within the team.

Norms concerning how to handle conflict and controversy are especially important for effective team decision making.

5. *Explain how to diagnose and remove barriers to poor team performance.*

When teams are ineffective, the source of the problem may be internal team processes. However, poor internal processes may be caused by factors in the team's external system. Managers who accurately diagnose the causes of work team problems will be able to take appropriate corrective actions.

Key Terms and Concepts ....

Adjourning stage	Group	Productive controversy
Behavioral norms	Groupthink	Quality circle
Cohesiveness	Informal group	Self-managing work team
Effectiveness criteria	Internal team processes	Storming stage
External system	Multidisciplinary work team	Task force
Feelings	Norming stage	Team proximity
Forming stage	Performing stage	Virtual work team
Free rider	Problem-solving work	Work team
Functional work team	team	

Questions for Discussion and Reflective Thinking ....

1. Explain why Motorola used a multifunctional team to design the RAZR phone.

2. What effectiveness criteria were most important for Motorola's RAZR team?

3. Choose two organizations that you are familiar with (e.g., your school, your employer, a local community group, or a department store in your town). For each organization, list the work teams that appear to be present, identify the types of teams (functional, multidisciplinary, problem-solving, self-managing, or virtual), and explain why the organization needs those particular types of teams.

4. Think about two teams in which you were a member. Pick a team that you think was very effective and one that was less effective. What role did the following factors have in shaping the effectiveness of these two teams: internal team processes, team design, and team member selection?

5. Describe how work teams develop. What dangers are present at each stage of development?

6. As the owner of a small business that offers marketing services, you believe that your staff needs to understand how to work effectively in teams, including teams whose members are mostly the employees of your clients. You plan to send several of your employees to a teamwork training program. You have found three consultants who provide team training. List four questions that you would want these consultants to address before deciding which one to hire.

7. Search the Internet for companies that offer team-building events for corporations. Pick three programs that you find especially interesting. Explain why you think the programs are helpful in building team cohesiveness and eventually improving business results. For your search, consider keywords such as "team building," "team bonding," "outdoor training programs," or "adventure training."

DEVELOPING YOUR COMPETENCIES

Virtual teams are becoming quite common. Nevertheless, many managers have had very little experience with virtual teams. Assume you are working at NetAd, a communication agency specializing in innovative Web-based advertising for customers from the health-care industry. As project manager you are heading a newly formed virtual brand team that is in charge of developing an Internet site for a new pharmaceutical product called IVYOUT, which is used to treat skin rashes caused by poison ivy and other toxic plants. Your office is in Parsippany, New Jersey, but you often work at home. The team members include

- two employees of your client—one who works in Basel, Switzerland, and one who works in Palo Alto, California;

- two NetAd colleagues who work in the same building as you;

- a freelance graphics design specialist who works in Orlando, Florida; and

- a software engineer who specializes in e-commerce Internet programming and works in Bangalore, India.

All of the team members speak English fluently, but English is a second language for four members of the team. This is the team's first project, and it also is the first time you have been responsible for managing a virtual team. The team is working under a tight schedule and you will not be able to hold a face-to-face start-up session. You know that it is important to help the team establish strong norms to guide their behavior. Your plan is to propose a list of about 20 norms for the team to consider adopting. You expect the team members to participate in modifying your draft, but you need something to get them started.

Using the worksheet on the next page, prepare the draft list of norms for your team to consider.

General Aspect of Team Life That the Norm Applies to	Norms Describing Positive Behaviors That Team Members Can Exhibit	Norms Describing Negative Behaviors That Team Members Should Not Exhibit	Norms That Apply Specifically to the Team Manager (Positive or Negative Behaviors)
Using e-mail communications			
Managing personal relationships among team members			
Managing conflict within the team			
Managing cultural differences			
Managing unanticipated individual problems that affect the team's work			
Managing due dates and deadlines			
Other:			

Questions

1. What competencies do you need to effectively manage your virtual team?
2. Imagine that one month has passed since the team started working together. One member of the team continues to exhibit some negative behaviors that everyone agreed should not be exhibited. How would you deal with this problem?

You may have never heard of Sabre, but if you ever booked a reservation through Travelocity.com, which Sabre owns, you've done business with them. More than 60,000 travel agents in 114 countries also use the company's services. Sabre's North American division relies heavily on multidisciplinary virtual teams, each with about eight members located all over the continent. Account executives sell the reservation system, field service technicians install it, training representatives teach customers how to use it, and so on. Members of the team occasionally work alongside each other at a location, but most of the time they work in isolation. A whole team meets face to face only about once per year. To coordinate their activities, teams use e-mail, telephones, videoconferencing, and Web-based conferencing.

According to an internal survey, one of the biggest challenges Sabre encountered in the management of virtual teams was how to measure and reward the performance of a virtual team. How do you manage people whom you do not see? Realizing that much of the success of its virtual team concept depended on a well-tuned performance management system, Sabre introduced a balanced scorecard to measure team performance in four categories:

- growth (measured against market share),
- profitability (cost versus revenue generated for each travel booking),
- process improvement (cycle time, order time, installation time), and
- customer satisfaction (regular customer surveys).

The customer satisfaction data were posted on the company's intranet. Results were compared against customer satisfaction goals that were set with input from the teams. Managers also assessed the performance of individual team members using objective measures such as number of installations, customer retention rates, number of persons trained, and the accuracy of financial contracts. By carefully monitoring electronic team discussions and e-mails, managers were also able to assess individual initiative, leadership activities, problem-solving effectiveness, and coaching efforts. Finally, the performance of team members is evaluated by their peers.

With its sophisticated approach to assessing team effectiveness, Sabre has done a great deal to create high-performing virtual teams. According to Sabre, the focus on results and statistical measures allows managers to judge people by what they really do, rather than what they appear to be doing.

Questions

1. Why do you think Sabre makes the results of its customer service surveys available on the company's intranet? Outline advantages and disadvantages of this practice. What consequences might this practice have for a team's development across time?

2. Review the team effectiveness criteria discuss in this chapter. Which effectiveness criteria are not measured by Sabre's performance management approach? Do you think they should change the way they measure team effectiveness? Explain your rationale.

3. Compare Google's work teams with Sabre's virtual teams. Do you think the Sabre teams go through the same stages of team development as the Google teams? Why or why not?

chapter 18

© Color Blind Images/Blend Images/Jupiter Images

Understanding Organizational Culture and Cultural Diversity

Learning Goals..

After studying this chapter, you should be able to:

1. Describe the core elements of a culture.

2. Compare and contrast four types of organizational culture.

3. Discuss why subcultures exist in organizations.

4. Describe several activities for successfully managing diversity.

Communication Competency

Planning and Administration Competency

Teamwork Competency

Managing Effectively

Self-Management Competency

Strategic Action Competency

Multicultural Competency

Challenge of Managing ....

Darden Restaurants

© William Perry/AP Photo

You may not recognize the corporate name of Darden Restaurants, but you probably know the restaurants that fall under their umbrella: Olive Garden, Red Lobster, Bahama Breeze chains, and Smokey Bones Barbeque and Grill. Founded by Bill Darden nearly 70 years ago, today Darden Restaurants is the world's largest casual dining company. It employs more than 140,000 people and serves about 300 million guests annually. In a company this large, diversity is a fact of life. At Darden, diversity also is a core value that supports the company's core purpose, which is "To nourish and delight everyone we serve."

Like many U.S. organizations, Darden's approach to managing diversity has evolved over time. For many years, their headquarters buildings, located in Orlando, Florida, were decorated to celebrate the Christmas season. Managers thought the decorations were appropriate because they were secular and not religious in nature (e.g., Christmas trees and Santa, not a nativity scene). Then some employees began to complain that the secular Christmas decorations failed to recognize the importance of other non-Christian holidays. And some Christians complained that the "Christ was being taken out of Christmas." This was a difficult situation for Darden. Should they stop celebrating holidays altogether, as one consultant recommended? Should they try to celebrate all holidays that were important to their employees, as another consultant recommended? After surveying employees, Darden decided to celebrate the holidays that employees said they wanted to celebrate. In one recent year, they celebrated 12 holidays in the months of October through February. Employees are encouraged to celebrate their own religious and/or cultural heritage by putting up decorations for the holidays they care about.

Darden's approach to managing diversity is grounded in a firm understanding of its customers. Strong brands like Red Lobster and Olive Garden take decades to build but their reputations can be quickly tarnished. Emerging brands like Bahama Breeze and Smokey Bones will grow only if guests leave feeling satisfied and they tell their friends about the experience.

Learning Content

In stating that diversity is a core value, Darden's management understands that they are inviting scrutiny from all of their stakeholders. Their actions in all arenas must reflect this value. To show their commitment to diversity as a core value, managers strive to:

▶ achieve minority and female representation at all levels in the company,

▶ "nourish and delight" guests from all backgrounds,

▶ increase supplier diversity,

▶ partner with the communities from which they draw employees and guests, and

▶ evaluate leaders' performance against diversity objectives.

As an example of how valuing diversity influences Darden's relationships with its stakeholders, consider its Community Alliance Project (CAP). CAP operates in 10 large cities (e.g., Atlanta, Cincinnati, Orlando, Miami), striving to ensure that Darden is considered a "neighbor of choice." Restaurant directors and managers serve as ambassadors to local organizations focused on race, gender, disability, age, and the gay and lesbian community. One of their tasks is to stay abreast of community needs and opportunities and pass along relevant information to the company's Diversity Affairs team. Through CAP, Darden sponsors activities such as

▶ Nulites, a youth development project of the National Urban League;

▶ LINC TELACU, a college scholarship program for Hispanic students in East Los Angeles and Chicago;

▶ Sphinx, a music program for inner-city schools in Detroit; and

▶ Bit Thought, a music appreciation and performance program in Dallas.

From the dining room to the board room, Darden promotes and celebrates diversity because it makes good business sense, and they also believe it is the right thing to do.[1]

To learn more about this organization, visit *www.dardenrestaurants.com.*

Describe the core elements of a culture.

The Elements of a Culture

A culture *is the unique pattern of shared assumptions, values, and norms that shape the socialization, symbols, language, narratives, and practices of a group of people.*[2] Organizational cultures are important because they influence the satisfaction and performance of organization members. At Enron, a culture of greed has been blamed for the unethical behaviors that eventually destroyed that company. At NASA, a "broken safety culture" was blamed for the loss of the *Columbia* space shuttle and its crew. At companies such as Darden, more positive cultures are part of the reason for the company's success.[3]

As illustrated in Figure 18.1, assumptions, values, and norms form the base of a culture but they can't be observed directly. They can only be inferred from a culture's more visible elements—its socialization activities, symbols, language, narratives, and practices. At Darden Restaurants, core values such as diversity—as well as other core

596 Part 5 Leading

values, such as teamwork and excellence—become visible through the everyday experiences of people who work for the company, eat in their restaurants, participate in the community events they sponsor, and so on.

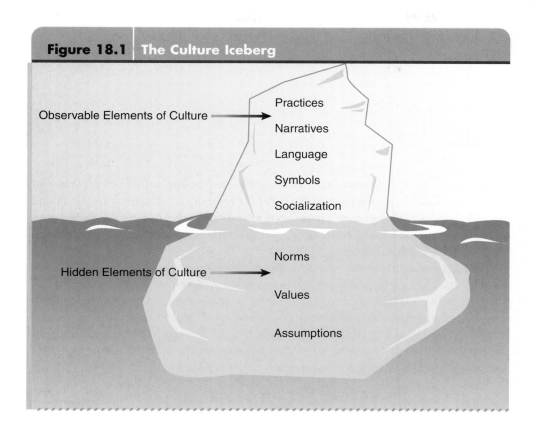

Figure 18.1 | The Culture Iceberg

Observable Elements of Culture →
- Practices
- Narratives
- Language
- Symbols
- Socialization

Hidden Elements of Culture →
- Norms
- Values
- Assumptions

Darden Restaurants values diversity. The visibility of diversity as a value at Darden Restaurants has resulted in the company being recognized by *Fortune*, *Black Enterprise*, and *Hispanic Business* as one of the best U.S. companies to work for. Procter & Gamble is another company that cares about its culture. When CEO A. G. Lafley first took over, he wanted to show that he valued teamwork and collaboration. To communicate these values, he completely rebuilt the executive floor to open it up and encourage conversations. He even added a "living room" area for casual gatherings. On other floors, "huddle rooms" were added, and mini espresso cafes created places for people to relax on cushy sofas and watch a bit of news on the flat-screen TVs.[4]

Assumptions

Shared assumptions *are the underlying thoughts and feelings that members of a culture take for granted and believe to be true.* At Darden, one shared assumption seems to be that guests who feel respected as individuals are more likely to enjoy their meals and return for meals in the future. Members of the loose-knit "open-source" community of Linux software programmers share the assumption that software code should be openly available so that anyone anywhere can modify it or create new code to enhance the software's capability. This assumption contrasts sharply with the assumption held by most software producers who believe that code should be proprietary and that secrecy is required in order to make a profit.

Snapshot

"I have a profound belief that ethics flow from actions. Whatever plans or words or principles you set up, if you don't follow through, they don't mean anything."

Keith Krach, CEO, Ariba

Values and Norms

Values *are the basic beliefs people hold about things that are important and meaningful and are stable over time.* Darden Restaurants lists the following as its core values:

▶ Integrity and fairness,

▶ Respect and caring,

▶ Diversity,

▶ Always learning—always teaching,

▶ Being "of service,"

▶ Teamwork, and

▶ Excellence.

At Southwest Airlines, "having fun" is a value shared by the airline's employees and customers alike. Nonprofit professional theaters typically value artistic creativity and independence as well as community education and outreach.[5] As we have emphasized throughout this book, many contemporary organizations are striving to ensure that all employees value ethical conduct.

Norms are rules that govern the behaviors of group members. In Chapter 17, we discussed norms as elements of the internal processes of work teams. When a norm is widely shared throughout the organization, it becomes an element of the organization's culture. The main function of norms in organizations is to regulate and standardize behavior. When members of an organization engage in behaviors that violate the norms, they can expect expressions of disapproval. When behavior conforms to the norms, members receive the approval of their peers and others in the organization.

Socialization

Socialization *is a process by which new members are brought into a culture.* The most powerful way to do so is through consistent role modeling, teaching, coaching, and enforcement by others in the culture. At the societal level, socialization takes place within the family, in schools and religious organizations, and through the media. At the industry level, socialization often occurs through organized activities conducted by industry trade associations. In the Linux open-source community, socialization occurs over the Internet, where norms such as "don't dump on others" and "make nice" are posted electronically.

In most organizations, socialization typically begins subtly during the hiring process. It then becomes more apparent during orientation and training events soon after the new hire begins work. Job applicants who go to Darden's Web site will quickly see that diversity is something the company cares about. The message is reinforced during the orientation process, when new employees hear about the company's commitment to diversity awareness and its importance to the company's success.

At Ritz-Carlton hotels, room-service waiters attend formal training sessions and also learn on the job by working with veteran waiters who serve as coaches. Both types of training teach new waiters about the hotel's service philosophy, which is captured by the saying "We are ladies and gentlemen serving ladies and gentlemen." The formal training sessions tell new employees the story of how the hotel began and ensure that they are familiar with each sentence of the firm's credo—three paragraphs that capture the firm's most important values and principles. The on-the-job coaching sessions teach new waiters how to deliver the excellent quality of service expected by the hotel and its clients. Emphasis is placed on *how* people do their jobs, not just getting the job done. For example, new waiters are taught how to use language that fits the Ritz-Carlton's image (e.g., "Please accept my apologies," rather than "I'm sorry," and "Certainly, my pleasure," instead of "okay"). Coaching also teaches new hires to think about situations from the customer's perspective, to imagine the customer's emotional reactions, and to anticipate (rather than respond to) each customer's concerns. Ultimately, the hotel's goal is to create a workforce whose attitudes and habits are perfectly aligned with the hotel's values.[6]

Symbols

A symbol *is anything visible that can be used to represent an abstract shared value or something having special meaning.* Symbols are the simplest and most basic observable form of cultural expression. They may take the form of logos, architecture, uniforms, awards, and many other tangible expressions. At US Airways, the "heritage logo" is an important symbol. Appearing on all of the company's airplanes, it depicts the fact that this company was created by merging US Air and America West. The logo was developed to acknowledge the firm's historical roots. At Quad/Graphics, the blue factory uniforms that are worn by *everyone* in the company are a symbol adopted by the founder as a way to remind everyone that they are all production workers.[7]

At GSD&M Advertising, the entire building serves as a symbol of the organizational culture. The GSD&M building is designed to look and feel like a small city. The business development department is located in the city's financial district. Employees go to the community center to socialize or have a meal. To speak with top-level managers, employees head for the city center, where windowless executive offices were located in order to make them as accessible as possible. As employees walk around their "city," they are constantly reminded of GSD&M's core values: community, winning, restlessness, freedom, responsibility, curiosity, and integrity. These words are carved in stone at the "city center," and they show up in various other forms throughout the work areas.

For some companies, a song or anthem is an important symbol. Consider this one, which was popular at IBM during its early years, when the founder, Thomas Watson, still ran the show. The lyrics were sung to the tune, "Singin' in the Rain":

> *Selling IBM, selling IBM.*
> *What a glorious feeling, the world is our friend.*
> *We're Watson's great crew; we're loyal and true.*
> *We're proud of our job, and we never feel blue.*[8]

Language

Language *is a shared system of vocal sounds, written signs, and/or gestures used to convey special meanings among members of a culture.* At the Mayo Clinic, a medical complex in Rochester, Minnesota, the use of language reinforces the value placed on teamwork. Mayo doctors work in patient-centered teams, which typically include other doctors and may also include social workers, spiritual advisers, and psychiatrists. At Mayo, all doctors use the term *consultants* to refer to each other. To describe the socialization practices that they've all been through, they say they have been "Mayo-ized."

At Commerce Bank, people use the word *Wow* a lot. *Wow* isn't a word many people associate with banking—but that's just the point. Commerce Bank built its organizational culture to be more like that of retailers Home Depot and Starbucks. The bank's goal is to wow customers, not just meet their basic needs. At Commerce, "wow" is so important that there's a Wow Department. There's also a Dr. Wow. Employees and customers are encouraged to send their compliments and complaints to Dr. Wow, who sorts through them and then sends them along to the appropriate staff member. In 2006, the company introduced a new WOW! Award, which it gives to recognize talented employees. Modeled after *American Idol*, the Commerce Idol contest was held before an audience of 6,000 people at Radio City Music Hall in New York City. The competition was open to all 12,000 employees in seven states, and there were 110 contestants. The winner, Shana Cope, drew enthusiastic applause for her rendition of Aretha Franklin's, "Baby, I Love You." The WOW! Awards celebrate the Commerce work culture, which emphasizes personal achievement.[9]

Narratives

Narratives are the unique stories, sagas, legends, and myths in a culture. They often describe the unique accomplishments and beliefs of leaders over time, usually in heroic and romantic terms. The basic story may be based on historical fact, but as the story gets told and retold, the facts may be embellished with fictional details.

The story of how Art Fry, a 3M employee, developed Post-It Notes is a well-known saga that's told over and over at 3M and many other innovative firms. According to the story, Fry became frustrated when the bits of paper he used to mark pages in his hymnal kept falling out. To solve the problem, he needed an adhesive that would stick long enough to keep his pages marked without leaving a residue on the hymnal. When he found such an adhesive in one of 3M's labs, he suggested the idea of marketing the product that eventually became Post-It Notes. But market surveys yielded negative results and potential distributors couldn't see the product's potential. Undaunted, Fry gave out samples to 3M secretaries and executives. Eventually, everyone—at 3M and elsewhere—was hooked on Fry's new product. Eventually, Fry was promoted to the highest level possible in the technical career ladder. At 3M, this story is used to teach employees three important lessons: (1) They should look everywhere for new ideas, (2) when they have a great idea, they should be persistent, and (3) 3M rewards employees for great ideas.

In organizations that value innovation, stories that illustrate the value of persistence are quite common. A manager in a jet engine plant likes to tell the story of how employees reacted when he first suggested using two-way radios to improve communication and speed up the production process. In this case, the innovation influenced the process used to put together the parts that make up a very complex product: "I got radios for everyone. All the major functions had radios. Two-way radios. And that was something that had never been done here before. And [people said] 'it will not work, it can't work, we've never done that.' Well, I went ahead and did it. Now, they won't give up the radios. We were asked to do the job one month early by our customer. We did it."[10]

 Shared

Practices

The most complex but observable cultural element is shared practices, which include taboos and ceremonies. Taboos *are culturally forbidden behaviors.* A taboo at Johnson & Johnson is to put profits ahead of ethical responsibilities to doctors, nurses, and patients. When people join the company, they receive a copy of the Johnson & Johnson credo (a statement of their values), which states this taboo. Johnson & Johnson doesn't just state the taboo and assume people will understand how to live the company credo—they give employees an entire booklet titled *Living the Credo: Making Good Decisions at Johnson & Johnson*. The Ethical Challenge describes some of the principles that Johnson & Johnson explains to employees in this book.[11]

Johnson & Johnson

The 200 operating companies of Johnson & Johnson create and sell products found in millions of homes around the world. Band-Aid, Johnson's Baby, Motrin, Mylanta, Shower-to-Shower, and Tylenol are just a few of their brands. Since its founding in 1886, the company has been a leader in health-care products. They see their first responsibility as being to serve doctors, nurses, patients, and patients' families and everyone else who is touched by their products. To earn and sustain the trust of these and other stakeholders, Johnson & Johnson promotes the importance of ethical decision making by all employees. Leaders are expected to make ethical choices under all circumstances, and employees are taught that every action should reflect conscious attention to ethics. To help employees recognize the types of ethical challenges they are likely to face, the company describes several in the handbook employees receive, titled *Living the Credo*. Here are some examples:

1. An approved prescription drug is known to have some serious side effects. It also is extremely effective in fighting a fatal infection and advanced forms of disease. You need to decide whether to disclose the risks, and how. You are worried that full disclosure may cause the drug to be pulled off the market, and the result will be that people who could have been saved will die.

2. Jean's business unit is about to launch a new medical device. An engineer informs him of a design defect. After extensive discussions, Jean concludes that the risks are minimal and the law doesn't require that they be disclosed. He thinks the engineer's judgment is simply wrong. Reporting the information will delay the launch, lead to a costly investigation, and the company's financial goals will not be met. On the other hand, if he does not report the defect and it is later determined to be significant, patients may suffer, the company may be fined, and customers may lose trust in the company's products.

3. A cost-cutting effort means that you must terminate someone in your unit, and it is up to you to decide who. Everyone is competent, so what criteria should you use to make your decision? You could try to decide who is least competent, but it would not be easy to document that decision. Or you could terminate the most recently hired person, but if you do it will reduce the diversity of your unit. You could also terminate the person who has the least long-term potential, but that would mean losing a valuable senior employee who is nearing retirement.

Johnson & Johnson recognizes that there are no clear answers to challenges such as these. The company's solution is to encourage employees to make their decisions carefully and always consider the moral consequences of their decisions. The company defines ethical decisions as those that are consistent with all six of its "Pillars of Character": trustworthiness, respect, responsibility, fairness, caring, and good citizenship. After considering these, employees are also encouraged to check their decisions against several other criteria, including these:

▶ *Role model test:* Think of someone you respect and ask yourself, "What would they do?"

▶ *Publicity test:* What would you do if you knew your decision would be reported on the evening news?

▶ *Golden rule:* How would *you* want to be treated?

▶ *Parenting perspective:* What would you hope your child would do? What would you do if you knew your child was looking over your shoulder?

By providing employees with concrete suggestions for how to approach ethical challenges, Johnson & Johnson strives to maintain a company culture that puts ethics first.

To learn more about this organization, visit *www.jnj.com.*

Ceremonies *are elaborate and formal activities designed to generate strong feelings.* Usually they are carried out as special events.[12] In most societies, ceremonies celebrate the birth, marriage, and death of the society's members. In many organizations, ceremonies are used to recognize special achievements and honor the retiring employee. At Ravenswood Winery, company meetings are held at a CawCaw. People gather around a barbeque pit to enjoy a meal and sample various company products. When Ravenswood was bought by Constellation Brands, a CawCaw was held to discuss the decision. According to Kimberly Dreyer, a Ravenswood manager, a CawCaw "gives people a chance to ask questions, cry, or jump for joy." It's an important part of their culture. According to Dreyer, Constellation Brands "saw that our approach worked. They knew that it was what made us unique, so they left the culture intact."[13]

2.

Compare and contrast four types of organizational culture.

Basic Types of Organizational Culture

Cultural elements and their relationships create a pattern that is distinct to an organization, just as a personality is unique to an individual. As with a classification of individuals that share some common characteristics, several general types of organizational culture can be described. One useful type is presented in Figure 18.2. The vertical axis reflects the relative *formal control* orientation, ranging from stable to flexible. The horizontal axis reflects the relative *focus of attention*, ranging from internal functioning to external functioning. The four quadrants represent four pure types of organizational culture: bureaucratic, clan, entrepreneurial, and market.[14] In a culturally homogeneous organization, one of these basic types of culture will dominate.

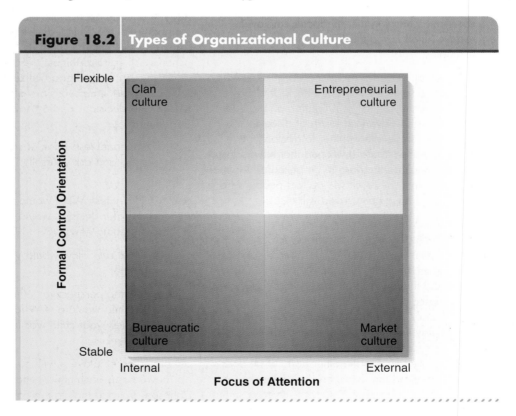

Figure 18.2 | **Types of Organizational Culture**

Different organizational cultures may be appropriate under different conditions, with no one type of culture being ideal for every situation. Some employees may prefer one over another. As you read about each type of culture, consider which best fits your preferences. An employee who works in an organization that fits his or her view of an ideal culture tends to be committed to the organization and optimistic about its future.[15]

Bureaucratic Culture

In a bureaucratic culture, *the behavior of employees is governed by formal rules and standard operating procedures, and coordination is achieved through hierarchical reporting relationships.* Recall that the long-term concerns of a bureaucracy are predictability, efficiency, and stability. The focus of attention is on the internal operations of the organization. To ensure stability, the tasks, responsibilities, and authority for all employees are clearly spelled out. Rules and processes that apply to most situations are developed, and employees are socialized to believe that their duty is to "go by the book" and follow legalistic procedures. Behavioral norms support formality over informality.[16]

Bureaucratic cultures often are found in organizations that produce standardized goods and/or services, such as Pizza Hut, the IRS, and Farmers Insurance Company. They are particularly common in local, state, and federal governments. Governments create rules in their efforts to ensure that all citizens are treated the same, regardless of their backgrounds, wealth, or status. These same values often are reflected in the organizational cultures of such organizations.

Clan Culture

An internal focus also characterizes a clan culture. Compared to a bureaucratic culture, however, in a clan culture, control over behavior is more subtle. Few formal rules and procedures exist. Instead, in a clan culture *the behaviors of employees are shaped by tradition, loyalty, personal commitment, extensive socialization, and self-management.* Members of the organization recognize an obligation beyond the simple exchange of labor for a salary. They understand that contributions to the organization (e.g., hours worked per week) may exceed any contractual agreements. The clan culture achieves unity with a long and thorough socialization process. Long-time employees serve as mentors and role models for newer members. These relationships perpetuate the organization's values and norms over successive generations of employees. Members of a clan culture are aware of their unique history and they have a shared image of the organization's style and manner of conduct. They have a strong sense of identification and recognize their need to work together. Shared goals, perceptions, and behavioral tendencies foster communication, coordination, and integration. Peer pressure to adhere to important norms is strong.

Analytical Graphics, chosen in 2006 as the Best Medium Company to Work For in America, has a clan culture. The tone is set by CEO Paul Graziani and Human Resources Director Lisa Velte. For Velte, maintaining the company's friendly and open atmosphere is a key area of responsibility. The company offers generous benefits that smooth the hassles of everyday life. Besides serving breakfast, lunch, and dinner to anyone who wants it, the company has an on-site workout room and an on-site laundry room. New hires are socialized through a long process of orientation, which includes having long lunches in small groups that include new hires, the founders, and the COO and CFO. These lunches are used to pass along this software company's history and teach new hires about the company's markets, products (navigation systems), and plans. They also serve to establish open lines of communication so employees will feel free to participate actively once they know their way around. On Fridays, everyone meets for a buffet lunch to receive updates about company performance. Employees working out in the field join these buffet meetings via teleconferencing.[17]

Entrepreneurial Culture

In an entrepreneurial culture, *the external focus and flexibility create an environment that encourages risk taking, dynamism, and creativity.* There is a commitment to

Snapshot

"There's a family mentality here as opposed to just being another number. That trickles down from the top. He [the CEO] knows everyone's name and says 'hi' everyday when I see him during morning workouts at the gym."

Andrew Smith, Accountant, Analytic Graphics Inc., Easton, Pennsylvania

experimentation, innovation, and being on the leading edge. An entrepreneurial culture suits a new company's start-up phase. An entrepreneurial culture also fits well with the demands faced by employees who are seeking to create and develop new products. GSD&M has an entrepreneurial culture. This culture doesn't just quickly react to changes in the environment; it creates change. Effectiveness means providing new and unique products and rapid growth. Individual initiative, flexibility, and freedom foster growth and are encouraged and well rewarded.

Regardless of whether an organization is a start-up company or a more established firm, this focus on the external environment will be evident in an entrepreneurial culture. However, for managing products and services that have already been brought to market and may be entering later stages of the product life cycle, a market culture may be more appropriate.

Market Culture

In a market culture, *the values and norms reflect the importance of achieving measurable and demanding goals, especially those that are financial and market based (e.g., sales growth, profitability, and market share).* Hard-driving competitiveness and a profits orientation prevail throughout the organization. EDS, Frito-Lay, and Oracle, among others, share many elements of a market culture.

A market culture doesn't exert much informal social pressure on an organization's members. Superiors' interactions with subordinates largely consist of negotiating performance–reward agreements and/or evaluating requests for resource allocations. Social relations among coworkers aren't emphasized, and few economic incentives are tied directly to cooperating with peers. Managers in one department are expected to cooperate with managers in other departments only to the extent necessary to achieve their performance goals.

The corporate culture at this new Mercedes-Benz plant in Alabama is a blend of German, Japanese, and U.S. auto-production customs. Will employees adapt?

© Dave Martin/AP Photo

Organizational Implications

Organizational culture has the potential to enhance organizational performance, individual satisfaction, the sense of certainty about how problems are to be handled, and other aspects of worklife. Many managers pay attention to culture. Some managers are concerned about building or maintaining their existing culture. Other managers are concerned about changing their organizational culture in order to improve their future performance.

When Mercedes-Benz decided to set up a new facility in Alabama to produce its M-Class SUV, CEO Andreas Renschler wanted to create a unique corporate culture. This new culture would incorporate the best elements of many different country cultures. He explained, "I strongly believe you have only one chance to establish a corporate culture and that it ultimately sets the tone for your entire organization. By design, we brought together people with a variety of experiences, with a lot of different ideas, and with different ways of thinking." Experts from Japan, the United States, and Germany all worked together to develop the new organization. When the Alabama facility was up and running, its own distinct culture was different from that of the Mercedes-Benz plants in Germany. The experiences of Mercedes-Benz are described in the Multicultural Competency feature.[18]

Mercedes-Benz

Mercedes-Benz is one of the world's most widely recognized brands. It stands for quality and luxury. Some people are surprised to learn that Mercedes-Benz manufactures some of its automobiles in Vance, Alabama. That's where Mercedes-Benz U.S. International (MBUSI) is located, and it's where the award-winning M-Class SUV was born. The facility was created by a team of executives and workers who came from three countries: Germany, the United States, and Japan. Each country has its own approach to designing and building automobiles.

In Germany, engineers are highly trained experts who develop their skills by working as an apprentice to a *Meister* (master in the profession). Workers accept the authority of the Meister and don't expect to be treated as equals to the Meister. Once they learn the skills they need, they expect to carry out their tasks without close supervision. This is a sign that they are respected and can be trusted to do a good job. Strong norms exist concerning the importance of producing automobiles of superior quality. In traditional U.S. automobile plants, managers control workers through division of labor and narrow spans of control. Henry Ford's assembly-line approach still dominates many production plants. At the Jeep plant in Ohio, relationships between managers and subordinates are relatively informal. People are quite direct in saying what they think. Americans tend to be driven to get things done, and they are more willing to begin production before working through every problem. In Japan, strong norms concerning the importance of quality are similar to those in Germany. However, quality is achieved using a system of team-based production and continuous improvement. Employees are generalists rather than specialists, and it is important to reach consensus. At MBUSI, elements of all three cultures have been blended together.

The creation of MBUSI began with U.S. executives spending 18 months in Germany, where they worked with German engineers to design the plant. When the Vance plant was built, German engineers spent two years there helping to train the Americans. Following the Japanese model, multidisciplinary teams are used to manage the operation. Each team is autonomous and self-managing. They are held accountable for meeting quality standards, controlling costs, and meeting production schedules. Relationships between managers and their subordinates are egalitarian and open. When Jack Duncan, a supervisor, noticed that workers had to "slant walk" zigzag style to reach a parts bin, his response was to brainstorm with the workers to find a better arrangement. They made the change, and it shaved 1 or 2 seconds off the production time for each SUV. According to Duncan, everyone is looking for small changes like that in the spirit of continuous improvement. Whether the hybrid organizational culture is a success is still open to debate. Initial demand for the M-Class SUV was stronger than expected, but quality problems at the plant caused disappointment among customers. Subsequently the company invested $600 million to improve the plant and double the size of the workforce. Reviews of its 2006 model were positive, suggesting the plant's quality problems have been repaired. But recently the machinists have been engaged in discussions about whether to unionize. Mercedes-Benz workers are represented by strong unions in Spain, Brazil, South Africa, and Germany, where the company was founded more than a century ago. The concerns of workers in Alabama don't seem to involve wages or benefits, which are problems at many American auto plants. Instead, the issue is the company culture. According to George Jones, a 38-year-old who inspects raw materials at the Mercedes-Benz plant, "It's about having a voice." Ultimately, workers will have to decide whether the culture at the plant is positive or in need of change.

To learn more about this organization, visit *www.mbusa.com.*

Building a Strong Culture. An organization is said to have a strong culture *when the more observable cultural elements project a single, consistent message.* In such organizations, managers and employees share a common behavioral style. They use the same basic approach to solve problems, meet goals, and deal with important customers, suppliers, and other stakeholders. They share common norms that guide how they relate to one another. Results are measured the same way throughout the organization. A common set of rules governs the use of rewards and punishments.[19] Commerce Bank, Southwest Airlines, and Johnson & Johnson all have strong cultures. A strong organizational culture results in predictable, well-specified behavior patterns. When an organization's business environment is relatively stable, strong cultures that support strategic goals contribute to firm performance.[20]

A strong organizational culture doesn't just happen. It's cultivated by management, learned and reinforced by employees, and passed on to new employees. Before it was acquired by Bank of America, MBNA was the world's largest independent credit card company. Founded less that 25 years ago in Wilmington, Delaware, MBNA was known as a company with a strong culture. People in Wilmington could easily see that MBNA's company culture was very different from the culture of DuPont, another big company headquartered there. The DuPont family and their company have been influential in Wilmington for more than 200 years. A realtor explained: "DuPonters have always kept a low profile. They don't buy fancy cars, even though they could afford to. The MBNAers do." Some people described the MBNA culture as hard driving and friendly. Some people called it intense. Some people described it as being "a cult." Even the way MBNAers looked and dressed was distinctive. One reporter described the men as being easy to spot because they looked like Secret Service agents—they tended to be youngish (mid-20s to mid-40s), physically fit, and trim. Now that the MBNA staff works for Bank of America, the culture of the new organization, MBNA America Bank, may begin to change. But after 25 years, the old culture is not likely to die quickly.[21]

Changing an Organizational Culture. Not all organizations have a strong culture, and many organizations have several subcultures. Such organizations may undergo cultural change in order to meld the different subcultures. In other words, one reason for change is to create a stronger, more consistent organizational culture. Another reason that organizations may want to change their organizational culture is because the external environment has changed. In the United States during the 1980s, many companies began changing their cultures to be more responsive to customers' expectations for high-quality products and excellent customer service.

During the 1990s, when unemployment levels reached historic lows and labor shortages made it difficult for organizations to take advantage of market opportunities, many top managers began to reassess how well their organizational cultures fit the expectations of their workforces. By 2002, a sharp economic decline and revelations about unethical and illegal accounting practices pressured many firms to reassess their organizational cultures. Going forward, rapid rates of globalization, the shift toward knowledge-based competition, and the continuation of merger and acquisition activities have focused attention on the importance of understanding, assessing, and melding differing organizational cultures.

Before an organization can change or improve its overall culture, it must first understand the culture that is present now in the organization. When an organization focuses on understanding its culture, it is likely to discover that it doesn't have *one* organizational culture. Instead, it probably has several subcultures. Next we discuss the reasons why an organization might have several different subcultures. Later in this chapter, we describe some steps that organizations are taking to change their organizational cultures.

Subcultures within Organizations

3.

Discuss why subcultures exist in organizations.

An organizational subculture *exists when assumptions, values, and norms are shared by some—but not all—organizational members.* Organizational subcultures occur for a variety of reasons. Here we discuss four reasons why many organizations have subcultures:

▶ The organization was created from a merger or acquisition.

▶ Departments within the organization have their own norms and values.

▶ Operations and facilities are located in several geographic regions.

▶ A diverse workforce creates subcultures.

Subcultures Due to Mergers and Acquisitions

When one firm acquires another firm, or when two firms merge, it is likely that the two firms will have had different cultures. In fact, incompatible cultures is the most frequently cited reason for why mergers and acquisitions (M&A) fail, as shown in Figure 18.3.[22] When the organizational cultures of the merged firms are similar, the chances of success increase. Likewise, the success of joint ventures and other strategic alliances is greater when the firms involved have similar organizational cultures.[23]

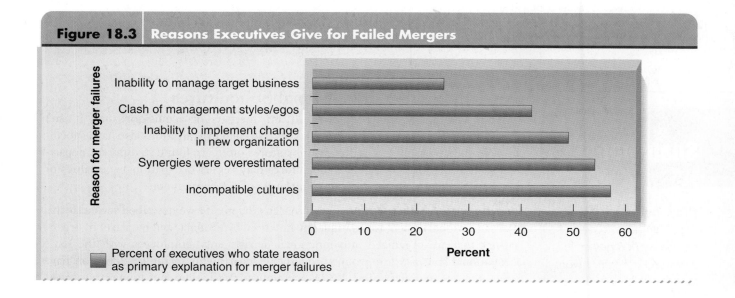

Figure 18.3 | Reasons Executives Give for Failed Mergers

When US Airways and America West joined forces, Larry LeSueur was given the responsibility of bringing these two cultures together. The fact that the two airlines were competitors made things difficult enough, but the companies also had different histories and different workforces. US Airways was a much larger and older company. Compared to America West, it was more bureaucratic. Employees of US Airways tended to be more senior and more experienced. Even the workspaces of the two companies had a different feel. As described in the Strategic Action Competency feature on the next page, LeSueur has begun to create a common culture by establishing new ceremonies and using new symbols.[24]

Within a year after America West merged with US Airways, the stock price had almost doubled. The market seemed to think this merger was a good idea. But how successful it really is won't be known for a while. CEO Doug Parker knows that success depends on bringing the two companies together into a seamless whole. Leading that effort is Larry LeSueur, vice president of culture integration. Formerly a vice president of America West, he's worked in a variety of jobs—from part-time ramp agent to director of reservations. Now he spends his time designing the culture of a new company.

To get employees involved immediately, he put together an event called Day One. Workers across the company decorated their workstations in ways that signaled the changes they were expected to make. In Philadephia, employees used a wedding theme to decorate. A bride and groom came dressed for the event and everyone celebrated by eating a wedding cake. The employees with the most creative workstations on Day One received prizes such as new furniture or a TV for the staff break room. In the months that followed, LeSueur and Parker held town meetings around the country. The events included a 20-minute speech by Parker and then two hours of questions and answers from employees.

Another ongoing initative is an e-mail campaign that addresses the company's new "guiding principles." Employees are invited to write in with their suggestions for changes that are needed in order to align everyday reality with the stated principles. Parker answers some of the e-mails himself and sends others on to the relevant local managers. Still on the agenda are manager training programs, which will help managers develop the skills they will need to be effective in a culture that expects employees to soar toward excellence.

To learn more about this organization, visit www2.usairways.com.

Snapshot

This is a teamwork business. You have to have people work together in some sort of team. I want to mold (the two companies) into one culture but still keep the best of both cultures. That's the only way this is going to work."

Doug Parker, CEO, US Airways Group

Departmental and Divisional Subcultures

Suppose a company hasn't experienced any mergers or acquisitions and it isn't involved in other forms of strategic alliances. Do such organizations also have subcultures? Yes, they usually do. Different subcultures often are found in different departments of an organization. These subcultures may reflect occupational specialties or they may be created by the managers in charge of the departments.

Occupational Subcultures. Recall that in Chapter 11 we described several forms of organizational design, for example, by function, by product, and by place. In organizations that are organized into functional departments, employees with the same occupational specialty are grouped together. Departments in the organization have names such as manufacturing, R&D, accounting, marketing, and human resources. Occupational socialization practices can be strong sources of cultural indoctrination, especially for professionals. For them, the socialization period begins in college and continues as long as they identify with their chosen professions. Professional associations often formulate their own mission statements, codes of ethics, and standards for professional practice. Together, these values and norms can create a shared world view that is understood and generally accepted within the profession, but is largely unknown to outsiders. Organizational designs that group members of a profession together reinforce and sustain occupation-based subcultures.

Subcultures Created by Managers. Differences in the personalities and leadership styles of managers are another reason units in an organization have different subcultures. A recent survey of employees found that when fun happened at work, it usually was because lower level managers made fun happen. Employees clearly believe that in most organizations some units have more appealing cultures than others. What makes a unit's culture more positive for employees? According to the survey, positive cultures are created by managers who:

▶ recognize personal milestones, such as birthdays and employment anniversaries,

▶ hold public celebrations for professional achievements,

▶ sponsor picnics and parties, and

▶ listen to their employees and recognize the efforts they put into work.[25]

Geographically Based Subcultures

Many organizations have facilities and operations spread across several geographic regions. As we described in Chapter 11, these organizations often rely on a geographic structure. If places in which units are located each have distinct cultures, then the organization is likely to have place-based, or regional, subcultures.

Regional subcultures are common in global organizations. At each location, the societal culture combines with the organization's culture to create a distinct subculture. The result is that different subcultures are found in each country where the company has operations. IBM has a strong organizational culture. But the IBM organizational culture is not identical all around the world. The subculture found at each IBM location is a combination of the IBM organizational culture and the culture of that country.[26]

It is easy to see why geographic locations create organizational subcultures within global firms. But some people are surprised to learn that domestic firms also have regional subcultures. In the United States, many people in Midwestern Minneapolis behave differently than those in West Coast Los Angeles—that's readily apparent to anyone who visits these cities. In Switzerland, four regional subcultures can be found within the country—each is a unique blend of elements from the traditional Swiss culture and the cultures of neighboring France, Italy, and Germany. In China, there are at least three regions with distinct local cultures: one in the southeast, another in the northeast, and a third covering much of the central and western parts of the country. The subculture of the southeast region is the most individualistic, whereas the subculture of the central and western areas is the most collectivistic. The culture of the northeast region falls between these two extremes. Thus, a manager whose company operates at several locations in China needs to understand the subcultures that are created by these regional differences.

Subcultures Due to Workforce Demographics

During the past decade, many U.S. employers began to realize that workforce demographics are another reason why an organization may have several subcultures. Workforce demographics *describe employee characteristics such as ethnicity, age, and gender.* The fact that people with different demographic backgrounds live side by side, however, doesn't mean that they share the same culture.

Ethnicity. In the United States, people from a variety of ethnic backgrounds are found in every region. Today, 1 in 10 workers in the United States is foreign born—the highest rate in 70 years. Millions of other workers are the children of recent immigrants. They were born in the United States and grew up in a family that was strongly influenced by the parents' home country culture. Many workers born in the United States still identify with the ethnic groups of their ancestors—even though their ancestors may have come to this country two, three, or several generations ago.

Snapshot

"My first conscious exposure to racism occurred when I came back to the States and went to public school. One of the children said something—I don't remember now what—but I remember what my grandmother said to me: 'They tried to put you in a box. Don't ever let anybody put you in a box.'"

Clifton R. Wharton, Jr., Former Chairman and CEO, TIAA-CREF

Others have more complicated backgrounds. Clifton R. Wharton was born in the United States, but he spent most of his childhood in Spain's Canary Islands. Because his father was a diplomat, he traveled widely and was fluent in Spanish and French by the time he was 10 years old. Then he was sent to Boston to become "Americanized." Eventually, Wharton became the first African American to head a major U.S. company—TIAA-CREF, a multibillion dollar pension fund.[27]

The dominant ethnic groups in the United States, as defined by the Census Bureau, are described in Table 18.1.[28] Note that each of the categories shown includes more specific geographic or ethnic groups that people may identify with more readily. For some people, ethnic origins may have a pervasive influence on their daily experiences, while for others their ethnic origins are much less salient than their "American" identity. Note also that the identity of many people is influenced by more than one ethnic group.

Table 18.1	Ethnic Identities as Measured in the U.S. Census	
Ethnic Category	Description	Percentage of Total Population
People choosing two or more ethnicities	Any combination of ethnic origins.	1.4
People choosing only one ethnicity		98.6
American Indian or Alaska Native	Origins in the original peoples of North, South, or Central America who maintain tribal affiliation and community attachment.	1.0
Asian	Origins in any of the original peoples of the Far East, Southeast Asia, or the Indian subcontinent, including Cambodia, China, India, Japan, Korea, Malaysia, Pakistan, the Philippines, Thailand, and Vietnam.	3.9
Black or African American	Origins in any of the black racial groups in Africa.	12.7
White Non-Hispanic	Origins in any of the original peoples of Europe, the Middle East, or North Africa.	68.9
Hispanic	Origins in Cuban, Puerto Rican, South American, Central American, or other Spanish culture, of white race.	12.0
Total Hispanic	Origins in Cuban, Puerto Rican, South American, Central American, or other Spanish culture, regardless of race.	13.0

Note: Respondents may identify themselves as belonging to more than one ethnic group.

Census counts of people in the categories shown in Table 18.1 are, at best, rough estimates of the proportion of workers who identify with each ethnic group's culture. Although their consequences are difficult to quantify, ethnic subcultures can have a significant impact on an organization.

Age. In a typical organization, employees of all ages can be found, from teenagers to people in their seventies. Employees within each generation tend to share experiences and values that are somewhat distinct from those of other generations. Different generational groups develop their own slang and they often develop symbols that have special meaning for them.[29] Of course, not all members of each generation are exactly alike. Also, people of different ages share many experiences and values. Nevertheless, age-based subcultures are found in many societies around the world.

Inaccurate stereotypes about older workers are a common source of problems for such workers. Older workers often experience age discrimination stemming from the inaccurate beliefs held by managers, who may be reluctant to hire or promote them. Misconceptions about older people are most common among people who have not yet reached middle age. How knowledgeable are you about aging? To find out, take the Quiz shown in Table 18.2.[30]

Table 18.2	Aging Facts Quiz

Circle T if you believe the statement is true, or F if you believe the statement is false.

T F 1. Physical strength declines with age.
T F 2. All five senses decline with age.
T F 3. Older people react more slowly than younger people.
T F 4. Over three-fourths of older people say they are healthy.
T F 5. The majority of older people are senile.
T F 6. Older people tend to be pretty much alike.
T F 7. The majority of older people have no capacity for sex.
T F 8. Older workers aren't as effective as younger workers.
T F 9. Older people take longer to learn something new.
T F 10. The majority of older people cannot adapt to change.
T F 11. The majority of older people are below the poverty line.
T F 12. The majority of older people say they are seldom bored.
T F 13. Drivers age 65+ have fewer accidents than those under age 65.
T F 14. The majority of older people say they are lonely.
T F 15. Older people become more religious as they age.
T F 16. At least 10% of older people live in institutions.
T F 17. Over 20% of the U. S. population is age 65 or older.

The correct answers are given at the end of this chapter on page 624.

Gender and Other Demographics. Differences in the way men and women are socialized and differences in the experiences they have at work are another source of organizational subcultures. Gender roles may seem to be more powerful in some ethnic communities than others, and they may be more powerful in some generations than others. Nevertheless, in many organizations, gender continues to be an important basis for the formation of subcultures. In San Diego, Fire Engine Company 22's unique culture is due to the fact that its four members are all women—a rarity in the United States. Women make up only 8 percent of firefighters across the country, and the culture of many engine crews is masculine. Women are the outsiders. But Fire Engine Company 22 is the opposite. Although the work and basic routines are the same regardless of the gender, the conversations and the feelings of camaraderie reflect women's interests and styles.[31]

Other workforce demographics that can be the basis for organizational subcultures include marital status, family status, sexual orientation, and physical abilities. All of these characteristics can shape the experiences, values, and concerns of people. Demographic similarity often provides a basis for people to develop personal relationships and enjoy feelings of camaraderie. In short, people with similar demographic characteristics often develop their own subcultures, and these exist side by side with other subcultures within many organizations.

Snapshot

"Revenues of U.S. Hispanic companies are growing at an average rate of 20 percent a year—three times faster than the rest of corporate America. The Hispanic demographic is a very unique customer base. It sticks together because it has some common denominators and loyalty to its products and to its people."

**Jay Garcia,
Managing Director,
Ramirez & Company**

Implications of Organizational Subcultures

Managers have many different views about whether subcultures are "good" or "bad" for business. Sometimes organizational subcultures coexist peacefully within an overall organizational culture; at other times subcultures are a major source of continuing conflict.

Advantages. Like Darden Restaurants, many management teams believe that the presence of distinct subcultures in an organization can be beneficial and should be valued. Being able to serve diverse customers is a key reason for valuing diverse employees. At Ford Motor Company, the rationale for valuing the perspectives present in different subcultures focuses on customers. According to Mary Ellen Heyde, director of Ford's lifestyle vehicles, "If you have a diverse workforce, then you know that the customer's point of view will always be represented." The design and marketing teams for Ford's Windstar minivan, which is bought mostly by women, included many women. Their involvement in the project accounts for features such as the "sleeping baby mode" for overhead lights. At UPS, bilingual support centers in Southern California serve the area's many foreign-born entrepreneurs. At Avon, selling to the growing Hispanic market meant creating a Latina-based line of cosmetics and accessories, supported by a targeted marketing campaign.[32]

Disadvantages. The presence of subcultures sometimes creates problems for employees and employers. Consider what often occurs after one firm acquires the other. Employees in the acquired firm may now be expected to give up the culture of their old company and adopt the culture of the company that acquired then. Suddenly, the old ways of doing things are unacceptable. Often, managers in the acquired firm feel that their level of status and influence has been reduced.

Like employees of an acquired firm, members of demographic minority groups often feel that their subculture is not valued as highly as the culture of the majority group. Consider the experience of Eula Adams. Adams was the first African American to become a partner at Touche (which is now Deloitte & Touche). That was in 1983. Adams began working at Touche 10 years earlier. There were about 800 partners at that time and none was African American. In fact, there were only about 10 African-American partners in the entire accounting profession. Remembering what it was like, he says, "The loneliness, especially in the early days, was the hardest. I lived in two worlds. I'd leave work and go home to one world, and then wake up and go back to work in that other world." Actually, the experiences of African Americans may not be much different today.[33] In general, research shows that employees who are part of a minority subculture often perceive that a glass ceiling exists, which limits their career opportunities.[34] Feeling that they are part of a separate culture and that they don't fit in also plays a role in the decisions gay and lesbian employees make about whether to be open about their own sexual orientation.[35]

To reduce the negative consequences of clashes between subcultures, many organizations are in the process of transforming themselves into multicultural organizations. A multicultural organization *has a workforce representing the full mix of cultures found in the population at large, along with a commitment to utilize fully these human resources.* Multicultural organizations strive to be inclusive and permit many subcultures to coexist. Inclusive organizations strive to ensure that no one subculture dominates the others. Next, we describe how U.S. managers are beginning to address the challenge of managing the diverse subcultures that often are present in organizations.

Managing Cultural Diversity and Inclusion

4.
Describe several activities for successfully managing diversity.

Cultural diversity *encompasses the full mix of the cultures and subcultures to which members of the workforce belong.* Subcultures with which employees may identify include all those described earlier in this chapter.

Today, efforts to manage diversity effectively usually involve finding ways to include and support people representing the wide variety of subcultures found in an organization, regardless of the basis for those subcultures: nationality, occupation, ethnicity, age, gender, sexual orientation, language, religion, and many other factors.[36]

Some experts believe that addressing such a broad variety of diversity issues may be detrimental to improving the treatment and career outcomes of ethnic minorities. Others believe that eventually the new, more inclusive approach to managing diversity is likely to pay off for members of all subcultures. The particular approach an organization takes to managing diversity depends partly on the goals it hopes to achieve.

Organizational Goals for Managing Cultural Diversity and Inclusion

We have already suggested that there are many reasons for managers to be concerned about managing diversity effectively. The three major goals that most organizations strive to achieve are complying with laws and regulations, creating a positive culture for employees, and creating economic value.

Legal Compliance. Complying with laws and regulations that prohibit discrimination, such as Title VII of the Civil Rights Act, is a necessary first step for any U.S. organization that seeks to manage diversity effectively. For multinational companies, international laws and the laws of local countries also come into play.[37] As we explained in Chapter 13, a variety of laws makes it illegal for employers to discriminate against employees on the basis of personal characteristics that are unrelated to their jobs. The basic premise of such laws and regulations is that employment decisions should be based on job-related qualifications, not membership in a demographic group. Other laws and regulations go further and state that employers should be proactive in their efforts to recruit, hire, and retain employees from demographic groups who traditionally have been underrepresented in their organizations. These laws and regulations support the use of affirmative action policies and practices. Affirmative action regulations are built on the basic premise that organizations should actively recruit job applicants to build a workforce that reflects the demographics of the qualified labor force locally. In other words, they should strive to create a culturally diverse workforce. To monitor the success of their affirmative action programs, employers generally assess various employment numbers and ratios. These measures include female and minority hiring numbers, offer/acceptance ratios, turnover and retention rates, promotion patterns, downsizing decisions, and compensation levels.

© Stewart Charles Cohen/Workbook Stock/Jupiter Images

While cultural diversity can benefit any organization by providing different perspectives, individuals must feel integrated into the larger organization to be successful.

During the past three decades, affirmative action practices have become common and relatively well accepted in many organizations. But recently, they have become controversial. In 2003, the affirmative action practices built into the University of Michigan's student admissions procedures were challenged in a case heard by the U.S. Supreme Court. Like many employers, the University of Michigan argued that it was appropriate to take into account their desire for a culturally diverse student body when making admissions decisions. They were sued by two white applicants who were denied admission. The applicants argued that it was illegal for the University of Michigan to take into account the ethnic background of applicants. Many employers supported the university's affirmative action practices. In fact, 30 prominent companies—Microsoft, General Motors, Steelcase, and Bank One—publicly wrote in support of the university. In their brief, they explained their thinking: They argued that having a culturally diverse workforce is essential to business success because diversity "facilitates unique and creative approaches to problem solving" and makes it possible for their organizations to "appeal to a variety of consumers." Furthermore, employers need educated workers. If universities do not provide education to a diverse group of students today, then the future success of these businesses was in jeopardy.[38] In deciding the case, the Supreme Court agreed with the logic presented by these 30 companies. Their ruling permitted the University of Michigan to strive to ensure that their student body is culturally diverse. At the same time, the Supreme Court made it clear that universities should not simply give points to non-white students. Each student's entire record should be considered in a wholistic approach when making admissions decisions.

Creating a Positive Culture. A positive organizational culture is one in which everyone feels equally integrated into the larger organization. Members of majority and minority subcultures feel respected; everyone has an equal chance to express views and influence decisions; and everyone has similar access to both formal and informal networks within the organization. Some organizations that initially monitored their diversity numbers primarily because of concerns about legal compliance discovered that the numbers could also be used to gain insights into other problems, such as low morale and high turnover.[39] Addressing such problems promotes a positive culture, which may in turn have benefits that reach far beyond avoiding legal problems. For Scott McQuillan, the culture of diversity and inclusion at Deloitte & Touche influences many aspects of his daily work, as described in the Planning and Administration Competency feature.[40]

Planning and Administration Competency

Deloitte & Touche

At the accounting firm of Deloitte and Touche, employment numbers alerted the partners to a disturbing trend about a decade ago. Only 5 percent of the company's partners were women, and the turnover rate for women throughout the firm was 30 percent. When Diana O'Brien left Deloitte and Touche to work elsewhere, she was just one of many women who did so. Subsequently, partners at Deloitte and Touche realized that they needed to change the company's culture. The changes they made were so successful that Diana O'Brien decided to return. "Before I left, I couldn't have a life and still do consulting. Now, enough has changed that I have been able to do that," she explained. One of the most significant changes was the company's flexible work arrangements, which included compressed workweeks, telecommuting, job sharing, and paid child-care leave. For Jeff McLane, the new policies made it possible to have a more balanced personal life, which included training to compete as an

Olympic cyclist. For Scott McQuillan, the company's culture of diversity and inclusion helps him achieve his business goals:

> The major task for my job is to go to college campuses and generate an interest in the organization and be able to win the war for talent; be able to go out and tell the story of the organization—all the opportunities we have, that we welcome all, that we want people to succeed both personally and professionally. That message is getting out to people with different backgrounds and talents. Campus recruiting has been the lifeblood of the organization. The Diversity & Inclusion Initiative has revamped the way we do things. We start recruiting earlier, we have branched out and go to conferences,

such as that of the National Association of Black Accountants and Latino and Hispanic organizations, to accomplish our goal to bring in a variety of people. The organization's culture has changed and been received very well, and we've gotten a lot of outside recognition. [The diversity and inclusion initiatives] really made us think about how we do things. One thing we've realized is that we [campus recruiting] can't do it by ourselves. We have to rely on other people—partners, senior managers and managers—to team with us. We need those others out there with clients to help tell our story.

To learn more about this organization, visit *www.deloitte.com*.

The most common methods used to assess organizational culture are employee surveys and focus groups. In addition to asking employees directly about the organization's culture, managers at companies such as Deloitte & Touche, Xerox, and Avon conduct cultural audits to evaluate the language used in organizational documents and advertising, the visible symbols that decorate public spaces, the types of awards given to employees, the types and quality of food available in the company cafeteria, policies regarding holidays and absences, and the types of social activity sponsored by the organization, among other items. Cultural audits often reveal that the organizational culture reflects the values and preferences of some subcultures while ignoring those of others. When such discrepancies are found, simple changes often can be made to create a more inclusive organizational culture.[41]

Creating Economic Value. A third reason that managers are striving to foster diversity is because they believe that diversity will create greater economic value. For Granite Broadcasting, which operates eight network-affiliated television stations, a diverse workforce helps ensure that the company is in tune with its diverse viewer audience. With a diverse workforce and positive organizational culture in place, Don Cornwell, CEO of Granite Broadcasting, thinks his company will be able to

▶ develop products and services for new markets,

▶ attract a broader range of customers,

▶ improve customer satisfaction and increase business from repeat customers, and

▶ reduce costs, including those associated with litigation.

To date, little research is available publicly to document the economic benefits of a diverse workforce and positive organizational culture.[42] Some managers use proprietary information to establish the economic benefits of diversity.

To retain talented employees, some organizations recognize the need to change their cultures.

© Andersen Ross/Brand X Pictures/Jupiter Pictures

Snapshot

"HP is committed to building a work environment where everyone has an opportunity to fully participate in creating business success. . . . We address our commitment [to diversity] through development programs targeted to the next generation of HP leaders, work-life initiatives for our employees, recruiting of diverse talent, and other efforts that help employees and managers foster an inclusive work environment. Additionally, we establish diversity goals to create accountability and drive our success. By weaving diversity into the fabric of our company, we create a mindset in every employee and manager that will allow them to think consciously about diversity and inclusion in everything they do."

Emily Duncan, VP Culture and Diversity, Hewlett-Packard

Others simply believe that there is a link and don't require research evidence to support their view. New Jersey radio station NJ 101.5 learned the hard way how costly it can be to ignore issues of diversity. After a DJ made several comments that were offensive to Asians, Hyundai Motor America and Cingular Wireless immediately suspended their advertising. The comments also touched off a wave of protests against the radio station, including a campaign to pressure elected officials and the Federal Communications Commission to take legal action against the company.[43]

Undoubtedly, personal experiences with customers and clients have convinced some CEOs that managing diversity poorly is risky business. Multimillion-dollar legal penalities and the negative effects such penalities have on stock prices also grab the attention of CEOs. To settle a publicized discrimination lawsuit, Texaco paid $175 million. The cost of the settlement itself was substantial. But that cost paled in comparison to the nearly $1 billion decline in market value that occurred when the evidence against the company was reported by the news media. The most costly evidence was a tape recording in which a high-level executive was heard making racist remarks that were apparently accepted without comment by the other executives who were present. Texaco's share price later recovered, and management has since earned praise for its efforts to improve the company's organizational culture. But the cost of this episode to the company and its employees was enormous.

The Process of Change

Organizations that succeed in managing diversity do so because senior managers are committed to achieving legal compliance, instituting a positive organizational culture, and using diversity to create economic value. As described in Chapter 12, considerable investments of time, money, and people are necessary to carry out successfully any type of large-scale organizational change.

Diagnosis. Before managers begin designing new approaches to managing diversity, they first need to be sure that they understand how current practices affect the amount and nature of diversity—both in the organization as a whole and within its smaller units. Traditional organizational practices tend to minimize cultural diversity in various ways. Recruiting practices emphasize finding candidates from "reliable" sources. Interviews screen out candidates who "don't fit." Socialization and training practices produce uniform ways of thinking and behaving. Attendance policies and pay practices standardize work schedules. Centralization often limits the amount of discretion that managers can exercise in addressing the special needs of employees. Many such practices were adopted by organizations for valid reasons. Standardization and centralization often evolve to increase efficiency and ensure the fair (equal) treatment of employees. Some types of homogeneity may be appropriate, or even essential, to effective operations and thus should be retained if justified after careful evaluation. But sometimes homogeneity is a sign that change is needed.

Once managers have analyzed their organization and agreed that they need to improve their approach to managing diversity, they can begin the process of planning for change. As described in Chapter 12, the planning process itself is the beginning of the change process. This is when a vision is formed and employees become involved in improving the organization.

Vision. Articulating and communicating a clear vision of how the future can be better are essential when developing a plan for change. Until leaders formulate a clear vision and persuade others to join them in being dedicated to that vision, they won't be able to generate the enthusiasm and resources needed for large-scale cultural change.

Most experts agree that the CEO is the key to articulating a vision of a new organizational culture that supports and builds on diversity. The CEO must be a tireless advocate and exemplar of the new culture. Otherwise, employees will not believe that change is important. In addition, the CEO may need to make a persuasive business case for changing the culture. The question to be answered is this: If the organization has been successful up to now, why does it need to change?

Involvement. For the plan to be effective, those who are affected must buy into it. The best way to ensure that they do so is through early involvement. The importance of involving employees should be obvious, but even experienced managers often forget to follow this principle. Xerox has a long record of enlightened diversity management. One of its earliest successes involved a caucus group for African-American employees. In fact, it was so successful that the company decided to create a caucus group for female employees. However, the first attempt to establish a women's caucus—in the mid-1970s—failed. One explanation for the failure was that the women's caucus was designed to duplicate the existing African-American caucus instead of being designed specifically to address the concerns of female employees. A few years later, female employees at Xerox began to establish caucus groups on their own. Eventually a dozen different women's caucuses emerged: Some are national, some are regional, and some are specific to one location; some are for minority women and others aren't; and some are for exempt employees and others are for nonexempt employees.

When IBM initiated a cultural change effort to increase diversity, one of the goals was to create a work environment in which all voices were heard. To explore what that might involve, IBM created eight diversity task forces representing

- Asians,
- blacks,
- gays, lesbians, bisexuals, and transgender individuals,
- Hispanics,
- Native Americans,
- people with disabilities,
- white men, and
- women.

The task forces were charged with reaching out to their constituencies to learn about their concerns and evaluating more than 2,000 suggestions that employees had sent in response to an e-mail asking for ideas about what changes were needed. After six months of outreach and research, the task forces reported their findings to the CEO.[44]

Timing. Planned organizational change usually follows an evolutionary—not revolutionary—path. Realistic expectations about how quickly change will occur are important to the long-term success of change efforts. Usually, change occurs more slowly than expected. The IBM change effort has been ongoing for a decade. At Xerox, becoming a multicultural organization has taken more than 30 years of continued effort. Table 18.3 on the following page describes some of the many practices that were developed in order to improve the organization's approach to managing diversity.

The list of methods that organizations can use to manage cultural diversity is quite long and varied. For most organizations, there are many things that might be done to improve how well diversity is managed. Thus managers need to target specific efforts and set priorities for implementing them.

Table 18.3	Actions Taken to Manage Diversity Effectively at Xerox Corporation

CAUCUS GROUPS
- Employee-initiated and employee-funded caucus groups (based on gender, ethnicity, sexual orientation, disability, area of expertise) sponsor activities such as training workshops, conferences, and mentoring programs for their members.
- Caucus groups are allowed to use company facilities for meetings during nonworking hours; allowed to use company's internal electronic mail for communications; and routinely meet with senior managers to discuss their concerns and seek mutually acceptable solutions.

MANAGEMENT RESOURCES PLANNING (MRP)
- MRP is a companywide formal succession planning process for identifying, developing, and tracking the flow of women and people of color through the company.
- The goal of MRP is to ensure upward mobility of women and minorities, and business unit leaders are responsible for the process.

BALANCED WORKFORCE STRATEGY
- Involves setting numerical targets that specify the percentages of white men, men of color, white women, and women of color to be hired and promoted into each major job category. Targets are based on labor market demographics.
- Incentive pay and promotions of managers are explicitly tied to their achievement of balanced workforce goals.

WORK AND FAMILY PROGRAMS
- A corporate dependent care development fund provides financial grants for small-scale company and employee-initiated projects to improve work–family balance.
- Alternative work schedules include job sharing, flextime, and compressed workweeks.
- A variety of family-friendly benefits are offered, including child-care and elder care resources and referral service, adoption assistance, and employee assistance programs.

MEASUREMENT
- Workforce demographics are tracked and monitored at all levels and within all units of the company.
- Annual employee surveys include questions that assess satisfaction with all aspects of work life, and results are analyzed to assess whether satisfaction differs by gender or ethnicity.

COMMUNITY OUTREACH AND DEVELOPMENT
- To combat early gender and ethnic occupational stereotyping, science education days are offered in the community to stimulate interest in science and technology among all members of the future workforce.
- Partnerships with schools provide academic counseling, part-time employment, mentoring, and tutoring to encourage at-risk students to complete high school.

We cannot discuss all of these possible changes here. Instead, we describe just two of the most common approaches used by managers who are attempting to manage diversity more effectively. An organization's choice of specific efforts will reflect the nature of diversity that is important for the organization, the goals set, the actions of other organizations in the industry, and so on. For United Technologies, diversity management helps improve teamwork among employees. As described in the Teamwork Competency feature, practices that improve the way employees feel at work benefit everyone.[45]

Diversity Training

Sending employees to diversity training sessions is perhaps the most common targeted action that organizations take when they initiate a diversity change program. All

United Technologies

United Technologies Corporation provides high-tech products and support to aerospace industries and to the building-systems industry. Its headquarters are in Hartford, Connecticut. With 153,000 employees worldwide, United Technologies is always competing to attract and retain the best talent available. It strives to be listed on the best-employer lists published in business magazines, and believes that having managing diversity effectively is one way to get on those best-employer lists.

At United Technologies, the diversity goals are

▶ making all associates feel valued,

▶ providing an inclusive environment,

▶ removing all attitudinal barriers, and

▶ building community.

To achieve these goals, United Technologies uses a variety of diversity management practices. During succession planning, a diversity manager participates to ensure that a diverse pool of employees is considered for career advancement. The company also provides performance appraisal training to help managers make judgments that accurately reflect each person's effort and contributions. It sponsors forums and symposia for women and minorities as well as employee mentoring networks. To recruit new talent, it partners with organizations such as the National Society of Black Engineers, the National Society of Hispanic MBAs, and the Society of Women Engineers. In five years, efforts such as these resulted in a substantial change in the company's workforce. For example, the percentage of women in executive positions increased 61 percent and the percentage of people of color in managerial positions increased 35 percent.

As the workforce changes, the company's efforts to build an inclusive culture will also evolve. The next challenge for United Technologies is to ensure that employees from all backgrounds feel comfortable and committed to working for the company. George David, chairman and CEO, explains: "We must treasure openness in every single thing we do, from ideas to beliefs to people. This is the business benefit of strong and committed diversity in our ranks. It's also a personal benefit, because this is how we learn. We remain totally committed to diversity within our workforce and to opportunities for advancement for all. I expect our entire team, advised by our diversity councils and staff, to embrace these practices and values."

To learn more about this organization, visit *www.utc.com*.

Darden Restaurants' executives, directors, restaurant general managers, and managers at the Restaurant Support Center attend diversity training as part of their leadership development.

Training programs vary greatly, but most attempt to provide basic information about cultural differences and similarities and sensitize participants to the powerful role that culture plays in determining their work behavior.

Awareness Training. Many of the diversity interventions offered by consultants and adopted by organizations during the 1990s focused on individual awareness training. Awareness training *is designed to provide accurate information about the many subcultures present in the organization.* A typical program is conducted over the course of one or two days. Activities may include information sharing intended to educate employees about differences between subcultures, educating employees about the negative consequences of stereotypes, and helping employees understand their own subculture's unique perspective.

Some organizations supplement formal training sessions with informal learning opportunities such as a Black History Month or a Gay and Lesbian Pride Week, using these times to focus on a group's history and cultural traditions. Ultimately, the goal of such change efforts is to eliminate unwanted employee behaviors and encourage behaviors that are consistent with a positive organizational culture.

Harassment Training. Another common type of training offered is harassment training. Harassment training *is aimed at ensuring that employees understand the meaning of harassment and the actions the company will take if someone complains of being harrassed.* Employees should understand, for example, that some of the jokes they hear on television and radio or receive via the Internet or e-mail may be unacceptable to repeat at work. Employees should also understand how to inform the company when they see harassment occur. Employees need to understand what the company's response will be if an employee engages in harassment. Many organizations terminate employees who create a negative atmosphere by engaging in harassment or other clearly inappropriate behavior.

Although there is scant research on the effectiveness of diversity training programs, the general consensus is that training programs *alone* do little to create positive change. Learning about how men and women differ, or about differences among generational groups, may have some value, but understanding differences is not sufficient to improve the functioning of diverse work units. Employees must also understand how the mix of subcultures influences the way their work teams and departments function. And they need practical tools to use to ensure that the team functions well. Similarly, managers need to understand how diversity influences communication patterns and they need practical tools to build and maintain effective communication. For these and other reasons, training entire teams and work units to manage and leverage their own diversity may prove more effective than training individuals about differences between subcultures.

Creating Family-Friendly Workplaces

To be competitive in the labor market, organizations need to survey their employees to determine their preferences. They should then consider offering a variety of options to meet employees' needs. In response to the influx of women with children and changing attitudes among men regarding child care, more and more employers address employees' family needs. A recent survey of more than 10,000 firms employing 10 or more workers showed that 63 percent offered financial assistance, benefits, scheduling help, or services related to child care. Figure 18.4 shows the most common practices used to create a family-friendly workplace.[46]

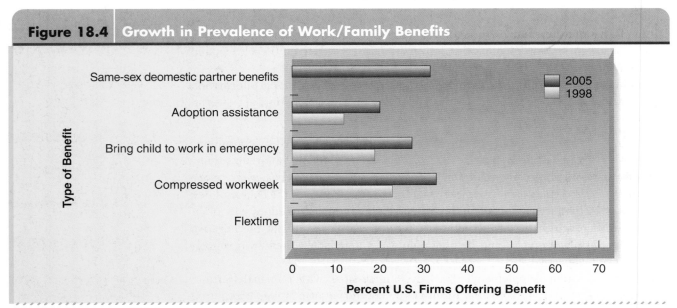

| Figure 18.4 | Growth in Prevalence of Work/Family Benefits |

Note: 1998 data are not available for same-sex partner benefits.

Some employers fear that childless employees may resent progressive policies to assist families. The formation of The Childfree Network—an advocacy group that serves as a voice for childless workers—is one indication that there is good reason to be prepared for some backlash from employees who feel they are not able to benefit from employers' investment in family-friendly workplaces. Research shows that employees without children are less positive about them. It is not clear that their more negative attitudes have any effects of the behavior of childless employees, however. Most of the evidence indicates that any backlash that occurs tends to be limited.[47]

Even if some backlash occurs, the benefits and services associated with child-care initiatives may outweigh the disadvantages. A study of nine Western European countries found that parental leave-taking is associated with improved children's health and survival. In the countries studied, on average, eligible employees (men and women) used 32 weeks of parental leave benefits. Longer leaves significantly reduced deaths among infants and young children.[48] In the United States, the company's bottom line provides a sufficient rationale: At the groundbreaking ceremonies for its $8 million child-care center, Dick Parker, director of administrative services for Merck and Company, observed: "You don't provide child care just because you want to be a good guy. You do it for business reasons. Merck decided to build the center for three reasons: retention, recruitment, and productivity. Child care will become more and more of a recruitment issue in the future. If employees are worried about their child care services, that will affect their productivity and retention."[49] For the same reasons, many employers are finding ways to help workers who care for elderly relatives, also.

Employee retention is a key reason why many companies help their employees solve child-care needs.

Holding Managers Accountable

When an organization offers a new product (good or service) in the marketplace, it almost always uses one or more numerical indicators to measure its success. How well the product does is important in determining managers' raises, bonuses, and promotions. When the development and sale of a product is successful, the people who contributed to that success often are recognized and rewarded. Many organizations apply these same principles to the introduction of diversity-related changes. Like Darden Restaurants, these companies include diversity and inclusion goals in the performance evaluations of their managers.

Challenges

Any organizational change effort can run into unanticipated problems, and diversity programs are no exception. Cultural awareness training programs may backfire if they seem to reinforce stereotypes or highlight cultural differences that employees have tried to erase in order to fit into the company's culture. Special skill-building programs offered only to some subgroups also can feed negative stereotyping, or they may be viewed as giving the target group an unfair advantage. Employees assigned to work in markets that match their cultural backgrounds may view that as limiting rather than maximizing the contributions that they can make. Affirmative action programs may create a stigma for all members of groups targeted to benefit. As a result, even the best qualified people are presumed to have acquired their positions because of their demographic attributes rather than on the basis of merit. Networking or caucus groups may lead to increased segregation and fragmentation. Problems seem to arise in organizations when employees become focused on their cultural differences rather than on their common goals.

Ultimately, managing diversity successfully involves developing a strong organizational culture that values cultural differences and ensures that the talents of all employees are used to their fullest extent. Implementing the variety of changes that may be needed to manage diversity more effectively will take many years in most organizations. Observers familiar with the change process at Coca Cola contend that the company is just getting started and that the benefits of their change efforts will not be fully realized for several more years.[50] During that time, many challenges will arise along the way. Among the most difficult challenges that companies face as they attempt to implement these changes are

- managing the reactions of members of the dominant culture, who may feel that they have lost some of the power they previously held and exercised;

- synthesizing the diversity of opinions from individuals and using them as the basis for reaching meaningful agreement on issues; and

- avoiding real and perceived tokenism and quota systems that can help the organization achieve its quantitative goals but can be destructive to developing a positive culture.[51]

Perhaps the biggest challenge to managers, however, is understanding that cultural diversity can have many organizational consequences. On the one hand, diversity can enhance a team's ability to solve problems creatively. On the other hand, the price of such creativity may be heightened conflict within the team. Similarly, changing the mix of men and women in a team or department toward a 50–50 split may improve the attitudes of the women involved while irritating the men. Managers shouldn't expect diversity-related initiatives to affect members of the organization in uniformly positive ways. They should consider carefully which improvements are most important for the organization to achieve, and be prepared for some resistance from employees who do not gain personally from those improvements.[52]

Chapter Summary

The thoughts, feelings, motivations, and behaviors of employees reflect an organization's culture and subcultures. Subcultures in an organization may reflect the influence of cultures within societies, occupations, and various other social groupings. The greater the variety of subcultures in an organization, the more difficult it is to create a strong overarching organizational culture and the greater is the need to actively manage cultural diversity.

Learning Goals

1. Describe the core elements of a culture.

A culture is the unique pattern of shared assumptions, values, and norms that shape the socialization activities, language, symbols, and practices that unite members of a group and maintain their distinction relative to nonmembers. Assumptions are the underlying thoughts and feelings that are taken for granted and believed to be true.

Values are basic beliefs about a condition that has considerable importance and meaning to individuals and is stable over time. Socialization is a systematic process by which new members are brought into a culture and taught the norms for behavior. A symbol is anything visible that can be used to represent an abstract shared value or something having special meaning. Language is a shared system of vocal sounds, written signs, and/or gestures used to convey special meanings among members. Narratives are the unique stories, legends, and myths in a culture. Shared practices include taboos (forbidden behaviors) and rites and ceremonies (formal activities that generate strong feelings).

2. Compare and contrast four types of organizational culture.

Each organization's culture is unique. Nevertheless, four general types of organizational culture that are useful for comparing organizations are bureaucratic, clan, entrepreneurial, and market cultures. They are characterized by differences in formal control (ranging from stable to flexible) and focus of attention (ranging from internal to external).

3. Discuss why subcultures exist in organizations.

The cultural diversity of a workforce reflects the range of subcultures to which employees belong. When two organizations merge, the subcultures of the original firms may become subcultures within the new organization. Subcultures also reflect departmental and occupational differences. Subcultures dues to the demographic characteristics of employees include those based on age, gender, and ethnicity. In multicultural organizations, no one subculture dominates the others. The organizational culture reflects a blending of all the subcultures found within the organization.

4. Describe several activities for successfully managing diversity.

Concern about effectively managing workforce diversity reflects three types of organizational goals: complying with EEO laws and regulations, creating a positive organizational culture that makes work enjoyable for all employees, and improving organizational performance. Managing cultural diversity in order to achieve these objectives is a long-term process requiring substantial investments of time, money, and people. Organizations use many activities to manage diversity effectively. Diversity training and family-friendly practices are two popular approaches to creating a positive culture for a diverse workforce. An organization's approach to managing diversity is determined by its specific goals and objectives as well as by the subcultures present within the organization.

Key Terms and Concepts ....

Awareness training	Harassment training	Socialization
Bureaucratic culture	Language	Strong culture
Ceremonies	Market culture	Symbol
Clan culture	Multicultural organization	Taboos
Cultural diversity	Narratives	Values
Culture	Organizational subculture	Workplace demographics
Entrepreneurial culture	Shared assumptions	

Questions for Discussion and Reflective Thinking ....

1. Describe the elements of Darden Restaurants' culture. Does this company seem to have a strong culture? Defend your opinion.

2. Review Figure 18.2. Which type of organizational culture would you prefer to work in? Why would you choose it?

3. Suppose Mercedes-Benz acquired an American auto company such as General Motors or Ford. What challenges would the new CEO face in creating a strong culture for the new organization? Explain. Visit *www.ford.com* and *www.gm.com* to learn more about the cultures of these two American auto companies.

4. Choose two occupations with which you are familiar. Describe how the subcultures associated with these two occupations are similar or different. What would be the implications of these similarities and differences for a team with 50 percent of the members coming from each occupational group?

5. MTV Networks Music is a music entertainment company with 22 worldwide destinations on the Web. MTV Web sites bring original online music and entertainment programming to many cultures and to many demographic segments of the population. Suppose that you're a manager at MTV. What types of diversity issues do you think you would face? To get a feel for MTV's promotions and programming, visit *www.mtv.com*.

6. Do you agree that employers should include diversity and inclusion goals in their evaluations of managers? Do you agree that achieving such goals should influence managers' pay? Explain the rationale for your opinions.

7. Reread ethical challenges that employees of Johnson & Johnson might face (in the Ethical Challenge feature on page 601). What would you do in each of these situations? Explain your rationale.

The answers to the Age Facts Quiz presented in Table 18.2 on page 611 are as follows:

1. Physical strength declines with age. (T)
2. All five senses decline with age. (T)
3. Older people react more slowly than younger people. (T)
4. Over three-fourths of older people say they are healthy. (T)
5. The majority of older people are senile. (F)
6. Older people tend to be pretty much alike. (F)
7. The majority of older people have no capacity for sex. (F)
8. Older workers aren't as effective as younger workers. (F)
9. Older people take longer to learn something new. (T)
10. The majority of older people cannot adapt to change. (F)
11. The majority of older people are below the poverty line. (F)
12. The majority of older people say they are seldom bored. (T)
13. Drivers age 65+ have fewer accidents than those under age 65. (T)
14. The majority of older people say they are lonely. (F)
15. Older people become more religious as they age. (F)
16. At least 10% of older people live in institutions. (F)
17. Over 20% of the U.S. population is age 65 or older. (F)

Questions

1. What are the workplace implications of your score?

2. People have inaccurate stereotypes about younger people, just as they have inaccurate stereotypes about older people. What are some common stereotypes about younger people that you think are inaccurate?

DEVELOPING YOUR COMPETENCIES

This exercise is designed to help you reflect on the role that culture has played in your life. It has three parts:

1. First, take a few minutes to write out answers to the following questions:
   a. Describe the earliest experience you can think of when you became aware of your cultural background. What happened?
   b. What is the most important way in which your cultural background has shaped you into the person you are today?
   c. Do you have any negative feelings about your cultural background? If so, what are they?
   d. Do you think other people you know have any negative feelings about your cultural background? Explain.
   e. Have you ever felt discriminated against because of your cultural background? If yes, what happened?
   f. How do you think employers should address issues of cultural diversity?

2. Next, share your answers with one or more members of your class. In this step, your objective is to simply describe yourselves to each other. Share as much information as you feel comfortable doing; you don't have to read everything you wrote.

3. Finally, after sharing your answers, discuss these questions:
   a. What seem to be the most significant differences in your cultural backgrounds?
   b. How have your differing cultural backgrounds shaped who you are as an individual and your life experiences (e.g., what you value, your interests, your goals, your experiences with your family and in school)?
   c. How are your cultural backgrounds likely to influence your experiences in the workplace? For example, will you feel like an insider or an outsider? Will your culture present any special opportunities or challenges?
   d. How can understanding cultural backgrounds help you become a more effective team member or manager?

James Dale spent 12 years of his life working with the Boy Scouts of America (BSA). As an assistant scoutmaster, he was proud of the work he was doing and the organization itself. In 1990, the Scouts learned he was gay and expelled him from the organization. In an interview with *The Advocate*, Dale was quoted as saying, "I think what the scouting program teaches is self-reliance and leadership. Giving your best to society. Leaving things better than you found them. Standing up for what's right. That's one of the ironies of this whole story—that when they found out that I was gay, suddenly I wasn't good enough anymore."

Searching for help, Dale turned to the courts. A state court ruled that the BSA's restriction was illegal and Dale should be allowed to serve as a scoutmaster. The court further concluded that there was no evidence that a gay scoutmaster could not care for or impart the BSA's values to his Scouts. When the BSA appealed this decision, the U.S. Supreme Court reversed the state supreme court's decision and ruled against Dale and for the Boy Scouts of America. In essence, the decision allowed the BSA to continue to be able to determine who could or could not join their organization.

The United Way realized that their antidiscrimination policies were in conflict with the national BSA policy that allowed discrimination against avowed gays. The national United Way organization issued a statement emphasizing that local United Way chapters determined their own antidiscrimination policies. Several independent United Way agencies had funding policies requiring agencies wishing to receive funds over which the United Way has discretion to agree to provide services without discriminating on the basis of age, gender, race, religion, sexual orientation, ethnicity, national origin, or disability.

United Way of Columbia-Willamette

Larry Norvell, the local head of the United Way of Columbia-Willamette (UWCW), knew that the time had come for his agency to face the issue of allocations to the local BSA organization, the Cascade Pacific Council of the Boy Scouts of America (CPCBSA). By this time, three board members had spoken to the media accusing the BSA of teaching hatred and intolerance. Besides these board members, Norvell had to work with several other stakeholders (agency heads, UWCW personnel, donors, board members, community people, etc.) who strongly felt that the agency's antidiscrimination policy should be applied to the local Boy Scout organization.

Norvell experienced his own personal struggles over the matter. He realized that as the head of the local United Way his task was to obtain donations for the numerous agencies in the Portland area that served the needy. It was not to pursue a personal agenda over an issue that could be construed as divisive.

Larry Norvell's Perspective

Larry Norvell stated his perspective in an interview:

Long before the Dale case, our allocation volunteers had raised questions about the Scouts' outreach to minorities and gays. We have an anti-discrimination policy within the United Way but don't impose it on agencies. It originated in 1984 when one of our board members became very concerned about the Boy Scouts and the gay issue. I wasn't here at the time, but I was told that the board didn't want lots of negative publicity during the campaign. They came up with a policy statement strongly encouraging agencies to have policies of anti-discrimination, including sexual orientation.

When the Dale story broke in the paper last summer [2000], my board chair told me to get on it. One board member, in particular, was very concerned. Other board members were equally concerned about the possibility of negative publicity occurring during our campaign.

There are a couple of board members who are particularly conflicted about this issue. I know it is going to be a difficult decision for them as well as the other board members, but I am convinced everyone will go into this with an open mind and make the best decision for us. We have to put aside any personal agendas. The central issue is, "How can the United Way best serve the community?" We have to look beyond the immediate situation. We can decide to not fund the Scouts because of our policy against any kind of discrimination, but we have to weigh the consequences for all of our stakeholders.

We have to consider the future implications of any decision that we make. If we adopt a policy that precludes allocation of United Way funds to any agency that discriminates, we might lose $2 million in contributions, which is about 10 percent of our total campaign.

A bigger issue is future controversy; how does a decision today set us up for the next controversial issue to affect our community? Several years ago we had a controversy over allocations to Planned Parenthood. Catholic Charities withdrew from the United Way in opposition to Planned Parenthood's stance on abortion. Should we take stances on community issues and run the risk of losing agencies, funding, and other types of support? And yet, these are exactly the types of agencies we are pledged to help.

Others argue that we represent 83,000 contributors in this community and those contributors do not speak with one voice. People make contributions to the United Way without advocating a particular moral set or philosophy. They're saying we want the United Way to be the big umbrella that makes decisions based on where the dollars can have the greatest impact.

Another thing to consider is that we have one of the most progressive donor-directed giving programs in the nation. Donors have the ability to direct their gifts to a specific agency or away from a specific agency. If people feel an agency such as the Boy Scouts is unacceptable to them, they can [tell us to] send their gift where they choose.

This past year we only had 11 agencies that were negatively designated and the Scouts were one. I believe they were negatively designated to the tune of about $380,000, most of which were corporate funds. In particular, Wells Fargo Bank and Portland General Electric asked us to withhold funds from the local BSA because of their companies' non-discrimination policies. In addition, we had 140 companies that told us they would not conduct their United Way campaigns until we resolve this Scout issue.

We also met with 30 to 40 key business leaders who told us, "United Way, why are you into this mess? We are not supporting you to weigh in on political or controversial issues."

Personally I don't want anyone discriminated against. I believe that people don't choose to be gay. I spoke with several ethicists about our situation. Does discrimination against gays fall in the context of a moral issue? Both said it did. But one told me that at least half of the energy devoted to the gay issue would be feelings-oriented rather than rational. He said I wouldn't be likely to persuade people with reason.

"I also spoke with African-American leaders and several Jewish leaders and asked for their advice. One advisor told me to look at how the United Way can serve the greater good. If the United Way weighed in for gays, who would be helped? Who would be hurt? Would it change the public's feelings about gays?

What about the poor elderly lady who lives in isolation and needs assistance—what if she isn't able to receive help from an agency because our contributions fall? Is taking a moral stance worth it? Can we really change The Scouts?

Larry Otto's Perspective

Larry Otto is the executive director of the CPCBSA. Otto also met with one of the case authors and provided numerous insights on the Boy Scouts' position:

I worry about the 30-year-old mother who may not send her son to Cub Scouts because of this controversy. I don't want her to keep her son out of Scouting. We're not homophobic. We don't sit around making cracks about gays. In fact, many of our people disagree with the BSA's national policy. We don't ask people about their sexual preference—it's inappropriate.

There was one individual—a young man who was registered in scouting as an adult volunteer leader. When he insisted on presenting me with his document declaring his homosexuality, I was required by BSA policy to deny his volunteer status with the BSA and sent him a letter stating this. He wasn't in our employ so we didn't fire him but simply denied him registration.

I'm Catholic. For decades Catholics have been told about approved birth control methods, which some follow and some ignore. The fact that someone uses pills doesn't mean that they're going to leave the church. We can't let specific issues blow communities apart. Look at the agencies that have strong ties to religious denominations—they don't welcome gays either yet they haven't been singled out for media attention or pressure from the United Way.

Look at all the positive things the Scouts do. For example, we annually serve more than 53,000 youth, operate nine summer camps that served nearly 13,000 boys, and operate three winter lodges serving 6,000 youth and a Sea Scout base serving 200 young men and women. Our outreach programs serve 16,000 boys and girls in "at-risk" neighborhoods. Our members contributed more than 1.3 million hours of service to the local communities in the Cascade Pacific Council. We planted more than two million trees and collected 500,000 pounds of usable clothing and household goods for Goodwill Industries and more than 361,000 pounds of food for local relief agencies.

What we're most proud of is that the Scouts have clearly had a positive impact on the lives of so many young people. We're here to help kids grow up to be good citizens.

You know, this all began when a *New York Times* article that was full of errors came out after the Supreme Court decision. . . . The gay issue just doesn't play in Middle America. Only a dozen or so United Way agencies, out of 1,400, have pressured the Scouts. Only around 30 percent of the public question what we did. The Mormons clearly line up behind us. Some of the other church groups are ambivalent but generally supportive. It's unfair to single the Scouts out.

Questions

1. Does Larry Norvell face an ethical challenge, in your opinion? Or can he simply handle this situation as a business decision? Explain.

2. If you were Larry Norvell, how would you prepare for your meeting with the United Way board to discuss the issue of whether to continue providing funds to the Boy Scouts. Identify the three *key* points that you would make and your rationale for each point.

3. If you were a board member, what would *your* position be on the question of whether the Columbia-Willamette United Way should continue to provide funds to the local Boy Scouts?

REFERENCES

Chapter 1

1. *Adapted from* J. Battelle. Turning the page bit by bit, Xerox Anne Mulcahy is digitizing the copier company she helped save. *Business 2.0*, July 2005, 98ff; K. Hammonds. What I know Now. *Fast Company*, March 2005, 96; Xerox: Back on track. *Fortune*, September 26, 2005, 24ff; D. Hellriegel and J. W. Slocum, Jr. *Organizational Behavior*, 11th ed. Cincinnati, OH: South-Western Publishing Company, 2007, 36–37; www.xerox.com (February 2006).

2. Our definition of competencies is adapted from the definition by M. W. McCall, Jr. *High Flyers: Developing the Next Generation of Leaders*. Boston: Harvard Business School Press, 1998; Career Planning Competency Model developed by Bowling Green State University, as described in its Web site, www.bgsu.edu (February 2006).

3. The lists incorporate the competencies identified by others, including D. Bartram. The great eight competencies: A criterion-centric approach to validation. *Journal of Applied Psychology*, 90, 2005, 1185–1203; A. R. Levenson, W. A. Van der Stede, and S. G. Cohen. Measuring the relationship between managerial competencies and performance. *Journal of Management*, 32, 2006, 360–380; B. Howland. *The Prospector*. Greensboro, NC: Center for Creative Leadership, 1999.

4. E. Scannell. Cracking Dell's code. *VARbusiness*, January 9, 2006, 26ff.

5. www.AmericanExpress.com (February 2006).

6. Zimbra unveils alternative to notes. *Computerworld*, September 12, 2005, 16.

7. S. Avery. Lean, but not mean, Rockwell Collins excels. *Purchasing*, September 1, 2005, 26–32.

8. www.starbucks.com (February 2006).

9. www.fedex.com (July 2006).

10. M. Kripalani. Wired villages. *Business Week*, October 14, 2002, 116.

11. Q. N. Huy. Emotional balancing of organizational continuity and radical change: The contribution of middle managers. *Administrative Science Quarterly*, 47, 2002, 31–69.

12. Personal conversation with Eric Daly, regional manager, State Farm Insurance Company, Dallas, TX, June 2006.

13. T. S. Bateman, H. O'Neill, and A. Kenworthy-U'Ren. A hierarchical taxonomy of top managers' goals. *Journal of Applied Psychology*, 87, 2002, 1134–1148.

14. Oracle: Now the hard part. *Business Week*, December 16, 2005, 23ff.

15. www.hbfuller.com (February 2006).

16. C. D. Stoltenberg. Enhancing professional competence through developmental approaches to supervision. *American Psychologist*, 60, 2005, 857–864.

17. J. A. Fernandez and L. Underwood. Succeeding in China: The voices of experience. *Organizational Dynamics*, 34, 2005, 402–417; G. Yeung and V. Mok. What are the impacts of implementing ISOs on competitiveness of manufacturing industry in China? *Journal of World Business*, 40, 2005, 139–157; Y. Luo. From foreign investors to strategic insiders: Shifting parameters, prescriptions, and paradigms for MNCs in China. *Journal of World Business*, 42, 2007, in press.

18. *Adapted from* D. Elliott. Can this man save the American auto industry? *Time*, January 30, 2006, 38–48.

19. Personal conversation with Rachel Cheeks, manager, PepsiCo, Dallas, TX, January 2006.

20. *Adapted from* www.containerstore.com (February 2006); D. Drickhamer. The Container Store. *Material Handling Management*, 60(6), 2005, 16–18.

21. M. Buckingham and D. Clifton. *Now, Discover Your Strengths*. New York: The Free Press, 2001; M. Buckingham and C. Coffman. *First, Break all the Rules*. New York: Simon and Schuster, 1999.

22. S. Yun, S. Faraj, and H. P. Sims, Jr. Contingent leadership and effectiveness of trauma resuscitation teams. *Journal of Applied Psychology*, 90, 2005, 1288–1296; M. A. Marks, L. A. DeChurch, J. E. Mathieu, F. J. Panzer, and A. Alonso. Teamwork in multiteam systems *Journal of Applied Psychology*, 90, 2005, 964–971; P. Lencioni.

The Five Dysfunctions of a Team. San Francisco, CA: Jossey-Bass, 2002.

23. *Adapted from* E. Levinson. Welcome to our world. *Fortune*, January 23, 2006, 114; U. Kher. Getting smart at being good. *Time*, December 17, 2005,1Aff; www.wholefoods.com (June 2006).

24. K. Dell. Lacost's riposte. *Time*, October 2005, A15–A17.

25. A. B. Bossard and R. B. Peterson. The repatriate experience as seen by American expatriates. *Journal of World Business*, 40, 2005, 9–28.

26. D. C. Thomas, M. B. Lazarova and K. Inkson. Global careers: New phenomenon or new perspectives? *Journal of World Business*, 40, 2005, 340–347; M. Dickmann and H. Harris. Developing career capital for global careers: The role of international assignments. *Journal of World Business*, 40, 2005, 399–408.

27. *Adapted from* S. Prasso. Battle for the face of China. *Fortune*, December 12, 2005, 157ff.

28. www.visa.com (June 2006).

29. J. M. Brett and L. K. Stroh. Working 61 plus hours a week: Why managers do it? *Journal of Applied Psychology*, 88, 2003, 67–78; S. W. Wellington. *Women of Color in Corporate Management: Opportunities and Barriers*. New York: Catalyst, 1999.

30. G. N. Powell and L. M. Graves. *Women and Men in Management*, 3rd ed. Thousand Oaks, CA: Sage, 2003.

31. M. W. McCall, Jr. *High Flyers: Developing the Next Generation of Leaders*. Boston: Harvard Business School Press, 1999.

32. *Adapted from* M. Arndt. George Buckley: The new skipper at 3M's helm. *Business Week*, December 19, 2005, 7; Good governance, the best investment. *Business Week Online*, June 15, 2004; D. DeFotis. Why 3M looks good. *Barron's*, June 20, 2005, 50ff.

Chapter 2

1. *Adapted from* www.starbucks.com (May 2006); R. W. Gunn and B. R. Gullickson. Mind-set. *Strategic Finance*, September

2005, 8–10; J. S. Harrison, E. Chan, C. Gauther, T. Joerchel, J. Nevarez, and M. Weng. Exporting a North American concept to Asia: Starbucks in China. *Cornell Hotel & Restaurant Administration Quarterly*, 46(2), 2005, 275–284.

2. M. Weber. *The Theory of Social and Economic Organization*, trans. by M. A. Henderson and T. Parsons. New York: Free Press, 1947. Also see M. Lounsbury and E. J. Carberry. From king to court jester: Weber's fall from grace in organizational theory. *Organization Studies*, 26(4), 2005, 501–526.

3. *Adapted from* www.kerr-mcgee.com (June 2006).

4. *Adapted from* T. Mucha. What works. *Business 2.0*, September 2005, 47–49.

5. Personnel communication with Tim Logan, Corporate Finance department, Caterpillar, May 2006.

6. Personal communication with Gerardo Gonzalez, chief operating officer, Dolex, June 2006.

7. M. M. Davis, N. J. Aquilano, and R. B. Chase. *Fundamentals of Operations Management*, 4th ed. Boston: Irwin McGraw-Hill, 2003.

8. Davis et al., 16.

9. Ibid.

10. S. Norman, B. Luthans, and K. Luthans. The proposed contagion effect of hopeful leaders on the resiliency of employees and organizations. *Journal of Leadership and Organizational Studies*, 12(2), 2005, 55–65; F. Luthans. Positive organizational behavior: Developing and managing psychological strengths. *Academy of Management Executive*, 16, 2002, 57–75.

11. H. Fayol. *General and Industrial Management*. London: Pitman & Sons, 1949. Also see D. Lamond. A matter of styles: Reconciling Henri and Henry. *Management Decision*, 42(2), 2004, 330–356.

12. F. Barber and R. Strack. The surprising economics of a "people business." *Harvard Business Review*, June 2005, 80–91; C. D. Cooper. Just joking around? Employee humor expression as an ingratiatory behavior. *Academy of Management Review*, 30, 2005, 751–764.

13. M. P. Follett. *Prophet of Management*. Boston: Harvard Business School Press, 1995.

14. J. Reed and R. Cunningham. *Team Member General Information Guidebook*. Austin, TX: Whole Foods Market, 1998.

15. C. Barnard. *The Functions of the Executive*. Cambridge, MA: Harvard University Press, 1938.

16. E. Mayo. *The Social Problems of an Industrial Civilization*. Boston: Harvard Business School, 1945.

17. G. C. Homans. *The Human Group*. New York: Harcourt, Brace and World, 1959.

18. *Adapted from* TDIndustries. Servant Leadership. www.tdindustries.com

(February 2006). Also see C. McLaughlin. A strong foundation. *Training*, 38(3), 2001, 80ff.

19. J. Swart and J. H. Powell. Men and measures: Capturing knowledge requirements in firms through qualitative system modeling. *Journal of Operational Research Society*, 57, 2006, 10–22.

20. C. Ranganathan and V. Sethi. Rationality in strategic information technology decisions: The impact of shared domain knowledge and IT unit structure. *Decision Sciences*, 33(1), 2002, 59–86.

21. *Adapted from* D. Lyons. Attack of the blogs. *Forbes*, November 14, 2005, 129–138. Also see B. Johnson, Counting cost of blogs. *Advertising Age*, October 24, 2005, 1ff.

22. E. N. Brockmann, J. J. Hoffman, and D. D. Dawley. A contingency theory of CEO successor choice and post-bankruptcy strategic change. *Journal of Managerial Issues*, 18(2), 2006, 213–233.

23. *Adapted from* R. Meredith. Split personality. *Forbes*, October 17, 2005, 114–116; The new face of Philips. *Business Week Online*, December 1, 2005.

24. B. W. Taylor and R. S. Russell. *Operations Management*, 5th ed. New York: John Wiley & Sons, 2006, 77–130.

25. W. E. Deming. Quality. *Productivity and Competitive Position*. Cambridge, MA: MIT Center for Advanced Engineering, 1982

26. D. A. Floyd. Statistical process control. *IIE Transactions*, 37, 2005, 1086–1088.

27. D. Dickson, R. C. Ford, and B. Laval. The top ten excuses for bad service. *Organizational Dynamics*, 34, 2005, 168–184.

28. A. Haasen. M-class: The making of the new Daimler-Benz. *Organizational Dynamics*, 26, 1998, 74–78.

29. L. L. Berry. The collaborative organization: Leadership lessons from Mayo Clinic. *Organizational Dynamics*, 33, 2004, 228–243; L. L. Berry and N. Bendpudi. Clueing in customer. When a company's offers are hard to judge, customers look for subtle indicators of quality. *Harvard Business Review*, 81(2), 2003, 100–107.

30. *Adapted from* K. Bonamici. Timberland. *Fortune*, January 23, 2006, 116ff; J. Reingold. Walking the walk. *Fast Company*, November 2005, 81ff; K. Bowers. Swartz's new rules for Timberland. *Footwear News*, October 24, 2005, 9ff; J. L. Krotz. Philanthropy: A new breed. Corporate board. *Town & Country*, June 2005, 190ff.

31. *Adapted from* A. J. Dubin. *Essentials of Management*. Cincinnati, OH: South-Western, 1997.

32. *Adapted from* M. L. Kirsche. Boots cuts 900 support jobs, adds Rx roles. *Drug Store News*, February 16, 2004, 7–9; Boots' scope expands with merger. *Chain Drug Review*, October 24, 2005, 1–3; A. Wilkinson. Baker gives retail a cutting edge: Boots chief executive gets tough and starts to

bring retail expertise to the company. *Marketing Week*, October 30, 2004, 11–12; D. Pinto. New CEO sharpens Boots' competitive edge. *Chain Drug Review*, February 2, 2004, 10–11; R. L. Daft. *Organizational Theory and Design*, 9th ed. Cincinnati, OH: South-Western, 2007, 359.

Chapter 3

1. *Adapted from* D. Ivanovich. Widespread water issues alleged. *Knight Ridder Tribune Business News*, January 24, 2006, 1; Halliburton Watch. www.halliburtonwatch.org (February 2006); D. Lesar. A tough job and Halliburton does it. *Los Angeles Times*, October 10, 2004, 5.

2. D. J. Lesar. Letter to all Halliburton employees. www.halliburton.com (February 2006).

3. C. H. Deutsch. New surveys show that big business has a P.R. problem. *New York Times*, December 9, 2005, C1.

4. Gallup Poll. Nurses remain atop honesty and ethics list. December 5, 2005. http://poll.gallup.com (February 2006).

5. R. Chun. Ethical character and virtue of organizations: An empirical assessment and strategic implications. *Journal of Business Ethics*, 57, 2005, 269–284; C. C. Verschoor. Integrity is a strategy for performance. *Strategic Finance*, 86(1), 2004, 15–18.

6. S. Burns. Hanging's too good for some bigwigs. *Houston Chronicle*, November 8, 2004, D3.

7. *Adapted from* Ex-Halliburton employee sentenced to prison. *Wall Street Journal*, November 21, 2005, 1; G. Witte. Former KBR worker admits to fraud. *Washington Post*, August 23, 2005, A11.

8. *Adapted from* K. Kranhold. U.S. firms raise ethics focus. *Wall Street Journal*, November 28, 2005, B4.

9. C. Jones, M. Parker, and R. T. Bos. *For Business Ethics*. New York: Routledge, 2006.

10. P. R. Harris, R. T. Moran, and S. Moran. *Managing Cultural Differences: Global Strategies for the 21st Century*, 6th ed. Burlington, MA: Butterworth-Heinemann, 2005.

11. M. J. Copeland and C. P. Schuster. *Global Business Practices—Adapting for Success*. Mason, OH: Thomson South-Western, 2007.

12. L. L. Nash. *Good Intentions Aside: A Manager's Guide to Resolving Ethical Problems*. Boston: Harvard Business School Press, 1993; C. E. Johnson. *Ethics in the Workplace: Tools and Tactics for Organizational Transformation*. Thousand Oaks, CA: Sage, 2007.

13. W. W. George. Restoring governance to our corporations: Crisis in the corporate world. *Vital Speeches of the Day*, 68, 2002, 793–794.

14. S. P. Huntington. *Who Are We: The Challenges to America's National Identity*. New York: Simon & Schuster, 2005.

15. J. Janove. Keep 'em at will, treat 'em for cause. *HR Magazine*, 50(5), 2005, 111–116.

16. *Adapted from* S. E. Jackson and R. S. Schuler. *Managing Human Resources through Strategic Partnerships*, 9th ed. Mason, OH: Thomson South-Western, 2006. Used with permission.

17. B. Mike and J. Grimshaw. Communicating legal compliance effectively. *Corporate Responsibility Management*, 2(4), 2006, 34–38.

18. *Adapted from Employment Law Briefs*. Washington, DC: Schmeltzer, Aptaker, and Shepard, November 2002, 1–4.

19. Ethics Resource Center. *2005 National Business Ethics Survey*. www.ethics.org (February 2006).

20. *Adapted from* F. Navran. Seven steps for changing the ethical culture of an organization. www.ethics.org (February 2006); J. Joseph. Integrating ethics and compliance programs: Next steps for successful implementation and change. www.ethics.org (February 2006).

21. L. Paine, R. Deshpandé, J. D. Margolis, and K. E. Bettcher. Up to code: Does your company's conduct meet world-class standards? *Harvard Business Review*, 83(2), 2005, 122–133.

22. *Citigroup Code of Conduct*. www.citigroup .com (February 2006).

23. L. Kohlberg. *The Psychology of Moral Development: The Nature and Validity of Moral Stages and the Idea of Justice*. New York: Harper & Row, 1984; G. D. Boxter and C. A. Rarick. Education and moral development of managers: Kohlberg's stages of moral development and integrative education. *Journal of Business Ethics*, 6, 1987, 243–248; M. Schminke, M. L. Ambrose, and D. O. Neubaum. The effect of leader moral development on ethical climate and employee attitudes. *Organizational Behavior and Human Decision Processes*, 97, 2005, 131–151; J. S. Reynolds. Moral awareness and ethical predispositions: Investigating the role of individual differences in the recognition of moral issues. *Journal of Applied Psychology*, 91, 2006, 233–243; C. Gopinath. Trusteeship as a moral foundation for business. *Business and Society Review*, 110, 2005, 331–345.

24. *Adapted from* T. Case. Non-traditional media: Monica Gadsby. *Mediaweek*, November 15, 2005, A36–A37; Monica Gadsby profile. www.tapestrypartners.com (February 2006).

25. M. J. Gundlach, S. C. Douglas, and M. J. Martinko. The decision to blow the whistle: A social information processing framework. *Academy of Management Review*, 28, 2003, 107–123; J. R. Mesmer-Magnus and C. Viswesvaran. Whistleblowing in organizations: An examination of the correlates of whistleblowing intentions, actions, and retaliation. *Journal of Business Ethics*, 62, 2005, 277–297.

26. C. C. Verschoor. To blow the whistle or not is a tough decision. *Strategic Finance*, 87(4), 2005, 21–23; L. Bowes-Sperry and A. M. O'Leary-Kelly. To act or not to act. The dilemma faced by sexual harassment observers. *Academy of Management Review*, 30, 2005, 288–306.

27. T. L. Mohr and D. Slovin. Making tough calls easy. *Security Management*, 49(3), 2005, 51–56.

28. *Adapted from* P. Dwyer and D. Carney. The year of the whistleblower. *Business Week*, December 16, 2002, 107–110.

29. *Source:* Marshall Sashkin. Used with permission. Undated.

30. M. Schminke, M. L. Ambrose, and T. W. Noel. The effect of ethical frameworks on perceptions of organizational justice. *Academy of Management Journal*, 40, 1997, 1198–1207; J. S. Mill. *Utilitarianism*. Indianapolis: Bobbs-Merrill, 1957 (originally published 1863).

31. M. A. Friedman. Friedman doctrine. The social responsibility of business is to increase its profits. *New York Times Magazine*, September 13, 1970, 32ff; S. Pearlstein. Social responsibility doesn't much sway the balance sheet. *Washington Post*, October 5, 2005, D1.

32. J. Q. Wilson. Adam Smith on business ethics. *California Management Review*, Fall 1989, 59–72; S. Gallagher. A strategic response to Friedman's critique of ethics. *Journal of Business Strategy*, 26, 2005, 56–61.

33. S. M. Puffer and D. J. McCarthy. Finding the common ground in Russian and American business ethics. *California Management Review*, Winter 1995, 29–46.

34. J. D. Aram. *Presumed Superior: Individualism and American Business*. Englewood Cliffs, NJ: Prentice Hall, 1993; D. Vogel. *The Market for Virtue: The Potential and Limits of Corporate Social Responsibility*. New York: Brookings Institution Press, 2005.

35. L. E. Lomasky. *Persons, Rights, and the Moral Community*. New York: Oxford University Press, 1997; W. H. Shaw and V. Berry. *Moral Issues in Business*, 10th ed. Mason, OH: Thomson South-Western, 2007.

36. A. Genn. These bills would expand OSHA standards. *St. Louis Daily Record*, February 10, 2006, 1, 3.

37. C. A. Sawyer. A different view. *Automotive Design & Production*, 118(2), 2006, 46–48.

38. K. Lundegaard and L. Meckler. Regulations push for anti-rollover system; NHTSA to propose requiring that all vehicles include stability control technology. *Wall Street Journal*, February 1, 2006, D1, D3.

39. T. Frankel. *Trust and Honesty: America's Business Culture at a Crossroad*. New York: Oxford University Press, 2006.

40. A. D. Moore (Ed.). *Information Ethics: Privacy, Property and Power*. Seattle: University of Washington Press, 2005.

41. Tips on keeping workplace surveillance from going too far. *HR Focus*, 83(1), 2006, 10–13; N. M. Firox, R. Taghi, and J. Souckova. E-mails in the workplace: The electronic equivalent of 'DNA' evidence. *Journal of American Academy of Business*, 8(2), 2006, 71–78.

42. *Adapted from Fidelity's Commitment to Privacy*. http://personal.fidelity.com (February 2006).

43. P. Jenkins. *Beyond Tolerance: Child Pornography Online*. New York: New York University Press, 2001.

44. J. E. Roemer. *Theories of Distributive Justice*. Cambridge, MA: Harvard University Press, 1998; F. Allhoff and A. Vaidya. *Business Ethics*. Thousand Oaks, CA: Sage, 2005.

45. E. Murphy and E. J. Graff. *Getting Even: Why Women Don't Get Paid Like Men and What to Do About It*. New York: Simon & Schuster/Touchstone, 2005.

46. B. R. Ellig. The evolution of executive pay in the United States. *Compensation & Benefits Review*, 38(1), 2006, 55–61; E. Woolard, Jr. CEOs are being paid too much. *Across the Board*, 43(1), 2006, 28–31.

47. M. A. Stein. S.E.C. wants companies to tell all on executive pay. *New York Times*, January 21, 2006, C2.

48. Z. S. Byrne. Fairness reduces the negative effects of organizational politics on turnover intentions, citizenship behavior and job performance. *Journal of Business and Psychology*, 20, 2005, 175–200.

49. A. B. Carroll and A. K. Buchholtz. *Business and Society—Ethics and Stakeholder Management*. Mason, OH: Thomson South-Western, 2006; J. W. Weiss. *Business Ethics: Stakeholders and Issues, A Management Approach*. Mason, OH: Thomson South-Western, 2006.

50. W. B. Werther, Jr., and D. Chandler. *Strategic Corporate Social Responsibility*. Thousand Oaks, CA: Sage, 2006.

51. L. S. Munilla and M. P. Miles. The corporate social responsibility continuum as a component of stakeholder theory. *Business and Society Review*, 110, 2005, 371–387; R. W. Clement. The lessons from stakeholder theory for U.S. business leaders. *Business Horizons*, 48(3), 2005, 255–264.

52. M. Wu. Corporate social performance, corporate financial performance, and firm size: A meta-analysis. *Journal of American Academy of Business*, 8, 2006, 163–172.

53. T. R. Harting, S. S. Harmeling, and S. Venkataraman. Innovative stakeholder relations: When "ethics pays" (and when it doesn't). *Business Ethics Quarterly*, 16, 2006, 43–68.

54. *Adapted from* Message from our Chairman and CEO. www.investor.jnj.com (February 2006); Our company. www.jnj.com (February 2006); Johnson & Johnson 2004 Annual Report. www.investor.jnj.com (May 2005).

55. Q& A with William C. Weldon. *Med Ad News*. September 2005, 128–129.

56. W. M. Lafferty and J. R. Meadowcroft (Eds.). *Implementing Sustainable Development Strategies and Initiatives in High Consumption Societies.* New York: Cambridge University Press, 2001.

57. Sustainability development issues. United Nations Division for Sustainable Development. www.un.org/esa (February 2006).

58. J. R. Ehrenfeld. The roots of sustainability. *MIT Sloan Management Review,* 46(2), 2005, 23–25; C. Giller and D. Roberts. Resources: Green gets going. *Fast Company,* March 2006, 73–78.

59. A better view of sustainable community. www.sustainablemeasures.com (February 2006); P. Hjorth and A. Bagheri. Navigating toward sustainable development. *Futures,* 38, 2006, 74–92.

60. Wells Fargo commits to ten-point plan for environmental sustainability. July 2005. www.greenbiz.com (February 2006).

61. K. Krebsbach. The green revolution. *US Banker,* December 2005, 28–32.

62. Wells Fargo & Company announces 10-point environmental commitment. July 11, 2005. www.wellsfargo.com (February 2006).

63. D. A. Rondinelli and T. London. How corporations and environmental groups cooperate: Assessing cross-sector alliances and collaborations. *Academy of Management Executive,* 17(1), 2003, 61–76.

64. *Adapted from* Best practices. *Calvert Online.* www.calvert.com (February 2006).

65. *Adapted from Johnson & Johnson 2004 Sustainability Report.* www.jnj.com (February 2006).

66. *Scenario 1:* James R. Harris. *The Harris Survey,* Auburn University; *scenario 2:* B. Z. Posner and W. H. Schmidt. Ethics in American companies: A managerial perspective. *Journal of Business Ethics,* 6, 1987, 383–391; *scenario 3:* D. J. Fritzsche and H. Becker. Linking management behavior to ethical philosophy: An empirical investigation. *Academy of Management Journal,* 27, 1984, 172–180.

67. *Adapted from* A. Bianco. *The Bully of Bentonville: How the High Cost of Wal-Mart's Everyday Low Prices Is Hurting America.* New York: Random House/Currency Books, 2006; A. Bernstein. Declaring war on Wal-Mart. *Business Week,* February 7, 2005, 31; T. A. Hemphill. Rejuvenating Wal-Mart's reputation. *Business Horizons,* 48(1), 2005, 11–21; L. Scott. *Wal-Mart: Twenty First Century Leadership,* October 24, 2005. Speech by Lee Scott, CEO of Wal-Mart, presented at Cox School of Business, Southern Methodist University (February 2006); T. P. Coates. Wal-Mart's urban romance. *Time,* September 5, 2005, 44–45; R. Berner. Can Wal-Mart fit into a white hat? *Business Week,* October 3, 2005, 94–96.

Chapter 4

1. *Adapted from* T. Eisenmann and J. Wong. *Electronic Arts in Online Gaming.* Boston: Harvard Business School, case 9-804-240, 2005; R. E. Ofek. *Home Video Games: Generation Seven.* Boston: Harvard Business School, case 9-505-072; 2005; www.writenews.com/ (March 2006).

2. R. A. Pitts and D. Lei. *Strategic Management: Building and Sustaining Competitive Advantage,* 4th ed. Cincinnati, OH: South-Western, 2006, 46.

3. W. A. McEachern. *Micro-Economics: A Contemporary Introduction,* 7th ed. Cincinnati, OH: South-Western, 2006, 2.

4. *Adapted from* T. L. Friedman. *The World Is Flat.* New York: Farrar, Straus and Giroux, 2005.

5. D. W. Conklin. Risks and rewards in HR business process outsourcing. *Long Range Planning,* 6, 2005, 579–599; R. Avon and J. V. Singh. Getting offshoring right. *Harvard Business Review,* 83(12), 2005, 135–143; D. DiMartino. Examining the upside of outsourcing. *Dallas Morning News,* March 1, 2006, D4.

6. B. Uzzi and S. Dunlap. How to build your network. *Harvard Business Review,* 83(12), 2005, 53–60.

7. W. Hoffman. The pig pursues RFID. *Traffic World,* January 30, 2006, 14–15; V. Godinez. Wal-Mart to expand RFID. *Dallas Morning News,* March 2, 2006, 8D.

8. www.ebay.com (March 2006).

9. A. C. Inkpen and E. W. K. Tsang. Social capital: Networks and knowledge transfer. *Academy of Management Review,* 30, 2005, 146–165; J. B. Quinn, P. Anderson, and S. Finkelstein. Leveraging intellect. *Academy of Management Executive,* 19(4), 2005, 78–94.

10. D. Day. *The City of Calgary Envirosystem Annual Report.* Calgary, Alberta: City of Calgary, 2005. Also see www.calgary.gov (March 2006).

11. J. W. Spencer, T. P. Murtha, and S. A. Lenway. How governments matter to new industry creation. *Academy of Management Review,* 30, 2005, 321–337.

12. R. L. Daft. *Organization Theory and Design,* 9th ed. Cincinnati, OH: South-Western, 2007, 156–161.

13. M. Toossi. Labor force projection to 2012: The graying of the U.S. workforce. www.bls.gov/opub/mlr/2004/02/art3exc.htm (March 2006); S. J. Peterson and B. K. Spiker. Establishing the positive contributory value of older workers. *Organizational Dynamics,* 34, 2005, 153–167.

14. M. Mittelstadt. Challenges, stakes are high for Hispanics. *Dallas Morning News,* March 2, 2006, 1D, 8D; M. Mittelstadt. Illegal immigrants make up 5% of the workforce. *Dallas Morning News,* March 8, 2006, 1D, 8D; www.agingstats.gov (March 2006).

15. P. A. Heslin. Experiencing career success. *Organizational Dynamics,* 34, 2005, 376–390; S. R. Barley and G. Kunda. Contracting: A new form of professional practice. *Academy of Management Perspectives,* 20, 2006, 45–66.

16. G. Hofstede and G. J. Hofstede. *Cultures and Organizations: Software of the Mind.* New York: McGraw-Hill, 2005. Also see M. Javidan, P. W. Dorfman, M S. deLuque, and R. J. House. In the eye of the beholder: Cross cultural lessons in leaderships from Project GLOBE. The *Academy of Management Perspectives,* 20, 2006, 67–90.

17. J. A. Clair, J. E. Beatty, and T. L. MacLean. Out of sight but not out of mind: Invisible social identities in the workplace. *Academy of Management Review,* 30, 2005, 78–95.

18. *Adapted from* R. C. Morais. Cracks in the wall. *Forbes,* February 27, 2006, 90–96.

19. G. Hofstede. *Culture's Consequences: Comparing Values, Behaviors Institutions and Organizations Across Cultures,* 2nd ed. London: Sage, 2001; A. A. Erumban and S. B. deJong. Cross-country differences in ICT adoption: A consequence of culture. *Journal of World Business,* 41, 2006, in press.

20. *Adapted from* Hofstede, *Culture's Consequences.* Also see D. A. Ralston, P. Hallinger, C. P. Egri, and S. Naothinsuhk. The effects of culture and life stage on workplace strategies of upward influence: A comparison of Thailand and the United States. *Journal of World Business,* 40, 2005, 321–337.

21. M. Chen. *Inside Chinese Business.* Boston: Harvard Business School Press, 2001.

22. S. C. Carr, K. Inkson, and K. Thorn. From global careers to talent flow. *Journal of World Business,* 40, 2005, 386–398; C. M. Vance. The personal quest for building global competence. *Journal of World Business,* 40, 2005, 374–385.

23. *Adapted from* C. Chandler. Mickey MAO. *Fortune,* April 18, 2005, 170–178.

24. M. E. Porter. *Competitive Strategy: Techniques for Analyzing Industries and Competitiveness.* New York: Free Press, 1980.

25. M. Krantz. Video game college is "boot camp" for designers. *USA Today,* February 16, 2006, 1ff; R. Hastings. Showtime for Netflix. *Business 2.0,* March 2005, 36–38; Personal communication with P. Raad, Hart eCenter, Southern Methodist University, Dallas, TX, June 2006.

26. www.nintendo.com (March 2006). Also see S. Woolley. Xbox. *Fortune,* June 6, 2005, 63–67.

27. J. Bonardi and G. D. Keim. Corporate political strategies for widely salient issues. *Academy of Management Review,* 30, 2005, 555–576.

28. P. H. Kim, R. L. Pinkley, and A. R. Fragale. Power dynamics in negotiation. *Academy of Management Review,* 30, 2005, 799–822.

29. M. Bennedsen and S. Feldmann. Lobbying legislatures. *Journal of Political Economy*, 110, 2002, 919–937.

30. P. Bernhagen and T. Brauninger. Structural power and public policy. *Political Studies*, 53(1), 2005 43–65; www.signonsandiego.com/uniontrib/20060217/news_1n17lobby.html (March 2006).

31. www.nam.org (March 2006).

32. Special Issue: New Orleans. *U.S. News and World Report*, February 27, 2006.

33. B. Nielsen. The role of knowledge embeddedness in the creation of synergies in strategic alliances. *Journal of Business Research*, 59, 2005,1194–2005; H. Merchant. The structure-performance relationship in international joint ventures: A comparative analysis. *Journal of World Business*, 40, 2005, 421–431.

34. D. Lei and J. W. Slocum, Jr. Strategic and organizational requirements for competitive advantage. *Academy of Management Executive*, 19, 2005, 31–45; W. H. Hoffmann. How to manage a portfolio of alliances. *Long Range Planning*, 38, 2005, 121–144.

35. K. H. Ehrhart and J. C. Ziegert. Why are individuals attracted to organizations? *Journal of Management*, 31, 2005, 901–919.

36. *Adapted from* www.aarp.org (March 2006).

37. R. Nolan and F. W. McFarlan. Information technology and the board of directors. *Harvard Business Review*, 83(10), 2005, 96–107; R. Sabherwal and S. Sabherwal. Knowledge management using information technology. *Decision Sciences*, 36, 2005, 531–568.

38. *Adapted from* E. Charnock. Digital sleuthing. *Fast Company*, March 2006, 66; and C. Johnson, B. Self, J. Franklin-Hodge, and J. Rospars. Online campaigning. *Fast Company*, March 2006, 112; www.bluestatedigital.com (March 2006).

39. C. Hall. Trying to alter the fashion industry. *Dallas Morning News*, February 26, 2006, D1–D6.

40. www.pitneybowes.com (March 2006). Also see T. Laseter, E. Rabinovich, and A. Huang. The hidden costs of clicks. *Business & Strategy*, 42(1), 2006, 26–31.

41. www.internationalcargosystems.com (March 2006).

42. *Used by permission from* P. Dorfman and J. Howell. *Cultural Values Questionnaire*. Las Cruces, NM: New Mexico State University, 2006.

43. *Adapted from* interviews with Eileen Albright, Lease Administrator–Western Region, Cinemark Theaters, Dallas, TX, June 2006; V. Godinez. Coming soon: Battle of video formats. *Dallas Morning News*, February 26, 2006, D1–D5; N. Denvir. Popcorn is salt of the box office: Concessions comprise 25% of revenue for such chains as Regal, AMC. *Hollywood Reporter*, December 10, 2004, 14–15; S.

Ault. Theater chains unspool DVD sales. *Video Business*, January 24, 2005, 5–7; G. Snyder. Who's on top? *Variety*, December 26, 2005, 7–9; J. Heilemann. Showtime for Netflix. *Business 2.0* March 2005, 36–38.

Chapter 5

1. *Adapted from* www.grupobimbo.com.mx (April 2R06).

2. Personal communication with M. Parekh, Senior Account Manager, Dell Preferred Corporate Accounts, Dell Computer, Dallas, TX, April 2006.

3. www.wto.org (April 2006).

4. T. L. Friedman. *The World Is Flat*. New York: Farrar, Straus and Giroux, 2005.

5. Ibid., 198.

6. D. C. Thomas, M. B. Lazarova, and K. Inkson. Global careers: New phenomenon or new perspective? *Journal of World Business*, 40, 2005, 340–348.

7. Friedman, *ibid.*, 184–185.

8. S. Jun and J. W. Gentry, An exploratory investigation of the relative importance of cultural similarity and personal fit in the selection and performance of expatriates. *Journal of World Business*, 40, 2005, 1–8; A. H. L. Slangen. National cultural distance and initial foreign acquisition performance: The moderating effect of integration. *Journal of World Business*, 41, 2006, 161–170.

9. D. J. Wood, J. M. Logsdon, P. G. Lewellyn, and K. Davenport. *Global Business Citizenship*. Armonk, NY: M. E. Sharpe, 2006.

10. R. Saner and L. Yiu. Swiss executives as business diplomats in the new Europe. *Organizational Dynamics*, 34, 2005, 298–312.

11. T. H. Becker, *Doing Business in the New Latin America*. Westport, CT: Praeger, 2004.

12. P. Kotler and G. Armstrong, *Principles of Marketing*, 10th ed. Upper Saddle River, NJ: Pearson/Prentice Hall, 2004, 616.

13. J. B. Cullen, *Multinational Management: A Strategic Approach*, 2nd ed. Cincinnati, OH: South-Western, 2002, 68–97.

14. Ibid.; G. Van Der Vegt, E. Nan De Vliert, and X. Huang. Location-level links between diversity and innovative climate depend on national power distance. *Academy of Management Journal*, 48, 2005, 1171–1182.

15. P. Ghemawat. Distance still matters. *Harvard Business Review*, 79(8), 2001, 137–146.

16. *Adapted from* A. Stevens, Grupo Bimbo. Unpublished paper, Cox School of Business, Dallas, TX, 2006.

17. M. R. Czinkota and I. A. Ronkainen. A forecast of globalization, international business and trade: Report from a Delphi study. *Journal of World Business*, 40, 2005, 111–123; T. H. Moran and G. T. West,

International Political Risk Management: Looking at the Future. Washington, DC: The World Bank, 2005.

18. www.transparency.org (April 2006). Also see P. Rodrigues, J. Doh, and L. Eden. The impact of corruption on entry strategy: Evidence from telecommunications projects in emerging economies. *Organization Science*, 17, 2006, 402–414.

19. China's candle exports to US set to be hit. *PTI–The Press Trust of India Ltd*, November 25, 2005.

20. Five largest sugar producers vow action to push put prices. *Asia Africa Intelligence Wire*, June 12, 2003.

21. M. Liu, J. Ansfield, and C. Simmons. The proxy war: Corruption scandals are a battleground for jousting among the nation's top leadership. *Newsweek International*, November 1, 2004, 34.

22. S. A. Zahra, R. L. Priem, and A. A. Rasheed. The antecedents and consequences of top management fraud. *Journal of Management*, 34, 2005, 803–829.

23. J. G. Tillen, The Foreign Corrupt Practices Act: Compliance issues in the tax and customs area. *Tax Executive*, 57(5), 2005, 446–453.

24. www.wto.org (April 2006).

25. www.usmcoc.org (April 2006); also see R. Morton. NAFTA: Twelve years later. *Logistics Today*, 47(2), 2006, 10–11.

26. M. Allen. Smaller firms reignite Baja's *maquiladora* corridor after decline. *San Diego Business Journal*, August 15, 2005, 16–18.

27. *Adapted from* K. A. Garrett. Mabe: At the vanguard in household appliances. *Business Mexico*, April 2005, 27–28; also www.mabe.com.mx (April 2006).

28. www.europa.eu (April 2006).

29. www.eurunion.org (April 2006); also see S. M. Puffer and D. J. McCarthy. Management challenges in the new Europe. *Organizational Dynamics*, 34, 2005, 197–201; J. U. Farley and P. Barwise. How European marketing management measures up to take on the future. *Organizational Dynamics*, 34, 2005, 273–284.

30. R. A. Pitts and D. Lei. *Strategic Management*, 4th ed. Cincinnati, OH: South-Western, 2006, 229–284.

31. www.californiasunshine.com (April 2006).

32. B. Cresti. U.S. domestic barter: An empirical investigation. *Applied Economics*, 37(17) 2005, 1951–1967; www.countertrade.org (April 2006).

33. J. Biediger, T. Decicco, T. Green, G. Hoffman, D. Lei, K. Mahadevan, J. Ojeda, J.W. Slocum, Jr., and K. Ward. Strategic action at Lenovo. *Organizational Dynamics*, 34, 2005, 89–102.

34. J. G. Combs, D. J. Ketchen, Jr., and R. D. Ireland. Effectively managing service organizations. *Organizational Dynamics*, 35, 2006, 357–371.

35. *Adapted from* www.singer.com (April 2006); also see F. F. Tocatli. Mexican franchising at its peak. *Franchising World*, March 2006, 23–25.

36. H. Merchant. The structure-performance relationship in international joint ventures: A comparative analysis. *Journal of World Business*, 40, 2005, 41–56, and J. W. Lu and D. Xu. Growth and survival of international joint ventures: An external-internal legitimacy perspective. *Journal of Management*, 32, 2006, 426–448.

37. R. E. Hoskisson, R. A. Johnson, L. Tiohanyi, and R. E. White. Diversified business groups and corporate refocusing in emerging economies. *Journal of Management*, 31, 2005, 941–965.

38. P. Ghemawat. Regional strategies for global leadership. *Harvard Business Review*, 83(12), 2005, 98–109; Y. Lou. Toward coopetition within a multinational enterprise: A perspective from foreign subsidiaries. *Journal of World Business*, 40, 2005, 71–90; Y. Zhang, J. M. George, and T. Chan. The paradox of dueling identities: The case of local senior executives in MNC subsidiaries. *Journal of Management*, 32, 2006, 400–425.

39. www.ici.com (April 2006).

40. D. A. Griffith and M. B. Myers. The performance implications of strategic fit. *Journal of International Business Studies*, 36, 2005, 254–270; A. S. Cui, D. A. Griffith, S. T. Cavusgil, and M. Dabic. The influence of market and cultural environmental factor on technology transfer between foreign MNCs and local subsidiaries: A Croatian illustration. *Journal of World Business*, 41, 2006, 100–111.

41. *Adapted from* www.yueyen.com (April 2006); L. T. Chang. In Chinese factory, rhythms of trade replace rural life. *Wall Street Journal*, December 31, 2004, A1, A5.

Chapter 6

1. *Adapted from* Entrepreneurship in action: Denise Devine. *BGS International Exchange*, Winter 2005, 8–9; P. Binzen. Sweetness is not a weakness for this food entrepreneur. *Philadelphia Inquirer*, July 1, 2002, B1.

2. *Adapted from* A. Abrams. *The Successful Business Plan: Secrets & Strategies*, 4th ed. Palo Alto, CA: Planning Shop, 2003, 2.

3. U1: Jake Burton. *Fast Company*, April 2000, 122; J. B. Carpenter, How we got started. www.fortune.com/sitelets/innovators/burton.html (November 1, 2002).

4. Burton Snowboards. *Hoover's*. www.hoovers.com. (February 2006); L. Jenkins. Big air, loud tunes: In the halfpipe, a techno cavalcade. *New York Times*, February 12, 2006, B.1.

5. Introducing the ultimate razor for your dome. Press release. www.headblade.com (February 2006).

6. HeadBlade: Ultimate head shaving razor. www.headblade.com (February 2006); M.

Hofman. The razor's edge. *Inc.*, March 2000, 86–87.

7. The Outsource Group, LLC. *Hoover's*. www.hoovers.com (February 2006); About us: The Outsource Group. www.outsourcegroup.net (February 2006).

8. B. R. Barringer and R. D. Ireland. *Entrepreneurship: Successfully Launching New Ventures*. Upper Saddle River, NJ: Pearson Education, 2006.

9. T. W. Zimmerer and N. W. Scarborough. *Essentials of Entrepreneurship and Small Business Management*, 4th ed. Upper Saddle River, NJ: Pearson Education, 2005. Also see J. Mair and I. Marti. Social entrepreneurship research: A source of explanation, prediction, and delight. *Journal of World Business*, 41, 2006, 36–44.

10. National Business Incubation Association. What defines business incubation? www.nbia.org (February 2006).

11. National Business Incubation Association. Business incubators. www.nbia.org (February 2006).

12. H. Totterman and J. Sten. Start-up: Business incubation and social capital. *International Small Business Journal*, 23, 2005, 487–511.

13. U.S. Small Business Administration. What is a small business? www.sba.gov (February 2006).

14. U.S. Small Business Administration. *Table of Small Business Size Standards*. www.sba.gov (February 2006).

15. About Kohler Co. www.kohler.com (February 2006).

16. Family Firm Institute. Facts and figures. www.ffi.org (February 2006).

17. D. Dahl. Meet the founders. *INC.*, November 2005, 126–127; S. Mulvehill. *Employee to Entrepreneur*. Delray Beach, FL: Business Publications, 2003.

18. Entrepreneurship in action, 9.

19. S. D. Saravathy. *Batten Briefings*, 1, Summer 2004, 8–11.

20. R. G. McGrath and I. MacMillan. *The Entrepreneurial Mindset*. Boston: Harvard Business School Press, 2000; B. A. Baron and G. D. Markham. Beyond social capital: How social skills can enhance entrepreneurs' success. *Academy of Management Executive*, 14(1), 2000, 106–116.

21. D.C. McClelland. Characteristics of successful entrepreneurs. *Journal of Creative Behavior*, 21, 1987, 219–233; O. C. Hansemark. Predictive validity of TAT and CMPS on the entrepreneurial activity "start of a new business": a longitudinal study. *Journal of Managerial Psychology*, 15, 2000, 634–654.

22. About radio one. www.radio-one.com (February 2006); B. Dumaine, J. Sloane, K. Powers, and J. Boorstein. How we got started. *FSB: Fortune Small Business*, September 2004, 92–101.

23. B. Murray and A. Fortinberry. *Creating Optimism*. New York: McGraw-Hill, 2005.

24. F. Luthans and C. M. Yousseff. Human, social, and now positive psychological capital management: Investing in people for competitive advantage. *Organizational Dynamics*, 33, 2004, 143–160.

25. Entrepreneurship in action, 9.

26. H. Page. Like father, like son? Entrepreneurial history repeats itself. *Entrepreneur*, 20, 1997, 45–53.

27. Adapted from B. Burlingham. *Small Giants: Companies that Choose to Be Great Instead of Big*. New York: Penguin USA, 2006; B. Burlingham. There is a choice. *INC.*, February 2006, 81–89; B. B. Buchholz. Jay Goltz's home-design empire started simply. *Chicago Tribune*, May 7, 2000, 26; J. Goltz and J. Oesterreicher. *The Street Smart Entrepreneur: 133 Tough Lessons I Learned the Hard Way*. Omaha, NE: Addicus Books, 1998; About Goltz Group. www.goltzgroup.com (February 2006).

28. Ernst & Young. *Ernst and Young Entrepreneurs of the Year 2005*. Fall 2005. www.ey.com/us (February 2006).

29. R. M. Nideffer. *Test of Attentional and Interpersonal Style*. San Diego, CA: Enhanced Performance Systems, 2006.

30. K. McFarland. The psychology of success. *INC.*, November 2005, 159.

31. V. Govindarajan and C. Trimble. *Ten Rules for Strategic Innovators: From Idea to Execution*. Boston: Harvard Business School Press, 2006.

32. S. Vyakarnam and J. Handelberg. Four themes of the impact of management teams on organizational performance: Implications for future research of entrepreneurial teams. *International Small Business Journal*, 23, 2005, 236–256.

33. *Adapted from* K. Johnson. Next level of leadership. *Quality Progress*, 38(8), 2005, 48–53; Summary of the Texas Nameplate Company Application for the Malcolm Baldrige National Quality Award. www.quality.nist.gov (April 2006); About us: Texas Nameplate Company. www.nameplate.com (April 2006).

34. B. A. Baron and G. D. Markham. Beyond social capital: How social skills can enhance entrepreneurs' success. *Academy of Management Executive*, 14, 2000, 106–115.

35. K. McFarland. The psychology of success. *INC.*, November 2005, 159.

36. Adapted from K. Sutliff Lang. The challenges of being an ethics officer for a small organization. *Ethics Today Online*. December 2005, 6–10. www.ethics.org (March 2006).

37. L. Kolodny. Building a global alliance. *INC.*, September 2005, 48–49.

38. U.S. Small Business Administration. Breaking into the trade game. www.sba.gov (February 2006).

39. *Adapted from* Astute Solutions. *Hoover's*. www.hoovers.com (March 2006); Astute Solutions: Company, management team, history, news, solutions. www.astutesolutions.com (March 2006).

40. S. Shane and F. Delmar. Planning for the market: Business planning before marketing and the continuation of organizing efforts. *Journal of Business Venturing*, 19, 2004, 767–785; J. D. Ryan and G. Hiduke. *Small Business: An Entrepreneur's Business Plan.* Mason, OH: Thomson South-Western, 2006.

41. *Adapted from* W. A. Sohlman. How to write a great business plan. *Harvard Business Review*, 77(7), 1997, 106.

42. Barnes & Noble. *Hoover's.* www.hoovers .com (March 2006); Barnes & Noble: Mission, history, and main businesses. www.barnesandnobleinc.com (March 2006).

43. E. Teixeira. *Franchising from the Inside Out.* Philadelphia, PA: Xlibris Corporation, 2005; International Franchise Association. Franchising frequently asked questions and answers. www.franchise.org (March 2006); J. G. Combs, D. J. Ketchen, Jr., and R. D. Ireland. Effectively managing service chain organizations. *Organizational Dynamics*, 35, 2006, 357–371.

44. Success stories: Fastsigns—SCORE points franchisee in right direction in Naperville, IL. www.score.org (March 2006).

45. About Fastsigns franchise. www.fastsigns .com (March 2006).

46. *Adapted from* S. Venkataraman. Ten principles of entrepreneurial creation. *Batten Briefings* (newsletter of the Batten Institute, Darden Business School, University of Virginia), Autumn 2002, 1, 6, 7.

47. P. J. Adelman and A. M. Marks. *Entrepreneurial Finance*, 4th ed. Upper Saddle River, NJ: Prentice-Hall, 2007.

48. N. M. Carter, M. Williams, and P. D. Reynolds. Discontinuance among new firms in retail: The influence of initial resources, strategy, and gender. *Journal of Business Venturing*, 12, 1997, 125–145.

49. J. Cardis, S. Kirschner, S. Richelson, J. Kirschner, and H. Richelson. *Venture Capital: The Definitive Guide for Entrepreneurs, Investors, and Practitioners.* New York: Wiley, 2001; H. Riquelme and J. Walson. Do venture capitalists' implicit theories on new business success/failure have empirical validity? *International Small Business Journal*, 20, 2002, 395–421.

50. N. Brodsky and B. Burlingham. My life as an angel. *INC* July 1997, 43–48.

51. T. S. Manolova, C. G. Brush, L. F. Edelman, and P. G. Greene. Internationalization of small firms: Personal factors revisited. *International Small Business Journal*, 20, 2002, 9–31.

52. B. M. Oviatt and P. Phillips McDougall. Global start-ups: Entrepreneurs on a worldwide stage. *Academy of Management Executive*, 9, 1995, 30–79.

53. *Adapted from* R. P. Roberts, Jr. Localizing the brand. *INC.*, October 2005, 54–56; S. Maben. Tapping foreign markets. *Knight Ridder Tribune News*, March 22, 2005, 1;

Henry Estate Winery. www.henryestate .com (March 2006).

54. J. G. Longenecker, C. W. Moore, J. W. Petty, and L. E. Palich. *Small Business Management: An Entrepreneurial Emphasis*, 13th ed. Mason, OH: Thomson South-Western, 2006.

55. M. Selz. Caught in the crossfire. *Wall Street Journal*, May 22, 1997, R15; E. J. Poza. *Family Business.* Mason, OH: Thomson South-Western, 2007.

56. ACT-1 Personnel Services. *Hoover's.* www.hoovers.com (March 2006); About ACT-1. www.act-1.com (March 2006); K. Greenberg. The pacesetter: ACT*1 personnel services. *Los Angeles Business Journal*, September 23, 2002, 3.

57. R. S. Levin. Midtown at the Oasis. *New York Enterprise Report* (online magazine), January 2006, 5–6. www.myreport.com. Also see J. Sandberg. Despite Success Stories: Working with a spouse is very risky business. *Wall Street Journal*, January 24, 2006, B1.

58. M. Daly. *5 Steps to Board Success: New Approaches to Board Effectiveness and Business Success.* Bloomington, IN: Authorhouse, 2005.

59. E. McFadzean, A. O'Laughlin, and E. Shaw. Corporate entrepreneurship and innovation part 1: The missing link. *European Journal of Innovation Management*, 8, 2005, 350–372.

60. V. Sathe. *Corporate Entrepreneurship: Top Managers and New Business Creation.* Cambridge University Press, 2003; M. H. Morris and D. F. Kuratko. *Corporate Entrepreneurship: Entrepreneurial Development Within Organizations.* Mason, OH: Thomson South-Western, 2002.

61. G. Pinchott III. *Intrapreneurship.* New York: Harper & Row, 1985; S. A. Zahra. (Ed.). *Corporate Entrepreneurship and Growth.* Northampton, MA: Edgar Elger, 2006.

62. For more information on Lou Dobbs entrepreneurship, go to www.cnn.com and click on "Lou Dobbs" (March 2006).

63. M. Buckingham and C. Coffman. *First, Break All the Rules: What the World's Great Managers Do Differently.* New York: Simon & Schuster, 1999; P. Burns. *Corporate Entrepreneurship: Building an Entrepreneurial Organization.* Hampshire, United Kingdom: Palgrave Macmillan, 2005; T. Elfring (Ed.). *Corporate Entrepreneurship and Venturing.* New York: Springer, 2005.

64. S. Venkataraman.

65. Entrepreneurial Quotient. Northwestern Mutual Life & Insurance Company. www.nmfn.com (March 2006).

66. *Adapted from* D. F. Kuratko and R. M. Hodgetts. *Entrepreneurship: Theory, Process, and Practice*, 6th ed. Mason, OH: Thomson South-Western, 2006, 24–25; About FAST-SIGNS. www.fastsigns.com (March 2006); B. Amaro. What about a franchise? *Sign Builder Illustrated*, October 2005, 43–46.

Chapter 7

1. *Adapted from* T. Lowry. Can MTV stay cool. *Business Week*, February 20, 2006, 51–60; MTV Networks Company. www.hoovers.com (March 2006); D. Carr. I want my ubiquitous conglomerate. *New York Times*, November 7, 2005, C1, C3; A. Romano. Cable powerhouse. *Broadcasting & Cable*, July 26, 2004, 5.

2. R. A. Burgelman, A. S. Gove, and P. E. Meza. *Strategic Dynamics: Concepts and Cases.* Burr Ridge, IL: Irwin/McGraw-Hill, 2006; S. Kaplan and E. D. Beinhocker. The real value of strategic planning. *MIT Sloan Management Review*, 44(2), 2003, 71–76.

3. T. Lowry. Can MTV stay cool. *Business Week*, February 2006, 58.

4. M. A. Hitt, R. D. Ireland, and R. E. Hoskisson. *Strategic Management: Concepts and Cases*, 7th ed. Mason, OH: Thomson South-Western, 2007; R. Adner and P. Zemsky. A demand perspective on sustainable competitive advantage. *Strategic Management Journal*, 27, 2006, 215–239.

5. Y. Sheffi. *The Resilient Enterprise: Overcoming Vulnerability for Competitive Advantage.* Cambridge, MA: The MIT Press, 2005; N. Hatch Woodward. Words to recover by. *HRM Magazine*, 50(12), 2005, 52–56.

6. M. D. Watkins and M. H. Bazerman. Predictable surprises: The disasters you should have seen coming. *Harvard Business Review*, March 2003, 72–80.

7. *Adapted from* W. Inman. Staying ahead of the storm. *Industrial Engineer*, 38(2), 2006, 28–33; Mississippi Power. www.southernco .com/mspower (March 2006).

8. Southern Company. *Hoover.* www.hoovers .com (March 2006).

9. S. R. Covey. Mission and margin. *Leadership Excellence*, 22(9), 2005, 3–5; F. Buytendijk. The five keys to building a high performance organization. *Business Performance Management Magazine*, February 2006, 24–30.

10. Vision and mission statements are from the Web sites for Lowe's, www.lowes.com (March 2006); eBay, www.ebay.com (March 2006); and Dell Computer, www.dell.com (March 2006).

11. J. Wegner. Goodyear's strategy has Lincoln, Nebraska workers worried. *Knight Ridder Tribune Business News*. September 26, 2005; About Goodyear. www.goodyear.com (March 2006); The Goodyear Tire & Rubber Company: 2005 company profile edition 3: SWOT analysis. *Just-Auto*, December 2005, 17–20.

12. D. O. Faulkner and A. Campbell (Eds.). *Oxford Handbook of Strategy.* New York: Oxford University Press, 2007.

13. N. Argyres and A. M. McGahan. An interview with Michael Porter. *Academy of Management Executive*, 16(2), 2002, 43–52.

14. Lowe's fact sheet for investors. www.lowes.com (March 2006); Lowe's Companies Inc. www.finance.yahoo.com (March 2006).

15. M. W. Peng, S. H. Lee, and D. Y. Wang. What determines the scope of a firm over time? A focus on institutional relatedness. *Academy of Management Review*, 30, 2005, 622–633.

16. *Johnson and Johnson Annual Reports*. www.jnj.com (March 2006).

17. Johnson and Johnson to acquire Animas Corporation for 7.63 times revenue. *Weekly Growth Report*, January 2, 2006, 5.

18. M.S. Gary. Implementation strategy and performance outcomes in related diversification. *Strategic Management Journal*, 26, 2005, 643–664.

19. R. E. Hoskisson and M. A. Hitt. *Downscoping: How to Tame the Diversified Firm*. New York: Oxford University Press, 1994.

20. C. Raulwald and K. Brune. DaimlerChrysler sells two units to Swedish equity firm EQT. *Wall Street Journal*, December 29, 2005, B2.

21. Management report: DaimlerChrysler. www.daimlerchrysler.com (March 6, 2006).

22. About us: Toys "R" Us. www.3.toysrus.com (March 2006).

23. Toys "R" Us. *Hoover's*. www.hoovers.com (March 2006); J. Verdon. New Toys "R" CEO gets mandate. *Knight Ridder Tribune Business News*, February 8, 2006, 1.

24. Dell, Inc. *Hoover's*. www.hoovers.com (March 2006).

25. Google Inc. *Hoover's*. www.hoovers.com (March 2006); About Google: Corporate information. www.google.com (March 2006).

26. What is mtvU? www.mtvu.com (March 2006); V. Heffernan. MTV's focus on colleges streams into your PC. *New York Times*, January 31, 2006, E1.

27. Business segments. www.jnj.com (March 2006).

28. Conglomerates. Yahoo! Finance. www.biz.yahoo.com (March 2006).

29. Our Company: GE. www.ge.com (March 2006).

30. G. Colvin. What makes GE great? *Fortune*, March 6, 2006, 90–104.

31. *Adapted from* J. R. Immelt. Letter to stakeholders. *GE 2005 Annual Report*. www.ge.com (March 2006); G. Colvin. The bionic manager. *Fortune*, September 19, 2005, 88–93.

32. D. Lei and R. A. Pitts. *Strategic Management: Building and Sustaining Competitive Advantage*. Mason, OH: Thomson South-Western, 2006; T. A. Olsen, M. Pinto, and S. Virji. Navigating growth in emerging markets: Six rules for improving decision making between corporate and local leadership. *Journal of Business Strategy*, 26(6), 2005, 37–45.

33. *GE 2005 Annual Report*. www.ge.com (March 2006); D. Fisher. GE turns green. *Forbes*, August 15, 2005, 8–10.

34. S. C. Abraham. *Strategic Planning: A Practical Guide for Competitive Success*.

Mason, OH: Thomson South-Western, 2006; L. Fuentelsaz and J. Gómez. Multipoint competition, strategic similarity and entry into geographic markets. *Strategic Management Journal*, 27, 2006, 477–499.

35. B. Stone. Cisco plans its home invasion. *Newsweek*, March 20, 2006, 44–45.

36. IBM announces completion of acquisition of Micromuse Inc. *Telecomworldwide*, February 16, 2006, 1; C. Forelle. IBM's acquisition of Micromuse fills another gap in software unit. *Wall Street Journal*, December 22, 2005, B4, B6.

37. AT&T Inc. *Hoover's*. www.hoovers.com (March 2006); D. C. Chmielewski. Telecom marriage could spur others. *Los Angeles Times*, March 7, 2006, C12–C13; S. Nowlin. Whitacre trumps the art of the big deal. *Knight Ridder Tribune Business News*, March 8, 2006, 1, 3.

38. Merck Consumer Pharmaceuticals Co. www.jnj.com (March 2006).

39. H. A. Simon, F. F. Bilstein, and F. Luby. *Manage for Profits, Not for Market Share*. Boston: Harvard Business School Press, 2006; C. Homburg and M. Bucerius. Is speed of integration really a success factor of mergers and acquisitions? An analysis of the role of internal and external relatedness. *Strategic Management Journal*, 27, 2006, 347–367.

40. Wm. Wrigley Jr. Company completes Kraft confections acquisition. Investor information: Press release. June 29, 2005. www.wrigley.com (March 2006).

41. J. Adamy. Father, son and gum. *Wall Street Journal*, March 11, 2006, A1, A10.

42. Berkshire Hathaway, Inc. *Hoover's*. www.hoovers.com (March 2006).

43. Berkshire Hathaway decides on eventual successor to CEO Buffet. *Los Angeles Times*, March 6, 2006, C2.

44. Business Wire. *Hoover's*. www.hoovers.com (March 2006); S. Jordon. Berkshire seals purchase of PR company. *Knight Ridder Tribune News*, March 2, 2006, 1.

45. J. F. Reda, S. Reifler, and L. G. Thatcher. *Compensation Committee Handbook*. New York: Wiley, 2005.

46. *Adapted from* Stock options. *Wikipedia: The Free Encyclopedia*. www.en.wikipedia.org (March 2006).

47. S. Sum Lee and B. Fen Cheng. Do executive stock option grants have value implications for firm performance? *Review of Quantitative Finance and Accounting*, 26, 2006, 249–274.

48. J. Dow and C. C. Raposo. CEO compensation, change, and corporate compensation. *Journal of Finance*, 60, 2005, 2701–2727.

49. *Adapted from* M. Flood. Whistle-blower tells jury of blatant lies. *Houston Chronicle*, March 16, 2006, A1, A16; B. Nichols. Enron witness becomes pariah. *Knight Ridder Tribune Business News*, March 16, 2006, C1, C3.

50. J. Barney and W. Hesterly. *Strategic Management and Competitive Advantage: Concepts and Cases*. Upper Saddle River, NJ: Prentice Hall, 2006; J. R. Hough. Business segment performance redux: A multilevel approach. *Strategic Management Journal*, 27, 2006, 45–61.

51. M. A. Carpenter and W. G. Sanders. *Strategic Management: Concepts and Cases*. Upper Saddle River, NJ: Prentice Hall, 2007; R. R. Wiggins and T. W. Ruefli. Schumpeter's ghost: Is hypercompetition making the best of times shorter? *Strategic Management Journal*, 26, 2005, 887–911.

52. *Lowe's 2005 Annual Report*. www.lowes.com (March 2006).

53. J. Birger. Second-mover advantage. *Fortune*, March 20, 2006, 20–21; A. Baldwin, Satisfaction for 2 firms: Lowe's and Wachovia outrank bigger competitors in customer service. *Knight Ridder Tribune Business News*, February 21, 2006, 1.

54. S. E. Jackson and R. S. Schuler. *Managing Human Resources—Through Strategic Partnerships*, 9th ed. Mason, OH: Thomson South-Western, 2006.

55. Career opportunities: Lowe's. www.lowes.com (March 2006).

56. Our Company Goals: Eden Foods. www.edenfoods.com (March 2006); Eden Foods, Inc. *Hoover's*. www.hoovers.com (March 2006).

57. J. Collins. *Good to Great: Why Some Companies Make the Leap . . . and Others Don't*. Glenview, IL: HarperCollins, 2002.

58. About Bain. www.bain.com (March 2006).

59. C. Clapper. Branching out. *Aftermarket Business*, November 2005, 100–101.

60. D. Brown and S. Wilson. *The Black Book of Outsourcing: How to Manage the Changes, Challenges, and Opportunities*. New York: Wiley, 2005.

61. FAQ Research. *Finance and Accounting Outsourcing Market Overview and Analysis of 14 Service Providers*. Cambridge, MA: FAQ Research, 2006.

62. P. Engardio. The future of outsourcing. *Business Week*, January 30, 2006, 50–64.

63. Business plan checklists. *Plan Ware*. www.planware.org (March 2006).

64. T. W. Porter and S. C. Harper. Tactical implementation: The devil is in the details. *Business Horizons*, 46(1), 2003, 53–60.

65. R. S. Kaplan and D. P. Norton. The office of strategy management. *Harvard Business Review*, 83(10), 2005, 72–80.

66. *Adapted from* Engaging to improve results at Bombardier Aerospace. *Strategic Communication Management*, 9(3), 2005, 18–22.

67. Profile: Bombardier Aerospace. www.bombardier.com (March 2006).

68. M. E. Porter. *Competitive Advantage: Creating and Sustaining Superior Performance*, 2nd ed. New York: Free Press, 1998; M. E. Porter. *Michael E. Porter on Competition*. Boston: Harvard Business

School Press, 1998; O. Akan, R. S. Allen, M. M. Helms, and S. A. Spralls III. Critical tactics for implementing Porter's generic strategies. *Journal of Business Strategy*, 27(1), 2006, 43–53.

69. *Adapted from* T. Siegel Bernard. Enterprise: Entrepreneur heads south to launch firm; Leather goods maker finds savings—and obstacles—in Argentine start-up. *Wall Street Journal*, February 21, 2006; B6; About Qara Argentina. www.qara.com (March 2006).

70. E*Trade Web site. www.us.etrade.com (March 2006).

71. Our vision: IKEA. www.ikea.com (March 2006).

72. IKEA. *Wikipedia: The Free Encyclopedia*. www.en.wikipedia.org (March 2006).

73. W. Chan Kim and R. Mauborgne. *Blue Ocean Strategy: How to Create Uncontested Market Space and Make Competition Irrelevant*. Boston: Harvard Business School Press, 2005.

74. *Adapted from* D. C. Hambrick and J. W. Fredrickson. Are you sure you have a strategy? Reprinted in *Academy of Management Executive*, 15(4), 2005, 51–62.

75. *Adapted from* Harley-Davidson, Inc. *Hoover's*. www.hoovers.com (March 2006); H. L. Kuglin, F. A. Kuglin, and J. W. Slocum, Jr. A route to building competitive advantage: Harley Davidson. *Nanyang Business Review*, 4(1), 2005, 23–43; Harley-Davidson-CEO interview. *CEO Wire*, August 23, 2005 (online magazine, no pagination); H. Scott, P. Cheese, and S. Cantrell. Focusing HR on growth at Harley-Davidson. *Strategic HR Review*, 5(2), 2006, 28–31; Harley-Davidson. www.harley-davidson.com. Click on "Company" (March 2006); J. B. Kelleher. Harley wants a diversified ride. *Houston Chronicle*, March 16, 2006, D1, D4; Harley-Davidson 2004 Annual Report. www .harley-davidson.com (March 2006).

Chapter 8

1. Adapted from C. M. Dalton. From canning jars to aerospace: An interview with R. D. Hoover, chairperson, chief executive officer, and president of Ball Corporation. *Business Horizons*, 49, 2006, 97–104; About Ball. www.ball.com (April 2006); *Ball Corporation 2005 Annual Report*. www.ball.com (April 2006).

2. C. R. Henderson and C. L. Hooper. *Making Great Decisions in Business and Life*. Chicago Park, CA: Chicago Park Press, 2006; M. R. LeGault. *Think! Why Crucial Decisions Can't Be Made in the Blink of an Eye*. New York: Threshold Editions, 2006.

3. *Ball Corporation 2005 Annual Report*. www.ball.com (April 2006).

4. C. M. Dalton. From canning jars . . . . *Business Horizons*, 49, 2006, 103.

5. J. Pfeffer and R. I. Sutton. Evidence-based management. *Harvard Business Review*,

84(1), 2006, 62–75; J. Pfeffer and R. I. Sutton. *Hard Facts, Dangerous Half-Truths and Total Nonsense: Profiting from Evidence-Based Management*. Boston: Harvard Business School Press, 2006.

6. About Avis. www.avis.com (April 2006); T. Mucha. The payoff for trying harder. *Business 2.0*, July 2002, 84–86; S. Deaver and C. Beasty. Secret of my success. *Customer Relationship Management*, 9(12), 2005, 44–45.

7. Brand Keys Awards. www.brandkeys.com (April 2006).

8. Risk. *Wikipedia: The Free Encyclopedia*. http://en.wikipedia.org (April 2006); P. Taylor-Gooby and J. O. Zinn. Current directions in risk research: New developments in psychology and sociology. *Risk Analysis*, 26, 2006, 397–411.

9. Probability. *Mathworld*. http://mathworld.wolfram.com (April 2006).

10. *Adapted from* Form 10-K for the Ball Corporation. Filed with the U.S. Securities and Exchange Commission. February 3, 2006. www.sec.gov/edgar (April 2006).

11. Uncertainty. *Wikipedia: The Free Encyclopedia*. http://en.wikipedia.org (April 2006); B. Hoijer, R. Lidskog, and Y. Uggla. Facing dilemmas: Sense-making and decision-making in late modernity. *Futures*, 38, 2006, 350–366.

12. I. I. Mitroff. *Why Some Companies Emerge Stronger and Better from a Crisis: 7 Essential Lessons for Surviving Disaster*. New York: AMACOM, 2005.

13. *Adapted from* D. Gill. . . . Or your money back. *INC.*, September 2005, 46–47; About Shoes For Crews. www.shoesforcrews.com (April 2006).

14. R. Bohn. Stop fighting fires. *Harvard Business Review*, 78(4), 2000, 83–91.

15. T. Francis, K. J. Dunham, and A. Frangos. New fortified homes aim to withstand nature's assaults. *Wall Street Journal*, November 13, 2005, B1, B6.

16. M. H. Bazerman and D. Chugh. Decisions without blinders. *Harvard Business Review*, 84(1), 2006, 88–97.

17. R. Hallowell, D. E. Bowen, and C. I. Knoop. Four seasons goes to Paris. *Academy of Management Executive*, 16(4), 2002, 7–24; Four Seasons Hotels and Resorts 2005 Annual Report. www.fourseasons.com (April 2006).

18. Introducing the RC9800i. www .homecontrol.phillips.com (April 2006).

19. D. L. Goetsch and S. B. Davis. *Quality Management*, 5th ed. Upper Saddle River, NJ: Prentice Hall, 2006.

20. J. E. Bauer, G. L. Duffy, and R. T. Westcott (Eds.). *The Quality Improvement Handbook*, 2nd ed. Milwaukee, WI: ASQ Quality Press, 2006.

21. J. Amy. Dunkin' Donuts tries to go upscale, but not too far. *Wall Street Journal*, April 8–9, 2006, A1, A7; P. Frumkin. Dunkin'

Donuts explores lunch with panini sandwiches. *Nation's Restaurant News*, July 25, 2005, 12; K. Hein. Enter a new espresso king. *Brandweek*, February 21, 2005, 12–13.

22. About Us: Dunkin' Brands. www .duncanbrands.com (April 2006).

23. H. E. Aldrich and M. Ruff. *Organizations Evolving*, 2nd ed. Thousand Oaks, CA: Sage, 2006; L. Selden and I. C. MacMillan. Manage customer-centric innovation—systematically. *Harvard Business Review*, 84(4), 2006, 108–116.

24. W. Sparks. Gary Hamel: A lab grows at London Business School. *Business Week*, August 15, 2005, 12.

25. *Adapted from* G. Hamel. Innovation now. *Fast Company*, December 2002, 115–123; L. L. Berry, V. Shankar, J. Turner Parish, S. Cadwallader, and T. Dotzel. Creating new markets through service innovation. *Sloan Management Review*, 47(2), 2006, 56–63.

26. *Adapted from* G. Hamel. The why, what, and how of management innovation. *Harvard Business Review*, 84(2), 2006, 72–84.

27. About Whirlpool Corporation. www.whirlpool.com (April 2006).

28. R. M. Dawes and R. Hastie. *Rational Choice in an Uncertain World: The Psychology of Judgment and Decision Making*. Thousand Oaks, CA: Sage Publications, 2001.

29. J. Baron. *Thinking and Deciding*, 3rd ed. New York: Cambridge University Press, 2001.

30. M. Ray and R. Myers. *Creativity in Business*. Garden City, NY: Doubleday, 1986, 94–96.

31. Adapted from C. D. Charitou and C. C. Markides. Responses to disruptive strategic innovation. *MIT Sloan Management Review*, Winter 2003, 55–63; About Edward Jones. www.edwardjones.com (April 2006).

32. T. Skinner. *Beyond the Summit: Setting and Surpassing Extraordinary Business Goals*. New York: Viking, 2003.

33. D. P. Baron. *Business and Its Environment*, 5th ed. Upper Saddle River, NJ: Prentice Hall, 2006.

34. DuPont's Experimental Station. www2.dupont.com (April 2006).

35. G. T. Doran and J. Gunn. Decision making in high tech firms: Perspectives of three executives. *Business Horizons*, 45(6), 2002, 9.

36. *Adapted from* R. C. Ford, C. P. Heaton, and S. W. Brown. Delivering excellent service: Lessons from the best firms. *California Management Review*, Fall 2001, 39–56.

37. K. R. Brousseau, M. J. Driver, G. Hourihan, and R. Larsson. The seasoned executive's decision making style. *Harvard Business Review*, 84(2), 2006,111–120.

38. L. Buchanan and A. O'Connell. A brief history of decision making. *Harvard Business Review*, 84(1), 2006, 32–41; G. Morse. Decisions and desire. *Harvard Business Review*, 84(1), 2006, 42–51.

39. H. A. Simon. *Administrative Behavior: A Study of Decision-Making Processes in*

Administrative Organizations, 4th ed. New York: Free Press, 1997; C. R. Sunstein. Boundedly rational borrowing. *University of Chicago Law Review*, 73, 2006, 249–260; M. Klaes and E. M. Sent. A conceptual history of the emergence of bounded rationality. *History of Political Economy*, 37, 2005, 27–60.

40. T. D. Gilovich, D. W. Griffin, and D. Kahneman (Eds.). *Heuristics and Biases: The Psychology of Intuitive Judgment*. New York: Cambridge University Press, 2002; F. Gino. Let me give you some advice. *Harvard Business Review*, 84(3), 2006, 24–25; M. Muramatsu and Y. Hanoch. Emotion as a mechanism for boundedly rational agents: The fast and frugal way. *Journal of Economic Psychology*, 26, 2005, 201–221.

41. G. Klein and K. E. Weick. Decisions: Making the right ones, learning from the wrong ones. *Across the Board*, June 2000, 16–22; L. R. Beach and T. Connolly. *The Psychology of Decision Making: People in Organizations*, 2nd ed. Thousand Oaks, CA: Sage, 2005.

42. Doran and Gunn, Decision making in high tech firms.

43. E. H. Foreman. How additional information can lead to inferior decisions—A paradox. *Decision Line*, July 1993, 3; J. L. Pollack. *Thinking about Acting: Logical Foundations for Rational Decision Making*. New York: Oxford University Press, 2006.

44. L. W. Busenitz. Entrepreneurial risk and strategic decision making: It's a matter of perspective. *Journal of Applied Behavioral Science*, 35, 1999, 325–340; J. J. Janney and G. R. Dess. The risk concept for entrepreneurs reconsidered: New challenges to the conventional wisdom. *Journal of Business Venturing*, 21, 2006, 385–400.

45. M. Harvey and M. Novicevic. The trials and tribulations of addressing global organizational ignorance. *European Management Journal*, 17, 1999, 431–443.

46. J. M. Roach. Simon says: Decision making is a "satisficing" experience. *Management Review*, January 1979, 8–9.

47. *Adapted from* Satisficing. *Wikipedia: The Free Dictionary*. http://en.wikipedia.org (April 2006).

48. *Adapted from* J. G. Lamkin. Ethics in action: Aligning decisions with organizational values. In *1998 Annual: Volume 2, Consulting*. San Francisco: Jossey-Bass/Pfeiffer, 1998, 75–80.

49. P. M. Todd and G. Gigerenzer. Bounding rationality to the world. *Journal of Economic Psychology*, 24, 2003, 143–165; S. Huck (Ed.). *Advances in Understanding Strategic Behavior: Game Theory, Experiments and Bounded Rationality*. New York: Palgrave Macmillan, 2005.

50. J. Frooman. Stakeholder influence strategies. *Academy of Management Review*, 24, 1999, 191–205; J. Pfeffer. *Managing with Power: Politics and Influence in Organizations*.

Boston: Harvard Business School Press, 1992; G. Kassinis and N. Vafeas. Stakeholder pressures and environmental performance. *Academy of Management Journal*, 49, 2006, 145–159.

51. A. L. Gabbin and R. C. Richardson. Professional responsibility and the fate of whistleblowers. *CPA Journal*, 76(4), 2006, 14–15.

52. C. J. Loomis. The tragedy of General Motors. *Fortune*, February 20, 2006, 59–70; D. C. Smith. Iacocca on Detroit. *Ward's Auto World*, 42(3), 2006, 30–33.

53. S.R. Clegg, D. Courpasson, and N. Phillips. *Power and Organizations*. Thousand Oaks, CA: Sage, 2006.

54. J. Pfeffer. *New Directions for Organization Theory*. New York: Oxford University Press, 1997; C. A. Schriesheim and L. L. Neider (Eds.). *Power and Influence in Organizations: New Empirical and Theoretical Perspectives*. Greenwich, CT: Information Age Publishing, 2006.

55. *Adapted from* M. Brandel. Bad boss. *Computerworld*. January 23, 2006, 31–34; K. K. Reardon. *It's All Politics: Winning in a World Where Hard Work and Talent Aren't Enough*. New York: Doubleday, 2005.

56. *Adapted from* V. Liberman. Companies are quizzing employees about their ethics. What are they finding out? *Across the Board*, November/December 2003, 47–50.

57. *Adapted from* T. Ward. *Dan's Golf Date*. Copyright © 1993 by Thomas Ward.

Chapter 9

1. *Adapted from* Profile: The Office of Michael Rosenfeld, Inc., Architects. www.quickbase.com (May 2006); About us: OMR Architects. www.omr-architects.com (May 2006).

2. Knowledge management. *Wikipedia: The Free Encyclopedia*. http://en.wikipedia.org (May 2006): D. Rooney, G. Hearn, and A. Ninan (Eds.). *Handbook on the Knowledge Economy*. Northampton, MA: Edward Elgar Publishing, 2006.

3. M. Grossman. An overview of knowledge management approaches. *Journal of American Academy of Business*, 8, 2006, 242–247; K. Dalkir. *Knowledge Management in Theory and Practice*. Burlington, MA: Elsevier Butterworth-Heinemann, 2005.

4. A. Back, E. Enkel, and G. Krogh. *Knowledge Networks for Business Growth*. New York: Springer Verlag, 2006.

5. M. J. English and W. H. Baker, Jr. Rapid knowledge transfer: The key to success. *Quality Progress*, 39(2), 2006, 41–48.

6. J. Kluge, W. Stein, and T. Licht. *Knowledge Unplugged: The McKinsey & Company Global Survey on Knowledge Management*. Basingstoke, Hampshire, UK: Palgrave Macmillan, 2002.

7. *Adapted from* S. Thurn. Companies struggle to pass on knowledge that workers acquire. *Wall Street Journal*, January 23, 2006, B1, B3.

8. Adapted from J. Lamont. Getting personal with content management. *KMworld*, 15(3), 2006, 12–16.

9. *Adapted from* RFID. *Wikipedia: The Free Dictionary*. http://en.wikipedia.org (May 2006).

10. *Adapted from* The end of privacy. *Consumer Reports*, 71(6), 2006, 33–39; RFID-controversy. *Wikipedia: The Free Encyclopedia*. http://en.wikipedia.com (May 2006); C. M. Roberts. Radio frequency identification (RFID). *Computers & Security*, 25, 2006, 18–26; A. R. Peslak. An ethical exploration of privacy and radio frequency identification. *Journal of Business Ethics*, 59, 2005, 327–345.

11. R. W. Coff, D. C. Coff, and R. Eastvold. The knowledge-leveraging paradox: How to achieve scale without making knowledge imitable. *Academy of Management Review*, 31, 2006, 452–465; C. J. Collins and K. G. Smith. Knowledge exchange and combination: The role of human resource practices in the performance of high-technology firms. *Academy of Management Journal*, 49, June 2006, 544–560.

12. M. Corso, A. Martini, L. Pellegrini, S. Massa, and S. Testa. Managing dispersed workers: The new challenge in knowledge management. *Technovation*, 26, 2006, 583–594.

13. *Adapted from* L. Grensing-Pophal. Knowledge set free. *Credit Union Management*, 27(4), 2006, 62–66; About BECU. www.becu.org (May 2006).

14. Y. Park and S. Kim. Knowledge management system for fourth generation R&D: KNOVATION. *Technovation*, 26, 2006, 595–602; B. Kahin and D. Foray (Eds.). *Advancing Knowledge and the Knowledge Economy*. Cambridge, MA: MIT Press, 2006.

15. M. Minsky. *The Emotion Machine: Commonsense Thinking: Artificial Intelligence and the Future of the Human Mind*. New York: Simon & Schuster, 2006; S. Hsien Lao. Expert system methodologies and applications. *Expert Systems with Applications*, 28, 2005, 93–103.

16. E. Turban and J. E. Aronson. *Business Intelligence and Decision Support Systems*, 8th ed. Upper Saddle River, NJ: Prentice Hall, 2007.

17. *Adapted from* About us: DeepGreen Financial. www.deepgreenfinancial.com (May 2006); T. H. Davenport. Decision evolution. *CIO*, October 1, 2004, 1–2.

18. Wiki. *Wikipedia: The Free Dictionary*. http://en.wikipedia.org (May 2006).

19. *Adapted from* J. Rivkin. Why you need a wiki. *Profit*, 25(1), 2006, 59–60; Corporate overview: Black & McDonald. www.blackandmcdonald.com (May 2006).

20. D. Hislop. *Knowledge Management in Organizations*. New York: Oxford University Press, 2005; M. Alavi, T. R. Kayworth, and D. E. Leidner. An empirical examination of the influence of organizational culture on

knowledge management practices. *Journal of Management Information Systems*, 22, 2005–06, 191–224.

21. *Adapted from* A. Perrin, P. Vidal, and J. McGill. Valuing knowledge sharing in Lafarge. *Knowledge and Process Management*, 13, 2006, 26–34; Lafarge at a glance. www.lafarge.com (May 2006).

22. R. S. Kaplan and D. P. Norton. *Alignment: Using the Balanced Scorecard to Create Corporate Synergies*. Boston: Harvard Business School Press, 2006; P. R. Niven. *Balanced Scorecard Diagnostics: Maintaining Maximum Performance*. New York: Wiley, 2005.

23. Balanced scorecard. *Wikipedia: The Free Encyclopedia*. http://en.wikipedia.com (May 2006); M. Souissi. Going beyond compliance: The role of the balanced scorecard. *Journal of Corporate Accounting & Finance*, May/June 2006, 75–78; P. R. Niven. Driving focus and alignment with the balanced scorecard. *Journal for Quality and Participation*, 28(4), 2005, 21–25.

24. M. A. Huselid, B. E. Becker, and R. W. Beatty. *The Workforce Scorecard: Managing Human Capital to Execute Strategy*. Boston: Harvard Business School Press, 2006.

25. *Adapted from* G. H. Anthes. Balanced scorecard. *Computerworld*, February 17, 2003, 34–35; *Southwest Airlines Annual Report*. www.southwest.com/investor (May 2006); J. McGregor. The world's most innovative companies. *Business Week*, April 24, 2006, 62–68.

26. S. C. Voelpel, M. Leibold, R. A. Eckhoff, and T. H. Davenport. The tyranny of the balanced scorecard in the innovation economy. *Journal of Intellectual Capital*, 17, 2006, 43–60; M. W. Meyer. *Rethinking Performance Management: Beyond the Balanced Scorecard*. New York: Cambridge University Press, 2003.

27. S. Millett. Technology forecasts. www.battelle.org/forecasts (May 2006).

28. J. E. Hanke and D. W. Wichern. *Business Forecasting*, 8th ed. Upper Saddle River, NJ: Prentice Hall, 2005.

29. C. Russell. *Best Customer: Demographics of Consumer Demand*, 3rd ed. Ithaca, NY: New Strategist Publications, 2005.

30. J. S. Armstrong. *Principles of Forecasting: A Handbook for Researchers and Practitioners*. Norwell, MA: Kluwer Academic Publishers, 2001.

31. C. Okoli and S. D. Pawlowski. The Delphi method as a research tool: An example, design considerations and applications. *Information & Management*, 42, 2004, 15–29.

32. Adapted from M. R. Czinkota and I. A. Ronkainen. A forecast of globalization, international business and trade: Report from a Delphi study. *Journal of World Business*, 40, 2005, 111–123.

33. M. Laguna and J. Marklund. *Business Process Modeling, Simulation, and Design*. Upper Saddle River, NJ: Prentice Hall, 2004.

34. Crystal Ball boasts ExperCorp's new venture planning for recreation markets. www.decisioneering.com (May 2006).

35. I. Wilson and W. Ralston. *Scenario Planning Handbook: Developing Strategies in Uncertain Times*. Mason, OH: Thomson South-Western, 2006.

36. C. Selin. Trust and the illusive force of scenarios. *Futures*, 38, 2006, 1–14.

37. L. Fahey. Competitor scenarios. *Strategy & Leadership*, 31(1), 2003, 32–44.

38. F. Roubelat. Scenarios to challenge strategic paradigms: Lessons from 2025. *Futures*, 38, 2006, 519–527.

39. J. Van der Veer (Ed.). *Shell Global Scenarios to 2025*. Netherlands: Royal Dutch Shell Group, 2005.

40. About Shell scenarios. www.shell.com (May 2006).

41. Creativity. *Wikipedia: The Free Dictionary*. http://en.wikipedia.org (May 2006); M. A. Runco. Creativity. *Annual Review of Psychology*, S5, 2004, 657–687.

42. This section draws on A. G. Robinson and D. M. Schroeder. *Ideas Are Free: How the Idea Revolution Is Liberating People and Transforming Organizations*. San Francisco: Berrett-Kohler, 2004; J. Mauzy and R. A. Harriman. *Creativity, Inc.: Building an Inventive Organization*. Boston: Harvard Business School Press, 2003.

43. P. Israel. *Edison: A Life of Invention*. New York: John Wiley & Sons, 1999.

44. A. F. Osborn. *Applied Imagination*, 3rd ed. New York: Scribner's, 1963.

45. P. B. Paulus and H.-C. Yang. Idea generation in groups. A basis for creativity in organizations. *Organizational Behavior and Human Decision Processes*, 82(1), 2000, 76–87.

46. Osborn, *Applied Imagination*, 229–290; M. Michalko. *Thinkpak: A Brainstorming Card Deck*, rev. ed. Berkeley, CA: Ten Speed Press, 2006.

47. Osborn, *Applied Imagination*, 155–158; C. Fleetham. Irrational secrets to innovation. *HR Magazine*, 50(12), 2005, 96–99.

48. Osborn, *Applied Imagination*, 156.

49. *Adapted from* Osborn, *Applied Imagination*, 166–196.

50. *Adapted from* T. Kelley and J. Littman. *The Ten Faces of Innovation: IDEO's Strategies for Defeating the Devil's Advocate and Driving Creativity throughout Your Organization*. New York: Random House, 2005; J. Myerson. *IDEO: Masters of Innovation*. London: Laurence King Publishing, 2005; About IDEO. www.ideo.com (May 2006).

51. S. D. Williams. Self-esteem and the self-censorship of creative ideas. *Personnel Review*, 31(4), 2002, 495–303; J. A. Goncalo and B. M. Staw. Individualism—collectivism and group creativity. *Organizational Behavior and Human Decision Processes*, 100, 2006, 96–109.

52. D. Staw. Evaluating electronic workshops through analyzing the "brainstormed" ideas. *Journal of the Operational Research Society*, 54, 2003, 692–705; A. R. Dennis and B. A. Reinicki. Beta versus VHS and the acceptance of electronic brainstorming technology. *MIS Quarterly*, 28, 2004, 1–20.

53. D. S. Kerr and U. S. Murthy. Divergent and convergent idea generation in teams: A comparison of computer-mediated and face-to-face communication. *Group Decision and Negotiation*, 13, 2004, 381–399.

54. D. C. Summers. *Quality*, 4th ed. Upper Saddle River, NJ: Prentice Hall, 2005.

55. D. L. Goetsch and S. B. Davis. *Quality Management*, 5th ed. Upper Saddle River, NJ: Prentice Hall, 2006.

56. J. M. Kerr. *The Best Practices Enterprise: A Guide to Achieve Sustainable World-class Performance*. Fort Lauderdale, FL: J. Ross Publishing, 2006.

57. American Society for Quality. http://asq.org (May 2006); M. T. Howell. *Actionable Performance Measurement: A Key to Success*. Milwaukee, WI: Quality Press, 2006.

58. P. Smith. Hits and myths. *Safety and Health Practitioner*, 24(3), 2006, 49–54; W. A. Taylor and G. H. Wright. The contribution of management and information infrastructure to TQM success. *Omega*, 34, 2006, 372–384.

59. W. E. Deming. *The New Economics for Industry, Government, and Education*. Cambridge, MA: Center for Advanced Engineering Study, Massachusetts Institute of Technology, 1993; G. R. Russell. The Deming cycle extended to software development. *Production and Inventory Management Journal*, 39(3), 1998, 32–37.

60. *Adapted from* E. Tilden. PDSA-proposed operational definition. http://deming.eng.clemson.edu (May 2006); R. Reid and C. Chesterson. Applying Deming's process improvement techniques to banking. *Journal of Organizational Excellence*, 21, 2001, 41–56.

61. U. Gonzalez Booch and F. T. Enriquez. TQM and QFD: Exploiting a customer complaint management system. *International Journal of Quality & Reliability Management*, 22, 2005, 30–37.

62. This section is adapted from *Baldrige National Quality Program Criteria for Performance Excellence*. Gaithersburg, MD: National Institute of Standards and Technology, 2006; Baldrige National Quality Program. www.baldrige.nist.gov (May 2006); M. G. Brown. *Baldrige Award Winning Quality: How to Interpret the Baldrige Criteria for Performance Excellence*, 15th ed. University Park, IL: Productivity Press, 2006.

63. *Adapted from* Sunny Fresh Foods: 2005 Baldrige Award recipient. www.baldrige.nist.gov (May 2006).

64. Overview: Sunny Fresh Foods. www.sunnyfreshfoods.com (May 2006).

65. This section is adapted from R. M. Kerchner's What's beyond ISO. www.qualitydigest.com (May 2006); How does

the Baldrige award differ from ISO 9000? www.nist.gov (May 2006); ISO 9000. *Wikipedia: The Free Dictionary.* http://en.wikipedia.com (May 2006).

66. L. P. Martin. Inventory of barriers to creative thought and innovation action. Reprinted from J. William Pfeiffer (Ed.). *The 1990 Annual: Developing Human Resources.* San Diego: University Associates, 1990, 138–141. Used with permission.

67. *Adapted from* DynMcDermott Petroleum Operations Company: 2005 Baldrige Award recipient. www.baldrige.nist.gov (May 2006); DynMcDermott Petroleum Operations Company: Malcolm Baldrige National Quality Award application (63 pages). Available at www.dynmcdermott .com (May 2006).

Chapter 10

1. *Adapted from* About PepsiCo. www .pepsico.com (June 2006); R. Gamble, S. Kelly, and J. Labate. Corporate governance winner: PepsiCo. Inc. www.treasuryandrisk .com (June 2006); Investors—corporate governance guidelines. www.pepsico.com (June 2006); S. Wagner and L. Dittmar. The unexpected benefits of Sarbanes-Oxley. *Harvard Business Review,* 84(4), 2006, 133–140.

2. R. N. Anthony and V. Govindarajan. *Management Control Systems,* 12th ed. Columbus, OH: McGraw-Hill/Irwin, 2006.

3. R. Simons. *Levers of Organization Design: How Managers Use Accountability Systems for Greater Performance and Commitment.* Boston: Harvard Business Press, 2005.

4. R. Steurer. Mapping stakeholder theory anew: From the "stakeholder theory of the firm" to three perspectives on business-society relations. *Business Strategy and the Environment,* 15, 2006, 55–69.

5. About the Environmental Protection Agency. www.epa.gov (June 2006).

6. S. Sisaye. Management control systems and organizational development: New directions for managing work teams. *Leadership and Organization Development Journal,* 26, 2005, 51–61.

7. Y. Gendron, R. Suddaby, and H. Lam. An examination of the ethical commitment of professional accountants to auditor independence. *Journal of Business Ethics,* 64, 2006, 169–193.

8. J. Graham. Cypress melds into one. *EBN,* December 17, 2001, 30–31; Management: T. J. Rodgers. www.cypress.com (June 2006).

9. PepsiCo's code of conduct: Business gifts and payments. www.pepsico.com (June 2006).

10. N. A. Theobald and S. Nicholson-Crotty. The many faces of span of control: Organizational structure across multiple goals. *Administration & Society,* 36, 2005, 648–660.

11. *This section is adapted from* COSO–Committee of Sponsoring Organizations of the Treadway Commission. Internal control-integrated framework. www.coso.org (June 2006).

12. J. Kausek. *The Management System Auditor's Handbook.* Milwaukee, WI: ASQ Quality Press, 2006.

13. F. J. Reh. Pareto's principle—The 80–20 rule. *Business Credit,* 107(7), 2005, 76–77.

14. International standard. *Wikipedia: The Free Encyclopedia.* http://en.wikipedia.org (June 2006).

15. International Organization for Standardization. *Wikipedia: The Free Dictionary.* http://en.wikipedia.org (June 2006).

16. S. Ekanayake. Agency theory, national culture and management control systems. *Journal of American Academy of Business,* 4, 2004, 49–54.

17. R. W. Brislin and E. S. Kim. Cultural diversity in people's understanding and uses of time. *Applied Psychology: An International Review,* 52, 2003, 363–382.

18. K. L. Turner and M. V. Makhija. The role of organizational controls in managing knowledge. *Academy of Management Review,* 31, 2006, 197–217.

19. *Adapted from* Office of Federal Housing Enterprise Oversight. *Report of the Special Examination of Fannie Mae, 2006.* www.ofheo.gov (June 2006); T. O'Hara, K. Day, and A. Shin. Report slams Fannie Mae. *Houston Chronicle,* May 24, 2006, D1, D4.

20. *Adapted from* Press release: Fannie Mae agrees to comprehensive settlement with OFHEO and SEC. www.fanniemae.com (June 2006).

21. E. J. Watson. The persistence of bureaucracy: A meta-analysis of Weber's model of bureaucratic control. *Organization Studies,* 26, 2005, 569–600.

22. N. Khatri, A. Baveja, S. A. Boren, and A. Mammo. Medical errors and quality of care: From control to commitment. *California Management Review,* 48(3), 2006, 115–141; A. Neely and M. Al Najjar. Management learning not management control: The true role of performance measurement? *California Management Review,* 48(3), 2006, 99–114.

23. Pepsi Spain. www.pepsi.sk (June 2006).

24. PepsiCo company Web sites. www .pepsico.com/PEP_Company (June 2006).

25. A. V. Douglas. Capital structure, compensation and incentives. *Review of Financial Studies,* 19, 2006, 605–632; M. J. Conyon. Executive compensation and incentives. *Academy of Management Perspectives,* 20, 2006, 25–44.

26. M. A. Stiffler. Incentive compensation management: Making pay for performance a reality. *Performance Improvement,* 45(1), 2006, 25–30; A. Cox. The outcomes of variable pay systems: Tales of multiple costs and unforeseen consequences. *International Journal of Human Resource Management,* 16, 2005, 1475–1497.

27. I. St. Johns-Brooks. Performance-based pay gains wider acceptance. *Global Benefits and Compensation International,* 35(7), 2006, 29. *Towers Perrin 2005–2006 Worldwide Total Remuneration Study.* www.towersperrin.com (June 2006).

28. J. S. Heywood, U. Jerjahn, and G. Tsertsvadze. Getting along with colleagues—Does profit sharing help or hurt? *Kyklos,* 58, 2005, 557–573.

29. R. Lawton. Eight dimensions of quality. *Quality Progress,* 39(4), 2006, 55–62.

30. I. Morgan and J. Rao. Aligning service strategy through super-measure management. *Academy of Management Executive,* 16(4), 2002, 121–131; Fairfield Inn. http://marriott.com/fairfieldinn (June 2006).

31. P. B. Miller and P. R. Bahnson. *Quality Financial Reporting.* New York: McGraw-Hill, 2002.

32. Chief financial officer. *Wikipedia: The Free Dictionary.* http://en.wikipiedia.org (June 2006).

33. K. G. Palepu, P. M. Healy, and V. L. Bernard. *Business Analysis & Valuation, Text and Cases,* 3rd. ed. Mason, OH: Thomson South-Western, 2004.

34. C. P. Stickney, P. Brown, and J. M. Wahlen. *Financial Reporting, Statement Analysis, and Valuation: A Strategic Perspective,* 6th ed. Mason, OH: Thompson South-Western, 2007.

35. L. G. Elddenburg and S. K. Wolcott. *Cost Management: Measuring, Monitoring, and Motivating Performance.* New York: Wiley, 2005.

36. R. J. Parker and L. Kyj. Vertical information sharing in the budgeting process. *Accounting Organizations and Society,* 31, 2006, 27–45.

37. R. J. Herzog. Performance budgeting: Descriptive, allegorical, mythical, and idealistic. *International Journal of Organization Theory and Behavior,* 9, 2006, 72–91.

38. *Adapted from* The pros of a modern budgeting process. *Business Performance Management Magazine,* 4(1), 2006, 38–39; Western Container Corporation. www .themanufacturer.com (June 2006).

39. P. Waurzyniak. Automation integration. *Manufacturing Engineering,* 136(5), 2006, 105–116.

40. P. Waurzyniak. Machine controllers: Smarter and faster. *Manufacturing Engineering,* 135(6), 2005, 61–73.

41. T. Aeppel. Working without workers. *Wall Street Journal,* November 19, 2002, B1; Air Products and Chemicals, Inc. www .airproducts.com (June 2006).

42. National Association of Corporate Directors. Frequently asked questions in corporate governance. www.nacdonline.org (June 2006); Y. Luo. *Global Dimensions of Corporate Governance.* Boston: Blackwell Publishing, 2007.

43. J. Gimpert. Internal audit chief: Sarbanes-Oxley put internal auditing in the limelight. *Financial Executive*, 24(4), 2006, 15–17.

44. Y. Luo. *Global Dimensions of Corporate Governance*. Malden, MA: Blackwell, 2006.

45. Corporate governance glossary. www.corp-gov.org (June 2006).

46. R. C. Smith and I. Walter. *Governing the Modern Corporation: Capital Markets, Corporate Control, and Economic Performance.* New York: Oxford University Press, 2006.

47. J. Charkham. *Keeping Better Company: Corporate Governance Ten Years On*, 2nd ed. New York: Oxford University Press, 2006; S. Benn and D. Dunphy (Eds.). *Corporate Governance and Sustainability: Challenges for Theory and Practice*. New York: Routledge, 2007.

48. S. Green, *Manager's Guide to the Sarbanes-Oxley Act: Improving Internal Controls to Prevent Fraud*. New York: Wiley, 2004.

49. American Corporate Counsel Association. Sarbanes-Oxley Act. www.acca.com (June 2006).

50. U.S. Securities and Exchange Commission. Sarbanes-Oxley Act of 2002: Frequently asked questions and answers. www.sec.gov (June 2006).

51. *Adapted from* C. Wofford and T. W. White. Key issues in whistleblower case law under Sarbanes-Oxley. *Corporate Governance Advisor*, 14(2), 2006, 1–8.

52. D. A. Nadler, B. Behan, M. Nadler, and J. W. Lorsch. *Building Better Boards: A Blueprint for Effective Governance.* San Francisco: Jossey-Bass, 2006; R. Charan. *Boards That Deliver: Advancing Corporate Governance From Compliance to Competitive Advantages.* San Francisco: Jossey-Bass, 2005.

53. *Adapted from* PepsiCo corporate governance guidelines. www.pepsico.com (June 2006).

54. K. Brooker. The PEPSI Machine. *Fortune*, February 6, 2006, 68–70.

55. *Adapted from* PricewaterhouseCoopers: United States. *Questions That May Be Asked at 2006 Shareholders' Meetings.* www.pwcglobal.com (June 2006).

56. R. A. Cook, L. S. Corman, and S. Wilhelm. A question of theft. In R. J. Hart (Ed.) *Society for Case Research 2006 Proceedings*, 2006. This case incident was prepared by Roy A. Cook, Suzanne Wilhelm, and Lawrence S. Corman, and is intended to be used as a basis for class discussion rather than to illustrate either effective or ineffective handling of the situation. The name of an individual has been disguised to preserve that person's desire for anonymity. © 2006 by Roy A. Cook, Suzanne Wilhelm, and Lawrence S. Corman. Used with permission.

Chapter 11

1. *Adapted from* www.lowes.com (May 2006); personal conversation with H. Johnson, Vice President, Internal Auditing, Lowe's, May 2006; C. Waxer. How Lowe's grows. *CIO*, 19(5), 2005, 1–2.

2. D. Lei and J. W. Slocum, Jr. Strategic and organizational requirements for competitive advantage. *Academy of Management Executive*, 19, 2005, 31–45.

3. R. A. Pitts and D. Lei. *Strategic Management: Building and Sustaining Competitive Advantage*, 4th ed. Cincinnati, OH: Thomson Learning, 2006, 442.

4. P. Lawrence and J. Lorsch. *Organization and Environment*. Homewood, IL: Richard D. Irwin, 1969.

5. J. Hamm. The five messages leaders must manage. *Harvard Business Review*, 84(5), 2006, 114–123; P. Puranam, H. Singh, and M. Zollo Organizing for innovation: Managing the coordination-autonomy dilemma in technology acquisitions. *Academy of Management Journal*, 49, 2006, 263–280.

6. J. R. Galbraith. *Designing Organizations*. San Francisco: Jossey-Bass, 2002.

7. N. Bennett and S. A. Miles. Second in command: The misunderstood role of the chief operating officer. *Harvard Business Review*, 84(5), 2006, 70–80.

8. Y. Yoo, R. J. Boland, Jr., and K. Lyytinen. From organization design to organization designing. *Organizational Science*, 17, 2006, 215–230.

9. *Adapted from* P. Elkind and B. McLean. The luckiest people in Houston. *Fortune*, April 17, 2006, 59ff; B. McLean and P. Elkind. Skilling time. *Fortune*, May 1, 2006, 36ff; B. McLean and P. Elkind. The guiltiest guys in the room. *Fortune*, June 12, 2006, 26–28; Nichols, B. Unmistakable message. *Dallas Morning News*, May 26, 2006, 1A, 17A; S. Reddy and B. M. Case. Decision expected to reinforce strict corporate accountability. *Dallas Morning News*, May 26, 2006, 1A, 16A.

10. L. G. Hrebiniak. Obstacles to effective strategy implementation. *Organizational Dynamics*, 35, 2006, 12–31.

11. D. Mehri. The darker side of lean: An insider's perspective on the realities of the Toyota production system, *The Academy of Management Perspective*, 20 (2), 2006, 21–42; Y. Sunaoshi, M. Kotabe, and J. Y. Murray. How technology transfer really occurs on the factory floor: A case of a major Japanese automotive die manufacturer in the United States. *Journal of World Business*, 40, 2005, 57–70; Y. S. Pak and Y. Park. Characteristics of Japanese FDI in the East and West: Understanding the strategic moves of Japanese investment. *Journal of World Business*, 40, 2005, 254–266.

12. *Adapted from* www.americanstandard.com (May 2006).

13. Wm. G. Ouchi. Power to the principals: Decentralization in three large school districts. *Organization Science*, 17, 2006, 298–307.

14. *Adapted from* www.katespade.com (May 2006).

15. H. L. Kuglin, F. A. Kuglin, and J. W. Slocum, Jr. A route to building competitive advantage: Harley-Davidson. *Nanyang Business Review*, 4(1), 2005, 23–43; www.harleydavidson .com (May 2006).

16. www.generaldynamics.com (May 2006).

17. Pitts and Lei, *Strategic Management*, 394–395, 402–414.

18. G. Westerman, F. W. McFarlan, and M. Iansiti. Organization design and effectiveness over the innovation life cycle. *Organization Science*, 17, 2006, 230–239.

19. M. G. Jacobides and S. Billinger. Designing the boundaries of the firm: "Make or buy" to the dynamic benefits of vertical architecture. *Organization Science*, 17, 2006, 249–261; R. E. Miles, G. Miles, and C. C. Snow. Collaborative entrepreneurship: A business model for continuous innovation. *Organizational Dynamics*, 35, 2006, 1–12.

20. *Adapted from* www.dreamworksanimation .com (May 2006).

21. T. Burns and G. M. Stalker. *The Management of Innovation*. London: Tavistock, 1961, 119–122; W. D. Sine, H. Mitsuhashi, and D. A. Kirsch. Revisiting Burns and Stalker: Formal structure and new venture performance in emerging economic sectors. *Academy of Management Journal*, 49, 2006, 121–132.

22. *Adapted from* www.flextronics.com (May 2006); Flextronics: Few rules, fast responses. *Business Week*, October 23, 2000, 148ff; S. Moore. Flextronics bulks up sales. *Modern Plastics*, September 2001, 49ff.

23. J. D. Thompson. *Organizations in Action*. New York: McGraw-Hill, 1967, 51–67.

24. Used by permission by Professor Robert T. Keller, College of Business Administration, University of Houston, Houston, TX, May 2006.

25. *Adapted from* www.fedexkinkos.com (May 2006); G. Walker. Kinko's. Unpublished paper, Cox School of Business, Southern Methodist University, Dallas, TX, May 2003.

Chapter 12

1. D. Ulrich, S. Kerr, and R. N. Ashkenas. *The GE Work-Out.* New York: McGraw-Hill, 2002; R. H. Schaffer. *Rapid Results: How 100-Day Projects Can Build the Capacity for Large-Scale Change.* San Francisco: Jossey-Bass. www.gp.com (June 2006); D. Fisher. Koch Industries: Mr Big. *Forbes*, March 13, 2006, 100–104.

2. For a practical guide on change management, see S. L. Cowan. *Change Management.* New York: ASTD, 2006.

3. J. P. Kotter and D. S. Cohen. *The Heart of Change*. Boston: Harvard Business School Press, 2002; M. Beer and N. Nohria. *Breaking the Code of Change*. Boston:

Harvard Business School Press, 2000; R. A. Johnson. Antecedents and outcomes of corporate refocusing. *Journal of Management*, 22, 1996, 439–483.

4. C. Sulter. On the road again. *Fast Company*, January 2002, 58; Lessons on leadership: Follow these leaders. *Fortune*, December 12, 2005; http://www.hoovers.com/yellow (June 2006); A. Zuckerman. What every executive needs to know about trucking trends. www.worldtrademag.com (May 2006).

5. K. Lewin. *Field Theory in Social Science*. New York: Harper & Row, 1951; C. Hendry. Understanding and creating organizational change through learning theory. *Human Relations*, 49, 1996, 621–641.

6. This and other stage models are reviewed in A. A. Armenakis and A. G. Bedeian. Organizational change: A review of theory and research in the 1990s. *Journal of Management*, 25, 1999, 293–315.

7. D. A Garvin and M. A. Roberto. Change through persuasion. *Harvard Business Review*, February 2005, 104–112.

8. R. C. Wood and G. Hamel. The World Bank's innovation market. *Harvard Business Review*, November 2002, 104–112; 2006 Global Development Marketplace, www.worldbank.org (June 2006).

9. D. E. Myers. *Tempered Radicals: How People Use Difference to Inspire Change at Work*. Boston: Harvard Business School Press, 2001.

10. Turning an industry inside out: A conversation with Robert Redford. *Harvard Business Review*, May 2002, 57–62.

11. P. Burrows. Stalking high tech. *Business Week*, June 19, 2006.

12. For a description of the turnaround at IBM UK, see R. Balgobin and N. Pandit. Stages in the turnaround process: The case of IBM UK. *European Management Journal*, 19, 2001, 301–316.

13. Schaffer and Ashkenas. *Rapid Results.*

14. M. Conlin. Square feet. Oh, how square. *Business Week*, July 3, 2006, 100–101.

15. W. W. Burke. *Organizational Change: Theory and Practice*. Thousand Oaks, CA: Sage, 2002; M. S. Poole, A. H. Van de Ven, K. Dooley, and M. E. Holmes. *Organizational Change Processes*. Oxford, UK: Oxford University Press, 2000.

16. K. Brooker and D. Burke. The Pepsi machine. *Fortune*, February 6, 2006, 68–72.

17. S. Fox and Y. Amichai-Hamburger. The power of emotional appeals in promoting organizational change programs. *Academy of Management Executive*, 15(4), 2001, 84–95. For more details about the role of top management in communicating during organizational change, see Delta Consulting Group. *Strategic Communication: A Key to Implementing Change*. New York: Delta Consulting Group, 1999.

18. D. M. Rousseau and S. A. Tijoriwala. What's a good reason to change? Motivated reasoning and social accounts in promoting organizational change. *Journal of Applied Psychology*, 84, 1999, 514–528.

19. Follow these leaders: Bill Zollars. *Fortune*, December 12, 2005, 15.

20. P. J. Kiger. Corporate crunch. *Workforce Management*, April 2005, 32–38.

21. L. Herscovitch and J. P. Meyer. Commitment to organizational change: Extension of a three-component model. *Journal of Applied Psychology*, 87, 2002, 474–487.

22. T. D. Ludwig and E. S. Geller. Assigned versus participative goal setting and response generalization: Managing injury control among professional pizza deliverers. *Journal of Applied Psychology*, 82, 1997, 253–261.

23. P. Prasad and A. Prasad. Stretching the iron cage: The constitution and implications of routine workplace resistance. *Organization Science*, 11, 2000, 387–403; R. Maurer. *Beyond the Wall of Resistance*. Austin, TX: Bard Books, 1996.

24. R. Kegan and L. L. Lahey. The real reason people won't change. *Harvard Business Review*, November 2001, 84–93; J. A. Clair, R. Dufresne, N. Jackson, and J. Ladge. Being the bearer of bad news: Challenges facing downsizing agents in organizations. *Organizational Dynamics*, 35, 2006, 145–159.

25. P. J. Kiger. Corporate crunch. *Workforce Management*, April 2005, 32–38.

26. J. Clarke, C. Ellett, J. Bateman, and J. Rugutt. Faculty receptivity/resistance to change, personal and organizational efficacy, decision deprivation and effectiveness in research universities. Paper presented at the Twenty-First Annual Meeting of the Association for the Study of Higher Education, Memphis, TN, 1996.

27. J. Dean, P. Brandes, and R. Dharwadkar. Organizational cynicism. *Academy of Management Review*, 23, 1998, 341–352; A. E. Reichers, J. P. Wanous, and J. T. Austin. Understanding and managing cynicism about organizational change. *Academy of Management Executive*, 11, 1997, 48.

28. C. Axtell, T. Wall, C. Stride, K. Pepper, C. Clegg, P. Gardner, and R. Bolden. Familiarity breeds content: The impact of exposure to change on employee openness and well-being. *Journal of Occupational and Organizational Psychology*, 2002, 75, 217–231.

29. J. E. Mathieu and D. M. Zajkac. A review and meta-analysis of the antecedents, correlates, and consequences of organizational commitment. *Psychological Bulletin*, 108, 1990, 171–194; J. Ross. Retaining top performers during change. *Harvard Management Update*, February 2006, 3–6; C. D. Ruta. The application of change management theory to HR portal implementation in subsidiaries of multinational corporations. *Human Resource Management*, 44(Spring), 2005, 35–53.

30. T. G. Cummings. *Organization Development and Change*. Mason, OH: South-Western, 2005.

31. Open source. http://en.wikipedia.org (June 2006); K. L. Miller. The new Big Blue attitude. *Newsweek*, December 19, 2005, 21–24.

32. T. Hindle. The new organization. *The Economist*, January 21, 2006, 21.

33. G. Hamel. The why, what, and how of management innovation. *Harvard Business Review*, February 2006, 72–84.

34. V. B. Wayman and S. Werner. The impact of workforce reductions on financial performance: A longitudinal perspective. *Journal of Management*, 26, 2000, 341–363.

35. W. F. Cascio. Financial consequences of employment-change decisions in major U. S. corporations. *Academy of Management Journal*, 40, 1997, 1175–1189; J. Brockner, G. Spreitzer, A. Mishra, L. Pepper, and J. Weinburg. Perceived control as an antidote to the negative effects of layoffs on survivors' organizational commitment and job performance. *Administrative Science Quarterly*, 48, 2004, 75–100; L. Uchitell. *The Disposable American: Layoffs and Their Consequences*. New York: Knopf, 2006.

36. E. Brynjolfsson, A. A. Renshaw, and M. V. Alstyne. The matrix of change. *Sloan Management Review*, Winter 1997, 37–54; M. Hammer and J. Champy. *Reengineering the Corporation*. New York: HarperCollins, 1993; M. Hammer. *Beyond Reengineering: How the Process-Centered Organization Is Changing Our Lives*. New York: HarperBusiness, 1996; J. Champy. *Reengineering Management: The Mandate for New Leadership*. New York: HarperBusiness, 1996.

37. J. Guaspari. Dispatch from the front: A shining example. *Across the Board*, May/June 2002, 67–68; M. E. Ruquest. National Grange Mutual rated No. 1 in business ease by agents, workers. *National Underwriter*, December 15, 2003, 9; M. E. Ruquest. Making things easier for agents. *National Underwriter, P & C*. May 10, 2004, 21.

38. J. Waclawski and A. H. Church (Eds.). *Organization Development: A Data-Driven Approach to Organizational Change*. San Francisco: Jossey Bass, 2002; T. G. Cummings (Ed.). *Handbook of Organization Development*. Newbury Park, CA: Sage, 2006.

39. J. Waclawski and S. G. Rogelberg. Interviews and focus groups: Quintessential organizational development techniques. In J. Waclawski and A. H. Church (Eds.). *Organization Development: A Data-Driven Approach to Organizational Change*. San Francisco: Jossey Bass, 2002, 103–126.

40. A. I. Kraut. *Getting Action from Organizational Surveys*. San Francisco: Jossey-Bass, 2006.

41. M. A. West. Sparkling fountains or stagnant ponds: An integrative model of cre-

activity an innovation implementation in work groups. *Applied Psychology: An International Review*, 51, 2001, 355–424; C. K. W. D Dreu and M. A. West. Minority dissent and team innovation: The importance of participation in decision-making. *Journal of Applied Psychology*, 86, 2001, 1191–1201; D. Barrett. *Leadership Communication*. New York: McGraw-Hill, 2006; IBM Case Studies, www-306 .ibm.com. (June 2006).

42. S. F. Gale. For ERP success, create a culture change. *Workforce*, September 2002, 83–88; L. Berlin. *The Man behind the Microchip: Robert Noyce and the Invention of Silicon Valley*. New York: Oxford University Press, 2005.

43. For a discussion of various facets of innovation, see M. Beyerlein, S. Beyerlein, and F. Kennedy (Eds.). *Innovation through Collaboration*. New York: Elsevier, 2006.

44. R. Gupta and J. Wendler. Leading change: An interview with the CEO of P&G. *The McKinsey Quarterly*, www.mckinseyquarterly .com (August 1, 2005); L. Huston and N. Sakkab. Connect and develop: Inside Procter & Gamble's new model for innovation. *Harvard Business Review*, March 2006, 58–66.

45. 2006 CEO of the year: Man with a mission. *Chief Executive*, April/May 2006. www.chiefexecutive.net (August 22, 2006).

46. F. Warner. In a word, Toyota drives for innovation. *Fast Company*, August 2002, 36–38; T. Hindle. Inculcating culture: The Toyota way. *The Economist*. January 21, 2006, 11.

47. M. Conlin. The easiest commute of all. *Business Week*, December 12, 2005, 78–80.

48. For an example of how adopting the balanced scorecard might stimulate organization to adopt administrative and structural innovations, see R. S. Kaplan and D. P. Norton. How to implement a new strategy without disrupting your organization. *Harvard Business Review*, March 2006, 100–109.

49. J. McGregor. Dawn of the idea czar. *Business Week*, April 10, 2006, 98–99.

50. A. C. Edmondson. The local and variegated nature of learning in organizations: A group-level perspective. *Organization Science*, 13, 2002, 128–146; S. E. Jackson, M. A. Hitt, and A. S. DeNisi, *Managing Knowledge for Sustained Competitive Advantage*. San Francisco: Jossey-Bass, 2003; A creative corporate toolbox. *Business Week*, August 1, 2005, 73–75; B. Nussbaum. How to build innovative companies. *Business Week*, August 1, 2005, 61–68; S. D. Anthony, M. Eyring, and L. Gibson. Mapping your innovation strategy. *Harvard Business Review*, May 2006, 104–113.

51. P. Senge, *The Fifth Discipline: The Art and Practice of the Learning Organization*. New York: Doubleday, 1990; see also Society for Organizational Learning, www.sol.org; E. E. Lawler III and C. G. Worley. *Built to Change*. San Francisco: Wiley & Sons, 2006.

52. M. Albert. Managing change at HP Lab: Perspectives for innovation, knowledge management, and becoming a learning organization. *The Business Review, Cambridge*. Summer 2006, 17–22.

53. J. G. C. Navarro and B. R. Moya. Business performance management and unlearning process. *Knowledge and Process Management*, 12, 2006, 161–170.

54. Y.-T. Cheng and A. H. Van de Ven. Learning the innovation journey: Order out of chaos. *Organization Science*, 7, 1996, 593–614; M. Goldsmith, H. Morgan, and A. J. Ogg (Eds.). *Leading Organizational Learning*. San Francisco: Jossey-Bass, 2004.

55. J.-L. Denis, L. Lamothe, and A. Langley. The dynamics of collective leadership and strategic change in pluralistic organizations. *Academy of Management Journal*, 44, 2001, 809–837.

56. For suggestions about how to encourage people to share their knowledge, see K. Husted and S. Michailova. Diagnosing and fighting knowledge-sharing hostility. *Organizational Dynamics*, 31(1), 2002, 60–73; see also M. Baer and M. Frese. Innovation is not enough: Climates for initiative and psychological safety, process innovations and firm performance. *Journal of Organizational Behavior*, 2003, 24, 45–68.

57. C. Kim and R. Maubourgne. Fair process: Managing in the knowledge economy. *Harvard Business Review*, July/August 1997, 65–75; R. Pascale, M. Millimann, and L. Gioja. Changing the way we change. *Harvard Business Review*, November/December 1997, 127–139.

58. Whole Foods Market: Our core values. www.wholefoodsmarket.com (June 2006).

59. M. Hertz. KM in the legal profession. *KM Review*, February 2006, 2–3.

60. J. P. MacDuffie. The road to "Root Cause": Shop-floor problem-solving at three auto assembly plants. *Management Science*, 43, 1997, 479–502.

61. T. A. Stewart and L. O'Brien. Execution without excuses. *Harvard Business Review*, March 2005, 102–111.

62. To learn more about such arrangements, see the Special Research Forum on Building Effective Networks, *Academy of Management Review*, 31, 2006, 560–738.

63. J. D. Wolpert. Breaking out of the innovation box. *The Innovative Enterprise*, August 2002, 77–83; J. E. Perry-Smith. Social yet creative: The role of social relationships in facilitating individual creativity. *Academy of Management Journal*, 49, 2006, 85–101.

64. For specific measures that can be used, see M. S. Huselid, B. E. Becker and R. W. Beatty. *The Workforce Scorecard*, Boston: Harvard Business School Press, 2005.

65. See L. B. Cardinal. Technological innovation in the pharmaceutical industry: The use of organizational control in managing research and development. *Organization Science*, 12, 2001, 19–36.

66. J. S. Brown and P. Duguid. Capturing knowledge without killing it. *Harvard Business Review*, May/June 2000, 73–80.

67. M. Schilling. *Strategic Management of Technological Innovation*. New York: McGraw-Hill, 2005.

68. *Adapted from* J. E. Jones and A. G. Banet, Jr. Critical consulting incidents inventory. In J. W. Pfeiffer and J. E. Jones (Eds.). *The 1978 Annual Handbook for Group Facilitators*. LaJolla, CA: University Associates, 1978, 91–94.

69. *Adapted from* T. Lowry. Can MTV stay cool? *Business Week*, February 20, 2006, 51–60; J. Hibbard. Electronic media: Judy McGrath. *Television Week*, April 10, 2006, 36.

Chapter 13

1. A. Barrett. Star search. *Business Week*, October 10, 2005, 68–78.

2. D. K. Datta, J. P. Guthrie, and P. W. Wright. Human resource management and labor productivity: Does industry matter? *Academy of Management Journal*, 48, 2005, 135–145.

3. See B. S. Klaas, T. W. Gainey, J. A. McClendon, and H. Yang. Professional employer organizations and their impact on client satisfaction with human resource outcomes: A field study of human resource outsourcing in small and medium enterprises. *Journal of Management*, 31, 2005, 234–254.

4. S. E. Jackson and R. S. Schuler. *Managing Human Resources through Strategic Partnerships*, 9th ed. Mason, OH: South-Western, 2006. Used with permission.

5. D. P. Lepak, H. Liao, Y. Chung, and E. Harden. A conceptual review of human resource management systems in strategic human resource management research. In Joseph, J. Martocchio (Ed.). *Research in Personnel and Human Resource Management*, Vol. 25. Oxford: Elsevier, 2006, 219–272.

6. M. Buckingham and C. Coffman. *First Break All the Rules*. New York: Simon and Schuster, 1999; L. Grant. Happy workers, happy returns. *Fortune*, January 12, 1998, 81; G. E. Fryzell and J. Wang. The Fortune Corporation 'Reputation' Index: Reputation for what? *Journal of Management*, 20, 1994, 1–14; M. J. Schmit and S. P. Allscheid. Employee attitudes and customer satisfaction: Making the theoretical and empirical connections. *Personnel Psychology*, 48, 1995, 521–536.

7. D. Brady. The Immelt revolution. *Business Week*, March 28, 2005, 64–73.

8. R. J. Grossman. Blind Investment: If people are a company's biggest asset, why don't Wall Street analysts pay more attention to them? *HR Magazine*, January 2005, 40–47.

9. Ethical practice 2006: J. M. Smucker & Co. *Workforce Management*, March 13, 2006, 19.

10. M. A. Konovsky. Understanding procedural justice and its impact on business organizations. *Journal of Management*, 26, 2000, 489–511.

11. J. C. Morrow, P. C. Morrow, and E. J. Mullen. Intraorganizational mobility and work-related attitudes. *Journal of Organizational Behavior* 17, 1996, 363–374.

12. *EEOC Charge statistics, 1992–2005.* www .eeoc.gov/stats/charges.html (June 2006).

13. C. Waxer. Life's a balancing act for Cirque du Soleil. *Workforce Management*, January 2005, 52–53.

14. *Adapted from* G. W. Florkowski. *Managing Global Legal Systems.* United Kingdom: Routledge, 2006.

15. D. Creedman. Six easy pieces. *Workforce Management*, May 2005, 59–62.

16. U. S. Department of Labor. *Contingent and alternative employment arrangements.* February 2005. www.bls.gov/cps (June 2006).

17. I. Speizer. Shopper's special. *Workforce Management*, September 2004, 51–54; www.traderjoes.com (June 2006).

18. J. Zeppe. Temp-to-hire is becoming full-time practice at firms. *Workforce Management*, June 2005, 82–84.

19. A. Bernstein. Too many workers? Not for long. *Business Week*, May 2002, 126–130.

20. For a full discussion, see L. Uchitelle. *The Disposable American: Layoffs and Their Consequences.* New York: Knopf, 2006.

21. For research on what managers can do to reduce some of the negative effects of layoffs, see J. Brockner, G. Spreitzer, A. Mishra, W. Hochwarter, and J. Weinberg. Perceived control as an antidote to the negative effects of layoffs on survivors' organizational commitment and job performance. *Administrative Science Quarterly*, 49, 2004, 76–100; A. Molinsky and J. D. Margollis. The emotional tightrope of downsizing: Hidden challenges for leaders and their organizations. *Organizational Dynamics*, 35, 2006, 145–159.

22. E. E. Lawler III and G. E. Ledford. New approaches to organizing: Competencies and the decline of the bureaucratic model. In C. L. Cooper and S. E. Jackson (Eds.). *Creating Tomorrow's Organizations: Handbook for Future Research in Organizations.* Chichester, UK: John Wiley & Sons, 1997, 231–249.

23. J. S. Shippmann, R. A. Ash, and Associates. The practice of competency modeling. *Personnel Psychology*, 53, 2000, 703–740.

24. J. S. MacNeil. Hey, look us over. *Growth*, October 2002, 146.

25. For a comprehensive review, see J. A. Breaugh and M. Starke. Research on employee recruitment: So many studies, so many remaining questions. *Journal of Management*, 26, 2000, 405–434.

26. F. Hansen. Continental's global recruiting takes off with a tech upgrade. *Workforce Management*, February 27, 2006, 34–37.

27. For suggestions about how to avoid such problems, see I. Kotlyar. If recruitment means building trust, where does technology fit in? *Canadian HR Reporter*, October 7, 2002, 21–24.

28. J. Marquez. The insider: Recruiting. *Workforce Management*, June 2005, 24–25.

29. W. C. Taylor. To hire sharp employees, recruit in sharp ways. *New York Times*, April 23, 2006, BU3.

30. A. Van Vianen. Person–organization fit: The match between newcomers' and recruiters' preferences for organizational cultures. *Personnel Psychology*, 53, 2000, 113–149; T. A. Judge and D. M. Cable. Applicant personality, organizational culture, and organizational attraction. *Personnel Psychology*, 50, 1997, 359–394; R. W. Griffeth, P. W. Hom, L. S. Fink, and D. J. Cohen. Comparative tests of multiple models of recruiting sources effects. *Journal of Management*, 23, 1997, 19–36.

31. For more details, see J. F. Kehoe (Ed.). *Managing Selection in Changing Organizations.* San Francisco: Jossey-Bass, 2000; C. J. Collins and C. K. Stevens. The relationships between early recruitment-related activities and application decisions of new labor-market entrants: A brand equity approach to recruitment. *Journal of Applied Psychology*, 27, 2002, 1121–1133.

32. B. S. Bell, D. Weichman, and A. M. Ryan. Consequences of organizational justice expectations in a selection system. *Journal of Applied Psychology*, 91, 2006, 455–466.

33. S. Caudron. Who are you really hiring? *Workforce*, November 2002, 28–32.

34. W.-C. Tsai, C.-C. Chen, and S.-F. Chiu. Exploring boundaries of the effects of applicant impression management tactics in job interviews. *Journal of Management*, 31, 2005, 108–125.

35. C. Daniels. To hire a lumber expert, click here. *Fortune*, April 3, 2000, 267–270.

36. R. A. Posthuma, F. P. Morgeson, and M. A. Campoin. Beyond employment interview validity: A comprehensive narrative review of recent research and trends over time. *Personnel Psychology*, 55, 2002. 1–81.

37. S. L. Rynes, K. G. Brown, and A. E. Colbert. Seven misconceptions about human resource practices: Research findings versus practitioner beliefs. *Academy of Management Executive*, 16(3), 2002, 92–103; F. L. Schmidt and J. E. Hunter. The validity and utility of selection methods in personnel psychology: Practical and theoretical implications of 85 years of research findings. *Psychological Bulletin*, 124, 1998, 252–274.

38. D. Bartram. The eight great competencies: A criterion-centric approach to validation. *Journal of Applied Psychology*, 90, 2005, 1185–1203; N. M. Dudley, K. A. Orvis, J. E. Lebiecki, and J. M. Cortina. A meta-analytic investigation of conscientiousness in the prediction of job performance: Examining the intercorrelations and the incremental validity of narrow traits. *Journal of Applied Psychology*, 91, 2006, 40–57.

39. H. Cooper-Thomas and N. Anderson. Newcomer adjustment: The relationship between organizational socialization tactics, information acquisition and attitudes. *Journal of Occupational and Organizational Psychology*, 75, 2002, 423–437.

40. E. Tahmincioglu. True blue. *Workforce Management*, February 2005, 47–50.

41. C. Lachnit. Hire right: Do it the Ritz way. *Workforce*, April 2002, 16; B. Lampton. My pleasure: The Ritz-Carlton Hotel. *Expert*, 2003, 3 (accessed online at www.expertmagazine.com, June 2006); additional information obtained from the company Web site at www .ritzcarlton.com.

42. For a review, see P. J. Taylor, D. F. Russ-Eft, and D. W. L. Chun. A meta-analytic review of behavior modeling training. *Journal of Applied Psychology*, 90, 2005, 692–709.

43. *Adapted from* C. Huff. Accent on training. *Workforce Management*, March 2005, 54. See also E. Frauenheim. Culture of understanding. *Workforce Management*, November 2005, 26–30.

44. R. E. DeRouin, B. A. Fritzche, and E. Salas. E-learning in organizations. *Journal of Management*, 31, 2005, 920–940; R. C. Clark. Harnessing the virtual classroom. *ASTD*, November 2005, 41–43; I. Speizer. Value-minded. *Workforce Management*, July 2005, 55–60.

45. R. C. Clark. Harnessing the virtual classroom. *TD*, November 2005, 41–43; R. Jana. On-the-job video gaming. *Business Week*, March 27, 2006, 43.

46. R. J. Grossman. Developing talent. *HR Magazine*, January 2005, 40–46.

47. See C. O. Trevor. Interactions among actual ease-of-movement determinants and job satisfaction in the determination of voluntary turnover. *Academy of Management Journal*, 44, 2001, 621–638.

48. For a recent review, see G. P. Latham, J. Almost, S. Mann, and C. Moore. New developments in performance management. *Organizational Dynamics*, 34, 2005, 77–87.

49. For an excellent discussion of how performance standards can affect employees' satisfaction and motivation, see P. Bobko, and A. Colella. Employee reactions to performance standards: A review and research propositions. *Personnel Psychology*, 47, 1994, 1–29.

50. A. G. Walker and J. W. Smither. A five-year study of upward feedback: What managers do with their results matters. *Personnel Psychology*, 52, 1999, 393–423.

51. See J. W. Smither (Ed.). *Performance Appraisal: State of the Art in Practice.* San Francisco: Jossey-Bass, 1998.

52. D. Grote. Forced ranking: Behind the scenes. *Across the Board.* November/December 2002, 40–45.

53. A. S. DeNisi and A. N. Kluger. Feedback effectiveness: Can 360-degree appraisals be improved? *Academy of Management Executive,* 14, 2000, 129–139.

54. D. P. Shuitt. Former Pepsico executives do a 360 in managing Yum Brands' workforce. *Workforce Management,* April 2005, 59–60.

55. Society for Human Resource Management. Workers redefine what leads to job satisfaction, poll shows. *HR News,* January 2003, 5.

56. A. E. Barber and R. D. Bretz, Jr. Compensation, attraction and retention. In S. L. Rynes and B. Gerhart (Eds.). *Compensation in Organizations: Current Research and Practice.* San Francisco: Jossey-Bass, 2000; M. L. Williams, M. A. McDaniel, and N. T. Nguyen. A meta-analysis of the antecedents and consequences of pay level satisfaction. *Journal of Applied Psychology,* 91, 2006, 392–413.

57. R. Batt. Managing customer services: Human resource practices, quit rates, and sales growth. *Academy of Management Journal,* 45, 2002, 587–597.

58. M. V. Rafter. Welcome to the club. *Workforce Management,* March 2005, 41–46.

59. E. Frauenheim. Studies: More workers look to switch jobs. *Workforce Management,* February 13, 2006, 12.

60. R. L. Heneman, G. E. Ledford, and M. T. Gresham. The changing nature of work and its effects on compensation design and delivery. In S. L. Rynes and B. Gerhart (Eds.). *Compensation in Organizations: Current Research and Practice.* San Francisco: Jossey-Bass, 2000; J. D. Shaw, N. Gupta, A. Mitra, and G. E. Ledford, Jr. Success and survival of skill-based pay plans. *Journal of Management,* 31, 2005, 28–49.

61. C. Garvey. Philosophizing compensation: Develop an overarching statement to ensure that your pay practices are applied consistently and effectively. *HR Magazine,* January 2005, 73–75.

62. G. Ruiz. Bank of America ties bonuses to overall success. *Workforce Management,* October 2005, 14–15.

63. Jackson and Schuler. *Managing Human Resources .* Used with permission.

64. G. Weber. Preserving the counter culture. *Workforce Management,* February 2005, 28–34.

65. *Source:* S. M. Nkomo, M. D. Fottler, and R. B. McAfee. *Applications in Human Resource Management: Cases, Exercises and Skill Builders.* Mason, OH: South-Western, 2005. Reprinted with permission.

Chapter 14

1. A. E. Smith. Houston, do you read me? *Incentive,* 180(2), 2006. www.incentivemag.com (May 2006); J. Schwartz. To return shuttle to space, NASA calls on cool leader. *New York Times,* April 17, 2005, 21.

2. For a detailed discussion of unproductive behavior in organizations, see R. W. Griffin and Y. P. Lopez. "Bad behavior" in organizations: A review and typology for future research. *Journal of Management,* 31, 2005, 988–1005.

3. T. A. Judge, C. J. Thoresen, J. E. Bono, and G. K. Patton. The job satisfaction–job performance relationship: A qualitative and quantitative review. *Psychological Bulletin,* 127, 2001, 376–407; see also S. C. Payne and S. S. Webber. Effects of service provider attitudes and employment status on citizenship behaviors and customers' attitudes and loyalty behavior. *Journal of Applied Psychology,* 91, 2006, 365–378; D. A. Harrison, D. A. Newman, and P. L. Roth. How important are job attitudes? Meta-analytic comparisons of integrative behavioral outcomes and time sequences. *Academy of Management Journal,* 49, 2006, 305–325.

4. For a more detailed model of motivation, see E. A. Locke and G. P. Latham. What should we do about motivation theory? Six recommendations for the twenty-first century. *Academy of Management Review,* 29, 2004, 388–403.

5. J. K. Harter, F. L. Schmidt, and T. L. Hayes. Business-unit-level relationship between employee satisfaction, employee engagement, and business outcomes: A meta–analysis. *Journal of Applied Psychology,* 87, 2002, 268–279.

6. J. P. Cable and D.S. DeRue. The convergent and discriminant validity of subjective fit perceptions. *Journal of Applied Psychology,* 87, 2002, 875–884; C. Hult. Organizational commitment and person–environment fit in six western countries. *Organization Studies,* 26, 2005, 249–270.

7. B. Buckingham and C. Coffman. *First, Break All the Rules.* New York: Simon & Schuster, 1999.

8. E. A. Locke and G. P. Latham. *A Theory of Goal Setting and Task Performance.* Upper Saddle River, NJ: Prentice-Hall, 1990.

9. S. Hamm. Motivating the troops. *Business Week,* November 21, 2005, 88–90.

10. P. J. Kiger. How performance management reversed NCCI's fortunes. *Workforce,* May 2002, 48–51.

11. G. P. Latham and G. H. Seijts. The effects of proximal and distal goals on performance on a moderately complex task. *Journal of Organizational Behavior,* 20, 1999, 421–429.

12. A. D. Stajkovic and F. Luthans. Self-efficacy and work-related performance: A meta-analysis. *Psychological Bulletin,* 124, 1998, 240–261.

13. N. W. Van Yperen and O. Janssen. Fatigued and dissatisfied or fatigued but satisfied: Goal orientations and responses to high job demands. *Academy of Management Journal,* 45, 2002, 1161–1171.

14. G. P. Latham and E. A. Locke. Enhancing the benefits and overcoming the pitfalls of goal setting. *Organizational Dynamics,* 35, 2006, in press; B. S. Wiese and A. M. Freund. Goal progress makes one happy or does it? Longitudinal findings from the work domain. *Journal of Occupational Psychology,* 78, 2005, pp. 1–19.

15. S. Caudron. How HR drives profits. *Workforce,* December 2001, 26–31.

16. E. A. Locke and G. P. Latham. Building a practically useful theory of goal setting and task motivation: A 35-year odyssey. *American Psychologist,* 57, 2002, 705–717.

17. L. Roberson, E. A. Deitch, A. P. Brief, and C. J. Block. Stereotype threat and feedback seeking in the workplace. *Journal of Vocational Behavior,* 62, 2003, 176–188.

18. M. Tuckey, N. Brewer, and P. Williamson. The influence of motives and goal orientation on feedback seeking. *Journal of Occupational and Organizational Psychology,* 75, 2002, 195–216.

19. J. E. Sawyer, W. R. Latham, R. D. Pritchard, and W. R. Bennett, Jr. Analysis of work group productivity in an applied setting: Application of a time series panel design. *Personnel Psychology,* 52, 1999, 927–967.

20. For an example of how using feedback can improve workplace safety, see D. Zohar. Modifying supervisory practices to improve subunit safety: A leadership-based intervention model. *Journal of Applied Psychology,* 87, 2002, 156–163.

21. C. Garvey. Steer teams with the right pay. *HR Magazine,* May 2002, 71–78.

22. G. H. Seijts and G. P. Latham. Learning versus performance goals: When should each be used? *Academy of Management Executive,* 19, 2005, 124–131.

23. B. F. Skinner. *Contingencies of Reinforcement.* New York: Appleton-Century-Crofts, 1969; B. F. Skinner. *Beyond Freedom and Dignity.* New York: Bantam, 1971; B. F. Skinner. *About Behaviorism.* New York: Knopf, 1974.

24. A. D. Stajkovic and F. Luthans. Differential effects of incentive motivators on work performance. *Academy of Management Journal,* 4, 2001,580–590.

25. F. Luthans and D. Strajkovic. Reinforce for performance: The need to go beyond pay and even rewards. *Academy of Management Executive,* 12, 1999, 49–57; A. D. Strajkovic and F. Luthans. A meta-analysis of the effects of organizational behavior modification on task performance, 1975–1995. *Academy of Management Journal,* 40, 1997, 1122–1149.

26. S. E. Markham, K. D. Scott, and G. H. McKee. Recognizing good attendance: A longitudinal, quasi-experimental field study. *Personnel Psychology,* 55, 2002, 639–660.

27. P. A. Rivera. A cure for sick leave abuse? *The Dallas Morning News,* March 4, 2003, 3D.

28. J. Marquez. The insider: Health care benefits. *Workforce Management,* September 2005, 66–69.

29. S. E. Seibert, J. M. Crant, and M. L. Kraimer. Proactive personality and career success. *Journal of Applied Psychology*, 84, 1999, 416–427; J. B. Vancouver and D. V. Day. Industrial and organizational psychology research on self-regulation: From constructs to applications. *Applied Psychology: An International Review*, 54, 2005, 155–185.

30. A. Bandura and E. A. Locke. Negative self-efficacy and goal effects revisited. *Journal of Applied Psychology*, 88, 2003, 87–99.

31. W. Van Erde and H. Thierry. Vroom's expectancy models and work-related criteria: A meta-analysis. *Journal of Applied Psychology*, 81, 1996, 575–586.

32. S. Bates. Murky corporate goals can undermine recovery. *HR Magazine*, November 2002, 14.

33. J. M. Brett and L. K. Stroh. Working 61 plus hours a week: Why do managers do it? *Journal of Applied Psychology*, 88, 2003, 67–78.

34. T. R. Zenger and C. R. Marshall. Determinants of incentive intensity in group-based rewards. *Academy of Management Journal*, 43, 2000, 149–163.

35. *Adapted from* J. Marquez. McDonald's rewards program leaves room for some local flavor. *Workforce Management*, April 10, 2006, 26.

36. T. Shanker. New incentives for pilots of remote plane. *New York Times*, October 17, 2002, A22.

37. G. P. Latham. The importance of understanding and changing employee outcome expectancies for gaining commitment to an organizational goal. *Personnel Psychology*, 54, 2001, 707–716.

38. For more about how employees weigh the costs and benefits of unethical behavior, see M. J. Gundlach, S. C. Douglas, and M. J. Martinko. The decision to blow the whistle: A social information processing framework. *Academy of Management Review*, 28, 2003, 107–123.

39. N. Bynes. The art of motivation. *Business Week*, May 1, 2006, 57–62.

40. M. E. Schweitzer, L. Ordonez, and B. Douma. Goal setting as a motivator of unethical behavior. *Academy of Management Journal*, 47, 2004, 422–432.

41. *Source:* J. R. Hackman and G. R. Oldham. *Work Redesign*. Reading, MA: Addison-Wesley, 1980, 83. Reprinted with permission. Also see N. G. Dodd and D. C. Ganster. The interactive effects of variety, autonomy, and feedback on attitudes and performance. *Journal of Organizational Behavior*, 17, 1996, 329–347.

42. P. W. Mulvey, G. E. Ledford, and P. V. LeBlanc. Rewards of work: How they drive performance, retention and satisfaction. *WorldatWork Journal*, Third Quarter, 2000, 6–28.

43. www.wholefoodsmarket.com (May 2006); R. Forrester. Empowerment: Rejuvenating a potent idea. *Academy of Management Executive*, 14(3), 2000, 67–77. S. Caudron.

How HR drives profits. *Workforce*, December 2001, 26–31.

44. R. W. Renn and R. J. Vandenberg. The critical psychological states: An underrepresented component in job characteristics model research. *Journal of Management*, 21, 1995, 279–303; S. P. Brown and T. W. Leigh. A new look at psychological climate and its relationship to job involvement, effort, and performance. *Journal of Applied Psychology*, 81, 1996, 358–368.

45. R. A. Roe, I. L. Zinovieva, E. Dienes, and L. A. T. Horn. A comparison of work motivation in Bulgaria, Hungary, and the Netherlands: Test of a model. *Applied Psychology: An International Review*, 49, 2000, 658–687.

46. B. P. Sunoo. Blending a successful workforce. *Workforce*, March 2000, 44–48.

47. F. Herzberg, B. Mausner, and B. Snyderman. *The Motivation to Work*. New York: John Wiley & Sons, 1959 ; see also, F. Herzberg. One more time: How do you motivate employees? *Harvard Business Review*, January 2003, 87–96.

48. *Adapted from* T. Henneman. Jack in the Box going upmarket in benefits as well as at its eateries. *Workforce Management*, March 2005, 76–77; www.nraef.org (May 2006).

49. C. L. Jurkiewicz and T. K. Massey, Jr. What motivates municipal employees: A comparison study of supervisor and non-supervisory employees. *Public Personnel Management*, 26, 1997, 367–376.

50. J. Wiscombe. Rewards get results. *Workforce*, April 2002, 42–48.

51. T. Henneman. What's the payoff? *Workforce Management*, October 12, 2005, 41–50.

52. *Adapted from* J. Wiscombe. Rewards get results. *Workforce*, April 2002, 42–48; Fortune 100 Best Companies to Work For. *Fortune*, March 13, 2006; money.cnn.com/magazines/fortune/best-companies.

53. J. S. Adams. Toward an understanding of equity. *Journal of Abnormal and Social Psychology*, 67, 1963, 422–436.

54. R. T. Mowday and K. A. Colwell. Employee reactions to unfair outcomes in the workplace: The contributions of Adam's equity theory to understanding work motivation. In L. W. Porter, G. A. Bigley, and R. M Steers (Eds.). *Motivation and Work Behavior* (7th ed.). Burr Ridge, IL: Irwin/McGraw-Hill, 2003, 65–82.

55. A. S. Tsui, J. L. Pearce, L. W. Porter, and A. M. Tripoli. Alternative approaches to the employee–organization relationship: Does investment in employees pay off? *Academy of Management Journal*, 40, 1997, 1089–1121.

56. P. D. Sweeney and D. B. McFarlin. Wage comparisons with similar and dissimilar others. *Journal of Occupational and Organizational Psychology*, 78, 2005, 113–131.

57. H. Baum. Care for the little guy. *Harvard Business Review*, January 2003, 45.

58. For a recent study of how laid-off executives react to they reemployment situation, see D. C. Feldman, C. R. Leana, and M. C. Bolino. Underemployment and relative deprivation among re-employed executives. *Journal of Occupational and Organizational Psychology*, 75, 2002, 453–471.

59. J. D. Shaw, N. Gupta, and J. E. Delery. Pay dispersion and workforce performance: Moderating effects of incentives and interdependence. *Strategic Management Journal*, 23, 2002, 491–512; S. J. Wayne, L. M. Shore, W. H. Bommer, and L. E. Tetrick. The role of fair treatment and rewards in perceptions of organizational support and leader-member exchange. *Journal of Applied Psychology*, 87, 2002, 590–598.

60. See R. Kanfer and P. L. Ackerman. Individual differences in work motivation: Further explorations of a trait framework. *Applied Psychology: An International Review*, 49, 2000, 470–482.

61. A. H. Maslow. *Motivation and Personality*, 2nd ed. New York: Harper & Row, 1970. For a recent discussion of self-actualization, see S. A. Haslam, R. A. Eggins, and K. J. Reynolds. The ASPIRe model: Actualizing social and personal identity resources to enhance organizational outcomes. *Journal of Occupational and Organizational Psychology*, 77, 2003, 83–113.

62. U1: Richard Branson. *Fast Company*. August 2000, 78.

63. *Adapted from* A. Bourdain. Management by fire: A conversation with Chef Anthony Bourdain. *Harvard Business Review*, July 2002, 57–61.

64. H. Chura. Sabbaticals aren't just for academics anymore. *New York Times*, April 22, 2006, C6.

65. C. P. Alderfer. *Existence, Relatedness and Growth: Human Needs in Organizational Settings*. New York: Free Press, 1972.

66. For a discussion of this and other common pitfalls, see S. Kerr. An academy classic: On the folly of rewarding A, while hoping for B. *Academy of Management Executive*, 9, 1995, 7–16.

67. A. N. Kluger and A. S. DeNisi. The effects of feedback interventions on performance: A historical review, a meta-analysis, and a preliminary feedback intervention theory. *Psychological Bulletin*, 119, 1996, 254–284.

68. J. Mackintosh. How BMW put the Mini back on track. *Financial Times*, March 19, 2003, 14.

Chapter 15

1. C. Kathy. Newsmaker profile: John Thompson: Man with a plan. *San Francisco Chronicle*, January 29, 2002, 14; A. Saita. Profile: John Thompson. *Information-Security*, February 2003, infosecuritymag.techtarget.com (July 2006); H. K. Chang. Execution and customer focus are leadership keys, says Symantec's Thompson. Address given at Stanford Graduate School

of Business, March 2005, www.gsb
.stanford.edu (July 2006); C. Taylor.
John Thompson: Symantec, U.S. *Time
Magazine—Europe*, July 19, 2004,
www.time.com (July 2006); L. Hooper.
John Thompson, Symantec. *CRN*,
November 11, 2005; www.crn.com (July
2006); K. McLaughlin. Thompson outlines
Symantec's 2006 strategy. *CRN*, May 8,
2006, www.crn.com (July 2006); The 50
who matter now. *Business 2.0*, July 2006,
83–98.

2. R. L. Daft. *The leadership experience*. Mason,
OH: Thomson South-Western, 2002. For
more detailed discussions of leadership, see
also D. N. Den Hartog and P. L.
Koopman. Leadership in organizations. In
N. Anderson, D. S. Ones, H. K. Sinangil,
and C. Viswesvaran (Eds.). *Handbook of
Industrial, Work and Organizational
Psychology*, Vol. 2. Thousand Oaks, CA:
Sage, 2001, 166–187. See also J. M.
Polodny, R. Khurana, and M. Hill-Popper.
Revisiting the meaning of leadership.
Research in Organizational Behavior, 26,
2005, 1–36.

3. Interview with Stanley O'Neal. *Fortune*,
December 12, 2005 (n.p.).

4. J. O. Whitney, T. Parker, and S. Noble.
*Power plays: Shakespeare's lessons in leadership
and management*. Old Tappan, NJ: Simon &
Schuster, 2000; B. Lee and S. R. Covey.
The power principle: Influence with honor.
New York: Fireside, 1998.

5. J. Hamm. The five messages leaders must
manage. *Harvard Business Review*, May
2006, 115–129.

6. G. Farrell. A CEO and a gentleman: Ken
Chenault combines fierce drive with concern for people. *USA Today*, April 25, 2005,
1B.

7. T. A. Judge, R. Ilies, J. E. Bono, and M. W.
Gerhardt. Personality and leadership: A
qualitative and quantitative review. *Journal
of Applied Psychology*, 87, 2002, 765–780.

8. For a history of work on emotional intelligence, see C. Cherniss. Emotional intelligence: What it is and why it matters.
Retrieved from the Consortium for
Research on Emotional Intelligence Web
site, www.eiconsortium.org (June 2006).

9. J. E. Barbuto and M. E. Burbach. The
emotional intelligence of transformational
leaders. A field study of elected officials.
Journal of Applied Social Psychology, 32, 2006,
29–55; C.-S. Wong and K. S. Law. The
effects of leader and follower emotional
intelligence on performance and attitude.
Leadership Quarterly, 13, 2002, 243–274; S.
Cote and C. T. H. Miners. Emotional
intelligence, cognitive intelligence and job
performance. *Administrative Science
Quarterly*, 51, 2006, 1–28.

10. Leadership lessons from survivors:
Climbing on the mountain's schedule, not
ours. Retrieved from the Knowledge@
Wharton: Leadership and Change Web

site, knowledge.wharton.upenn.edu (June
2006).

11. P. Balkundi and D. A. Harrison. Ties, leaders, and time in teams: Strong inference
about network structure's effects on team
viability and performance. *Academy of
Management Journal*, 49, 2006, 49–68.

12. For an alternative perspective, see R. M.
Kramer. The great intimidators. *Harvard
Business Review*, February 2006, 88–96.

13. R. J. Sternberg and V. Vroom. The person
versus the situation in leadership.
Leadership Quarterly, 13, 2002, 301–323.

14. D. McGregor. The human side of enter-
prise. *Management Review*, 46(11), 1957,
22–28, reprinted in *Reflections: The SOL
Journal*, Fall 2000, 6–14; G. Heil, D. C.
Stephens, D. McGregor, and W. G. Bennis.
*Douglas McGregor, Revisited: Managing the
Human Side of the Enterprise*. New York:
John Wiley & Sons, 2000.

15. R. R. Blake and J. S. Mouton. *The
Managerial Grid*. Houston: Gulf, 1985; L.
S. Pheng and B. S. K. Lee. "Managerial
Grid" and Zhuge Liang's "Art of
Management": Integration for effective
project management. *Management Decisions*,
35, 1997, 382–392.

16. B. Grow. Renovating Home Depot.
Business Week, March 6, 2006, 50–58.

17. G. Ruiz. Playing together. *Workforce
Management*, June 26, 2006, 27–34.

18. R. F. Littrell. Desirable leadership behaviors of multi-cultural managers in China.
Journal of Management Development, 21,
2002, 5–74.

19. G. A. Yukl. *Leadership in Organizations*, 6th
ed. Upper Saddle River, NJ: Prentice Hall,
2005.

20. L. D. Shaeffer. The leadership journey.
Harvard Business Review, October 2002,
42–47.

21. P. Hersey, K. H. Blanchard, and D. E.
Johnson. *Management of Organizational
Behavior: Leading Human Resources*, 9th ed.
Upper Saddle River, NJ: Prentice Hall,
2006.

22. P. Hersey, K. H. Blanchard, and D. E.
Johnson, *Management of Organizational
Behavior: Leading Human Resources*, 8th ed.
Upper Saddle River, NJ: Prentice Hall,
2001, 182. Copyright © 2001, Center for
Leadership Studies, Escondido, CA. Used
with permission.

23. K. Brooker. It took a lady to save Avon.
Fortune, October 15, 2001, 203–208; P.
Sellers. True grit. *Fortune*, October 14,
2002, 101–110; Business Week Staff. The
best (& worst) managers of the year.
Business Week, January 13, 2003, 8–11;
Executive sweet: Andrea Jung Asian
American Wonder Woman,
www.goalsea.com/WW/Jungandrea/
jungandrea.html (June 2006); A conversa-
tion with Andrea Jung. *Business Week*,
February 6, 2006, 104.

24. D. Brady. The glass ceiling's iron girders.
Business Week, March 25, 2005; C. R.
Schoenberger. Technicolor dreams. *Forbes*,
July 4, 2005; The cow in the ditch: How
Ann Mulcahy rescued Xerox. Retrieved
from Knowledge@Wharton Web site,
knowledge.wharton.upenn.edu (November
16, 2005).

25. R. E. deVries, R. A. Roe, and T. C. B.
Tallieu. Need for leadership as a moderator
of the relationships between leadership and
individual outcomes. *Leadership Quarterly*,
13, 2002, 121–137.

26. *Adapted from* V. H. Vroom. Leadership and
the decision-making process. *Organizational
Dynamics*, Spring 2000, 82–94.

27. V. H. Vroom. Leadership and the decision-
making process. *Organizational Dynamics*,
Spring 2000, 82–94. Used with permission.

28. *Adapted from* Vroom. Leadership and the
decision-making process.

29. A. Sornech. The effects of leadership style
and team process on performance and
innovation in functionally heterogeneous
teams. *Journal of Management*, 32, 2006,
132–157.

30. For an interesting example, see S. Yun, S.
Faraj, and H. P. Sims, Jr. Contingent leadership and effectiveness in trauma resuscitation teams. *Journal of Applied Psychology*,
90, 2005, 1288–1296.

31. K. R. Xin and L. H. Pelled.
Supervisor–subordinate conflict and perceptions of leadership behavior: A field
study. *Leadership Quarterly*, 14, 2003,
25–40.

32. K. R. Brousseau, M. J. Driver, G.
Hourihan, and Rikard Larsson. The sea-
soned executive's style. *Harvard Business
Review*, February 2006, 111–121.

33. F. J. Yammarino, W. D. Spangler, and A. J.
Dubinsky. Transformational and contingent
reward leadership: Individual dyad and
group levels of analysis. *Leadership
Quarterly*, 9, 1998, 27–54; B. M. Bass and
R. E. Riggio. *Transformational leadership*,
2nd ed. Mahwah, NJ: Lawrence Erlbaum,
2006.

34. J. R. McColl-Kennedy and R. D.
Anderson. Impact of leadership style and
emotions on subordinate performance.
Leadership Quarterly, 13, 2002, 545–559.

35. B. M. Bass, D. J. Jung, B. J. Avolio, and Y.
Berson. Predicting unit performance by
assessing transformational and transactional
leadership. *Journal of Applied Psychology*, 88,
2003, 207–218; K. T. Durks and D. L.
Ferrin. Trust in leadership: Meta-analytic
findings and implications for research and
practice. *Journal of Applied Psychology*, 87,
2002, 611–628.

36. *Adapted from* H. H. Friedman, M.
Lingbert, and K. Giladi. Transformational
leadership: Instituting revolutionary change
in accounting. *National Public Accountant*,
May 2000, 8–11; B. J. Avolio. *Full*

Leadership Development: Building the Vital Forces in Organizations. Thousand Oaks, CA: Sage, 1999; B. J. Avolio and B. M. Bass (Eds.), *Developing Potential across a Full Range of Leadership*. Mahwah, NJ: Erlbaum Associates, 2002.

37. P. LaBarre. Hospitals are about healing; This one is about changing lives. *Fast Company*, May 2002, 64–78.

38. D. De Cremer and D. van Knippenberg. How do leaders promote cooperation? The effects of charisma and procedural fairness. *Journal of Applied Psychology*, 87, 2002, 858–866.

39. M. Schminke, M. L. Ambrose, and D. O. Neubaum. The effect of leader moral development on ethical climate and employee attitudes. *Organizational Behavior and Human Decision Processes*, 2005, 97, 135–151; M. E. Brown, L. K. Treviño, and D. A. Harrison. Ethical leadership: A social learning perspective for construct development and testing. *Organizational Behavior and Human Decision Processes*, 97, 2005, 117–134; R. Piccolo and J. A. Colquitt. Transformational leadership and job behaviors: The mediating role of core job characteristics. *Academy of Management Journal*, 49, 2006, 327–341.

40. C. E. Johnson. *Meeting the Ethical Challenges of Leadership. Casting Light or Shadow*. Thousand Oaks, CA: Sage, 2002; S. S. Tzafrir and S. L. Dolan. Trust me: A scale for measuring manager–employee trust. *Management Research*, Spring 2004, 2, 115–152; see also In the spotlight: William D. Harvey, Alliant Energy. *American Gas*, February 2006, 36–38.

41. J. Muller. The impatient Mr. Ghosn. *Forbes*, May 22, 2006, 104–108.

42. R. Kark, B. Shamir, and G. Chen. The two faces of transformational leadership: Empowerment and dependency. *Journal of Applied Psychology*, 88, 2003, 246–255; K. S. Groves. Linking leader skills, follower attitudes, and contextual variables via an integrated model of charismatic leadership. *Journal of Management*, 31, 2005, 255–277; B. Erdogan, R. C. Liden and M. L. Kraimer. Justice and leader–member exchange: The moderating role of organizational culture. *Academy of Management Journal*, 49, 2006, 395–406.

43. J. Guyon. The soul of a money making machine. *Fortune*, October 3, 2005, 113–120.

44. J. A. Byne. Jeff Immelt: The *Fast Company* interview. *Fast Company*, July 2005, 80–86.

45. S. Caudron. Where have all the leaders gone? *Workforce*, December 2002, 29–32; see also W. C. Byham, A. B. Smith, and M. J. Paese. *Grow Your Own Leaders: How to Identify, Develop, and Retain Leadership Talent*. Upper Saddle River, NJ: Prentice Hall, 2002.

46. J. M. Coh, R. Khurana, and L. Reeves. Growing talent as if your business depended on it. *Harvard Business Review*, October 2005, 62–70.

47. The cow in the ditch: How Ann Mulcahy rescued Xerox. Retrieved from Knowledge@Wharton Web site, knowledge.wharton.upenn.edu (November 16, 2005).

48. J. Mullick. Holding a seat for top talent. *Workforce Management*, March 2005, 45–46.

49. E. White. What would you do? Ethics courses get context. *Wall Street Journal*, June 12, 2006, B3; C. Huff. Framing a culture. *Workforce Management*, May 9, 2006, 28–36.

50. D. C. Feldman and M. J. Lankau. Executive coaching: A review and agenda for future research. *Journal of Management*, 2005, 31, 829–848; D. P. Shuitt. Huddling with the coach. *Workforce Management*, February 2006, 53–57.

51. A. Marsh. The art of work. *Fast Company*, August 2005, 77–79.

52. L. Deen. One on one with Grace Lieblein. *Hispanic Engineer & Information Technology Online*. www.hispanicengineer.com (June 2006).

53. For tips on getting a mentor, see M. Heffernan and S.-N. Joni. Of protégés and pitfalls. *Fast Company*, August 2005, 81–83.

54. *Adapted from* M. Javidan, P. W. Dorfman, M. S. de Loupe, and R. J. House. In the eye of the beholder: Cross cultural lessons in leadership from GLOBE. *Academy of Management Perspectives*, February 2006, 67–90. See also D. Nilsen, B. Kowske, and K. Anthony. Managing globally. *HR Magazine*, August 2005, 11–15.

55. *Adapted from* J. Marquez. Companies send employees on volunteer projects abroad to cultivate leadership skills. *Workforce Management*, November 2005, 50–52.

56. N. S. Schutte, J. M. Malouf, L. E. Hall, D. J. Haggerty, J. T. Cooper, C. J. Golden, and L. Dornheim. Development and validation of a measures of emotional intelligence. *Personality and Individual Differences*, 25, 1998, 167–177.

57. S. E. Ante. The new Blue. *Business Week*, March 17, 2003, 80–88; S. E. Ante and I. Sager. IBM's new boss. *Business Week*, February 11, 2002, www.businessweek.com (June 2006); S. Palmisano. The information puzzle: Issues 2006. *Newsweek*, December 2, 2005; C. Barker. IBM boss spells out a better future. http://news.com.com (June 12, 2006); C. Noon. Palmisano's IBM continues passage to India. *Forbes*, June 9, 2006, www.forbes.com; S. Hamm. Innovation: The view from the top. *Business Week*, April 3, 2006, 52–54.

Chapter 16

1. *Adapted from* M. Myser. Marketing made easy. *Business 2.0*, June 2006, 43–45, and www.staples.com (June 2006).

2. J. Penrose, R. W. Rasberry, and R. Myers. *Business Communication for Managers*. Mason, OH: Thomson South-Western, 2004.

3. A. Molinsky and J. Margolis. The emotional tightrope of downsizing: Hidden challenges for leaders and their organizations. *Organizational Dynamics*, 35, 2006, 145–159.

4. D. A. Whetten and K. S. Cameron. *Developing Management Skills*, 6th ed. Upper Saddle River, NJ: Pearson/Prentice Hall, 2005, 207–246.

5. Personal communication with R. Sorrentino, Partner, Deloitte Consulting, June 2006.

6. M. N. Ruderman and P. J. Ohlott. Coaching women leaders. In S. Ting and P. Scisco (Eds.). *The CCL Handbook of Coaching: A Guide for the Leader Coach*. San Francisco, CA: Jossey-Bass, 2006, 65–91; A. Varma, S. M. Toh, and P. Budhwar. A new perspective on the female expatriate experience: The role of host country national categorization. *Journal of World Business*, 41, 2006, 112–120.

7. V. Manusov and A. R. Trees. "Are you kidding me?" The role of nonverbal cues. *Journal of Communication*, 52, 2002, 640–657.

8. Sorrentino, Personal communication.

9. S. E. Jones and C. D. LeBaron. Research of the relationship between verbal and nonverbal communications. *Journal of Communication*, 52, 2002, 499–523.

10. L. DeLay and M. Dalton. Coaching across cultures. In Ting and Scisco, *The CCL Handbook*, 122–148; M. Janssens, T. Cappellen, and P. Zanoni. Successful female expatriates as agents: Positioning oneself through gender, hierarchy, and culture. *Journal of World Business*, 41, 2006, 133–148.

11. *Adapted from* J. W. Gibson and R. M. Hodgetts. *Organizational Communication: A Managerial Perspective*. Orlando, FL: Academic Press, 1986, 99.

12. Based on E. Hall. *Understanding Cultural Differences*. Yarmouth, ME: Intercultural Press, 1989; M. Munter. *Guide to Managerial Communication*, 6th ed. Upper Saddle River, NJ: Prentice Hall, 2002; Workplace potpourri: Strict etiquette in Japanese firms lives on. *Manpower Argus*, August 1996, 11.

13. A. M. Konrad. Engaging employees through high-involvement work practices. *Ivey Business Journal Online*, March/ April 2006, 1–6; G. L. Stewart. A meta-analytic review of relationships between team design features and team performance. *Journal of Management*, 32, 2006, 29–56.

14. M. Chen. *Inside Chinese Business*. Boston: Harvard Business Press, 2001, 88–91.

15. I. Ross. Good ch'i helps businesses prosper: Feng shui practitioners hail ancient Chinese practice as savior to workplace balance. *Northern Ontario Business*, 22(11),

2002, 15–16; K. R. Carter. *Move Your Stuff, Change Your Life: How to Use Feng Shui to Get Love, Money and Happiness.* New York: Fireside Books, 2000.

16. H. Aguinis and C. A. Henle. Effects of nonverbal behavior on perceptions of female employees' power base. *Journal of Social Psychology*, 141, 2001, 537–548.

17. *Adapted from* R. Parloff. Not exactly. *Fortune*, May 1, 2006, 108–116.

18. J. R. Carlson and R. W. Zmud. Channel exposition theory and the experiential nature of media richness perceptions. *Academy of Management Journal*, 42, 1999, 153–170.

19. www.llbean.com (June 2006)

20. A. Dragoon. The amazing traveling show. *CIO*, November 1, 2002, 96–101.

21. J. S. Lubin. Dear boss: I'd rather not tell you my name, but. . . . *Wall Street Journal*, June 18, 1997, B1.

22. L. Gratton and S. Ghosal. Improving the quality of conversations. *Organizational Dynamics*, 31, 2002, 209–223.

23. D. J. Monetta. The power of affinity group. *Management Review*, 87(10),1998, 70–71.

24. *Adapted from* A. Kamenetz. The network unbound. *Fast Company*, June 2006, 69–73.

25. *Adapted from* Whetten and Cameron, *Developing Management Skills*, 23–24. Used with permission.

26. P. A. Heslin, G. P. Latham, and D. VandeWalle. The effect of implicit person theory on performance appraisals. *Journal of Applied Psychology*, 90, 2005, 842–856.

27. Personal communication with Allison Connally, Director, Human Resources Manager, SW Real Estate, Dallas, TX, June 2006.

28. D. Butcher and M. Clarke. Organizational politics. *Organizational Dynamics*, 31, 2002, 35–46.

29. Ting and Scisco, *The CCL Handbook*.

30. L. DeLay and M. Dalton, Coaching across cultures.

31. *Adapted from* M. Chen, *Inside Chinese Business*, 130–136.

32. W. L. Cron, J. W. Slocum, D. VandeWalle, and F. Fu. The role of goal orientation on negative emotions and goal setting when initial performance falls short of one's performance goal. *Human Performance*, 18(1), 2005, 55–80.

33. Whetten and Cameron, *Developing Management Skills*, 228–229.

34. These guidelines are abridged from *Ten Commandments for Good Communications.* New York: American Management Association, 1955.

35. D. V. Newman. Impersonal interactions and ethics of the World-Wide-Web. *Ethics and Information Technology*, 3(4), 2001, 239–247.

36. www.brook.edu/its/cei/cei_hp.htm (June 2006).

37. *Adapted from* K. D. Kelsey. Computer ethics: An overview of the issues. *Ethics: Easier Said Than Done*, December 15, 1991, 30–33; T. E. Webber. Does anything go? *Wall Street Journal*, December 8, 1997, R29–31.

38. www.cpsr.org (June 2006); R. Brenner. Email ethics. *Canyon Consulting*, 5(14), 2005.

39. B. C. Stahl. Responsibility for information assurance and privacy: A problem for individual ethics? *Journal of Organizational and End User Computing*, July/September 2004, 59–78.

40. *Adapted from* J. S. Osland, D. A. Kolb, and I. M. Rubin. *Organizational Behavior: An Experiential Approach*, 7th ed. Upper Saddle River, NJ: Prentice Hall, 2001,150–151. Used with permission; J. I. Castican and M. A. Schmeidler. Communication climate inventory. In J. W. Pfeiffer and L. D. Goodstein (Eds.). *The 1984 Annual: Developing Human Resources.* Copyright © 1984 by Pfeiffer and Company, San Diego, CA. Used with permission.

41. *Adapted from* L. L. Berry. Clueing in customers. *Harvard Business Review*, 81(2) 2003, 100–107; L. Berry. Communicating without words. *Healthcare Design*, September 2002, 15–18; S. H. Haeckel, L. P. Carbone, and L. L. Berry. How to lead the customer experience. *Marketing Management*, January/February 2003, 18–23.

Chapter 17

1. *Adapted from* Small groups, big ideas. *Workforce Management*, February 26, 2006, 22–27; A. Deutschman. The fabric of creativity. *Fast Company*, December 2004, 54–62.

2. See H. Oh, M.-H. Chung, and G. Labianca. Group social capital and group effectiveness: The role of informal socializing ties. *Academy of Management Journal*, 2004, 47, 860–875.

3. C. R. Emery and L. D. Fredenall. The effect of teams on firm profitability and customer satisfaction. *Journal of Service Research*, 4, 2002, 217–229; L. Gordon. Winning with teamwork. *American Machinist*, September 2006, 38–39.

4. A. Ignatius and L. A. Locke. In search of the real Google. *Time*, February 20, 2006, 36–49; A. Deutschman. Can Google stay Google? *Fast Company*, August 2005, 62–68; A. Ehrbar. Breakaway brands. *Fortune*, October 31, 2005, 153–170; http://www.google.com/intl/en/corporate/culture.html (February 18, 2006); M. Conlin. Champions of innovation. *BW*, June 2006, 18–25.

5. M. A. West and G. Hirst. Cooperation and teamwork for innovation. In M. A. West, D. Tjosvold, and K. G. Smith (Eds.). *International Handbook of Organizational Teamwork and Cooperative Working.* Chichester, England: John Wiley & Sons, 2003, 297–319.

6. S. Saeed. A "personnel" decision. *American Gas*, March 2006, 22.

7. R. L. Cross, A. Yan, and M. R. Louis. Boundary activities in "boundaryless" organizations: A case study of a transformation to a team-based structure. *Human Relations*, 2000, 56, 841–859. For several excellent articles describing the work of multinational multidisciplinary teams, see the entire issue of the *Journal of World Business*, Vol. 31, 2003.

8. *Adapted from* A. M. Thayer. The genomics evolution. *Chemical & Engineering News*, 81(49), 2003, 17–26.

9. For a description of the change process, see P. C. Palmes. *The magic of self-directed work teams. A case-study in courage and culture change.* Milwaukee, WI: American Society for Quality, 2006.

10. B. L. Kirkman and B. Rosen. Powering up teams. *Organizational Dynamics*, Winter 2000, 48–66; J. E. Mathieu, L. L. Gibson, and T. M. Ruddy. Empowerment and team effectiveness: An empirical test of an integrated model. *Journal of Applied Psychology*, 91, 2006, 97–108.

11. B. L. Kirkman and J. E. Mathieu. The dimensions and antecedents of team virtuality. *Journal of Management*, 31, 2005, 700–718; J. M. Kumar. Working as a designer in a global team. *Interactions*, March/April 2006, 25–27.

12. M. Lu, M. B. Watson-Manheim, K. M. Chudoba, and W. Wynn. *Journal of Global Information Technology Management*, 9, 2006, 4–24; M. Janssens and J. M. Brett. Cultural intelligence in global teams: A fusion model of collaboration. *Group and Organization Management*, 31, 2006, 124–154.

13. *Adapted from* S. E. Jackson, K. E. May, and K. Whitney. Understanding the dynamics of diversity in decision making teams. In R. A. Guzzo, E. Salas, and Associates (Eds.). *Team Effectiveness and Decision Making in Organizations.* San Francisco: Jossey-Bass, 1995, 204–261; see also J. R. Hackman. *Leading Teams: Setting the Stage for Great Performances.* Boston: Harvard Business School, 2002; G. L. Stewart. A meta-analytic review of relationships between team design features and team performance. *Journal of Management*, 32, 2006, 29–54.

14. J. R. Hackman and R. Wageman. A theory of team coaching. *Academy of Management Review*, 30, 2005, 269–287.

15. G. Weissman. Scientists are on a roll as they reinvent the ball. *Financial Times*, March 3, 2006, 8.

16. G. L. Stewart. A meta-analytic review of relationships between team design features and team performance. *Journal of Management*, 32, 2006, 29–54.

17. M. Hoegl and H. G. Gemuenden. Teamwork quality and the success of innovative projects: A theoretical concept and empirical evidence. *Organization Science*, 12, 2001, 435–449; S. W. Lester, B. M. Meglino, and M. A. Korsgaard. The antecedents and consequences of group

potency: A longitudinal investigation of newly formed work groups. *Academy of Management Journal*, 45, 2002, 352–368; D. J. Beal, R. R. Cohen, M. J. Burke, and C. L. McLendon. Cohesion and performance in groups: A meta-analytic clarification of construct relations. *Journal of Applied Psychology*, 88, 2003, 989–1004.

18. K. T. Dirks. The effects of interpersonal trust on work group performance. *Journal of Applied Psychology*, 84, 1999, 445–555; T. L. Simons and R. S. Peterson. Task conflict and relationship conflict in top management teams: The pivotal role of intragroup trust. *Journal of Applied Psychology*, 85, 2000, 102–111; P. H. Kim, R. L. Pinkley, and A. R. Fragale. Power dynamics in negotiations. *Academy of Management Review*, 30, 2005, 799–823.

19. *Adapted and modified from* B. W. Tuckman, and M. A. C. Jensen. Stages of small-group development revisited. *Group and Organization Studies*, 2, 1977, 419–442; B. W. Tuckman. Developmental sequence in small groups. *Psychological Bulletin*, 63, 1965, 384–389; C. J. G. Gersick. Marking time: Predictable transitions in task groups. *Academy of Management Journal*, 32, 1989, 274–309; A. Chang, P. Bordia, and J. Duck. Punctuated equilibrium and linear progression: Toward a new understanding of group development. *Academy of Management Journal*, 46, 2003, 106–117.

20. K. A. Jehn and E. A. Mannix. The dynamic nature of conflict: A longitudinal study of intragroup conflict and group performance. *Academy of Management Journal*, 44, 2001, 238–251; M. A. Marks, J. E. Matthieu, and S. J. Zaccaro. A temporally based framework and taxonomy of team processes. *Academy of Management Review*, 26, 2001, 356–375.

21. M. J. Waller, M. E. Zeller-Bruhn, and R. C. Giambatista. Watching the clock: Group pacing behavior under dynamic deadlines. *Academy of Management Journal*, 45, 2002, 1046–1055.

22. M. J. Stevens and M. A. Campion. The knowledge, skill, and ability requirements for teamwork: Implications for human resource management. *Journal of Management*, 20, 1994, 503–530; A. M. O'Leary, J. J. Martocchio, and D. D. Frink. A review of the influence of group goals on group performance. *Academy of Management Journal*, 37, 1994, 1285–1301.

23. E. D. Pulakos, D. W. Dorsey, and R. A. Mueller-Hanson. PDRI's Adaptability Research Program SIOP presentation. *The Industrial Psychologist*, 43, 2005, 25–32.

24. A. Lashinsky. RAZR's edge. *Fortune*, June 12, 2006, 124–132.

25. For a more detailed discussion, see M. A. West. The human team: Basic motivations and innovations. In N. Anderson, D. S. Ones, H. K. Sinangil, and C. Viswesvaran (Eds.). *Handbook of Industrial, Work, and Organizational Psychology*, Vol. 2, London: Sage, 2001, 270–288; M. A. Korsgaard, S. E. Brodt, and H. J. Sapienza. Trust, identity, and attachment: Promoting individuals' cooperation in groups. In West et al., *International Handbook of Organizational Teamwork and Cooperative Working*, 113–130.

26. J. W. Bishop and E. D. Scott. An examination of organizational and team commitment in a self-directed team environment. *Journal of Applied Psychology*, 85, 2000, 439–450.

27. Beal et al., Cohesion and performance in groups .

28. S. F. Gale. No sacred cows, small or large. *Workforce*, February 2003, 60–62.

29. R. R. Hirschfeld, M. H. Jordan, H. S. Field, W. F. Giles, and A. A. Armenakis. Become team players: Team members' mastery of teamwork knowledge as a predictor of team task proficiency and observed team effectiveness. *Journal of Applied Psychology*, 91, 2006, 467–474.

30. A. Zander. *Making Groups Effective*, 2nd ed. San Francisco: Jossey-Bass, 1994.

31. B. Mullen, T. Anthony, E. Salas, and J. E. Driskell. Group cohesiveness and quality of decision making: An integration of tests of the groupthink hypothesis. *Small Group Research*, 25, 1994, 189–204; S. M. Miranda. Avoidance of groupthink: Meeting management using group support systems. *Small Group Research*, 25, 1994, 105–136.

32. K. M. Eisenhardt, J. L. Kahwajy, and L. J. Bourgeois III. Conflict and strategic choice: How top management teams disagree. *California Management Review*, 39, 1997, 42–62.

33. Hay Group. *Top Teams: Why Some Work and Some Don't.* Philadelphia, PA: Hay, 2001.

34. A. Malhotra and A. Majchrzak. Teams across borders. *Financial Times*, March 30, 2006 (Supplement: Mastering Uncertainty), 11.

35. For a discussion of how managers should use problem diagnosis and coaching to improve team performance, see Hackman and Wageman, A theory of team coaching.

36. R. Wageman. How leaders foster self-managing team effectiveness: Design choices versus hands-on coaching. *Organization Science*, 12, 2001, 557–577.

37. D. C. Ganster and D. J. Dwyer. The effects of understaffing on individual and group performance in professional and trade occupations. *Journal of Management*, 21, 1995, 175–190.

38. A. P. Hare. Group size. *American Behavioral Scientist*, 24, 1981, 695–708; G. G. Rutte. Social loafing in teams. In West et al., *International Handbook of Organizational Teamwork and Cooperative Working*, 361–378.

39. E. Sundstrom, K. P. DeMeuse, and D. Futrell. Work teams: Applications and effectiveness. *American Psychologist*, 45, 1990, 120–133; K. G. Smith and Associates. Top management team demography and process: The role of social integration and communication. *Administrative Science Quarterly*, 39, 1994, 412–438.

40. B. L. Kirkman and D. I. Shapiro. The impact of cultural values on job satisfaction and organizational commitment in self-managing work teams: The mediating role of employee resistance. *Academy of Management Journal*, 44, 2001, 557–569.

41. For a comparison of the United States and several European countries, see J. B. Leslie and E. VanVelsor. *A Cross-National Comparison of Effective Leadership and Teamwork: Toward a Global Workforce.* Greensboro, NC: Center for Creative Leadership, 1998; see also C. B. Gibson and M. E. Zellmer-Bruhn. Metaphors and meaning: An intercultural analysis of the concept of teamwork. *Administrative Science Quarterly*, 46, 2001, 274–303; P. C. Earley and C. B. Gibson. *Multinational Work Teams: A New Perspective*. Mahwah, NJ: Lawrence Erlbaum, 2002.

42. G. A. Neuman and J. Wright. Team effectiveness: Beyond skills and cognitive ability. *Journal of Applied Psychology*, 84, 1999, 376–389; S. Taggar. Individual creativity and group ability to utilize creative resources: A multilevel model. *Academy of Management Journal*, 45, 2002, 315–330.

43. G. Colvin. Why dream teams fail. *Fortune*, June 12, 2006, 87–92.

44. A. Edmondson, R. Bohmer, and G. Pisano. Speeding up team learning. *Harvard Business Review*, October 2001, 125–132.

45. The new right stuff. *Fortune*, June 12, 2006, 16–20.

46. R. R. Hirschfeld, M. H. Jordan, H. S. Field, W. F. Giles, and A. A. Armenakis. Becoming team players: Team members' mastery of teamwork knowledge as a predictor of team task proficiency and observed team effectiveness. *Journal of Applied Psychology*, 91, 2006, 467–474.

47. M. A. Marks, M. J. Sabella, C. S. Burke, and S. J. Zaccaro. The impact of cross-training on team effectiveness. *Journal of Applied Psychology*, 87, 2002, 3–13.

48. S. M. Gully, K. A. Incalcaterra, A. Joshi, and J. M. Beaubien. A meta-analysis of team-efficacy, potency, and performance: Interdependence and level of analysis as moderators of observed relationships. *Journal of Applied Psychology*, 87, 2002, 819–832.

49. D. S. DeRue and F. P. Morgeson. Developing taxonomy of team leadership behavior in self-managing teams. Paper presented at the Twentieth Annual Conference of the Society for Industrial and Organizational Psychology, Los Angeles, CA, 2005.

50. C. K. W. De Dreu and M. A. West. Minority dissent and team innovation: The importance of participation in decision making. *Journal of Applied Psychology*, 86, 2001, 1191–2000; L. Thompson. Improving the creativity of organizational work groups. *Academy of Management Executive*, 17, 2003, 96–111.

51. S. S. K. Lam and J. Schaubroeck. Improving group decisions by better pooling information: A comparative advantage of group decision support systems. *Journal of Applied Psychology*, 85, 2000, 565–573; For more about the challenges faced by virtual teams, see F. Agarwal. Teamwork in the netcentric organization. In West et al., *International Handbook of Organizational Teamwork and Cooperative Working*.

52. J. McAdams and E. J. Hawk. Making group incentives work. *WorldatWork*, Third Quarter, 2000, 28–39; G. Parker, J. McAdams, and D. Zielinski. *Rewarding Teams: Lessons from the Trenches*. San Francisco: Jossey-Bass, 2000; see also M. D. Johnson, J. R. Hollenbeck, D. R. Ilgen, D. Jundit, and C. J. Meyer. Cutthroat cooperation: Asymmetrical adaptation to changes in team reward structures. *Academy of Management Journal*, 49, 2006, 103–119.

53. B. L. Kirkman, B. Rosen, C. B. Gibson, P. E. Tesluk, and S. O. McPherson. Five challenges to virtual team success: Lessons from Sabre, Inc. *Academy of Management Executive*, 16(3), 2002, 67–79; for more suggestions about leading virtual teams, see the entire issue of *Organizational Dynamics*, 31(4), 2003, which is devoted to this topic. See also S. A. Furst, M. Reeves, B. Rosen, and R. S. Blackburn. Managing the life cycle of virtual teams. *Academy of Management Executive*, 18, 2004, 6–20.

Chapter 18

1. www.dardenrestaurants.com (June 2006); World's largest casual dining company honors its best suppliers with top award. *Fortune*, May 22, 2006; see also V. Liberman. Tough issues. *Across the Board*. May/June 2002, 22–29.

2. N. M. Ashkanasy and C. R. A. Jackson. Organizational culture and climate. In N. Anderson, D. S. Ones, H. K. Sinangil, and C. Viswesvaran (Eds.). *Handbook of Industrial, Work, and Organizational Psychology*, Vol. 2. London: Sage, 2001, 398–415.

3. S. E. Seibert, S. R. Silver, and W. A. Randolph. Taking empowerment to the next level: A multi-level model of empowerment, performance and satisfaction. *Academy of Management Journal*, 47, 2004, 332–449; U. Fairbairn. HR as a strategic partner: Culture change as an American Express story. *Human Resource Management*, 44(1), 2005, 79–84.

4. J. Schlosser. Another space race. *Fortune*, June 12, 2006, 120.

5. G. B. Voss, D. M. Cable, and Z. G. Voss. Linking organizational values to relationships with external constituencies. A study of nonprofit professional theatres. *Organizational Science*, 11, 2000, 330–347.

6. P. Hemp. My week as a room-service waiter at the Ritz. *Harvard Business Review*, June 2002, 50–62.

7. K. Bonamici. Decoding the dress code. *Fortune*, January 11, 2006, 130–131.

8. C. Lachnit. Cheesy corporate cheers. *Workforce*, October 2002, 19.

9. J. Ridgeway, Bank selects its "idol." *Courier News*, May 25, 2006, 3.

10. A. R. Jassawalla and H. C. Sashittal. Cultures that support product-innovation processes. *Academy of Management Executive*, 16(3), 2002, 42–54.

11. M. Josephson. *Living the credo: Making good decisions at Johnson & Johnson*. Josephson Institute of Ethics, 2003; www.jnj.com (June 2006).

12. H. M. Trice and J. M. Beyer. Cultural leadership in organizations. *Organization Science*, 2, 1991, 149–169.

13. S. F. Gale. Big corporation embraces quirky culture. *Workforce*. February 2003, 61.

14. *Adapted from* R. Hooijberg and F. Petrock. On cultural change: Using the competing values framework to help leaders execute a transformational strategy. *Human Resource Management*, 32, 1993, 29–50, R. E. Quinn. *Beyond Rational Management: Mastering the Paradoxes and Competing Demands of High Performance*. San Francisco: Jossey-Bass, 1988.

15. S. G. Harris and K. W. Mossholder. The affective implications of perceived congruence with culture dimensions during organizational transformation. *Journal of Management*, 22, 1996, 527–547.

16. D. A. Morand. The role of behavioral formality and informality in the enactment of bureaucratic versus organic organizations. *Academy of Management Review*, 20, 1995, 831–872.

17. L. Rubis. Cultural consistency amid change at Analytic Graphics. *HR Magazine*, July 2005, 58–59; Best Small & Medium Companies to Work for in America. Retrieved from www.greatplacetowork.com (August 2006).

18. G. Apfelthaler, H. J. Muller, and R. R. Rehder. Corporate global culture as a competitive advantage: Learning from Germany and Japan in Alabama and Austria? Journal of World Business, 37, 2002, 108–118; R. J. Newman. Productivity payoff. U.S. News& World Report, February 24, 2003; D. Sherman. 2006 Mercedes-Benz M-class. Automobile. www.automobilemag.com (June 2006); W. Glanz. Alabama auto union drive launched. *The Washington Times*, March 27, 2006. Retrieved from www.wpherald.com (June 2006).

19. E. H. Schein. What is culture? In P. J. Frost, L. F. Moore, M. R. Louis, C. C. Lundberg, and J. Martin (Eds.). *Reframing Organizational Culture*. Newbury Park, CA: Sage, 1991, 243–253.

20. J. B. Sorensen. The strength of corporate culture and the reliability of firm performance. *Administrative Science Quarterly*, 47, 2002, 70–91; B. Schneider, A. N. Salvaggio, and M. Subirats. Climate strength: A new direction for climate research. *Journal of Applied Psychology*, 87, 2002, 220–229.

21. N. Varchaver. Who's the king of Delaware? *Fortune*, May 13, 2002, 125–130; www.mbna.com/.

22. Towers Perrin. *The Role of Human Capital in M&A: A White Paper Based on Opinions of 132 Senior Executives Worldwide*. London: Towers Perrin, 2002; see also P. Pauntler. *The Effects of Mergers and Postmerger Integration*. Federal Trade Commission, 2003.

23. J. P. van Oudenhove and K. I. van der Zee. Successful international cooperation: The influence of cultural similarity, strategic differences, and international experience. *Applied Psychology: An International Review*, 51, 2002, 633–653.

24. E. Tahmincioglu. On the same flight plan. *Workforce Management*, January 16, 2006, 22–28.

25. B. McConnell. Fun at work good for business, HR pros say in survey. *HR News*, January 2003, 18.

26. L. Saari and M. Erez. Cross-cultural diversity and employee attitudes. Paper presented at the annual conference of the Society for Industrial and Organizational Psychology, Toronto, April 2002.

27. C. Daniels. Pioneers. *Fortune*, August 22, 2005, 73–88.

28. www.gov.census (June 2006); A. Kane. Minority milestone. *The Denver Post*, May 10, 2006, 1; A. Zolli. Demographics: The population hourglass. *Fast Company*, March 2006, 57–64.

29. L. C. Lancaster and D. Stillman. *When Generations Collide*. New York: Harper Business, 2002; T. Gutner. A balancing act for Gen X women. *Business Week*, January 21, 2002, 82; W. G. Bennis and R. J. Thomas. *Geeks and Geezers: How Era, Values and Defining Moments Shape Leaders*. Boston: Harvard Business School Press, 2002.

30. *Adapted from* A. Abramson and M. Silverstein. *Images of Aging in America 2004*. Washington, DC: AARP and University of Southern California, 2006.

31. S. Kershaw. Answering the fire bell in the company of women. *New York Times*, January 23, 2006, A1, A14.

32. S. Ali. Reaching the Hispanic market. *Sunday Star Ledger*, April 10, 2005 (Section 3), 1, 7.

33. C. Daniels. The most powerful black executives in America. *Fortune*, July 22, 2002, 60–80.

34. S. Foley, D. L. Kidder, and G. N. Powell. The perceived glass ceiling and just perceptions: An investigation of Hispanic law associates. *Journal of Management*, 28, 2002, 471–496.

35. K. H. Griffeth and M. R. Hebl. The disclosure dilemma for gay men and lesbians: "Coming out" at work. *Journal of Applied Psychology*, 87, 2002, 1191–1999; M. M. Clark. Religion versus sexual orientation. *HR Magazine*, August 2004, 54–58.

36. R. R. Thomas. *Building on the Promise of Diversity*. New York: Amacom, 2006,

37. G. M. Combs, S. Nadkarni, and M. W. Combs. Implementing affirmative action in multinational corporations. *Organizational Dynamics*, 32, 2005, 346–360.

38. R. O. Crockett. Memo to the Supreme Court: "Diversity is good for business." *Business Week*, January 27, 2003, 96; L. Greenhouse. Justices look for nuance in race-preference case. *New York Times*, April 2, 2003, A1, A15.

39. B. Leonard. Gallup: Workplace bias still prevalent. *HR Magazine*, February 2006, 34. See also Q. M. Roberson and C. K. Stevens. Making sense of diversity in the workplace: Organizational justice and language abstractions in employees' accounts of diversity-related incidents. *Journal of Applied Psychology*, 91, 2006, 379–399.

40. *Adapted from* K. Townsend. Female partners double thanks to gender initiative. *Financial Times*, May 8, 2000, 35; Diversity means encouragement and support. www.deloitte.com/dtt/article/0,1002,sid%253D48823%2526cid%253D69423,00.html (June 2006).

41. Q. M. Roberson and C. K. Stevens. Making sense of diversity in the workplace: Organizational justice and language abstraction in employees' accounts of diversity-related incidents. *Journal of Applied Psychology*, 91, 2006, 379–391.

42. T. Kochan, K. Bezrukova, R. Ely, S. E. Jackson, A. Joshi, K. A. Jehn, J. Leonard, D. Levine, and D. Thomas. The effects of diversity on business performance: Report of the diversity research network. *Human Resource Management Journal*, 42, 2003, 3–22.

43. S. Din. Radio station loses ads after racial slurs. *The Star-Ledger*, May 11, 2005, 19.

44. D. A. Thomas. Diversity as strategy. *Harvard Business Review*, September 2004, 98–108.

45. S. F. Gale. Diversity as a recruitment strategy. *Workforce*, February 2002, 68–69; The Black Collegian Online. www.black-collegian.com/career/top100_diversity2005.shtml (June 2006).

46. M. E. Burke. *SHRM 2005 Benefits Survey Report*. Alexandria, VA: Society for Human Resource Management, 2005.

47. A. Hayashi. Mommy-track backlash. *Harvard Business Review*, March 1997, 3–42; J. Rothauser, J. A. Gonzalez, N. E. Clarke, and L. L. O'Dell. Family-friendly backlash—fact or fiction? The case of organizations' on-site child care centers. *Personnel Psychology*, 51, 1998, 685–706.

48. Parental leave: Healthier kids. *Business Week*, January 18, 1999, 30.

49. C. M. Loder. Merck and Co. breaks new ground for employee child care centers. *Star Ledger*, May 1999, 12.

50. S. Day. Anti-bias task force gives Coca Cola good marks, but says challenges remain. *New York Times*, September 26, 2002, C3

51. J. R. W. Joplin and C. S. Daus. Challenges of leading a diverse workforce. *Academy of Management Executive*, 11(3), 1997, 32–47; J. E. Slaughter, E. F. Sinar, and P. D. Bachiochi. Black applicants' reactions to affirmative action plans: Effects of plan content and previous experience with discrimination. *Journal of Applied Psychology*, 87, 2002, 333–344.

52. S. E. Jackson and A. Joshi. Research on domestic and international diversity in organizations: A merger that works. In N. Anderson, D. S. Ones, H. K. Sinangil, and C. Viswesvaran (Eds.). *Handbook of Work and Organizational Psychology*. Thousand Oaks, CA: Sage, 2001, 206–231.

53. *Adapted from* H. Feldman and A. Osland. The United Way and Boy Scouts of America: Controversy in Portland, Oregon. In P. F. Buller and R. S. Schuler (Eds.). *Managing Organizations and People*, 7th ed. Mason, OH: Thomson South-Western, 2006. Used with permission.

ORGANIZATION INDEX

V

W

X

Y

Z

NAME INDEX

Note: The *n* in selected entries designates a reference. The page number with the R– prefix indicates the page where the note can be found in its entirety. The number following the *n*. is the appropriate footnote number. The number in parentheses indicates the page on which the note reference appears.

A

Abraham, S. C., R–8*n*. 34 (225)
Abrams, A., R–6*n*. 2 (184)
Abramson, A., R–23*n*. 30 (611)
Ackerman, P. L., R–18*n*. 60 (483)
Adams, Eula, 612
Adams, J. S., R–18*n*. 53 (481)
Adamy, J., R–8*n*. 41 (227)
Adelman, P. J., R–7*n*. 47 (199)
Adner, R., R–7*n*. 4 (215)
Adolf, Mary M., 479
Aeppel, T., R–12*n*. 41 (341)
Agarwal, F., R–23*n*. 51 (586)
Agulnis, H., R–21*n*. 16 (538)
Akan, O., R–9*n*. 68 (239)
Al Najjar, M., R–12*n*. 22 (335)
Alavi, M., R–10*n*. 20 (292)
Albert, M., R–15*n*. 52 (409)
Albright, Eileen, 146, R–5*n*. 43 (146)
Alderfer, C. P., R–18*n*. 65 (486)
Aldrich, H. E., R–9*n*. 23 (264)
Ali, S., R–23*n*. 32 (612)
Allair, Paul, 3
Allen, M., R–5*n*. 26 (166)
Allen, R. S., R–9*n*. 68 (239)
Allhoff, F., R–3*n*. 44 (96)
Allscheid, S. P., R–15*n*. 6 (425)
Almost, J., R–16*n*. 48 (444)
Alonso, A., R–1*n*. 22 (21)
Alpaslan, M. C., 258
Alstyne, M. V., R–14*n*. 36 (402)
Amaro, B., R–7*n*. 66 (210)
Ambrose, M. L., R–3*n*. 23 (87), R–3*n*. 30 (91),
    R–20*n*. 39 (515)
Amichai-Hamburger, Y., R–14*n*. 17 (395)
Amy, J., R–9*n*. 21 (263)
Anderson, N., R–16*n*. 39 (440), R–19*n*. 2 (497),
    R–22*n*. 25 (578), R–23*n*. 2 (596),
    R–24*n*. 52 (622)
Anderson, P., R–4*n*. 9 (118)
Anderson, R. D., R–19*n*. 34 (514)
Ansfield, J., R–5*n*. 21 (163)
Ante, S. E., R–20*n*. 57 (527)
Anthes, G. H., R–11*n*. 25 (295)
Anthony, K., R–20*n*. 54 (521)
Anthony, R. N., R–12*n*. 2 (322)
Anthony, S. D., R–15*n*. 50 (409)
Anthony, T., R–22*n*. 31 (579)
Apfelthaler, G., R–23*n*. 18 (605)
Aquilano, N. J., R–2*n*. 7 (49)
Aram, J. D., R–3*n*. 34 (93)
Argyres, N., R–7*n*. 13 (218)
Armenakis, A. A., R–14*n*. 6 (390), R–22*n*. 29 (579),
    R–22*n*. 46 (584)
Armstrong, G., R–5*n*. 12 (155)
Armstrong, J. S., R–11*n*. 30 (297)
Armstrong, Neil, 457
Arndt, M., R–1*n*. 32 (37)
Arnholt, Chris, 577
Aronson, J. E., R–10*n*. 16 (291)
Asacker, Tom, 94
Ash, R. A., R–16*n*. 23 (435)
Ashkanasy, N. M., R–23*n*. 2 (596)
Ashkenas, R. N., R–13*n*. 1 (388), R–14*n*. 13 (393)
Ashley, Stephen, 333
Ault, S., R–5*n*. 43 (146)
Austin, J. T., R–14*n*. 27 (399)
Avery, S., R–1*n*. 7 (10)
Avolio, B. J., R–19*n*. 35 (514), R–19*n*. 36 (514),
    R–20*n*. 36 (514)
Avon, R., R–4*n*. 5 (117)
Axtell, C., R–14*n*. 28 (399)
Ayub, Tahir, 522

B

Bachiochi, P. D., R–24*n*. 51 (622)
Bachmann, John, 267
Back, A., R–10*n*. 4 (287)
Baer, M., R–15*n*. 56 (412)
Bagheri, A., R–4*n*. 59 (102)
Bahnson, P. R., R–12*n*. 31 (337)
Baker, Richard, 74
Baker, W. H., Jr., R–10*n*. 5 (288)
Baldrige, Malcolm, 310–14
Baldwin, A., R–8*n*. 53 (229)
Balgobin, R., R–14*n*. 12 (392)
Balkundi, P., R–19*n*. 11 (502)
Bandura, A., R–18*n*. 30 (467)
Banet, A. G., Jr., R–15*n*. 68 (417)
Barahona, Arturo, 580
Barber, A. E., R–17*n*. 56 (447)
Barber, F., R–2*n*. 12 (53)
Barbuto, J. E., R–19*n*. 9 (499)
Barker, C., R–20*n*. 57 (527)
Barley, S. R., R–4*n*. 15 (121)
Barnard, C., R–2*n*. 15 (54)
Barnard, Chester, 54–55
Barnevik, Percy, 373
Barney, J., R–8*n*. 50 (228)
Baron, B. A., R–6*n*. 20 (188), R–6*n*. 34 (193)
Baron, D. P., R–9*n*. 33 (269)
Baron, J., R–9*n*. 29 (266)
Barrett, A., R–15*n*. 1 (422)
Barrett, D., R–15*n*. 41 (405)
Barringer, B. R., R–6*n*. 8 (185)
Bartram, D., R–1*n*. 3 (5), R–16*n*. 38 (440)
Barwise, P., R–5*n*. 29 (169)
Basil, Thomas, 572
Bass, B. M., R–19*n*. 33 (514), R–19*n*. 35 (514),
    R–19*n*. 36 (514)
Bateman, J., R–14*n*. 26 (398)
Bateman, T. S., R–1*n*. 13 (13)
Bates, S., R–18*n*. 32 (469)
Batt, R., R–17*n*. 57 (447)
Battelle, J., R–1*n*. 1 (4)
Bauer, J. E., R–9*n*. 20 (263)
Baum, H., R–18*n*. 57 (482)
Baum, Herb, 482
Baveja, A., R–12*n*. 22 (335)
Bazerman, R. M. H., R–7*n*. 6 (215), R–9*n*. 16 (261)
Beach, L. R., R–10*n*. 41 (272)
Beal, D. J., R–22*n*. 17 (574), R–22*n*. 27 (578)
Bean, Leon Leonwood, 541
Beard, Shane, 198
Beasty, C., R–9*n*. 6 (256)
Beatty, J. E., R–4*n*. 17 (122)
Beatty, R. W., R–11*n*. 24 (295), R–15*n*. 64 (414)
Beaubien, J. M., R–22*n*. 48 (584)
Becker, B. E., R–11*n*. 24 (295), R–15*n*. 64 (414)
Becker, H., R–4*n*. 66 (109)
Becker, T. H., 158, R–5*n*. 11 (155)
Bedeian, A. G., R–14*n*. 6 (390)
Beer, M., R–13*n*. 3 (388)
Behan, B., R–13*n*. 52 (344)
Beinhocker, E. D., R–7*n*. 2 (215)
Bell, B. S., R–16*n*. 32 (438)
Bendpudi, N., R–2*n*. 29 (66)
Benn, S., R–13*n*. 47 (342)
Bennedsen, M., R–5*n*. 29 (133)
Bennett, N., R–13*n*. 7 (362)
Bennett, W. R., Jr., R–17*n*. 19 (464)
Bennis, W. G., R–19*n*. 14 (503), R–23*n*. 29 (611)
Berbauer, David, 51
Berlin, L., R–15*n*. 42 (405)
Bernard, V. L., R–12*n*. 33 (337)
Berner, R., R–4*n*. 67 (110)
Bernhagen, P., R–5*n*. 30 (133)
Bernstein, A., R–4*n*. 67 (110), R–16*n*. 19 (433)
Bernstein, Nancy, 374

Berrondo, Luis, 167
Berry, L., R–21*n*. 41 (561)
Berry, L. L., R–2*n*. 29 (66), R–9*n*. 25 (264),
    R–21*n*. 41 (561)
Berry, V., R–3*n*. 35 (93)
Berson, Y., R–19*n*. 35 (514)
Bettcher, K. E., 86, R–3*n*. 21 (85)
Beyer, J. M., R–23*n*. 12 (601)
Beyerlein, M., R–15*n*. 43 (406)
Beyerlein, S., R–15*n*. 43 (406)
Bezos, Jeff, 27, 140, 264
Bezrukova, K., R–24*n*. 42 (615)
Bianco, A., R–4*n*. 67 (110)
Biediger, J., R–5*n*. 33 (171)
Bigley, G. A., R–18*n*. 54 (481)
Bilstein, F. F., R–8*n*. 39 (226)
Binzen, P., R–6*n*. 1 (184)
Birger, J., R–8*n*. 53 (229)
Bischmann, Joanne, 251
Bishop, J. W., R–22*n*. 26 (578)
Blackburn, R. S., R–23*n*. 53 (592)
Blake, R. R., R–19*n*. 15 (504)
Blake, Robert, 504
Blanchard, K. H., 507, R–19*n*. 21 (506),
    R–19*n*. 22 (506)
Blanco, Kathleen, 134
Bland-Baker, Cynthia, 48
Block, C. J., R–17*n*. 17 (464)
Bobko, P., R–16*n*. 49 (445)
Bohmer, R., R–22*n*. 44 (583)
Bohn, R., R–9*n*. 14 (260)
Boland, R. J., Jr., R–13*n*. 8 (363)
Bolden, R., R–14*n*. 28 (399)
Bolino, M. C., R–18*n*. 58 (482)
Bommer, W. H., R–18*n*. 59 (483)
Bonamici, K., R–2*n*. 30 (67), R–23*n*. 7 (599)
Bonardi, J., R–4*n*. 27 (132)
Bono, J. E., R–17*n*. 3 (458), R–19*n*. 7 (499)
Boone, Garrett, 18
Boorstein, J., R–6*n*. 22 (189)
Bordia, P., R–22*n*. 19 (574)
Boren, S. A., R–12*n*. 22 (335)
Bos, R. T., R–2*n*. 9 (80)
Bossard, A. B., R–1*n*. 25 (24)
Bourdain, Anthony, 485, R–18*n*. 63 (485)
Bourgeois, L. J., III, R–22*n*. 32 (579)
Boussard, Gerard, 431, 432
Bowen, D. E., 262, R–9*n*. 17 (261)
Bowers, K., R–2*n*. 30 (67)
Bowes-Sperry, L., R–3*n*. 26 (90)
Boxter, G. D., R–3*n*. 23 (87)
Brady, D., R–15*n*. 7 (425), R–19*n*. 24 (509)
Brady, Janet, 423
Brandel, M., R–10*n*. 55 (277)
Brandes, P., R–14*n*. 27 (399)
Branson, Richard, 485, R–18*n*. 62 (485)
Brauninger, T., R–5*n*. 30 (133)
Brautigam, Kurt, 216
Breaugh, J. A., R–16*n*. 25 (436)
Brenner, R., R–21*n*. 38 (556)
Brenner, Rick, 558
Brett, J. M., R–1*n*. 29 (27), R–18*n*. 33 (469),
    R–21*n*. 12 (572)
Bretz, R. D., Jr., R–17*n*. 56 (447)
Brewer, N., R–17*n*. 18 (464)
Brief, A. P., R–17*n*. 17 (464)
Brill, Ed, 60
Brislin, R. W., R–12*n*. 17 (331)
Brockmann, E. N., R–2*n*. 22 (61)
Brockner, J., R–14*n*. 35 (402), R–16*n*. 21 (434)
Brodsky, N., R–7*n*. 50 (200)
Brodsky, Norm, 200
Brodt, S. E., R–22*n*. 25 (578)
Brooker, K., R–13*n*. 54 (346), R–14*n*. 16 (395),
    R–19*n*. 23 (508)

Brousseau, K.,
Brousseau, K. R., R–9n. 37 (270), R–19n. 32 (514)
Brown, D., R–8n. 60 (235)
Brown, J. S., R–15n. 66 (414)
Brown, K. G., R–16n. 37 (439)
Brown, M. E., R–20n. 39 (515)
Brown, M. G., R–11n. 62 (310)
Brown, Michael, 8
Brown, P., R–12n. 34 (337)
Brown, S. P., R–18n. 44 (476)
Brown, S. W., R–9n. 36 (270)
Browning, Lorrie, 500
Brune, K., R–8n. 20 (220)
Brush, C. G., R–7n. 51 (200)
Brynjolfsson, E., R–14n. 36 (402)
Bucerius, M., R–8n. 39 (226)
Buchan, Carl, 357
Buchanan, L., R–9n. 38 (271)
Buchholtz, A. K., R–3n. 49 (98)
Buchholz, B. B., R–6n. 27 (190)
Buckingham, B., R–17n. 7 (460)
Buckingham, M., R–1n. 21 (20), R–7n. 63 (205),
    R–15n. 6 (425)
Buckley, Dan, 8
Buckley, George, 37
Budhwar, P., R–20n. 6 (533)
Buffet, Warren, 227
Buller, P. F., R–24n. 53 (626)
Burbach, M. E., R–19n. 9 (499)
Burgelman, R. A., R–7n. 2 (215)
Burke, C. S., R–22n. 47 (584)
Burke, D., R–14n. 16 (395)
Burke, M. E., R–24n. 46 (620)
Burke, M. J., R–22n. 17 (574)
Burke, W. W., R–14n. 15 (394)
Burlingham, B., R–6n. 27 (190), R–7n. 50 (200)
Burns, P., R–7n. 63 (205)
Burns, S., R–2n. 6 (79)
Burns, Scott, 79
Burns, T., R–13n. 21 (376)
Burrows, P., R–14n. 11 (391)
Burton, Jake, R–6n. 3 (184)
Busenitz, L. W., R–10n. 44 (273)
Bush, George W., 160, 319
Butcher, D., R–21n. 28 (549)
Buytendijk, F., R–7n. 9 (216)
Byham, W. C., R–20n. 45 (517)
Byne, J. A., R–20n. 44 (517)
Bynes, N., R–18n. 39 (472)
Byrne, Z. S., R–3n. 48 (97)

C

Cable, D. M., R–16n. 30 (438), R–23n. 5 (598)
Cable, J. P., R–17n. 6 (460)
Cadwallader, S., R–9n. 25 (264)
Cameron, K. S., R–20n. 4 (531), R–21n. 25 (544),
    R–21n. 33 (552)
Campbell, A., R–7n. 12 (218)
Campion, M. A., R–16n. 36 (439), R–22n. 22 (576)
Canter, Charles, 360
Cantrell, S., R–9n. 75 (251)
Cappellen, T., R–20n. 10 (535)
Cappelli, Peter, 426
Carberry, E. J., R–2n. 2 (43)
Carbone, L. P., R–21n. 41 (561)
Cardinal, L. B., R–15n. 65 (414)
Cardis, J., R–7n. 49 (200)
Carlson, J. R., R–21n. 18 (539)
Carney, D., R–3n. 28 (90)
Carpenter, J. B., R–6n. 3 (184)
Carpenter, Jake Burton, 184
Carpenter, M. A., R–8n. 51 (229)
Carr, D., R–7n. 1 (214)
Carr, S. C., R–4n. 22 (127)
Carroll, A. B., R–3n. 49 (98)
Carter, Ben, 77
Carter, K. R., R–21n. 15 (537)
Carter, N. M., R–7n. 48 (199)
Cascio, W. F., R–14n. 35 (402)
Case, B. M., R–13n. 9 (363)
Case, T., R–3n. 24 (89)
Castican, J. I., R–21n. 40 (559)
Caudron, S., R–16n. 33 (438), R–17n. 15 (463),
    R–18n. 43 (476), R–20n. 45 (517)

Cavusgil, S. T., R–6n. 40 (176)
Champy, J., R–14n. 36 (402)
Chan, Derek, 374
Chan, E., R–2n. 1 (40)
Chan, Kim W., R–9n. 73 (243)
Chan, T., R–6n. 38 (175)
Chandler, C., R–4n. 23 (127)
Chandler, D., R–3n. 50 (99)
Chang, A., R–22n. 19 (574)
Chang, Horace, 539, 544
Chang, K., R–18n. 1 (496)
Chang, L. T., R–6n. 41 (181)
Charan, R., R–13n. 52 (344)
Charitou, C. D., R–9n. 31 (267)
Charkham, J., R–13n. 47 (342)
Charnock, E., R–5n. 38 (139)
Charnock, Elizabeth, 139
Chase, R. B., R–2n. 7 (49)
Cheeks, Rachel, 17, R–1n. 19 (17)
Cheese, P., R–9n. 75 (251)
Chemiss, C., R–19n. 8 (499)
Chen, C.-C., R–16n. 34 (439)
Chen, G., R–20n. 42 (517)
Chen, M., R–4n. 21 (126), R–20n. 14 (537),
    R–21n. 31 (550)
Chenault, Kenneth, 9, 498–99
Cheney, Dick, 313
Cheng, Y.-T., R–15n. 54 (410)
Chesterson, C., R–11n. 60 (309)
Childers, Mark, 408
Chin, S.-F., R–16n. 34 (439)
Chizen, Bruce, 496, 517, 547
Chmielewski, D. C., R–8n. 37 (226)
Chudoba, K. M., R–21n. 12 (572)
Chugh, D., R–9n. 16 (261)
Chun, D. W. L., R–16n. 42 (441)
Chun, R., R–2n. 5 (79)
Chung, M.-H., R–21n. 2 (564)
Chung, Y., R–15n. 5 (424)
Chura, H., R–18n. 64 (486)
Church, A. H., R–14n. 38 (403), R–14n. 39 (403)
Clair, J. A., R–4n. 17 (122), R–14n. 24 (398)
Clapper, C., R–8n. 59 (234)
Clark, M. M., R–24n. 35 (612)
Clark, R. C., R–16n. 44 (442), R–16n. 45 (442)
Clarke, J., R–14n. 26 (398)
Clarke, M., R–21n. 28 (549)
Clarke, N. E., R–24n. 47 (621)
Clegg, C., R–14n. 28 (399)
Clegg, S. R., R–10n. 53 (277)
Clement, R. W., R–3n. 51 (99)
Clifton, D., R–1n. 21 (20)
Clinton, Bill, 419
Coates, T. P., R–4n. 67 (110)
Coblin, Jim, 487
Coder, C. M., R–24n. 49 (621)
Coff, D. C., R–10n. 11 (289)
Coff, R. W., R–10n. 11 (289)
Coffman, C., R–1n. 21 (20), R–7n. 63 (205),
    R–15n. 6 (425), R–17n. 7 (460)
Coh, J. M., R–20n. 46 (517)
Cohen, D. J., R–16n. 30 (438)
Cohen, D. S., R–13n. 3 (388)
Cohen, R. R., R–22n. 17 (574)
Cohen, S. G., R–1n. 3 (5)
Colbert, A. E., R–16n. 37 (439)
Colella, A., R–16n. 49 (445)
Collins, C. J., R–10n. 11 (289), R–16n. 31 (438)
Collins, Eileen, 460–61
Collins, Ellen, 533
Collins, J., R–8n. 57 (234)
Colquitt, J. A., R–20n. 39 (515)
Colvin, G., R–8n. 30 (222), R–8n. 31 (222),
    R–22n. 43 (583)
Colwell, K. A., R–18n. 54 (481)
Combs, G. M., R–24n. 37 (613)
Combs, J. G., R–5n. 34 (172), R–7n. 43 (197)
Combs, M. W., R–24n. 37 (613)
Confucius, 126
Conklin, D. W., R–4n. 5 (117)
Conlin, M., R–14n. 14 (393), R–15n. 47 (408),
    R–21n. 4 (565)
Connally, Allison, R–21n. 27 (548)
Connolly, T., R–10n. 41 (272)
Consolino, Ron, 240

Conyon, M. J., R–12n. 25 (336)
Cook, R. A., R–13n. 56 (353)
Cooper, C. D., R–2n. 12 (53)
Cooper, C. L., R–16n. 22 (435)
Cooper, J. T., R–20n. 56 (526)
Cooper-Thomas, H., R–16n. 39 (440)
Cope, Shana, 600
Copeland, M. J., R–2n. 11 (80)
Corman, L. S., R–13n. 56 (353)
Cornwell, Don, 615
Corso, M., R–10n. 12 (289)
Cortina, J. M., R–16n. 38 (440)
Cote, S., R–19n. 9 (499)
Couric, Katie, 23
Courpasson, D., R–10n. 53 (277)
Covey, S. R., R–7n. 9 (216), R–19n. 4 (497)
Cowan, S. L., R–13n. 2 (388)
Cox, A., R–12n. 26 (336)
Crant, J. M., R–18n. 29 (467)
Creedman, D., R–16n. 15 (431)
Cresti, B., R–5n. 32 (171)
Crockett, R. O., R–24n. 38 (614)
Cron, W. L., R–21n. 32 (551)
Cross, R. L., R–21n. 7 (569)
Crownover, Dale, 193
Cuban, Mark, 514
Cui, A. S., R–6n. 40 (176)
Cullen, J. B., R–5n. 13 (156), R–5n. 14 (157)
Cummings, T. G., R–14n. 30 (400),
    R–14n. 38 (403)
Cunningham, R., R–2n. 14 (54)
Czinkota, M. R., R–5n. 17 (160), R–11n. 32 (298)

D

Dabic, M., R–6n. 40 (176)
Daft, R. L., R–2n. 32 (74), R–4n. 12 (119),
    R–19n. 2 (497)
Dahl, D., R–6n. 17 (188)
Dale, James, 626
Dalkir, K., R–10n. 3 (287)
Dalton, C. M., R–9n. 1 (254), R–9n. 4 (255)
Dalton, M., R–20n. 10 (535), R–21n. 30 (550)
Daly, Eric, 12, R–1n. 12 (12)
Daly, M., R–7n. 58 (204)
Damaschke, Bill, 374
Daniels, Aubrey, 465
Daniels, C., R–16n. 35 (439), R–23n. 27 (610),
    R–23n. 33 (612)
Darden, Bill, 595
Darrouzet, John, 193
Datta, D. K., R–15n. 2 (422)
Daus, C. S., R–24n. 51 (622)
Davenport, K., R–5n. 9 (154)
Davenport, T. H., R–10n. 17 (291), R–11n. 26 (296)
David, George, 619
Davidson, Diane, 567
Davis, M. M., R–2n. 7 (49)
Davis, S. B., R–9n. 19 (263), R–11n. 55 (307)
Dawes, R. M., R–9n. 28 (266)
Dawley, D. D., R–2n. 22 (61)
Day, D., R–4n. 10 (119)
Day, D. V., R–18n. 29 (467)
Day, Jerry, 282
Day, K., R–12n. 19 (332)
Day, S., R–24n. 50 (622)
De Cremer, D., R–20n. 38 (515)
De Dreu, C. K. W., R–15n. 41 (405), R–23n. 50 (585)
de Loupe, M. S., R–20n. 54 (521)
Dean, Howard, 139
Dean, J., R–14n. 27 (399)
DeAngelo, Joe, 505
Deaver, S., R–9n. 6 (256)
DeChurch, L. A., R–1n. 22 (21)
Dechy, Natalie, 23
Decicco, T., R–5n. 33 (171)
Deen, L., R–20n. 52 (521)
Deitch, E. A., R–17n. 17 (464)
deJong, S. B., R–4n. 19 (123)
DeLay, L., R–20n. 10 (535), R–21n. 30 (550)
Delery, J. E., R–18n. 59 (483)
Dell, K., R–1n. 24 (23)
Dell, Michael, 264, 412
Delmar, F., R–7n. 40 (195)
deLuque, M. S., R–4n. 16 (121)
DeMeuse, K. P., R–22n. 39 (581)

Deming, W. Edwards, 63–64, 69, 309, R–2n. 25 (63), R–11n. 59 (309)
Den Hartog, D. N., R–19n. 2 (497)
Denis, J.-L., R–15n. 55 (411)
DeNisi, A. S., R–15n. 50 (409), R–17n. 53 (446), R–18n. 67 (487)
Dennis, A. R., R–11n. 52 (307)
Denvir, N., R–5n. 43 (146)
DeRouin, R. E., R–16n. 44 (442)
DeRue, D. S., R–17n. 6 (460), R–22n. 49 (584)
Deshpandé, R., 86, R–3n. 21 (85)
Dess, G. R., R–10n. 44 (273)
Deutsch, C. H., R–2n. 3 (78)
Deutschman, A., R–21n. 1 (564), R–21n. 4 (565)
Devine, Denise, 183–84, 188, 189, 195, 208, R–6n. 1 (184)
deVries, R. E., R–19n. 25 (509)
Dharwadkar, R., R–14n. 27 (399)
Dickmann, M., R–1n. 26 (25)
Dickson, D., R–2n. 27 (65)
Dickson, William, 55–56
Dienes, E., R–18n. 45 (476)
Dietzen, Scott, 15
DiMartino, D., R–4n. 5 (117)
Din, S., R–24n. 43 (616)
Dirks, K. T., R–22n. 18 (574)
Dittmar, L., R–12n. 1 (322)
Dittmar, Lee, 83
Dobbs, Lou, 204–5, R–7n. 62 (205)
Dodd, N. G., R–18n. 41 (474)
Doh, J., R–5n. 18 (161)
Dolan, S. L., R–20n. 40 (515)
Dooley, K., R–14n. 15 (394)
Doran, G. T., R–9n. 35 (269), R–10n. 42 (272)
Dorfman, P., R–5n. 42 (144)
Dorfman, P. W., R–4n. 16 (121), R–20n. 54 (521)
Dormit, Marco Antonio Slim, 158
Dornheim, L., R–20n. 56 (526)
Dorsey, D. W., R–22n. 23 (577)
Dotzel, T., R–9n. 25 (264)
Douglas, A. V., R–12n. 25 (336)
Douglas, S. C., R–3n. 25 (90), R–18n. 38 (472)
Douma, B., R–18n. 40 (472)
Dow, J., R–8n. 48 (227)
Dragoon, A., R–21n. 20 (541)
Dreyer, Kimberly, 602
Drickhamer, D., R–1n. 20 (17)
Driesenga, Daniel, 192
Driskell, J. E., R–22n. 31 (579)
Driver, M. J., R–9n. 37 (270), R–19n. 32 (514)
Drucker, Peter, 290
Dubin, A. J., R–2n. 31 (73)
Dubinsky, A. J., R–19n. 33 (514)
Duck, J., R–22n. 19 (574)
Duck, Jeanie, 575
Dudley, N. M., R–16n. 38 (440)
Duffy, G. L., R–9n. 20 (263)
Dufresne, R., R–14n. 24 (398)
Dugas, Richard, 47
Duguid, P., R–15n. 66 (414)
Dumaine, B., R–6n. 22 (189)
Duncan, Emily, 616
Duncan, Jack, 605
Duncan, Russell, 453
Dunham, K. J., R–9n. 15 (260)
Dunlap, S., R–4n. 6 (117)
Dunphy, D., R–13n. 47 (342)
Durks, K. T., R–19n. 35 (514)
Dwyer, D. J., R–22n. 37 (581)
Dwyer, P., R–3n. 28 (90)

E

Earley, P. C., R–22n. 41 (582)
Eastvold, R., R–10n. 11 (289)
Eckert, Robert, 503, 505, 524–25
Eckhoff, R. A., R–11n. 26 (296)
Edelman, L. F., R–7n. 51 (200)
Eden, L., R–5n. 18 (161)
Edison, Thomas, 303
Edmondson, A., R–22n. 44 (583)
Edmondson, A. C., R–15n. 50 (409)
Edwards, Bill, 360
Eggins, R. A., R–18n. 61 (483)

Egri, C. P., R–4n. 20 (123)
Ehrbar, A., R–21n. 4 (565)
Ehrenfeld, J. R., R–4n. 58 (101)
Ehrhart, K. H., R–5n. 35 (135)
Eisenhardt, K. M., R–22n. 32 (579)
Eisenmann, T., R–4n. 1 (114)
Eisner, Michael, 127
Ekanayake, S., R–12n. 16 (331)
Elddenburg, L. G., R–12n. 35 (338)
Elfring, T., R–7n. 63 (205)
Elkind, P., R–13n. 9 (363)
Ellett, C., R–14n. 26 (398)
Ellig, B. R., R–3n. 46 (97)
Elliott, D., R–1n. 18 (17)
Ellison, Larry, 12, 13
Ely, R., R–24n. 42 (615)
Ely, Richard T., 41
Emery, C. R., R–21n. 3 (565)
Engardio, P., R–8n. 62 (235)
English, M. J., R–10n. 5 (288)
Enkel, E., R–10n. 4 (287)
Enriquez, F. T., R–11n. 61 (310)
Erdogan, B., R–20n. 42 (517)
Erez, M., R–23n. 26 (609)
Erumban, A. A., R–4n. 19 (123)
Eskew, Michael, 44
Eyring, M., R–15n. 50 (409)

F

Fahey, L., 301, R–11n. 37 (301)
Fairbairn, U., R–23n. 3 (596)
Falvey, David, 370
Faraj, S., R–1n. 22 (21), R–19n. 30 (513)
Farley, J. U., R–5n. 29 (169)
Farrell, G., R–19n. 6 (499)
Farrell, John, 466
Fastow, Andrew, 228, 363
Faulkner, D. O., R–7n. 12 (218)
Fayol, H., R–2n. 11 (51)
Fayol, Henri, 51, 53
Feldman, D. C., R–18n. 58 (482), R–20n. 50 (520)
Feldman, H., R–24n. 53 (626)
Feldmann, R., R–5n. 29 (133)
Fen Cheng, B., R–8n. 47 (227)
Fernandez, J. A., R–1n. 17 (16)
Ferrin, D. L., R–19n. 35 (514)
Fettig, Jeff, 264, 265
Field, H. S., R–22n. 29 (579), R–22n. 46 (584)
Filo, David, 11
Fink, L. S., R–16n. 30 (438)
Finkelstein, S., R–4n. 9 (118)
Firox, N. M., R–3n. 41 (95)
Fischman, Bruce, 60
Fisher, D., R–8n. 33 (224), R–13n. 1 (388)
Fitzgerald, Kevin, 13
Fleetham, C., R–11n. 47 (305)
Flood, M., R–8n. 49 (228)
Florkowski, G. W., R–16n. 14 (429)
Floyd, D. A., R–2n. 26 (64)
Foley, S., R–24n. 34 (612)
Follett, Mary Parker, 53–54, R–2n. 13 (53)
Foray, D., R–10n. 14 (290)
Ford, Bill, 16–17, 91
Ford, Henry, 49, 50, 400, 605
Ford, R. C., R–2n. 27 (65), R–9n. 36 (270)
Forelle, C., R–8n. 36 (226)
Foreman, E. H., R–10n. 43 (273)
Forrester, R., R–18n. 43 (476)
Fortinberry, A., R–6n. 23 (189)
Fottler, M. D., R–17n. 65 (453)
Fox, Michael, 374
Fox, S., R–14n. 17 (395)
Fragale, A. R., R–4n. 28 (133), R–22n. 18 (574)
Francis, T., R–9n. 15 (260)
Frangos, A., R–9n. 15 (260)
Frankel, T., R–3n. 39 (94)
Franklin-Hodge, J., R–5n. 38 (139)
Frauenheim, E., R–16n. 43 (441), R–17n. 59 (448)
Fredenall, L. D., R–21n. 3 (565)
Fredrickson, J. W., 244, 246, R–9n. 74 (243)
Fredrickson, Jim, 243
Frese, M., R–15n. 56 (412)
Freund, A. M., R–17n. 14 (463)
Friedman, H. H., R–19n. 36 (514)

Friedman, Milton, 91–92, R–3n. 31 (91)
Friedman, Thomas L., 116, 152, 180, R–4n. 4 (116), R–5n. 4 (151), R–5n. 7 (153)
Frink, D. D., R–22n. 22 (576)
Fritz, David, 341
Fritzche, B. A., R–16n. 44 (442)
Fritzsche, D. J., R–4n. 66 (109)
Frooman, J., R–10n. 50 (275)
Frost, P. J., R–23n. 19 (606)
Frumkin, P., R–9n. 21 (263)
Fry, Art, 600
Fryzell, G. E., R–15n. 6 (425)
Fu, F., R–21n. 32 (551)
Fuentelsaz, L., R–8n. 34 (225)
Furst, S. A., R–23n. 53 (592)
Futrell, D., R–22n. 39 (581)

G

Gabbin, A. L., R–10n. 51 (276)
Gadsby, Monica, 89
Gaetano, Joy, 573
Gagnon, Marc, 541
Gainey, T. W., R–15n. 3 (423)
Galbraith, J. R., R–13n. 6 (362)
Gale, S. F., R–15n. 42 (405), R–22n. 28 (578), R–23n. 13 (602), R–24n. 45 (618)
Gallagher, S., R–3n. 32 (93)
Gamble, R., R–12n. 1 (322)
Gandhi, 44, 63
Ganster, D. C., R–18n. 41 (474), R–22n. 37 (581)
Gantt, Henry, 50
Garcia, Jay, 612
Gardner, P., R–14n. 28 (399)
Garrett, K. A., R–5n. 27 (167)
Garvey, C., R–17n. 21 (464), R–17n. 61 (448)
Garvin, D. A., R–14n. 7 (390)
Gary, M. S., R–8n. 18 (220)
Gasparrini, Paolo, 26
Gasquet, Richard, 23
Gates, Bill, 122, 123, 546
Gauther, C., R–2n. 1 (40)
Geffen, David, 374
Geller, E. S., R–14n. 22 (397)
Gemuenden, H. G., R–21n. 17 (574)
Gendron, Y., R–12n. 7 (325)
Genn, A., R–3n. 36 (94)
Gentry, J. W., R–5n. 8 (153)
George, J. M., R–6n. 38 (175)
George, W. W., R–2n. 13 (82)
George, William W., 79, 81–82
Gerhardt, M. W., R–19n. 7 (499)
Gerhart, B., R–17n. 56 (447), R–17n. 60 (448)
Gersick, C. J. G., R–22n. 19 (574)
Ghemawat, P., R–5n. 15 (158), R–6n. 38 (175)
Ghosal, S., R–21n. 22 (543)
Ghosn, Carlos, 509, 516
Giambatista, R. C., R–22n. 21 (576)
Gibson, C. B., R–22n. 41 (582), R–23n. 53 (592)
Gibson, J. W., R–20n. 11 (535)
Gibson, L., R–15n. 50 (409)
Gibson, L. L., R–21n. 10 (571)
Gigerenzer, G., R–10n. 49 (274)
Giladi, K., R–19n. 36 (514)
Gilbreth, Frank and Lillian, 50, 51, 52
Giles, W. F., R–22n. 29 (579), R–22n. 46 (584)
Gill, D., R–9n. 13 (258)
Giller, C., R–4n. 58 (101)
Gilovich, T. D., R–10n. 40 (271)
Gimpert, J., R–13n. 43 (341)
Gino, F., R–10n. 40 (271)
Gioja, L., R–15n. 57 (412)
Glanz, W., R–23n. 18 (605)
Glisan, Ben, 363
Godinez, V., R–4n. 7 (117), R–5n. 43 (146)
Goetsch, D. L., R–9n. 19 (263), R–11n. 55 (307)
Golden, C. J., R–20n. 56 (526)
Goldsmith, M., R–15n. 54 (410)
Goltz, Jay, 190–91, R–6n. 27 (190)
Golub, Harvey, 498
Gómez, J., R–8n. 34 (225)
Gompers, Samuel, 41
Goncalo, J. A., R–11n. 51 (307)
Gonzalez, Gerardo, 48, R–2n. 5 (48)
Gonzalez, J. A., R–24n. 47 (621)

Gonzalez Booch, U., R–11n. 61 (310)
Goodman, Shira, 529–30, 540, 541, 544
Goodnight, Jim, 303
Goodstein, L. D., R–21n. 40 (559)
Gopinath, C., R–3n. 23 (87)
Gordon, L., R–21n. 3 (565)
Gore, Wilbert L., 563–64
Gould, Andrew, 421, 422
Gove, A. S., R–7n. 2 (215)
Govindarajan, V., R–6n. 31 (192), R–12n. 2 (322)
Graff, E. J., R–3n. 45 (97)
Graham, J., R–12n. 8 (326)
Graham, Jon, 80
Grant, L., R–15n. 6 (425)
Gratton, L., R–21n. 22 (543)
Grauman, Kevin, 185
Graves, L. M., R–1n. 30 (27)
Greehy, Bill, 517
Green, S., R–13n. 48 (343)
Green, T., R–5n. 33 (171)
Greenberg, K., R–7n. 56 (202)
Greene, P. G., R–7n. 51 (200)
Greene, Todd, 184–85
Greenhouse, L., R–24n. 38 (614)
Grensing-Pophal, L., R–10n. 13 (290)
Gresham, M. T., R–17n. 60 (448)
Griffeth, K. H., R–24n. 35 (612)
Griffeth, R. W., R–16n. 30 (438)
Griffin, D. W., R–10n. 40 (271)
Griffin, R. W., R–17n. 2 (458)
Griffith, D. A., R–6n. 40 (176)
Grimshaw, J., R–3n. 17 (83)
Grossman, M., R–10n. 3 (287)
Grossman, R. J., R–15n. 8 (426), R–16n. 46 (443)
Grote, D., R–17n. 52 (445)
Grove, Andy, 118
Groves, K. S., R–20n. 42 (517)
Grow, B., R–19n. 16 (505)
Guaspari, J., R–14n. 37 (402)
Gullickson, B. R., R–1n. 1 (40)
Gully, S. M., R–22n. 48 (584)
Gundlach, M. J., R–3n. 25 (90), R–18n. 38 (472)
Gunn, J., R–9n. 35 (269), R–10n. 42 (272)
Gunn, R. W., R–1n. 1 (40)
Gunz, Rainer, 297
Gupta, N., R–17n. 60 (448), R–18n. 59 (483)
Gupta, R., R–15n. 44 (407)
Gurjar, Nandita, 442
Guthrie, J. P., R–15n. 2 (422)
Gutner, T., R–23n. 29 (611)
Guyon, J., R–20n. 43 (517)
Guzzo, R. A., R–21n. 13 (573)

H

Haasen, A., R–2n. 28 (65)
Hackman, Barbara, 346
Hackman, J. R., R–18n. 41 (474), R–21n. 13 (573),
    R–21n. 14 (573), R–22n. 35 (581)
Haeckel, S. H., R–21n. 41 (561)
Haggerty, D. J., R–20n. 56 (526)
Haldeman, Charles (Ed), 509
Hall, C., R–5n. 39 (140)
Hall, E., R–20n. 12 (535)
Hall, L. E., R–20n. 56 (526)
Hallinger, P., R–4n. 20 (123)
Hallowell, R., 262, R–9n. 17 (261)
Hambrick, D. C., 244, 246, R–9n. 74 (243)
Hambrick, Don, 243
Hamel, G., R–9n. 25 (264), R–9n. 26 (264), R–14n.
    8 (390), R–14n. 33 (401)
Hamm, J., R–13n. 5 (361), R–19n. 5 (497)
Hamm, S., R–17n. 9 (461), R–20n. 57 (527)
Hammer, M., R–14n. 36 (402)
Hammonds, K., R–1n. 1 (4)
Handelberg, J., R–6n. 32 (192)
Hanke, J. E., R–11n. 28 (297)
Hanoch, Y., R–10n. 40 (271)
Hansemark, O. C., R–6n. 21 (189)
Harden, E., R–15n. 5 (424)
Hare, A. P., R–22n. 38 (581)
Harmeling, S. S., R–3n. 53 (99)
Harper, S. C., R–8n. 64 (238)
Harriman, R. A., R–11n. 42 (303)

Harris, H., R–1n. 26 (25)
Harris, James R., R–4n. 66 (109)
Harris, P. R., R–2n. 10 (80)
Harris, S. G., R–23n. 15 (602)
Harrison, D. A., R–17n. 3 (458), R–19n. 11 (502),
    R–20n. 39 (515)
Harrison, J. S., R–2n. 1 (40)
Hart, R. J., R–13n. 56 (353)
Harter, J. K., R–17n. 5 (459)
Harting, T. R., R–3n. 53 (99)
Harvey, M., R–10n. 45 (273)
Haslam, S. A., R–18n. 61 (483)
Hastie, R., R–9n. 28 (266)
Hastings, R., R–4n. 25 (129)
Hatch Woodward, N., R–7n. 5 (215)
Hawk, E. J., R–23n. 52 (587)
Hayashi, A., R–24n. 47 (621)
Hayden, Melanie, 550–51
Hayes, T. L., R–17n. 5 (459)
Healy, P. M., R–12n. 33 (337)
Hearn, G., R–10n. 2 (287)
Heaton, C. P., R–9n. 36 (270)
Hebl, M. R., R–24n. 35 (612)
Heffernan, M., R–20n. 53 (521)
Heffernan, V., R–8n. 26 (220)
Heil, G., R–19n. 14 (503)
Heilemann, J., R–4n. 21 (146)
Hein, K., R–9n. 21 (263)
Hellriegel, D., R–1n. 1 (4)
Helms, M. M., R–9n. 68 (239)
Hemp, P., R–23n. 6 (599)
Hemphill, T. A., R–4n. 67 (110)
Henderson, Bruce D., 129
Henderson, C. R., R–9n. 2 (254)
Henderson, M. A., R–2n. 2 (43)
Hendrickson, Andy, 374
Hendry, C., R–14n. 5 (389)
Heneman, R. L., R–17n. 60 (448)
Henle, C. A., R–21n. 16 (538)
Henneman, T., R–18n. 48 (478), R–18n. 51 (480)
Henry, Scott, III, 201–2
Hense, F., R–16n. 26 (437)
Herbold, Robert J., 332
Hermann, Eliza, 275
Herscovitch, L., R–14n. 21 (396)
Hersey, P., 507, R–19n. 21 (506), R–19n. 22 (506)
Hertz, M., R–15n. 59 (412)
Herzberg, Frederick, 477, R–18n. 47 (477)
Herzog, R. J., R–12n. 37 (339)
Heslin, P. A., R–4n. 15 (121), R–21n. 26 (545)
Hesterly, W., R–8n. 50 (228)
Heyde, Mary Ellen, 612
Heywood, J. S., R–12n. 28 (336)
Hibbard, J., R–15n. 69 (419)
Hiduke, G., R–7n. 40 (195)
Hill, Mike, 66
Hill-Popper, M., R–19n. 2 (497)
Hindle, T., R–14n. 32 (401), R–15n. 46 (408)
Hinman, Doyle, 201–2
Hirai, Kazuo, 114
Hirschfeld, R. R., R–22n. 29 (579),
    R–22n. 46 (584)
Hirst, G., R–21n. 5 (567)
Hislop, D., R–10n. 20 (292)
Hitler, Adolph, 515
Hitt, M. A., R–7n. 4 (215), R–8n. 19 (220),
    R–15n. 50 (409)
Hjorth, P., R–4n. 59 (102)
Hochwarter, W., R–16n. 21 (434)
Hock, Dee, 26–27
Hodgetts, R. M., R–7n. 66 (210), R–20n. 11 (535)
Hoegl, M., R–21n. 17 (574)
Hoffman, G., R–5n. 33 (171)
Hoffman, J. J., R–2n. 22 (61)
Hoffman, W., R–4n. 7 (117)
Hoffmann, W. H., R–5n. 34 (135)
Hofman, G., R–6n. 6 (185)
Hofstede, G., R–4n. 16 (121), R–4n. 19 (123),
    R–4n. 20 (123)
Hofstede, G. J., R–4n. 16 (121)
Hofstede, Geert, 123
Hoijer, B., R–9n. 11 (257)
Holden, Melvin "Kip," 134
Hollenbeck, J. R., R–23n. 52 (587)
Holloway, Tom, 457, 458

Holmes, M. E., R–14n. 15 (394)
Hom, P. W., R–16n. 30 (438)
Homans, G. C., R–2n. 17 (55)
Homburg, C., R–8n. 39 (226)
Hooijberg, R., R–23n. 14 (602)
Hooper, C. L., R–9n. 2 (254)
Hooper, L., R–19n. 1 (496)
Hoover, David, 270
Hoover, R. David, 253–55
Horn, L. A. T., R–18n. 45 (476)
Horowitz, Bradley, 543
Hosack, Dale, 339, 340
Hoskisson, R. E., R–6n. 37 (174), R–7n. 4 (215),
    R–8n. 19 (220)
Hough, J. R., R–8n. 50 (228)
Hourihan, G., R–9n. 37 (270), R–19n. 32 (514)
House, R. J., R–4n. 16 (121), R–20n. 54 (521)
Howard, Timothy, 332
Howell, J., R–5n. 42 (144)
Howell, M. T., R–11n. 57 (308)
Howland, B., R–1n. 3 (5)
Howroyd, Janice Bryant, 202
Hrebiniak, L. G., R–13n. 10 (364)
Hsien Lao, S., R–10n. 15 (290)
Hu Jintao, 163
Huang, A., R–5n. 40 (140)
Huang, X., R–5n. 14 (157)
Huck, S., R–10n. 49 (274)
Hudson, Cliff, 15, 19
Hueston, John, 228
Huff, C., R–16n. 43 (441), R–20n. 49 (519)
Hughes, Catherine, 189–90
Hult, C., R–17n. 6 (460)
Hunter, J. E., R–16n. 37 (439)
Huntington, S. P., R–2n. 14 (82)
Huselid, M. A., R–11n. 24 (295)
Huselid, M. S., R–15n. 64 (414)
Husted, K., R–15n. 56 (412)
Huston, L., R–15n. 44 (407)
Huy, Q. N., R–1n. 11 (12)
Hyman, Chris, 273

I

Iansiti, M., R–13n. 18 (372)
Iger, Robert, 127–28
Ignatius, A., R–21n. 4 (565)
Ilgen, D. R., R–23n. 52 (587)
Ilies, R., R–19n. 7 (499)
Immelt, Jeffrey R., 7, 222–23, 425, 503, 517, 520,
    R–8n. 31 (222)
Incalcaterra, K. A., R–22n. 48 (584)
Inkpen, A. C., R–4n. 9 (118)
Inkson, K., R–1n. 26 (25), R–4n. 22 (127),
    R–5n. 6 (152)
Inman, W., R–7n. 7 (215)
Ireland, R. D., R–5n. 34 (172), R–6n. 8 (185),
    R–7n. 4 (215), R–7n. 43 (197)
Israel, P., R–11n. 43 (303)
Ivanovich, D., R–2n. 1 (78)

J

Jackson, C. R. A., R–23n. 2 (596)
Jackson, N., R–14n. 24 (398)
Jackson, S. E., R–3n. 16 (82), R–8n. 54 (229),
    R–15n. 4 (423), R–15n. 50 (409), R–16n. 22
    (435), R–16n. 63 (448), R–21n. 13 (573),
    R–14n. 24 (398), R–24n. 52 (622),
    R–24n. 42 (615)
Jacobides, M. G., R–13n. 19 (373)
Jana, R., R–16n. 45 (442)
Janney, J. J., R–10n. 44 (273)
Janove, J., R–3n. 15 (82)
Janssen, O., R–17n. 13 (462)
Janssens, M., R–20n. 10 (535), R–21n. 12 (572)
Jassawalla, A. R., R–23n. 10 (600)
Javidan, M., R–4n. 16 (121), R–20n. 54 (521)
Jehn, K. A., R–22n. 20 (574), R–24n. 42 (615)
Jellicone, Roger, 577
Jenkins, L., R–6n. 4 (184)
Jenkins, P., R–3n. 43 (96)
Jensen, M. A. C., R–22n. 19 (574)
Jerjahn, U., R–12n. 28 (336)

Lundberg, C. C., R–23n. 19 (606)
Lundegaard, K., R–3n. 38 (94)
Luo, Y., R–1n. 17 (16), R–12n. 42 (341),
    R–13n. 44 (341)
Luthans, B., R–2n. 10 (51)
Luthans, F., R–2n. 10 (51), R–6n. 24 (189), R–17n.
    12 (462), R–17n. 24 (465), R–17n. 25 (466)
Luthans, K., R–2n. 10 (51)
Lyons, D., R–2n. 21 (60)
Lyytinen, K., R–13n. 8 (363)

M

Maben, S., R–7n. 53 (201)
MacDowell, Harold, 56
MacDuffie, J. P., R–15n. 60 (412)
Mackey, John, 22, 23, 54
Mackintosh, J., R–18n. 68 (493)
MacLean, T. L., R–4n. 17 (122)
MacMillan, I., R–6n. 20 (188)
MacMillan, I. C., R–9n. 23 (264)
MacNeil, J. S., R–16n. 24 (436)
Madden, John, 130
Mahadevan, K., R–5n. 33 (171)
Mair, J., R–6n. 9 (185)
Majchrzak, A., R–22n. 34 (580)
Makhija, M. V., R–12n. 18 (331)
Malhotra, A., R–22n. 34 (580)
Malouf, J. M., R–20n. 56 (526)
Mammo, A., R–12n. 22 (335)
Mann, S., R–16n. 48 (444)
Mannix, E. A., R–22n. 20 (574)
Manolova, T. S., R–7n. 51 (200)
Manusov, V., R–20n. 7 (534)
Mao, 63
Margolis, J., R–20n. 3 (531)
Margolis, J. D., 86, R–3n. 21 (85), R–16n. 21 (434)
Markham, G. D., R–6n. 20 (188), R–6n. 34 (193)
Markham, S. E., R–17n. 26 (466)
Markides, C. C., R–9n. 31 (267)
Marklund, J., R–11n. 33 (299)
Marks, A. M., R–7n. 47 (199)
Marks, M. A., R–1n. 22 (21), R–22n. 20 (574),
    R–22n. 47 (584)
Marks, Michael, 377
Marquez, J., R–16n. 28 (438), R–17n. 28 (467),
    R–18n. 35 (469), R–20n. 55 (521)
Marsh, A., R–20n. 51 (521)
Marshall, C. R., R–18n. 34 (469)
Marshall, Rice, 321
Marti, I., R–6n. 9 (185)
Martin, J., R–23n. 19 (606)
Martin, L. P., R–12n. 66 (317)
Martinez, Kevin, 67
Martini, A., R–10n. 12 (289)
Martinko, M. J., R–3n. 25 (90), R–18n. 38 (472)
Martinuzzi, A., 103
Martocchio, Joseph J., R–15n. 5 (424),
    R–22n. 22 (576)
Maslow, Abraham, 483–86, R–18n. 61 (483)
Massa, S., R–10n. 12 (289)
Massey, T. K., Jr., R–18n. 49 (479)
Mathieu, J. E., R–1n. 22 (21), R–14n. 29 (399),
    R–21n. 10 (571), R–21n. 11 (571),
    R–22n. 20 (574)
Mauborgne, R., R–9n. 73 (243)
Mauborgne, R., R–15n. 57 (412)
Maurer, R., R–14n. 23 (398)
Mausner, B., R–18n. 47 (477)
Mauzy, J., R–11n. 42 (303)
May, K. E., R–21n. 13 (573)
May, Kenneth, 77, 385
Mayberry, Rory, 77
Mayer, Marrissa, 566
Mayo, E., R–2n. 16 (55)
Mayo, Elton, 55–56
Mayo, William, 561
McAdams, J., R–23n. 52 (587)
McAfee, R. B., R–17n. 65 (453)
McCall, M. W., Jr., R–1n. 2 (4), R–1n. 31 (28)
McCann, Renetta, 89
McCarthy, D. J., R–3n. 33 (93), R–5n. 29 (169)
McClelland, D. C., R–6n. 21 (189)
McClelland, David, 189

McClendon, J. A., R–15n. 3 (423)
McColl-Kennedy, J. R., R–19n. 34 (514)
McConnell, B., R–23n. 25 (609)
McDaniel, M. A., R–17n. 56 (447)
McDougall, P. Phillips, R–7n. 52 (200)
McEachern, W. A., R–4n. 3 (116)
McFadzean, E., R–7n. 59 (204)
McFarlan, F. W., R–5n. 37 (138), R–13n. 18 (372)
McFarland, K., R–6n. 30 (192), R–6n. 35 (194)
McFarlin, D. B., R–18n. 56 (482)
McGahan, A. M., R–7n. 13 (218)
McGill, J., R–11n. 21 (292)
McGill, Jimmy, 14
McGrath, Judy, 213–14, 215, 218, 419
McGrath, R. G., R–6n. 20 (188)
McGregor, D., R–19n. 14 (503)
McGregor, Douglas, 502–4
McGregor, J., R–11n. 25 (295), R–15n. 49 (409)
McGuire, Pam, 321
McKee, G. H., R–17n. 26 (466)
McKeever, Jeffrey, 272
McLane, Jeff, 614
McLaughlin, C., R–2n. 18 (56)
McLaughlin, K., R–19n. 1 (496)
McLean, B., R–13n. 9 (363)
McLendon, C. L., R–22n. 17 (574)
McMahon, Jeff, 363
McNerney, James, 37
McPherson, S. O., R–23n. 53 (592)
McQuillan, Scott, 614, 615
Meadowcroft, J. R., R–4n. 56 (101)
Meckler, L., R–3n. 38 (94)
Meglino, B. M., R–21n. 17 (574)
Mehri, D., R–13n. 11 (365)
Meir, Golda, 44
Merchant, H., R–5n. 33 (134), R–6n. 36 (173)
Meredith, R., R–2n. 23 (62)
Mesmer-Magnus, J. R., R–3n. 25 (90)
Meyer, C. J., R–23n. 52 (587)
Meyer, J. P., R–14n. 21 (396)
Meyer, M. W., R–11n. 26 (296)
Meza, P. E., R–7n. 2 (215)
Michailova, S., R–15n. 56 (412)
Michalko, M., R–11n. 46 (304)
Mike, B., R–3n. 17 (83)
Miles, G., R–13n. 19 (373)
Miles, M. P., R–3n. 51 (99)
Miles, R. E., R–13n. 19 (373)
Miles, S. A., R–13n. 7 (362)
Mill, J. S., R–3n. 30 (91)
Miller, High, 176
Miller, K. L., R–14n. 31 (401)
Miller, P. B., R–12n. 31 (337)
Millett, S., R–11n. 27 (297)
Millett, Stephen, 296–97
Millimann, M., R–15n. 57 (412)
Minerich, Carolyn A., 191
Miners, C. T. H., R–19n. 9 (499)
Minsky, M., R–10n. 15 (290)
Miranda, S. M., R–22n. 31 (579)
Mishra, A., R–14n. 35 (402), R–16n. 21 (434)
Mitra, A., R–17n. 60 (448)
Mitroff, I. I., 258, R–9n. 12 (257)
Mitsuhashi, H., R–13n. 21 (376)
Mittelstadt, M., R–4n. 14 (120)
Mohr, T. L., R–3n. 27 (90)
Mok, V., R–1n. 17 (16)
Molinsky, A., R–16n. 21 (434), R–20n. 3 (531)
Monetta, D. J., R–21n. 23 (543)
Montero, Sylvia, 500–501, 520
Moore, A. D., R–3n. 40 (95)
Moore, C., R–16n. 48 (444)
Moore, C. W., R–7n. 54 (202)
Moore, L. F., R–23n. 19 (606)
Moore, S., R–13n. 22 (377)
Morais, R. C., R–4n. 18 (122)
Moran, R. T., R–2n. 10 (80)
Moran, S., R–2n. 10 (80)
Moran, T. H., R–5n. 17 (160)
Morand, D. A., R–23n. 16 (603)
Morgan, H., R–15n. 54 (410)
Morgan, I., R–12n. 30 (337)
Morgeson, F. P., R–16n. 36 (439), R–22n. 49 (584)
Morris, M. H., R–7n. 60 (204)

Morris, Mary Ann, 561
Morris, Steve, 550
Morrow, J. C., R–16n. 11 (427)
Morrow, P. C., R–16n. 11 (427)
Morse, G., R–9n. 38 (271)
Morton, R., R–5n. 25 (166)
Moss, Bernard, 493
Mossholder, K. W., R–23n. 15 (602)
Mott, Richard, 442
Mouton, J. S., R–19n. 15 (504)
Mouton, Jane, 504
Mowday, R. T., R–18n. 54 (481)
Moya, B. R., R–15n. 53 (410)
Mucha, T., R–2n. 4 (47), R–9n. 6 (256)
Mudd, Dan, 333–34
Mueller-Hanson, R. A., R–22n. 23 (577)
Mulally, Allen, 17
Mulcahy, Anne, 3–4, 7, 13, 16, 19, 23, 27, 509, 518
Mullen, B., R–22n. 31 (579)
Mullen, E. J., R–16n. 11 (427)
Muller, H. J., R–23n. 18 (605)
Muller, J., R–20n. 41 (516)
Mullick, J., R–20n. 48 (518)
Mulvehill, S., R–6n. 17 (188)
Mulvey, P. W., R–18n. 42 (474)
Munilla, L. S., R–3n. 51 (99)
Munter, M., R–20n. 12 (535)
Muramatsu, M., R–10n. 40 (271)
Murdoch, Rupert, 544
Murphy, E., R–3n. 45 (97)
Murray, B., R–6n. 23 (189)
Murray, J. Y., R–13n. 11 (365)
Murtha, T. P., R–4n. 11 (119)
Murthy, U. S., R–11n. 53 (307)
Myers, D. E., R–14n. 9 (390)
Myers, M. B., R–6n. 40 (176)
Myers, R., R–9n. 30 (267), R–20n. 2 (531)
Myerson, J., R–11n. 50 (306)
Myser, M., R–20n. 1 (530)

N

Nadkarni, S., R–24n. 37 (613)
Nadler, D. A., R–13n. 52 (344)
Nadler, M., R–13n. 52 (344)
Nagin, Ray, 134
Nan De Vliert, E., R–5n. 14 (157)
Naothinsuhk, S., R–4n. 20 (123)
Nardelli, Robert, 19, 505
Nash, L. L., R–2n. 12 (80)
Navarro, J. G. C., R–15n. 53 (410)
Navran, F., R–3n. 20 (84)
Neeleman, David, 549
Neely, A., R–12n. 22 (335)
Neider, L. L., R–10n. 54 (277)
Neishi, Ken, 578
Neubaum, D. O., R–3n. 23 (87), R–20n. 39 (515)
Neuman, G. A., R–22n. 42 (583)
Nevarez, J., R–2n. 1 (40)
Newman, D. A., R–17n. 3 (458)
Newman, D. V., R–21n. 35 (554)
Newman, R. J., R–23n. 18 (605)
Nguyen, N. T., R–17n. 56 (447)
Niblock, Robert, 358, 360, 362
Nichols, B., R–8n. 49 (228), R–13n. 9 (363)
Nicholson-Crotty, S., R–12n. 10 (327)
Nideffer, R. M., R–6n. 29 (192)
Nielsen, B., R–5n. 33 (134)
Nilsen, D., R–20n. 54 (521)
Ninan, A., R–10n. 2 (287)
Niven, P. R., R–11n. 22 (293), R–11n. 23 (293)
Nixon-Gardiner, Bonnie, 391–92
Nkomo, S. M., R–17n. 65 (453)
Noble, S., R–19n. 4 (497)
Noel, T. W., R–3n. 30 (91)
Nohria, N., R–13n. 3 (388)
Nolan, R., R–5n. 37 (138)
Noon, C., R–20n. 57 (527)
Norcross, Melissa, 77–78
Norman, S., R–2n. 10 (51)
Norton, D. P., R–8n. 65 (238), R–11n. 22 (293),
    R–15n. 48 (408)
Norvell, Larry, 626–27

SUBJECT INDEX

A

Absenteeism, 466
Acceptable controls, 326
Acceptance theory of authority, 55
Accountability: and corporate governance, 341; criminal, 343; for cultural diversity, 621; and vertical design, 362–63
Accounting practices, corporate, 83
Accounts receivable, 331
Accuracy: of financial information, 343; of performance appraisals, 445–46
Achievement, need for, 189
Acquisitions, subcultures due to, 607–8; illustrated, 607
Act stage, of Deming cycle, 310
Acting locally, 331
Action plan, for organizational change, 395–97
Active inertia, 261
Active listening, 552
Adaptive decisions, 261–63; continuous improvement, 263; convergence, 262
Adjourning stage, 577
Administrative innovation, 408
Administrative law judges (ALJs), 344
Administrative management, 51, 52
Affiliation needs, 484
Affinity groups, 543, 564
Affirmative action, 613–14, 621–22
Affordable loss principle, 199
Age-based subcultures, 610–11
Age discrimination, 611
Age Discrimination in Employment Act, 428
Aging Facts Quiz, 611
Alabama, 605
Alexander Hamilton Corporate Governance Award, 321, 322, 346
Alignment, 311
Alliance strategy, 173–74, 226, 277
Alliances, 134–35, 151; defined, 134; global strategic, 173
Americans with Disabilities Act, 120, 428
America's Best Places to Work, 17, 425
America's Most Admired Company, 222
Annual meetings, 342
Annual reports, 342
Anticipatory change, 393
Arenas, 243–44
Assumptions, as element of culture, 597
Attentional styles, 192
Audit committee, 346
Auditability, 343
Auditors, 337
Audits, cultural, 615
Authority: acceptance theory of, 55; centralization and decentralization of, 366–68; charismatic, 44; defined, 362; protection of, 48; rational-legal, 44; traditional, 44; and vertical design, 362–63
Authority levels, as communication hurdle, 547–48
Authority principle, 51
Authority structure, 44
Auto industry, 94, 135, 138, 155, 167, 179–80, 233, 239–40, 241, 567, 605
Automation, defined, 339
Automation-based controls, 339–41
Autonomy, 205, 476
Availability bias, 272
Awareness training, 619–20

B

Baby boomers, 120, 136, 358
Backsliding, 390
Backtranslation, 549–50
Backward integration strategy, 131, 225–26
Balanced Budget Act, 136–37

Balanced scorecard model, 293–96, 592; assessment, 294–96; concerns with, 296; defined, 293; illustrated, 294; knowledge perspectives, 293–94; outcomes and activities, 293–94; potential benefits of, 295; vision and strategies, 293–94
Balancing work and life issues, 26, 27, 28
Baldrige National Quality Program, 310–14; Board of Examiners, 313; categories, 311–12; cooperative process, 313–14; effectiveness, 314; illustrated, 311; and ISO 9000, 314; Quality Award, 310–11, 441; systems perspective, 311, 312, illustrated, 311
Baldrige National Quality Program: Criteria for Performance Excellence, 312
Baldrige Quality Program (BOP), 311
Baldrige Quality Program for Performance Excellence, 311
Bamboo ceiling, 365
Barriers to delegation, 364–66
Barriers to entry, 129–30, 233
Base pay, 447–48
Basic skills training, 441–42
Baton Rouge, Louisiana, 134
Behavior modification, 465, 491–92; defined, 465; illustrated, 465
Behavioral models of leadership, 502–6; managerial grid, 504–5; Theory X and Theory Y, 502–4
Behavioral norms, 578–80
Behavioral viewpoint, 53–57, 68; Barnard's contributions, 54–55; basic assumptions of, 57; defined, 53; Follett's contributions, 53–54; Hawthorne contributions, 55–56; lessons from, 57
Benchmarking, 307–9; defined, 307; effectiveness, 308–9; illustrated, 308; stages, 307–8
Benefits, 429–31, 448–49; Equal Pay Act, 430–31; Fair Labor Standards Act, 430; illustrated, 449
Best Companies to Work For, 39, 56, 425, 427, 479, 509, 563
Best Managed Companies, 10
Best Medium Company to Work For in America, 603
Best Places to Work in the Federal Government, 458
Bill of Rights, 93
Blogs, 59–60, 123, 412
Boards of directors, 135; defined, 342; evaluation of CEO, 345; executive compensation, 345; family-owned business, 203, 204; fiduciary responsibility and control, 345–46; independent directors, 345; as internal control, 344–47; resource allocation, 345; self-assessment, 345
Body language, 534, 535
Borderless competition, 117–18
Bounded rationality model, 271–74; decision biases, 271–72; defined, 271; illustrated, 271; inadequate problem definition, 272–73; limited information, 273; limited search for alternatives, 273; satisficing, 273–74
Brainstorming, 304–5, 306; basic rules, 304–5; defined, 304; electronic, 307; guidelines for leading, 305; illustrated, 305
Brand image, 60, 509
Brand loyalty, 265
Brazil, 156
Bribery, 163–64
Budget, 19, 20, 340; capital, 339; cash, 339; labor, 339; materials, 339; research and development, 339; sales, 339
Budgetary control, 338–39
Bulgaria, 365–66, 476
Bureaucratic continuum, illustrated, 46
Bureaucratic culture, 603
Bureaucratic management, 43–49; authority structure, 44; benefits of bureaucracy, 47; characteristics of, 52; costs of bureaucracy, 48; defined, 43; division of labor, 44; hierarchical structure,

44; illustrated, 46; impersonality, 44; insights from, 48–49; lifelong career commitment, 44, 46; and mechanistic controls, 335; ranking organizations by bureaucratic orientation, 46; rationality, 46; rules, 43
Business: deciding to buy, start, or franchise, 196–99; family-owned, 187, 202–4; international, illustrated, 171; international, strategies for, 170–76; small, 187
Business angel, 200
Business incubator, 186
Business leaders, loss of trust in, 78–79
Business-level strategy, 228–29
Business plan, 195–96, 198; defined, 195; essential components for new ventures, 196; illustrated, 196
Buy strategy, 197
Bylaws, 342

C

Cable television, 146
Calgary, Alberta, Canada, 119, 120
Call centers, 152–53
Canada, 119, 120, 125, 126, 166–67
Canada–United States Free Trade Agreement, 166, 167
Capital budget, 339
Capital requirements, 130, 233
Capitalist theory, 91
Career development, 27–28, 443–44; illustrated, 443. *See also* Training.
Cartel, 163
Cash budget, 339
Casinos, 59
Catalyst Award, 426
Caucus groups, 618
Caveat emptor, 94
Celebrities, 130
Cell phones, 134
Census Population Survey, 432
Centralization, 366–68
Ceremonies, 601–2
Certainty, 255–56
Certification, of financial statements, 343
Certified public accountant (CPA), 276
Chad, 161
Chalk Talks, 410
Change. *See* Organizational change.
Change tactics exercise, 417–18
Channels, 539–44; defined, 539; downward, 540–41; horizontal, 542; illustrated, 540; informal, 542–43; upward, 541–42
Charisma, 497
Charismatic authority, 44
Charismatic leader, 385, 515
Chief financial officer (CFO), 337
Child-care initiatives, 621
Child labor, 50, 430
Childless workers, 621
China, 9, 16, 25–26, 40, 62–63, 110, 117, 122–23, 127–28, 133, 151, 152, 155, 162, 163, 165, 181, 201–2, 218, 243, 391–92, 537, 539, 550–51, 609
Citigroup Code of Conduct, 86–87
Civil Rights Act, 82, 428, 429, 613
Clan culture, 335, 603
Classic capitalist theory, 91
Clean Air Act, 119, 120, 324
Closed system, 58
Co-optation, 277
Coaching, 444, 520–21
Coalition, 277
Code of ethics, 85–87, 392, 416
Coercion, 497
Cognitive ability test, 439
Cohesiveness, 578

Collective bargaining, 53
Collectivism, 125, 128, 145, 157–58
College admissions, 614
Columbia space shuttle, 596
Commitment to Privacy Policy, 95–96
Communication, 486–87, 529–30; channels, 539–44; and corporate governance, 341; defined, 531; ethical issues in, 553–56; feedback, 544–46, 551–52; formal, 15, 16–17, 19; fostering, 551–53; gender differences, 533–34; gender differences, table of, 533; guidelines for personal communications competencies, 552–53; hurdles to, 547–52, illustrated, 547, 548; informal, 15, 16, 19, 542–43; listening, 534, 552; and managerial approach, 460–61; message, 534–39; organizational, 414; perception, 546–47; principles of, 532; process, 530–47, illustrated, 531; receiver (decoder), 532–34; sender (encoder), 532
Communication competency, 5, 6, 15–18; defined, 15; dimensions of, 19; entrepreneurs, 193–94; illustrated, 5; in Self-Assessment Inventory, 34
Communication Inventory, 559–60
Communism, 152
Communities-of-practice, 410, 411, 413
Comparable worth, 430
Comparative advantage, 239
Comparative financial control, 337–38
Compensation, 447–49; base pay, 447–48; benefits, 448–49; Equal Pay Act, 430–31; executive, 97, 227–28, 345, 482; Fair Labor Standards Act, 430; importance of pay fairness, 447–49; incentives, 227–28, 336, 448; legal and regulatory issues, 429–31; monetary, 447; nonmonetary, 447
Competency: core, 234–35; defined, 4; levels of, 367. *See also* Communication Competency, Multicultural Competency, Planning and Administration Competency, Self-Management Competency, Strategic Action Competency, Teamwork Competency.
Competency inventories, 434–35
Competition: borderless, 117–18. *See also* Generic competitive strategies model.
Competitive advantage, gaining and sustaining, 423–25
Competitive forces, 128–32, 232–34; competitors, 129; customers, 130–31; illustrated, 129; new entrants, 129–30; substitute goods and services, 130; suppliers, 131–32
Competitor scenario, 301
Competitors, 129, 232
Complete controls, 325
Complexity, 170, 171
Computer ethics, 554–55; table of, 554
Concentration stage, 303
Concrete information bias, 272
Conflicts of interest, 93
Conglomerates, 222, 223, 227
Conglomeration diversification strategy, 227
Constitution, U.S., 93
Consult individually style, 510
Consult team style, 510
Container traffic, 151
Contingency models of leadership, 506–14; Situational Leadership®, 506–10; Vroom-Jago, 510–14
Contingency planning, 215–16
Contingency viewpoint, 61–63, 69; defined, 61; illustrated, 61; learning from, 63; variables of, 61–62
Contingent workers, 432–33
Continued Dumping and Subsidy Act, 162
Continuous improvement, 263
Control, 321–22; acceptable, 326; automation-based, 339–41; budgetary, 338–39; and centralization/decentralization, 367; comparative financial, 337–38; complete, 325; corrective, 323; corrective control model, 329–34; defined, 322; external, 342–44; financial, 337–39; foundations of, 322–29; group, 324; illustrated, 324, 325, 335; individual self-controls, 325; interaction with planning, 322; internal, 327–29; machine, 339–40; market, 336–37; mechanistic, 335; objective, 325;

optimal amount of, 327; organic, 335; organizational, 324; preventive, 322–23; primary methods of, 334–41, illustrated, 334; sources and types of, 323–25, illustrated, 324; span of, 361–62; stakeholder, 323–24; and strategic goals, 325–26; timely controls, 326
Controlling, 10
Convergence, 262
Coordination principles, 53–54
Core competencies, 234–35
Corporate accounting practices, 83
Corporate and Criminal Fraud Accountability Act, 83
Corporate culture, 292–93, 604–5
Corporate entrepreneurs, 204–5
Corporate entrepreneurship, 204–6
Corporate governance, 341–47; boards of directors, 344–47; and communication, 341; defined, 341–42; external control, 342–44; internal control, 342, 344–47; issues and activities, 342; Sarbanes-Oxley Act, 342–44
Corporate-level strategy, 223–28; core focus, 223–25; corporate growth strategies, 225–27, illustrated, 225; defined, 223; executive compensation and corporate growth, 227–28
Corporate scandals, 83, 302, 325, 332, 343, 363
Corporation, defined, 341
Corrective control model, 329–34; defined, 329; illustrated, 330
Corrective controls, 323
Corruption, 161–62, 227–28
Corruption Perception Index, 161; illustrated, 162
Cost-benefit analysis, 327
Cost leadership strategy, 242
Countertrade, 170–71
Country club style, 505
Creativity: aids for, 302–7; defined, 302; Osborn's model of, 304–7; Personal Creativity Inventory, 303–4, 317–18; stages of creative process, 303–4, illustrated, 303; and work teams, 567
Credit laws, 132
Criminal crises, 258
Crises, 257–58; table of, 258
Critical psychological states, 474–75
Cultural audits, 615
Cultural barriers, and knowledge management, 292–93
Cultural distance, 158–60; defined, 158; industries affected by, illustrated, 159
Cultural diversity, 17, 595–96; challenges of, 621–22; change process, 616–18; defined, 613; economic benefits of diverse workforce, 615–16; family-friendly workplaces, 620–21, illustrated, 620; holding managers accountable, 621; managing, 613–22; organizational goals, 613–16; training, 618–20
Cultural forces, 153–60; cultural distance, 158–60; illustrated, 153; language, 154–55; time orientation, 154; value systems, 156–58; views of social change, 153–54
Cultural history exercise, 625
Cultural knowledge and understanding, 24, 26
Cultural openness and sensitivity, 24–25, 26
Cultural values, 80–82, 121–23, 158; gender role orientation, 126, 145; illustrated, 124, 125, 156; individualism, 125–26; long-term orientation, 126–27; managerial implications, 127–28; power distance, 123–24; questionnaire, 123, 127, 144–45; uncertainty avoidance, 124–25
Culture, 121–28; as barrier to delegation, 365; cultural contact continuum, illustrated, 537; defined, 80, 121, 596; elements of, 596–602; enabling, 292–93; entrepreneurial, 603–4; and ethical conduct, 80–82; as hurdle to communication, 550–51; importance to managers, 121–28; and internal team processes, 580; multicultural competency, 24–26; and nonverbal messages, 535, illustrated, 537; organizational, 602–6; and team performance, 582. *See also* Organizational culture; Subcultures.
Culture, elements of, 596–602; assumptions, 597; illustrated, 597; language, 599–600; narratives, 600; practices, 600–602; socialization, 598–99; symbols, 599; values and norms, 598
Current ratio, 337–38

Customer convenience, 118
Customer loyalty index, 256
Customer monitoring, 336–37
Customer perspective, of balanced scorecard model, 293–94, 296
Customers: bargaining power of, 130–31, 233; and business-level strategy, 229, 233; as competitive force, 130–31; as focus of Baldrige quality program, 312; as knowledge management target, 288–89; and learning organizations, 413; and strategies for learning organizations

D

Debt-to-worth ratio, 338
Decentralization, 366–68
Decide style, 510
Decision aids, 585
Decision making, 253–55; defined, 254; framework for, illustrated, 260; slow, 48
Decision-making conditions, 255–59; certainty, 255–56; illustrated, 255; objective probability, 257; risk, 256–57; subjective probability, 257; uncertainty, 257–59
Decisions: adaptive, 261–63; decision rules, illustrated, 262; innovative, 264–65; rational, 266; routine, 261; types of, 259–65; types of problems, 259–60; types of solutions, 260
Declaration of Human Rights, 93
Decoding, 532–34
Delegate style, 510–11
Delegating style, 506, 507, 509
Delegation, 364–66; barriers to delegation, 364–66; effective delegation, 364
Delphi method, 297–99; Delphi questionnaires, 297–98; phases, 298–99
Deming cycle, 309–10; act stage, 310; defined, 309; do stage, 310; effectiveness, 310; illustrated, 309; plan stage, 309–10; study stage, 310
Deming Prize, 64
Demographics. *See* Workforce demographics.
Departmental subcultures, 608–9
Derailment, 27–28
Deregulation, 128, 185, 233
Development, 27–28, 443–44; defined, 440; illustrated, 443. *See also* Training.
Development Marketplace, 390
Developmental stages of teams, 574–77; adjourning stage, 577; forming stage, 575; illustrated, 575; norming stage, 576; performing stage, 576–77; storming stage, 575–76
Differentiation, 360; focused strategy, 240–42; product, 130; strategy, 239–40
Differentiators, 245
Digital sleuthing, 139
Disclosure, 104, 342, 343
Discovery space shuttle, 584
Discrimination against women and minorities, 82; illustrated, 81
Dismissal: lawful and unlawful reasons for, illustrated, 82
Distribution, technology's impact on, 140–41
Distributive justice principle, 96–97
Diversification: defined, 219; questions in considering, 219–21; strategies and planning, 219–23, illustrated, 221; types of strategies, 221–23
Diversity training, 618–20; awareness training, 619–20; harassment training, 620
Division of labor, 44, 360
Divisional structures. *See* Product design.
Divisional subcultures, 608–9
Do stage, of Deming cycle, 310
Dominant-business strategy, 222
Downscoping, 220
Downsizing, 16–17, 402
Downward channels, 540–41
Dumping, 162

E

E-learning, 442–43
Easy Button (Staples), 529–30

Ecometrics, 67
Economic climate, 161
Economic crises, 258
Economic logic, 245
Economic value, 116
Economics, 116
Economies of scale, 129–30, 233, 242
Economy, 116–20; borderless competition, 117–18; customer convenience, 118; environmental stewardship, 119–20; global, 150–53, illustrated, 150; human capital, 118; illustrated, 116; outsourcing, 116–17
Effectiveness criteria, 573
Effectiveness determinants, 573–74; illustrated, 574
Effectiveness framework for teams, 572–74
Efficiency, 93, 242
80/20 rule, 330–31
Electronic brainstorming, 307
Electronic Industry Code of Conduct, 392, 416
Emotion, 550–51, 552, 578
Emotional intelligence, 499–502; components of, illustrated, 500; defined, 499; questionnaire, 526–27; self-awareness, 499–501; self-control, 501; social awareness, 501–2; social skill, 502
Employee benefits, 429–31, 448–49; illustrated, 449
Employee motivation and satisfaction, 458–60; defined, 458; guidelines for managers, 486; illustrated, 459; individual differences approach, 460, 483–86; job design approach, 459, 474–77; managerial approach, 459, 460–74; organization approach, 460, 477–83
Employee network groups, 543
Employee referrals, 437–38
Employee selection, 438–40; defined, 438; interviews, 439; interviews, table of questions, 439; reference checks, 438; résumés, 438; tests, 439–40
Employee surveys, 404–5, 615
Employee turnover, 331, 447–48, 479
Employees: and human resources management, 424; lawful and unlawful reasons for dismissal, illustrated, 82
Employment-at-will, 82
Employment law, 613–14; equal employment opportunity, 427–29; federal employment laws and regulations, table of, 428
Employment tests, 439–40
Empowerment, 412
Encoding, 532
"Engineer as an Economist, The" (Towne), 41
Enterprise resource planning (ERP) software, 405–6
Entertainment industry, 146–47, 374–75
Entrepreneurial culture, 603–4
Entrepreneurial Quotient exercise, 188–89, 209
Entrepreneurs, 183–84, 241; assessing affordable loss, 199; attributes of, illustrated, 188; business angel, 200; business incubation, 186; business plan, 195–96; buy strategy, 197; corporate, 204–6; deciding to buy, start, or franchise, 196–99; defined, 184–85; economic and technological conditions, 186; and environment, 185–86; family businesses, 187, 202–4, illustrated, 203; finding funds, 199–200; franchise strategy, 197–98; going global, 200–202, illustrated, 201; meaning and scope, 184–87; open and free markets, 185; planning essentials, 195–204; small-business owners, 187; start-up strategy, 197; venture capitalist, 200
Entrepreneurs, competencies of, 187–95; communication competency, 193–94; multicultural competency, 194–95; planning and administration competency, 192; self-management competency, 188–91; specialized knowledge, 195; strategic action competency, 191–92; teamwork competency, 192–93
Environment, 114–28; assessing, 394–95; and centralization/decentralization, 367; competitive forces, 128–32; economy, 116–20; and entrepreneurship, 185–86; general environment, 115, 128; impact of changing demographics on organizations, 120–21; organization design and, 360; political-legal forces, 132–37; protecting, 91–92; technological forces, 137–41

Environmental forces of rational model, illustrated, 266
Environmental protection, 91–92
Environmental scanning, 394–95
Environmental stewardship, 119–20
Equal Credit Opportunity Act, 132
Equal Employment Opportunity (EEO), 82, 427–29; enforcement of, 429; in global arena, 429, illustrated, 430
Equal Employment Opportunity Commission (EEOC), 429
Equal Pay Act, 96–97, 428, 430–31
Equator Principles, 103
Equity ratios, 481
Equity theory, 480–82
Ernst & Young Entrepreneur of the Year, 185
ERP (enterprise resource planning) software, 405–6
Escape clause, 165
Esteem needs, 484
Ethical Challenge, 16, 60, 80, 122, 155, 194, 228, 274, 289, 344, 363, 391, 426, 473, 520, 539, 580, 601
Ethical behaviors questionnaire, 281, 473–74
Ethical judgments, 91–98; combining approaches, 98, illustrated, 98; justice approach, 96–98; moral rights approach, 93–96, 98; utilitarian approach, 91–93, 98
Ethical leaders, 515
Ethical Practice Award, 426
Ethics, 26, 27, 28; codes of ethics, 85–87, 392, 416; and communication, 84, 553–56; computer ethics, 554–55; cultural influences, 80–82, 122; defined, 80; expectancy theory and, 470–74; fostering an ethical organizational culture, 84–85; Halliburton, 77–78, 79; importance of, 78–80; individual influences, 87–91; legal and regulatory influences, 82–83; organization influences, 83–87; ratings of various professions, 78–79; shaping, 80–91, illustrated, 81; stages of moral development, 87–89, illustrated, 88; talking about, 84–85; whistle-blowing, 90–91
Ethnicity, 609–10
Euro, 168
European Community, 168
Evidence management, 561
Exception reporting, 551
Exchange rates, 150–51
Executive compensation, 97, 227–28, 345, 482
Executive management, 41
Executives, ratings of ethical standards, 78
Expectancy, 468
Expectancy theory, 468–74; applying, 470–72, illustrated, 471; defined, 468; and ethics, 470–74; illustrated, 469
Expectations, and corporate governance, 341
Experienced meaningfulness, 474
Experienced responsibility, 475
Experiential training, 586
Expert System, 513
Expert systems, 290–91
Expertise, 497
Explicit knowledge, 287
Exporting strategy, 170–71
Exports, 151, 166–67, 200, 201–2
External control, and corporate governance, 342–44
External system, 581
Extinction, 467
Extortion, 163–64
Extrapolation, 297
Extraversion, 440
Eye contact, 535

F

Facilitate style, 510
Fact-finding stage, 304
Factory system, 42
Fair Labor Standards Act, 428, 430
Fairness: pay fairness, 447–49; principle of, 97; as social value, 427; treating people fairly, 480–83
Family and Medical Leave Act, 27, 428
Family business, 187, 202–4; illustrated, 203
Family-friendly workplaces, 27, 620–21; illustrated, 620

Fast-food industry, 479
Feedback, 58, 475, 476, 487; characteristics of, 545–46; communication, 544–46, 551–52; defined, 544; and goal setting, 464; performance feedback sessions, 445; questionnaire, 545; from surveys, 404–5
Feelings, of team members, 578
Feng shui, 128, 537
Fiefdom Syndrome, The (Herbold), 332
50 Most Important African-Americans in Technology, 495
Film production, 374–75
Finance strategies, 229
Financial controls, 337–39; budgetary control, 338–39; comparative financial control, 337–38
Financial incentive system, 50, 51
Financial information, accuracy of, 343
Financial management, 19, 20
Financial perspective, 293–94, 296
Financial ratios, 337–38
Financial statements, 325; certification of, 343
Fire fighting, 259–60, 611
Firefighters, 611
Firms: dominant-business, 222; related-business, 222; single-business, 221–22; unrelated-business, 222
First-line managers, 11–12, 54
Flow of information, 551
Focus groups, 403, 540, 615; defined, 403; illustrated, 404
Focused cost leadership strategy, 242–43
Focused differentiation strategy, 240–42
Forces: competitive, 128–32, 232–34; cultural, 153–60; environmental, 128–41; legal and regulatory, 82–83; political-legal, 132–37, 160–64; technological, 137–41
Forecasting, 296–302; defined, 296; Delphi method, 297–99; scenarios, 300–302; simulation, 299–300
Foreign conflict, 160–61
Foreign Corrupt Practices Act, 164
Foreign exchange rates, 150–51
Formal communication, 15, 16–17, 19
Formal position, 497
Formal training, 518–20
Forming stage, 575
Fortune 500 companies, 257, 370, 479, 495, 521, 543
Forward integration strategy, 225
France, 40, 122, 124–25, 126
Franchise strategy, 172–73, 197–98
Free rider, 579
Free will, 55
Freedom of conscience and speech, 96
Frustration-regression hypothesis, 486
Functional design, 368–70; illustrated, 369
Functional foremanship, 50
Functional-level strategy, 229–30; defined, 229; illustrated, 230
Functional managers, 8
Functional work team, 569
Functions of the Executive, The (Barnard), 54
Funding, 199–200

G

Gambler's fallacy bias, 272
Gambling casinos, 59
Gantt chart, 50
Gender differences, in communication, 533–34
Gender norms, 580
Gender role orientation, 126, 145
Gender roles, 611
Gender subcultures, 611
General Agreement on Tariffs and Trade (GATT), 165
General environment, 115, 128
General goals, 267
General managers, 8
Generic competitive strategies model, 239–43; cost leadership strategy, 242; defined, 239; differentiation strategy, 239–40; focused cost leadership strategy, 242–43; focused differentiation strategy, 240–42; illustrated, 240
Genomics, 569–70

292–93; enabling technology, 290–92; Information Age drivers, 287–88; main components, 287; targets, 288–90; teams as targets, 288; workforce as targets, 289–90

Knowledge management (KM) software, 286

Korea, 122

Kwankye, 16

L

Labor budget, 339

Labor division, 44, 360

Labor force, diversity of, 120–21

Labor-management relations, 41

Labor markets, 152–53

Labor Movement in America, The (Ely), 41

Labor unions, 41, 50, 53, 57, 133, 163, 168, 367, 605

Language: and communication, 552; as cultural force, 154–55; defined, 599; as element of culture, 599–600

Language training, 441–42

Law and order stage, 88

Law of small numbers bias, 272

Laws: credit, 132; defined, 82; employee dismissal, 82; employment, 613–14; equal employment, 429. *See also* Legal and regulatory environment.

Layoffs, 16–17, 396, 433–34; consequences of, illustrated, 434; growth rate of workforce, illustrated, 434

Leaders: charismatic, 385, 515; confident, 517; considerate, 517; ethical, 515; global, 521–22; personal characteristics, 499–502; self-awareness, 499–501; self-control, 501; social awareness, 501–2; social skill, 502; thoughtful, 516; trustworthy, 515; visionary, 515

Leadership, 495–96; across cultures, illustrated, 522; and Baldrige quality program, 312; bases of influence, 497; behavioral models, 502–6; contingency models, 506–14; creating change, 498–99; defined, 497; meaning of, 497–99; and multicultural competency, 521–22; and rewards, 497; servant leadership, 56; shared, 411; shared purposes, 497; training, 518–20, 584–86; transformational, 514–17; trust and confidence in, 517. *See also* Vroom-Jago leadership model.

Leadership assessment and training, 518–20

Leadership development, 517–22; coaching and mentoring, 520–21; formal assessment and training, 518–20; on-the-job learning, 518; special assignments, 521–22

Leading, 10

Learning: e-learning, 442–43; on-the-job, 518

Learning and growth perspective, 293–94, 296

Learning framework for managing, illustrated, 29

Learning goals/motivation, 464

Learning organizations, 409–14; characteristics of, illustrated, 411; community, 412; continuous learning, 412–13; culture of innovation, 412–13; customer-focused strategy, 413; defined, 409; illustrated, 411; intensive use of information, 413–14; organic organization design, 413; shared leadership, 411

Legal and regulatory environment, 427–31; compensation and benefits, 429–31; equal employment opportunity, 427–29; table of federal employment laws and regulations, 428. *See also* Laws.

Legal and regulatory forces, on ethical conduct, 82–83

Licensing strategy, 171–72

Lifelong career commitment, 44, 46

Light pollution, 119

Lights-out system, 341

Line managers, 424

Listening, 534, 552

Living the Credo, 600, 601

Lobbying, 133–34, 136, 277

Long-term care, 137

Long-term orientation, 126–27, 145

Louisiana, 134, 297, 517

Low-context cultures, 535

M

Machine control, 339–40

Macroenvironment, 115

Malaysia, 166

Malcolm Baldrige National Quality Award, 193, 310–11, 313, 314, 319

Management, 7–8; administrative, 51, 52; behavioral viewpoint, 53–57; bureaucratic, 43–49; contingency viewpoint, 61–63; defined, 7; functions of, 9–10, illustrated, 9; history of viewpoints, illustrated, 43; levels of, 11–14, illustrated, 11; proactive, 104; quality viewpoint, 63–68; systems viewpoint, 57–60; traditional viewpoint, 40–52; viewpoints and competencies, 68–69, illustrated, 68

Management by objectives (MBO), 463

Management Challenges for the 21st Century (Drucker), 290

Management innovation, 264

Managerial approach, 459, 460–74; communication, 460–61; motivating with goals and reward expectations, 468–74; offering incentives and rewards, 464–67; performance versus learning goals, 464; setting goals, 461–64

Managerial competencies, 4–6; communication, 15–18; core competencies, 14–30; and decision making, 254–55; defined, 4, 14; developing, 14–15; exploring, 28–30; key, 6, illustrated, 5; learning, 5; management viewpoints and, 68–69, illustrated, 68; model of, illustrated, 5; multicultural, 24–26; planning and administration, 18–20; self-management, 26–28; strategic action, 22–24; and team member selection, 583; teamwork, 20–22; what it takes to be a great manager, 14–15

Managerial grid, 504–5; country club style, 505; impoverished style, 504; middle-of-the-road style, 505; produce or perish style, 505; team style, 505

Managerial Values Profile questionnaire, 91, 92

Managers, 7; defined, 7; first-line, 11–12; functional, 8; general, 8; holding accountable for cultural diversity, 621; middle, 12–13; subcultures created by, 608–9; top, 13–14, 23; types, 7, 8

Managing, 7–8

Managing an Organization exercise, 73

Manufacturing, technology's impact on, 140

Manufacturing industry, 134

Maquiladora plants, 166–67

Market: defined, 222; as focus of Baldrige quality program, 312; labor, 152–53; niche, 184–85, 210, 240–42; open and free, 185; time to, 567

Market controls, 336–37; customer monitoring, 336–37; incentive compensation, 336

Market culture, 604

Market development strategy, 237

Market influencing, 342

Market penetration strategy, 236–37

Marketing, 130

Marketing strategies, 229

Mass customization, 140

Materials budget, 339

Measurement, analysis, and knowledge management (Baldrige quality program), 312

Measuring by attribute, 66

Measuring by variable, 65–66

Mechanistic controls, 335

Mechanistic system, 376–77; defined, 376; illustrated, 376; versus organic system, 376

Media All-Star for Non-traditional Media Award, 89

Media Planning Executive of the Year, 89

Meeting times, 331

Meetings, 565, 584–85

Mentoring, 444, 520–21

Mergers, subcultures due to, 607–8; illustrated, 607

Message, 534–39; defined, 534; nonverbal, 534–38; verbal, 538; written, 538–39

Mexico, 122, 126, 149–50, 154, 156–58, 159–60, 166–68, 173, 178

Middle managers, 12–13

Middle-of-the-road style, 505

Mill Improvement Process (Georgia-Pacific), 411

Minimum wage, 430

Mission, 217; defined, 217; developing, 230–32

Monetary compensation, 447

Monopolies, 40–41

Moral development stages, 87–89; illustrated, 88

Moral rights approach, 93–96, 289; freedom of conscience and speech, 96; interrelated elements in, illustrated, 94; life and safety, 93–94; and natural duty principle, 97–98; privacy, 95–96; truthfulness, 94

Most Admired Company, 509

Most favored nation, 133, 165

Motivation, 457–60; defined, 458; illustrated, 459. *See also* Employee motivation and satisfaction.

Motivator factors, 479

Movie industry, 146–47

Movie theater industry, 374–75

Multicultural competency, 5, 6, 24–26; dimensions of, 26; entrepreneurs, 194–95; global teams, 572; illustrated, 5; and leadership, 521–22; in Self-Assessment Inventory, 35

Multicultural organizations, 612

Multidisciplinary work teams, 413, 569–70, 605

Multidomestic strategy, 174–75

Muslim countries, 126

N

N-Geners, 118

Narratives, 600

National Business Ethics Survey, 83

National identity, 82

National Labor Relations Act, 428

National responsiveness, 170

Natural disasters, 258. *See also* Hurricane Katrina; Hurricane Rita.

Natural duty principle, 97–98

Needs: for achievement, 189; affiliation, 484; defined, 483; esteem, 484; hierarchy of, 483–85; physiological, 484; security, 484; self-actualization, 584

Negative reinforcement, 467

Negotiation, 15, 17, 19, 133; defined, 17, 133

Net Generation, 118

Netherlands, 476

Network design, 373–75; as administrative innovation, 408; and channels, 542; illustrated, 375; and organic design, 413

Network groups, 543

New entrants, 129–30, 233

New Orleans, Louisiana, 134, 297, 517

Niche, 184–85, 210, 240–42

Nigeria, 122, 331

Nobel Prize, 271

Non-compete clause, 197

Nonmonetary compensation, 447

Nonverbal cues, 158, 552

Nonverbal messages, 534–38

Norming stage, 576

Norms: behavioral, 578–80; as element of culture, 598; gender, 580; performance, 579; social, 158

Norms for Virtual Teams exercise, 590–91

North American Free Trade Agreement (NAFTA), 119, 165, 166–68, 178

Noticing, 267

O

Obedience and punishment stage, 87

Objective controls, 325

Objective probability, 257

Occupational Safety and Health Act (OSHA), 93–94, 428

Office space, 393, 535–37

Offshoring, 117

Oil industry, 163

Older workers, 136–37, 610–11

On-the-job learning, for leaders, 518

100 Best Companies to Work for in America, 39, 56, 425, 427

100 Best Corporate Citizens, 509

Oobeya, 408

Open-source community, 597, 598

Open-source software, 401

Open system, 58

Related-business strategy, 222
Related diversification strategy, 226–27
Relationship behavior, 506
Reliable process, 234
Report of the Special Examination of Fannie Mae, 334
Representation, 135, 136
Reputation crises, 258
Research and development budget, 339
Resistance to change, 397–99
Resistol glue, 14
Resource allocation, 218–19
Resource commitment, 170, 171
Responsibility, 362
Restructuring, 401
Results: and Baldrige quality program, 312; controlling and diagnosing, 239; knowledge of, 475; from performance appraisals, 444–45
Résumés, 438
Retail industry, 400–401
Return on investment (ROI) ratio, 337
Reward systems, 587
Rewards, 487; and leadership, 497; motivating with, 468–74, 487; offering, 464–67
RFID (radio-frequency identification), 117–18, 289
Richness of information, 539–40
Risk: and decision making, 256–57; defined, 256; illustrated, 258; political risk, 160–62
Risk assessment, 327–28
Routine decisions, 261
Rules, 43, 48
Russia, 159, 171

S

Sabbatical leaves, 486
Sales budget, 339
Sales productivity, 331
Sales-to-assets ratio, 338
Sandbox Wisdom (Asacker), 94
Sarbanes-Oxley Act, 83, 90, 342–44; criminal accountability, 343; general provisions, 343; whistle-blower protection, 343–44
Satisfaction, 458–60; defined, 458; illustrated, 459. *See also* Employee motivation and satisfaction.
Satisfaction-progression hypothesis, 486
Satisficing, 273–74
Scandals, 83, 302, 325, 332, 343, 363
Scapegoating, 276
Scenarios, 300–302; compared with contingency planning, 300; competitor, 301; defined, 300; illustrated, 301; planning process, 301–2; "What if?" questions, 300–301
Scientific management, 49–51; characteristics of, 52; insight from, 50–51
Scorecard. *See* Balanced scorecard model.
Secretary of Labor, 344
Security needs, 484
Selective perception, 546
Selective perception bias, 272
Selectivity principle, 330
Self-actualization needs, 485
Self-Assessment Inventory, 5, 30, 32–36
Self-awareness, 499–501; and development, 26, 27, 28
Self-confidence, 189
Self-control, 501
Self-management, 467
Self-management competency, 5, 6, 26–28; defined, 26; desire for independence, 189; digital sleuthing, 139; dimensions of, 28; entrepreneurs, 188–91; illustrated, 5, 188; need for achievement, 189; reactions to change, 397–98; in Self-Assessment Inventory, 35; self-confidence, 189; self-sacrifice, 189–90
Self-managing work team, 570–71; illustrated, 571, 585
Self-sacrifice, 189–90
Selling style, 506, 507, 508–9
Semantics, 549–50
Sender, 532
Sequential interdependence, 378
Serial development, 567
Servant leadership, 56
Shared assumptions, 597
Shared leadership, 411

Shared practices, 600–602
Shared purposes, 497
Shareholder meetings, governance questions at, 350–52
Shareholder value, 104–5
Shell Global Scenarios to 2025, 302
Shoe industry, 181
Shop management and accounting, 41
Sigma, 64–65, 168
Sign industry, 210
Simulations, 299–300; defined, 299; illustrated, 300; spreadsheet simulations, 299–300
Single-business strategy, 221–22
Situational approach. *See* Contingency viewpoint.
Situational contingency, 507, 511
Situational Leadership® Model, 506–10; assessment, 509–10; choosing a leadership style, 508–9; defined, 506; illustrated, 507; leadership styles, 506; situational contingency, 507
Six Sigma training, 37
Skill variety, 476
Skunkworks, 582
Small business, 187
Social awareness, 501–2
Social change, 153–54
Social contract stage, 88–89
Social networks, 543–44, 553
Social norms, 158
Social performance, evaluating, 103–5
Social responsibility. *See* Stakeholder social responsibility.
Social skill, 502
Social value, of human resources, 427
Socialization, 135–36, 137; defined, 135, 598; as element of culture, 598–99
Soft information, 414
Solution-finding stage, 306
Solution types, and decision making, 260
Source of advantage, 239
Space, 535, 536
Space shuttle, 460–61, 584, 596
Spain, 40
Span of control, 361–62
Special assignments, 521–22
Specialization, 50, 360, 548–49
Spirit Award, 479
Spreadsheet simulations, 299–300
Stages of moral development, 87–89; illustrated, 88
Stakeholder controls, 323–24
Stakeholder social responsibility, 98–105; communication and engagement, 104; creating shareholder value, 104–5; defined, 99; disclosure, 104; evaluating social performance, 103–5; proactive management, 104; reasons for embracing, 99; stakeholder pressures, 101, illustrated, 102; stakeholders, 99–101; sustainable development, 101–3
Stakeholders, 99–101; defined, 99; and goals, 269; illustrated, 100; pressures of, 101, illustrated, 102; primary, 99; secondary, 99
Standards, 10, 331
Standards of professionalism, 325
Start-up strategy, 197
Statistical process control, 64
Status, defined, 547
Status level, as hurdle to communication, 547–48
Stereotyping, 546–47
Stock options, 227
Storming stage, 575–76
Strategic action competency, 5, 6, 22–24; defined, 22; dimensions of, 24; entrepreneurs, 191–92; illustrated, 5; in Self-Assessment Inventory, 35
Strategic actions, 23, 24
Strategic business unit (SBU), 225
Strategic goals, and control, 325–26
Strategic levels, 223–30; business-level strategy, 228–29; corporate-level strategy, 223–28; functional-level strategy, 229–30; illustrated, 224
Strategic planning, 215–19; and Baldrige quality program, 312; contingency planning, 215–16; core competencies, 234–35; core components, illustrated, 217; defined, 215; diagnosing opportunities and threats, 232–34; diagnosing strengths and weaknesses, 234–36; exercise for, 250; illustrated, 231, 235, 236; organic growth

strategies, 236; organizational goals, 218; outsourcing strategy, 235–36; resource allocation, 218–19; strategic plan, 237; strategies, 218; tactical plans, 237–38; tasks and process, 230–39; vision and mission, 216–17
Strategic target, 239
Strategies: alliance, 173–74, 226, 277; backward integration, 131, 225–26; business-level, 228–29; buy, 197; conglomeration diversification, 227; corporate-level, 223–28; cost leadership, 242; customer-focused, learning organizations, 413; defined, 218; differentiation, 239–40; dominant-business, 222; exporting, 170–71; finance, 229; focused cost leadership, 242–43; focused differentiation, 240–42; forward integration, 225; franchising, 172–73, 197–98; functional-level, 229–30; generic competitive, 239–43; global, 175–76; horizontal integration, 226; integrated, 243–46; international business, 170–76; licensing, 171–72; market development, 237; market penetration, 236–37; marketing, 229; multidomestic, 174–75; operations, 229; organic growth, 236; outsourcing, 235–36; political, 133–37; product development, 237; related-business, 222; related diversification, 226–27; single-business, 221–22; start-up, 197; technology's role, 138–39; unrelated-business, 222
Strengths, diagnosing, 234–36
Strong culture, 606
Structural redesign, 401–2
Study stage, of Deming cycle, 310
Subcultures, 606, 607–12; age-based, 610–11; created by managers, 608–9; defined, 607; departmental and divisional, 608–9; due to mergers and acquisitions, 607–8, illustrated, 607; due to workforce demographics, 609–11; ethnic identities, table of, 610; ethnicity-based, 609–10; gender-based, 611; geographically based, 609; implications, 612; occupational, 608; reasons for, 607
Subjective probability, 257
Subordinates, optimal number of, 362
Subsidiaries, 344
Subsidy, 163
Substitute goods and services, 130, 234
Subteams, 581
Sugar industry, 143, 163
Supernets, 137
Suppliers, 131–32, 233–34
Supply chain management system, 117–18
Survey feedback, 404–5
Surveys, 404–5, 539–40, 615
Sustainability, 101, 102
Sustainable development, 101–3
Sweatshops, 391
Sweden, 156
Symbols: defined, 599; as element of culture, 599
Synergy, 329
Synthesis, 311
Systems: closed, 58; concepts, 57–58; defined, 57; expert, 290–91; external, 581; integration through, 376–77; mechanistic, 376–77; open, 58; organic, 376–77; types, 58; value system, 122, 156–58
Systems analysis, 57
Systems perspective, 311, 312
Systems viewpoint, 57–60, 69; defined, 58; illustrated, 58; learning from, 59–60; qualitative techniques, 58–59; and sustainable development, 102; system concepts, 57–58; system types, 58

T

Taboos, 600
Tacit knowledge, 287, 414
Tactical planning, 219, 237–38
Tariff, 162, 165, 166
Tariff concession, 165
Task behavior, 506
Task forces, 568–69
Task identity, 476